EVALUATING POLICY REGIMES

EVALUATING POLICY REGIMES

New Research in Empirical Macroeconomics

Ralph C. Bryant
Peter Hooper
Catherine L. Mann

The Brookings Institution
Washington, D.C.

Library of Congress Cataloging-in-Publication data:

Evaluating policy regimes: new research in empirical macroeconomics /
   [edited by] Ralph C. Bryant ... [et al.].
      p.   cm.
   Includes bibliographical references and indexes.
   ISBN 0-8157-1150-6 (cloth: alk. paper)—ISBN
   0-8157-1149-2 (pbk.: alk. paper)
      1. Macroeconomics.   2. Economic policy—Mathematical models.
   3. Monetary policy—Mathematical models. I. Bryant, Ralph C.,
   1938–
   HB172.5.E93   1993
   339.5'01'5118—dc20   92-44908
                                                              CIP

9 8 7 6 5 4 3 2 1

The paper used in this publication meets the minimum requirements of
the American National Standard for Information Sciences—Permanence of
paper for Printed Library Materials, ANSI Z39.48-1984

₿ BROOKINGS INSTITUTION

The Brookings Institution is an independent organization devoted to nonpartisan research, education, and publication in economics, government, foreign policy, and the social sciences generally. Its principal purposes are to aid in the development of sound public policies and to promote public understanding of issues of national importance.

The Institution was founded on December 8, 1927, to merge the activities of the Institute for Government Research, founded in 1916, the Institute of Economics, founded in 1922, and the Robert Brookings Graduate School of Economics and Government, founded in 1924.

The Board of Trustees is responsible for the general administration of the Institution, while the immediate direction of the policies, program, and staff is vested in the President, assisted by an advisory committee of the officers and staff. The by-laws of the Institution state: "It is the function of the Trustees to make possible the conduct of scientific research, and publication, under the most favorable conditions, and to safeguard the independence of the research staff in the pursuit of their studies and in the publication of the results of such studies. It is not a part of their function to determine, control, or influence the conduct of particular investigations or the conclusions reached."

The President bears final responsibility for the decision to publish a manuscript as a Brookings book. In reaching his judgment on the competence, accuracy, and objectivity of each study, the President is advised by the director of the appropriate research program and weighs the views of a panel of expert outside readers who report to him in confidence on the quality of the work. Publication of a work signifies that it is deemed a competent treatment worthy of public consideration but does not imply endorsement of conclusions or recommendations.

The Institution maintains its position of neutrality on issues of public policy in order to safeguard the intellectual freedom of the staff. Hence interpretations or conclusions in Brookings publications should be understood to be solely those of the authors and should not be attributed to the Institution, to its trustees, officers, or other staff members, or to the organizations that support its research.

Foreword

ECONOMISTS have long debated the theoretical merits of alternative approaches to the conduct of economic policy, typically referred to as different "policy regimes." Some of the debate focuses on issues that are primarily "domestic" for individual nations. In the case of monetary policy, for example, should authorities try to achieve targets for growth of the money supply, for nominal income, or some other objective? Other parts of the debate, such as that over exchange-rate arrangements, arise because the economies of many nations influence one another through trade in goods and services and capital movements. Theory alone cannot determine which approach for conducting monetary policy works best or how policies in one country influence others. Policymakers and economists can reach an informed consensus on which economic interventions to use only after the effects of each approach have been carefully examined with such tools as multicountry empirical models.

This book breaks new ground by combining theoretical and empirical evaluation of alternative policy regimes. It draws on the expertise of leading researchers on the systemic behavior of the global economy. A large body of new empirical evidence was generated for the project. Many parts of the book use "stochastic simulation," an evaluation procedure in which the response to a large number of policy interventions is repeatedly estimated. This technique is at the frontier of empirical economic analysis.

The book constitutes another installment of a continuing worldwide research project to improve empirical knowledge about the interdependence of national economies. The project and the publication of this book reflect the support and assistance of many people and institutions. Particular thanks and credit are due to the modeling groups and individuals whose contributions are the core of the project: staff members of the National Institute for Economic and Social Research in London and of the London Business School who jointly maintain versions of the global economic model known as GEM (especially Ray Barrell and David A. Currie); the team of economists responsible for the

INTERMOD model sponsored by the Canadian Department of Finance and subsequently supported also by the Bank of Canada (especially Guy Meredith and Mary Macgregor); Patrick Minford and several associates at the University of Liverpool, who developed and maintain the LIVERPOOL model; staff members of the Division of International Finance at the Federal Reserve Board responsible for the MCM multicountry model (especially Jaime R. Marquez); staff members of the Division of Research and Statistics at the Federal Reserve Board responsible for the MPS model (especially Flint Brayton); Warwick J. McKibbin, who has extended and refined the MSG model originally developed by McKibbin and Jeffrey D. Sachs; staff members of the Research Department of the International Monetary Fund responsible for the MULTIMOD model (especially Paul R. Masson and Steven A. Symansky); Joseph E. Gagnon and Ralph W. Tryon, who developed and maintain the MX3 model in the Division of International Finance at the Federal Reserve Board; staff members of the Economics Department at the Organization for Economic Cooperation and Development responsible for the INTER-LINK multicountry model (especially Pete Richardson); and economists working at Stanford University with John B. Taylor on the TAYLOR multicountry model (especially Peter J. Klenow). Three of these participating model groups stem from the Federal Reserve Board staff, as do two of the three editors and several authors of key chapters. These facts indicate the vital role played in the project by staff members of the Federal Reserve. Among the model group participants, Paul R. Masson and Steven A. Symansky made especially valuable contributions during the planning stages for the project. Others who gave professional advice to the project organizers include Henry J. Aaron, Barry P. Bosworth, Neil Ericcson, Ray C. Fair, John F. Helliwell, Gerald Holtham, Andrew Hughes Hallett, Donald L. Kohn, Bennett T. McCallum, Richard Portes, Charles L. Schultze, Christopher A. Sims, John B. Taylor, Peter A. Tinsley, Edwin M. Truman, and David Vines.

The administration of the project was organized under the auspices of the Brookings Institution by the three editors, with extensive assistance from three of the other authors. Ralph C. Bryant is a senior fellow in the Brookings Economic Studies program. Peter Hooper is an assistant director in the Division of International Finance at the Federal Reserve Board; during part of the project, he was also a visiting fellow at Brookings. Catherine L. Mann is a senior economist in the Division of International Finance at the Federal Reserve Board; during the course of the project she also served on the staffs of the World Bank and the Council of Economic Advisers. Warwick J. McKibbin, a senior fellow at Brookings, and Ralph W. Tryon and Dale W. Henderson, both of the staff of the Division of International Finance at the Federal Reserve Board, contributed substantially to the organization and management of the project in addition to being participants and authors.

Glenn Y. Yamagata, Britt Nesheim, Paul R. Bergin, Peter D. Fishman, and Daniel W. Brodkey provided research assistance and computer support. Jim McEuen, Rozlyn Coleman, and Caroline Lalire edited the manuscript; Laura Kelly and Roshna Kapadia verified its factual content. Evelyn M. E. Taylor and Ruby M. Brooks provided administrative assistance and secretarial support. Robert Elwood prepared the index.

This project received generous financial support from the Ford Foundation; the John D. and Catherine T. MacArthur Foundation; and the Toyko Club Foundation for Global Studies. The Board of Governors of the Federal Reserve System provided major support in the form of staff and computer time.

The views expressed in this book are those of the editors and authors. They should not be attributed to the other persons acknowledged, to the supporting organizations and foundations, to the Board of Governors of the Federal Reserve System, or to the trustees, officers, or staff members of the Brookings Institution.

Bruce K. MacLaury
President

Washington, D.C.
July 1993

Contents

PART THREE: Stochastic Simulations of Monetary-Policy Regimes

PART FOUR: Other Approaches to Monetary-Policy Regimes

PART FIVE: Applications and Extensions of Stochastic Simulation
           Techniques to Particular Economic Sectors

1
Introduction and Overview

CHAPTER 1

Evaluating Policy Regimes and Analytical Models: Background and Project Summary

Ralph C. Bryant, Peter Hooper, and Catherine L. Mann

SINCE THE MID-1980S, researchers in a worldwide network sponsored by the Brookings Institution have been collaborating to assess and to improve empirical knowledge about the interdependence of national economies. A fundamental premise has driven this research: before progress can be made on virtually any of the important positive and normative issues of macroeconomic policy facing national governments, analytical understanding of interactions among national economies must first improve. The initial research effort yielded a two-volume publication completed in 1987. Several other publications followed.[1] This new volume reports another, substantial installment of the continuing research effort.

This volume evaluates alternative regimes for the conduct of national monetary policies. ("Regimes" are defined and discussed below.) Many policymakers and economists contend that some simplified approach to monetary policy would lead to superior performances by individual national economies and the world economy as a whole. Yet suggested candidates for the "best" approach are numerous and controversial. Some analysts, for example, argue for money targeting. Others favor exchange-rate targeting. Still others advocate some form of nominal-income targeting. Is one suggested approach demonstrably better than the others? This question—obviously vital for central banks and other government institutions—is the primary focus of this book.

In particular, the research summarized here examines the stabilization properties of alternative monetary-policy regimes. It analyzes how well various

---

1. The initial volumes were published as Bryant, Henderson, and others, eds., *Empirical Macroeconomics for Interdependent Economies* (Brookings, 1988; referred to here as *EMIE*). Subsequent studies include Bryant, Holtham, and Hooper, eds., *External Deficits and the Dollar: The Pit and the Pendulum* (Brookings, 1988); Hooper and others, eds., *Financial Sectors in Open Economies: Empirical Analysis and Policy Issues* (Board of Governors of the Federal Reserve System, 1990); and Bryant, Currie, and others, *Macroeconomic Policies in an Interdependent World* (Brookings, Centre for Economic Policy Research, and IMF, 1989). See below for further discussion.

regime types perform in achieving desired outcomes for target variables and other macroeconomic variables in the face of unexpected shocks to economies. The analysis takes place in an explicitly multicountry, multiregion context, in keeping with the focus of the broader research effort on attaining a better understanding of the domestic and cross-border consequences of policy actions and nonpolicy shocks in the world economy as a whole.

Most previous evaluations of alternative monetary-policy regimes have been theoretical rather than empirical. Theoretical analysis alone, conducted in terms of highly simplified models, is valuable but insufficient. What is needed is a careful examination of the robustness of alternative approaches in the context of a range of empirical models. The research reported in this volume begins to redress the paucity of empirical analyses in previous work.

The analysis here is representative of the most useful and most advanced work on policy regimes being carried out in macroeconomics. In several respects, especially in its use of the evaluative techniques of stochastic simulation, it pushes outward the frontier of our empirical knowledge.

A principal conclusion of the book is that some simplifed regimes for monetary policy are markedly less promising than others for achieving the stabilization objectives customarily sought by policymakers. Most notably, for a wide variety of circumstances, neither money targeting nor exchange-rate targeting performs as well as a regime that targets either nominal GNP or the sum of real GNP and the inflation rate.

This introduction to the book first summarizes the key issues involved in evaluating policy regimes and clarifies the relationships among those issues. It next gives some background about the research agenda underlying the project. The chapter then provides a reader's guide to parts 2 through 5 of the volume. Part 2 is a distillation of the new theoretical and empirical research. Parts 3 through 5 contain revised versions of related papers first presented at a conference held at Brookings in March 1990. The final sections of the chapter highlight key generalizations emerging from the project and identify ways in which future research should refine the analysis.

Economic Policymaking and Policy Regimes

Basic Features and Definitions

Government policymakers seek to attain ultimate objectives. These goals can be stated in terms of desired time paths for future values of certain *ultimate-target variables*. Policymakers have at their disposal certain *instruments* of economic policy — variables that the policymakers can, and do, control precisely at each point in time. No slippage exists between the values of instrument settings desired by policymakers and the values actually implemented. But there are many sources of slippage between the instrument settings and the desired values for ultimate-target variables. Great uncertainty exists about how national economies evolve domestically and how they interact with each other in the larger world economy. Economies are buffeted more or less continuously by various types of *shocks*, disturbances for which the consequences are uncertain. Policymakers are even uncertain about the effects of their own instruments on ultimate-target variables. Given this pervasive uncertainty, policymakers cannot achieve their ultimate objectives precisely. The basic task facing policymakers is to choose time paths for instrument settings that are judged most likely to bring about the best feasible combination of time paths for the ultimate-target variables.[2]

Policymakers have some discretion about *instrument choice*—that is, the selection of particular variables to use as operating instruments. With monetary policy, for example, the policy authority faces a basic choice between selecting a "price" or a "quantity" as its primary instrument variable. In particular, it can choose either a short-term market interest rate (such as the rate at which commercial banks lend immediately available funds to each other) or the amount of a central-bank liability (such as the aggregate deposits of commercial banks at the central bank). Both variables are potential instruments. Once one of the two is selected as the primary actual instrument, however, the other cannot be controlled precisely.

Instrument variation is the manner in which policymakers vary the settings of their actual policy instruments over time. Policymakers have substantially more discretion about instrument variation than about instrument choice. Moreover, the policymakers' either-or selection of particular instruments, although not of trivial import, is much less significant than their medium- and long-run decisions about instrument variation.

Described more completely, the task facing policymakers is to choose particular instruments and to develop procedures for intertemporal instrument variation such that the economy is most likely to attain the best feasible combination of time paths for ultimate-target variables.

The way in which policymakers resolve the issues of instrument choice and instrument variation constitutes an *operating regime* for policy. Alternative selections of instruments and alternative procedures for varying them over time give rise to different operating regimes. Much of this book is devoted to a comparison and evaluation of alternative operating regimes for monetary policy.

---

2. Actual policymaking may not always correspond well with this summary characterization. For example, some policymakers may make successive static decisions for individual periods rather than focus deliberately and systematically on time paths.

Ultimate and Intermediate Targets

Ultimate targets are macroeconomic objectives deemed to influence directly the welfare of individuals and the society. Ultimate-target variables are pursued in their own right as final goals of policy. The volume of output, aggregate employment, and the rate of inflation of the average price level are often regarded as ultimate-target variables.

Most endogenous variables in economic systems are not ultimate-target variables but rather are *intermediate variables*. Policymakers typically do not pursue intermediate variables as final goals of policy; more precisely, policymakers tend not to have preferences with respect to intermediate variables directly, and such variables do not usually appear as arguments in the policymakers' *loss function*.[3] Intermediate variables are influenced by the behavior of private-sector decisionmakers as well as by the actual instrument variables of policymakers. Intermediate variables are part of the "transmission mechanism"—a euphemism for complex chains of behavioral causation—between instruments and ultimate-target variables. Policymakers influence, but cannot precisely control, intermediate variables.[4]

When conducting economic policy, policymakers can follow either a single-stage or a two-stage decisionmaking procedure. In a single-stage procedure, the policymakers in effect reason backward from the desired paths for their ultimate-target variables directly to the most appropriate time sequences of the settings for their policy instruments. Alternatively, the policymakers can choose a two-stage procedure, termed an *intermediate-target strategy*. Such a strategy entails the selection of a particular intermediate variable as an *intermediate-target variable*—for the moment, identify it only generally with the label Z—as a fulcrum for decisionmaking.[5] In effect, an intermediate-target strategy disaggregates the complete decision problem facing the policymakers into two subordinate problems, with decisions at the two levels made sequentially. An upper-level decision involves reasoning backward from the desired time paths for the ultimate targets to a target path for Z. The lower-level decision takes the target path for Z as given and determines time paths for the instrument settings designed to keep the actual value of Z tracking as closely as possible along its target path. Typically, different periodicities of decisionmaking are employed for the two levels. Calculations of the target path for Z are revised

---

3. The phrase "loss function"—or, synonymously, "social welfare function"—is shorthand for how policymakers evaluate the disutility (welfare) associated with alternative conceivable economic outcomes. As typically specified in analytical discourse, the function identifies which ultimate-target variables are deemed important by the policymakers and indicates the relative weights attached to those variables.

4. Long-term interest rates, broadly defined monetary aggregates, equity prices, mortgage loans outstanding, and stocks of inventories are examples of intermediate variables.

5. An intermediate-target strategy can focus on more than one intermediate-target variable. For simplicity the text discusses only the single-variable case.

only periodically. But lower-level decisions are revised more or less continuously in response to observed discrepancies between the actual value of Z and its target path. A given upper-level specification of the target path for Z thus becomes a surrogate for the ultimate objectives and is the week-by-week "operating objective" of lower-level policy actions.

Why might policymakers focus on an intermediate target rather than directly on their ultimate targets? Why disaggregate their overall decision problem into two stages, with different periodicities of decisionmaking, rather than use a single-stage operating regime? Protagonists have given a variety of rationales for intermediate targeting, in particular for the conduct of monetary policy. Critics have challenged all of them. Most notably, several decades of controversy about "monetarism," which entails the use of the money stock as an intermediate target of monetary policy, featured debates about these rationales. But macroeconomic variables other than the money stock—for example, nominal GNP or a long-term interest rate—have also been proposed as candidates for Z, and these intermediate-target strategies, too, have generated interest and criticism. Although the debate about the advisability of targeting intermediate variables has not been resolved, much energy has been devoted to analysis of regimes that target intermediate variables. The alternative simplified regimes for monetary policy studied in this volume can be interpreted as examples of intermediate-target regimes.[6]

Discretion and Rules

Important differences in judgment about operating regimes for economic policies arise more from differences in views about intertemporal instrument variation than from differences in views about instrument choice or, even, from differences in views about targeting intermediate variables. Most prominently, judgments differ about the role that "activism" should play in the conduct of policy (especially monetary policy). Controversy about the appropriate degree of activism is often couched in terms of the relative merits of "rules" versus "discretion."

Activist approaches to instrument variation tend to be defended in the policy community but are often criticized in academic circles. Advocates of activist discretion stress the probable need for policymakers to adjust their instrument decisions to new information about the evolution of the economy or to changed perceptions of how the economy does or should function. Critics of activist discretion emphasize the probable beneficial effects of "commitment" of policy to an announced rule. *Discretion* gives policymakers flexibility with

---

6. For discussion of monetarism and intermediate-target strategies for monetary policy, see for example M. Friedman (1959, 1968, 1982); Kareken, Muench, and Wallace (1973); Waud (1973); B. Friedman (1975, 1977, 1990); Bryant (1980, 1983); and McCallum (1985, 1990).

respect to their future actions. *Commitment* to a rule is like a binding contract that specifies in advance the actions that policymakers will (and will not) take.

Clarity requires a distinction between the terms "regime" and "rule." In conventional language as commonly used in economics, "rule" has at least two connotations. Sometimes, as in the preceding paragraph, "rule" is used as an antonym for activist discretion. In that connotation, a rule for policy is a determinate, often simple and rigid, procedure indicating how policy shall be implemented. Such a rule gives little or no scope to policymakers for activist discretion today or in the future. At other times, "rule" has a looser, more general connotation: it may indicate only a prescribed guide for conduct, which need not be simple and rigid and which might or might not allow policymakers substantial scope for discretion in the future. In this second usage, a "rule" for policy is virtually a synonym for "operating regime" as defined above.

To avoid confusion, we reserve the word "rule" for situations in which the first, "nondiscretionary" connotation is dominant. In our usage, therefore, "operating regime" is the broader term. Some regimes may take the form of (nondiscretionary, nonactivist) rules, but other regimes do not.

Any systematic procedure for making decisions can in principle be described by its originators in a manner that permits its replication and implementation by others. With an elastic stretching of conventional language, any systematic procedure, no matter how complex, could thus in some broad sense be construed as a set of decision "rules." Conversely, any systematic procedure for making decisions must be initially selected from a menu of alternative procedures. If the original selection should be judged not to be working well, it may be abandoned. Thus any systematic procedure, no matter how simple or rigid, presumes some degree of "discretionary" choice.

Nevertheless, to label every systematic method of conducting monetary policy a "rule," or alternatively to describe every operating regime as "discretionary," is more likely to foster confusion than insight. In everyday discourse it is more straightforward to identify a policy regime as a (nondiscretionary) rule if the regime permits little or no flexibility for the policymakers to adjust the settings on their instruments in response to new data, to changes in their perceptions of how the economy works, or to alterations in their ultimate objectives. Analogously, the more flexibility of this type available to policymakers, the greater the degree of discretion (potential activism) permitted by a regime.[7]

7. When alternative policy regimes are arrayed along a spectrum, many differences among them are more a matter of degree than of kind. No important substantive issue turns on where the semantic dividing line is drawn between rules and discretion. A distinction between "rule" and "regime" is less clarifying in technical discourse than in conventional language. In technical discourse describing an analytical model, *any* approximation of the manner in which policymakers define their goals and adjust the settings on their instruments—even a highly complex regime that is unambiguously discretionary (in the sense of conventional language)—will be written technically as a "rule." When economists discuss policy in technical discourse, therefore, it often makes little difference whether they use "regime" or "rule" to describe their analytical

The debate about nonactivist rules versus activist discretion is venerable.[8] But it took on new force and relevance in the 1970s and 1980s, when inflation rates rose dramatically and economic theory began to focus more intensively on expectations, issues of "time consistency" and reputation, and the potential benefits of credible commitment to an announced policy rule. An operating regime announced by policymakers may be described as time consistent if there is no incentive for the policymakers to change the regime even though they are free to do so. If society is afflicted with an inflation bias, it was increasingly argued in the 1970s and 1980s, policymakers acting in the interests of the society should tie their own hands by credible commitment to a rule that will, if followed, prevent inflation. The rationale is analogous to Ulysses's behavior in putting wax in his sailors' ears and having them tie him to the mast as their ship sailed by the Sirens' rocks.

In the early 1990s, the debate about rules and discretion—with its associated themes of commitment, credibility, and time consistency—is one of the most controversial and salient issues about the conduct of economic policies by national governments. That debate partially overlaps with the debate about intermediate-target regimes, moreover, since proponents of intermediate targeting often appeal to the alleged benefits of credible commitments to a simple rule.[9]

Primary Emphasis in This Project

This book does not present a consensus view on all the controversial issues of instrument choice and instrument variation, much less resolve them. In particular, most of the research does not add to the analysis of the potential benefits of credible commitment to policy rules (chapters 7 and 8 are exceptions). Nor does it take a general stand on the relative merits of intermediate-target and single-stage operating regimes.

Rather, the focus of the research is on the stabilization properties of alternative operating regimes. The book's authors study which types of regime may prove most useful and most robust in buffering ultimate-target variables against a variety of nonpolicy shocks.

The stabilization properties of alternative operating regimes are intrinsically important. And they must be assessed alongside the potential benefits of

representations of policy behavior. In some of the chapters in this book (for example, chapters 7, 8, and 11), the authors prefer to use "rule" rather than "regime"; for the purposes of their chapters, "rule" and "regime" are often synonyms.

8. See, for example, Simons (1936) and M. Friedman (1948, 1959).

9. In the recent literature on the issues of rules versus discretion, time consistency, and reputation, the most pertinent references include Kareken, Muench, and Wallace (1973), Kydland and Prescott (1977), Barro and Gordon (1983), Barro (1986), Rogoff (1987), Fischer (1990), Canzoneri (1985), Flood and Isard (1989), and Canzoneri and Henderson (1991). Barro (1986) and Fischer (1990) are helpful overviews.

policymakers' commitment, for credibility and time-consistency reasons, to regimes that are rules or that embody limited scope for discretion. When policymakers choose between regimes, a trade-off may even exist between stabilization and commitment properties (Henderson and Zhu 1990).

The research reported here has been guided by a conviction that an accumulation of empirical knowledge about the stabilization properties of alternative regimes is a necessary (though not sufficient) condition for developing more of a consensus about the appropriate conduct of monetary policy.

Analytical Representations of the Conduct of Monetary Policy

Analysts studying alternative approaches to economic policy must be able to summarize adequately those alternatives when conducting their research. For many alternatives, especially those involving significant discretion, procedures for instrument variation are likely to be complex when implemented in real life. The researcher must nonetheless be able to capture the key features of an approach in a summary analytical representation.

Instrument Choice and Pegging Rules

The theory of economic policy has concentrated more on instrument choice and the choice of intermediate-target variables than on procedures for intertemporal instrument variation. The efforts to compare alternative procedures for instrument variation, moreover, have focused on highly simplified rules.[10] Indeed, the typical goal in theoretical studies has been to evaluate "pegging" rules for alternative choices of the policy instruments or intermediate targets. A *pegging rule* keeps the instrument or intermediate-target variable at an unchanged— "pegged"—setting during the course of the theoretical analysis. This type of study has been presumed to give some guidance for the more complex problems of instrument variation faced by policymakers in real life.

For monetary policy, this theoretical literature concentrated on two prominent debates about instrument choice.[11] Policymakers were construed as se-

10. "Rule" rather than "regime" is the more accurate term here. The focus of the theoretical studies on simplified, nondiscretionary rules can be partially explained by the difficulties that arise in accurately representing, in analytically tractable form, the differences among operating regimes that permit discretionary instrument variation.

11. The language and selection of variables in some of the theoretical studies can be construed as saying that the pegging rules pertain to intermediate targets (for example, the money stock). The theoretical analyses, however, treated these intermediate variables as if policymakers can control them precisely. In actual policymaking, although instruments can be and are controlled precisely ("pegged"), intermediate variables cannot be (see the further discussion below).

lecting, for domestic monetary policy, either a regime that pegs a short-term interest rate or a regime that pegs a monetary-aggregate quantity. The analogous price-versus-quantity selection for external monetary policy was framed as the choice between fixed and flexible exchange rates. Some additional studies also considered a regime in which policymakers attempt to keep the value of nominal GNP unchanged.

Analysis has often proceeded by presuming that policymakers choose an instrument peg and then maintain that peg while various types of shocks occur. Alternatively, the analysis may peg the value of an intermediate-target variable (requiring the actual instrument to change to whatever value is consistent with the peg for the intermediate target). The analysis shows how the alternative pegging rules perform in cushioning ultimate-target variables against the effects of the shocks. The conclusions typically drawn take the generic form that, given a shock of type A, one of the regimes outperforms the others, whereas if a shock of type B occurs, the ranking of preferred regimes may change, with still different rankings possibly being relevant for shocks C or D.

These theoretical studies recognized that economies are buffeted by a variety of shocks, and that shocks cannot be predicted in advance, or even reliably identified until after their occurrence. Hence the problem facing policymakers is, at least in part, to identify regimes that will perform robustly in the face of a variety of unpredictable shocks. Chapter 2 in this book consolidates and extends the traditional theoretical analysis.[12]

Partial Adjustment of Instruments to Targets

The analysis of pegging rules in the context of theoretical models is informative. Yet policymaking alternatives in real life, even those characterized by limited discretion, cannot accurately be described as pegging behavior. Only the values of actual instruments themselves can be pegged (continuously and precisely controlled).

Consider an intermediate-target variable Z—for example, nominal GNP or the broadly defined money stock (inclusive of deposits at private financial institutions). Unlike in theoretical analysis, where the theorist is able to manipulate the model to calculate exactly the amount of instrument adjustment necessary to keep Z at a prescribed (desired) value, the real-life policymaker inevitably experiences slippage between actual and desired values. Given uncertainty about

---

12. This prevailing approach to the analysis of regimes for monetary policy, applied to domestic monetary policy in a closed economy, is usually attributed to Poole (1970). For other contributions, including extension of the analysis to open economies, see for example Boyer (1978), Henderson (1979), Bryant (1980), Henderson (1984), Bean (1983), Taylor (1985), Aizenman and Frenkel (1986), and Argy (1991). Additional references are provided in chapter 2.

the current state of the economy and about how it responds to various shocks and policy actions, the policymaker can never accurately calculate a sequence of instrument settings that would *continuously* prevent significant deviations of Z from a desired target path.

If a temporal reference period for evaluating control is extended to a sufficiently lengthy interval (measured, say, in calendar quarters or years), the policymaker can probably be successful at *average control*. This possibility involves bringing the *average* value of Z, measured over the extended interval, close to the *average* value of its target path for the same period. To achieve this control of the intertemporal average, the policymaker must continuously monitor the inescapable short-run deviations of Z from its target path and make frequent, short-run adjustments in instrument settings to try to move Z toward its average target value. Policymakers wishing to target an intermediate variable in this fashion typically face an awkward trade-off: the more intense the effort to achieve close average control of Z, the greater the likelihood that they must accept higher variability in their instrument settings.

Averaging the value of Z over an extended interval washes out shorter-run fluctuations. Comparing the discrepancy between such an average and the period average of the target path nets temporary overshoots and temporary shortfalls. For example, if Z remains below the target path for several months and then rises above the target path for several months, the averages of actual Z and its target path may be nearly identical for the extended period as a whole. The longer the period over which the averages are taken, the smaller the weight assigned to the variance of Z about the target path.

The concept of average control invites the relatively superficial observation that the policymaker can closely control Z over a longer-run period. This observation is superficial because it entirely begs two important questions: whether, and if so by how much, the variability of Z during the reference period matters; and whether, and if so by how much, the required variability in instrument settings is a matter for concern.

Neither of these two questions arises in the traditional theoretical analysis of pegging rules. The theorist comparing alternative rules, having analytical control of and full information about his model, can achieve *exact targeting* for each Z variable in the alternative rules. Stated another way, the theorist postulates *full instrument adjustment:* policymakers are assumed to change their instrument settings, costlessly, by exactly the amount needed to eliminate any deviation of Z from its desired (pegged) value.

When researchers using empirical models study alternative policy regimes, like the theorists they can try to implement full instrument adjustment in the context of their models. Such pegging of an intermediate-target variable will be possible provided that the model is sufficiently stable to be solved for the requisite change in instrument values.

More frequently, however, researchers with empirical models experiment with *inexact targeting* of the Z variables. That is, they incorporate "reaction functions" (analytical approximations of the policy operating regimes) in the model that assume only *partial instrument adjustment:* policymakers are deemed to adjust their instrument settings so as to reduce partially, but not necessarily to eliminate completely, the deviations of an intermediate-target variable from a desired time path. The assumption of partial rather than full instrument adjustment is common in research with empirical models both because it is thought to correspond better to the actual behavior of policymakers and because an attempt to impose full instrument adjustment leads in many models to problems of instrument instability.

Suppose the following simplified reaction function is being considered for incorporation into an empirical model:

$$X_t = X_{t-1} + \beta(Z_t - Z_t^*).$$

Here X is a policy instrument; Z is the intermediate-target variable; Z^* denotes the desired target value for Z; and β is the policymakers' feedback or response parameter, summarizing the strength of the responsiveness of X to deviations of Z from Z^*. If the feedback coefficient β is set at a very high (in the limit, infinite) value and if the model behaves stably under this assumption, simulations with the model will result in nearly exact targeting of Z (virtually full instrument adjustment). Alternatively, with β set at a finite value, Z will be targeted inexactly. The smaller in absolute size is β, the more partial will be the extent of instrument adjustment.

Need for Empirical Research on Policy Regimes

Most of the research done so far to evaluate alternative policy regimes has been theoretical rather than empirical. The theoretical research has yielded much insight. Some of it is a precondition for useful further research.

Yet theoretical analysis alone, conducted in terms of highly simplified models with the assumption of full instrument adjustment, cannot resolve all the issues at stake. Only after the robustness of alternative approaches to policy has been carefully examined in the context of a range of more comprehensive empirical models will a convergence of views become possible. As stressed at the beginning of this overview, the present volume is an effort to redress the paucity in previous research of empirical analyses of alternative policy regimes.

The empirical research here uses the techniques of both deterministic and stochastic simulation, with an emphasis on the latter. The distinction between deterministic and stochastic simulations and the basic ideas underlying stochastic simulation are summarized later in this chapter. Chapters 3 and 5 provide a comprehensive overview.

Economic Policymaking and Uncertainty

As policymakers conduct economic policy, they and their advisers confront great uncertainty. They require some analytical framework that describes the links between their instrument settings and the behavior of ultimate-target variables. Yet there is no consensus, either within or outside the economic profession, on the most appropriate way of characterizing an economy's behavior.

The Competing-Model Problem

Rival models are put forward, often embodying significantly different analytical views. Basic disagreements exist, for example, about how to summarize the behavior of private economic agents, how to describe the behavior of the policy authorities themselves, how to treat expectations of future economic developments, and how to specify assumptions for the current and future values of the driving forces not treated endogenously in a model. Policymakers will accordingly be uncertain about which of the competing models represents the least inadequate approximation of the "true" model (the actual relationships that will in reality determine the consequences of their actions).

Such analytical ignorance and controversy—for brevity, "model uncertainty"—is a major obstacle to sound policymaking. Model uncertainty is a critical issue in most or all scientific and quasi-scientific disciplines. It is arguably the paramount issue in the conduct of macroeconomic policy.

When considering the competing-model problem, one should at the outset dismiss a point of view that, while often encountered, undermines constructive thinking about model uncertainty. This unconstructive response is that, since all existing models are seriously defective, they should all, at least for the time being, be discarded and ignored.

Policymakers necessarily rely on some form of analytical model. Models can be explicit and systematic (for example, models whose builders have tried to design them in accordance with best-practice theory and econometric techniques). Or models can be casually, sometimes even carelessly, devised—or even implicitly presumed (for example, a back-of-envelope incomplete sketch). Modeling attempts, in other words, can be more or less successful. Yet a model of *some* sort is a logical prerequisite for decisions by policymakers on what to do with their instruments.

The logical necessity for some type of analytical model is not acknowledged by those who argue that all existing models are so uncertain and unreliable that policymakers should avoid using any of them. Yet a moment's reflection is sufficient to see that such an attitude is a foolish reaction to the problem of model uncertainty. Were a policymaker to insist that he makes decisions without relying on any type of model, he would be lying, quibbling over semantics, or severely deceiving himself. It is plainly not a realistic option for policymakers simply to ignore all models. They cannot set all their policy instruments at "zero" values, so to speak, and decide to have no policy at all. If a policymaker chooses to ignore all explicit models, in essence he chooses to use an implicit model—which is typically still more flawed and unreliable than the explicit models. Explicit models can at least be analyzed, criticized, and improved. Implicit models can be badly wrong, and can stay wrong because they are not subjected to criticism.

The only sensible responses to the competing-model problem are to conduct better evaluations of existing models, to improve the existing models (or to build new improved ones), and—in the meantime while attempts at model evaluation and improvement are going forward—to learn how better to select and combine the existing models in current policy analysis. The emphasis in this project on model comparison and evaluation, as was true for its predecessor projects, stems from the conviction that research along these lines is a necessary precondition for improving economic policymaking under uncertainty.

Implications of Model Uncertainty for Policy Choice

The competing claims of rival models and the other dimensions of model uncertainty would not vex policymakers greatly if policymakers could safely downplay uncertainty. But they cannot safely do so. In any practical policy situation, uncertainty should be explicitly taken into account when formulating and implementing decisions.

Uncertainty about the consequences of policymakers' own actions—about the time paths of the policy "multipliers" associated with the policymakers' instruments—is an especially critical type of uncertainty. In contrast with other forms of uncertainty for which it may sometimes be sensible to form expectations of the uncertain coefficients or variables and treat those expected values as if they were certain, policymakers should never ignore uncertainty about policy multipliers. Even if it were feasible to use policy doses of any size (which of course it is not), it would be inappropriate to select those instrument settings that would be dictated by focusing on only the expected values of multipliers and ignoring their variances and covariances. All available instruments should be fully utilized, moreover, no matter how few the target variables that are the objective of policy and no matter how plentiful the number of instruments. As a general presumption, the more uncertain are its multipliers, the less aggressively should an individual policy instrument be used. More broadly stated, the greater the uncertainty associated with the values of policy multipliers, the less active policymakers should be in adjusting the settings on their instruments.[13]

---

13. The basic reference for these generalizations is the seminal article by Brainard (1967). Many subsequent researchers have confirmed the importance of this line of inquiry.

The International Dimensions of Uncertainty

Even policymakers in a hypothetical, completely closed national economy would be confounded by numerous types of "domestic" uncertainty. Increasingly, however, "international" uncertainties associated with the interdependence of national economies have been growing in relative importance.

Despite the pervasive trend toward increasing interdependence in the world economy, neither policymakers, businessmen, nor economists have developed a commonly accepted analytical framework for assessing the macroeconomic interactions among national economies. Consequently, little analytical agreement exists about how policy actions and nonpolicy disturbances originating in one nation spill across borders to influence economic developments in other nations. This lack of agreement is even more pronounced than the disagreement among analysts about how individual national economies behave.

Increasing economic interdependence would substantially complicate policymaking even if governments had reliable estimates of the cross-border spillovers. Typically, larger cross-border spillovers reduce the effects of a country's policy instruments on national variables relative to their effects on variables in other countries, and hence reduce the autonomy of home economic policy. Externally originating forces constrain the ability of a government to achieve its goals, thereby diminishing the degree of control that a nation's policymakers can exert over national target variables. The closer intertwining of economies renders policy decisions in any single nation more difficult (Bryant 1980).

The difficulties for policy are still greater because of the great uncertainty about the empirical magnitudes, and sometimes even the directions, of the cross-border spillovers. A nation's policymakers know that policy actions and nonpolicy shocks originating abroad will constrain their own policy choices, and that their actions will alter outcomes and policy choices abroad, but in forms and magnitudes that cannot be well estimated. In such circumstances of enhanced uncertainty, appropriate decisionmaking becomes especially difficult.

Inadequate empirical knowledge about the functioning of the world economy is also a serious impediment to any attempts to achieve intergovernmental cooperation for economic policies. Theorists have shown a strong presumptive case for governments sometimes cooperating in framing their individual national policies, thereby internalizing external diseconomies and hence avoiding Pareto-suboptimal outcomes that could otherwise result. But how can governments cooperate when existing knowledge about how countries' actions influence each other is so uncertain? More of a consensus about the direction and quantitative size of cross-border interactions is a necessary—albeit far from sufficient—condition for significant progress in facilitating cooperation for national macroeconomic policies.

The preceding points all lead to the conclusion that an improved analytical understanding of macroeconomic interactions among national economies—a compelling illustration of the general need for progress in model evaluation and improvement—must be achieved before policymakers and analysts can hope to resolve the many controversial issues that afflict the conduct of macroeconomic policies. Unquestionably, progress in evaluating alternative policy regimes requires this improved understanding.

Summary of This Project

The first in the sequence of model-evaluation research projects sponsored by the Brookings Institution originated in 1984, led to a major conference in 1986, and resulted in the publication of *Empirical Macroeconomics for Interdependent Economies (EMIE)*.[14] One offshoot of this initial project was the establishment of an informal network among the modeling groups around the world that were constructing or maintaining empirical multicountry models. The *EMIE* project also established the viability and usefulness of getting model groups to prepare simulations under commonly specified assumptions, thereby facilitating evaluation and comparison of the models' strengths and weaknesses.

The collaborative research was extended in 1987 with a workshop devoted to the imbalance in the current account of the U.S. balance of payments. Model groups and other participants analyzed the reasons for the U.S. external deficit and evaluated policy options for correcting it. Model simulations prepared under commonly specified assumptions were again used to study the issues.[15]

Most of the same model groups participated in a further conference held in May 1988 under the auspices of the Board of Governors of the Federal Reserve System. The focus of the research presented there was on the financial structures of national economies and the cross-border consequences of changes in monetary policies. Model-based empirical analysis featured prominently in the conference papers, published subsequently as *Financial Sectors in Open Economies* (Hooper and others 1990).

At a conference in December 1988, with many of the modeling groups again represented, papers were presented that consolidated or extended the earlier work. Three of the papers used the techniques of stochastic simulation

14. Bryant, Henderson, and others (1988). Empirical research on the international linkages of economies has a long history. References to pioneering efforts in the early decades following World War II and to, for example, the research sponsored by Project LINK are given in the first chapter of *EMIE*.

15. The results of the research are described in *External Deficits and the Dollar: The Pit and the Pendulum* (Bryant, Holtham, and Hooper 1988).

to evaluate alternative policy regimes.[16] These papers attracted considerable interest, not least among the other modeling groups. In the spring of 1989, consultations were held among the modeling groups about further collaborative research. By the summer of 1989 it had been decided to hold a working conference in March 1990 to emphasize the comparison of alternative regimes for monetary policy. The conference was to have not only the substantive goal of evaluating policy regimes but also a procedural goal: to explore the techniques of stochastic simulation and to initiate a cross-model comparison of stochastic simulation results.

Stochastic Simulation

How do the techniques of stochastic simulation differ from the more familiar techniques of deterministic simulation? The essence of the difference is simple. To solve an empirical model, some assumption must be made about the error terms ("residuals") appearing in its behavioral equations. When only a single set of values for the residuals is used (including the assumption that the residuals are zero), the simulation is said to be deterministic. In contrast, when a researcher uses many sets of values for the residuals and solves the model for each set, the resulting collection of model outcomes is described as a stochastic simulation.[17]

In deterministic simulations, the residuals in the model equations are typically held constant at the values that, in the absence of the experimental shock being studied, would force the model to track baseline or historical values of endogenous variables.[18] For stochastic simulations, in contrast, it is typically necessary to make assumptions about the probability distribution of the residuals. The required probability distribution can be generated from historical data for a particular sample period. Alternatively, it can be generated in some other manner to reflect a pattern of residuals thought to be appropriate given the analytical issues motivating the study. Once the pattern of residuals (technically, the variance-covariance matrix of the residuals) has been chosen, the researcher then makes N repeated "draws" of the sets of residuals and, for each of the

16. The papers from the December 1988 conference were published in Bryant, Currie, and others, eds., *Macroeconomic Policies for an Interdependent World* (Brookings, Centre for Economic Policy Research, and IMF 1989). The papers that presented results for stochastic simulation are those by Frenkel, Goldstein, and Masson (1989), Taylor (1989), and McKibbin and Sachs (1989). Bryant, Helliwell, and Hooper (1989) consolidated the comparative empirical results available at the time of the December 1988 conference.

17. A more complex type of stochastic simulation can postulate alternative sets of values for both the residuals of the model and its estimated coefficients. The stochastic simulation experiments discussed in this book entail only alternative sets of values for the model residuals. For general background on the solution of empirical macroeconomic models, see Fair (1984, chap. 7).

18. If the shock being studied takes the form of a change in one or a few of the model's residuals, the residuals in all the remaining model equations are held constant at the values that would cause the model, in the absence of the shock, to replicate the baseline.

N draws, derives a new solution for the endogenous variables in the model. By analyzing the values for key variables across the N individual model solutions taken together—for example, calculating the root-mean-squared deviation of a key ultimate-target variable from a given baseline value—the researcher can summarize the properties of the stochastic simulation as a whole. (The stochastic simulation is thus a collection of N comparably designed deterministic simulations, with N being a number sufficiently large to make the summary properties of the stochastic simulation insensitive to the value of N.) The details of stochastic simulation techniques are discussed in chapter 3 below.

The potential benefits of using stochastic rather than merely deterministic simulations are especially compelling when the objective of the research is—as in this volume—to compare and evaluate alternative policy regimes. Policy-makers need to be, and typically are, interested not only in the estimated mean effects of nonpolicy shocks and of their own policy actions; they also need estimates of the possible variance of outcomes. In effect, they require analysis of the robustness of the ranking of alternative policy regimes to different drawings from the mix of shocks and policy actions that can be experienced by the economy. The traditional presentation of mean paths for macroeconomic variables with the paths contingent on a particular shock or policy action—obtained from a single deterministic simulation of a model—does not capture any of the uncertainty associated with the mean paths. Nor does a single deterministic simulation of a particular policy regime shed light on the robustness of that regime. The techniques of stochastic simulation, by virtue of their using a large number of different types of shocks, can reveal much more about the likely performance of a regime in the face of the variety of shocks characteristic of the real world.

Policy Regimes Used in the Study

Although conceptually appealing, the techniques of stochastic simulation have not yet become widely used in empirical policy analysis. For one thing, the techniques are computationally intensive. Another impediment to their more widespread use has been a lack of consensus on some of the details of the procedures to be followed (see chapter 3). For those reasons, and because of widespread questions about the adequacy of empirical models, it was apparent at the outset of planning for this project that the design of the simulations would have to be simple. In particular, prospective participants agreed that the types of policy regimes to be studied with stochastic simulation would have to be limited in number and highly simplified in design.

In that spirit, a collective decision was taken to focus on regimes for monetary policy alone (rather than for both monetary and fiscal policies), and to select a small number of simple regimes for monetary policy. These regimes could serve as benchmarks for analytical comparison but, of course, would not be intended as realistic representations of how monetary policy is or should be conducted in actual practice. Similarly, the decision not to include alternative regimes for fiscal policy was driven solely by the need to keep the exercise simplified and manageable; in no way did it presume that alternative fiscal regimes are unimportant either practically or analytically.

Four simplified monetary-policy regimes were selected for empirical study: a version of money targeting, nominal-income targeting, a regime that targets the sum of real GNP and the inflation rate, and a particular form of exchange-rate targeting. For all four regimes, the short-term rate of interest was specified as the primary instrument for monetary policy. Each regime can be interpreted as an intermediate-target regime, with (respectively) the money stock, nominal GNP, real GNP plus inflation, and a bilateral dollar exchange rate as the key intermediate-target variable. Chapter 3 gives detailed information about these regimes and about how they were implemented in the empirical models.

Chapter 2 presents a theoretical analysis of these four regimes (plus a fifth, interest-rate targeting). In chapter 2, the regimes are implemented in the form of the pegging rules traditionally used in the theoretical literature. Stated in terms of the definitions presented earlier, the theoretical analysis postulates full instrument adjustment (exact targeting). In contrast, in the remainder of the book the empirical implementation of the policy regimes incorporates partial instrument adjustment (inexact targeting). As will become clear in part 2, the differences between full and partial instrument adjustment are sometimes highly significant for interpreting differences between the theoretical conclusions in chapter 2 and the empirical results in chapters 4 and 5.

Participating Models

Consultations about the project were held with a large number of prominent teams actively maintaining empirical multicountry models. Detailed guidelines for the preparation of commonly specified simulations were circulated in the summer of 1989. In the event, initial results for stochastic simulations were prepared by early 1990 for eight models. These models, and in alphabetical order the mnemonics used to refer to them in this book, are

> **GEM:** A version of the Global Economic Model developed by the National Institute for Economic and Social Research (NIESR) in London and jointly maintained with the London Business School (LBS). Ray Barrell and David Currie, working with colleagues from both the NIESR and LBS, coordinated the model simulations prepared for the project.

INTERMOD: A policy-simulation model originally developed by a Canadian team under the direction of John Helliwell (following the IMF effort to construct MULTIMOD), sponsored by the Canadian Department of Finance and subsequently supported also by the Bank of Canada. Two versions of the model were used (see below). Guy Meredith and Mary MacGregor managed the models for this project.

LIVERPOOL: The model developed by Patrick Minford and several associates at the University of Liverpool.

MPS: The model, primarily of the U.S. economy but also with an external sector, developed by the domestic divisions of the Federal Reserve Board (following earlier work by teams of economists at MIT, the University of Pennsylvania, and the Federal Reserve, financed by the Social Science Research Council). Flint Brayton and colleagues ran the simulations for this project.

MSG: An updated version of a policy-simulation model originally developed by Warwick McKibbin and Jeffrey Sachs at Harvard University, run for the purposes of this project by Warwick McKibbin at the Brookings Institution.

MULTIMOD: The policy-simulation model developed in the Research Department of the International Monetary Fund, managed for this project by Paul Masson and Steven Symansky.

MX3: A policy-simulation model developed in the Division of International Finance of the Federal Reserve Board and managed for this project by Joseph Gagnon and Ralph Tryon.

TAYLOR: The multicountry policy-simulation model developed by John Taylor and associates at Stanford University, run for this project by Peter Klenow.

A number of other modeling groups were also consulted during the preparation of the conference in 1989. Because of the intensive computations required to carry out the suggested stochastic simulations, or because of other pressing demands on their work schedules, these other groups were unable to join fully in the exercise. Representatives of many of these groups, however, attended the subsequent conference—held at Brookings on March 8–9, 1990—and participated in the dialogue.

Four of the participating models—GEM, MPS, MX3, and TAYLOR—have a quarterly periodicity. The remaining models—INTERMOD, LIVERPOOL, MSG, and MULTIMOD—are annual. The MPS model in the version used for the project treats expectations adaptively. The LIVERPOOL, MSG, MULTIMOD, MX3, and TAYLOR models treat expectations as model-consistent (rational). The INTERMOD model can treat expectations either as adaptive or model-consistent, and that modeling group submitted simulations for both versions of the model (referred to, respectively, as INTERMOD-A and INTERMOD-C). The GEM model uses forward-looking expectations in its treatment of exchange rates and adaptive expectations for the other variables. The participating models have noteworthy differences in country and regional coverage and in their specifications of macroeconomic behavior, and these are discussed in the chapters that follow.

Deterministic Simulations

By the time of the conference held in March 1990, some preliminary analysis had been done on the stochastic simulations, and a preconference overview had been prepared. Extensive discussion of the results took place at the conference.

The conference organizers and a large majority of the modeling groups and discussants, however, felt hampered in their interpretation of the stochastic simulation results by not having access to deterministic simulations for selected key shocks. After further consultation at the conference and in subsequent weeks, therefore, it was decided to ask the modeling groups to prepare some deterministic simulations for the project. These simulations were to be generated with the same policy regimes used for the stochastic simulations. The shocks studied in the deterministic simulations were chosen so as to shed light on the consistency between theory and the empirical models and to elucidate differences across the models.

These deterministic simulations were carried out and sent to the project organizers in the summer and fall of 1990. In addition to results from the eight model groups listed above, another model group also submitted deterministic simulations:

MCM: The Multicountry Model developed by the staff of the Division of International Finance of the Federal Reserve Board, with Jaime Marquez responsible for generating the simulations.

The group responsible for the INTERLINK model developed and maintained in the Economics and Statistics Department of the Organization for Economic Cooperation and Development (OECD) in Paris, led by Pete Richardson, was unable to submit stochastic or deterministic simulations for the collaborative research. That group, however, did participate in the planning for the project. And Richardson analyzes deterministic simulations conducted with the INTERLINK model in chapter 12 of this volume.

During the final months of 1990 and in 1991–92, considerable further work was done to digest and interpret the large body of empirical results prepared for the project. Dale Henderson and Warwick McKibbin worked together to summarize, and to extend, the theoretical knowledge pertinent for interpretation of the empirical results. Ralph Bryant, Peter Hooper, and Catherine Mann worked together to provide further evaluation and interpretation of the empirical data for the deterministic and stochastic simulations. This extensive postconference analysis is summarized in part 2 of the book.

Guide to the Book

Apart from this overview chapter, the book is divided into four further parts. The first is a detailed comparison and evaluation of the simulation experiments prepared for the project, preceded by an analysis that reviews and extends existing theory (part 2). The next three parts contain revised and edited versions of papers originally prepared for the 1990 conference. One group of papers contains applications of the techniques of stochastic simulation to the evaluation of monetary-policy regimes (part 3). Another group uses other approaches to study regimes for monetary policy (part 4). A further set of papers applies or extends the techniques of stochastic simulation to particular economic sectors (part 5). In addition, two annexes to the book provide selected reference tables.

The discussion that follows here identifies the chapters of the book and indicates the ground that each covers. We do not try to summarize the main points and conclusions of a chapter. Rather, our purpose is merely to provide the reader with a guide to the volume.

Contents of Part 2

The initial contribution toward understanding the simulation experiments is "An Assessment of Some Basic Monetary-Policy Regime Pairs: Analytical and Simulation Results from Simple Multiregion Macroeconomic Models," by Dale W. Henderson and Warwick J. McKibbin (chapter 2). This paper provides a review and extensions of the theoretical literature on policy regimes in the tradition of Poole (1970). Of special value for this project, the authors focus on the case of two open economies interacting with each other. Their analysis compares the performance of five regimes—interest-rate targeting, money targeting, nominal-income targeting, real-GNP-plus-inflation targeting, and a version of exchange-rate targeting—when economies experience shocks to money demand, goods demand, productivity, and the exchange rate. Henderson and McKibbin use a theoretical model that can include oil as an intermediate production input; they can therefore also consider oil shocks in their analysis. The initial sections of the chapter solve variants of their expositional model analytically. Later sections use the techniques of numerical simulation to solve the model, enabling the authors to extend their conclusions to alternative specifications of wage and price dynamics. Readers will find this chapter a basic reference source on the theory of open-economy policy regimes in addition to its role in providing theoretical background for the interpretation of the empirical research in this volume.

Chapter 3, "Design and Implementation of the Empirical Simulations," prepared by Ralph C. Bryant, Peter Hooper, and Catherine L. Mann, describes the empirical research done for the project and provides the necessary background for its interpretation. The chapter summarizes some contrasting features of the participating models, defines the alternative policy regimes, presents the design for the stochastic and the deterministic simulations, and identifies problems of comparability arising from the way in which the stochastic and deterministic simulations were implemented. The chapter also reviews the basic mechanics of stochastic simulation techniques and discusses differences in detailed application of the techniques as followed by the participating model groups.

Chapter 4, "Deterministic Simulations with Simple Policy Regimes," is an analytical survey prepared by Peter Hooper and Ralph C. Bryant. Using the deterministic simulations generated for the project, the analysis assesses the comparative performance of the alternative regimes for monetary policy in the face of different types of shocks to aggregate demand, aggregate supply, and the demand for money. The main emphasis is on a few key ultimate-target variables—real GNP, employment, the price level and inflation, interest rates, and exchange rates—for the three largest industrial countries: the United States, Japan, and Germany. Drawing on a variety of interpretive charts and tables, the analysis seeks to identify some degree of consensus about the properties of the regimes across the participating models. The chapter also discusses the degree to which the model-based deterministic simulations conform to the predictions of theory as surveyed by Henderson and McKibbin in chapter 2.

In "Stochastic Simulations with Simple Policy Regimes" (chapter 5), Ralph C. Bryant, Catherine L. Mann, and Peter Hooper continue the evaluation of the empirical results prepared for the project, but with a focus on the stochastic simulations. The chapter presents the simulation results in a cross-model, comparative context and interprets them in the light of the theory summarized in chapter 2 and the deterministic simulations surveyed in chapter 4. The discussion focuses both on individual models and on the general tendencies across all the participating models, identifying consensus where possible but also noting the main exceptions and contrasts.

When the analyses of chapters 2, 4, and 5 are taken together, some relatively robust conclusions about the alternative regimes do emerge. The most important of these conclusions are summarized in the final sections of this overview chapter. The three chapters themselves also contain concluding sections summarizing some of their key points.

The analytical approaches of chapters 2, 4, and 5 are complementary, sharing some things in common but differing in others. The theory in chapter

2 stems from a simplified and stylized version of the empirical macroeconomic models that generated the simulations for chapters 4 and 5. Given the differing nature of the techniques, deterministic and stochastic simulations necessarily yield somewhat different types of conclusions. Although chapters 2, 4, and 5 discuss the relevant issues in detail, we call the reader's attention here to several contrasting aspects of the approaches in these chapters. First, the theoretical exposition in chapter 2 specifies a three-region world where the "United States" and the "Rest of the OECD" are oil-consuming regions that are mirror images of each other; the third highly simplified region, "OPEC," is the oil producer. In contrast, the empirical models incorporate a larger number of country or regional blocks (although differences in the degree of country/regional aggregation among the empirical models themselves are also great). Some of the empirical models explicitly model OPEC oil producers, although still only in a sketchy way. Second, chapter 2's theory examines monetary policy regimes under five alternative hypotheses about how wages and prices are set. Wages are intertemporally sticky under each hypothesis. Under four of the five hypotheses, prices are perfectly flexible; under the fifth, however, prices too are sticky. The empirical models incorporate varying degrees of wage and price stickiness. As already noted, the empirical models also differ among themselves in the treatment of expectations as adaptive or model-consistent (rational). Third, the theoretical model of chapter 2 assumes full instrument adjustment (exact targeting), whereas the empirical simulations implement feedback equations that embody only partial instrument adjustment. Finally, the theory in chapter 2 and the analysis of the deterministic simulations in chapter 4 both study situations in which the nonpolicy shocks that occur are explicitly and clearly defined. The nonpolicy shocks underlying the stochastic simulations analyzed in chapter 5 cannot be explicitly and clearly categorized. For each empirical model, the stochastic shocks stem from the entire set of historical residuals; because of differences in the models' structures, the stochastic shocks differ significantly from one model to another.

Chapter 6 is a compendium of selected comments and reflections from invited contributors. These individuals—John Helliwell, John Taylor, Christopher Sims, Bennett McCallum, Ray Fair, and Donald Kohn—attended the March 1990 conference and offered comments then on what had and had not been achieved by the project to that time. Each of these contributors was also given an opportunity to read drafts of chapters 1 through 5, the material subsequently generated to interpret and evaluate the project.

Contents of Part 3

The papers in part 3 apply the techniques of stochastic simulation to the evaluation of monetary-policy regimes or deal with other analytical aspects of stochastic simulations.

Paul R. Masson and Steven A. Symansky, in "Evaluating Policy Regimes under Imperfect Credibility" (chapter 7), focus on the possibility that private-sector expectations of policy behavior can be strongly influenced by the reputation of policymakers and by the credibility of their operating regime. (In contrast, most of the empirical data generated for this project were based on the working assumption that the postulated policy regimes were fully credible.) With their MULTIMOD model, Masson and Symansky implement an index of credibility designed to reflect the probability that a policy regime in force may be abandoned in favor of a simple alternative regime. Their analysis offers suggestive evidence that the performance of policy regimes can be significantly influenced by the endogenous formation of private-sector expectations.

Chapter 8, "The Importance of Federal Reserve Credibility: Evidence from the TAYLOR Model" by Peter J. Klenow, also addresses issues of policymakers' credibility, but in this case with an emphasis on the empirical importance of the time-inconsistency problem. Klenow conducts stochastic simulations with the TAYLOR model, focusing on Federal Reserve policy in the United States and on nominal-income targeting as the preferred policy regime. He investigates the incentives that the Federal Reserve has to deviate from the preferred policy regime by surprising private-sector agents, thereby generating higher than optimal inflation. His paper offers empirical estimates of the possible magnitude of "excess inflation" that may result when the Federal Reserve cannot credibly commit itself to a nominal-GNP target consistent with the optimal inflation rate.

During the period 1989–90, a small multicountry simulation model known as MX3 was developed in the Division of International Finance at the Federal Reserve Board. Chapter 9, "Stochastic Behavior of the World Economy under Alternative Policy Regimes," is an essay by Joseph E. Gagnon and Ralph W. Tryon that uses stochastic simulation techniques with the MX3 model to examine the simple policy regimes proposed for this project. After describing the structure and theoretical underpinnings of the model, the paper analyzes the properties of the model's forecasts under alternative policy regimes for the ten years following the estimation period. The paper also discusses the construction of true model residuals during the estimation period.

Chapter 10, "Stochastic Simulations of Alternative Monetary Regimes Using the McKibbin-Sachs Global (MSG2) Model" by Warwick J. McKibbin, is another application of stochastic simulation techniques to the problem of evaluating simplified regimes for monetary policy. McKibbin uses the model developed jointly by himself and Jeffrey Sachs as the analytical framework into which the alternative monetary regimes are embedded. Among other issues, McKibbin compares the simplified regimes studied in this project with more complex regimes derived by optimization techniques. Because of the problem of time consistency associated with the complex "optimal" discretionary regimes, commitment to a simplified regime can deliver relatively large gains in credibility, which in turn can lead to better performance of the simplified regime. This dominance of the simplified over the "optimal" regime can occur despite the greater flexibility of the latter in adjusting to shocks.

Several of the greatest obstacles encountered when trying to conduct stochastic simulations with a large multicountry model stem from the sheer size of the model; the difficulties of specifying the shocks to be used and the computational burdens of carrying out the calculations tend to increase more than proportionately with the number of a model's behavioral equations. Accordingly, it can be very useful, when feasible, to carry out such calculations with a smaller, structural representation (a "maquette") of the larger model. Chapter 11, "Policy Analysis and Model Reduction Techniques" by a team of authors working with the GEM model (Nicos Christodoulakis, David Currie, Anthony Garratt, David Kemball-Cook, Paul Levine, Ray Barrell, Jonathan Ireland, and Peter Westaway), addresses this problem. The authors produce a smaller, linearized version of GEM—referred to as MINIGEM—and discuss the linearization algorithm used to do so. The paper then reports the results of carrying out some simple policy analyses with the linear MINIGEM.

Contents of Part 4

The initial paper in part 4, chapter 12, is an essay by Pete Richardson entitled "Simulating the OECD INTERLINK Model under Alternative Monetary-Policy Regimes." Richardson uses the OECD's INTERLINK model, for which he has had immediate supervisory responsibility in recent years, as a laboratory for studying a variety of possible simplified monetary-policy regimes, including variants of the regimes suggested for this project. The approach followed is to conduct carefully chosen deterministic simulations that bring out the contrasting consequences of the postulated regimes. Richardson finds that simple monetary-policy regimes in the context of the INTERLINK model can be used to stabilize output and inflation responses. As for experiments with other models, however, the stabilizing properties are sensitive to the type of shocks studied, and the trade-offs among target variables can be better mediated by more flexible and realistic specifications of the regimes.

In their paper "The European Monetary System: Achievements and Survival" (chapter 13), Andrew Hughes Hallett, Patrick Minford, and Anupam Rastogi use the LIVERPOOL world model to study the interaction of monetary policies with the exchange-rate system in force in Europe since the late 1970s. They focus on the likely relative stability of several alternative designs for the European Monetary System (EMS), basing their inferences on simulations of the model and strategic optimization algorithms used in conjunction with it. Their analysis suggests that the use of national monetary policies under the existing EMS may generate unstable outcomes for the economies. They argue that flexibility in intra-European exchange rates would permit independent monetary policies without concomitant instability, or would at least produce—whatever assumptions are made about monetary policies (for example, cooperation by EMS central banks, cooperation among central banks on a worldwide scale, or implementation of completely rigid money supply rules)—markedly less instability than generated by the EMS exchange-rate arrangements. The authors believe their analysis to hold for a wide range of variations in assumed EMS arrangements, including capital controls, limited or no parity changes, and negligible wage sensitivity to devaluation risk. They therefore conclude that exchange rate flexibility would be a superior European regime.[19]

Contents of Part 5

The final papers in the book address diverse subjects but share an interest in applying or extending stochastic simulation techniques to difficult analytical problems in economics.

Jaime Marquez and Neil R. Ericsson, in their paper "Evaluating Forecasts of the U.S. Trade Balance" (chapter 14), generalize existing methodology for evaluating model forecasts and apply the methodology to forecasts from six econometric models of the U.S. merchandise trade balance. The authors argue that forecast errors from deterministic simulations are an unreliable basis for assessing model performance. They show that forecasts generated by stochastic simulation are a computationally feasible alternative that can allow for uncertainty not only from disturbances but also from coefficient estimation. The paper derives confidence intervals and forecast-based test statistics; the estimates of the confidence intervals are large and generally increasing with the forecast horizon. In the authors' view, model-based forecasts must be seen as random variables; accounting for their distributional properties is thus essential for appropriate interpretation of the forecasts.

Chapter 15 is an essay by Flint Brayton, William Kan, Peter A. Tinsley, and Peter von zur Muehlen entitled "Modeling and Policy Use of Auction Price Expectations." It is often presumed that auction prices—for example, primary commodity prices and the term structure of interest rates—embody agents' expectations of future inflation. Hence analysts have proposed auction price indexes as indicators for short-run monetary policy. The aim of this essay is to evaluate these proposals empirically, making use of stochastic simulations performed with the MPS econometric model of the U.S. economy. For one set

---

19. At the original conference at which first drafts of the papers in this volume were initially presented, Peter Pauly and Christian Petersen presented a draft paper entitled "Monetary Feedback Rules for Oil Price Shocks and Defense Cuts." This paper reported simulations carried out with a version of the GEM model. The paper could not be included in this volume because the authors, owing to pressing other commitments, were unable to revise the paper in time for this volume's publication.

of stochastic policy experiments, in which expectations are based on historical autoregressions, the authors find commodity prices to be moderately useful as policy indicators in circumstances where aggregate measurements of current economic activity are reported with a lag. For a second set of simulation experiments, the authors based expectations on autoregressions estimated with data generated by simulation so as to be consistent with each monetary-policy rule analyzed. Accounting for the policy dependence of agents' expectations in this manner does not appreciably alter the authors' evaluation of the relative performance of the alternative policies.

Appraising the sustainability of a nation's external payments imbalances, including the consequences of such imbalances for trends in the nation's exchange rate, is fraught with analytical difficulties. Ellen Meade and Charles Thomas tackle this subject for the United States in chapter 16, "Using External Sustainability to Forecast the Dollar." The authors reject the current-account approach taken in several earlier studies, in part because those studies did not allow for substantial uncertainties about the appropriate model of the current account, the preferences of foreign investors for U.S. assets, and the determination of exchange rates. Their own approach, making use of stochastic simulation techniques, emphasizes external sustainability not in terms of a particular value for the dollar but rather in terms of a range of values. The authors conclude that the levels of the dollar prevailing at the time their paper was written "are likely to be well within the 'sustainable' range."

Annexes

The volume concludes with reference tables for the various model simulations generated for the project. Annex A supplements the material in chapter 4 with tables that provide summary statistics for key variables generated in the deterministic simulations. Annex B contains reference tables for the stochastic simulations, providing further background detail for the discussion in chapter 5.

Generalizations from the Project Research

This project, uniquely, uses three different approaches to analyze the questions of how an economy responds to shocks and which monetary policy regime best stabilizes macroeconomic variables in the face of shocks. Each approach— theoretical analysis, empirical deterministic simulations, and empirical stochastic simulations—generates somewhat different insights into the main questions. Remarkable similarity, however, exists in the overall conclusions.

In what follows, we identify several points made in part 2 of the book that warrant highlighting in this overview of the project. These generalizations appear to be robust despite the great diversity among the structures of the participating models and despite some nonstandardized aspects of the empirical experiments. The hope of reaching such robust generalizations is, of course, the primary motivation for undertaking this type of research.

Overall Performance of Nominal-Income Targeting and Real-GNP-plus-Inflation Targeting

One conclusion about regime preference, already identified in the initial paragraphs of this chapter, emerges clearly from all three approaches used in this study. Either nominal-income targeting or real-GNP-plus-inflation targeting, in contrast to money targeting or exchange-rate targeting, best stabilizes national economies if the loss functions of policymakers stress real ultimate-target variables such as output or employment, or if the loss functions stress a combination of such real variables and nominal ultimate-target variables such as the rate of inflation or the price level. This preference for either nominal-income targeting or real-GNP-plus-inflation targeting is evident in a large majority of the cases studied in the theoretical analysis. In the deterministic simulations, one or the other of these regimes is preferred in nearly three-fourths of the shock/model/country combinations considered. The proportion of cases favoring these regimes is even higher—more than five-sixths—in the stochastic simulations.[20]

The preference for nominal-income targeting or real-GNP-plus-inflation targeting—and more specifically, the preference against money targeting—is strongest of all for money-demand shocks. In both the theoretical analysis and the deterministic simulations, money-demand shocks are always best neutralized under one or the other of these two regimes.

Across the major countries considered in the empirical analysis, the preference for nominal-income targeting or real-GNP-plus-inflation targeting appears strongest for the United States. For Germany and Japan, regime preferences are somewhat more mixed; exchange-rate targeting is sometimes preferred to nominal-income targeting or real-GNP-plus-inflation targeting.

Situations leading to departures from the overall generalization about regime preference also appear to be consistent across the three methodological approaches. The theoretical analysis suggests, and the two types of empirical simulation tend to confirm, that money targeting or exchange-rate targeting could be the preferred regime under one or (especially) several of the following

---

20. As will be explained and emphasized in later chapters, "preferred regime" is used as shorthand for indicating the regime type with smallest deviations from baseline in the analyses conducted for this project. This shorthand does not prejudge in any way the critical issue of which variables are, or should be, included in policymakers' loss functions.

three conditions: (1) if productivity or other supply shocks are the most prevalent disturbances to economies, (2) if policymakers' loss functions place great weight on stabilization of the inflation rate or the price level and place little or no weight on stabilization of output or employment, and (3) if policymakers' loss functions give significant weight to the stabilization of financial variables such as interest rates and exchange rates.

Stabilizing the Inflation Rate versus Stabilizing the Price Level

Nominal-income targeting and real-GNP-plus-inflation targeting tend to have similarly favorable consequences for real ultimate-target variables such as output and employment. The consequences for nominal ultimate-target variables, however, differ importantly between the two regimes. The nominal-income targeting regime tends to stabilize the price level. Real-GNP-plus-inflation targeting tends to stabilize the rate of inflation while permitting the price level to drift.

The reason for the different price paths under the two regimes is straightforward. After a shock has caused an initial change in the price level and inflation rate, nominal-income targeting in effect requires a further change in the price level that offsets the initial change, thereby bringing the price level back toward baseline. This offsetting change works to minimize departures of the price level from baseline over the whole period of analysis. Yet it simultaneously increases deviations of the inflation rate from baseline. Thus, if policymakers' main objective is the price level, nominal-income targeting is preferred. If the rate of inflation is the primary objective, real-GNP-plus-inflation targeting tends to be preferred.

This ranking of the two regime types in terms of effects on nominal ultimate targets is observed in the theoretical analysis (in a striking way, for example, when productivity shocks occur and wages are set in one-period contracts or according to a standard Phillips curve). The ranking is strongly confirmed in the deterministic simulations. It is supported less strongly, if at all, in the stochastic simulations.

Stabilization of Financial-Market Variables

The nominal-income targeting and real-GNP-plus-inflation targeting regimes can be differentiated from each other still more sharply if it is assumed that policymakers' loss functions include financial-market variables such as interest rates or exchange rates. Moreover, if the weight on financial-market variables in the loss functions is sufficiently great, the general preference for these two regime types over money targeting and exchange-rate targeting can be overturned.

All three approaches in this project yield the result that, among the regime types considered, real-GNP-plus-inflation targeting causes the largest amount of variability in financial-market variables. Hence policymakers are likely to prefer nominal-income targeting over real-GNP-plus-inflation targeting if they attach sufficiently great importance to stabilization of financial-market variables.[21]

The deterministic simulations show that if stabilization of interest rates or exchange rates were the policymakers' sole or predominant goal, they might often have reason to prefer money targeting or exchange-rate targeting instead of the two regime types that otherwise are usually preferred. Opportunities for an analogous overturning of the otherwise strong preference for nominal-income targeting or real-GNP-plus-inflation targeting can be observed in the stochastic simulations.

These points about financial-market variables and regime preference reflect a broader and increasingly well understood generalization about the consequences of unpredictable nonpolicy shocks: policymakers can aspire to smooth the postshock paths of some macroeconomic variables, but only at the expense of tolerating variability in others. Shocks must manifest themselves *somewhere* in economies (just as when a balloon is punched, some other part of the balloon's surface must give way). In effect, policymakers have some degree of choice about *which* variables will act as shock absorbers (so to speak, "less critical" variables), thereby cushioning other variables deemed to be of greatest importance (presumably their ultimate targets). When shocks occur, it is neither sensible nor feasible to try to cushion *all* macroeconomic variables.

Supply Shocks and Employment as an Ultimate-Target Variable

The theoretical analysis in this project makes an important contribution by carefully investigating productivity shocks and by assessing the stabilizing properties of alternative regimes in terms of their effects on employment rather than on output. In the presence of money-demand or goods-demand shocks, there tends to be a one-to-one correlation between effects on output and effects on employment. Under typical assumptions, it thus makes no difference whether analysis focuses on output or employment as the primary real ultimate-target variable. For shocks on the supply side of economies, however, the choice between these two target variables does make an important difference. The effects of a productivity shock on output and on employment, for example, are often in opposite directions. An unexpected decline in productivity

---

21. In the theoretical analysis of chapter 2, whether real-GNP-plus-inflation targeting causes the largest variability in financial-market variables depends on the values of certain parameters.

can initially increase labor demand even as it decreases output. Because of these opposite forces, the consequences can be quite different depending on whether policymakers try to stabilize output or employment.[22]

Fewer than half the empirical models participating in the simulation exercises include separate equations for employment variables and hence were able to report employment results. To judge from the limited empirical sample, however, the distinction between employment stabilization and output stabilization suggested by the theory can be empirically significant and can influence regime preference, especially for shocks to the supply side of economies.

The theoretical analysis shows that the overall preference for nominal-income targeting or real-GNP-plus-inflation targeting, described earlier, is least likely to be sustained in circumstances in which economies are dominated by shocks to productivity (more generally, by supply shocks). The probability of money targeting or exchange-rate targeting being preferred increases further if supply shocks are predominant and if policymakers attach high weight to inflation in their loss functions.

Implications for the Conduct of Policy

Each of the generalizations just summarized has direct or indirect implications for the operational conduct of national monetary policies. When using this research to try to draw specific recommendations for actual policy decisions, however, one should be cautious. The research presented in this volume is relatively abstract. It focuses on simplified formulations of a limited set of policy regimes. The empirical simulations stem from a diverse group of models. No one of the models may be regarded as fully reliable, and the simulation results do not lead to uniform or unanimous conclusions. For these reasons, and because our commonsense goal for the project has been to assess the general stabilization properties of regime types rather than to develop specific recommendations about particular regimes, the implications for policy that we emphasize here pertain to the further studies that policymakers may wish to commission to analyze and refine alternative approaches to the conduct of monetary policy.[23]

22. Under conditions of inelastic labor supply, policymakers confronted with supply shocks will probably prefer to focus on employment stabilization rather than on output stabilization. Chapter 2 thus ranks regimes according to how well they stabilize employment.

23. Abstract research can only aspire to reach abstract conclusions. Yet, without doubt, the place to begin thinking about alternative regimes for the conduct of monetary policy is with the abstract, most basic points. Robert Solow, in his exposition of growth theory (1970), likened his contribution to a parable and remarked that "you expect a parable to have a moral, but hardly to contain concrete instructions for the conduct of life" (p. 77).

One implication of the main generalization summarized above suggests research areas that do not warrant primary emphasis. For the many tests considered in this project, neither money targeting nor exchange-rate targeting emerged frequently as the preferred policy regime. A conservative interpretation of this evidence, therefore, is that in future analysis of monetary-policy regimes, the burden of proof should fall on the shoulders of protagonists of money targeting and exchange-rate targeting.

Two caveats should temper this point about the future burden of proof. First, the project did find exceptions to the general preference for real-GNP-plus-inflation targeting or nominal-income targeting. Protagonists of either money targeting or exchange-rate targeting can find support for their preference in circumstances, for example, in which productivity or other supply shocks predominate over demand-side or financial shocks or in which policymakers assign dominant weight to the goal of fighting inflation. The second caveat concerns exchange-rate targeting. Whereas it seems appropriate in the case of all countries to place the burden of proof on those who favor a money-targeting regime, a bias against exchange-rate targeting may not necessarily be justified for countries that are members of, or are planning to join, an existing or potential currency union. The complex pros and cons of belonging to the EMS, for example, have not been systematically addressed in this project. Moreover, among the three major industrial countries that were the focus of the empirical research here, Germany—the most "open" of the three and a member of the EMS—showed a somewhat greater preference for exchange-rate targeting than did either Japan or the United States. More research to categorize the types of shocks hitting national economies and to assess the relative importance of policymakers' objectives in different nations will help to shed light on the salience of the two caveats discussed in this paragraph.

The preceding implication, its caveats notwithstanding, has an obvious converse. Because nominal-income targeting and real-GNP-plus-inflation targeting emerge well ahead in the horse races carried out for this project, these two regime types deserve the most attention in future examinations, by policymakers and academic analysts alike, of alternative approaches to the conduct of monetary policy.

This project has shed some light on the differences between nominal-income targeting and real-GNP-plus-inflation targeting. Yet a soundly based policy choice between these two relatively similar types of regime requires more refined research efforts in the future. The tentative results here suggest that nominal-income targeting may be relatively more attractive to countries that place a heavy weight on achieving stability of the price level as the primary goal of monetary policy. On the basis of statements in recent years by central-bank policymakers, Canada, New Zealand, and perhaps Germany may be examples of such countries. Conversely, real-GNP-plus-inflation targeting may be relatively better suited for countries—for example, the United States and, possibly, Japan—for which the stated goals of monetary policy appear to include stabilization of real-sector variables as well as of inflation.

As a final implication for policy, we observe again that the improved degree of stabilization of ultimate-target variables (output, employment, price level, inflation rate) that policymakers might enjoy from nominal-income targeting or real-GNP-plus-inflation targeting could well come at the cost of significantly greater variation of interest rates and exchange rates. Greater variability in financial variables is particularly likely in the case of real-GNP-plus-inflation targeting. Interest rates and exchange rates could be more stable under money targeting and, especially, under exchange-rate targeting. How much weight to give to interest-rate stabilization or exchange-rate stabilization is an issue that will and should continue to be debated in both the policy arena and in academic research.

Future Research

Before concluding this overview, it is appropriate to identify ways that future research might refine the evaluation of policy regimes carried out for this project. Such research is needed to enhance the comparability and persuasiveness of conclusions derived from this type of analysis.

Still more can be done to standardize, across analysts and models, the formulation and implementation of the policy regimes studied. Greater efforts could be made to standardize the structural specification of the regimes. Within those specifications, it would also be helpful to achieve more standardization for the values of feedback parameters. Improved standardization would help to eliminate some of the sources of uncertainty associated with comparing and interpreting empirical results obtained from different models.[24]

To be sure, the experience obtained in this project suggests that complete standardization may be elusive. A trade-off may exist between obtaining standardized results and obtaining any results at all. Some models may not be able to converge for particular specifications of operating regimes or for particular values of key parameters. A fuller standardization of regime specification in experiments comparing different models may require some fundamental modifications in the equation structures of individual models.

Future research should also use less simplified, more realistic specifications of the policy regimes. For example, policymakers in practice frequently pay

---

24. Questions of standardization are discussed at length in chapter 3, and in passing in chapters 4 and 5.

attention to several ultimate-target or intermediate-target variables rather than to merely one. The limited experience in this project with the real-GNP-plus-inflation targeting regime illustrates the potential efficacy of regimes with more than one objective; such regimes can be successfully implemented in model simulations and may often exhibit superior stabilization properties relative to simpler, single-objective regimes. Future studies of multiple-variable regimes could generate insights with more immediate application to monetary policies as they are conducted in actual practice.

In a similar vein, specification of policy regimes in future research can be more realistic in the handling of the problems of intertemporal aggregation. The design of policy regimes to be studied could more carefully align the details of the regimes with the timing of the actual receipt of data by policymakers. Specifically, researchers might try to represent more realistically the lags between changes in target variables and the policymakers' perceptions of the changes (see Bennett McCallum's comments in chapter 6).[25] More also needs to be done to enhance the comparability of the specification of policy regimes and shocks for models with different time frequencies. In particular, more careful attention needs to be paid to the design of mutually consistent regimes for annual, quarterly, and monthly models.

For future studies using stochastic simulation, it would be helpful to achieve greater standardization not only in the specification of the regimes but also in the details of the techniques themselves. Chapter 3 discusses this highly technical matter and indicates its importance for future collaborative research. Among other things, researchers could define more narrowly the types of shocks considered, thereby improving the transparency and comparability of stochastic simulations. For example, as suggested by John Helliwell and Ray Fair in their comments in chapter 6, the variance-covariance matrices derived from the models could be "unbundled." That is, different subsets of shocks could be segregated—such as a set of shocks just for goods demand, or a set for supply equations only—that would permit greater uniformity across participating models in the types of shocks entering the experiments. This unbundling could serve, in effect, as a halfway house between deterministic simulations of single, well-defined shocks and stochastic simulation of the entire range of shocks represented in the full matrices of the models' residuals.

Greater emphasis on supply-side shocks, with clarification of the specification and manner of implementation of the shocks in differing models, is

---

25. Recent research by Gagnon and Tryon (1992) suggests that improvements of this type might not have major effects on conclusions drawn from empirical simulations. In particular, in tests run with the MX3 model, Gagnon and Tryon found that the introduction of errors in the observation of target variables (of a magnitude comparable to errors normally made in forecasting the variables) did not significantly affect the outcomes for different policy regimes.

still another respect in which future studies can improve on the research presented here. The theoretical analysis in chapter 2 demonstrates the potential importance of supply-side shocks for the ranking of alternative policy regimes. Experience with this project has shown, however, that the supply-side characteristics of empirical models differ substantially—indeed, in some models these characteristics are not well developed. Careful specification and standardization of supply shocks across models will require a greater convergence in analytical views than now exists.

The preceding point has a corollary: future research should also pay greater attention to the distinction between changes in output and changes in employment. As already summarized, and as will be amplified in later chapters, this distinction is often uninteresting for the analysis of goods-demand and money-demand shocks but becomes critically important for the study of supply shocks. A significant impediment to a full analysis of the employment effects of shocks is that some researchers have not included equations for wages and employment variables in their empirical models.

Finally, we emphasize three areas of fundamental salience for future research. The first is the treatment of expectations. Modeling groups that have incorporated forward-looking behavior into their models by using the techniques of rational, model-consistent expectations merit substantial commendation. Such models, well-represented in this project, have significantly advanced the ability of the profession to describe and understand forward-looking behavior. Nevertheless, analysts need still more innovative ways of handling expectations. The older approach of adaptive expectations and the newer approach of model-consistent expectations are opposite extremes; neither corresponds well with the complexity and heterogeneity of actual economic behavior. The economic profession requires practical methods of modeling expectations that fall in between these extremes, some of them no doubt drawing on the emerging literature about learning.

Second, model groups need to pay much closer attention to the "closure rules" used for characterizing the intertemporal behavior of governments. The issue of closure rules arises even for monetary policies, but it is especially important for the modeling of fiscal policies. Alternative specifications in the models for tax-rate or government-expenditure reaction functions can lead to large differences in system properties and simulation results. An appreciation of the potential importance of this issue led to an attempt to standardize fiscal closure rules for the purposes of this project (discussed in chapter 3). In retrospect, the attempt was inadequate. In practice, moreover, standardization proved elusive. Spotty empirical evidence from a few of the models suggests that cross-model differences in the treatment of this issue can cause major cross-model differences in simulation results. The comments by Christopher

Sims in chapter 6 strongly emphasize the need to improve the handling of this issue in future research.

A third fundamental point is perhaps the most important of all: existing research on model comparison and evaluation, including this project, has badly neglected the examination of how well extant empirical models fit historical data. Policymakers presumably ought to give much more weight to conclusions derived with the aid of models carefully validated against actual data than to conclusions based on unvalidated models. In practice, however, few resources have been allocated to model validation. Despite the complex reasons for this neglect, which include weak incentives for model groups to carry out validation efforts and to publicize the results, the neglect cannot be justified. As organizers of several of the efforts to compare and evaluate models, we have over the past decade become steadily more aware of this gap in research and more convinced that it ought to be remedied. Among the invited contributors whose comments are included in chapter 6, Ray Fair, John Helliwell, and Christopher Sims likewise feel strongly about this issue. What needs to be done for future research is to find some incentive-compatible way to induce model groups to devote more resources to model validation.

Concluding Observations

This research project has advanced understanding of the effects of monetary policies in open economies along several critical lines. Building on earlier research comparing monetary transmission mechanisms and the effects of changes in monetary policy in different models, the present project has focused more explicitly on the effectiveness of alternative monetary-policy regimes in achieving macroeconomic objectives in the face of various economic shocks. In earlier research, the evaluation of alternative monetary-policy regimes was limited largely to small models and theoretical analysis. In this project, we have not only broadened the theoretical treatment of regime evaluation but have also marshaled a large body of empirical evidence generated by a variety of different models, including some of medium and large size. In addition, the project has significantly extended research on model comparison and evaluation along methodological lines: assessment has moved from analysis based on single, sustained shocks in deterministic simulations to analysis of transitory shocks in deterministic simulations and in stochastic simulations. Stochastic simulation techniques, in particular, have facilitated evaluation of the robustness of alternative policy regimes in the face of the various types of shocks characteristic of real-world economies.

These considerable achievements, seen from the perspective of project participants, represent a significant contribution to knowledge and to public debate. The diversity of models and techniques used in the project, although creating potential and sometimes actual impediments to clear interpretation of the evidence, nonetheless has on balance been a source of strength. The diversity has added to the robustness and plausibility of the conclusions when it has been possible to discern agreement across the models and the alternative analytical techniques. Enough agreement has been found, moreover, to enhance substantially the understanding of the properties of several representative types of monetary-policy regimes.

Nonetheless, as with the earlier publications in this continuing research effort, this volume should be judged as an interim stocktaking. Ample disagreement about some of the details remains among the various analytical approaches used in the project. The evaluation of monetary-policy regimes needs to be refined and extended along the lines suggested above. Empirical models of the macroeconomic interactions among national economies continue to differ in major ways. The models need to be structurally improved and better validated in the light of historical data. Not least, the central issue about the conduct of monetary policy that has been relatively neglected in this volume—the relative merits of credible commitment to a simple policy rule versus the pursuit of more activist discretion—needs further theoretical exploration and empirical analysis.

The status of the research may be likened to reaching an intermediate camp on a long expedition to ascend a high mountain. Looking back after several days of hard climbing, one can see evidence of much progress. The starting point on a marshy lowland is far below in the distance. The vistas from the current promontory are much more spacious and revealing than those observable in the early parts of the journey. Looking up, however, the prospect for tomorrow's climb remains daunting. The final goal is more clearly in view. But many pitches and ridges lie ahead—including some steep scrambling—before the summit itself can be attained.

References

Aizenman, J., and J. A. Frenkel. 1986. "Targeting Rules for Monetary Policy." *Economic Letters* 21:183–87.

Argy, V. 1991. "Nominal Income Targeting: A Critical Evaluation." Working Paper WP/91/92. International Monetary Fund.

Barro, R. J. 1986. "Recent Developments in the Theory of Rules versus Discretion." *Economic Journal* (Annual Conference Papers) 96:23–37.

Barro, R. J., and D. B. Gordon. 1983. "Rules, Discretion, and Reputation in a Model of Monetary Policy." *Journal of Monetary Economics* 12:101–21.

Bean, C. 1983. "Targeting Nominal Income: An Appraisal." *Economic Journal* 93:806–19.

Boyer, R. S. 1978. "Optimal Foreign Exchange Market Intervention." *Journal of Political Economy* 86:1045–55.

Brainard, W. C. 1967. "Uncertainty and the Effectiveness of Policy." *American Economic Review* 57 (*Papers and Proceedings, 1966*):411–25.

Bryant, R. C. 1980. *Money and Monetary Policy in Interdependent Nations*. Brookings.

——. 1983. *Controlling Money: The Federal Reserve and Its Critics*. Brookings.

Bryant, R. C., D. Currie, J. A. Frenkel, P. R. Masson, and R. Portes, eds. 1989. *Macroeconomic Policies in an Interdependent World*. Washington: Brookings, Centre for Economic Policy Research, and International Monetary Fund.

Bryant, R. C., J. F. Helliwell, and P. Hooper. 1989. "Domestic and Cross-Border Consequences of U.S. Macroeconomic Policies." In Bryant, Currie, and others (1989), 59–115. Unabridged version available as Brookings Discussion Paper in International Economics 68 (January 1989).

Bryant, R. C., D. W. Henderson, G. Holtham, P. Hooper, and S. A. Symansky, eds. 1988. *Empirical Macroeconomics for Interdependent Economies*. Brookings.

Bryant, R. C., G. Holtham, and P. Hooper. 1988. *External Deficits and the Dollar: The Pit and the Pendulum*. Brookings.

Canzoneri, M. B. 1985. "Monetary Policy Games and the Role of Private Information." *American Economic Review* 75:1056–70.

Canzoneri, M. B., and D. W. Henderson. 1991. *Monetary Policy in Interdependent Economies: A Game-Theoretic Approach*. MIT Press.

Fair, R. C. 1984. *Specification, Estimation, and Analysis of Macroeconometric Models*. Harvard University Press.

Fischer, S. 1990. "Rules versus Discretion in Monetary Policy." In *Handbook of Monetary Economics,* vol. 2, edited by B. M. Friedman and F. H. Hahn. Amsterdam; New York: North-Holland, Elsevier. Originally available as NBER Working Paper 2518 (February 1988).

Flood, R. P., and P. Isard. 1989. "Monetary Policy Strategies." *IMF Staff Papers* 36:612–32.

Frenkel, J. A., M. Goldstein, and P. R. Masson. 1989. "Simulating the Effects of Some Simple Coordinated versus Uncoordinated Policy Rules." In Bryant, Currie, and others (1989), 203–39.

Friedman, B. M. 1975. "Targets, Instruments, and Indicators of Monetary Policy." *Journal of Monetary Economics* 1:443–73.

——. 1977. "The Inefficiency of Short-Run Monetary Targets for Monetary Policy." *Brookings Papers on Economic Activity* 2:293–335.

——. 1990. "Targets and Instruments of Monetary Policy." In *Handbook of Monetary Economics*, vol. 2. Originally available as NBER Working Paper 2668 (July 1988).

Friedman, M. 1948. "A Monetary and Fiscal Framework for Economic Stability." *American Economic Review* 38:245–64. Reprinted in M. Friedman, *Essays in Positive Economics* (University of Chicago Press), 1953.

——. 1959. *A Program for Monetary Stability.* Fordham University Press.

——. 1968. "The Role of Monetary Policy." *American Economic Review* 58:1–17.

——. 1982. "Monetary Policy: Theory and Practice." *Journal of Money, Credit and Banking* 14:98–118.

Gagnon, J. E., and R. W. Tryon. 1992. "Price and Output Stability under Alternative Monetary Policy Rules." Draft manuscript, Board of Governors of the Federal Reserve System.

Henderson, D. W. 1979. "Financial Policies in Open Economies." *American Economic Review* 69 (*Papers and Proceedings, 1978*):232–39.

——. 1984. "Exchange Market Intervention Operations: Their Role in Financial Policy and Their Effects." In *Exchange Rate Theory and Practice*, edited by J. F. O. Bilson and R. C. Marston, 357–406. University of Chicago Press.

Henderson, D. W., and Ning Zhu. 1990. "Uncertainty and the Choice of Instruments in a Two-County Monetary-Policy Game." *Open Economies Review* 1:39–65.

Hooper, P., and others, eds. 1990. *Financial Sectors in Open Economies: Empirical Analysis and Policy Issues.* Board of Governors of the Federal Reserve System.

Kareken, J. H., T. Muench, and N. Wallace. 1973. "Optimal Open Market Strategy: The Use of Information Variables." *American Economic Review* 63:156–72.

Kydland, F. E., and E. C. Prescott. 1977. "Rules Rather Than Discretion: The Inconsistency of Optimal Plans." *Journal of Political Economy* 85:473–92.

McCallum, B. T. 1985. "On Consequences and Criticisms of Monetary Targeting." *Journal of Money, Credit, and Banking* 17 (pt. 2):570–97.

——. 1990. "Targets, Indicators, and Instruments of Monetary Policy." In *Monetary Policy for a Changing Financial Environment,* edited by W. S. Haraf and P. Cagan, 44–70. Washington: American Enterprise Institute.

McKibbin, W. J., and J. D. Sachs. 1989. "Implications of Policy Rules for the World Economy." In Bryant, Currie, and others (1989), 151–94.

Poole, W. 1970. "Optimal Choice of Monetary Policy Instruments in a Simple Stochastic Macro Model." *Quarterly Journal of Economics* 84:197–216.

Rogoff, K. 1987. "Reputational Constraints on Monetary Policy." In *Bubbles and Other Essays,* edited by Karl Brunner and Alan Meltzer, 141–82. Carnegie-Rochester Conference Series on Public Policy 26. Amsterdam: North-Holland.

Simons, H. C. 1936. "Rules versus Authorities in Monetary Policy." *Journal of Political Economy* 44:1–30. Reprinted in *Economic Policy for a Free Society.* University of Chicago Press, 1948.

Solow, R. M. 1970. *Growth Theory: An Exposition.* Oxford University Press.

Taylor, J. B. 1985. "What Would Nominal GNP Targeting Do to the Business Cycle?" In *Understanding Monetary Regimes,* edited by K. Brunner and A. H. Meltzer, 61–84. Carnegie-Rochester Conference Series on Public Policy 22. Amsterdam: North-Holland.

——. 1989. "Policy Analysis with a Multicountry Model." In Bryant, Currie, and others (1989), 122–41.

Waud, R. N. 1973. "Proximate Targets and Monetary Policy." *Economic Journal* 83:1–20.

2
Comparison and Evaluation of Model Simulations

CHAPTER 2

An Assessment of Some Basic Monetary-Policy Regime Pairs: Analytical and Simulation Results from Simple Multiregion Macroeconomic Models

Dale W. Henderson and Warwick J. McKibbin

THIS CHAPTER is an assessment of some basic monetary-policy regime pairs based on analytical and simulation results from simple multiregion macroeconomic models. All our models are versions of a three-region model with two oil-consuming regions, the United States (US) and the rest of the OECD (ROECD), and an oil-producing cartel (OPEC). We compare the performance of five regime pairs for the US and the ROECD. There are four "matched" regime pairs under which the interest rate, the money supply, nominal income, or the unweighted sum of real output and inflation, respectively, is kept constant in each region. In addition, there is a fifth "unmatched" regime pair under which the exchange rate and the US money supply are kept constant. We provide a unified exposition of the existing theory of monetary-policy regimes for open economies and some extensions. It is designed to set the stage for the discussion in later chapters of simulation results from empirical models of open economies.

Previous Theoretical Analysis

The prevailing approach to analyzing monetary-policy regimes is usually attributed to Poole (1970). Poole investigates the effects of temporary money-demand and goods-demand shocks on output under interest-rate-constant and money-supply-constant regimes in a closed economy. For money-demand

We would like to give special thanks to Ralph Bryant for encouraging us to write this chapter and helping us to make it better in so many ways. We have benefited from the comments of Peter Hooper, Catherine Mann, Juergen von Hagen, and participants in seminars at the Board of Governors of the Federal Reserve System, Indiana University, and the University of Pittsburgh. We are responsible for any failure to recognize good advice and for all remaining errors.

shocks, he finds that output is more stable under an interest-rate-constant regime because the goods market is insulated from the shocks. In contrast, for goods-demand shocks, he finds that output is more stable under a money-supply-constant regime because the effects of the induced movements in the interest rate partially offset the impact effects of the shocks on the goods market.[1] When Poole's analysis is extended to models with employment, it is found that stabilizing output and stabilizing employment amount to the same thing for both money-demand shocks and goods-demand shocks.

Roper and Turnovsky (1980) apply the prevailing approach to a single open economy under the assumptions that home (-currency) and foreign (-currency) bonds are perfect substitutes and that exchange-rate expectations are rational. Under rational expectations, keeping the home interest rate constant is necessary and sufficient for keeping the exchange rate fixed.[2] Like Poole, Roper and Turnovsky conclude that for money-demand shocks, output is more stable under an interest-rate-constant regime (fixed-exchange-rate regime) whereas for goods-demand shocks, output is more stable under a money-supply-constant regime (flexible-exchange-rate regime).[3]

Corden (1981), Meade (1978), and Tobin (1980) suggest that a nominal-income-constant regime might be better than either an interest-rate-constant regime or a money-supply-constant regime.[4] Comparisons of regimes including nominal-income-constant regimes are provided by Bean (1983), Taylor (1985), Aizenman and Frenkel (1986), and Asako and Wagner (1992) for closed economies and by McKibbin and Sachs (1988 and 1989), Frenkel, Goldstein, and Masson (1989), Frankel (1991), and Frankel and Chinn (1993) for open economies.[5]

1. These findings were actually first obtained by Bailey (1962). Poole (1970) summarizes Bailey's findings and extends the analysis of monetary-policy regimes by deriving the optimal combination policy under which either the interest rate or the money supply is used as a policy instrument, the other is used as an information variable, and the policy instrument is varied in response to movements in the information variable.

2. If home and foreign bonds are perfect substitutes, the home interest rate must equal the foreign interest rate plus the difference between (the logarithms of) the expected future exchange rate and the current exchange rate. Roper and Turnovsky (1980) assume that all shocks are temporary and that the foreign interest rate is constant. Under these assumptions, the expected future exchange rate is a constant. Therefore, keeping the home interest rate constant is necessary and sufficient for keeping the current exchange rate fixed.

Roper and Turnovsky is an extension of Boyer (1978), who assumes that exchange-rate expectations are static. With static expectations, the expected future exchange rate is always equal to the current exchange rate, so the home interest rate must always be equal to the constant foreign interest rate. Therefore, the home interest rate is constant whether or not the current exchange rate is kept fixed.

3. Henderson (1979) considers the case in which home and foreign bonds are imperfect substitutes. Under this assumption, keeping the home interest rate fixed does not in general keep the exchange rate fixed. He finds that for asset-demand shocks, output is more stable when the interest rate and the exchange rate are kept constant; for goods-demand shocks, output is more stable when the public's holdings of money and home bonds are kept constant. Bryant (1980) and Henderson (1984) allow for two countries.

4. Argy (1991) surveys the literature on the nominal-income-constant regime.

5. The Aizenman and Frenkel (1986), Frankel and Chinn (1993), and Asako and Wagner (1992) comparisons are most similar to the comparisons of Poole (1970) and Roper and Turnovsky (1980). The Taylor

It is more difficult to summarize the comparisons including nominal-income-constant regimes than to summarize the Poole and Roper and Turnovsky comparisons. One very robust result is that under a basic nominal-income-constant regime, money-demand and goods-demand shocks do not affect output and the price of output.[6]

Primarily as a result of the oil shocks of the 1970s, supply shocks such as oil shocks and productivity shocks have been added to the standard list of shocks to consider when comparing monetary policy regimes.[7] For supply shocks, stabilizing output and stabilizing employment do not result in equivalent outcomes. Also, greater emphasis has been placed on the price level or the inflation rate as an ultimate target of monetary policy. For supply shocks, a nominal-income-constant regime is often but not always superior for stabilizing employment and the price level or inflation.

Our Assessment

Our assessment is a unified exposition of the main implications of the prevailing approach to the analysis of basic monetary-policy regimes. We present the central results of existing contributions.[8] We also extend existing contributions in several important ways—for example, by adding oil to the analysis and by examining alternative hypotheses about how wages and output prices are set.

As stated above, we use different versions of a basic model with three regions: the US, the ROECD, and OPEC. For theoretical clarity and simplicity, we assume that the the US and ROECD are mirror images of each other.

To avoid misunderstanding, we must be explicit about what we mean by the term "monetary-policy regime." Throughout part 2 of this book, it is assumed that the monetary policymaker in each region adjusts an instrument of monetary policy to reduce or eliminate deviations of an intermediate-target variable from a desired value. The name of the monetary-policy regime in a region is determined by the intermediate-target variable in that region. For example, a region has a nominal-income regime if the policymaker for that region tries to reduce or eliminate deviations of nominal income from a desired value.

(1985); McKibbin and Sachs (1988 and 1989); Frenkel, Goldstein, and Masson (1989); and Frankel (1991) comparisons are empirical. The Bean (1983) comparison addresses the common argument that a nominal-income-constant regime may be inferior because information on nominal income is received with a longer lag than information on interest rates and money supplies. He assumes that information on nominal income becomes available with a one-period lag and considers both temporary and permanent shocks.

6. It has been argued that nominal income is a better intermediate target than the interest rate or the money supply because it is more closely related to the ultimate objectives of monetary policy.

7. Canzoneri and Gray (1985) consider strategic aspects of monetary policymaking in a three-region model with oil.

8. However, we do not provide a systematic summary of existing contributions.

In this chapter, we assume that policymakers practice *full instrument adjustment* (FIA). Under FIA, a policymaker adjusts his instrument in each period by the full amount required to eliminate the deviation of his intermediate-target variable from its desired value. In contrast, in the simulations discussed in chapters 3–5, it is assumed that policymakers practice *partial instrument adjustment* (PIA). Under PIA, each policymaker adjusts his instrument in each period by enough to reduce, but not eliminate, the deviation of his intermediate-target variable from its desired value.[9]

We assume in this chapter that the nominal interest rate is the instrument of monetary policy in each region. Similarly, in the simulations discussed in chapters 3–5, it is assumed that a short-term nominal interest rate is the instrument of monetary policy in each region. Because we assume FIA in this chapter, our results for each regime pair would have been the same if we had assumed a monetary aggregate to be the instrument of monetary policy. For the simulations discussed in chapters 3–5, however, because PIA rather than FIA is assumed, the results reported there might have been significantly different with a monetary-aggregate instrument.

We consider five pairs of monetary-policy regimes for the US and the ROECD, referred to for brevity as the II, MM, YY, CC, and ME regime pairs. In the abbreviation for each regime pair, the first letter indicates the regime in the US and the second letter indicates the regime in the ROECD. There are four "matched" regime pairs in which the regimes in the two regions are the same and one "unmatched" regime pair in which the regimes in the two regions are different. Under the matched II regime pair, the policymaker in each region keeps his interest-rate instrument itself constant. Under all the other regime pairs, the policymaker in each region adjusts his interest-rate instrument to keep his intermediate-target variable constant. Under the matched MM, YY, and CC regime pairs, respectively, the intermediate target in each region is the money supply, nominal income, or the sum of real output and inflation.[10] Under the unmatched ME regime pair, the US intermediate target is the US money supply while the ROECD intermediate target is the nominal exchange rate between the dollar and the ROECD currency.

In the course of the chapter, we consider five alternative hypotheses about how nominal wages and output prices are set and refer to them as "wage-price hypotheses." We devote most attention to the hypothesis that we

---

9. See chapter 1 for further discussion of the terms "regime" and "intermediate target" and of the difference between FIA and PIA.

10. The pair of letters CC is chosen to represent the regime pair in which the intermediate target in each country is the sum of real output and inflation because a *combination* of inflation and output is the intermediate target. For simplicity, we assume that observations on nominal incomes, real outputs, output prices, money supplies, and interest rates for a period become available at exactly the same time. Actually, observations on nominal income, real output, and output prices become available later; this difference must be taken into account in choosing among a YY regime pair or a CC regime pair and other regime pairs. See note 5.

call the Contract hypothesis, under which wages are set in one-period, non-overlapping contracts. But we also consider four other wage-price hypotheses that we call the Phillips, Taylor, Barro-Grossman 1 (BG1), and Barro-Grossman 2 (BG2) hypotheses. Under the Contract hypothesis and the first three of the four other hypotheses, wages are sticky but output prices are perfectly flexible and move to clear goods markets in each period, while employments are determined by marginal productivity conditions. Under the BG2 hypothesis, in contrast to the Contract hypothesis and the remaining three of the other hypotheses, prices, as well as wages, are sticky, while employments are determined by the production functions. Wages under the Phillips hypothesis are set according to expectations-augmented Phillips curves. Under the Taylor hypothesis, wages are set in two-period, overlapping contracts.[11] Wages under the BG1 hypothesis and wages and prices under the BG2 hypothesis are set so as to close part of the gap between actual and market-clearing values and to keep up with the expected change in market-clearing values.

We spell out the consequences for key variables of eleven shocks in all. There are nine basic shocks. These basic shocks are divided into three general types: money-demand shocks, goods-demand shocks, and productivity shocks. For each of the three general types of shocks, we define and analyze three variants. The tenth shock is a shock to the exchange-rate risk premium, and the eleventh shock is a shock to the global supply of oil. For the first ten shocks, we obtain results without oil for all five alternative wage-price hypotheses, and for all eleven shocks, we obtain results with oil for the Contract hypothesis. The eleven shocks are representative of shocks analyzed in previous theoretical research and of the shocks studied in the simulations described in chapters 4 and 5.

The three variants of each of the three general types of shock are symmetric shocks, asymmetric shocks, and region-specific shocks. *Symmetric shocks* have impact effects that are identical in size and sign on markets for corresponding items from each of the two regions—for example, equal increases in the demands for US and ROECD money. *Asymmetric shocks* have impact effects that are equal in size but opposite in sign on markets for corresponding items from each of the two regions—for example, an increase in the demand for US goods and a reduction in the demand for ROECD goods by the same amounts. *Region-specific shocks* have impact effects on markets for items from only one of the two regions—for example, a decrease in US productivity with no change in ROECD productivity. We begin with an analysis of symmetric and asymmetric shocks not only because they are intrinsically interesting but also because the results of this analysis can be used in the analysis of region-specific shocks.

---

11. Reinhart (1990) analyzes nominal-income targeting in a model with overlapping wage contracts.

After this overview section there are seven further sections. We first present the three-region model from which we derive all the models used in the chapter. In the subsequent five sections, we assume that nominal wages and output prices are set according to the Contract hypothesis. The first of these sections is a discussion of models for sums of and differences between variables. In the next three of these sections, we assume that oil is neither consumed nor produced. We consider the effects of symmetric and asymmetric shocks under the matched II, MM, and YY regime pairs in the first, the effects of region-specific shocks under these same regime pairs in the second, and the effects of examples of symmetric, asymmetric, and region-specific shocks under the unmatched ME regime pair in the third.[12] In the last of these five sections, we spell out the implications of including oil in the analysis; in that section, we also demonstrate that it makes a difference whether the elasticity of substitution among factors of production is unitary or nonunitary. In the final section, we show what happens when wages and prices are set according to the four other wage-price hypotheses (Phillips, Taylor, BG1, and BG2).

The text is supplemented with several appendixes. A typical appendix is a collection of algebraic results or a discussion of detailed points omitted from the text. Appendix E contains reference tables that summarize the rankings of regime pairs under the Contract wage-price hypothesis. Appendix M is a discussion of simulation results for a shock to the exchange-rate risk premium.

Summary of Main Conclusions

We recognize that some readers will be more interested in our main conclusions than in the details of the arguments that we use to establish them. Therefore, we present a summary of our main conclusions at the outset. In addition, we begin each section with a summary of the conclusions of that section.[13]

Throughout the chapter, we "rank" regime pairs on the basis of their stabilization properties. For a particular variable and a particular shock, one regime pair "dominates" another if the variable moves less under that regime pair, and one regime pair "is ranked the same as" another if the variable moves by the same amount under both. We rank the regime pairs for those variables typically used as ultimate targets by policymakers: employment, output, and the inflation rate or price level. The stabilization properties of a regime pair are determined by comparing outcomes under that regime pair with a shock to outcomes in a "baseline" with no shock.

12. The reason that we do not provide a separate discussion of the CC regime pair is given in the section entitled "Symmetric and Asymmetric Shocks with Matched Regime Pairs."

13. In order to fully appreciate the implications of some of the conclusions in these summaries, it may be necessary to go through the arguments used to establish them.

We present both analytical and simulation results for the Contract wage-price hypothesis, whereas we report mostly simulation results for the four other wage-price hypotheses. For the Contract hypothesis, we are often able to draw definitive conclusions about whether one regime pair dominates another for all parameter values that are admissible in the model. For the other wage-price hypotheses, however, we are usually only able to draw conclusions about whether one pair dominates another for the parameter values used in the simulations.

In the body of the chapter, we rank regime pairs both on the basis of impact effects in the period in which a shock initially occurs and on the basis of sums of squared deviations of variables from baseline over the whole adjustment path. Here we emphasize the results for rankings based on sums of squared deviations. We believe these rankings are more relevant for policymakers' choice among regimes.

We first summarize some general results about rankings of regimes that apply to all or most of the variables in the model. Then we summarize separately results for the stabilization of employments under all the wage-price hypotheses and results for the stabilization of inflation rates and price levels under the Contract hypothesis. We also summarize the implications of including oil under the Contract hypothesis.

General Results

In accordance with the analysis by Poole (1970), the II regime pair dominates the MM pair for all money-demand shocks under all wage-price hypotheses. All variables except money supplies are stabilized perfectly under the II pair, since all markets other than money markets are insulated from the shocks. It follows that the YY and CC regime pairs rank the same as the II regime pair for all money-demand shocks under each wage-price hypothesis. The II, YY, and CC regimes also dominate the ME regime pair for all money-demand shocks with one exception. The exception is a region-specific shock to ROECD money demand. For this shock, the US money supply and the exchange rate remain constant when the US and ROECD interest rates are kept constant, so the ME regime ranks the same as the II regime.

For symmetric shocks to money demands, goods demands, and productivities, the effects under the MM and ME pairs are identical because the ROECD must keep its money supply unchanged in order to keep the exchange rate fixed. However, for asymmetric and region-specific shocks, the effects under these two regime pairs are not identical.

Under the YY and CC regime pairs for all money-demand and goods-demand shocks the impact effects on all variables are identical under all wage-price hypotheses. The reason that this result is obtained is that wages do not change in the initial period, either because they are fixed (as under all hypotheses except the Taylor hypothesis), or because there is no reason for them to change (as under the Taylor hypothesis). For all productivity shocks under all the wage-price hypotheses except the Taylor hypothesis, the impact effects on all variables are identical except for those on nominal interest rates. The reason that this result is obtained is that wages do not change in the initial period under all the wage-price hypotheses except the Taylor hypothesis because they are not allowed to, but wages can and must change under the Taylor hypothesis.

The explanation for why the impact effects on nominal interest rates are different under the YY and CC regime pairs is straightforward under the Contract wage-price hypothesis. The impact effects on nominal interest rates are different because expectations of inflation are different under the two regime pairs. Under both regime pairs outputs are expected to return to their baseline values. Therefore, under the YY regime pair it is expected that policymakers acting to stabilize nominal incomes will act so that output prices move from their post-shock levels back to their baseline values. In contrast, under the CC regime pair it is expected that policymakers acting to stabilize sums of real incomes and inflations will act to keep output prices constant at their post-shock values.

Results for Stabilization of Employments without Oil

In early analyses of the stabilization properties of alternative monetary policy regimes, regimes were ranked according to how well output was stabilized. Supply shocks, like productivity shocks and oil shocks, were not included in the analyses because they had not yet become a central concern. In the absence of supply shocks, stabilizing output has the same consequences for all the variables in the model as stabilizing employment. When supply shocks became a central concern, as noted above, it was recognized that for such shocks stabilizing output does not have the same consequences as stabilizing employment.

One possible objective for monetary policy is to minimize the squared deviations of employment from its natural level, the level that would result if wages and prices were perfectly flexible given the values of the shocks. We assume that the notional supply of labor is perfectly inelastic and nonstochastic. Under this assumption, the natural level of employment is constant. Hence stabilizing employment is equivalent to minimizing the squared deviations of employment from its natural level.

For the stabilization of employments without oil, in accordance with the analysis of Poole (1970), for symmetric and asymmetric goods-demand shocks, the MM regime pair dominates the II pair under all wage-price hypotheses. The induced movements in real interest rates and the real exchange rate partially offset the impact effects of the shocks on the demands for goods.

For all goods-demand shocks under all wage-price hypotheses, not only do the YY and CC regime pairs dominate the other pairs, but employments are completely unaffected under those pairs. This result is obtained because wages do not change. With unchanged wages, there is a one-to-one relationship between nominal incomes and employments. Under both the YY and CC pairs, nominal incomes and, therefore, employments are stabilized.

For all productivity shocks under the Contract wage-price hypothesis, the YY and CC regime pairs are ranked the same and dominate the other pairs for the region or regions in which the shocks have their impact effects. Employments are perfectly stabilized under the YY and CC pairs. However, under the other wage-price hypotheses with more wage stickiness or wage and price stickiness, whether the YY and CC regime pairs dominate all the other pairs depends on parameter values. Since the rankings of regime pairs in theoretical models are ambiguous under wage-price hypotheses other than the simple Contract hypothesis, it is all the more important to obtain rankings of regimes from empirical models of the kind used to produce the simulation results in chapters 3–5.

The results for employment stabilization without oil can be summarized succinctly. For all money-demand and goods-demand disturbances, the YY and CC regime pairs are ranked the same and dominate the other pairs. For productivity disturbances, the YY and CC pairs are ranked the same under all but one wage-price hypothesis. Under two wage-price hypotheses, however, neither the YY nor the CC pair performs best in response to productivity disturbances for the parameter values used in the simulations. Across all types of shocks, the YY pair is preferred in the largest number of cases. The CC pair, often ranked equally, is a close second. Under two of the five wage-price hypotheses, however, it is better to adopt some regime pair other than the YY or CC pair for employment stabilization if productivity shocks are important enough.

Results for Stabilization of Inflation Rates and Price Levels
under the Contract Hypothesis without Oil

Other possible objectives for monetary policy are stabilization of the inflation rate or the level of either output prices or consumer prices (CPIs). When policymakers seek to stabilize inflation or the price level, a variety of conclusions about the rankings of policy regimes is possible, even when attention is restricted to the Contract wage-price hypothesis. The Contract hypothesis is the simplest of the five wage-price hypotheses analyzed in the body of the chapter. Accordingly, here we summarize the results for this hypothesis alone.

The US CPI is equal to the US output price plus the average propensity to import times the real exchange rate. The ROECD CPI is equal to the ROECD output price minus the average propensity to import times the real exchange rate. For symmetric shocks, the real exchange rate remains unchanged, so the conclusions for output prices and CPIs are the same. However, for asymmetric and region-specific shocks, the real exchange rate changes, so the conclusions for output prices and CPIs are different.

Under the II, MM, YY, and ME pairs, output prices return to their pre-shock level in the period following a temporary shock. Under the CC pair, in contrast, output prices remain at their post-shock level in the period following a shock. Under all regime pairs, the real exchange rate returns to its pre-shock level in the period following a shock.

A number of results follow for the stabilization of inflation rates and of levels of output prices and CPIs under the Contract hypothesis without oil. First, for money-demand and goods-demand shocks, the ranking of regime pairs for stabilization of inflation rates and of levels of output prices is the same as the ranking for stabilization of employments. A one-to-one relationship exists between movements in employments and movements in output prices in the period in which the shock hits. Employments and output prices do not move at all under the YY and CC pairs.

Second, for asymmetric goods-demand shocks and if the average propensity to import is close enough to one-half, the II pair is preferred to the MM pair, which is preferred to the YY pair for the stabilization of inflation rates and of levels of CPIs. The reason that this result is obtained is that the real exchange rate changes least under the II pair, more under the MM pair, and most under the YY pair. Thus, the very changes that make the YY pair rank first for employment stabilization make it rank last for CPI stabilization.

Third, for symmetric productivity shocks, the YY pair may or may not dominate the II and MM pairs for stabilization of inflation rates and of levels of output prices and CPIs. The YY pair dominates the CC pair for the stabilization of levels of output prices and CPIs. In contrast, the CC pair dominates the YY pair for the stabilization of inflation rates for output prices and CPIs. Under both the YY and CC pairs, output prices change by the same amount in the period in which the shocks hit. Under the YY pair, output prices return to their pre-shock levels in the period following the shocks. Under the CC pair, however, output prices remain at their post-shock level in the period following the shocks.

Results with Oil under the Contract Hypothesis

When oil is included in the analysis, conclusions can depend on the elasticity of substitution among factors of production. For all symmetric shocks, the results with and without oil are the same for any given value of the elasticity of substitution. If the elasticity of substitution is equal to one, for all nine basic shocks, the YY and CC regime pairs dominate the other pairs for employment stabilization; employments are completely unaffected under these pairs.

If the elasticity of substitution is less than one, the YY and CC pairs still dominate the other pairs for employment stabilization for the parameters used in the simulations. However, employments are no longer stabilized perfectly for asymmetric and region-specific shocks to goods demand and to productivity. For those cases, oil utilizations enter the relationships between nominal incomes and employments, and the induced changes in the real exchange rate affect oil utilizations.

The results for oil suggest that some important variables might be affected more by shocks under the YY and CC regime pairs if other imported intermediate goods were included in the model. It seems likely that the difference in results would be greater for regions in which the elasticity of output with respect to imported intermediate inputs is higher.

Another interesting result is that, for each of the five regime pairs, a symmetric reduction in productivity and a decrease in the global supply of oil have effects that are the same in both qualitative and quantitative terms if the elasticity of substitution is equal to one. These two kinds of shocks have effects that are the same in qualitative but not quantitative terms if the elasticity of substitution is less than one. Therefore, it is reasonable to analyze shocks to the global supply of oil by examining the results for symmetric productivity shocks.

Future Research

The analysis in this chapter yields many clear conclusions about the stabilization properties of monetary-policy regimes. However, it should come as no surprise that we do not find that one regime pair dominates every other pair in all circumstances. Furthermore, it is clear that the task of analyzing the stabilization properties of monetary-policy regimes is far from being finished.

As we stress in the final section of the chapter, when we change from one assumption about the dynamic behavior of wages and prices to another, conclusions about the ranking of regimes can be substantially modified, and sometimes overturned completely. Throwing more light on the consequences of different assumptions about wage-price dynamics should, in our view, be a major goal for future theoretical and empirical research.

Though we point out above the distinction between full and partial instrument adjustment (FIA and PIA), we consider only FIA in this chapter. Obtaining a better understanding of the implications of PIA should be another goal of future research. We make some progress toward reaching this goal in Henderson and McKibbin (forthcoming), where we consider PIA as well as FIA.

We conclude this overview by reemphasizing a point made in chapter 1. Our goal here in chapter 2, and the central goal of the book itself, is to advance the understanding of the stabilization properties of monetary-policy regimes. This improved understanding is a necessary condition—a vital underpinning— for intelligent choices about monetary policy regimes. Intelligent choices also require better understanding of other dimensions of the conduct of monetary policy *not* addressed in this chapter. For example, policymakers must evaluate the credibility and commitment properties of alternative regimes and must weigh the relative merits of single-stage as well as intermediate-target operating regimes. In open economies, decisions by one nation's monetary authorities are strategically interdependent with decisions made by other nations' monetary authorities; policymakers must accordingly consider the potential benefits and risks of international coordination of their policies, as emphasized in, for example, Canzoneri and Henderson (1991) and McKibbin and Sachs (1991). Only when the stabilization properties of regimes are assessed in conjunction with those other important dimensions of policy choice is it possible to wisely select the most appropriate method for conducting monetary policy.

The Model

For easy reference, the equations of our three-region model are collected together in table 2-1, and the definitions of the variables and parameters are given in table 2-2.[14] Variables with no symbol over them are US variables, variables with asterisks over them are ROECD variables, and variables with tildes over them are OPEC variables. All variables in the model are logarithms except interest rates. All the shocks are identically and independently distributed with zero means.

The US specializes in the production of a single final good that is an imperfect substitute for the single final good produced in the ROECD. The US and ROECD production functions (equations 2-1) have identical parameters; output in each region increases with its employment and its oil utilization and decreases with its productivity shock. These production functions are log linearizations of CES production functions in the neighborhood of the expected

---

14. Our specifications of the monetary-policy-regime pairs are in appendix B.

Table 2-1. *The Model*

Production functions for US and ROECD:

$$(2\text{-}1) \qquad y = \alpha n + \beta o - x, \qquad \overset{*}{y} = \alpha \overset{*}{n} + \beta \overset{*}{o} - \overset{*}{x}$$

Sum of oil utilizations equals oil production:

$$(2\text{-}2) \qquad o + \overset{*}{o} = 2\tilde{b}$$

Real product wage equals marginal product of labor conditions for US and ROECD:

$$(2\text{-}3) \quad w - p = \omega - \left[\frac{1-\alpha}{\sigma}\right]n + \left[\frac{\beta}{\sigma}\right]o - x, \qquad \overset{*}{w} - \overset{*}{p} = \omega - \left[\frac{1-\alpha}{\sigma}\right]\overset{*}{n} + \left[\frac{\beta}{\sigma}\right]\overset{*}{o} - \overset{*}{x},$$

$$\omega = \ln \alpha$$

Real product oil price equals marginal product of oil conditions for US and ROECD:

$$(2\text{-}4) \qquad \bar{p} - p = \zeta + \left[\frac{\alpha}{\sigma}\right]n - \left[\frac{1-\beta}{\sigma}\right]o - x, \qquad \overset{*}{\bar{p}} - \overset{*}{p} = \zeta + \left[\frac{\alpha}{\sigma}\right]\overset{*}{n} - \left[\frac{1-\beta}{\sigma}\right]\overset{*}{o} - \overset{*}{x},$$

$$\zeta = \ln \beta$$

Law of one price for oil:

$$(2\text{-}5) \qquad \bar{p} = \overset{*}{\bar{p}} + e$$

Consumer price indexes for US and ROECD:

$$(2\text{-}6) \qquad q = (1-\gamma)p + \gamma(e + \overset{*}{p}) = p + \gamma z, \qquad \overset{*}{q} = \gamma(p - e) + (1-\gamma)\overset{*}{p} = \overset{*}{p} - \gamma z$$

Consumer price index for OPEC:

$$(2\text{-}7) \qquad \tilde{q} = \frac{1}{2}p + \frac{1}{2}(e + \overset{*}{p}) = p + \frac{1}{2}z$$

Real exchange rate:

$$(2\text{-}8) \qquad z = e + \overset{*}{p} - p$$

Open interest parity:

$$(2\text{-}9) \qquad i = \overset{*}{i} + e_{+1|} - e$$

Real interest rates for US and ROECD:

$$(2\text{-}10) \qquad r = i - q_{+1|} + q, \qquad \overset{*}{r} = \overset{*}{i} - \overset{*}{q}_{+1|} + \overset{*}{q}$$

Real interest rate for OPEC:

$$(2\text{-}11) \qquad \tilde{r} = i - \tilde{q}_{+1|} + \tilde{q} = \frac{1}{2}(r + \overset{*}{r})$$

Money market equilibrium conditions for US and ROECD:

$$(2\text{-}12) \qquad p + \phi y - \lambda i + v - m = 0, \qquad \overset{*}{p} + \phi \overset{*}{y} - \lambda \overset{*}{i} + \overset{*}{v} - \overset{*}{m} = 0$$

Goods market equilibrium conditions for US and ROECD:

$$
\begin{aligned}
& -[1 - (1-\gamma)\epsilon]y + \gamma\epsilon\overset{*}{y} - (1-\tau)vr - \tau v\overset{*}{r} + \delta z \\
& \quad - \beta\kappa\epsilon(o + \bar{p} - p) + \beta\kappa\epsilon(\overset{*}{o} + \overset{*}{\bar{p}} - \overset{*}{p}) + u = 0, \\
(2\text{-}13) \qquad & \gamma\epsilon y - [1 - (1-\gamma)\epsilon]\overset{*}{y} - \tau vr - (1-\tau)v\overset{*}{r} - \delta z \\
& \quad + \beta\kappa\epsilon(o + \bar{p} - p) - \beta\kappa\epsilon(\overset{*}{o} + \overset{*}{\bar{p}} - \overset{*}{p}) + \overset{*}{u} = 0, \\
& \tau = \gamma + \beta\kappa, \qquad \kappa = \frac{1}{2} - \gamma, \qquad \delta = 2\eta + \gamma\epsilon + \beta\kappa\epsilon
\end{aligned}
$$

Table 2-2. *Definitions of Variables and Parameters*

$y, \overset{*}{y}$	outputs	e	nominal exchange rate (\$/ROECD)
$n, \overset{*}{n}$	employments	$q, \overset{*}{q}, \tilde{q}$	consumer price levels (CPIs)
$o, \overset{*}{o}$	oil utilizations	z	real exchange rate
$x, \overset{*}{x}$	productivity shocks	$i, \overset{*}{i}$	nominal interest rates
$\tilde{b}$	oil shock	$r, \overset{*}{r}, \bar{r}$	real interest rates
$w, \overset{*}{w}$	nominal wages	$v, \overset{*}{v}$	money-demand shocks
$p, \overset{*}{p}$	output prices	$u, \overset{*}{u}$	goods-demand shocks
$\tilde{p}, \overset{*}{\tilde{p}}$	oil prices	$\pi, \overset{*}{\pi}$	output price inflation

α	ratio of wage bills to outputs
β	ratio of oil bills to outputs
γ	marginal and average propensities to import out of spendings
δ	absolute value of elasticity of output demands with respect to the real exchange rate with incomes measured in US good changng (different from η)
ϵ	marginal propensity to consume out of incomes
η	absolute value of elasticity of output demands with respect to the real exchange rate with incomes measured in US good constant (different from δ)
υ	semi-elasticity of spending with respect to the real interest rate
ϕ	elasticity of demand for money with respect to income
λ	semi-elasticity of demand for money
σ	elasticity of substitution between factors of production
τ	fraction of change in world spending due to a change in a region's real interest rate that falls on demand for the other region's good

rate of output which is defined below.[15] α and β are, respectively, the ratio of the wage bill to output and the ratio of the oil bill to output. Increases in x and $\overset{*}{x}$ represent, respectively, *decreases* in US and ROECD productivity.

OPEC produces only oil that is used as a factor of production in the US and the ROECD. According to equation 2-2, oil utilizations must sum to production, which rises with an oil production shock. Units for oil are chosen so that one-half of OPEC oil production with no shock is equal to zero.

To fulfill one condition for profit maximization, firms in the US and the ROECD must employ labor up to the point at which real product wages are equal to marginal products of labor, as shown in equations 2-3. These conditions are log linearizations of the marginal productivity conditions for CES production functions with the elasticity of substitution σ in the neighborhood of expected output, which is defined below. Real product wages are equal to nominal wages minus output prices. Marginal products of labor are declining functions of employments and productivity shocks and increasing functions of oil utilizations.

15. We assume that each country has the same fixed amount of capital or land. Units are chosen so that these fixed amounts are equal to zero, so they do not appear in equations 2-1, 2-3, and 2-4.

As stated above, we consider five alternative hypotheses about how nominal wages are set. Under all these hypotheses workers agree to supply whatever amount of labor firms want at the prevailing nominal wage.

To fulfill another condition for profit maximization, firms must use oil up to the point at which real product prices of oil are equal to marginal products of oil (equations 2-4). Real product prices of oil are equal to oil prices minus output prices. Marginal products of oil are declining functions of oil utilizations and productivity shocks and increasing functions of employments.

The law of one price holds for oil (equation 2-5). The nominal exchange rate, e, is the dollar price of ROECD currency.

Residents of all three regions consume both US and ROECD goods. CPIs are weighted averages of US and ROECD output prices expressed in the same currency (equations 2-6 and 2-7). In both the US and the ROECD, the average propensity to import is γ ($0 \leq \gamma \leq 1/2$). In OPEC, residents allocate half of their expenditure to US goods and half to ROECD goods. We refer to the relative price of the ROECD good in terms of the US good, z, as the real exchange rate (equation 2-8). We assume that CPIs in the previous period were equal to zero, so that CPIs and inflation rates are the same thing in the current period.[16]

The model includes four kinds of financial assets: dollar bonds, ROECD-currency bonds, US money, and ROECD money. Since OPEC-currency bonds and OPEC money are assumed not to exist, the only exchange rate in the model is the dollar price of ROECD currency. The residents of all three regions may hold both types of bonds. Open interest parity (equation 2-9) holds. A variable with a $+1|$ subscript represents the value of the variable expected to prevail in the next period based on today's information. (Expected) real interest rates are equal to (nominal) interest rates minus expected rates of CPI inflation (equations 2-10 and 2-11). The second equality in equation 2-11 can be derived from equations 2-6, 2-7, 2-9, and 2-10. All US money is held by US residents, and all ROECD money is held by ROECD residents. The money-market-equilibrium conditions (equations 2-12) are conventional. The demand for each money is subject to a shock, v for US money and $\overset{\star}{v}$ for ROECD money.

The excess demands for US goods and for ROECD goods must equal zero (equations 2-13).[17] The excess demand for each good falls with the output of that good and rises with the output of the other good. For both the US and

---

16. More exactly, we assume that $p_{-1} = \overset{\star}{p}_{-1} = z_{-1} = 0$, where a variable with the subscript -1 represents the value of the variable in the previous period. This assumption implies that CPIs in period -1 are equal to zero.

17. Equations 2-13 are log-linearizations of the goods-market-equilibrium conditions at expected outputs where expected outputs are defined below.

the ROECD, an increase in the oil bill measured in home goods lowers the demand for home goods and raises the demand for foreign goods. Residents of the US, the ROECD, and OPEC increase spending by the same fraction (0 $< \epsilon < 1$) of increases in income. In both the US and the ROECD, the marginal propensity to import is equal to the average propensity, γ. In OPEC the marginal propensity to spend on both US and ROECD goods is equal to the average propensity to spend of $1/2$. Demands for both goods fall with increases in real interest rates. Residents of the US, the ROECD, and OPEC decrease spending by the same amount (ν) for each percentage point increase in the real interest rate available to them. A depreciation of the dollar in real terms (an increase in z) shifts world demand from ROECD goods to US goods.[18] The demand for each good is subject to a shock, u for the US good and $\overset{*}{u}$ for the ROECD good.

It is useful to define the natural and (unconditional) expected values of employments and outputs in the US and the ROECD.[19] Natural employments and outputs in a given period are the outputs and employments that would result if wages and prices were perfectly flexible given the realized values of shocks. We assume that in the absence of wage contracts, workers' supply of labor would be perfectly inelastic at zero in each region.[20] Therefore, in each country natural employment is constant and equal to zero. As shown below, in each country natural output varies because of productivity shocks and oil production shocks. Expected employments and outputs are the employments and outputs that would result if wages and prices were perfectly flexible and the shocks took on their expected values of zero. Under our assumptions, in each country expected output is constant and equal to zero. Since the US and the ROECD are mirror images of each other, each of them uses one-half of OPEC oil production when the shocks take on their expected values of zero. Since the production functions are the same, and expected employments and expected oil uses are the same and equal to zero, expected outputs are the same and equal to zero in the two regions.

18. World demand shifts for three reasons. First, residents of the US, the ROECD, and OPEC substitute spending on US goods for spending on ROECD goods by the same amount (η) with their incomes measured in US goods held constant. Second, the US-goods value of ROECD output rises, creating excess demand for US goods and excess supply of ROECD goods of $\gamma \epsilon$. Third, the US-goods value of the ROECD oil bill rises increasing demand for US goods and reducing demand for ROECD goods by $\beta \kappa \epsilon$.

19. The distinction between unconditional and conditional expected employments and outputs is not important except in the last section of the chapter, where we consider other wage-price hypotheses in addition to the Contract hypothesis.

20. That is, we assume that the notional supply of labor is perfectly inelastic and nonstochastic. The usual criterion for ranking regimes for employment stabilization is the variance of employment around natural employment. Applying this criterion is much easier if natural employment is constant. Others, including Bean (1983), Marston (1984), and Aizenman and Frenkel (1986), have considered the case in the which the notional supply of labor varies with the real consumption wage.

Models for Sums and Differences
under the Contract Hypothesis

In analyzing the effects of the various shocks under the different monetary policy regimes, it is convenient and instructive to employ models for sums of and differences between corresponding US and ROECD variables. The model of sums (where a subscript s is used to indicate the sum of variables) yields results for symmetric shocks, and the model of differences (where a subscript d is used to indicate the difference between variables) yields results for asymmetric shocks. In addition, results from these models can be combined to yield results for region-specific shocks. Using models for sums and differences simplifies our analysis considerably because we assume that the US and the ROECD are mirror images of each other.[21]

In this section, we discuss models for sums and differences under the Contract hypothesis. First, we spell out the Contract hypothesis. Then we obtain some intermediate results. Next we derive models for sums and differences with oil ($\beta > 0$) and without oil ($\beta = 0$) and show how the models without oil can be represented graphically.[22] Then we explain how we obtain our algebraic results for the models without oil. Finally, we explain how to read the tables of simulation results for the Contract hypothesis.

The Contract Hypothesis

Under the Contract wage-price hypothesis, firms and workers set wages for each period so that the expected values of employments based on information available in the previous period are equal to natural employments of zero as shown in equations 2-14 in table 2-3.[23] Under the Contract hypothesis, wages in the current period are independent of wages in the previous period. However, as we explain below, under the other wage-price hypotheses, they are not.

Intermediate Results

We make use of several intermediate results that are displayed in table 2-4. The values of the endogenous variables in period 0 depend on the values of

---

21. As far as we know, the technique of using models of sums of and differences between individual country variables in the analysis of the effects of shocks in models with two mirror-image countries was first used by Aoki (1981).

22. We show how the models with oil can be represented graphically in the section entitled "Including Oil."

23. Equations 2-23 are obtained by taking expectations of equations 2-3 and setting $n_{t|t-1} = \overset{*}{n}_{t|t-1} = o_{t|t-1} = \overset{*}{o}_{t|t-1} = x_{t|t-1} = \overset{*}{x}_{t|t-1} = 0$.

Table 2-3. *The Alternative Wage- and Price-Setting Hypotheses*

Contract hypothesis

$$\text{(2-14)} \qquad w_t - p_{t|t-1} = \omega, \qquad \overset{*}{w}_t - \overset{*}{p}_{t|t-1} = \omega$$

Phillips hypothesis

$$\text{(2-15)} \qquad w_{t+1} - w_t = \theta n_t + p_{t+1|t} - p_t, \qquad \overset{*}{w}_{t+1} - \overset{*}{w}_t = \theta \overset{*}{n}_t + \overset{*}{p}_{t+1|t} - \overset{*}{p}_t$$

Taylor hypothesis

$$\text{(2-16)} \qquad \tilde{w}_t = \mu(n_{t+1|t} + n_t) + \frac{1}{2}(\tilde{w}_{t+1|t} + \tilde{w}_{t-1})$$

$$\overset{*}{\tilde{w}}_t = \mu(\overset{*}{n}_{t+1|t} + \overset{*}{n}_t) + \frac{1}{2}(\overset{*}{\tilde{w}}_{t+1|t} + \overset{*}{\tilde{w}}_{t-1})$$

$$\text{(2-17)} \qquad w_t = \frac{1}{2}(\tilde{w}_t + \tilde{w}_{t-1}), \qquad \overset{*}{w}_t = \frac{1}{2}(\overset{*}{\tilde{w}}_t + \overset{*}{\tilde{w}}_{t-1})$$

Barro-Grossman 1 (BG1) and Barro-Grossman 2 (BG2) hypothesis for wage setting

$$\text{(2-18)} \qquad w_{t+1} - w_t = \varphi(\bar{w}_t - w_t) + \bar{w}_{t+1|t} - \bar{w}_t$$

$$\overset{*}{w}_{t+1} - \overset{*}{w}_t = \varphi(\overset{*}{\bar{w}}_t - \overset{*}{w}_t) + \overset{*}{\bar{w}}_{t+1|t} - \overset{*}{\bar{w}}_t$$

Barro-Grossman 2 (BG2) hypothesis for price setting

$$\text{(2-19)} \qquad p_{t+1} - p_t = v(\bar{p}_t - p_t) + \bar{p}_{t+1|t} - \bar{p}_t$$

$$\overset{*}{p}_{t+1} - \overset{*}{p}_t = v(\overset{*}{\bar{p}}_t - \overset{*}{p}_t) + \overset{*}{\bar{p}}_{t+1|t} - \overset{*}{\bar{p}}_t$$

Table 2-4. *Intermediate Results*

$$\text{(2-20)} \qquad z_{+1|} = p_{+1|} = q_{+1|} = \overset{*}{p}_{+1|} = q_{+1|} = 0$$

$$\text{(2-21)} \qquad w = \overset{*}{w} = \omega$$

$$\text{(2-22)} \qquad z = -(i_d + p_d)$$

$$\text{(2-23)} \qquad r = (1-\gamma)(i+p) + \gamma(\overset{*}{i} + \overset{*}{p}), \qquad \overset{*}{r} = \gamma(i+p) + (1-\gamma)(\overset{*}{i} + \overset{*}{p})$$

$$\text{(2-24)} \qquad r_s = i_s + p_s$$

$$\text{(2-25)} \qquad r_d = (1-2\gamma)(i_d + p_d)$$

$$\text{(2-26)} \qquad q = p - \gamma(i_d + p_d), \qquad \overset{*}{q} = \overset{*}{p} + \gamma(i_d + p_d)$$

$$\text{(2-27)} \qquad q_s = p_s$$

$$\text{(2-28)} \qquad q_d = (1-2\gamma)p_d - 2\gamma i_d$$

several variables expected to prevail in period $+1$ and of the wages set in the contracts. Under two assumptions made earlier and two additional assumptions these values are given by equations 2-20 and 2-21.[24] The definition of the real exchange rate (equation 2-8), open interest parity (equation 2-9), and the expression for $e_{+1|}$ in equation 2-20 imply equation 2-22. The definitions of real interest rates (equation 2-10) and CPIs (equation 2-6) and the expressions for $p_{+1|}$, $\overset{*}{p}_{+1|}$, and $z_{+1|}$ in equation 2-20 and z in equation 2-22 imply equations 2-23, which in turn imply equations 2-24 and 2-25. The definitions of price levels (equations 2-6) and the expression for the real exchange rate given by equation 2-22 imply equations 2-26, which in turn imply equations 2-27 and 2-28.

The Equations for the Schedules

In this section we derive the equations for the schedules used in the graphical representation of the models for sums and for differences, with and without oil, and explain the schedules for the models without oil. For each model we use four schedules: an aggregate-demand schedule, a money-market-equilibrium schedule, an aggregate-supply schedule, and a nominal-income-constant schedule. We choose these schedules because we can use them to analyze all three of the II, MM, and YY regime pairs.

The schedules for the models of sums and of differences without oil have the same qualitative properties, so we use figures 2-1 through 2-5 to represent both models. The schedules in these figures have the subscript h, which can take on the values of s for sums and d for differences.

The equations for the *aggregate-demand schedules* for sums and for differences with oil are equation 2-29 in table 2-5 and equation 2-39 in table 2-6. These equations are the sum of and difference between equations 2-13 in table 2-1, with r_s and r_d eliminated using equations 2-24 and 2-25 in table 2-4.[25] The equations for the aggregate-demand schedules without oil

24. The two assumptions made earlier are (1) that natural employments are equal to zero and (2) that all shocks are identically and independently distributed with zero means. The two additional assumptions are (1) that agents expect that in every future period the interest rate in each country will be set according to one of the four pairs of reaction functions described in appendix B, and (2) that there are no speculative bubbles. The method of proof is similar to the one used in appendix A of Canzoneri and Henderson (1991) and in the appendix to Obstfeld (1985).

25. There is an important difference between the assumptions underlying the textbook aggregate-demand schedule and those underlying our AD_s and AD_d schedules. In deriving the textbook aggregate-demand schedule, it is assumed that the nominal interest rate moves in order to keep the money market in equilibrium. In algebraic terms, the nominal interest rate is eliminated from the aggregate-demand equation using the money-market-equilibrium condition. In deriving our AD_s and AD_d schedules, it is assumed that nominal interest rates and, therefore, the exchange rate are constant. Dornbusch (1984) uses two aggregate-demand schedules, one drawn on the assumption that the nominal interest rate and the exchange rate move in order to keep asset markets in equilibrium, and one drawn on the assumption that the nominal interest rate and the exchange rate are constant.

(designated AD rather than ADO) are obtained by setting $\beta = 0$. The equation for the aggregate-demand schedule for sums without oil (AD_s) is just equation 2-29 in table 2-5 (AD_s and ADO_s do not differ). The equation for the aggregate-demand schedule for differences without oil (AD_d) is equation 2-40 in table 2-6.

The AD_s and AD_d schedules show the pairs of p_s and y_s for which the sum of excess demands for goods is zero, and the pairs of p_d and y_d for which the difference between excess demands for goods is zero, respectively. Both AD_s and AD_d are represented by $AD_{h,o}$ in figure 2-1. Their slopes are negative and may be greater or less than one in absolute value. For the AD_s schedule with slope $-(1 - \epsilon)/v$, increases in both p_s and y_s reduce the sum of excess demands: an increase in p_s raises r_s, and an increase in y_s raises the sum of demands by less than the sum of supplies. For the AD_d schedule with slope $-[1 - (1 - 2\gamma)\epsilon]/[(1 - 2\gamma)^2 v + 2\delta]$, increases in both p_d and y_d reduce the difference between excess demands: an increase in p_d not only increases r_d but also causes the dollar to appreciate in real terms, and an increase in y_d raises the difference between demands by less than it raises the difference between supplies. We emphasize the case shown in figure 2-1 in which the slope of AD_h is greater than one in absolute value but discuss the other case when the results are different.

Figure 2-1. *Explanation of Schedules*

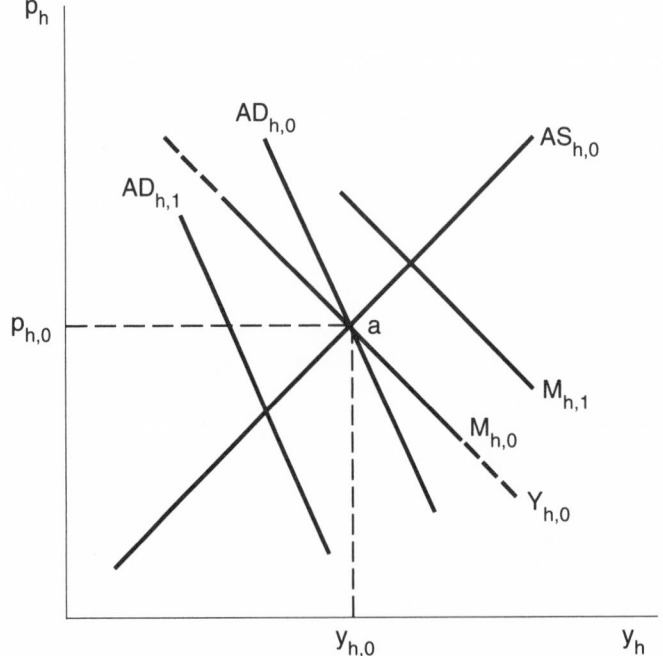

Table 2-5. *The Model for Sums under the Contract Hypothesis*

(2-29)	$-(1-\epsilon)y_s - v(i_s + p_s) + u_s = 0$	(ADO_s and AD_s schedule)
(2-30)	$p_s + \phi y_s - \lambda i_s + v_s - m_s = 0$	(M_s schedule)
(2-31)	$y_s = \alpha n_s + \beta 2\tilde{b} - x_s$	
(2-32)	$-p_s = -[(1-\alpha)/\sigma]n_s + (\beta/\sigma)2\tilde{b} - x_s$	
(2-33)	$\tilde{p}_s - p_s = (\alpha/\sigma)n_s - [(1-\beta)/\sigma]2\tilde{b} - x_s$	
(2-34)	$-(1-\alpha)y_s + \alpha\sigma p_s + \beta 2\tilde{b} - [1-\alpha(1-\sigma)]x_s = 0$	(ASO_s schedule)
(2-35)	$-(1-\alpha)y_s + \alpha\sigma p_s - [1-\alpha(1-\sigma)]x_s = 0$	(AS_s schedule)
(2-36)	$p_s + y_s = \overline{p + y_s}$	(Y_s schedule)
(2-37)	$p_s + y_s = \{\alpha + [(1-\alpha)/\sigma]\}n_s - [\beta - (\beta/\sigma)]2\tilde{b}$	
(2-38)	$p_s + y_s = \{\alpha + [(1-\alpha)/\sigma]\}n_s$	

An increase in i_s shifts the AD_s schedule down by the same amount, say from $AD_{s,0}$ to $AD_{s,1}$, because unit increases in i_s and p_s reduce the sum of excess demands by the same amount. An increase in i_d shifts the AD_d schedule down by the same amount for an analogous reason.

The equations for the *money-market-equilibrium schedules* for sums (M_s) and for differences (M_d), both with and without oil, are equation 2-30 in table 2-5 and equation 2-41 in table 2-6. These equations are the sum of and difference between equations 2-12.

The M_s and M_d schedules show the pairs of p_s and y_s for which the sum of excess demands for money is zero and the pairs of p_d and y_d for which the difference between excess demands is zero, respectively. Both M_s and M_d are represented by M_h in figure 2-1. The slopes of both M_s and M_d are negative and equal to $-\phi$, which may be greater than, equal to, or less than one in absolute value. The M_s schedule slopes downward because increases in both p_s and y_s raise the sum of excess demands, and the M_d schedule slopes downward for analogous reasons. We emphasize the case shown in figure 2-1 in which M_h has a slope of negative one and is flatter than AD_h but discuss other cases when the results are different.

An increase in i_s shifts the M_s schedule up because it reduces the sum of excess demands for money, so p_s must rise in order to return this sum to its previous value. An increase in i_d shifts the M_d schedule up for analogous reasons.

Deriving the *aggregate-supply schedules* involves more steps. To derive the aggregate-supply schedule for sums with oil, we sum the production functions (equations 2-1), the first-order conditions for labor (equations 2-3) with w set

Table 2-6. *The Model for Differences under the Contract Hypothesis*

(2-39)	$-[1 - (1 - 2\gamma)\epsilon + \beta Q]y_d - [(1 - 2\gamma)^2 v$
	$+ 2\delta + \beta R](i_d + p_d) + u_d = 0$ (ADO$_d$ schedule)
	$Q = 2\kappa\epsilon, \qquad R = -v(2\kappa)^2 + 2\kappa\epsilon, \qquad 2\kappa = 1 - 2\gamma$
(2-40)	$-[1 - (1 - 2\gamma)\epsilon]y_d - [(1 - 2\gamma)^2 v + 2\delta](i_d + p_d) + u_d = 0$ (AD$_d$ schedule)
(2-41)	$p_d + \phi y_d - \lambda i_d + v_d - m_d = 0$ (M$_d$ schedule)
(2-42)	$y_d = \alpha n_d + \beta o_d - x_d$
(2-43)	$-p_d = -[(1 - \alpha)/\sigma]n_d + (\beta/\sigma)o_d - x_d$
(2-44)	$\tilde{p}_d - p_d = e - p_d = z = -(i_d + p_d) = (\alpha/\sigma)n_d - [(1 - \beta)/\sigma]o_d - x_d$
(2-45)	$(1 - \alpha - \beta)n_d = (1 - \beta)\sigma p_d + \beta\sigma(i_d + p_d) - \sigma x_d$
(2-46)	$(1 - \alpha - \beta)o_d = \alpha\sigma p_d + (1 - \alpha)\sigma(i_d + p_d) - \sigma x_d$
(2-47)	$-(1 - \alpha - \beta)y_d + \alpha\sigma p_d + \beta\sigma(i_d + p_d)$
	$-[1 - (\alpha + \beta)(1 - \sigma)]x_d = 0$ (ASO$_d$ schedule)
(2-48)	$-(1 - \alpha)y_d + \alpha\sigma p_d - [1 - \alpha(1 - \sigma)]x_d = 0$ (AS$_d$ schedule)
(2-49)	$p_d + y_d = \overline{p + y}_d$ (Y$_d$ schedule)
(2-50)	$p_d + y_d = \{\alpha + [(1 - \alpha)/\sigma]\}n_d - [\beta - (\beta/\sigma)]o_d$
(2-51)	$p_d + y_d = \{\alpha + [(1 - \alpha)/\sigma]\}n_d$

equal to ω from equation 2-21, and the first-order conditions for oil (equations 2-4) and note that, in equilibrium, o_s must equal $2\tilde{b}$ from equation 2-2 to obtain equations 2-31 through 2-33. The equation for the aggregate-supply schedule for differences with oil (ASO_s) is equation 2-34, which is obtained by solving equation 2-32 for n_s and substituting the result into equation 2-31. The aggregate-supply schedule for sums without oil (AS_s) is equation 2-35, which is obtained by setting $\beta = 0$ in equation 2-34.

To derive the aggregate-supply schedule for differences with oil, we first find the difference between the production functions (equations 2-1), the first-order conditions for labor (equations 2-3) with w set equal to ω from equation 2-21, and the first-order conditions for oil (equations 2-4). We then eliminate $\tilde{p}_d$, using equation 2-5, and z, using equation 2-22, to obtain equations 2-42 through 2-44. The equation for the aggregate-supply schedule for differences with oil (ASO_d) is equation 2-47, which is obtained by solving equations 2-43 and 2-44 for the expressions for n_d and o_d in equations 2-45 and 2-46 and substituting these expressions into equation 2-42. The aggregate-supply schedule for differences without oil (AS_d) is equation 2-48, which is obtained by setting $\beta = 0$ in equation 2-47.

The AS_s and AS_d schedules show what y_s will be produced for each p_s and what y_d will be produced for each p_d without oil, respectively. Both AS_s and AS_d are represented by AS_h in figure 2-1, and the slopes of both schedules are positive and equal to $(1-\alpha)/\alpha\sigma$. The AS_s schedule slopes upward because an increase in p_s causes the sum of real wages to fall, so n_s and, therefore, y_s increase, and the AS_d schedule slopes upward for an analogous reason.

The equations for the *nominal-income-constant schedules* for sums (Y_s) and differences (Y_d) are equations 2-36 in table 2-5 and 2-49 in table 2-6. The Y_s and Y_d schedules show the pairs of p_s and y_s for which $p_s + y_s$ is a constant and the pairs of p_d and y_d for which $p_d + y_d$ is a constant, respectively. Both Y_s and Y_d are represented by Y_h in figure 2-1, and both have slopes of minus one. The $Y_{h,0}$ schedule coincides with the $M_{h,0}$ schedule in figure 2-1, which is drawn under the assumption that $\phi = 1$.

The Y_s and Y_d schedules have another interpretation without oil. Adding equation 2-31 and minus one times equation 2-32 yields equation 2-37. Without oil ($\beta = 0$), equation 2-37 becomes equation 2-38. Thus, there is a one-to-one relationship between the sum of nominal incomes and the sum of employments, and a Y_s schedule gives the pairs of p_s and y_s for which n_s is constant. Adding equation 2-42 and minus one times equation 2-43 yields equation 2-50. Without oil ($\beta = 0$), equation 2-50 becomes equation 2-51. Hence, a one-to-one relationship exists between $p_d + y_d$ and n_d, and a Y_d schedule gives the pairs p_d and y_d for which n_d is constant.

Algebraic Results

Algebraic results for the effects of symmetric shocks on y_s, αn_s, and q_s and for the effects of asymmetric shocks on y_d, αn_d, and q_d are reported in appendix D. Algebraic results for $\overset{\star}{n}$ and n can be obtained by combining results for n_s and n_d as shown in table 2-7, and those for y and $\overset{\star}{y}$ and q and $\overset{\star}{q}$ can be obtained in an analogous way.

Equations 2-29, 2-30, 2-35, 2-36, 2-38, and 2-27 are a system of six equations in the seven variables p_s, y_s, n_s, q_s, i_s, m_s, and $\overline{p + y_s}$. The algebraic results for sums for the II, MM, or YY regime pairs, respectively, are obtained by making i_s, m_s, or $\overline{p + y_s}$ exogenous and solving for the six remaining variables. The results are shown in appendix D. Equations 2-40, 2-41, 2-48, 2-49, 2-51, and 2-28 are a system of six equations in the seven variables p_d, y_d, n_d, q_d, i_d, m_d, and $\overline{p + y_d}$. The results for differences for the II, MM, or YY regime pairs, respectively, are obtained by making i_d, m_d, or $\overline{p + y_d}$ exogenous and solving for the six remaining variables. The results are shown in appendix D.

Table 2-7. *Expressions for the Effects of Shocks on Region-Specific Variables*

(2-52) $$2n_{v_s}^{\mathrm{MM}} = 2\mathring{n}_{v_s}^{\mathrm{MM}} = n_{s,v_s}^{\mathrm{MM}} = \frac{1}{2}\left([n_v^{\mathrm{MM}} + \mathring{n}_v^{\mathrm{MM}}] + [n_{\mathring{v}}^{\mathrm{MM}} + \mathring{n}_{\mathring{v}}^{\mathrm{MM}}]\right)$$

(2-53) $$2n_{v_d}^{\mathrm{MM}} = -2\mathring{n}_{v_d}^{\mathrm{MM}} = n_{d,v_d}^{\mathrm{MM}} = \frac{1}{2}\left([n_v^{\mathrm{MM}} - \mathring{n}_v^{\mathrm{MM}}] - [n_{\mathring{v}}^{\mathrm{MM}} - \mathring{n}_{\mathring{v}}^{\mathrm{MM}}]\right)$$

(2-54) $$2n_v^{\mathrm{MM}} = n_{s,v_s}^{\mathrm{MM}} + n_{d,v_d}^{\mathrm{MM}}$$

$$= \frac{1}{2}\left([n_v^{\mathrm{MM}} + \mathring{n}_v^{\mathrm{MM}}] + [n_{\mathring{v}}^{\mathrm{MM}} + \mathring{n}_{\mathring{v}}^{\mathrm{MM}}]\right) + \frac{1}{2}\left([n_v^{\mathrm{MM}} - \mathring{n}_v^{\mathrm{MM}}] - [n_{\mathring{v}}^{\mathrm{MM}} - \mathring{n}_{\mathring{v}}^{\mathrm{MM}}]\right)$$

(2-55) $$2\mathring{n}_v^{\mathrm{MM}} = n_{s,v_s}^{\mathrm{MM}} - n_{d,v_d}^{\mathrm{MM}}$$

$$= \frac{1}{2}\left([n_v^{\mathrm{MM}} + \mathring{n}_v^{\mathrm{MM}}] + [n_{\mathring{v}}^{\mathrm{MM}} + \mathring{n}_{\mathring{v}}^{\mathrm{MM}}]\right) - \frac{1}{2}\left([n_v^{\mathrm{MM}} - \mathring{n}_v^{\mathrm{MM}}] - [n_{\mathring{v}}^{\mathrm{MM}} - \mathring{n}_{\mathring{v}}^{\mathrm{MM}}]\right)$$

(2-56) $$n_v^{\mathrm{MM}} = \mathring{n}_{\mathring{v}}^{\mathrm{MM}}$$

(2-57) $$n_{\mathring{v}}^{\mathrm{MM}} = \mathring{n}_v^{\mathrm{MM}}$$

Note: n_v^{MM} effect of increase in v on n under the MM regime pair

$\mathring{n}_v^{\mathrm{MM}}$ effect of increase in v on $\mathring{n}$ under the MM regime pair

$n_{\mathring{v}}^{\mathrm{MM}}$ effect of increase in $\mathring{v}$ on n under the MM regime pair

$\mathring{n}_{\mathring{v}}^{\mathrm{MM}}$ effect of increase in $\mathring{v}$ on $\mathring{n}$ under the MM regime pair

Simulation Results for the Contract Hypothesis

Simulation results for the Contract hypothesis are presented with a standard layout that we explain using table 2-8 for reference. Each table contains results for the effects of one kind of shock, without and with oil, obtained using the parameter values in appendix A. The columns are divided into two groups of five each. In the left-hand group we report results without oil ($\beta = 0$) for the II, MM, YY, CC, and ME regimes; the right-hand group contains results with oil ($\beta = 0.10$) for the same five regimes. The rows are divided into three groups that show effects on US variables (top), ROECD variables (bottom), and nominal and real exchange rates (middle).[26] All the numbers are first-period effects and are either actual deviations (D) or percent deviations (%) from baseline. The baseline is a shock-free simulation in which all variables are at steady-state, equilibrium values. For example, the numbers in the upper portion of the first column of table 2-8 indicate that a symmetric 10 percent increase in money demands under the MM regime without oil causes US output to fall by 2.93 percent, US consumer-price inflation to fall by 1.26 percentage points, and the US nominal interest rate to rise by 7.27 percentage points, all relative to the baseline simulation.

---

26. Recall that the nominal exchange rate is the dollar price of ROECD currency; therefore, a rise in the exchange rate is a depreciation of the dollar.

Table 2-8. *First-Period Impact of a Symmetric Increase in Money Demand*

	Regime pair									
	Oil excluded (β = 0)					Oil included (β = 0.1)				
Variable[a]	MM	II	YY	CC	ME	MM	II	YY	CC	ME
US economy										
Output (%)	-2.93	0	0	0	-2.93	-2.93	0	0	0	-2.93
CPI inflation (D)	-1.26	0	0	0	-1.26	-1.26	0	0	0	-1.26
Output price (%)	-1.26	0	0	0	-1.26	-1.26	0	0	0	-1.26
Nominal interest rate (D)	7.27	0	0	0	7.27	7.27	0	0	0	7.27
Real interest rate (D)	6.01	0	0	0	6.01	6.01	0	0	0	6.01
Nominal wage (%)	0	0	0	0	0	0	0	0	0	0
Employment (%)	-4.19	0	0	0	-4.19	-4.19	0	0	0	-4.19
Money (%)	0	10	10	10	0	0	10	10	10	0
Nominal exchange rate ($/R)(%)	0	0	0	0	0	0	0	0	0	0
Real exchange rate ($/R)(%)	0	0	0	0	0	0	0	0	0	0
ROECD economy										
Output (%)	-2.93	0	0	0	-2.93	-2.93	0	0	0	-2.93
CPI inflation (D)	-1.26	0	0	0	-1.26	-1.26	0	0	0	-1.26
Output price (%)	-1.26	0	0	0	-1.26	-1.26	0	0	0	-1.26
Nominal interest rate (D)	7.27	0	0	0	7.27	7.27	0	0	0	7.27
Real interest rate (D)	6.01	0	0	0	6.01	6.01	0	0	0	6.01
Nominal wage (%)	0	0	0	0	0	0	0	0	0	0
Employment (%)	-4.19	0	0	0	-4.19	-4.19	0	0	0	-4.19
Money (%)	0	10	10	10	0	0	10	10	10	0

a. % is percent deviation from unchanged baseline; D is deviation from unchanged baseline in percentage points.

Symmetric and Asymmetric Shocks
with Matched Regime Pairs

In this section we use the models of sums and differences derived in the previous section to discuss the effects of symmetric and asymmetric money-demand, goods-demand, and productivity shocks under the II, MM, and YY matched regime pairs and the Contract hypothesis.

Under the Contract hypothesis, all endogenous variables move in the same way under the YY and CC regime pairs except for nominal interest rates for productivity shocks, as we show in appendix C. Therefore, we do not discuss the CC regime pair separately in this and the following three sections. In the final section we show that there can be important differences between outcomes under the YY and CC regime pairs under wage-price hypotheses other than the Contract hypothesis. There would probably also be important differences between outcomes under these two pairs if shocks were permanent rather than temporary.

With symmetric shocks, mirror-image regions, and matched regime pairs, the world of our model can be viewed as a closed economy. It should, therefore, come as no surprise that our results for symmetric money-demand and goods-demand shocks under the II and MM regime pairs are the same as Poole's results for analogous shocks and regimes in a closed economy.

In the discussion of each kind of shock, we begin with a statement of our conclusions regarding the rankings of regimes and proceed to provide explanations for those conclusions. In the explanations we first derive the results for a symmetric shock of a given type and then discuss the differences between these results and those for an asymmetric shock of the same type. We refer to graphical, algebraic, and simulation results. Graphical results are in figures 2-2 through 2-5. Algebraic results for employments, outputs, and CPIs for symmetric and asymmetric shocks appear in appendix D. Simulation results for several variables are in tables 2-8 through 2-13. The rankings of regimes for employments and CPIs for symmetric, asymmetric, and region-specific shocks are summarized in tables in appendix E, where the symbol $\underset{p}{>}$ means "dominates," the symbol $\underset{p}{=}$ means "is ranked the same as," and the symbol $\underset{p}{\lessgtr}$ means "is not rankable relative to."

Money-Demand Shocks

For symmetric or asymmetric money-demand shocks, outcomes are the same under the II and YY regime pairs, and either of these pairs dominates the MM pair for all variables. The result for a symmetric shock is identical to Poole's result for a money-demand shock in a closed economy. The logic behind the

Figure 2-2. *Money-Demand Shock*

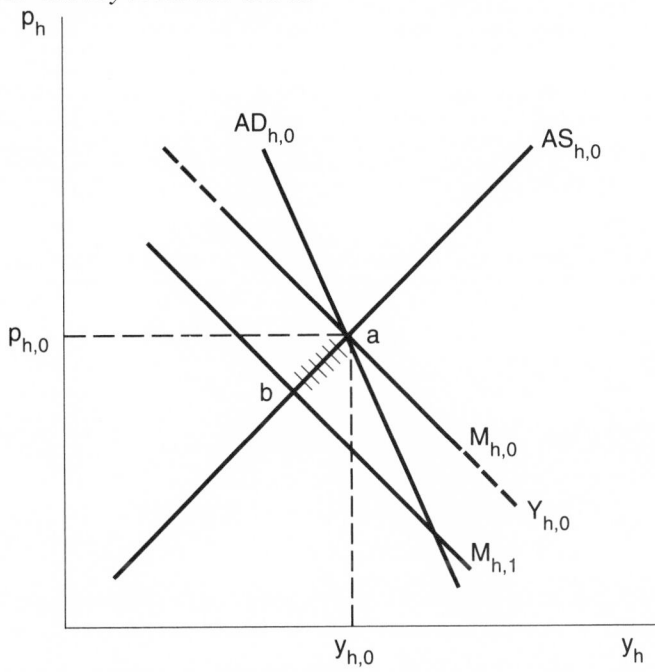

results for both symmetric and asymmetric shocks is the same as the logic behind Poole's result. Under the II and YY pairs, all markets other than the money markets are insulated from the shocks. The results for money-demand shocks are in figure 2-2, tables 2-8 and 2-9, and appendixes D and E.

A *symmetric increase in the demands for US and ROECD money,* an increase in v_s, causes the M_s schedule to shift down from $M_{s,0}$ to $M_{s,1}$ as shown in figure 2-2 (with $h = s$). An increase in v_s increases the sum of excess demands; thus, p_s must be lower for given values of y_s, m_s, and i_s in order to keep this sum equal to zero. The increase in the sum of money demands creates an excess demand for money at the original values of p_s, y_s, m_s, and i_s corresponding to point a, so there is upward pressure on i_s . If i_s is increased, the M_s schedule shifts up and the AD_s schedule shifts down until they meet along the marked part of the $AS_{s,0}$ schedule between points a and b.

Under the II and YY regime pairs, i_s is kept unchanged. Under the II pair, i_s must be kept unchanged by definition.[27] Under the YY pair, it must be kept unchanged in order to keep the economy on the $Y_{s,0}$ schedule. If i_s

27. For a symmetric shock, i_d remains constant. Therefore, keeping i_s unchanged keeps i and $\hat{i}$ unchanged.

Table 2-9. *First-Period Impact of an Asymmetric Money-Demand Shock (US Demand Increasing)*

	Regime pair									
	Oil excluded (β = 0)					Oil included (β = 0.1)				
Variable[a]	MM	II	YY	CC	ME	MM	II	YY	CC	ME
US economy										
Output (%)	-3.68	0	0	0	-2.93	-3.61	0	0	0	-2.93
CPI inflation (D)	-2.88	0	0	0	-1.26	-2.93	0	0	0	-1.26
Output price (%)	-1.58	0	0	0	-1.26	-1.64	0	0	0	-1.26
Nominal interest rate (D)	5.92	0	0	0	7.27	5.93	0	0	0	7.27
Real interest rate (D)	3.04	0	0	0	6.01	3	0	0	0	6.01
Nominal wage (%)	0	0	0	0	0	0	0	0	0	0
Employment (%)	-5.26	0	0	0	-4.19	-5.26	0	0	0	-4.19
Money (%)	0	10	10	10	0	0	10	10	10	0
Nominal exchange rate ($/R)(%)	-11.84	0	0	0	0	-11.86	0	0	0	0
Real exchange rate ($/R)(%)	-8.68	0	0	0	0	-8.57	0	0	0	0
ROECD economy										
Output (%)	3.68	0	0	0	-2.93	3.61	0	0	0	-2.93
CPI inflation (D)	2.88	0	0	0	-1.26	2.93	0	0	0	-1.26
Output price (%)	1.58	0	0	0	-1.26	1.64	0	0	0	-1.26
Nominal interest rate (D)	-5.92	0	0	0	7.27	-5.93	0	0	0	7.27
Real interest rate (D)	-3.04	0	0	0	6.01	-3	0	0	0	6.01
Nominal wage (%)	0	0	0	0	0	0	0	0	0	0
Employment (%)	5.26	0	0	0	-4.19	5.26	0	0	0	-4.19
Money(%)	0	-10	-10	-10	-20	0	-10	-10	-10	-20

a. % is percent deviation from unchanged baseline; D is deviation from unchanged baseline in percentage points.

were increased, the new equilibrium would lie on the AS_0 schedule between points a and b below the $Y_{s,0}$ schedule. To keep i_s unchanged, the money supply must be allowed to increase by enough to shift the M_s schedule from $M_{s,1}$ back to $M_{s,0}$. So i_s, y_s, and p_s and, therefore, $p_s + y_s, n_s$, and $q_s = p_s$ remain unchanged. In terms of the algebraic expressions in appendix D, $y_{s,v_s}^{jj} = \alpha n_{s,v_s}^{jj} = q_{s,v_s}^{jj} = 0$, where $jj = $ II, YY and where, for example, n_{s,v_s}^{II} represents the effect of a symmetric increase in money demands on the sum of employments under the II regime pair.

Under the MM regime pair, i_s must be increased in order to keep m_s constant. The new equilibrium lies somewhere on the marked part of the $AS_{s,0}$ schedule between points a and b and below the $Y_{s,0}$ schedule. In the new equilibrium, i_s is higher and y_s and p_s and, therefore, $p_s + y_s, n_s$, and q_s are lower. Since y_s is lower, $i_s + p_s$ and, therefore, r_s must be higher in order to keep the sum of excess demands for goods equal to zero. The new equilibrium lies on an AD_s schedule below $AD_{s,0}$. $i_s + p_s$ would be unchanged if the new equilibrium were at the point on the new AS_s schedule that is directly below point a. However, since the new equilibrium lies to the northwest of the point on the new AS_s that is directly below point a, the fall in p_s must be less in absolute value than the rise in i_s. For symmetric shocks, the real exchange rate remains unchanged, and corresponding variables in each region move in the same direction with each moving by half as much as their sum.[28]

The analysis of an *asymmetric money-demand shock* with US money demand increasing and ROECD money demand decreasing is analogous to the analysis of a symmetric money-demand shock. It is conducted using figure 2-2 with $h = d$. Under the II and YY regime pairs, i_d is kept constant; y_d and p_d and, therefore, $p_d + y_d$, n_d, and q_d remain unchanged. Under the MM pair, i_d is increased; y_d and p_d, and, therefore, $p_d + y_d, n_d$, and q_d are lower. Since y_d is lower $i_d + p_d$ must be higher and, therefore, r_d must be higher and the dollar must appreciate in real terms in order for the difference between excess demands for goods to remain equal to zero.

There are two main differences between the results for asymmetric shocks and those for symmetric shocks. For asymmetric shocks, (1) the real exchange rate changes, and (2) corresponding variables in each region move in opposite directions, with each moving by half as much as their difference.[29]

---

28. For example, the effects of an increase in v_s on n and $\mathring{n}$ under the MM regime ($n_{v_s}^{MM}$ and $\mathring{n}_{v_s}^{MM}$) can be obtained directly from the effect of an increase in v_s on n_s as shown in equation 2-52 in table 2-7, where n_v^{MM}, $\mathring{n}_v^{MM}$, $n_{\mathring{v}}^{MM}$, and $\mathring{n}_{\mathring{v}}^{MM}$ are defined below equation 2-57 and equations 2-56 and 2-57 hold because the two countries are mirror images of each other. See the next note.

29. For example, the effects of an increase in v_d on n and $\mathring{n}$ under the MM regime ($n_{v_d}^{MM}$ and $\mathring{n}_{v_d}^{MM}$) can be obtained directly from the effect of an increase in v_d on n_d as shown in equation 2-53 in table 2-7. See the previous note.

Goods-Demand Shocks

For symmetric goods-demand shocks, the YY regime pair dominates the MM regime pair, which dominates the II regime pair for both employments and CPIs. For asymmetric goods-demand shocks, the ranking is the same for employments, but the ranking for CPIs depends on parameter values, so that, for example, the YY regime pair may not dominate the other pairs.[30]

The result that for symmetric shocks the MM pair dominates the II pair is the same as Poole's result for a goods-demand shock in a closed economy. The logic behind both this result and the result that for asymmetric shocks the MM pair dominates the II pair for employments is the same as the logic behind Poole's result. Under the MM pair, larger induced movements in real interest rates and, for asymmetric shocks, the real exchange rate offset more of the impact effects of the shocks on the goods markets.

The result that for asymmetric shocks the ranking for CPIs depends on parameter values is important because the YY pair unambiguously dominates the II and MM pairs in many other cases.

The results for symmetric and asymmetric goods-demand shocks are in figure 2-3, tables 2-10 and 2-11, and appendixes D and E.

A *symmetric increase in the demands for US and ROECD goods*, an increase in u_s, causes the AD_s schedule to shift up from $AD_{s,0}$ to $AD_{s,1}$ in figure 2-3 (with $h = s$). A positive u_s tends to increase the sum of excess demands for goods; thus for a given value of y_s, p_s must be higher, causing r_s to be higher in order to keep this sum equal to zero. At point b, where the $AD_{s,1}$ and $AS_{s,0}$ schedules intersect, the sum of excess demands for money is positive, so there is upward pressure on i_s. If i_s is increased, the AD_s schedule shifts down from $AD_{s,1}$ and the M_s schedule shifts up from $M_{s,0}$ until they meet at some point along the marked part of the $AS_{s,0}$ schedule between points a and b.

Under the II regime pair, i_s is kept constant, so the new equilibrium is at the intersection of the $AD_{s,1}$ and $AS_{s,0}$ schedules at point b, which is above the $Y_{s,0}$ schedule. In the new equilibrium, p_s and y_s and, therefore, $p_s + y_s, n_s$, and q_s are all higher. Since i_s is kept constant, the increase in y_s and the associated increase in p_s must be large enough to fully offset the effect of the disturbance on the goods market. m_s must rise by enough to satisfy money demand at an unchanged i_s and higher p_s and y_s.

Under the MM regime pair, i_s is increased in order to prevent an increase in m_s. The new equilibrium lies on the marked part of the $AS_{s,0}$ schedule

30. Melitz (1983) was among the first to point out that, because of exchange-rate effects, the ranking of regimes for measures of real economic activity like employments could be different from the ranking for CPIs.

between points a and b and above the $Y_{s,0}$ schedule. i_s, p_s, and y_s and, therefore, $p_s + y_s$, n_s, and q_s are all higher. p_s and y_s must be higher given that i_s is higher in order for the money market to remain in equilibrium at an unchanged value of m_s. However, the increases in all the variables but i_s are smaller under the MM pair than under the II pair, because smaller increases in p_s and y_s are required to reequilibrate the goods markets when i_s is increased.

Under the YY regime pair, the new equilibrium is at the same point as the initial equilibrium was, point a on the $Y_{s,0}$ schedule. To keep $p_s + y_s$ constant, i_s must be increased by enough to shift the AD_s schedule all the way back to its original position. Not only $p_s + y_s$ and n_s but also p_s and y_s individually remain unchanged under the YY pair. The increase in i_s must be larger under the YY pair than under the MM pair because $p_s + y_s$ rises under the MM pair.

The analysis of an *asymmetric shock to goods demands* with the demand for US goods increasing and the demand for ROECD goods decreasing is analogous to the analysis of a symmetric shock. It is conducted using figure 2-3 (with $h = d$). y_d, p_d and, therefore, $p_d + y_d$ and n_d rise more under the II pair than under the MM pair and not at all under the YY pair. i_d is kept constant under the II pair, increased under the MM pair, and increased more under the YY pair.

Figure 2-3. *Goods-Demand Shock*

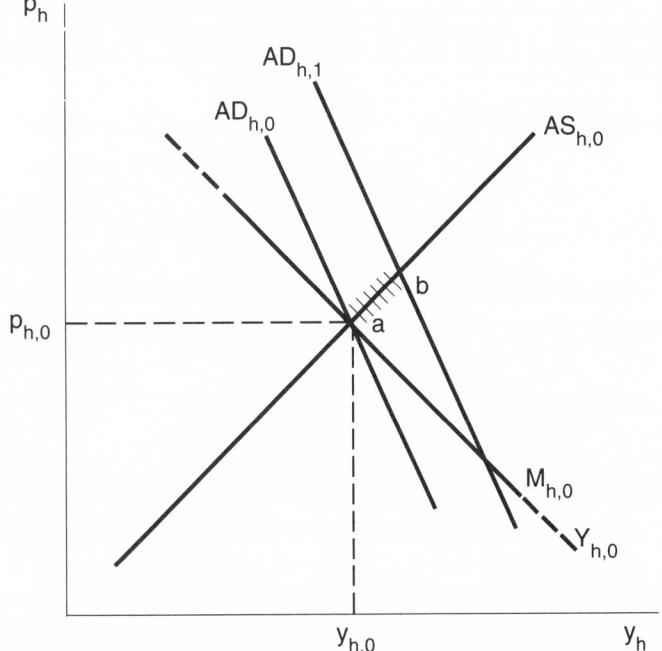

Table 2-10. First-Period Impact of a Symmetric Increase in Goods Demand

	Regime pair									
	Oil excluded (β = 0)					Oil included (β = 0.1)				
Variable[a]	MM	II	YY	CC	ME	MM	II	YY	CC	ME
US economy										
Output (%)	11.73	20.17	0	0	11.73	11.73	20.17	0	0	11.73
CPI inflation (D)	5.03	8.65	0	0	5.03	5.03	8.65	0	0	5.03
Output price (%)	5.03	8.65	0	0	5.03	5.03	8.65	0	0	5.03
Nominal interest rate (D)	20.94	0	50	50	20.94	20.94	0	50	50	20.94
Real interest rate (D)	25.96	8.65	50	50	25.96	25.96	8.65	50	50	25.96
Nominal wage (%)	0	0	0	0	0	0	0	0	0	0
Employment (%)	16.75	28.82	0	0	16.75	16.75	28.82	0	0	16.75
Money (%)	0	28.82	-40	-40	0	0	28.82	-40	-40	0
Nominal exchange rate ($/R)(%)	0	0			0	0	0			0
Real exchange rate ($/R)(%)	0	0			0	0	0			0
ROECD economy										
Output (%)	11.73	20.17	0	0	11.73	11.73	20.17	0	0	11.73
CPI inflation (D)	5.03	8.65	0	0	5.03	5.03	8.65	0	0	5.03
Output price (%)	5.03	8.65	0	0	5.03	5.03	8.65	0	0	5.03
Nominal interest rate (D)	20.94	0	50	50	20.94	20.94	0	50	50	20.94
Real interest rate (D)	25.96	8.65	50	50	25.96	25.96	8.65	50	50	25.96
Nominal wage (%)	0	0	0	0	0	0	0	0	0	0
Employment (%)	16.75	28.82	0	0	16.75	16.75	28.82	0	0	16.75
Money (%)	0	28.82	-40	-40	0	0	28.82	-40	-40	0

a. % is percent deviation from unchanged baseline; D is deviation from unchanged baseline in percentage points.

Table 2-11. *First-Period Impact of an Asymmetric Goods-Demand Shock (US Demand Increasing)*

| | Regime pair | | | | | | | | | |
| | Oil excluded (β = 0) | | | | | Oil included (β = 0.1) | | | | |
Variable[a]	MM	II	YY	CC	ME	MM	II	YY	CC	ME
US economy										
Output (%)	5.92	12.49	0	0	7.26	7.21	13.15	1.85	1.85	8.33
CPI inflation (D)	-1.39	3.75	-6.02	-6.02	1.51	-2.51	2.3	-6.86	-6.86	0.24
Output price (%)	2.54	5.35	0	0	3.11	0.58	3.29	-1.85	-1.85	1.22
Nominal interest rate (D)	10.57	0	20.08	20.08	12.97	9.74	0	18.54	16.69	11.94
Real interest rate (D)	9.17	3.75	14.06	14.06	14.47	7.23	2.3	11.68	11.68	12.18
Nominal wage (%)	0	0	0	0	0	0	0	0	0	0
Employment (%)	8.45	17.85	0	0	10.37	7.8	16.43	0	0	9.55
Money (%)	0	17.85	-16.06	-16.06	0	0	16.43	-14.83	-13.35	0
Nominal exchange rate ($/R)(%)	-21.14	0	-40.16	-40.16	0	-19.49	0	-37.08	-37.08	0
Real exchange rate ($/R)(%)	-26.21	-10.71	-40.16	-40.16	-10.71	-20.66	-6.57	-33.37	-33.37	-6.57
ROECD economy										
Output (%)	-5.92	-12.49	0	0	-17.73	-7.21	-13.15	-1.85	1.85	-17.96
CPI inflation (D)	1.39	-3.75	6.02	6.02	-5.99	2.51	-2.3	6.86	6.86	-4.37
Output price (%)	-2.54	-5.35	0	0	-7.6	-0.58	-3.29	1.85	1.85	-5.35
Nominal interest rate (D)	-10.57	0	-20.08	-20.08	12.97	-9.74	0	-18.54	-16.69	11.94
Real interest rate (D)	-9.17	-3.75	-14.06	-14.06	6.98	-7.23	-2.3	-11.68	-11.68	7.57
Nominal wage (%)	0	0	0	0	0	0	0	0	0	0
Employment (%)	-8.45	-17.85	0	0	-25.32	-7.8	-16.43	0	0	-23.31
Money (%)	0	-17.85	16.06	16.06	-35.7	0	-16.43	14.83	13.35	-32.87

a. % is percent deviation from unchanged baseline; D is deviation from unchanged baseline in percentage points.

The results for the difference between CPIs, q_d, depend on the results for p_d and i_d and the value of γ, the average propensity to import (see equation 2-28). q_d definitely rises under the II pair and definitely falls under the YY pair. But whether it rises or falls under the MM pair depends on parameter values. For example, it definitely rises if $\gamma = 0$ and definitely falls if $\gamma = 1/2$.

The ranking of regime pairs for q_d depends on parameter values. For example, if $\gamma = 0$, q_d rises more under the II pair than under the MM pair and remains unchanged under the YY pair. But if $\gamma = 1/2$, q_d falls more under the YY pair than under the MM pair and remains unchanged under the II pair. Note that for the simulation results in table 2-11, γ is high enough (0.15) that deviations of CPI inflation from baseline for the YY pair are worse than for either the II or the MM pair.

Productivity Shocks

For symmetric and asymmetric productivity shocks, the YY regime pair dominates the MM and II regime pairs for employments. But either the MM or II pair, or both, may dominate the YY pair for CPIs. Indeed, all other rankings for employments and all rankings for CPIs depend on parameter values. For symmetric shocks, the crucial parameters are the slopes of the AD_s and M_s schedules. For asymmetric shocks, the crucial parameters are γ and the slopes of the AD_d and M_d schedules. The results for symmetric and asymmetric productivity shocks are in figures 2-4 and 2-5, tables 2-12 and 2-13, and appendixes D and E.

A *symmetric decrease in productivity* in the US and the ROECD, an increase in x_s, causes the AS_s schedule to shift up from $AS_{s,0}$ to $AS_{s,1}$ in figures 2-4 and 2-5 (with $h = s$). To keep y_s constant, p_s must be higher so that n_s will rise by enough to offset the effect of the increase in x_s. The pair of y_s and p_s that clears the goods market is given by the intersection of the $AS_{s,1}$ and $AD_{s,0}$ schedules at point b. Whether there is upward or downward pressure on i_s depends on what happens to the sum of excess demands for money at point b. What happens to the sum of excess demands for money depends on the relative slopes of the AD_s and M_s schedules.

If the AD_s schedule is steeper than the M_s schedule as in figure 2-4, the sum of excess demands for money is positive at point b, so there is upward pressure on i_s. If i_s is increased, the AD_s schedule shifts down and the M_s schedule shifts up until they meet somewhere on the marked part of the $AS_{s,1}$ schedule between points b and c. For the parameter values used to generate the simulation results in table 2-12, $\phi = 1$ and the AD_s schedule is steeper than the M_s schedule.

In contrast, if the AD_s schedule is flatter than the M_s schedule, as in figure 2-5, the sum of excess demands for money is negative at point b, so there is

Figure 2-4. *Productivity Shock 1*

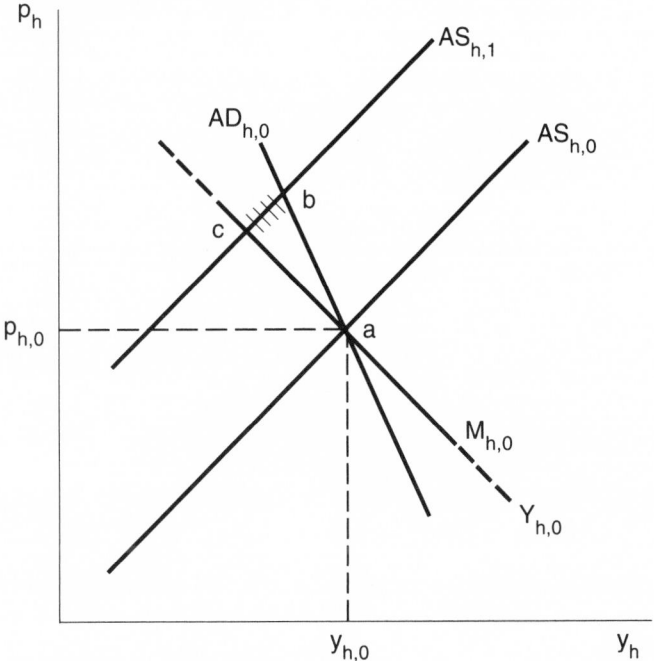

Figure 2-5. *Productivity Shock 2*

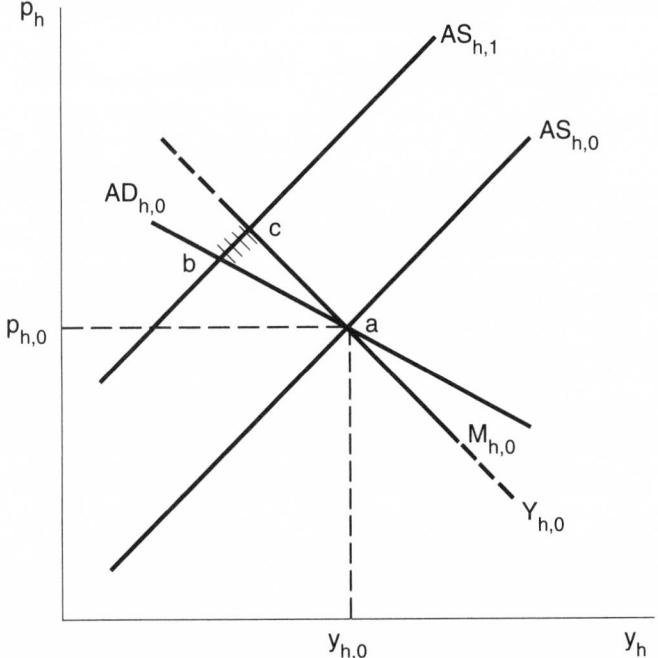

Table 2-12. *First-Period Impact of a Symmetric Decrease in Productivity*

| | Regime pair | | | | | | | | | |
| | Oil excluded (β = 0) | | | | | Oil included (β = 0.1) | | | | |
Variable[a]	MM	II	YY	CC	ME	MM	II	YY	CC	ME
US economy										
Output (%)	-7.54	-5.76	-10	-10	-7.54	-7.54	-5.76	-10	-10	-7.54
CPI inflation (D)	11.06	11.82	10	10	11.06	11.06	11.82	10	10	11.06
Output price (%)	11.06	11.82	10	10	11.06	11.06	11.82	10	10	11.06
Nominal interest rate (D)	4.4	0	10.5	20.5	4.4	4.4	0	10.5	20.5	4.4
Real interest rate (D)	15.45	11.82	20.5	20.5	15.45	15.45	11.82	20.5	20.5	15.45
Nominal wage (%)	0	0	0	0	0	0	0	0	0	0
Employment (%)	3.52	6.05	0	0	3.52	3.52	6.05	0	0	3.52
Money (%)	0	6.05	-8.4	-16.4	0	0	6.05	-8.4	-16.4	0
Nominal exchange rate ($/R)(%)	0	0	0	0	0	0	0	0	0	0
Real exchange rate ($/R)(%)	0	0	0	0	0	0	0	0	0	0
ROECD economy										
Output (%)	-7.54	-5.76	-10	-10	-7.54	-7.54	-5.76	-10	-10	-7.54
CPI inflation (D)	11.06	11.82	10	10	11.06	11.06	11.82	10	10	11.06
Output price (%)	11.06	11.82	10	10	11.06	11.06	11.82	10	10	11.06
Nominal interest rate (D)	4.4	0	10.5	20.5	4.4	4.4	0	10.5	20.5	4.4
Real interest rate (D)	15.45	11.82	20.5	20.5	15.45	15.45	11.82	20.5	20.5	15.45
Nominal wage (%)	0	0	0	0	0	0	0	0	0	0
Employment (%)	3.52	6.05	0	0	3.52	3.52	6.05	0	0	3.52
Money (%)	0	6.05	-8.4	-16.4	0	0	6.05	-8.4	-16.4	0

a. % is percent deviation from unchanged baseline; D is deviation from unchanged baseline in percentage points.

Table 2-13. *First-Period Impact of an Asymmetric Productivity Shock (US Productivity Decreasing)*

	Regime pair									
	Oil excluded (β = 0)					Oil included (β = 0.1)				
Variable[a]	MM	II	YY	CC	ME	MM	II	YY	CC	ME
US economy										
Output (%)	-9.47	-8.89	-10	-10	-9.35	-9.29	-8.7	-9.82	-9.82	-9.18
CPI inflation (D)	6.88	7.33	6.46	6.46	7.13	6.75	7.23	6.32	6.32	7.02
Output price (%)	10.23	10.48	10	10	10.28	10.06	10.32	9.82	9.82	10.12
Nominal interest rate (D)	0.94	0	1.79	11.79	1.15	0.96	0	1.83	11.65	1.18
Real interest rate (D)	7.82	7.33	8.25	8.25	8.29	7.71	7.23	8.15	8.15	8.2
Nominal wage (%)	0	0	0	0	0	0	0	0	0	0
Employment (%)	0.75	1.59	0	0	0.92	0.77	1.62	0	0	0.94
Money (%)	0	1.59	-1.43	-9.43	0	0	1.62	-1.47	-9.32	0
Nominal exchange rate ($/R)(%)	-1.88	0	-3.57	-3.57	0	-1.93	0	-3.66	-3.66	0
Real exchange rate ($/R)(%)	-22.33	-20.95	-23.57	-23.57	-20.95	-22.04	-20.65	-23.3	-23.3	-20.65
ROECD economy										
Output (%)	9.47	8.89	10	10	8.42	9.29	8.7	9.82	9.82	8.23
CPI inflation (D)	-6.88	-7.33	-6.46	-6.46	-7.53	-6.75	-7.23	-6.32	-6.32	-7.43
Output price (%)	-10.23	-10.48	-10	-10	-10.68	-10.06	-10.32	-9.82	-9.82	-10.53
Nominal interest rate (D)	-0.94	0	-1.79	-11.79	1.15	-0.96	0	-1.83	-11.65	1.18
Real interest rate (D)	-7.82	-7.33	-8.25	-8.25	-6.38	-7.71	-7.23	-8.15	-8.15	-6.25
Nominal wage (%)	0	0	0	0	0	0	0	0	0	0
Employment (%)	-0.75	-1.59	0	0	-2.25	-0.77	-1.62	0	0	-2.3
Money (%)	0	-1.59	1.43	9.43	-3.18	0	-1.62	1.47	9.32	-3.25

a. % is percent deviation from unchanged baseline; D is deviation from unchanged baseline in percentage points.

downward pressure on i_s. If i_s is decreased, the AD_s schedule shifts up and the M_s schedule shifts down until they meet somewhere on the marked part of the $AS_{s,1}$ schedule between points b and c.

Under the II regime pair, i_s is kept constant, so the new equilibrium must be at the intersection of the $AS_{s,1}$ and $AD_{s,0}$ schedules at point b in figure 2-5. y_s falls, and p_s and, therefore, q_s rise.

If the AD_s schedule is steeper than the M_s schedule as in figure 2-4, the new equilibrium lies above the $Y_{s,0}$ schedule, so $p_s + y_s$ and, therefore, n_s must rise. The conclusion that symmetric reductions in productivity increase employments may seem counterintuitive, but it can be explained. The pair of y_s and p_s consistent with unchanged factor use following the symmetric productivity shock is given by the intersection of the $AS_{s,1}$ and $Y_{s,0}$ schedules at point c in figure 2-4. This pair implies an excess demand for goods. Therefore, y_s must fall by less, and p_s must rise by more, than the amounts consistent with unchanged factor use, and so n_s must rise.

If the AD_s schedule is flatter than the M_s schedule as in figure 2-5, the new equilibrium lies below the $Y_{s,0}$ schedule, so $p_s + y_s$ and, therefore, n_s must fall. The pair of y_s and p_s consistent with unchanged factor use following the symmetric productivity shock given by point c implies an excess supply of goods. Therefore, y_s must fall by more, and p_s must rise by less, than the amounts consistent with unchanged factor use, and so n_s must fall.

Under the MM regime pair, i_s is changed by enough to keep m_s unchanged, so the new equilibrium lies on the marked part of the $AS_{s,1}$ schedule between points b and c in figure 2-4. Since the slope of the AD_s schedule is greater than one in absolute value, i_s must be increased. y_s falls by more, p_s rises by less, and, therefore, $p_s + y_s, n_s$, and q_s rise by less than under the II regime pair. If the slope of the AD_s schedule is less than one in absolute value, i_s must be decreased. y_s falls by less, p_s rises by more, and, therefore, $p_s + y_s$ and n_s fall by less and q_s rises by more than under the II regime pair.

Under the YY regime pair, $p_s + y_s$ is kept constant, so the new equilibrium must be on the $Y_{s,0}$ schedule just as the initial equilibrium was. i_s is adjusted so that the AD_s schedule passes through the intersection of the $AS_{s,1}$ and $Y_{s,0}$ and schedules at point c. Since the new equilibrium is on the $Y_{s,0}$ schedule, employments are unchanged. Since employments are unchanged, y_s falls and p_s rises by amounts that are equal in absolute value to the increase in x_s. It is worth emphasizing that the equilibrium decrease in y_s is the same as the decrease in y_s that would take place if wages were flexible and all markets cleared.[31] If the AD_s schedule is steeper than the M_s schedule (figure 2-4), i_s

---

31. According to the sum of equations 2-1 with $\beta = 0$, if n_s remains unchanged at zero, the amount by which y_s must change for a given change in x_s is uniquely determined. With perfectly flexible wages, n_s remains unchanged, because wages adjust. With one-period wage contracts, n_s remains unchanged under the YY regime, because policymakers adjust i_s by enough.

is increased by more, y_s falls by more, and p_s and, therefore, q_s rise by less than under the MM regime pair. If instead, the AD_s schedule is flatter than the M_s schedule (figure 2-5), i_s is decreased by more, y_s falls by less, and p_s and, therefore, q_s rise by more than under the MM regime pair. This is a case in which both the II and MM pairs dominate the YY pair for stabilization of CPIs.

So far we have been assuming that the slope of the M_s schedule is equal to one in absolute value. The following *additional results for symmetric productivity shocks* can be proved for cases in which the slope of M_s is greater or less than one in absolute value. First, if the slopes of both the M_s and AD_s schedules are greater than one in absolute value, the YY regime pair dominates both other regime pairs for CPIs (q_s). Whether the II or MM pair is preferred for employments (n_s) and for CPIs depends on whether the AD_s schedule is flatter or steeper than the M_s schedule. Second, if the slopes of the M_s and AD_s schedules are less than one in absolute value, then the II and MM pairs both dominate the YY pair for q_s. Whether the II or the MM pair is preferred for n_s while the other is preferred for q_s depends on whether the AD_s schedule is steeper or flatter than the M_s schedule. Third, if the slope of the AD_s schedule is greater than one in absolute value and the slope of the M_s schedule is less than one in absolute value, then the ranking of the MM and II regime pairs for n_s is ambiguous, the YY pair is preferred to the II pair for q_s, and the ranking of the MM and YY pairs for q_s is ambiguous. Fourth, if the slope of the M_s schedule is greater than one in absolute value and the slope of the AD_s schedule is less than one in absolute value, the ranking of the MM and II pairs for n_s is ambiguous, the II pair is preferred to the YY pair for q_s, and the ranking of the MM and YY pairs for q_s is ambiguous.

The analysis of an *asymmetric productivity shock* with US productivity falling and ROECD productivity rising, an increase in x_d, is analogous to the analysis of a symmetric productivity shock and is conducted using figures 2-4 and 2-5 with $h = d$. The results depend on whether the AD_d schedule is steeper or flatter than the M_d schedule and on the value of γ, the average propensity to import.

Suppose the AD_d schedule is steeper than the M_d schedule as in figure 2-4. y_d falls least under the II pair, more under the MM pair, and most under the YY pair; p_d rises most under the II pair, less under the MM pair, and least under the YY pair. $p_d + y_d$ and n_d rise most under the II pair, less under the MM pair, and not at all under the YY pair. i_d is kept constant under the II pair, is increased under the MM pair, and is increased by more under the YY pair.

For the difference between CPIs, q_d, the signs of changes under the MM and YY regime pairs and the ranking of pairs depend on the results for p_d and i_d and the value of γ, just as they do in the case of an asymmetric goods-demand shock. For example, when $\gamma = 0$, q_d rises most under the II pair, less under the MM pair, and least under the YY pair. However, when $\gamma = 1/2$, q_d falls more under the YY pair than under the MM pair and remains unchanged under the II pair.

Although for q_d the signs of the changes under the MM and YY pairs and the ranking of pairs depend on γ for both an asymmetric productivity shock and an asymmetric goods-demand shock, the critical values of γ at which the signs and rankings change are different for the two kinds of shocks. For productivity shocks, the total effect on p_d is the sum of the increase on impact and the increase induced by the rise in employment. But for goods-demand shocks, the total effect on p_d is just the increase induced by the rise in employment.

Suppose the AD_d schedule is flatter than the M_d schedule (figure 2-5). y_d falls most under the II pair, less under the MM pair, and least under the YY pair; p_d rises least under the II pair, more under the MM pair, and most under the YY pair. $p_d + y_d$, and n_d fall most under the II pair, less under the MM pair, and not at all under the YY pair. i_d is kept constant under the II pair, is decreased under the MM pair, and is decreased by more under the YY pair. Therefore, q_d rises least under the II pair, more under the MM pair, and most under the YY pair no matter what the value of γ. This is another case in which both the MM pair and the II pair are better than the YY pair for CPIs.

It is possible to prove additional results for an asymmetric productivity shock for cases in which the slope of the M_d schedule is greater or less than one in absolute value. Those results are analogous to the additional results for a symmetric productivity shock for cases in which the slope of the M_s schedule is greater or less than one in absolute value. We do not report those results here.

Region-Specific Shocks with Matched Regime Pairs

In this section, we consider the effects of three region-specific shocks to behavioral relations in the US—a money-demand shock, a goods-demand shock, and a productivity shock—under the II, MM, and YY matched regime pairs and the Contract hypothesis. In general, the effects of these shocks on employments, outputs, and CPIs in the two regions are neither symmetric nor asymmetric. With mirror-image regions and matched regime pairs, a region-specific shock in the US and the corresponding region-specific shock in the ROECD have effects that are mirror images of each other. Hence we do not provide a separate discussion of region-specific shocks in the ROECD with matched regime pairs.[32]

---

32. However, entries for region-specific shocks in the ROECD with matched regime pairs are included in the tables of simulation results and in the table that summarizes rankings.

In the discussion of each region-specific shock, just as in the discussion of symmetric and asymmetric shocks, we first state our general conclusions regarding the rankings of regimes and then provide explanations for those conclusions. In most cases, the analysis of region-specific shocks is more complicated than the analysis of symmetric and asymmetric shocks, and the results are more ambiguous. In the explanations, we rely on algebraic and simulation methods and do not use graphical methods. Since it is usually difficult to derive the effect of a shock on each variable, we report effects only for employments and CPIs in the two regions.[33]

The analysis of region-specific shocks is based on the analysis of symmetric and asymmetric shocks. The algebraic results for region-specific shocks can be obtained by combining expressions from appendix D. For example, as is shown in table 2-7, the expression for the effect of an increase in the demand for US money on US employment under a given regime pair can be obtained by adding the effect of a symmetric increase in money demands on the sum of employments to the effect of an asymmetric change in money demands (US money demand increasing and ROECD money demand decreasing) on the difference between employments. The other expressions needed for the analysis of region-specific shocks can be obtained in an analogous way.

US Money-Demand Shock

For a shock to the demand for US money, the rankings of regime pairs are independent of parameter values. The II and YY pairs are ranked the same, and either of them dominates the MM pair. Under the II and YY pairs, neither employment nor the CPI is affected in either region because the US policymaker prevents the shock from being transmitted to markets other than the US money market by keeping the US interest rate from changing. In contrast, under the MM pair, employment and the CPI change in both regions. The results for region-specific money-demand shocks are in tables 2-14, 2-15, and 2-16.

First, we explain the approach and notation used in the algebraic analysis of region-specific shocks. As examples, we refer to the expressions for the effects of an increase in the demand for US money on US and ROECD employments under the MM regime pair. A one-unit increase in the demand for US money, an increase in v, can be represented by equal one-half unit increases in v_s and v_d, since $2v = v_s + v_d$. Under the MM pair the effects of an increase in v on n (n_v^{MM}) and $\overset{*}{n}$ ($\overset{*}{n}_v^{\text{MM}}$) are given by equations 2-54 and 2-55 in

---

33. Of course, for money-demand and goods-demand shocks there are one-to-one relationships between the effect on employment and the effects on output price and output.

Table 2-14. *The Effect of an Increase in the Demand for US Money*
(v) *on ROECD Employment* ($\overset{\star}{n}$)

(2-58)
$$2\alpha \overset{\star}{n}{}_v^{MM} = \alpha\left[n_{s,v_s}^{MM} - n_{d,v_d}^{MM}\right] = -\frac{v/\lambda}{E} + \frac{v[(1-2\gamma)^2 + 2\delta/v]/\lambda}{J}$$

$$= \left[\frac{1/\lambda}{EJ}\right]v\{(1-\epsilon)[\delta/v - 2(1-\gamma)\gamma] - \epsilon\gamma\} = \left[\frac{1/\lambda}{EJ}\right]M$$

$$E = 1 - \epsilon + v(A + D/\lambda), \qquad J = 1 - (1-2\gamma)\epsilon + v[(1-2\gamma)^2 + 2\delta/v](A + D/\lambda)$$

table 2-7, respectively. Equations 2-56 and 2-57 in table 2-7 hold because the US and the ROECD are mirror images of each other. General expressions for n_{s,v_s}^{MM} and n_{d,v_d}^{MM} are given by equations 2-52 and 2-53 in table 2-7, respectively. Expressions for n_{s,v_s}^{MM} and n_{d,v_d}^{MM} in terms of the parameters of the model are obtained from appendix D. Other expressions for the effects of region-specific shocks on variables for individual regions are analogous.

Now, we discuss the effects of an increase in the demand for US money, an increase in v, on employments and CPIs in the US and the ROECD. We established in the previous section that under the II and YY regime pairs, increases in v_s have no effects on n_s and q_s, while increases in v_d have no effects on n_d and q_d. Thus, for example, $n_{s,v_s}^{II} = n_{d,v_d}^{II} = 0$. Therefore, from the expressions for $n_v^{II}, \overset{\star}{n}{}_v^{II}, q_v^{II}, \overset{\star}{q}{}_v^{II}, n_v^{YY}, \overset{\star}{n}{}_v^{YY}, q_v^{YY}$, and $\overset{\star}{q}{}_v^{YY}$ analogous to equations 2-54 and 2-55, it follows that under the II and YY pairs, increases in v have no effects on $n, \overset{\star}{n}, q$, and $\overset{\star}{q}$.

We also established that under the MM regime pair increases in v_s affect n_s and q_s and increases in v_d affect n_d and q_d. As we show below, the effects of equal increases in v_s and v_d on the sum of and difference between n_s and n_d and the sum of and difference between q_s and q_d do not cancel, so an increase in v affects $n, \overset{\star}{n}, q$, and $\overset{\star}{q}$ under the MM pair. Since an increase in v has no effects on employments and CPIs under the II or the YY pairs, either of these pairs dominates the MM pair.

In the remainder of this subsection, we spell out the effects of an increase in v under the MM pair. We want not only to verify that these effects exist but also to have information about them available for use in our subsequent discussion of the effects of shocks under the unmatched ME regime pair.

Under the MM pair, US employment (n) decreases. We establish in the previous section that $n_{s,v_s}^{MM} < 0$ and that $n_{d,v_d}^{MM} < 0$, that is, that under the MM regime pair an increase in v_s causes a decrease in n_s that corresponds to symmetric decreases in n and $\overset{\star}{n}$, while an increase in v_d causes a decrease in n_d that corresponds to a decrease in n and an increase in $\overset{\star}{n}$ that are equal in absolute value. From equation 2-54, it follows that n_v^{MM} is negative.

ROECD employment ($\overset{\star}{n}$) may rise or fall, and this result should not be surprising. The effects of an increase in v are the same as those of a decrease in the US money supply, and it is well known that the effect of a decrease in one region's money supply on employment in the other region is ambiguous.[34] As stated above, an increase in v causes n to fall. If an increase in v causes $\overset{\star}{n}$ to rise, we say that US money-demand shocks have a negative transmission effect on ROECD employment.[35]

The effect of an increase in v on $\overset{\star}{n}$ is given by equation 2-58 in table 2-14, where expressions for n_{s,v_s}^{MM} and n_{d,v_d}^{MM} are obtained from appendix D. Since both n_{s,v_s}^{MM} and n_{d,v_d}^{MM} are negative, $\overset{\star}{n}_v^{\mathrm{MM}}$ is positive if and only if n_{d,v_d}^{MM} is larger in absolute value.[36] The sign of n_v^{MM} depends on the sign of M which, in turn, depends critically on the ratio δ/v, where δ is the absolute value of the elasticity of output demands with respect to the real exchange rate, and v the responsiveness of expenditure to changes in the real interest rate in each region.[37] If δ/v is large enough, $\overset{\star}{n}_v^{\mathrm{MM}}$ is positive ($M > 0$), and shocks to the demand for US money have a negative transmission effect on ROECD employment. This possibility is illustrated by the simulation results in table 2-15.[38] In contrast, if δ/v is small enough, $\overset{\star}{n}_v^{\mathrm{MM}}$ is negative ($M < 0$), and shocks to the demand for US money have a positive transmission effect on ROECD employment.[39]

34. In discussions of the effects of monetary policy, it is usual to consider the effects of an increase in the money supply instead of a decrease. Under three assumptions, Mundell (1968) uses a two-region model to derive the result that an increase in the money supply in one region raises output in that region and lowers output in the other region. Since, under his assumptions, an increase in the money supply in one region has a negative transmission effect on economic activity in the other, Mundell calls this policy a "beggar thy neighbor policy."

Mundell assumes (1) that the level of the exchange rate does not enter the money-market equilibrium conditions either directly or indirectly through a price index, (2) that bonds denominated in different currencies are perfect substitutes, and (3) that exchange-rate expectations are static. The last two assumptions taken together imply that the interest rates in the two regions must always be the same.

For some time it has been recognized that changing any of Mundell's assumptions can lead to a result different from his. We assume that exchange-rate expectations are rational, not static, but retain Mundell's other two assumptions, and obtain the result that an increase in the US money supply may lead to either a decrease or an increase in output in the ROECD.

35. It is usual to say that a region-specific shock with an impact effect on the market for an item from a given region has a negative transmission effect on economic activity in the other region when it moves economic activity in the given region in one direction and economic activity in the other region in the opposite direction.

36. In appendix F, we explain in more detail why $\overset{\star}{n}_v^{\mathrm{MM}}$ may be either positive or negative.

37. For a more precise definition of δ, see table 2-2.

38. These simulation results confirm that it is possible to have $\overset{\star}{n}_v^{\mathrm{MM}} > 0$ when the slopes of the AD_s and AD_d schedules are greater than one in absolute value, because, as stated above, the parameters used in the simulations imply that these slopes are greater than one in absolute value. See the next note.

39. It is also possible to have $\overset{\star}{n}_v^{\mathrm{MM}} < 0$ when the slopes of the AD_s and AD_d schedules are greater than or equal to one in absolute value. For the slopes of the AD_s and AD_d schedules to be greater than or equal to one in absolute value, we must have $\epsilon + v \leq 1$ and $(1 - 2\gamma)\epsilon + v[(1 - 2\gamma)^2 + 2\delta/v] \leq 1$. If $\epsilon + v = 1$, $\gamma = 1/2$, and $2\delta < \epsilon$, the slope of the AD_s schedule is equal to one in absolute value, the slope of the AD_d schedule is greater than one in absolute value, and $\overset{\star}{n}_v^{\mathrm{MM}} < 0$. See the previous footnote.

Table 2-15. *First-Period Impact of a Region-Specific Increase in US Money Demand*

	Regime pair									
	Oil excluded (β = 0)					Oil included (β = 0.1)				
Variable[a]	MM	II	YY	CC	ME	MM	II	YY	CC	ME
US economy										
Output (%)	-3.31	0	0	0	-2.93	-3.27	0	0	0	-2.93
CPI inflation (D)	-2.07	0	0	0	-1.26	-2.09	0	0	0	-1.26
Output price (%)	-1.42	0	0	0	-1.26	-1.45	0	0	0	-1.26
Nominal interest rate (D)	6.59	0	0	0	7.27	6.6	0	0	0	7.27
Real interest rate (D)	4.52	0	0	0	6.01	4.5	0	0	0	6.01
Nominal wage (%)	0	0	0	0	0	0	0	0	0	0
Employment (%)	-4.73	0	0	0	-4.19	-4.72	0	0	0	-4.19
Money (%)	0	10	10	10	0	0	10	10	10	0
Nominal exchange rate ($/R)(%)	-5.92	0	0	0	0	-5.93			0	0
Real exchange rate ($/R)(%)	-4.34	0	0	0	0	-4.29			0	0
ROECD economy										
Output (%)	0.38	0	0	0	-2.93	0.34	0	0	0	-2.93
CPI inflation (D)	0.81	0	0	0	-1.26	0.84	0	0	0	-1.26
Output price (%)	0.16	0	0	0	-1.26	0.19	0	0	0	-1.26
Nominal interest rate (D)	0.67	0	0	0	7.27	0.67	0	0	0	7.27
Real interest rate (D)	1.48	0	0	0	6.01	1.5	0	0	0	6.01
Nominal wage (%)	0	0	0	0	0	0	0	0	0	0
Employment (%)	0.54	0	0	0	-4.19	0.53	0	0	0	-4.19
Money (%)	0	0	0	0	-10	0	0	0	0	-10

a. % is percent deviation from unchanged baseline; D is deviation from unchanged baseline in percentage points.

Table 2-16. *First-Period Impact of a Region-Specific Increase in ROECD Money Demand*

	Regime pair									
	Oil excluded (β = 0)					Oil included (β = 0.1)				
Variable[a]	MM	II	YY	CC	ME	MM	II	YY	CC	ME
US economy										
Output (%)	0.38	0	0	0	0	0.34	0	0	0	0
CPI inflation (D)	0.81	0	0	0	0	0.84	0	0	0	0
Output price (%)	0.16	0	0	0	0	0.19	0	0	0	0
Nominal interest rate (D)	0.67	0	0	0	0	0.67	0	0	0	0
Real interest rate (D)	1.48	0	0	0	0	1.5	0	0	0	0
Nominal wage (%)	0	0	0	0	0	0	0	0	0	0
Employment (%)	0.54	0	0	0	0	0.53	0	0	0	0
Money (%)	0	0	0	0	0	0	0	0	0	0
Nominal exchange rate ($/R)(%)	5.92	0	0	0	0	5.93	0	0	0	0
Real exchange rate ($/R)(%)	4.34	0	0	0	0	4.29	0	0	0	0
ROECD economy										
Output (%)	-3.31	0	0	0	0	-3.27	0	0	0	0
CPI inflation (D)	-2.07	0	0	0	0	-2.09	0	0	0	0
Output price (%)	-1.42	0	0	0	0	-1.45	0	0	0	0
Nominal interest rate (D)	6.59	0	0	0	0	6.6	0	0	0	0
Real interest rate (D)	4.52	0	0	0	0	4.5	0	0	0	0
Nominal wage (%)	0	0	0	0	0	0	0	0	0	0
Employment (%)	-4.73	0	0	0	0	-4.72	0	0	0	0
Money (%)	0	10	10	10	10	0	10	10	10	10

a. % is percent deviation from unchanged baseline; D is deviation from unchanged baseline in percentage points.

Under the MM regime pair, The US CPI (q) decreases. We establish in the previous section that $q_{s,v_s}^{MM} < 0$ and $q_{d,v_d}^{MM} < 0$. From an expression analogous to equation 2-54, it follows that q_v^{MM} is negative.

The ROECD CPI ($\overset{*}{q}$) may rise or fall depending on parameter values. We know that $\overset{*}{q}_v^{MM} = \overset{*}{p}_v^{MM} - \gamma z_v^{MM}$, and $\overset{*}{p}_v^{MM} = A\alpha \overset{*}{n}_v^{MM}$.[40] If parameter values are such that $\overset{*}{n}_v^{MM}$ is positive, $\overset{*}{q}$ rises because $\overset{*}{p}$ rises, and the dollar appreciates in real terms as illustrated by the simulation results in table 2-15. However, if parameter values are such that $\overset{*}{n}_v{}^{MM}$ is negative and γ is small enough, $\overset{*}{q}$ may fall because $\overset{*}{p}$ falls, and the decline in $\overset{*}{p}$ may be large enough to outweigh the effect of the real dollar appreciation.

US Goods-Demand Shock

For a shock to the demand for the US good, some rankings of regime pairs are independent of parameter values, but others are not. For stabilization of US employment, the YY regime pair dominates the MM pair, and the MM pair dominates the II pair. For stabilization of ROECD employment, the YY pair ranks at least as high as either the MM pair or the II pair and almost certainly dominates either of them, but the ranking of the MM and the II pairs depends on parameter values. For stabilization of the US and ROECD CPIs, all the rankings depend on parameter values. The results for the effects of region-specific increases in the demands for goods are in tables 2-17 through 2-19, and appendix E (2E-3 and 2E-4).

As we state above, for US employment, the YY pair dominates the MM pair, which dominates the II pair. We establish in the previous section that $n_{s,u_s}^{II} > n_{s,u_s}^{MM} > n_{s,u_s}^{YY} = 0$ and $n_{d,u_d}^{II} > n_{d,u_d}^{MM} > n_{d,u_d}^{YY} = 0$. Therefore, from an expression analogous to equation 2-54, it follows that $n_u^{II} > n_u^{MM} > n_u^{YY} = 0$. Hence US employment is stabilized perfectly under the YY pair. The MM pair dominates the II pair because the induced increase in the US nominal interest rate causes an additional increase in the US real interest rate and additional real appreciation of the dollar, both of which offset part of the impact effect of the shock on the excess demand for the US good.

For ROECD employment, the YY pair ranks at least the same as the II and MM pairs and almost certainly dominates both of them, but the ranking of the MM and the II pairs depends on parameter values. From the rankings in the last paragraph and an expression analogous to equation 2-55, it is clear that $|\overset{*}{n}_u^{II}|, |\overset{*}{n}_u^{MM}| \geq \overset{*}{n}_u^{YY} = 0$. However, the ranking of $\overset{*}{n}_u^{II}$ and $\overset{*}{n}_u^{MM}$ is less clear cut. Expressions for $\overset{*}{n}_u^{II}$ and $\overset{*}{n}_u^{MM}$ are given in equations 2-59 and 2-60 in table 2-17.

---

40. The first equality follows from equations 2-6, and the second follows from equations 2-3 and 2-21 with $\beta = 0$.

Table 2-17. *The Effects of an Increase in Demand for US Goods* (u) *on* $\overset{\star}{n}$, q, *and* $\overset{\star}{q}$

(2-59) $\quad 2\alpha \overset{\star}{n}_u^{II} = \dfrac{2}{BG}(\gamma\epsilon + NA) = \dfrac{2}{BG}\{\gamma\epsilon + [-2(1-\gamma)\gamma v + \delta]A\}$

(2-60) $\quad 2\alpha \overset{\star}{n}_u^{MM} = \dfrac{2}{EJ}[\gamma\epsilon + N(A + D/\lambda)] = \dfrac{2}{EJ}\{\gamma\epsilon + [-2(1-\gamma)\gamma v + \delta](A + D/\lambda)\}$

$\qquad B = 1 - \epsilon + vA, \qquad G = 1 - (1 - 2\gamma)\epsilon + [(1 - 2\gamma)^2 v + 2\delta]A$

$\qquad E = 1 - \epsilon + v(A + D/\lambda) \quad J = 1 - (1 - 2\gamma)\epsilon + [(1 - 2\gamma)^2 v + 2\delta](A + D/\lambda)$

(2-61) $\quad 2\alpha\left[\overset{\star}{n}_u^{II} - \overset{\star}{n}_u^{MM}\right] = \alpha\left(\left[n_{s,u_s}^{II} - n_{s,u_s}^{MM}\right] - \left[n_{d,u_d}^{II} - n_{d,u_d}^{MM}\right]\right)$

$\qquad\qquad = \left[\dfrac{1}{B} - \dfrac{1}{E}\right] - \left[\dfrac{1}{G} - \dfrac{1}{J}\right] = \dfrac{vD/\lambda}{BE} - \dfrac{[(1-2\gamma)^2 v + 2\delta]D/\lambda}{GJ}$

(2-62) $\quad 2q_u^{II} = A\left[\dfrac{1}{1 - \epsilon + vA}\right] + (1 - 2\gamma)A\left[\dfrac{1}{1 - (1 - 2\gamma)\epsilon + [(1 - 2\gamma)^2 v + 2\delta]A}\right] > 0$

(2-63) $\quad 2q_u^{MM} = A\left(\dfrac{1}{1 - \epsilon + v\left[A + \frac{D}{\lambda}\right]}\right) + \left[(1 - 2\gamma)A - \dfrac{2\gamma D}{\lambda}\right]$

$\qquad\qquad \times \left(\dfrac{1}{1 - (1 - 2\gamma)\epsilon + [(1 - 2\gamma)^2 v + 2\delta]\left[A + \frac{D}{\lambda}\right]}\right)$

(2-64) $\quad 2q_u^{YY} = -2\gamma\left[\dfrac{1}{(1 - 2\gamma)^2 v + 2\delta}\right] \le 0$

(2-65) $\quad 2\overset{\star}{q}_u^{II} = A\left[\dfrac{1}{1 - \epsilon + vA}\right] - (1 - 2\gamma)A\left[\dfrac{1}{1 - (1 - 2\gamma)\epsilon + [(1 - 2\gamma)^2 v + 2\delta]A}\right]$

(2-66) $\quad 2\overset{\star}{q}_u^{MM} = A\left(\dfrac{1}{1 - \epsilon + v\left[A + \frac{D}{\lambda}\right]}\right) - \left[(1 - 2\gamma)A - \dfrac{2\gamma D}{\lambda}\right]$

$\qquad\qquad \times \left(\dfrac{1}{1 - (1 - 2\gamma)\epsilon + [(1 - 2\gamma)^2 v + 2\delta]\left[A + \frac{D}{\lambda}\right]}\right)$

(2-67) $\quad 2\overset{\star}{q}_u^{YY} = 2\gamma\left[\dfrac{1}{(1 - 2\gamma)^2 v + 2\delta}\right] \ge 0$

$\overset{\star}{n}_u^{II}$ and $\overset{\star}{n}_u^{MM}$ are positive if and only if the expressions $\gamma\epsilon + NA$ and $\gamma\epsilon + N(A + D/\lambda)$ are positive, respectively. These expressions are the effects of the increases in y and p associated with a unit increase in αn on the excess demand for ROECD goods under the II and MM pairs, respectively.[41] We will assume that $\overset{\star}{n}_u^{II}$ and $\overset{\star}{n}_u^{MM}$ are positive as they are in the simulation results in table 2-18.[42]

41. For more detailed explanations of $\gamma\epsilon + NA$ and $\gamma\epsilon + N(A + D/\lambda)$, see appendix G.

42. Note that if it is possible for $\overset{\star}{n}_u^{II}$ to be positive and $\overset{\star}{n}_u^{MM}$ to be negative for cases in which $-2(1 - \gamma)\gamma v + \delta$ is negative, because this term receives a higher weight in $\overset{\star}{n}_u^{MM}$.

$\overset{\star}{n}{}^{II}_u$ may be greater or less than $\overset{\star}{n}{}^{MM}_u$. The difference between $\overset{\star}{n}{}^{II}_u$ and $\overset{\star}{n}{}^{MM}_u$ is given by equation 2-61 in table 2-17. Under our assumptions, if $\nu = 0$, then $0 < \overset{\star}{n}{}^{II}_u < \overset{\star}{n}{}^{MM}_u < n^{II}_{s,u_s} = n^{MM}_{s,u_s}$, since the increase in i_s induced by the increases in y_s and p_s associated with a unit rise in αn_s under the MM pair has no effect on the sum of excess demands, and $n^{MM}_{d,u_d} < n^{II}_{d,u_d}$, since the increase in i_d induced by the increases in y_d and p_d resulting from a unit increase in αn_d causes the real appreciation of the dollar to be greater. Therefore, $0 < 2\overset{\star}{n}{}^{II}_u = \left[n^{II}_{s,u_s} - n^{II}_{d,u_d} \right] < 2\overset{\star}{n}{}^{MM}_u = \left[n^{MM}_{s,u_s} - n^{MM}_{d,u_d} \right]$ because more of the effect of the increase in u_s is offset by the effect of the increase in u_d under the II pair.

However, if ν is positive, $\overset{\star}{n}{}^{II}_u$ may be greater than $\overset{\star}{n}{}^{MM}_u$, as it is in the simulation results in table 2-18. For example, $\overset{\star}{n}{}^{II}_u > \overset{\star}{n}{}^{MM}_u$ if $\nu > 0$, $\gamma = 0$, and D/λ is large enough.[43] In this case, an increase in u_s has a smaller effect on n_s under the MM pair because the induced increase in i_s helps to accomplish the necessary reduction in the sum of excess demands.

For the US CPI, all the rankings of regime pairs depend on parameter values. We establish in the previous section that $q^{II}_{s,u_s} > q^{MM}_{s,u_s} > q^{YY}_{s,u_s} = 0$ and that the rankings of effects of an increase in u_d on q_d depend on parameter values. For $\gamma = 0$, $q^{II}_{d,u_d} > q^{MM}_{d,u_d} > q^{YY}_{d,u_d} = 0$, and, for $\gamma = 1/2$, $0 = q^{II}_{d,u_d} > q^{MM}_{d,u_d} > q^{YY}_{d,u_d}$. Therefore, from an expression analogous to equation 2-54, it is clear that if $\gamma = 0$, $q^{II}_u > q^{MM}_u > q^{YY}_u = 0$.

However, if γ is larger, the rankings may be different.[44] Expressions for q^{II}_u, q^{MM}_u, and q^{YY}_u are given in equations 2-62 through 2-64. If $\gamma = 1/2$ and δ is small enough, $|q^{YY}_u| > q^{II}_u, |q^{MM}_u|$. In this case, if q^{MM}_u is positive, q^{II}_u is larger. But if q^{MM}_u is negative, q^{II}_u may be larger or smaller. If $\gamma = 0.15$ as in the simulations, it is possible to have $q^{II}_u > |q^{YY}_u| > q^{MM}_u$ as shown in table 2-18.

For the ROECD CPI, just as for the US CPI, all the rankings of regime pairs depend on parameter values. Expressions for $\overset{\star}{q}{}^{II}_u$, $\overset{\star}{q}{}^{MM}_u$, and $\overset{\star}{q}{}^{YY}_u$ are given in equations 2-65 through 2-67. If $\gamma = 0$, $\overset{\star}{q}{}^{jj}_u = \overset{\star}{p}{}^{jj}_u = A\alpha \overset{\star}{n}{}^{jj}_u$; $jj = $ II, MM, YY.[45] In this case, $\overset{\star}{q}{}^{YY}_u = 0$, since $\overset{\star}{n}{}^{YY}_u = 0$; $\overset{\star}{q}{}^{II}_u$ and $\overset{\star}{q}{}^{MM}_u$ are both positive under our assumption that $\overset{\star}{n}{}^{II}_u$ and $\overset{\star}{n}{}^{MM}_u$ are both positive; the ranking of $\overset{\star}{q}{}^{II}_u$ and $\overset{\star}{q}{}^{MM}_u$ is the same as the ranking of $\overset{\star}{n}{}^{II}_u$ and $\overset{\star}{n}{}^{MM}_u$, which is ambiguous as explained above.

However, if $\gamma = 1/2$, then $\overset{\star}{q}{}^{II}_u$, $\overset{\star}{q}{}^{MM}_u$ and $\overset{\star}{q}{}^{YY}_u$ are all positive, and if δ is small enough, $\overset{\star}{q}{}^{YY}_u$ is larger than both $\overset{\star}{q}{}^{II}_u$ and $\overset{\star}{q}{}^{MM}_u$.[46] In this case, $\overset{\star}{q}{}^{II}_u$ may be

---

43. Another set of parameters for which $\overset{\star}{n}{}^{II}_u > \overset{\star}{n}{}^{MM}_u$ is $\nu > 0$, $\gamma = \frac{1}{2}$, $\epsilon + \nu = 1$, and $2\delta < 1$.

44. Also, if δ is large enough, $\overset{\star}{q}{}^{II}_u > \overset{\star}{q}{}^{MM}_u > |\overset{\star}{q}{}^{YY}_u| \geq 0$.

45. The first equality follows from equations 2-6 with $\gamma = 0$, and the second equality follows from equations 2-3 and 2-21 with $\beta = 0$.

46. Also, if δ is large enough, $\overset{\star}{q}{}^{II}_u > \overset{\star}{q}{}^{MM}_u > \overset{\star}{q}{}^{YY}_u \leq 0$.

Table 2-18. *First-Period Impact of a Region-Specific Increase in US Goods Demand*

	Regime pair									
	Oil excluded (β = 0)					Oil included (β = 0.1)				
Variable[a]	MM	II	YY	CC	ME	MM	II	YY	CC	ME
US economy										
Output (%)	8.82	16.33	0	0	9.49	9.47	16.66	0.93	0.93	10.03
CPI inflation (D)	1.82	6.2	−3.01	−3.01	3.27	1.26	5.47	−3.43	−3.43	2.63
Output price (%)	3.78	7	0	0	4.07	2.8	5.97	−0.93	−0.93	3.12
Nominal interest rate (D)	15.75	0	35.04	35.04	16.95	15.34	0	34.27	33.34	16.44
Real interest rate (D)	17.57	6.2	32.03	32.03	20.22	16.6	5.47	30.84	30.84	19.07
Nominal wage (%)	0	0	0	0	0	0	0	0	0	0
Employment (%)	12.6	23.33	0	0	13.56	12.27	22.63	0	0	13.15
Money (%)	0	23.33	−28.03	−28.03	0	0	22.63	−27.42	−26.67	0
Nominal exchange rate ($/R)(%)	−10.57	0	−20.08	−20.08	0	−9.74	0	−18.54	−18.54	0
Real exchange rate ($/R)(%)	−13.1	−5.35	−20.08	−20.08	−5.35	−10.33	−3.29	−16.69	−16.69	−3.29
ROECD economy										
Output (%)	2.9	3.84	0	0	−3	2.26	3.51	−0.93	−0.93	−3.12
CPI inflation (D)	3.21	2.45	3.01	3.01	−0.48	3.77	3.17	3.43	3.43	0.33
Output price (%)	1.24	1.65	0	0	−1.29	2.22	2.68	0.93	0.93	−0.16
Nominal interest rate (D)	5.18	0	14.96	14.96	16.95	5.6	0	15.73	16.66	16.44
Real interest rate (D)	8.4	2.45	17.97	17.97	16.47	9.37	3.17	19.16	19.16	16.77
Nominal wage (%)	0	0	0	0	0	0	0	0	0	0
Employment (%)	4.15	5.49	0	0	−4.29	4.48	6.19	0	0	−3.28
Money (%)	0	5.49	−11.97	−11.97	−17.85	0	6.19	−12.58	−13.33	−16.43

a. % is percent deviation from unchanged baseline; D is deviation from unchanged baseline in percentage points.

Table 2-19. *First-Period Impact of a Region-Specific Increase in ROECD Goods Demand*

	Regime pair									
	Oil excluded (β = 0)					Oil included (β = 0.1)				
Variable[a]	MM	II	YY	CC	ME	MM	II	YY	CC	ME
US economy										
Output (%)	2.9	3.84	0	0	2.23	2.26	3.51	-0.93	-0.93	1.7
CPI inflation (D)	3.21	2.45	3.01	3.01	1.76	3.77	3.17	3.43	3.43	2.39
Output price (%)	1.24	1.65	0	0	0.96	2.22	2.68	0.93	0.93	1.9
Nominal interest rate (D)	5.18	0	14.96	14.96	3.99	5.6	0	15.73	16.66	4.5
Real interest rate (D)	8.4	2.45	17.97	17.97	5.75	9.37	3.17	19.16	19.16	6.89
Nominal wage (%)	0	0	0	0	0	0	0	0	0	0
Employment (%)	4.15	5.49	0	0	3.19	4.48	6.19	0	0	3.6
Money (%)	0	5.49	-11.97	-11.97	0	0	6.19	-12.58	-13.33	0
Nominal exchange rate ($/R)(%)	10.57	0	20.08	20.08	0	9.74	0	18.54	18.54	0
Real exchange rate ($/R)(%)	13.1	5.35	20.08	20.08	5.35	10.33	3.29	16.69	16.69	3.29
ROECD economy										
Output (%)	8.82	16.33	0	0	14.73	9.47	16.66	0.93	0.93	14.84
CPI inflation (D)	1.82	6.2	-3.01	-3.01	5.51	1.26	5.47	-3.43	-3.43	4.7
Output price (%)	3.78	7	0	0	6.31	2.8	5.97	-0.93	-0.93	5.19
Nominal interest rate (D)	15.75	0	35.04	35.04	3.99	15.34	0	34.27	33.34	4.5
Real interest rate (D)	17.57	6.2	32.03	32.03	9.49	16.6	5.47	30.84	30.84	9.19
Nominal wage (%)	0	0	0	0	0	0	0	0	0	0
Employment (%)	12.6	23.33	0	0	21.04	12.27	22.63	0	0	20.03
Money (%)	0	23.33	-28.03	-28.03	17.85	0	22.63	-27.42	-26.67	16.43

a. % is percent deviation from unchanged baseline; D is deviation from unchanged baseline in percentage points.

larger or smaller than $\overset{\star}{q}_u^{MM}$.[47] If $\gamma = 0.15$ as in the simulations, it is possible to have $\overset{\star}{q}_u^{MM} > \overset{\star}{q}_u^{YY} > \overset{\star}{q}_u^{II} > 0$, as shown in table 2-18.

US Productivity Shock

For a shock to US productivity, some rankings of regime pairs are independent of parameter values, but most are not. For the stabilization of US and ROECD employments, the YY pair ranks at least as high as the II and MM pairs and almost certainly dominates both of them. As we established in the previous section, $n_{s,x_s}^{YY} = n_{d,x_d}^{YY} = 0$. It follows that $0 = n_x^{YY} \leq |n_x^{II}|, |n_x^{MM}|$ and $0 = \overset{\star}{n}_x^{YY} \leq |\overset{\star}{n}_x^{II}|, |\overset{\star}{n}_x^{MM}|$. But, as we demonstrate in appendix H, for stabilization of US and ROECD employments, the rankings of the MM and the II pairs depend on parameter values, and for stabilization of US and ROECD CPIs, all rankings depend on parameter values. For the parameters used in the simulations, the YY pair dominates the MM pair, and the MM pair dominates the II pair for both employment and both CPIs, as we report in table 2-20. Other results for region-specific reductions in productivity are in table 2-21 and appendix E.

The Unmatched ME Regime Pair

In this section we compare the effects of symmetric shocks and some asymmetric and region-specific shocks under the unmatched ME regime pair to the effects of the same shocks under the matched regime pairs. Under the ME regime pair, the US money supply and the exchange rate between the dollar and the ROECD currency are kept fixed.

Understanding the properties of the unmatched ME regime pair is at least as important as understanding those of the matched regime pairs. The ME regime pair is patterned after common interpretations of the Bretton Woods system and the European Monetary System (EMS). According to these interpretations, under the Bretton Woods system the US money supply was kept equal to a target value, and dollar values of other currencies were kept fixed. Similarly, under the EMS, the German money supply is kept equal to a target value, and mark values of other currencies are kept fixed.

Our comparison of the unmatched ME regime pair with the matched regime pairs draws on our analysis of the matched regime pairs. For symmetric shocks, results are easy to obtain and unambiguous. But for many asymmetric and region-specified specific shocks, results are difficult to obtain and ambiguous.

---

47. If ν and $1 - \epsilon$ both approach zero with ν remaining equal to $1 - \epsilon$, then $\overset{\star}{q}_u^{II} > \overset{\star}{q}_u^{MM}$, since $q_{s,u_s}^{II} > q_{s,u_s}^{MM} > 0, q_{d,u_d}^{MM} < q_{d,u_d}^{II} = 0$, and $q_{s,u_s}^{II} - q_{s,u_s}^{MM}$ rises without limit as ν approaches zero. However, if ν alone approaches zero with $1 - \epsilon$ remaining unchanged, then $\overset{\star}{q}_u^{II} < \overset{\star}{q}_u^{MM}$, since $q_{s,u_s}^{II} - q_{s,u_s}^{MM}$ approaches zero.

Table 2-20. *First-Period Impact of a Region-Specific Decrease in US Productivity*

	Regime pair									
	Oil excluded (β = 0)					Oil included (β = 0.1)				
Variable[a]	MM	II	YY	CC	ME	MM	II	YY	CC	ME
US economy										
Output (%)	-8.51	-7.33	-10	-10	-8.45	-8.41	-7.23	-9.91	-9.91	-8.36
CPI inflation (D)	8.97	9.57	8.23	8.23	9.09	8.9	9.52	8.16	8.16	9.04
Output price (%)	10.64	11.15	10	10	10.67	10.56	11.07	9.91	9.91	10.59
Nominal interest rate (D)	2.67	0	6.14	16.14	2.78	2.68	0	6.17	16.07	2.79
Real interest rate (D)	11.63	9.57	14.38	14.38	11.87	11.58	9.52	14.33	14.33	11.83
Nominal wage (%)	0	0	0	0	0	0	0	0	0	0
Employment (%)	2.14	3.82	0	0	2.22	2.14	3.84	0	0	2.23
Money (%)	0	3.82	-4.91	-12.91	0	0	3.84	-4.93	-12.86	0
Nominal exchange rate ($/R)(%)	-0.94	0	-1.79	-1.79	0	-0.96	0	-1.83	-1.83	0
Real exchange rate ($/R)(%)	-11.17	-10.48	-11.79	-11.79	-10.48	-11.02	-10.32	-11.65	-11.65	-10.32
ROECD economy										
Output (%)	0.97	1.56	0	0	0.44	0.87	1.47	-0.09	-0.09	0.34
CPI inflation (D)	2.09	2.24	1.77	1.77	1.76	2.15	2.29	1.84	1.84	1.81
Output price (%)	0.41	0.67	0	0	0.19	0.5	0.75	0.09	0.09	0.26
Nominal interest rate (D)	1.73	0	4.36	4.36	2.78	1.72	0	4.33	4.43	2.79
Real interest rate (D)	3.82	2.24	6.12	6.12	4.54	3.87	2.29	6.17	6.17	4.6
Nominal wage (%)	0	0	0	0	0	0	0	0	0	0
Employment (%)	1.38	2.23	0	0	0.63	1.37	2.21	0	0	0.61
Money (%)	0	2.23	-3.49	-3.49	-1.59	0	2.21	-3.47	-3.54	-1.62

a. % is percent deviation from unchanged baseline; D is deviation from unchanged baseline in percentage points.

Table 2-21. *First-Period Impact of a Region-Specific Decrease in ROECD Productivity*

	Regime pair									
	Oil excluded (β = 0)					Oil included (β = 0.1)				
Variable[a]	MM	II	YY	CC	ME	MM	II	YY	CC	ME
US economy										
Output (%)	0.97	1.56	0	0	0.91	0.87	1.47	-0.09	-0.09	0.82
CPI inflation (D)	2.09	2.24	1.77	1.77	1.96	2.15	2.29	1.84	1.84	2.02
Output price (%)	0.41	0.67	0	0	0.39	0.5	0.75	0.09	0.09	0.47
Nominal interest rate (D)	1.73	0	4.36	4.36	1.62	1.72	0	4.33	4.43	1.61
Real interest rate (D)	3.82	2.24	6.12	6.12	3.58	3.87	2.29	6.17	6.17	3.62
Nominal wage (%)	0	0	0	0	0	0	0	0	0	0
Employment (%)	1.38	2.23	0	0	1.3	1.37	2.21	0	0	1.29
Money (%)	0	2.23	-3.49	-3.49	0	0	2.21	-3.47	-3.54	0
Nominal exchange rate ($/R)(%)	0.94	0	1.79	1.79	0	0.96	0	1.83	1.83	0
Real exchange rate ($/R)(%)	11.17	10.48	11.79	11.79	10.48	11.02	10.32	11.65	11.65	10.32
ROECD economy										
Output (%)	-8.51	-7.33	-10	-10	-7.98	-8.41	-7.23	-9.91	-9.91	-7.88
CPI inflation (D)	8.97	9.57	8.23	8.23	9.29	8.9	9.52	8.16	8.16	9.24
Output price (%)	10.64	11.15	10	10	10.87	10.56	11.07	9.91	9.91	10.79
Nominal interest rate (D)	2.67	0	6.14	16.14	1.62	2.68	0	6.17	16.07	1.61
Real interest rate (D)	11.63	9.57	14.38	14.38	10.92	11.58	9.52	14.33	14.33	10.85
Nominal wage (%)	0	0	0	0	0	0	0	0	0	0
Employment (%)	2.14	3.82	0	0	2.89	2.14	3.84	0	0	2.91
Money (%)	0	3.82	-4.91	-12.91	1.59	0	3.84	-4.93	-12.86	1.62

a. % is percent deviation from unchanged baseline; D is deviation from unchanged baseline in percentage points.

Thus, we include in our comparison all symmetric shocks, but only a subset of the asymmetric and region-specific shocks considered for the matched pairs. This subset is asymmetric shocks to money demands and goods demands, and region-specific shocks to US money demand and ROECD money demand. Our objective is to highlight some of the important similarities and differences between the ME pair and the matched pairs. The ME regime pair appears in the tables of rankings in appendix E only for the shocks included in our comparison.

Symmetric Shocks

Under our assumptions, all symmetric shocks have the same effects under the ME regime pair as they do under the MM regime pair. A constant US money supply is one of the two defining characteristics for each of the ME and MM pairs. A constant nominal exchange rate between the dollar and the ROECD currency is the other defining characteristic for the ME pair and, as we established in the section before last, for symmetric shocks it emerges as an outcome for the MM pair. Thus, the two regime pairs are equivalent for symmetric shocks, since both defining characteristics for the ME pair are properties of the MM pair. This equivalence is illustrated by the results in tables 2-8, 2-10, and 2-12 and is reflected in the summary tables of rankings in appendix E.

The Method Used to Compare the ME, II, and MM Regime Pairs

For each asymmetric or region-specific shock that we consider, we use the same method to compare the ME regime pair with the II and MM regime pairs. First, we compare the effects of the asymmetric or region-specific shock under the ME and II regime pairs, and then we compare the effects under the ME and MM regime pairs.

Under the II regime pair, a constant exchange rate emerges as an outcome. Under this pair, both interest rates are kept constant at their no-shock levels. Because we consider only temporary shocks, the expected value of next period's exchange rate is unaffected by shocks. With interest rates and the expected value of next period's exchange rate constant, open interest parity implies that the current exchange rate must remain constant. In general, to keep interest rates constant, it is necessary to change both the US and ROECD money supplies.

A constant exchange rate and a constant US money supply are the two defining characteristics for the ME regime pair. To move from the II equilibrium to the ME equilibrium, it is necessary to move the US money supply from its level in the II equilibrium back to its no-shock level and to make a parallel movement in the ROECD money supply so that the exchange rate remains constant at its no-shock level. The conclusion that a parallel movement in the ROECD money supply is needed follows from the analysis of the section before last. There we established that symmetric increases in money demands leave the exchange rate unchanged under all matched regime pairs including the MM pair. Symmetric reductions in the US and ROECD money supplies have the same effects as symmetric increases in money demands under the MM pair.

Symmetric changes in US and ROECD money supplies have effects on employments and CPIs in the US and the ROECD, so outcomes under the ME pair are different from outcomes under the II pair. The total change in the ROECD money supply under the ME pair is the algebraic sum of the change in the ROECD money supply under the II pair and an amount equal to the change in the US money supply required to move from the II equilibrium to the ME equilibrium.

Under both the ME and MM regime pairs, the US money supply is kept constant. A constant US money supply and a constant ROECD money supply are the two defining characteristics for the MM regime pair. Thus, to move from the ME equilibrium to the MM equilibrium, it is necessary to move the ROECD money supply from its level in the ME equilibrium back to its no-shock level. We explained earlier in this section why there must usually be a net change in the ROECD money supply from its no-shock level under the ME pair in order to keep the exchange rate constant and describe one way to determine the size of any required change.

Because a change in the ROECD money supply has effects on employments and CPIs in the US and the ROECD, outcomes under the MM pair are different from outcomes under the ME pair. Conclusions about the effects of a change in the ROECD money supply follow from the analysis of the previous section. According to that analysis, a region-specific increase in the demand for ROECD money under the MM regime pair decreases ROECD employment and the ROECD CPI and may raise or lower US employment and the US CPI. A reduction in the ROECD money supply has the same effects as a region-specific increase in the demand for ROECD money under the MM pair.

An Asymmetric Money-Demand Shock under the ME and II Regime Pairs

Under the ME regime pair, even with mirror-image regions, asymmetric shocks do not in general have asymmetric effects, equal and opposite effects on US and ROECD variables. For an asymmetric money-demand shock with US money demand increasing and ROECD money demand decreasing, an increase in v_d, the ME regime pair is dominated by the II pair (and by the YY pair which is ranked the same as the II pair) for employments and CPIs in both regions. This conclusion is illustrated by the simulation results in table 2-9. An asymmetric money-demand shock under the ME pair leads to the same outcomes as a symmetric increase in money demands under both the ME and MM pairs, as can be confirmed by comparing tables 2-8 and 2-9.

We established in the section before last that under the II pair, an increase in v_d does not affect any variables except money supplies in the two regions. The US money supply rises, while the ROECD money supply falls.

To move from the II equilibrium to the ME equilibrium, it is necessary to reduce the US money supply back to its no-shock level and to reduce the ROECD money supply one for one with the US money supply. Since the reduction in the sum of money supplies causes employments and CPIs to fall in both regions, the ME pair is dominated by the II pair.

In accordance with the general principle that we stated in the previous subsection, the ROECD money supply falls by twice as much under the ME pair as under the II pair. The total reduction in the ROECD money supply is the sum of the reduction required to reach the II equilibrium, which is equal to the reduction in the demand for ROECD money, and an amount equal to the reduction in the US money supply required to move from the II equilibrium to the ME equilibrium, which is also equal to the reduction in the demand for ROECD money. In effect, the ROECD policymaker must convert the asymmetric money-demand shock into a symmetric increase in excess demands for money. That is, an asymmetric money-demand shock, an increase in v_d, under the ME pair leads to the same outcomes as a symmetric increase in money demands, an increase in v_s, under both the ME and MM pairs.

In the analysis below, we need expressions for $n_{v_d}^{\text{ME}}$, $q_{v_d}^{\text{ME}}$, $\overset{\star}{n}_{v_d}^{\text{ME}}$, and $\overset{\star}{q}_{v_d}^{\text{ME}}$. In order to derive these expressions we need the expressions for n_{s,v_d}^{ME}, n_{d,v_d}^{ME}, q_{s,v_d}^{ME}, and q_{d,v_d}^{ME} given in equations 2-68 through 2-71 in table 2-22. In those equations, $n_{s,v_d}^{\text{II}} = n_{d,v_d}^{\text{II}} = q_{s,v_d}^{\text{II}} = q_{d,v_d}^{\text{II}} = 0$ are the effects of an increase in v_d on n_s, n_d, q_s, and q_d under the II pair; $-n_{s,v_s}^{\text{MM}} > 0$ and $-q_{s,v_s}^{\text{MM}} > 0$ are the effects of an increase in m_s on n_s and q_s under the MM pair; $-2m_{v_d}^{\text{II}} = -1$ is the reduction in m_s per unit change in v_d required to move from the II equilibrium to the ME equilibrium since $m_{v_d}^{\text{II}} = 1/2$ is the increase in m per unit change in v_d required under the II pair; $-n_{d,v_d}^{\text{MM}} > 0$ and $-q_{d,v_d}^{\text{MM}} > 0$ are the effects of an increase in m_d on n_d and q_d under the MM pair; and no change in m_d is required to move from the II equilibrium to the ME equilibrium.

The required expressions for $n_{v_d}^{\text{ME}}$, $\overset{\star}{n}_{v_d}^{\text{ME}}$, $q_{v_d}^{\text{ME}}$, and $\overset{\star}{q}_{v_d}^{\text{ME}}$ are given in equations 2-72 and 2-73, where n_{s,v_d}^{ME}, n_{d,v_d}^{ME}, q_{s,v_d}^{ME}, and q_{d,v_d}^{ME} are given by equations 2-68 through 2-71.

An Asymmetric Money-Demand Shock under the ME and MM Regime Pairs

For an asymmetric money-demand shock, in both regions the ranking of the MM and ME pairs for employment stabilization is the same, and the ranking of these pairs for CPI stabilization is the same. For employments, the ME pair dominates if and only if an increase in the demand for US money raises ROECD employment. For CPIs, the ME pair dominates if and only if an increase in demand for US money raises the ROECD CPI. For the parameters used in the simulations, the ME pair dominates for both employments and for both CPIs, as shown in table 2-9, and an increase in the demand for US money raises ROECD employment and the ROECD CPI, as stated above and as shown in table 2-15.

Under the ME pair, the US money supply is kept constant at its no-shock level. We established above that under this pair both employments, both CPIs and the ROECD money supply fall. To move from the ME equilibrium to the MM equilibrium, the ROECD money supply must be increased by enough to return it to its no-shock level.

In the analysis below we need expressions for $n_{v_d}^{MM}$, $\overset{*}{n}_{v_d}^{MM}$, $q_{v_d}^{MM}$, and $\overset{*}{q}_{v_d}^{MM}$. These expressions are given in equations 2-74 through 2-77 in table 2-22. The terms $2n_v^{MM}$, $2\overset{*}{n}_v^{MM}$, and $2\overset{*}{q}_v^{MM}$ are the negatives of twice the effects of an increase in $\overset{}{m}$ on n, $\overset{*}{n}$, q, and $\overset{*}{q}$, [48] respectively, and $2m_{v_d}^{II} = 1$ is the increase in $\overset{}{m}$ per unit change in v_d required to move from the ME equilibrium to the MM equilibrium (since $m_{v_d}^{II} = \frac{1}{2}$ is the increase in m per unit change in v_d required under the II pair). These expressions confirm the conclusions stated above regarding the effects of an increase in v_d under the MM pair.

For both employments, the ranking of the ME and MM regime pairs is the same. The differences between the absolute values of the decreases in n under the ME and MM pairs and between the absolute value of the decrease in $\overset{*}{n}$ under the ME pair and the increase in this variable under the MM pair are given in equation 2-78 in table 2-22. Similarly, for both CPIs the ranking of regime pairs is the same. The difference between the absolute values of the decreases in q under the ME and MM pairs and between the absolute value of the decrease in $\overset{*}{q}$ under the ME pair and the increase in this variable under the MM pair are given in equation 2-79 in table 2-22.

For employments, the ME pair dominates if and only if an increase in the demand for US money raises ROECD employment, and for CPIs the ME pair dominates if and only if an increase in the demand for US money raises the ROECD CPI. The effects of a region-specific shock to US money demand

---

48. The expressions for $2n_v^{MM}$, $2\overset{*}{n}_v^{MM}$, $2q_v^{MM}$, $and\ 2\overset{*}{q}_v^{MM}$ are analogous to the expressions in equations 2-54 and 2-55 in table 2-7.

Table 2-22. *The Effects of an Asymmetric Money-Demand Shock* (v_d) *under the ME Regime Pair*

(2-68)	$n_{s,v_d}^{ME} = n_{s,v_d}^{II} + \left[-n_{s,v_s}^{MM}\right]\left[-2m_{v_d}^{II}\right] = 0 + \left[-n_{s,v_s}^{MM}\right][-1] = n_{s,v_s}^{MM} < 0$
(2-69)	$n_{d,v_d}^{ME} = n_{d,v_d}^{II} + \left[-n_{d,v_d}^{MM}\right][0] = 0 + 0 = 0$
(2-70)	$q_{s,v_d}^{ME} = q_{s,v_d}^{II} + \left[-q_{s,v_s}^{MM}\right]\left[-2m_{v_d}^{II}\right] = 0 + \left[-q_{s,v_s}^{MM}\right][-1] = q_{s,v_s}^{MM} < 0$
(2-71)	$q_{d,v_d}^{ME} = q_{d,v_d}^{II} + \left[-q_{d,v_d}^{MM}\right][0] = 0 + 0 = 0$
(2-72)	$2n_{v_d}^{ME} = n_{s,v_d}^{ME} + n_{d,v_d}^{ME} = 2\mathring{n}_{v_d}^{ME} = n_{s,v_d}^{ME} - n_{d,v_d}^{ME} = n_{s,v_s}^{MM} < 0$
(2-73)	$2q_{v_d}^{ME} = q_{s,v_d}^{ME} + q_{d,v_d}^{ME} = 2\mathring{q}_{v_d}^{ME} = q_{s,v_d}^{ME} - q_{d,v_d}^{ME} = q_{s,v_s}^{MM} < 0$
(2-74)	$2n_{v_d}^{MM} = 2n_{v_d}^{ME} + \left[-2n_{v_d}^{MM}\right]\left[2m_{v_d}^{II}\right] = n_{s,v_s}^{MM} + \left(-\left[n_{s,v_s}^{MM} - n_{d,v_d}^{MM}\right]\right) = n_{d,v_d}^{MM} < 0$
(2-75)	$2\mathring{n}_{v_d}^{MM} = 2\mathring{n}_{v_d}^{ME} + \left[-2\mathring{n}_{v_d}^{MM}\right]\left[2m_{v_d}^{II}\right] = n_{s,v_s}^{MM} + \left(-\left[n_{s,v_s}^{MM} + n_{d,v_d}^{MM}\right]\right) = -n_{d,v_d}^{MM} > 0$
(2-76)	$2q_{v_d}^{MM} = 2q_{v_d}^{ME} + \left[-2q_{v_d}^{MM}\right]\left[2m_{v_d}^{II}\right] = q_{s,v_s}^{MM} + \left(-\left[q_{s,v_s}^{MM} - q_{d,v_d}^{MM}\right]\right) = q_{d,v_d}^{MM} < 0$
(2-77)	$2\mathring{q}_{v_d}^{MM} = 2\mathring{q}_{v_d}^{ME} + \left[-2\mathring{q}_{v_d}^{MM}\right]\left[2m_{v_d}^{II}\right] = q_{s,v_s}^{MM} + \left(-\left[q_{s,v_s}^{MM} + q_{d,v_d}^{MM}\right]\right) = -q_{d,v_d}^{MM} > 0$
(2-78)	$2\left[\left\|n_{v_d}^{ME}\right\| - \left\|n_{v_d}^{MM}\right\|\right] = 2\left[\left\|\mathring{n}_{v_d}^{ME}\right\| - \mathring{n}_{v_d}^{MM}\right] = \left\|n_{s,v_s}^{MM}\right\| - \left\|n_{d,v_d}^{MM}\right\| \gtreqless 0$
(2-79)	$2\left[\left\|q_{v_d}^{ME}\right\| - \left\|q_{v_d}^{MM}\right\|\right] = 2\left[\left\|\mathring{q}_{v_d}^{ME}\right\| - \mathring{q}_{v_d}^{MM}\right] = \left\|q_{s,v_s}^{MM}\right\| - \left\|q_{d,v_d}^{MM}\right\| \gtreqless 0$
(2-80)	$\mathring{n}_v^{MM} = n_{s,v_s}^{MM} - n_{d,v_d}^{MM} = -\left[\left\|n_{s,v_s}^{MM}\right\| - \left\|n_{d,v_d}^{MM}\right\|\right] \gtreqless 0$
(2-81)	$\mathring{q}_v^{MM} = q_{s,v_s}^{MM} - q_{d,v_d}^{MM} = -\left[\left\|q_{s,v_s}^{MM}\right\| - \left\|q_{d,v_d}^{MM}\right\|\right] \gtreqless 0$

on ROECD employment and the ROECD CPI under the MM regime pair ($\mathring{n}_v^{MM}$ and $\mathring{q}_v^{MM}$) are given by equations 2-80 and 2-81 in table 2-22, respectively. The second equalities in both equations hold because n_{s,v_s}^{MM}, n_{d,v_d}^{MM}, q_{s,v_s}^{MM}, and q_{d,v_d}^{MM} are all negative. We showed in the previous section how the signs of $\mathring{n}_v^{MM}$ and $\mathring{q}_v^{MM}$ depend on parameter values. Equations 2-78 through 2-81 imply that $\left|n_{v_d}^{ME}\right| - \left|n_{v_d}^{MM}\right| < 0$ and that $\left|q_{v_d}^{ME}\right| - \left|q_{v_d}^{MM}\right| < 0$ if and only if $\mathring{n}_v^{MM} > 0$ and $\mathring{q}_v^{MM} > 0$, respectively.

An Asymmetric Goods-Demand Shock under the ME
and II Regime Pairs

For an asymmetric goods-demand shock with the demand for US goods increasing and the demand for ROECD goods decreasing, an increase in u_d, the ME regime pair dominates the II pair for US employment, but the II pair dominates the ME pair for ROECD employment and for the ROECD CPI. The ranking of the ME and II pairs for the US CPI depends on parameter values, as shown in appendix I. For the parameters used in the simulations, the ME pair dominates for the US CPI, as shown in table 2-11.

We established in the section before last that under the II pair an increase in v_d raises both US employment and the US CPI and lowers both ROECD employment and the ROECD CPI. The US money supply rises, and the ROECD money supply falls.

To move from the II equilibrium to the ME equilibrium, it is necessary to move the US money supply back to its no-shock level and to move the ROECD money supply one for one with the US money supply. Symmetric reductions in the two money supplies cause symmetric decreases in employments and CPIs in the two regions. Now we can compare the outcomes for employments and CPIs in the ME, II, and no-shock equilibria. ROECD employment and the ROECD CPI are lower in the ME equilibrium than in the II equilibrium, and, as stated above, are lower in the II equilibrium than in the no-shock equilibrium.

In the ME equilibrium, US employment is lower than in the II equilibrium but higher than in the no-shock equilibrium. The reductions in US output and the US output price associated with a move from the II equilibrium to the ME equilibrium are smaller than the increases in US output and the US output price under the II pair because the rise in the US interest rate associated with the move offsets part of the initial excess demand for US money.

In the ME equilibrium, the US CPI is lower than in the II equilibrium and may be higher or lower than in the no-shock equilibrium. If the US CPI is higher in the ME equilibrium than in the no-shock equilibrium, then the ME pair dominates the II pair for the US CPI. However, if the US CPI is lower in the ME equilibrium than in the no-shock equilibrium, the ranking of the ME and II pairs depends on parameter values. It is possible for there to be a decrease in the US CPI under the ME pair that is greater in absolute value then the increase under the II pair because the appreciation of the dollar in real terms is the same under the two pairs, but the US output price rises by less under the ME regime.

In accordance with the general principle that we stated earlier in this section, the ROECD money supply falls by twice as much under the ME pair as under the II pair. The total reduction in the ROECD money supply is the sum of the reduction in the demand for ROECD money caused by the falls in $\overset{*}{y}$ and $\overset{*}{p}$ under the II pair and an amount equal to the reduction in the US money supply required to move from the II equilibrium to the ME equilibrium, which is also equal to the reduction in the demand for ROECD money caused by the falls in $\overset{*}{y}$ and $\overset{*}{p}$ under the II pair.

An Asymmetric Goods-Demand Shock under the ME and MM Regime Pairs

For an asymmetric goods-demand shock, the MM pair dominates the ME pair for US employment stabilization if and only if an increase in the ROECD money supply lowers US employment. The MM pair always dominates the ME pair for ROECD employment stabilization. The ranking of the MM and ME pairs for both CPIs depends on parameter values, as shown in appendix I. For the parameters used in the simulations, the MM pair dominates for stabilization of both employments and both CPIs, as shown in table 2-11.

For US employment, the MM pair dominates the ME pair if and only if an increase in $\overset{*}{m}$ lowers n. We showed earlier that an increase in u_d has a positive effect on n under the MM pair and that an increase in u_d also has a positive effect on n under the ME pair. To move from the ME equilibrium to the MM equilibrium, $\overset{*}{m}$ must be increased by enough to return it to its no-shock level. Therefore, an increase in u_d causes a smaller rise in n under the MM pair than under the ME pair if and only if an increase in $\overset{*}{m}$ lowers n.

For ROECD employment, the MM pair always dominates the ME pair. We show earlier that an increase in u_d lowers $\overset{*}{n}$ under the MM pair and that an increase in u_d also lowers $\overset{*}{n}$ under the ME pair. To move from the ME equilibrium to the MM equilibrium, $\overset{*}{m}$ must be increased by enough to return it to its no-shock level. Therefore, ROECD employment must fall by less under the MM pair.

An Asymmetric Goods-Demand Shock under the ME and YY Regime Pairs

For an asymmetric goods-demand shock, the YY regime pair dominates the ME pair for stabilization of both employments. We show above that US and ROECD employments remain unchanged under the YY pair and change under all other pairs, including the ME pair. However, for stabilization of both CPIs, the ranking of the YY and ME pairs depends on parameter values, as shown in appendix I. For the parameters used in the simulations, the YY pair is dominated by all other pairs including the ME pair for stabilization of both CPIs, as shown in table 2-11.

A Shock to US Money Demand under the ME and II Regime Pairs

Under the unmatched ME pair, a region-specific shock in the US and the corresponding region-specific shock in the ROECD do not have effects that are mirror images of each other. First we consider an increase in the demand for US money, an increase in v. For all variables except money supplies, the outcomes for a one-unit increase in the demand for US money under the ME pair are the same as those for an asymmetric money-demand shock with US money demand rising by one unit under the ME pair, which, in turn, are the same as those for a symmetric increase in money demand under both the ME and MM pairs. These conclusions can be confirmed by comparing tables 2-8, 2-9, and 2-15.

The ME pair is dominated by the II pair (and the YY pair which is ranked the same as the II pair) for stabilization of both employments and both CPIs, as shown in table 2-15. We established in the last section that under the II pair, an increase in v does not affect any variables except the US money supply, which increases. The increase in the US money supply necessitated by a one-unit increase in v under the II pair is the same as the increase in the US money supply required for a two-unit increase in $v_d = v - \overset{\star}{v}$ brought about by a one-unit increase in v and a one-unit decrease in $\overset{\star}{v}$, as can be confirmed by comparing tables 2-9 and 2-15.

To move from the II equilibrium to the ME equilibrium, it is necessary to reduce the US money supply back to its no-shock level and to reduce the ROECD money supply one for one with the US money supply so that the exchange rate remains fixed. The reduction in each money supply is equal in absolute value to the increase in US money demand. The reduction in m_s causes employments and CPIs to fall in both regions, so the ME pair is dominated by the II pair. For both an increase in v and an increase in v_d, the ROECD policymaker must convert the US money-demand shock into a symmetric increase in excess demands for money under the ME pair.

Since under the II pair the increase in US money demand for a unit increase in v is the same as for a two-unit increase in v_d, the effects of a unit increase in v under the ME pair are the same as those of a two-unit increase in v_d under this pair for all variables except the ROECD money supply. This is shown in equations 2-82 and 2-83 in table 2-23, where the expressions for $n_{v_d}^{ME}$, $\overset{\star}{n}_{v_d}^{ME}$, $q_{v_d}^{ME}$, and $\overset{\star}{q}_{v_d}^{ME}$ are restatements of equations 2-72 and 2-73 in table 2-22. The decrease in the ROECD money supply under the ME pair is smaller for a unit increase in v than for a two-unit increase in v_d because no decrease in the ROECD money supply is required to reach the II equilibrium for the increase in v.

Table 2-23. *The Effects of an Increase in US Money Demand* (v)
under the ME Regime Pair

(2-82)	$2n_v^{ME} = 2\mathring{n}_v^{ME} = 4n_{v_d}^{ME} = 4\mathring{n}_{v_d}^{ME} = 2n_{s,v_s}^{MM} < 0$
(2-83)	$2q_v^{ME} = 2\mathring{q}_v^{ME} = 4q_{v_d}^{ME} = 4\mathring{q}_{v_d}^{ME} = 2q_{s,v_s}^{MM} < 0$
(2-84)	$2n_v^{MM} = 2n_v^{ME} + (-2n_{\mathring{v}}^{MM})[m_v^{II}]$
	$= 2n_{s,v_s}^{MM} + (-[n_{s,v_s}^{MM} - n_{d,v_d}^{MM}]) = n_{s,v_s}^{MM} + n_{d,v_d}^{MM} < 0$
(2-85)	$2q_v^{MM} = 2q_v^{ME} + (-2q_{\mathring{v}}^{MM})[m_v^{II}]$
	$= 2q_{s,v_s}^{MM} + (-[q_{s,v_s}^{MM} - q_{d,v_d}^{MM}]) = q_{s,v_s}^{MM} + q_{d,v_d}^{MM} < 0$
(2-86)	$2\mathring{n}_v^{MM} = 2\mathring{n}_v^{ME} + (-2\mathring{n}_{\mathring{v}}^{MM})[m_v^{II}]$
	$= 2n_{s,v_s}^{MM} - (-[n_{s,v_s}^{MM} + n_{d,v_d}^{MM}]) = n_{s,v_s}^{MM} - n_{d,v_d}^{MM} \lessgtr 0$
(2-87)	$2\mathring{q}_v^{MM} = 2\mathring{q}_v^{ME} + (-2\mathring{q}_{\mathring{v}}^{MM})[m_v^{II}]$
	$= 2q_{s,v_s}^{MM} - (-[q_{s,v_s}^{MM} + q_{d,v_d}^{MM}]) = q_{s,v_s}^{MM} - q_{d,v_d}^{MM} \lessgtr 0$
(2-88)	$2\left[|n_v^{ME}| - |n_v^{MM}|\right] = |n_{s,v_s}^{MM}| - |n_{d,v_d}^{MM}| = -\mathring{n}_v^{MM} \lessgtr 0$
(2-89)	$2\left[|q_v^{ME}| - |q_v^{MM}|\right] = |q_{s,v_s}^{MM}| - |q_{d,v_d}^{MM}| = -\mathring{q}_v^{MM} \lessgtr 0$
(2-90)	$2\left[|\mathring{n}_v^{ME}| - |\mathring{n}_v^{MM}|\right] = |2n_{s,v_s}^{MM}| - |n_{s,v_s}^{MM} - n_{d,v_d}^{MM}| \lessgtr 0$
(2-91)	$2\left[|\mathring{q}_v^{ME}| - |\mathring{q}_v^{MM}|\right] = |2q_{s,v_s}^{MM}| - |q_{s,v_s}^{MM} - q_{d,v_d}^{MM}| \lessgtr 0$

A Shock to US Money Demand under the ME and MM Regime Pairs

For stabilization of US employment, the ME pair dominates the MM pair if
and only if an increase in the demand for US money raises ROECD employment. For stabilization of the US CPI, the ME pair dominates the MM pair
if and only if an increase in demand for US money raises the ROECD CPI.
For stabilization of both ROECD employment and the ROECD CPI, the rankings of the MM and ME pairs depend on parameter values. For the parameters
used in the simulations, the ME pair dominates the MM pair for US employment and for the US CPI, as shown in table 2-15, and an increase in the
demand for US money raises ROECD employment and the ROECD CPI, as
stated above and as shown in table 2-15. Also, for these parameters, the MM
pair dominates the ME pair for stabilization of ROECD employment and the
ROECD CPI.

Under the ME pair, the US money supply is kept constant at its no-shock
level. We established in the previous subsection that under this pair both em-

ployments, both CPIs, and the ROECD money supply fall in response to an increase in US money demand.

To move from the ME equilibrium to the MM equilibrium, the ROECD money supply must be increased by enough to return it to its no-shock level. Expressions for n_v^{MM}, $\overset{*}{n}_v^{\text{MM}}$, q_v^{MM}, and $\overset{*}{q}_v^{\text{MM}}$ are given by equations 2-84 through 2-87, in table 2-23, where $m_v^{\text{II}} = 2m_{v_d}^{\text{II}} = 1$ is the increase in the US money supply required under the II pair for a unit increase in v and a two-unit increase in v_d and where the terms in parentheses are explained in the discussion of equations 2-74 through 2-77 in table 2-22. These expressions are consistent with the conclusions regarding the effects of an increase in v under the MM pair that we derived in the previous section.

As we stated above, for US employment the ME pair dominates if and only if an increase in the demand for US money raises ROECD employment, and for the CPI the ME pair dominates if and only if an increase in demand for US money raises the ROECD CPI. The differences between the absolute values of the decreases in n and q under the ME and MM pairs are given in equations 2-88 and 2-89, where the expressions for $n_v^{*\text{MM}}$ and $q_v^{*\text{MM}}$ are given in equations 2-80 and 2-81.

For both ROECD employment and the ROECD CPI, the ranking of the ME and MM pairs depends on parameter values. The differences between the absolute values of the decreases in $\overset{*}{n}$ and $\overset{*}{q}$ under the ME pair and the absolute values of the changes in $\overset{*}{n}$ and $\overset{*}{q}$ under the MM pair are given by equations 2-90 and 2-91. If $\nu = 0$, then $n_{s,v_s}^{\text{MM}} = q_{s,v_s}^{\text{MM}} = 0$, as can be confirmed from equations 2D-5 and 2D-6 in appendix D, so the MM pair is worse. However, if $\gamma = \delta = 0$, then $n_{s,v_s}^{\text{MM}} = n_{d,v_d}^{\text{MM}}$ and $q_{s,v_s}^{\text{MM}} = q_{d,v_d}^{\text{MM}}$, as can be confirmed from equations 2D-5, 2D-6, 2D-14, and 2D-15 in appendix D, so the MM pair is better.

A Shock to ROECD Money Demand

For an increase in the demand for ROECD money, an increase in $\overset{*}{v}$, the ME pair is ranked the same as the II pair (and YY pair which is ranked the same as the II pair) and, therefore, dominates the MM pair.

Under the ME pair, the US money supply is kept fixed. To keep the exchange rate fixed, the ROECD interest rate must remain fixed so the ROECD money supply must be allowed to increase by an amount equal to the increase in $\overset{*}{v}$. Therefore, under the ME pair, an increase in $\overset{*}{v}$ has no effect on any variable except the ROECD money supply. We established in the previous section that a region-specific increase in money demand does not affect any variables except money supplies under the II pair whereas it affects employments and CPIs in both regions under the MM pair.

Including Oil

In this section, we investigate the implications of including oil in the analysis. We use the three-region model with $\beta > 0$ rather than $\beta = 0$. We consider what happens not only when the elasticity of substitution among factors of production (σ) is unitary but also when it is non-unitary.

The role of oil as a factor of production in the US and the ROECD together with the assumed behavior of OPEC is outlined above. Here we explain how the model works when oil is included, highlight differences between the results with oil and the results without it, and demonstrate that some of the results with oil depend on whether σ is unitary or not.[49] As in the discussion of symmetric and asymmetric shocks without oil, we use graphical, algebraic, and simulation methods.

In each table of simulation results under the Contract hypothesis, the results for a single shock under all five regime pairs with oil included are presented in the right-hand block of columns. In the simulations we assume that the factor income share of oil, β, is 0.10. For reasons explained below, most of the graphical and algebraic analysis in this section is conducted under the assumption that the average and marginal propensities to import in the US and the ROECD, γ, are equal to $1/2$. We have performed simulation experiments with $\gamma = 1/2$, and the results confirm the predictions of the graphical and algebraic analysis.[50] Here, however, we report simulation results for $\gamma = 0.15$ in order to provide some information about the implications of assuming a more realistic value of γ.

Symmetric Shocks and the Schedules for Sums with Oil

Adding oil to the model does not affect any of the results for symmetric shocks to money demands, goods demands, and productivities. This initially surprising conclusion, a consequence of some strong assumptions, is evident from the simulation results for symmetric shocks in tables 2-8, 2-10, and 2-12. The conclusion can be confirmed and the role of the strong assumptions clarified by an explanation of why all the conditions for equilibrium for the model for sums with oil are the same as the corresponding conditions without oil when there is no oil shock.[51]

---

49. Although we call the included factor of production oil for concreteness, our analysis applies to any factor that is produced outside the US-ROECD block and is fixed in total supply in each period.

50. These results are available from the authors on request.

51. We consider shocks to the world supply of oil later in this section.

The equation for the aggregate-demand schedule for sums (equation 2-29 in table 2-5) is the same with and without oil because we make the assumption that OPEC's propensity to spend out of income is the same as the equal propensities to spend out of income in the US and the ROECD (ϵ). Under this assumption, changes in the oil bill of either the US or the ROECD have no effect on the sum of excess demands for goods.

The equation for the money-market equilibrium schedule (equation 2-30) is the same with and without oil because we assume that OPEC residents hold no money.

The equation for the aggregate-supply schedule for sums with oil (equation 2-34) is the same as the equation for the aggregate-supply schedule without oil (equation 2-35) when there is no oil shock, that is, when the exogenous oil supply takes on its mean value of zero ($2\tilde{b} = 0$). When we add oil to the model, for both the US and the ROECD we assume that the share of income going to labor (α) is unchanged and that the share of income going to capital is reduced from $1 - \alpha$ to $1 - \alpha - \beta$, where β is the share of income going to oil. We assume that the supply of capital is fixed. When there is no oil shock, the world supply of oil is fixed although the supply of oil to any region is variable. Therefore, any symmetric shock will have the same effect on aggregate production with and without oil. The only variable factor whose total supply can change is labor, and labor enters the model in the same way with and without oil.

The equation relating the sum of nominal incomes to the sum of employments with oil (equation 2-37) is the same as the equation relating the sum of nominal incomes to the sum of employments without oil (equation 2-38) when there is no oil shock ($2\tilde{b} = 0$).

Without oil, equations 2-29, 2-30, 2-35, 2-36, and 2-38 are five equations in the six variables p_s, y_s, n_s, i_s, m_s, and $\overline{p + y}_s$. One of the three variables i_s, m_s, or $\overline{p + y}_s$ is exogenous depending on the regime pair. With oil, equations 2-29, 2-30, 2-34, 2-36, and 2-37 are the same five equations in the same six variables when there is no oil shock ($2\tilde{b} = 0$). Therefore, adding oil to the model does not affect any of the results for symmetric shocks to money demands, goods demands, and productivities.

The sum of oil prices, $\tilde{p}_s$, varies to keep the sum of demands for oil equal to the exogenous supply (equation 2-33), but $\tilde{p}_s$ does not enter anywhere else in the equilibrium conditions for the model for sums.[52]

---

52. $\tilde{p}_s$ is determined recursively by equation 2-33 given the values for n_s and p_s determined jointly with y_s, i_s, m_s, and $\overline{p + y}_s$ by equations 2-29, 2-30, 2-34, 2-36, and 2-37 with one of the three variables i_s, m_s, and $\overline{p + y}_s$ exogenous.

The Schedules for Differences with Oil

Adding oil to the model does affect the results for asymmetric shocks. We can analyze the effects of asymmetric shocks in the model with oil using appropriately modified versions of four schedules for differences— the aggregate-demand schedule, the money-market-equilibrium schedule, the aggregate-supply schedule, and the nominal-income-constant schedule—and an additional schedule. First we explain the schedules that we use in the analysis, and then we show how the results for asymmetric shocks are affected.

The *aggregate-demand schedule for differences* with oil (ADO_d) is given by equation 2-39. In general, the slope of the ADO_d schedule is different from the slope of the aggregate-demand schedule for differences without oil (AD_d) given by equation 2-40.[53] However, the slope of the ADO_d schedule is the same as the slope of the AD_d schedule in the special case of $\gamma = 1/2$. In this special case, $Q = R = 0$, so the ADO_d schedule and AD_d schedule are both given by equation 2-40, just as they are when $\beta = 0$. We want to focus our analysis on the supply effects of including oil. Therefore, in our graphical and algebraic analysis we limit our attention to the special case of $\gamma = 1/2$ and label the aggregate-demand schedule for differences with oil AD_d.[54]

Although the slope of the AD_d schedule may be greater or less than one in absolute value, even in the special case with $\gamma = 1/2$, in the text we consider only the case in which it is greater than one. The AD_d schedule is represented by the $AD_{d,0}$ schedule in figure 2-6. Recall from the earlier analysis without oil that an increase in i_d shifts the AD_d schedule down by the amount of the increase in i_d.

---

53. With oil, the negative effect of an increase in y_d on the difference between excess demands is larger in absolute value. An increase in y_d increases the difference between the US oil bill and the ROECD oil bill, thereby shifting world demand away from US goods and toward ROECD goods ($2\beta\kappa\epsilon > 0$), because residents of both the US and the ROECD allocate a larger fraction of their spending to the goods produced in their countries than OPEC does. This difference tends to make the *AD* schedule steeper.

An increase in i_d or p_d causes a reduction in the difference between excess demands because it raises r_d and causes the dollar to appreciate in real terms. With oil, the negative effect of an increase in r_d is smaller in absolute value. An increase in r_d has no effect on the real interest rate faced by OPEC, which puts equal weights on r and $\check{r}$ in its spending function. This difference also tends to make the *AD* curve steeper.

With oil, the negative effect of an appreciation of the dollar in real terms is greater in absolute value. A decrease in z lowers the value of the ROECD oil bill in terms of US goods, thereby reducing demand for US goods because OPEC allocates a larger fraction of its spending to US goods than does the ROECD. This difference tends to make the *AD* curve flatter. None of the differences affects the conclusion about how much the *AD* curve shifts down when i_d increases.

54. As stated in the beginning of this section, in the simulations reported on in the tables it is assumed that $\gamma = 0.15$. Given this value of γ and the values of the other parameters (see appendix A), the ADO_d schedule is steeper than the AD_d schedule. The slopes of the AD_d and ADO_d schedules can be obtained from the results for the case of an asymmetric productivity shock under the II regime (see table 2-13) because those schedules do not shift in that case. The slope of the AD_d schedule is $-(10.48)/(8.89) = -1.179$, and the slope of the ADO_d schedule is $-(10.32)/(8.70) = -1.186$.

Figure 2-6. *Explanation of Schedules: Oil*

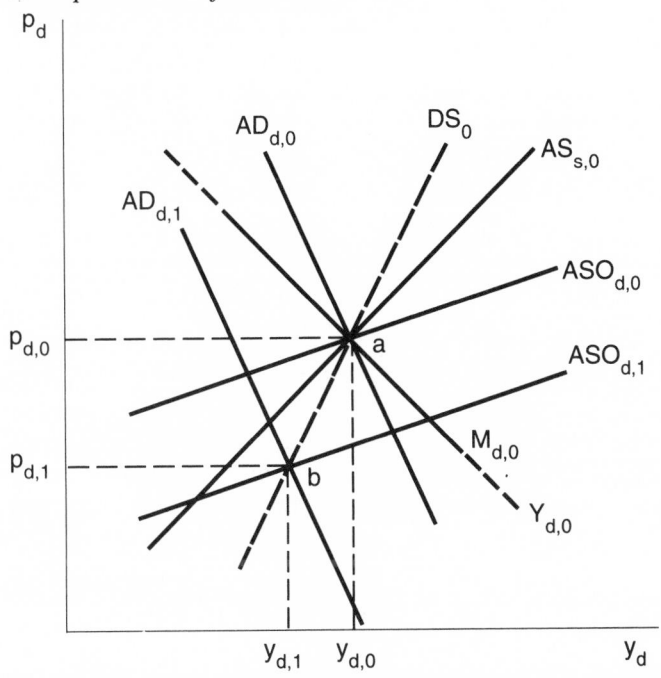

The *money-market-equilibrium schedule for differences* (M_d), given by equation 2-41, is the same with and without oil because we assume that OPEC residents hold no money. Although the slope of the M_d schedule may be greater than, equal to, or less than one in absolute value, in the text we consider only the case in which it is equal to one. The M_d schedule is represented by the $M_{d,0}$ schedule in figure 2-6. Recall from the earlier analysis that an increase in i_d shifts the M_d schedule up.

The *aggregate-supply schedule for differences* with oil (ASO_d) is given by equation 2-47. The ASO_d schedule is represented by the $ASO_{d,0}$ schedule in figure 2-6. The ASO_d schedule shows how y_d responds to a change in p_d. It has a positive slope in p_d, y_d space. An increase in p_d causes the difference between relative prices of both labor and oil in the US and the ROECD to fall, so the use of both factors and, therefore, output increase in the US and decrease in the ROECD.

An increase in p_d with z held constant causes the difference between real wages to fall (equation 2-43). When the difference between real wages falls, both n_d and o_d must increase in order to maintain equilibrium in the factor markets by reducing the difference between marginal products of labor and by keeping the difference between the marginal products of oil constant.

An increase in p_d also reduces the difference between the relative prices of oil in the US and the ROECD, $\tilde{p}_d - p_d$, which is equal to z (equation 2-44). When z falls, both o_d and n_d must increase in order to maintain equilibrium in the factor markets by reducing the difference between marginal products of oil and by keeping the difference between marginal products of labor constant.

The ASO_d schedule is flatter than the aggregate-supply schedule for differences without oil (AS_d), as shown in figure 2-6. A given increase in p_d generates a larger increase in y_d with oil, for two reasons. First, with z held constant the increase in p_d leads to increases in both n_d and o_d, and the increase in n_d is larger with oil than without it because o_d increases. Second, the increase in p_d leads to a fall in z, which causes additional increases in n_d and o_d.

An increase in i_d, say from $i_{d,0}$ to $i_{d,1}$, shifts the ASO_d schedule down, say from $ASO_{d,0}$ to $ASO_{d,1}$, but by less than the increase in i_d. An increase in i_d raises y_d only by causing z to fall, but an increase in p_d raises y_d both by causing z to fall and by lowering the difference between real wages.

The *nominal-income-constant schedule for differences* (Y_d), given by equation 2-49, is the same with and without oil. The Y_d schedule is represented by the $Y_{d,0}$ schedule in figure 2-6.

The Y_d schedule also has another interpretation in the important special case in which the elasticity of substitution among factors of production (σ) is unitary. If $\sigma = 1$, equation 2-50 reduces to $p_d + y_d = n_d$, so even with oil there is a one-to-one relationship between the difference between nominal incomes and the difference between employments. Thus, in this case, a Y_d schedule gives the pairs of p_d and y_d for which n_d is constant. Throughout most of this section we assume that $\sigma = 1$, but we relax this assumption in the last subsection.

It is useful for what follows to derive a fifth schedule, the *DS schedule*. The *DS* schedule is represented by the DS_0 schedule in figure 2-6. This schedule shows the pairs of p_d and y_d for which aggregate demand equals aggregate supply given that the interest rate is varying. Suppose that for interest rate i_0 the aggregate-demand schedule $AD_{d,0}$ intersects the aggregate-supply schedule with oil $ASO_{d,0}$ at point a, which corresponds to the pair $p_{d,0}$ and $y_{d,0}$. We have established that an increase in i_d, say to $i_{d,1}$, shifts the AD_d schedule down by the amount of the increase in i_d and shifts the ASO_d schedule down by less than the amount of the increase. Let the shifted schedules be $AD_{d,1}$ and $ASO_{d,1}$. Then the intersection of the shifted schedules is at the point b, corresponding to the pair $p_{d,1}$ and $y_{d,1}$. The DS_0 schedule is obtained by connecting the points a and b. The *DS* schedule is upward sloping and steeper than the ASO_d schedule and is steeper or flatter than the AS_d schedule depending on whether the slope of the AD_d schedule is greater than one, as in figure 2-6, or less than one in absolute value.[55]

Asymmetric Money-Demand Shock

A shift up in money demand in the US matched by a shift down in money demand in the ROECD, an increase in v_d, causes the M_d schedule to shift down from $M_{d,0}$ to $M_{d,1}$, as shown in figure 2-7 (see above). The increase in the difference between money demands puts upward pressure on i_d at the original values of p_d and y_d. As will be seen, including oil makes a difference for the effects of a shock if and only if the shock causes the real exchange rate to change. For an asymmetric money-demand shock, the only regime pair under which the real exchange rate changes is the MM regime pair.

Under the II and YY regime pairs, i_d is kept constant. To keep i_d constant, m_d must be allowed to increase by enough to shift the M_d schedule from $M_{d,1}$ back to $M_{d,0}$, so i_d, y_d, and p_d remain unchanged. With oil just as without it, under the II and YY regime pairs an asymmetric shock to money demand does not affect any variables except money supplies.

Under the MM regime pair, i_d is increased in order to prevent m_d from rising. The M_d schedule shifts up and the ASO_d and AD_d schedules shift down until they meet at some point along the marked part of the DS_0 schedule, between points a and b, below the $Y_{d,0}$ schedule. i_d is higher, and y_d and p_d and, therefore, $p_d + y_d$, n_d, and q_d are lower. Since y_d is lower, $i_d + p_d$ and, therefore, r_d must be higher and the dollar must appreciate in real terms so that the difference between excess demands for goods remains equal to zero. n_d tends to fall because p_d falls but tends to rise because the dollar appreciates in real terms. The first effect outweighs the second. With oil, just as without it, the MM regime pair is inferior to the II and YY regime pairs.

The increase in i_d sufficient to shift the AD_d schedule and the M_d schedule until they meet on the DS_0 schedule is less than sufficient to shift these schedules until they meet on the $AS_{d,0}$ schedule. For an equilibrium on the $AS_{d,0}$ schedule to be reached, i_d must continue to rise, so the increase in i_d is

---

55. When $\sigma = 1$, the slope of the AS_d schedule is $(1 - \alpha)/\alpha$, as can be seen in equation 2-48. The algebraic representation of the DS schedule is obtained by solving equation 2-40 for the interest rate, substituting the result into equation 2-47 with $\sigma = 1$, and collecting terms:

$$P_d = \left(\left[\frac{1-\alpha}{\alpha}\right] - \left[1 - \frac{1-(1-2\gamma)\epsilon}{F}\right]\left[\frac{\beta}{\alpha}\right]\right)y_d - \left[\frac{\beta}{\alpha F}\right]u_d + \left[\frac{1}{\alpha}\right]x_d.$$

The slope of the AD_d schedule is $-[1 - (1 - 2\gamma)\epsilon]/F$ from equation 2-40, where F is defined in appendix A.

Figure 2-7. *Asymmetric Money-Oil Demand Shock: Oil*

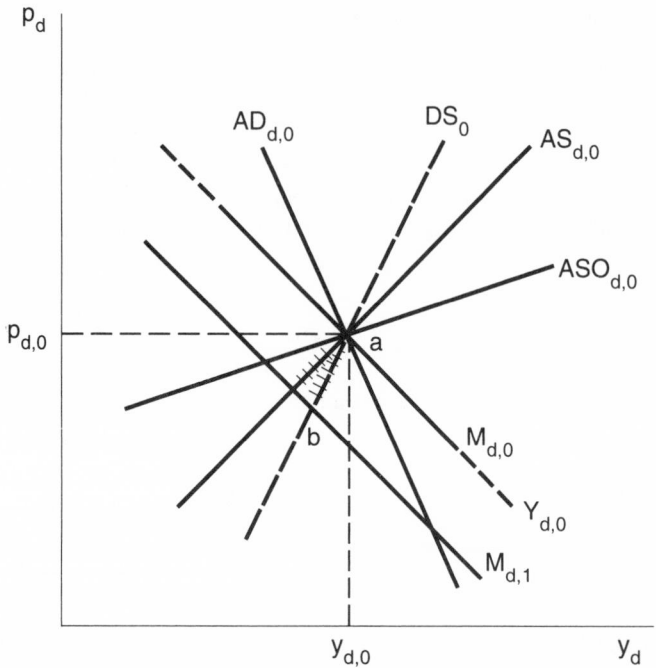

smaller with oil than without it.[56] The DS_0 schedule is steeper than the $AS_{d,0}$ schedule, so the decrease in y_d is smaller and the decrease in p_d is larger with oil than without it.[57] In addition, the decrease in n_d is larger with oil than without it.[58] In terms of figure 2-7, the decrease in n_d must be larger because the intersection of the M_d, AD_d, and ASO_d schedules must lie on a Y_d schedule farther from the $Y_{d,0}$ schedule. In terms of economics, there are two effects that tend to make the decrease in n_d greater with oil—a given decrease in p_d is associated with a larger reduction in n_d, and p_d falls by more—and one effect that tends to make it smaller—the dollar appreciates in real terms. The first two effects dominate the third.

56. i_d rises less with oil either if the AD_d schedule has a slope greater than one in absolute value and the AD_d schedule is steeper than the M_d schedule or if the AD_d schedule has a slope less than one in absolute value and the AD_d schedule is flatter than the M_d schedule.

57. y_d falls by less with oil and p_d falls by more with oil if and only if the DS schedule is steeper than the AS_d schedule. As shown in note 55, the DS schedule is steeper than the AS_d schedule if and only if the AD_d schedule has a slope greater than one in absolute value.

58. Changes in i_d shift the M_d and AD_d schedules and the intersections of the shifting schedules trace out a new schedule in p_d, y_d space which we call the MD schedule (not shown). The MD schedule lies between the AD_d and M_d schedules, has a negative slope, and may have a slope greater or less than one in absolute value. Under the assumptions of the text the MD schedule has a slope greater than one in absolute value. n_d falls more with oil if and only if the slope of the MD schedule is greater than one in absolute value.

In the simulation results in table 2-9, outputs change marginally less and output prices change marginally more with oil. Because of rounding, it is not clear from table 2-9, but n_d falls slightly less with oil than without it.[59] The difference between the theoretical prediction for n_d and the simulation result is possible because the two are based on different assumptions about γ.

In the graphical analysis, we assume that $\gamma = 1/2$. Under this assumption, the increase in i_d is smaller and the decrease in p_d is larger with oil.[60] In addition, q_d is independent of p_d, so the effect of adding oil on the change in q_d depends entirely on the effect of adding oil on the change in i_d. Since the increase in i_d is smaller with oil, the fall in q_d is also smaller. If $\gamma < 1/2$ as in the simulations, q_d varies not only inversely with i_d but also directly with p_d. In the simulation results in table 2-9, both the increase in i_d and the decrease in p_d are larger with oil, so the fall in q_d is unambiguously larger. The difference between the theoretical prediction for i_d and the simulation result is possible because the two are based on different assumptions about γ.

Asymmetric Goods-Demand Shock

A shift up in the demand for US goods matched by a shift down in the demand for ROECD goods, an increase in u_d, increases the difference between excess demands for goods. It causes the AD_d schedule to shift up from $AD_{d,0}$ to $AD_{d,1}$, as shown in figure 2-8. The increase in u_d puts upward pressure on y_d and p_d and (with the money supply constant) on i_d.

Under the II regime pair, i_d is kept constant, so the new equilibrium is at the intersection of $AD_{d,1}$ and $AS_{d,0}$ schedules at point b without oil and at the intersection of the $AD_{d,1}$ and $ASO_{d,0}$ schedules at point c with oil. The difference between money supplies is allowed to increase by enough to shift the M_d schedule from $M_{d,0}$ until it passes through the appropriate intersection.

In the new equilibrium, y_d, p_d, and n_d are all higher with or without oil.[61] The increase in p_d raises $i_d + p_d$, so r_d rises and the dollar appreciates in real terms. With oil, the increase in y_d is greater and the increase in p_d is smaller because the ASO_d schedule is flatter than the AS_d schedule. In the simulation results in table 2-11, y and $\overset{*}{y}$ change by more and p and $\overset{*}{p}$ change by less with oil than without it.

---

59. It is clear from table 2-15 that employment falls by slightly less. The results in table 2-15 are the sum of the symmetric-shock results in table 2-8, where adding oil makes no difference, and the asymmetric-shock results in table 2-9.

60. See notes 56 and 57.

61. The results reported in this paragraph are independent of whether the slope and the AD_d schedule is greater or less than one in absolute value.

Figure 2-8. *Asymmetric Goods-Demand Shock: Oil*

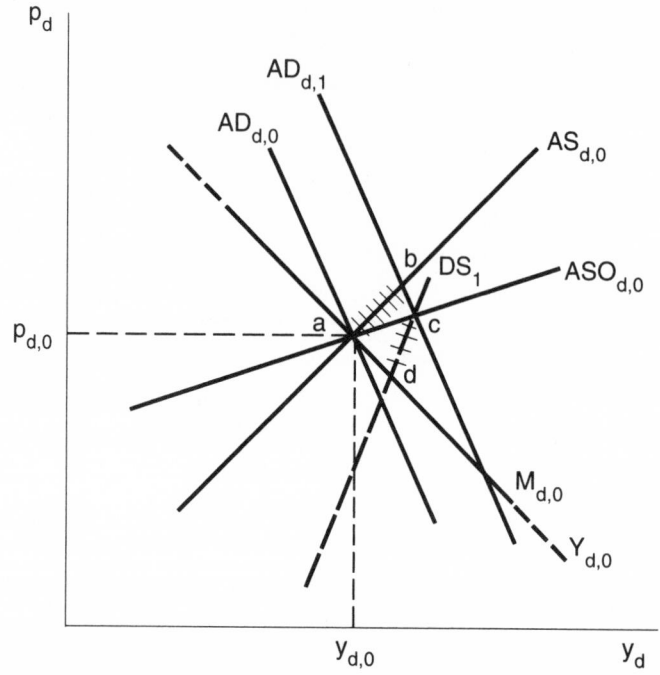

Under the II regime pair, the increase in n_d is less with oil.[62] The Y_d schedule that passes through point c passes below point b. n_d tends to rise more with oil because a given increase in p_d gives rise to a larger increase in n_d, but n_d tends to rise less because the increase in p_d is less. The second effect outweighs the first. In the simulation results in table 2-11, n and $\overset{*}{n}$ change by less with oil.

In the graphical analysis, we assume that $\gamma = 1/2$. Under this assumption, the increase in p_d is less with oil. In addition, q_d is independent of p_d, so there is no change in q_d with or without oil. If $\gamma < 1/2$, there is a one to one relationship between changes in p_d and changes in q_d. In the simulation results in table 2-11, the increases in p and q and the decreases in $\overset{*}{p}$ and $\overset{*}{q}$ under the II pair are smaller with oil than without it.

Under the MM regime pair, i_d is increased in order to prevent m_d from rising. Thus, the new equilibrium without oil lies on the marked part of the $AS_{d,0}$ schedule between points a and b, and the new equilibrium with oil lies on the marked part of the DS_1 schedule between points c and d. Under this regime

---

62. The increase in n_d is less with oil if and only if the slope of the AD_d schedule is greater than one in absolute value.

pair and our assumption that the M_d schedule has a slope equal to negative one, all the results for the effects of adding oil depend on whether the slope of the AD_d schedule is greater than or less than one in absolute value. In both cases the intersections of the AD_d schedule and the AS_d and ASO_d schedules following the shift in demand are points of excess demand for money, so i_d must be increased.

If the slope of the AD_d schedule is greater than one in absolute value, the increase in i_d sufficient to shift the AD_d schedule and M_d schedule until they meet on the DS schedule is less than sufficient to shift these schedules until they meet on the AS_d schedule. For an equilibrium on the AS_d schedule to be reached, i_d must continue to rise. Therefore, the increase in i_d is smaller and the increase in y_d is larger in the equilibrium with oil.[63] In addition, the increase in n_d is smaller in the equilibrium with oil.[64] If p_d increases with oil, then the increase with oil must be smaller. If p_d decreases with oil, then the decrease can be less or greater in absolute value than the increase without oil.[65] In the simulation results in table 2-11, i_d rises by less, y_d rises by more, n_d rises by less, and p_d rises by less with oil.

In the graphical analysis, we assume that $\gamma = 1/2$. Under this assumption and with oil, i_d rises by less, while p_d may rise by less or fall by more or less in absolute value than p_d rises without oil. In addition, q_d is independent of p_d, so q_d falls less with oil (since i_d rises by less). If $\gamma < 1/2$ as in the simulations, q_d varies not only inversely with i_d but also directly with p_d. In this case it is much more difficult to draw conclusions because of the many possibilities for the effect of including oil on the change in p_d. q_d may rise or fall with and without oil, and we have not been able to draw any general conclusions about what difference oil makes for the change in q_d.[66] In the simulation results in table 2-11, q_d falls by more with oil because the effect of the decrease in the rise in p_d is greater than the effect of the decrease in the rise in i_d.

The most important result of this section is apparent in the simulation results in table 2-11: including oil can alter the ranking of regime pairs. Without oil,

---

63. i_d rises less and y_d rises more with oil if and only if the AD_d schedule is steeper than the M_d schedule. See note 56.

64. n_d rises less with oil if and only if the slope of the MD schedule described in note 58 is greater than one in absolute value.

65. When the slope of the AD_d schedule is less than one in absolute value, i_d, y_d, and n_d increase by more in the equilibrium with oil and the qualitative results for p_d are the same as when the slope of the AD_d schedule is greater than one in absolute value.

66. Suppose the slope of the AD_d schedule is less than one in absolute value. If $\gamma = 1/2$, then q_d falls more with oil (since i_d rises by more). However, if $\gamma < 1/2$, the qualitative results for q_d are the same when the slope of the AD_d schedule is less than one in absolute value as when it is greater than one in absolute value.

the MM pair is preferred to the II pair for stabilization of CPIs. However, with oil the II pair is preferred for stabilization of CPIs because the appreciation of the dollar in real terms is enough less under that pair.

Under the YY regime pair, the new equilibrium is on the $Y_{d,0}$ schedule just as the initial equilibrium was. i_d is increased so that AD_d and ASO_d schedules shift down the DS_1 schedule until they intersect on the $Y_{d,0}$ schedule. Since the new equilibrium is on the original $Y_{d,0}$ schedule, employments are unchanged with oil just as they are without it. i_d may be increased by less or more with oil than without it, depending on whether the AD_d schedule is steeper or flatter than the $Y_{d,0}$ schedule.

Without oil, n_d, p_d, and y_d all remain unchanged under the YY regime pair. However, with oil n_d and $p_d + y_d$ remain unchanged but y_d rises and p_d falls (no matter whether i_d rises less or more). The reason is that, with oil, the appreciation of the dollar in real terms affects the supply side of the economy. Since n_d is unchanged and the dollar appreciates in real terms,[67] o_d must rise, thereby increasing y_d in order to decrease the difference between the marginal productivity conditions for oil (equation 2-44). p_d must fall because the increase in o_d increases the difference between marginal productivity conditions for labor (equation 2-43). The increase in y_d is the one that would take place if wages were flexible and all markets cleared.[68]

Asymmetric Productivity Shock

A shift down in productivity in the US matched by a shift up in productivity in the ROECD, an increase in x_d, decreases the difference between aggregate supplies of goods. It causes the AS_d schedule to shift up from $AS_{d,0}$ to $AS_{d,1}$, as shown in figure 2-9. It also causes the ASO_d schedule to shift up from $ASO_{d,0}$ to $ASO_{d,1}$. For a given value of y_d, p_d and, therefore, $i_d + p_d$ must be higher so that n_d and o_d will rise by enough to offset the effect of the rise in x_d.

---

67. The dollar appreciates in real terms because $i_d + p_d$ rises even though p_d falls. The new equilibrium lies on a new AD_d schedule (not shown in figure 2-8) that lies below $AD_{d,1}$. $i_d + p_d$ would be unchanged if the new equilibrium were at the point on the new AD_d schedule that lies directly below the intersection of $AD_{d,1}$ and the $ASO_{d,0}$ schedule. However, since the new equilibrium lies to the northwest of this point on the new AD_d schedule, the fall in p_d must be less in absolute value than the rise in i_d.

68. y_d can be written in terms of n_d and $i_d + p_d$ by obtaining expressions for o_d and p_d from equations 2-43 and 2-44 and substituting the expression for o_d into equation 2-42. Substituting this expression for y_d into the equation for the difference between excess demands for goods (equation 2-39) yields an equation in n_d, $i_d + p_d$, and u_d because not only z but also r_d depend only on $i_d + p_d$. If n_d remains unchanged at zero, the amounts by which $i_d + p_d$ and, therefore, all the other real variables must change for a given increase in u_d are uniquely determined. With perfectly flexible wages, n_d remains unchanged, because wages adjust. With fixed wages, n_d remains unchanged under the YY regime, because policymakers increase i_d by enough.

Figure 2-9. *Asymmetric Productivity Shock: Oil*

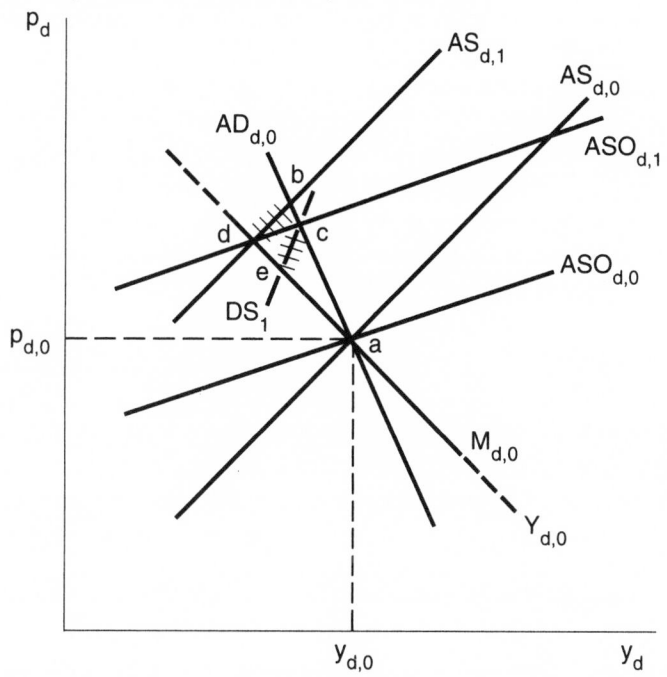

The AS_d and ASO_d schedules shift to the northwest by the same distance along the $Y_{d,0}$ schedule, which has a slope equal to one in absolute value. A decrease in y_d and an increase in p_d and the associated appreciation of the dollar in real terms that are equal in absolute value to the increase in x_d keep employments unchanged without oil and keep employments and oil usages unchanged with oil. These conclusions can be confirmed from the difference between production functions (equation 2-42 in table 2-6) and the difference between first-order conditions for the factors of production (equations 2-43 and 2-44).

Following the increase in x_d, the pair of y_d and p_d that clears the goods market is given by the intersection of the $AS_{d,1}$ and $AD_{d,0}$ schedules at point b without oil and by the intersection of the $ASO_{d,1}$ and $AD_{d,0}$ schedules at point c with oil. There is an increase in the difference between excess demands for money at these points, so there is upward pressure on i_d.[69]

Under the II regime pair, i_d is kept constant, so the new equilibrium without oil is at point b, and the new equilibrium with oil is at point c. The

69. In contrast, if the slope of the AD_d schedule is less than one in absolute value, there is a reduction in the difference between excess demands for money, so there is downward pressure on i_d.

difference between money supplies is allowed to change by enough to shift the M_d schedule from $M_{d,0}$ until it passes through the appropriate point.

The combination of Y_d and p_d consistent with unchanged factor use following the asymmetric productivity shock is given by the intersection of the $AS_{d,1}$, $ASO_{d,1}$, and $Y_{d,0}$ schedules at point d. This combination implies an increase in the difference between excess demands for goods. Therefore, y_d must fall by less, while p_d and $i_d + p_d$ must rise by more, than the amounts consistent with unchanged factor use. With oil, given additional increases in p_d and $i_d + p_d$ are associated with larger increases in y_d, so y_d falls by less and p_d rises by less with oil. In the simulation results in table 2-13, outputs and output prices change by less under the II pair with oil than without it. Each additional increase in p_d causes a larger increase in n_d with oil, but p_d rises by less. The latter consideration dominates, so n_d rises by less with oil. The Y_d schedule passing through point c (not shown in figure 2-9) is closer to $Y_{d,0}$ than the Y_d schedule passing through point b (not shown).[70] In the simulation results in table 2-13, employments change by more under the II pair with oil than without it. The difference between the theoretical prediction and the simulation result for n_d is possible because the two are based on different assumptions about γ.

In the graphical analysis, $\gamma = 1/2$. With this assumption, the increase in p_d is less with oil.[71] Because q_d is independent of p_d, there is no change in q_d with or without oil. If $\gamma < 1/2$, however, there is a one-to-one relationship between changes in p_d and changes in q_d. In the simulation results in table 2-13, output prices and CPIs change by less under the II pair with oil than without it.

Under the MM regime pair, i_d is increased in order to keep m_d constant. Thus, the new equilibrium without oil lies on the marked part of the $AS_{d,1}$ schedule between points b and d, while the new equilibrium with oil lies on the marked part of the DS_1 schedule between points c and e.

There is an increase in the difference between excess demands for moneys at points b and c, so i_d must be increased. The increase in i_d sufficient to shift the $AD_{d,0}$ schedule and $M_{d,0}$ schedule until they meet on the DS_1 schedule is less than sufficient to shift these schedules until they meet on the $AS_{d,1}$ schedule. For an equilibrium on the $AS_{d,1}$ schedule to be reached, i_d must continue to rise. Therefore, the increase in i_d is smaller with oil.[72] Also, the increase in p_d and the decrease in y_d are smaller with oil.[73] In addition, the

70. If the AD_d schedule has a slope less than one in absolute value, y_d and n_d fall by more and p_d rises by more with oil.

71. If the slope of the AD_d schedule is less than one, the increase in q_d is greater with oil. See the previous note.

72. i_d rises less with oil if and only if the AD_d schedule is steeper than the M_d schedule.

73. The increase in p_d and the decrease in y_d are smaller with oil if and only if the slope of the AD_d schedule is greater than one in absolute value.

increase in n_d is smaller with oil.[74] In the simulation results for the MM pair in table 2-13, p_d rises less and and y_d falls less with oil than without it. However, i_d and n_d rise by more with oil. The difference between the theoretical predictions and the simulation results for i_d and n_d is possible because the two are based on different assumptions about γ.

With $\gamma = 1/2$ as in the graphical analysis, q_d falls less with oil because i_d rises by less. If $\gamma < 1/2$, however, q_d may rise or fall with and without oil. We have not been able to draw any general conclusions about what difference oil makes for the change in q_d. In the simulation results for the MM pair in table 2-13, q_d rises by less with oil because p_d rises by less and i_d rises by more.

Under the YY regime pair, both the initial equilibrium and the new equilibrium lie on the $Y_{d,0}$ schedule. Without oil, i_d is increased such that the AD_d schedule shifts along the $AS_{d,1}$ schedule until the $AD_{d,0}$ and $AS_{d,1}$ schedule intersect on the $Y_{d,0}$ schedule. With oil, i_d is increased such that the AD_d and ASO_d schedules shift along the DS_1 schedule until they intersect on the $Y_{d,0}$ schedule.[75] Since the new equilibrium is always on the original $Y_{d,0}$ schedule, employments are unchanged both without and with oil as confirmed by the simulation results in table 2-13.

Under the YY regime pair, it is always true following an increase in x_d that y_d falls and p_d rises by amounts that are equal to each other in absolute value. The equilibrium decrease in y_d is equal to the decrease in y_d that would take place if wages were flexible and all markets cleared.[76] Without oil, y_d falls and p_d rises by amounts that are equal in absolute value to the increase in x_d. With oil, y_d falls and p_d rises by amounts that are less in absolute value than the increase in x_d.[77] The increase in i_d required to shift the AD_d and ASO_d schedules down along the DS_1 schedule causes the dollar to appreciate in real terms, thereby increasing o_d and y_d and reducing p_d for a given value of n_d (for reasons given above). In the simulation results for the YY pair in table 2-13, outputs and output prices change less with oil than without it.

Assuming that $\gamma = 1/2$, as we do in the graphical analysis, implies that i_d and p_d rise less with oil. Because q_d is independent of p_d, q_d falls by less with oil. If $\gamma < 1/2$, however, q_d may rise or fall with and without oil, and we again have not been able to draw any general conclusions about what

74. n_d rises less with oil if and only if the slope of the MD schedule described in note 58 is greater than one in absolute value.

75. i_d must be increased or decreased depending on whether the AD schedule is steeper or flatter than the Y_d schedule.

76. See note 68.

77. In contrast, if the slope of the AD_d schedule is less than one in absolute value, y_d falls and p_d rises by amounts greater in absolute value than the increase in x_d.

difference oil makes for the change in q_d. In the simulation results for the YY pair in table 2-13, i rises by more and $\overset{*}{i}$ falls by more with oil, while q rises by less and $\overset{*}{q}$ falls by less with oil. The difference between the theoretical predictions and the simulation results for i_d and q_d is possible because, again, the two are based on different assumptions about γ.

Region-Specific Shocks

As we explain above, the effects of region-specific shocks can be expressed as sums of or differences between the effects of symmetric and asymmetric shocks. For example, for any US variable under the MM regime pair, adding the effect of the symmetric money shock from table 2-8 to the effect of the asymmetric money shock from table 2-9 and dividing by two yields the effect of a region-specific increase in US money demand. Because there is no change in the effects of a symmetric shock from including oil, any change in the effects of a region-specific shock must be due to a change in the effects of an asymmetric shock. We have just discussed the changes in the effects of asymmetric shocks that result from including oil. Accordingly, there is no need to discuss the changes in results for region-specific shocks, and we will not do so. For completeness, however, we include the results for region-specific shocks with oil in the tables for region-specific shocks (tables 2-15, 2-16, and 2-18 through 2-21).

A Shock to the Supply of Oil

An exogenous fall in the world oil supply is equivalent to a symmetric fall in productivity when the elasticity of substitution among factors of production, σ, is unitary. As we state above, equations 2-29, 2-30, 2-34, 2-36, and 2-37 are five equations in the six variables p_s, y_s, n_s, i_s, m_s, and $\overline{p + y}_s$, and one of the three variables i_s, m_s, or $\overline{p + y}_s$ is exogenous depending on the regime pair. In general, the oil supply enters equations 2-34 and 2-37, while the productivity shock enters only equation 2-34. However, if $\sigma = 1$, the oil supply no longer enters equation 2-37. In this case, both the oil supply and the productivity shock enter only in equation 2-34. The equivalence of a fall in the world oil supply of $1/2\beta$ units and a global (symmetric) decrease in productivity of one unit when $\sigma = 1$ is clear from a comparison of the simulation results in the right-hand columns of tables 2-12 and 2-24.

A Non-Unitary Elasticity of Substitution among Factors of Production

Until now, we have been operating under the assumption that the elasticity of substitution among factors of production, σ, is unitary. This assumption

Table 2-24. *First-Period Impact of a Fall in OPEC Oil Supply*

	Regime pair									
	Oil excluded (β = 0)					Oil included (β = 0.1)				
Variable[a]	MM	II	YY	CC	ME	MM	II	YY	CC	ME
US economy										
Output (%)	0	0	0	0	0	−7.54	−5.76	−10	−10	−7.54
CPI inflation (D)	0	0	0	0	0	11.06	11.82	10	10	11.06
Output price (%)	0	0	0	0	0	11.06	11.82	10	10	11.06
Nominal interest rate (D)	0	0	0	0	0	4.4	0	10.5	20.5	4.4
Real interest rate (D)	0	0	0	0	0	15.45	11.82	20.5	20.5	15.45
Nominal wage (%)	0	0	0	0	0	0	0	0	0	0
Employment (%)	0	0	0	0	0	3.52	6.05	−8.4	−16.4	3.52
Money (%)	0	0	0	0	0	0	6.05	0	0	0
Nominal exchange rate ($/R)(%)	0	0	0	0	0	0	0	0	0	0
Real exchange rate ($/R)(%)	0	0	0	0	0	0	0	0	0	0
ROECD economy										
Output (%)	0	0	0	0	0	−7.54	−5.76	−10	−10	−7.54
CPI inflation (D)	0	0	0	0	0	11.06	11.82	10	10	11.06
Output price (%)	0	0	0	0	0	11.06	11.82	10	10	11.06
Nominal interest rate (D)	0	0	0	0	0	4.4	0	10.5	20.5	4.4
Real interest rate (D)	0	0	0	0	0	15.45	11.82	20.5	20.5	15.45
Nominal wage (%)	0	0	0	0	0	0	0	0	0	0
Employment (%)	0	0	0	0	0	3.52	6.05	−8.4	−16.4	3.52
Money (%)	0	0	0	0	0	0	6.05	0	0	0

a. % is percent deviation from unchanged baseline; D is deviation from unchanged baseline in percentage points.

implies that the production function is Cobb-Douglas. In this subsection, we explain three implications of departing from the assumption that $\sigma = 1$. In the discussion, we refer to the simulation results in tables 2-25 through 2-27, which are based on the assumption that $\sigma = 0.6$.

First, the results for the effects of symmetric shocks are quantitatively but not qualitatively different. In particular, adding oil does not change the effects of symmetric shocks. It is clear from equation 2-32 (table 2-5), the sum of the marginal productivity conditions for labor, that the coefficient on n_s is different when $\sigma \neq 1$. Nevertheless, the argument used above to establish that adding oil does not change the effects of symmetric shocks goes through without modification when $\sigma \neq 1$. Table 2-25 contains the results for a symmetric decrease in productivity when $\sigma = 0.6$. This table is directly comparable to table 2-12. A comparison of these tables confirms that changing σ changes the results quantitatively. The results in table 2-25 confirm that adding oil does not change the effects of symmetric shocks.

Second, a symmetric productivity shock is no longer equivalent to a global reduction in the supply of oil. Consider equation 2-37 (table 2-5), which is one of the five equilibrium conditions that we referred to above. As we noted above, with $\sigma = 1$, the world oil supply does not enter equation 2-37. However, with $\sigma \neq 1$, the world supply of oil does enter equation 2-37, while the symmetric productivity shock does not. Thus, with $\sigma \neq 1$, the world oil supply and the symmetric productivity shock no longer enter the equilibrium conditions in the same way. A comparison of the simulation results for a symmetric productivity shock in table 2-25 with those for a fall in OPEC oil supply in table 2-26 confirms that the two shocks no longer have the same effects when $\sigma \neq 1$.

Third, stabilizing nominal incomes under the YY regime pair no longer stabilizes employments for asymmetric shocks. This result follows from equations 2-50 and 2-51 (table 2-6). From these equations it is clear that either with no oil ($\beta = 0$) and σ equal to any value or with oil ($\beta > 0$) and $\sigma = 1$, there are one-to-one relationships between nominal incomes and employments. For these cases, therefore, stabilizing nominal incomes stabilizes employments. With oil and $\sigma \neq 1$, however, there are no longer one-to-one relationships between nominal incomes and employments. In the example of the simulation results for an asymmetric productivity shock in table 2-27, employments vary under the YY regime pair even though nominal incomes are stabilized. With oil included and $\sigma \neq 1$, we no longer obtain the previously robust result that employments are perfectly stabilized under the YY regime pair and the Contract hypothesis for all kinds of shocks.

Table 2-25. *First-Period Impact of a Symmetric Decrease in Productivity with Elasticity of Substitution between Factors* = −0.6.

	Regime pair									
	Oil excluded ($\beta = 0$)					Oil included ($\beta = 0.1$)				
Variable[a]	MM	II	YY	CC	ME	MM	II	YY	CC	ME
US economy										
Output (%)	−7.86	−6.2	−10	−10	−7.86	−7.86	−6.2	−10	−10	−7.86
CPI inflation (D)	11.53	12.71	10	10	11.53	11.53	12.71	10	10	11.53
Output price (%)	11.53	12.71	10	10	11.53	11.53	12.71	10	10	11.53
Nominal interest rate (D)	4.59	0	10.5	20.5	4.59	4.59	0	10.5	20.5	4.59
Real interest rate (D)	16.11	12.71	20.5	20.5	16.11	16.11	12.71	20.5	20.5	16.11
Nominal wage (%)	0	0	0	0	0	0	0	0	0	0
Employment (%)	3.06	5.43	0	0	3.06	3.06	5.43	0	0	3.06
Money (%)	0	6.51	−8.4	−16.4	0	0	6.51	−8.4	−16.4	0
Nominal exchange rate ($/R)(%)	0	0				0	0			
Real exchange rate ($/R)(%)	0	0				0	0			
ROECD economy										
Output (%)	−7.86	−6.2	−10	−10	−7.86	−7.86	−6.2	−10	−10	−7.86
CPI inflation (D)	11.53	12.71	10	10	11.53	11.53	12.71	10	10	11.53
Output price (%)	11.53	12.71	10	10	11.53	11.53	12.71	10	10	11.53
Nominal interest rate (D)	4.59	0	10.5	20.5	4.59	4.59	0	10.5	20.5	4.59
Real interest rate (D)	16.11	12.71	20.5	20.5	16.11	16.11	12.71	20.5	20.5	16.11
Nominal wage (%)	0	0	0	0	0	0	0	0	0	0
Employment (%)	3.06	5.43	0	0	3.06	3.06	5.43	0	0	3.06
Money (%)	0	6.51	−8.4	−16.4	0	0	6.51	−8.4	−16.4	0

a. % is percent deviation from unchanged baseline; D is deviation from unchanged baseline in percentage points.

Table 2-26. *First-Period Impact of a Fall in OPEC Oil Supply with Elasticity of Substitution between Factors* = −0.6

	Regime pair									
	Oil excluded (β = 0)					Oil included (β = 0.1)				
Variable[a]	MM	II	YY	CC	ME	MM	II	YY	CC	ME
US economy										
Output (%)	0	0	0	0	0	−10.92	−8.61	−13.89	−13.89	−10.92
CPI inflation (D)	0	0	0	0	0	16.01	17.66	13.89	13.89	16.01
Output price (%)	0	0	0	0	0	16.01	17.66	13.89	13.89	16.01
Nominal interest rate (D)	0	0	0	0	0	6.37	0	14.58	28.47	6.37
Real interest rate (D)	0	0	0	0	0	22.38	17.66	28.47	28.47	22.38
Nominal wage (%)	0	0	0	0	0	0	0	0	0	0
Employment (%)	0	0	0	0	0	−1.31	1.98	−5.56	−5.56	−1.31
Money (%)	0	0	0	0	0	0	9.04	−11.67	−22.78	0
Nominal exchange rate ($/R)(%)	0	0				0	0			
Real exchange rate ($/R)(%)	0	0				0	0			
ROECD economy										
Output (%)	0	0	0	0	0	−10.92	−8.61	−13.89	−13.89	−10.92
CPI inflation (D)	0	0	0	0	0	16.01	17.66	13.89	13.89	16.01
Output price (%)	0	0	0	0	0	16.01	17.66	13.89	13.89	16.01
Nominal interest rate (D)	0	0	0	0	0	6.37	0	14.58	28.47	6.37
Real interest rate (D)	0	0	0	0	0	22.38	17.66	28.47	28.47	22.38
Nominal wage (%)	0	0	0	0	0	0	0	0	0	0
Employment (%)	0	0	0	0	0	−1.31	1.98	−5.56	−5.56	−1.31
Money (%)	0	0	0	0	0	0	9.04	−11.67	−22.78	0

a. % is percent deviation from unchanged baseline; D is deviation from unchanged baseline in percentage points.

Table 2-27. *First-Period Impact of an Asymmetric Productivity Shock (US Productivity Decreasing) with Elasticity of Substitution between Factors* = −0.6.

	Regime pair									
	Oil excluded (β = 0)					Oil included (β = 0.1)				
Variable[a]	MM	II	YY	CC	ME	MM	II	YY	CC	ME
US economy										
Output (%)	−9.56	−9.06	−10	−10	−9.47	−9.35	−8.83	−9.83	−9.83	−9.25
CPI inflation (D)	6.94	7.47	6.46	6.46	7.18	6.81	7.34	6.32	6.32	7.04
Output price (%)	10.32	10.67	10	10	10.38	10.15	10.49	9.83	9.83	10.19
Nominal interest rate (D)	0.95	0	1.79	11.79	1.14	0.99	0	1.89	11.72	1.17
Real interest rate (D)	7.89	7.47	8.25	8.25	8.32	7.79	7.34	8.21	8.21	8.21
Nominal wage (%)	0	0	0	0	0	0	0	0	0	0
Employment (%)	0.63	1.35	0	0	0.76	0.73	1.47	0.07	0.07	0.86
Money (%)	0	1.62	−1.43	−9.43	0	0	1.66	−1.51	−9.38	0
Nominal exchange rate ($/R)(%)	−1.9	0	−3.57	−3.57	0	−1.98	0	−3.78	−3.78	0
Real exchange rate ($/R)(%)	−22.53	−21.35	−23.57	−23.57	−21.35	−22.27	−20.98	−23.44	−23.44	−20.98
ROECD economy										
Output (%)	9.56	9.06	10	10	8.64	9.35	8.83	9.83	9.83	8.4
CPI inflation (D)	−6.94	−7.47	−6.46	−6.46	−7.77	−6.81	−7.34	−6.32	−6.32	−7.64
Output price (%)	−10.32	−10.67	−10	−10	−10.97	−10.15	−10.49	−9.83	−9.83	−10.79
Nominal interest rate (D)	−0.95	0	−1.79	−11.79	1.14	−0.99	0	−1.89	−11.72	1.17
Real interest rate (D)	−7.89	−7.47	−8.25	−8.25	−6.63	−7.79	−7.34	−8.21	−8.21	−6.47
Nominal wage (%)	0	0	0	0	0	0	0	0	0	0
Employment (%)	−0.63	−1.35	0	0	−1.94	−0.73	−1.47	−0.07	−0.07	−2.07
Money (%)	0	−1.62	1.43	9.43	−3.24	0	−1.66	1.51	9.38	−3.32

a. % is percent deviation from unchanged baseline; D is deviation from unchanged baseline in percentage points.

Other Wage-Price Hypotheses

In this section, we consider the effects of the basic shocks for the different regime pairs under four other wage-price hypotheses in addition to the Contract hypothesis. These other hypotheses are what we call the Phillips, Taylor, Barro-Grossman 1 (BG1), and Barro-Grossman 2 (BG2) hypotheses. Instead of the Contract hypothesis, we use each of the other hypotheses in turn to close the model. Some of these other hypotheses imply wage- and price-setting behavior like that incorporated in the empirical multicountry models used to produce the simulations discussed in chapters 3–5 of this book. To simplify the analysis, we revert to the assumption that oil is absent ($\beta = 0$).

Under the Phillips, Taylor, and BG1 hypotheses, just as under the Contract hypothesis, wages are sticky, but output prices are perfectly flexible and move to clear goods markets in each period. Under these hypotheses, employments are determined by the marginal productivity conditions for labor (equations 2-3 with $\beta = 0$). However, under the BG2 hypothesis, both wages and prices are sticky. Under this hypothesis, the marginal productivity conditions for labor no longer hold, and employments are determined by inverting the production functions (equations 2-1 with $\beta = 0$).

Most of the shocks considered in this book are temporary shocks, and all of the shocks considered in this chapter are temporary shocks unless we explicitly state otherwise. The results for temporary shocks can be quite different from the results for permanent shocks. Many readers may be more familiar with the latter. Therefore, we provide a comparison of the effects of permanent and temporary symmetric shocks to money demands under the Phillips hypothesis, using both phase-diagram and simulation analysis.

Most of the analysis in this section is simulation analysis conducted using the parameter values given in appendix A. One reason for using simulation analysis is that under some of the other wage-price hypotheses, analytical solutions are difficult or even impossible to obtain. We provide summary statistics for employments, inflation rates, and outputs derived from simulations for all five alternative wage-price hypotheses. We also provide graphs of the full adjustment paths for eight variables under the Phillips hypothesis.

The Four Other Hypotheses

In this subsection, we describe the four other wage-price hypotheses. Under the *Phillips* hypothesis, wages are determined by expectations-augmented Phillips curves that embody the natural-rate hypothesis. Wages for period $t + 1$ are set in period t and are equal to wages in period t plus a constant times the gaps between actual and natural levels of employments plus expected rates of output price inflation between periods t and $t + 1$. See equations 2-15 in table 2-3, where n_t and $\overset{*}{n}_t$ represent not only actual employments in period t but also the amounts by which employments exceed their natural levels of zero.[78]

Under the *Taylor* hypothesis, wage contracts are overlapping.[79] Half the workers and firms in each region enter into two-period contracts in each period. In period t, the workers and firms negotiating contracts agree on a single contract nominal wage $(\tilde{w}_t, \overset{*}{\tilde{w}}_t)$ that the workers will receive in both period t and period $t + 1$. Workers agree to supply whatever amount of labor the firms want in those periods at the agreed wage. $\tilde{w}_t$ and $\overset{*}{\tilde{w}}_t$ are set according to the rules in equations 2-16, where $n_{t+1|t} + n_t$ and $\overset{*}{n}_{t+1|t} + \overset{*}{n}_t$ are the sums of the expected excess demand for labor in period $t + 1$ and the excess demand for labor in period t in the US and in the ROECD, respectively. These sums represent demand pressure. If the sums representing demand pressures are equal to zero, $\tilde{w}_t$ and $\overset{*}{\tilde{w}}_t$ are set so as to maintain the relative wage of the contracting workers over the life of the contract. $\tilde{w}_t$ and $\overset{*}{\tilde{w}}_t$ are set equal to the average of the wage being received in period t by workers who negotiated contracts in period $t - 1$ $(\tilde{w}_{t-1}, \overset{*}{\tilde{w}}_{t-1})$ and the wage it is expected that these same workers will receive when they negotiate new contracts in period $t + 1$ $(\tilde{w}_{t+1|t'}, \overset{*}{\tilde{w}}_{t+1|t})$. If the sums representing demand pressures are positive or negative, $\tilde{w}_t$ and $\overset{*}{\tilde{w}}_t$ are set so as to raise or lower the relative wage of the contracting workers.

Average wages, w_t and $\overset{*}{w}_t$, are the averages of the contract wages negotiated in periods t and $t - 1$, as shown in equations 2-17. In what follows, for convenience we refer to w_t and $\overset{*}{w}_t$ simply as wages. The values of w_t and $\overset{*}{w}_t$ generated by the Taylor hypothesis are used in the marginal productivity conditions for labor in the same way as the values of w_t and $\overset{*}{w}_t$ generated by the other hypotheses under which prices are perfectly flexible (Contract, Phillips, and BG1).

Under the Taylor hypothesis in contrast to the other hypotheses, w_t and $\overset{*}{w}_t$ are affected by period t shocks.[80] However, it is still appropriate to say that w_t and $\overset{*}{w}_t$ are sticky because they do not adjust instantaneously to keep employments at their full employment values.

---

78. Some analysts might prefer that expected output-price changes in equation 2-15 be replaced by expected CPI changes. We do not explore this alternative formulation.

79. This hypothesis is based on Taylor (1980). See appendix J for further discussion.

80. It is possible to construct an alternative Taylor hypothesis for which w_t is unaffected by shocks in period t. Under the alternative hypothesis the contract wage in period t in, for example, the US is generated by the following rule:

$$\tilde{w}_t = \theta(n_{t+1|t-1} + n_{t|t-1}) + \frac{1}{2}(\tilde{w}_{t+1|t-1} + \tilde{w}_{t-1}).$$

In contrast to the rule in the text, under this rule $\tilde{w}_t$ is determined on the basis of information available in period $t - 1$. When shocks are temporary, $\tilde{w}_t$ never changes under the alternative Taylor hypothesis. Therefore, the effects of shocks are the same as under the Contract hypothesis.

Under the *BG1* hypothesis, wages are set according to an adjustment mechanism of the type suggested by Barro and Grossman (1976). Wages in period $t + 1$ are set in period t and are equal to wages in period t plus a constant times the gaps between market-clearing wages ($\bar{w}_t$, $\overset{\star}{\bar{w}}_t$) and actual wages in period t plus expected changes in market-clearing wages between period t and period $t + 1$ (see equations 2-18). $\bar{w}_t$ and $\overset{\star}{\bar{w}}_t$ are the wages that clear labor markets at time t, conditional on the values of policy-instrument variables at time t. In explaining how $\bar{w}_t$ and $\overset{\star}{\bar{w}}_t$ are determined, we refer to two versions of the model, one with perfectly flexible wages and the other with wages determined according to the BG1 hypothesis. We continue to assume that interest rates are the policy instruments of the monetary authorities. Under the II regime pair, because interest rates are held fixed, $\bar{w}_t$ and $\overset{\star}{\bar{w}}_t$ can be determined using only the version of the model with perfectly flexible wages. The values of actual wages and the other variables besides interest rates can then be determined separately using the version of the model with wages determined according to the BG1 hypothesis. Under regime pairs other than the II pair, however, $\bar{w}_t$, $\overset{\star}{\bar{w}}_t$, actual wages, and the other variables besides interest rates must be jointly determined with interest rates, using both versions of the model, because interest rates must be varied in order to hit the intermediate targets that define those regime pairs. It is important to stress that $\bar{w}_t$ and $\overset{\star}{\bar{w}}_t$ vary over time and are not constant, long-run equilibrium wages.

The *BG2* hypothesis is different from all the other hypotheses because, under the BG2 hypothesis, prices as well as wages are sticky. In particular, not only wages but also prices are set according to Barro-Grossman (1976) type adjustment mechanisms as shown by equations 2-18 and 2-19, respectively. Variables with bars over them in these equations represent the market-clearing values of those variables. $\bar{w}_t$ and $\overset{\star}{\bar{w}}_t$ and $\bar{p}_t$ and $\overset{\star}{\bar{p}}_t$ are the wages and output prices that clear the labor and goods markets at time t, respectively, conditional on the values of policy-instrument variables at time t. The procedure for determining market-clearing wages and prices under the BG2 hypothesis is analogous to the procedure for determining market-clearing wages under the BG1 hypothesis.

Permanent and Temporary Money-Demand Shocks
under the Phillips Hypothesis

Results for temporary shocks can differ substantially from the results for permanent shocks. To set the stage for the simulation analysis of temporary shocks, we provide a comparison of the effects of permanent and temporary symmetric increases in money demand under the Phillips hypothesis. We present both phase-diagram results and simulation results. As we would expect, permanent and temporary symmetric shocks to money demand have no effects under the II, YY, and CC regime pairs, but do have effects under the equivalent MM and ME pairs.

The model for sums of variables under the Phillips hypothesis and the MM regime pair is presented in table 2-28. Equations 2-92 through 2-96 are the sums of equations 2-1, 2-3, 2-12, 2-13, and 2-15, respectively, with $\beta = 0$, with r_s eliminated using the sums of equations 2-6 and 2-10, and with time subscripts included for clarity. In table 2-28, the symbol Δ in front of a variable indicates the difference between that variable and the value of the same variable in the previous period. For example, $\Delta p_{s,t+1} = p_{s,t+1} - p_{s,t}$. For simplicity, we assume that there are no shocks after period 0. Under this assumption, the values of all variables after period 0 are equal to their expected values based on information available in period 0. For example, $p_{s,t|0} = p_{s,t}$ for all $t > 0$. Also for simplicity, we assume that the sum of money supplies is constant and given by $\hat{m}_s = 0$ instead of including the sum of the reaction functions in equations 2B-1 in appendix B among the equilibrium conditions and letting $\psi \to \infty$.[81]

The model in table 2-28 can be reduced to two difference equations in $w_{s,t}$ and $n_{s,t}$: a wage-change equation (equation 2-97) and an employment-change equation (equation 2-98). The *wage-change equation* is obtained by beginning with equation 2-96, eliminating $\Delta p_{s,t+1}$ using equation 2-95, eliminating $i_{s,t}$ from the resulting expression using equation 2-94, and eliminating $y_{s,t}$ and $p_{s,t}$ from the resulting expression using equations 2-92 and 2-93, respectively. According to equation 2-97, a unit increase in $w_{s,t}$ raises $\Delta w_{s,t+1}$ by $1/\lambda$ units because it raises $p_{s,t}$ by one unit from equation 2-93, and therefore raises $i_{s,t}$ from equation 2-94 and $\Delta p_{s,t+1}$ from equation 2-95 by $1/\lambda$ units. A unit increase in $n_{s,t}$ causes $\Delta w_{s,t+1}$ to rise for three reasons: (1) it raises $\Delta w_{s,t+1}$ directly by θ units; (2) it raises $y_{s,t}$ by α units from equation 2-92 and therefore raises $\Delta p_{s,t+1}$ from equation 2-95 by $(1-\epsilon)\alpha/\nu$ units; and (3) it raises $p_{s,t}$ by $(1 - \alpha)/\sigma$ units from equation 2-93 and $y_{s,t}$ by α units from equation 2-92 and, therefore, raises $i_{s,t}$ from equation 2-94 and $\Delta p_{s,t+1}$ from equation 2-95 by $[(1 - \alpha)/\lambda\sigma + \phi\alpha/\lambda]$ units.

The *employment-change equation* is obtained by differencing equation 2-93 and eliminating $\Delta w_{s,t+1} - \Delta p_{s,t+1}$ using equation 2-96. A unit increase in $n_{s,t}$ increases the real wage by θ units from equation 2-96, so $\Delta n_{s,t+1}$ must fall by $\theta\sigma/(1 - \alpha)$ units from the equation obtained by differencing equation 2-93.

---

81. In Henderson and McKibbin (forthcoming), we obtain results for the MM regime pair by including the sum of the reaction functions in equations 2B-1 in appendix B among the equilibrium conditions and letting $\psi \to \infty$. Those results are the same as the ones presented.

Table 2-28. *The Model for Sums under the Phillips Hypothesis and the MM Regime Pair*

Full model

(2-92)
$$y_{s,t} = \alpha n_{s,t} - x_{s,t}$$

(2-93)
$$w_{s,t} - p_{s,t} = 2\omega - \left[\frac{1-\alpha}{\sigma}\right] n_{s,t} - x_{s,t}$$

(2-94)
$$p_{s,t} + \phi y_{s,t} - \lambda i_{s,t} + v_{s,t} - \hat{m}_s = 0, \qquad \hat{m}_s = 0$$

(2-95)
$$-(1-\epsilon)y_{s,t} - v(i_{s,t} - \Delta p_{s,t+1}) + u_{s,t} = 0$$

(2-96)
$$\Delta w_{s,t+1} = \theta n_{s,t} + \Delta p_{s,t+1}$$

Wage-change equation

(2-97)
$$\Delta w_{s,t+1} = \left[\frac{1}{\lambda}\right]w_{s,t} + \Omega n_{s,t} + \left[\frac{1}{\lambda}\right]v_{s,t} - \left[\frac{1}{v}\right]u_{s,t} - \left[\frac{1-\epsilon}{v} - \frac{1-\phi}{\lambda}\right]x_{s,t} - \left[\frac{2\omega}{\lambda}\right]$$

$$\Omega = \left[\theta + \frac{1-\alpha}{\lambda\sigma} + \frac{\phi\alpha}{\lambda} + \frac{(1-\epsilon)\alpha}{v}\right]$$

Employment-change equation

(2-98)
$$\Delta n_{s,t+1} = -\left[\frac{\theta\sigma}{1-\alpha}\right]n_{s,t} - \left[\frac{\sigma}{1-\alpha}\right](x_{s,t+1} - x_{s,t})$$

Stable path

(2-99)
$$\left[\frac{\sigma}{1-\alpha}\right]\left[\theta + \frac{1-\alpha}{\lambda\sigma}\right](w_{s,t} - \hat{w}_{s,t}) = -\Omega(n_{s,t} - \hat{n}_{s,t})$$

We assume that $n_{s,t}$ can jump at time t but that $w_{s,t}$ cannot. Therefore, to ensure that there is a unique path to stationary equilibrium, it is necessary to assume that $-1 < 1 - \theta\sigma/(1-\alpha) < 1$.[82] However, we make the still stronger assumption that $0 < 1 - \theta\sigma/(1-\alpha) < 1$ in order to rule out paths along which $n_{s,t}$ and $w_{s,t}$ alternate between positive and negative values for two reasons: (1) we do not think such paths are interesting, and (2) we cannot illustrate them using our diagrammatic framework.

We analyze the system made up of the two difference equations 2-97 and 2-98, using the phase diagram in figure 2-10. A W schedule shows the pairs of $w_{s,t}$ and $n_{s,t}$ for which $\Delta w_{s,t+1}$ is equal to zero for given values of $v_{s,t}$, $u_{s,t}$, and $x_{s,t}$. As explained above, increases in both $w_{s,t}$ and $n_{s,t}$ tend to raise $\Delta w_{s,t+1}$, so an increase in $n_{s,t}$ must be matched by a decrease in $w_{s,t}$ if

---

82. We discuss why this assumption is necessary in appendix K.

Figure 2-10. *Money-Demand Shocks: Phillips*

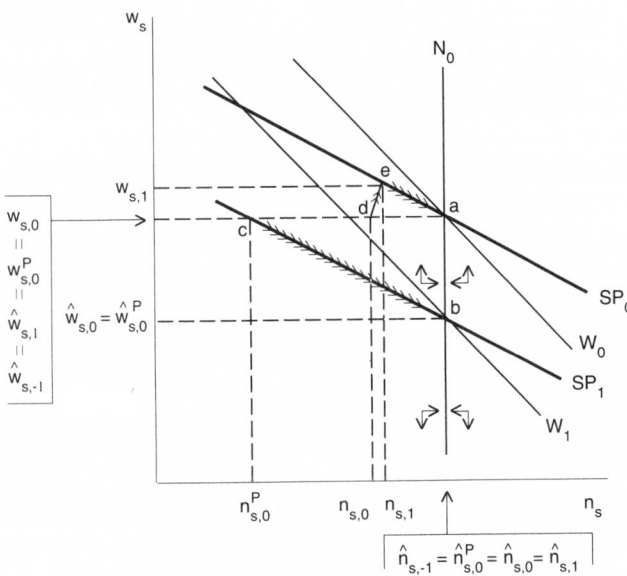

$\Delta w_{s,t+1}$ is to remain equal to zero. An N schedule gives the unique value of $n_{s,t}$ for which $\Delta n_{s,t+1}$ is equal to zero for given values of $x_{s,t+1}$ and $x_{s,t}$.

The vertical arrows show how $w_{s,t}$ changes when the $n_{s,t}$, $w_{s,t}$ pair is above or below the W_1 schedule. The horizontal arrows show how $n_{s,t}$ changes when the $n_{s,t}$, $w_{s,t}$ pair is to the right or left of the N_0 schedule. For example, if the $n_{s,t}$, $w_{s,t}$ pair is above the W_1 schedule and to the right of the N_0 schedule, $w_{s,t}$ rises and $n_{s,t}$ falls. An analogous set of vertical arrows (not drawn) show how $w_{s,t}$, changes when the $n_{s,t}$, $w_{s,t}$ pair is above or below the W_0 schedule.

The schedules labeled SP_0 and SP_1 are, respectively, the unique stable paths to the stationary equilibria at points a and b. As indicated by the arrows of motion, the unique stable path to a stationary equilibrium must have a negative slope and must be flatter than the corresponding W schedule. The equation for the stable path is equation 2-99, where $\hat{w}_{s,t}$ and $\hat{n}_{s,t}$ are the values of $w_{s,t}$ and $n_{s,t}$ for which $\Delta w_{s,t+1} = \Delta n_{s,t+1} = 0$, given the values of the exogenous variables in period t.

The effects of a *permanent symmetric increase in money demands*, an increase in $v_{s,t}$ for all $t \geq 0$, are shown in figure 2-10.[83] Suppose that the

---

83. In phase-diagram analysis it is conventional to refer to the period in which the shock hits as period 0, while in simulation analysis it is conventional to refer to the period in which the shock hits as period 1. We have followed these different conventions in the presentation of our results.

economy is initially in stationary equilibrium at point a. The increase in $v_{s,t}$ causes the W schedule to shift down permanently by the same amount, say from W_0 to W_1, so the new stationary equilibrium is at point b and the new stable path is SP_1. In period 0, $w_{s,0}^P$ is predetermined, so it cannot change from its previous stationary-equilibrium value of $\hat{w}_{s,-1} = 2\omega$. A variable with a superscript P represents the value of that variable after a permanent shock. However, $n_{s,t}$ can change, and it jumps down from its previous stationary-equilibrium value of $\hat{n}_{s,-1} = 0$ to $n_{s,0}^P$ the level corresponding to point c on the SP_1 schedule. Over time the economy moves along SP_1 to point b. $w_{s,t}$ gradually falls to its new, lower stationary-equilibrium value of $(\hat{w}_{s,0}^P = \hat{w}_{s,-1} - v_{s,0})$, and $n_{s,t}$ gradually rises to its new stationary-equilibrium value, which is the same as its original value ($\hat{n}_{s,0} = \hat{n}_{s,-1} = 0$).

The different effects of a *temporary symmetric increase in money demands*, an increase in $v_{s,0}$, are also shown in figure 2-10. The W schedule shifts down from W_0 to W_1 in period 0 when the shock occurs and then back up to W_0 in period 1. The stationary equilibrium remains at point a.

The equilibrium position of the economy in period 0 following the increase in money demands is determined by three requirements. First, if the economy is to reach its stationary equilibrium at point a, it must be on the SP_0 schedule in period 1. Second, $w_{s,0}$ cannot change from $\hat{w}_{s,-1}$, so the equilibrium must lie on the horizontal line through point a in period 0. Third, the movement of the economy between periods 0 and 1 is determined by the arrows of motion for the W_1 and N_0 schedule shown in figure 2-10. The point that is consistent with these three requirements must lie on the horizontal line through point a between point a and the intersection of that line with the W_1 schedule.

We assume that the economy is at point d in period 0. In period 1 the economy moves to point e on SP_0, and over time it moves down SP_0 to the stationary equilibrium at a. $w_{s,t}$ remains constant at $\hat{w}_{s,-1}$ in period 0, rises above $\hat{w}_{s,-1} = \hat{w}_{s,1}$ in period 1, and falls back to $\hat{w}_{s,1}$ over time. $n_{s,t}$ falls below $\hat{n}_{s,-1} = \hat{n}_{s,0} = \hat{n}_{s,1}$ in period 0, rises to a value that is still below $\hat{n}_{s,1}$ in period 1, and continues to rise back to $\hat{n}_{s,1}$ over time. The fall in n_s in period 0 must be less for a temporary shock than for a permanent shock.

Simulation results for the effects on eight variables of a temporary symmetric increase in money demands under the Phillips hypothesis for all five regime pairs are presented in figure 2-11. Variables are plotted as deviations from their pre-shock (baseline) levels.[84] As we stated above, the temporary symmetric increase in money demands has no effects under the II, YY, and CC pairs, but does have effects (in this case the same ones) under the MM and ME pairs.

---

84. Recall that different conventions are used in presenting phase diagram and simulation results. (See the previous note.) Period 1 in figure 2-11 corresponds to period 0 in figure 2-10 and in the text discussion.

The paths for US employment and the US wage under the MM regime pair in figure 2-11 conform exactly to what we predict for $w_{s,t}$ and $n_{s,t}$ using the phase-diagram analysis in figure 2-10. The wage path is striking because the wage rises above its baseline level before falling back to that level. The output-price path is even more striking: the output price first falls below its baseline level and then rises above it before falling gradually back to it. We can provide some insight about why these paths arise.

The sum of employments in the period of the shock, $n_{s,0}$, and the sums of wages and employments in the first period after the shock, $w_{s,1}$ and $n_{s,1}$, are jointly determined by three equations from table 2-28: the difference equations for $w_{s,t}$ and $n_{s,t}$ (equations 2-97 and 2-98) with $t = 0$, and the equation for the stable path (equation 2-99) with $t = 1$ and with $v_{s,0} > 0$, $w_{s,0} = \hat{w}_{s,-1} = \hat{w}_{s,1} = 2\omega$, $\hat{n}_{s,1} = 0$, and $u_{s,0} = x_{s,0} = 0$, given. According to equation 2-98, both $n_{s,0}$ and $n_{s,1}$ must be on the same side of $n_{s,1}$. They cannot be above $\hat{n}_{s,1}$. If they were, $w_{s,1}$ would have to be below $\hat{w}_{s,1}$ to satisfy equation 2-99 and would have to be above $\hat{w}_{s,1}$ to satisfy equation 2-97 given that $v_{s,0} > 0$. They can be below $n_{s,1}$, however, because a value of $w_{s,1}$ above baseline can satisfy both equation 2-99 and equation 2-97, given that $v_{s,0} > 0$.

From equation 2-93, $p_{s,0}$ must be below baseline because $n_{s,0}$ must be below $\hat{n}_{s,1}$ and $\hat{w}_{s,0}$ is fixed at $\hat{w}_{s,-1}$. $p_{s,1}$ must be above baseline even though $n_{s,1}$ is below $\hat{n}_{s,1}$ because $w_{s,1}$ must be enough above $\hat{w}_{s,1}$. Consider the net effect on $p_{s,1}$ of having $n_{s,1}$ below $\hat{n}_{s,1}$, using equation 2-93. The direct effect of having $n_{s,1}$ below $\hat{n}_{s,1}$ by one unit is to lower $p_{s,1}$ by $(1 - \alpha)/\sigma$ units. But if $n_{s,1}$ is below $\hat{n}_{s,1}$ by one unit, $w_{s,1}$ must be above $\hat{w}_{s,1}$ by

$$\left[\frac{1 - \alpha}{\sigma}\right] \Omega \left[\theta + \frac{1 - \alpha}{\lambda \sigma}\right]^{-1} > \frac{1 - \alpha}{\sigma}$$

units from equation 2-99. Therefore, the net effect of having $n_{s,1}$ below $\hat{n}_{s,1}$ must be to have $p_{s,1}$ above baseline.

Nominal interest rates are above real interest rates in period 0, reflecting the rise in expected rates of inflation between periods 0 and 1. The high nominal interest rate is consistent with equilibrium in the money market, and the high real interest rate is consistent with equilibrium in the goods market.

After period 1 (period 2 in the simulation graphs in figures 2-11), all variables except rates of inflation adjust monotonically back to their baseline values. After period 2 (period 3 in the simulation graphs), rates of inflation also adjust back to baseline values. For each kind of temporary shock to be discussed below, all the variables exhibit analogous behavior subsequent to the first period after the shock. Accordingly, in what follows, we do not discuss what happens subsequent to the first period after the shock.

Figure 2-11. *Symmetric Increase in Money Demand under the Phillips Hypothesis*

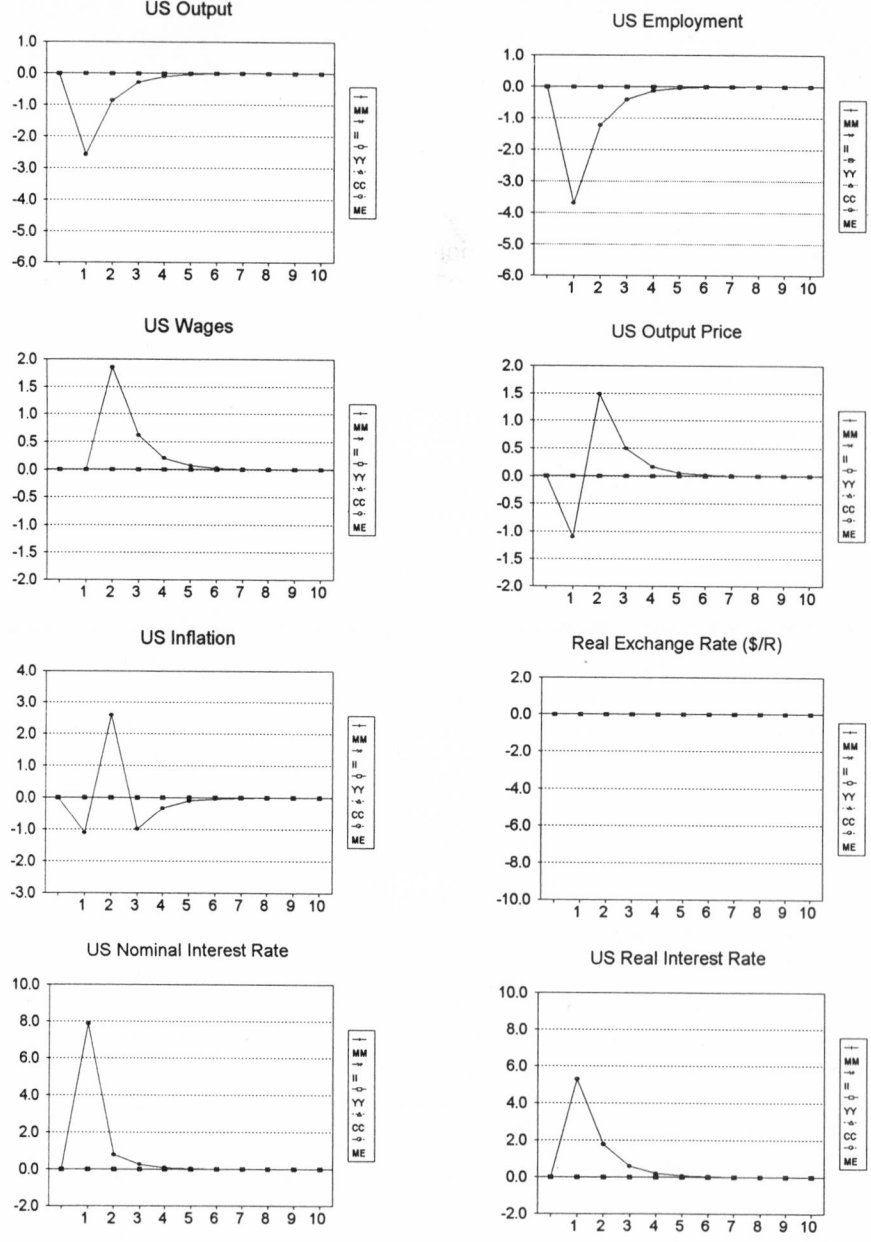

The Information Provided about the Simulations

With five wage-price hypotheses, several kinds of shocks, and five regime pairs, the number of simulations to be compared is quite large. To simplify our discussion, we therefore rely primarily on two summary statistics for each variable: the impact effect (the change for the period in which the shock occurs) and the sum of squared deviations from baseline over the entire simulation period. We also refer to a third summary statistic, the discounted sum of squared deviations from baseline. We report these summary statistics for employment, CPI inflation, and output for each shock and regime pair, for each region under each hypothesis.

Again to simplify, we adopt some abbreviated terminology. "Inflation" will mean "CPI inflation." "Statistic" will refer to any of the three types of summary statistic. "Ranking" will be shorthand for "ranking of regime pairs." "Contract" will be shorthand for "the Contract hypothesis"; "Phillips," "Taylor," "BG1," and "BG2" will be analogous shorthand for the other wage-price hypotheses. We will also adopt the convention that if two regime pairs are tied under one hypothesis but one of the pairs dominates under another hypothesis, the ranking of pairs is taken to be the same under the two hypotheses.[85]

The simulation statistics are reported in tables 2-29 through 2-40. Each table has results for one shock. In each table there are three groups of columns: one for employments, one for inflations, and one for outputs. Within a group, there is a column for each of the five regime pairs: MM, II, YY, CC, and ME. The top half of each table refers to the US, and the bottom half to the ROECD. Within each half, the three types of statistics are included, labeled "Impact Effect," "Sum of Squared Deviations," and "Discounted Sum of Squared Deviations," respectively. We present each statistic for each of the five hypotheses: Contract, Phillips, Taylor, BG1, and BG2.

The first type of statistic is the impact effect (IE). For IEs, we ask whether the rankings under the four other hypotheses are the same as the ranking under Contract. Comparisons of rankings for IEs are of interest because they can be aids in understanding the differences in results among the various hypotheses. However, it would definitely not make sense to base a choice among regime pairs solely on the rankings for IEs.[86]

The second type of statistic is the sum of squared deviations of a variable from baseline (SSD). We use SSD to convey information about the effects of a shock over the whole adjustment path. Under Contract, the ranking for SSD

---

85. For example, if the MM and ME regime pairs are ranked the same under Contract but the ME pair dominates the MM pair under Taylor, the ranking of the MM and ME pairs is taken to be the same under both Contract and Taylor.

86. For Contract, the IEs are a subset of the simulation results presented previously in tables 2-8 through 2-13, 2-15, 2-16, and 2-18 through 2-21.

for a variable is always the same as the ranking for IE. But under the other hypotheses, the ranking is not always the same. For SSDs, just as for IEs, we ask whether the rankings under the other hypotheses are the same as the ranking under Contract. It might make sense to base a choice among regime pairs on the rankings for SSDs.

Under Contract, the SSDs for employments and outputs are just the squares of the IEs because there are no effects on these variables beyond the first (impact) period. For the II, MM, YY, and ME pairs, CPIs return to baseline in period 2 (the first period after the shock).[87] Thus, the SSDs for inflations under the II, MM, YY, and ME pairs are twice the squares of the IEs. For the CC pair, the SSDs for inflations are equal to the square of the IEs for CPIs in period 1 plus the squares of $\gamma = 0.15$ times the IEs for the real exchange rate in period 1 (because output prices remain at their period 1 levels in period 2, but the nominal exchange rate changes between period 1 and period 2 in such a way that the real exchange rate returns to its pre-shock level in period 2).

The SSD resulting from a unit shock of a given kind has an interesting interpretation if the shock is independent of all other shocks. In this case, the SSD for a variable caused by a unit shock of a given kind is equal to the effect of a unit increase in the variance of a shock of that kind on the steady-state variance of the variable. We derive this result in appendix L.

The final type of statistic is the discounted sum of squared deviations of a variable from baseline (DSSD). For our illustrative DSSDs, the discount rate is 10 percent a year. Under some circumstances, the DSSD can be used in measuring a policymaker's loss. It is often assumed that a policymaker's loss function takes the form of a weighted sum of discounted sums of squared deviations of target variables from their paths of desired values. Under this assumption, if the path of desired values for a target variable is unaffected by shocks, the DSSD for that target variable measures the unweighted contribution of movements in that target variable to a policymaker's loss.

Suppose that the desired values for target variables are the values that would result if wages and prices were perfectly flexible. Suppose further that notional labor supplies are perfectly inelastic and nonstochastic. With those assumptions, the values of employments that would result if wages and prices were perfectly flexible are unaffected by shocks. However, the values of outputs are affected by productivity shocks, and the values of inflations are affected by goods-demand shocks and productivity shocks, with the effects depending on the regime pair. Therefore, strictly speaking, when notional labor supplies are perfectly inelastic and nonstochastic, DSSDs for employments could be used in

---

87. In this paragraph and hereafter, we refer to particular periods using the conventions of simulation analysis rather than phase-diagram analysis. Hence the impact period is period 1 (as in figures 2-11 through 2-19) rather than period 0 (as in the phase-diagram analysis).

measuring a policymaker's losses, while DSSDs for outputs and inflations could not be. The last point notwithstanding, it is often simply assumed that desired values for inflations are constant, usually zero. Of course, with that further assumption, DSSDs for inflations can be used in measuring a policymaker's losses.[88]

In this subsection, we make no further mention of rankings using DSSDs. The reason is that for individual variables the rankings of SSDs and DSSDs are always the same for the discount rate that we have chosen. The possibility remains that the ranking of a weighted sum of SSDs for two or more variables might be different from the ranking of a weighted sum of DSSDs for the same variables with the same weights, but we have not attempted to find an example of such a difference in rankings.

Under all the hypotheses except Contract, a temporary shock can have effects that last for many periods. To provide an example of the kinds of dynamic paths that can be generated by temporary shocks, we present complete paths for several variables under Phillips. We choose Phillips because it is most closely related to the wage-price hypotheses in the empirical multicountry models used to produce the simulations discussed in chapters 3–5. However, as we confirm below using the statistics, the dynamic paths generated under Phillips can be quite different from those generated under the other hypotheses, even though the same long-run equilibrium is reached under all hypotheses.

The full dynamic paths resulting from temporary shocks under Phillips are presented in figures 2-11 through 2-19. Each of these figures contains results for one shock. In each figure there are eight panels, one for each of eight variables. In each panel there are graphs of the deviations from baseline for the variable shown in that panel under all five regime pairs.

General Patterns

Before we proceed to a more detailed discussion of the simulation results, we draw attention to some general patterns. We take these patterns for granted in the detailed discussion. Some of them are to be expected on the basis of the analysis of Contract above. Others follow immediately from the nature of a particular wage-price hypothesis.

For all money-demand shocks for the II, YY, and CC pairs and for a money-demand shock in the ROECD for the ME pair, there are no effects on

---

88. As an example, consider the case of a symmetric money-demand shock under the MM regime pair and the Contract hypothesis. According to table 2-29, the DSSDs for each employment and each inflation are 17.54 and 2.88, respectively. Therefore, if employment and inflation were given equal weight and if the same loss function (including the 10 percent discount rate) were appropriate for each region, a possible measure of the loss for the policymaker in each region would be the sum of these two figures, 20.42.

any variable under any wage-price hypothesis. All markets other than money markets are insulated from the money-demand shocks.

For all goods-demand shocks for the YY and CC pairs, there are no effects on employments under any wage-price hypothesis.

Under Taylor for all productivity shocks, there are IEs on employments under the CC pair as well as under the MM and II pairs. This result is possible because wages in period 1 are sticky but not fixed (as we explain below for the case of a symmetric productivity shock).

For the YY and CC pairs, all results for all shocks, including productivity shocks, are identical under BG1 and Contract. The explanation for this outcome is that the paths of wages are the same under BG1 and Contract (as we explain below in the case of a symmetric productivity shock).

For region-specific productivity shocks for the YY and CC pairs, employment is unaffected under all wage-price hypotheses in the region other than the one in which the shocks have their impact effect.

Under BG2, for all productivity shocks, there are IEs on employments in the region or regions in which the shocks have their impact effects under the YY and CC pairs (for which effects are the same) as well as under the MM and II pairs. In period 1, output prices are predetermined, so stabilizing nominal income or keeping the sums of deviations of outputs and inflation rates from baseline equal to zero is equivalent to keeping outputs equal to baseline. Therefore, employments must change if productivities change.

Under BG2, there are no IEs on inflations either for symmetric shocks under any regime pair or for asymmetric and region-specific shocks under the II and ME pairs because output prices are predetermined in period 1 and the nominal exchange rate does not change.

It is more difficult to generalize about rankings for productivity shocks than for money-demand and goods-demand shocks.

Money-Demand Shocks

For a *symmetric money-demand shock* with money demands increasing, the statistics are reported in table 2-29. This shock has effects on employments and inflations only under the MM and ME pairs, for which the effects are the same under all the wage-price hypotheses (for reasons given above). The ranking for both IEs and SSDs under the four other hypotheses is the same as under Contract: II $\underset{p}{=}$ YY $\underset{p}{=}$ CC $\underset{p}{>}$ MM $\underset{p}{=}$ ME, where again the symbol $\underset{p}{>}$ means "dominates," and the symbol $\underset{p}{=}$ means "ranks the same as." The adjustment paths under Phillips, which we discussed above, are shown in figure 2-11.

For an *asymmetric money-demand shock* with the demand for US money increasing, the statistics are reported in table 2-30. For both regions for both

IEs and SSDs, the ranking is the same for employments and inflations under all the other hypotheses as it is under Contract: $\text{II} \underset{p}{=} \text{YY} \underset{p}{=} \text{CC} \underset{p}{\geq} \text{ME} \underset{p}{\geq} \text{MM}$. For Contract, we explain above why the ME pair dominates the MM pair for employments and inflations in both regions (for the parameters used in the simulations).

The adjustment paths under Phillips are shown in figure 2-12. As we explain above, under the ME pair an asymmetric money-demand shock with the demand for US money increasing is converted into a symmetric increase in excess demands for moneys. Therefore, the paths for an asymmetric money-demand shock under the ME pair are identical to the paths for a symmetric money-demand shock under the MM and ME pairs.

The paths for US variables for the MM pair are qualitatively the same as the paths for US variables under the ME pair. But employment, output, the output price, and inflation all move by more because the decrease in the ROECD interest rate required to move from the ME pair to the MM pair has a contractionary effect on the US. From the analysis under Contract, it is to be expected that, in general, there will be differences between the paths for the MM and ME pairs for asymmetric shocks.

Of course, the adjustment paths for ROECD variables (not shown in figure 2-12) are identical to the those for US variables under the ME pair and are the mirror images of those for US variables under the MM pair.

For *region-specific money-demand shocks* with US or ROECD money demand increasing, the statistics are reported in tables 2-31 and 2-32, respectively. For a shock to US money demand (table 2-31), the rankings for both IEs and SSDs for employment and inflation in each region are the same under all five wage-price hypotheses: $\text{II} \underset{p}{=} \text{YY} \underset{p}{=} \text{CC} \underset{p}{\geq} \text{ME} \underset{p}{\geq} \text{MM}$ for the US and $\text{II} \underset{p}{=} \text{YY} \underset{p}{=} \text{CC} \underset{p}{\geq} \text{MM} \underset{p}{\geq} \text{ME}$ for the ROECD.[89] For Contract, we explain above why the ME pair dominates the MM pair for the US and why the MM pair dominates the ME pair for the ROECD (for the parameters used in the simulations).

The adjustment paths for US variables under Phillips for a shock to US money demand are shown in figure 2-13. As we expect, under the ME pair the adjustment paths are the same as they would be for a symmetric increase in money demands under the MM and ME pairs. The effects on employment, output, output price, and inflation in the US are greater under the MM pair because the decrease in the ROECD interest rate required to move from the ME pair to the MM pair is contractionary for the US.

---

89. There is one exception to this statement. For a US money-demand shock under BG2, the ME pair dominates the MM pair for the ROECD for the IE on inflation because the exchange rate changes under the MM pair but not under the ME pair.

Table 2-29. *Symmetric Increase in Money Demand*

Summary statistic and wage-price hypothesis	Employment					Inflation					Output				
	MM	II	YY	CC	ME	MM	II	YY	CC	ME	MM	II	YY	CC	ME
						US variables									
Impact effect															
Contract	−4.19	0.00	0.00	0.00	−4.19	−1.26	0.00	0.00	0.00	−1.26	−2.93	0.00	0.00	0.00	−2.93
Phillips	−3.69	0.00	0.00	0.00	−3.69	−1.11	0.00	0.00	0.00	−1.11	−2.58	0.00	0.00	0.00	−2.58
Taylor	−4.10	0.00	0.00	0.00	−4.10	−1.51	0.00	0.00	0.00	−1.51	−2.87	0.00	0.00	0.00	−2.87
BG1	−3.43	0.00	0.00	0.00	−3.43	−1.03	0.00	0.00	0.00	−1.03	−2.40	0.00	0.00	0.00	−2.40
BG2	−4.21	0.00	0.00	0.00	−4.21	0.00	0.00	0.00	0.00	0.00	−2.95	0.00	0.00	0.00	−2.95
Sum of squared deviations															
Contract	17.54	0.00	0.00	0.00	17.54	3.16	0.00	0.00	0.00	3.16	8.59	0.00	0.00	0.00	8.59
Phillips	15.33	0.00	0.00	0.00	15.33	9.03	0.00	0.00	0.00	9.03	7.51	0.00	0.00	0.00	7.51
Taylor	16.94	0.00	0.00	0.00	16.94	3.60	0.00	0.00	0.00	3.60	8.30	0.00	0.00	0.00	8.30
BG1	15.68	0.00	0.00	0.00	15.68	13.61	0.00	0.00	0.00	13.61	7.68	0.00	0.00	0.00	7.68
BG2	23.62	0.00	0.00	0.00	23.62	10.29	0.00	0.00	0.00	10.29	11.57	0.00	0.00	0.00	11.57
Discounted sum of squared deviations															
Contract	17.54	0.00	0.00	0.00	17.54	2.88	0.00	0.00	0.00	2.88	8.59	0.00	0.00	0.00	8.59
Phillips	15.00	0.00	0.00	0.00	15.00	7.51	0.00	0.00	0.00	7.51	7.35	0.00	0.00	0.00	7.35
Taylor	16.91	0.00	0.00	0.00	16.91	3.37	0.00	0.00	0.00	3.37	8.29	0.00	0.00	0.00	8.29
BG1	14.82	0.00	0.00	0.00	14.82	11.12	0.00	0.00	0.00	11.12	7.26	0.00	0.00	0.00	7.26
BG2	22.33	0.00	0.00	0.00	22.33	8.04	0.00	0.00	0.00	8.04	10.94	0.00	0.00	0.00	10.94

ROECD variables

Impact effect															
Contract	-4.19	0.00	0.00	0.00	-4.19	-1.26	0.00	0.00	0.00	-1.26	-2.93	0.00	0.00	0.00	-2.93
Phillips	-3.69	0.00	0.00	0.00	-3.69	-1.11	0.00	0.00	0.00	-1.11	-2.58	0.00	0.00	0.00	-2.58
Taylor	-4.10	0.00	0.00	0.00	-4.10	-1.51	0.00	0.00	0.00	-1.51	-2.87	0.00	0.00	0.00	-2.87
BG1	-3.43	0.00	0.00	0.00	-3.43	-1.03	0.00	0.00	0.00	-1.03	-2.40	0.00	0.00	0.00	-2.40
BG2	-4.21	0.00	0.00	0.00	-4.21	0.00	0.00	0.00	0.00	0.00	-2.95	0.00	0.00	0.00	-2.95
Sum of squared deviations															
Contract	17.54	0.00	0.00	0.00	17.54	3.16	0.00	0.00	0.00	3.16	8.59	0.00	0.00	0.00	8.59
Phillips	15.33	0.00	0.00	0.00	15.33	9.03	0.00	0.00	0.00	9.03	7.51	0.00	0.00	0.00	7.51
Taylor	16.94	0.00	0.00	0.00	16.94	3.60	0.00	0.00	0.00	3.60	8.30	0.00	0.00	0.00	8.30
BG1	15.68	0.00	0.00	0.00	15.68	13.61	0.00	0.00	0.00	13.61	7.68	0.00	0.00	0.00	7.68
BG2	23.62	0.00	0.00	0.00	23.62	10.29	0.00	0.00	0.00	10.29	11.57	0.00	0.00	0.00	11.57
Discounted sum of squared deviations															
Contract	17.54	0.00	0.00	0.00	17.54	2.88	0.00	0.00	0.00	2.88	8.59	0.00	0.00	0.00	8.59
Phillips	15.00	0.00	0.00	0.00	15.00	7.51	0.00	0.00	0.00	7.51	7.35	0.00	0.00	0.00	7.35
Taylor	16.91	0.00	0.00	0.00	16.91	3.37	0.00	0.00	0.00	3.37	8.29	0.00	0.00	0.00	8.29
BG1	14.82	0.00	0.00	0.00	14.82	11.12	0.00	0.00	0.00	11.12	7.26	0.00	0.00	0.00	7.26
BG2	22.33	0.00	0.00	0.00	22.33	8.04	0.00	0.00	0.00	8.04	10.94	0.00	0.00	0.00	10.94

Table 2-30. Asymmetric Money-Demand Shock (US Demand Increasing)

Summary statistic and wage-price hypothesis	Employment					Inflation					Output				
	MM	II	YY	CC	ME	MM	II	YY	CC	ME	MM	II	YY	CC	ME
						US variables									
Impact effect															
Contract	-5.26	0.00	0.00	0.00	-4.19	-2.88	0.00	0.00	0.00	-1.26	-3.68	0.00	0.00	0.00	-2.93
Phillips	-5.22	0.00	0.00	0.00	-3.69	-2.95	0.00	0.00	0.00	-1.11	-3.66	0.00	0.00	0.00	-2.58
Taylor	-4.98	0.00	0.00	0.00	-4.10	-3.01	0.00	0.00	0.00	-1.51	-3.48	0.00	0.00	0.00	-2.87
BG1	-5.23	0.00	0.00	0.00	-3.43	-3.01	0.00	0.00	0.00	-1.03	-3.66	0.00	0.00	0.00	-2.40
BG2	-7.30	0.00	0.00	0.00	-4.21	-2.00	0.00	0.00	0.00	0.00	-5.11	0.00	0.00	0.00	-2.95
Sum of squared deviations															
Contract	27.70	0.00	0.00	0.00	17.54	16.61	0.00	0.00	0.00	3.16	13.57	0.00	0.00	0.00	8.59
Phillips	30.69	0.00	0.00	0.00	15.33	23.67	0.00	0.00	0.00	9.03	15.04	0.00	0.00	0.00	7.51
Taylor	25.02	0.00	0.00	0.00	16.94	16.86	0.00	0.00	0.00	3.60	12.26	0.00	0.00	0.00	8.30
BG1	36.52	0.00	0.00	0.00	15.68	27.91	0.00	0.00	0.00	13.61	17.90	0.00	0.00	0.00	7.68
BG2	70.97	0.00	0.00	0.00	23.62	19.35	0.00	0.00	0.00	10.29	34.78	0.00	0.00	0.00	11.57
Discounted sum of squared deviations															
Contract	27.70	0.00	0.00	0.00	17.54	15.17	0.00	0.00	0.00	2.88	13.57	0.00	0.00	0.00	8.59
Phillips	30.04	0.00	0.00	0.00	15.00	21.01	0.00	0.00	0.00	7.51	14.72	0.00	0.00	0.00	7.35
Taylor	24.96	0.00	0.00	0.00	16.91	15.50	0.00	0.00	0.00	3.37	12.23	0.00	0.00	0.00	8.29
BG1	34.53	0.00	0.00	0.00	14.82	24.54	0.00	0.00	0.00	11.12	16.92	0.00	0.00	0.00	7.26
BG2	67.09	0.00	0.00	0.00	22.33	16.50	0.00	0.00	0.00	8.04	32.88	0.00	0.00	0.00	10.94

ROECD variables

Impact effect

Contract	5.26	0.00	0.00	-4.19	2.88	0.00	0.00	0.00	-1.26	3.68	0.00	0.00	0.00	-2.93
Phillips	5.22	0.00	0.00	-3.69	2.95	0.00	0.00	0.00	-1.11	3.66	0.00	0.00	0.00	-2.58
Taylor	4.98	0.00	0.00	-4.10	3.01	0.00	0.00	0.00	-1.51	3.48	0.00	0.00	0.00	-2.87
BG1	5.23	0.00	0.00	-3.43	3.01	0.00	0.00	0.00	-1.03	3.66	0.00	0.00	0.00	-2.40
BG2	7.30	0.00	0.00	-4.21	2.00	0.00	0.00	0.00	0.00	5.11	0.00	0.00	0.00	-2.95

Sum of squared deviations

Contract	27.70	0.00	0.00	17.54	16.61	0.00	0.00	0.00	3.16	13.57	0.00	0.00	0.00	8.59
Phillips	30.69	0.00	0.00	15.33	23.67	0.00	0.00	0.00	9.03	15.04	0.00	0.00	0.00	7.51
Taylor	25.02	0.00	0.00	16.94	16.86	0.00	0.00	0.00	3.60	12.26	0.00	0.00	0.00	8.30
BG1	36.52	0.00	0.00	15.68	27.91	0.00	0.00	0.00	13.61	17.90	0.00	0.00	0.00	7.68
BG2	70.97	0.00	0.00	23.62	19.35	0.00	0.00	0.00	10.29	34.78	0.00	0.00	0.00	11.57

Discounted sum of squared deviations

Contract	27.70	0.00	0.00	17.54	15.17	0.00	0.00	0.00	2.88	13.57	0.00	0.00	0.00	8.59
Phillips	30.04	0.00	0.00	15.00	21.01	0.00	0.00	0.00	7.51	14.72	0.00	0.00	0.00	7.35
Taylor	24.96	0.00	0.00	16.91	15.50	0.00	0.00	0.00	3.37	12.23	0.00	0.00	0.00	8.29
BG1	34.53	0.00	0.00	14.82	24.54	0.00	0.00	0.00	11.12	16.92	0.00	0.00	0.00	7.26
BG2	67.09	0.00	0.00	22.33	16.50	0.00	0.00	0.00	8.04	32.88	0.00	0.00	0.00	10.94

Figure 2-12. *Asymmetric Money-Demand Shock under the Phillips Hypothesis*

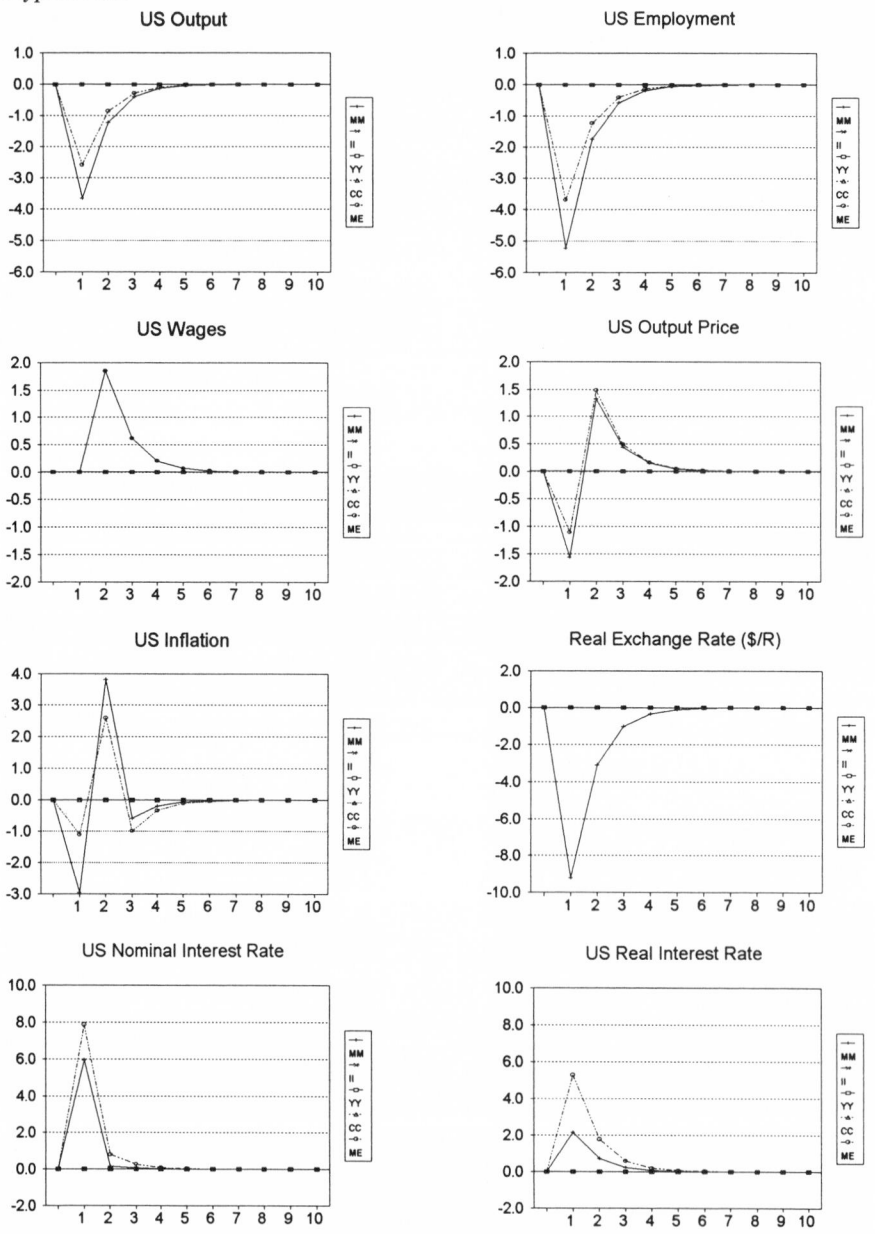

Figure 2-13. *Region-Specific Increase in US Money Demand under the Phillips Hypothesis*

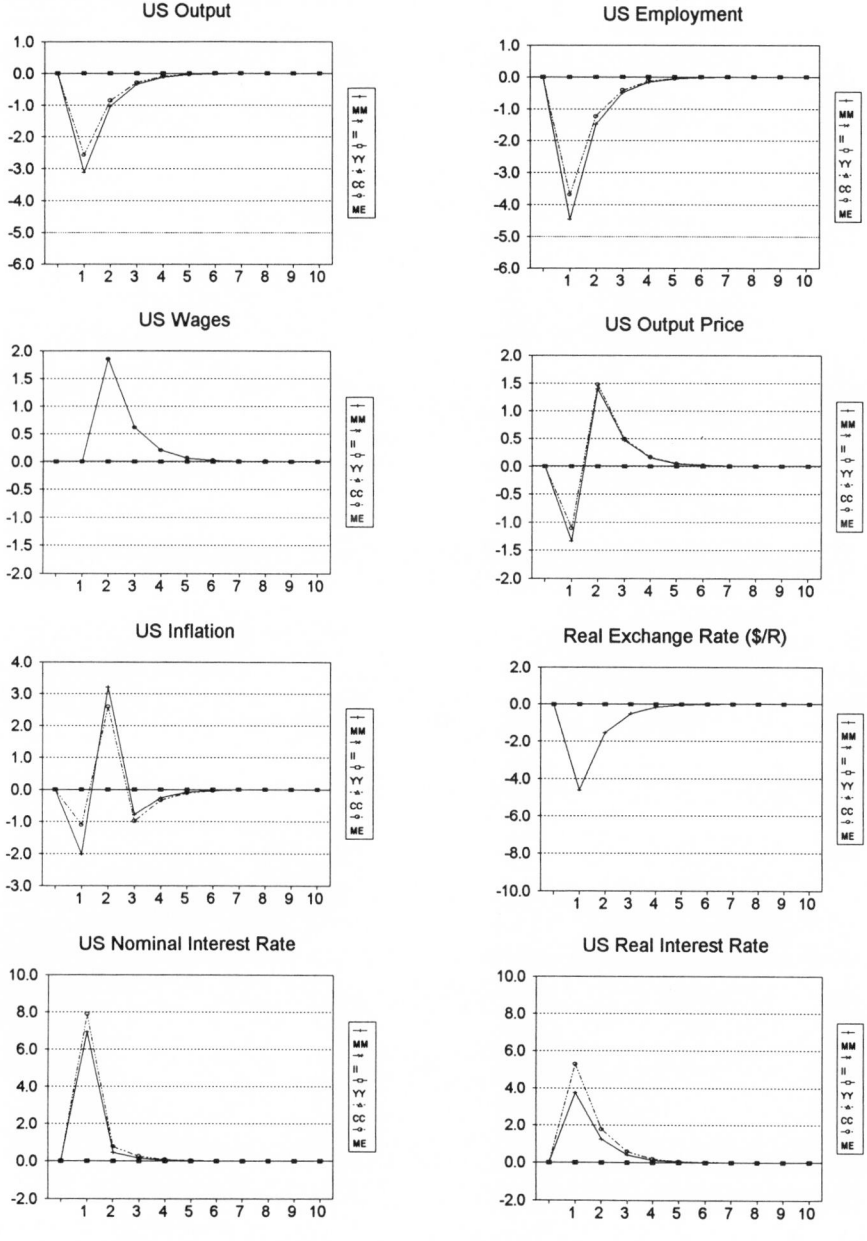

Table 2-31. Region-Specific Increase in US Money Demand

Summary statistic and wage-price hypothesis	Employment					Inflation					Output				
	MM	II	YY	CC	ME	MM	II	YY	CC	ME	MM	II	YY	CC	ME
						US variables									
Impact effect															
Contract	-4.73	0.00	0.00	0.00	-4.19	-2.07	0.00	0.00	0.00	-1.26	-3.31	0.00	0.00	0.00	-2.93
Phillips	-4.46	0.00	0.00	0.00	-3.69	-2.03	0.00	0.00	0.00	-1.11	-3.12	0.00	0.00	0.00	-2.58
Taylor	-4.54	0.00	0.00	0.00	-4.10	-2.26	0.00	0.00	0.00	-1.51	-3.18	0.00	0.00	0.00	-2.87
BG1	-4.33	0.00	0.00	0.00	-3.43	-2.02	0.00	0.00	0.00	-1.03	-3.03	0.00	0.00	0.00	-2.40
BG2	-5.75	0.00	0.00	0.00	-4.21	-1.00	0.00	0.00	0.00	0.00	-4.03	0.00	0.00	0.00	-2.95
Sum of squared deviations															
Contract	22.33	0.00	0.00	0.00	17.54	8.56	0.00	0.00	0.00	3.16	10.94	0.00	0.00	0.00	8.59
Phillips	22.35	0.00	0.00	0.00	15.33	15.08	0.00	0.00	0.00	9.03	10.95	0.00	0.00	0.00	7.51
Taylor	20.78	0.00	0.00	0.00	16.94	8.99	0.00	0.00	0.00	3.60	10.18	0.00	0.00	0.00	8.30
BG1	25.02	0.00	0.00	0.00	15.68	19.45	0.00	0.00	0.00	13.61	12.26	0.00	0.00	0.00	7.68
BG2	44.12	0.00	0.00	0.00	23.62	13.48	0.00	0.00	0.00	10.29	21.62	0.00	0.00	0.00	11.57
Discounted sum of squared deviations															
Contract	22.33	0.00	0.00	0.00	17.54	7.82	0.00	0.00	0.00	2.88	10.94	0.00	0.00	0.00	8.59
Phillips	21.87	0.00	0.00	0.00	15.00	13.07	0.00	0.00	0.00	7.51	10.72	0.00	0.00	0.00	7.35
Taylor	20.74	0.00	0.00	0.00	16.91	8.31	0.00	0.00	0.00	3.37	10.16	0.00	0.00	0.00	8.29
BG1	23.65	0.00	0.00	0.00	14.82	16.60	0.00	0.00	0.00	11.12	11.59	0.00	0.00	0.00	7.26
BG2	41.71	0.00	0.00	0.00	22.33	11.00	0.00	0.00	0.00	8.04	20.44	0.00	0.00	0.00	10.94

ROECD variables

Impact effect

Contract	0.54	0.00	0.00	-4.19	0.81	0.00	0.00	0.00	-1.26	0.38	0.00	-2.93
Phillips	0.77	0.00	0.00	-3.69	0.92	0.00	0.00	0.00	-1.11	0.54	0.00	-2.58
Taylor	0.44	0.00	0.00	-4.10	0.75	0.00	0.00	0.00	-1.51	0.31	0.00	-2.87
BG1	0.90	0.00	0.00	-3.43	0.99	0.00	0.00	0.00	-1.03	0.63	0.00	-2.40
BG2	1.54	0.00	0.00	-4.21	1.00	0.00	0.00	0.00	0.00	1.08	0.00	-2.95

Sum of squared deviations

Contract	0.29	0.00	0.00	17.54	1.32	0.00	0.00	0.00	3.16	0.14	0.00	8.59
Phillips	0.66	0.00	0.00	15.33	1.27	0.00	0.00	0.00	9.03	0.32	0.00	7.51
Taylor	0.20	0.00	0.00	16.94	1.25	0.00	0.00	0.00	3.60	0.10	0.00	8.30
BG1	1.09	0.00	0.00	15.68	1.31	0.00	0.00	0.00	13.61	0.53	0.00	7.68
BG2	3.18	0.00	0.00	23.62	1.34	0.00	0.00	0.00	10.29	1.56	0.00	11.57

Discounted sum of squared deviations

Contract	0.29	0.00	0.00	17.54	1.21	0.00	0.00	0.00	2.88	0.14	0.00	8.59
Phillips	0.65	0.00	0.00	15.00	1.19	0.00	0.00	0.00	7.51	0.32	0.00	7.35
Taylor	0.20	0.00	0.00	16.91	1.13	0.00	0.00	0.00	3.37	0.10	0.00	8.29
BG1	1.03	0.00	0.00	14.82	1.23	0.00	0.00	0.00	11.12	0.50	0.00	7.26
BG2	3.00	0.00	0.00	22.33	1.26	0.00	0.00	0.00	8.04	1.47	0.00	10.94

Table 2-32. Region-Specific Increase in ROECD Money Demand

Summary statistic and wage-price hypothesis	Employment					Inflation					Output				
	MM	II	YY	CC	ME	MM	II	YY	CC	ME	MM	II	YY	CC	ME
						US variables									
Impact effect															
Contract	0.54	0.00	0.00	0.00	0.00	0.81	0.00	0.00	0.00	0.00	0.38	0.00	0.00	0.00	0.00
Phillips	0.77	0.00	0.00	0.00	0.00	0.92	0.00	0.00	0.00	0.00	0.54	0.00	0.00	0.00	0.00
Taylor	0.44	0.00	0.00	0.00	0.00	0.75	0.00	0.00	0.00	0.00	0.31	0.00	0.00	0.00	0.00
BG1	0.90	0.00	0.00	0.00	0.00	0.99	0.00	0.00	0.00	0.00	0.63	0.00	0.00	0.00	0.00
BG2	1.54	0.00	0.00	0.00	0.00	1.00	0.00	0.00	0.00	0.00	1.08	0.00	0.00	0.00	0.00
Sum of squared deviations															
Contract	0.29	0.00	0.00	0.00	0.00	1.32	0.00	0.00	0.00	0.00	0.14	0.00	0.00	0.00	0.00
Phillips	0.66	0.00	0.00	0.00	0.00	1.27	0.00	0.00	0.00	0.00	0.32	0.00	0.00	0.00	0.00
Taylor	0.20	0.00	0.00	0.00	0.00	1.25	0.00	0.00	0.00	0.00	0.10	0.00	0.00	0.00	0.00
BG1	1.09	0.00	0.00	0.00	0.00	1.31	0.00	0.00	0.00	0.00	0.53	0.00	0.00	0.00	0.00
BG2	3.18	0.00	0.00	0.00	0.00	1.34	0.00	0.00	0.00	0.00	1.56	0.00	0.00	0.00	0.00
Discounted sum of squared deviations															
Contract	0.29	0.00	0.00	0.00	0.00	1.21	0.00	0.00	0.00	0.00	0.14	0.00	0.00	0.00	0.00
Phillips	0.65	0.00	0.00	0.00	0.00	1.19	0.00	0.00	0.00	0.00	0.32	0.00	0.00	0.00	0.00
Taylor	0.20	0.00	0.00	0.00	0.00	1.13	0.00	0.00	0.00	0.00	0.10	0.00	0.00	0.00	0.00
BG1	1.03	0.00	0.00	0.00	0.00	1.23	0.00	0.00	0.00	0.00	0.50	0.00	0.00	0.00	0.00
BG2	3.00	0.00	0.00	0.00	0.00	1.26	0.00	0.00	0.00	0.00	1.47	0.00	0.00	0.00	0.00

Impact effect

Contract	−4.73	0.00	0.00	0.00	0.00	0.00	−2.07	0.00	0.00	0.00	0.00	0.00	−3.31	0.00	0.00	0.00
Phillips	−4.46	0.00	0.00	0.00	0.00	0.00	−2.03	0.00	0.00	0.00	0.00	0.00	−3.12	0.00	0.00	0.00
Taylor	−4.54	0.00	0.00	0.00	0.00	0.00	−2.26	0.00	0.00	0.00	0.00	0.00	−3.18	0.00	0.00	0.00
BG1	−4.33	0.00	0.00	0.00	0.00	0.00	−2.02	0.00	0.00	0.00	0.00	0.00	−3.03	0.00	0.00	0.00
BG2	−5.75	0.00	0.00	0.00	0.00	0.00	−1.00	0.00	0.00	0.00	0.00	0.00	−4.03	0.00	0.00	0.00

Sum of squared deviations

Contract	22.33	0.00	0.00	0.00	0.00	0.00	8.56	0.00	0.00	0.00	0.00	0.00	10.94	0.00	0.00	0.00
Phillips	22.35	0.00	0.00	0.00	0.00	0.00	15.08	0.00	0.00	0.00	0.00	0.00	10.95	0.00	0.00	0.00
Taylor	20.78	0.00	0.00	0.00	0.00	0.00	8.99	0.00	0.00	0.00	0.00	0.00	10.18	0.00	0.00	0.00
BG1	25.02	0.00	0.00	0.00	0.00	0.00	19.45	0.00	0.00	0.00	0.00	0.00	12.26	0.00	0.00	0.00
BG2	44.12	0.00	0.00	0.00	0.00	0.00	13.48	0.00	0.00	0.00	0.00	0.00	21.62	0.00	0.00	0.00

Discounted sum of squared deviations

Contract	22.33	0.00	0.00	0.00	0.00	0.00	7.82	0.00	0.00	0.00	0.00	0.00	10.94	0.00	0.00	0.00
Phillips	21.87	0.00	0.00	0.00	0.00	0.00	13.07	0.00	0.00	0.00	0.00	0.00	10.72	0.00	0.00	0.00
Taylor	20.74	0.00	0.00	0.00	0.00	0.00	8.31	0.00	0.00	0.00	0.00	0.00	10.16	0.00	0.00	0.00
BG1	23.65	0.00	0.00	0.00	0.00	0.00	16.60	0.00	0.00	0.00	0.00	0.00	11.59	0.00	0.00	0.00
BG2	41.71	0.00	0.00	0.00	0.00	0.00	11.00	0.00	0.00	0.00	0.00	0.00	20.44	0.00	0.00	0.00

For a shock to ROECD money demand (table 2-32), the rankings for both IEs and SSDs for employment and inflation in each region are the same under all five wage-price hypotheses: $II \underset{p}{=} YY \underset{p}{=} CC \underset{p}{=} ME \underset{p}{>} MM$. Under Contract, we explain above why the ME pair is ranked the same as the II, YY, and CC pairs.

Goods-Demand Shocks

For a *symmetric goods-demand shock* with goods demands increasing, the statistics are presented in table 2-33. The ranking for both IEs and SSDs is the same under all five wage-price hypotheses: $YY \underset{p}{=} CC \underset{p}{>} MM \underset{p}{=} ME \underset{p}{>} II$. There are no effects on inflations for the YY and CC pairs under any hypothesis because both output prices and the nominal exchange rate remain constant. The MM and ME pairs, for which the effects are the same, dominate the II pair for reasons given in the analysis of Contract.

The adjustment paths for US variables under Phillips are displayed in figure 2-14. The variances of employment and inflation are smaller for the MM pair (and the ME pair) than for the II pair. For the US, the qualitative properties of the paths for employment, output, output price, and inflation generated by a symmetric increase in goods demands under the II and MM pairs are just the reverse of the qualitative properties of the paths generated by a symmetric increase in the demands for money under the MM pair as is clear from a comparison of figures 2-11 and 2-14. For the increase in goods demand, a real interest rate above baseline in period 1 is consistent with output being above baseline because of the shock to demand. But only a real interest rate below baseline for the rest of the adjustment period is consistent with output being above baseline during that time.

Table 2-34 contains the statistics for an *asymmetric goods-demand shock* with the demand for US goods increasing. For both IEs and SSDs, the rankings for employments are the same under all five wage-price hypotheses: $YY \underset{p}{=} CC \underset{p}{>} MM \underset{p}{>} ME \underset{p}{>} II$ for US employments, and $YY \underset{p}{=} CC \underset{p}{>} MM \underset{p}{>} II \underset{p}{>} ME$ for ROECD employments. For US employment, the rankings for asymmetric and symmetric goods-demand shocks are the same except that the MM pair is strictly preferred to the ME pair for the asymmetric shock. But for ROECD employments, the rankings for asymmetric and symmetric shocks are different because the ME pair ranks last.

Next we discuss the rankings for US inflation. We obtain an important result. Outcomes for US inflation are relatively bad under the YY and CC pairs because of real exchange-rate effects. For IEs, the ranking under all of the other hypotheses except BG2 is the same as under Contract: $MM \underset{p}{>} ME \underset{p}{>} II \underset{p}{>} YY \underset{p}{=} CC$. Under BG2, the II and ME pairs are ranked the

Figure 2-14. *Symmetric Increase in Goods Demand under the Phillips Hypothesis*

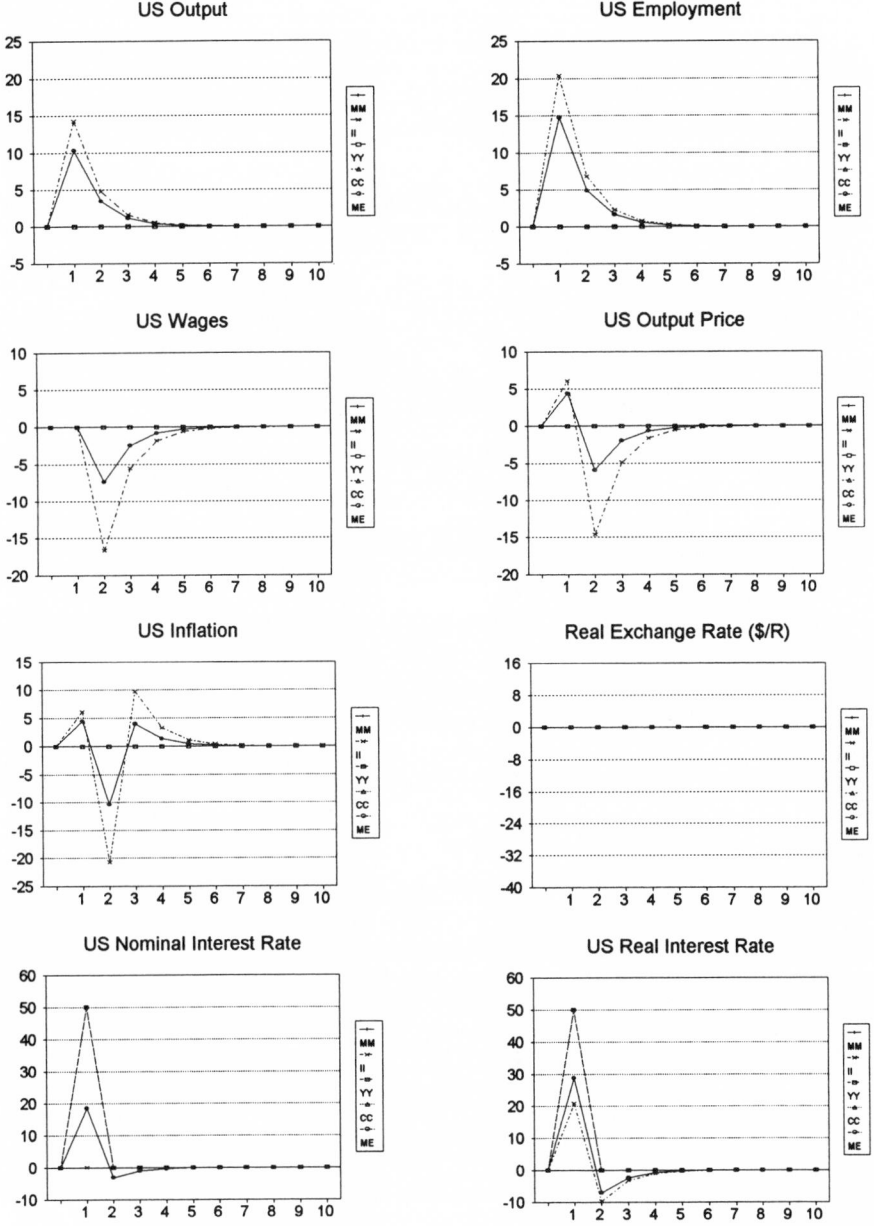

Table 2-33. *Symmetric Increase in Goods Demand*

US variables

Summary statistic and wage-price hypothesis	Employment					Inflation					Output				
	MM	II	YY	CC	ME	MM	II	YY	CC	ME	MM	II	YY	CC	ME
Impact effect															
Contract	16.75	28.82	0.00	0.00	16.75	5.03	8.65	0.00	0.00	5.03	11.73	20.17	0.00	0.00	11.73
Phillips	14.76	20.39	0.00	0.00	14.76	4.43	6.12	0.00	0.00	4.43	10.33	14.27	0.00	0.00	10.33
Taylor	16.41	29.80	0.00	0.00	16.41	6.03	11.35	0.00	0.00	6.03	11.49	20.86	0.00	0.00	11.49
BG1	13.72	15.77	0.00	0.00	13.72	4.12	4.73	0.00	0.00	4.12	9.60	11.04	0.00	0.00	9.60
BG2	16.84	17.42	0.00	0.00	16.84	0.00	0.00	0.00	0.00	0.00	11.79	12.20	0.00	0.00	11.79
Sum of squared deviations															
Contract	280.58	830.50	0.00	0.00	280.58	50.50	149.49	0.00	0.00	50.50	137.48	406.95	0.00	0.00	137.48
Phillips	245.21	467.60	0.00	0.00	245.20	144.54	574.72	0.00	0.00	144.54	120.15	229.12	0.00	0.00	120.15
Taylor	270.98	889.27	0.00	0.00	270.98	57.66	183.08	0.00	0.00	57.66	132.78	435.74	0.00	0.00	132.78
BG1	250.89	331.71	0.00	0.00	250.89	217.67	942.05	0.00	0.00	217.67	122.94	162.54	0.00	0.00	122.94
BG2	377.89	404.68	0.00	0.00	377.89	164.61	833.33	0.00	0.00	164.61	185.17	198.30	0.00	0.00	185.17
Discounted sum of squared deviations															
Contract	280.58	830.50	0.00	0.00	280.58	46.12	136.52	0.00	0.00	46.12	137.48	406.95	0.00	0.00	137.48
Phillips	240.00	457.67	0.00	0.00	240.00	120.08	464.57	0.00	0.00	120.08	117.60	224.26	0.00	0.00	117.60
Taylor	270.54	888.92	0.00	0.00	270.54	53.85	173.06	0.00	0.00	53.85	132.57	435.57	0.00	0.00	132.57
BG1	237.17	313.57	0.00	0.00	237.17	177.89	751.57	0.00	0.00	177.89	116.21	153.65	0.00	0.00	116.21
BG2	357.23	382.55	0.00	0.00	357.23	128.60	651.04	0.00	0.00	128.60	175.04	187.45	0.00	0.00	175.04

ROECD variables

Impact effect

Contract	16.75	28.82	0.00	0.00	16.75	5.03	8.65	0.00	0.00	5.03	11.73	11.73	20.17	0.00	11.73
Phillips	14.76	20.39	0.00	0.00	14.76	4.43	6.12	0.00	0.00	4.43	10.33	10.33	14.27	0.00	10.33
Taylor	16.41	29.80	0.00	0.00	16.41	6.03	11.35	0.00	0.00	6.03	11.49	11.49	20.86	0.00	11.49
BG1	13.72	15.77	0.00	0.00	13.72	4.12	4.73	0.00	0.00	4.12	9.60	9.60	11.04	0.00	9.60
BG2	16.84	17.42	0.00	0.00	16.84	0.00	0.00	0.00	0.00	0.00	11.79	11.79	12.20	0.00	11.79

Sum of squared deviations

Contract	280.58	830.50	0.00	0.00	280.58	50.50	149.49	0.00	0.00	50.50	137.48	137.48	406.95	0.00	137.48
Phillips	245.21	467.60	0.00	0.00	245.20	144.54	574.72	0.00	0.00	144.54	120.15	120.15	229.12	0.00	120.15
Taylor	270.98	889.27	0.00	0.00	270.98	57.66	183.08	0.00	0.00	57.66	132.78	132.78	435.74	0.00	132.78
BG1	250.89	331.71	0.00	0.00	250.89	217.67	942.05	0.00	0.00	217.67	122.94	122.94	162.54	0.00	122.94
BG2	377.89	404.68	0.00	0.00	377.89	164.61	833.33	0.00	0.00	164.61	185.17	185.17	198.30	0.00	185.17

Discounted sum of squared deviations

Contract	280.58	830.50	0.00	0.00	280.58	46.12	136.52	0.00	0.00	46.12	137.48	137.48	406.95	0.00	137.48
Phillips	240.00	457.67	0.00	0.00	240.00	120.08	464.57	0.00	0.00	120.08	117.60	117.60	224.26	0.00	117.60
Taylor	270.54	888.92	0.00	0.00	270.54	53.85	173.06	0.00	0.00	53.85	132.57	132.57	435.57	0.00	132.57
BG1	237.17	313.57	0.00	0.00	237.17	177.89	751.57	0.00	0.00	177.89	116.21	116.21	153.65	0.00	116.21
BG2	357.23	382.55	0.00	0.00	357.23	128.60	651.04	0.00	0.00	128.60	175.04	175.04	187.45	0.00	175.04

Table 2-34. *Asymmetric Goods-Demand Shock (US Demand Increasing)*

Summary statistic and wage-price hypothesis	Employment					Inflation					Output				
	MM	II	YY	CC	ME	MM	II	YY	CC	ME	MM	II	YY	CC	ME
						US variables									
Impact effect															
Contract	8.46	17.85	0.00	0.00	10.37	−1.40	3.75	−6.02	−6.02	1.51	5.92	12.49	0.00	0.00	7.26
Phillips	8.39	16.97	0.00	0.00	10.91	−1.28	3.56	−6.02	−6.02	1.75	5.87	11.88	0.00	0.00	7.64
Taylor	7.99	17.10	0.00	0.00	9.63	−1.19	4.35	−6.02	−6.02	1.58	5.59	11.97	0.00	0.00	6.74
BG1	8.41	16.53	0.00	0.00	11.21	−1.19	3.47	−6.02	−6.02	1.88	5.89	11.57	0.00	0.00	7.84
BG2	11.72	21.94	0.00	0.00	16.05	−2.81	0.00	−6.02	−6.02	0.00	8.20	15.36	0.00	0.00	11.23
Sum of squared deviations															
Contract	71.48	318.54	0.00	0.00	107.61	3.89	28.10	72.58	72.58	4.54	35.03	156.08	0.00	0.00	52.73
Phillips	79.20	324.12	0.00	0.00	133.87	2.64	68.69	72.58	72.58	7.66	38.81	158.82	0.00	0.00	65.60
Taylor	64.58	295.30	0.00	0.00	94.08	3.82	31.15	72.58	72.58	4.63	31.64	144.70	0.00	0.00	46.10
BG1	94.25	364.10	0.00	0.00	167.44	3.55	98.18	72.58	72.58	9.30	46.18	178.41	0.00	0.00	82.05
BG2	183.15	641.95	0.00	0.00	343.28	10.59	65.86	72.58	72.58	2.80	89.74	314.56	0.00	0.00	168.21
Discounted sum of squared deviations															
Contract	71.48	318.54	0.00	0.00	107.61	3.55	25.66	66.28	66.28	4.14	35.03	156.08	0.00	0.00	52.73
Phillips	77.52	317.24	0.00	0.00	131.02	2.31	58.01	66.28	66.28	6.84	37.98	155.45	0.00	0.00	64.20
Taylor	64.42	294.66	0.00	0.00	93.78	3.40	28.99	66.28	66.28	4.26	31.56	144.38	0.00	0.00	45.95
BG1	89.10	344.19	0.00	0.00	158.29	2.93	81.54	66.28	66.28	8.28	43.66	168.65	0.00	0.00	77.56
BG2	173.14	606.84	0.00	0.00	324.50	9.63	51.45	66.28	66.28	2.19	84.84	297.35	0.00	0.00	159.01

ROECD variables

Impact effect

Contract	−8.46	−17.85	0.00	0.00	−25.32	1.40	−3.75	6.02	6.02	−5.99	−5.92	−12.49	0.00	0.00	−17.73
Phillips	−8.39	−16.97	0.00	0.00	−23.04	1.28	−3.56	6.02	6.02	−5.38	−5.87	−11.88	0.00	0.00	−16.13
Taylor	−7.99	−17.10	0.00	0.00	−24.58	1.19	−4.35	6.02	6.02	−7.13	−5.59	−11.97	0.00	0.00	−17.21
BG1	−8.41	−16.53	0.00	0.00	−21.84	1.19	−3.47	6.02	6.02	−5.07	−5.89	−11.57	0.00	0.00	−15.29
BG2	−11.72	−21.94	0.00	0.00	−27.84	2.81	0.00	6.02	6.02	0.00	−8.20	−15.36	0.00	0.00	−19.49

Sum of squared deviations

Contract	71.48	318.54	0.00	0.00	641.18	3.89	28.10	72.58	72.58	71.76	35.03	156.08	0.00	0.00	314.18
Phillips	79.20	324.12	0.00	0.00	597.15	2.64	68.69	72.58	72.58	194.67	38.81	158.82	0.00	0.00	292.60
Taylor	64.58	295.30	0.00	0.00	608.79	3.82	31.15	72.58	72.58	81.32	31.64	144.70	0.00	0.00	298.31
BG1	94.25	364.10	0.00	0.00	636.20	3.55	98.18	72.58	72.58	288.67	46.18	178.41	0.00	0.00	311.74
BG2	183.15	641.95	0.00	0.00	1033.35	10.59	65.86	72.58	72.58	211.88	89.74	314.56	0.00	0.00	506.34

Discounted sum of squared deviations

Contract	71.48	318.54	0.00	0.00	641.18	3.55	25.66	66.28	66.28	65.54	35.03	156.08	0.00	0.00	314.18
Phillips	77.52	317.24	0.00	0.00	584.47	2.31	58.01	66.28	66.28	162.47	37.98	155.45	0.00	0.00	286.39
Taylor	64.42	294.66	0.00	0.00	607.68	3.40	28.99	66.28	66.28	75.88	31.56	144.38	0.00	0.00	297.76
BG1	89.10	344.19	0.00	0.00	601.41	2.93	81.54	66.28	66.28	236.91	43.66	168.65	0.00	0.00	294.69
BG2	173.14	606.84	0.00	0.00	976.84	9.63	51.45	66.28	66.28	165.53	84.84	297.35	0.00	0.00	478.65

same and are better than the other pairs. For SSDs for US inflation, the ranking under Phillips and Taylor is the same as under Contract. Under BG1, the II pair ranks last; under BG2, the ME pair ranks first.

Now we discuss the rankings for ROECD inflation. Of course, for the matched regime pairs, the rankings for ROECD inflation are identical to the rankings for US inflation under all hypotheses. Thus, the only question is whether the position of the ME pair is different. For IEs, the ranking of pairs under Phillips and BG1 is the same as under Contract. In this ranking the ME pair moves from second for US inflation to third for ROECD inflation; that is, $MM \underset{p}{>} II \underset{p}{>} ME \underset{p}{>} YY \underset{p}{=} CC$. Under Taylor, all the other pairs dominate the ME pair. Under BG2 the II and ME pairs dominate all the others. For SSDs for ROECD inflation, the ranking under each of the other hypotheses is different from Contract. Under all the other hypotheses, the ME pair ranks last instead of next to last. Under BG1, the II pair ranks below the YY and CC pairs.

It is interesting to note that if prices are sticky as under the BG2 hypothesis, then under the ME pair the outcomes for employments are very bad for both regions (though the outcome for the ROECD is much worse), while the outcome for inflation is very favorable for the US and very unfavorable for the ROECD.

The adjustment paths for US variables under Phillips are shown in figure 2-15. The adjustment paths for an asymmetric goods-demand shock are quite similar to those for a symmetric goods-demand shock. However, as we expect from the earlier analysis under Contract, there are some differences. The nominal exchange rate (not shown) changes under all but the II and ME pairs, and the real exchange rate changes under all pairs. As a consequence, US inflation changes even under the YY and CC pairs. As we expect for asymmetric shocks, the paths for the MM and ME pairs are not identical. Under the ME pair, for an asymmetric goods-demand disturbance, the paths for ROECD variables (not shown) are not the same as the paths for US variables (as they are for an asymmetric money-demand shock). Nor are they mirror images of the paths for US variables, as they are for the matched regime pairs.

For *region-specific goods-demand shocks* with US or ROECD goods demand increasing, the statistics appear in tables 2-35 and 2-36, respectively. Recall that the effects for region-specific shocks under matched regime pairs can be derived by adding and subtracting the results for symmetric and asymmetric shocks.

First consider the effects of a shock to the demand for US goods. For US employment under Contract, the ranking for a shock to the demand for US goods is the same as the ranking for an asymmetric goods-demand shock: $YY \underset{p}{=} CC \underset{p}{>} MM \underset{p}{>} ME \underset{p}{>} II$. The rankings under the four other hypotheses, for both IEs and SSDs, are the same as this ranking under Contract.

Figure 2-15. *Asymmetric Goods-Demand Shock under the Phillips Hypothesis*

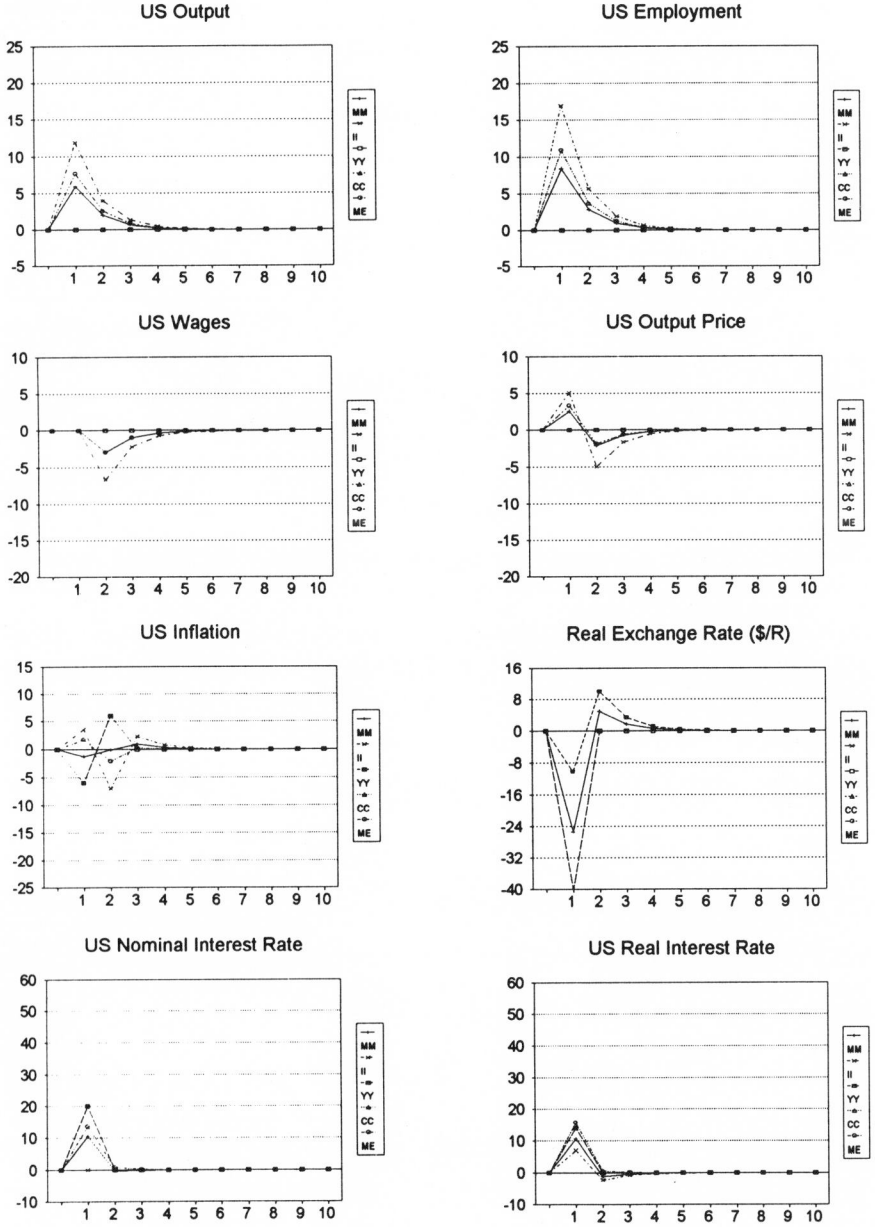

For ROECD employment, the equally ranked YY and CC pairs dominate under the other hypotheses as well as under Contract. The full ranking under Contract is $YY \underset{p}{=} CC \underset{p}{\geq} MM \underset{p}{\geq} ME \underset{p}{\geq} II$. Under Taylor, for both IEs and SSDs, the ranking is the same except that the positions of ME and MM are reversed. Under Phillips, BG1, and BG2, for both IEs and SSDs, the II pair is ranked ahead of both the MM and ME pairs instead of being ranked last.

For US inflation, for IEs the rankings under Phillips and Taylor are the same as under Contract, $MM \underset{p}{\geq} YY \underset{p}{=} CC \underset{p}{\geq} ME \underset{p}{\geq} II$. Under BG1, the ranking is the same except that the positions of the ME pair and the equally ranked YY and CC pairs are reversed. Under BG2, II and ME rank first, while YY and CC rank last. For SSDs for US inflation, the ranking under Taylor is the same as under Contract (both rankings being the same as for IEs). Under Phillips, BG1, and BG2, however, the positions of the MM pair and the equally ranked YY and CC pairs are reversed. In other words, the YY and CC pairs dominate the other pairs over the whole simulation period even though they are dominated by all other pairs in the impact period.

For ROECD inflation, only under Taylor for SSD is the ranking the same as under Contract, that is, $ME \underset{p}{\geq} II \underset{p}{\geq} YY \underset{p}{=} CC \underset{p}{\geq} MM$. For IEs, under Phillips, BG1, and BG2, the positions of the MM pair and the equally ranked YY and CC pairs are reversed; under Taylor, the positions of the II pair and the equally ranked YY and CC pairs are reversed. For SSDs, although the II pair ranks second under Contract and Taylor, it ranks last under Phillips, BG1, and BG2.

Adjustment paths for US variables under Phillips for an increase in the demand for US goods appear in figure 2-16. These paths are qualitatively similar to those for an asymmetric goods-demand shock (with the demand for US goods increasing) in figure 2-15.

Now consider the effect of a shock to the demand for ROECD goods. For this shock and the matched regime pairs, the rankings for the US and the ROECD for a shock to US goods demand given above apply, respectively, to the ROECD and the US. However, the position of the unmatched ME pair for a shock to ROECD goods demand may change because the ROECD is the region responsible for keeping the exchange rate constant. For example, for a shock to the demand for US goods (table 2-35), for US employment for both IEs and SSDs, $YY \underset{p}{=} CC \underset{p}{\geq} MM \underset{p}{\geq} ME \underset{p}{\geq} II$ under all five hypotheses. But for a shock to the demand for ROECD goods (table 2-36), for ROECD employment for both IEs and SSDs, the ME pair ranks last, not next to last, under the Phillips, BG1, and BG2 hypotheses.

Figure 2-16. *Region-Specific Increase in US Goods Demand under the Phillips Hypothesis*

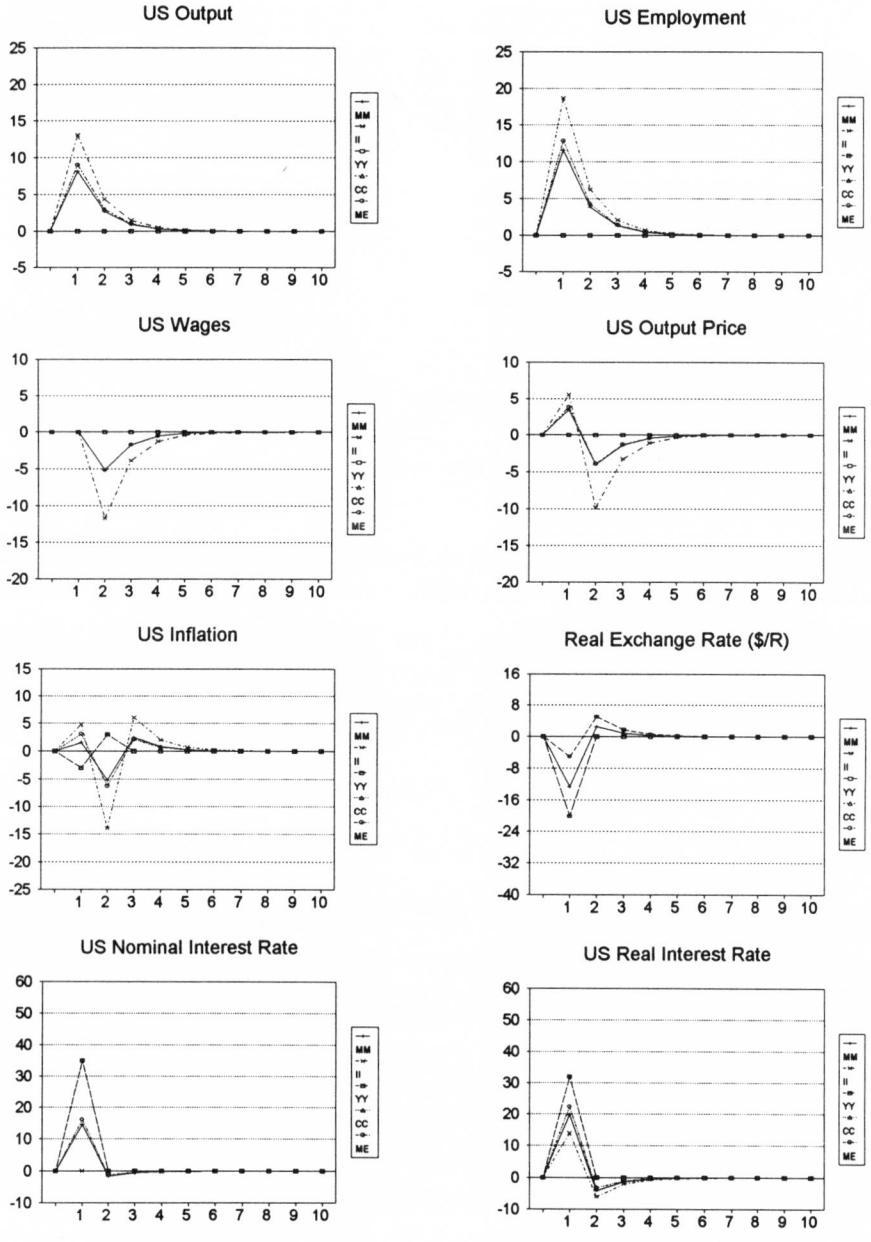

Table 2-35. Region-Specific Increase in U.S. Goods Demand

Summary statistic and wage-price hypothesis	Employment					Inflation					Output				
	MM	II	YY	CC	ME	MM	II	YY	CC	ME	MM	II	YY	CC	ME
						US variables									
Impact effect															
Contract	12.60	23.33	0.00	0.00	13.56	1.82	6.20	−3.01	−3.01	3.27	8.82	16.33	0.00	0.00	9.49
Phillips	11.58	18.68	0.00	0.00	12.84	1.57	4.84	−3.01	−3.01	3.09	8.10	13.08	0.00	0.00	8.99
Taylor	12.20	23.45	0.00	0.00	13.02	2.42	7.85	−3.01	−3.01	3.81	8.54	16.42	0.00	0.00	9.11
BG1	11.06	16.15	0.00	0.00	12.46	1.46	4.10	−3.01	−3.01	3.00	7.74	11.30	0.00	0.00	8.72
BG2	14.28	19.68	0.00	0.00	16.44	−1.40	0.00	−3.01	−3.01	0.00	9.99	13.78	0.00	0.00	11.51
Sum of squared deviations															
Contract	158.82	544.43	0.00	0.00	183.93	6.59	76.80	18.15	18.15	21.33	77.82	266.77	0.00	0.00	90.13
Phillips	150.78	392.58	0.00	0.00	185.36	36.59	257.79	18.15	18.15	53.52	73.88	192.37	0.00	0.00	90.82
Taylor	150.01	551.77	0.00	0.00	171.02	8.34	91.07	18.15	18.15	23.70	73.50	270.37	0.00	0.00	83.80
BG1	163.18	347.72	0.00	0.00	207.07	61.56	408.14	18.15	18.15	77.10	79.96	170.38	0.00	0.00	101.46
BG2	271.80	516.50	0.00	0.00	360.38	49.35	341.93	18.15	18.15	52.60	133.18	253.09	0.00	0.00	176.58
Discounted sum of squared deviations															
Contract	158.82	544.43	0.00	0.00	183.93	6.02	70.14	16.57	16.57	19.48	77.82	266.77	0.00	0.00	90.13
Phillips	147.58	384.25	0.00	0.00	181.42	29.61	210.63	16.57	16.57	45.10	72.31	188.28	0.00	0.00	88.90
Taylor	149.73	551.32	0.00	0.00	170.66	7.87	85.73	16.57	16.57	22.06	73.37	270.15	0.00	0.00	83.62
BG1	154.25	328.70	0.00	0.00	195.74	49.39	328.48	16.57	16.57	63.89	75.58	161.06	0.00	0.00	95.91
BG2	265.94	488.26	0.00	0.00	340.67	38.19	267.14	16.57	16.57	41.09	125.90	239.25	0.00	0.00	166.93

ROECD variables

Impact effect

Contract	4.15	5.49	0.00	0.00	3.21	−4.29	2.45	3.01	3.01	−0.48	2.90	3.84	0.00	−3.00
Phillips	3.19	1.71	0.00	0.00	2.86	−4.14	1.28	3.01	3.01	−0.48	2.23	1.20	0.00	−2.90
Taylor	4.21	6.35	0.00	0.00	3.61	−4.09	3.50	3.01	3.01	−0.55	2.95	4.45	0.00	−2.86
BG1	2.66	−0.38	0.00	0.00	2.65	−4.06	0.63	3.01	3.01	−0.48	1.86	−0.26	0.00	−2.84
BG2	2.56	−2.26	0.00	0.00	1.40	−5.50	0.00	3.01	3.01	0.00	1.79	−1.58	0.00	−3.85

Sum of squared deviations

Contract	17.21	30.09	0.00	0.00	20.61	18.37	11.99	18.15	18.15	0.47	8.43	14.74	0.00	9.00
Phillips	11.42	3.28	0.00	0.00	37.00	19.26	63.92	18.15	18.15	0.95	5.60	1.61	0.00	9.44
Taylor	17.77	40.51	0.00	0.00	22.40	16.87	16.04	18.15	18.15	0.51	8.71	19.85	0.00	8.27
BG1	9.40	0.19	0.00	0.00	49.05	22.01	111.97	18.15	18.15	1.28	4.61	0.09	0.00	10.79
BG2	8.72	6.81	0.00	0.00	38.26	40.36	107.66	18.15	18.15	0.75	4.27	3.34	0.00	19.78

Discounted sum of squared deviations

Contract	17.21	30.09	0.00	0.00	18.82	18.37	10.95	16.57	16.57	0.43	8.43	14.74	0.00	9.00
Phillips	11.18	3.21	0.00	0.00	31.59	18.85	50.66	16.57	16.57	0.82	5.48	1.57	0.00	9.24
Taylor	17.75	40.47	0.00	0.00	20.76	16.83	15.29	16.57	16.57	0.47	8.70	19.83	0.00	8.25
BG1	8.88	0.18	0.00	0.00	41.02	20.81	88.08	16.57	16.57	1.08	4.35	0.09	0.00	10.20
BG2	8.24	6.44	0.00	0.00	30.93	38.16	84.11	16.57	16.57	0.58	4.04	3.16	0.00	18.70

Table 2-36. Region-Specific Increase in ROECD Goods Demand

Summary statistic and wage-price hypothesis	Employment					Inflation					Output				
	MM	II	YY	CC	ME	MM	II	YY	CC	ME	MM	II	YY	CC	ME
						US variables									
Impact effect															
Contract	4.15	5.49	0.00	0.00	3.19	3.21	2.45	3.01	3.01	1.76	2.90	3.84	0.00	0.00	2.23
Phillips	3.19	1.71	0.00	0.00	1.93	2.86	1.28	3.01	3.01	1.34	2.23	1.20	0.00	0.00	1.35
Taylor	4.21	6.35	0.00	0.00	3.39	3.61	3.50	3.01	3.01	2.22	2.95	4.45	0.00	0.00	2.37
BG1	2.66	−0.38	0.00	0.00	1.26	2.65	0.63	3.01	3.01	1.12	1.86	−0.26	0.00	0.00	0.88
BG2	2.56	−2.26	0.00	0.00	0.40	1.40	0.00	3.01	3.01	0.00	1.79	−1.58	0.00	0.00	0.28
Sum of squared deviations															
Contract	17.21	30.09	0.00	0.00	10.17	20.61	11.99	18.15	18.15	6.19	8.43	14.74	0.00	0.00	4.98
Phillips	11.42	3.28	0.00	0.00	4.18	37.00	63.92	18.15	18.15	22.58	5.60	1.61	0.00	0.00	2.05
Taylor	17.77	40.51	0.00	0.00	11.51	22.40	16.04	18.15	18.15	7.45	8.71	19.85	0.00	0.00	5.64
BG1	9.40	0.19	0.00	0.00	2.10	49.05	111.97	18.15	18.15	36.39	4.61	0.09	0.00	0.00	1.03
BG2	8.72	6.81	0.00	0.00	0.21	38.26	107.66	18.15	18.15	31.11	4.27	3.34	0.00	0.00	0.10
Discounted sum of squared deviations															
Contract	17.21	30.09	0.00	0.00	10.17	18.82	10.95	16.57	16.57	5.66	8.43	14.74	0.00	0.00	4.98
Phillips	11.18	3.21	0.00	0.00	4.09	31.59	50.66	16.57	16.57	18.37	5.48	1.57	0.00	0.00	2.01
Taylor	17.75	40.47	0.00	0.00	11.50	20.76	15.29	16.57	16.57	6.99	8.70	19.83	0.00	0.00	5.64
BG1	8.88	0.18	0.00	0.00	1.99	41.02	88.08	16.57	16.57	29.20	4.35	0.09	0.00	0.00	0.97
BG2	8.24	6.44	0.00	0.00	0.20	30.93	84.11	16.57	16.57	24.31	4.04	3.16	0.00	0.00	0.10

ROECD variables

Impact effect

Contract	12.60	23.33	0.00	0.00	21.04	1.82	6.20	−3.01	−3.01	5.51	8.82	16.33	0.00	14.73
Phillips	11.58	18.68	0.00	0.00	18.90	1.57	4.84	−3.01	−3.01	4.91	8.10	13.08	0.00	13.23
Taylor	12.20	23.45	0.00	0.00	20.49	2.42	7.85	−3.01	−3.01	6.58	8.54	16.42	0.00	14.35
BG1	11.06	16.15	0.00	0.00	17.78	1.46	4.10	−3.01	−3.01	4.59	7.74	11.30	0.00	12.45
BG2	14.28	19.68	0.00	0.00	22.34	−1.40	0.00	−3.01	−3.01	0.00	9.99	13.78	0.00	15.64

Sum of squared deviations

Contract	158.82	544.43	0.00	0.00	442.51	6.59	76.80	18.15	18.15	60.67	77.82	266.77	0.00	216.83
Phillips	150.78	392.58	0.00	0.00	401.92	36.59	257.79	18.15	18.15	168.65	73.88	192.37	0.00	196.94
Taylor	150.01	551.77	0.00	0.00	423.02	8.34	91.07	18.15	18.15	68.98	73.50	270.37	0.00	207.28
BG1	163.18	347.72	0.00	0.00	421.53	61.56	408.14	18.15	18.15	251.89	79.96	170.38	0.00	206.55
BG2	271.80	516.50	0.00	0.00	665.26	49.35	341.93	18.15	18.15	187.50	133.18	253.09	0.00	325.98

Discounted sum of squared deviations

Contract	158.82	544.43	0.00	0.00	442.51	6.02	70.14	16.57	16.57	55.40	77.82	266.77	0.00	216.83
Phillips	147.58	384.25	0.00	0.00	393.38	29.61	210.63	16.57	16.57	140.46	72.31	188.28	0.00	192.76
Taylor	149.73	551.32	0.00	0.00	422.28	7.87	85.73	16.57	16.57	64.39	73.37	270.15	0.00	206.92
BG1	154.25	328.70	0.00	0.00	398.48	49.39	328.48	16.57	16.57	206.32	75.58	161.06	0.00	195.26
BG2	256.94	488.26	0.00	0.00	628.88	38.19	267.14	16.57	16.57	146.48	125.90	239.25	0.00	308.15

Productivity Shocks

For a *symmetric productivity shock* with productivities decreasing, the statistics are in table 2-37. Under the YY and CC pairs, all results for all shocks, including a symmetric productivity shock, are the same under BG1 and Contract because the paths of wages are the same under the two hypotheses. It follows from equations 2-18 that under BG1 if market-clearing wages do not change in period 1, then actual wages and market-clearing wages change by the same amount between periods 1 and 2.

Under the YY pair, market-clearing wages do not change in period 1, because output prices increase by the amount of the productivity shock. Market-clearing wages do not change in period 2, because output prices return to their baseline values. Since market-clearing wages remain unchanged, actual wages remain unchanged under BG1 just as actual wages do under Contract.

Under the CC pair just as under the YY pair, market-clearing wages do not change in period 1, because output prices increase by the amount of the productivity shock. However, market-clearing wages change by the amount of the productivity shock in period 2, because the policymakers act so as to keep output prices in period 2 equal to output prices in period 1, which are above baseline by the amount of the productivity shock. Since market-clearing wages remain unchanged in period 1 and rise by the amount of the productivity shock in period 2, actual wages rise under BG1, just as actual wages rise under Contract.

For IEs, for employments and inflations in both regions under Contract, YY $\underset{p}{\geqq}$ CC $\underset{p}{>}$ MM $\underset{p}{=}$ ME $\underset{p}{>}$ II, where the symbol $\underset{p}{\geqq}$ means "dominates or is ranked the same as." The IE rankings for employments and inflations in both regions under Taylor and BG1, and for employments in both regions under Phillips, are the same as under Contract. Under Phillips, the signs of the impact effects on employments under the MM, ME, and II pairs are different from those under all the other hypotheses. The IE rankings for inflations, moreover, are quite different under Phillips than under Contract: II $\underset{p}{>}$ MM $\underset{p}{=}$ ME $\underset{p}{>}$ YY $\underset{p}{=}$ CC. Under BG2, for employments, the II pair is ranked first for the impact effects, while the YY and CC pairs are ranked last. For inflations under BG2, all pairs are ranked the same.

Under Taylor, there are IEs on employments under the CC pair as well as under the MM, ME, and II pairs. We obtain this result because wages in period 1 are sticky but not fixed. For employments to be unchanged, output prices must be above baseline by the amount of the shock in period 1 and equal to baseline in period 2; outputs must be below baseline by the amount of the shock in period 1 and equal to baseline in period 2; nominal wages must remain equal to baseline in both periods 1 and 2. These requirements are met under the YY pair because the required values for output prices and outputs are consistent with unchanged nominal incomes. However, these requirements cannot be met under the CC pair. To meet the requirements for period 2, the sums of the deviations of outputs from their expected values and output price inflations would have to be negative. These sums must be kept equal to zero under the CC pair, but in order to keep them equal to zero, policymakers must lower interest rates in period 2, raising employments and contract wages set in period 2 above baseline. Since wages in period 1 depend on contract wages set in period 2, they rise. Increases in period-1 wages reduce period-1 employments below baseline, causing output prices to rise by more and outputs to fall by more than the amount of the productivity disturbance.

Now consider the SSD statistics for the symmetric productivity shock. For employments, only under BG1 are the rankings the same as under Contract: YY $\underset{p}{=}$ CC $\underset{p}{>}$ MM $\underset{p}{=}$ ME $\underset{p}{>}$ II. Under Phillips, we obtain an important result. The equally ranked MM and ME pairs dominate the equally ranked YY and CC pairs: MM $\underset{p}{=}$ ME $\underset{p}{>}$ YY $\underset{p}{=}$ CC $\underset{p}{>}$ II. That is, for the form of sticky wages embodied in Phillips, the YY and CC pairs are not the best regime pairs for stabilizing employments even when prices are perfectly flexible. Under Taylor, the CC pair yields the worst results for SSD: YY $\underset{p}{>}$ MM $\underset{p}{=}$ ME $\underset{p}{>}$ II $\underset{p}{>}$ CC. Under BG2, we obtain another important result. The II pair yields the best results, while the equally ranked YY and CC pairs yield the worst results: II $\underset{p}{>}$ MM $\underset{p}{=}$ ME $\underset{p}{>}$ YY $\underset{p}{=}$ CC. That is, when both prices and wages are sticky, the YY and CC pairs seem very unattractive, and the II pair seems more attractive.

For inflations, the SSD rankings are the same under all five wage-price hypotheses: CC $\underset{p}{>}$ YY $\underset{p}{>}$ MM $\underset{p}{=}$ ME $\underset{p}{>}$ II.

The adjustment paths under Phillips are shown in figure 2-17. In the first period, outputs fall and output prices rise under all regime pairs. First-period employments remain constant under the YY and CC pairs but fall under the other pairs because the demand for output falls by more under these pairs.

We consider the YY and CC pairs in detail. Under these pairs in period 1, outputs fall by the amount of the productivity disturbance, and output prices rise by the amount of the productivity disturbance, while employments remain unchanged. Policymakers under these regime pairs see to it that real interest rates rise by just enough to offset the net increases in the excess demand for goods that result from the decreases in outputs and increases in output prices (given the parameters used in the simulations). Expected inflation between periods 1 and 2 is negative under both the YY and CC pairs but more negative under the YY pair, so nominal interest rates must fall by more under the YY pair in order to be consistent with the required rise in the real interest rate.

Since employments remain constant in period 1, real wages must be below baseline in period 1 from the marginal productivity conditions because of the

Table 2-37. *Symmetric Decrease in Productivity*

Summary statistic and wage-price hypothesis	Employment					Inflation					Output				
	MM	II	YY	CC	ME	MM	II	YY	CC	ME	MM	II	YY	CC	ME
						US variables									
Impact effect															
Contract	3.52	6.05	0.00	0.00	3.52	11.06	11.82	10.00	10.00	11.06	−7.54	−5.76	−10.00	−10.00	−7.54
Phillips	−8.76	−24.98	0.00	0.00	−8.76	7.37	2.51	10.00	10.00	7.37	−16.13	−27.48	−10.00	−10.00	−16.13
Taylor	3.45	6.26	0.00	−1.51	3.45	11.27	12.38	10.00	11.06	11.27	−7.59	−5.62	−10.00	−11.06	−7.59
BG1	2.88	3.31	0.00	0.00	2.88	10.86	10.99	10.00	10.00	10.86	−7.98	−7.68	−10.00	−10.00	−7.98
BG2	11.11	7.14	14.29	14.29	11.11	0.00	0.00	0.00	0.00	0.00	−2.22	−5.00	0.00	0.00	−2.22
Sum of squared deviations															
Contract	12.37	36.63	0.00	0.00	12.37	244.44	279.22	200.00	100.00	244.44	56.82	33.22	100.00	100.00	56.82
Phillips	1117.32	1327.33	1250.00	1250.00	1117.37	2664.33	4629.18	1483.33	712.50	2664.41	770.15	1100.04	712.50	712.50	770.18
Taylor	11.95	39.22	0.00	53.60	11.95	247.02	286.10	200.00	147.39	247.02	57.61	31.59	100.00	147.39	57.61
BG1	11.06	14.63	0.00	0.00	11.06	282.19	376.36	200.00	100.00	282.19	65.09	60.80	100.00	100.00	65.09
BG2	164.61	68.03	272.11	272.11	164.61	71.70	140.08	33.33	33.33	71.70	25.10	33.33	33.33	33.33	25.10
Discounted sum of squared deviations															
Contract	12.37	36.63	0.00	0.00	12.37	223.23	254.99	182.65	100.00	223.23	56.82	33.22	100.00	100.00	56.82
Phillips	918.47	1192.87	1011.12	1011.12	918.51	2105.27	3598.03	1200.26	595.45	2105.33	672.72	1034.15	595.45	595.45	672.74
Taylor	11.93	39.20	0.00	44.53	11.93	226.17	263.04	182.65	142.95	226.17	57.60	31.58	100.00	142.95	57.60
BG1	10.46	13.83	0.00	0.00	10.46	253.48	330.65	182.65	100.00	253.48	64.80	60.40	100.00	100.00	64.80
BG2	155.61	64.31	257.23	257.23	155.61	56.02	109.44	26.04	26.04	56.02	20.69	31.51	26.04	26.04	20.69

ROECD variables

Impact effect

Contract	3.52	6.05	0.00	0.00	3.52	11.06	11.82	10.00	10.00	11.06	-7.54	-5.76	-10.00	-10.00	-10.00	-7.54
Phillips	-8.76	-24.98	0.00	0.00	-8.76	7.37	2.51	10.00	10.00	7.37	-16.13	-27.48	-10.00	-10.00	-10.00	-16.13
Taylor	3.45	6.26	0.00	-1.51	3.45	11.27	12.38	10.00	11.06	11.27	-7.59	-5.62	-10.00	-10.00	-11.06	-7.59
BG1	2.88	3.31	0.00	0.00	2.88	10.86	10.99	10.00	10.00	10.86	-7.98	-7.68	-10.00	-10.00	-10.00	-7.98
BG2	11.11	7.14	14.29	14.29	11.11	0.00	0.00	0.00	0.00	0.00	-2.22	-5.00	0.00	0.00	0.00	-2.22

Sum of squared deviations

Contract	12.37	36.63	0.00	0.00	12.37	244.44	279.22	200.00	100.00	244.44	56.82	33.22	100.00	100.00	100.00	56.82
Phillips	1117.32	1327.33	1250.00	1250.00	1117.37	2664.33	4629.18	1483.33	712.50	2664.41	770.15	1100.04	712.50	712.50	712.50	770.18
Taylor	11.95	39.22	0.00	53.60	11.95	247.02	286.10	200.00	147.39	247.02	57.61	31.59	100.00	147.39	100.00	57.61
BG1	11.06	14.63	0.00	0.00	11.06	282.19	376.36	200.00	100.00	282.19	65.09	60.80	100.00	100.00	100.00	65.09
BG2	164.61	68.03	272.11	272.11	164.61	71.70	140.08	33.33	33.33	71.70	25.10	33.33	33.33	33.33	33.33	25.10

Discounted sum of squared deviations

Contract	12.37	36.63	0.00	0.00	12.37	223.23	254.99	182.65	100.00	223.23	56.82	33.22	100.00	100.00	100.00	56.82
Phillips	918.47	1192.87	1011.12	1011.12	918.51	2105.27	3598.03	1200.26	595.45	2105.33	672.72	1034.15	595.45	595.45	595.45	672.74
Taylor	11.93	39.20	0.00	44.53	11.93	226.17	263.04	182.65	142.95	226.17	57.60	31.58	100.00	142.95	100.00	57.60
BG1	10.46	13.83	0.00	0.00	10.46	253.48	330.65	182.65	100.00	253.48	64.80	60.40	100.00	100.00	100.00	64.80
BG2	155.61	64.31	257.23	257.23	155.61	56.02	109.44	26.04	26.04	56.02	20.69	31.51	26.04	26.04	26.04	20.69

Figure 2-17. *Symmetric Decrease in Productivity under the Phillips Hypothesis*

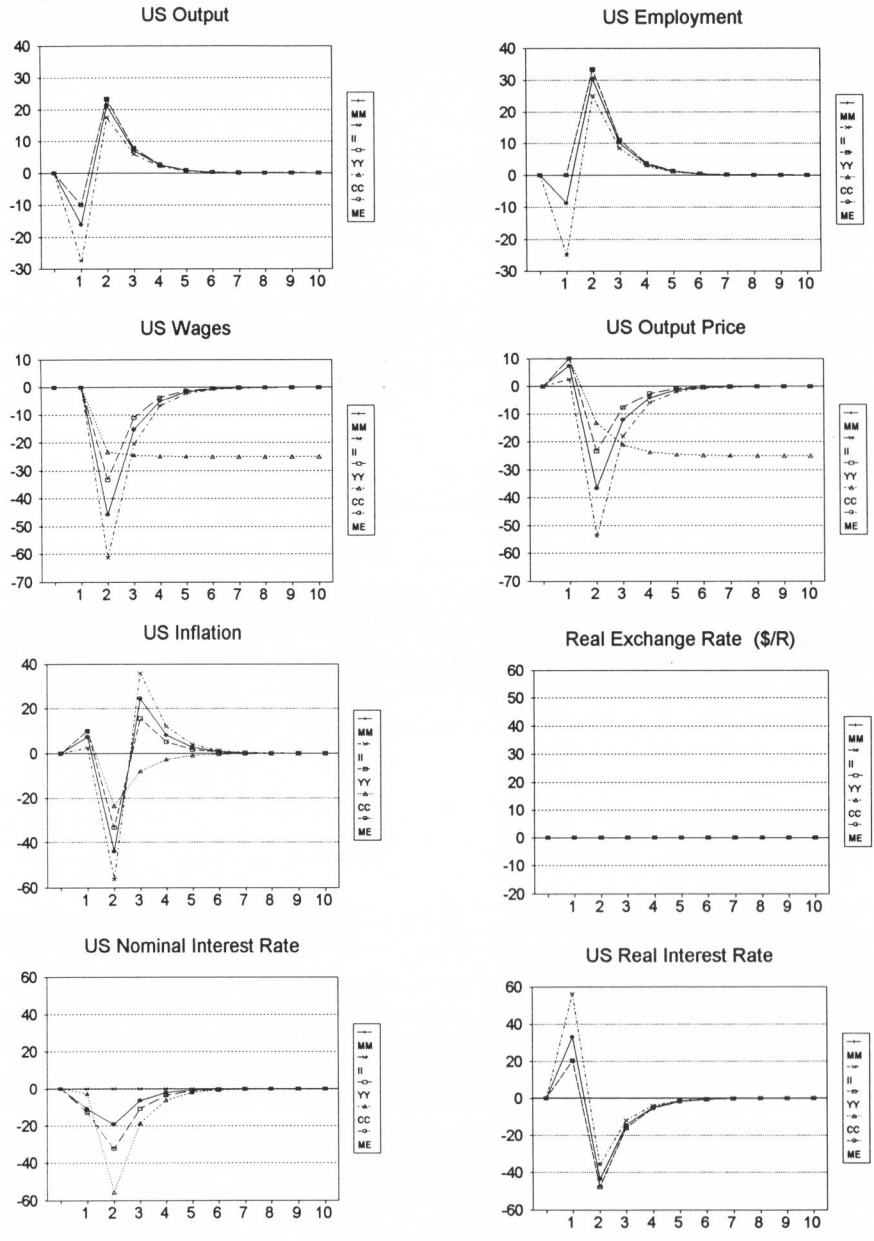

negative productivity shocks; they must be the same in period 1 and period 2 from the Phillips curves. Therefore, employments must be above baseline in period 2 from the marginal productivity conditions because there are no negative productivity shocks. If employments are above baseline, then outputs must be above baseline. Under the YY pair, nominal incomes are kept constant. Thus, if outputs are above baseline, then output prices must be below baseline. In contrast, under the CC pair, the unweighted sums of outputs and inflations are kept constant. Thus, if outputs are above baseline, then output prices must fall. For the parameters used in the simulations, the required fall in output prices is great enough that output prices are below baseline. Under both the YY and CC pairs, real wages must be below baseline, so wages must be below baseline by more than output prices.

As shown in figure 2-17, period-2 employments are farther above baseline for the YY and CC pairs than under the II and MM pairs, a result that is consistent with the fact that for US employment the SSD under Phillips in table 2-37 is larger for the YY and CC pairs than for the MM pair.

It is evident from the graphs of the US output price and US inflation in figure 2-17 that the difference between the YY and CC pairs can have important implications. Under the YY pair, because policymakers keep nominal incomes equal to their baseline values, they act to return output-price levels to baseline as outputs return to baseline. However, under the CC pair, because policymakers keep sums of output and output price inflation equal to baseline values, they do not attempt to return output price levels to their baseline values as outputs return to baseline. Therefore, output price levels and nominal wages are permanently changed under the CC pair.

We report statistics in table 2-38 for an *asymmetric productivity shock* with US productivity falling. For IEs, under Contract for US employment and US inflation, YY $\underset{p}{=}$ CC $\underset{p}{>}$ MM $\underset{p}{>}$ ME $\underset{p}{>}$ II. For ROECD employment and ROECD inflation, the ranking is the same except that the ME and II pairs are reversed. For employments in both regions, the IE rankings under Phillips and BG1 are the same as under Contract. For both inflations, the ranking under BG1 is the same as under Contract. Under Phillips, for US inflation, II $\underset{p}{>}$ ME $\underset{p}{>}$ YY $\underset{p}{=}$ CC $\underset{p}{=}$ MM. For ROECD inflation, the ranking is the same except that the ME and II pairs are reversed. For an asymmetric productivity shock just as for a symmetric productivity shock, employments remain unchanged under the YY and CC pairs for Contract, Phillips, and BG1. The signs of the first-period employment effects for the MM, II, and ME pairs under Phillips are the opposite of those under all the other hypotheses.

Under Taylor, the IE ranking is the same as under Contract except for the CC pair. The CC pair ranks fourth for US employment, fifth for US inflation, third for ROECD employment, and fourth for ROECD inflation.

Table 2-38. *Asymmetric Productivity Shock (US Productivity Decreasing)*

Summary statistic and wage-price hypothesis	Employment					Inflation					Output				
	MM	II	YY	CC	ME	MM	II	YY	CC	ME	MM	II	YY	CC	ME
						US variables									
Impact effect															
Contract	0.75	1.59	0.00	0.00	0.92	6.88	7.33	6.46	6.46	7.13	−9.47	−8.89	−10.00	−10.00	−9.35
Phillips	−0.01	−3.39	0.00	0.00	−1.00	8.20	6.29	8.20	8.20	7.00	−10.01	−12.37	−10.00	−10.00	−10.70
Taylor	0.71	1.52	0.00	−1.51	0.86	6.89	7.39	6.46	7.50	7.14	−9.50	−8.93	−10.00	−11.06	−9.40
BG1	0.75	1.47	0.00	0.00	1.00	6.89	7.31	6.46	6.46	7.17	−9.48	−8.97	−10.00	−10.00	−9.30
BG2	14.18	12.88	14.29	14.29	13.63	0.36	0.00	0.39	0.39	0.00	−0.08	−0.98	0.00	0.00	−0.46
Sum of squared deviations															
Contract	0.57	2.52	0.00	0.00	0.85	94.56	107.56	83.56	54.29	101.79	89.74	79.00	100.00	100.00	87.49
Phillips	1249.73	1178.26	1250.00	1250.00	1226.10	821.29	923.88	687.94	438.73	771.09	712.52	724.74	712.50	712.50	714.80
Taylor	0.51	2.34	0.00	53.60	0.75	94.63	107.98	83.56	61.69	101.82	90.29	79.84	100.00	147.39	88.37
BG1	0.75	2.88	0.00	0.00	1.33	97.61	114.02	83.56	54.29	103.38	89.89	80.82	100.00	100.00	86.69
BG2	267.93	221.20	272.11	272.11	247.61	18.59	22.69	14.96	28.03	17.56	32.83	28.07	33.33	33.33	30.54
Discounted sum of squared deviations															
Contract	0.57	2.52	0.00	0.00	0.85	86.35	98.23	76.31	52.12	92.96	89.74	79.00	100.00	100.00	87.49
Phillips	1010.90	955.28	1011.12	1011.12	991.98	668.59	739.11	563.61	341.09	622.90	595.50	615.48	595.45	595.45	600.08
Taylor	0.51	2.33	0.00	44.53	0.74	86.45	98.71	76.31	59.99	93.00	90.29	79.83	100.00	142.95	88.37
BG1	0.71	2.73	0.00	0.00	1.25	88.91	103.49	76.31	52.12	94.36	89.87	80.75	100.00	100.00	86.65
BG2	253.28	209.10	257.23	257.23	234.07	14.67	17.73	11.83	20.27	13.72	25.65	22.14	26.04	26.04	23.91

ROECD variables

Impact effect

Contract	−0.75	−1.59	0.00	0.00	−2.25	−6.88	−7.33	−6.46	−6.46	−7.53	9.47	8.89	10.00	10.00	8.42
Phillips	0.01	3.39	0.00	0.00	5.77	−8.20	−6.29	−8.20	−8.20	−5.57	10.01	12.37	10.00	10.00	14.04
Taylor	−0.71	−1.52	0.00	1.51	−2.19	−6.89	−7.39	−6.46	−7.50	−7.63	9.50	8.93	10.00	11.06	8.47
BG1	−0.75	−1.47	0.00	0.00	−1.94	−6.89	−7.31	−6.46	−6.46	−7.45	9.48	8.97	10.00	10.00	8.64
BG2	−14.18	−12.88	−14.29	−14.29	−12.13	−0.36	0.00	−0.39	−0.39	0.00	0.08	0.98	0.00	0.00	1.51

Sum of squared deviations

Contract	0.57	2.52	0.00	0.00	5.08	94.56	107.56	83.56	54.29	113.50	89.74	79.00	100.00	100.00	70.94
Phillips	1249.73	1178.26	1250.00	1250.00	1143.21	821.29	923.88	687.94	438.73	1095.45	712.52	724.74	712.50	712.50	740.95
Taylor	0.51	2.34	0.00	53.60	4.82	94.63	107.98	83.56	61.69	114.33	90.29	79.84	100.00	147.39	71.74
BG1	0.75	2.88	0.00	0.00	5.04	97.61	114.02	83.56	54.29	125.46	89.89	80.82	100.00	100.00	75.25
BG2	267.93	221.20	272.11	272.11	196.27	18.59	22.69	14.96	28.03	28.48	32.83	28.07	33.33	33.33	26.32

Discounted sum of squared deviations

Contract	0.57	2.52	0.00	0.00	5.08	86.35	98.23	76.31	52.12	103.65	89.74	79.00	100.00	100.00	70.94
Phillips	1010.90	955.28	1011.12	1011.12	931.10	668.59	739.11	563.61	341.09	869.70	595.50	615.48	595.45	595.45	637.02
Taylor	0.51	2.33	0.00	44.53	4.81	86.45	98.71	76.31	59.99	104.60	90.29	79.83	100.00	142.95	71.73
BG1	0.71	2.73	0.00	0.00	4.76	88.91	103.49	76.31	52.12	113.27	89.87	80.75	100.00	100.00	75.12
BG2	253.28	209.10	257.23	257.23	185.54	14.67	17.73	11.83	20.27	22.25	25.65	22.14	26.04	26.04	21.06

Under BG2, the IE rankings are different from the ranking under Contract in several respects. Just as for a symmetric productivity shock, the YY and CC pairs are ranked last and the II and ME pairs dominate the MM pair for employments. For US employment, II $\gtrsim_p$ ME $\gtrsim_p$ MM $\gtrsim_p$ YY $=_p$ CC. For ROECD employment, the ranking is the same except that the II and ME pairs are reversed. For inflation in both regions, the II and ME pairs are ranked first, while the YY and CC pairs are ranked last.

For the SSD statistics, for asymmetric shocks just as for symmetric shocks, only under BG1 are the employment rankings the same as under Contract. For US employment under Contract and BG1, YY $=_p$ CC $\gtrsim_p$ MM $\gtrsim_p$ ME $\gtrsim_p$ II; for ROECD employment under Contract and BG1, the ranking is the same except that the positions of the ME and II pairs are reversed. Under Phillips and BG2, the SSD rankings are quite different than under Contract: for US employment, II $\gtrsim_p$ ME $\gtrsim_p$ MM $\gtrsim_p$ YY $=_p$ CC, and for ROECD employment, the ranking is the same except that the II and ME pairs are reversed. The only difference between the SSD rankings for employments in both regions under Taylor and Contract is that the CC pair ranks last, not first.

For inflations, the SSD rankings under Taylor and BG1 are the same as under Contract: for US inflation, CC $\gtrsim_p$ YY $\gtrsim_p$ MM $\gtrsim_p$ ME $\gtrsim_p$ II, while for ROECD inflation, the ranking is the same except that the ME and II pairs are reversed. Under Phillips, the inflation rankings are the same except that the MM pair and ME pair are reversed for US inflation. Under BG2, for US inflation and ROECD inflation, the CC pair ranks last and next to last, respectively, rather than first, and for US inflation the positions of the MM and ME pairs are reversed.

Figure 2-18 contains the adjustment paths for US variables under Phillips. The movements following an asymmetric productivity shock are similar to the movements following a symmetric productivity shock. Once again, it is evident that the YY and CC pairs have quite different implications for inflations following productivity shocks. Also, for an asymmetric productivity shock, the real exchange rate changes, and the effects under the MM and ME pairs are not the same (see also table 2-38).

For *region-specific productivity shocks* with US and ROECD productivities decreasing, the statistics are in tables 2-39 and 2-40, respectively. First we consider the effect of a reduction in US productivity. For US employment, the IE rankings under all the other hypotheses except BG2 are the same as the ranking under Contract: YY $\gtreqless_p$ CC $\gtrsim_p$ MM $\gtrsim_p$ ME $\gtrsim_p$ II; the ranking under BG2 is II $\gtrsim_p$ ME $\gtrsim_p$ MM $\gtrsim_p$ YY $=_p$ CC. For SSDs for employment, as we expect, only under BG1 is the ranking the same as under Contract. Under Taylor, CC ranks last, not first. Under Phillips, II $\gtrsim_p$ MM $\gtrsim_p$ ME $\gtrsim_p$ YY $=_p$ CC.

Figure 2-18. *Asymmetric Productivity Shock under the Phillips Hypothesis*

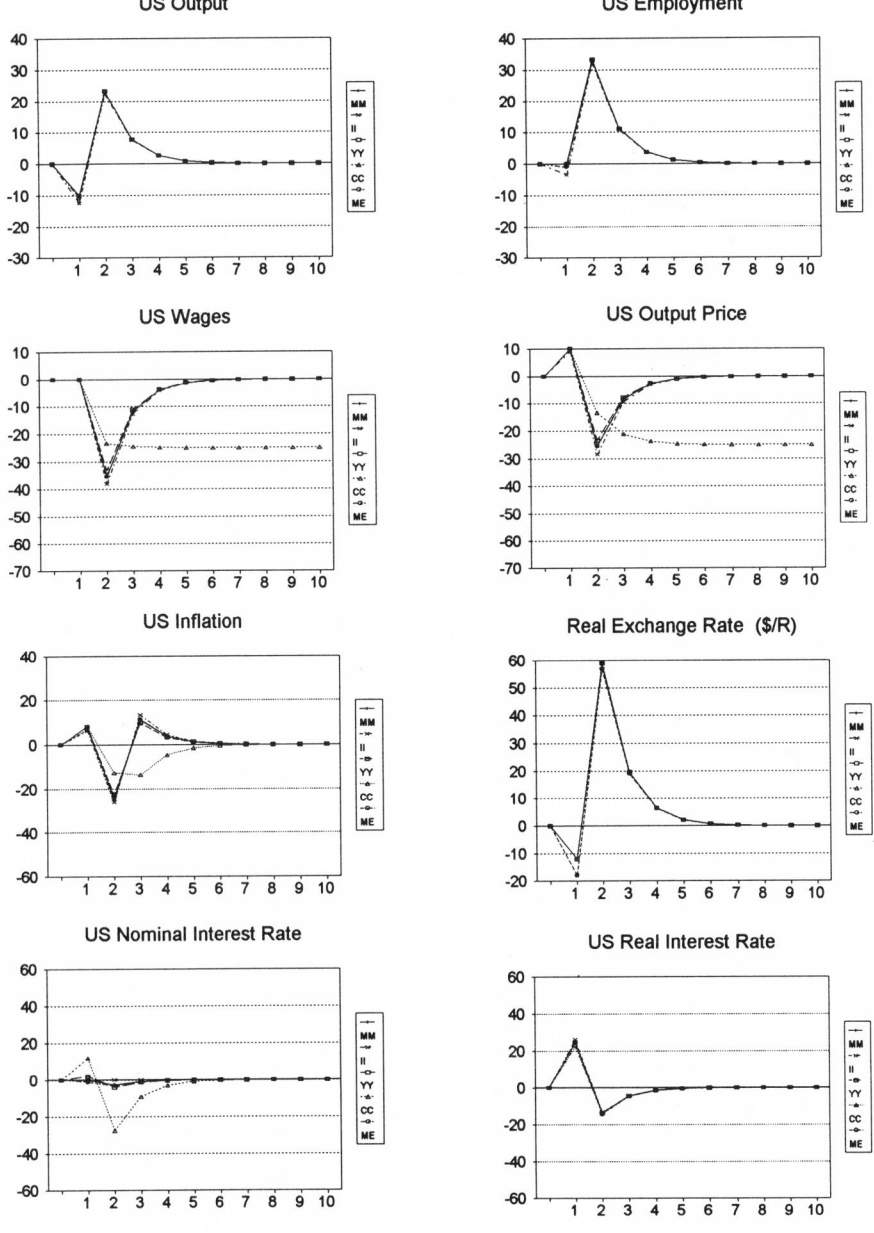

Table 2-39. *Region-Specific Decrease in US Productivity*

Summary statistic and wage-price hypothesis	Employment					Inflation					Output				
	MM	II	YY	CC	ME	MM	II	YY	CC	ME	MM	II	YY	CC	ME
						US variables									
Impact effect															
Contract	2.14	3.82	0.00	0.00	2.22	8.97	9.58	8.23	8.23	9.10	−8.51	−7.33	−10.00	−10.00	−8.45
Phillips	−4.39	−14.18	0.00	0.00	−4.88	7.78	4.40	9.10	9.10	7.19	−13.07	−19.93	−10.00	−10.00	−13.42
Taylor	2.08	3.89	0.00	−1.51	2.15	9.08	9.89	8.23	9.28	9.20	−8.55	−7.28	−10.00	−11.06	−8.49
BG1	1.81	2.39	0.00	0.00	1.94	8.88	9.15	8.23	8.23	9.02	−8.73	−8.33	−10.00	−10.00	−8.64
BG2	12.64	10.01	14.29	14.29	12.37	0.18	0.00	0.19	0.19	0.00	−1.15	−2.99	0.00	0.00	−1.34
Sum of squared deviations															
Contract	4.56	14.59	0.00	0.00	4.93	160.76	183.35	135.53	70.89	165.43	72.34	53.65	100.00	100.00	71.33
Phillips	1161.99	1121.71	1250.00	1250.00	1154.79	1600.26	2401.95	1046.84	536.82	1569.51	730.78	848.16	712.50	712.50	734.19
Taylor	4.35	15.17	0.00	53.60	4.66	161.85	186.35	135.53	93.59	166.49	73.03	52.96	100.00	147.39	72.17
BG1	4.39	7.63	0.00	0.00	5.01	177.62	224.40	135.53	70.89	181.38	76.75	70.26	100.00	100.00	75.31
BG2	213.14	133.64	272.11	272.11	204.00	40.75	68.89	23.17	29.70	40.06	27.43	25.32	33.33	33.33	26.79
Discounted sum of squared deviations															
Contract	4.56	14.59	0.00	0.00	4.93	146.81	167.44	123.77	70.35	151.07	72.34	53.67	100.00	100.00	71.33
Phillips	943.61	945.77	1011.12	1011.12	938.66	1277.01	1881.10	851.27	437.60	1249.21	623.78	761.95	595.45	595.45	628.29
Taylor	4.34	15.16	0.00	44.53	4.74	148.07	170.96	123.77	91.96	152.30	73.03	52.96	100.00	142.95	72.16
BG1	4.15	7.21	0.00	0.00	4.74	160.41	199.58	123.77	70.35	163.95	76.63	70.05	100.00	100.00	75.18
BG2	201.48	126.33	257.23	257.23	192.84	31.93	53.82	18.18	22.40	31.30	21.72	21.74	26.04	26.04	21.32

ROECD variables

Impact effect

Contract	1.38	2.23	0.00	0.63	2.09	2.24	1.77	1.77	1.76	0.97	1.56	0.00	0.44
Phillips	−4.38	−10.80	0.00	−1.50	−0.41	−1.89	0.90	0.90	0.90	−3.06	−7.56	0.00	−1.05
Taylor	1.37	2.37	0.00	0.63	2.19	2.50	1.77	1.78	1.82	0.96	1.66	0.00	0.44
BG1	1.07	0.92	0.00	0.47	1.99	1.84	1.77	1.77	1.71	0.75	0.65	0.00	0.33
BG2	−1.53	−2.87	0.00	−0.51	−0.18	0.00	−0.19	−0.19	0.00	−1.07	−2.01	0.00	−0.36

Sum of squared deviations

Contract	1.91	4.98	0.00	0.40	8.73	10.04	6.25	6.25	6.20	0.94	2.44	0.00	0.20
Phillips	21.54	131.09	0.00	2.52	142.55	374.58	38.80	38.80	86.14	10.55	64.23	0.00	1.23
Taylor	1.88	5.61	0.00	0.40	8.98	10.69	6.25	10.95	6.31	0.92	2.75	0.00	0.20
BG1	1.52	1.13	0.00	0.29	12.28	20.79	6.25	6.25	7.88	0.74	0.55	0.00	0.14
BG2	3.13	10.97	0.00	0.35	4.40	12.50	0.98	0.98	2.45	1.53	5.38	0.00	0.17

Discounted sum of squared deviations

Contract	1.91	4.98	0.00	0.40	7.98	9.17	5.71	5.71	5.67	0.94	2.44	0.00	0.20
Phillips	21.08	128.30	0.00	2.46	109.92	287.47	30.67	30.67	67.53	10.33	62.87	0.00	1.21
Taylor	1.88	5.61	0.00	0.40	8.25	9.91	5.71	9.51	5.79	0.92	2.75	0.00	0.20
BG1	1.43	1.07	0.00	0.28	10.79	17.50	5.71	5.71	7.00	0.70	0.52	0.00	0.14
BG2	2.96	10.37	0.00	0.33	3.41	9.77	0.26	0.76	1.92	1.45	5.08	0.00	0.16

Table 2-40. *Region-Specific Decrease in ROECD Productivity*

Summary statistic and wage-price hypothesis	Employment					Inflation					Output				
	MM	II	YY	CC	ME	MM	II	YY	CC	ME	MM	II	YY	CC	ME
						US variables									
Impact effect															
Contract	1.38	2.23	0.00	0.00	1.30	2.09	2.24	1.77	1.77	1.96	0.97	1.56	0.00	0.00	0.91
Phillips	-4.38	-10.80	0.00	0.00	-3.88	-0.41	-1.89	0.90	0.90	0.18	-3.06	-7.56	0.00	0.00	-2.72
Taylor	1.37	2.37	0.00	0.00	1.29	2.19	2.50	1.77	1.78	2.06	0.96	1.66	0.00	0.00	0.91
BG1	1.07	0.92	0.00	0.00	0.94	1.99	1.84	1.77	1.77	1.85	0.75	0.65	0.00	0.00	0.66
BG2	-1.53	-2.87	0.00	0.00	-1.26	-0.18	0.00	-0.19	-0.19	0.00	-1.07	-2.01	0.00	0.00	-0.88
Sum of squared deviations															
Contract	1.91	4.98	0.00	0.00	1.68	8.73	10.04	6.25	6.25	7.69	0.94	2.44	0.00	0.00	0.82
Phillips	21.54	131.09	0.00	0.00	16.94	142.55	374.58	38.80	38.80	148.24	10.55	64.23	0.00	0.00	8.30
Taylor	1.88	5.61	0.00	0.00	1.68	8.98	10.69	6.25	10.95	7.92	0.92	2.75	0.00	0.00	0.83
BG1	1.52	1.13	0.00	0.00	1.18	12.28	20.79	6.25	6.25	11.41	0.74	0.55	0.00	0.00	0.58
BG2	3.13	10.97	0.00	0.00	2.11	4.40	12.50	0.98	0.98	4.57	1.53	5.38	0.00	0.00	1.03
Discounted sum of squared deviations															
Contract	1.91	4.98	0.00	0.00	1.68	7.98	9.17	5.71	5.71	7.02	0.94	2.44	0.00	0.00	0.82
Phillips	21.08	128.30	0.00	0.00	16.58	109.92	287.47	30.67	30.67	114.91	10.33	62.87	0.00	0.00	8.13
Taylor	1.88	5.61	0.00	0.00	1.68	8.25	9.91	5.71	9.51	7.29	0.92	2.75	0.00	0.00	0.82
BG1	1.43	1.07	0.00	0.00	1.12	10.79	17.50	5.71	5.71	9.97	0.70	0.52	0.00	0.00	0.55
BG2	2.96	10.37	0.00	0.00	2.00	3.41	9.77	0.76	0.76	3.57	1.45	5.08	0.00	0.00	0.98

ROECD variables

Impact effect

Contract	2.14	3.82	0.00	0.00	2.89	8.97	9.58	8.23	8.23	9.29	−8.51	−7.33	−10.00	−10.00	−7.98
Phillips	−4.39	−14.18	0.00	0.00	−7.27	7.78	4.40	9.10	9.10	6.47	−13.07	−19.93	−10.00	−10.00	−15.09
Taylor	2.08	3.89	0.00	−1.51	2.82	9.08	9.89	8.23	9.28	9.45	−8.55	−7.28	−10.00	−11.06	−8.03
BG1	1.81	2.39	0.00	0.00	2.41	8.88	9.15	8.23	8.23	9.16	−8.73	−8.33	−10.00	−10.00	−8.31
BG2	12.64	10.01	14.29	14.29	11.62	0.18	0.00	0.19	0.19	0.00	−1.15	−2.99	0.00	0.00	−1.87

Sum of squared deviations

Contract	4.56	14.59	0.00	0.00	8.33	160.76	183.35	135.53	70.89	172.76	72.34	53.67	100.00	100.00	63.68
Phillips	1161.99	1121.71	1250.00	1250.00	1127.77	1600.26	2401.95	1046.84	536.82	1793.80	730.78	848.16	712.50	712.50	754.33
Taylor	4.35	15.17	0.00	53.60	7.99	161.85	186.35	135.53	93.59	174.36	73.03	52.96	100.00	147.39	64.48
BG1	4.39	7.63	0.00	0.00	7.76	177.62	224.40	135.53	70.89	195.95	76.75	70.26	100.00	100.00	70.03
BG2	213.14	133.64	272.11	272.11	180.09	40.75	68.89	23.17	29.70	47.64	27.43	25.32	33.33	33.33	25.54

Discounted sum of squared deviations

Contract	4.56	14.59	0.00	0.00	8.33	146.81	167.44	123.77	70.35	157.77	72.34	53.67	100.00	100.00	63.68
Phillips	943.61	945.77	1011.12	1011.12	922.34	1277.01	1881.10	851.27	437.60	1419.98	623.78	761.95	595.45	595.45	653.67
Taylor	4.34	15.16	0.00	44.53	7.98	148.07	170.96	123.77	91.96	159.60	73.03	52.96	100.00	142.95	64.47
BG1	4.15	7.21	0.00	0.00	7.34	160.41	199.58	123.77	70.35	176.38	76.63	70.05	100.00	100.00	69.82
BG2	201.68	126.33	257.23	257.23	170.24	31.93	53.82	18.18	22.40	37.22	21.72	21.74	26.04	26.04	20.71

Under BG2, the ranking is the same as under Phillips except that the positions of MM and ME pairs are reversed.

For ROECD employment, for both IEs and SSDs, the rankings under all the other hypotheses except BG1 are the same as the ranking under Contract: $\text{YY} \underset{p}{=} \text{CC} \underset{p}{\geq} \text{ME} \underset{p}{\geq} \text{MM} \underset{p}{\geq} \text{II}$. Under BG1, MM ranks last, not next to last, for both IEs and SSDs.

For US inflation, the rankings under BG1 for IEs and SSDs and under Taylor for SSDs are the same as under Contract: $\text{CC} \underset{p}{\gtreqqless} \text{YY} \underset{p}{\geq} \text{MM} \underset{p}{\geq} \text{ME} \underset{p}{\geq} \text{II}$. For IEs, under Taylor, the CC pair ranks next to last, not first. Under Phillips and BG2, the ME and II pairs rank higher and the equally ranked YY and CC pairs rank lower: $\text{II} \underset{p}{\gtreqqless} \text{ME} \underset{p}{\geq} \text{MM} \underset{p}{\geq} \text{YY} \underset{p}{=} \text{CC}$. For SSDs, under Phillips the MM and ME pairs are reversed. Under BG2, $\text{YY} \underset{p}{\geq} \text{CC} \underset{p}{\geq} \text{ME} \underset{p}{\geq} \text{MM} \underset{p}{\geq} \text{II}$.

For ROECD inflation, no other hypothesis has the same ranking as Contract, for either IEs or SSDs. The ranking under Contract is $\text{ME} \underset{p}{\geq} \text{YY} \underset{p}{=} \text{CC} \underset{p}{\geq} \text{MM} \underset{p}{\geq} \text{II}$. For IEs, under Phillips, the MM pair ranks first, not next to last; under Taylor, the positions of the ME pair and the equally ranked YY and CC pairs are reversed; under BG1, the positions of the II and MM pairs are reversed; predictably, under BG2, $\text{ME} \underset{p}{=} \text{II} \underset{p}{\geq} \text{MM} \underset{p}{\geq} \text{YY} \underset{p}{=} \text{CC}$. For SSDs, under Phillips, BG1, and BG2, the ME pair and the equally ranked YY and CC pairs are reversed; under Taylor, the YY pair ranks first, instead of being tied for second, and the CC pair ranks last, instead of being tied for second.

Adjustment paths for US variables under Phillips appear in figure 2-19. These paths are qualitatively similar to those for an asymmetric productivity shock with US productivity falling shown in figure 2-18.

Finally, we consider the effects of a reduction in ROECD productivity (table 2-40). For the matched regime pairs, under all five wage-price hypotheses, the rankings for the region in which the shock has its impact effect and the other region are the same, no matter in which region the shock has its impact effect. However, under some hypotheses the position of the unmatched ME pair in the rankings for both the region in which the shock has its impact effect and the other region changes depending on whether the region in which the shock has its impact effect is the one that pegs the exchange rate. Unfortunately, it is very difficult to generalize about how the position of the ME pair changes.

Figure 2-19. *Region-Specific Decrease in US Productivity under the Phillips Hypothesis*

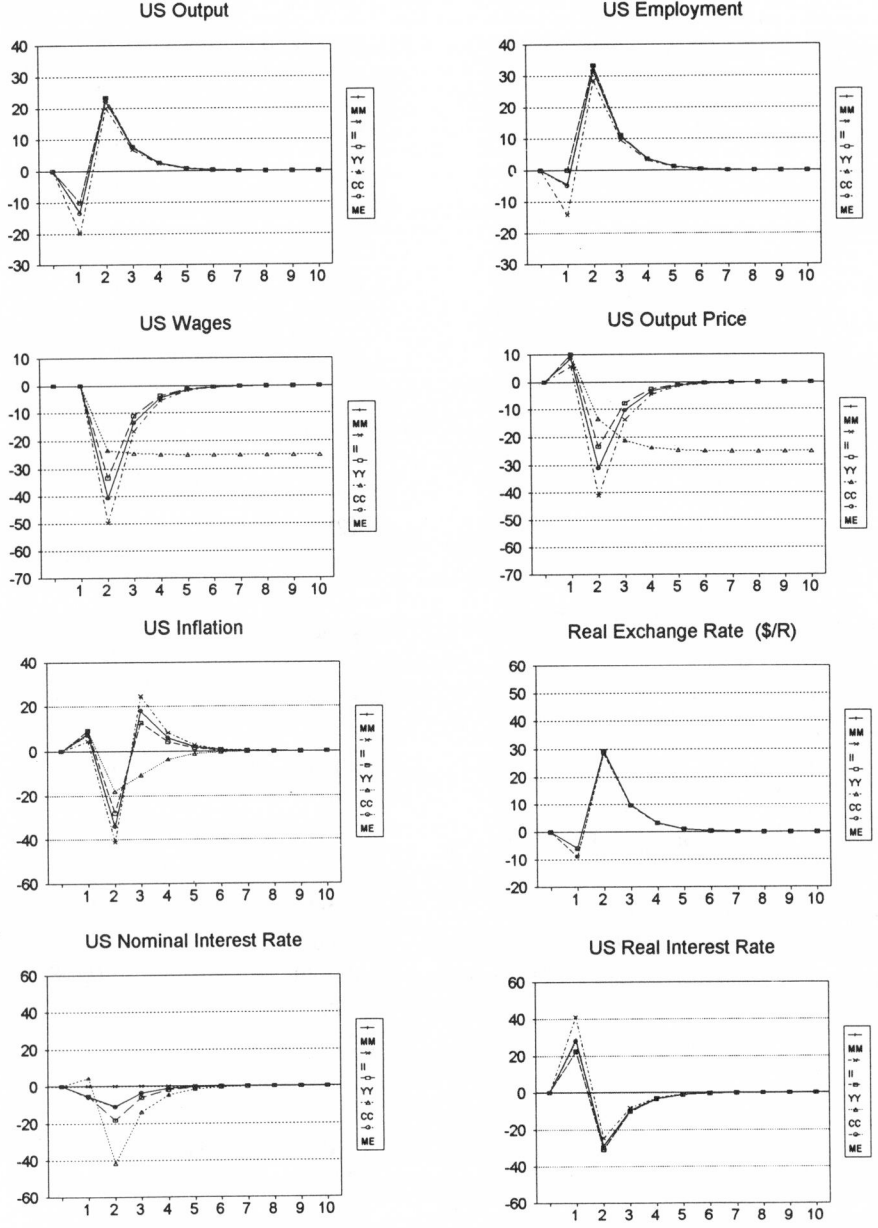

Appendix A: Values of Parameters and Combinations Used in Simulations

Parameter	No Oil ($\sigma = 1$)	Oil ($\sigma = 1$)
α	0.7	0.7
β	0	0.1
γ	0.15	0.15
δ	0.2	0.2207
ϵ	0.59	0.59
η	0.05575	0.05575
υ	0.2	0.2
ϕ	1.0	1.0
λ	0.8	0.8
σ	1.0	1.0
τ	0.15	0.185
$A = (1 - \alpha)/\alpha\sigma$	0.4286	0.4286
$B = 1 - \epsilon + \upsilon A$	0.4957	0.4957
$C = 1 - \epsilon - \upsilon$	0.21	0.21
$D = A + \phi$	1.4286	1.4286
$E = 1 - \epsilon + \upsilon(A + D/\lambda)$	0.8529	0.8529
$F = (1 - 2\gamma)^2\upsilon + 2\delta$	0.498	0.5393
$G = 1 - (1 - 2\gamma)\epsilon + FA$	0.8004	0.8181
$H = 1 - (1 - 2\gamma)\epsilon - F$	0.089	0.0477
$J = 1 - (1 - 2\gamma)\epsilon + F(A + D/\lambda)$	1.69	1.7814
$K = (1 - 2\gamma)AF + 2\gamma G$	0.3895	0.4072
$L = (1 - 2\gamma)\lambda A - 2\gamma D$	−0.1878	−0.1878
$M = (1 - \epsilon)\upsilon\{[\delta/\upsilon - 2(1 - \gamma)\gamma] - \epsilon\gamma\}$	0.04339	0.05186
$N = -2(1 - \gamma)\gamma\upsilon + \delta \gtrless 0$	0.149	0.1697
θ	0.2	. . .
μ	0.25	. . .
φ	0.6 BG1, 0.5 BG2	. . .
υ	0.5	. . .

Appendix B: Reaction Functions for Regime Pairs

In this appendix, we present the reaction functions for the MM, YY, CC, and ME regime pairs:

MM Regime Pair

$$i - \hat{\imath} = \psi(m - \hat{m}), \qquad \hat{\imath} = \hat{m} = 0,$$

(2B-1)

$$\overset{\star}{\imath} - \overset{\star}{\hat{\imath}} = \psi(\overset{\star}{m} - \overset{\star}{\hat{m}}), \qquad \overset{\star}{\hat{\imath}} = \overset{\star}{\hat{m}} = 0,$$

YY Regime Pair

$$i - \hat{\imath} = \rho\left(p + y - \overline{\widehat{p + y}}\right), \qquad \overline{\widehat{p + y}} = 0,$$

(2B-2)

$$\overset{\star}{\imath} - \overset{\star}{\hat{\imath}} - \rho(\overset{\star}{p} + \overset{\star}{y} - \overline{\widehat{\overset{\star}{p + y}}}), \qquad \overline{\widehat{\overset{\star}{p + y}}} = 0,$$

CC Regime Pair

$$i - \hat{\imath} = \iota(y + \pi - \overline{\widehat{y + \pi}}), \qquad \overline{\widehat{y + \pi}} = 0$$

(2B-3)

$$\overset{\star}{\imath} - \overset{\star}{\hat{\imath}} = \iota(\overset{\star}{y} + \overset{\star}{\pi} - \overline{\widehat{\overset{\star}{y + \pi}}}), \qquad \overline{\widehat{\overset{\star}{y + \pi}}} = 0,$$

ME Regime Pair

(2B-4) $\qquad i - \hat{\imath} = \xi(m - \hat{m}), \qquad \overset{\star}{\imath} - \overset{\star}{\hat{\imath}} = \chi(e - \hat{e}), \qquad \hat{e} = 0.$

In this chapter, we consider only full instrument adjustment. Under full instrument adjustment, $\psi, \rho, \iota, \xi,$ and $\chi \to \infty$ for the MM, YY, CC, and ME regime pairs. Variables with hats over them represent desired values for intermediate-target variables.

The II regime pair is the limit of either the MM or YY regime pair as either ψ or ρ approaches zero.

Appendix C: Comparison of the CC and YY Regime Pairs under the Contract Hypothesis

In this appendix, we demonstrate that—under the Contract hypothesis in the model without oil—all endogenous variables move in the same way under the CC and YY regime pairs except nominal interest rates for productivity shocks.[90] As an example, we interpret the results for nominal interest rates for symmetric shocks.

Under the CC regime pair, in each period the policymaker in each country keeps the unweighted sum of the deviation of output from its (unconditional) expected value and of the inflation rate for the output price equal to zero:

$$(2C\text{-}1) \qquad y - \hat{y} + \pi = y + \pi = y + (p - p_{-1}) = p + y - p_{-1} = 0,$$

$$(2C\text{-}2) \qquad \overset{*}{y} - \overset{\hat{*}}{y} + \overset{*}{\pi} = y + \overset{*}{\pi} = \overset{*}{y} + (\overset{*}{p} - \overset{*}{p}_{-1}) = \overset{*}{p} + \overset{*}{y} - \overset{*}{p}_{-1} = 0.$$

A variable with a hat over it indicates the expected value of the variable. Under our assumptions, $\hat{y} = \overset{\hat{*}}{y} = 0$. That is, under our assumptions, in each period nominal income is kept equal to the output price in the previous period in each region.

In the rest of this appendix, just as in the text, we use p and $\overset{*}{p}$ to represent output prices in the specific period we analyze, while p_{-1} and $\overset{*}{p}_{-1}$ represent output prices in the previous period. We also assume that $p_{-1} = \overset{*}{p}_{-1} = 0$. Therefore, in the specific period we analyze, nominal income is kept equal to zero in each region under both the CC and YY regime pairs.

Under the CC regime pair, agents expect that in every future period interest rates will be set according to the reaction functions in equations 2B-3 with $\iota \rightarrow \infty$. Therefore, it can be shown that[91]

$$(2C\text{-}3) \qquad z_{+1|} = 0, \; p_{+1|} = q_{+1|} = p, \qquad \overset{*}{p}_{+1|} = \overset{*}{q}_{+1|} = \overset{*}{p}, \; e_{+1|} = p_d,$$

$$(2C\text{-}4) \qquad\qquad\qquad\qquad w = \overset{*}{w} = \omega.$$

The expression for $e_{+1|}$ in equation 2C-3 implies that the expression for the real exchange rate is not equation 2-22 but rather

$$(2C\text{-}5) \qquad\qquad\qquad\qquad z = -i_d.$$

The expressions for $p_{+1|}$, $\overset{*}{p}_{+1|}$, and $e_{+1|}$ in equation 2C-3 imply that the expressions for real interest rates given are not equations 2-23 but rather

---

90. The same result holds in the model with oil included ($\beta > 0$), but we do not prove it in this chapter.

91. The method of proof is similar to the one used in appendix A of Canzoneri and Henderson (1991) and in the appendix to Obstfeld (1985).

(2C-6) $r = (1 - \gamma)i + \gamma \overset{\star}{i}, \qquad \overset{\star}{r} = \gamma i + (1 - \gamma)\overset{\star}{i}.$

Adding the second equation in equations 2C-6 to and subtracting it from the first equation yield expressions for the sum of and difference between real interest rates:

(2C-7) $r_s = i_s,$

(2C-8) $r_d = (1 - 2\gamma)i_d.$

Price levels are obtained by substituting the expression for the real exchange rate given by equation 2C-5 into equations 2-6 to obtain

(2C-9) $q = p - \gamma i_d, \qquad \overset{\star}{q} = \overset{\star}{p} + \gamma i_d.$

Adding the second equation in equations 2C-9 to and subtracting it from the first yield

(2C-10) $q_s = p_s,$

(2C-11) $q_d = p_d - 2\gamma_d^i.$

The equations for the aggregate-demand schedules for sums and differences under the CC regime pair—the AD_s^{CC} and AD_d^{CC} schedules—are different from the equations for the aggregate-demand schedules for the other symmetric regime pairs (the AD_s and AD_d schedules) given by equations 2-29 and 2-40. Adding the second equation in equations 2-13 to and subtracting it from the first equation and eliminating r_s using equation 2C-7, r_d using equation 2C-8, and z using equation 2C-5 yield

(2C-12) $-(1 - \epsilon)y_s - \nu i_s + u_s = 0, \qquad (AD_s^{CC} \text{schedule}),$

(2C-13) $-[1 - (1 - 2\gamma)\epsilon]y_d$

$\qquad\qquad - [(1 - 2\gamma)^2\nu + 2\delta]i_d + u_d = 0, \qquad (AD_d^{CC}\text{schedule}).$

The aggregate-supply schedules for sums and differences for the CC regime pair are the same as those for the other matched regime pairs, and are given by equations 2-35 and 2-48. Equations 2-36 and 2-49, which state that the sum of and difference between nominal incomes are constants hold under both the CC and YY regime pairs.

As shown in the text, our model implies the unique relationships between sums of employments and sums of nominal incomes, and between differences between employments and differences between nominal incomes, given by equations 2-38 and 2-51. Therefore, n_s and n_d are given by equations 2D-8 and 2D-17 under both the CC and YY regime pairs.

Under both the CC and YY regime pairs, y_s and p_s are obtained by solving equations 2-35 and 2-36, while y_d and p_d are obtained by solving equations 2-48 and 2-49. The results are given by equations 2D-7, 2D-9, 2D-16, and

$$(2C\text{-}14) \qquad p_d^{CC} = p_d^{YY} = \left[\frac{A}{A+1}\right](p+y_d) + x_d.$$

Substituting equation 2D-7 into equation 2C-12 and equation 2D-16 into equation 2C-13 and solving for i_s and i_d yield

$$(2C\text{-}15) \qquad i_s^{CC} = \left[\frac{1}{\nu}\right]u_s + \left[\frac{1-\epsilon}{\nu}\right]x_s - \left[\frac{1}{A+1}\right]\left[\frac{1-\epsilon}{\nu}\right]\overline{p+y_s},$$

$$(2C\text{-}16) \qquad i_d^{CC} = \left[\frac{1}{(1-2\gamma)^2\nu + 2\delta}\right]u_d + \left[\frac{1-(1-2\gamma)\epsilon}{(1-2\gamma)^2\nu + 2\delta}\right]x_d$$
$$- \left[\frac{1}{A+1}\right]\left[\frac{1-(1-2\gamma)\epsilon}{(1-2\gamma)^2\nu + 2\delta}\right]\overline{p+y_d}.$$

Substituting equations 2C-14 and 2C-16 into equation 2C-11 confirms that q_d is given by equation 2D-18 under both the CC and YY regime pairs.

To compare the effects of shocks on nominal interest rates under the CC and YY regime pairs, it is necessary to derive expressions for i_s and i_d under the YY pair. Substituting the expressions for y_s in equation 2D-7 and for $q_s = p_s$ in equation 2D-9 into equation 2-29 and the expressions for y_d in equation 2D-16 and for p_d in equation 2C-14 into equation 2-40, and then solving for i_s and i_d yield

$$(2C\text{-}17) \quad i_s^{YY} = \left[\frac{1}{\nu}\right]u_s + \left[\frac{1-\epsilon}{\nu} - 1\right]x_s - \left[\frac{1}{A+1}\right]\left[\frac{1-\epsilon}{\nu} - A\right]\overline{p+y_s},$$

$$(2C\text{-}18) \quad i_d^{YY} = \left[\frac{1}{(1-2\gamma)^2\nu + 2\delta}\right]u_d + \left[\frac{1-(1-2\gamma)\epsilon}{(1-2\gamma)^2\nu + 2\delta} - 1\right]x_d$$
$$- \left[\frac{1}{A+1}\right]\left[\frac{1-(1-2\gamma)\epsilon}{(1-2\gamma)^2\nu + 2\delta} - A\right]\overline{p+y_d}.$$

Now we compare the effects of shocks on i_s and i_d under the CC regime pair given by equations 2C-15 and 2C-16 with those under the YY regime given by equations 2C-17 and 2C-18. For either a symmetric or asymmetric money-demand shock (v_s or v_d) and for either a symmetric or asymmetric goods-demand shock (u_s or u_d), i_s and i_d change by the same amounts under the CC and YY regime pairs.

For a symmetric productivity shock (x_s), the results depend on whether the absolute value of the slope of the AD_s schedule under the YY pair $[(1 - \epsilon)/\nu]$ is greater or less than one. If $(1 - \epsilon)/\nu > 1$, i_s changes in the same direction under both pairs, and the absolute value of the change in i_s is greater under the CC pair. If $(1 - \epsilon)/\nu < 1$, i_s changes in opposite directions under the two pairs, and the absolute value of the change in i_s is greater or less under the CC pair depending on whether $(1 - \epsilon)/\nu$ is greater or less than $1/2$.

Similarly, for an asymmetric productivity shock (x_d), the results depend on whether the absolute value of the slope of the AD_d schedule under the YY pair $\{[1 - (1 - 2\gamma)\epsilon]/[(1 - 2\gamma)^2\nu + 2\delta]\}$ is greater or less than one. If $[1 - (1 - 2\gamma)\epsilon]/[(1 - 2\gamma)^2\nu + 2\delta] > 1$, i_d changes in the same direction under both pairs, and the absolute value of the change is greater under the CC pair. If $[1 - (1 - 2\gamma)\epsilon]/[(1 - 2\gamma)^2\nu + 2\delta] < 1$, i_d changes in opposite directions under the two pairs, and the absolute value of the change is greater or less under the CC pair depending on whether $[1-(1-2\gamma)\epsilon]/[(1-2\gamma)^2\nu+2\delta]$ is greater or less than $1/2$.

Now we interpret the results for nominal interest rates for symmetric shocks. For symmetric money-demand and goods-demand shocks, stabilizing the sum of nominal incomes ($p_s + y_s = 0$) implies stabilizing both the sum of outputs ($y_s = 0$) and the sum of output prices ($p_s = 0$) under both the CC and YY regime pairs. The same change in r_s is required to keep the sum of excess demands for goods equal to zero under both regime pairs. Under the CC pair, private agents expect the sum of output prices to remain at its post-shock level next period ($p_{s,+1|} = p_s$), so $r_s = i_s$, as shown by equation 2C-7. In contrast, under the YY pair, private agents expect the sum of output prices to return to its pre-shock level of zero next period ($p_{s,+1|} = 0$), so $r_s = i_s + p_s$ as shown by equation 2-24. However, stabilizing nominal incomes implies that $p_s = 0$; that is, the sums of pre-shock and post-shock output prices are the same. Therefore, the same change in i_s is needed to achieve the required change in r_s under both the CC and YY regime pairs.

For symmetric decreases in productivity, stabilizing the sum of nominal incomes implies allowing a decrease in y_s and an increase in p_s both of which are equal in absolute value to the increase in x_s under both regime pairs. The same rise in r_s is required to keep the sum of excess demands for goods equal to zero under both regime pairs.

Under the CC pair, the rise in p_s does not affect r_s from equation 2C-7. Therefore, i_s must rise by the full amount needed to achieve the required rise in r_s.

In contrast, under the YY pair, the rise in p_s causes a rise in r_s from equation 2-24, and, as stated above, the results depend on whether the absolute value of the slope of the AD_s schedule under the YY pair is greater or less than one. If the absolute value of the slope is greater than one, the rise in

r_s caused by the rise in p_s is less than the required rise. Therefore, i_s must increase under the YY pair, but only by enough that the sum of the increases in i_s and p_s is equal to the required rise in r_s. Therefore, the rise in i_s must be smaller under the YY pair than under the CC pair. For the parameters used to generate the simulation results reported in table 2-12, the absolute value of the slope is greater than one; hence i and $\overset{*}{i}$ increase under both the CC and YY pairs, and they increase by more under the CC pair.

If the absolute value of the slope of the AD_s schedule is less than one, the rise in r_s caused by the rise in p_s under the YY pair is more than the required rise. Therefore, i_s must fall under the YY pair by enough to make the sum of the decrease in i_s and the rise in p_s equal to the required rise in r_s. In this case, the rise in i_s under the CC pair may be greater or less in absolute value than the fall in i_s under the YY pair, depending on whether the absolute value of the slope of the AD_s schedule is greater or less than $1/2$.

Appendix D: Reduced Forms for Sums and Differences

Sums: Reduced Forms for y_s, αn_s, and q_s

II Regime

(2D-1) $$By_s^{\text{II}} = u_s - \nu(A + 1)x_s - \nu \bar{i}_s$$

(2D-2) $$B\alpha n_s^{\text{II}} = u_s + Cx_s - \nu \bar{i}_s$$

(2D-3) $$Bq_s^{\text{II}} = Au_s + (B + AC)x_s - A\nu \bar{i}_s$$

MM Regime

(2D-4) $$\lambda E y_s^{\text{MM}} = -\nu v_s + \lambda u_s - \nu(1 + \lambda)(A + 1)x_s + \nu \bar{m}_s$$

(2D-5) $$\lambda E \alpha n_s^{\text{MM}} = -\nu v_s + \lambda u_s + [\lambda C + \nu(\phi - 1)]x_s + \nu \bar{m}_s$$

(2D-6) $$\lambda E q_s^{\text{MM}} = -A\nu v_s + \lambda A u_s + [\lambda E + \lambda CA + \nu(\phi - 1)A]x_s + A\nu \bar{m}_s$$

YY Regime

(2D-7) $$(A + 1)y_s^{\text{YY}} = -(A + 1)x_s + \overline{p + y}_s$$

(2D-8) $$(A + 1)\alpha n_s^{\text{YY}} = \overline{p + y}_s$$

(2D-9) $$(A + 1)q_s^{\text{YY}} = (A + 1)x_s + A(\overline{p + y}_s)$$

Definitions of combinations of parameters

$$A = (1 - \alpha)/\alpha\sigma > 0 \qquad D = A + \phi$$

$$B = 1 - \epsilon + \nu A > 0 \qquad E = 1 - \epsilon + \nu[A + (A + \phi)/\lambda] > 0$$

$$C = 1 - \epsilon - \nu \gtrless 0$$

Differences: Reduced Forms for y_d, αn_d, and q_d

II Regime

(2D-10)
$$G y_d^{\text{II}} = u_d - (A+1)F x_d - F \bar{\imath}_d$$

(2D-11)
$$G \alpha n_d^{\text{II}} = u_d + H x_d - F \bar{\imath}_d$$

(2D-12)
$$G q_d^{\text{II}} = (1 - 2\gamma) A u_d + (1 - 2\gamma)(G + AH) x_d$$
$$-[(1 - 2\gamma)AF + 2\gamma G] \bar{\imath}_d$$

MM Regime

(2D-13)
$$\lambda J y_d^{\text{MM}} = -F v_d + \lambda u_d + F(1 + \lambda)(A + 1) x_d + F \bar{m}_d$$

(2D-14)
$$\lambda J \alpha n_d^{\text{MM}} = -F v_d + \lambda u_d + [\lambda H + F(\phi - 1)] x_d + F \bar{m}_d$$

(2D-15)
$$\lambda J q_d^{\text{MM}} = -K v_d + L u_d + [(1 - 2\gamma)\lambda J$$
$$+ (\phi - 1)K + HL] x_d + K \bar{m}_d$$

YY Regime

(2D-16)
$$(A + 1)F y_d^{\text{YY}} = -(A + 1)F x_d + F(\overline{p + y_d})$$

(2D-17)
$$(A + 1)F \alpha n_d^{\text{YY}} = F(\overline{p + y_d})$$

(2D-18)
$$(A + 1)F q_d^{\text{YY}} = -2\gamma(A + 1)u_d$$
$$+ [(1 - 2\gamma)F - 2\gamma H](A + 1) x_d$$
$$+ [(1 - 2\gamma)AF - 2\gamma G]\overline{p + y_d}$$

Definitions of combinations of parameters

$$A = (1 - \alpha)/\alpha\sigma > 0 \qquad\qquad J = 1 - (1 - 2\gamma)\epsilon + F(A + D/\lambda) > 0$$

$$F = (1 - 2\gamma)^2 \nu + 2\delta > 0 \qquad D = A + \phi$$

$$G = 1 - (1 - 2\gamma)\epsilon + AF > 0 \qquad K = (1 - 2\gamma)AF + 2\gamma G > 0$$

$$H = 1 - (1 - 2\gamma)\epsilon - F \gtrless 0 \qquad L = (1 - 2\gamma)\lambda A - 2\gamma D \gtrless 0$$

Appendix E. Rankings of Regime Pairs under the Contract Hypothesis

Table 2E-1. *Rankings of Regime Pairs for Symmetric Shocks with $\phi = 1$[a]*

Goal variables	Assumption[b]	Money demand (v_s)	Goods demand (u_s)	Productivity (x_s)
Employment ($n, \hat{n}$)	| slope AD_s | > 1	$II \underset{p}{=} YY \underset{p}{\gtrsim} MM \underset{p}{=} ME$	$YY \underset{p}{\gtrsim} MM \underset{p}{=} ME \underset{p}{\gtrsim} II$	$YY \underset{p}{\gtrsim} MM \underset{p}{=} ME \underset{p}{\gtrsim} II$
	| slope AD_s | < 1	$II \underset{p}{=} YY \underset{p}{\gtrsim} MM \underset{p}{=} ME$	$YY \underset{p}{\gtrsim} MM \underset{p}{=} ME \underset{p}{\gtrsim} II$	$YY \underset{p}{\gtrsim} MM \underset{p}{=} ME \underset{p}{\gtrsim} II$
Consumer prices ($q, \hat{q}$)	| slope AD_s | > 1	Same as for $n, \hat{n}$	Same as for $n, \hat{n}$	$YY \underset{p}{\gtrsim} MM \underset{p}{=} ME \underset{p}{\gtrsim} II$
	| slope AD_s | < 1	Same as for $n, \hat{n}$	Same as for $n, \hat{n}$	$II \underset{p}{\gtrsim} MM \underset{p}{=} ME \underset{p}{\gtrsim} YY$

Key: $\underset{p}{\gtrsim}$ means "dominates"; $\underset{p}{=}$ means "ranks the same as."

a. ϕ is the income elasticity of money demand in both regions.

b. \| slope AD_s \| is the absolute value of the slope of the aggregate demand schedule in the model of sums of variables.

Table 2E-2. *Rankings of Regime Pairs for Asymmetric Shocks with $\phi = 1$[a]*

Goal variable	Assumptions[b]	γ	Money demand (v_d)	Goods demand (u_d)	Productivity (x_d)
US employment (n)	|slope AD_d| > 1	$\gamma = 0$	$II \underset{p}{=} YY \underset{p}{\gtrsim} ME \underset{p}{\gtrsim} MM$	$YY \underset{p}{\gtrsim} MM \underset{p}{\gtrsim} ME \underset{p}{\gtrsim} II$	$YY \underset{p}{\gtrsim} MM \underset{p}{\gtrsim} II$
		$\gamma = \frac{1}{2}$	$II \underset{p}{=} YY \underset{p}{\gtrsim} ME \underset{p}{\lessgtr} MM$	$YY \underset{p}{\gtrsim} MM \underset{p}{\lessgtr} ME \underset{p}{\gtrsim} II$	$YY \underset{p}{\gtrsim} MM \underset{p}{\gtrsim} II$
	|slope AD_d| < 1	$\gamma = 0$	$II \underset{p}{=} YY \underset{p}{\gtrsim} ME \underset{p}{\gtrsim} MM$	$YY \underset{p}{\gtrsim} MM \underset{p}{\gtrsim} ME \underset{p}{\gtrsim} II$	$YY \underset{p}{\gtrsim} MM \underset{p}{\gtrsim} II$
		$\gamma = \frac{1}{2}$	$II \underset{p}{=} YY \underset{p}{\gtrsim} ME \underset{p}{\lessgtr} MM$	$YY \underset{p}{\gtrsim} MM \underset{p}{\lessgtr} ME \underset{p}{\gtrsim} II$	$YY \underset{p}{\gtrsim} MM \underset{p}{\gtrsim} II$
US consumer price (q)	|slope AD_d| > 1	$\gamma = 0$	Same as for n	Same as for n	$YY \underset{p}{\gtrsim} MM \underset{p}{\gtrsim} II$
		$\gamma = \frac{1}{2}$	$II \underset{p}{=} YY \underset{p}{\gtrsim} ME \underset{p}{\lessgtr} MM$	$II \underset{p}{\gtrsim} MM \underset{p}{\lessgtr} ME > YY$	$II \underset{p}{\gtrsim} MM \underset{p}{\gtrsim} YY$
	|slope AD_d| < 1	$\gamma = 0$	Same as for n	Same as for n	$II \underset{p}{\gtrsim} MM \underset{p}{\gtrsim} YY$
		$\gamma = \frac{1}{2}$	$II \underset{p}{=} YY \underset{p}{\gtrsim} ME \underset{p}{\lessgtr} MM$	$II \underset{p}{\gtrsim} MM \underset{p}{\lessgtr} ME \underset{p}{\gtrsim} YY$	$II \underset{p}{\gtrsim} MM \underset{p}{\gtrsim} YY$
ROECD employment ($\hat{n}$)	|slope AD_d| > 1	$\gamma = 0$	$II \underset{p}{=} YY \underset{p}{\gtrsim} ME \underset{p}{\gtrsim} MM$	$YY \underset{p}{\gtrsim} MM \underset{p}{\gtrsim} II \underset{p}{\gtrsim} ME$	$YY \underset{p}{\gtrsim} MM \underset{p}{\gtrsim} II$
		$\gamma = \frac{1}{2}$	$II \underset{p}{=} YY \underset{p}{\gtrsim} ME \underset{p}{\lessgtr} MM$	$YY \underset{p}{\gtrsim} MM \underset{p}{\gtrsim} II \underset{p}{\gtrsim} ME$	$YY \underset{p}{\gtrsim} MM \underset{p}{\gtrsim} II$
	|slope AD_d| < 1	$\gamma = 0$	$II \underset{p}{=} YY \underset{p}{\gtrsim} ME \underset{p}{\gtrsim} MM$	$YY \underset{p}{\gtrsim} MM \underset{p}{\gtrsim} II \underset{p}{\gtrsim} ME$	$YY \underset{p}{\gtrsim} MM \underset{p}{\gtrsim} II$
		$\gamma = \frac{1}{2}$	$II \underset{p}{=} YY \underset{p}{\gtrsim} ME \underset{p}{\lessgtr} MM$	$YY \underset{p}{\gtrsim} MM \underset{p}{\gtrsim} II \underset{p}{\gtrsim} ME$	$YY \underset{p}{\gtrsim} MM \underset{p}{\gtrsim} II$
ROECD consumer price ($\hat{q}$)	|slope AD_d| > 1	$\gamma = 0$	Same as for $\hat{n}$	Same as for $\hat{n}$	$YY \underset{p}{\gtrsim} MM \underset{p}{\gtrsim} II$
		$\gamma = \frac{1}{2}$	$II \underset{p}{=} YY \underset{p}{\gtrsim} ME \underset{p}{\lessgtr} MM$	$II \underset{p}{\gtrsim} MM \underset{p}{\lessgtr} ME \underset{p}{\gtrsim} YY$	$II \underset{p}{\gtrsim} MM \underset{p}{\gtrsim} YY$
	|slope AD_d| < 1	$\gamma = 0$	Same as for $\hat{n}$	Same as for $\hat{n}$	$II \underset{p}{\gtrsim} MM \underset{p}{\gtrsim} YY$
		$\gamma = \frac{1}{2}$	$II \underset{p}{=} YY \underset{p}{\gtrsim} ME \underset{p}{\lessgtr} MM$	$II \underset{p}{\gtrsim} MM \underset{p}{\lessgtr} ME \underset{p}{\gtrsim} YY$	$II \underset{p}{\gtrsim} MM \underset{p}{\gtrsim} YY$

Key: $\underset{p}{\gtrsim}$ means "dominates"; $\underset{p}{=}$ means "ranks the same as"; $\underset{p}{\lessgtr}$ means "is not rankable relative to."

a. ϕ is the income elasticity of money demand in both regions.

b. \|slope AD_d\| is the absolute value of the slope of the aggregate demand schedule in the model of differences between variables. γ is the average and marginal propensity to import.

Table 2E-3. *Rankings of Regime Pairs for Region-Specific Shocks in the US, with* $\phi = 1$ *and* $|slope\ AD_s|$ *and* $|slope\ AD_d| > 1^a$

Goal variables	Assumption[b]	Type of shock		
		Money demand (v)	Goods demand (u)	Productivity (x)
US employment (n)	$\gamma = 0$	$II \underset{p}{=} YY \underset{p}{\gtrsim} ME \underset{p}{\gtrsim} MM$	$YY \underset{p}{\gtrsim} MM \underset{p}{\gtrsim} II$	$YY \underset{p}{\gtrsim} MM \underset{p}{\gtrsim} II$
	$\gamma = 1/2$	$II \underset{p}{=} YY \underset{p}{\gtrsim} ME \underset{p}{\gtrless} MM$	$YY \underset{p}{\gtrsim} MM \underset{p}{\gtrsim} II$	$YY \underset{p}{\gtrsim} MM \underset{p}{\gtrsim} II$
US consumer price (q)	$\gamma = 0$	Same as for n	Same as for n	$YY \underset{p}{\gtrsim} MM \underset{p}{\gtrsim} II$
	$\gamma = 1/2$	$II \underset{p}{=} YY \underset{p}{\gtrsim} ME \underset{p}{\lesssim} MM$	$II \underset{p}{\lesssim} MM \underset{p}{\lesssim} YY$	$II \underset{p}{\lesssim} MM \underset{p}{\lesssim} YY$
ROECD employment (ñ)	$\gamma = 0$	$II \underset{p}{=} YY \underset{p}{\gtrsim} ME \underset{p}{\lesssim} MM$	$YY \underset{p}{\gtrsim} MM \underset{p}{\lesssim} II$	$YY \underset{p}{\gtrsim} MM \underset{p}{\lesssim} II$
	$\gamma = 1/2$	$II \underset{p}{=} YY \underset{p}{\gtrsim} ME \underset{p}{\lesssim} MM$	$YY \underset{p}{\gtrsim} MM \underset{p}{\lesssim} II$	$YY \underset{p}{\gtrsim} MM \underset{p}{\lesssim} II$
ROECD consumer price (q̃)	$\gamma = 0$	Same as for ñ	Same as for ñ	Same as for ñ
	$\gamma = 1/2$	$II \underset{p}{=} YY \underset{p}{\gtrsim} ME \underset{p}{\lesssim} MM$	$II \underset{p}{\lesssim} MM \underset{p}{\lesssim} YY$	$II \underset{p}{\lesssim} MM \underset{p}{\lesssim} YY$

Key: $\underset{p}{\gtrsim}$ means "dominates"; $\underset{p}{=}$ means "ranks the same as"; $\underset{p}{\gtrless}$ means "is not rankable relative to."

a. ϕ is the income elasticity of money demand in both regions. $|slope\ AD_s|$ and $|slope\ AD_d|$ are, respectively, the absolute values of the slopes of the aggregate demand schedule in the model of sums of variables and in the model of differences between variables.

b. γ is the average and marginal propensity to import.

Table 2E-4. *Rankings of Regime Pairs for Region-Specific Shocks in the ROECD with* $\phi = 1$ *and* $|slope\ AD_s|$ *and* $|slope\ AD_d| > 1^a$

Goal variables	Assumption[b]	Type of shock		
		Money demand (v̌)	Goods demand (ǔ)	Productivity (x̌)
US employment (n)	$\gamma = 0$	$II \underset{p}{=} YY \underset{p}{=} ME \underset{p}{\gtrsim} MM$	$YY \underset{p}{\gtrsim} MM \underset{p}{\lesssim} II$	$YY \underset{p}{\gtrsim} MM \underset{p}{\lesssim} II$
	$\gamma = 1/2$	$II \underset{p}{=} YY \underset{p}{=} ME \underset{p}{\gtrsim} MM$	$YY \underset{p}{\gtrsim} MM \underset{p}{\lesssim} II$	$YY \underset{p}{\gtrsim} MM \underset{p}{\lesssim} II$
US consumer price (q)	$\gamma = 0$	Same as for n	Same as for n	Same as for n
	$\gamma = 1/2$	$II \underset{p}{=} YY \underset{p}{=} ME \underset{p}{\gtrsim} MM$	$II \underset{p}{\lesssim} MM \underset{p}{\lesssim} YY$	$II \underset{p}{\lesssim} MM \underset{p}{\lesssim} YY$
ROECD employment (ñ)	$\gamma = 0$	$II \underset{p}{=} YY \underset{p}{=} ME \underset{p}{\gtrsim} MM$	$YY \underset{p}{\gtrsim} MM \underset{p}{\gtrsim} II$	$YY \underset{p}{\gtrsim} MM \underset{p}{\gtrsim} II$
	$\gamma = 1/2$	$II \underset{p}{=} YY \underset{p}{=} ME \underset{p}{\gtrsim} MM$	$YY \underset{p}{\gtrsim} MM \underset{p}{\gtrsim} II$	$YY \underset{p}{\gtrsim} MM \underset{p}{\gtrsim} II$
ROECD consumer price (q̃)	$\gamma = 0$	Same as for ñ	Same as for ñ	$YY \underset{p}{\gtrsim} MM \underset{p}{\gtrsim} II$
	$\gamma = 1/2$	$II \underset{p}{=} YY \underset{p}{=} ME \underset{p}{\gtrsim} MM$	$II \underset{p}{\lesssim} MM \underset{p}{\lesssim} YY$	$II \underset{p}{\lesssim} MM \underset{p}{\lesssim} YY$

Key: $\underset{p}{\gtrsim}$ means "dominates"; $\underset{p}{=}$ means "ranks the same as."

a. ϕ is the income elasticity of money demand in both regions. $|slope\ AD_s|$ and $|slope\ AD_d|$ are, respectively, the absolute values of the slopes of the aggregate demand schedule in the model of sums of variables and in the model of differences between variables.

b. γ is the average and marginal propensity to import.

Appendix F: The Effect of an Increase in Demand for US Money on ROECD Employment under the MM Regime Pair

In this appendix, we explain in more detail why $\overset{*}{n}{}^{MM}_v$ may be either positive or negative. In particular, we interpret the expressions for $\alpha n^{MM}_{s,v_s}$ and $\alpha n^{MM}_{d,v_d}$ in equation 2-58 in table 2-14.

First we consider $\alpha n^{MM}_{s,v_s}$, noting that with no productivity shock $\alpha n_s = y_s$. The total reduction in αn_s caused by a unit increase in v_s is equal to the impact effect of a unit increase in v_s on the sum of excess demands for goods $(-\nu/\lambda)$ divided by the sum of the direct and indirect effects of a unit fall in y_s and the associated fall in p_s on this sum $[E = 1 - \epsilon + \nu(A + D/\lambda)]$. On impact, a unit increase in v_s causes i_s to rise by $1/\lambda$ and, therefore, causes the sum of excess demands to fall by ν/λ because r_s rises. Thus, a fall in y_s and the associated fall in p_s are required in order to raise the sum of excess demands back to zero. A one-unit fall in y_s increases the sum of excess demands directly by $1 - \epsilon$ because it reduces the sum of supplies by more than the sum of demands; the associated fall in p_s increases this sum directly by νA because it lowers r_s. These falls in y_s and p_s also cause i_s to fall by D/λ, so they increase the sum of excess demands indirectly by $\nu D/\lambda$ because they lower r_s.

Now we consider $\alpha n^{MM}_{d,v_d}$, recalling that with no productivity shock $\alpha n_d = y_d$. The total reduction in $\alpha n_d = y_d$ caused by a unit increase in v_d is equal to the impact effect of a unit increase in v_d on the difference between excess demands for goods $\{-\nu[(1 - 2\gamma)^2 + 2\delta/\nu]/\lambda\}$ divided by the sum of the direct and indirect effects of a unit fall in y_d and the associated fall in p_d on this difference $\{J = 1 - (1 - 2\gamma)\epsilon + \nu[(1 - 2\gamma)^2 + 2\delta/\nu](A + D/\lambda)\}$. On impact, a unit increase in v_d causes i_d to rise by $1/\lambda$ and, therefore, causes the sum of excess demands to fall by $\nu[(1 - 2\gamma)^2 + 2\delta/\nu]/\lambda$ because r_d rises and the dollar appreciates in real terms. A one-unit fall in y_d increases the difference between excess demands directly by $1 - (1 - 2\gamma)\epsilon$ because it reduces the difference between supplies by more than the difference between demands, and the associated fall in p_d increases this difference directly by $\nu[(1 - 2\gamma)^2 + 2\delta/\nu]A$ because it reduces r_d and causes the dollar to depreciate in real terms. These falls in y_d and p_d also cause i_d to fall by D/λ, so they increase the difference between excess demands indirectly by $\nu[(1 - 2\gamma)^2 + 2\delta/\nu] D/\lambda$ because they lower r_d and cause the dollar to depreciate in real terms.

For large enough δ/ν, $\overset{*}{n}{}^{MM}_v$ is positive, so US money-demand shocks have a negative transmission effect on ROECD employment. $\alpha n^{MM}_{d,v_d}$ rises without limit in absolute value as δ/ν rises without limit, so there must be a value of δ/ν large enough that n^{MM}_{d,v_d} is greater than n^{MM}_{s,v_s} in absolute value. An increase in δ/ν raises by the same proportion the absolute value of the impact effect of a unit increase in v_d on the difference between the excess demands for goods $\{\nu[(1 - 2\gamma)^2 + 2\delta/\nu]\lambda\}$ and the sum of the direct effects of a rise in p_d associated with a unit rise in y_d, as well as the indirect effects of a unit rise in y_d and the associated rise in p_d on the difference between excess demands $\{\nu[(1 - 2\gamma)^2 + 2\delta/\nu](A + D/\lambda)\}$. However, it does not affect the direct effect of an increase in y_d on the difference between excess demands $[1 - (1 - 2\gamma)\epsilon]$.

For small enough δ/ν, $\overset{*}{n}{}_v^{MM}$ is negative, so US money-demand shocks have a positive transmission effect on ROECD employment. For example, if δ/ν is small enough for the impact effects of unit increases in v_s and v_d on the sum of and difference between excess demands to be the same $\{[(1 - 2\gamma)^2 + 2\delta/\nu] = 1\}$, n_{s,v_s}^{MM} is greater than n_{d,v_d}^{MM} in absolute value. In this case, the sum of the direct effects of a rise in p_d associated with a unit rise in y_d and the indirect effects of a unit rise in y_d and the associated rise in p_d on the difference between excess demands $\{\nu[(1 - 2\gamma)^2 + 2\delta/\nu](A + D/\lambda)\}$ is the same as the sum of the direct effects of a rise in p_s associated with a unit rise in y_s and the indirect effects of a unit rise in y_s and the associated rise in p_s on the sum of excess demands $\nu(A + D/\lambda)$. However, the direct effect of a unit increase in y_d on the difference between excess demands $[1 - (1 - 2\gamma)\epsilon]$ is greater than the direct effect of a unit increase in y_s on the sum of excess demands $(1 - \epsilon)$.

Appendix G: The Effects of an Increase in the Demand for US Goods on ROECD Employment under the II and MM Regime Pairs

In this appendix, we provide derivations and interpretations of the terms which determine the signs of $\overset{*}{n}_u^{II}$ and $\overset{*}{n}_u^{MM}$. According to equations 2-59 and 2-60 in table 2-17, $\overset{*}{n}_u^{II}$ and $\overset{*}{n}_u^{MM}$ are positive if and only if $\gamma\epsilon + NA$ and $\gamma\epsilon + N(A + D/\lambda)$, respectively, are positive, where N, A, and D are defined in appendix A.

The term $\gamma\epsilon + NA$ represents the effect of the increases in y and p associated with a unit increase in αn on the excess demand for ROECD goods under the II regime pair. It can be obtained by substituting the expressions for $q_{+1|}$ and $\overset{*}{q}_{+1|}$ from equation 2-20 and the second expressions for q and $\overset{*}{q}$ from equations 2-6 into equations 2-10, substituting the resulting expressions for r and $\overset{*}{r}$ into the second equation in equations 2-13 with $\beta = 0$, and eliminating z, y, and p from the resulting expression using equations 2-22 and 2G-1 and 2G-2, respectively, where

(2G-1) $$y = \alpha n - x,$$

(2G-2) $$p = A\alpha n + x,$$

are obtained from equations 2-1 and 2-3 with $\beta = 0$ and equation 2-21.

$\gamma\epsilon + NA$ can be broken into two components: (1) the increase in excess demand resulting from the increase in y ($\gamma\epsilon > 0$), and (2) the ambiguous effect on excess demand resulting from the rise in $i + p$ induced by the increase in p $\{[-2(1-\gamma)\gamma\nu + \delta]A \gtreqless 0\}$. The rise in $i + p$ tends to reduce excess demand by causing r to rise $[-2(1-\gamma)\gamma\nu A < 0]$ and tends to increase excess demand by causing the dollar to appreciate in real terms ($\delta A > 0$). In the text we assume that $\gamma\epsilon + NA$ is positive, as it is for the parameter values in appendix A, since $\overset{*}{n}_u^{II}$ is positive in the simulation results in table 2-18.

The term $\gamma\epsilon + N(A + D/\lambda)$ represents the effect of the increases in y and p associated with a unit increase in αn on the excess demand for ROECD goods under the MM pair. It can be obtained by substituting the expressions for $q_{+1|}$ and $\overset{*}{q}_{+1|}$ from equation 2-20 and the second expressions for q and $\overset{*}{q}$ from equations 2-6 into equations 2-10, substituting the resulting expressions for r and $\overset{*}{r}$ into the second equation in equations 2-13 with $\beta = 0$, and eliminating z, i, y, and p from the resulting expression using equations 2-22, 2G-3, 2G-1, and 2G-2, respectively, where

(2G-3) $$i = (1/\lambda)p + (\phi/\lambda)y + (1/\lambda)v - (1/\lambda)m$$

is obtained by rearranging the first equation in equation 2-12.

$\gamma\epsilon + N(A + D/\lambda)$ can be broken into three components. The first two are the two components of $\gamma\epsilon + NA$ discussed above. There is one more: (3) the ambiguous effect on excess demand resulting from the additional rise in $i + p$ caused by the rise in i induced by the the rises in y and p $\{[-2(1 - \gamma)\gamma\nu + \delta]D/\lambda \gtreqless 0\}$. The additional rise in $i + p$ tends to reduce excess demand by causing r to rise $[-2(1 - \gamma)\gamma\nu D/\lambda < 0]$ and tends to increase excess demand by causing the dollar to appreciate in real terms $[\delta D/\lambda > 0]$. In the text we assume that $\gamma\epsilon + N(A + D/\lambda)$ is positive, as it is for the parameter values in appendix A, since $\overset{\star}{n}_u^{\mathrm{MM}}$ is positive in the simulation results in table 2-18.

Appendix H: The Effects of a Region-Specific Productivity Shock under the II, MM, and YY Regime Pairs

In this appendix, we demonstrate that, for a shock to US productivity, for US and ROECD employments the ranking of the MM and the II pairs depends on parameter values, and that for the US and ROECD CPIs, all rankings depend on parameter values.

Expressions for n_x^{II} and n_x^{MM} are given in equations 2H-1 and 2H-2:

(2H-1)
$$2\alpha n_x^{II} = \left[\frac{C}{B}\right] + \left[\frac{H}{G}\right],$$

(2H-2)
$$2\alpha n_x^{MM} = \left[\frac{C - (1 - \phi)v/\lambda}{E}\right] + \left[\frac{H - (1 - \phi)F/\lambda}{J}\right]$$

$$= \left[\frac{C}{E}\right] + \left[\frac{H}{J}\right] - (1 - \phi)\left[\frac{v/\lambda}{E}\right] + \left[\frac{F/\lambda}{J}\right],$$

$$C = 1 - \epsilon - v, \quad H = 1 - (1 - 2\gamma)\epsilon - [(1 - 2\gamma)^2 v + 2\delta].$$

Note that the slope of the AD_s schedule of equation 2-29 $[-(1 - \epsilon)/v]$ is greater than one in absolute value if and only if $C > 0$, that the slope of the AD_d schedule of equation 2-40 $\{-[1 - (1 - 2\gamma)\epsilon]/[(1 - 2\gamma)^2 v + 2\delta]\}$ is greater than one in absolute value if and only if $H > 0$, and that the slopes of the M_s schedule of equation 2-30 and the M_d schedule of equation 2-41 $(-\phi)$ are steeper than, equal to, or flatter than minus one as $1 - \phi \gtreqless 0$.

Consider the case in which $C, H > 0$ so that the slopes of the AD_s and AD_d schedules are both greater than one in absolute value. In this case n_x^{II} is always positive, and n_x^{MM} is positive if $1 - \phi$ is small enough that the slopes of the M_s and M_d schedules are close enough to minus one. If $n_x^{MM} > 0$, then $n_x^{II} > n_x^{MM}$, since $B < E$ and $G < J$. For the parameter values used in the simulations, $C, H > 0$, and $1 - \phi = 0$, and in the simulation results in table 2-20, n_x^{II} and n_x^{MM} are both positive, with n_x^{II} larger.

However, if $n_x^{MM} < 0$, then n_x^{MM} may be larger than n_x^{II} in absolute value. For example, if $C = H = 0$ and $1 - \phi > 0$ then $|n_x^{MM}| > |n_x^{II}| = 0$.

Expressions for $\overset{\star}{n}_x^{II}$ and $\overset{\star}{n}_x^{MM}$ are given by equations 2H-3 and 2H-4:

(2H-3)
$$2\alpha \overset{\star}{n}_x^{II} = \left[\frac{C}{B}\right] - \left[\frac{H}{G}\right] = \left[\frac{1 - \epsilon - v}{1 - \epsilon + vA}\right]$$

$$- \left[\frac{1 - (1 - 2\gamma)\epsilon - v[(1 - 2\gamma)^2 + 2\delta/v]}{1 - (1 - 2\gamma)\epsilon + v[(1 - 2\gamma)^2 + 2\delta/v]A}\right]$$

$$= \frac{2}{BG} \nu\{(1 - \epsilon)[\delta/\nu - 2(1 - \gamma)\gamma] - \epsilon\gamma\} = \left[\frac{2}{BG}\right]M.$$

(2H-4) $2\alpha \overset{\star}{n}_x^{\mathrm{MM}} = \left[\dfrac{C - (1 - \phi)\nu/\lambda}{E}\right] - \left[\dfrac{H - (1 - \phi)F/\lambda}{J}\right]$

$$= \left[\frac{C}{E}\right] - \left[\frac{H}{J}\right] - (1 - \phi)\left[\frac{\nu/\lambda}{E} - \frac{F/\lambda}{J}\right]$$

$$= \left[\frac{1 - \epsilon - \nu}{1 - \epsilon + \nu(A + D/\lambda)}\right]$$

$$- \left[\frac{1 - (1 - 2\gamma)\epsilon - [(1 - 2\gamma)^2\nu + 2\delta]}{1 - (1 - 2\gamma)\epsilon + [(1 - 2\gamma)^2\nu + 2\delta](A + D/\lambda)}\right]$$

$$+ (1 - \phi)2\alpha \overset{\star}{n}_v^{\mathrm{MM}}$$

$$= \left[\frac{2(1 + D/\lambda) + (1 - \phi)/\lambda}{EJ}\right]$$

$$\times \nu\{(1 - \epsilon)[\delta/\nu - 2(1 - \gamma)\gamma] - \epsilon\gamma\}$$

$$= \left[\frac{2(1 + D/\lambda) + (1 - \phi)/\lambda}{EJ}\right]M.$$

The signs of both $\overset{\star}{n}_x^{\mathrm{II}}$ and $\overset{\star}{n}_x^{\mathrm{MM}}$ depend on the sign of M as does the sign of $\overset{\star}{n}_v^{\mathrm{MM}}$ (which we discuss in the text when we analyze a region-specific shock to money demand).[92] The sign of M depends critically on the ratio δ/ν, which we define in the discussion of $\overset{\star}{n}_v^{\mathrm{MM}}$.[93] Both $\overset{\star}{n}_x^{\mathrm{II}}$ and $\overset{\star}{n}_x^{\mathrm{MM}}$ are positive for large enough δ/ν, and both are negative for small enough δ/ν.

No matter what the signs of $\overset{\star}{n}_x^{\mathrm{II}}$ and $\overset{\star}{n}_x^{\mathrm{MM}}$, their ranking depends on parameter values. Consider the case in which $1 - \phi = 0$. In this case, the difference between $\overset{\star}{n}_x^{\mathrm{II}}$ and $\overset{\star}{n}_x^{\mathrm{MM}}$ is given by equation 2H-5:

(2H-5) $\quad 2\alpha \left[\overset{\star}{n}_x^{\mathrm{II}} - \overset{\star}{n}_x^{\mathrm{MM}}\right] = \alpha\left(\left[n_{s,u_s}^{\mathrm{II}} C - n_{d,u_d}^{\mathrm{II}} H\right]\right.$

$$\left. - \left[n_{s,u_s}^{\mathrm{MM}} C - n_{d,u_d}^{\mathrm{MM}} H\right]\right)$$

$$= \left[\frac{1}{B} - \frac{1}{E}\right]C - \left[\frac{1}{G} - \frac{1}{J}\right]H$$

92. We have not yet discovered an intuitively appealing explanation for why the signs of $\overset{\star}{n}_x^{\mathrm{II}}$, $\overset{\star}{n}_x^{\mathrm{MM}}$, and $\overset{\star}{n}_v^{\mathrm{MM}}$ all depend on M. n_v^{MM} must always be negative, while $\overset{\star}{n}_v^{\mathrm{MM}}$ may be either positive or negative. However, n_x^{II} and n_x^{MM} may be either positive or negative, and no matter what the signs of n_x^{II} and n_x^{MM}, $\overset{\star}{n}_x^{\mathrm{II}}$ and $\overset{\star}{n}_x^{\mathrm{MM}}$ may be positive or negative.

93. As shown in the next two notes, M can be either positive or negative for $C \geq 0$ and $H \geq 0$.

$$= \frac{\nu CD/\lambda}{BE} - \frac{[(1 - 2\lambda)^2 \nu + 2\delta]HD/\lambda}{GJ},$$

where C and H are defined below equation 2H-2. Suppose $M > 0$, so that both $\overset{\star}{n}_x^{\mathrm{II}}$ and $\overset{\star}{n}_x^{\mathrm{MM}}$ are positive. As an example, $\overset{\star}{n}_x^{\mathrm{II}} > \overset{\star}{n}_x^{\mathrm{MM}}$ if $C > 0$ and $H = 0$, but $\overset{\star}{n}_x^{\mathrm{II}} < \overset{\star}{n}_x^{\mathrm{MM}}$ if $\nu = 0$ and $H > 0$.[94] For the parameter values used in the simulations, $M > 0$ and $\overset{\star}{n}_x^{\mathrm{II}} < \overset{\star}{n}_x^{\mathrm{MM}}$. Now suppose $M < 0$ so that both $\overset{\star}{n}_x^{\mathrm{II}}$ and $\overset{\star}{n}_x^{\mathrm{MM}}$ are negative. $|\overset{\star}{n}_x^{\mathrm{II}}| > |\overset{\star}{n}_x^{\mathrm{MM}}|$ if $C = 0$ and $H > 0$, but $|\overset{\star}{n}_x^{\mathrm{II}}| < |\overset{\star}{n}_x^{\mathrm{MM}}|$ if $C > 0$, $\gamma = 1/2$, and $\delta = 0$.[95]

Expressions for q_x^{II}, q_x^{MM}, and q_X^{YY} are given in equations 2H-6–2H-8:

(2H-6) $2q_x^{\mathrm{II}} = 1 + A\left[\dfrac{C}{B}\right] + (1 - 2\gamma) + (1 - 2\gamma)A\left[\dfrac{H}{G}\right] > 0,$

(2H-7) $2q_x^{\mathrm{MM}} = 1 + A\left[\dfrac{C}{E}\right] - (1 - \phi)A\left[\dfrac{\nu/\lambda}{E}\right] + (1 - 2\gamma)$

$$+ \left[(1 - 2\gamma)A - \frac{2\gamma D}{\lambda}\right]\left[\frac{H}{J}\right] - (1 - \phi)\left[\frac{K}{J}\right]$$

$$= 1 + A\left[\frac{C}{E}\right] + (1 - 2\gamma)$$

$$+ \left[(1 - 2\gamma)A - \frac{2\gamma D}{\lambda}\right]\left[\frac{H}{J}\right]$$

$$- (1 - \phi)\left[\frac{A\nu/\lambda}{E} + \frac{K}{J}\right],$$

(2H-8) $2q_x^{\mathrm{YY}} = 1 + (1 - 2\gamma) - 2\gamma\left[\dfrac{H}{F}\right].$

The ranking for the US CPI, q, is $q_x^{\mathrm{II}} > q_x^{\mathrm{MM}} > q_x^{\mathrm{YY}} > 0$ if the rankings for q_s and q_d are $q_{s,x_s}^{\mathrm{II}} > q_{s,x_s}^{\mathrm{MM}} > q_{s,x_s}^{\mathrm{YY}} > 0$ and $q_{d,x_d}^{\mathrm{II}} > q_{d,x_d}^{\mathrm{MM}} > q_{d,x_d}^{\mathrm{YY}} > 0$, respectively. We establish in the text that these rankings for q_s and q_d are implied if $C, H > 0$ and $1 - \phi$ and γ are small enough. For example, they are implied if $C, H > 0$ and $1 - \phi = \gamma = 0$. They are also implied for the parameters used in the simulations since $C, H > 0$, $1 - \phi = 0$, and γ is small enough as shown by the simulation results for q_s and q_d in tables 2-12 and 2-13, and those for q in table 2-20.

94. If $H = 0$, $M = [(1 - \epsilon)/2 + \eta\gamma](1 - \epsilon - \nu)$. Now $C = 1 - \epsilon - \nu$. Therefore, $M > 0$ if and only if $C > 0$. If $\nu = 0$, $M > 0$ for any value of H.

95. If $C = 0$, $M = -\nu[\gamma + 2\gamma\nu(1 - 2\gamma) - \delta]$ and $H = 2[\gamma + \gamma\nu(1 - 2\gamma) - \delta]$, so $M < 0$ if and only if $H > 0$. If $\delta = 0$, $M < 0$ for all values of C.

The ranking for q is also $q_x^{II} > q_x^{MM} > q_x^{YY} > 0$ if the rankings for q_s and q_d are $q_{s,x_s}^{II} > q_{s,x_s}^{MM} > q_{s,x_s}^{YY} > 0$ and $|q_{d,x_d}^{YY}| \geq |q_{d,x_d}^{MM}| \geq q_{d,x_d}^{II} \geq 0$, respectively, and if $|q_{d,x_d}^{YY}|$, $|q_{d,x_d}^{MM}|$, and q_{d,x_d}^{II} are small enough. As an example, these conditions are met if $C > 0$, $\gamma = 1/2$, and $H = 1 - \phi = 0$.

However, the ranking for q is $q_x^{YY} > q_x^{MM} > q_x^{II} > 0$ if the ranking for q_s is $q_{s,x_s}^{YY} > q_{s,x_s}^{MM} > q_{s,x_s}^{II} > 0$ and the ranking for q_d is $q_{d,x_d}^{YY} > q_{d,x_d}^{MM} > q_{d,x_d}^{II} > 0$. We establish in the text that this ranking for q_s is implied if $C < 0$ but q_{s,x_s}^{YY}, q_{s,x_s}^{MM}, $q_{s,x_s}^{II} > 0$ and $1 - \phi$ is small enough and that this ranking for q_d is implied if $C < 0$ but q_{d,x_d}^{YY}, q_{d,x_d}^{MM}, $q_{d,x_d}^{II} > 0$ and $1 - \phi$ and γ are small enough. As an example, these conditions are met if C, $H < 0$; q_{s,x_s}^{YY}, q_{s,x_s}^{MM}, $q_{s,x_s}^{II} > 0$; q_{d,x_d}^{YY}, q_{d,x_d}^{MM}, $q_{d,x_d}^{II} > 0$, and $1 - \phi = \gamma = 0$.

The ranking for q is $|q_x^{YY}| > |q_x^{MM}| > q_x^{II} > 0$ if the rankings for q_s and q_d are $1 = q_{s,x_s}^{YY} \leq q_{s,x_s}^{MM} \leq q_{s,x_s}^{II}$ and $|q_{d,x_d}^{YY}| > |q_{d,x_d}^{MM}| > q_{d,x_d}^{II} \geq 0$, respectively, and if $|q_{d,x_d}^{YY}|$ and $|q_{d,x_d}^{MM}|$ are large enough. For example, these conditions are met if $H > 0$, $C = 1 - \phi = 0$, $\gamma = 1/2$, and $\left[\frac{D}{\lambda}\right]\left[\frac{H}{J}\right] > 2$.[96]

Expressions for $\overset{\star}{q}_x^{II}$, $\overset{\star}{q}_x^{MM}$, and $\overset{\star}{q}_x^{YY}$ are given in equations 2H-9–2H-11:

$$(2H\text{-}9) \qquad 2\overset{\star}{q}_x^{II} = 1 + A\left[\frac{C}{B}\right] - (1 - 2\gamma) - (1 - 2\gamma)A\left[\frac{H}{G}\right],$$

$$(2H\text{-}10)\, 2\overset{\star}{q}_x^{MM} = 1 + A\left[\frac{C}{E}\right] - (1 - \phi)A\left[\frac{v/\lambda}{E}\right] - (1 - 2\gamma)$$

$$- \left[(1 - 2\gamma)A - \frac{2\gamma D}{\lambda}\right]\left[\frac{H}{J}\right] + (1 - \phi)\left[\frac{K}{J}\right]$$

$$= 1 + A\left[\frac{C}{E}\right] - (1 - 2\gamma)$$

$$- \left[(1 - 2\gamma)A - \frac{2\gamma D}{\lambda}\right]\left[\frac{H}{J}\right] - (1 - \phi)\left[\frac{Av/\lambda}{E} - \frac{K}{J}\right],$$

$$(2H\text{-}11) \qquad 2\overset{\star}{q}_x^{YY} = 1 - (1 - 2\gamma) + 2\gamma\left[\frac{H}{F}\right].$$

96. Note that if $H > 0$, then

$$\left[\frac{H}{F}\right] - \left[\frac{D}{\lambda}\right]\left[\frac{H}{J}\right] = H\left(\left[\frac{1}{F}\right] - \left[\frac{D}{\lambda}\right]\left[\frac{1}{J}\right]\right) > 0,$$

since $J = 1 - (1 - 2\gamma)\epsilon + F(A + D/\lambda) > FD/\lambda$. Note also that if D/λ is large,

$$\left[\frac{D}{\lambda}\right]\left[\frac{1}{J}\right]$$

rises without limit as δ approaches zero.

If $\gamma = 0$, then $0 = \overset{\star}{q}{}_x^{YY} \le |\overset{\star}{q}{}_x^{II}|, |\overset{\star}{q}{}_x^{MM}|$ but $|\overset{\star}{q}{}_x^{II}| \gtreqless |\overset{\star}{q}{}_x^{MM}|$. In this case, $\overset{\star}{q}{}_x^{jj} = \overset{\star}{p}{}_x^{jj} = A\alpha \overset{\star}{n}{}_x^{jj}$; $jj = $ II, MM, YY.[97] As explained above, $\overset{\star}{n}{}_x^{YY} = 0$, and $\overset{\star}{n}{}_x^{II}$ and $\overset{\star}{n}{}_x^{MM}$ are either both positive with $\overset{\star}{n}{}_x^{II} \gtreqless \overset{\star}{n}{}_x^{MM}$ if $M > 0$, or both negative with $|\overset{\star}{n}{}_x^{II}| \gtreqless |\overset{\star}{n}{}_x^{MM}|$ if $M < 0$. If $\gamma = 1/2$, at least two rankings are possible. If $C > 0$ and $1 - \phi = H = 0$, then $q_{s,x_s}^{II} > q_{s,x_s}^{MM} > q_{s,x_s}^{YY} = 1$, and $q_{d,x_d}^{II} = q_{d,x_d}^{MM} = q_{d,x_d}^{YY} = 0$, so $\overset{\star}{q}{}_x^{II} > \overset{\star}{q}{}_x^{MM} > \overset{\star}{q}{}_x^{YY} = 1$. However, if $H > 0$ and $1 - \phi = C = 0$, then $q_{s,x_s}^{YY} = q_{s,x_s}^{MM} = q_{s,x_s}^{II} = 1$, and $q_{d,x_d}^{YY} > q_{d,x_d}^{MM} > q_{d,x_d}^{II} = 0$, so $\overset{\star}{q}{}_x^{YY} > \overset{\star}{q}{}_x^{MM} > \overset{\star}{q}{}_x^{II} = 1$.[98] In the simulation, $\gamma = 0.15$, $\overset{\star}{n}{}_x^{II} > \overset{\star}{n}{}_x^{MM} > \overset{\star}{n}{}_x^{YY} = 0$, and $\overset{\star}{q}{}_x^{II} > \overset{\star}{q}{}_x^{MM} > \overset{\star}{q}{}_x^{YY} > 0$, as shown in table 2-20.

97. See note 45.

98. See note 96.

Appendix I: The Rankings of the ME, II, MM, and YY Regime Pairs for CPIs for an Asymmetric Goods-Demand Shock

In this appendix, we demonstrate that, for an asymmetric goods-demand shock, the ranking of the ME and II regime pairs for stabilization of the US CPI and the rankings of the ME and MM pairs and the rankings of the ME and YY regime pairs for stabilization of both the US CPI and the ROECD CPI depend on parameter values.

The ranking of the *ME and II regime pairs* for the *US CPI* depends on parameter values. The following expressions are helpful in explaining this conclusion:

$$(2\text{I-1}) \qquad 2q_{u_d}^{\text{II}} = q_{d,u_d}^{\text{II}} = (1 - 2\gamma)p_{d,u_d}^{\text{II}},$$

$$(2\text{I-2}) \qquad 2q_{u_d}^{\text{ME}} = 2q_{u_d}^{\text{II}} + [-2q_{v_s}^{\text{MM}}][-2m_{u_d}^{\text{II}}]$$

$$= q_{d,u_d}^{\text{II}} + [-q_{s,v_s}^{\text{MM}}][-m_{d,u_d}^{\text{II}}]$$

$$= (1 - 2\gamma)p_{d,u_d}^{\text{II}}$$

$$+ \left[\frac{vA/\lambda}{1 - \epsilon + vA + v(A + \phi)/\lambda}\right][-[(A + \phi)/A]p_{d,u_d}^{\text{II}}],$$

$$= \left[1 - 2\gamma - \frac{v(A + \phi)/\lambda}{1 - \epsilon + vA + v(A + \phi)/\lambda}\right]p_{d,u_d}^{\text{II}} \gtreqless 0,$$

where $A = (1 - \alpha)/\alpha\sigma$.

Equations 2I-1 give the effects of an increase in u_d on the US CPI under the II regime pair. The first equality in equations 2I-1 is analogous to equation 2-53 in table 2-7.

Equations 2I-2 give the effect of an increase in u_d on the US CPI under the ME regime pair. According to the first equality in equation 2I-2, the effect of an increase in u_d on q under the ME pair can be expressed as the sum of a positive and a negative effect: (1) the increase in q caused by an increase in u_d under the II pair and (2) the reduction in q caused by the reduction in m_s required to move from the II equilibrium to the ME equilibrium. Two times the first effect is equal to the effect of an increase in u_d on q_d under the II pair, which, in turn, is equal to $(1 - 2\gamma)p_{d,u_d}^{\text{II}}$ from equation 2-I1. Two times the second effect is equal to the product of two terms. The first term is two times the change in q caused by an increase in m_s, which is equal to the negative of two times the change in q caused by an increase in $v_s(-2q_{v_s}^{\text{MM}} > 0)$, which, in turn, is equal to the negative of the change in q_s caused by an increase in

$v_s(-q_{s,v_s}^{MM} > 0)$. The second term is the decrease in m_s required in order to move from the II equilibrium to the ME equilibrium, which is equal to the negative of two times the increase in m under the II pair $(-2m_{u_d}^{II} < 0)$, which in turn is equal to the negative of the change in m_d caused by the change in u_d $(-m_{d,u_d}^{II} < 0)$. An expression for q_{s,v_s}^{MM} is obtained from equation 2D-5 in appendix D. An expression for m_{d,u_d}^{II} is obtained from equations 2-41 and 2-48 in table 2-6.

As we established in the text and as equation 2I-1 confirms, q rises under the II pair because p_d rises. According to equation 2I-2, q may rise under the ME pair. For example, if $\gamma = 0$, q definitely rises. If q rises under the ME pair, it rises by less than under the II pair. However, q may fall under the ME pair. It falls if the expression in square brackets in the last line of equation 2-I1 is negative. If q falls under the ME pair, the absolute value of the fall in q under the ME pair may be smaller or greater than the rise in q under the II pair. For example, if $\gamma = \frac{1}{2}$, the absolute value of the fall in q under the ME pair is greater.

The ranking of the *MM and ME regime pairs* for the *US CPI* depends on parameter values. Equation 2I-2 and the following expression are helpful in explaining this conclusion:

$$(2I\text{-}3) \qquad 2q_{u_d}^{MM} = -2\overset{\star}{q}_{u_d}^{MM} = q_{d,u_d}^{MM} = (1 - 2\gamma)p_{d,u_d}^{MM} - 2\gamma i_{d,u_d}^{MM} \gtreqless 0.$$

Equations 2I-3 give the effects of an increase in u_d on the US and ROECD CPIs under the MM regime pair. The first two equalities in equation 2I-3 are analogous to equation 2-53 in table 2-7. The third equality in equation 2I-3 gives the effect of an increase in u_d on q_d under the MM pair and follows from equation 2-28.

As we establish in the text and as equation 2I-3 confirms, q may rise or fall under the MM pair because both p_d and i_d rise, and if q rises, it rises by less than p_d rises. As stated above, according to equation 2I-2, q may rise or fall under the ME pair; if it rises, it rises by less than p_d rises under the II pair.

If $\gamma = 0$, it can be shown that $q_{u_d}^{ME} > q_{u_d}^{MM} > 0$. If $\gamma = 1/2$ and v is small, then $|q_{u_d}^{MM}| > |q_{u_d}^{ME}|$ since q_{s,v_s}^{MM} is small. However, if $\gamma = 1/2$, it is possible that $|q_{u_d}^{MM}| < |q_{u_d}^{ME}|$. If $\gamma = 1/2$ and $1 - \epsilon = v$, then

$$(2I\text{-}4) \qquad\qquad 2q_{u_d}^{MM} = -i_{d,u_d}^{MM} = -(D/\lambda)\alpha n_{d,u_d}^{MM},$$

$$(2I\text{-}5) \qquad 2q_{u_d}^{ME} = [q_{s,v_s}^{MM}]2m_{u_d}^{II} = -\left[\frac{A/\lambda}{1 + A + D/\lambda}\right]2D\alpha n_{d,u_d}^{II}$$

$$= -\left[\frac{D}{\lambda}\right]\left[\frac{2A}{1 + A + D/\lambda}\right]\alpha n_{d,u_d}^{II}.$$

Since $n_{d,u_d}^{\mathrm{MM}} < n_{d,u_d}^{\mathrm{II}}$ then also $|q_{u_d}^{\mathrm{MM}}| < |q_{u_d}^{\mathrm{ME}}|$ if $2A/(1 + A + D/\lambda)$ is not too much less than one.

The ranking of the *MM and ME regime pairs* for the *ROECD CPI* also depends on parameter values. Equation 2I-3 and the following expression are useful in explaining this conclusion:

$$
(2\text{I-6}) \qquad
\begin{aligned}
2\overset{\star}{q}_{u_d}^{\mathrm{ME}} &= 2\overset{\star}{q}_{u_d}^{\mathrm{II}} + \left[-2\overset{\star}{q}_{v_s}^{\mathrm{MM}}\right]\left[-2m_{u_d}^{\mathrm{II}}\right] \\
&= -q_{d,u_d}^{\mathrm{II}} + \left[-q_{s,v_s}^{\mathrm{MM}}\right]\left[-2m_{u_d}^{\mathrm{II}}\right] \\
&= -(1 - 2\gamma)p_{d,u_d}^{\mathrm{II}} + \left[q_{s,v_s}^{\mathrm{MM}}\right]\left[2m_{u_d}^{\mathrm{II}}\right] < 0.
\end{aligned}
$$

Equations 2I-6 give the effect of an increase in u_d on the ROECD CPI under the ME regime pair. According to the first equality in the equation, the effect of an increase in u_d on $\overset{\star}{q}$ under the ME pair can be expressed as the sum of two negative effects: (1) the reduction in $\overset{\star}{q}$ caused by an increase in u_d under the II pair and (2) the reduction in $\overset{\star}{q}$ caused by the reduction in m_s required to move from the II equilibrium to the ME equilibrium. Two times the first effect is equal to the negative of the effect of an increase in u_d on q_d under the II pair, which in turn is equal to $-(1 - 2\gamma)p_{d,u_d}^{\mathrm{II}}$ from equation 2I-1. Two times the second effect is equal to the product of two terms. The first term is two times the change in $\overset{\star}{q}$ caused by an increase in m_s, which is equal to the negative of two times the change in $\overset{\star}{q}$ caused by an increase in v_s $(-2\overset{\star}{q}_{v_s}^{\mathrm{MM}} > 0)$, which, in turn, is equal to the negative of the change in q_s caused by an increase in v_s $(-q_{s,v_s}^{\mathrm{MM}} > 0)$. The second term is the decrease in m_s required to move from the II equilibrium to the ME equilibrium, which is two times the negative of the increase in m under the II pair $(-2m_{u_d}^{\mathrm{II}} < 0)$.

As we establish in the text and as equation 2I-3 confirms, $\overset{\star}{q}$ may fall or rise under the MM pair because both p_d and i_d rise, and if $\overset{\star}{q}$ falls, it falls by less than p_d rises. According to equation 2I-6, $\overset{\star}{q}$ must fall under the ME pair, and it must fall by more than p_d rises under the II pair. Therefore, if $\overset{\star}{q}$ falls under the MM pair, it falls by less than under the ME pair because $p_{d,u_d}^{\mathrm{II}} = A\alpha n_{d,u_d}^{\mathrm{II}} > p_{d,u_d}^{\mathrm{MM}} = A\alpha n_{d,u_d}^{\mathrm{MM}}$ (from equations 2D-11 and 2D-14). $\overset{\star}{q}$ definitely falls under the MM pair if γ is small enough.

If $\overset{\star}{q}$ rises under the MM pair, the rise may be smaller (as in the simulation results in table 2-11) or greater than the absolute value of the fall under the ME pair. For some value of γ between zero and $1/2$, $\overset{\star}{q}_{u_d}^{\mathrm{MM}}$ is positive and arbitrarily small, while $\overset{\star}{q}_{u_d}^{\mathrm{ME}}$ is negative and larger in absolute value. For $\gamma = 1/2$, $\overset{\star}{q}_{u_d}^{\mathrm{MM}}$ is positive, with its size dependent only on i_{d,u_d}^{MM}, while $\overset{\star}{q}_{u_d}^{\mathrm{ME}}$ is negative, with the size of its absolute value dependent only on $[q_{s,v_s}^{\mathrm{MM}}][2m_{u_d}^{\mathrm{II}}]$. q_{s,v_s}^{MM} approaches zero as ν approaches zero from equation 2D-6, and $i_{d,u_d}^{MM} = (D/\lambda)\alpha n_{d,u_d}^{MM}$ remains positive as ν approaches zero from equation 2D-14.

The ranking of the *ME and YY regime pairs* for *both CPIs* depends on parameter values. Equations 2I-2 and 2I-6 and the following expression are useful in establishing this result:

$$(2I\text{-}7) \qquad 2q_{u_d}^{YY} = -2\overset{\star}{q}_{u_d}^{YY} = q_{d,u_d}^{YY} = -2\gamma i_{d,u_d}^{YY}.$$

Equation 2I-7 gives the changes in the US and ROECD CPIs caused by an increase in u_d under the YY pair. If $\gamma = 0$, then $|q_{u_d}^{ME}| > |q_{u_d}^{YY}| = 0$. However, if $\gamma = 1/2$, then $|q_{u_d}^{YY}| > |q_{u_d}^{ME}| > 0$. In this case,

$$(2I\text{-}8) \quad |2q_{u_d}^{YY}| = \frac{1}{2\delta} > |2q_{u_d}^{ME}| = \left[\frac{\nu D/\lambda}{1 - \epsilon + \nu(A + D/\lambda)}\right]\left[\frac{1}{1/A + 2\delta}\right] > 0.$$

This result follows from equations 2D-18, 2I-2, and 2D-11 and the fact that $2m_{u_d}^{II} = 2A\alpha n_{d,u_d}^{II}$.

Appendix J: The Relationship between the Taylor Hypothesis and Taylor's Own Formulation

In this appendix, we explain the relationship between our specification of the "Taylor" hypothesis (table 2-3) and Taylor's own formulation. Taylor (1980) writes the following wage- and price-setting equations:

$$(2J\text{-}1) \qquad \tilde{w}_t = \mu(y_{t+1|t} + y_t) + \frac{1}{2}(\tilde{w}_{t+1|t} + \tilde{w}_{t-1}),$$

$$(2J\text{-}2) \qquad p_t = w_t = \frac{1}{2}(\tilde{w}_t + \tilde{w}_{t-1}),$$

where the equations are expressed in our notation. Taylor's equation 2J-1 is the same as our equations 2-16 except that his measure of demand pressure is $y_{t+1|t} + y_t$. According to equation 2J-2, the output price in period t is equal to w_t. Taylor writes no marginal productivity condition for labor.

One plausible interpretation of Taylor is that he implicitly assumes that the average product of labor is constant and equal to one so that

$$(2J\text{-}3) \qquad\qquad\qquad y_t = n_t.$$

Under this interpretation, equation 2J-1 is identical to equations 2-16. For Taylor, $p_t = w_t$ because labor is paid its constant average product of one, and n_t is determined by equation 2J-3. However, for us, p_t moves to clear the goods market, and n_t is determined by the condition that variable marginal productivities of labor equal real wages.

It is important to note that although the wage-setting hypothesis in Taylor's empirical Multicountry model—used in chapters 3–5 of this book—is closely related to the one in Taylor (1980), it is different in some important respects.

Appendix K: Derivation of the Stable Path for the Model for Sums under the Phillips Hypothesis and the MM Regime Pair

In this appendix, we derive the equation of the stable path to a stationary equilibrium for the model for sums under the Phillips hypothesis and the MM regime pair, equation 2-99 in table 2-28.

The characteristic equation of the system of two difference equations made up of equations 2-97 and 2-98 is

$$(2K\text{-}1) \qquad \begin{vmatrix} 1 + \dfrac{1}{\lambda} - \mu & \theta + \dfrac{1 - \alpha + \phi\sigma\alpha}{\lambda\sigma} + \dfrac{(1 - \epsilon)\alpha}{\nu} \\[3mm] 0 & 1 - \dfrac{\theta\sigma}{1 - \alpha} - \mu \end{vmatrix} = 0,$$

where μ represents a root of the characteristic equation. It is obvious from inspection that the roots of the characteristic equation are

$$(2K\text{-}2) \qquad \mu_1 = 1 - \frac{\theta\sigma}{1 - \alpha}, \qquad \mu_2 = 1 + \frac{1}{\lambda}.$$

In a system of two difference equations, the solutions for the variables imply a unique convergent path to a stationary equilibrium if and only if one root of the characteristic equation lies inside the unit circle and the other root lies outside it and is not allowed to enter the solutions for the periods after the period or periods in which any temporary shocks occur. We want to ensure that there is a unique convergent path to a stationary equilibrium and that variables do not alternate between positive and negative values, so we assume that

$$(2K\text{-}3) \qquad\qquad\qquad 0 < \mu_1 < 1,$$

and note that μ_2 lies outside the unit circle.

The form of the solutions for $w_{s,t}$ and $n_{s,t}$ that are consistent with a unique convergent path are

$$(2K\text{-}4) \qquad w_{s,t} - \hat{w}_{s,t} = Sk_1\mu_1^t, \qquad n_{s,t} - \hat{n}_{s,t} = Sk_2\mu_1^t,$$

where $\hat{w}_{s,t}$ and $\hat{n}_{s,t}$ are the values of $w_{s,t}$ and $n_{s,t}$ for which $w_{s,t+1} = w_{s,t}$ and $n_{s,t+1} = n_{s,t}$ in equations 2-97 and 2-98, S is a constant that depends on initial conditions, and k_1 and k_2 are the elements of the characteristic vector corresponding to μ_1.

To characterize the unique convergent path, we must determine the ratio of k_1 to k_2. The ratio of k_1 to k_2 is determined by the set of homogenous equations

(2K-5)
$$
\begin{bmatrix}
1 + \dfrac{1}{\lambda} - \mu_1 & \theta + \dfrac{1 - \alpha + \phi\sigma\alpha}{\lambda\sigma} + \dfrac{(1 - \epsilon)\alpha}{\nu} \\[4mm]
0 & 1 - \dfrac{\theta\sigma}{1 - \alpha} - \mu_1
\end{bmatrix}
\begin{bmatrix} k_1 \\ k_2 \end{bmatrix}
=
\begin{bmatrix} 0 \\ 0 \end{bmatrix}.
$$

Setting k_1 equal to unity and using the first equation to determine k_2 yields

(2K-6) $k_1 = 1,$

$$
k_2 = -\left[\frac{1}{\lambda} + \frac{\theta\sigma}{1 - \alpha} \right]\left[\theta + \frac{1 - \alpha + \phi\sigma\alpha}{\lambda\sigma} + \frac{(1 - \epsilon)\alpha}{\nu} \right]^{-1}.
$$

Equation 2-99 in table 2-28 is obtained by dividing the first equation in 2K-4 by the second, eliminating k_1 and k_2 using equations 2K-6, and rearranging.

Appendix L: The Relationship between the Effects of Increases in Variances of Shocks on Steady-State Variances of Variables and Sums of Squared Deviations of Variables Caused by Shocks

In this appendix, we use some examples to clarify the relationship between the effects of unit increases in the variances of shocks on the steady-state variances of the variables in linear, first-order, dynamic stochastic systems and the sums of squared deviations of the variables in such systems resulting from unit initial-period increases in the shocks.

We begin with a one-variable example. Suppose one variable, x, is generated by the linear, first-order, univariate dynamic process,

$$(2L\text{-}1) \qquad\qquad x_{t+1} = \alpha x_t + \epsilon_t,$$

where ϵ is identically and independently distributed. It can be shown that the steady-state variance of x, σ_x^2, is proportional to the variance of ϵ (σ_ϵ^2):

$$(2L\text{-}2) \qquad\qquad \sigma_x^2 = \left[\frac{1}{1 - \alpha^2}\right]\sigma_\epsilon^2.$$

Therefore, the effect of a unit increase in σ_ϵ^2 on σ_x^2 is $1/(1 - \alpha^2)$.

According to the impulse response function for x, the sequence of deviations of x from baseline in response to a unit change in ϵ_t is given by $\{1, \alpha, \alpha^2, \alpha^3, \ldots, \alpha^T\}$, where T goes to infinity. The sum of squared deviations of x from baseline caused by a unit initial period change in ϵ is therefore

$$(2L\text{-}3) \qquad \sum_{s=t}^{\infty} x_s^2 = 1 + \alpha^2 + \alpha^4 + \alpha^6 + \ldots = \frac{1}{1 - \alpha^2},$$

which is equal to the effect of a unit increase in σ_ϵ^2 on σ_x^2.

We now proceed to consider a two-variable example. Suppose two variables, x and y, are generated by the linear, first-order, bivariate dynamic process,

$$(2L\text{-}4) \qquad\qquad x_{t+1} = \alpha x_t + \epsilon_t,$$

$$(2L\text{-}5) \qquad\qquad y_{t+1} = \beta y_t + \delta x_t + \mu_t.$$

First, we consider the steady-state variances of x and y. From the discussion above it is clear that the steady-state variance of x, σ_x^2, is given by equation 2L-2. It can be shown that the steady-state variance of y, σ_y^2, is

$$(2L\text{-}6) \qquad \sigma_y^2 = \left[\frac{1}{1-\beta^2}\right]\left[\frac{1}{1-\alpha^2}\right]\left[\frac{(1+\beta\alpha)\delta^2}{1-\beta\alpha}\right]\sigma_\epsilon^2$$

$$+ \left[\frac{1}{1-\beta^2}\right]\sigma_\mu^2 + \left[\frac{1}{1-\beta^2}\right]\left[\frac{2\beta\delta}{1-\beta\alpha}\right]\rho_{\epsilon\mu}\sigma_\epsilon\sigma_\mu,$$

where σ_ϵ^2 is the variance of ϵ, σ_μ^2 is the variance of μ, and $\rho_{\epsilon\mu}$ is the coefficient of correlation between ϵ and μ.

Next, we consider the sums of squared deviations of x and y from baseline caused by an initial-period unit change in ϵ and an initial-period unit change in μ. As we show above, the sum of squared deviations of x from baseline caused by an initial-period unit change in ϵ is given by equation 2L-3. It can be shown that the sum of squared deviations of y from baseline caused by a unit initial-period change in ϵ is

$$(2L\text{-}7) \quad \sum_{s=t}^{\infty} y_{s,\epsilon}^2 = \delta^2[1 + (\alpha+\beta)^2 + (\alpha^3 + \alpha\beta + \beta^2)$$

$$+ (\alpha^2 + \alpha^2\beta + \alpha\beta^2 + \beta^3)$$

$$+ (\alpha^4 + \alpha^3\beta + \alpha^2\beta^2 + \alpha\beta^3 + \beta^4) + \ldots]$$

$$= \delta^2(1 + \beta^2 + \beta^4 + \beta^6 + \ldots)(1 + \alpha^2 + \alpha^4 + \alpha^6 + \ldots)$$

$$\times (1 + \alpha\beta + \alpha^2\beta^2 + \alpha^3\beta^3 + \ldots)(1 + \alpha\beta)$$

$$= \delta^2\left[\frac{1}{1-\beta^2}\right]\left[\frac{1}{1-\alpha^2}\right]\left[\frac{(1+\beta\alpha)}{1-\beta\alpha}\right].$$

The sum of squared deviations of x from baseline caused by an initial-period change in μ is clearly zero. It can be shown that the sum of squared deviations of y from baseline caused by a unit initial-period change in μ is

$$(2L\text{-}8) \qquad \sum_{s=t}^{\infty} y_{s,\mu}^2 = 1 + \beta^2 + \beta^4 + \beta^6 + \ldots = \frac{1}{1-\beta^2}.$$

It follows from the expressions for the steady-state variances of x and y (equations 2L-2 and 2L-6) and the expressions for the sums of squared deviations for x and y for unit initial-period changes in ϵ and μ (equations

2L-3, 2L-7, and 2L-8) that the effect of a unit increase in the variance of a particular shock on the steady-state variance of a given variable is equal to the sum of squared deviations in that variable caused by a unit initial-period change in the shock, provided that one or the other of two conditions holds: (1) if the equation for the variable contains no other variable, or (2) if the particular shock is independent of all other shocks ($\rho_{\epsilon\mu} = 0$).

Appendix M: A Shock to the Exchange-Rate Risk Premium

In this appendix, we discuss simulation results for a shock to the exchange-rate risk premium. We focus most of our attention on the results for the model, with oil excluded under the Contract hypothesis. The simulation results are presented in the left half of table 2M-1.[99] However, we also consider briefly the simulation results for the four wage-price hypotheses other than the Contract hypothesis (presented in table 2M-2). The shock to the exchange-rate risk premium is a temporary reduction in the risk premium on dollar assets sufficient to cause the dollar to appreciate by 10 percent *ceteris paribus*.

Under the *Contract hypothesis,* the dollar appreciates in both nominal and real terms under all the matched regime pairs. As should be expected, it appreciates by 10 percent in nominal terms under the II pair, as we show in table 2-41. Under the II pair, the shock causes the demand for goods, the output price, employment, and output to fall in the US and causes the corresponding magnitudes to rise in the ROECD. To keep interest rates unchanged, the US money supply must be allowed to decrease and the ROECD money supply must be allowed to increase. Under the MM pair, the US interest rate must be decreased and the ROECD interest rate must be increased in order to prevent money supplies from changing. Thus, the declines in output prices, employments, and outputs are less than under the II pair, and the nominal appreciation of the dollar required to reach the new equilibrium is less than 10 percent. Under the YY and CC pairs, the US interest rate must be decreased and the ROECD interest rate must be increased by more than under the MM pair in order to prevent nominal incomes from changing. There are no changes in output prices, employments, and outputs. Real dollar appreciation is smallest under the YY and CC pairs, greater under the MM pair, and greatest under the II pair, so CPIs change least under the YY and CC pairs, more under the MM pair, and most under the II pair. Thus, for both employments and CPIs, the YY and CC pairs dominate the MM pair, and the MM pair dominates the II pair.

Under the ME regime pair, the ROECD interest rate must be reduced in order to keep the dollar from appreciating in nominal terms. The increases in the ROECD nominal and real interest rates lower the demand for ROECD goods and cause the output price, employment, and output to fall in the ROECD. The rise in the ROECD real interest rate and the decline in ROECD output and the ROECD output price reduce the demand for US goods, causing the output price, employment, output, and the nominal and real interest rates to fall in

---

99. For completeness, we also present simulation results for this shock with oil included (right half of table 2M-2), but we do not discuss those results.

Table 2M-1. *First-Period Impact of an Exchange-Rate Shock*

| | Regime pair | | | | | | | | | |
| | Oil excluded ($\beta = 0$) | | | | | Oil included ($\beta = 0.1$) | | | | |
Variable[a]	MM	II	YY	CC	ME	MM	II	YY	CC	ME
US economy										
Output (%)	−1.06	−2.26	0	0	−0.66	−0.87	−2.02	0.12	0.12	−0.53
CPI inflation (D)	−1.25	−2.17	−0.42	−0.42	−0.4	−1.28	−2.24	−0.43	−0.43	−0.44
Output price (%)	−0.45	−0.96	0	0	−0.28	−0.57	−1.09	−0.12	−0.12	−0.38
Nominal interest rate (D)	−1.89	0	−3.59	−3.59	−1.19	−1.8	0	−3.33	−3.45	−1.13
Real interest rate (D)	−3.14	−2.17	−4.02	−4.02	−1.58	−3.08	−2.24	−3.76	−3.76	−1.57
Nominal wage (%)	0	0	0	0	0	0	0	0	0	0
Employment (%)	−1.51	−3.19	0	0	−0.95	−1.44	−3.11	0	0	−0.91
Money (%)	0	−3.19	2.88	2.88	0	0	−3.11	2.67	2.76	0
Nominal exchange rate ($/R)(%)	−6.22	−10	−2.81	−2.81	0	−5.97	−10	−2.34	−2.34	0
Real exchange rate ($/R)(%)	−5.31	−8.08	−2.81	−2.81	−0.75	−4.73	−7.64	−2.1	−2.1	−0.41
ROECD economy										
Output (%)	1.06	2.24	0	0	−2.41	1.11	2.42	−0.12	−0.12	−2.19
CPI inflation (D)	1.25	2.17	0.42	0.42	−0.92	1.38	2.41	0.43	0.43	−0.73
Output price (%)	0.45	0.96	0	0	−1.03	0.67	1.27	0.12	0.12	−0.79
Nominal interest rate (D)	1.89	0	3.59	3.59	8.81	2.22	0	4.33	4.45	8.87
Real interest rate (D)	3.14	2.17	4.02	4.02	7.89	3.6	2.41	4.76	4.76	8.14
Nominal wage (%)	0	0	0	0	0	0	0	0	0	0
Employment (%)	1.51	3.19	0	0	−3.45	1.78	3.68	0	0	−2.98
Money (%)	0	3.19	−2.88	−2.88	−10.5	0	3.68	−3.47	−3.56	−10.07

a. % is percent deviation from unchanged baseline; D is deviation from unchanged baseline in percentage points.

Table 2M-2. *Exchange-Rate Shock*

Summary statistic and wage-price hypothesis	Employment					Inflation					Output				
	MM	II	YY	CC	ME	MM	II	YY	CC	ME	MM	II	YY	CC	ME
						US variables									
Impact effect															
Contract	-1.51	-3.20	0.00	0.00	-0.95	-1.25	-2.17	-0.42	-0.42	-0.40	-1.06	-2.24	0.00	0.00	-0.66
Phillips	-1.50	-3.04	0.00	0.00	-0.71	-1.27	-2.14	-0.42	-0.42	-0.32	-1.05	-2.13	0.00	0.00	-0.50
Taylor	-1.43	-3.06	0.00	0.00	-0.97	-1.29	-2.28	-0.42	-0.42	-0.49	-1.00	-2.14	0.00	0.00	-0.68
BG1	-1.51	-2.96	0.00	0.00	-0.59	-1.29	-2.12	-0.42	-0.42	-0.28	-1.05	-2.07	0.00	0.00	-0.41
BG2	-2.10	-3.93	0.00	0.00	-0.56	-1.00	-1.50	-0.42	-0.42	0.00	-1.47	-2.75	0.00	0.00	-0.39
Sum of squared deviations															
Contract	2.29	10.21	0.00	0.00	0.90	3.13	9.43	0.36	0.36	0.32	1.12	5.00	0.00	0.00	0.44
Phillips	2.54	10.39	0.00	0.00	0.57	3.95	12.41	0.36	0.36	1.05	1.24	5.09	0.00	0.00	0.28
Taylor	2.07	9.46	0.00	0.00	0.94	3.16	9.69	0.36	0.36	0.37	1.01	4.64	0.00	0.00	0.46
BG1	3.02	11.67	0.00	0.00	0.46	4.43	14.22	0.36	0.36	1.65	1.48	5.72	0.00	0.00	0.23
BG2	5.87	20.57	0.00	0.00	0.42	3.36	10.38	0.36	0.36	1.36	2.88	10.08	0.00	0.00	0.21
Discounted sum of squared deviations															
Contract	2.29	10.21	0.00	0.00	0.90	2.86	8.61	0.33	0.33	0.29	1.12	5.00	0.00	0.00	0.44
Phillips	2.48	10.17	0.00	0.00	0.56	3.54	11.02	0.33	0.33	0.86	1.22	4.98	0.00	0.00	0.27
Taylor	2.06	9.44	0.00	0.00	0.94	2.90	8.91	0.33	0.33	0.35	1.01	4.63	0.00	0.00	0.46
BG1	2.86	11.03	0.00	0.00	0.44	3.94	12.48	0.33	0.33	1.33	1.40	5.40	0.00	0.00	0.21
BG2	5.55	19.44	0.00	0.00	0.40	2.93	8.88	0.33	0.33	1.06	2.72	9.53	0.00	0.00	0.19

ROECD variables

Impact effect

Contract	1.51	3.20	0.00	0.00	−3.45	1.25	2.17	0.42	0.42	−0.92	1.06	2.24	0.00	0.00	−2.41
Phillips	1.50	3.04	0.00	0.00	−3.09	1.27	2.14	0.42	0.42	−0.82	1.05	2.13	0.00	0.00	−2.16
Taylor	1.43	3.06	0.00	0.00	−3.36	1.29	2.28	0.42	0.42	−1.10	1.00	2.14	0.00	0.00	−2.35
BG1	1.51	2.96	0.00	0.00	−2.90	1.29	2.12	0.42	0.42	−0.77	1.05	2.07	0.00	0.00	−2.03
BG2	2.10	3.93	0.00	0.00	−3.63	1.00	1.50	0.42	0.42	0.00	1.47	2.75	0.00	0.00	−2.54

Sum of squared deviations

Contract	2.29	10.21	0.00	0.00	11.89	3.13	9.43	0.36	0.36	1.70	1.12	5.00	0.00	0.00	5.82
Phillips	2.54	10.39	0.00	0.00	10.74	3.95	12.41	0.36	0.36	4.75	1.24	5.09	0.00	0.00	5.26
Taylor	2.07	9.46	0.00	0.00	11.38	3.16	9.69	0.36	0.36	1.93	1.01	4.64	0.00	0.00	5.58
BG1	3.02	11.67	0.00	0.00	11.22	4.43	14.22	0.36	0.36	7.10	1.48	5.72	0.00	0.00	5.50
BG2	5.87	20.57	0.00	0.00	17.59	3.36	10.38	0.36	0.36	5.30	2.88	10.08	0.00	0.00	8.62

Discounted sum of squared deviations

Contract	2.29	10.21	0.00	0.00	11.89	2.86	8.61	0.33	0.33	1.55	1.12	5.00	0.00	0.00	5.82
Phillips	2.48	10.17	0.00	0.00	10.51	3.54	11.02	0.33	0.33	3.95	1.22	4.98	0.00	0.00	5.15
Taylor	2.06	9.44	0.00	0.00	11.36	2.90	8.91	0.33	0.33	1.81	1.01	4.63	0.00	0.00	5.57
BG1	2.86	11.03	0.00	0.00	10.61	3.94	12.48	0.33	0.33	5.81	1.40	5.40	0.00	0.00	5.20
BG2	5.55	19.44	0.00	0.00	16.63	2.93	8.88	0.33	0.33	4.14	2.72	9.53	0.00	0.00	8.15

the US. For the output price, employment, and output in the US, outcomes are better under the ME regime pair than under the II and MM pairs. But, for the corresponding variables in the ROECD, outcomes are worse under the ME pair than under any other pair. These results are obtained under the ME pair because the ROECD interest rate must be increased substantially, while the US interest rate is decreased only a little under the ME pair, and because the value for the marginal and average propensity to import out of spending used in the simulations is relatively low ($\gamma = 0.15$). For the CPI in the US, the outcome is better under the ME pair than under any other pair because both the fall in the output price and real dollar appreciation are less. For the CPI in the ROECD, the outcome under the ME pair is better than the outcomes under the MM and II pairs because real dollar appreciation is enough less and the ROECD output price falls instead of rising. It is worse than the outcomes under the YY and CC pairs, however, though real dollar appreciation is less, because the fall in the output price is so large.

For the Contract hypothesis and for *the four other wage-price hypotheses,* the results for each variable under the YY regime pair are exactly the same. These results are exactly the same, moreover, as those under the CC regime pair, as we show in table 2-42. The ranking of regime pairs is the same for the Contract, Phillips, and Taylor hypotheses. The YY and CC pairs are ranked the same and dominate the MM and II pairs. For the US the ME pair dominates the MM and II pair. But for the ROECD, the ME pair is worse than the MM and II pairs. The ranking of regime pairs is the same under the BG1 and BG2 hypotheses, and this ranking is the same as the ranking for the Contract, Phillips, and Taylor hypotheses except that the ME pair ranks above the II pair for the ROECD.

References

Aizenman, J., and J. A. Frenkel. 1986. "Targeting Rules for Monetary Policy." *Economics Letters* 21:183–87.

Aoki, M. 1981. *Dynamic Analysis of Open Economies*. Academic Press.

Argy, V. 1991. "Nominal Income Targeting: A Critical Evaluation." Working Paper WP/91/92. International Monetary Fund.

Asako, K., and H. Wagner. 1992. "Nominal Income Targeting versus Money Supply Targeting." *Scottish Journal of Political Economy* 39:167–87.

Bailey, M. J. 1962. *National Income and the Price Level*, 1st ed. McGraw-Hill.

Barro, R. J., and H. I. Grossman. 1976. *Money, Employment, and Inflation*. Cambridge, U.K.: Cambridge University Press.

Bean, C. 1983. "Targeting Nominal Income: An Appraisal." *Economic Journal* 93:806–19.

Boyer, R. S. 1978. "Optimal Foreign Exchange Market Intervention." *Journal of Political Economy* 86:1045–55.

Bryant, R. C. 1980. *Money and Monetary Policy in Interdependent Nations*. Brookings.

Canzoneri, M. B., and J. A. Gray. 1985. "Monetary Policy Games and the Consequences of Non-cooperative Behavior." *International Economic Review* 26:547–64.

Canzoneri, M. B., and D. W. Henderson. 1991. *Monetary Policy in Interdependent Economies: A Game Theoretic Approach*. MIT Press.

Corden, M. 1981. "Comments: On Monetary Targets." In *Monetary Targets*, edited by B. Griffiths and G. Wood, 86–94. St. Martin's Press.

Dornbusch, R. 1984. "Comment." In *Exchange Rate Theory and Practice*, edited by J. F. O. Bilson and R. C. Marston, 398–402. University of Chicago Press.

Frankel, J. A. 1991. "International Nominal Income Targeting: A Proposal for Overcoming Obstacles to Policy Coordination." In *International Trade and Global Development: Essays in Honor of Jagdish Bhagwati*, edited by A. Koekkoek and L. B. M. Mennes, 211–36. London: Routledge House.

Frankel, J. A., and M. Chinn. 1993. "The Stabilizing Properties of a Nominal GNP Rule in an Open Economy." *Journal of Money, Credit, and Banking* (forthcoming).

Frankel, J. A., M. Goldstein, and P. R. Masson. 1989. "Simulating the Effects of Some Simple Coordinated versus Uncoordinated Policy." In *Macroeconomic Policies in an Interdependent World*, edited by R. C. Bryant, D. A. Currie, and others, 203–39. Washington: Brookings, Centre for Economic Policy Research, and International Monetary Fund.

Henderson, D. W. 1979. "Financial Policies in Open Economies." *American Economic Review* 69 (*Papers and Proceedings, 1978*):232–39.

———. 1984. "Exchange Market Intervention Operations: Their Role in Financial Policy and Their Effects." In *Exchange Rate Theory and Practice*, edited by J. F. O. Bilson and R. C. Marston, 357–406. University of Chicago Press.

Henderson, D. W., and W. J. McKibbin. Forthcoming. "A Comparison of Some Basic Monetary Policy Regimes for Open Economies: Implications of Different Degrees of Instrument Adjustment and Wage Persistence." In Carnegie-Rochester Series on Public Policy 39. Amsterdam: North-Holland.

Marston, R. C. 1984. "Real Wages and the Terms of Trade: Alternative Indexation Rules for an Open Economy." *Journal of Money, Credit, and Banking* 16:285–301.

McKibbin, W. J., and J. D. Sachs. 1988. "Comparing the Global Performance of Alternative Exchange Rate Regimes." *Journal of International Money and Finance* 7:387–410.

——. 1989. "Implications of Policy Rules for the World Economy." In *Macroeconomic Policies in an Interdependent World,* edited by R. C. Bryant, D. A. Currie, and others, 151–94. Washington: Brookings, Centre for Economic Policy Research, and International Monetary Fund.

——. 1991. *Global Linkages: Macroeconomic Interdependence and Cooperation in the World Economy.* Brookings.

Meade, J. E. 1978. "The Meaning of Internal Balance." *Economic Journal* 88:423–35.

Melitz, J. 1983. "Optimal Stabilization and the Proper Exercise of the Monetary Policy Instruments under Flexible Exchange Rates." In *Recent Issues in the Theory of Flexible Exchange Rates,* edited by E. Classen and P. Salin, 231–55. Amsterdam: North-Holland.

Mundell, R. A. 1968. *International Economics.* Macmillan.

Obstfeld, M. 1985. "Floating Exchange Rates: Experience and Prospects." *Brookings Papers on Economic Activity* 2:369–464.

Poole, W. 1970. "Optimal Choice of Monetary Policy Instruments in a Simple Stochastic Macro Model." *Quarterly Journal of Economics* 84:197–216.

Reinhart, V. 1990. "Targeting Nominal Income in a Dynamic Model." *Journal of Money Credit and Banking* 22:427–43.

Roper, D. E., and S. J. Turnovsky. 1980. "Optimal Exchange Market Intervention in a Simple Stochastic Macro Model." *Canadian Journal of Economics* 13:296–309.

Taylor, J. B. 1980. "Aggregate Dynamics and Staggered Contracts." *Journal of Political Economy* 88:1–24.

——. 1985. "What Would Nominal GNP Targeting Do to the Business Cycle?" In *Understanding Monetary Regimes,* edited by K. Brunner and A. H. Meltzer, 61–84. Carnegie-Rochester Conference Series on Public Policy 22. Amsterdam: North-Holland.

Tobin, J. 1980. "Stabilization Policy Ten Years After." *Brookings Papers on Economic Activity* 1:19–72.

CHAPTER 3

Design and Implementation
of the Empirical Simulations

Ralph C. Bryant, Peter Hooper, and Catherine L. Mann

THIS CHAPTER describes the design and implementation of the collaborative empirical research giving rise to this volume. The information here is necessary background for a full understanding of the analysis in chapters 4 and 5.

We begin by summarizing some key features of the models that participated in the project. Next we describe the alternative policy regimes that are the focus of the empirical experiments. Although the regimes are simplified, not all model groups followed the guidelines for implementing the regimes in exactly the same way. Thus we identify differences in implementation that may affect the comparability of results across models. The chapter then turns to the mechanics of stochastic simulation. We describe the basic procedures followed and discuss differences in details of the approaches taken by the participating models. We also discuss what can be learned from examination of the historical residual matrices underlying the stochastic simulations actually implemented by the different models. The material in these sections, important for a clear understanding of the stochastic simulations, is necessarily technical. The final section of the chapter defines the specific shocks used to conduct the deterministic simulations.[1]

Summary Description of the Participating Models

The models participating in the project, identified in chapter 1, are with one exception multicountry models. They were constructed for the primary purpose of analyzing macroeconomic interactions among major countries or regions of the world. Most models incorporate separate representations of the largest industrial economies, with other national economies aggregated in a few regional blocs. Typically, the country or bloc sectors in these multicountry models have

---

1. Readers primarily concerned with the conclusions emerging from the analysis may wish to go directly to chapters 4 and 5, returning to this chapter as they require information about how the simulations were designed and carried out.

fewer equations and less disaggregated detail than large econometric models constructed for a single national economy. The multicountry models, however, explicitly specify the economic links among country or bloc sectors—in particular trade flows, traded-goods prices, and exchange rates—thereby enabling models to address analytical issues about economic interdependence that cannot be analyzed in single-country models.

The participating models share several broad features. For example, they tend to have structural frameworks derived from the so-called neoclassical synthesis in macroeconomics. Aggregate demand is modeled in some variant of the IS-LM framework, with aggregate supply usually characterized by factor-market disequilibrium and some form of "stickiness" in wages and prices. Differences in structural design among the models, however, are numerous and significant.

Half of the participating models have an annual frequency. The other half are quarterly. Most of the models were estimated with data from the 1970s through the latter 1980s. The MPS model was estimated with data going back to the early 1960s, and the LIVERPOOL model with data going back to 1956–57. The authors of the MSG model used empirical studies reported in the literature and country data from the mid-1980s to calibrate the values of the MSG model's parameters.

Most models contain several (four to nine) small- to medium-scale models of individual countries. The most common focus is on the Group of Seven (G7) largest countries (the United States, Japan, Canada, Germany, France, the United Kingdom, and Italy). Smaller industrial countries and developing countries are typically included as additional regional blocs, usually with highly aggregated specifications. The TAYLOR and MX3 models do not contain regional blocks for smaller industrial or developing countries. The MSG and MX3 models distinguish individual country sectors only for the United States, Japan, and Germany. The fourth bloc in the MX3 model is an aggregation of the United Kingdom, Canada, France, and Italy. The MSG model splits the Organization for Economic Cooperation and Development (OECD) countries other than the United States, Japan, and Germany into two blocs—countries in the European Monetary System (EMS) and an aggregate rest-of-OECD (ROECD) bloc—and also contains regional models for OPEC (Organization of Petroleum Exporting Countries) and other developing countries. The MCM model separately distinguishes five of the G7 countries and a small bloc for OPEC oil-producing countries; all other countries are grouped into an abbreviated rest-of-world (ROW) bloc. The GEM model, in the version used for the simulations in this project, contains more geographical disaggregation than the other models; it has separate sectors for nine individual countries (the G7 plus Belgium and the Netherlands) and seven other regional blocs encompassing the rest of the world.[2] The MPS model is the exception to the generalization that the models were constructed primarily to analyze the macroeconomic interactions among the major countries in the world economy. The MPS model is a large-scale model of the U.S. economy with only a small, rudimentary rest-of-world sector. The MPS model was initially designed primarily for analysis of the U.S. domestic economy. Even with the MPS model, however, it was later felt necessary to incorporate some of the most important features of interdependence between the U.S. economy and other parts of the world economy, albeit at a very aggregative level (see, for example, Brayton and Mauskopf 1985, 1987).

Differences in the regional disaggregations of the models are associated with differences in model size. The smallest of the models are TAYLOR and MX3, each of which contains some 100 to 150 equations; the largest are GEM (with some 640 equations) and MCM (with over 900 equations). Multicountry models of still larger size—such as the OECD INTERLINK model, the world model of the Japanese Economic Planning Agency, and Project LINK—were unable to participate in the project to the extent of implementing the stochastic simulations (either because of personnel or other resource constraints, or because of the technical difficulties of carrying out stochastic simulations in very large models).[3]

For their treatments of expectations, the GEM, INTERMOD, LIVER-POOL, MSG, MULTIMOD, MX3, and TAYLOR models impose forward-looking, model-consistent (rational) expectations. The INTERMOD model has two variants, however, one in which expectations are model-consistent (INTERMOD-C) and the other in which expectations are treated adaptively (INTERMOD-A). For this project, the GEM model's use of rational expectations is limited to exchange rates only.[4] In the other models with rational expectations, forward-looking variables enter into the determination of interest rates as well as exchange rates and, in many cases, wages, prices, consumption, and investment. The MCM and MPS models (and INTERMOD-A) specify expectations as adaptive.

Exchange rates and interest rates are determined endogenously in all the models. Most models impose some form of the uncovered interest-parity (UIP)

---

2. In the simulations in part 2 of this volume (both stochastic and deterministic), the GEM model reported is the version developed by the National Institute of Economic and Social Research and jointly maintained with the London Business School. Chapter 11 also makes use of a smaller, linearized version of GEM, referred to as MINIGEM (see the further discussion in that chapter).

3. With the exception of MCM, models that had been unable to participate in implementing the stochastic simulations were not requested to submit the deterministic simulations. Note, however, that a number of closely related deterministic simulations generated with the OECD INTERLINK model are reported in chapter 12.

4. The model-consistent treatment of expectations limited only to exchange rates applies both to the full National Institute GEM model used for the simulations discussed in chapters 3–5 and to the small linearized version of GEM discussed in chapter 11.

condition as a key equation determining exchange rates. The MPS model determines the weighted average exchange rate of the United States by means of portfolio-balance equations for asset demands and a balance of payments clearing condition.

The LIVERPOOL model and, to a lesser extent, the MSG model are exceptions to the generalization that the specification of the models' equations assumes factor-price disequilibrium and stickiness in wages and prices. LIVERPOOL presumes that wages and prices are fully flexible and that labor and product markets clear continuously. In the MSG model, wages are sticky, but product-market prices are fully flexible.

Table 3-1 summarizes some of the salient differences among the models that have been identified here. The reader can use this table as a convenient reference for the attributes of the participating models.

We do not try here to provide a careful bibliography of references to the various models. Rather, we have included only one or two key sources for each model in the list of references at the end of the chapter.[5] Readers seeking additional references on the models may consult the reference lists in the cited papers; in Bryant, Helliwell, and Hooper (1989); or in the supplemental volume to *Empirical Macroeconomics for Interdependent Economies* (*EMIE:* Bryant, Henderson, and others 1988).

Specification of Alternative Policy Regimes

For both the stochastic and deterministic simulations prepared for the project, model groups were asked to focus on four types of monetary policy regime. All four are highly simplified. (For a definition of "regime" and a general discussion of the underlying issues at stake in evaluating alternative regimes, see chapter 1.)

For each regime type, model groups were asked to assume that the monetary authority selects a short-term interest rate as its instrument and uses that instrument to target one or more key variables of policy interest. The specific variables targeted under the alternative regimes are a monetary aggregate, some combination of gross output and prices, or bilateral nominal U.S. dollar ex-

---

5. For the GEM model, see Barrell and Wren-Lewis (1990) and Barrell and Gurney (1991); for INTERMOD, Helliwell and others (1990) and Meredith (1989); for LIVERPOOL, Minford (1985) and Minford, Agenor, and Nowell (1986); for MCM, Stevens and others (1984) and Edison, Marquez, and Tryon (1987); for MPS, Brayton and Mauskopf (1985, 1987) and Mauskopf (1990); for MSG, McKibbin (1988) and McKibbin and Sachs (1991); for MULTIMOD, Masson and others (1988) and Masson, Symansky, and Meredith (1990); for MX3, Gagnon (1991) and chapter 9 in this volume; and for TAYLOR, Taylor (1988, 1989a, 1989b, 1992).

Table 3-1. *Main Attributes of Participating Models*

Attribute	GEM	INTERMOD	LIVERPOOL	MCM	MPS
Frequency of time-series observations	Quarterly	Annual	Annual	Quarterly	Quarterly
In-sample estimation period	1970:1–1989:4	1972–87	1957 through early- or mid-1980s (some variation across individual countries)	1970–82	1960:1–1984:4
Countries/regions represented in model	United States Germany Japan United Kingdom Canada France Italy Belgium Netherlands 7 additional regional blocs	United States Germany Japan United Kingdom Canada France Italy Small industrial countries bloc High-income oil exporters bloc Developing countries bloc	United States Germany Japan United Kingdom Canada France Italy Netherlands Belgium 3 other blocs (trade only)	United States Germany Japan United Kingdom Canada OPEC bloc Aggregate rest-of-world (ROW) bloc	United States (in detail) Aggregate ROW bloc (simplified)
Size of model (approximate number of equations)	625-50 including identities	472 including identities		929 including identities	325 including identities
Key types of exogenous variables	Money supplies, government expenditures, and others	Targeted money supplies, real government expenditures, targeted stocks of government debt, technical change, real oil price, G7 oil production, G7 oil exports, demographic variables, steady-state real interest rates		Money supplies, government expenditures, oil prices, oil production, demographic variables	Monetary-policy variables (federal funds rate or reserve aggregate), some categories of government expenditure, tax parameters, population measures, farm-sector variables
Treatment of expectations	Typically adaptive, but model-consistent for exchange rates	Both adaptive (INTERMOD-A) and model-consistent (INTERMOD-C)	Model-consistent	Adaptive	Adaptive
Model sectors in which expectations are forward looking	Exchange rates only	Consumption, investment, long-term interest rate, exchange rates, inflation, developing-country debt			

(continued)

Table 3-1 (continued)

Attribute	MSG	MULTIMOD	MX3	TAYLOR
Frequency of time series observations	Annual	Annual	Quarterly	Quarterly
In-sample estimation period	Calibrated on 1986 data	1974–88	1976:4–1988:4	1972:1–1984:4
Countries/regions represented in the model	United States Germany Japan REMS bloc (rest of European monetary system) ROECD bloc (rest of OECD industrial countries) OPEC bloc Non-oil developing-countries bloc	United States Germany Japan United Kingdom Canada France Italy Small industrial countries bloc Creditor developing-countries bloc Debtor developing-countries bloc	United States Germany Japan ROW bloc (composed by aggregating United Kingdom, Canada, France, and Italy)	United States Germany Japan United Kingdom Canada France Italy
Size of model (approximate number of equations)	Approximately 500 including identities	Approximately 460 including identities	143 equations including identities (10 behavioral equations, 4 government policy reaction functions, and 22 identities per main bloc)	112 equations including identities (98 stochastic)
Key types of exogenous variables	Population growth, technical change, oil supply, lending to developing countries	Targeted money supplies, real government expenditures, targeted stocks of government debt, technical change, real oil price, demographic variables, steady-state real interest rates, targeted ratio of interest payments to exports for developing countries	Labor force, production technology, real government expenditures	Money supplies, government expenditures, trend outputs
Treatment of expectations	Model-consistent	Model-consistent	Model-consistent	Model-consistent
Model sectors in which expectations are forward looking	Consumption, investment, wages, exchange rates, short- and long-term interest rates, share markets	Consumption, investment, long-term interest rate, exchange rates, inflation, developing-country debt	Consumption, investment, exchange rates, contract prices, long-term interest rates	Consumption, investment, wages, inflation, short- and long-term interest rates, exchange rates

change rates. Two variants for the combination of gross output and prices are considered: the level of nominal gross national product (the level of real GNP multiplied by the price level, as measured by the GNP deflator) or an additive combination of the level of real GNP and the inflation rate for the GNP deflator.[6] Hence we postulate four alternative regime types, on which policymakers concentrate their attention:

    1:    Target variable is a monetary aggregate

   2A: Target variable is the level of nominal GNP

   2B: Target variable is the sum of the level of real GNP plus the inflation rate

    3:    Target variable is a bilateral nominal dollar exchange rate.

The numbers in this list—1, 2A, 2B, and 3—are used throughout the following discussion, and in chapters 4 and 5, for summary identification of the types of policy regimes.

For regime type 1, "money targeting," the simulation guidelines asked model groups to adjust their models to assume that the monetary authorities in each country focus on deviations of the monetary base or some other narrow monetary aggregate from a desired path. The monetary aggregate is an "intermediate target" of policy action. Some central banks—including those of the United States, Germany, Japan, Canada, and the United Kingdom—implemented some variant of money targeting (sometimes only in weak form or with escape clauses) during the 1970s or 1980s.

Regime type 2A, representative of the specification for nominal-income targeting most frequently encountered in the academic literature on policy regimes, presumes that the monetary authorities target the level of nominal GNP or GDP (the product of the price level and the level of real output). We refer to this regime as "nominal-income targeting."

Regime type 2B, referred to here as "real-GNP-plus-inflation targeting," is an alternative specification giving equal weight to the level of real output and the inflation rate. One of the motives for requesting the model groups to use this regime in their simulations was that such a specification seems consistent with the stated dual objectives of many central banks to achieve a sustainable growth in real economic activity while avoiding inflation.

Under regime 2A, deviations of the price *level* from a targeted path for the price level receive the same weight as deviations of real output from a

---

6. The distinction between GNP and GDP (gross domestic product) is not made in all the participating models. For the purposes of the empirical results, we have substituted GDP for GNP when the latter was not available and regarded the two as largely interchangeable.

targeted path for real output. Any incipient sustained movement of the price level away from its targeted path is resisted by policy action. Under regime 2B, in contrast, the policymakers are assumed to focus on the path of the level of real output and on the inflation *rate*, not the price level; regime 2B thus permits sustained deviations of the price level away from a baseline path. In effect, regime 2B treats past episodes of upward or downward adjustment in the price level as bygones, not subject to correction. Ex ante, policy is deemed to try only to move the rate of change of prices to a target rate.

For regime type 3, "exchange-rate targeting," the simulation guidelines requested the model groups to adjust their models so that non-U.S. countries target the bilateral exchange rates of their currencies in relation to the U.S. dollar, while the United States targets its own money supply independently of dollar exchange rates. Regime 3 implies that, taken together, the monetary policies of the major industrial countries have the joint objective of stabilizing exchange rates in the world economy. (Seen from the perspective of the United States, there is some similarity, but not identity, between regimes 1 and 3.) Under regimes 1, 2A, and 2B, bilateral U.S. dollar exchange rates are allowed to float freely. However, for regimes 1, 2A, and 2B, countries in the EMS other than Germany are assumed to peg their currencies to the deutsche mark, whereas the German policy authorities target money or nominal income. One or another variant of regime 3 has been strongly espoused by some European countries from time to time.

Each policy regime was specified as an extremely simple equation—in effect, a rudimentary "reaction function"—in which the policy instrument responds over time, with a given feedback parameter, to deviations of the targeted variables from desired time paths. For the analytical purposes of the simulations (both deterministic and stochastic), the desired paths were assumed coincident with the baseline paths for the targeted variables.[7] The reaction-function equations thus took the generic form:

$$X_t - X_t^* = \beta[f(T_t, T_t^*)],$$

where X is the policy instrument of the monetary authorities, T is a targeted variable, the (*) asterisk superscript denotes baseline values, $f(\ldots)$ is some function of the deviations of T from T^*, and β is the monetary authority's feedback or response parameter, denoting the strength of the responsiveness of X to deviations of T from T^*. For simplicity, all variables in the reaction functions are dated contemporaneously.

---

7. As discussed in chapter 2, this assumption can be problematic when the shocks being analyzed are productivity or other supply-side shocks.

The suggested policy regimes took the explicit form:

(3-1)   (Regime 1) $RS_t - RS_t^* = -5 \log(M_t^*/M_t)$

(Regime 2A) $RS_t - RS_t^* = 1.5 \log[(PY)_t/(PY)_t^*]$

(Regime 2B) $RS_t - RS_t^* = 1.5 \, [(\pi_t - \pi_t^*) + \log(Y_t/Y_t^*)]$

(Regime 3) $RS_t - RS_t^* = 2.5 \log(E_t^*/E_t),$

where

RS = the short-term nominal interest rate measured in percentage points per year divided by 100

M = the monetary base (or some other narrow monetary aggregate)

P = the price level (GNP or GDP deflator)

Y = real GNP or GDP

π = the rate of inflation in the price level P (expressed as percent per year)

E = the nominal exchange rate, measured in U.S. dollars per unit of local currency,

and where an asterisk superscript denotes a target (baseline) value.

When the guidelines for the simulations were drafted, it was recognized that the particular values for the feedback coefficients (the values of β) inevitably involved some degree of arbitrariness, especially because these values had been initially tested in only one model.[8] It was also expected that some models might not be able to run the stochastic simulations successfully with these specific regimes. The model groups were asked to make a good-faith effort to conform to the prescribed regimes and feedback coefficients. But they were also encouraged to test alternative regime specifications if such alternatives were needed to obtain meaningful results.[9]

When preparing their stochastic simulations, many of the model groups did adopt variations on the regime specifications (see below). For the preparation of the deterministic simulations, the model groups were asked to use *both* the originally prescribed regimes (as specified in equations 3-1) and the particular variants of the regimes that were used to prepare their stochastic simulations.

8. The prescribed values for the feedback coefficients had been obtained from some preliminary simulations of the MULTIMOD model carried out in 1989.

9. The value of a feedback coefficient appropriate for annual models would differ from the value of the analogous coefficient appropriate for quarterly models if the models with different frequencies used different measures of their variables (for example, if quarterly models measured inflation at quarterly rather than annual rates).

The regimes in equations 3-1 correspond roughly to four of the regimes studied in the theoretical analysis of chapter 2: regime 1 is an empirical analog of the theoretical MM regime, regime 2A of the YY regime, regime 2B of the CC regime, and regime 3 of the ME regime. Notwithstanding the conceptual similarity, there is of course also a major difference. The theoretical analysis in chapter 2, by design, achieved *exact* targeting of the variables on which each regime focused. The simulations carried out in the empirical models, with equations 3-1 defining the regimes, are characterized by *inexact* targeting. This important difference will be discussed further in chapter 4.

In addition to the four regimes in equations 3-1, model groups were asked, when carrying out the deterministic simulations, to use a fifth regime for the single case of a sustained shock to the U.S. money supply (described below). This fifth regime presumed exact money targeting—that is, making the simulation values of the money stock *precisely* equivalent to the values along the baseline path. This regime and shock produce results roughly comparable to the simulations carried out for the earlier model-comparison conferences in which national money stocks had been exogenously fixed along paths identical to the baseline paths.

For all of the regime types, the guidelines requested that fiscal policies for each country be held unchanged from their baseline paths *during the ten years of the simulation period*. In particular, real government expenditures and nominal tax rates were to be kept exogenous for the simulation period, equal to their values along the baseline path. It was recognized, of course, that the models incorporating forward-looking expectations would not be able to obtain sensible solutions (if any could be obtained at all) without making adjustments *beyond the ten-year horizon* in tax-rate reaction functions or in other aspects of fiscal policies. This issue is discussed further below.

Before proceeding, we reemphasize what was said in chapter 1. The regimes for the conduct of monetary policy summarized above can serve as useful benchmarks for analytical comparison. Yet they are only simplified representations of some major regime types from which policymakers may choose in realistic policy situations. Because of their simplicity, the regimes studied here should be considered as no more than rough approximations of how monetary policy might be conducted in actual practice.

Two examples illustrate the point. First, the regimes studied in this project assume that policymakers focus on a single target variable (or, in the case of regime 2B, on two variables only). In operational practice, policymakers can and typically do pay attention to a variety of key macroeconomic variables. (Chapters 4 and 5 take this fact into account when interpreting the empirical results of the project.)

Second, in operational practice policymakers receive data for most macroeconomic variables only with a lag. Data for interest rates, exchange rates, and prices for many financial assets are available almost contemporaneously. But data for real-sector variables trickle in slowly. For example, estimated data for real and nominal GNP, and economywide measures of the price level— the variables that are the focus of regimes 2A and 2B—come to policymakers with lags of one to three months, and even then the estimates are subject to substantial subsequent revision.

The regimes used here postulate that policymakers can react to contemporaneous values of the key target variables. Policymakers do tend to have access to *forecasts* for the contemporaneous values of target variables. But techniques for forecasting are not fully reliable, and in any event they too are primarily based on the lagged data. In practice, therefore, any regime for characterizing monetary policy in a more realistic way would have to specify lagged values for the right-hand-side target variables.[10]

The assumption of contemporaneously available data for target variables is a bigger practical problem for models that are specified with a monthly or quarterly frequency than for annual models. But the difficulty is nonetheless present even for annual models.[11]

Differences in Implementing the Policy Regimes

When preparing their simulations, almost every model group departed in some way from the original specifications of the policy regimes. For ease of reference, regimes 1, 2A, 2B, and 3 shown in equations 3-1 above will be referred to here and in the following chapters as "O" (original) regimes. Variants of the original regimes, as modified by the model groups, will be referred to as "X" (alternative) regimes and will be labeled, respectively, as 1X, 2AX, 2BX, and 3X.

To the extent that the model groups implemented the O regimes, simulation results can be more directly compared across the models. The particular forms of X regimes tend to be unique to each model. Moreover, the underlying reasons for the deviations of X from O regimes vary considerably across the models. Divergence among models in the implementation of policy regimes makes standardization of interpretation of the results more difficult. In the next paragraphs, therefore, we briefly describe the most important discrepancies.

---

10. Bennett McCallum sharply criticized this aspect of the design of the project at the March 1990 conference, and his comments in chapter 6 amplify his views on this point.

11. Suppose that data for a target variable reach policymakers with a lag of exactly one quarter. In a quarterly model, the right-hand-side variables for a policy regime would simply have a time subscript of $t - 1$. For an annual model, done with careful intertemporal aggregation, the right-hand side of the reaction function would in effect contain both the current-year and the past-year value of the target variable, with the current year receiving three-fourths and the past year one-fourth of the total weight given to the variable.

Table 3-2. *Summary of Regime Implementation by Model: Deterministic and Stochastic Simulations*

Model group	Money targeting (1)	(1X)	Nominal-income targeting (2A)	(2AX)	Real-GNP-plus-inflation targeting (2B)	(2BX)	Exchange-rate targeting (3)	(3X)
			Deterministic simulations[a]					
GEM		✓	✓		✓			
INTERMOD-A	✓		✓		✓		✓	
INTERMOD-C	✓		✓	✓	✓		✓	
LIVERPOOL	✓	✓	✓	✓	✓	✓	✓	✓
MCM		✓	✓		✓			✓
MPS	✓	✓	✓	✓	✓	✓		
MSG	✓	✓	✓	✓	✓	✓	✓	✓
MULTIMOD	✓	✓	✓		✓			✓
MX3	✓		✓		✓			
TAYLOR		✓	✓	✓	✓	✓		✓
			Stochastic simulations					
GEM		✓	✓		✓			
INTERMOD-A	✓		✓	✓	✓	✓	✓	
INTERMOD-C	✓		✓		✓	✓	✓	
LIVERPOOL	✓	✓	✓	✓	✓	✓	✓	✓
MCM								
MPS		✓	✓	✓	✓			
MSG	✓	✓	✓	✓	✓	✓	✓	✓
MULTIMOD	✓	✓	✓		✓			✓
MX3	✓		✓	✓	✓			
TAYLOR		✓	✓		✓			✓

a. Several of the model groups—LIVERPOOL, MPS, MSG, MX3, and TAYLOR—also submitted deterministic simulations for one shock in which policymakers are assumed to fix the value of the money stock on an exogenous target path ("exact money targeting").

Table 3-2 provides an overview of which model groups implemented which regimes. Only about half of the groups were able to run the bulk of both the deterministic and stochastic simulations using the O regimes. In most of the cases where a model group could not or did not use an O regime, an X regime was substituted. Some significant omissions exist. No results at all are available for one of the regime types from three models: the MPS group could not implement exchange-rate targeting because of its structure; the GEM group did not report results for this regime in any variant; and the MX3 group was not able to implement exchange-rate targeting in any variant despite repeated efforts to do so. The MCM group was unable to participate in the stochastic simulations exercise, but did submit deterministic simulations (however, only for X variants of the regimes).

Thus stochastic simulation results for all four types of regimes are available only for six (INTERMOD-A, INTERMOD-C, LIVERPOOL, MSG, MULTI-

MOD, and TAYLOR) of the nine models that ran stochastic simulations. Deterministic simulation results for all regime types are available only for seven (the preceding six plus MCM) of the ten models that ran deterministic simulations.

Several model groups—notably INTERMOD-C, MSG, MULTIMOD—had difficulties when initially trying to implement real-GNP-plus-inflation targeting for the stochastic simulations. That regime appeared to be unstable in those models. Upon further experimentation after the March 1990 conference, however, those groups did successfully implement either the original 2B specification or a 2BX variant.[12] If one is willing to abstract from the important differences between O and X regimes and between the different X regimes, therefore, it is possible to compare results for money targeting, nominal-income targeting, and real-GNP-plus-inflation targeting across nine models for the stochastic simulations and across ten models for the deterministic simulations.

A few of the detailed differences among models in the implementation of the policy regimes are probably inconsequential or only second order in importance, and we omit discussion of them. Other differences, however, do appear to be meaningful and warrant identification here.

The TAYLOR group implemented each of the four regime types with the *real* (inflation-adjusted) rather than the nominal short-term interest rate specified as the policy instrument manipulated by the monetary authority. Instead of using $RS_t - RS_t^*$ on the left-hand side of the policy reaction functions as in equations 3-1, in other words, the TAYLOR group specified the left-hand side, in effect, as $RS_t - \pi_t - (RS_t^* - \pi_t^*)$, where π_t is expected inflation. In his submission to the project organizers, Peter Klenow observed that he was compelled to modify the regimes in this way because output in Japan, or sometimes in Canada or France, was invariably driven to zero after several years of each stochastic simulation when he attempted to implement the regimes with the nominal short-term interest rate as the policy instrument. Klenow indicated that he might have altered the O specification of the regimes only for Japan (or Canada, or France) and thereby still obtained solutions for the model. In the interest of symmetry across the countries, however, he modified each country's regime to use the real interest rate as the policy instrument. Klenow also experienced difficulties in implementing the O specification for exchange-rate targeting, even after using the real rather than nominal short-term interest rate as the policy instrument. He therefore added a term in real GNP to the regime to get convergence. Whatever

12. The experience with the MSG model is instructive. Warwick McKibbin initially thought that the real-GNP-plus-inflation targeting regime was inherently incompatible with the MSG model. He conjectured that a regime without a price-level or nominal variable as an explicit anchor would cause the price level to be indeterminate, and therefore that the model could not converge. But subsequent rethinking, and revision of how he implemented the regime, did permit McKibbin to submit MSG results for regime 2B (and, analogously with his treatment of the other regimes, for a 2BX regime).

the need or rationale for these alterations in the TAYLOR regimes, the modified specifications constitute a major divergence from the other models.[13]

The LIVERPOOL group reported results for the four O regimes but also submitted results for four X variants. The LIVERPOOL X variants incorporate a major, conceptual respecification: rather than treating the nominal short-term interest rate as the policy instrument, the X regimes assume that a key monetary aggregate, M, is the policy instrument.[14] For example, rather than the O specification for regime 2A in equations 3-1, the LIVERPOOL 2AX specification is

$$(3\text{-}2) \quad \log(M_t/M_t^*) = -(1/1.5)\log[(PY)_t/(PY)_t^*] - (1/1.5)[RS_t - RS_t^*].$$

The LIVERPOOL group also used a different specification for their 3X regime. They fixed the bilateral dollar exchange rate precisely to the baseline (target) path:

$$(3\text{-}3) \qquad\qquad \log(E_t) = \log(E_t^*),$$

which differs from the approximate exchange-rate targeting in the O specification. As can be verified by examining the LIVERPOOL model results in annexes A and B, very different outcomes are obtained for that model depending on whether the simulations are based on the O or X specifications. The differences between O and LIVERPOOL X results are especially striking for real-GNP-plus-inflation targeting and exchange-rate targeting for the stochastic simulations.[15]

McKibbin submitted results for the MSG model for both O and X regimes. His X regimes, however, differ in concept from all those used by other model groups. The X variants for MSG are "optimal" for that simplified regime type in the sense that the feedback coefficients are calculated by choosing a value for the coefficient to minimize a loss function that gives equal weight to output loss and inflation loss, subject to the constraint that the simple rule is followed. For each regime type, the feedback coefficient in the X variant has a very large value. The simulations with the MSG X regimes therefore result in virtually exact targeting of the key variable or variables in the regime (money in 1X, nominal GNP in 2AX, bilateral dollar exchange rates in 3X, and the simple

---

13. Klenow further observed that "in my experience with the TAYLOR model, real-interest-rate rules far outperform nominal-interest-rate rules in stabilizing output and prices. I find this result intuitively appealing." It is not intuitive how policymakers can use a real interest rate as their policy instrument in actual practice.

14. At the time of the March 1990 conference, the LIVERPOOL group had only been able to implement and present results for a version of their X regimes. The O and (somewhat revised) X regimes used in this volume were submitted to the project organizers later in 1990.

15. The LIVERPOOL group also used an alternative method for drawing and processing their shocks in the stochastic simulations, as will be explained below.

sum of real GNP and the inflation rate in 2BX). Any comparisons of the results from the MSG X regimes with the results from other models' X or O regimes, therefore, should take this conceptual difference into account (for further discussion, see chapter 10).

Two other examples of differing implementations of the regimes seem sufficiently important to mention here. Both pertain to money targeting, in one case for the MPS model and in the other case for MULTIMOD.

The quarterly MPS model contains lagged responses of money demand to both interest rates and measures of real activity and prices, and substantial lagged responses of changes in real output to changes in interest rates. These features cause a complex dynamic response of real output and prices to changes in the stock of money. The MPS group found that the O specification of money targeting performed very poorly in their model and, accordingly, found it necessary to make several amendments to get "reasonable" solutions. The MPS 1X specification thus adds the first- and fourth-quarter differences of deviations in money from baseline to the level deviation of money from baseline:

$$(3\text{-}4) \qquad RS_t - RS_t^* = \delta_0 \log(M_t^*/M_t) + \delta_1 \Delta \log(M_t^*/M_t) + \delta_4 \Delta_4 \log(M_t^*/M_t).$$

The MPS preferred values for the three coefficients of this amended regime were $\delta_0 = -0.25$, $\delta_1 = -0.50$, and $\delta_4 = -1.5$.

The MULTIMOD group also had initial difficulty in getting the O specification of money targeting to work in their model, apparently in large part because the money-demand functions in MULTIMOD are extremely interest-inelastic in the short run. In any event, the MULTIMOD group did submit results for regime 1 but also submitted results for a 1X specification that they regarded as more plausible (in the context of their model). Their 1X specification incorporates the money-targeting reaction function typically used in MULTIMOD simulations run in the course of the model's regular use for analytical purposes at the IMF. The essential idea behind MULTIMOD's regular reaction function is that policymakers focus on a target path for the money stock but choose to dampen interest-rate fluctuations in the short run. Specifically, the policy authority acts as if it identifies a "long-run equilibrium" value of the short-term interest rate, $RSBAR_t$, that is consistent with the money stock being on its target path (in this context, the baseline) after lags have worked themselves out:

$$(3\text{-}5a) \qquad\qquad RS_t - RS_t^* = \gamma(RSBAR_t - RS_t^*);$$

γ is a response coefficient indicating the speed of reaction. The value of $RSBAR_t$ is calculated, in effect, by inverting the money demand function, setting M_t equal to M_t^*, and solving for the value of RS_t after the lags in that function have worked themselves out. The end result is a rule of the form:

$$(3\text{-}5b) \qquad RS_t - RS_t^* = \gamma\left\{[1/(-\alpha_2)][(1 - \alpha_3)\log(M_t^*/P_t) - \alpha_0\right.$$
$$\left. -\alpha_1 \log Y_t] - RS_t^*\right\},$$

where α_0, α_1, α_2, and α_3 are the parameters of the money-demand function. In practice, the short-run elasticity of money demand with respect to interest rates, α_2, takes on a low value of -0.005, so that the LM curves in each country are quite steep.[16]

Because they constitute changes in the form of the reaction-function equations, the preceding differences among the models in the implementation of regimes presumably have the greatest significance for interpreting cross-model differences in the results. But another set of differences in the model regimes, in the values used for the feedback coefficients, also needs to be taken into account.

Under its 1X money-targeting regime the TAYLOR model, apart from its specification of the policy instrument as the real rather than the nominal short-term interest rate, would not solve for several countries when the feedback coefficient was set as high as -5. To obtain solutions, the coefficient for money targeting was substantially lowered to -0.5 (for all countries).

The MULTIMOD and INTERMOD groups both had difficulty in implementing the O regimes for nominal-income targeting for the stochastic simulations. With the original feedback coefficient value of 1.5, half or more of the attempted stochastic simulations proved to be unstable.[17] Both groups thus lowered the feedback coefficient significantly; the MULTIMOD group used a value of 0.5 for its 2AX regime, and the INTERMOD group lowered the coefficient to 0.7 for its 2AX regime (both adaptive and consistent). MULTIMOD

16. MULTIMOD's money-demand functions were estimated with data pooled across all the industrial countries, and each country is constrained to have an identical function. For the simulations prepared with regime 1X for this project, the value of γ was set at 0.25. It can be shown that the MULTIMOD reaction function 3-5b is equivalent, for the purposes of this project, to the function

$$RS_t - RS_t^* = 0.01(\gamma/\alpha_2) \log(M_t^*/M_t).$$

With values of $\gamma = 0.25$ and $\alpha_2 = -.005$, the function is effectively

$$RS_t - RS_t^* = -0.5 \log(M_t^*/M_t),$$

which differs from the O specification in equation 3-1 by having a feedback coefficient only one-tenth the size of the standard coefficient.

17. "Unstable" in the sense that the solution process would fail to converge (because, for example, some of the variables were being forced to values less than zero, which is arithmetically impossible for variables appearing in the model as logarithms). The INTERMOD group experienced these problems only for the version of the model using model-consistent expectations.

had an analogous problem with exchange-rate targeting. That group had to cut the feedback coefficient in half, from 2.5 to 1.25, before obtaining satisfactory simulations.[18]

The GEM model group did not report any results for O regimes. For each of their X alternatives, they greatly lowered the value of the O feedback coefficient. For their money targeting regime 1X, the GEM group used a feedback coefficient of -0.25 (only one-twentieth of the O coefficient value of -5). The GEM feedback coefficients for their 2AX and 2BX regimes were both 0.25 (one-sixth of the O coefficient values of 1.5).

As a final illustration, the MPS and MULTIMOD groups found that they obtained poor results for real-GNP-plus-inflation targeting when they imposed the O specification, which in effect forces the same feedback coefficient on the output and inflation-rate terms. The MPS and MULTIMOD groups accordingly specified several 2BX variants with unequal coefficients on the two terms:

$$(3-6) \qquad RS_t - RS_t^* = \theta_1 \log(Y_t/Y_t^*) + \theta_2(\pi_t - \pi_t^*).$$

The 2BX regime for MPS used in the main tables in chapters 4 and 5 has values for θ_1 and θ_2, respectively, of 1.5 and 0.75—that is, with a weight on output twice as large as that on inflation.[19] For their 2BX regime, the MULTIMOD group used values for θ_1 and θ_2, respectively, of 0.5 and 7.0—that is, with a much smaller weight on output than on inflation.[20]

The preceding summary of regime implementation brings out a regrettable fact about the empirical experiments undertaken for the project. Efforts to achieve standardization in policy regimes across the models were only partially successful. The difficulties in attaining standardization were greater than had been anticipated at the outset. Indeed, the very notion of regime standardization in a context with numerous and heterogenous models contains inherent ambiguities. (Standardization of regimes is certainly not the same thing as an analytically valid standard for evaluating policy regimes.) These difficulties signal that caution must be used in interpreting the simulation results.

The lack of full standardization in implementing the monetary-policy regimes can be attributed to two sets of factors. First, some model groups did

18. Ironically, the values of the feedback coefficients specified for the O regimes in the original guidelines (prepared before the March 1990 conference) had been obtained from trial simulations with an earlier version of the MULTIMOD model. By the time that the final MULTIMOD simulations were prepared for this project, the model had changed sufficiently to make the original feedback coefficients no longer workable!

19. The MPS group also reported simulations obtained with other pairs of values; see chapter 5 for discussion.

20. As pointed out in chapter 5, MULTIMOD's stochastic simulation results favor real-GNP-plus-inflation targeting markedly less than is the case for other models. This difference between MULTIMOD and the other models may be attributable in part to the large departure from the guidelines identified in the text.

not have sufficient financial, personnel, or computing resources to experiment long enough to get the O regimes to work successfully in the context of their models. For this project, as with the earlier projects of this collaborative research effort, it has been necessary for each model group to cover its own costs in preparing the research results. As is always the case, each group also faced competing demands for its time, usually of higher priority, during the period when the research was being carried out. A secondary consideration also played a role: the original guidelines sent to the model groups were not explicit enough (viewed with the wisdom of hindsight) in a few details of the instructions.

Second, and more important, for the stochastic simulations the O specifications of the policy regimes may in some cases have been incompatible with the structures of individual models. The details of incompatibility (where located, in which sectors and equations of a model) and the particular reasons for failure of an O regime proved difficult, sometimes impossible, for the model group to track down. For example, the MX3 group could not successfully implement exchange-rate targeting regardless of the variants tried; the group's efforts included changing the feedback-response coefficient in the regime and omitting all shocks to the exchange-rate equations in the stochastic simulations. The reason or reasons for failure were never fully determined, although the difficulties were found to originate in the Japanese sector of the model (for further discussion, see chapter 9). Similarly, as already pointed out, the TAYLOR model would not converge for several of the O regimes because of problems originating in the Japanese (or French, or Canadian) sectors of the model. Particular problems were experienced with exchange-rate targeting; in the end, the TAYLOR 3X regimes contain not only the bilateral dollar exchange rate but also real GNP as an explicit target variable.

A related reason for a model group's inability to implement the O regimes as set out in the stochastic-simulation guidelines may have been that the values of the feedback coefficients, combined with the magnitude of the shocks drawn from the model's covariance matrix, caused a large number of replications to violate economic constraints (nonnegativity, for example) or to fail to converge within set bounds of the simulation software (number of periods to achieve convergence criteria). In principle, such convergence problems could be caused by the magnitude of the shocks drawn in the stochastic simulation or by an inappropriately valued feedback coefficient, not by incompatibility between the regime specification and the model's structure.

For situations of this latter type, changes in the feedback coefficients—adopting an X variant rather than staying with the O regime—resulted in convergence of the stochastic simulations after more trials. The GEM, INTERMOD, MCM, MPS, MULTIMOD, and TAYLOR groups all engaged in this type of experimentation before settling on particular X variants for some or

Table 3-3. *Feedback-Coefficient Values Used by Model Groups That Submitted Simulation Results for X-Variant Regimes Only*[a]

Model group	Money targeting (1/1X)	Nominal-income targeting (2A/2AX)	Real-GNP-plus-inflation targeting (2B/2BX)	Exchange-rate targeting (3/3X)
GEM	−0.25	0.25	0.25	n.a.
MCM	[−5.0]	0.20	0.20	[2.5]
MULTIMOD[b]	−0.50	0.50	0.5; 7.0	1.25
TAYLOR[c]	−0.50	[1.5]	[1.5]	1.5; [2.5]
"O" specification in guidelines[a]	−5.0	1.5	1.5	2.5

n.a. Not available.

a. Values in brackets denote cases in which the feedback coefficient for a model does *not* differ from the O-specification value in the project guidelines (that is, the value according to the "original" regime specifications in equations 3-1, discussed in the text and reproduced in the last row of this table).

b. The MULTIMOD value for money targeting is that group's 1X regime. See the text for discussion of MULTIMOD's 2BX regime; the first of the two coefficients refers to the term on output, the second to the term on inflation.

c. See the text for discussion of the alternative specifications for all four regime types for the TAYLOR model. For the TAYLOR 3X regime, the first coefficient refers to a term in nominal GNP (a departure from the guidelines); the second coefficient is the O-specification value (see footnote a) for the feedback coefficient on the exchange rate.

all of the regimes. For convenient reference, we have included in table 3-3 a summary of the differing feedback coefficients used by those models that submitted results only for X-variant regimes.

In a few instances, most notably for the MSG model and for a few other models for nominal-income targeting, model groups submitted results not only for the O specification of a regime but also for an X specification with a different value of the feedback coefficient. For these instances, it appears generally true that an increase in the feedback coefficient on the target variable in the policy regime stabilizes the target variable in the face of the historical shocks but tends to destabilize other macroeconomic variables of interest that are not target variables in the policy regime. How much the other variables of interest are destabilized appears to depend in a complex way on the shocks, model, and feedback coefficient of the regime.[21] A discussion of these results for changed feedback coefficients appears in chapter 5.

As explained earlier, the project guidelines had requested participating model groups to keep fiscal policies, defined in terms of real government expenditures and nominal tax rates, unchanged from their baseline paths during the initial ten years of the simulation period. Models incorporating forward-looking, model-consistent expectations were to make adjustments in their

21. For the MSG model, specifications that "optimize" the feedback coefficient in a regime achieve the minimum value of the policymakers' loss function perfectly, by design. Such specifications of a regime might not be preferred as a first-best regime by policymakers, however, if policymakers care about other variables that are not included as target variables in the regime, or if policymakers use a loss function that differs in other ways from the one used to calculate the optimal coefficients.

tax reaction functions or other aspects of the terminal conditions for fiscal policies only *after* the first ten years of the simulation period.[22]

In the event, model groups differed significantly in the ways that they did, or did not, implement these guidelines for unchanged fiscal policies. In earlier research on model specification, model groups had not reached a consensus on the most appropriate form of intertemporal "closure rules" for fiscal and monetary policies. Unfortunately, even our weak efforts to standardize the intertemporal aspects of fiscal policies for this project were not successful. Models such as MULTIMOD and MSG, for example, appear *not* to have suppressed their normal tax-rate reaction functions during the initial ten-year simulation period. INTERMOD and LIVERPOOL are examples of models that did follow the instructions, raising tax rates only after the completion of the initial ten years.

As more has been learned about the simulation properties of empirical models, in particular those making use of model-consistent expectations, evidence has accumulated that different specifications for tax-rate or government-expenditure reaction functions can lead to significant differences in simulation results. Without greater standardization of the reaction functions specified for fiscal policies, it may be impossible to diagnose the many other causes of differences in results across models.[23]

In hindsight, we wish that more strenuous efforts had been made to ensure greater conformity to a common specification of unchanged fiscal policies. The differences among the participating models in implementation of the fiscal assumptions may well be an important contributing factor to some of the differences in the models' results. Given the information available, however, this conjecture cannot be verified or refuted.

It will be important in future model-comparison projects to try to eliminate noncomparabilities of this sort. At clearly specified times during or after the simulation horizon, all models should implement tax-rate increases or expenditure decreases in reaction to increases in the stock of government debt or increases in interest payments on government debt (and vice versa for reductions in government debt or interest payments), with the size of these reactions being standardized.

---

22. The reason that such adjustments are necessary at some point during the simulation horizon for rational-expectations models is well known. Models with forward-looking expectations typically cannot reach a convergent solution without making some explicit assumption about how the intertemporal budget constraint facing a government is ultimately met. If an attempt were made to keep real government expenditures and nominal tax rates *indefinitely* at their baseline values, some types of shocks would lead to violation of the transversality conditions of agents holding government debt, and hence to nonconvergent behavior of the model.

23. Christopher Sims identified this aspect of the design of the simulation guidelines as a problem in his remarks at the 1990 conference, and his comments in chapter 6 amplify his views on this point.

In the preceding discussion of differences in implementation of the regimes, we have candidly identified a variety of problems. But it would be inappropriate to stress these problems so much that the entire exercise of comparing the regimes across different models is called into doubt. Although the glass is partly empty, it is nonetheless more than half full.

Certainly, the comparability of regimes *within a model* is not typically compromised by nonstandardization across models. Even for a model group that implemented only their own X variants of the regime types, analysis can validly assess the performance of the alternative regimes for that model.

Still more important, it is possible that robust generalizations about regime types can emerge *despite* heterogeneity among the models and differences in implementation of the regimes. If such robustness should emerge, moreover, the resulting conclusions would have enhanced, not diminished, value for policymakers. Uncertainty about the types of shocks currently buffeting the economy and uncertainty stemming from the rival claims of competing models are the essence of life for policymakers. The great merit of undertaking comparative projects like this one is the potential for identifying approaches to policy decisions that will be relatively robust in the presence of *both* sources of uncertainty.

The Mechanics of Stochastic Simulation

Stochastic simulation uses the residuals from a model's equations to generate multiple forecast paths of key variables of interest. The average properties of these multiple forecast paths can be summarized with statistical measures such as the root-mean-squared deviations (RMSDs) of the forecast paths from the baseline path. When a stochastic simulation is performed for each of several alternative policy regimes, a comparison of such statistics across the regimes gives the policymaker information about the likely consequences (for a variety of macroeconomic variables of interest) of implementing one or another regime given the set of shocks drawn from the model's residuals.

In this project, historical residuals (generated by the model for the period of the 1970s and 1980s; see below) are the raw material for generating the multiple forecast paths. Together with the structure of the model itself, the residuals are the common elements of policy experiments conducted across alternative regimes. The characteristics of the model that determine its residuals—the model's theoretical structure, data aggregation, and method of econometric estimation—are thus the critical determinants of the forecast paths. Econometric issues such as the manner of forming expected variables and the treatment of autoregressive elements, moreover, will influence the determination of the residuals. Technical issues such as methods of inverting covariance matrices and drawing shocks will likewise arise when computing the set of economic shocks to be passed through the model when carrying out stochastic simulations. Adjustments to the raw matrix of historical residuals may be desirable or necessary to obtain these shocks.

The issues identified in the preceding paragraph will be discussed below using examples drawn from the stochastic simulations prepared for this project. First, however, we describe the basic steps involved using a simplified example.

Basic Procedures for Stochastic Simulation

Assume a model with m stochastic equations of the general form $\mathbf{Y_t} = \alpha\mathbf{Y_t} + \beta\mathbf{X_t} + \gamma\mathbf{Y_{t-1}} + \mathbf{u_t}$, where $\mathbf{Y_t}$, $\mathbf{Y_{t-1}}$, and $\mathbf{u_t}$ are $m \times 1$ column vectors, $\mathbf{X_t}$ is a $k \times 1$ column vector, α and y are $m \times m$ matrices, and β is a $m \times k$ matrix. For a historical sample period of T observations, each variable Y_i will have an associated vector of T residuals, $u_i = (u_{i1} \ldots u_{iT})$. The estimated variance-covariance matrix of the historical residuals, $\hat{\mathbf{\Sigma}}$, is an $m \times m$ matrix computed as $(1/T)\, \hat{\mathbf{U}}\hat{\mathbf{U}}'$, where $\hat{\mathbf{U}}$ is the $m \times T$ matrix of values of the estimated error terms. If the u_i were independent and identically distributed (IID), then the set of shocks to use in a stochastic simulation could be obtained directly from a simple transformation of $\hat{\mathbf{\Sigma}}$. To generate the shocks to be used, the researcher would first decompose the matrix $\hat{\mathbf{\Sigma}}$ into two triangular matrices that, when multiplied together, yield the original matrix $\hat{\mathbf{\Sigma}}$; if the rank condition were to hold (if T were greater than m), there would be a unique such decomposition, $\hat{\mathbf{\Sigma}} = \mathbf{PP}'$, where $\mathbf{P}$ is lower triangular and $\mathbf{P}'$ is upper triangular. To carry out an initial "trial" for the first period of a simulation horizon, the researcher would next draw m values from a distribution for a standard normal random variable with a mean of 0 and variance 1; defining these values as the vector $\mathbf{e_1}$, he would then compute the $m \times 1$ vector $\mathbf{u_1^*} = \mathbf{Pe_1}$. Using the values $\mathbf{u_1^*}$ and the values for $\alpha, \beta, \gamma, \mathbf{X_1}$, and $\mathbf{Y_0}$, the researcher would solve the model for period 1 to obtain $\mathbf{Y_1}$, the solution values for the initial trial. Another set of draws from the standard normal distribution would be made to obtain $\mathbf{e_2}$ and $\mathbf{u_2^*}$, which in turn would be used to solve the model for $\mathbf{Y_2}$ for the second trial period.[24] The process would be repeated for successive periods until a stipulated horizon is reached, say period N. The solution path for the N periods would constitute the first N replications or trials of the stochastic

---

24. The solution values $\mathbf{Y_2}$ depend on $\mathbf{Y_1}$, which in turn depend on $\mathbf{u_1^*}$. More generally, the solution values $\mathbf{Y_t}$ for period t during the simulation horizon depend on past solution values, and hence on past as well as current values of $\mathbf{e}$ and $\mathbf{u^*}$. For rational-expectations models, solution values for period t can be obtained only by solving the model over an extended future period, where the terminal date is far enough in the future not to greatly influence the solution values for period t. When the model is initially solved for period 1, agents are assumed to expect no new shocks in period 2 and beyond; when the period-2 shocks are applied to obtain the solution values for period 2, agents are assumed to expect no shocks in period 3 and beyond; and so on.

simulation. Finally, the preceding process—successive draws from the normal distribution and computation of the $\mathbf{u}_t^*$, use of the $\mathbf{u}_t^*$ to solve the model for period t, with the initial simulation period then moving forward to period $t + 1$—would be repeated S times, yielding in total NS sets of solution values. These solution values would then be used to calculate summary statistics for the stochastic simulation as a whole (for example, RMSDs of key variables from their baseline paths).

Several of the assumptions of the simplified example in the preceding paragraph tend to be violated when the techniques are applied to actual models. First, for models with rational expectations, it can be difficult to create the covariance matrix $\hat{\boldsymbol{\Sigma}}$. For such models, it would be preferable to calculate the residuals $\mathbf{u}_t$ from whole-model simulations and use those residuals to form $\hat{\boldsymbol{\Sigma}}$. Some of the groups with rational-expectations models, however, created the covariance matrix by stacking the u_i generated from estimation of the individual equations of the model one at a time.

Second, most of the u_i for most of the models are probably not identically and independently distributed. For these circumstances, several of the model groups decided to "whiten" the u_i before computing the covariance matrix $\hat{\boldsymbol{\Sigma}}$. The transformation used to whiten the u_i—for example, a first-order correction for serial correlation: $u_{it} = \rho u_{i,t-1} + v_t$—in effect becomes part of the $\hat{\boldsymbol{\Sigma}}$ matrix. The matrix from which the stochastic shocks are drawn becomes $\hat{\boldsymbol{\Sigma}}_\mathbf{v} = (1/T)\hat{\mathbf{V}}\hat{\mathbf{V}}'$, where $\hat{\mathbf{V}}$ is an $m \times T$ matrix of values of the whitened residuals v_t.[25]

Third, most models in practice have a larger number of equations than observation periods in their historical data sample. Hence with $m > T$, the rank condition does not hold, and the matrix $\hat{\boldsymbol{\Sigma}}$ or $\hat{\boldsymbol{\Sigma}}_\mathbf{v}$ is singular and cannot be straightforwardly decomposed into the triangular components $\mathbf{P}$ and $\mathbf{P}'$. Several alternative procedures exist to obtain a matrix $\mathbf{P}$ to premultiply the draws from the normal distribution. One model group (MPS), moreover, used a different, "bootstrapping" procedure to draw its shocks, in effect drawing them directly from the $\hat{\mathbf{V}}$ matrix.

The following subsections discuss these issues in more detail, identifying differences in procedures across the model groups.

Methods of Estimating the Model

Several important problems arise in the creation of the historical residual matrix from which the matrix of shocks is derived. These are the econometric technique used to generate the matrix, the treatment of future values of expected

---

25. In practice the whitening process may result in the loss of one or two time series observations, thereby causing the T dimension of $\hat{\mathbf{V}}$ to be slightly smaller than the T dimension of the $\hat{\mathbf{U}}$ matrix.

variables, and the treatment of autoregressive components of the individual equations.

To be internally consistent, a model with rational expectations should use full-model simulations to generate the expected variables needed for the calculation of historical residuals. A model-consistent estimate of the structural residuals cannot be obtained from the individual equations alone if those equations have expectations of future variables included as explanatory variables; model-consistent expectations must be obtained from solutions of the entire model. Yet calculation of the residuals in this whole-model approach is a computer-intensive task.

Of those participating models using rational expectations, only TAYLOR and MX3 used full-model simulations to generate the historical residuals. And even those two models differed in the formation of their baseline paths in a manner that affects the elements of the historical residual matrix.

Peter Klenow included "perfect tracking residuals" in each equation in the TAYLOR model so that the equations would hold exactly when all variables and expected variables were equal to baseline values. For derivation of the model-consistent forecast, these perfect tracking residuals became integral parts of the residual matrix, and therefore were incorporated in the $\hat{\Sigma}$ and $\mathbf{P}$ matrices.

Joseph Gagnon and Ralph Tryon did not include such perfect tracking residuals in the baseline paths of variables for the MX3 model. The MX3 baseline paths are derived from the paths of the fundamental forcing variables of, for example, labor and capital. But some of the equations in the MX3 model contain autoregressive components that were not excluded from the residuals used for computation of the $\hat{\Sigma}$ and $\mathbf{P}$ matrices. Thus the representative shocks used in the MX3 stochastic simulations may not have been independent and identically distributed.

The residual matrix used for computation of $\hat{\Sigma}$ and $\mathbf{P}$ for the MSG model had substantially smaller dimensions than for the other models. Warwick McKibbin generated his residuals from three key equations—consumption, money demand, and production—for each of the three largest industrial countries (United States, Japan, and Germany). He also incorporated the residual from the model's oil-price equation. His procedures and the smallness of the dimensions of the matrices allowed him to calculate the shock matrix analytically and directly.

All the remaining model groups formed their $\hat{\Sigma}$ or $\hat{\Sigma}_v$ matrix by stacking the estimated residuals obtained from single-equation estimation of the model's equations.[26]

---

26. In the case of GEM, the single-equation residuals stacked to form the variance-covariance matrix were from the full National Institute GEM model (not the residuals from the linearized MINIGEM model discussed in chapter 11).

Forming Expected Variables

Methods of generating the expectations for forward-looking variables varied among model groups. For in-sample rational-expectations calculations, Klenow assumed that agents in the TAYLOR model had perfect foresight about the actual values of exogenous variables for future periods. For the MX3 model, Gagnon and Tryon made a similar assumption about expectations of non-policy exogenous variables; for policy exogenous variables, however, agents were assumed to make use of first-order, nonstationary autoregressions.[27] The LIVERPOOL group projected future values of exogenous variables in line with forecast values for those variables made (for other purposes) around the time they implemented the simulation exercise.

The remaining model groups estimated the values of expected future variables from regressions incorporating lagged terms, but with differences across models in the lagged variables that were used. The INTERMOD group used a lagged-instrumental-variables approach, replacing the values for forward-looking variables appearing in the model with an ordinary least squares (OLS) projection of their future values.[28] For MULTIMOD and the MSG model, a time-series approach was used: the expected values of forward-looking variables were replaced with forecasts obtained from autoregressive time-series equations.[29] In the MPS model, expectations of forward-looking variables were formed adaptively from weighted averages of lagged values of the variables in question.

Formation of the expected future values of variables in asset-market equations sometimes deviated from this approach. The INTERMOD and MULTIMOD groups used the current observed value of the exchange rate for the expected future value, consistent with the random walk hypothesis of exchange-rate movements. In MULTIMOD, the interest-parity and money-demand residuals for EMS countries other than Germany were eliminated from the historical matrix.[30] Ray Barrell, Jonathan Ireland, and Peter Westaway of the GEM group at the National Institute formed expected values for exchange rates with a method dependent on uncovered-interest-parity relationships and on terminal

---

27. Gagnon and Tryon also made adjustments for unanticipated regime shifts, but these adjustments do not appear to be particularly important to their results. See chapter 9 for more details.

28. The INTERMOD procedure regressed actual future values of the forward-looking variables on the following set of instruments: a constant term, the lagged capital stock, capacity output, the lagged long-term interest rate, real government spending, lagged real GDP, a 1980 dummy, and a linear time trend.

29. For MSG, no residuals were calculated or used from the model's exchange-rate equations.

30. The MULTIMOD group assumed that full monetary union prevailed among the countries participating in the exchange-rate mechanism (ERM) of the EMS. With a single European currency, interest parity among the EMS countries implies that interest rates are equal and in effect only a single money-demand function, that for Germany, is relevant. Consequently, the MULTIMOD group set the errors in the interest-parity equations and money-demand equations for EMS countries other than Germany to zero. (The group verified that there was negligible covariation between the estimated money-demand residuals for the non-German EMS countries and other estimated residuals in the model.)

conditions requiring current account balances (changes in net foreign assets) to return to baseline.[31]

Treatment of Autoregressive Components

In theoretical analyses (for example, as in chapter 2), it is frequently assumed that the shocks hitting the economy are independent and identically distributed. As already noted, for empirical models this assumption tends not to be satisfied. The historical residuals used to form the matrix $\hat{\Sigma}$ contain autoregressive components stemming from the original equation estimation. To obtain an adjusted matrix of shocks, $\hat{\Sigma}_v$, several of the model groups modified the non-IID u_i of the historical residual matrix to generate new residual series that did have the IID property.

The MULTIMOD and INTERMOD groups used similar whitening methods to create $\hat{\Sigma}_v$ matrices of IID shocks from the historical residuals. The MULTIMOD group regressed each historical residual on a constant, the lagged value of the residual, and a time trend ($u_{it} = \alpha + \rho u_{i,t-1} + \gamma t + v_t$) and then used the resulting estimates of v_t to form $\hat{\Sigma}_v$. The INTERMOD group followed the same procedure except for the addition of a coefficient and a term in time squared in the regression estimating the v_t.

For the MX3 model, Gagnon and Tryon assumed that the historical shocks incorporated in $\hat{\Sigma}$ were IID except for the residuals from the exchange-rate and U.S. output-price equations. For those equations, the u_i were whitened by running the regression $u_{it} = \rho u_{i,t-1} + v_t$; the resulting estimates for v_t were used in the construction of $\hat{\Sigma}_v$. Gagnon and Tryon also introduced autoregressive errors into the equations for their policy reaction variables (monetary bases and government expenditures).

The LIVERPOOL group created a $\hat{\Sigma}$ directly from the variances of the single equations in the model, some of which were first-differenced and some of which had estimated autocorrelation coefficients. Covariances were ignored; thus, by assumption, the matrix was constructed as diagonal.

For the TAYLOR model, Klenow assumed that the u_i in the $\hat{\Sigma}$ matrix of historical residuals were IID. Thus no transformation of the $\hat{\Sigma}$ matrix was performed. As already noted, Klenow's $\hat{\Sigma}$ matrix embodies perfect tracking residuals.

For the MSG model, McKibbin solved for $\hat{\Sigma}$ analytically, assuming that the residuals from the model equations were IID.

---

31. The approach and associated equations are described further in Barrell and Gurney (1991). The GEM group observes that "no other variables were solved forward in this exercise. The exchange rate itself was not shocked, and hence there were no problems specifying its future path; but because the current-balance ratio in the terminal condition and the interest rate in the UIP condition are both endogenous, the current exchange rate responded in a forward-looking manner to all shocks."

The GEM group indicated that they carried out some experimental simulations that took into account serial correlation in the estimated residuals. The GEM simulations discussed in chapter 5, however, are based on the assumption that the residuals are IID.

In principle, as emphasized by Christopher Sims in correspondence with project participants after the 1990 conference, large amounts of serial correlation and cross-equation correlation in the structural residuals of a model are indications of model weakness. They imply that much of the observed inertia and cross-variable interaction among economic variables is not well captured by the model's equations. In future model-comparison exercises based on stochastic simulations, it would be beneficial to ask the model groups to provide detail about the covariance properties of their structural residuals before autoregressive adjustments. It might also be helpful to suggest some standardization in procedures for making such adjustments.

Inverting the Adjusted Variance-Covariance Matrix

The procedure most commonly used to draw the shocks for each stochastic simulation exercise requires a decomposition of the adjusted historical matrix into two triangular components, $\hat{\Sigma}_v = \mathbf{P}'\mathbf{P}$ (see above). The typical decomposition to obtain $\mathbf{P}$ requires that $\hat{\Sigma}_v$ be inverted. But the rank condition on $\hat{\Sigma}_v$ frequently does not hold, so that the matrix is singular and cannot be inverted; that is, the number of stochastic equations for which residuals have been created is greater than the number of data observations in the historical sample period.[32]

The model groups that faced this problem adjusted the $\hat{\Sigma}_v$ matrix in several different ways to make it invertible. These adjustments add noise (as opposed to bias) to the diagonal elements of the matrix, which in turn can affect the resulting stochastic simulations. The differences in the way in which the model groups made a singular matrix nonsingular, however, are probably much less important to the comparisons across models than are the many other differences in the creation of the $\hat{\Sigma}_v$ matrix of shocks.

For the MULTIMOD and INTERMOD models, very small numbers (for example, 0.000001) were added to each diagonal element of the $\hat{\Sigma}_v$ matrix to obtain a nonsingular and invertible matrix. Klenow for the TAYLOR model used a modified Cholesky decomposition technique to obtain the lower triangular matrix $\mathbf{P}$.[33]

---

32. For further discussion, see Fair (1984, chapter 7) and Ireland and Westaway (1991).

33. The $\hat{\Sigma}$ or $\hat{\Sigma}_v$ matrix is symmetric and at least positive-semidefinite. When the covariance matrix is singular, however, it is not positive definite. The usual Cholesky procedure to obtain a decomposition of $\hat{\Sigma}$ requires $\hat{\Sigma}$ to be positive definite. Klenow reported that he therefore used a less widely known, modified Cholesky decomposition that applies to positive-semidefinite matrices; see Faddeeva (1959).

Not all the model groups faced the rank problem or needed to invert the matrix. For MX3, the rank condition held. McKibbin solved for the $\hat{\Sigma}$ matrix for the MSG model analytically and thus did not need to invert it to draw the stochastic shocks. Neither the MPS nor LIVERPOOL groups inverted a $\hat{\Sigma}_v$ matrix in their procedure to obtain shocks; they chose to follow an alternative procedure (see below) in part because the rank condition did not hold.[34] GEM used a method proposed by McCarthy for drawing shocks, which also does not require inversion of the $\hat{\Sigma}$ or $\hat{\Sigma}_v$ matrix.[35]

Drawing the Shocks and Implementing the Replications

After preparation of the $\hat{\Sigma}$ or $\hat{\Sigma}_v$ matrix, the INTERMOD, MULTIMOD, TAYLOR, and MX3 groups drew random shocks from a standard normal distribution and multiplied by the lower triangular matrix $\mathbf{P}$ to create the shocks used for each trial of their stochastic simulations. (Their procedure was akin to the simplified example discussed above.) The specific draws of shocks were applied identically to each policy regime.

The groups using quarterly models made 400 drawings of shocks, 10 for each of the 40 quarters of the ten-year period 1990–99 ($N = 40$ and $S = 10$). The groups with annual models did 40 simulations for each of the ten years ($N = 10$ and $S = 40$), again for a total of 400 drawings of shocks and 400 periods simulated. Each drawing of the shocks was identically applied to all of the policy regimes being studied.

The MPS model group did not select their shocks in the preceding way. Instead, to perform a single trial, they randomly selected a particular historical quarter and then inserted the vector of shocks for that quarter into the model. For certain asset-market equations of the model, the elements of the vector of shocks were replaced with shocks drawn from independent normal distributions with variances equal to the error variance of the original estimate of that equation.[36] In general, the MPS group carried out only 100 trials for each policy regime. For some regimes, where they carried out 300 trials, the results varied little from those for only 100.

The LIVERPOOL procedure for drawing shocks also differed somewhat from that used by other model groups. As noted, the LIVERPOOL group as-

34. The LIVERPOOL group was not able to carry out the full tracking exercise (involving forecasting the past from each year of the period) required to generate the historical residuals over the 1973–87 period. It used single-equation residuals, with the variance-covariance matrix assumed to be diagonal.

35. McCarthy's method for drawing values of the error terms is discussed in McCarthy (1972); see also Ireland and Westaway (1991) and Fair (1984, chapter 7.3).

36. These equations were the portfolio-balance equations for U.S. holdings of foreign-currency assets and for foreign holdings of dollar assets. These relationships were important for the determination of the dollar's exchange value in the model but fit very poorly and had not been reestimated for several years.

sumed a diagonal $\hat{\Sigma}$ matrix, where the diagonal elements were the standard errors of the stochastic equations of the model and the off-diagonal elements (the covariances among the equation errors) were assumed to be zero. In addition to ignoring the covariances, "to economize computer time," the LIVERPOOL group scaled down their shocks before inserting them into the model and then multiplied the resulting solution by the square of the scale factor. This procedure of scaling down the shocks before running a trial and scaling up the resulting simulation path assumes that the model is approximately linear within the bounds of the single equation errors.[37]

For the MSG model, McKibbin also followed a different procedure (see chapter 10 for details). In practice, he derived the solution paths for the model's variables analytically. In effect, the linearized equations of the MSG model can be written as a function of state variables and the shocks (after substituting out the "jumping" variables using the equation for the stable manifold): $\mathbf{Y_t} = \boldsymbol{\phi}\mathbf{Z_t} + \boldsymbol{\psi}\mathbf{v_t}$. The variance-covariance matrix for $\mathbf{Y_t}$ ($\hat{\boldsymbol{\Sigma}}_y$, which is the analytical representation of the mean forecast path and squared deviation from the mean path) can then be derived from the $\hat{\boldsymbol{\Sigma}}_v$ matrix and the coefficients on the shocks: $\hat{\boldsymbol{\Sigma}}_y = \boldsymbol{\psi}\hat{\boldsymbol{\Sigma}}_v\boldsymbol{\psi}'$.

The GEM group reported their results for only 40 replications, carried out over only five years. In their covering note to the project organizers, the GEM group observed that "we decided to use this shorter simulation period to overcome our problems with computer time."[38]

Characteristics of Shocks Applied by Model Groups

Some of the main attributes of the participating models were identified in table 3-1. As another point of reference, serving as a reminder from the preceding section, table 3-4 summarizes how the model groups handled several of the procedural issues about the historical residuals and the preparation of the stochastic simulations. All the differences among the models displayed in tables 3-1 and 3-4 can lead to differences among the models' historical residuals and variance-covariance matrices, and hence to differences in the patterns of "representative" shocks used in their stochastic simulations.

---

37. The assumed linearity between shocks and path would appear to hold only when the shock matrix is diagonal and the model is linear. Although most of the participating models are thought to be approximately linear in their behavior, the shock matrices in other models (where the full covariance matrix was calculated) are not diagonal.

38. The GEM group indicated that they implemented their shocks unscaled (unlike LIVERPOOL) and that they reported only those simulations "that converged in the time allowed. Nonconvergence appeared to be more a consequence of model ordering (and shortage of time) than an indication of serious underlying problems."

Table 3-4. *Summary Features of Implementation of Stochastic Simulations: Differences among the Participating Models*

Item	GEM	INTERMOD	LIVERPOOL	MPS
Derivation of the historical residuals				
Technique of model estimation[a]	Instrumental variables/ordinary least squares (OLS) where suitable	Instrumental variables/OLS	Instrumental variables/generalized method of moments/OLS	Instrumental variables/OLS
Time period for model estimation	Varies with data availability (in general, 1966:1–1989:4; but often 1972:1–1989:4	1972–87	1957–81 (United States, Canada, France, Italy, United Kingdom); 1956–85 (Japan); 1961–83 (Germany)	Varies by equation; for most equations, early or mid-1960s through mid- to late 1980s
Method of calculating residuals for variance-covariance matrix (whole-model simulation, simulation equation-by-equation, or simulation with the subset of model equations)[b]	Equation by equation, for 360 estimated equations	Equation by equation	Equation by equation	Equation by equation
Formation of the variance-covariance matrix used for draws				
Types/number of equations for which residuals were included in variance-covariance matrix	360 stochastic equations	80 stochastic equations	Not available	All (about 125) stochastic equations
Adjustment for autoregressive residuals?	Residuals were not adjusted for autoregressive responses	Autocorrelation correction and trend adjustments applied to historical residuals before formation of variance-covariance matrix	See text	Autocorrelation correction applied to historical residuals before formation of variance-covariance matrix
Treatment of expectations (of exogenous variables where whole-model methods were used; of endogenous variables where equation-by-equation methods were used)	Model-consistent/perfect-foresight assumptions were made for exchange rates	Lagged-instrumental-variables approach for estimation of values of expected future variables for model-consistent expectations (INTERMOD-C); no leads in adaptive-expectations version of model (INTERMOD-A)	Perfect foresight for future values of exogenous variables	Adaptive expectations
Adjustments made to variance-covariance matrix to render the matrix positive definite	McCarthy method (see text)	Very small numbers added to main diagonal of Σ_v matrix	No adjustment (matrix is assumed to be diagonal)	Shocks drawn by bootstrap method from a randomly chosen historical quarter

Item	MSG	MULTIMOD	MX3	TAYLOR
Derivation of the historical residuals				
Technique of model estimation[a]	Most coefficients calibrated from theory and 1986 data, or studies in literature	Instrumental variables/OLS/three stage least squares (Zellner)	Generalized method of moments/ instrumental variables/OLS	Instrumental variables/OLS
Time period for model estimation	Not applicable	1974–88	1976:4–1988:4	1972:1–1984:4
Method of calculating residuals for variance-covariance matrix (whole-model simulation, simulation equation-by-equation, or simulation with subset of model equations)[b]	Equation by equation	Equation by equation	Whole model	Whole model
Formation of the variance-covariance matrix used for draws				
Types/number of equations for which residuals were included in variance-covariance matrix	10 stochastic equations (consumption, money demand, and production for each of 3 countries, plus OPEC oil price)	92 stochastic equations (including consumption; investment; imports of manufactures, commodities, oil; manufactures exports; price deflators; long-term interest rates; money demands and interest parity for Germany and non-EMS countries)	31 stochastic equations (price deflator, exchange rate, consumption, fixed investment, inventory investment, export price and volume, money demand for each of 4 regions)	All 98 stochastic equations (short- and long-term interest rates, exchange-rates, exports, imports, wages, prices, import and export prices, consumption, investment)
Adjustment for autoregressive residuals?	Residuals assumed not to require an autoregressive adjustment	Autocorrelation correction and trend adjustment applied to historical residuals before formation of variance-covariance matrix	Autocorrelation correction applied to small subset of the historical residuals before formation of variance-covariance matrix	First-order autoregressive adjustment of residuals in exchange-rate equations
Treatment of expectations (of exogenous variables where whole-model methods were used; of endogenous variables where equation-by-equation methods were used)	Expected values of forward-looking variables replaced with forecasts from auto-regressive time series equations	Expected values of forward-looking variables replaced with forecasts from autoregressive time series equations	Perfect foresight for nonpolicy exogenous variables; autoregressive expectations for policy variables	Perfect foresight for all exogenous variables
Adjustments made to variance-covariance matrix to render the matrix positive definite	Not relevant	Very small numbers added to main diagonal of Σ_v matrix	No adjustment necessary (rank condition satisfied)	Modified Cholesky decomposition

a. The technique of estimation is one of the factors determining how much of the cross-equation correlations is included in the residuals.
b. This choice of method helps to determine the range and type of shocks actually used in the stochastic simulations.

One obvious distinction among the models is a difference in time frequency: four of the models that ran the stochastic simulations are quarterly, and the other five are annual (with INTERMOD-A and INTERMOD-C counted as two models). This difference in frequency could give rise to significant differences in the characteristics of shocks. Historical residuals associated with a quarterly model, for example, may exhibit greater intertemporal correlation than those from an annual model. Quarterly models may therefore need to pay more attention to appropriate adjustment for autoregressive elements.

The estimation sample period used by a model group is a second factor influencing the model's historical residuals, and hence the $\hat{\Sigma}$ covariance matrix. Model groups with residuals generated from greatly differing time periods could have notable differences in historical residuals.

Model groups were asked to generate their residuals using data from the period 1973–87, or a period as close as possible to those years. In practice, groups deviated from the recommended period. The largest deviations were the inclusion by the MPS and LIVERPOOL model groups of residuals generated from data before the 1970s, whereas the sample periods for the other models began in 1972 or later. Moreover, the MPS estimation period ended in 1984 and the LIVERPOOL period ended at various dates during 1981–85, thereby excluding data from the later 1980s that were used in the other models. Arguably, the decade of the 1960s experienced fewer and smaller shocks than the 1970s and 1980s. The second half of the 1980s may also have experienced somewhat different shocks—for example, in types of financial innovations—than those prevalent in the early 1980s. If so, the matrices of shocks derived from the MPS and LIVERPOOL models could be significantly different from those for the other models. The estimation period for the MX3 model excluded the first oil-shock years, and the MX3 shock matrix might therefore omit some important shocks.

The degree of a model's disaggregation and its number of stochastic equations is a further set of factors conditioning the matrix of the model's shocks. The magnitudes of the diagonal and off-diagonal elements, and the complexity of covariance relationships, can all be affected. For example, models that incorporate linkages between industrial and developing countries or between industrial and OPEC countries provide potentially more complex channels for the transmission of shocks between individual G7 countries. As an illustration, shocks from the traded-goods sectors in country blocs seem notably important in MULTIMOD; that model disaggregates across regions more than most of the other models and includes probably the richest specification of the developing countries. As a contrasting illustration, the MPS model has the most highly developed set of relationships for the government sector of the U.S. economy and, accordingly, assigns more importance to U.S. fiscal shocks and fiscal linkages.

Not least important, as suggested earlier, the estimation technique used to construct a model and the model group's methods of adjusting the historical residuals can critically influence the nature of the shocks drawn for stochastic simulation. Except for the MSG model,[39] the models were originally estimated using single-equation techniques—that is, OLS, instrumental variables, or some variation of these two. Some MULTIMOD equations were estimated with Zellner techniques. None of the models was estimated using full information maximum likelihood (FIML). The use of FIML would allow correlations between the errors of individual equations of a model to be incorporated into the estimated coefficients and the estimated matrix of residuals. It is not clear in general whether FIML estimation techniques would yield larger or smaller off-diagonal terms in the variance-covariance matrix for a model, but FIML would at least permit a more complex (and potentially more accurate) pattern of relationships between the model's variables and its estimated errors.

In principle, it is possible to glean considerable information from an explicit examination of a model's variance-covariance matrix of historical residuals. After the initial project conference, therefore, each model group submitting stochastic simulation results was asked to provide empirical details about the variance-covariance matrix used for drawing its shocks. In practice, however, the objective of close analysis and direct comparison of the models' covariance matrices proved to be unattainable. Future model-comparison projects will be able to improve on our experience in this regard, and we therefore summarize briefly here the reasons for our lack of success.

One difficulty in comparing shocks across equations within an individual model, or across equations in different models, is a problem with units. Some equations may be specified with the left-hand-side variables as levels (for example, consumption in billions of local currency units), others as the natural logarithm of the variables, and still others as the percentage change in the variables. Thus the elements of the $\hat{\Sigma}$ or $\hat{\Sigma}_v$ matrix for an individual model, and even more so for two different models, may be measured in different units. Interpretation of the elements of the matrices must start with appropriate adjustments for these unit differences. In practice, we did not always have sufficient information to make such adjustments.

Apart from the problem with units, an even more serious difficulty was incomplete, and noncomparable, information about the elements of the $\hat{\Sigma}$ or $\hat{\Sigma}_v$ matrices. A majority of models drew their shocks from a full matrix with nonzero off-diagonal elements. Only five model groups—INTERMOD, MPS, MSG, MX3, and TAYLOR—however, reported the full matrix (the off-diagonal

---

39. Many of the coefficients in the MSG model were calibrated on a 1986 cross section of data. The remainder, rather than being independently estimated, were extracted from other published research.

as well as diagonal elements). The MULTIMOD group drew from a full matrix, but reported only the main diagonal. When submitting their results, the MULTIMOD group observed that some of the off-diagonal elements in their matrix were "large." As noted earlier, all off-diagonal elements were assumed to be zero by the LIVERPOOL group. The GEM group did not report any information about their variance-covariance matrix.[40]

Of the five model groups reporting full matrices to the project organizers, only the INTERMOD and MSG groups reported the matrix literally as a variance-covariance matrix. The other three—MPS, MX3, and TAYLOR—reported the off-diagonal elements in the form of correlation coefficients, not covariances. The correlation coefficient between two residual series u_a and u_b is defined as $\rho_{ab} = \text{cov}(a, b)/(\sigma_a \cdot \sigma_b)$, where $\text{cov}(a, b)$ is the (off-diagonal) covariance between u_a and u_b, and σ_a and σ_b are the standard deviations of the respective residual series (the square roots of the main-diagonal elements of the $\hat{\Sigma}$ or $\hat{\Sigma}_v$ matrix). Correlation coefficients measure the degree of cross-correlation between equation errors and thus are a guide to the complexity of the transmission mechanism of shocks across equations. Because the correlation coefficients scale the covariances by the square roots of the main diagonal elements, however, the correlation coefficients cannot be used directly to appraise the magnitude of the covariances between shocks.

Suppose that appropriate adjustments could systematically be made for the unit problem.[41] Suppose, however, that information were available only for the main diagonal elements of the $\hat{\Sigma}$ or $\hat{\Sigma}_v$ matrix. In such circumstances, examination of the main diagonal elements could reveal which types of shocks were large—"quantitatively important"—*relative to the own-variable means*. Such an assessment, however, would be of limited relevance. What an analyst will wish to appraise, at least as much, is a measure of the quantitative importance of shocks *as they affect key ultimate-target variables*. For that more basic assessment, it is necessary to take into account both the off-diagonal elements of the covariance matrix and the structural specifications of the model equations themselves.

Table 3-5 presents part of a hypothetical variance-covariance matrix, showing the elements and corresponding correlation coefficients for five variables. The main diagonal elements indicate that money-demand shocks are quantitatively the most important in terms of own-variable means (a standard deviation of $0.06 = 0.0036^{1/2}$, or 6 percentage points), followed in declining order by

40. The GEM group observed that "our variance-covariance matrix was too large to report, but there did not appear to be any regularity problems, and off-diagonal elements were not large."

41. For example, imagine that all equations in a model are estimated with variables expressed as natural logarithms, or that the standard deviations of the equation residuals are scaled by the means of the left-hand-side variables.

Table 3-5. *Portion of Illustrative Variance-Covariance Matrix*

Variable	GDP deflator	Consumption	Investment	Money demand	U.S. dollar exchange rate
	Numerical values of elements of the matrix				
GDP deflator	.00010				
Consumption	.00012	.00090			
Investment	.00035	.00000	.00250		
Money demand	−.00015	−.00027	−.00120	.00360	
U.S. dollar exchange rate	.00009	.00005	.00038	−.00045	.00090
	Correlation coefficients of the series of residuals[a]				
GDP deflator	1.00				
Consumption	0.40	1.00			
Investment	0.70	0.00	1.00		
Money demand	−0.25	−0.15	−0.40	1.00	
U.S. dollar exchange rate	0.30	0.05	0.25	−0.25	1.00

a. The correlation coefficient between two residual series u_a and u_b is defined as $\rho_{ab} = \mathrm{cov}(a, b)/(\sigma_a \cdot \sigma_b)$, where $\mathrm{cov}(a, b)$ is the (off-diagonal) covariance between u_a and u_b, and σ_a and σ_b are the standard deviations of the respective residual series (the square roots of the main-diagonal elements of the covariance matrix).

shocks to investment expenditures, the dollar exchange rate, consumption, and the GDP deflator (standard deviations of, respectively, 5, 3, 3, and 1 percentage points). Judged from the perspective of ultimate-target variables such as gross output, employment, or the general price level, however, money-demand shocks might not be as important as, say, investment shocks. In this illustrative $\hat{\Sigma}$, money-demand shocks have a negative covariance with investment, consumption, and price-deflator shocks. Investment and consumption shocks have a relatively high positive correlation with shocks to the price level. In these circumstances, the net effect on output, employment, or the general price level of a typical incremental shock to money demand might be smaller than the effects of a typical incremental shock to investment or consumption spending.[42]

The illustrative data in table 3-5 suggest the potential importance of taking into account the off-diagonal elements in a model's covariance matrix. Our inability to examine the off-diagonal elements for five of the nine models inhibited a systematic effort to study the characteristics of the shocks applied by the model groups in the stochastic simulations.

Even if we had been able to obtain the full variance-covariance matrices for all the models, a systematic comparison would still have been very difficult for another reason. The equation specifications and structural designs of the models are different in various ways, which in turn means that cross-model

42. The effects are also, of course, conditioned by the particular operating regime for monetary policy in force. For example, under nominal-income targeting or real-GNP-plus-inflation targeting, money-demand shocks—even if large—tend to have no effects on prices or outputs (see chapters 2 and 4).

comparisons of historical residuals and covariance matrices cannot proceed straightforwardly equation by equation. The consequences for key target variables of any particular drawing of stochastic shocks cannot be analyzed in a given model without taking into account the model's entire variance-covariance matrix *and* the particular features of its equation specifications. Imagine, for example, a covariance matrix for which the ith residual has "smaller" main diagonal and off-diagonal elements than the jth residual. It could be true that the jth residual pertains to a variable in the model that has a poorly specified equation but that also has only minor effects on other variables in the model and, hence, on output, employment, and the price level. The ith residual, although associated with "smaller" elements in the covariance matrix, could actually play a highly significant role in influencing output, employment, and the price level because of the importance of the channels of transmission for the ith variable in that particular model.

One implication is that future exercises attempting to compare stochastic simulations across models should try to achieve somewhat greater standardization—difficult though that will be—in the size and nature of the variance-covariance matrices from which "representative" shocks are drawn. At the most fundamental level, representative shocks will always be model specific. That fact, however, need not prevent improvements in project design that will enhance the comparability and usefulness of the results.

To keep this last observation in perspective, we emphasize again our earlier point about robustness. If a given policy regime should emerge from comparative analysis as dominant—apparently achieving policy objectives more successfully than other regimes despite heterogeneity among the models and despite nonstandardization of the experimental procedures—that fact can appropriately be interpreted as supporting evidence of the regime's robustness and efficacy.

Design of the Deterministic Simulations

At the inception of the project in 1989, a set of guidelines was circulated to model groups that described the procedures to be followed for the preparation of stochastic simulations. The guidelines spelled out details for the specification of the alternative policy regimes and procedures to be followed in implementing the simulations. Model groups were asked to prepare the simulations for the ten-year period 1990–99.

Following the March 1990 conference, participating model groups agreed to prepare a set of deterministic simulations to facilitate interpretation of the stochastic simulations already prepared. The deterministic simulations were to be implemented over the same period used for the stochastic simulations. Model groups were asked to use the same baseline solution paths as their benchmark point of reference and to implement the same policy regimes (O and X variants).

To conform with the types of shocks used in the stochastic simulations, the deterministic shocks were specified as one-period, transitory disturbances. Hence the shocks were injected for the first period of the simulation only—1990:1 in quarterly models, or the year 1990 in annual models—after which the shocked variables returned to and remained on their baseline paths.[43]

A menu of aggregate-demand, aggregate-supply, and money-demand shocks was specified in the guidelines for the deterministic simulations. This menu was motivated by the objective of shedding light on the consistency between theory and empirical models as well as by the goal of elucidating the reasons for cross-model differences in the stochastic simulations. At the time the model groups agreed to do the deterministic simulations, it was understood that some groups might be unable to generate the full list of simulations requested. The list of shocks was therefore ranked in order of priority.

The shocks used in previous model-comparison exercises had been sustained shocks, with the disturbances typically assumed to persist over many periods—in most cases, indefinitely. In part to provide a more explicit link with the past exercises, the menu of deterministic simulations for this exercise included a single shock requesting a sustained rather than transitory specification (shock F, a persistent increase in the U.S. money supply).

The full menu of deterministic shocks requested from the model groups, ranked in descending order of priority, was as follows (the letters preceding the shocks are used to reference the results in chapter 4).

A: *U.S. aggregate-demand shock*. Real U.S. government expenditures transitorily increased by 1 percent of baseline U.S. real GNP

B: *Global aggregate-demand shock* (with "global" referring to only the three largest components of the world economy). Real government expenditures in each of the "Group of Three"—G3—countries (the United States, Germany, and Japan) transitorily increased, simultaneously, by 1 percent of each country's baseline real GNP

---

43. Because of this specification of the transitory shocks, direct comparisons of the effects of the shocks between the annual and the quarterly models are not possible. Roughly speaking, the size of the shock administered to the annual models is four times as large as that for the quarterly models (lasting in the annual models for four quarters rather than one). If the quarterly models had been asked to specify their deterministic shocks as lasting for four quarters, the deterministic simulations for the quarterly models would then have been inconsistent with the specifications of their stochastic simulations. Notwithstanding the differences in size of shocks between the annual-model and quarterly-model deterministic simulations, it is still valid and interesting to compare the performance of regimes across both the annual and quarterly models (see chapter 4).

C: *U.S. aggregate-supply shock.* Implemented as a transitory downward shift in the U.S. production function equal to 1 percent of baseline U.S. real GNP[44]

D: *Japanese money-demand shock.* The residual in the Japanese money-demand equation transitorily increased by an amount equal to 1 percent of the baseline value of the Japanese money stock; the relevant money stock is that definition of money used within the model as an (intermediate) target for monetary policy

E: *"Global" supply shock (oil price increase).* The world U.S. dollar price of oil transitorily increased (exogenously) by 25 percent (roughly $5 per barrel)

F: *Sustained U.S. money-supply shock.* The U.S. money stock (definition of money targeted by policy in the model) to be increased by 1 percent above the baseline path and held 1 percent above the baseline path for the entire simulation period and thereafter (note that this shock is the only one in the list that specifies a sustained, rather than transitory, one-period shock)

G: *German aggregate-demand shock.* German real government expenditures transitorily increased by 1 percent of baseline German real GNP

H: *German aggregate-supply shock.* Implemented as a transitory downward shift in the German production function equal to 1 percent of baseline German real GNP (analogous to the U.S. aggregate supply shock, shock C)

I: *Japanese aggregate-demand shock.* Japanese real government expenditures transitorily increased by 1 percent of baseline Japanese real GNP

J: *Japanese aggregate-supply shock.* Implemented as a transitory downward shift in the Japanese production function equal to 1 percent of baseline Japanese real GNP (analogous to shocks C and H)

K: *German money-demand shock.* The residual in the German money-demand equation transitorily increased by an amount equal to 1 percent of the baseline value of the German money stock (definition of money targeted by policy in the model)

L: *U.S. money-demand shock.* The residual in the U.S. money-demand equation transitorily increased by an amount equal to 1 percent of the baseline value of the U.S. money stock (definition of money targeted by policy in the model).

---

44. One of the complexities associated with implementing this productivity shock in the models, and the analogous German and Japanese shocks H and J, is that not all of the models include a specific production

As anticipated, some of the model groups could not take the time to implement all of the listed shocks. Table 3-6 identifies, by shock and model, which of the deterministic simulations were submitted to the project organizers. With the inclusion of the MCM model, and with INTERMOD-A and INTERMOD-C counted as separate models, a total of ten model groups participated in the deterministic simulations. Results for shocks A and C are available for all ten models; shock B for nine models; and shocks D, E, and F for (differing combinations of) eight models. All twelve shock simulations are available for five models—INTERMOD-A, INTERMOD-C, LIVERPOOL, MSG, and MULTIMOD. Because the structure of the MPS model focuses on the United States, shocks originating in foreign countries (shocks D and G–K) cannot be straightforwardly implemented in MPS. The MX3 model does not separately model the oil price, and thus could not run shock E. GEM, MCM, and TAYLOR are the models for which several of the shock simulations are not available.

As discussed earlier in this chapter, some of the participating models have individual-country submodels for only three countries—the United States, Japan, and Germany. That fact is the reason for the focus of the design of the deterministic simulations, and of their interpretation in chapter 4, on these G3 (the three largest industrial) countries.

---

function. Moreover, in principle the shock should affect not only the production function (or its nearest representation), but also the price (and in some cases wage) markup equations or marginal productivity conditions in the models. In the TAYLOR model (which does not include an explicit production function), for example, the exogenous capacity output variable in the wage equation was lowered 1 percent, and the residual in the price equation was raised by an amount equal to 1 percent times the wage coefficient. Because of structural differences in the supply sides of the different models, the model groups were given considerable discretion, following consultations with the project organizers, about the precise manner of implementing shocks C, H, and J in their models.

Table 3-6. *Summary of Deterministic Simulations Implemented, by Model and Type of Shock*

Type of Shock	GEM	INTERMOD-A	INTERMOD-C	LIVERPOOL	MCM	MPS	MSG	MULTIMOD	MX3	TAYLOR
A. U.S. aggregate demand	✓	✓	✓	✓	✓	✓	✓	✓	✓	✓
B. "Global" aggregate demand	✓	✓	✓	✓	✓		✓	✓	✓	✓
C. U.S. aggregate supply	✓	✓	✓	✓	✓	✓	✓	✓	✓	✓
D. Japanese money demand		✓	✓	✓	✓		✓	✓	✓	✓
E. Oil price increase	✓	✓	✓	✓	✓	✓	✓	✓		
F. U.S. money supply		✓		✓		✓	✓		✓	✓
G. German aggregate demand	✓	✓	✓	✓			✓	✓	✓	
H. German aggregate supply	✓	✓	✓	✓			✓	✓	✓	
I. Japanese aggregate demand	✓	✓	✓	✓			✓	✓	✓	
J. Japanese aggregate supply		✓	✓	✓			✓	✓	✓	
K. German money demand		✓	✓	✓			✓	✓	✓	
L. U.S. money demand		✓	✓	✓		✓	✓	✓	✓	

a. See table 3-2 for availability of results for deterministic simulation by type of regime. All shocks other than F are one-period, transitory disturbances (one year for annual models, one quarter for quarterly models). Shock F involves a sustained rather than transitory increase in the U.S. money supply; the model groups checked on the row for shock F are those that implemented the regime for exact money targeting.

References

Barrell, R., and A. Gurney. 1991. "Fiscal and Monetary Policy Simulations with Forward-Looking Exchange Rates Using the National Institute Global Econometric Model." Discussion Paper 200. London: National Institute of Economic and Social Research.

Barrell, R., and S. Wren-Lewis. 1990. "The National Institute World Model" (model structure and equation listing). London: National Institute of Economic and Social Research.

Brayton, F., and E. Mauskopf. 1985. "The Federal Reserve Board MPS Quarterly Econometric Model of the U.S. Economy." *Economic Modelling* 2: 170–292.

———. 1987. "Structure and Uses of the MPS Quarterly Econometric Model of the United States." *Federal Reserve Bulletin* 73: 93–109.

Bryant, R. C., D. A. Currie, J. A. Frenkel, P. R. Masson, and R. Portes, eds. 1989. *Macroeconomic Policies in an Interdependent World.* Washington: Brookings, Centre for Economic Policy Research, International Monetary Fund.

Bryant, R. C., J. F. Helliwell, and P. Hooper. 1989. "Domestic and Cross-Border Consequences of U.S. Macroeconomic Policies." In Bryant, Currie, and others (1989), 59–115. Unabridged version available as Brookings Discussion Paper in International Economics 68 (January 1989).

Bryant, R. C., D. W. Henderson, G. Holtham, P. Hooper, and S. A. Symansky, eds. 1988. *Empirical Macroeconomics for Interdependent Economies.* Brookings.

Edison, H. J., J. R. Marquez, and R. W. Tryon. 1987. "The Structure and Properties of the Federal Reserve Board Multicountry Model." *Economic Modelling* 4:115–315.

Faddeeva, V. N. 1959. *Computational Methods of Linear Algebra.* New York: Dover.

Fair, R. C. 1984. *Specification, Estimation, and Analysis of Macroeconometric Models.* Harvard University Press.

Gagnon, J. E. 1991. "A Forward-Looking Multicountry Model for Policy Analysis: MX3." *Economic and Financial Computing* 1: 311–61.

Helliwell, J. F., G. Meredith, P. Bagnoli, and Y. Durand. 1990. "INTERMOD 1.1: A G-7 Version of the IMF's MULTIMOD." *Economic Modelling* 7: 3–62.

Ireland, J., and P. Westaway. 1991. "Stochastic Simulation and Forecast Uncertainty in a Large Forward-Looking Model." London: National Institute of Economic and Social Research.

McCarthy, M. D. 1972. "Notes on the Generation of Pseudo-Structural Errors for Use in Stochastic Simulation Studies." In *Econometric Models of Cyclical Behavior*, edited by B. G. Hickman, 85–91. Columbia University Press.

McKibbin, W. J. 1988. "Policy Analysis with the MSG2 Model." *Australian Economic Papers* 27 (Supplement): 126–50.

McKibbin, W. J., and J. D. Sachs. 1991. *Global Linkages: Macroeconomic Interdependence and Cooperation in the World Economy.* Brookings.

Masson, P. R., S. A. Symansky, R. Haas, and M. Dooley. 1988. "MULTIMOD: A Multi-Region Econometric Model." In *Staff Studies for the World Economic Outlook*, 50–104. International Monetary Fund.

Masson, P. R., S. A. Symansky, and G. Meredith. 1990. *MULTIMOD Mark II: A Revised and Extended Model*. Occasional Paper 71. International Monetary Fund.

Mauskopf, E. 1990. "The Transmission Channels of Monetary Policy: How Have They Changed?" *Federal Reserve Bulletin* (December): 985–1008.

Meredith, G. 1989. "INTERMOD 2.0: Model Specification and Simulation Properties." Working Paper 89-7. Ottawa: Working Group on International Macroeconomics, Department of Finance.

Minford, P. 1985. "The Effects of American Policies—A New Classical Interpretation." In *International Economic Policy Coordination*, edited by W. H. Buiter and R. C. Marston, 84–118. Cambridge University Press for the Centre for Economic Policy Research.

Minford, P., P.-R. Agenor, and E. Nowell. 1986. "A New Classical Macroeconometric Model of the World Economy." *Economic Modelling* 3: 154–76.

Richardson, P. 1988. "The Structure and Simulation Properties of OECD's Interlink Model." *OECD Economic Studies* 10: 57–122.

Stevens, G., R. Berner, P. Clark, E. Hernandez-Cata, H. Howe, and S. Kwack. 1984. *The U.S. Economy in an Interdependent World: A Multicountry Model*. Board of Governors of the Federal Reserve System.

Taylor, J. B. 1988. "The Treatment of Expectations in Large Multicountry Econometric Models." In Bryant, Henderson, and others (1988), 161–82.

———. 1989a. "Policy Analysis with a Multicountry Model." In Bryant, Currie, and others (1989), 122–41.

———. 1989b. "The Current Account and Macroeconomic Policy: An Econometric Analysis." In *The U.S. Trade Deficit: Causes, Consequences, and Cures*, edited by A. E. Burger, 131–85. Twelfth Annual Economic Policy Conference Proceedings, Federal Reserve Bank of Saint Louis. Boston: Kluwer.

———. 1993. *Macroeconomic Policy in a World Economy: From Econometric Design to Practical Operation*. Norton.

CHAPTER 4

Deterministic Simulations with Simple Policy Regimes

Peter Hooper and Ralph C. Bryant

THIS CHAPTER analyzes the deterministic simulations prepared for the project. The emphasis is on the differences in responses to standardized transitory shocks under the alternative policy regimes and on differences in responses across the participating multicountry models.

The deterministic simulations are of substantial interest in their own right. The various shocks studied—changes to both real and financial variables and to aggregate demand and aggregate supply—are representative of the most important economic disturbances experienced by actual economies. Although the postulated policy regimes—money targeting, nominal-income targeting, real-GNP-plus-inflation targeting, and exchange-rate targeting—are specified in the models in simple form, the simulations nonetheless provide suggestive evidence about economic performance under alternative approaches to monetary policy. Because the participating models are multicountry in structure, it is possible to consider how the effects of the shocks differ across individual countries and how shocks originating in one country are transmitted to others. The simulations provide clues to the properties of the various models and help to identify and interpret cross-model differences. The deterministic simulations also permit one to study the extent to which the model-based results conform to the predictions of theory as outlined in chapter 2, at least with respect to the directions of effects of various types of shocks and the relative magnitudes of the effects across different policy regimes.

The deterministic simulations were prepared after the original generation of the stochastic simulations (see chapters 1 and 3). A main objective of taking this additional step was to permit a better understanding of the sources of differences across models in the stochastic simulation results. The shocks chosen for study in the deterministic simulations, therefore, were selected to be representative of the types of one-time transitory shocks included by the models in their stochastic simulations. In contrast to the heterogeneous shocks imposed in the stochastic simulations, the shocks in the deterministic simulations were much more standardized across the models, thus allowing for more direct comparisons of the models' properties (chapter 3).

261

The deterministic simulations are useful in still another way: they serve as a link to previous model-comparison exercises involving deterministic simulations, such as those discussed in *Empirical Macroeconomics for Interdependent Economies (EMIE)*.[1] This linkage to past studies is loose, however, for two reasons. First, whereas the deterministic simulations in past exercises typically involved *sustained* shocks to monetary and fiscal policies, the new simulations discussed here are, with one exception, *transitory* shocks to various private-sector variables under alternative monetary policy regimes. Second, the group of models included in the present study differs noticeably from that in the previous exercises. For example, models with forward-looking, model-consistent expectations are much more heavily represented in these new simulations than in the earlier studies.

Although the focus here on transitory shocks limits the direct comparisons that can be made with previous model-comparison efforts, it also adds a new dimension to empirical analysis of macroeconomic disturbances. It allows us to assess the *persistence* of the effects of transitory shocks on key variables and to consider whether such persistence is significantly affected by alternative policy regimes or by the treatment of expectations.

We begin our analyses of the deterministic simulations by surveying the results of each shock for a common monetary policy regime, nominal-income targeting. This survey compares results, presented in graphs, across all of the models. The remainder of the chapter then assesses the performance of the alternative policy regimes in the face of different types of shocks, emphasizing the effects on real income, inflation, interest rates, and exchange rates in the United States, Japan, and Germany. Initially, we assess performance by directly comparing the results across models for each of the various types of shocks. Subsequently, we search for some degree of consensus by aggregating the results across the models, first through ordinal and then through cardinal rankings of the regimes by the individual models. Throughout the chapter, we try to assess how the empirical results in these simulations do or do not conform with the theoretical results discussed in chapter 2.

Effects of Shocks under Nominal-Income Targeting

In this initial section, we illustrate the simulation results provided by each of the models for the various types of standardized shocks. (Table 3-4 in chapter 3 provides a reference list of the shocks actually implemented.) The discussion and the associated charts presenting individual model outcomes pertain only

---

1. Bryant, Henderson, and others (1988). Other model-comparison evaluations include Bryant, Holtham, and Hooper (1988); Hooper and others (1990); and Bryant, Helliwell, and Hooper (1989).

to results for a single regime, nominal-income targeting (2A or 2AX). We restrict this preliminary survey to one of the regime types merely to keep the illustration within manageable limits. Any of the other three regime types could have served equally well as the focus.

We begin with the effects of a shock to U.S. aggregate demand, describing them in somewhat more detail than the effects of subsequent shocks. We first consider the effects in the initial period ("impact" effects) when a shock is imposed (the first quarter or year of the simulation, depending on the periodicity of the model) and then consider the ongoing effects in subsequent periods after the shock has been removed.

U.S. Aggregate Demand Shock

The shock to U.S. aggregate demand, shock A, is a transitory increase in real U.S. government expenditures equal to 1 percent of baseline U.S. real GNP in the first period of the simulation.

The theory reviewed in chapter 2 indicates that under exact nominal-income targeting (that chapter's YY regime, with full instrument adjustment), a transitory exogenous increase in goods demand occurring simultaneously in all countries has no effect on real outputs, employments, and domestic product prices, because interest rates rise enough to keep nominal incomes on track while nominal and real exchange rates do not change. A country-specific shock to goods demand will appreciate the shocked country's currency and affect consumer prices at home and abroad. When oil or other intermediate goods are taken into account, even outputs and product prices can be affected, although employments remain unchanged.

A key difference between the predictions of the theory for exact nominal-income targeting and the simulation outcomes for inexact nominal-income targeting generated by the empirical models considered here is that the partial-instrument-adjustment regime specified for the empirical simulations allows for slippage between current nominal income and its targeted (baseline) path. Specifically, the prescribed empirical regime calls for countries' short-term interest rates to rise $1\frac{1}{2}$ percentage points for every percentage point by which nominal income exceeds its target baseline value; that is, the feedback parameter for regime 2A is set at a value of 1.5. Given that output and inflation respond only gradually to changes in interest rates in most empirical models, a feedback parameter of this magnitude allows for a considerable deviation between actual and targeted nominal GNP in the short run.

An illustration of the difference that high and low feedback coefficients for instrument adjustment can make in empirical models—a difference consistent with the theory in chapter 2—is given in figure 4-1. The three panels show what

Figure 4-1. *Effects of Increase in U.S. Aggregate Demand (Shock A): MSG Model Results under Nominal-Income Targeting with Alternative Feedback Coefficients*

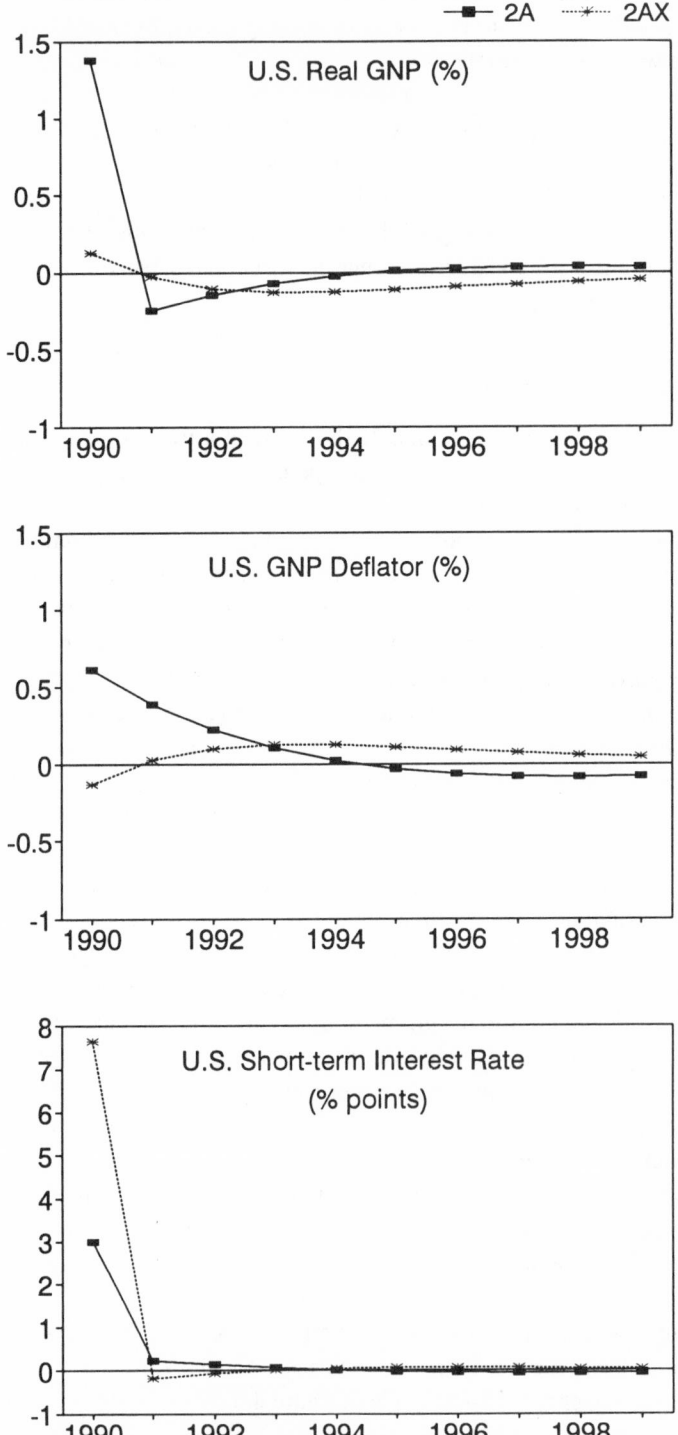

the MSG model reports for the effects of the U.S. aggregate demand shock on U.S. real GNP, the U.S. GNP deflator, and the U.S. nominal short-term interest rate, respectively, under two variants of regime 2A. The line with the filled-square symbol shows the effects under the O (original) specification of regime 2A (with a feedback parameter of 1.5); the line with the asterisk symbol shows the effects under regime 2AX as specified by the MSG model group, where the feedback parameter was given an extremely high value. Under the prescribed regime 2A, output and product prices both deviate significantly and positively from their baseline values in the early part of the simulation. But under the MSG model's regime 2AX, which entails much more precise targeting of nominal income, interest rates initially rise much more and keep output and product prices from deviating significantly from baseline (in fact, real GNP and prices do deviate slightly from their baseline paths, but in offsetting directions, so that nominal GNP remains essentially unchanged).

In the results for nominal-income targeting discussed in this section of the chapter, we are able to report simulations run under the prescribed regime 2A for all but three of the models. The GEM, MCM, and MULTIMOD model groups reported results for their own variants of the regime type (2AX), but not for the O specification (2A). Each of these three groups reduced the feedback parameter for the regime to values below 1.5, which permitted (at least in principle) greater slippage between actual and target values of nominal GNP than regime 2A itself would have permitted.[2]

The presence of such slippage in all of the models has the effect of making the initial-period effects of the transitory shock to aggregate demand qualitatively similar to those of the sustained shock to aggregate demand considered in *EMIE*. In the *EMIE* results, the sustained shock (an exogenous increase in real government spending) led to an initial increase in real GNP, prices, and interest rates. The home currency appreciated, and the current account fell. Over time, real GNP returned toward its baseline path as the rise in interest rates crowded out domestic spending and as net exports fell.[3] In the simulations here for a transitory shock to government spending, the results follow much the same pattern, at least in the first period of the simulation. Beyond the initial period, when the transitory increase in spending is reversed, output returns much more quickly to baseline (and often moves below baseline for a time).

2. The feedback parameter was reduced by the MCM and MULTIMOD groups because their models were unable to run the simulation for all countries with the prescribed value of 1.5. The INTERMOD group reported results for regime 2A for the deterministic simulations, but for the stochastic simulations discussed in chapter 5 was able to report results for only a 2AX variant with a reduced feedback parameter.

3. In the *EMIE* simulations, the monetary policy regime held money stocks unchanged from their baseline paths (exact money targeting). For that reason too, significant "slippage" (deviation of variables from their baseline paths) occurred. Under exact money targeting, interest rates need to rise only enough to hold the demand for money unchanged in the face of a shock to aggregate demand, thereby permitting significant variation in target variables such as real GNP and prices (see chapter 2).

The effects of the transitory shock to U.S. aggregate demand on key U.S. variables are shown in figure 4-2. This chart and those that follow in this section are divided into eight panels. Each row of two panels shows the results for one variable. Panels on the left-hand side contain results for the annual models; those on the right-hand side, results for the quarterly models. The curve for each model is plotted with a particular symbol, identified in the figure's legend. These model symbols are used uniformly throughout the charts in this section. All the results are presented in percentage, or percentage-point, deviations from baseline over the entire ten-year simulation period.

The positive impact effect on U.S. real GNP—the top two panels in figure 4-2—is generally in the range of $\frac{3}{4}$ to $1\frac{1}{4}$ percent for both annual and quarterly models. The LIVERPOOL model is a notable exception, showing very little effect on GNP; the LIVERPOOL model also shows U.S. GNP to be comparatively unresponsive to permanent spending shocks in the *EMIE* results because interest rates have relatively strong crowding-out effects in the U.S. bloc of that model. At the other end of the range, the MSG model simulates an increase in real GNP of nearly $1\frac{1}{2}$ percent on impact, contrary to the *EMIE* results, where it was at the low end of the range.[4]

Only four of the models—GEM, MCM, MPS, and MSG—are able to report effects on employment (shown in the second two panels in figure 4-2). For the MSG model, the only annual model in this group, employment rises substantially more than output. In MSG, demand for labor is boosted by a substantial rise in prices, which causes a significant decline in real wages. For the three quarterly models in the group, employment rises noticeably less than real output. This result presumably reflects the relatively brief duration of the shock in the quarterly models and the presence of lags in the response of employment to changes in output in these models.

The increase in aggregate demand induces a modest increase in the U.S. price level—on the order of 0.1 to 0.2 percent on impact—in most of the models. The MSG model, in which prices are flexible rather than sticky, has a price increase substantially higher than that for other models. Prices in the LIVERPOOL model rise only a little because, according to the LIVERPOOL group, "the only effect on money demand is through a small (from strong crowding out) rise in interest rates partly offset by the small rise in output."

The increases in income and prices are associated with sizable upward shifts in interest rates (figure 4-3). In half of the models the increase in

---

4. The version of the MSG model used for the *EMIE* simulations was significantly different from the version used for this project; the *EMIE* version had sticky prices and no supply side. Moreover, the *EMIE* simulations assumed exact money targeting, so the monetary-policy regime is different between the *EMIE* results and those discussed here. The newer MSG results are all the more puzzling because, as shown in the theory in chapter 2, output effects under nominal-income targeting should (other things being equal) be smaller than those under money targeting.

Figure 4-2. *Effects of Increase In U.S. Aggregate Demand (Shock A, Regime 2A/2AX)*

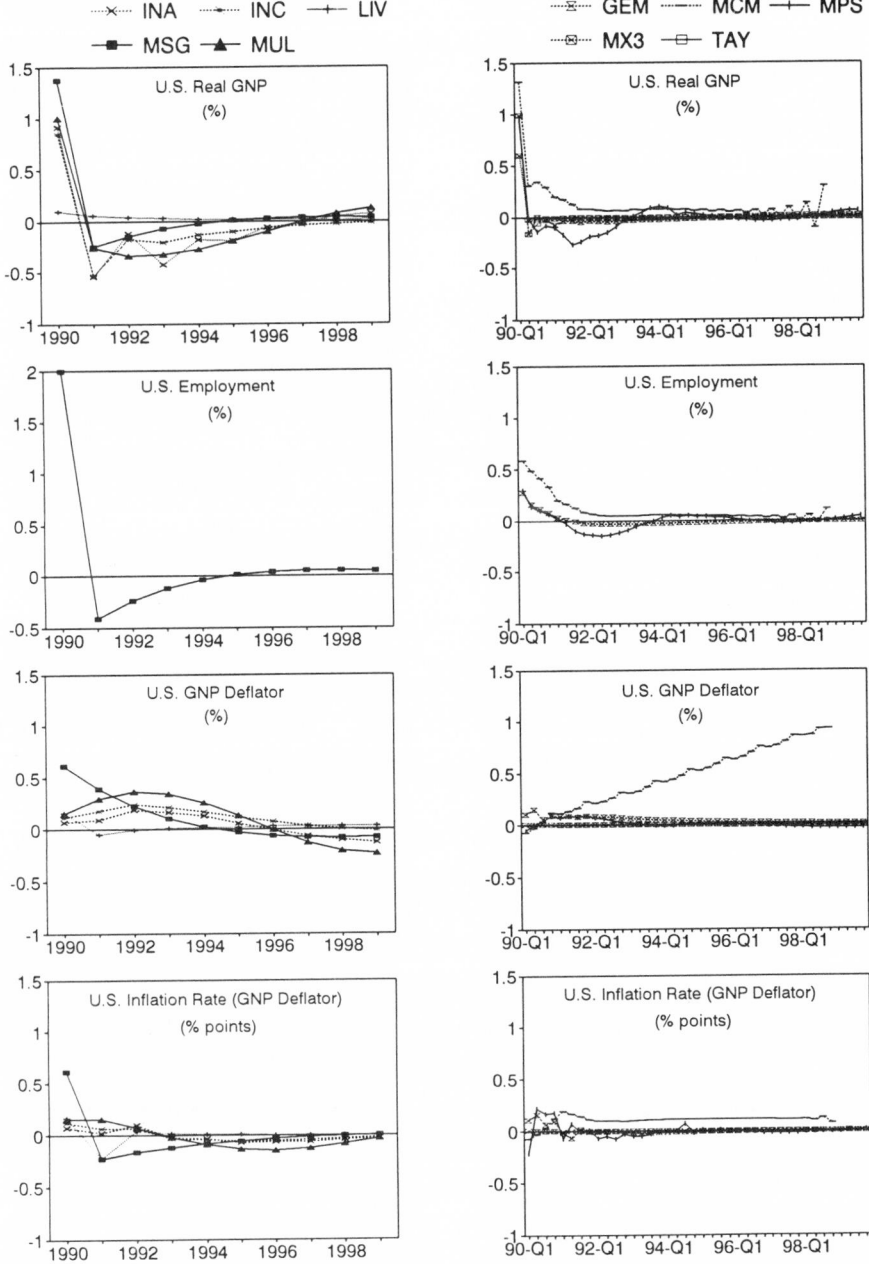

Figure 4-3. *Effects of Increase in U.S. Aggregate Demand (Shock A, Regime 2A/2AX)*

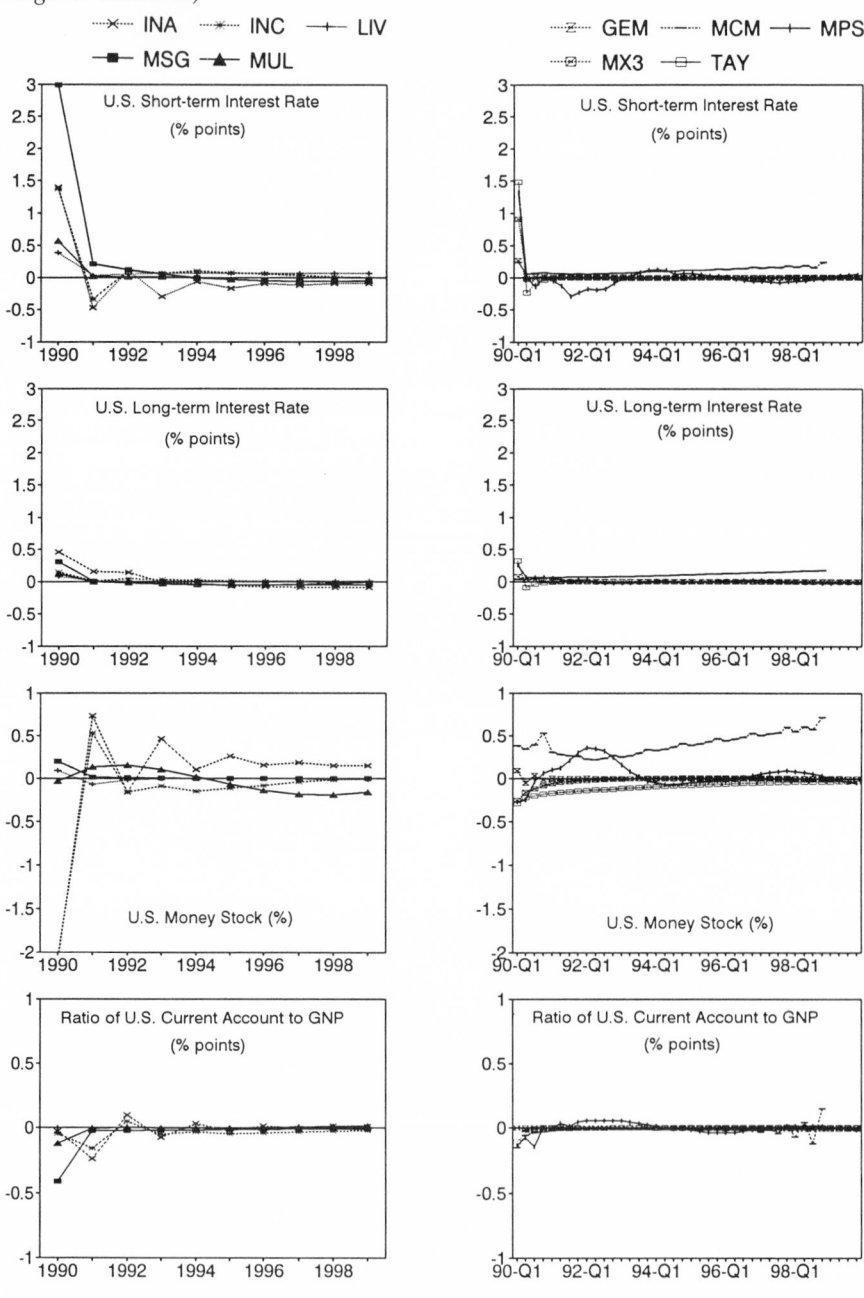

short-term interest rates exceeds 125 basis points on impact. Four of these models exhibit increases in the range of 130 to 150 basis points, and a fifth, the MSG model, shows an increase of 300 basis points. The high sensitivity in the MSG case reflects in part the greater response of income and prices to the fiscal shock in that model. The three models that used their own variation of the nominal-income targeting regime (2AX) report much smaller increases in interest rates (25 basis points for both GEM and MCM, and about 60 basis points for MULTIMOD), reflecting the lower feedback parameters used in their alternative specifications. The LIVERPOOL model, which did implement the prescribed regime 2A, also reports a fairly small increase in interest rates, reflecting the relatively small responses of output and prices to the aggregate demand shock in that model. Initial increases in long-term interest rates are much smaller than those in short-term rates in all models and are generally on the order of 10 to 30 basis points.

In most cases, the U.S. money stock falls because the depressing effects of higher interest rates on the demand for money offset the stimulative effects of higher nominal income. The exceptions (cases in which the money stock rises) are the three models with reduced feedback parameters and the LIVER-POOL model. In these cases the relatively small increases in interest rates are not enough to offset the stimulus to money demand from rising income and prices.

Higher interest rates generally cause the dollar to appreciate against both the deutsche mark and the yen, by anywhere from $\frac{1}{4}$ percent to $1\frac{1}{2}$ percent on impact (figure 4-4).[5] The GEM model is an exception, showing a small depreciation of the dollar initially, in part reflecting the relatively small increase in U.S. interest rates predicted by that model. Appreciation of the dollar and, more important, the expansion in the domestic economy lead to a first-period decline in the U.S. current account balance in most cases (see the bottom two panels of figure 4-3, which plot percentage-point deviations in the ratio of the current account to nominal GNP). The initial decline in the current account is generally on the order of 0.1 to 0.2 percent of GNP, and 0.4 percent for the MSG model.

Previous model-comparison exercises have documented the typically "positive" transmission of fiscal shocks to output and prices in foreign countries

---

5. In expository theoretical models in the Mundell-Fleming tradition, the direction of movement of the exchange value of a country's currency after an expansionary fiscal action is ambiguous, depending in part on the degree of substitutability between assets denominated in the home and foreign currencies. The greater the degree of that substitutability, the higher the probability that an expansionary fiscal action will appreciate the home currency. In the simplified theoretical model in chapter 2, under the MM, YY, and CC regimes the currency of the United States appreciates after a positive, country-specific shock to U.S. goods demand. With the exception of MPS, all the empirical models participating in the deterministic simulations tend to treat financial assets denominated in different currencies as perfect substitutes.

Figure 4-4. *Effects of Increase in U.S. Aggregate Demand (Shock A, Regime 2A/2AX)*

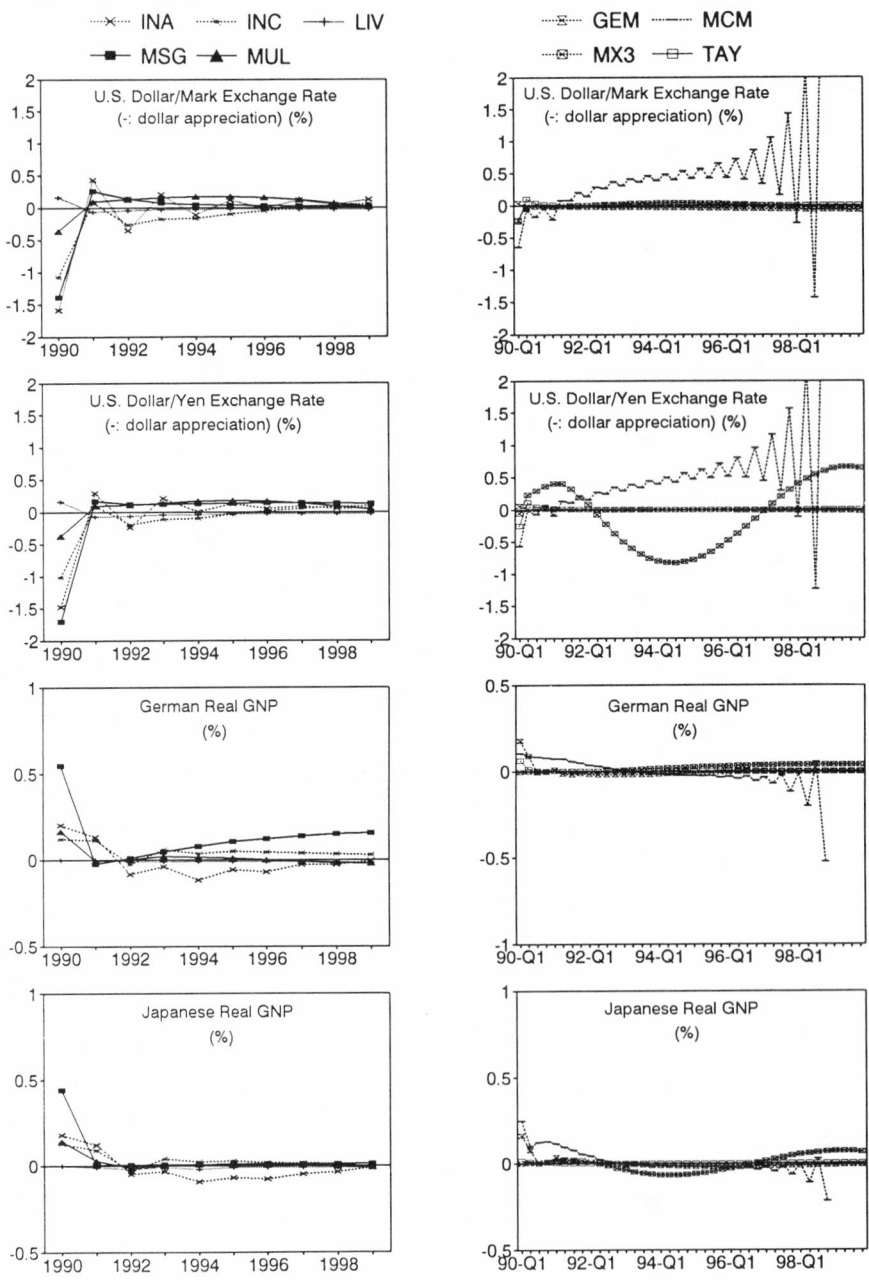

when money stocks are held unchanged on baseline paths.[6] In the present simulations, generated with inexact nominal-income targeting, the U.S. aggregate demand shock raises real GNP in both Germany and Japan by about 0.1 to 0.2 percent (figure 4-4), and prices in those countries by negligible amounts. The annual models generally show greater effects on these foreign variables for the first year than the quarterly models show for the first quarter, presumably because of the influence of lags in the transmission of shocks across countries. The LIVERPOOL model is generally below the others, and the MSG model above the others, in the magnitude of these transmission effects.

In the second period of the simulation, when the positive shock is removed and demand is depressed by the first-period increase in interest rates and exchange rates, U.S. real GNP falls below the baseline path by $\frac{1}{4}$ to $\frac{1}{2}$ percent for annual models, and somewhat less for quarterly models (figure 4-2).[7] The annual models with rational expectations (with the exception of the LIVERPOOL model) then show a gradual return, over a period of at least several years, to the baseline path from below. The quarterly models with rational expectations return to baseline almost immediately. The two quarterly models with adaptive expectations show somewhat different patterns. The MCM model has real GNP remaining above (but returning toward) the baseline for about eight quarters following the shock, then leveling off slightly above the baseline. In the MPS model real GNP continues falling below baseline for several quarters and then cycles moderately above before returning to the baseline path. The adaptive-expectations version of INTERMOD (an annual model) tends to remain somewhat further below baseline than INTERMOD-C for much of the remaining simulation period. For those models that report it, employment generally follows the pattern of output in the long run.

With several exceptions, price levels return toward baseline after the first period. In three of the annual models the U.S. inflation rate remains above baseline for several years (figure 4-2). At least half of the models have the inflation rate remaining above baseline for several years before falling below baseline, so that the positive effect on the price level first builds up over

6. In the theoretical analysis in chapter 2, a positive shock to the demand for goods in the U.S. bloc of the model definitely raises output and prices abroad under the II and MM regimes. For the YY regime (exact nominal-income targeting), foreign output and product prices do not change, but the dollar appreciation raises foreign consumer prices. The ME regime causes negative transmission of a U.S. goods demand shock to foreign output and prices. The *EMIE* empirical simulations correspond best to the case of the MM regime (exact money targeting).

7. The decline in GNP in the second period is larger in the annual models than in the quarterly models, at least in part because of the difference in the periodicity of the models. The one-period positive shock to demand in the annual models causes interest rates to rise for one year, whereas the same shock in the quarterly models causes interest rates to rise for only one quarter. Given the presence of lags in the adjustment of expenditures to interest rates, a rise in interest rates for one year no doubt depresses those expenditures more than a comparable rise in interest rates for only one quarter.

time and then diminishes. Because of their flexible-price specifications, the
MSG and LIVERPOOL models show a more abrupt shift from positive to
negative, with the inflation rate falling below baseline in the second period and
returning toward the baseline thereafter. At one extreme, the MX3 and TAYLOR
models show no effect on the inflation rate (or the price level) throughout the
simulation. At the other extreme, the MCM model shows a persistently positive
inflation rate: the shock sets off a continuous increase in the price level that is
accommodated by an increase in money growth. This result reflects the very
weak feedback parameter used in that model's 2AX regime. The rise in interest
rates induced by the shock to nominal GNP is too small to prevent the model
from jumping up to a higher inflation path, at least over the ten-year simulation
period we consider.[8]

U.S. interest rates and money (figure 4-3) return fairly quickly to a rather
narrow range around the baseline path after the first period in most cases, as do
exchange rates and the U.S. current account. One exception is the MCM model,
where interest rates and money tend to drift away slightly from the baseline
on the positive side. Exchange rates and German and Japanese outputs (figure
4-4) also return very near to baseline within two to three years, with a few
prominent exceptions.[9]

The longer-run instability of the dollar-yen exchange rate for the MCM
and MX3 models, and the dollar-deutsche-mark exchange rate for the MCM
model, is particularly striking. This behavior in the MCM model is related at
least in part to the longer-term U.S. monetary expansion that is kicked off in
that model. The MCM "sawtooth" cycling of exchange rates appears to induce
some cycling of foreign real GNPs toward the end of the simulation.[10] The
MX3 model exhibits strong cycling behavior in the dollar-yen exchange rate
because of properties specific to the Japanese sector of that model (the dollar-
deutsche-mark rate shows only very faint evidence of cycling). The reasons
for this cycling are not apparent to the MX3 modeling group, but the presence of

8. The MCM model group picked the maximum feedback parameter that would allow that model to run
all the shocks across all the countries under nominal-income targeting. Although a higher parameter value may
well have been desirable for the United States in the case of the aggregate demand shock, for some shocks it
would have been too high for certain other countries.

9. The sustained deviation of German real GNP from baseline in the results for the MSG model is due
to that model's specification of hysteresis in the German labor market, where the natural rate of unemployment
takes a long time to fall back after the initial shock.

10. The MCM model was designed and is used primarily for near-term quarterly policy simulation. Its
longer-term stability properties were not examined rigorously when the model was constructed. The MCM
group, when commenting on these exchange-rate results, observed that the application of static policy rules
to a dynamic model can generate this type of outcome. There is no guarantee that a model will exhibit
stable responses, they noted, if the model is expanded to include policy rules that are not derived from the
model's structure. The fact that the MCM group needed to adjust the reaction coefficients when using the
commonly specified regimes can be seen as evidence of a potential inconsistency between the model and those
regimes.

the cycle provides a clue about why the model was unable to run simulations under an exchange-rate targeting regime (see chapter 3).[11]

Two of the models with adaptive expectations, INTERMOD-A and MPS, show some variables cycling up and down over much of the simulation period. This cycling is more striking in INTERMOD-A, especially in later simulations. Cycling is less pronounced in the MPS model, where U.S. real GNP follows a damped cycle with a periodicity of several years, and the cycling of output is associated with moderate cycles in inflation, interest rates, and money demand. The cycling of output arises in part because aggregate demand is affected by movements in real interest rates with a long lag, while prices and inflation adjust to movements in demand with a lag (in part reflecting the backward-looking treatment of expectations). The interaction of the different lags produces the observed cycling. The same sort of reactions could be at work in the INTERMOD-A model as well, although the adjustment lags in that model are undoubtedly shorter, inasmuch as the periodicity of the cycles in INTERMOD-A (two years) is less than in the MPS model.[12] It is noteworthy that the same model with forward-looking expectations, INTERMOD-C, shows very little evidence of cycling, which suggests that forward-looking expectations play an important role in damping such cobweb-type reactions.

Other Aggregate Demand Shocks

The qualitative patterns of effects resulting from the shocks to aggregate demand in Germany and Japan, and in the G3 as a whole, are similar to the patterns just discussed.[13] For example, the effects of a German fiscal expansion—shock G—on German real GNP (top panel of figure 4-5), and the effects of a Japanese fiscal expansion—shock I—on Japanese real GNP (top panel of figure 4-6), are broadly similar to the effects of the U.S. fiscal expansion on U.S. real GNP (figure 4-2). The initial percentage effects on German real GNP in shock G are smaller than the corresponding effects on U.S. real GNP in shock A (by about $\frac{1}{4}$ percentage point on average for most of the models). The LIVERPOOL model, however, predicts a much larger effect (0.6 percent for the German case, compared with 0.1 percent for the U.S. case). For the Japanese fiscal action in shock I, most of the models have an initial impact on Japanese real GNP of about the same size as the average shock-A effects on

---

11. The MX3 group reports that, judged on the basis of simulations of the model over long horizons, the cycles appear to dampen out but do so very slowly.

12. INTERMOD-A also shows significant cycling of deutsche mark and yen exchange rates (as a result of the cycling in U.S. interest rates), which influences the patterns of Japanese and German real GNP seen in this shock. The MPS model does not include equations for German and Japanese variables.

13. Three of the quarterly models—MCM, MPS, and TAYLOR—did not run the German and Japanese aggregate demand shocks. All but one of the models (MPS) was able to run the global demand shock.

Figure 4-5. *Effects of Increase in German Aggregate Demand (Shock G, Regime 2A/2AX)*

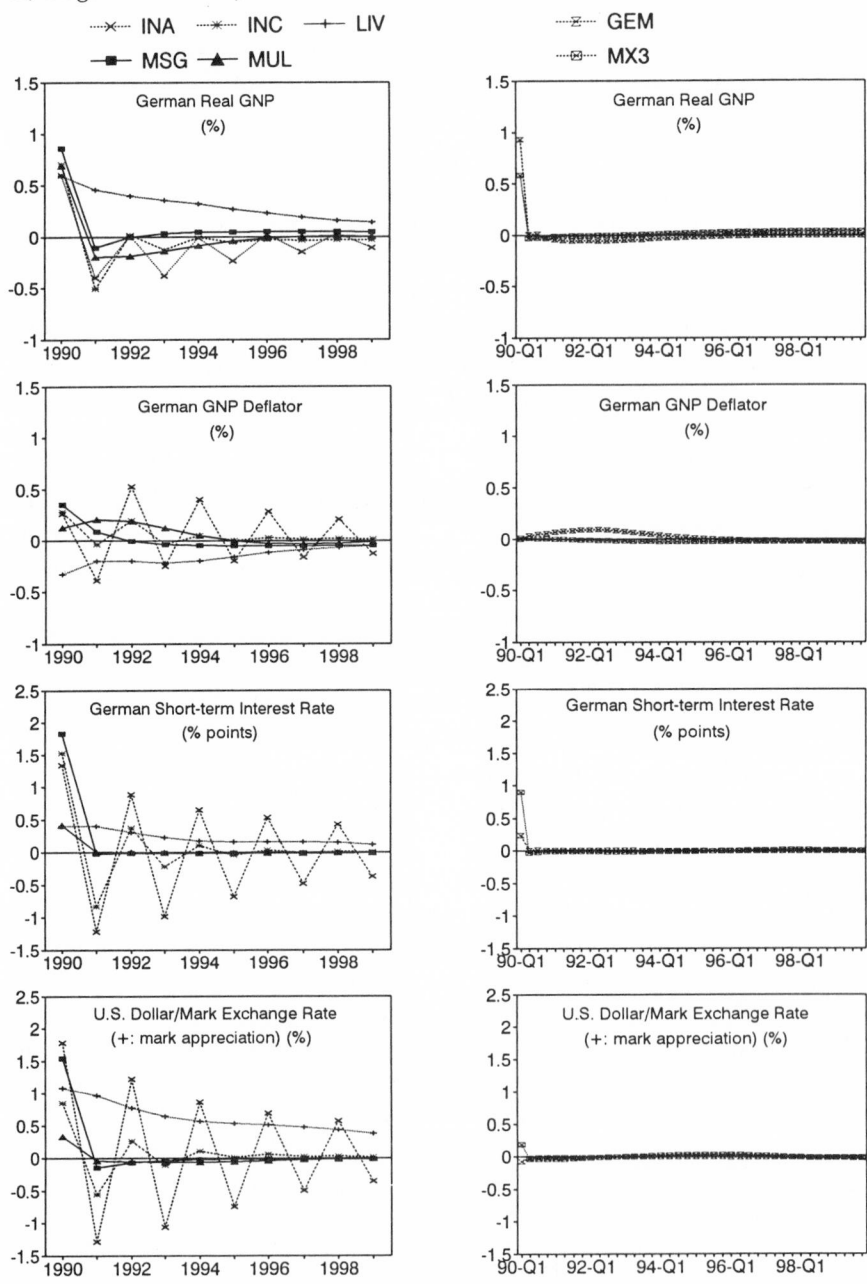

Figure 4-6. *Effects of Increase in Japanese Aggregate Demand (Shock I, Regime 2A/2AX)*

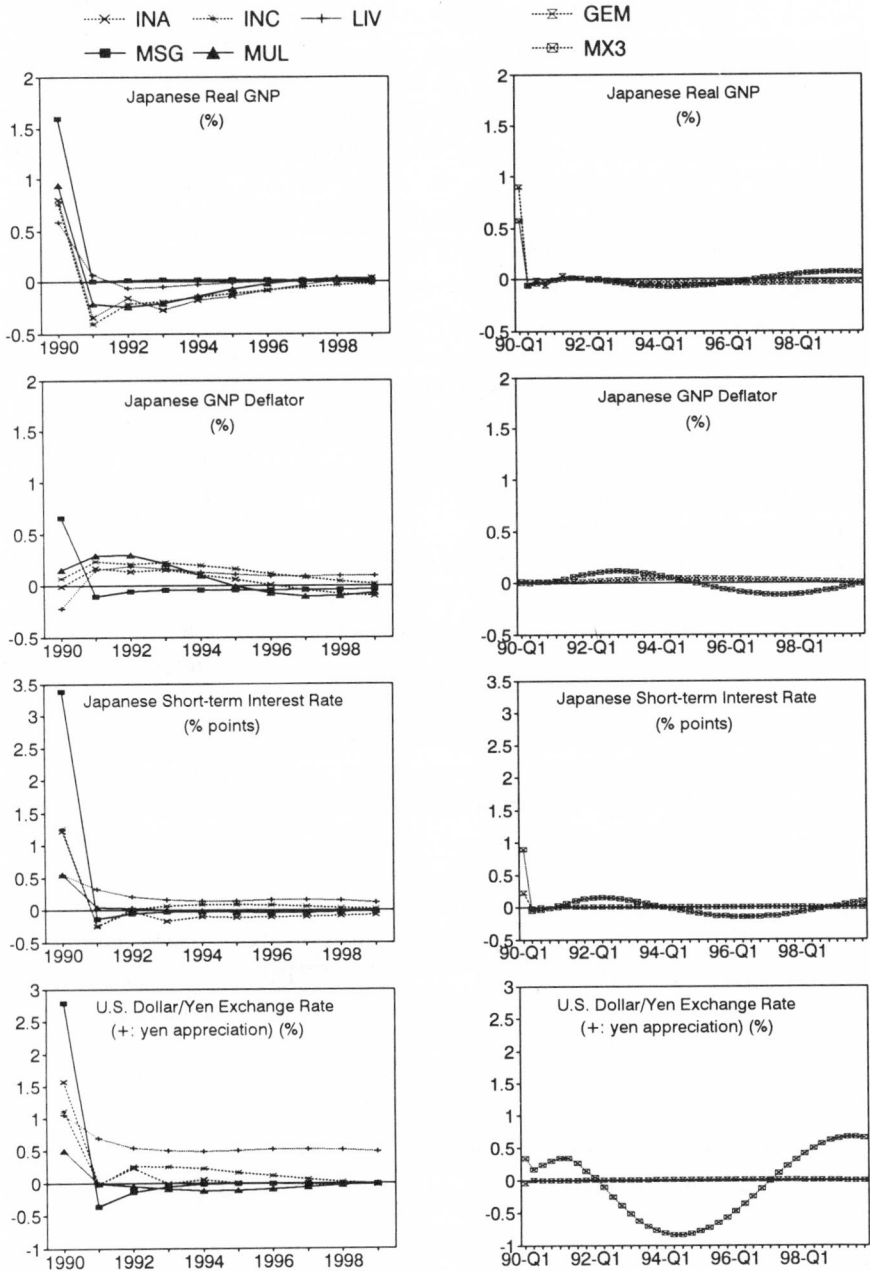

U.S. real GNP (roughly 1 percent), although the MSG model is again somewhat higher at 1.7 percent and the MX3 model somewhat lower at 0.6 percent.

In both the shock-G and shock-I simulations, own-country real GNP drops below baseline in the second period of the simulation and thereafter returns gradually to the baseline from below. As in the case of shock A, INTERMOD-A shows own-country real GNP falling less below baseline in the second period and remaining below baseline longer thereafter than does INTERMOD-C; these differences, however, are fairly small.[14] The LIVERPOOL model shows German real GNP returning to baseline much more slowly than do other models, and much more slowly than the same model shows for U.S. and Japanese real GNP.

Most of the models show both German and Japanese prices rising slightly above baseline initially and then returning to the baseline path. Own-country interest rates and the exchange values of own-country currencies rise significantly on impact; as in the case of the U.S. shock, the MSG model shows the greatest initial sensitivity of interest rates and (for Japan, at least) exchange rates. By comparison, GEM, LIVERPOOL, and MULTIMOD show much less increase in German and Japanese interest rates and less appreciation of the deutsche mark and yen in the initial period. In most cases, interest rates and exchange rates return fairly quickly to baseline in subsequent periods.

Three models stand out from the rest in the case of the German or Japanese aggregate demand shocks (or both). First, INTERMOD-A again shows persistent but diminishing two-year cycles in output, prices, interest rates, and exchange rates; this cycling is especially pronounced in the case of Germany. Second, as in the case of the U.S. shock, the MX3 model produces longer-term cycling of the dollar-yen exchange rate, and this cycling is now also clearly evident for other Japanese variables in the case of the Japanese aggregate demand shock. Third, unlike its results for the analogous U.S. shock, the LIVERPOOL model has both German and Japanese prices falling below baseline initially; German prices return only gradually to baseline from below (mirroring the path of real GNP), whereas Japanese prices rebound quickly and then return gradually to baseline from above.[15] In addition, LIVERPOOL shows interest rates remaining persistently above baseline, and own-country currencies persistently appreciated above baseline, for both countries.

As would be expected, when an aggregate demand shock is applied to the G3 simultaneously (the "global" shock B), the own-country effects on outputs and prices are similar to, but somewhat larger than, the single country shocks. See figures 4-7, 4-8, and 4-9, which respectively present the effects of the global demand shock on U.S., German, and Japanese variables. The

14. Neither of the large adaptive-expectations models (MCM, MPS) ran simulations G and I.

15. The LIVERPOOL group reports that the Japanese and German wage equations have lagged wage coefficients that are high (over 0.7 and over 0.9, respectively).

Figure 4-7. *Effects of Increase in Global Demand (Shock B, Regime 2A/2AX)*

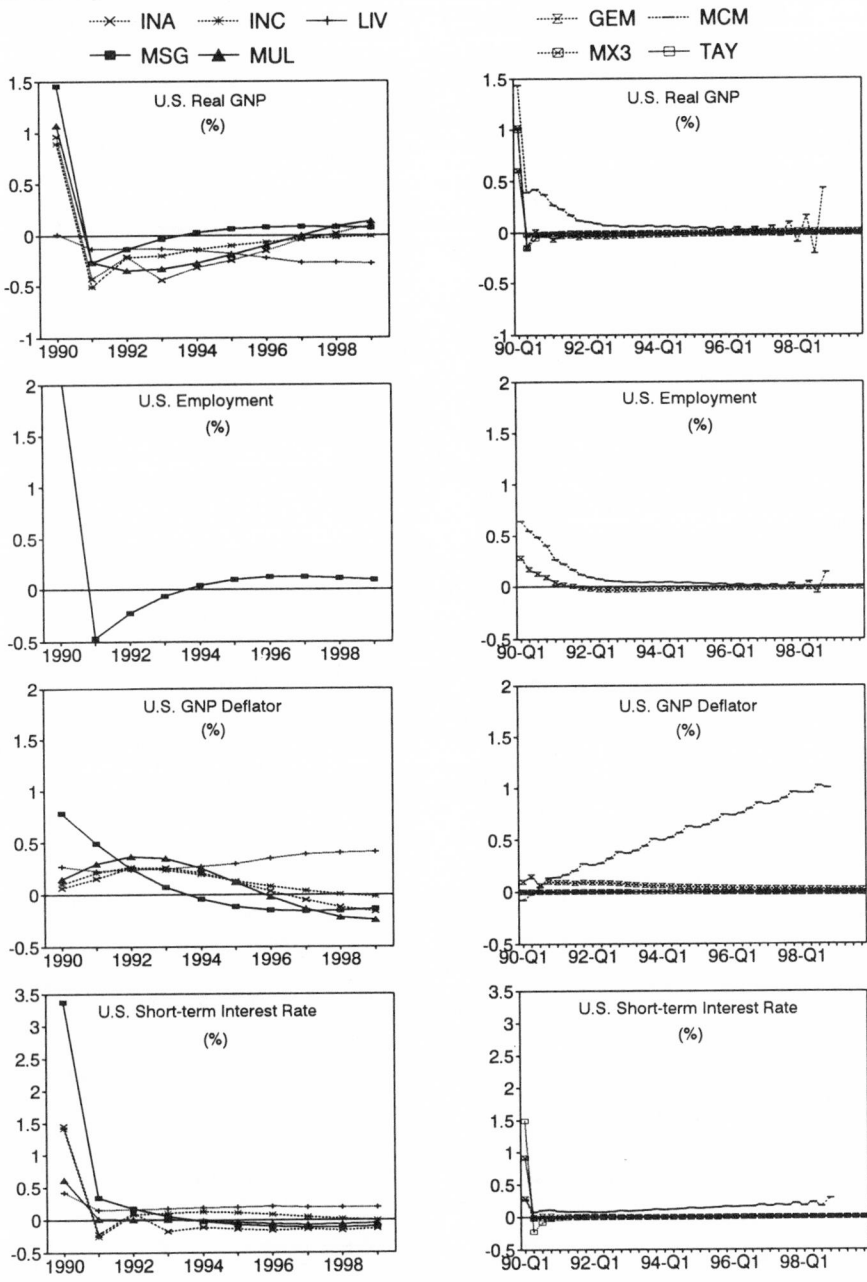

Figure 4-8. *Effects of Increase in Global Demand (Shock B, Regime 2A/2AX)*

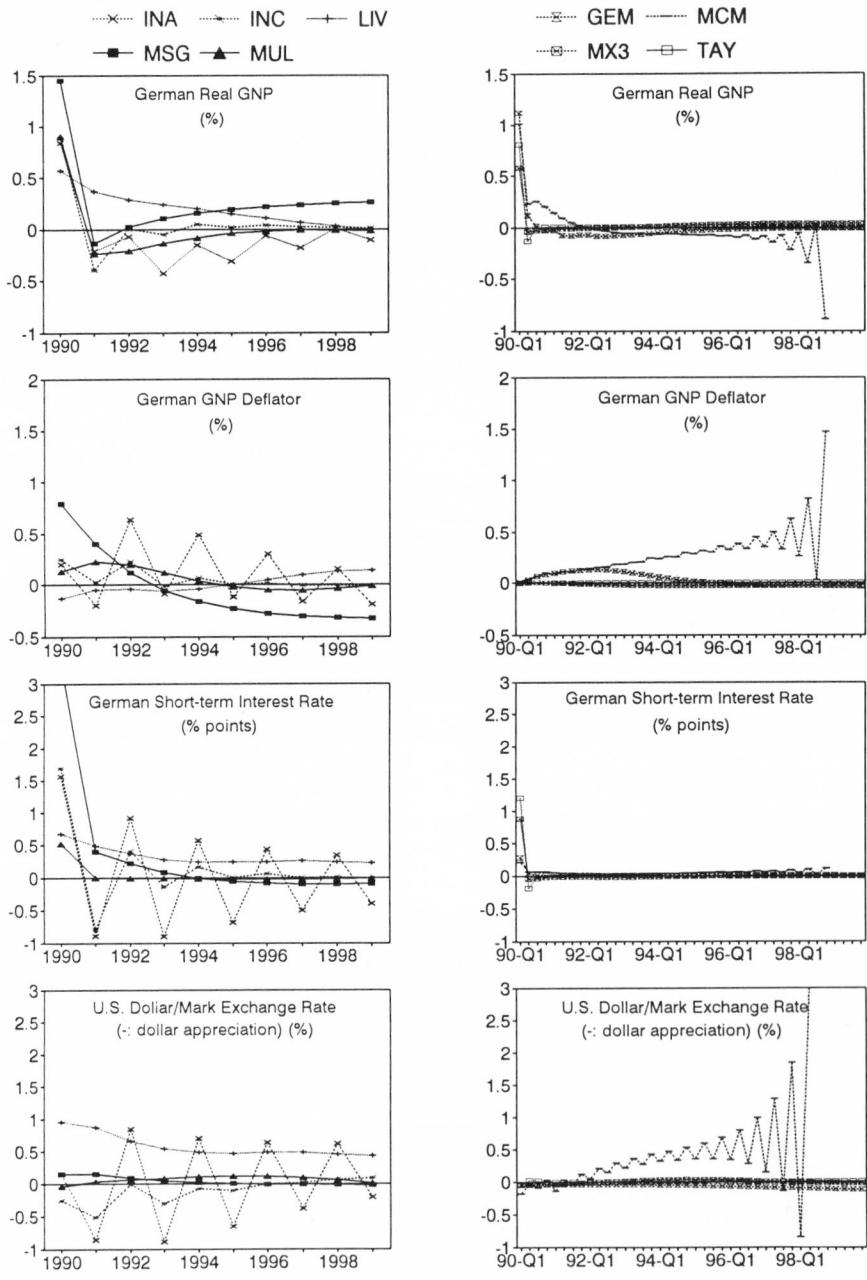

Figure 4-9. *Effects of Increase in Global Demand (Shock B, Regime 2A/2AX)*

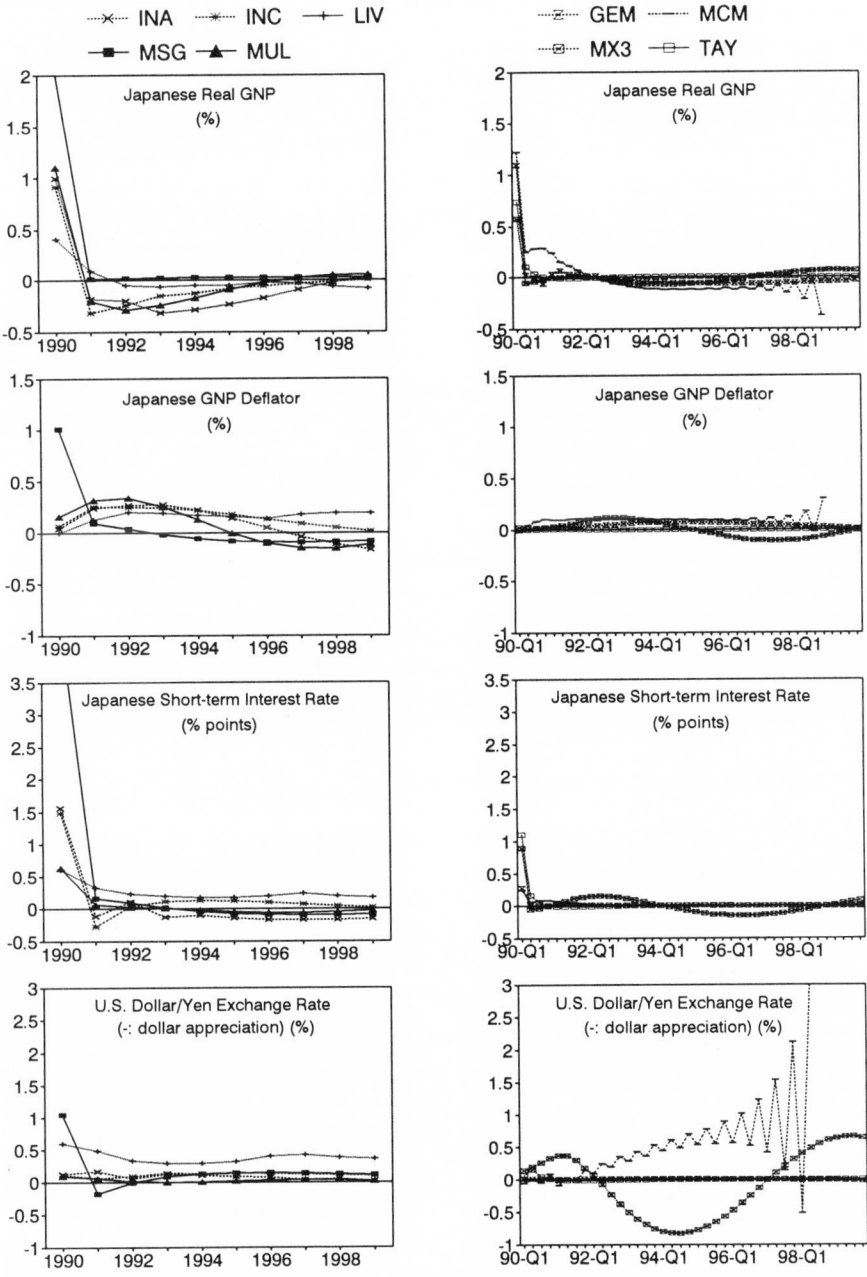

additional effect of the combined shock (relative to the own-country case) is to raise the initial effects on U.S. real GNP, prices, and interest rates by a little less than 0.1 percentage point each, on average, for the seven models that ran all four aggregate demand shocks. The average incremental effect on Japanese variables is 0.1 to 0.2 percentage point, and on German variables 0.2 to 0.3 percentage point.

The most visible difference between the single-country and global demand shocks is, as expected from chapter 2, in the behavior of exchange rates. In most cases, whereas home currencies appreciate in the case of a single-country demand shock, exchange rates move very little on impact in the global demand shock; increases in interest rates in all three countries largely offset one another. The MSG model is a notable exception, showing a significant appreciation of the yen for the global demand shock (although noticeably less than in the case of the Japanese demand shock), as Japanese interest rates rise more than U.S. rates.

The INTERMOD-A model again shows a strong two-year cycle in German variables, the MX3 model a longer cycle in Japanese variables, and the MCM model the same longer-run instabilities that showed up in the U.S. aggregate demand shock. Two new longer-term deviations from baseline are for the MSG model, which shows German real GNP and prices deviating persistently from baseline (although in offsetting directions), and for the LIVERPOOL model, which shows a similar picture for U.S. real GNP and prices (although in opposite directions to the MSG result).[16]

Aggregate Supply Shocks

Deterministic simulations were done for two types of transitory aggregate supply shocks (see chapter 3). One type involved shifting down the production function, or potential output, for one period by an amount equal to 1 percent of baseline real GNP. The equation specifications for aggregate supply variables differ substantially from model to model. It was recognized in advance, therefore, that there could be nontrivial variations in the implementation of this shock across the models. The second type of supply shock was a temporary 25 percent increase in the U.S. dollar price of oil (roughly $5 per barrel).

The theoretical analysis in chapter 2 explains how a transitory exogenous decline in productivity occurring simultaneously in all countries puts upward pressure on prices, causes outputs to fall, and induces increases in nominal interest rates. With exact nominal-income targeting (that chapter's YY regime) and with wage contracts and flexible prices, a country-specific shock to U.S. productivity leaves U.S. employment unchanged and appreciates the dollar in

---

16. The MSG deviations are due to that model's assumption of hysteresis in German labor markets.

real terms against the ROECD currency. Because of the shock's heterogeneous effects on macroeconomic variables, policymakers' preferences for nominal-income targeting versus other regime types may critically depend on the relative weights they assign in their loss function to output, inflation, and employment. Most analysts would agree that the appropriate response to a productivity shock is to let output change while stabilizing employment. As shown in chapter 2, however, changes in consumer prices may be smaller under some other regimes than under nominal-income targeting.

All ten models submitted results for the U.S. aggregate supply shock (shock C) under regime 2A/2AX (nominal-income targeting with partial instrument adjustment). Six of the models show an initial decline in U.S. real GNP, ranging between 0.1 percent and 0.8 percent (top two panels of figure 4-10). The MPS and INTERMOD-C models show small increases in real GNP initially.[17] The TAYLOR model reports a large (0.75 percent) increase in real GNP on impact. After the first period, almost all models show real GNP returning toward (sometimes rising above) the baseline and fluctuating within a range of ±0.3 percent of the baseline path. The MSG model shows a sustained positive deviation from baseline over the ten-year horizon (although gradually trending back toward baseline in the more distant future).

Employment rises initially by about $\frac{1}{2}$ percent in the several models that report that variable. The temporary negative shock to productivity and the associated increase in product prices reduce real wages (because nominal wages are sticky) and stimulate demand for factors of production.[18] Employment then falls to or below baseline in the second period and thereafter fluctuates in a fairly narrow range around the baseline in most cases (figure 4-10, second two panels).

The annual models report an initial increase in the U.S. price level of between 0.5 percent and 1.3 percent, followed by a fairly quick return to baseline or, in some cases, to as much as 0.5 percent below baseline. The MSG model, in particular, shows a sustained negative deviation from baseline during the fourth to tenth year. The quarterly models generally show much smaller initial effects on prices and, with the exception of MCM and MPS, return to baseline much more quickly. This result presumably reflects the fact that a transitory shock lasting for one quarter has a lesser effect on the in-flation process than a transitory shock lasting for one year. The three models with adaptive expectations tend to show more persistent positive effects on

---

17. The MPS group explains the initial small increase in real GNP in their model as follows. Output in the MPS model is largely demand-determined in the short run, and prices respond only gradually. The supply shock, imposed as a reduction in labor productivity, causes employment to be higher, and this in turn shifts the distribution of income toward labor and away from capital. The short-run spending propensity out of labor income is higher than that for capital income, which causes aggregate demand to increase.

18. Chapter 2 spells out conditions for the rise in employment.

Figure 4-10. *Effects of Decrease in U.S. Aggregate Supply (Shock C, Regime 2A/2AX)*

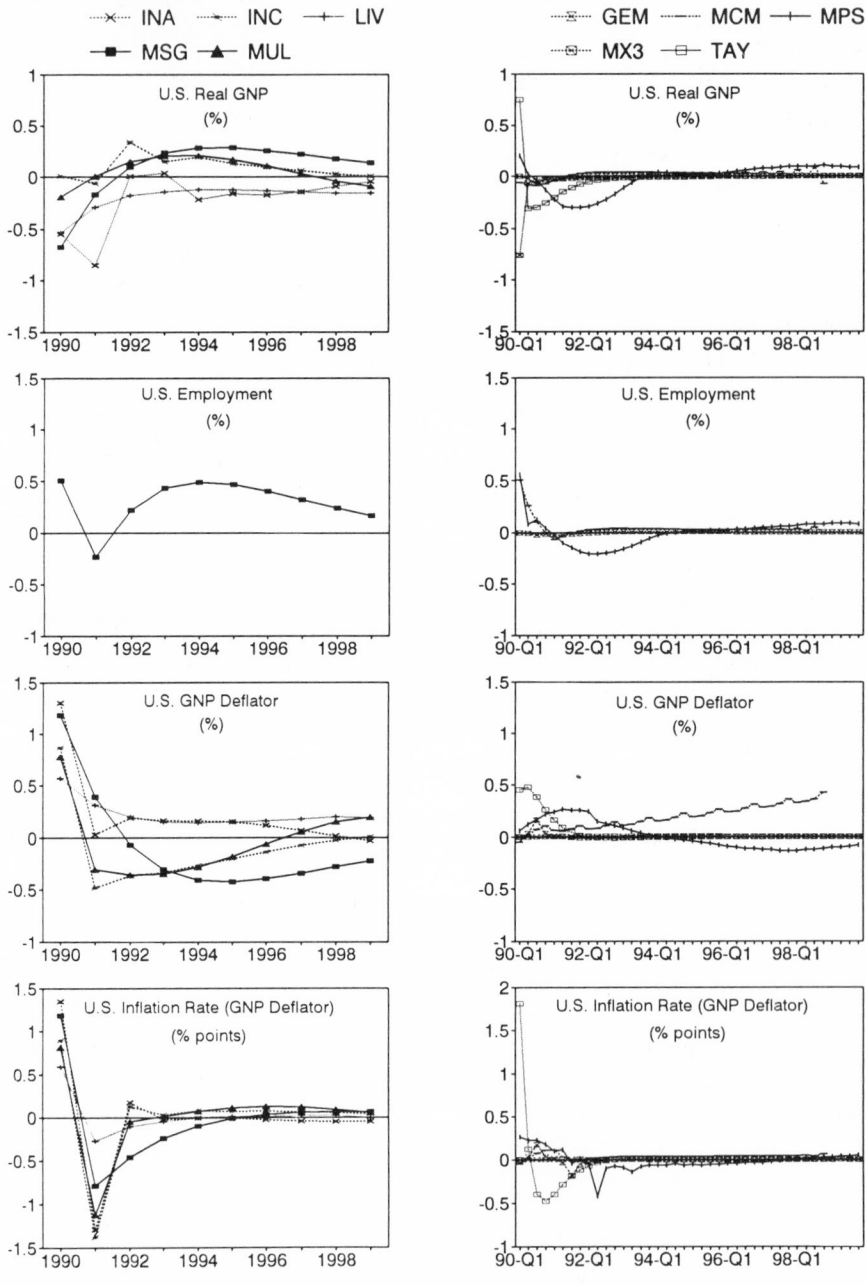

Figure 4-11. *Effects of Decrease in U.S. Aggregate Supply (Shock C, Regime 2A/2AX)*

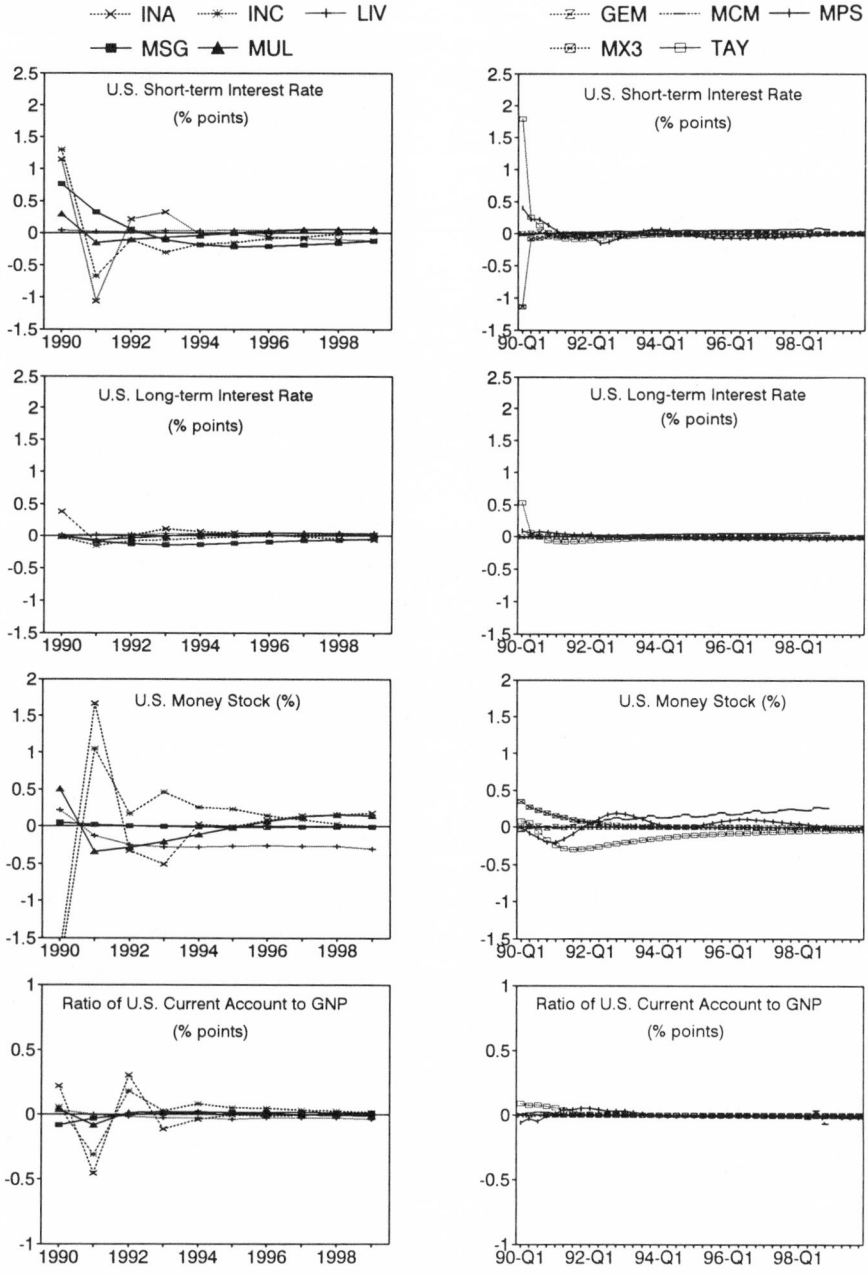

the price level than the models using rational expectations. (This result can be seen most dramatically in a comparison of the result for INTERMOD-A and INTERMOD-C.)

With the rise in the price level generally greater than the decline in real output, nominal income rises in most models, and short-term interest rates rise initially (figure 4-11). Long-term rates rise significantly only in the TAYLOR model (probably reflecting the effects of the increase in real output in that model), and in the INTERMOD-A model. Higher interest rates result in a small appreciation of the dollar in nominal terms in most cases (the dollar-deutsche-mark and dollar-yen exchange rates are shown in the top four panels of figure 4-12). With the rise in U.S. prices, the dollar appreciates significantly in real terms, consistent with the theoretical results in chapter 2.

The effects of the supply shock on the U.S. current account and foreign real GNP are generally quite small (figures 4-11 and 4-12).[19] In one case, the MSG model, the current account falls, and German and Japanese real GNP rise initially. This result reflects a tendency in the MSG model for relatively more of the shortfall in domestic supply relative to domestic demand to be made up by foreign producers through increased imports.[20] In other models, such as INTERMOD-A and LIVERPOOL, which show a slight increase in the current account or a slight decline in foreign real GNP, U.S. domestic demand may have adjusted downward more rapidly in response to the supply shock, resulting in a net decline in demand for imports.

The qualitative patterns of effects resulting from the German and Japanese negative supply shocks (shocks H and J) are broadly similar to those for the U.S. supply shock C (see figures 4-13 through 4-16). For each supply shock, most models reporting results show an initial decline in real GNP followed by a return toward baseline (and in some cases above baseline for a time). The results of several models suggest that the decline in German real GNP is proportionately greater than that of either U.S. or Japanese real GNP in response to the domestic supply shock. The MSG model results also suggest that the initial increase in German employment is proportionately somewhat less than for the other countries, possibly indicating the negative effects of a greater degree of labor market rigidity in Germany.

Prices, inflation, and interest rates in Germany and Japan rise initially; effects on current accounts and U.S. real GNP are essentially negligible. The INTERMOD-A model does show a moderate initial improvement in the German

---

19. In the theoretical analysis of chapter 2, under exact nominal-income targeting a downward shift in one country's productivity does not cause changes in the other country's output, product prices, and employment (or, when oil is included in the analysis, has only slight effects). The country in which the shock does not originate prefers the YY or the CC regime to the MM regime.

20. Forward-looking agents know that the shock is transitory and therefore buffer their consumption by importing more.

Figure 4-12. *Effects of Decrease in U.S. Aggregate Supply (Shock C, Regime 2A/2AX)*

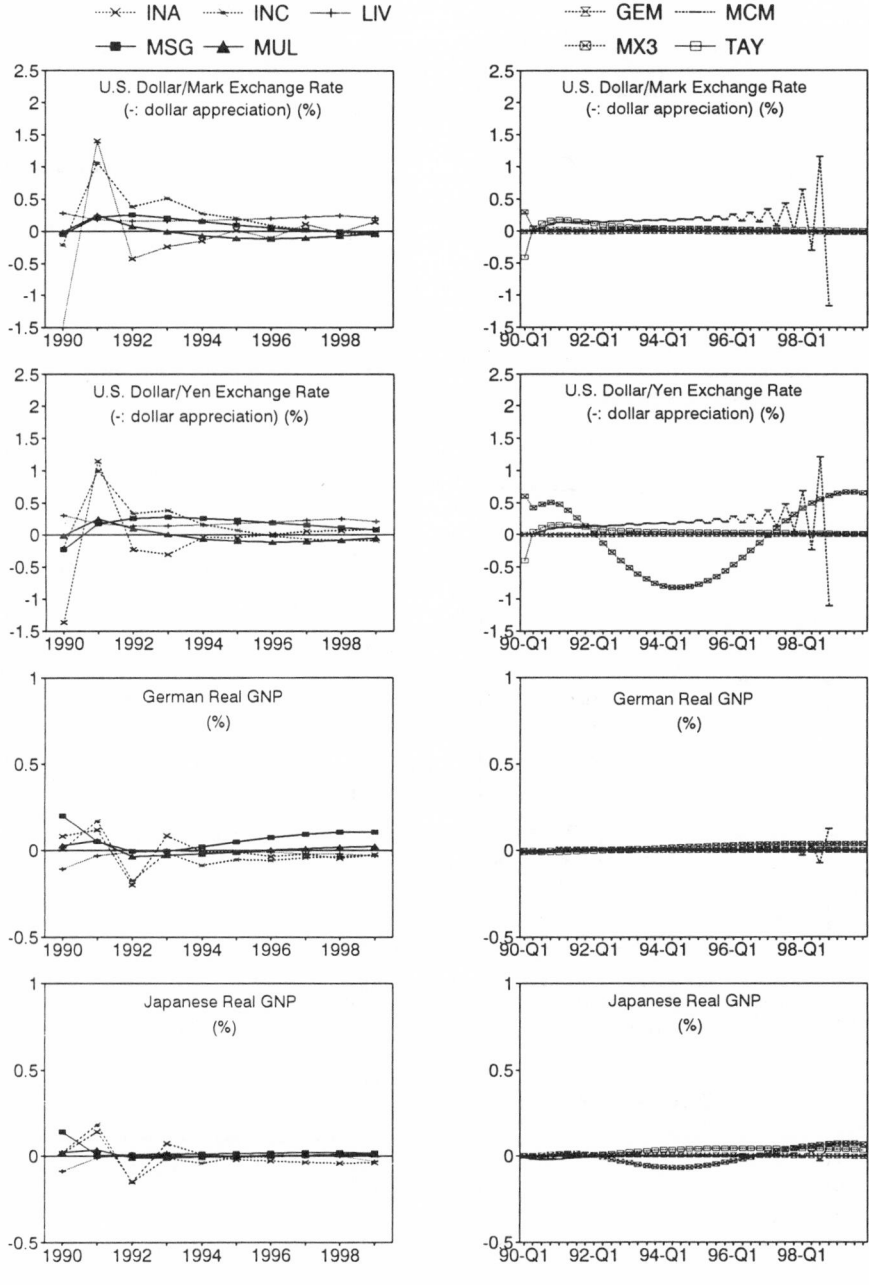

Figure 4-13. *Effects of Decrease in German Aggregate Supply (Shock H, Regime 2A/2AX)*

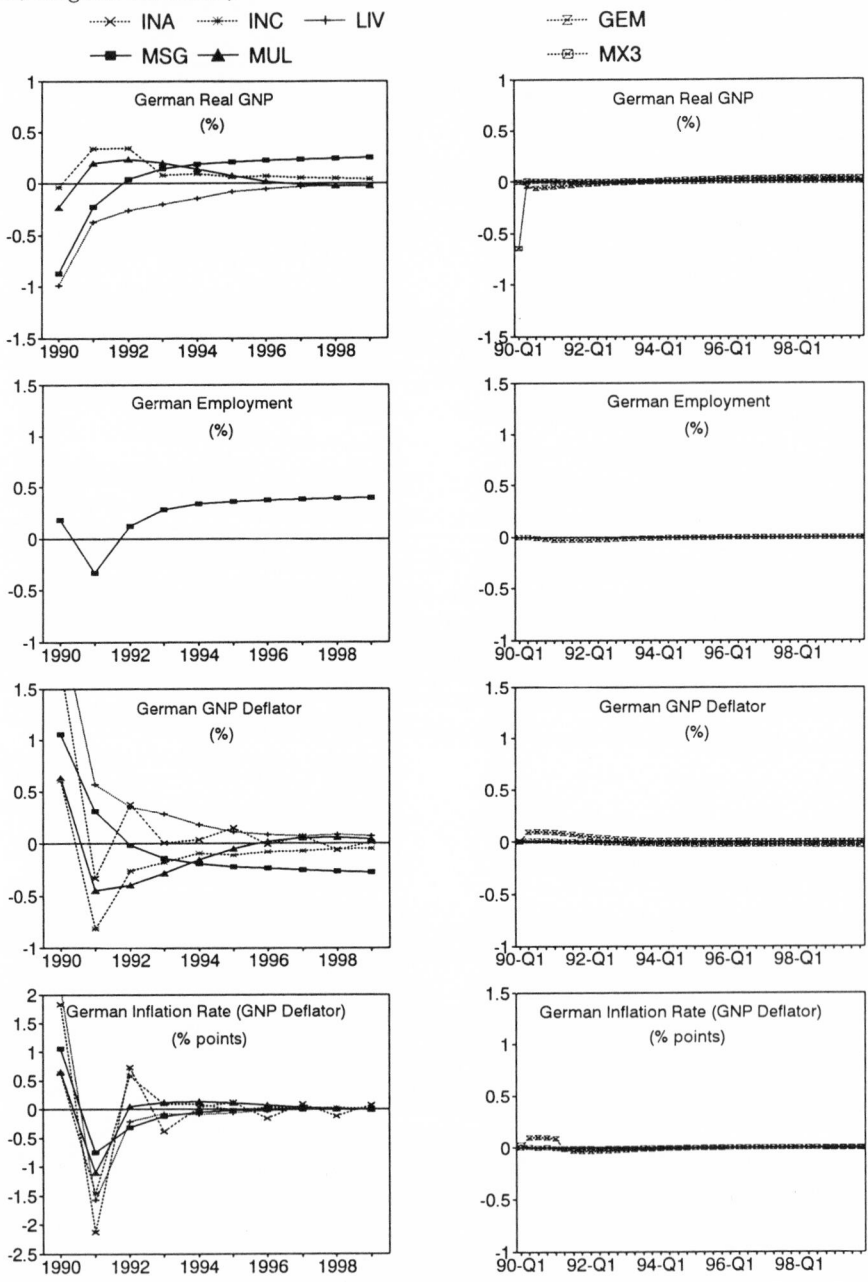

Figure 4-14. *Effects of Decrease in German Aggregate Supply (Shock H, Regime 2A/2AX)*

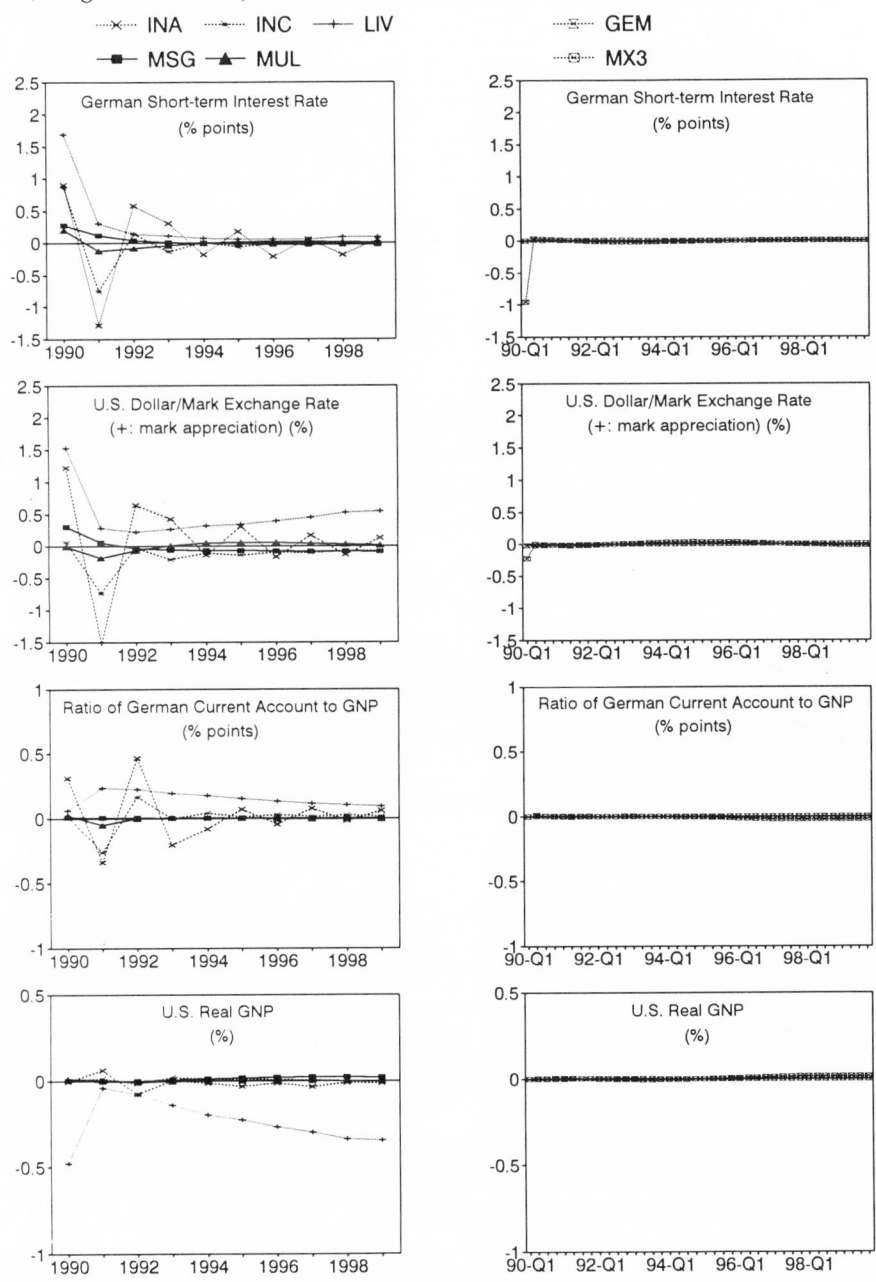

Figure 4-15. *Effects of Decrease in Japanese Aggregate Supply (Shock J, Regime 2A/2AX)*

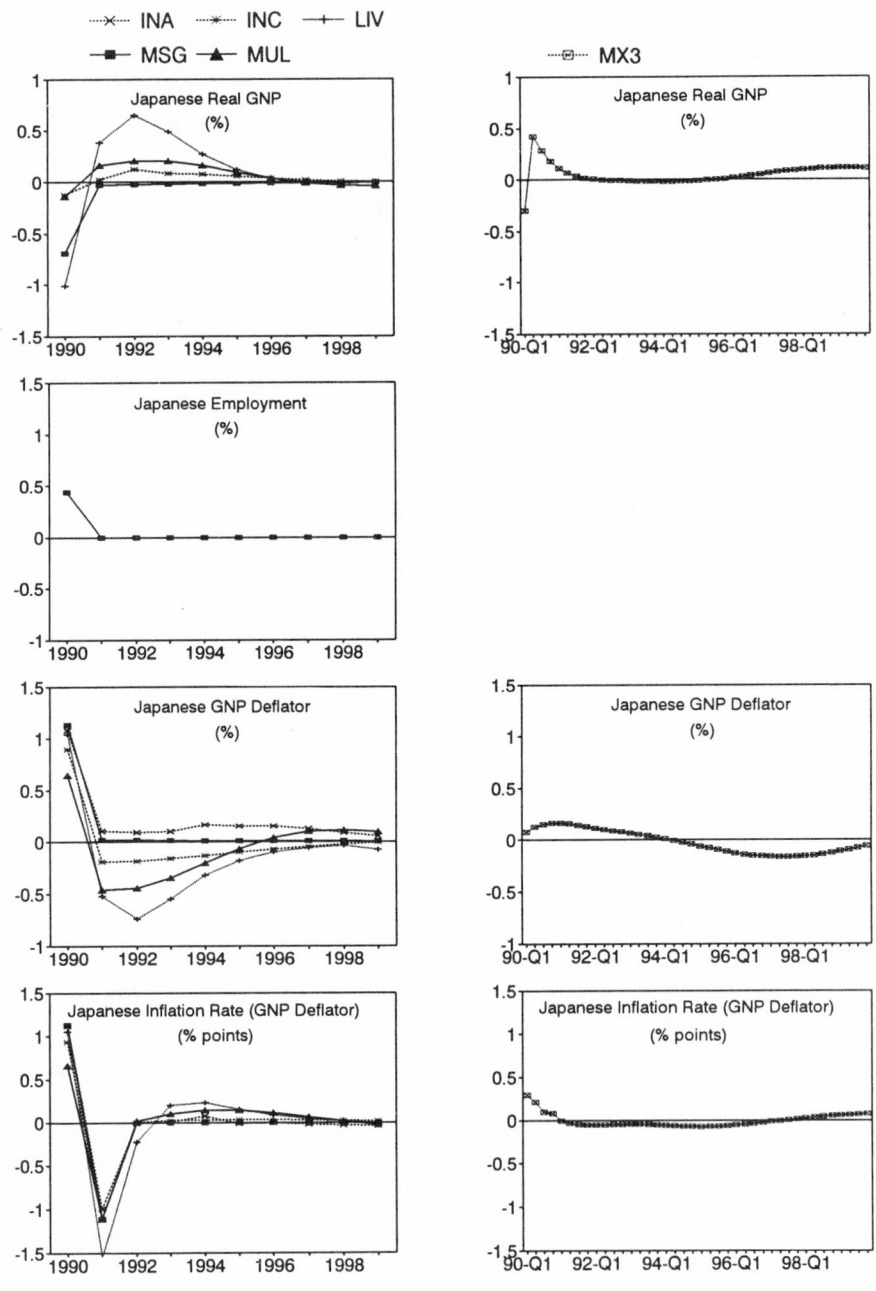

Figure 4-16. *Effects of Decrease in Japanese Aggregate Supply (Shock J, Regime 2A/2AX)*

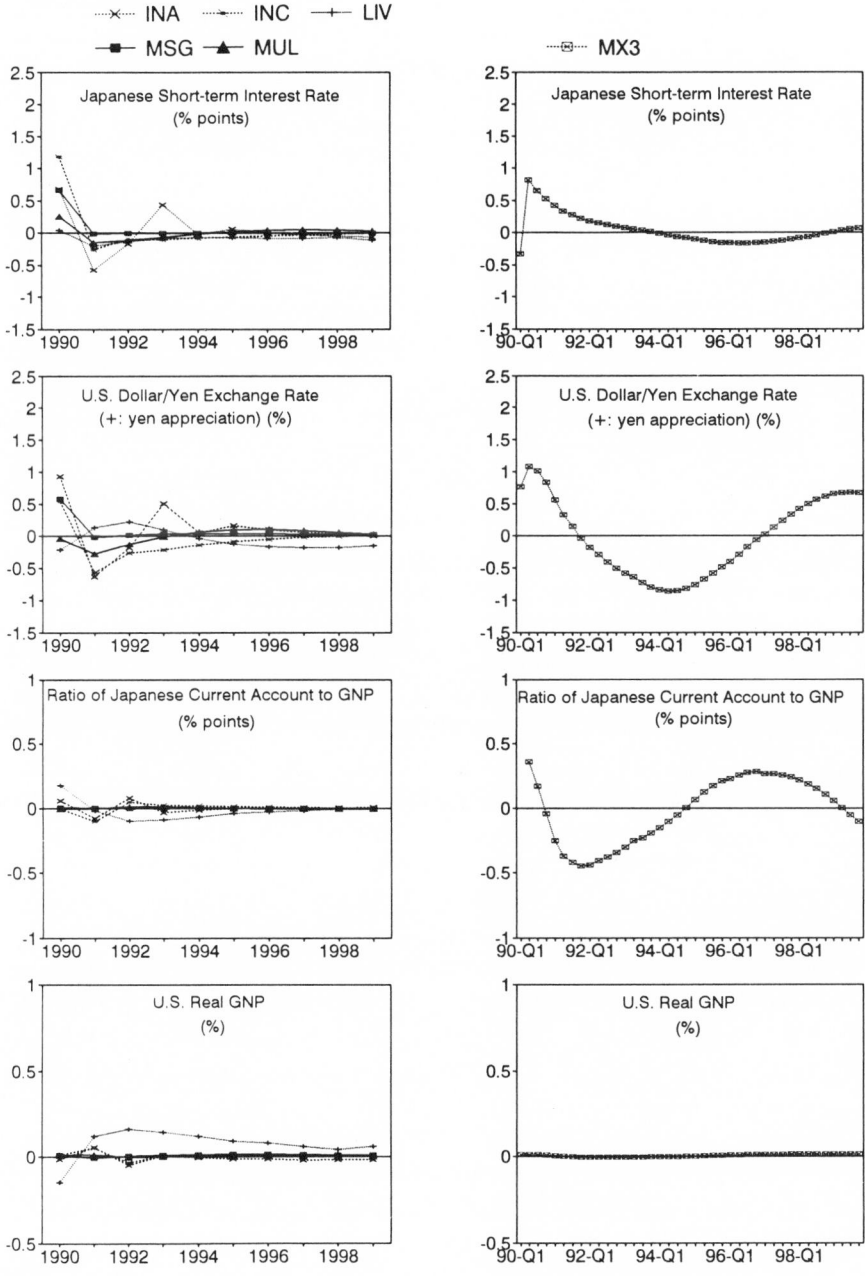

current account, reflecting the relatively large decline in German real GNP (hence import demand) predicted by that model.

For the transitory oil price increase (shock E), the simulation results submitted by the model groups exhibit less consensus about the consequences. Figures 4-17–4-19 show the effects on key variables for the United States, Germany, and Japan, respectively.

In the expository theoretical model of chapter 2, a transitory increase in world oil prices has effects that are analogous to those from a transitory global (symmetric) downward shift in productivity. In effect, an exogenous fall in the global supply of oil has the same effects—reductions in outputs, increases in product prices and interest rates—that occur when there is an exogenous fall in output per unit of non-oil input. In one of the empirical models (MSG), the results for the oil price shock are roughly consistent with the sum of the effects of the negative supply shocks (C, H, and J) in each of the countries. For most of the empirical models, however, the effects of the oil price shock are significantly different from those of the shocks to productivity. To some extent these differences result from the model groups having implemented the oil price shock differently from the productivity shocks. The differences also appear to stem from structures in the empirical models that are more complex than the simplified theoretical model considered in chapter 2.

The GEM, LIVERPOOL, MSG, and MCM models indicate that the transitory oil price increase has initial negative effects on real GNPs in most cases (Germany is an exception in MCM), consistent with the predictions of the theoretical model. (In the LIVERPOOL and MCM models, the fall in U.S. output is significantly greater under the oil price shock than under the productivity shock.) However, MULTIMOD, both versions of INTERMOD, and the MPS models show initial *positive* effects on GNPs under the oil price shock (except that in INTERMOD-A, the effect for Japan is essentially zero). The MULTIMOD group reported that the rise in outputs in their model results from significantly stronger exports to both oil-exporting countries and countries to which the oil producers recycle funds through international lending. Much the same sort of effect is probably at work in the INTERMOD models as well. The MULTIMOD group also reported that, whereas real outputs rise, real incomes fall because of the worsening of the terms of trade; the group observed that in a more recent, revised version of MULTIMOD, transitory oil price increases have a net negative effect on real GNP initially. Although the MPS model shows a small initial increase in U.S. real GNP in response to both the oil and U.S. productivity shocks, the explanations for the initial increase are different. For the productivity shock, the output increase is a demand phenomenon (as discussed in note 17). For the oil price shock, a supply response—higher oil prices stimulating oil exploration—appears to be more important.

Figure 4-17. *Effects of Increase in World Oil Price (Shock E, Regime 2A/2AX)*

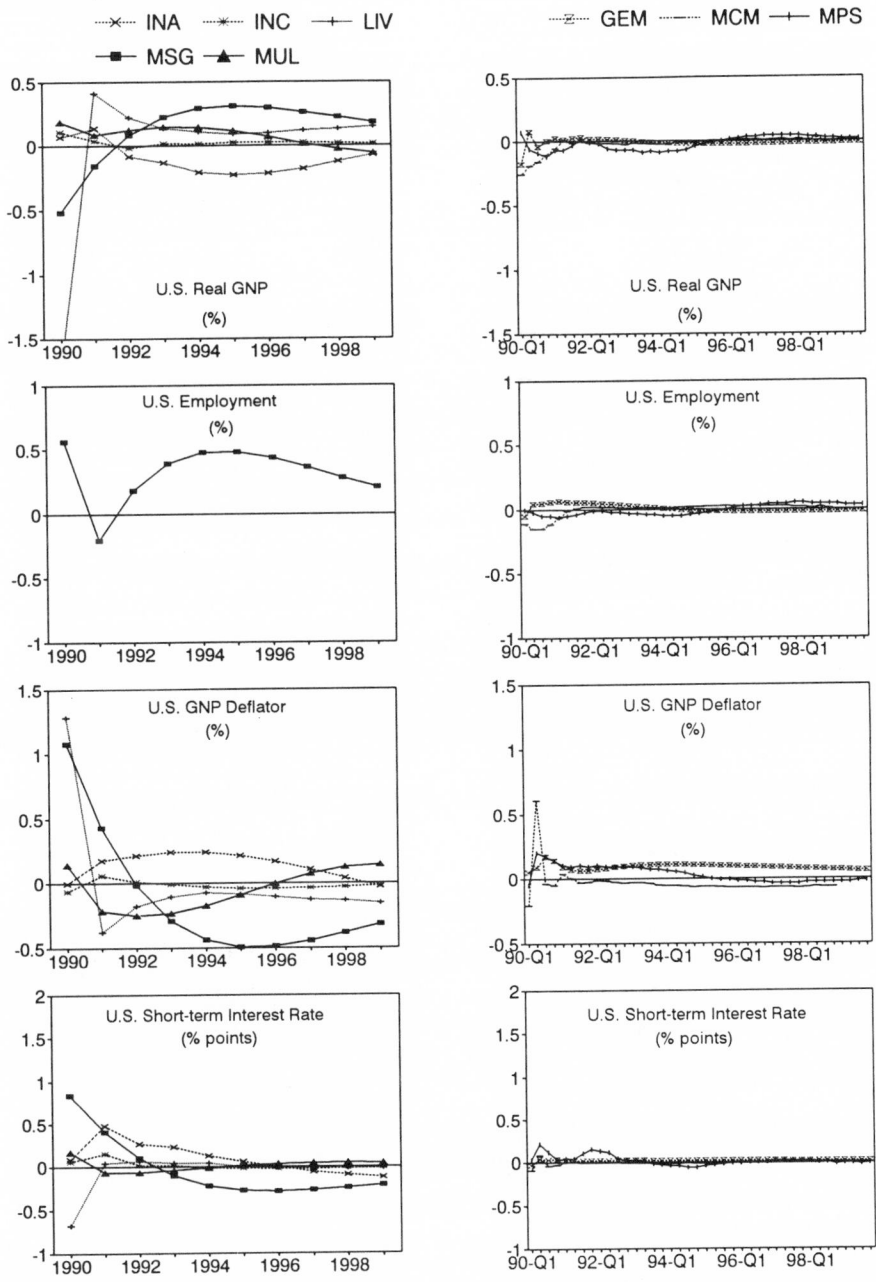

Figure 4-18. *Effects of Increase in World Oil Price (Shock E, Regime 2A/2AX)*

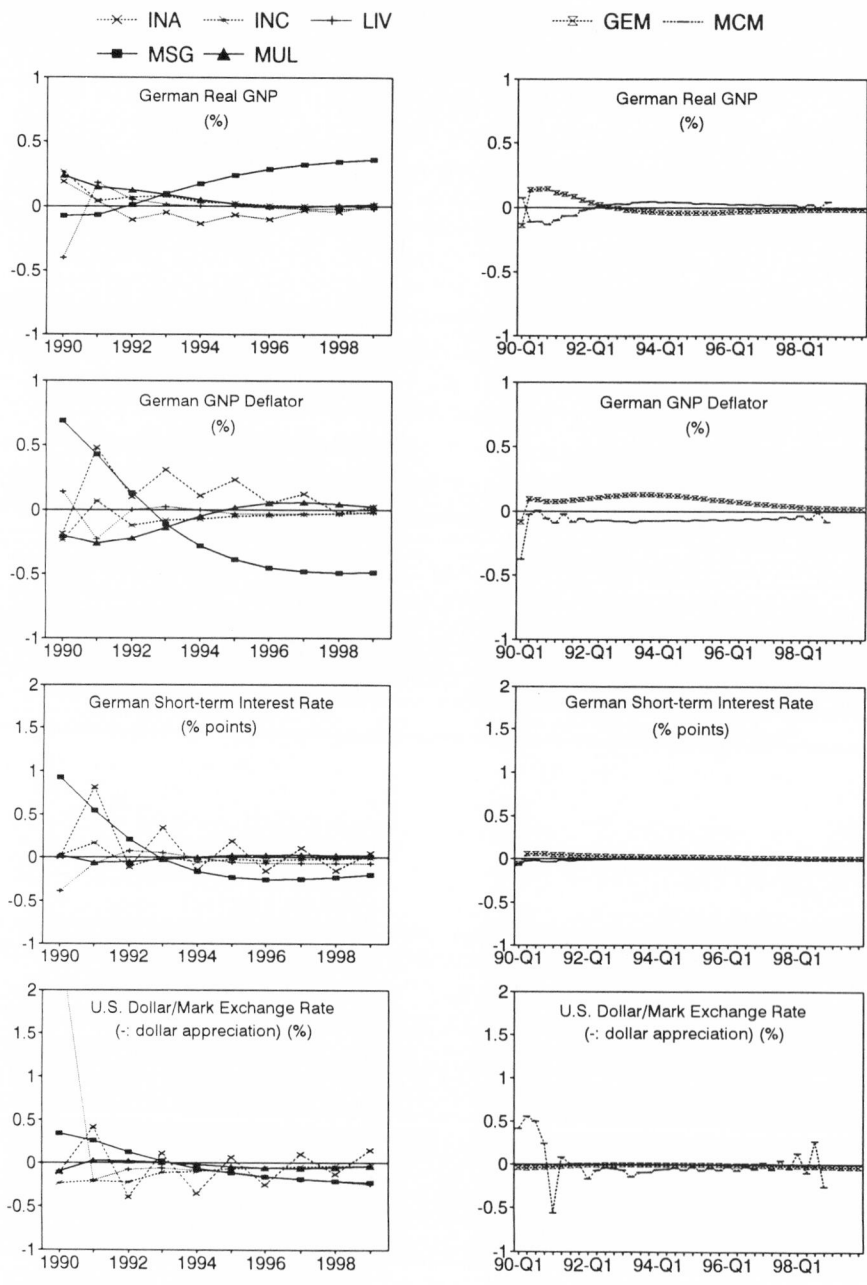

Figure 4-19. *Effects of Increase in World Oil Price (Shock E, Regime 2A/2AX)*

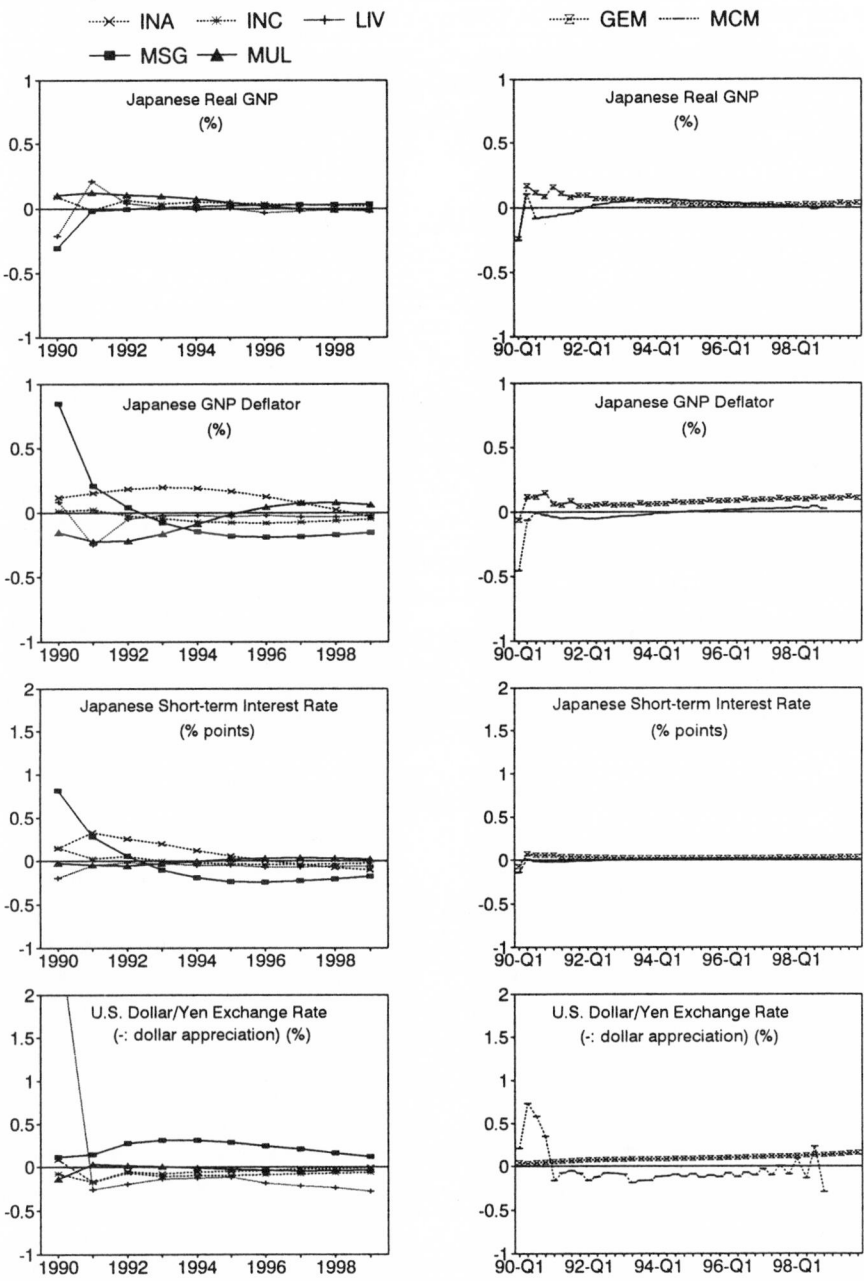

All but two of the models indicate that the initial effects of the oil price shock on the GNP deflators in all three countries are negligible to slightly negative. The small effects on prices can perhaps be explained in part by the fact that the GNP deflator does not include import prices. Presumably a domestic price index—such as the consumer price index, which does include import prices—would show a much larger positive effect. The two models with large initial price effects are LIVERPOOL and MSG, which unlike the other models use flexible-price specifications for product prices.[21]

The LIVERPOOL and MSG models suggest that the negative effects on U.S. output and positive effects on U.S. prices are proportionately greater than those on output and prices in Germany and Japan. This difference seems consistent with the view that the U.S. economy is more dependent on (and has lower indirect taxes on) both energy and oil than the other two economies. The remaining models, however, do not appear to support the view that the United States is significantly more vulnerable to a transitory oil price shock than either Japan or Germany. Those models may place relatively greater emphasis on the terms-of-trade effects of an oil price shock. Terms-of-trade effects tend to weigh in favor of the United States because of its lesser dependence on imported oil.

Given the small changes in real GNP and GNP deflators in most cases, the models generally report relatively small changes in interest rates under nominal-income targeting in the face of an oil price shock. The MSG model is a notable exception in showing a positive direction for all three G3 countries, reflecting the relatively large increases in prices predicted by that model. Interest rates in the LIVERPOOL model are also an exception, showing initial decreases below baseline, particularly for the United States, because of that model's prediction of a large decline in U.S. real GNP. The relatively large LIVERPOOL actual and expected decline in U.S. prices in the second period of the simulation, however, implies a significant second-year increase in U.S. real interest rates. The MCM and MSG models both have the dollar depreciating moderately against the deutsche mark and the yen, whereas other models show relatively little change in exchange rates.

Money Demand Shocks

The shocks to money demand in the United States, Germany, and Japan (shocks L, K, and D, respectively) involve exogenous increases in money demand equal

---

21. The large price effects for MSG unambiguously reflect the flexible-price specification of that model. The prices reported for LIVERPOOL are consumer prices rather than GNP deflators, but the LIVERPOOL model assumes that GNP deflators vary proportionally with consumer prices.

to 1 percent of the baseline monetary base (or some other narrow monetary aggregate), for one period only.

Under nominal-income targeting, as anticipated by the theoretical analysis in chapter 2, these shocks have zero to negligible effects on all key variables except the money stock. Accordingly, no charts are included here for the effects of these money demand shocks under regime 2A/2AX. With one exception, for all three shocks each of the models shows real GNP, prices, and interest rates—in both the country where the shock originates and in foreign countries—lying on the zero line.[22] In general, the money stock is allowed to expand enough to accommodate the shift in demand without significantly affecting incomes, prices, interest rates, and exchange rates.

The effects of money-demand shocks are quite different, however, under money targeting (regime 1/1X). As described in chapter 2, a positive shock to money demand under money targeting could be expected to raise interest rates and depress output, employment, and prices in the home country. The expected effects on foreign output and prices are ambiguous. The reason for this theoretical ambiguity is that, whereas the decline in real income in the home country reduces demand for imports and increases net exports, the rise in home interest rates causes the home currency to appreciate, thereby inducing expenditure switching, which works to reduce net exports. Theory gives no guidance about whether the income effect or the relative price effect dominates in the transmission of the near-term real effects of monetary shocks across countries.

The effects of the shock to U.S. money demand on key U.S. variables under money targeting are shown in figure 4-20. The effects on GNP, prices, and interest rates generally conform to the theory, with GNP and prices falling initially (by less than $\frac{1}{4}$ percent on average) and interest rates rising ($\frac{1}{4}$ to $1\frac{1}{4}$ percentage points). The quantitative effects on GNP are somewhat less than those obtained with the parameterized theoretical model presented in chapter 2, in part because somewhat greater flexibility in the money stock is allowed by the targeting rule used here (as indicated in the third pair of panels in figure 4-20) than in the theoretical analysis (which assumes exact money targeting). With one or two exceptions, after the initial declines, real GNPs, prices, and interest rates return to baseline fairly quickly. A notable exception is the MPS model, in which the shock to U.S. money demand under money targeting sets off large cyclical swings in U.S. real GNP, prices, and interest rates. These cycles are qualitatively similar to those observed for that model for goods-demand shocks

22. The sole exception is for Japanese variables in the MX3 model, which show the same moderate cycling behavior observed in other simulations.

Figure 4-20. *Effects of Increase in U.S. Money Demand (Shock L)*
under Money Targeting (Regime 1/1X)

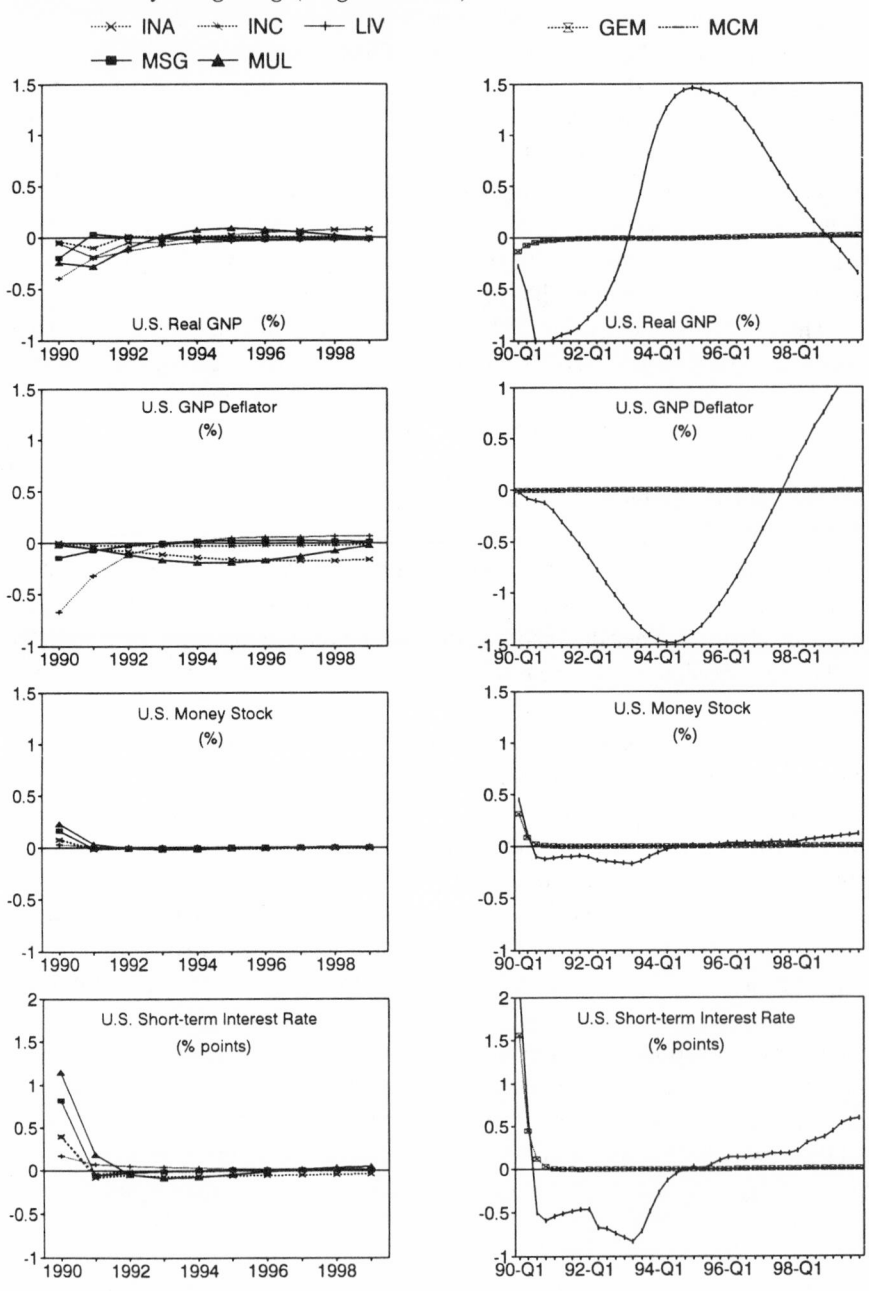

Figure 4-21. *Effects of Increase in U.S. Money Demand (Shock L) under Money Targeting (Regime 1/1X)*

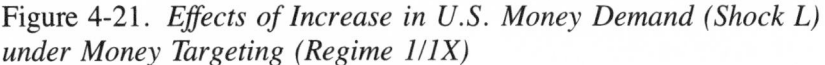

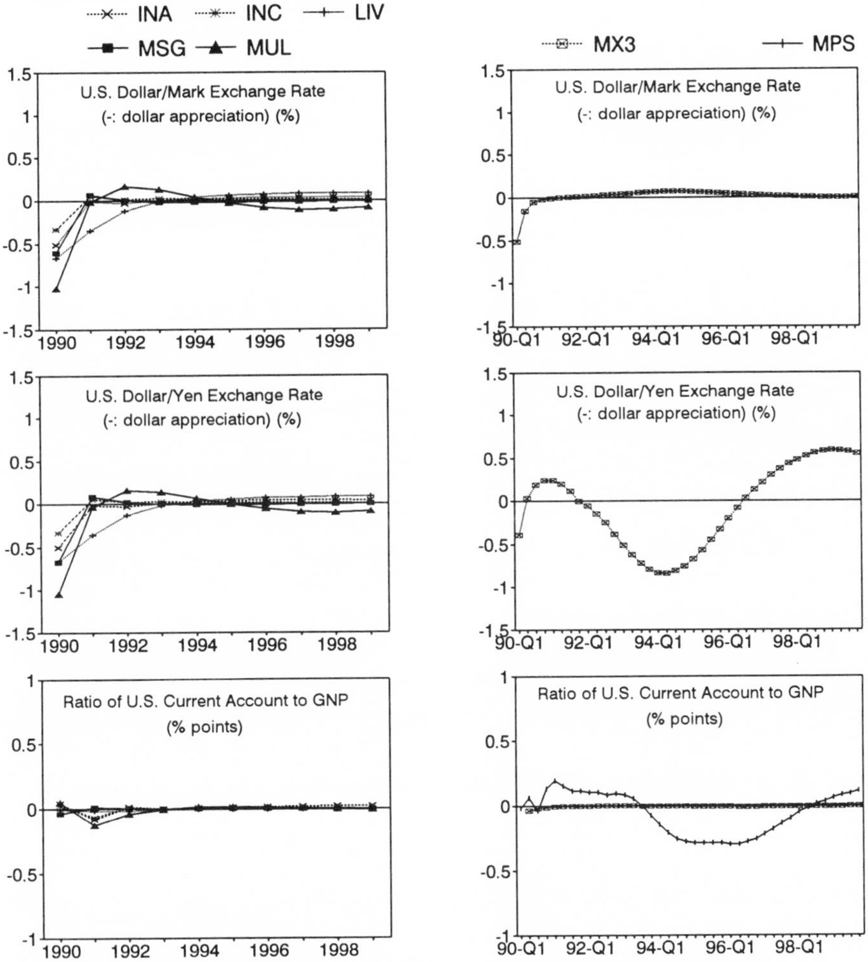

under nominal-income targeting, and presumably reflect the same underlying dynamic interactions among interest rates, aggregate demand, and prices. The quantitative differences between the cycles, however, are substantial. Under nominal-income targeting, the oscillations are damped over time; under money targeting, they are unstable.

The effects of the U.S. money-demand shock on exchange rates and the U.S. current account under money targeting are shown in figure 4-21. All

Figure 4-22. *Effects of Increase in U.S. Money Demand (Shock L)*
under Money Targeting (Regime 1/1X)

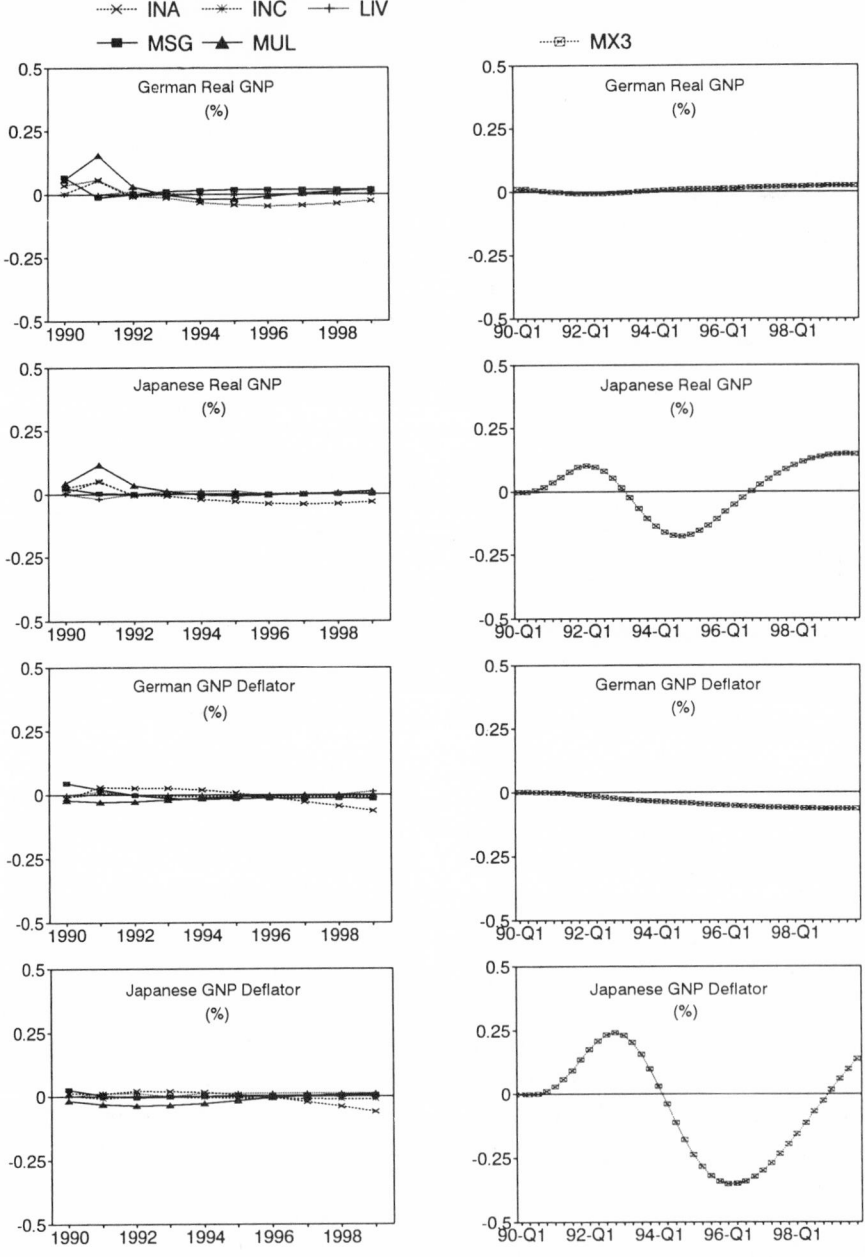

models show a significant initial appreciation of the dollar against the deutsche mark and the yen because of the rise in U.S. interest rates. The MX3 model exhibits the same cycling in the dollar-yen exchange rate as observed in other simulations. The effect on the U.S. current account is generally small, with several models showing a moderate decline in the second period. The current account behaves differently in the MPS model, first rising above baseline for several years and then falling below baseline. In that model, the effects of the large cycle in real GNP on import demand dominates the effects of the appreciation of the dollar on net exports.[23]

The effects of the U.S. money-demand shock on German and Japanese real GNP (figure 4-22) are somewhat less ambiguous. In most cases the effects on both German and Japanese GNP are slightly positive in the first period and increase somewhat in the second period. This result is consistent with the results for the parameterized theoretical model in chapter 2 and the results of earlier model-comparison exercises.[24] The depreciation of foreign currencies against the dollar generally causes prices abroad to rise somewhat.

The effects of the German and Japanese money-demand shocks (shocks K and D) under money targeting are not shown here graphically. For those few models that ran all three shocks, the effects of the German and Japanese shocks on own-country and foreign variables look very much the same as the results for the U.S. shock presented in figures 4-20–4-22.

Sustained Shock to U.S. Money Supply

Four of the participating models — MPS, MSG, MX3, and TAYLOR — correctly ran shock F, a permanent 1 percent increase in the U.S. money supply under a regime of exact money targeting (full instrument adjustment).[25] On the

---

23. The MPS model contains only an effective (weighted average) exchange rate for the dollar and does not identify bilateral exchange rates against the deutsche mark and the yen.

24. Although the empirical results in *EMIE* were ambiguous on this point, the more recent results surveyed in Bryant, Helliwell, and Hooper (1989) suggested that a U.S. monetary contraction has a slight positive effect on real GNP abroad, since the positive effects of the depreciations of foreign currencies outweigh the negative effects of the decline in U.S. real GNP. The net positive effect on foreign GNP can be reconciled with the more ambiguous effect on the U.S. current account because the appreciation of the dollar has a greater negative effect on U.S. real net exports than it has on the nominal current account. That is, the appreciation tends to reduce U.S. import prices, which reduces nominal imports (hence the current account) but stimulates real imports (hence foreign real GNP).

25. The LIVERPOOL model group submitted results for shock F, but with the money stock increasing above baseline in the first year by 1 percent, in the second year by 2 percent, in the third year by 3 percent, and so on. These LIVERPOOL results are not shown in figures 4-23 and 4-24.

Figure 4-23. *Effects of Sustained Increase in U.S. Money Supply (Shock F) with Exact Money Targeting*

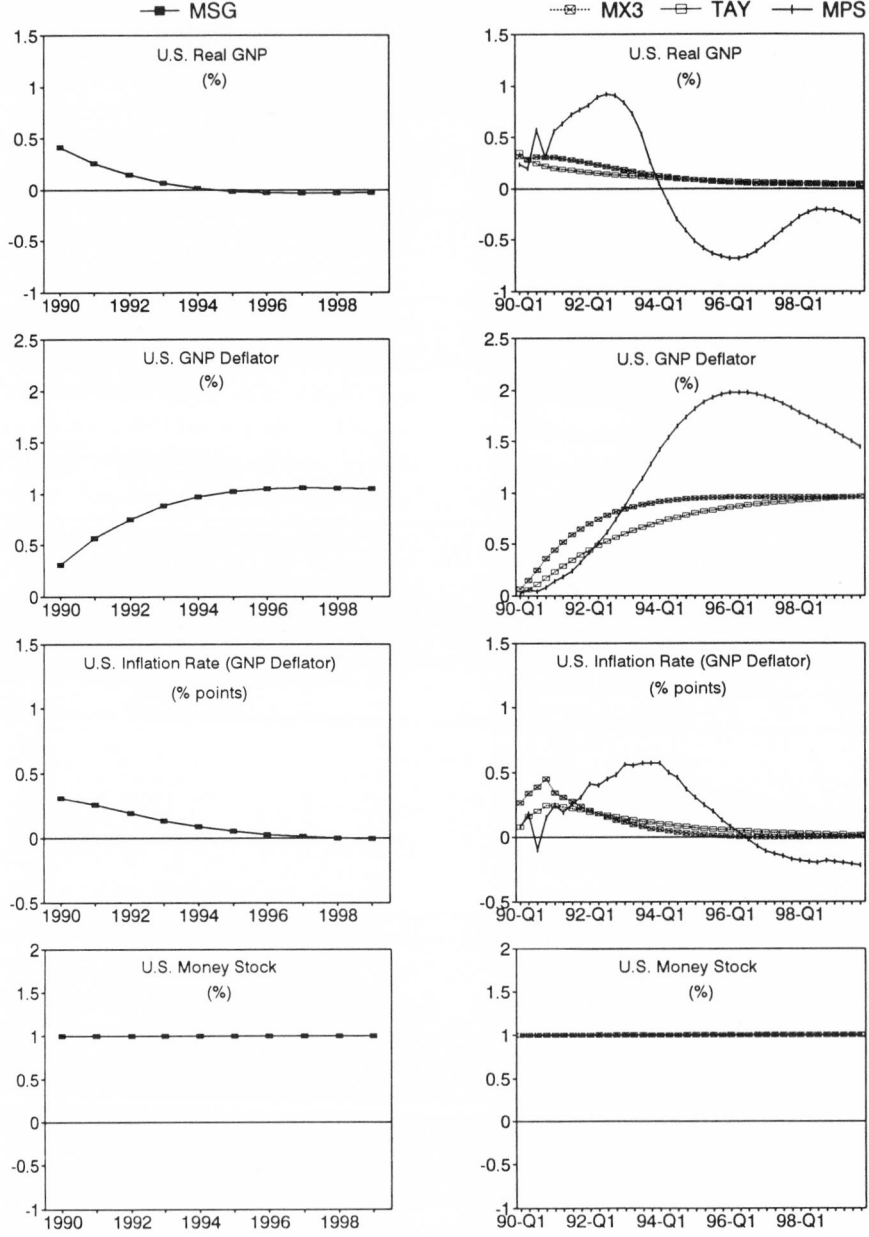

Figure 4-24. *Effects of Sustained Increase in U.S. Money Supply (Shock F) with Exact Money Targeting*

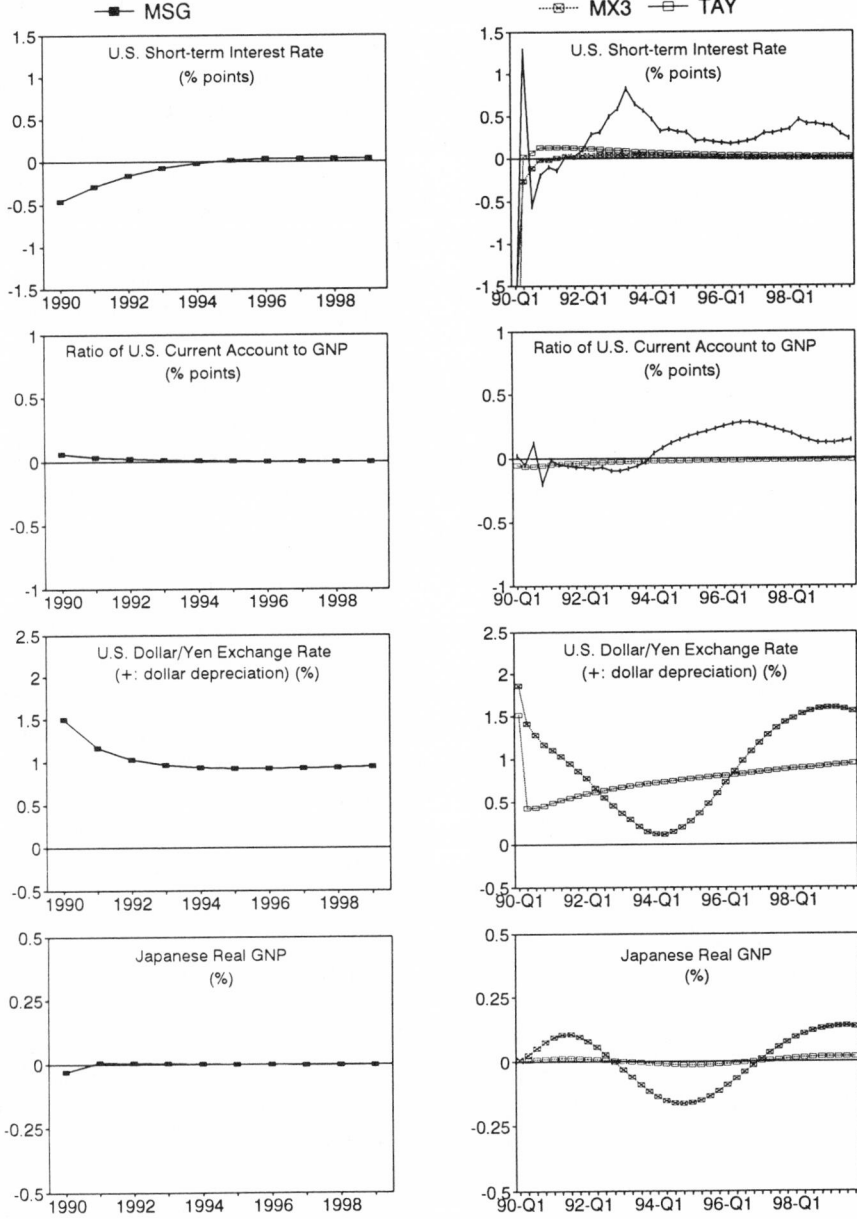

whole, the results lie within the range of outcomes observed in previous model-comparison exercises and, for three of the four models, tolerably close to the average outcome in earlier exercises (as calculated in Bryant, Helliwell, and Hooper 1989). In that average outcome of earlier results, a permanent 1 percent increase in U.S. money raises U.S. real GNP by about $\frac{1}{4}$ percent over a year or two, after which real GNP returns gradually to its baseline path.[26] In the meantime, the price level gradually rises to a level about 1 percent above its baseline path and then remains there. U.S. interest rates fall sharply on impact (by 1 percent or more), and the dollar depreciates by somewhat more. The dollar depreciation stimulates U.S. real net exports, but the rise in U.S. output and prices has the opposite effect on the current account. As a result, the net effects on the U.S. current account, and hence on real GNP and prices in other major countries, are fairly small.

The results of the new simulations done for this project are shown in figures 4-23 and 4-24. For the most part, the models tend to conform to the view that money is neutral with respect to real GNP in the medium to longer term. Three of the four models (MSG, MX3, and TAYLOR) show U.S. real GNP increasing about $\frac{1}{3}$ to $\frac{2}{5}$ percent during the first year or two of the simulation, after which it returns gradually to baseline (top panels of figure 4-23). The same three models also show U.S. prices rising gradually to about 1 percent above baseline. U.S. short-term interest rates decline sharply on impact, particularly in the quarterly models, and the dollar depreciates 1 to 2 percent (figure 4-24).

The MPS model shows more extreme movements in real GNP and prices than the other three models. Real GNP rises to a peak level about 1 percent above baseline after about ten quarters and then declines and cycles below the baseline path for much of the rest of the simulation period. Prices in that model rise to a level more than 2 percent above the baseline path midway through the ten-year simulation before returning toward the path followed by the other models.

Effects of Selected Shocks under Alternative Policy Regimes

The preceding discussion and charts give the reader some feeling for the type of information available from the results for the deterministic simulations. But that discussion focuses primarily on nominal-income targeting, and even then gives only skimpy attention to most of the shocks and types of variables.

The empirical data for the deterministic simulations are in fact a large multiple of that surveyed in the preceding section. The complete data base

---

26. The monetary shocks reported in *EMIE* are not strictly comparable with shock F in the present simulation exercise because the *EMIE* shock was four times as large and was phased in gradually over four quarters in the quarterly models. Bryant, Helliwell, and Hooper (1989), which covers a larger set of models and simulations than those included in *EMIE*, "standardized" the *EMIE* results to a 1 percent shock.

encompasses up to twelve shocks and up to nine regimes for each of ten models (some 450 simulations in all). For each simulation, it is possible to consider the effects on a variety of macroeconomic variables for each of the G3 countries (sometimes for other countries as well), with either ten (annual) or forty (quarterly) observations per variable. The overall data base comprises more than 225,000 observations.

Detailed tables, included as annex A to this volume, present some — of course, not all — of the data for the deterministic simulations. Each table in annex A, pertaining to a single model, exhibits data for selected variables for an individual country across all types of regimes run by that model group. The tables are ordered by model, and then by country within the tables for a particular model. Table 4-1, for the MULTIMOD model for three U.S. variables, illustrates how the data are presented. The three vertical panels report data for real GNP, the price level (GNP deflator), and the inflation rate (GNP deflator), all measured as deviations from a baseline simulation. The other key variables shown in the annex A tables are short-term interest rates, long-term interest rates, the ratio of the current account balance to nominal GNP, and the yen-dollar and deutsche-mark-dollar bilateral exchange rates. Data points for annual models, as in table 4-1, are shown for each variable for the first, second, fifth, and tenth year of the simulations. For quarterly models, the data points are for the first, sixth, eighteenth, and thirty-eighth quarters.[27] As in table 4-1, the annex A tables are divided horizontally into panels, one for each type of shock. Within each panel, the rows refer to regime types. For a model group running both the O and an X specification for each regime type, data are available for eight regimes. In the illustrative table 4-1, only five regime types are available. In table 4-1, we show panels for only the aggregate demand shocks (A, I, G, and B). The annex tables contain panels for all the shocks implemented by the model groups.

The focus of the rest of this chapter is an assessment of the alternative regimes, in particular how well they perform in damping the effects of shocks on key ultimate-target variables. In subsequent sections, we search for some degree of consensus across the models by presenting various methods of ranking the regimes overall, using summary tables or summary statistics that try to distill various features of the large mass of data. In this section, however, we continue to use a more straightforward charting method for comparing the regimes. It is obviously impractical to use this method for all of the shocks and variables, and we therefore concentrate on only a limited set for purposes of illustration.

Accordingly, we again examine the effects of only a few of the shocks: those to U.S. aggregate demand, U.S. aggregate supply, and Japanese and U.S.

---

27. These quarterly observations were chosen to conform with the counterpart observations from the annual models. The first quarter is the shock or impact period. The sixth, eighteenth, and thirty-eighth quarters correspond roughly to the mid-points of the second, fifth, and tenth years of the simulation.

Table 4-1. *Illustration of Annex A Tables for Deterministic Simulations, MULTIMOD Model: Effects on U.S. Real GNP, U.S. Price Level, and U.S. Inflation Rate*

Shock and re-gime	Real GNP[a]				GNP deflator[a]				Inflation rate[b]			
	1st yr.	2nd yr.	5th yr.	10th yr.	1st yr.	2nd yr.	5th yr.	10th yr.	1st yr.	2nd yr.	5th yr.	10th yr.
Shock A: U.S. aggregate demand												
1	0.994	−0.283	−0.226	0.087	0.142	0.286	0.300	−0.109	0.149	0.150	−0.062	−0.049
1X	0.986	−0.299	−0.226	0.117	0.132	0.252	0.179	−0.083	0.138	0.125	−0.086	0.004
2A	...	...	...	...	...	...	...	...	...	...	...	...
2AX	1.002	−0.259	−0.273	0.130	0.149	0.296	0.260	−0.235	0.156	0.153	−0.091	−0.031
2B	...	...	...	...	...	...	...	...	...	...	...	...
2BX	0.871	−0.443	−0.103	0.010	0.113	0.221	0.228	0.181	0.118	0.112	−0.034	0.010
3	...	...	...	...	...	...	...	...	...	...	...	...
3X	0.966	−0.280	−0.205	0.103	0.129	0.241	0.156	−0.074	0.135	0.117	−0.067	0.009
Shock I: Japanese aggregate demand												
1	0.041	−0.007	0.004	0.001	0.003	0.003	−0.003	−0.004	0.003	0.001	−0.003	0.002
1X	0.037	−0.014	0.008	−0.002	0.003	0.003	−0.009	0.002	0.003	0.000	−0.004	0.004
2A	...	...	...	...	...	...	...	...	...	...	...	...
2AX	0.044	−0.007	0.002	0.001	0.001	0.002	−0.005	−0.002	0.002	0.001	−0.003	0.003
2B	...	...	...	...	...	...	...	...	...	...	...	...
2BX	0.036	0.003	0.002	0.001	0.005	0.007	0.016	0.014	0.005	0.002	0.004	−0.002
3	...	...	...	...	...	...	...	...	...	...	...	...
3X	0.040	−0.015	0.004	−0.001	0.002	0.002	−0.004	0.001	0.002	0.001	−0.002	0.001
Shock G: German aggregate demand												
1	0.028	0.002	0.000	0.000	0.001	0.001	−0.002	0.000	0.001	−0.000	−0.001	0.001
1X	0.024	−0.003	0.005	−0.003	0.001	0.000	−0.006	0.003	0.001	−0.001	−0.001	0.002
2A	...	...	...	...	...	...	...	...	...	...	...	...
2AX	0.030	0.000	0.001	0.002	−0.000	−0.001	−0.004	0.001	−0.000	−0.001	−0.001	0.002
2B	...	...	...	...	...	...	...	...	...	...	...	...
2BX	0.021	0.013	0.002	0.004	0.003	0.005	0.013	0.009	0.003	0.002	0.004	−0.003
3	...	...	...	...	...	...	...	...	...	...	...	...
3X	0.028	−0.005	−0.002	0.001	0.000	0.001	−0.001	0.000	0.000	0.001	−0.001	0.000
Shock B: "Global" aggregate demand												
1	1.063	−0.288	−0.221	0.088	0.145	0.289	0.293	−0.113	0.152	0.150	−0.066	−0.046
1X	1.046	−0.318	−0.222	0.112	0.136	0.257	0.174	−0.075	0.143	0.126	−0.089	0.005
2A	...	...	...	...	...	...	...	...	...	...	...	...
2AX	1.073	−0.268	−0.275	0.138	0.151	0.299	0.254	−0.246	0.158	0.154	−0.095	−0.029
2B	...	...	...	...	...	...	...	...	...	...	...	...
2BX	0.931	−0.419	−0.107	0.018	0.121	0.231	0.256	0.204	0.127	0.114	−0.025	0.006
3	...	...	...	...	...	...	...	...	...	...	...	...
3X	1.048	−0.306	−0.199	0.104	0.133	0.248	0.149	−0.074	0.139	0.120	−0.093	0.013

Source: Annex A, table A-MUL-1. See text for further explanation.
a. Percent deviation from baseline.
b. GDP deflator, deviation from baseline in percentage points.

money demand (shocks A, C, D, and L). Our attention is also restricted to a few key variables: real GNP, the price level and inflation rate (GNP deflator), short-term interest rates, and a bilateral exchange rate.[28] The results are again presented in multipanel charts, although the format differs from the charts presented in the preceding section. Each chart, containing usually eight panels, now examines a single variable for a particular shock. Each panel pertains to an individual model, showing for that model the effects under the types of policy regime available for that model. The regime types are identified by symbols placed on the curves (see the chart legends); these symbols are used uniformly throughout this series of charts.

To prepare the individual panels of these charts, we used the O regimes (1, 2A, 2B, 3) if available for that model. When an O regime was not available, the model's corresponding X regime was used instead. For example, for MULTIMOD the regimes used were 1, 2AX, 2BX, and 3X; for the TAYLOR model, it was 1X, 2A, 2B, and 3X. Only X regimes could be used for the MCM model. (See chapter 3 for a detailed discussion of the O and X regimes and table 3-2 for a reference list of regimes available, by model group.) The results for two of the models, GEM and MX3, are not included in many of these charts. For these two models, no results are available for exchange-rate targeting; for the other regime types, moreover, the results differ very little across regimes in almost all cases for the shocks considered in this section.

U.S. Aggregate Demand Shock

The theoretical analysis in chapter 2 indicates that the nominal-income (YY) or real-GNP-plus-inflation (CC) regimes are equally preferred for purposes of minimizing the effects of country-specific goods-demand shocks on real GNP, employment, and inflation. The more powerful macroeconomic stabilization effects of these regimes, however, come at the cost of considerably more variation in interest rates (and exchange rates) than under either the money (MM) or exchange-rate (ME) regimes. In this section we consider whether the empirical results bear out the theory. The reader should keep in mind that the theory in chapter 2 and the empirical simulations considered here are not fully comparable because of differences in the treatment of policy regimes between the two.[29]

The effects of the U.S. aggregate demand shock on U.S. real GNP across the different models and regimes are shown in figure 4-25. In the pattern that

28. Employment data are available for the simulations for only four of the models. Chapter 2 focuses on consumer prices as well as output prices (GNP deflators). Simulation data are not available for consumer prices.

29. Recall that the analysis in chapter 2 is based on exact targeting, whereas the empirical results presented here are based on inexact targeting.

Figure 4-25. *Effects of Increase in U.S. Aggregate Demand (Shock A) on U.S. Real GNP*

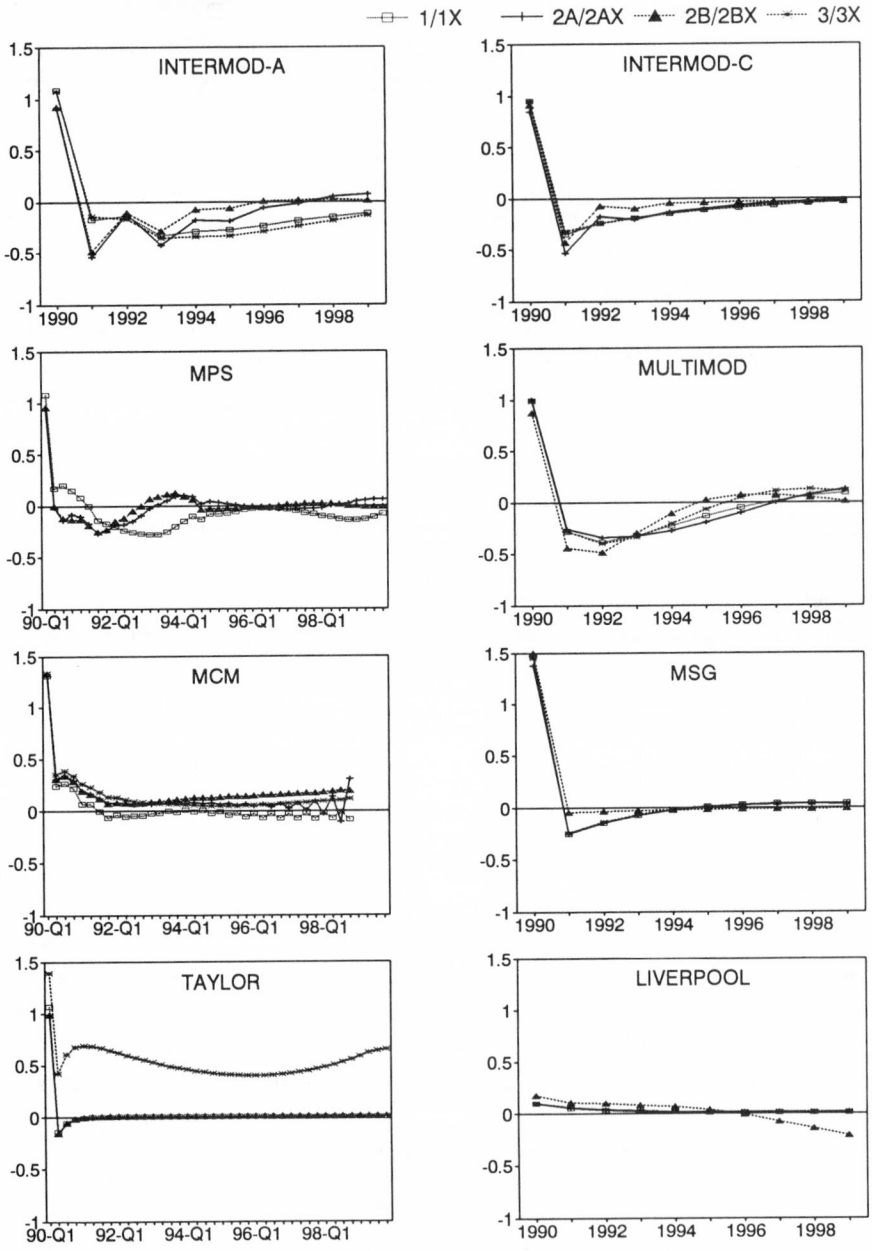

emerges most often across models, all regimes show significant positive effects in the first period somewhere in the neighborhood of 1 percent of baseline GNP. The effects under the nominal-income targeting and real-GNP-plus-inflation targeting regimes are generally somewhat less than those under either money targeting or exchange-rate targeting. In addition, all four regimes show significant reversal of the initial positive effects beyond the first period, with real GNP often moving below its baseline path in the second period after the demand shock is removed. Declines in real GNP in the second period tend to be greater under nominal-income targeting and real-GNP-plus-inflation targeting than under money targeting and exchange-rate targeting. Beyond the second period, real GNP tends to return to the baseline path faster under regimes 2A/2AX and 2B/2BX than under regimes 1/1X or 3/3X.

Several exceptions to the general pattern can be seen in the chart. First, the TAYLOR model shows results under regimes 1X, 2A, and 2B all moving in tandem, whereas under regime 3X, real GNP remains substantially above baseline throughout the simulation. Second, the MCM model shows real GNP deviating from baseline the *least* under regime 1X (money targeting), especially after the first period.[30] Third, and most prominently, the LIVERPOOL model shows both a much smaller deviation of real GNP from baseline in the initial period than other models under all regimes, and a significantly different "ordering" of the regimes in terms of the degree of deviation from baseline. In particular, regime 2B shows a persistently greater deviation from baseline than the other regimes, initially in a positive direction and, after about five years, in a negative direction. The persistent deviation of real GNP below baseline in the longer run under regime 2B in the LIVERPOOL model is related to an offsetting deviation of the inflation rate above baseline, as noted below.

Two of the models with adaptive expectations—INTERMOD-A and MPS—exhibit somewhat larger differences between nominal-income targeting and real-GNP-plus-inflation targeting on the one hand, and money targeting and exchange-rate targeting on the other, particularly during the first two periods of the simulation. Under money targeting and exchange-rate targeting, real GNP appears to fall less in the second period under adaptive expectations than it does under model-consistent expectations (compare the results for INTERMOD-A and INTERMOD-C).

---

30. This result seems directly contradictory to the theory in chapter 2. Recall from our discussion in the preceding section that this result reflects primarily the use of a very low feedback parameter in regimes 2AX and 2BX by the MCM modeling group. The low feedback parameters on those regimes means that regime 1 (with the originally prescribed parameter) actually holds GNP and prices closer to their target values. From one perspective, this outcome may be seen as weighting the results unfairly in favor of regime 1. From another perspective, however, this particular model is telling us that regimes 2A and 2B (as originally specified) cannot be used consistently across all shocks and countries without causing instability in some of the model's variables.

The effects of the aggregate demand shock on U.S. inflation are shown in figure 4-26. Most of the models show an initial increase in the inflation rate for up to several periods, often followed by a decline to below the baseline for an extended time. In most models the eventual adjustment of inflation in a negative direction is least pronounced under real-GNP-plus-inflation targeting. In some cases, the inflation rate returns fairly quickly to baseline without falling below that path; in others, it remains somewhat above baseline. In the LIVERPOOL model, the inflation rate rises steadily relative to the baseline in the second half of the simulation under real-GNP-plus-inflation targeting, apparently offsetting the steady decline in real GNP that takes place at the same time in that model. This result suggests the possibility that regime 2B might be inherently unstable in that model.[31]

Unlike the other models, the MPS and MCM models show the inflation rate dropping *below* the baseline initially under all regimes. This behavior can be traced in part to the sensitivity of the GNP deflator in those models to shifts among expenditure categories: the shock apparently increases spending in sectors with relatively low price levels initially. With increases in aggregate demand slow to raise prices because expectations are adaptive in the MCM and MPS models, the initial shift in the composition of expenditures is enough to cause the deflator to fall initially. In contrast to the GNP deflators, fixed-weight price indexes, which are not sensitive to shifts in the composition of expenditures, show increases in the first period of this shock in both models.[32] The TAYLOR model stands out from the rest in that it exhibits no effect on inflation under any of the regimes except exchange-rate targeting.

Differences across regimes show up more clearly in terms of movements in the price level. As shown in figure 4-27, under most of the regimes (and across most models) the price level rises initially as inflation moves up and then declines toward the baseline as inflation falls below its baseline path. Real-GNP-plus-inflation targeting is usually a clear exception to this pattern: the price level generally remains noticeably above baseline in that case, and in some models (INTERMOD-C, LIVERPOOL, and MCM) prices even continue rising relative to baseline. The persistent deviation of the price level from baseline in this case reflects the tendency toward price-level "drift" inherent in the specification of regime 2B/2BX. When targeting the inflation rate rather than the price level (the price level is the implicit target variable in regime

31. As noted in chapter 3, the MULTIMOD and MSG groups initially believed regime 2B to be unstable but subsequently found ways to implement it. The LIVERPOOL group conjectures that real-GNP-plus-inflation targeting is not unstable in their model but, rather, is characterized by very long cycles.

32. In the initial period for this simulation in the MCM model, the absorption price deflator falls and the import price deflator increases more than the export price deflator. The absorption price deflator, determined in a behavioral equation, falls initially because the downward effects on U.S. wages of the dollar's appreciation are stronger than the upward effects of the increase in aggregate demand.

Figure 4-26. *Effects of Increase in U.S. Aggregate Demand (Shock A)*
on U.S. Inflation Rate (GNP Deflator)

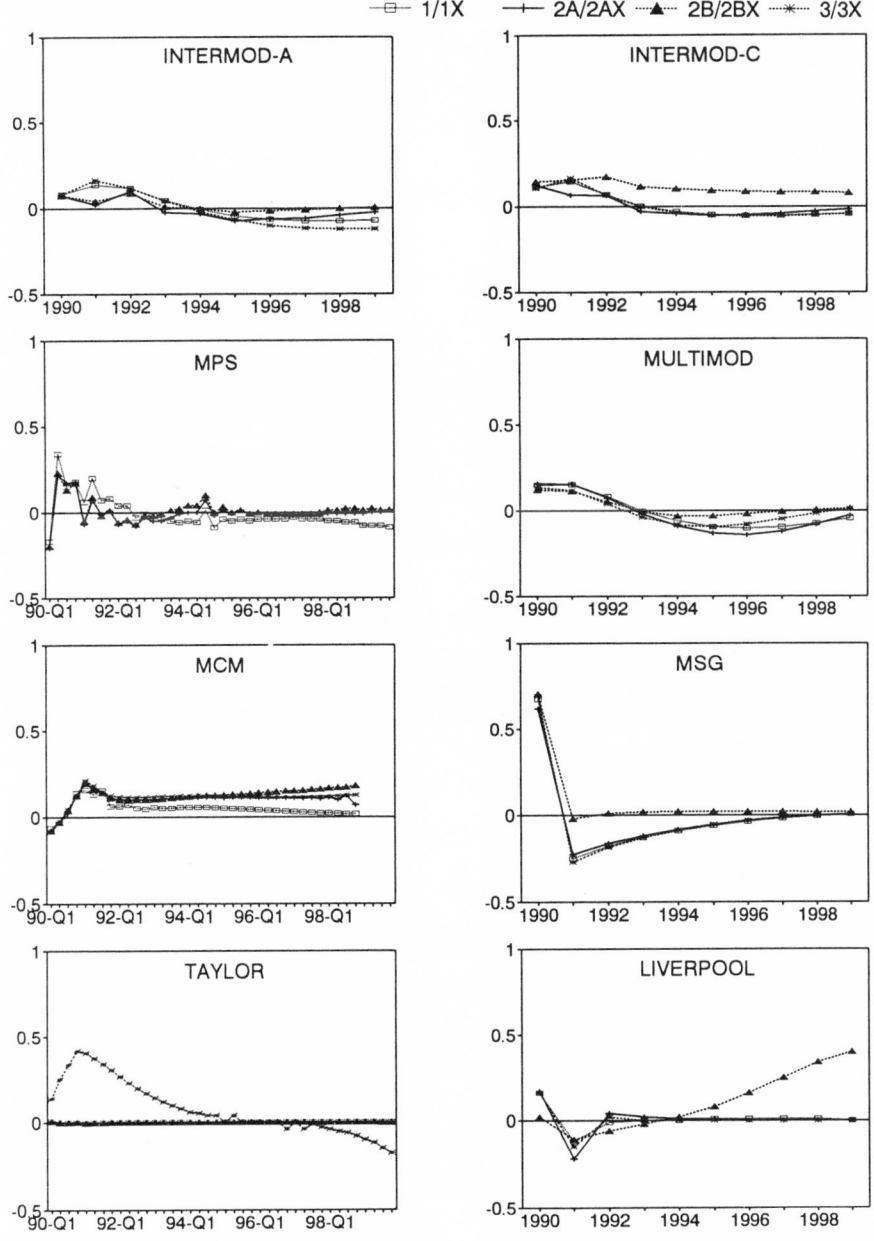

Figure 4-27. *Effects of Increase in U.S. Aggregate Demand (Shock A)*
on U.S. Price Level (GNP Deflator)

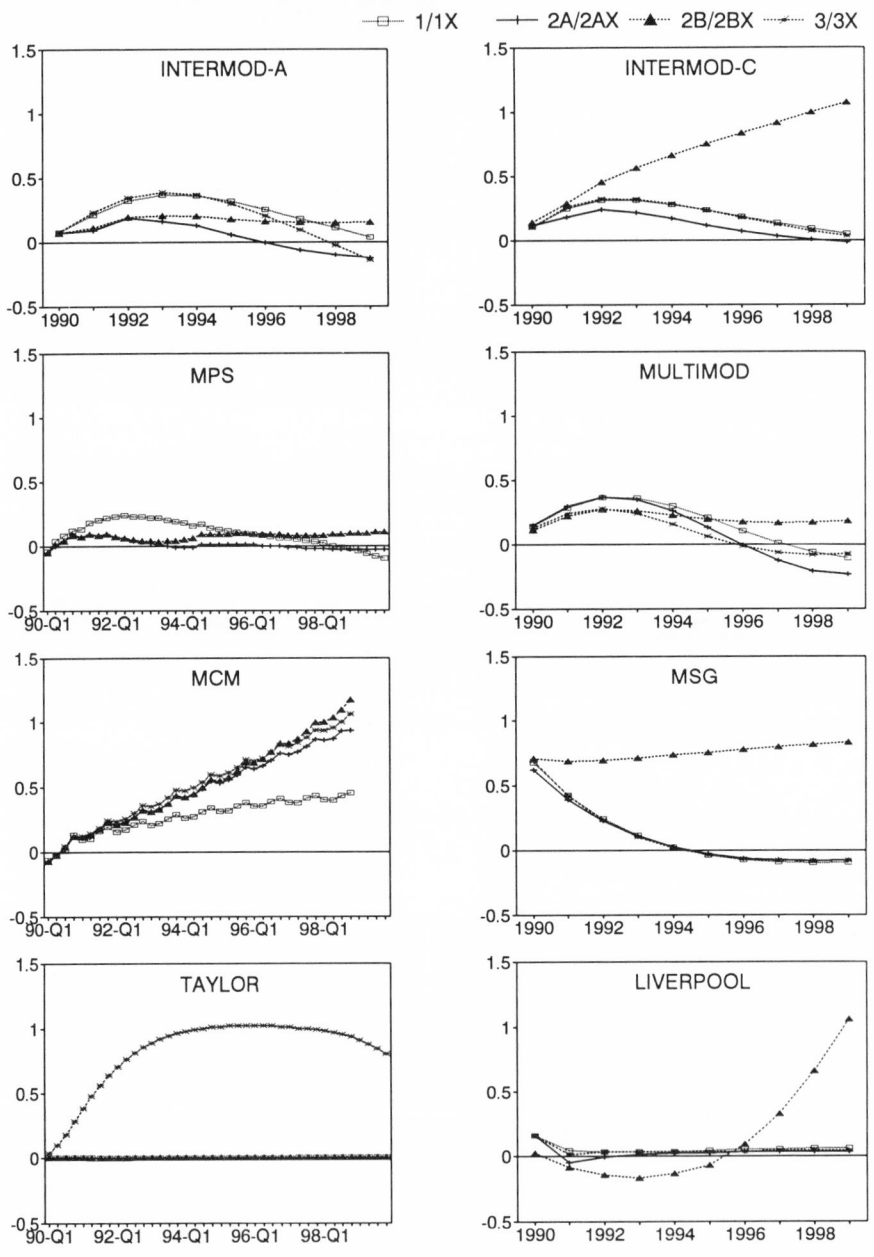

2A/2AX), there is no tendency to drive the inflation rate below its baseline for a time in order to unwind the initial increase in the price level. This tendency toward price-level drift under real-GNP-plus-inflation targeting also shows up, although slightly less pronounced, in the effects of German and Japanese aggregate demand shocks (G and I) on the price levels of those countries.

Distinctions among the other three regime types are generally less clear in all three countries. In the U.S. case, as shown in figure 4-27, deviations of the price level from baseline appear to be minimized under nominal-income targeting in several of the models. The MCM and TAYLOR models are outliers in this respect. In the MCM model, price-level deviations are clearly minimized under money targeting; that model also shows some seasonality in the effects of the shock on the price level.[33] The Taylor model shows a large deviation of the price level under exchange-rate targeting but no deviation at all under the other three regimes.

The models appear to be somewhat more in agreement about the relative effects, across different regimes, of the aggregate demand shock on U.S. short-term interest rates (figure 4-28). The smaller effects on real GNP and, initially at least, on the price level under nominal-income targeting and real-GNP-plus-inflation targeting are generally achieved at the cost of greater initial movements in interest rates, both initially and in the longer term. Consistent with the predictions of the theoretical models in chapter 2, in most cases interest rates deviate from baseline the most (especially on impact) under those two regimes. Movements in interest rates are generally much less pronounced under money targeting and exchange-rate targeting. The differences between 2A/2AX and 2B/2BX on the one hand and 1/1X and 3/3X on the other are particularly pronounced for the INTERMOD-A, INTERMOD-C, and MPS models. The MULTIMOD and MSG models show the same pattern, but the differences are more subdued. The similar effects on U.S. variables of money targeting and exchange-rate targeting in some cases probably reflect the fact that, under exchange-rate targeting as specified in the guidelines for the simulations, the United States actually targets money (as in regime 1/1X), whereas other countries target their bilateral dollar exchange rates.

In most of the models, the exchange rates appear to deviate from baseline most under nominal-income targeting and real-GNP-plus-inflation targeting and least under exchange-rate targeting (see figure 4-29, which shows the

---

33. This seasonality was masked in the results for the inflation rate because the MCM model group reported its inflation rate in terms of four-quarter changes in prices rather than quarter-to-quarter changes expressed at an annual rate.

Figure 4-28. *Effects of Increase in U.S. Aggregate Demand (Shock A) on U.S. Short-Term Interest Rate*

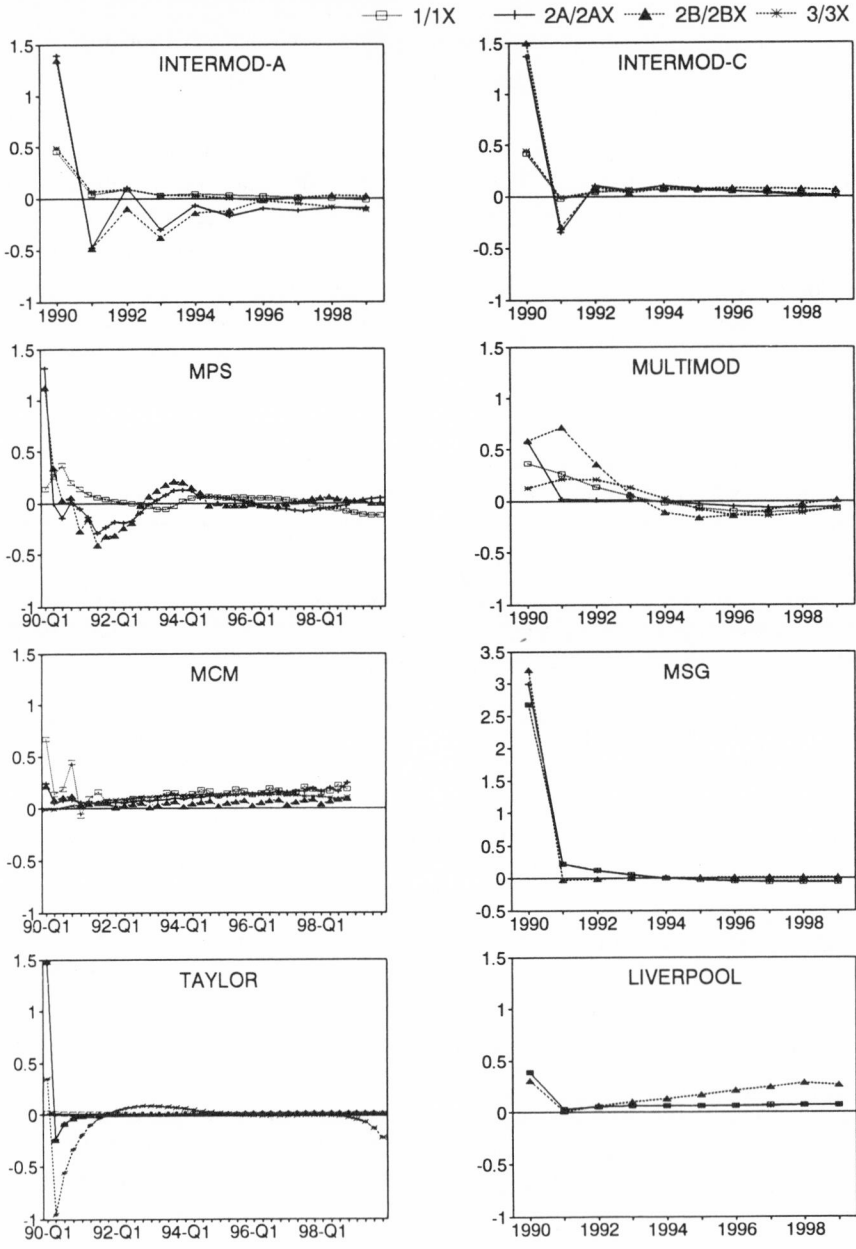

Figure 4-29. *Effects of Increase in U.S. Aggregate Demand (Shock A)*
on U.S. Dollar–Yen Exchange Rate (−: Dollar Appreciation)

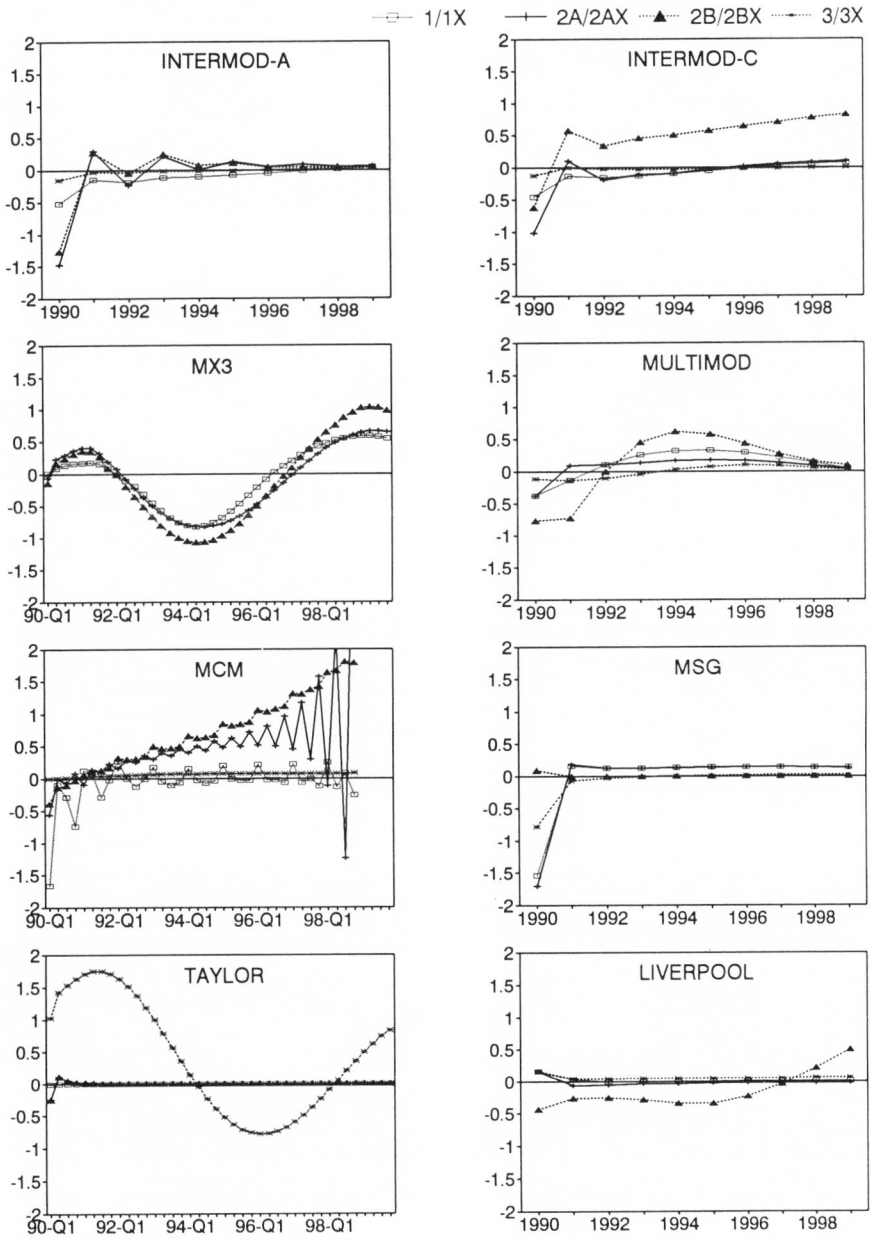

Figure 4-30. *Effects of Increase in U.S. Aggregate Demand (Shock A) on Japanese Real GNP*

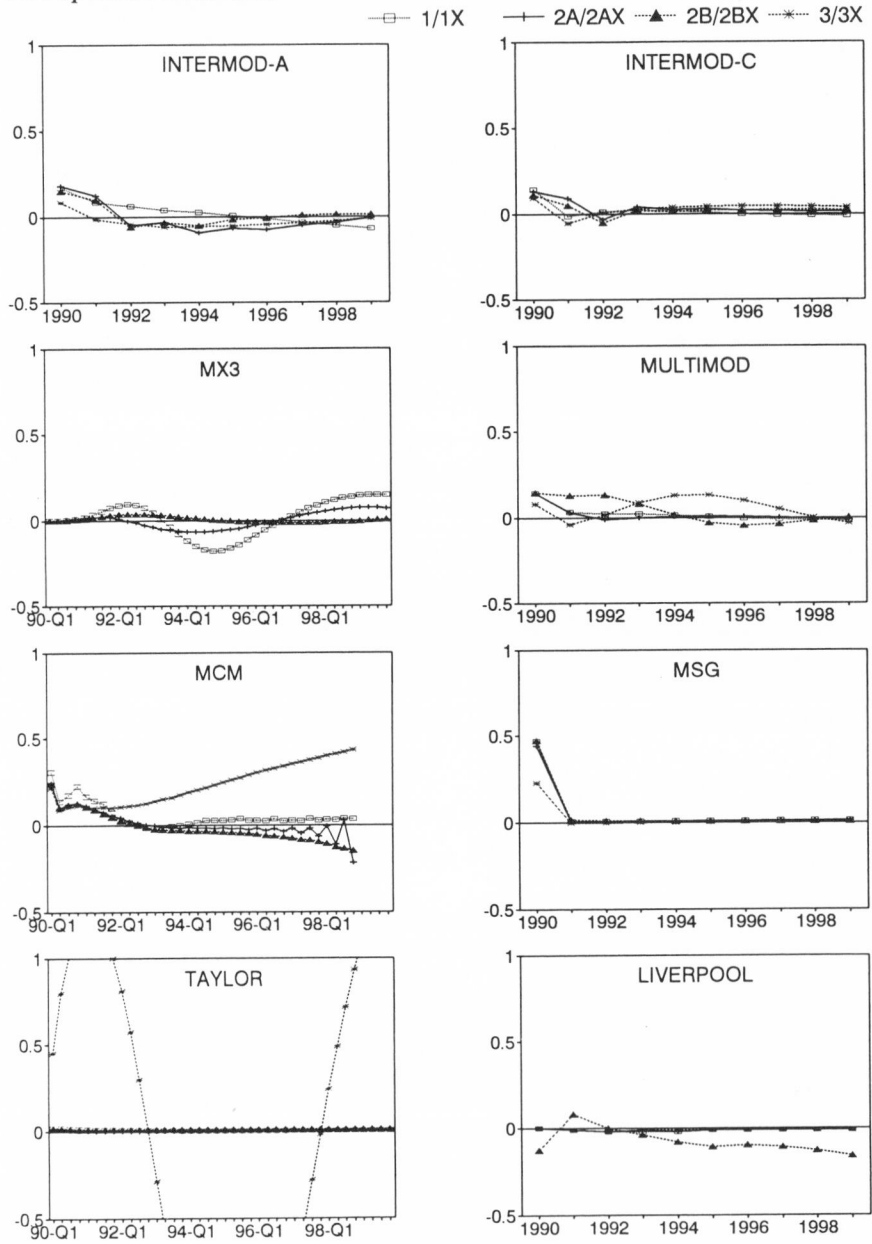

dollar-yen rate). These effects are broadly consistent with the theoretical expectations developed in chapter 2 (compare, for example, table 2-15).[34]

To distinguish more clearly between the performance of the money-targeting and exchange-rate-targeting regimes, we show in figure 4-30 the effects of the U.S. goods-demand shock on Japanese real GNP. For most models, exchange-rate targeting minimizes the initial effects of the shock on Japanese output. Money targeting, together with the other two regimes, generally results in a noticeably larger initial effect on Japanese output.[35] This result reflects the importance of the exchange rate as a channel for transmitting the effects of the U.S. shock to other countries.

U.S. Aggregate Supply Shock

The theoretical results in chapter 2 are not as clear-cut with respect to regime selection in the case of supply shocks as they are in the case of demand shocks. The theoretical models suggest that pegging either nominal income (regime YY) or real GNP plus inflation (regime CC) is preferred for minimizing effects on employment. If employment is kept constant, output falls by the full amount of the decrease in productivity.

When a productivity shock occurs, policymakers should probably prefer a change in output to occur with it. At any rate, it could easily be counterproductive to resist a change in output. If wages and prices were fully flexible, output would fall in response to a negative productivity shock; given the shock, that hypothetical outcome would arguably be a "welfare-maximizing" benchmark against which to evaluate other outcomes. Whereas goods-demand or money-demand shocks tend to move prices and output in the same direction (so that nominal-income targeting or real-GNP-plus-inflation targeting tends to offset those movements, and the preshock baseline is an appropriate path to return to), the productivity shock tends to move output and prices in opposite directions, and the preshock baseline for output is no longer an appropriate benchmark.

In the analysis in chapter 2, interest rates move by significantly larger amounts in response to supply shocks under the YY and CC regimes than under the MM and ME regimes. Moreover, movements in interest rates induced by supply shocks are larger for the CC regime than for the YY regime because the price level does not return to baseline under the CC regime, whereas it must do so under the YY regime. (For goods-demand and money-demand shocks, interest-rate effects are identical under the YY and CC regimes; not

34. The results for the TAYLOR model are puzzling, because the yen-dollar exchange rate varies substantially more under exchange-rate targeting (that model's regime 3X) than under real-GNP-plus-inflation targeting (regime 2BX). The exchange-rate results for the MSG model are also puzzling in this way.

35. The TAYLOR model is again a notable exception, given the puzzling behavior of the dollar-yen exchange rate under that model's regime 3X.

only is nominal income stabilized, but prices and output separately are also stabilized.)

Once again, the theoretical analysis of chapter 2 and the empirical simulations cannot be compared without an allowance for the differences between full and partial instrument adjustment. The empirical simulations, with their inexact targeting, permit somewhat different movements of the targeted variables than is entailed by the exact pegging of target variables in chapter 2.

The existence of any consistent pattern of differences across regimes is difficult to discern in the empirical results in the case of the negative shock to U.S. aggregate supply (shock C), at least by means of visual inspection of charts of the simulation results. The initial effects on real GNP (figure 4-31) are generally smaller to begin with than in the case of the demand shock, as are the differences in these effects across regimes. In several of the models (INTERMOD-A, MPS, MSG, and MULTIMOD), real GNP tends to bounce back more strongly above its baseline path after an initial decline under real-GNP-plus-inflation targeting than under other regimes. In the TAYLOR model, real GNP follows a significantly higher path throughout the simulation period under exchange-rate targeting than under the other regimes, analogously to its behavior under exchange-rate targeting in the aggregate demand shock.

At first glance, the effect of the supply shock on U.S. inflation differs little across regimes in most models (see figure 4-32). Two notable exceptions are the LIVERPOOL and MSG models. In the LIVERPOOL model, inflation remains well above baseline under regime 2B, whereas it returns to near baseline fairly quickly under other regimes. This result may again be related to the effects of jointly targeting real GNP and inflation in that model, since real GNP tends to remain below baseline under regime 2B in that model. In the MSG model the effect on inflation under regime 2B is persistently negative after the initial increase, possibly to balance the tendency for real GNP to remain above baseline in the longer run in that case.

Once again, differences across regimes show through more clearly in the effects of the supply shock on the price level (figure 4-33). Price-level drift is again evident in a number of models under real-GNP-plus-inflation targeting. In the INTERMOD-A and LIVERPOOL models, prices tend to rise continuously relative to baseline in the medium to longer run under that regime. In the INTERMOD-C and MSG models, however, the price level moves in the opposite direction, falling continuously. In the TAYLOR model, the price level remains consistently above baseline only under nominal-income targeting — an unexpected result, given the importance attached to the price level under nominal-income targeting. And in the MPS model, the price level tends to deviate most from the baseline under money targeting.

The one variable about which most models could agree in the case of the supply shock is the U.S. short-term interest rate. In six of the eight models

Figure 4-31. *Effects of Decrease in U.S. Aggregate Supply (Shock C) on U.S. Real GNP*

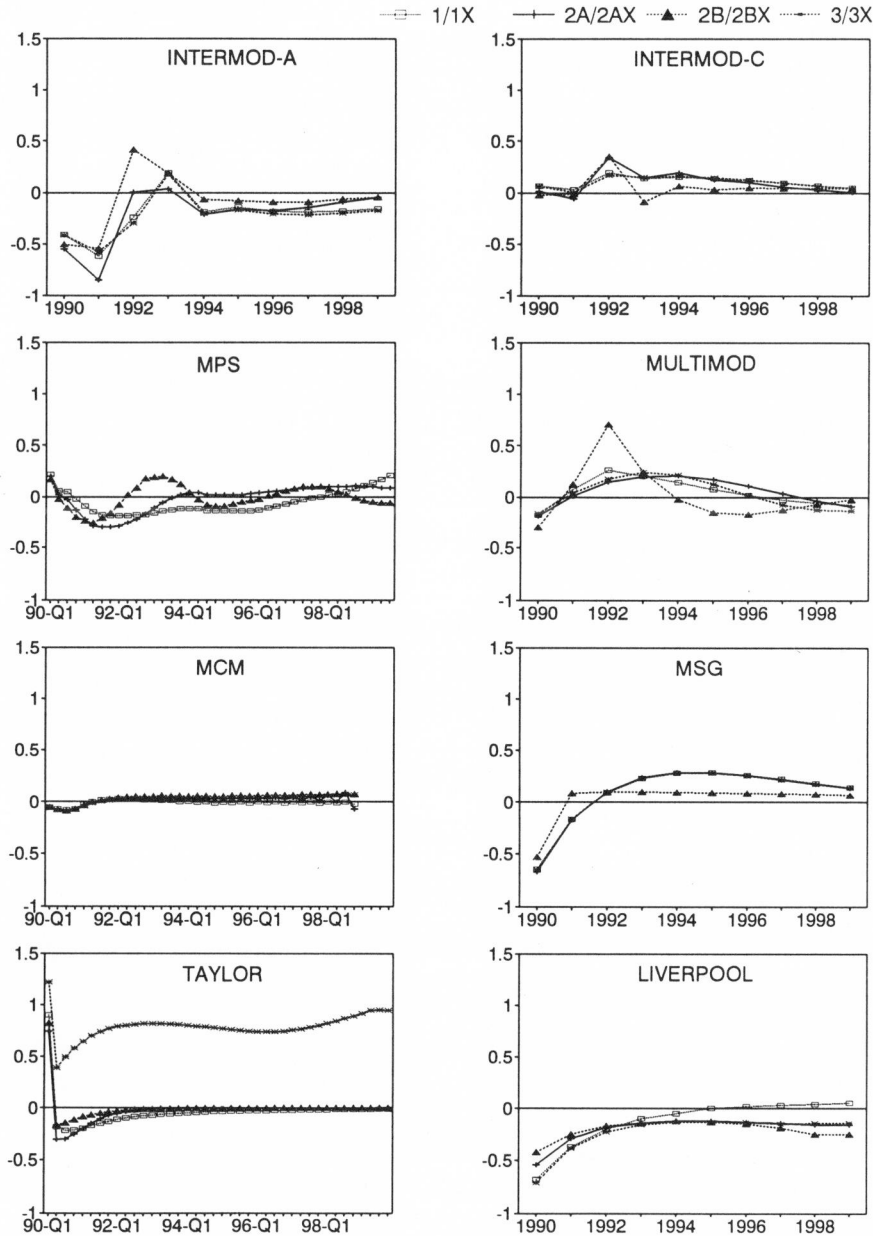

Figure 4-32. *Effects of Decrease in U.S. Aggregate Supply (Shock C)
on U.S. Inflation Rate (GNP Deflator)*

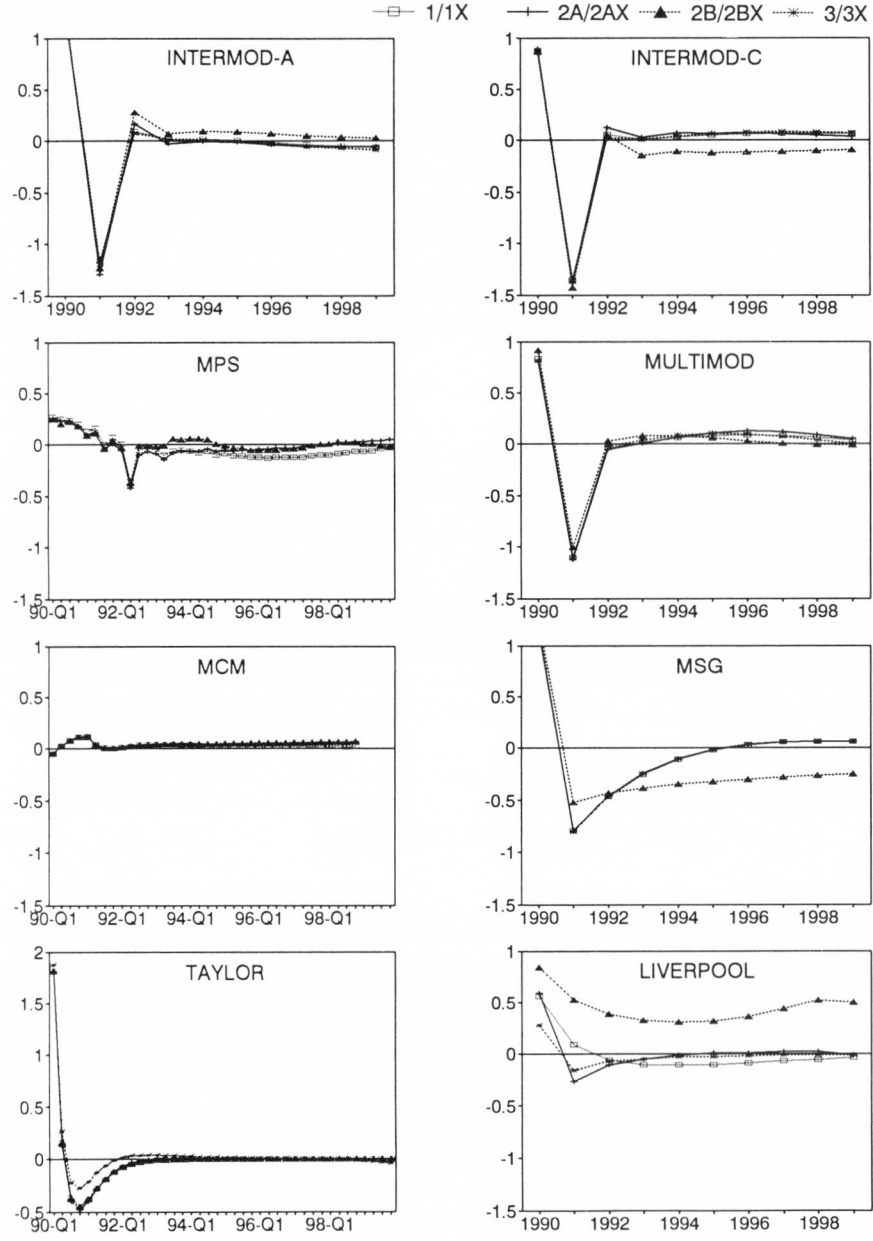

Figure 4-33. *Effects of Decrease in U.S. Aggregate Supply (Shock C) on U.S. Price Level (GNP Deflator)*

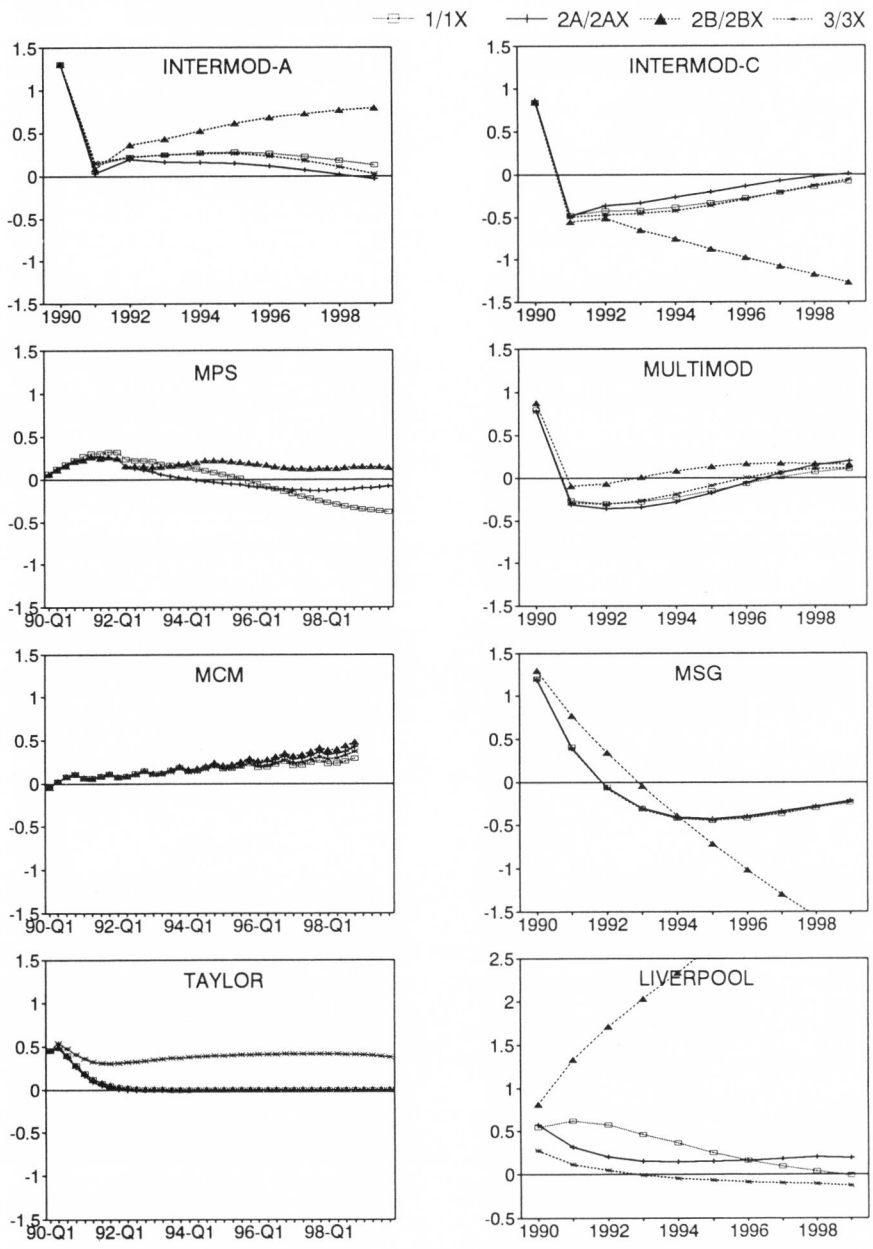

Figure 4-34. *Effects of Decrease in U.S. Aggregate Supply (Shock C) on U.S. Short-Term Interest Rate*

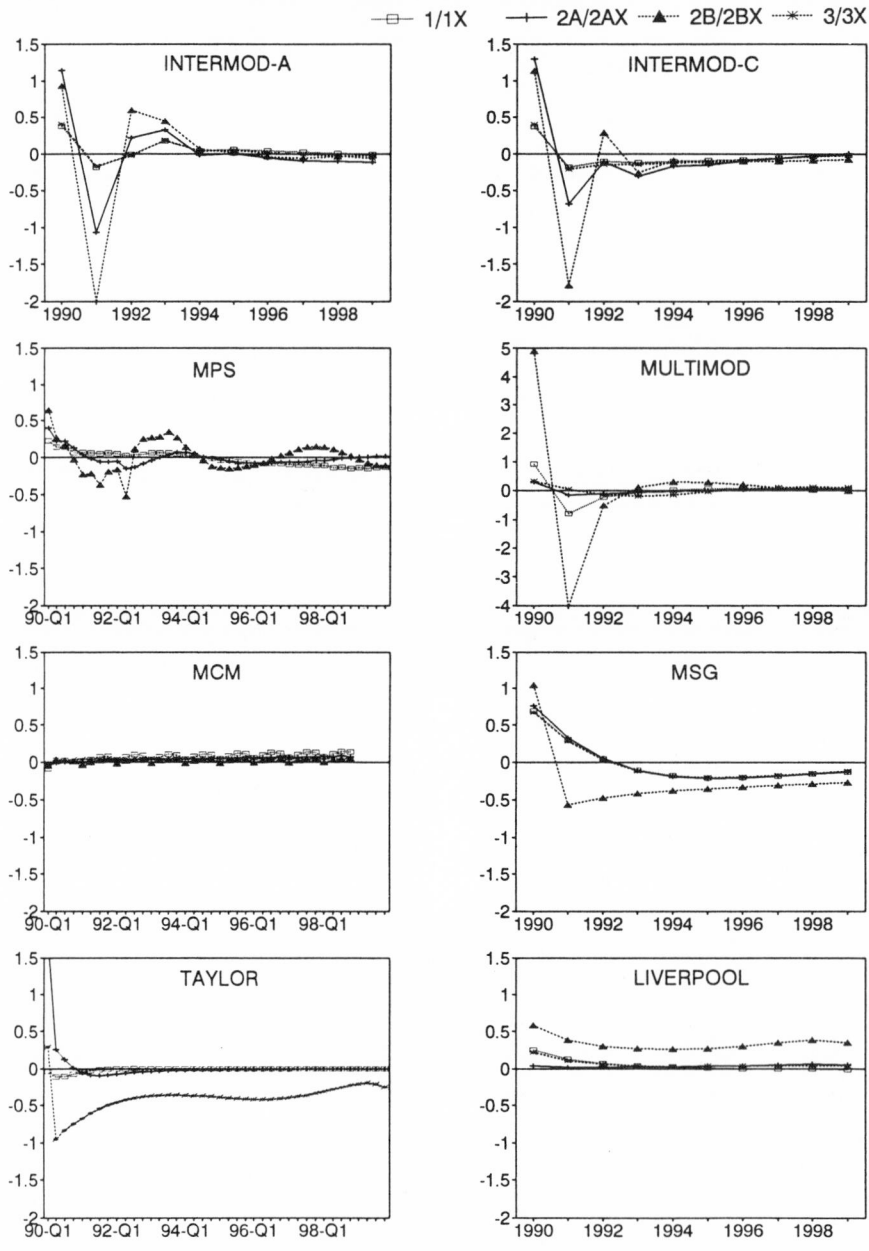

Figure 4-35. *Effects of Decrease in U.S. Aggregate Supply (Shock C) on U.S. Dollar–Yen Exchange Rate (−: Dollar Appreciation)*

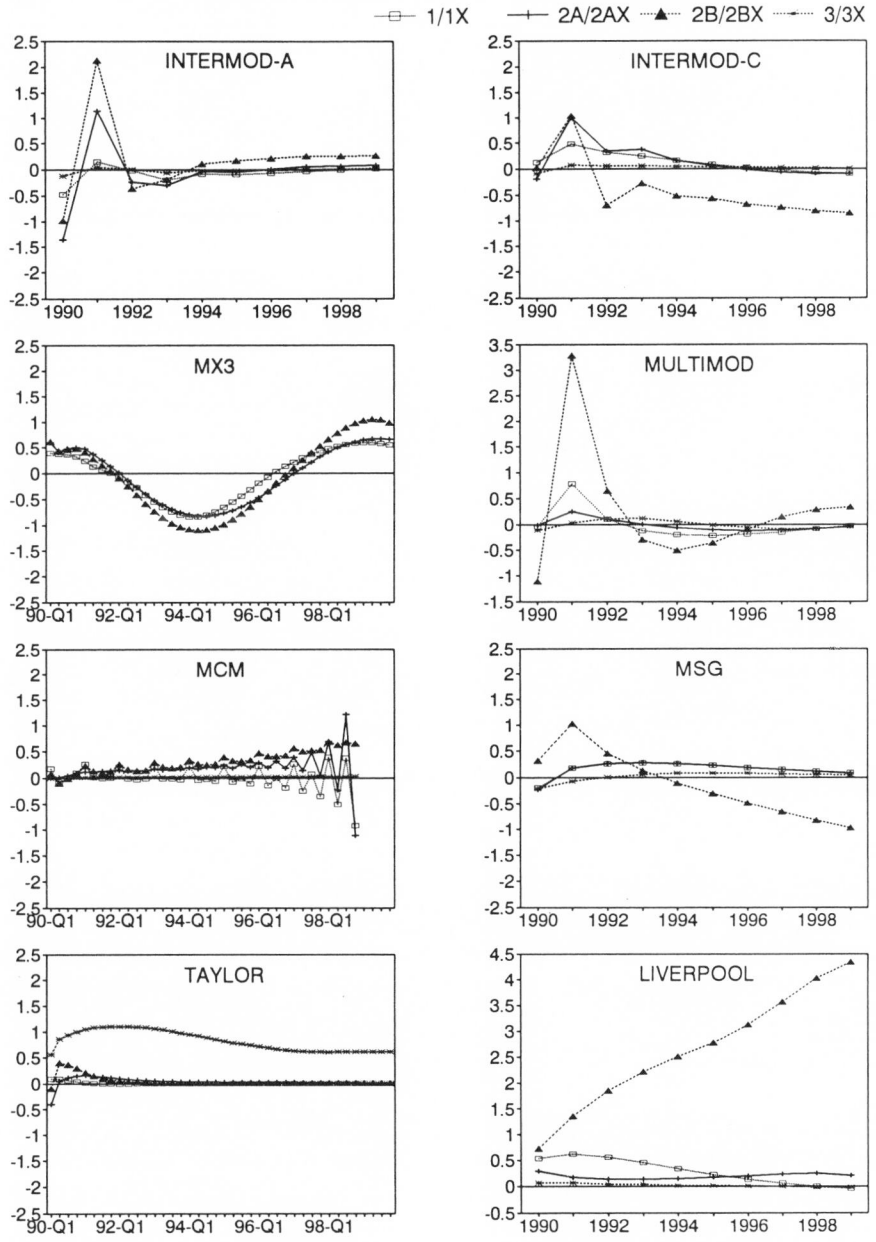

Figure 4-36. *Effects of Decrease in U.S. Aggregate Supply (Shock C) on Japanese Real GNP*

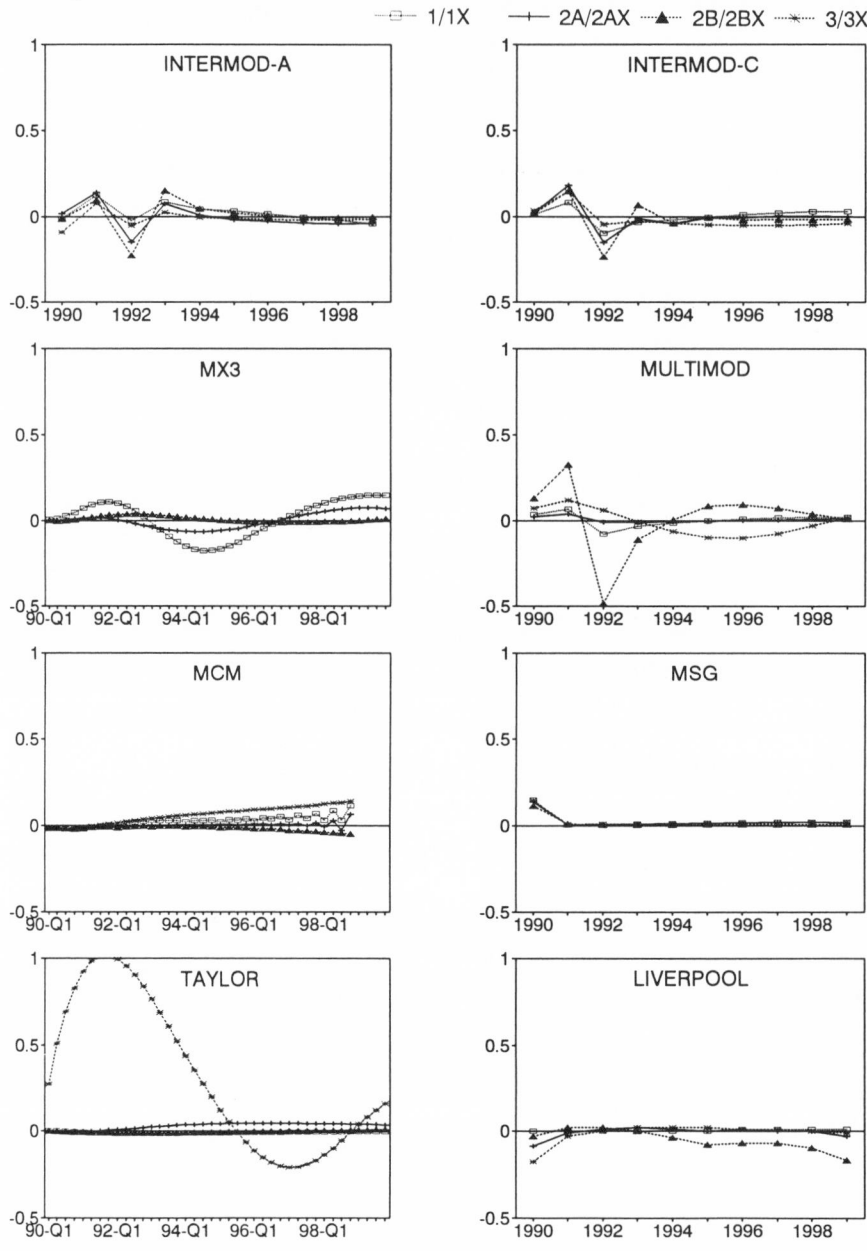

shown in figure 4-34, interest rates clearly exhibit the greatest deviation from baseline under real-GNP-plus-inflation targeting. In a seventh, the TAYLOR model, regimes 2AX and 2BX are tied for greatest deviation, at least in the initial stages of the simulation. (The eighth model, MCM, shows very little movement in interest rates under any of the regimes.) Nominal-income targeting also produces the second largest deviations from baseline in both INTERMOD models and the MPS model.

Exchange rates, too, show the greatest deviation from baseline under real-GNP-plus-inflation targeting in most cases (see figure 4-35). In the LIVERPOOL, MSG, MULTIMOD, and INTERMOD models, that deviation is relatively extreme. Exchange-rate targeting, not surprisingly, generally does best in damping deviations in exchange rates. The one notable (and puzzling) exception is again the TAYLOR model, in which the dollar-yen exchange rate exhibits the greatest variation under exchange-rate targeting.[36]

The cross-border transmission effects of the shock are illustrated in figure 4-36 for Japanese real GNP. The analysis in chapter 2 suggests that, for output in foreign countries, nominal-income targeting and real-GNP-plus-inflation targeting should initially show the least deviation from baseline. (See, for example, the simulation results for the corresponding country-specific productivity shock in table 2-16.) To judge from the effects on Japanese output shown in figure 4-36, some of the empirical models (for example, MSG and LIVERPOOL) agree on this ranking of the regimes. But others, notably MULTIMOD and TAYLOR, do not.

Japanese and U.S. Money Demand Shocks

For the reasons discussed in the theoretical analysis of chapter 2, money-demand shocks typically have zero to negligible effects on all key variables (except the money stock) under nominal-income targeting and real-GNP-plus-inflation targeting (chapter 2's YY and CC regimes). The effects of money-demand shocks on policymakers' target variables under money targeting and exchange-rate targeting (chapter 2's MM and ME regimes), however, can be significant. Moreover, the effects on an individual country's target variables depend on whether the money-demand shock originates at home or abroad. Recall that a U.S. money-demand shock in chapter 2 has qualitatively similar consequences for U.S. variables under both the MM and ME regimes but that the ME regime causes markedly larger deviations of ROECD variables from baseline than those under the MM regime (illustrated in table 2-14). In contrast, for a money-demand shock originating in the ROECD, the MM regime has

---

36. Simulation data for the dollar-yen exchange rate are not available for the MPS model. The second panel on the left-hand side of figure 4-35 shows instead the available data for MX3.

destabilizing effects on policymakers' target variables in both the ROECD and the United States, whereas key variables in both countries remain unaffected under the ME regime (table 2-17).

Apart from the differences between exact and inexact targeting, chapter 2's MM and ME regimes correspond to, respectively, money targeting and exchange-rate targeting as implemented for the empirical simulations discussed in this chapter. Earlier, in figures 4-20–4-22, we illustrated a few of the effects under money targeting of the transitory shock to U.S. money demand (shock L). Figures 4-37–4-41 show the consequences of the transitory shock to Japanese money demand (shock D) under all four regime types. In a comparable format, figures 4-42–4-44 return briefly to the U.S. money-demand shock (shock L).[37]

Among the eight models that ran the shock to Japanese money demand, all but MX3 exhibit the theoretically expected results under nominal-income targeting, real-GNP-plus-inflation targeting, and exchange-rate targeting. In particular, because the Japanese money stock expands sufficiently to accommodate the increase in money demand under all three of these regimes, Japanese interest rates (figure 4-37), Japanese output (figure 4-38), the Japanese price level (figure 4-39), and yen exchange rates (illustrated by the dollar-yen exchange rate in figure 4-40) differ little if at all from their baseline paths. The results for money targeting are also as expected: because the Japanese money stock is held unchanged in the face of the demand shift, the short-term interest rate rises sharply, output and prices decline, and the yen appreciates in external value.[38] Figure 4-41 shows the effects of the Japanese money-demand shock on U.S. real GNP. The results here also tend to conform with theoretical expectations (with MX3 again an exception, and possibly also TAYLOR): the United States is not influenced by the shock under any regime other than money targeting. The time patterns of the changes to U.S. real GNP under money targeting differ among the models, some showing increases and others decreases, and still others exhibiting a cyclical movement. The quantitative sizes of the effects in all cases are fairly small.[39] Perhaps the most interesting aspect of the evidence shown in figures 4-37–4-41 is its corroboration of the theoretical prediction that both U.S. and non-U.S. policymakers prefer exchange-rate targeting to money targeting when money-demand shocks originate outside the United States.

---

37. The choice of panels in figures 4-37–4-44 is dictated by the availability of simulation results for the different models. Simulations for shock D are not available for GEM and MPS. Shock L simulations are not available for GEM, MCM, and TAYLOR.

38. The atypical cycling behavior of Japanese variables in the MX3 model, already identified earlier in the chapter, occurs not only under money targeting but also under nominal-income targeting and real-GNP-plus-inflation targeting. (MX3 results for exchange-rate targeting are not available; see chapter 3.)

39. The vertical scales in figure 4-41 are smaller than those in earlier charts showing the cross-border effects on real GNPs.

Figure 4-37. *Effects of Increase in Japanese Money Demand (Shock D)*
on Japanese Short-Term Interest Rate

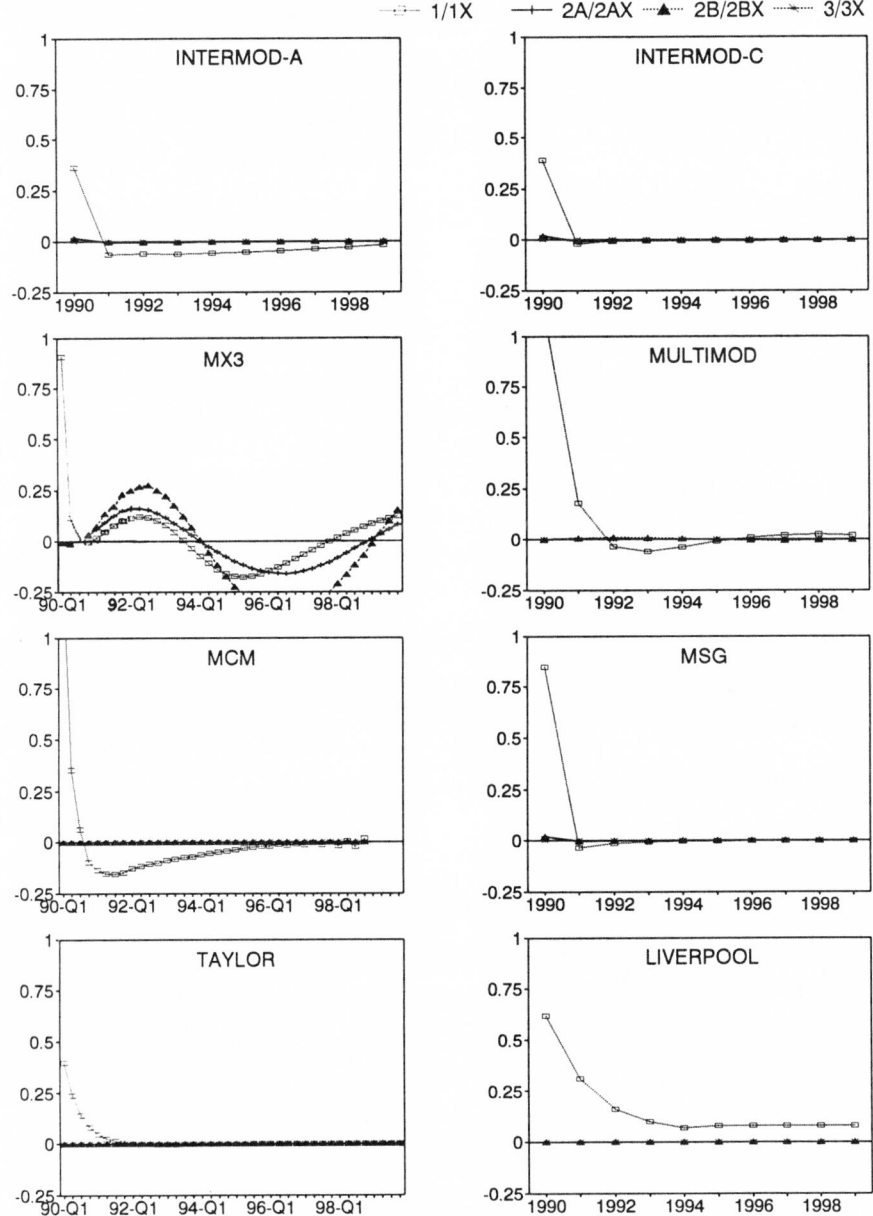

Figure 4-38. *Effects of Increase in Japanese Money Demand (Shock D) on Japanese Real GNP*

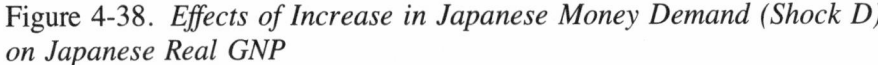

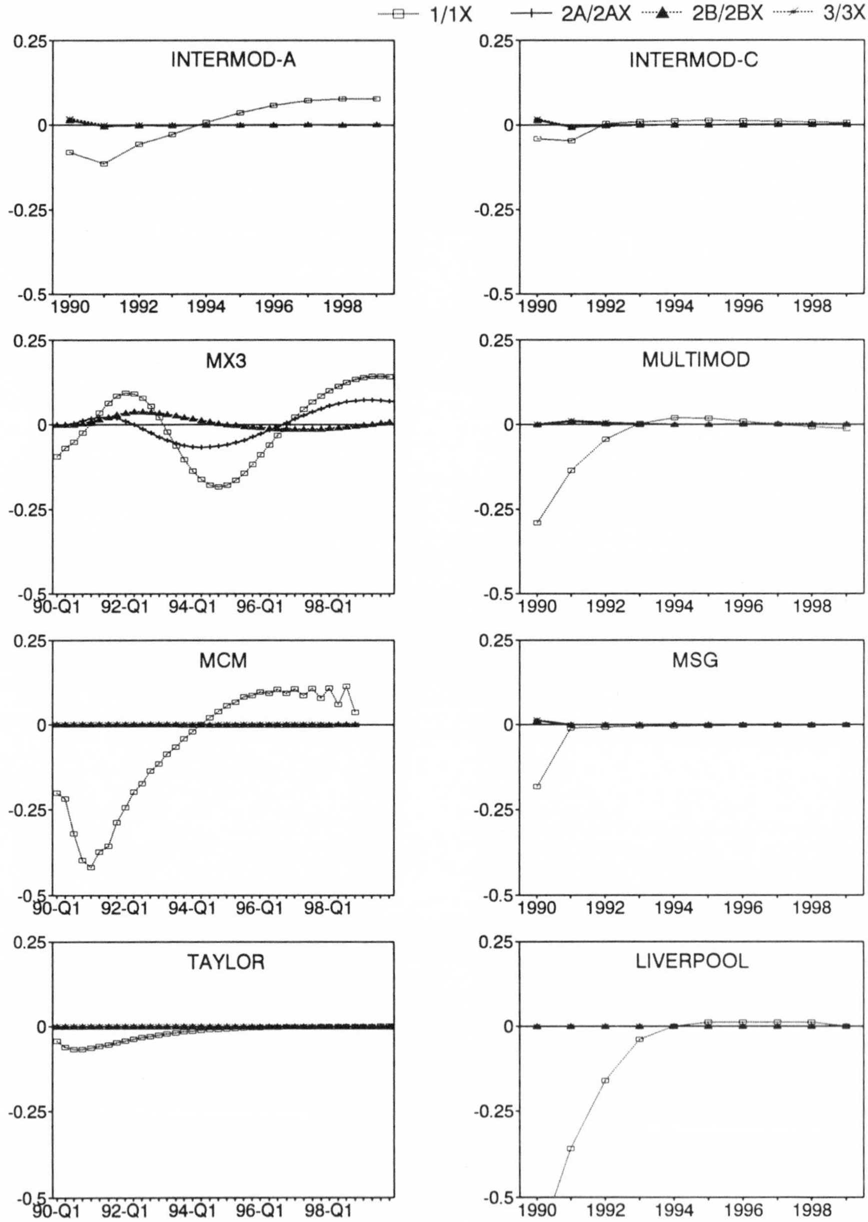

Figure 4-39. *Effects of Increase in Japanese Money Demand (Shock D) on Japanese Price Level (GNP Deflator)*

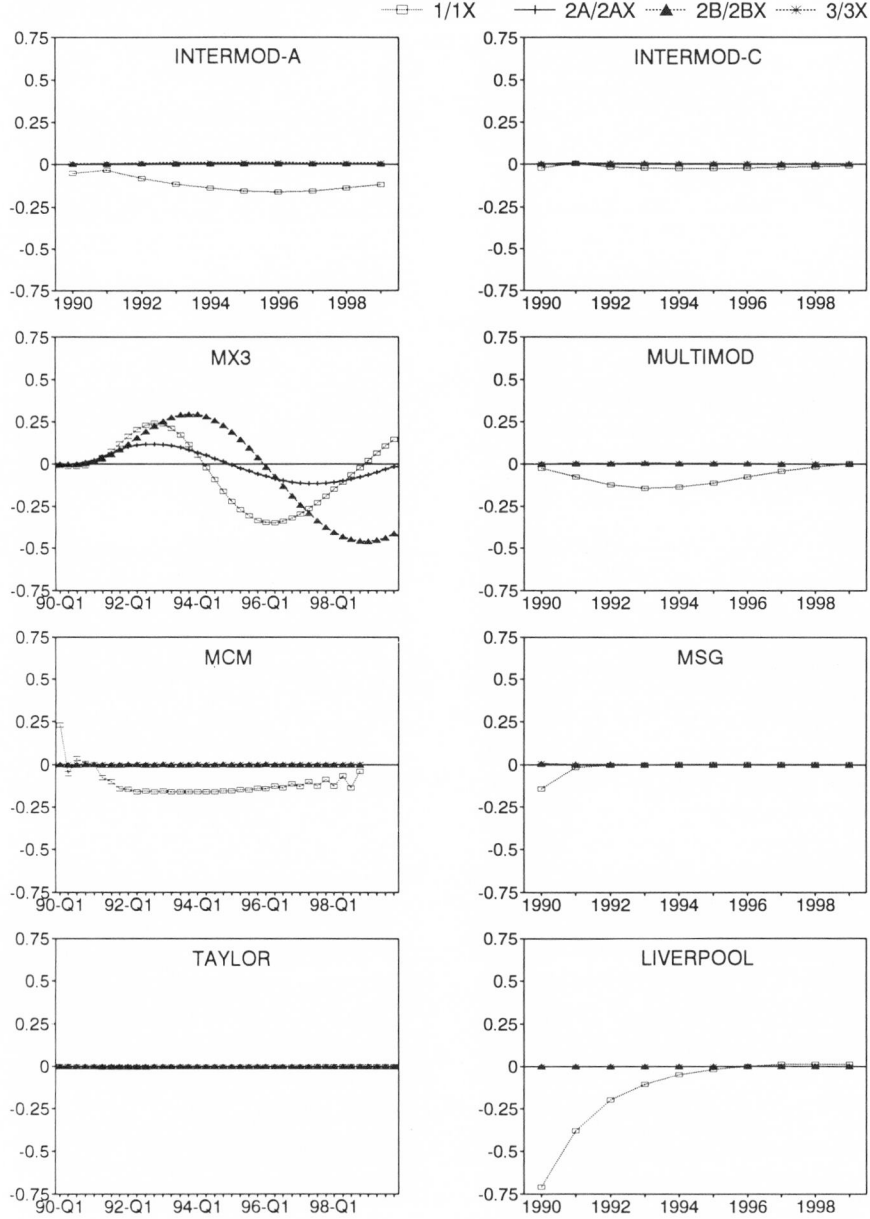

Figure 4-40. *Effects of Increase in Japanese Money Demand (Shock D) on U.S. Dollar–Yen Exchange Rate (−: Dollar Appreciation)*

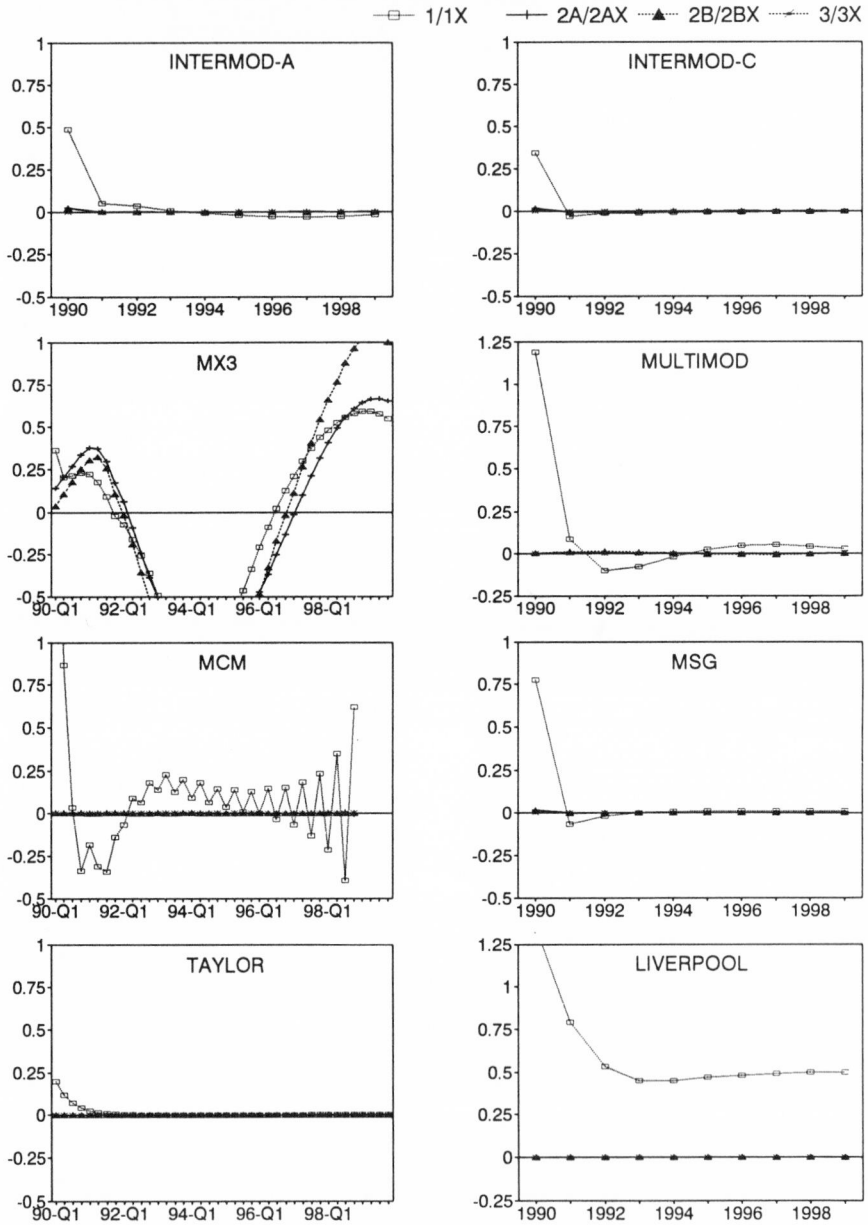

Figure 4-41. *Effects of Increase in Japanese Money Demand (Shock D) on U.S. Real GNP*

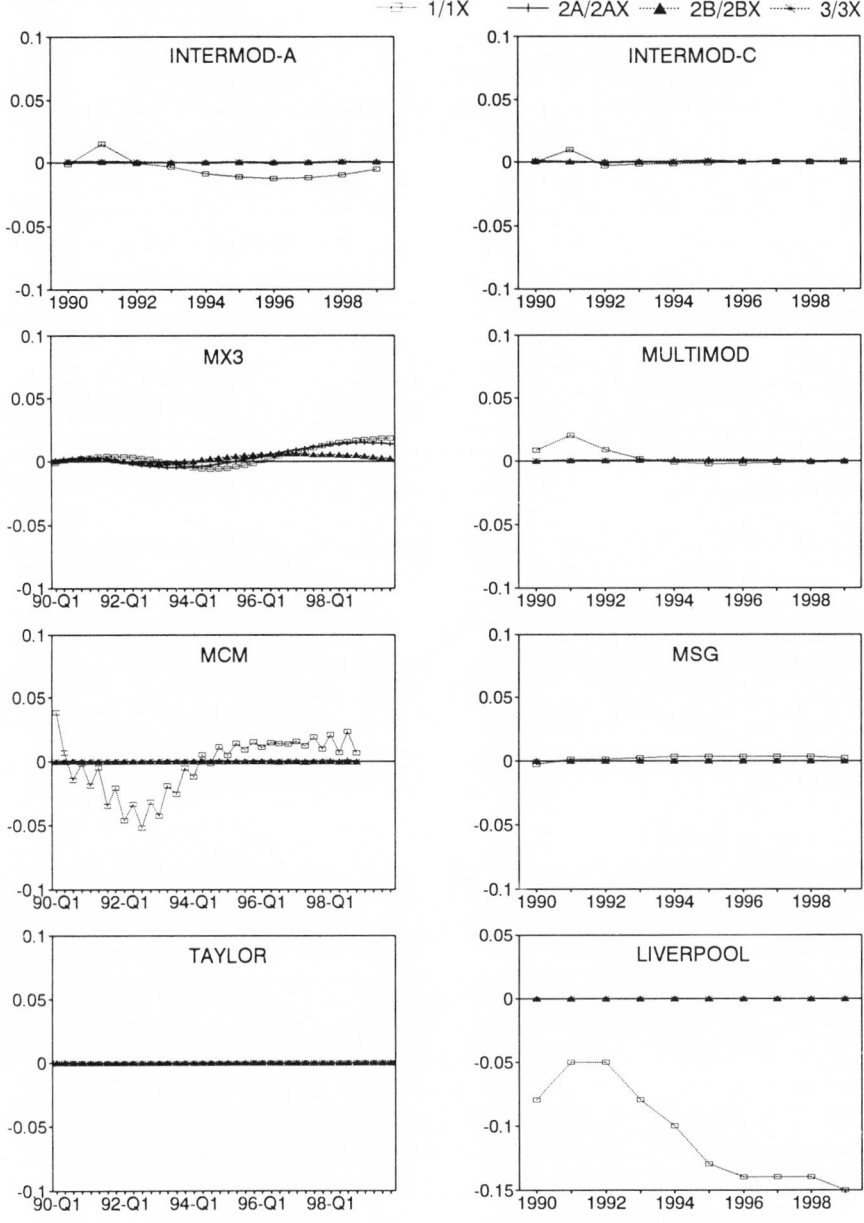

Consider now the effects of a transitory shock to U.S. money demand (shock L) on the U.S. short-term interest rate (figure 4-42), U.S. real GNP (figure 4-43), and Japanese real GNP (figure 4-44). Among the models that ran this shock, there is almost unanimous agreement that none of these variables deviates from its baseline path under nominal-income targeting or real-GNP-plus-inflation targeting.[40] The models also tend to agree that these variables deviate significantly from baseline, at least initially, under both money targeting and exchange-rate targeting. These empirical results broadly confirm the analysis in chapter 2 that a money-demand shock originating in the United States has roughly comparable adverse effects in the United States under both money targeting and exchange-rate targeting but that the adverse effects transmitted abroad tend to be smaller under money targeting than under exchange-rate targeting.[41]

When the shock to U.S. money demand is not accommodated by an increase in the U.S. money supply (that is, under money targeting and exchange-rate targeting), the result tends to be an immediate and often substantial increase in U.S. interest rates. Interest rates rise more in the two quarterly models shown (MPS and MX3), presumably because the initial shock is "larger" when it is concentrated in the first quarter than when it is spread over the first year, as in the annual models.[42] MULTIMOD shows the interest rate rising more initially under regime 1 than under the 3X regime run by that model. This difference probably can be attributed in part to the lower feedback parameter used by MULTIMOD in regime 3X.[43] After its initial increase, the U.S. short-term interest rate returns to the baseline and sometimes falls below the baseline. The MPS model and, to a lesser extent, MULTIMOD show some evidence of longer-term cycles in the interest rate.

In all models, the rise in interest rates under money targeting and exchange-rate targeting causes U.S. real GNP (figure 4-43) and U.S. prices (not shown in a chart) to fall below baseline for a time. It also causes the dollar to appreciate against the yen. Under money targeting, the MPS model shows relatively large

---

40. The sole exception (see figure 4-44) is the MX3 results for Japanese GNP, which exhibit the puzzling, implausible cycling behavior discussed earlier in this chapter and in chapter 3.

41. The LIVERPOOL model does not confirm the analysis of chapter 2. Neither the MX3 or MPS model groups reported results for exchange-rate targeting, so a comparison between money targeting and exchange-rate targeting is not possible for those models.

42. More to the point, lags in the response of money demand to changes in interest rates are longer (in the number of periods—quarters or years) in quarterly models than in annual models, so that interest rates have to rise more initially to equilibrate the money market.

43. The MULTIMOD group reduced the feedback parameter for regime 3 by half (see table 3-3), which presumably causes interest rates to rise significantly less than they would have risen under the original specification. The results under regime 3X in MULTIMOD were about the same as those under MULTIMOD's regime 1X (for which the feedback parameter was cut to one-tenth of the O specification). Three of the models that ran the O specifications for both money targeting and exchange-rate targeting (INTERMOD-A, INTERMOD-C, and MSG) show the interest rate rising the same amount under both regimes.

Figure 4-42. *Effects of Increase in U.S. Money Demand (Shock L) on U.S. Short-Term Interest Rate*

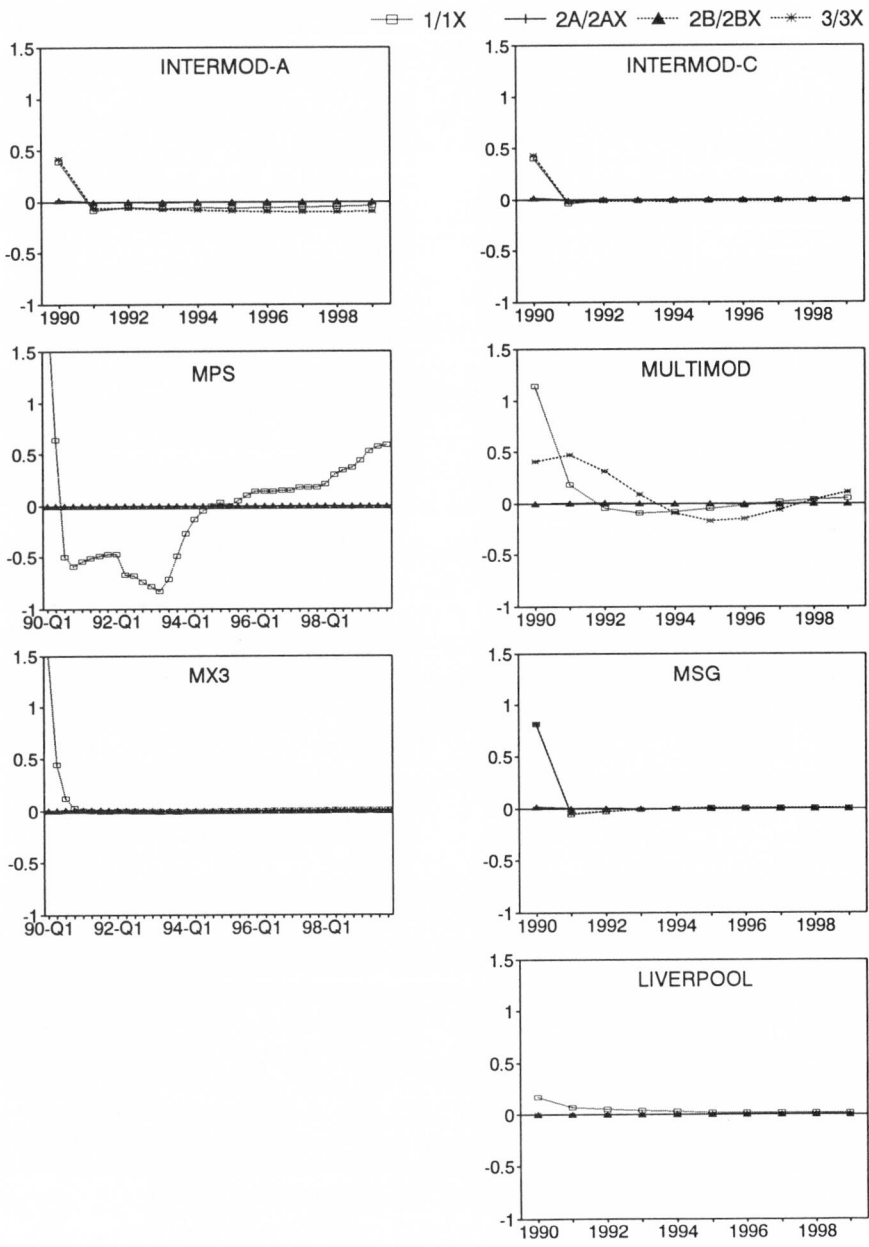

Figure 4-43. *Effects of Increase in U.S. Money Demand (Shock L) on U.S. Real GNP*

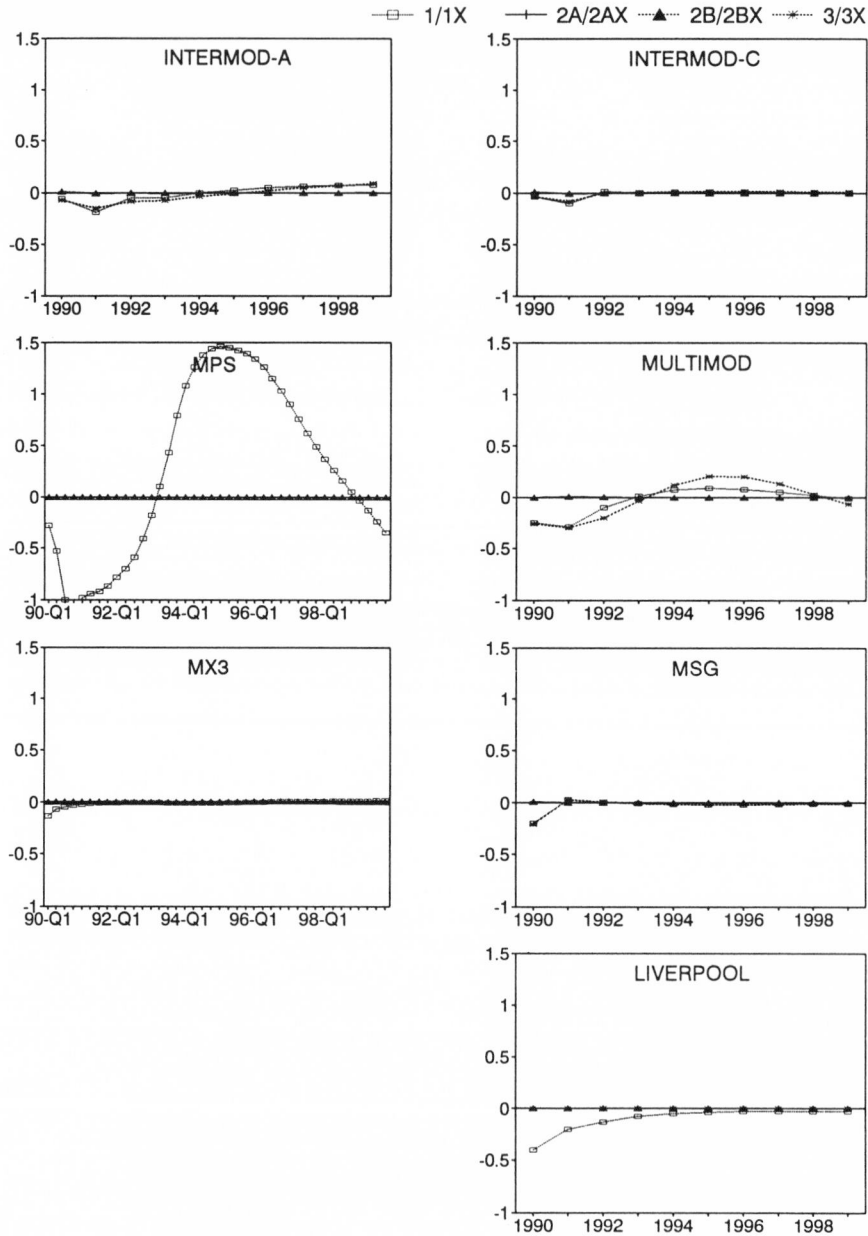

Figure 4-44. *Effects of Increase in U.S. Money Demand (Shock L) on Japanese Real GNP*

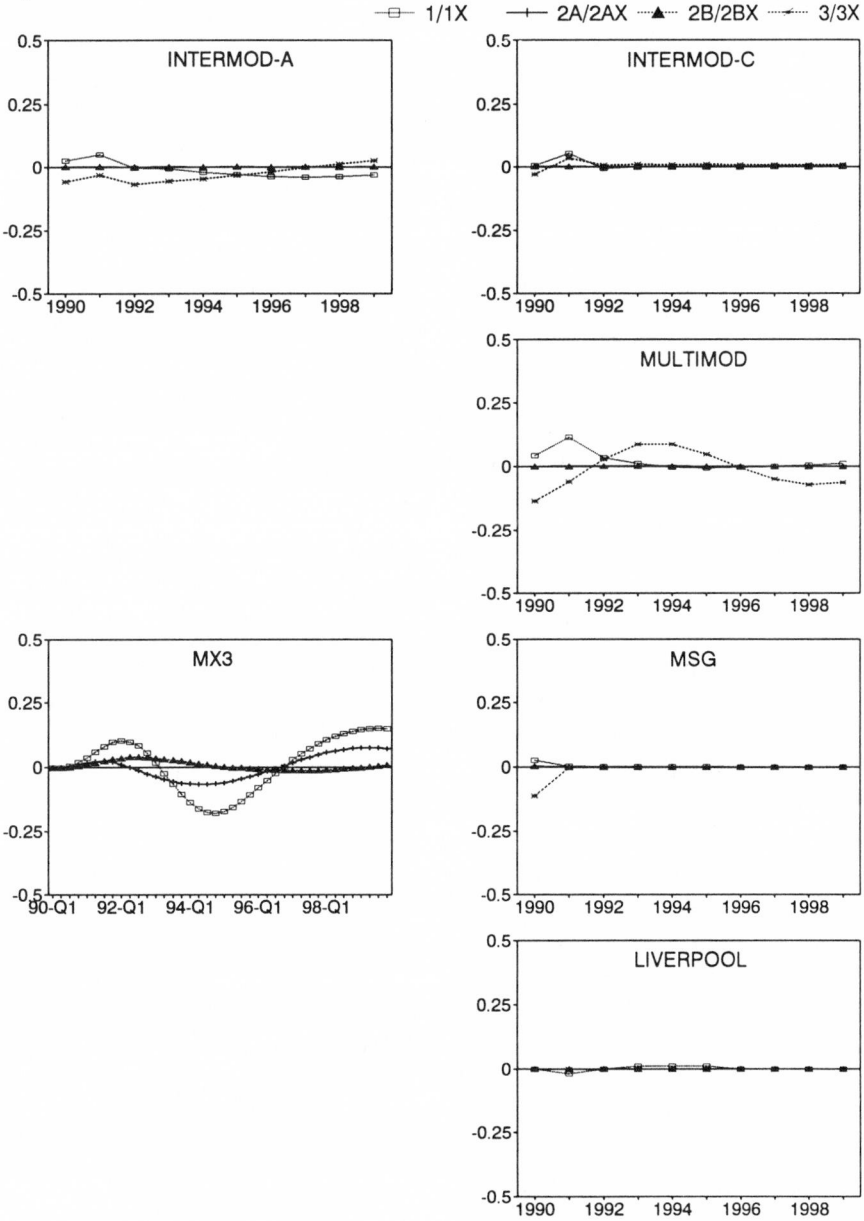

declines in real GNP and prices for several years following the onset of the shock. The lack of forward-looking expectations in that model may contribute to these relatively large declines, but it is probably not the major factor. The adaptive-expectations version of INTERMOD shows somewhat greater declines in real GNP and prices than does the version with model-consistent expectations, but the difference is small relative to the much greater declines predicted by the MPS model. Most of the models have real GNP returning to baseline within a couple of years and show prices returning to baseline somewhat later. The MPS and MULTIMOD models, however, show evidence of longer-term cycling.[44]

As noted, the cross-border effects of the U.S. money-demand shock on Japanese real GNP (figure 4-44) are minimized under nominal-income targeting and real-GNP-plus-inflation targeting. Except for the LIVERPOOL and MX3 models, Japanese output in the short run rises somewhat above baseline under money targeting and falls below baseline by a larger amount under exchange-rate targeting. This pattern is consistent with the predictions from the theoretical model in chapter 2.

Methodology for Overall Ranking of Regimes

In the preceding section, we considered qualitatively the comparative results across regimes for three types of shocks. Although a significant amount of agreement among the models with respect to the ranking of regimes in these cases is evident, diversity of opinion is also prominent. We turn next, therefore, to a more quantitative analysis and ranking of the regimes across the larger set of shocks and countries.

Our objective in the remainder of the chapter is to draw, from the entire range of deterministic simulations, some quantitative inferences about which regimes minimize the effects of various types of shocks on key variables. Given the large size of the complete data base, this objective would obviously be unattainable in the absence of procedures for summarizing and distilling the data.

---

44. The cycling in MULTIMOD under money targeting and exchange-rate targeting is relatively minor. The large oscillations observed for MPS are characteristic of MPS simulations under a broad range of policy regimes for all types of shocks. As explained by the MPS group, the oscillations stem from key features of that model's structure: a long nonmonotonic response of real output to real interest rates and lagged responses of prices and inflation to the level of real output. Under nominal-income targeting, the oscillatory responses to shocks are damped over time. Under money targeting, the oscillatory responses are explosive over time. The difference in outcomes under the two regimes in the MPS model can be understood, in part, by thinking of money targeting as very inexact nominal-income targeting; because money demand responds only gradually to income, money targeting introduces additional lags into the system when compared with nominal-income targeting.

Our efforts at distillation have proceeded in several ways. First, the number of observations per variable has been compressed by expressing the results for that variable from any one simulation in terms of a small number of summary statistics. Second, we have attempted to discern a model "consensus" by aggregating results across models. One factor that leads us to try to identify a consensus is the considerable effort that went into standardizing the simulations prepared for this exercise. Nevertheless, we fully recognize that such aggregation is fraught with pitfalls. As a partial safeguard, we use two alternative quantitative procedures to identify a consensus among the models.

As a third aspect of our distillation procedures, we restrict attention here to six types of key variables—real GNP, employment, the price level, the inflation rate, interest rates, and exchange rates—for each of the G3 countries, the United States, Japan, and Germany. The summary statistics we calculate are the root cumulative squared deviation *(RCSD)*, and the root cumulative squared percentage deviation *(RCS%D)*, of variables from their baseline paths. The *RCS%D* is computed in the case of variables expressed as levels (income, employment, price levels, exchange rates), and the *RCSD* is computed for variables already expressed in percentage points (inflation rates and interest rates). Thus, for simulation J the *RCS%D* for income *(Y)* relative to its baseline path (Y^B) through T years of the simulation is defined as

$$RCS\%D_J(Y_T) = \sqrt{\sum_{t=1}^{T}\left[100\left(\frac{Y_t - Y_t^B}{Y_t^B}\right)^2\right]}.$$

Similarly, the *RCSD* for the short-term interest rate *(RS)* relative to its baseline path (RS^B) is defined as

$$RCSD_J(RS_T) = \sqrt{\sum_{t=1}^{T}(RS_t - RS_t^B)^2}.$$

Note that by squaring the deviations from baseline before cumulation and thereafter taking the square root of the sum of those cumulated squared deviations, large deviations receive proportionately much greater weight than small deviations.[45]

The $RCS\%D_T$ and $RCSD_T$ statistics summarize the cumulative squared percentage deviation and squared absolute deviation caused by a shock over

45. These statistics were chosen in part to be consistent with the summary statistics calculated for the stochastic simulation results presented in chapter 5.

the first T years of the simulation. We compute these statistics for four different time periods: for the first or "impact" period of the simulation (in which case the statistics are equal to the absolute value of the actual deviation in that period), for the first two years, for the first five years, and for all ten years of the simulation. Roughly speaking, the value of the statistic for $T = 10$ years, for example, can be viewed as a measurement of the total area in one of the preceding charts between the simulated path of a variable and its baseline path over the entire simulation period. For the quarterly models, the cumulative-deviation statistics were computed for the first, sixth, eighteenth, and thirty-sixth quarters of the simulation period.[46]

A representative sample of these summary statistics for an individual model, MULTIMOD, is shown in table 4-2. The table shows the statistics for the effects of five different shocks—those to U.S. aggregate demand (A), global aggregate demand (B), U.S. aggregate supply (C), the oil price (E), and U.S. money demand (L)—on U.S. real GNP, the U.S. price level (GNP deflator), and the U.S. inflation rate (GNP deflator) under each of the different regimes implemented by the MULTIMOD group (1, 1X, 2AX, 2BX, 3X).

As can be seen in the first column of the top panel, for example, the shock to U.S. aggregate demand results in roughly a 1 percent change in U.S. real GNP on impact. The exact amount of the impact varies from a low of 0.871 percent under regime 2BX to a high of 1.002 percent under regime 2AX, with regimes 1, 1X, and 3X showing an impact effect of about 0.99 percent. After two years (as indicated at the top of column 2), the *RCS%D* of real GNP from its baseline path amounts to 0.977 percent under regime 2BX, and about 1.03 percent under most of the other regimes. After five years, the total deviation cumulates to 1.134 percent under regime 2BX, and to roughly 1.17 percent under most of the other regimes.

Beyond five years, the cumulative deviation rises only slightly further under any of the regimes, indicating that real GNP has returned to (and remains) very near its baseline path after five years. In this particular case, more than three-fourths of the cumulative squared deviation over the entire ten-year period

---

46. As noted earlier, the sixth and eighteenth quarters correspond roughly to the mid-points of the second and fifth years of the simulation. The thirty-sixth quarter, however, falls two quarters short of the mid-point of the final year. The thirty-sixth rather than thirty-eighth quarter was used for the cumulative "full-period" results in the case of all the quarterly models because one of the quarterly models, MCM, reported results for only nine years (thirty-six quarters). Most of the quantitative results in the final sections of the chapter are based on the cumulative-deviation statistics for the whole simulation period. Given the use of the thirty-sixth quarter for the quarterly models, we were concerned that the results for the annual models and the quarterly models might not be sufficiently comparable. A check for the stability of results between five years and ten years, however, indicated that the possible bias introduced by a slightly shorter time period for the quarterly models was likely to be very small. In the nearly 700 cases considered in this check (across 10 models, 5 shocks, 6 variables and 3 countries—not all the models ran all the shocks across all three countries), we found only 35 instances when the ordinal ranking of regimes changed between the fifth and tenth years (or eighteenth and thirty-sixth quarters) of the simulations. The chances of a change in ranking between the thirty-sixth and thirty-eighth quarters of the simulation are much smaller still.

Table 4-2. *Illustration of Tables for Root Cumulative Squared Deviations, MULTIMOD Model: Statistics for U.S. Real GNP, U.S. Price Level, and U.S. Inflation Rate*

Shock and regime	Real GNP[a]				GNP deflator[a]				Inflation rate[b]			
	1st yr.	2nd yr.	5th yr.	10th yr.	1st yr.	2nd yr.	5th yr.	10th yr.	1st yr.	2nd yr.	5th yr.	10th yr.
					Shock A: U.S. aggregate demand							
1	0.994	1.034	1.168	1.182	0.142	0.319	0.673	0.724	0.149	0.211	0.234	0.306
1X	0.986	1.030	1.192	1.213	0.132	0.284	0.519	0.543	0.138	0.186	0.213	0.261
2A	. . .	. . .	. . .	. . .	. . .	. . .	. . .	. . .	. . .	. . .	. . .	. . .
2AX	1.002	1.035	1.169	1.199	0.149	0.331	0.658	0.751	0.156	0.219	0.249	0.351
2B	. . .	. . .	. . .	. . .	. . .	. . .	. . .	. . .	. . .	. . .	. . .	. . .
2BX	0.871	0.977	1.134	1.140	0.113	0.248	0.504	0.643	0.118	0.163	0.174	0.179
3	. . .	. . .	. . .	. . .	. . .	. . .	. . .	. . .	. . .	. . .	. . .	. . .
3X	0.986	1.025	1.167	1.186	0.129	0.273	0.484	0.505	0.135	0.179	0.207	0.248
					Shock B: "Global" aggregate demand							
1	1.063	1.101	1.225	1.238	0.145	0.323	0.670	0.718	0.152	0.214	0.237	0.306
1X	1.046	1.093	1.249	1.269	0.136	0.291	0.522	0.542	0.143	0.191	0.219	0.262
2A	. . .	. . .	. . .	. . .	. . .	. . .	. . .	. . .	. . .	. . .	. . .	. . .
2AX	1.073	1.106	1.237	1.266	0.151	0.335	0.657	0.758	0.158	0.221	0.252	0.357
2B	. . .	. . .	. . .	. . .	. . .	. . .	. . .	. . .	. . .	. . .	. . .	. . .
2BX	0.931	1.021	1.134	1.136	0.121	0.261	0.540	0.713	0.127	0.171	0.180	0.184
3	. . .	. . .	. . .	. . .	. . .	. . .	. . .	. . .	. . .	. . .	. . .	. . .
3X	1.048	1.092	1.231	1.251	0.133	0.281	0.488	0.510	0.139	0.184	0.214	0.256
					Shock C: U.S. aggregate supply							
1	0.175	0.191	0.413	0.432	0.796	0.840	0.964	0.986	0.833	1.381	1.382	1.391
1X	0.170	0.174	0.432	0.501	0.782	0.832	0.950	0.971	0.818	1.374	1.377	1.387
2A	. . .	. . .	. . .	. . .	. . .	. . .	. . .	. . .	. . .	. . .	. . .	. . .
2AX	0.191	0.191	0.381	0.445	0.776	0.835	1.014	1.061	0.812	1.386	1.388	1.408
2B	. . .	. . .	. . .	. . .	. . .	. . .	. . .	. . .	. . .	. . .	. . .	. . .
2BX	0.300	0.326	0.815	0.859	0.875	0.880	0.887	0.955	0.915	1.359	1.364	1.366
3	. . .	. . .	. . .	. . .	. . .	. . .	. . .	. . .	. . .	. . .	. . .	. . .
3X	0.160	0.165	0.408	0.474	0.779	0.830	0.944	0.963	0.815	1.372	1.376	1.385
					Shock E: Oil price							
1	0.191	0.220	0.328	0.342	0.144	0.257	0.470	0.501	0.150	0.401	0.405	0.425
1X	0.192	0.215	0.350	0.391	0.140	0.262	0.466	0.489	0.146	0.402	0.408	0.428
2A	. . .	. . .	. . .	. . .	. . .	. . .	. . .	. . .	. . .	. . .	. . .	. . .
2AX	0.185	0.205	0.316	0.350	0.140	0.262	0.469	0.518	0.147	0.404	0.410	0.440
2B	. . .	. . .	. . .	. . .	. . .	. . .	. . .	. . .	. . .	. . .	. . .	. . .
2BX	0.181	0.268	0.475	0.481	0.170	0.220	0.286	0.293	0.178	0.368	0.371	0.372
3	. . .	. . .	. . .	. . .	. . .	. . .	. . .	. . .	. . .	. . .	. . .	. . .
3X	0.190	0.209	0.317	0.352	0.142	0.256	0.435	0.454	0.149	0.399	0.405	0.422
					Shock L: U.S. money demand							
1	0.246	0.379	0.398	0.419	0.021	0.063	0.291	0.421	0.022	0.046	0.097	0.133
1X	0.260	0.427	0.505	0.625	0.048	0.138	0.535	0.705	0.050	0.098	0.171	0.253
2A	. . .	. . .	. . .	. . .	. . .	. . .	. . .	. . .	. . .	. . .	. . .	. . .
2AX	0.000	0.007	0.007	0.008	0.000	0.000	0.002	0.003	0.000	0.001	0.001	0.002
2B	. . .	. . .	. . .	. . .	. . .	. . .	. . .	. . .	. . .	. . .	. . .	. . .
2BX	0.000	0.006	0.007	0.007	0.000	0.000	0.002	0.003	0.000	0.001	0.001	0.002
3	. . .	. . .	. . .	. . .	. . .	. . .	. . .	. . .	. . .	. . .	. . .	. . .
3X	0.256	0.391	0.457	0.561	0.052	0.153	0.558	0.698	0.055	0.111	0.176	0.264

Source: Annex A, table A-MUL-1. See text for definition of the statistics and further explanation.
a. Underlying data are percent deviations from baseline.
b. GDP deflator, underlying data are deviations from baseline in percentage points.

takes place on impact, in the very first period of the simulation. This is a good example of a case where the "persistence" of the effects of the transitory shock to aggregate demand is not very strong (that is, real GNP returns close to its baseline path fairly quickly).

The other two blocs of columns in the table show the cumulative effects, over time, on the U.S. price level and U.S. inflation rate. The shock-A results for inflation under regime 2AX provide an illustration of significant persistence of effects, where the cumulative deviation of inflation after ten years is noticeably greater than after five years. Successive panels further down the table show the effects of the other shocks on the same variables under the alternative regimes.

One other point that is illustrated in table 4-2 is the occasional occurrence of "regime switching" over time. For example, in the case of the effects of the U.S. aggregate supply shock on the U.S. inflation rate (third panel of rows in the table, right-hand columns), regime 2BX yields the largest deviation on impact but shows the smallest deviation thereafter. More generally across the broader set of models, when switching does occur, it is less clear-cut. Such switching often entails effects across different regimes that are quite similar in magnitude on impact but divergent thereafter. In the case of the effects of the oil shock on real GNP (fourth panel of rows in the table), for example, regime 2BX has a slight edge in a near five-way tie on impact, but clearly loses out to several other regimes as time goes by. Evidence of regime switching in the longer run is very limited.[47]

Tables analogous to 4-2 were produced for key variables for all of the model-shock combinations across each of the three major countries. The results of these calculations were used as inputs into a second stage of distillation of the results.

Ordinal Rankings of Regime Performance

Our next step in the analysis was to aggregate across models. This aggregation was done using two different methods. One involved an "ordinal" ranking of the results by model. The second generated a "cardinal" ranking, obtained by actually averaging summary statistics presented in table 4-2 and others like it.

Tables 4-3–4-11 present the first part of the procedure for an ordinal ranking of the regimes. In these nine tables—three tables each for the United States, Japan, and Germany—we identify the regimes that produce the minimum $RCS\%D$ or $RCSD$ over the whole simulation period for real GNP,

---

47. As indicated in the preceding footnote, in only about 5 percent of the cases considered did we find evidence of regime switching between the fifth and tenth years of the simulation.

employment, inflation, the price level, interest rates, and exchange rates in each of the shocks for each of the models.[48] Table 4-3 presents the results for the U.S. and global shocks and effects on U.S. real GNP and employment. Table 4-4 does the same for U.S. inflation and the price level, and table 4-5 for U.S. short-term and long-term interest rates. Tables 4-6–4-8 do the same for the effects of the Japanese and global shocks on Japanese variables, and tables 4-9–4-11 the same again for German and global shocks on German variables. In the tables focusing on Japanese and German variables, the bilateral exchange rates against the U.S. dollar (dollar per yen or dollar per deutsche mark) are substituted for the long-term interest rate.[49]

When identifying preferred regimes to appear in these tables, we selected from among O regimes and X regimes equally in instances when both variants were reported for the same regime type. For example, if a model group implemented all eight regimes (1, 1X, 2A, 2AX, 2B, 2BX, 3, 3X), our selection of the regime minimizing cumulative deviations from baseline was chosen from all eight. If a model group reported results for 1, 1X, 2AX, 2BX, 3, and 3X, our selection was based on comparison of these six regimes, and so on.

Two other special features of the construction of these tables need to be noted. First, in cases where the preferred regime has a statistical value that is at least 10 percent smaller than that of the second-place regime, the preferred regime is printed in bold type. Thus, for example, if for a given shock the values of the ten-year $RCS\%D$ (in parentheses) for the four regimes were regime 1 (1.15), regime 2A (1.00), regime 2B (1.11), regime 3 (1.20), the table would show regime 2A in bold type, since its value (1.00) was more than 10 percent less than that of the second-place regime (1.11).[50] Second, in cases where the value of the second-place regime differs from the regime in first place by less than 1 percent, both regimes are shown. Under this somewhat arbitrary rule, for example, values of 1.10 and 1.11 would be considered "ties," but values of 0.90 and 0.91 would not. In a few cases, application of this rule yields three-way or even four-way ties.

In reviewing the results for U.S. real GNP and employment in table 4-3, one is struck first by the preponderance of occurrences of nominal-income targeting or real-GNP-plus-inflation targeting across shocks and most models. Only two models, MCM and GEM, appear to prefer money targeting for a

48. For the quarterly models, as discussed earlier, the identification of preferred regime pertains to the time interval from the impact quarter through the thirty-sixth quarter of the simulation period.

49. Throughout the tables, the price levels and the inflation rates pertain to GNP or GDP deflators, not to consumer prices.

50. For calculation of whether the preferred regime reduces the value of the $RCSD$ or $RCS\%D$ by more than 10 percent relative to the "next-best" regime, the next-best regime had to be a different type of regime. For example, for a model where the magnitudes of the $RCS\%D$s were ranked in ascending order across regimes as 2BX, 2B, 2A, 2AX, 1, and 3X, the preferred regime 2BX was compared with 2A rather than 2B to determine whether to boldface the cell in table 4-3.

majority of the shocks; a third, MULTIMOD, prefers money targeting in the case of supply shocks.[51] Exchange-rate targeting is favored in only two cases: the global demand shock in the LIVERPOOL model and the aggregate supply shock in the INTERMOD-C model (where it ties with money targeting).[52]

A comparison of results for U.S. real GNP and employment between models with adaptive (or backward-looking) expectations and those with model-consistent (or forward-looking) expectations is inconclusive. INTERMOD-A gives slightly stronger preference to real-GNP-plus-inflation targeting than does INTERMOD-C, and the MPS model (an adaptive-expectations model) generally agrees with this preference. But the only other adaptive-expectations model, MCM, does not favor real-GNP-plus-inflation targeting for any of the shocks, whereas at least one model with model-consistent expectations (MSG) gives clear preference to that regime type across most of the shocks.

With respect to the U.S. inflation rate and price level (shown in table 4-4), money targeting (1X) is again strongly preferred by the MCM. That regime is given some preference by the TAYLOR model in the case of goods-demand shocks and by the MX3 and LIVERPOOL models in the case of aggregate supply and oil shocks respectively. Exchange-rate targeting is preferred fairly strongly by the LIVERPOOL model in most cases, and in several cases by the MULTIMOD model. Otherwise, nominal-income targeting and real-GNP-plus-inflation targeting together appear to reign supreme across most shocks and models.

The ranking of regimes minimizing the *RCSD* statistic changes substantially for U.S. interest rates (table 4-5). All but three of the models, MCM, MSG, and MULTIMOD, prefer money targeting more often than not, particularly in the case of demand shocks. The GEM, MX3, TAYLOR, and INTERMOD-C models favor money targeting in a large majority of cases. Among the exceptions, the MCM favors real-GNP-plus-inflation targeting slightly over nominal-income targeting, the MSG model favors exchange-rate targeting more often than not, and MULTIMOD shows a strong preference for nominal-income targeting. It is noteworthy that the MCM model, which shows a strong preference for money targeting in the case of U.S. real GNP and inflation, does not favor that regime even once for U.S. interest rates. With respect to short-term interest

51. Here and elsewhere below we speak of a model "preferring" or "favoring" a regime only in a descriptive sense, to indicate the particular regime associated with lowest *RCS%D* or *RCSD*. Our shorthand language here of "preferred regime" is not intended to prejudge in any way which variables are, or should be, included in policymakers' loss functions. Variability in short-term interest rates (the assumed instrument of monetary policy in these simulations) could be justified for inclusion in policymakers' loss functions either because policymakers attribute direct costs to such variability or as an analytical device for penalizing "instrument instability."

52. The results in tables 4-3 through 4-11 are somewhat biased against selection of the exchange-rate targeting regime inasmuch as three of the ten models did not report simulations with that regime. Before drawing quantitative inferences from the results, we adjust for this bias in the preparation of summary tables presented later in this chapter.

Table 4-3. *Identification of the Type of Regime Minimizing the Cumulative Deviation from Baseline after Ten Years: United States, Real GNP and Employment*[a]

| | Type of shock and U.S. variable | | | | | | | | | |
| | U.S. aggregate demand (A) | | "Global" aggregate demand (B) | | U.S. aggregate supply (C) | | Oil price (E) | | U.S. money demand (L) | |
Model	Real GNP	Employment	Real GNP	Employment	Real GNP	Employment	Real GNP	Employment	Real GNP	Employment
GEM	1X/2AX/2BX	2BX	1X/2AX/2BX	2BX	1X	1X	2BX	1X	…	…
INTERMOD A	2B	…	**2B**	…	2B	…	**2B**	…	**2B**	…
INTERMOD C	2B	…	2B	…	1/3	…	**2B**	…	2A/2B	…
LIVERPOOL	**1X**	…	3	…	**2BX**	…	2BX	…	2A/2B/3	…
MCM	**1X**	**1X**	**1X**	**1X**	**1X**	**1X**	**2AX**	**2AX**	**2A**	**2A/2B**
MPS	**2BX**	**2BX**	…	…	**2BX**	**2BX**	**2BX**	**2BX**	**2BX**	**2BX**
MSG	**2BX**	**2BX**	**2BX**	**2BX**	**2B**	**2BX**	**2B**	2BX	2BX	**2BX**
MULTIMOD	2BX	…	2BX	…	1	…	1	…	2BX	…
MX3	2A/2B	…	2A/2B	…	2A/2B	…	…	…	**2B**	…
TAYLOR	2A/2AX/2B/2BX	…	2A/2AX/2B/2BX	…	2B	…	…	…	…	…

a. Boldface denotes cases where the preferred regime had a *RCSD* or *RCS%D* at least 10 percent less than other regimes; multiple entries denote ties.

Table 4-4. *Identification of the Type of Regime Minimizing the Cumulative Deviation from Baseline after Ten Years: United States, Inflation Rate and Price Level (GNP Deflator)*[a]

	U.S. aggregate demand (A)		"Global" aggregate demand (B)		U.S. aggregate supply (C)		Oil price (E)		U.S. money demand (L)	
Model	Inflation rate	Price level	Inflation rate	Price level	Inflation rate	Price level	Inflation rate	Price level	Inflation rate	Price level
GEM	2BX	**2AX**	2BX	**2AX**	1X/2AX/2BX	1X/2AX/2BX	1X/2AX/2BX	1X	...	...
INTERMOD A	**2B**	**2A**	**2B**	**2A**	1/3	2A	**2B**	**2A**	**2B**	**2A**
INTERMOD C	**2A**	**2A**	**2A**	**2A**	1/2AX/3	2A	1/2AX/3	2B	**2B**	2B
LIVERPOOL	**3X**	**3X**	**3X**	**3X**	**3X**	**3X**	1X	1X	2A/2B/3	2A/2B/3
MCM	**1X**	**1X**	**1X**	**1X**	**1X**	1X	2AX	1X	...	...
MPS	2B	**2AX**	...	...	2B/2BX	2AX	2A/2AX/2B/2BX	2AX	**2A**	**2B**
MSG	**2BX**	**2AX**	**2AX**	**2AX**	**2BX**	**2AX**	**2BX**	**2AX**	**2BX**	**2AX**
MULTIMOD	**2BX**	3X	**2BX**	3X	2BX	2BX/3X	**2BX**	**2BX**	2AX/2BX	2AX
MX3	**2A**	**2A**	**2A**	**2A**	1	1	...	...	2A	2A
TAYLOR	**1X**	**2A**	**1X**	1X	3X	2A	...	...	...	...

a. Boldface denotes cases where the preferred regime had a *RCSD* or *RCS%D* at least 10 percent less than other regimes; multiple entries denote ties.

Table 4-5. *Identification of the Type of Regime Minimizing the Cumulative Deviation from Baseline after Ten Years: United States, Short-Term and Long-Term Interest Rates*[a]

| | U.S. aggregate demand (A) | | "Global" aggregate demand (B) | | U.S. aggregate supply (C) | | Oil price (E) | | U.S. money demand (L) | |
Model	Short-term interest rate	Long-term interest rate	Short-term interest rate	Long-term interest rate	Short-term interest rate	Long-term interest rate	Short-term interest rate	Long-term interest rate	Short-term interest rate	Long-term interest rate
GEM	**1X**	**1X**	**1X**	**1X**	**1X**	**1X**	1X	**2BX**	...	...
INTERMOD A	1	1	1	3	1	1/3	**2B**	**2B**	2B	2B
INTERMOD C	1	1	1	1	1	1	1	3	**2AX**	**2AX**
LIVERPOOL	**2BX**	1/1X/2A/3	1	1X	**2A**	1	1	1/1X	2A/2B/3	2A/2B/3
MCM	**2BX**	**2BX**	2AX/2BX	2AX/2BX	**2BX**	**2BX**	**2AX**	**2AX**		
MPS	1X	1	...	...	1X	2A	1X	2AX	**2A**	**2A**
MSG	1/3	3	1/3	**2B**	3	3X	3	2AX	2A	2A/2B
MULTIMOD	3X	**2AX**	3X	**2AX**	**2AX**	**2AX**	**2AX**	**2AX**	**2AX**	**2AX**
MX3	1	...	1	...	1	...	...	...	**2B**	...
TAYLOR	**1X**	**1X**	**1X**	**1X**	**1X**	**1X**	...	...	...	...

a. Boldface denotes cases where the preferred regime had a $RCS‰D$ or $RCS\%D$ at least 10 percent less than other regimes; multiple entries denote ties.

Table 4-6. *Identification of the Type of Regime Minimizing the Cumulative Deviation from Baseline after Ten Years: Japan, Real GNP and Employment*[a]

	Japanese aggregate demand (I)		"Global" aggregate demand (B)		Japanese aggregate supply (J)		Oil price (E)		Japanese money demand (D)	
Model	Real GNP	Employment	Real GNP	Employment	Real GNP	Employment	Real GNP	Employment	Real GNP	Employment
GEM	2AX/2BX	2BX	2BX	2BX	...	...	2AX	2AX	...	...
INTERMOD A	2B	...	2B	...	2B/3	...	**2B**	...	2A/2B	...
INTERMOD C	2B	...	2A/2B	...	**3**	...	**2B**	...	2A	...
LIVERPOOL	2AX	...	**2A**	...	**3X**	...	2AX	...	2A/2B/3	...
MCM	...	...	1X	1X	...	...	1X/2AX	**1X**	3X	**3X**
MPS	...	...	...	...	...	...	...	...	...	...
MSG	**2AX**	**2AX**	**2AX**	**2AX**	**2B**	**2AX**	**3**	**2AX**	**2AX**	**2AX**
MULTIMOD	2BX	...	**2BX**	...	3X	...	3X	...	**2BX**	...
MX3	2B	...	2B	...	2A	...	...	...	**2B**	...
TAYLOR	...	...	2A	...	...	...	...	...	**1X**	...

a. Boldface denotes cases where the preferred regime had a *RCSD* or *RCS%D* at least 10 percent less than other regimes; multiple entries denote ties.

Table 4-7. *Identification of the Type of Regime Minimizing the Cumulative Deviation from Baseline after Ten Years: Japan, Inflation Rate and Price Level (GNP-GDP Deflator)*[a]

	Japanese aggregate demand (I)		"Global" aggregate demand (B)		Japanese aggregate supply (J)		Oil price (E)		Japanese money demand (D)	
	Type of shock and Japanese variable									
Model	*Inflation rate*	*Price level*	*Inflation rate*	*Price level*	*Inflation rate*	*Price level*	*Inflation rate*	*Price level*	*Inflation rate*	*Price level*
GEM	**2BX**	**2AX**	**2BX**	**2AX**	...	...	2AX/2BX	**2BX**	...	**2A**
INTERMOD A	**2B**	**2A**	**2B**	**2A**	**2B**	**2A**	**2B**	**2A**	**2B**	**2A**
INTERMOD C	**2AX**	**2A**	2A	**2A**	2A	2A	2A/2AX	**2A**	**2AX**	2AX
LIVERPOOL	**1X**	1	**1X**	**1X**	**1X**	**1X**	**1X**	**1X**	2A/2B/3	2A/2B/3
MCM	...	...	**2BX**	**1X**	...	...	2AX	2AX/3X	**2BX**	**2BX**
MPS	...	...	...	...	...	...	...	...	...	...
MSG	**2BX**	**2AX**	**2BX**	**2AX**	**2BX**	**2AX**	**2BX**	**2AX**	**2BX**	**2AX**
MULTIMOD	**2BX**	3X	**2BX**	1X	3X	2BX/3X	**2BX**	3X	2AX	2AX
MX3	**2A**	**2A**	**2A**	**2A**	**2A**	2A	...	...	**2A**	**2A**
TAYLOR	...	...	**2A**	2AX	...	...	...	...	2A/2AX/2B/2BX/3X	1X

a. Boldface denotes cases where the preferred regime had a *RCSD* or *RCS%D* at least 10 precent less than other regimes; multiple entries denote ties.

Table 4-8. *Identification of the Type of Regime Minimizing the Cumulative Deviation from Baseline after Ten Years: Japan, Short-Term Interest Rate and Dollar-Yen Exchange Rate*[a]

	Type of shock and Japanese variable									
	Japanese aggregate demand (I)		"Global" aggregate demand (B)		Japanese aggregate supply (J)		Oil price (E)		Japanese money demand (D)	
Model	Short-term interest rate	Dollar-yen exchange rate	Short-term interest rate	Dollar-yen exchange rate	Short-term interest rate	Dollar-yen exchange rate	Short-term interest rate	Dollar-yen exchange rate	Short-term interest rate	Dollar-yen exchange rate
GEM	**1X**	**2AX**	**1X**	**2AX**	...	...	**1X**	**2BX**	...	...
INTERMOD A	3	3	3	3	3	3	1	1/3	3	3
INTERMOD C	3	3	3	3	3	3	3	3	3	3
LIVERPOOL	1	**3X**	3	**3X**	2A	**3X**	**2A**	3	2A/2B/3	2A/2B/3
MCM	...	...	**2AX/2BX**	**3X**	...	...	**2AX**	**3X**	**2AX**	**3X**
MPS	...	...	...	...	...	...	...	...	...	...
MSG	3	**3X**	3	**3X**	3	**3X**	3	**3X**	3	3/**3X**
MULTIMOD	**3X**	**3X**	**3X**	**1X**	**3X**	**3X**	**2AX**	**3X**	**3X**	**3X**
MX3	1	1	1	1	1	1	...	...	**2A**	1
TAYLOR	...	...	**1X**	**1X**	...	...	...	...	**1X**	**1X**

a. Boldface denotes cases where the preferred regime had a RCSD or RCS%D at least 10 percent less than other regimes; multiple entries denote ties.

Table 4-9. *Identification of the Type of Regime Minimizing the Cumulative Deviation from Baseline after Ten Years: Germany, Real GNP and Employment*[a]

	Type of shock and German variable									
	German aggregate demand (G)		"Global" aggregate demand (B)		German aggregate supply (H)		Oil price (E)		German money demand (K)	
Model	Real GNP	Employment	Real GNP	Employment	Real GNP	Employment	Real GNP	Employment	Real GNP	Employment
GEM	1X/2AX/2BX	2BX	1X/2AX/2BX	2BX	**2BX**	**2BX**	1X/2AX	2AX	...	...
INTERMOD A	**2A**	...	2A	...	2B	...	**2B**	...	**2A**	...
INTERMOD C	2A	...	2A	...	3	...	3	...	2A/2B	...
LIVERPOOL	3X	...	1	...	**3X**	...	2AX	...	2A/2B/3	...
MCM	...	...	2BX	2BX	...	...	3X	**2BX**	...	...
MPS	...	...	...	...	...	...	...	...	...	...
MSG	**2BX**	**2BX**	**2BX**	**2BX**	**2B**	2B	**2B**	**2BX**	**2BX**	**2BX**
MULTIMOD	2AX	...	**2BX**	...	3X	...	3X	...	2AX	...
MX3	2B	...	2B	...	2B	...	...	...	**2B**	...
TAYLOR	...	...	2A/2AX/2B/2BX	...	...	...	...	...	...	...

a. Boldface denotes cases where the preferred regime had a *RCSD* or *RCS%D* at least 10 percent less than other regimes; multiple entries denote ties.

Table 4-10. *Identification of the Type of Regime Minimizing the Cumulative Deviation from Baseline after Ten Years: Germany, Inflation Rate and Price Level (GNP-GDP Deflator)*[a]

	German aggregate demand (G)		"Global" aggregate demand (B)		German aggregate supply (H)		Oil price (E)		German money demand (K)	
Model	Inflation rate	Price level	Inflation rate	Price level	Inflation rate	Price level	Inflation rate	Price level	Inflation rate	Price level
GEM	2BX	**2AX**	2BX	**2AX**	1X/2AX/2BX	1X/2AX/2BX	1X/2AX	**2AX**	…	…
INTERMOD A	3	1	1	**2B**	3	1	3	**2A**	3	**2B**
INTERMOD C	3	1	3	3	3	1/2AX	3	2A/2AX	3	3
LIVERPOOL	2A	**2A**	**2A**	**2A**	**2AX**	**2AX**	2BX	**2A**	2A/2B/3	2A/2B/3
MCM	…	…	1X	1X	…	…	2AX	3X	…	…
MPS	…	…	…	…	…	…	…	…	…	…
MSG	2AX/2BX	1X	2BX	**2AX**	2BX	**2AX**	2BX	**2AX**	**2BX**	**2A**
MULTIMOD	**3X**	**3X**	2BX/3X	1X	3X	3X	**2BX**	2BX	**3X**	**3X**
MX3	**2A**	**2A**	**2A**	**2A**	**2A**	**2A**	…	…	**2A**	**2A**
TAYLOR	…	…	**1X**	**1X**	…	…	…	…	…	…

a. Boldface denotes cases where the preferred regime had a *RCSD* or *RCS%D* at least 10 percent less than other regimes; multiple entries denote ties.

Table 4-11. *Identification of the Type of Regime Minimizing the Cumulative Deviation from Baseline after Ten Years: Germany, Short-Term Interest Rate and Dollar–Deutsche Mark Exchange Rate*[a]

	Type of shock and German variable									
	German aggregate demand (G)		"Global" aggregate demand (B)		German aggregate supply (H)		Oil price (E)		German money demand (K)	
Model	Short-term interest rate	Dollar-DM exchange rate	Short-term interest rate	Dollar-DM exchange rate	Short-term interest rate	Dollar-DM exchange rate	Short-term interest rate	Dollar-DM exchange rate	Short-term interest rate	Dollar-DM exchange rate
GEM	**1X**	**1X**	**1X**	**2BX**	**1X**	**1X**	**1X**	**2AX**	...	...
INTERMOD A	3	3	3	3	3	3	1	3	3	3
INTERMOD C	3	3	3	3	3	3	3	3	3	3
LIVERPOOL	3	**3X**	**2B**	**3X**	3	**3X**	1	3	2A/2B/3	2A/2B/3
MCM	...	...	2AX/2BX	**3X**	3	...	**2AX**	**3X**	...	...
MPS	...	...	...	...	...	...	...	...	...	...
MSG	3	**3X**	3	**3X**	3	**3X**	3	**3X**	3	3/3X
MULTIMOD	**3X**	**3X**	**1X**	**2AX**	**3X**	**3X**	**2AX**	**3X**	**3X**	**3X**
MX3	1	1	1	**2A**	1	1	...	...	**2A**	**2A**
TAYLOR	...	...	**1X**	**1X**	...	...	...	...	...	...

a. Boldface denotes cases where the preferred regime had a *RCSD* or *RCS%D* at least 10 percent less than other regimes; multiple entries denote ties.

rates versus long-term interest rates, the deviation-minimizing regimes do differ in a number of cases, but no consistent pattern of differences is evident.

The ranking of deviation-minimizing regimes for Japan appears to be fairly similar to that for the United States, at least for real GNP, employment, the inflation rate, and the price level. In particular, nominal-income targeting and real-GNP-plus-inflation targeting are preferred noticeably more often than money targeting and exchange-rate targeting in tables 4-6 and 4-7.[53] A significant difference does arise, however, in the case of Japanese interest rates (table 4-8). Exchange-rate targeting becomes the deviation-minimizing regime for more than half of the cases reported, substantially more than any other regime. Only the GEM, MX3, and TAYLOR models retain a preference for money targeting with respect to interest rates in the Japanese case. Not surprisingly, exchange-rate targeting is even more strongly preferred (in about three-fourths of the cases reported) for minimizing fluctuations in the $RCS\%D$ for the dollar-yen exchange rate.

The ranking results for German variables (tables 4-9–4-11) are similar in many respects to those for Japan. Somewhat greater preference, however, is given to exchange-rate targeting, especially in the case of prices and inflation for a number of shocks, particularly by MULTIMOD, INTERMOD-A, and INTERMOD-C.

In about half the cases reported across all models, countries, and shocks, the deviation-minimizing regime is a pronounced rather than merely marginal favorite on the basis of our 10 percent rule of thumb. In roughly 10 percent of the cases, however, the models do not identify a dominant regime among the candidates, as indicated by the number of two-way, three-way, and four-way ties reported.

Summary of Ordinal Rankings

To extend the preceding analysis, a summary of the ordinal rankings was prepared by aggregating the results in tables 4-3–4-11 across models. This aggregation is presented in tables 4-12–4-14 (one table each for the United States, Japan, and Germany). Table 4-12, for example, reports for each U.S. shock and U.S. variable the percentage of models that prefer each regime. The percentages shown in these tables are derived by first assigning a value of 1.0 to a type of regime each time it appears alone in a cell in tables 4-3–4-11. (Regimes 1 and 1X, for example, are the same "type" of regime.) In the case of ties (that is, when more than one type of regime appears in a cell), the value 1.0 is divided among the regime types that appear in the ties. The percentages

---

53. One notable difference with the U.S. results is that the LIVERPOOL model gives a strong preference to regime 1X (instead of 3X) in the case of the Japanese inflation rate and price level.

Table 4-12. *Ordinal Summary of Preferred Regimes across Models That Ran All Four Types of Regimes: U.S. Variables*[a]

	Percent of models preferring regime					
			Real-GNP-plus-inflation targeting (2B/2BX)	Exchange-rate targeting (3/3X)	Number of model cases	
U.S. variable and shock	Money targeting (1/1X)	Nominal-income targeting (2A/2AX)			No.	%
U.S. real GNP						
U.S. aggregate demand (A)	29	7	64	0	7	100
"Global" aggregate demand (B)	14	7	64	14	7	100
U.S. aggregate supply (C)	36	0	57	7	7	100
Oil price (E)	17	17	67	0	6	100
U.S. money demand (L)	0	17	77	7	5	100
U.S. employment						
U.S. aggregate demand (A)	50	0	50	0	2	100
"Global" aggregate demand (B)	50	0	50	0	2	100
U.S. aggregate supply (C)	50	0	50	0	2	100
Oil price (E)	0	50	50	0	2	100
U.S. money demand (L)	0	0	100	0	1	100
U.S. inflation rate[b]						
U.S. aggregate demand (A)	29	14	43	14	7	100
"Global" aggregate demand (B)	29	29	29	14	7	100
U.S. aggregate supply (C)	26	5	29	40	7	100
Oil price (E)	22	22	50	6	6	100
U.S. money demand (L)	0	17	77	7	5	100
U.S. price level[b]						
U.S. aggregate demand (A)	14	57	0	29	7	100
"Global" aggregate demand (B)	29	43	0	29	7	100
U.S. aggregate supply (C)	14	57	7	21	7	100
Oil price (E)	33	33	33	0	6	100
U.S. money demand (L)	0	67	27	7	5	100
U.S. short-term interest rate						
U.S. aggregate demand (A)	50	0	29	21	7	100
"Global" aggregate demand (B)	64	7	7	21	7	100
U.S. aggregate supply (C)	43	29	14	14	7	100
Oil price (E)	33	33	17	17	6	100
U.S. money demand (L)	0	67	27	7	5	100
U.S. long-term interest rate						
U.S. aggregate demand (A)	48	19	14	19	7	100
"Global" aggregate demand (B)	43	21	21	14	7	100
U.S. aggregate supply (C)	50	14	14	21	7	100
Oil price (E)	17	50	17	17	6	100
U.S. money demand (L)	0	57	37	7	5	100
U.S. real GNP + inflation						
U.S. aggregate demand (A)	29	11	54	7	7	100
"Global" aggregate demand (B)	21	18	46	14	7	100
U.S. aggregate supply (C)	31	2	43	24	7	100
Oil price (E)	19	19	58	3	6	100
U.S. money demand (L)	0	17	77	7	5	100

a. The regime type with maximum percentage value is denoted with shading. For cases in which the maximum percentage is also a majority (half or more of the model cases—that is, 50 percent or higher), the percentage value is shown in boldface type.

b. GNP deflator.

Table 4-13. *Ordinal Summary of Preferred Regimes across Models That Ran All Four Types of Regimes: Japanese Variables*[a]

	Percent of models preferring regime				Number of model cases	
Japanese variable and shock	Money targeting (1/1X)	Nominal-income targeting (2A/2AX)	Real-GNP-plus-inflation targeting (2B/2BX)	Exchange-rate targeting (3/3X)	No.	%
Japanese real GNP						
Japanese aggregate demand (I)	0	40	60	0	5	100
"Global" aggregate demand (B)	14	50	36	0	7	100
Japanese aggregate supply (J)	0	0	30	70	5	100
Oil price (E)	8	25	33	33	6	100
Japanese money demand (D)	14	40	26	19	7	100
Japanese employment						
Japanese aggregate demand (I)	0	100	0	0	1	100
"Global" aggregate demand (B)	50	50	0	0	2	100
Japanese aggregate supply (J)	0	100	0	0	1	100
Oil price (E)	50	50	0	0	2	100
Japanese money demand (D)	0	50	0	50	2	100
Japanese inflation rate[b]						
Japanese aggregate demand (I)	20	20	60	0	5	100
"Global" aggregate demand (B)	14	29	57	0	7	100
Japanese aggregate supply (J)	20	20	40	20	5	100
Oil price (E)	17	33	50	0	6	100
Japanese money demand (D)	0	38	52	10	7	100
Japanese price level[b]						
Japanese aggregate demand (I)	20	60	0	20	5	100
"Global" aggregate demand (B)	43	57	0	0	7	100
Japanese aggregate supply (J)	20	60	10	10	5	100
Oil price (E)	17	58	0	25	6	100
Japanese money demand (D)	14	62	19	5	7	100
Japanese short-term interest rate						
Japanese aggregate demand (I)	20	0	0	80	5	100
"Global" aggregate demand (B)	14	7	7	71	7	100
Japanese aggregate supply (J)	0	20	0	80	5	100
Oil price (E)	17	50	0	33	6	100
Japanese money demand (D)	14	19	5	62	7	100
Dollar-yen exchange rate						
Japanese aggregate demand (I)	0	0	0	100	5	100
"Global" aggregate demand (B)	29	0	0	71	7	100
Japanese aggregate supply (J)	0	0	0	100	5	100
Oil price (E)	8	0	0	92	6	100
Japanese money demand (D)	14	5	5	76	7	100
Japanese real GNP + inflation						
Japanese aggregate demand (I)	10	30	60	0	5	100
"Global" aggregate demand (B)	14	39	46	0	7	100
Japanese aggregate supply (J)	10	10	35	45	5	100
Oil price (E)	13	29	42	17	6	100
Japanese money demand (D)	7	39	39	14	7	100

a. The regime type with maximum percentage value is denoted with shading. For cases in which the maximum percentage is also a majority (half or more of the model cases—that is, 50 percent or higher), the percentage value is shown in boldface type.

b. GNP deflator.

Table 4-14. *Ordinal Summary of Preferred Regimes across Models That Ran All Four Types of Regimes: German Variables*[a]

German variable and shock	Percent of models preferring regime				Number of model cases	
	Money targeting (1/1X)	Nominal-income targeting (2A/2AX)	Real-GNP-plus-inflation targeting (2B/2BX)	Exchange-rate targeting (3/3X)	No.	%
German real GNP						
German aggregate demand (G)	0	**60**	20	20	5	100
"Global" aggregate demand (B)	14	36	**50**	0	7	100
German aggregate supply (H)	0	0	40	**60**	5	100
Oil price (E)	0	17	33	**50**	6	100
German money demand (K)	0	**57**	37	7	5	100
German employment						
German aggregate demand (G)	0	0	**100**	0	1	100
"Global" aggregate demand (B)	0	0	**100**	0	2	100
German aggregate supply (H)	0	0	**100**	0	1	100
Oil price (E)	0	0	**100**	0	2	100
German money demand (K)	0	0	**100**	0	1	100
German inflation rate[b]						
German aggregate demand (G)	0	30	10	**60**	5	100
"Global" aggregate demand (B)	43	14	21	21	7	100
German aggregate supply (H)	0	20	20	**60**	5	100
Oil price (E)	0	17	**50**	33	6	100
German money demand (K)	0	7	27	**67**	5	100
German price level[b]						
German aggregate demand (G)	**60**	20	0	20	5	100
"Global" aggregate demand (B)	43	29	14	14	7	100
German aggregate supply (H)	30	**50**	0	20	5	100
Oil price (E)	0	**67**	17	17	6	100
German money demand (K)	0	27	27	47	5	100
German short-term interest rate						
German aggregate demand (G)	0	0	0	**100**	5	100
"Global" aggregate demand (B)	29	7	21	43	7	100
German aggregate supply (H)	0	0	0	**100**	5	100
Oil price (E)	33	33	0	33	6	100
German money demand (K)	0	7	7	**87**	5	100
Dollar-DM exchange rate						
German aggregate demand (G)	0	0	0	**100**	5	100
"Global" aggregate demand (B)	14	14	0	**71**	7	100
German aggregate supply (H)	0	0	0	**100**	5	100
Oil price (E)	0	0	0	**100**	6	100
German money demand (K)	0	7	7	**87**	5	100
German real GNP + inflation						
German aggregate demand (G)	0	**45**	15	40	5	100
"Global" aggregate demand (B)	29	25	36	11	7	100
German aggregate supply (H)	0	10	30	**60**	5	100
Oil price (E)	0	17	42	42	6	100
German money demand (K)	0	32	32	37	5	100

a. The regime type with maximum percentage value is denoted with shading. For cases in which the maximum percentage is also a majority (half or more of the model cases—that is, 50 percent or higher), the percentage value is shown in boldface type.

b. GNP deflator.

are then computed by summing the total values assigned to each regime in any given column (across models) and dividing by the total number of models reporting results in that column. The second to last column in the table reports the number of model cases included in the calculation of the percentages in each row.

Tables 4-12–4-14 are based on averages of the seven models that ran shocks under all four types of regime. Three models—GEM, MPS, and MX3—did not run simulations under exchange-rate targeting (regime 3 or 3X) and are therefore excluded from the comparisons in tables 4-12–4-14. For some shocks, particularly those specific to Japan and Germany, the results are based on fewer than seven models, since some of the models did not run all of the shocks (see table 3-6 in chapter 3).

Analogous sets of summary statistics, encompassing all ten participating models but restricted to only three regime types (1/1X, 2A/2AX, and 2B/2BX), are shown in tables 4-15–4-17. In the large majority of cases where regime 3/3X is not the preferred regime among the seven-model results (reported in tables 4-12–4-14), the ten-model results in tables 4-15–4-17 provide a more comprehensive basis for selecting among the other three regimes.

The deviation-minimizing regimes can be spotted quickly in tables 4-12–4-17, variable by variable, because of two features of the tables' construction. The maximum percentage values for each variable are denoted by shading; cases where the maximum percentage is also a majority (half or more of the model cases—that is, 50 percent or higher) are denoted in bold print.

Consider first table 4-12, the comparison across all four regime types for the United States. In that table it can be seen at a glance that real-GNP-plus-inflation targeting is always preferred (across all shocks considered in the table) for real GNP, and in all cases the preference is strong (50 percent or greater). For the U.S. demand shock (A), for example, regime 2B/2BX is preferred by 64 percent (four and one-half out of seven) of the model cases for minimizing real GNP deviations, while money targeting (regime 1/1X) is preferred by 29 percent (two out of seven), and real GNP plus inflation targeting (regime 2A/2AX) by 7 percent (one-half out of seven) model cases.[54] For minimizing deviations of U.S. employment, regime 2B/2BX is preferred for the four goods-market demand and supply shocks, but that preference is shared equally (50 percent) with regime 1/1X in three of those cases and with regime 2A/2AX in the other one. In the case of the U.S. inflation rate, regime 2B/2BX is preferred for four of the five shocks, but only weakly so for aggregate demand shocks. The one exception to the choice of regime 2B/2BX for U.S. inflation is under the aggregate supply shock, in which case exchange-rate targeting (regime 3/3X) is given a weak preference (the only instance in which that regime is selected

---

54. The one-half entry, of course, reflects a tie between regimes 2A and 2B in one case.

Table 4-15. *Ordinal Summary of Preferred Regimes across Models for Regime Types Other Than Exchange-Rate Targeting: U.S. Variables[a]*

	Percent of models preferring regime			Number of model cases	
U.S. variable and shock	Money targeting (1/1X)	Nominal-income targeting (2A/2AX)	Real-GNP-plus-inflation targeting (2B/2BX)	No.	%
U.S. real GNP					
U.S. aggregate demand (A)	23	13	63	10	100
"Global" aggregate demand (B)	15	15	70	9	100
U.S. aggregate supply (C)	40	5	55	10	100
Oil price (E)	13	13	75	8	100
U.S. money demand (L)	0	29	71	7	100
U.S. employment					
U.S. aggregate demand (A)	25	0	75	4	100
"Global" aggregate demand (B)	33	0	67	3	100
U.S. aggregate supply (C)	50	0	50	4	100
Oil price (E)	25	25	50	4	100
U.S. money demand (L)	0	25	75	2	100
U.S. inflation rate[b]					
U.S. aggregate demand (A)	30	20	50	10	100
"Global" aggregate demand (B)	33	33	33	9	100
U.S. aggregate supply (C)	42	12	47	10	100
Oil price (E)	23	29	48	8	100
U.S. money demand (L)	0	43	57	7	100
U.S. price level[b]					
U.S. aggregate demand (A)	20	80	0	10	100
"Global" aggregate demand (B)	44	56	0	9	100
U.S. aggregate supply (C)	23	63	13	10	100
Oil price (E)	38	38	25	8	100
U.S. money demand (L)	0	64	36	7	100
U.S. short-term interest rate					
U.S. aggregate demand (A)	80	0	20	10	100
"Global" aggregate demand (B)	89	6	6	9	100
U.S. aggregate supply (C)	70	20	10	10	100
Oil price (E)	63	25	13	8	100
U.S. money demand (L)	0	64	36	7	100
U.S. long-term interest rate					
U.S. aggregate demand (A)	72	17	11	9	100
"Global" aggregate demand (B)	63	19	19	8	100
U.S. aggregate supply (C)	56	33	11	9	100
Oil price (E)	13	63	25	8	100
U.S. money demand (L)	0	67	33	6	100
U.S. real GNP + inflation					
U.S. aggregate demand (A)	27	17	57	10	100
"Global" aggregate demand (B)	24	24	52	9	100
U.S. aggregate supply (C)	41	8	51	10	100
Oil price (E)	18	21	61	8	100
U.S. money demand (L)	0	36	64	7	100

a. The regime type with maximum percentage value is denoted with shading. For cases in which the maximum percentage is also a majority (half or more of the model cases—that is, 50 percent or higher), the percentage value is shown in boldface type.

b. GNP deflator.

Table 4-16. *Ordinal Summary of Preferred Regimes across Models for Regime Types Other Than Exchange-Rate Targeting: Japanese Variables*[a]

	Percent of models preferring regime			Number of model cases	
Japanese variable and shock	Money targeting (1/1X)	Nominal-income targeting (2A/2AX)	Real-GNP-plus-inflation targeting (2B/2BX)	No.	%
Japanese real GNP					
Japanese aggregate demand (I)	0	36	64	7	100
"Global" aggregate demand (B)	11	39	50	9	100
Japanese aggregate supply (J)	33	33	33	6	100
Oil price (E)	21	36	43	7	100
Japanese money demand (D)	13	38	50	8	100
Japanese employment					
Japanese aggregate demand (I)	0	50	50	2	100
"Global" aggregate demand (B)	33	33	33	3	100
Japanese aggregate supply (J)	0	100	0	1	100
Oil price (E)	33	67	0	3	100
Japanese money demand (D)	0	50	50	2	100
Japanese inflation rate[b]					
Japanese aggregate demand (I)	14	29	57	7	100
"Global" aggregate demand (B)	11	33	56	9	100
Japanese aggregate supply (J)	22	39	39	6	100
Oil price (E)	14	36	50	7	100
Japanese money demand (D)	0	50	50	8	100
Japanese price level[b]					
Japanese aggregate demand (I)	29	71	0	7	100
"Global" aggregate demand (B)	33	67	0	9	100
Japanese aggregate supply (J)	17	67	17	6	100
Oil price (E)	14	57	29	7	100
Japanese money demand (D)	13	69	19	8	100
Japanese short-term interest rate					
Japanese aggregate demand (I)	100	0	0	7	100
"Global" aggregate demand (B)	78	6	17	9	100
Japanese aggregate supply (J)	67	33	0	6	100
Oil price (E)	57	43	0	7	100
Japanese money demand (D)	13	69	19	8	100
Japanese long-term interest rate					
Japanese aggregate demand (I)	57	29	14	7	100
"Global" aggregate demand (B)	89	11	0	9	100
Japanese aggregate supply (J)	67	33	0	6	100
Oil price (E)	57	29	14	7	100
Japanese money demand (D)	25	31	44	8	100
Japanese real GNP + inflation					
Japanese aggregate demand (I)	7	32	61	7	100
"Global" aggregate demand (B)	11	36	53	9	100
Japanese aggregate supply (J)	28	36	36	6	100
Oil price (E)	18	36	46	7	100
Japanese money demand (D)	6	44	50	8	100

a. The regime type with maximum percentage value is denoted with shading. For cases in which the maximum percentage is also a majority (half or more of the model cases—that is, 50 percent or higher), the percentage value is shown in boldface type.

b. GNP deflator.

Table 4-17. *Ordinal Summary of Preferred Regimes across Models for Regime Types Other Than Exchange-Rate Targeting: German Variables*[a]

	Percent of models preferring regime			Number of model cases	
German variable and shock	Money targeting (1/1X)	Nominal-income targeting (2A/2AX)	Real-GNP-plus-inflation targeting (2B/2BX)	No.	%
German real GNP					
German aggregate demand (G)	12	55	33	7	100
"Global" aggregate demand (B)	15	31	54	9	100
German aggregate supply (H)	14	14	71	7	100
Oil price (E)	7	36	57	7	100
German money demand (K)	0	50	50	6	100
German employment					
German aggregate demand (G)	0	0	100	2	100
"Global" aggregate demand (B)	0	0	100	3	100
German aggregate supply (H)	0	0	100	2	100
Oil price (E)	0	33	67	3	100
German money demand (K)	0	0	100	1	100
German inflation rate[b]					
German aggregate demand (G)	29	36	36	7	100
"Global" aggregate demand (B)	44	22	33	9	100
German aggregate supply (H)	40	40	19	7	100
Oil price (E)	36	21	43	7	100
German money demand (K)	0	58	42	6	100
German price level[b]					
German aggregate demand (G)	57	43	0	7	100
"Global" aggregate demand (B)	33	56	11	9	100
German aggregate supply (H)	26	55	19	7	100
Oil price (E)	14	71	14	7	100
German money demand (K)	0	75	25	6	100
German short-term interest rate					
German aggregate demand (G)	100	0	0	7	100
"Global" aggregate demand (B)	78	6	17	9	100
German aggregate supply (H)	86	14	0	7	100
Oil price (E)	71	29	0	7	100
German money demand (K)	0	67	33	6	100
Dollar-DM exchange rate					
German aggregate demand (G)	71	29	0	7	100
"Global" aggregate demand (B)	56	22	22	9	100
German aggregate supply (H)	86	14	0	7	100
Oil price (E)	43	43	14	7	100
German money demand (K)	0	67	33	6	100
German real GNP + inflation					
German aggregate demand (G)	20	45	35	7	100
"Global" aggregate demand (B)	30	27	44	9	100
German aggregate supply (H)	27	27	45	7	100
Oil price (E)	21	29	50	7	100
German money demand (K)	0	54	46	6	100

a. The regime type with maximum percentage value is denoted with shading. For cases in which the maximum percentage is also a majority (half or more of the model cases—that is, 50 percent or higher), the percentage value is shown in boldface type.

b. GNP deflator.

for the United States). For the U.S. price level, regime 2A/2AX is preferred for all five shocks and strongly so for three of the five. This result reflects the greater weight placed on stabilizing the price level in that regime than in the others.

Regime preferences for minimizing interest-rate deviations are split between money targeting and nominal-income targeting; regime 1/1X is generally preferred for demand shocks and the U.S. supply shock, whereas regime 2A/2AX is preferred for the oil price and U.S. money-demand shocks. In the final rows of the table, we also report results for a simple loss function combining real GNP and inflation with equal weights; this loss function is one of those used in chapter 5. For this loss function, real-GNP-plus-inflation targeting clearly dominates (by a majority of the models in three out of five shocks).

With one or two exceptions, the rankings for the United States for the seven-model results in table 4-12 are confirmed by the ten-model results reported in table 4-15 (where the ranking is across only regime types 1/1X, 2A/2AX, and 2B/2BX). For the ten models the preference for regime 2B/2BX (relative to 1/1X and 2A/2AX) is strengthened somewhat for employment and inflation in the case of aggregate demand shocks. The preference for regime 2A/2AX in the case of the price level is also strengthened, across all shocks.

In the case of Japan (table 4-13), nominal-income targeting is strongly preferred, across nearly all shocks, for minimizing price-level variation; real-GNP-plus-inflation targeting is strongly preferred for minimizing inflation deviations; and, with only one exception, exchange-rate targeting is strongly preferred for minimizing variation in interest rates and exchange rates. The ranking results for Japanese real GNP are mixed. Regime 2B/2BX is favored for the Japanese aggregate demand shock; regime 2A/2AX is preferred for the global demand and Japanese money-demand shocks; and exchange-rate targeting is preferred for supply shocks. Regime 2A/2AX tends to be favored for minimizing employment deviations for the small number of model cases available. For the loss function combining real GNP and inflation, however, regime 2B/2BX is a winner in four out of five cases (the Japanese supply shock being the exception—in which case regime 3/3X is selected). This result for the simple loss function is confirmed by the ranking comparison for the larger group of models in table 4-16. As shown in that table, when exchange-rate targeting is dropped from the comparison for the larger set of models, regime 2B/2BX comes through more clearly as the choice for real GNP across all shocks; it also gains ground on regime 2A/2AX for employment.

The German results exhibit still more diversity across regimes (tables 4-14 and 4-17). Real-GNP-plus-inflation targeting and nominal GNP targeting are preferred in several instances for real GNP and employment, whereas exchange-rate targeting is preferred in others, doing well particularly for GNP in the presence of the supply shocks. Regime 3/3X also wins convincingly for minimizing variation in inflation and interest rates for three shocks (German goods demand, German supply, and German money demand) and for minimizing variation in the dollar-deutsche-mark exchange rate in all cases. Regimes 1/1X and 2A/2AX are preferred about evenly with respect to the price level. For minimizing deviations in real GNP and inflation together, preferences are split among regimes 2B/2BX, 3/3X, and 2A/2AX for most shocks, with the favored regime having less than 50 percent of the model cases. The ranking comparisons in table 4-17 are less meaningful in the German case because of the frequency with which exchange-rate targeting is chosen in the rankings for the smaller group of models.

In sum, if one were to select a "globally preferred" regime type for the United States, the ordinal rankings summarized in tables 4-12–4-17 point fairly strongly to real-GNP-plus-inflation targeting, unless variation in either interest rates or the price level (as opposed to the inflation rate) is assumed to figure prominently in policymakers' loss functions. Real-GNP-plus-inflation targeting is consistently picked ahead of the other regime types for purposes of damping the effects of each of the shocks on U.S. real GNP and inflation together. Regime 2B/2BX also appears to be favored for Japan on this basis. In the case of Germany, however, there is no clear favorite for a regime type that minimizes deviations from either demand shocks or supply shocks (or both). All four types of regime are preferred for different variables under different types of shocks. Exchange-rate targeting, while not predominant in the German case, figures much more prominently in that country than in the United States and somewhat more than in Japan.

These summary observations should be interpreted with caution. In about 50 percent of the cases considered (across models, shocks, and variables), the ordinal ranking of regimes at the individual model level is based on a relatively flat distribution of summary statistics.[55] That is, in as many as half the cases, inadequate weight might be given to a regime type that was narrowly edged out of first place in some models and strongly preferred over all other regime types by other models. For this reason we have chosen also to consider a second method of aggregating the results across models that gives more weight to differences in the degree of preferences across models.

Cardinal Rankings of Regime Performance

We turn now to "cardinal" rankings of regime performance across the models, again drawing from the larger set of summary statistics presented in table 4-2 and the analogous tables for each model. The cardinal rankings are computed by averaging across models the *RCS%D* and *RCSD* statistics for each shock

---

55. Recall that only about half of the ordinal selections or "preferences" at the individual model level were significant in the sense that they passed our "10 percent rule" as described at the beginning of this section.

and variable over the whole simulation period. These results are presented in tables 4-18–4-23. A separate table is shown for each of the G3 countries, first comparing results for the seven models that ran all four types of regime (tables 4-18–4-20) and then comparing all ten models but excluding the results for exchange-rate targeting (tables 4-21–4-23). As with tables 4-12–4-17, shading is used to indicate the regime type that yields the minimum *RCSD* or *RCS%D* (in tables 4-18–4-23, the arithmetic mean across the models). Bold print is again used to denote a degree of significance in the regime selection; that is, numbers in bold identify cases in which the *RCSD* or *RCS%D* under the preferred regime is at least 10 percent less than that of the second-place regime.

For the United States, the cardinal rankings (table 4-18) are consistent with the ordinal rankings in many respects. Real-GNP-plus-inflation targeting is selected on average as the deviation-minimizing regime for real GNP and employment for most shocks. Nominal-income targeting is most often preferred for minimizing deviations in the price level. Money targeting tends to minimize deviations most often for interest rates. Exchange-rate targeting never emerges as the preferred regime. In addition, regimes 2A/2AX and 2B/2BX are always strongly preferred for money-demand shocks across all variables. However, the extent to which those two regimes are ranked about equally (and to which both are strongly preferred over the other regimes) for all variables under money-demand shocks shows up much more clearly in the cardinal rankings than in the ordinal rankings.

The cardinal rankings differ more substantively from the ordinal rankings in several other respects. Nominal-income targeting is slightly preferred for min-imizing deviations in both real GNP and the sum of real GNP plus inflation in the case of the U.S. aggregate demand shock (whereas real-GNP-plus-inflation targeting is clearly favored in the ordinal rankings). In the case of employment under aggregate demand shocks, preference shifts from money targeting in the ordinal rankings to regimes 2A/2AX and 2B/2BX in the cardinal rankings. And, the choice for the price level under aggregate demand shocks shifts from nominal-income targeting in the ordinal results (table 4-12) to money targeting in the cardinal results (table 4-18).

The ten-model results for the United States in table 4-21 generally tend to confirm the seven-model results in table 4-18. However, the preference for money targeting with respect to the price level in table 4-18 disappears in table 4-21 and is switched back to nominal-income targeting for the aggregate demand shocks.

For Japan too, the cardinal rankings of regimes, though somewhat more dispersed than the ordinal rankings, tend to confirm those rankings in most cases. One notable exception is that the regime of preference for both Japanese inflation and inflation plus GNP shifts from 2B/2BX in the ordinal rankings (table 4-13) to regime 2A/2AX in the cardinal rankings for most of the shocks.

Table 4-18. *Cardinal Summary of Preferred Regimes across Models That Ran All Four Types of Regimes: U.S. Variables*[a]

| U.S. variable and shock | Average root cumulative squared deviation from baseline | | | | Number of model cases |
	Money targeting (1/1X)	Nominal-income targeting (2A/2AX)	Real-GNP-plus-inflation targeting (2B/2BX)	Exchange-rate targeting (3/3X)	
U.S. real GNP					
U.S. aggregate demand (A)	1.0584	0.9043	0.9381	1.4118	7
"Global" aggregate demand (B)	1.1896	1.0189	0.9470	1.5199	7
U.S. aggregate supply (C)	0.6661	0.6820	0.6345	1.2210	7
Oil price (E)	0.6792	0.6733	**0.5333**	0.9083	6
U.S. money demand (L)	0.2940	0.0066	0.0062	0.2214	5
U.S. employment					
U.S. aggregate demand (A)	1.4377	0.6691	0.6705	1.5380	2
"Global" aggregate demand (B)	1.6335	0.6179	0.6388	1.7375	2
U.S. aggregate supply (C)	0.8728	0.8531	0.7063	0.8879	2
Oil price (E)	0.7748	0.7273	**0.5448**	0.7706	2
U.S. money demand (L)	0.3615	0.0022	0.0017	0.3540	1
U.S. inflation rate[b]					
U.S. aggregate demand (A)	0.2649	0.2530	0.3032	0.4846	7
"Global" aggregate demand (B)	0.3287	0.2571	0.3147	0.5324	7
U.S. aggregate supply (C)	1.2875	1.2799	1.2550	1.2341	7
Oil price (E)	0.7437	0.8011	**0.6748**	0.9661	6
U.S. money demand (L)	0.2478	0.0013	0.0008	0.1099	5
U.S. price level[b]					
U.S. aggregate demand (A)	**0.6790**	0.7556	1.3229	1.6713	7
"Global" aggregate demand (B)	**0.8695**	0.9520	1.3939	1.8603	7
U.S. aggregate supply (C)	1.1958	1.1056	1.6653	1.2834	7
Oil price (E)	0.8792	**0.7381**	0.9148	0.9662	6
U.S. money demand (L)	0.3778	0.0022	0.0029	0.3101	5
U.S. short-term interest rate					
U.S. aggregate demand (A)	**0.8118**	1.2194	1.3707	0.9230	7
"Global" aggregate demand (B)	**0.8937**	1.2475	1.5307	1.0163	7
U.S. aggregate supply (C)	**0.4709**	0.8202	2.1460	0.8034	7
Oil price (E)	0.5063	**0.4366**	1.2250	0.9504	6
U.S. money demand (L)	0.5164	0.0090	0.0120	0.5023	5
U.S. long-term interest rate					
U.S. aggregate demand (A)	**0.2563**	0.3219	0.3530	0.3349	7
"Global" aggregate demand (B)	**0.2949**	0.3226	0.3766	0.4078	7
U.S. aggregate supply (C)	**0.2035**	0.2568	0.4689	0.5604	7
Oil price (E)	0.2151	**0.2001**	0.2882	0.3213	6
U.S. money demand (L)	0.1131	0.0019	0.0021	0.1365	5
U.S. real GNP + inflation					
U.S. aggregate demand (A)	1.3234	1.1573	1.2413	1.8964	7
"Global" aggregate demand (B)	1.5183	1.2760	1.2617	2.0522	7
U.S. aggregate supply (C)	1.9536	1.9619	1.8895	2.4551	7
Oil price (E)	1.4228	1.4744	**1.2080**	1.8744	6
U.S. money demand (L)	0.5418	0.0079	0.0070	0.3313	5

a. The regime type with minimum *RCSD* or *RCS%D* ("preferred" regime) is denoted with shading. For cases in which the *RCSD* or *RCS%D* under the preferred regime is at least 10 percent less than the second-place regime, the value is shown in boldface type.

b. GNP deflator.

Table 4-19. *Cardinal Summary of Preferred Regimes across Models That Ran All Four Types of Regimes: Japanese Variables*[a]

Japanese variable and shock	Average root cumulative squared deviation from baseline				Number of model cases
	Money targeting (1/1X)	Nominal-income targeting (2A/2AX)	Real-GNP-plus-inflation targeting (2B/2BX)	Exchange-rate targeting (3/3X)	
Japanese real GNP					
Japanese aggregate demand (1)	1.1253	0.7511	0.7635	1.3564	5
"Global" aggregate demand (B)	1.2460	0.8973	0.8842	2.1937	7
Japanese aggregate supply (J)	0.6609	0.6717	0.8421	0.5351	5
Oil price (E)	0.2666	0.2598	0.2924	0.5935	6
Japanese money demand (D)	0.4038	0.0065	0.0061	0.0093	7
Japanese employment					
Japanese aggregate demand (I)	2.1650	0.0000	0.2770	3.4900	1
"Global" aggregate demand (B)	1.6341	0.1754	0.2769	1.9908	2
Japanese aggregate supply (J)	0.4220	0.0000	0.1050	0.6940	1
Oil price (E)	0.2946	0.0398	0.0456	0.3325	2
Japanese money demand (D)	0.3420	0.0005	0.0013	0.0107	2
Japanese inflation rate[b]					
Japanese aggregate demand (I)	0.3397	0.3219	0.3197	0.5636	5
"Global" aggregate demand (B)	0.3553	0.2203	0.2672	1.0370	7
Japanese aggregate supply (J)	1.2319	1.1821	1.2570	1.3563	5
Oil price (E)	0.3780	0.3621	0.3648	0.4981	6
Japanese money demand (D)	0.2423	0.0017	0.0015	0.0031	7
Japanese price level[b]					
Japanese aggregate demand (I)	0.5324	0.4062	1.1135	1.0875	5
"Global" aggregate demand (B)	0.6056	0.4441	0.8496	2.1346	7
Japanese aggregate supply (J)	0.9456	0.8945	1.7997	1.1263	5
Oil price (E)	0.5350	0.3866	0.8112	0.7817	6
Japanese money demand (D)	0.3656	0.0024	0.0033	0.0055	7
Japanese short-term interest rate					
Japanese aggregate demand (I)	0.9581	1.3345	1.6557	0.1752	5
"Global" aggregate demand (B)	1.0324	1.4259	1.6848	1.0879	7
Japanese aggregate supply (J)	0.4995	0.5983	2.6066	0.0994	5
Oil price (E)	0.3624	0.3575	0.9917	0.6265	6
Japanese money demand (D)	0.7326	0.0084	0.0111	0.0004	7
Dollar-yen exchange rate					
Japanese aggregate demand (I)	1.5939	1.5381	1.6927	0.0254	5
"Global" aggregate demand (B)	0.5262	1.3321	1.5118	1.0008	7
Japanese aggregate supply (J)	0.5770	0.6543	2.6481	0.0196	5
Oil price (E)	1.1255	0.9251	1.3536	0.1924	6
Japanese money demand (D)	1.3793	0.0100	0.0116	0.0002	7
Japanese real GNP + inflation					
Japanese aggregate demand (I)	1.4651	1.0730	1.0832	1.9200	5
"Global" aggregate demand (B)	1.6013	1.1176	1.1514	3.2307	7
Japanese aggregate supply (J)	1.8928	1.8538	2.0991	1.8914	5
Oil price (E)	0.6446	0.6220	0.6572	1.0916	6
Japanese money demand (D)	0.6461	0.0082	0.0076	0.0124	7

a. The regime type with minimum *RCSD* or *RCS%D* ("preferred" regime) is denoted with shading. For cases in which the *RCSD* or *RCS%D* under the preferred regime is at least 10 percent less than the second-place regime, the value is shown in boldface type.

b. GNP deflator.

Table 4-20. *Cardinal Summary of Preferred Regimes across Models That Ran All Four Types of Regimes: German Variables*[a]

German variable and shock	Average root cumulative squared deviation from baseline				Number of model cases
	Money targeting (1/1X)	Nominal-income targeting (2A/2AX)	Real-GNP-plus-inflation targeting (2B/2BX)	Exchange-rate targeting (3/3X)	
German real GNP					
German aggregate demand (G)	0.9553	0.8056	0.9380	1.1173	5
"Global" aggregate demand (B)	1.1118	0.9418	0.9537	1.4388	7
German aggregate supply (H)	0.6921	0.6953	0.9460	0.6031	5
Oil price (E)	0.4019	0.3816	0.3304	0.5573	6
German money demand (K)	0.2376	0.0076	0.0078	0.0112	5
German employment					
German aggregate demand (G)	1.1897	0.7938	0.4300	2.0204	1
"Global" aggregate demand (B)	1.4099	0.5598	0.4087	1.5276	2
German aggregate supply (H)	1.0324	0.9286	0.6942	1.0952	1
Oil price (E)	0.6818	0.4777	0.2706	0.6719	2
German money demand (K)	0.4181	0.0052	0.0036	0.0117	1
German inflation rate[b]					
German aggregate demand (G)	0.3108	0.6106	0.4935	0.3544	5
"Global" aggregate demand (B)	0.3112	0.5168	0.3654	0.4609	7
German aggregate supply (H)	1.3605	1.4275	1.4755	1.4391	5
Oil price (E)	0.5308	0.5233	0.4531	0.6257	6
German money demand (K)	0.3339	0.0066	0.0036	0.0026	5
German price level[b]					
German aggregate demand (G)	0.4043	0.5064	0.7969	0.6425	5
"Global" aggregate demand (B)	0.7094	0.7873	1.2134	1.4043	7
German aggregate supply (H)	1.0246	1.0015	1.8136	1.1538	5
Oil price (E)	0.6636	0.4912	0.6113	0.9222	6
German money demand (K)	0.3355	0.0043	0.0035	0.0050	5
German short-term interest rate					
German aggregate demand (G)	0.7228	1.2842	1.2665	0.1673	5
"Global" aggregate demand (B)	0.8632	1.3936	1.4336	0.8697	7
German aggregate supply (H)	0.4270	0.7225	2.1007	0.0973	5
Oil price (E)	0.4444	0.4837	1.0156	0.6301	6
German money demand (K)	0.5453	0.0126	0.0117	0.0002	5
Dollar-DM exchange rate					
German aggregate demand (G)	1.0740	1.5395	1.5182	0.0133	5
"Global" aggregate demand (B)	0.5813	1.3179	1.8073	0.6201	7
German aggregate supply (H)	0.5321	0.8794	2.7792	0.0133	5
Oil price (E)	0.9222	0.9402	1.1416	0.1844	6
German money demand (K)	0.7672	0.0129	0.0105	0.0001	5
German real GNP + inflation					
German aggregate demand (G)	1.2661	1.4163	1.4315	1.4717	5
"Global" aggregate demand (B)	1.4230	1.4587	1.3191	1.8997	7
German aggregate supply (H)	2.0525	2.1227	2.4215	2.0422	5
Oil price (E)	0.9326	0.9050	0.7835	1.1830	6
German money demand (K)	0.5715	0.0142	0.0114	0.0138	5

a. The regime type with minimum *RCSD* or *RCS%D* ("preferred" regime) is denoted with shading. For cases in which the *RCSD* or *RCS%D* under the preferred regime is at least 10 percent less than the second-place regime, the value is shown in boldface type.

b. GNP deflator.

Table 4-21. *Cardinal Summary of Preferred Regimes across Models for Regime Types Other Than Exchange-Rate Targeting: U.S. Variables*[a]

	Average root cumulative squared deviation from baseline			
U.S. variable and shock	Money targeting (1/1X)	Nominal-income targeting (2A/2AX)	Real-GNP-plus-inflation targeting (2B/2BX)	Number of model cases
U.S. real GNP				
U.S. aggregate demand (A)	1.0358	0.9005	0.9200	10
"Global" aggregate demand (B)	1.1145	0.9762	0.9196	9
U.S. aggregate supply (C)	0.6226	0.6464	0.5694	10
Oil price (E)	0.6181	0.5745	**0.4606**	8
U.S. money demand (L)	0.6596	0.0105	**0.0075**	7
U.S. employment				
U.S. aggregate demand (A)	0.9882	0.5397	0.5241	4
"Global" aggregate demand (B)	1.2229	0.5402	0.5501	3
U.S. aggregate supply (C)	0.6421	0.6413	0.5180	4
Oil price (E)	0.5458	0.4643	**0.3561**	4
U.S. money demand (L)	1.3347	0.0011	**0.0009**	2
U.S. inflation rate[b]				
U.S. aggregate demand (A)	0.8230	0.7029	0.7244	10
"Global" aggregate demand (B)	0.9544	0.8212	0.7654	9
U.S. aggregate supply (C)	0.5675	0.5747	0.5346	10
Oil price (E)	0.6902	0.6807	**0.5752**	8
U.S. money demand (L)	0.4238	0.0069	0.0078	7
U.S. price level[b]				
U.S. aggregate demand (A)	0.4212	0.1922	0.2087	10
"Global" aggregate demand (B)	0.4253	0.1859	0.2004	9
U.S. aggregate supply (C)	0.3172	0.2714	0.2734	10
Oil price (E)	0.3665	0.3042	0.3201	8
U.S. money demand (L)	0.6778	0.0050	0.0078	7
U.S. short-term interest rate				
U.S. aggregate demand (A)	**0.6525**	1.1178	1.2257	10
"Global" aggregate demand (B)	**0.7279**	1.1037	1.3254	9
U.S. aggregate supply (C)	**0.3935**	0.7541	1.7079	10
Oil price (E)	0.4352	0.3913	1.0162	8
U.S. money demand (L)	0.9103	0.0102	0.0112	7
U.S. long-term interest rate				
U.S. aggregate demand (A)	**0.6651**	0.9920	1.1106	9
"Global" aggregate demand (B)	**0.7867**	1.1038	1.3515	8
U.S. aggregate supply (C)	**0.3939**	0.6626	1.7009	9
Oil price (E)	0.4183	0.3558	0.9537	8
U.S. money demand (L)	0.5777	0.0075	0.0100	6
U.S. real GNP + inflation				
U.S. aggregate demand (A)	1.8588	1.6034	1.6444	10
"Global" aggregate demand (B)	2.0689	1.7974	1.6850	9
U.S. aggregate supply (C)	1.1901	1.2211	1.1041	10
Oil price (E)	1.3083	1.2552	**1.0358**	8
U.S. money demand (L)	1.0834	0.0174	**0.0153**	7

a. The regime type with minimum *RCSD* or *RCS%D* ("preferred" regime) is denoted with shading. For cases in which the *RCSD* or *RCS%D* under the preferred regime is at least 10 percent less than the second-place regime, the value is shown in boldface type.

b. GNP deflator.

Table 4-22. *Cardinal Summary of Preferred Regimes across Models for Regime Types Other Than Exchange-Rate Targeting: Japanese Variables*[a]

	Average root cumulative squared deviation from baseline			
Japanese variable and shock	*Money targeting (1/1X)*	*Nominal-income targeting (2A/2AX)*	*Real-GNP-plus-inflation targeting (2B/2BX)*	*Number of model cases*
Japanese real GNP				
Japanese aggregate demand (I)	1.0653	0.7596	0.7616	7
"Global" aggregate demand (B)	1.1979	0.8946	0.8773	9
Japanese aggregate supply (J)	0.7762	0.6747	0.8327	6
Oil price (E)	0.3246	0.2880	0.3176	7
Japanese money demand (D)	0.4285	0.0371	0.0193	8
Japanese employment				
Japanese aggregate demand (I)	1.1701	0.0827	0.2198	2
"Global" aggregate demand (B)	1.1636	0.1861	0.2511	3
Japanese aggregate supply (J)	0.4220	0.0000	0.1050	1
Oil price (E)	0.2463	0.0573	0.0625	3
Japanese money demand (D)	0.3420	0.0005	0.0013	2
Japanese inflation rate[b]				
Japanese aggregate demand (I)	0.9405	0.5892	0.6715	7
"Global" aggregate demand (B)	1.0819	0.7431	0.7891	9
Japanese aggregate supply (J)	0.8182	0.6397	0.9664	6
Oil price (E)	0.2735	0.2651	0.2928	7
Japanese money demand (D)	0.4696	0.0439	0.1088	8
Japanese price level[b]				
Japanese aggregate demand (I)	0.5144	0.0973	0.2740	7
"Global" aggregate demand (B)	0.5493	0.1281	0.2542	9
Japanese aggregate supply (J)	0.4305	0.1185	0.5932	6
Oil price (E)	0.1872	0.0822	0.0783	7
Japanese money demand (D)	0.2366	0.0617	0.1775	8
Japanese short-term interest rate				
Japanese aggregate demand (I)	0.7784	1.1418	1.4553	7
"Global" aggregate demand (B)	0.8801	1.2612	1.5282	9
Japanese aggregate supply (J)	0.5915	0.7482	2.6038	6
Oil price (E)	0.3298	0.3377	0.8735	7
Japanese money demand (D)	0.7760	0.0885	0.1796	8
Dollar-yen exchange rate				
Japanese aggregate demand (I)	1.5408	1.5347	1.7988	7
"Global" aggregate demand (B)	0.7342	1.3706	1.6149	9
Japanese aggregate supply (J)	1.0087	1.1346	3.1784	6
Oil price (E)	1.1466	0.8685	1.1981	7
Japanese money demand (D)	1.5541	0.3820	0.4847	8
Japanese real GNP + inflation				
Japanese aggregate demand (I)	2.0058	1.3488	1.4331	7
"Global" aggregate demand (B)	2.2798	1.6376	1.6664	9
Japanese aggregate supply (J)	1.5943	1.3144	1.7991	6
Oil price (E)	0.5982	0.5531	0.6104	7
Japanese money demand (D)	0.8981	0.0809	0.1281	8

a. The regime type with minimum *RCSD* or *RCS%D* ("preferred" regime) is denoted with shading. For cases in which the *RCSD* or *RCS%D* under the preferred regime is at least 10 percent less than the second-place regime, the value is shown in boldface type.

b. GNP deflator.

Table 4-23. *Cardinal Summary of Preferred Regimes across Models for Regime Types Other Than Exchange-Rate Targeting: German Variables*[a]

| German variable and shock | Average root cumulative squared deviation from baseline | | | |
	Money targeting (1/1X)	Nominal-income targeting (2A/2AX)	Real-GNP-plus-inflation targeting (2B/2BX)	Number of model cases
German real GNP				
German aggregate demand (G)	0.9085	0.7975	0.8903	7
"Global" aggregate demand (B)	1.0615	0.9271	0.9336	9
German aggregate supply (H)	0.6096	0.6082	0.7835	7
Oil price (E)	0.3966	0.3794	0.3377	7
German money demand (K)	0.2216	0.0291	**0.0124**	6
German employment				
German aggregate demand (G)	0.7452	0.5447	**0.3611**	2
"Global" aggregate demand (B)	1.0711	0.5019	**0.3966**	3
German aggregate supply (H)	0.5526	0.5029	**0.3777**	2
Oil price (E)	0.5189	0.3818	**0.2519**	3
German money demand (K)	0.4181	0.0052	**0.0036**	1
German inflation rate[b]				
German aggregate demand (G)	0.7166	**0.6072**	0.7066	7
"Global" aggregate demand (B)	0.9004	**0.7657**	0.7777	9
German aggregate supply (H)	0.5328	0.5337	0.7196	7
Oil price (E)	0.3826	0.3653	**0.3220**	7
German money demand (K)	0.2051	**0.0111**	0.0200	6
German price level[b]				
German aggregate demand (G)	0.2476	0.1735	0.1622	7
"Global" aggregate demand (B)	0.4417	0.2099	0.2116	9
German aggregate supply (H)	0.2147	0.1863	0.1883	7
Oil price (E)	0.2835	0.2144	0.1947	7
German money demand (K)	0.1094	**0.0240**	0.0633	6
German short-term interest rate				
German aggregate demand (G)	**0.5801**	1.0791	1.0742	7
"Global" aggregate demand (B)	**0.7242**	1.2138	1.2507	9
German aggregate supply (H)	**0.3624**	0.6577	1.6418	7
Oil price (E)	**0.3954**	0.4394	0.8927	7
German money demand (K)	0.6290	**0.0207**	0.0282	6
Dollar-DM exchange rate				
German aggregate demand (G)	**0.8122**	1.1502	1.1732	7
"Global" aggregate demand (B)	**0.5234**	1.0879	1.4623	9
German aggregate supply (H)	**0.4184**	0.6703	2.0593	7
Oil price (E)	0.8368	0.8240	1.0796	7
German money demand (K)	0.7008	**0.0306**	0.0622	6
German real GNP + inflation				
German aggregate demand (G)	1.6251	1.4047	1.5969	7
"Global" aggregate demand (B)	1.9619	1.6928	1.7113	9
German aggregate supply (H)	1.1424	1.1419	1.5031	7
Oil price (E)	0.7792	0.7448	0.6596	7
German money demand (K)	0.4267	0.0401	**0.0323**	6

a. The regime type with minimum *RCSD* or *RCS%D* ("preferred" regime) is denoted with shading. For cases in which the *RCSD* or *RCS%D* under the preferred regime is at least 10 percent less than the second-place regime, the value is shown in boldface type.

b. GNP deflator.

Another difference is that money targeting gets a noticeably stronger preference for stabilizing interest rates and exchange rates in the cardinal results than in the ordinal results, although this difference is much less evident when the often preferred exchange-rate targeting regime is dropped (compare tables 4-16 and 4-22).

For Germany, the ordinal rankings of regime performance exhibited considerable dispersion to begin with, and that dispersion persists and may even increase in the cardinal rankings, shown in table 4-20. When compared with the ordinal rankings (table 4-14), money targeting and real-GNP-plus-inflation targeting gain, whereas exchange-rate targeting loses ground. The gain in real GNP plus inflation targeting is primarily for inflation and real GNP in the case of supply shocks.

One result that comes through more clearly in the cardinal than in the ordinal rankings is the poor performance of regime 1/1X (money targeting) in the case of money-demand shocks. For the United States, the $RCS\%D$s for nominal-income targeting and real-GNP-plus-inflation targeting across all variables are very small, whereas those for both money targeting and exchange-rate targeting are substantially greater (generally at least fifty times as large—see table 4-18). Recall that for the United States exchange-rate targeting is actually much the same as money targeting, since under exchange-rate targeting the United States is assumed to target money while other countries target their currencies' bilateral exchange rates against the U.S. dollar. For Germany and Japan (tables 4-19 and 4-20), nominal-income targeting, real-GNP-plus-inflation targeting, *and* exchange-rate targeting all show very small effects in the case of money-demand shocks, whereas the effects under money targeting are comparatively large.

Overall, the cardinal rankings tend to obscure the view (based on the ordinal rankings and the theory in chapter 2) that regime type 2B is globally preferred, at least for the United States and Japan. In general, real-GNP-plus-inflation targeting loses ground in the cardinal rankings, whereas money targeting clearly gains in the United States and Japan, particularly for inflation and the price level. In the German case, where there was no favorite to begin with, exchange-rate targeting is the bigger loser in the cardinal rankings, whereas real GNP plus inflation targeting and money targeting gain.

We did not expect a priori that cardinal rankings of regimes would be fully consistent with the ordinal rankings. As noted earlier, the ordinal rankings give equal weight to each model's deviation-minimizing regime, no matter how strongly or narrowly that regime emerges as first best. But the cardinal rankings, which are obtained by calculating average $RCS\%D$ or $RCSD$ statistics across the models, do give greater weight to models where the distance between first best and second place is large rather than small. Models that exhibit a wide dispersion of results across regime types, in other words, can have a much greater influence on the cardinal rankings than models whose dispersion of results across regimes is narrow.

The shifts in rankings that occurred between the ordinal and cardinal results probably can be attributed to a few models. The large deviations of inflation and, to a lesser extent, real GNP in the longer run under regime 2B in the LIVERPOOL model (see figures 4-26 and 4-25) may have had much to do with that regime being ranked lower in the cardinal results than in the ordinal results, particularly with respect to the loss function combining real GNP and inflation. Similarly, the INTERMOD-C and MSG models (as well as the LIVERPOOL model) weighed in heavily against regime type 2B for the price level (see figure 4-27). In addition, the MCM model gave relatively strong preference to the price level under money targeting (stemming partly from longer-term instabilities that developed in that model under the alternative regimes that incorporated reduced feedback parameters). Finally, exchange-rate targeting may have lost ground in the cardinal results, in part because of the relative instability of the TAYLOR model under that type of regime.

Summary Conclusions

This analysis of the deterministic shocks prepared for the project has shown that the participating models for the most part exhibit simulation properties that appear qualitatively similar to those presented in *EMIE* and its successor exercises. The simulation properties are also broadly, but not uniformly, consistent with the predictions of the theory reviewed in chapter 2.

Close comparisons with previous model-comparison exercises are not possible because of our focus this time on transitory shocks. Nonetheless, the directions of the initial effects of shocks to aggregate demand, money, and oil prices on such key variables as real output and prices are consistent with the effects of sustained shocks considered in the previous exercises. In addition, both demand and supply shocks in the United States exhibit effects on U.S. domestic variables that are broadly similar to the effects of demand and supply shocks in Germany and Japan on the domestic variables of those two countries. The results from at least one model, however, suggest a somewhat greater degree of labor-market rigidity in Germany than in the other two countries in the case of supply shocks.

The analysis of transitory shocks in this project has afforded us the opportunity to observe the persistence of the effects of those shocks. One would expect a priori, as seen in chapter 2, that most variables would settle back down to the vicinity of their baseline paths after the elapse of several periods. For the most part, such damping behavior is observed. Yet several models exhibit longer-term cycling, particularly of financial-sector variables such as interest rates and exchange rates, that in some instances appears to extend well beyond the ten-year simulation period. In some cases, longer-term cycling can be traced to particular dynamics within the models, especially in the treatment of expectations (for example, in the results for INTERMOD-A and MPS, both models with adaptive expectations). In other cases (the MCM and MX3 models, for example) the reasons for cycling are not immediately apparent.

Although the models agree more often than not on the direction of the effects of shocks on key variables, the magnitudes of effects, particularly in the short run, vary substantially, much the same as in the *EMIE* results. The ranges of effects of course reflect differences in the specifications and estimated coefficients of the participating models. One key difference among the models is their periodicity. Quarterly models generally, but not invariably, show smaller initial effects and a more rapid return to baseline than the annual models, largely because the one-period shocks are in effect sustained for four quarters in the annual models rather than for only a single quarter in the quarterly models. Another key difference is the treatment of expectations. As noted earlier, models with adaptive expectations in some cases produce larger initial effects and more persistent deviations from baseline paths over time than models with rational, model-consistent expectations.

Significant quantitative differences can sometimes also be traced to differences in the way the model groups implemented the prescribed policy regimes. The degree of "slippage" allowed between the actual and targeted value of the central intermediate-target variable in the prescribed regimes also results in some qualitative differences among the model results, and especially with the theory in chapter 2. The analysis in chapter 2 assumes full instrument adjustment (exact targeting), whereas the empirical simulations specify partial instrument adjustment. Hence nominal income, and thus also real income and prices, for example, are permitted to deviate substantially from their target values under the empirical implementations of the nominal-income targeting regime.

When analyzing the central question of what the deterministic simulations have to say about the relative performance of the alternative policy regimes, we have pursued two different approaches to try to distill a very large set of empirical results and to glean summary generalizations. One approach is to aggregate the individual models' ordinal rankings of regimes in terms of their performance in minimizing the deviations of key variables from their baseline values. In essence, this approach gives equal weight to each model's preferred regime, with zero weight given to a regime that came in a close second. The second approach calculates indicators of a cardinal ranking across the models by averaging the actual magnitudes of the models' root-mean-squared deviations from baseline.

The ordinal rankings point consistently to real-GNP-plus-inflation targeting (2B/2BX) as the regime preferred for the United States to minimize deviations of real GNP in the face of all types of shocks. ("Preferred," as emphasized earlier, is only shorthand for indicating the regime type with lowest root cumulative squared deviations from baseline and does not prejudge in any way which variables are, or should be, included in policymakers' loss functions.)

For employment, the results for the United States are somewhat more mixed. Only four of the models, moreover, were able to report results for employment. Real-GNP-plus-inflation targeting is preferred for employment in the case of goods demand shocks, and nominal-income targeting is preferred in the case of a U.S. money-demand shock. For a U.S. productivity shock, however, two of the four models reporting results for employment picked money targeting, and two picked real-GNP-plus-inflation targeting for minimizing employment deviations.[56]

For Germany, real-GNP-plus-inflation targeting and nominal-income targeting are also generally preferred for real-sector variables, with two notable exceptions. In the cases of real GNP under supply shocks and employment under money demand, exchange-rate targeting is preferred. For Japan, nominal-income targeting is generally preferred in most cases for real-sector variables, although exchange-rate targeting is preferred for real GNP in the case of supply shocks.

The regime of choice for preventing the rate of inflation from reflecting shocks is real-GNP-plus-inflation targeting in both the United States and Japan. Exchange-rate targeting tends to do better in Germany. For the price level, nominal-income targeting (which allows for less price-level drift than the other regimes) is strongly preferred in the United States and Japan. But in Germany, money targeting and exchange-rate targeting are chosen more often than either nominal-income targeting or real-GNP-plus-inflation targeting for stabilizing the price level. As noted in chapter 2, the choice of regime for stabilizing consumer prices can be influenced by the degree of openness of the economy. More open economies (as in Germany), being more exposed to the effects of changes in exchange rates, may have a preference for exchange-rate targeting to insulate their consumer prices from the effects of shocks that affect exchange rates.

When attention is focused not on real-sector variables or on goods prices but on financial variables (short-term and long-term interest rates for the United States and short-term interest rates and exchange rates for Germany and Japan),

---

56. In the theoretical results in chapter 2, money targeting is never preferred to nominal-income targeting for minimizing deviations of employment in the face of shocks to productivity.

a somewhat different mix of regimes emerges as preferred for minimizing deviations from baseline. For U.S. interest rates, the stabilizing regime is split between money targeting (preferred in the case of aggregate demand shocks) and nominal-income targeting (preferred in the case of supply shocks and a U.S. money-demand shock). For stabilizing both German and Japanese interest rates, exchange-rate targeting is strongly preferred in a majority of the model cases where all four regime types could be compared. Exchange-rate targeting is of course also the regime that best minimizes deviations from baseline of the yen-dollar and deutsche-mark-dollar exchange rates in all cases.

The distribution of preferences across regimes is fairly flat in a number of models. This fact led us to calculate data for the cardinal ranking of the regimes, thereby trying to factor in the quantitative degree to which a model preferred one regime type over the others. In the cardinal rankings, models that show sharp preferences for particular regimes are given greater weight in the aggregate selection index. In some cases, sharp preferences by a particular model reflect "outlier" results that are not readily understandable and that might represent modeling errors of one sort or another. Accordingly, we have somewhat less confidence in the final rankings based on the cardinal results than in those based on the ordinal analysis.

The aggregate cardinal rankings tend to give somewhat greater weight than the ordinal rankings to nominal-income targeting for real-sector variables in the United States and for inflation in Japan. In general, however, the cardinal rankings tend to support the conclusions that real-GNP-plus-inflation targeting is preferred in most cases for stabilizing real-sector variables and inflation in the United States and to a lesser extent in Germany, whereas nominal-income targeting is preferred for stabilizing real-sector variables in Japan and price levels in all three countries.

For stabilization of financial variables, according to the cardinal rankings, money targeting appears to be the preferred regime for the Unites States (especially in the case of goods-demand shocks). Exchange-rate targeting is strongly preferred for interest-rate stabilization for both Germany and Japan, and of course for stabilizing exchange rates. Real-GNP-plus-inflation targeting is typically the regime type with the *largest* deviations of interest rates and exchange rates from baseline (especially for supply shocks).

Almost unanimous agreement exists in the ordinal and cardinal rankings about the very poor performance for all three countries of the money-targeting regime in the case of shocks to money demand. This result fully supports the predictions of the theoretical model analyzed in chapter 2. The results of the deterministic simulations also suggest that in Germany and Japan, any of the three regimes other than money targeting work about equally well in very nearly fully offsetting the effects of money-demand shocks. In the United

States, nominal-income-targeting and real-GNP-plus-inflation targeting perform equally well in offsetting the effects of money-demand shocks.[57]

References

Bryant, R. C., J. F. Helliwell, and P. Hooper. 1989. "Domestic and Cross-Border Consequences of U.S. Macroeconomic Policies." In *Macroeconomic Policies in an Interdependent World*, edited by R. C. Bryant, D. A. Currie, and others, 59–115. Washington: Brookings, Centre for Economic Policy Research, and International Monetary Fund. Unabridged version available as Brookings Discussion Paper in International Economics 68 (January 1989).

Bryant, R. C., D. W. Henderson, G. Holtham, P. Hooper, and S. A. Symansky, eds. 1988. *Empirical Macroeconomics for Interdependent Economies*. Brookings.

Bryant, R. C., G. Holtham, and P. Hooper. 1988. *External Deficits and the Dollar: The Pit and the Pendulum*. Brookings.

Hooper, P., K. H. Johnson, D. L. Kohn, D. E. Lindsey, R. D. Porter, and R. Tryon, eds. 1990. *Financial Sectors in Open Economies: Empirical Analysis and Policy Issues*. Board of Governors of the Federal Reserve System.

57. Recall that, by design in our simulations, for the United States alone, "exchange-rate targeting" is essentially the same as money targeting. Also, as discussed in chapter 2, if sufficiently great weight is placed on stabilizing the inflation rate, exchange-rate targeting could under certain conditions be equivalent, or even preferred, to nominal-income targeting in the face of a money-demand shock.

CHAPTER 5

Stochastic Simulations
with Simple Policy Regimes

Ralph C. Bryant, Catherine L. Mann, and Peter Hooper

STOCHASTIC SIMULATION of macroeconomic models is a promising method of systematically evaluating alternative operating regimes for the conduct of macroeconomic policies. Stochastic simulation techniques, in contrast to a deterministic simulation, impose a variety of shocks on a number of different variables in a model (rather than a single shock on a single variable), thereby revealing considerably more about the likely robustness of a policy regime when confronted by the complex shocks that characterize the real world (chapter 1).

Despite the inherent appeal of the approach, the techniques of stochastic simulation have so far been infrequently used in empirical policy analysis.[1] An early obstacle to their widespread use was the computational intensity of the required calculations. The rapid fall in the relative price of computer-intensive calculations in the past decade has effectively eliminated this impediment. But another obstacle, equally serious and not yet fully resolved, has been a lack of consensus on the details of the appropriate computational procedures. One objective of the research project giving rise to this book was to review procedures for conducting stochastic simulations and to try to generate greater consensus about their implementation.

Stochastic simulation involves a less precisely controlled experiment and depends even more heavily on the historical validity of the simulated model than does deterministic simulation. These factors make the interpretation of stochastic simulations more difficult, which is a third reason that has hampered the use of stochastic simulation for policy analysis. A deterministic simulation imposes a single specific shock on a model under a particular policy regime; this tightly controlled experiment generates only one forecast path for each of the model's variables. In a stochastic simulation, although the particular policy regime is controlled exactly, an entire set of shocks is randomly drawn from a

---

1. The important research efforts of a few economists—for example, Fair (1984, 1988), Frenkel-Goldstein-Masson (1989), McKibbin and Sachs (1989), and Taylor (1989, 1992)—are exceptions to this generalization.

matrix of residuals for the model's equations (in the case of this project, histori-cal residuals). The shocks in a stochastic simulation cannot be straightforwardly characterized (for example, they are a complex mixture of expenditure, supply, and financial shocks); and an entire collection of forecast paths is generated for each of the model's variables. A stochastic simulation experiment thus en-capsulates much more information about the attributes of the model itself (its theoretical structure, data, and econometric estimation technique) as well as of the residuals from the model (in this project, the portion of the historical data that the model does not explain).

If a model is well specified, its residuals do represent in a reasonable way a time series of historical shocks. For such a model, if the pattern of future distur-bances were to prove similar to the past pattern, stochastically simulated paths of key variables under alternative policy regimes would accurately indicate the likely robustness of those regimes. In a poorly specified model, however, the residuals will not reasonably reflect the actual history of real-world shocks. Rather, its residuals will be a complex combination of historical shocks and biased noise caused by the inadequate model specification. Stochastically sim-ulated paths from such a model, in effect making use of "dirty" residuals, could lead to faulty inferences about the effectiveness and robustness of alternative policy regimes.[2] It is the important role of a model's residuals that differentiates stochastic simulation from deterministic simulation and makes the original esti-mation techniques used to construct the model, and its historical performance, even more important in stochastic simulation.

Interpreting the output from stochastic simulation experiments is more difficult than for deterministic simulations. For a typical deterministic simula-tion, when a standardized shock is imposed on a single variable, the effects of the shock and its interaction with a particular policy regime can typically be traced through the model system (as, for example, in chapter 4). A single pass through the model during a stochastic simulation, because it imposes a whole set of shocks drawn from the matrix of historical residuals, perturbs most or all of the behavioral equations in the model system simultaneously, and by different amounts depending on the historical residual matrix. Just for the single pass, tracing through the effects of the set of shocks on the model system is substantially more difficult. The stochastic simulation as a whole, of course, involves many repetitive passes through the model, each with a differ-ent draw of the shocks from the historical residual matrix. Tracing the effects of a set of shocks in a single pass through the model might be manageable if the covariances between shocks could plausibly be assumed to be zero. But the ma-

2. Of course, deterministic simulations conducted with an inadequately specified model could also lead to incorrect inferences.

trix of historical residuals usually has nonzero off-diagonal elements. These covariances substantially increase the complexity of the simulated paths for the model's variables and make it nearly impossible, in practice, to trace the effects of the shocks through the model system.

Policymakers often want to compare forecasts or policy inferences across alternative models. In the face of substantial uncertainty about the way the world economy functions, policymakers would be unwise to rely solely on a single model (chapter 1). Several previous model-comparison projects (identified in chapter 1) have been devoted to understanding why models differ under the same set of deterministic shocks. Those earlier projects focused primarily on the theoretical structures and broad properties of the models. For example, analysis tried to explain cross-model differences in observed outcomes for specific deterministic simulations by reference to characteristics of key model equations or the alternative treatments of expectations.

The research for this project also aspired to improve understanding of differences across the participating models. The cross-model comparisons possible here relate to differences in the stochastic simulations of the various policy regimes. Understanding why the stochastic simulations differ across the models requires, in principle, examining both the models and their historical residuals.

The complexity of simulated paths generated by stochastic simulation, for the reasons given, renders interpretation and understanding of the results difficult. Yet it is this very complexity that makes stochastic simulation dominate deterministic simulation for assessing the robustness of policy regimes. It may not be possible to explain in detail why a particular policy regime performs more satisfactorily than others in buffering ultimate-target variables in the face of diverse shocks. But evidence that the regime appears to do so, for a wide range of model specifications and shocks, could be valuable evidence for policymakers seeking to identify the most appropriate procedure for conducting economic policy.

This chapter provides an assessment of the stochastic simulation results generated for the project. It begins with a description of the summary statistics used in characterizing the data. It then analyzes the overall performance of the regime types, making generalizations where possible and noting also the main exceptions and contrasts among the participating models. Primary attention is focused on the variability of output, inflation, and the price level. Later in the chapter we also examine the consequences of the alternative regimes for the variability of other variables such as interest rates. Certain special topics—for example, differences in the results for model-consistent and adaptive expectations—are considered. As in chapter 4, we try where possible to relate the results of the empirical simulations to the predictions of the theory drawn from the simplified two-country models presented in chapter 2.

Descriptive Summary Statistics

Even for small models, and still more so for large ones, stochastic simulations generate large amounts of computer output. For this project, it was of course not feasible to collect detailed data on all the stochastic simulations, much less to try to interpret all the detail. Rather, the model groups were asked to report deviations from baseline for only a few key macroeconomic variables for each of the major industrial countries. The variables selected were levels and growth rates for real GNP and nominal GNP, price levels and inflation rates (for the GNP deflator), levels and changes in short-term nominal interest rates, levels of nominal bilateral dollar exchange rates, and the levels of ratios of current-account balances as a percentage of nominal GNP.

At the time the guidelines for the stochastic simulations were developed, model groups typically were not giving separate emphasis to employment as a key macroeconomic variable. Output and employment were presumed to be highly correlated, and a focus on output was regarded as doing double duty for both output and employment. Furthermore, two of the three model groups that had led the way with stochastic simulation techniques (MULTIMOD and TAYLOR) and three of the other groups (INTERMOD, LIVERPOOL, and MX3) were not able to report data for employment because their models did not incorporate separate variables for aggregate employment. Given that situation, and because the model groups and organizers wished to keep the reporting of the simulation results to the necessary minimum, none of the groups was requested to supply stochastic-simulation statistics for employment variables.

Viewed with the wisdom of hindsight, the omission of employment data is regrettable. As shown by the discussion of productivity shocks in chapter 2, in some circumstances analysts and policymakers are better advised to focus on employment rather than on output as a target variable. By the time the guidelines for the deterministic simulations were developed, the separate importance of employment was beginning to be more widely recognized. For the deterministic simulations discussed in chapter 4, therefore, all four model groups having employment variables in their models were asked to submit employment data. For the analysis in this chapter, however, no data at all are available for employment.

Annex B provides a comprehensive reporting of the stochastic simulation results for the key variables that are available, in tables B-I-1–B-I-35. Each table presents the results of one model for a particular country across all four simplified policy regimes (money targeting, nominal-income targeting, real-GNP-plus-inflation targeting, and exchange-rate targeting). The tables are ordered by major country and, within the country, by model. For example, the nine different model results for the United States are in tables B-I-1–B-I-9, those for Japan are in tables B-I-10–B-I-17, and so on. Separate tables are included for the INTERMOD-A and INTERMOD-C results. MPS results are available only for the United States. The MSG and MX3 results are limited to the United States, Japan, and Germany. For exchange-rate targeting, the MPS model does not have results because of that model's structure, the MX3 model does not have results because the model was unstable for that regime, and the GEM model did not report results for that regime.[3]

Table 5-1, whose format resembles the annex B-I tables, illustrates how the results are presented. The table shows summary statistics for the INTERMOD-C model, for U.S. variables, for the full simulation period of ten years. (The annex B tables provide separate results, when available, for the full ten years and the final five years.) With four types of regimes, and with a model group possibly implementing both the O specification and its own X variant, as many as eight sets of results per country may be available. In the example of table 5-1, data exist for only five of the eight possible columns.[4]

The statistics in table 5-1 and the annex B-I tables, except for the final two rows, are average root-mean-squared deviations of variables from baseline, either percentage deviations (*RMS%D*s) for level variables, or absolute deviations measured in percentage points (*RMSD*s) for variables such as GNP growth, inflation, and interest rates. These summary statistics are defined as follows. For each regime and for each time period t, the model groups generated S simulated values for each of the model's endogenous variables.[5] For a variable such as the level of a country's real or nominal GNP, define the mean squared deviations for period t under regime J as

$$\sigma_{Jt}^2(Y) = \frac{1}{S} \sum_{i=1}^{S} \left(\frac{(Y_{Jit} - Y_{Jt}^B)}{Y_{Jt}^B} \right)^2,$$

where the Y_{Jit} are the different simulated values for period t and Y_{Jt}^B is the period-t baseline value. Loosely speaking, one can think of this expression as a period-t "variance." For an interest rate measured in percentage points or an

---

3. As explained in chapter 3, at the outset of the project it was recognized that the functional form of the policy regimes and the particular parameter values specified in the guidelines might not be feasible for individual models. Model groups were thus asked to identify problems encountered in trying to implement the original (O) specification of the regimes, and, if they used an alternative (X) specification, to detail how they chose the X specification. Every model group departed in some way from the O specifications of the regimes. See table 3-2 for a convenient summary of regime implementation by model, for both the deterministic and stochastic simulations.

4. The INTERMOD group did not have 1X and 3X regimes; for the version of the model with model-consistent expectations, the group was unable to implement the O specification for nominal-income targeting (regime 2A).

5. $S = 10$ for quarterly models, and $S = 40$ for annual models (see chapter 3).

Table 5-1. *Illustrative Listing of Stochastic Simulation Results: INTERMOD-C, Variables for the United States*

Root-mean-squared deviations (*RMS%D* or *RMSD*) from baseline[a]

	Regime							
	Money targeting		Nominal-income targeting		Real-GNP-plus-inflation targeting		Exchange-rate targeting	
Variable	*(1)*	*(1X)*	*(2A)*	*(2AX)*	*(2B)*	*(2BX)*	*(3)*	*(3X)*
Real GNP								
Level (percent)	3.03			28.2	2.31	2.46	2.88	
Growth (percentage points)	2.85			2.69	2.53	2.69	2.76	
Nominal GNP								
Level (percent)	4.56		3.53		8.08	8.68	4.43	
Growth (percentage points)	2.48		2.31		2.85	3.05	2.42	
GNP deflator								
Level (percent)	5.00		3.92		8.27	8.78	4.94	
Change (percentage points)	1.42		1.19		2.02	2.23	1.41	
Short-term interest rate								
Level (percentage points)	2.88		2.59		4.37	3.92	2.90	
Change (percentage points)	2.08		1.42		3.70	3.17	2.05	
Current account/GNP ratio								
Level (percentage points)	0.82			0.81	1.04	0.98	0.68	
Loss: GNP + inflation	4.45		4.01		4.33	4.69	4.29	
Loss: GNP + inflation + change in short-term interest rate	6.53		5.43		8.03	7.86	6.34	

Source: Annex B, table B-I-2, full-period (ten-year) simulations.
a. Shading indicates the regime yielding lowest *RMSD* from baseline.

inflation rate measured as the period-to-period percentage change in the GNP deflator, the analogous period-*t* "variance" is:

$$\sigma^2_{Jt}(I) = \frac{1}{S} \sum_{i=1}^{S} \left(I_{Jit} - I^B_{Jt}\right)^2 ,$$

where the I_{Jit} are the simulated values and the I^B_{Jt} are the period-*t* baseline values.[6] Note that the squared deviations are taken around the baseline value (not, as would be the case for a true variance, around the mean of the simulated values). When calculated for each of the *t* periods over the whole simulation horizon, these statistics provide a time-series respresentation of the dispersion of the simulated outcomes for a variable around that variable's baseline path.

To avoid examining and reporting the entire time series of "variances" for each individual variable, model groups were asked to summarize the results by

6. For each time period, there are *S* different values for Y_{Jit} but only a single value for Y^B_{Jt}. In principle, the values for the baseline path could differ across regimes (it could be that Y^B_{Jt} for regime *J* will not be equal to Y^B_{Kt} for regime *K*). If that were so, it would be appropriate to use the own-regime baseline in the calculations of the summary statistics. In practice, model groups appear to have coded the various regimes into their models in such a way that the baselines were identical across regimes.

calculating a simple average of the mean squared deviations for only two time periods: the whole simulation of ten years, and the second half of the simulation (years six through ten). For the variable Y, for example, the average for all N periods is:[7]

$$\overline{\sigma_J^2}(Y) = \frac{1}{N} \sum_{t=1}^{N} \sigma_{Jt}^2(Y).$$

The final step in calculating the summary statistic was to take the square root of the preceding averages to obtain a measure of root-mean-squared deviations.

The complete definitions of the summary statistics, for the case of the whole simulation horizon, are therefore:

$$(5\text{-}1) \qquad RMS\%D_J(Y) = \sqrt{\left(\frac{1}{N}\right)\sum_{t=1}^{N}\left[\left(\frac{1}{S}\right)\sum_{i=1}^{S}\left(\frac{Y_{Jit} - Y_{Jt}^B}{Y_{Jt}^B}\right)^2\right]}$$

and

$$(5\text{-}2) \qquad RMSD_J(I) = \sqrt{\left(\frac{1}{N}\right)\sum_{t=1}^{N}\left[\left(\frac{1}{S}\right)\sum_{i=1}^{S}\left(I_{Jit} - I_{Jt}^B\right)^2\right]}.$$

These statistics (and the analogous ones for the final five years) are the raw material for the analysis that follows. In table 5-1, a particular entry on each row of the table is shaded, indicating which regime—for that particular variable/model/country combination—yields the lowest average root-mean-squared deviation (*RMS%D* or *RMSD*) from baseline for the full ten-year simulation period. The shading identifies, in other words, the regime that best insulated that particular variable, on average, from the full array of stochastic shocks.

The summary statistics for root-mean-squared deviations for several variables can be used separately, or combined, to calculate values for a variety of "loss functions," calibrating the relative disutility of outcomes under the different regimes.[8] For the overview here, we eschew complex calculations and focus instead (analogously with the discussion in chapter 4) on four highly

---

7. $N = 10$ for annual models and $N = 40$ for quarterly models (see chapter 3).

8. Chapter 2 investigated from a theoretical perspective, and chapter 4 from an empirical perspective, which policy regime would minimize the variance of output, or employment, or inflation, given a wide variety of single, specific shocks. The illustrative loss functions derived from the stochastic simulations are simple empirical analogs to those in chapter 2, with the empirical analysis making use of more complex models and shocks.

simplified loss functions. The two simplest are the *RMS%D* for real GNP alone (first row of data in the tables) and the *RMSD* for inflation alone (sixth row of data in the tables). A focus on these measures gives exclusive weight to either output variability or inflation variability. (As noted above, it would have been revealing to be able to report here also a *RMS%D* for employment alone.)

In practice, policymakers presumably include several types of variables in their loss function. Our third and fourth illustrative functions accordingly include more than one variable, but without complex weighting of the relative importance of the variables. The third function is merely the unweighted sum of the *RMS%D* for real GNP and the *RMSD* of the inflation rate. The fourth function adds to the third (again with an equal weight) the *RMSD* of the period-to-period change in the short-term interest rate. Volatility in the interest rate might be included in the loss function because, for example, the policymakers believe that such volatility imposes costs on private-sector behavior.[9] The calculations for the third and fourth loss functions are shown in the final two rows of table 5-1, and in a corresponding position in the annex B-I tables.

These four loss functions are merely illustrative. To state the obvious, moreover, any judgment about the likely superiority of one policy regime over another that is derived from a comparison of loss-function values can depend critically on the particular variables included in the loss function, on the relative weights assigned to each, and on the specific way that the variables are represented (for example, whether positive and negative deviations of the variables from target values are treated symmetrically or asymmetrically). We accordingly examine several functions rather than one and use them only as rough-and-ready yardsticks for comparing outcomes under the different policy regimes. Initially, we concentrate the discussion on the loss functions for real GNP alone, inflation alone, or the two together. Later in the discussion, we note how inferences may be altered if considerations such as interest-rate variability are taken into account.

The amount of detail in the B-I tables in annex B makes comparisons across countries or models difficult (quite apart from the underlying problem of differences between the O and the X regimes, and among the various X regimes). We have therefore also included some additional summary tables in annex B; these tables recompile or process further some of the data from the B-I tables. The B-II tables (B-II-1–B-II-9) facilitate, for each model separately,

---

9. More generally, policymakers may believe that volatility in a variety of variables can impose costs on the economy—even though those variables do not serve as ultimate-target variables per se in the policy regime. Other variables that might be perceived in this way include nominal or real exchange rates. See below for further discussion.

a comparison across countries and regimes of the values of the four illustrative loss functions. Finally, the annex includes a set of B-III tables, one for each country. These tables, constructed so as to give money targeting an index value of unity, give a better sense of the cardinal magnitudes of the values of loss functions across regimes. The B-III tables also facilitate a rough-and-ready comparison of the results across the models.

When interpreting the tables in annex B, readers should not forget the difficulties of making valid cross-model comparisons. Regrettably, as stressed in chapter 3, efforts to achieve standardization in the implementation of policy regimes across the models were only partially successful. Most notably, the MX3, MPS, and GEM model groups either could not or did not complete simulations for exchange-rate targeting. Several model groups—TAYLOR and LIVERPOOL especially, but also MPS and MULTIMOD—implemented X variants of the regimes that incorporated major substantive modifications to the O specifications. In other cases, model groups changed the feedback coefficients on the policy regimes so as to obtain satisfactory simulation results. The MSG group, in addition to implementing the O regimes, generated results for X variants in which the feedback coefficients in the policy regimes were set at very high values.

Overall Performance of Regime Types

Do the stochastic simulation results suggest a single best regime—common across models and across countries—that minimizes output variability? Is there a best regime for minimizing inflation variability? Can the same regime best accomplish both objectives? If the answers to these questions appeared to be yes, then it might be tempting to argue that policymakers in all countries should adopt the preferred type of regime (not necessarily the simplified variants used in this study) without regard for country-specific shocks and despite economists' disagreements about the appropriate models to describe national economies and their interactions.

As with the analysis of the deterministic simulations in the preceding chapter, no single regime emerges unequivocally as best for minimizing output variability, or inflation variability, for all the models and all the countries.[10] The estimated *RMS%D*s and *RMSD*s vary widely across the models, and to a lesser extent across countries. As expected, the calculated "performance" of

---

10. Recall also the important point that, when productivity shocks are taken into account, employment variability might be a more appropriate focus for policy attention than output variability.

Table 5-2. *Identification of the Regime Minimizing Three Simple Illustrative Loss Functions*[a]

Country and loss function	Model								
	GEM	INTERMOD-A	INTERMOD-C	LIVERPOOL	MPS	MSG	MULTIMOD	MX3	TAYLOR
United States									
Loss: Real GNP alone	2BX	**2B**	**2B**	3X	**2BX**	**2BX**	**2BX**	**2B**	**2AX**
Loss: Inflation alone	2BX	2A	**2AX**	**3X**	2AX	**2AX**	**2BX**	2AX	**2BX**
Loss: Real GNP + inflation	2AX/2BX	**2B**	2AX	**3X**	**2BX**	**2BX**	**2BX**	**2B**	**2AX**
Japan									
Loss: Real GNP alone	**2BX**	**2B**	**2B**	**2A**	n.a.	**2AX**	**1**	2B	**2BX**
Loss: Inflation alone	2AX	**2A**	2AX	**1X**	n.a.	**1X**	1X/2BX	2AX	3X
Loss: Real GNP + inflation	2BX	**2B**	1/2AX	1X/2A	n.a.	**2AX**	1	2AX	**2BX**
Germany									
Loss: Real GNP alone	2BX	**2B**	**2B**	2AX	n.a.	**2BX**	**2AX**	**2B**	2AX
Loss: Inflation alone	2AX	**2B**	2AX	**1X**	n.a.	**2A**	**2BX**	**2AX**	1X/2BX
Loss: Real GNP + inflation	2AX	**2B**	2AX	**1X**	n.a.	**2BX**	2AX	2B	2BX
United Kingdom									
Loss: Real GNP alone	n.a.	**2B**	**2B**	**2AX**	n.a.	n.a.	**3X**	n.a.	**2AX**
Loss: Inflation alone	n.a.	2A	**2AX**	**2A**	n.a.	n.a.	**2BX**	n.a.	3X
Loss: Real GNP + inflation	n.a.	**2B**	**2AX**	**2A**	n.a.	n.a.	3X	n.a.	2AX
Canada									
Loss: Real GNP alone	n.a.	**2B**	**2B**	3X	n.a.	n.a.	1X/2AX	n.a.	**2BX**
Loss: Inflation alone	n.a.	2A/2B	**2AX**	**2A**	n.a.	n.a.	**2BX**	n.a.	2AX/2BX
Loss: Real GNP + inflation	n.a.	**2B**	2AX	**2A**	n.a.	n.a.	1X/2AX	n.a.	**2BX**

Source: B-I tables in annex B.

n.a. Results not available.

a. When the RMSDs for two regimes differ by 1 percent or less, the table identifies the regimes as tied. When an entry in a cell is in boldface type, that regime is associated with a reduction in the value of the loss function by 10 percent or more relative to the second-best type of regime. See the text for further explanation.

the regimes can be influenced in important ways by which loss function is used as a yardstick. Nonetheless, some generalizations comparing the regime types can be made.

Summary perspectives on the results that emphasize rank ordering can help in the identification of such generalizations. We provide the first overview of this type in table 5-2.[11] Each participating model has a separate column in this table. Five groupings of rows are included, for five main industrial countries: the United States, Japan, Germany, the United Kingdom, and Canada. Within each country grouping, the individual rows refer to the first three of the illustrative loss functions. For a particular model, country, and loss function, the cells in the table identify which policy regime ranks as "preferred" (has the lowest value for the loss function). When the *RMS%D*s or *RMSD*s for two or more regimes differ from each other by 1 percent or less, the table shows the regimes as tied for first place. In addition to identifying which regime is preferred, the table provides a rough indication of cardinal ranking: when the preferred regime is associated with a reduction in the value of the loss function by more than 10 percent relative to the second best type of regime, the preferred regime is shown in boldface type.[12]

If the cells in table 5-2 are interpreted as repeated "heats" in a horse race among the types of regime, the overall outcome of this hypothetical race does not favor the four horses equally.[13] Rather, as suggested by the theory in chapter 2 and confirmed by the deterministic simulations in chapter 4, two of the regime types—nominal-income targeting (2A/2AX) and real-GNP-plus-inflation targeting (2B/2BX)—emerge considerably more often (in over four-fifths of the available cases) as the winner of individual heats. Money targeting (1/1X) and exchange-rate targeting (3/3X) are much less favored as the

11. Tables 5-2–5-4 provide analogous information to that in tables 4-3–4-17 for the deterministic simulations in chapter 4.

12. Designation of the preferred regime distinguishes (when the relevant data are available) between the O and the X regimes. Hence for a model running both the 2B and 2BX regimes, for example, the table differentiates whether 2B or 2BX minimizes the loss function. For the calculation of whether the preferred regime reduces the value of the loss function by more than 10 percent relative to the "next-best" regime, however, the next-best regime must be a different type of regime (the same procedure used in the tables for chapter 4). For example, for a model where the magnitudes of the loss function, with the regimes ranked in ascending order, are 2BX,2B,2A,2AX,1,3X, the preferred regime 2BX is compared with 2A rather than 2B to determine whether to boldface the cell in table 5-2. Readers may consult the B-III tables in annex B for full information about the relative cardinal magnitudes.

13. The heats are not statistically independent and are not always a "fair" race, for reasons apparent from the discussion in chapter 3. Participating model groups implemented the stochastic simulations in varying ways; not all model groups generated results for both O and X rules; the X variants differ in significant ways across the models; in some cases a model group did not or could not implement a regime type (the MX3, GEM, and MPS groups for exchange-rate targeting); the results for the loss function combining real GNP and inflation are not separate heats from those for real GNP alone or inflation alone; and so on. We use the analogy of heats in a horse race only for rough interpretations of table 5-2 and succeeding tables. Readers wishing to make more sophisticated calculations have the requisite raw material in the tables in annex B.

preferred regime, together accounting for less than one-fifth of the available cases. Between nominal-income targeting and real-GNP-plus-inflation targeting, the latter appears a bit more often than the former.[14]

As is shown by the distinction between cells that are and are not boldfaced, moreover, whenever money targeting or exchange-rate targeting do appear in table 5-2 as a preferred regime, those two regime types only infrequently emerge as markedly better. For the less than one-fifth of cases where either 1/1X or 3/3X is preferred, only about one-third of those cases exhibit a value of the loss function 10 percent or more less than the next closest type of regime. Of the much more numerous cases where nominal-income targeting or real-GNP-plus-inflation targeting is preferred, some two-thirds are boldfaced, implying a pronounced rather than modest margin of superiority.

Those model groups whose stochastic simulation results most strongly support the relative superiority of (taken together) nominal-income targeting and real-GNP-plus-inflation targeting are GEM, INTERMOD-A, INTERMOD-C, MPS, MSG, and MX3. The TAYLOR results provide somewhat less strong evidence for that ranking. The two model groups whose results are least consistent with, even contradict, the dominant ranking are MULTIMOD and LIVERPOOL (see further discussion below).

The generalization that money targeting performed relatively poorly overall is more robust than the assertion that exchange-rate targeting fared poorly overall. Three of the models for which nominal-income targeting and real-GNP-plus-inflation targeting performed well—MPS, MX3, and GEM—either could not or did not report results for exchange-rate targeting. This fact causes the heats for those models to bias the overall race against exchange-rate targeting.[15] Note, however, that the difficulty some model groups had in implementing the exchange-rate targeting regime could be considered a strike against that regime. A superior regime should be robust when confronted with heterogeneous model specifications, different values for its feedback parameters, and multiple draws from the distribution of historical shocks.

The preceding conclusions emerge even more sharply when the data are summarized in the manner of tables 5-3 and 5-4. Table 5-3 contrasts all four types of regimes for the subset of six models for which results for all types of regime (either O or X) are available. Table 5-4 contrasts only money

---

14. Specifically, results are available for 105 of the 135 cells in table 5-2. (Thirty cells exist for which the model groups could not or did not generate simulation data.) Of these 105 cases, regimes 1, 1X, or 3X are preferred in only 17 cases. An equal favoring of all four types of regime would have caused money targeting and exchange-rate targeting to emerge in about half the cases. Of the 88 cases where 2A, 2AX, 2B, or 2BX perform best, nominal-income targeting is preferred in $41\frac{1}{2}$ and real-GNP-plus-inflation targeting in $46\frac{1}{2}$ (counting a two-way tie in a cell as $\frac{1}{2}$ for each of the tied regimes).

15. If attention is restricted to only the six models that successfully implemented all four regime types, there are eighty-four cells in table 5-2 for which data are available. Exchange-rate targeting is preferred in eight and money targeting in nine of those cases (still only one-fifth of the total).

Table 5-3. *Ordinal Summary of Performance of All Four Regime Types across Participating Models: Models That Implemented All Four Types of Regime*

	Regime								Total number of model cases	
	Money targeting (1/1X)		Nominal-income targeting (2A/2AX)		Real-GNP-plus-inflation targeting (2B/2BX)		Exchange-rate targeting (3/3X)			
Country and loss function	Number[a]	Percent[b]	Number[a]	Percent[b]	Number[a]	Percent[b]	Number[a]	Percent[b]	Number[c]	Percent
United States										
Loss: Real GNP alone	0	0	1	17	4	67	1	17	6	100
Loss: Inflation alone	0	0	3	50	2	33	1	17	6	100
Loss: Real GNP + inflation	0	0	2	33	3	50	1	17	6	100
Japan										
Loss: Real GNP alone	1	17	2	33	3	50	0	0	6	100
Loss: Inflation alone	3	50	2	33	0	0	1	17	6	100
Loss: Real GNP + inflation	2	33	2	33	2	33	0	0	6	100
Germany										
Loss: Real GNP alone	0	0	3	50	3	50	0	0	6	100
Loss: Inflation alone	2	33	2	33	2	33	0	0	6	100
Loss: Real GNP + inflation	1	17	2	33	3	50	0	0	6	100
United Kingdom										
Loss: Real GNP alone	0	0	2	40	2	40	1	20	5	100
Loss: Inflation alone	0	0	3	60	1	20	1	20	5	100
Loss: Real GNP + inflation	0	0	3	60	1	20	1	20	5	100
Canada										
Loss: Real GNP alone	0	0	1	20	3	60	1	20	5	100
Loss: Inflation alone	0	0	3	60	2	40	0	0	5	100
Loss: Real GNP + inflation	1	20	2	40	2	40	0	0	5	100
Total, five countries										
Loss: Real GNP alone	1	4	9	32	15	54	3	11	28	100
Loss: Inflation alone	5	18	13	46	7	25	3	11	28	100
Loss: Real GNP + inflation	4	14	11	39	11	39	2	7	28	100

Source: Derived from B-I tables for six models (INTERMOD-A, INTERMOD-C, LIVERPOOL, MSG, MULTIMOD, and TAYLOR) in annex B. See the text for further explanation.

a. Number of models ranking this regime type as first best (lowest $RMS\%D$ or $RMSD$ from baseline) for the given country and loss-function combination.

b. Proportion, expressed as percent, of total cases for the given country and loss-function combination. Rounded to nearest whole percent.

c. Number of available model cases for the given country and loss-function combination.

Table 5-4. *Ordinal Summary of Performance of Three Regime Types across Participating Models (Money Targeting, Nominal-Income Targeting, and Real-GNP-plus-Inflation Targeting)*[a]

	Regime							
	Money targeting (1/1X)		Nominal-income targeting (2A/2AX)		Real-GNP-plus-inflation targeting (2B/2BX)		Total number of model cases	
Country and loss function	Number[b]	Percent[c]	Number[b]	Percent[c]	Number[b]	Percent[c]	Number[d]	Percent
United States								
Loss: Real GNP alone	0	0	2	22	7	77	9	100
Loss: Inflation alone	0	0	6	67	3	33	9	100
Loss: Real GNP + inflation	0	0	3½	39	5½	61	9	100
Japan								
Loss: Real GNP alone	1	13	2	25	5	63	8	100
Loss: Inflation alone	2½	31	4	50	1½	19	8	100
Loss: Real GNP + inflation	2	25	3	38	3	38	8	100
Germany								
Loss: Real GNP alone	0	0	3	38	5	63	8	100
Loss: Inflation alone	1½	19	4	50	2½	31	8	100
Loss: Real GNP + inflation	1	13	3	38	4	50	8	100
United Kingdom								
Loss: Real GNP alone	1	20	2	40	2	40	5	100
Loss: Inflation alone	0	0	3½	70	1½	30	5	100
Loss: Real GNP + inflation	1	20	3	60	1	20	5	100
Canada								
Loss: Real GNP alone	½	10	1½	30	3	60	5	100
Loss: Inflation alone	0	0	3	60	2	40	5	100
Loss: Real GNP + inflation	½	10	2½	50	2	40	5	100
Total, five countries								
Loss: Real GNP alone	2½	7	10½	30	22	63	35	100
Loss: Inflation alone	4	11	20½	59	10½	30	35	100
Loss: Real GNP + inflation	4½	13	15	43	15½	44	35	100

Source: Derived from B-I tables for all nine participating models (GEM, INTERMOD-A, INTERMOD-C, LIVERPOOL, MPS, MSG, MULTIMOD, MX3, and TAYLOR) in annex B. See the text for further explanation.

a. For purposes of this table, only three regime types are considered. (Exchange-rate targeting is excluded because of the smaller number of model groups that could or did implement exchange-rate targeting.) If an individual model implementing all four regime types reported its lowest *RMS%D* or *RMSD* for exchange-rate targeting, this table indicates which of the three remaining regime types had the next-lowest *RMS%D* or *RMSD*.

b. Number of models ranking this regime type as best of the three types (lowest *RMS%D* or *RMSD* from baseline) for the given country and loss-function combination.

c. Proportion, expressed as percent, of total cases for the given country and loss-function combination. Rounded to nearest whole percent.

d. Number of available model cases for the given country and loss-function combination.

targeting, nominal-income targeting, and real-GNP-plus-inflation targeting for all nine of the models participating in the stochastic simulations. For the different country/loss-function combinations, the tables record the number and proportion (percentage) of times a regime shows the lowest *RMS%D* or *RMSD*.

Among the models that implemented all four regime types, either real-GNP-plus-inflation targeting or nominal-income targeting performed better in a large majority of the available cases (last three rows in table 5-3). If exclusive attention is paid to minimizing output variability, real-GNP-plus-inflation targeting emerged as best in fifteen, and nominal-income targeting in nine, of the twenty-five total cases (54 percent and 32 percent, respectively; together, 86 percent). When exclusive attention is paid to minimizing the variability of the inflation rate, the comparable figures for real-GNP-plus-inflation targeting and nominal-income targeting are seven and thirteen out of twenty-five total cases (25 percent and 46 percent, respectively; together, 71 percent).

A similar pattern of dominance for regimes 2B/2BX and 2A/2AX is also apparent for the wider set of nine models (table 5-4), where the comparison is restricted to money targeting, nominal-income targeting, and real-GNP-plus-inflation targeting. Either real-GNP-plus-inflation targeting or nominal-income targeting dominates in 93 percent of the cases where the loss function contains real GNP alone, in 89 percent of the cases where the loss function focuses on inflation alone, or in 87 percent of the cases where the loss function is the simple sum of the root-mean-squared deviations from baseline of real GNP and inflation (last three rows of table 5-4).

For the deterministic simulations analyzed in chapter 4, our cross-country comparison focused on the Group of Three (G3) countries: the United States, Japan, and Germany. To minimize variability in real-sector variables such as output or employment or in the price level and inflation, real-GNP-plus-inflation targeting appeared preferable for the United States, with nominal-income targeting probably second best. Nominal-income targeting or real-GNP-plus-inflation targeting appeared preferable for Japan. The probability of money targeting or exchange-rate targeting emerging in chapter 4 as the preferred regime was significantly higher for Germany than for the United States or Japan. Exchange-rate targeting seemed often to minimize deviations of German variables from baseline, in particular for the German inflation rate.

The stochastic simulations analyzed here are not fully consistent with the inferences reached in chapter 4. To be sure, tables 5-2 and 5-3 confirm that nominal-income targeting or real-GNP-plus-inflation targeting tend to be preferred in general when the loss function contains output, inflation, or a simple combination of the two. Consistent with chapter 4, moreover, the preference for real-GNP-plus-inflation targeting seems relatively robust for the United States. The stochastic results for the preferred regime for Japan, however, are mixed, with money targeting emerging as preferred for minimizing inflation deviations. For Germany, there is little apparent consistency between the deterministic and stochastic results; in particular, in contrast with chapter 4, exchange-rate targeting is conspicuously absent in the rows of tables 5-2 and 5-3 for Germany. There is no apparent basis, so far in this chapter, for suggesting that German evaluation of policy regimes should be any different from that in the United States or Japan.[16]

The United Kingdom, although not adhering to the exchange-rate mechanism of the European Monetary System (EMS) until recent years, is markedly closer to Europe and its institutional arrangements than is the United States, Japan, or Canada. On a priori grounds, one might expect to observe different conclusions about regime types for the United Kingdom (and even more so for France) than for the other non-European countries considered in tables 5-2–5-4. Exchange-rate targeting is occasionally preferred for the United Kingdom. From this particular evidence, however, there seems little basis for distinguishing a preferred regime type for the United Kingdom different from that for other countries. The overall evidence still points to the superiority of nominal-income targeting or real-GNP-plus-inflation targeting.

Price and Inflation Variability versus Output Variability

Nominal-income targeting and real-GNP-plus-inflation targeting at first glance appear to have performed about equally well in tables 5-2–5-4. But a closer look reveals an important difference. The 2B/2BX regime performs better than the 2A/2AX regime for minimizing the variability of real GNP. The opposite tendency tends to hold for minimizing the variability of the price level and, to a lesser extent, of the inflation rate: real-GNP-plus-inflation targeting performs *less* well than nominal-income targeting. This difference, for reasons already given in chapters 2 and 4, can be traced to the key difference between the two regime types.

Nominal-income targeting presumes that policymakers give equal weight to minimizing deviations of output and the price *level* from desired paths. In contrast, real-GNP-plus-inflation targeting presumes that policymakers focus on output and the inflation *rate*, not on the price level. Under nominal-income targeting, other things being equal, a cumulative movement of the price level

---

16. For the United States, Japan, and Germany, there are seventy-five cells in table 5-2 for which stochastic simulations are available; twelve out of the seventy-five, about the same proportion as for the large group of five countries, indicate money targeting or exchange-rate targeting as preferred. Of the eight cases where money targeting is preferred, five and a half are for Japan and two and a half for Germany. Of the four cases of exchange-rate targeting, three are for the United States (all for the LIVERPOOL model) and one is for Japan.

away from its desired path requires stronger and stronger policy action to reverse that tendency. With real-GNP-plus-inflation targeting, a substantial drift over time can occur in the level of prices, measured ex post, without triggering policy action. As noted in chapter 3 and clearly observed in the deterministic simulations in chapter 4, past episodes of upward (or downward) adjustment in the price level are treated essentially as bygones, not subject to subsequent correction.

Suppose for an extended period that inflationary pressures in an economy, not attributable to monetary policy, would tend to produce a positive inflation rate, with the price level drifting upward over time. The inherent features of the two regimes imply that nominal-income targeting would prove unambiguously superior to real-GNP-plus-inflation targeting in inhibiting the upward drift in the price level (preventing cumulative inflation over the longer run). It seems at least possible, on a priori grounds, that nominal-income targeting could perform less well than real-GNP-plus-inflation targeting in moderating variability in the inflation rate over shorter runs.[17]

The inference that nominal-income targeting is better for minimizing deviations of the price level from baseline is broadly supported by the stochastic simulations. In two-thirds of the cases (twenty-three and a half of the thirty-five for which data are available), price-level variability is least for nominal-income targeting. But regime 2A/2AX and regime 2B/2BX do about equally well in minimizing variability in the inflation rate; 2A/2AX is the preferred regime in 54 percent of the cases (nineteen of thirty-five).[18]

These stochastic simulation results are roughly consistent with the analogous generalizations in earlier chapters. Chapter 2 gives clear examples, it will be remembered, where the price level stays permanently away from baseline under the CC regime, whereas it is forced to return to baseline under the YY regime. In chapter 4, as in this chapter, regime 2A/2AX is preferred over 2B/2BX for keeping the price level close to baseline (unambiguously for Japan, somewhat less clearly for the United States and Germany). Chapter 4 and this chapter show slightly different results, however, about the performance of the two regime types in minimizing inflation variability in the shorter run. For the deterministic simulations, regime 2B/2BX more often than not outperforms

---

17. Suppose that the inflation rate were to fluctuate narrowly around a constant rate in each period, and that that rate were modest and close to the target rate that policymakers specify for regime 2B/2BX. In such circumstances, the *RMSD* of the inflation rate could be quite small, even though the cumulative difference between the beginning and ending price level would be substantial. Regime 2A/2AX might therefore do markedly better at preventing a cumulative drift in prices, but at the expense of greater variability in the inflation rate.

18. If attention is restricted to the six models that implemented all four regime types, nominal-income targeting performs best in minimizing variability in the price level in 63 percent of the cases (seventeen and a half of twenty-eight) and performs best in minimizing inflation variability in 46 percent (thirteen of twenty-eight). The figures for price-level results are not shown in tables 5-2–5-4 but are available in annex B.

2A/2AX in minimizing deviations of the inflation rate from baseline (at least for the United States and Japan). For the stochastic simulations, the results for the inflation rate for the two regimes are mixed; no clear winner emerges for the G3 countries. For the United Kingdom and Canada, the 2B/2BX regime is somewhat preferred for minimizing both price-level and inflation-rate deviations.

Because real-GNP-plus-inflation targeting treats past episodes of inflation as bygones, policymakers using that regime will presumably have greater latitude to concentrate their policy on preventing deviations in the level of output from a desired path. In the empirical results here, which are supported by the deterministic simulations in chapter 4, it is true that regime 2B/2BX is preferred more often when the loss function includes only real GNP. Out of the thirty-five available model/country combinations, regime 2B/2BX emerges as best in twenty-two cases (63 percent); regime 2A/2AX is preferred in eight and a half cases (24 percent), 3/3X in three cases, and 1/1X in only one and a half cases.

Exceptions and Contrasts among Models

Given the numerous differences among the participating models in structure, and given the cross-model differences in implementation of the stochastic simulations, one should undoubtedly expect substantial diversity in the empirical results. We now identify some of the more important differences across the models, emphasizing the model/country combinations that are exceptions.

In the MULTIMOD results for Japan, money targeting (1 or 1X) is the preferred, or equivalently preferred, regime for all three of the illustrative loss functions shown in table 5-2. For Canada also, regime 1X is preferred (ranked equivalently to nominal-income targeting) if the loss function includes only real GNP or both real GNP and inflation. For the United Kingdom, exchange-rate targeting (MULTIMOD's regime 3X) is preferred for two of the three loss functions. In contrast, the MULTIMOD results for Germany tend to show nominal-income targeting as the preferred regime, whereas for the United States they show real-GNP-plus-inflation targeting as preferred. Thus MULTIMOD, unlike most of the models, reports considerable diversity in the preferred regime across the five countries.[19] (In the deterministic simulations of chapter 4, MUL-

---

19. The conceptual specifications of the country submodels in MULTIMOD are identical; furthermore, many of the parameter values are common across countries (imposed in the estimation process). The restriction that key parameters be identical across countries could result in significant differences in the MULTIMOD residuals across countries, which might contribute to an explanation of this diversity in preferred regime for the MULTIMOD stochastic results. It is also noteworthy, however, that a similar approach to the estimation of parameters was taken by the INTERMOD group, and an analogous diversity in the preferred regime across countries is not apparent for INTERMOD. (It may be that the INTERMOD group imposed fewer common constraints across regions than the MULTIMOD group during the estimation process.)

TIMOD also tends to exhibit more diversity than most other models in preferred regime across country/shock combinations.)

LIVERPOOL is the other participating model whose stochastic simulation results frequently favor exchange-rate targeting or money targeting. Like MULTIMOD, LIVERPOOL shows considerable diversity in the preferred regime across countries. Unlike any other model, LIVERPOOL consistently finds exchange-rate targeting (LIVERPOOL variant 3X) to be superior for the United States. Moreover, for two of the three loss functions, the LIVERPOOL model's preference for the United States to follow regime 3X is pronounced (boldfaced in table 5-2).[20] The other case in table 5-2 in which LIVERPOOL prefers regime 3X is for Canada when real GNP alone is in the loss function; for that case, however, the preference is weak rather than pronounced, since regime 2A performs almost as well as 3X. If policy emphasis is placed exclusively on inflation, the LIVERPOOL model argues that money targeting is preferred for Japan and Germany. (In the deterministic simulations of chapter 4, LIVERPOOL also shows a preference for money targeting or exchange-rate targeting more often than other models. Some interesting differences exist, however, between that model's deterministic and stochastic simulations. For example, when the loss function depends exclusively on inflation, the LIVERPOOL stochastic results for Germany favor money targeting, whereas the LIVERPOOL deterministic results tend to favor nominal-income targeting.)

Of the relatively small number of cases in table 5-2 where money targeting or exchange-rate targeting emerges as the loss-minimizing regime, LIVERPOOL and MULTIMOD together account for three-fourths of them (thirteen out of seventeen). Were it not for these two models, the combined dominance in the overall results of nominal-income targeting and real-GNP-plus-inflation targeting would be much more pronounced.[21]

The other models with occasional instances in table 5-2 of money targeting or exchange-rate targeting emerging as preferred, or tied for first place, are TAYLOR, MSG, and INTERMOD-C. Exchange-rate targeting in the TAYLOR model (variant 3X) does modestly better than other regimes in minimizing

---

20. Recall that regime 3/3X assumes that countries other than the United States peg their currencies to the U.S. dollar while the United States itself implements money targeting. For the LIVERPOOL group, regime 3X entails actual fixing of bilateral dollar exchange rates (as in the Bretton Woods system without realignments). Since none of the other model groups used an X specification that tightly fixed exchange rates, the LIVERPOOL 3X results for exchange-rate targeting are not comparable with those of other models.

21. Recall that most of the cases in which 1/1X or 3/3X is preferred are instances in which the next-closest type of regime has nearly as low a value of the loss function. It is also pertinent to recall—see chapter 3—that MULTIMOD (especially for real-GNP-plus-inflation targeting, their regime 2BX, but also for 1X, 2AX, and 3X) and LIVERPOOL (for all its X regimes) are among the most prominent examples of model groups deviating from the prescribed O specifications for the regimes. We do not have a feasible way to determine how much of the differences in simulation results between MULTIMOD and LIVERPOOL vis-à-vis the other models can be attributed to the greater departure of those two models from the standardized guidelines.

Table 5-5. *Variability in Real GNP, Price Level, and Inflation: Real-GNP-plus-Inflation Targeting Compared with Nominal-Income Targeting*

Index value for *RMS%D* or *RMSD* of regime 2B/2BX (regime 2A or 2AX = 1.0)

Country and variable	GEM	INTERMOD-A	INTERMOD-C	LIVERPOOL	MPS	MSG	MULTIMOD	MX3	TAYLOR
				Model					
United States									
Real GNP, level	0.93	0.70	0.87	3.65	0.69	0.72	0.87	0.25	1.33
Real GNP, growth	0.94	0.89	1.00	2.77	1.01	0.63	0.96	0.94	1.03
GNP deflator, level	0.98	0.84	2.24	32.62	1.94	2.78	0.53	2.47	0.93
GNP deflator, change	0.98	0.83	1.87	8.70	1.04	1.78	0.57	1.50	0.86
Loss: GNP + inflation	0.95	0.74	1.17	6.41	0.84	1.14	0.76	0.41	1.14
Japan									
Real GNP, level	0.83	0.53	0.53	5.23	n.a.	1.08	1.08	0.91	0.84
Real GNP, growth	1.05	0.83	0.86	5.93	n.a.	1.06	1.38	0.85	0.93
GNP deflator, level	1.04	1.20	3.24	38.65	n.a.	2.00	1.04	3.38	2.41
GNP deflator, change	1.08	1.04	2.20	11.55	n.a.	1.30	0.97	1.14	0.97
Loss: GNP + inflation	0.94	0.70	1.07	7.97	n.a.	1.10	1.03	1.00	0.88
Germany									
Real GNP, level	0.95	0.73	0.87	14.10	n.a.	1.42	1.15	0.69	1.06
Real GNP, growth	1.08	0.89	0.94	7.72	n.a.	1.35	1.07	0.64	1.01
GNP deflator, level	1.59	0.75	3.73	114.34	n.a.	2.02	0.83	5.23	1.08
GNP deflator, change	1.33	0.69	2.02	38.88	n.a.	2.89	0.81	1.38	0.84
Loss: GNP + inflation	1.08	0.72	1.15	25.93	n.a.	1.60	1.03	0.90	0.93
United Kingdom									
Real GNP, level	n.a.	0.68	0.93	4.00	n.a.	n.a.	1.30	n.a.	1.16
Real GNP, growth	n.a.	0.77	1.01	3.00	n.a.	n.a.	1.14	n.a.	0.99
GNP deflator, level	n.a.	0.92	7.47	22.64	n.a.	n.a.	0.90	n.a.	1.02
GNP deflator, change	n.a.	0.85	3.68	18.86	n.a.	n.a.	0.83	n.a.	1.00
Loss: GNP + inflation	n.a.	0.74	1.87	6.13	n.a.	n.a.	1.11	n.a.	1.07
Canada									
Real GNP, level	n.a.	0.66	0.69	4.88	n.a.	n.a.	1.26	n.a.	0.60
Real GNP, growth	n.a.	0.83	0.90	7.89	n.a.	n.a.	1.16	n.a.	0.99
GNP deflator, level	n.a.	0.99	5.13	28.63	n.a.	n.a.	0.75	n.a.	0.97
GNP deflator, change	n.a.	0.87	3.48	17.69	n.a.	n.a.	0.74	n.a.	0.90
Loss: GNP + inflation	n.a.	0.72	1.59	9.45	n.a.	n.a.	1.04	n.a.	0.64

Source: B-I tables in annex B, full-period (ten-year) simulations.
n.a.: Not available.

inflation variability for Japan and the United Kingdom. With exclusive emphasis on inflation in the loss function, money targeting (variant 1X) emerges as preferred for Japan in MSG, and as tied with 2BX for Germany in TAYLOR. Money targeting (1) and nominal-income targeting (2AX) perform about equally well for Japan in INTERMOD-C when the loss function gives equal weight to output and inflation.

The MULTIMOD and LIVERPOOL results, together with those for TAYLOR, are also the primary exceptions to the generalizations that nominal-income targeting is the overall preferred regime for controlling price-level variability, whereas real-GNP-plus-inflation targeting functions best overall for controlling output variability. TAYLOR and MULTIMOD both report regime 2A/2AX as preferred for keeping the price level close to baseline for only one of the five countries (LIVERPOOL is four out of five). When the illustrative loss function includes only real GNP, regime 2B/2BX never emerges as preferred overall for LIVERPOOL and fails to do so for TAYLOR for three of the five countries and for MULTIMOD for four of the five countries.

Table 5-5 facilitates a direct comparison between nominal-income targeting and real-GNP-plus-inflation targeting. The figures in this table are ratios: the root-mean-squared deviation (*RMS%D* or *RMSD*) of the 2B/2BX regime divided by the corresponding root-mean-squared deviation of the 2A/2AX regime (in other words, index values with the 2A/2AX regime equal to unity). A cell with a value greater than unity indicates greater variability (higher *RMS%D* or *RMSD*) for the real-GNP-plus-inflation targeting regime (relative to nominal-income targeting). Data are presented for the level and growth rate of GNP, the level of the GNP deflator and its inflation rate, and finally for the loss function that combines real GNP and inflation.

Reinforcing the inferences from the ordinal rankings in the earlier tables, table 5-5 reveals that there are five models for which real-GNP-plus-inflation targeting is consistently preferred over nominal-income targeting for stabilizing real GNP; these are GEM, INTERMOD-A, INTERMOD-C, MPS, and MX3. This dominance of the 2B/2BX regime over 2A/2AX, however, is not observed for two of three countries for MSG, three of the five countries for TAYLOR, four of the five countries for MULTIMOD, and any of the countries for LIVERPOOL.

The results for INTERMOD in table 5-5 are fully consistent with the generalizations about minimizing output variability: typically by a substantial margin, for both INTERMOD-A and INTERMOD-C, real-GNP-plus-inflation targeting outperforms nominal-income targeting for all five countries. For INTERMOD-C, furthermore, regime 2B or 2BX consistently does worse than 2A or 2AX in minimizing variability of the price level. The INTERMOD-A results, however, exhibit a contrary tendency for variability of the price level: for four of the five countries (Japan is the exception), INTERMOD-A shows 2B/2BX performing *better* than 2A/2AX. For the loss function combining real GNP and inflation, the INTERMOD-C results invariably show 2A/2AX as the preferred regime, whereas INTERMOD-A invariably favors 2B/2BX. For INTERMOD, therefore, the choice of monetary policy regimes is contingent on whether the model does or does not treat expectations as rational. Nominal-income targeting is favored when expectations are assumed to be rational, whereas the assumption of adaptive expectations yields outcomes favoring real-GNP-plus-inflation targeting. More is said below about this interesting difference between the consistent-expectations and adaptive-expectations versions of INTERMOD.

Money Targeting versus Exchange-Rate Targeting

A money-targeting or an exchange-rate-targeting regime seldom emerges as first best for keeping output or even inflation close to policymakers' desired paths. Nonetheless, given the prominence of these two regime types in policy debates, it is interesting to consider how they fare against each other.

For the MSG model, exchange-rate targeting performs substantially less well than money targeting for minimizing either output or inflation deviations; this finding is robust across all three of the countries for which results are reported.[22] The INTERMOD model, with a few exceptions, tends to find relatively small differences between the two regime types. For INTERMOD-C, exchange-rate targeting is usually mildly preferred for reducing output deviations, whereas money targeting is preferred for reducing inflation deviations; with INTERMOD-A, exchange-rate targeting is much better than money targeting for reducing output deviations for Japan but somewhat worse for Germany and the United Kingdom. The comparison for TAYLOR is also mixed: for the United States, exchange-rate targeting is strongly preferred for reducing output deviations but does somewhat worse than money targeting for reducing inflation deviations. The opposite is true for the TAYLOR model for Japan, where exchange-rate targeting is markedly worse for stabilizing output but marginally better for controlling the inflation rate; for Germany, money targeting is preferred for reducing both output and inflation deviations. The MULTIMOD results differ across countries: exchange-rate targeting is mildly better than money targeting for the United States, for both output and inflation; as seen earlier, exchange-rate targeting is the first-best regime for stabilizing output in the United Kingdom; for Japan, money targeting is the first-best regime for both

---

22. The statement in the text compares regimes 1 and 3 for the MSG model. When the MSG 1X and 3X regimes are compared, the differences between the two for the United States are small (a consequence of the "exact-targeting" nature of the X regimes implemented by the MSG group).

variables; money targeting also tends to outperform exchange-rate targeting in Germany and Canada. The LIVERPOOL model always prefers money targeting over exchange-rate targeting when the LIVERPOOL regimes are specified with the short-term interest rate as the policy instrument (regimes 1 and 3); in contrast, when the LIVERPOOL regimes are specified with the money stock treated as the policy instrument (variants 1X and 3X), money targeting often (but not invariably) performs worse than exchange-rate targeting.

Plainly, the comparison between money targeting and exchange-rate targeting is mixed. For output and inflation variability, we have not uncovered any generalization about the relative performance of these two regime types that seems robust across the participating models or across the countries for which data were reported.

Extending the Loss Function to Non-Price, Non-Output Variables

We have so far focused on variability in real GNP and in the inflation rate (or the price level). These two classes of macroeconomic variables perhaps should be the main center of attention; they are widely regarded by policymakers as the "ultimate-target" variables most closely correlated with basic measures of aggregate and individual economic welfare.

Output and inflation, however, cannot be the exclusive focus. For reasons given earlier, employment may be a better surrogate for welfare than output when productivity shocks are prevalent. And many policymakers include variables other than output, employment, and inflation in their loss functions (implicitly, if not explicitly). Policymakers may believe that other non-price, non-output variables—for example, a nation's external position—are important indicators of national economic welfare. Alternatively, policymakers may incorporate such variables in their rankings of outcomes because volatility in those variables is perceived as imposing costs on the economy. When interest rates or exchange rates are used as policy instruments, for example, costs may be incurred (or at least policymakers may believe that costs are incurred) if those instruments have to be changed frequently by large amounts rather than being held on smoother paths.

Whatever the details of the rationalization, attention needs to be paid to non-price, non-output variables in empirical analysis of policy regimes. As shown in chapters 2 and 4, moreover, conclusions about the relative performance of policy regimes can change significantly when these variables are considered. In particular, the apparent relative dominance of nominal-income targeting and real-GNP-plus-inflation targeting may be called more into question.

Table 5-6. *Non-Output, Non-Price Variables: Identification of Regime with Lowest Root-Mean-Squared Deviation*[a]

Country and variable					Model				
	GEM	INTERMOD-A	INTERMOD-C	LIVERPOOL	MPS	MSG	MULTIMOD	MX3	TAYLOR
United States									
Short-term interest rate	2AX/2BX	1	**2AX**	**3X**	**2A**	2A	**2AX**	1	**1X**
Change in interest rate	**1X**	**2AX**	**2AX**	**3X**	**1X**	1	**2AX**	1	n.a.
Bilateral dollar exchange rate	n.a.	n.a.	n.a.	n.a.	**2A**[b]	n.a.	n.a.	n.a.	n.a.
Current account/GNP ratio	2BX	1/3	3	3X	2AX	**2B**	1/2AX/2BX	1/2A/2AX	**2AX**
Japan									
Short-term interest rate	**2AX**	3	3	**3X**	n.a.	**3X**	2AX	1	1/2AX/2BX
Change in interest rate	**1X**	3	3	**3X**	n.a.	**3X**	1X/2AX	1	n.a.
Bilateral dollar exchange rate	**2AX**[c]	3	3	**3X**	n.a.	**3X**	**3X**	1/2A[c]	3X
Current account/GNP ratio	2BX	2BX	2BX	**2AX**	n.a.	**2AX**	2AX/2BX	1/2B	2BX
Germany									
Short-term interest rate	**1X**	3	3	**3X**	n.a.	**3X**	**2AX**	2A	**1X**
Change in interest rate	**1X**	3	3	**3X**	n.a.	**3X**	**2AX**	**2A**	n.a.
Bilateral dollar exchange rate	**2AX**[c]	3	3	**3X**	n.a.	**3X**	**3X**	2A[c]	**3X**
Current account/GNP ratio	1X	1	3	2AX	n.a.	**2BX**	2AX/2BX	**2A**	2AX
United Kingdom									
Short-term interest rate	n.a.	3	3	**2A**	n.a.	n.a.	2AX	n.a.	**1X**
Change in interest rate	n.a.	3	3	**2A**	n.a.	n.a.	**2AX**	n.a.	n.a.
Bilateral dollar exchange rate	n.a.	3	3	**3X**	n.a.	n.a.	**3X**	n.a.	**3X**
Current account/GNP ratio	n.a.	1	2AX	**3X**	n.a.	n.a.	3X	n.a.	2BX
Canada									
Short-term interest rate	n.a.	3	2AX	**2A**	n.a.	n.a.	2AX	n.a.	**1X**
Change in interest rate	n.a.	3	2AX	**2A**	n.a.	n.a.	1X	n.a.	n.a.
Bilateral dollar exchange rate	n.a.	3	3	**3X**	n.a.	n.a.	**3X**	n.a.	**3X**
Current account/GNP ratio	n.a.	1	3	**3X**	n.a.	n.a.	1	n.a.	**2BX**

Source: B-1 tables in annex B, full-period (ten-year) simulations.

n.a.: Not available.

a. When the *RMS%Ds* or *RMSDs* for two regimes differ by 1 percent or less, the table identifies the regimes as tied. When an entry in a cell is in boldface type, that regime is associated with a reduction in the value of the loss function by 10 percent or more relative to the second-best type of regime. See the text for further explanation. The MPS model did not implement regime 3/3X; see table C-1-4 in annex C.

b. The exchange rate in the MPS model is a weighted-average exchange rate for the U.S. dollar vis-à-vis the currencies of Group of Ten countries.

c. The GEM model group did not report results for regime 3/3X. The MX3 group was unable to implement regime 3/3X in their model.

Table 5-6 is constructed in a manner analogous to table 5-2 but is derived from simulation results for the short-term interest rate, bilateral dollar exchange rates, and the ratio of the nominal current account to nominal GNP. For each model/country/variable combination, the table again identifies the regime that minimizes *RMS%D*s or *RMSD*s. Ties for highest ordinal ranking are indicated when the *RMS%D*s or *RMSD*s for regimes differ by 1 percent or less. Boldfaced cells indicate reductions of more than 10 percent relative to the regime type with the next lowest value.

Consider first exchange-rate variability.[23] One would of course expect that exchange-rate targeting would result in less deviation of an exchange rate from its target (baseline) path than for the other regimes. And that presumption is consistently borne out in the empirical results here (as shown in the third row of table 5-6, for each country), as it was in chapter 4. It may be seen from examination of the B-1 tables in annex B that the *RMS%D*s for the regimes other than exchange-rate targeting (for bilateral dollar exchange rates for countries other than the United States) are often a large multiple of those for regime 3/3X. The GEM, MX3, and MPS models at first may seem to be an exception. Remember, however, that results for exchange-rate targeting are not available for GEM, MX3, and MPS. Hence the entries for those models in table 5-6 (as in table 5-2) cannot be interpreted as full heats in a hypothetical horse race; the 3/3X "horse" for those models could not or did not enter the starting gate.[24]

If policymakers were to take exchange-rate variability into account in their loss function, then that inclusion could make regime 3/3X appear more attractive than it otherwise would be. Whether this point would be quantitatively significant would depend, of course, on the weight attached to exchange-rate variability in the loss function.

An analogous point applies to the current account of the balance of payments. As shown in table 5-6, no one of the four regime types is markedly better than the others in minimizing deviations from baseline of the ratio of the current account to GNP. For the six model groups that successfully implemented all four regime types, data are available for twenty-eight cases for the current account ratio; for these cases each of the regime types, including exchange-rate targeting and money targeting, appears about equally with the lowest *RMSD*. Hence exchange-rate targeting or money targeting has a somewhat higher

---

23. In the original guidelines for the stochastic simulations, model groups were requested to submit root-mean-squared deviations not only for the level but also for the period-to-period *change* in bilateral dollar exchange rates. Only two groups submitted the *RMSD*s for exchange-rate changes, however, so that the tables and discussion here can focus only on deviations from baseline of the level of the exchange rate.

24. When the table shows for GEM that regime 2AX has the lowest *RMS%D* for the bilateral dollar exchange rate for Japan and Germany, for example, the correct interpretation is that regime 2AX has smaller deviations of the exchange rate from baseline than the GEM variant regimes 1X and 2BX.

probability of emerging as the preferred regime if policymakers include the current account as a target or constraint variable in their loss function.[25]

Interest-Rate Variability

The apparent dominance of nominal-income targeting and real-GNP-plus-inflation targeting might be even more questionable if policymakers are concerned about variability in interest rates. For the stochastic simulations discussed here, the model groups specified the nominal short-term interest rate as the instrument of monetary policy.[26] Inclusion of interest-rate variability in an illustrative loss function can be justified either as an acknowledgment of policymakers' concern about the costs of such variability or as an analytical device for penalizing "instrument instability."[27]

Table 5-6 reports the regime with lowest *RMSD* from baseline for both the level of the short-term interest rate (first row for each country) and its period-to-period change (second row). As was true for the deterministic simulations in chapter 4 and for the reasons identified in chapter 2, interest rates are often less variable under money targeting or exchange-rate targeting than under either nominal-income targeting or real-GNP-plus-inflation targeting. For all the available model results for both the level and period-to-period change, either money targeting or exchange-rate targeting has the lowest *RMSD* more than three-fifths of the time; out of sixty-five available cases, money targeting accounts for sixteen and five-sixths and exchange-rate targeting for twenty-four (a total of forty and five-sixths). If attention is restricted to the six models that successfully implemented all four regime types, the proportion for exchange-rate targeting and money targeting together is similarly high (thirty-one and five-sixths out of fifty-one cases). Furthermore, as is indicated by the cells in table 5-6 that are boldfaced, many of the instances in which exchange-rate targeting or money targeting minimizes variation in interest rates are cases where the variation is substantially less than that for the next closest type of regime.

As noted earlier, the last rows of the panels in the B-I tables in annex B contain an illustrative loss function that includes, in addition to output and inflation variability, an equally weighted term for the *RMSD* of the change in the short-term interest rate. The regime that minimizes this loss function for the various model/country combinations is identified in table 5-7. Exchange-rate targeting or money targeting is preferred in a larger proportion of the cases

---

25. Japan may be an exception to this generalization (see the eighth row of table 5-6).

26. The TAYLOR and the LIVERPOOL X regimes are exceptions (see chapter 3).

27. The problem of instrument instability is identified and discussed in, for example, Holbrook (1972). Some numerical examples are given in chapter 4 of Bryant, Henderson, and others (1988, *EMIE*).

for the loss function underlying table 5-7 than for the loss functions used for table 5-2. Data are available for thirty of the cells in the table; in ten of those instances, a third, regime 1, 1X, 3, or 3X is preferred.[28]

This result also has a corollary: as attention is shifted from a loss function that excludes to one that includes interest-rate variability, a "reversal" in ranking—a change of preferred regime—becomes possible (for some models, likely). Eight instances of such reversal occur in these empirical results. The relevant cells are shaded in table 5-7. Six of the eight reversals are instances in which the preferred regime shifts away from nominal-income targeting toward exchange-rate targeting or money targeting.[29] For example, for the United States MULTIMOD shifts from regime 2BX to 3X; for Japan, MX3 shifts from 2AX to 1 and INTERMOD-A shifts from 2B to 3. Such reversals imply substantial variability in interest rates.

How much weight in their loss function might policymakers give to interest-rate variation? We conjecture that the simplified, illustrative loss function underlying the calculations behind table 5-7, which gives the same weight to interest-rate variation as to deviations of output and inflation from desired paths, exaggerates the weight that would normally be given in actual practice. Nonetheless, this illustration empirically demonstrates the general point that incorporation of interest-rate variability in the loss function can significantly influence the evaluation of alternative regimes.

Can the regime types be ranked unambiguously in terms of the differing amounts of interest-rate variability to which they give rise? On the basis of these stochastic simulations, no overall generalization seems possible about the relative performances of exchange-rate targeting, money targeting, and nominal-income targeting. Among these three, the relative magnitudes of interest-rate variability appear to be contingent on the particular model, on the particular country, or on both. For example, for INTERMOD-C the ranking of *RMSD*s for period-to-period changes in the interest rate of the three regime types is $3 < 2AX < 1$ for Japan, Germany, and the United Kingdom but changes to $2AX < 3 < 1$ for the United States and Canada. Period-to-period changes for MULTIMOD are ranked $2AX < 1X < 3X$ for the United States, $1X < 2AX < 3X$ for Japan, and $2AX < 3X < 1X$ for Germany. And so on.

Table 5-6 provides a modest basis for distinguishing among the three regime types across countries in the ability of the regimes to minimize variability in

---

28. If attention is restricted to the five models that implemented all regime types and that reported data for the *RMSD* of the period-to-period change in the interest rate (INTERMOD-A, INTERMOD-C, LIVERPOOL, MSG, and MULTIMOD; period-to-period change data are not available for TAYLOR), the proportion is again about one-third (eight out of twenty-three).

29. The exceptions are the LIVERPOOL model for Japan and the MSG model for Germany, which prefer nominal-income targeting rather than money targeting or exchange-rate targeting when the loss function incorporates interest-rate variability.

Table 5-7. *Including Interest-Rate Variation: Identification of the Regime Minimizing Fourth Illustrative Loss Function (Real GNP + Inflation + Change in Interest Rate)*[a]

Country	Model								
	GEM	INTERMOD-A	INTERMOD-C	LIVERPOOL	MPS	MSG	MULTIMOD	MX3	TAYLOR
United States	2AX/2BX	2BX	**2AX**	**3X**	2BX	2BX	3X	**2B**	n.a.
Japan	2BX	3	2AX	**2A**	n.a.	2A	1X	1	n.a.
Germany	1X	2BX	3	**3X**	n.a.	**2A**	**2AX**	**2A**	n.a.
United Kingdom	n.a.	**2BX**	2AX	**2A**	n.a.	n.a.	3X	n.a.	n.a.
Canada	n.a.	**2BX**	2AX	**2A**	n.a.	n.a.	1X	n.a.	n.a.

Source: B-l tables in annex B, full-period (ten-year) simulations.

n.a.: Not available.

a. Shading of a cell indicates an instance of "regime switching" when analysis moves from the loss function used in table 5-2 to the loss function in this table containing the change in the short-term interest rate. When an entry in a cell is in boldface type, that regime is associated with a reduction in the value of the loss function by more than 10 percent relative to the second-best type of regime. See the text for further explanation.

interest rates. Exchange-rate targeting, for example, is favored more than any other regime for minimizing deviations in both levels and changes in interest rates for Germany and Japan. In contrast, exchange-rate targeting is not preferred for that purpose in the United States (with the single exception of LIVERPOOL).

When the relative magnitudes of interest-rate variability under nominal-income targeting and real-GNP-plus-inflation targeting are contrasted, a robust generalization does emerge: real-GNP-plus-inflation targeting tends to entail considerably more interest-rate variation than do the other regime types. Real-GNP-plus-inflation targeting also tends to generate larger root-mean-squared deviations for exchange rates. (A clue to this generalization was already apparent in table 5-6, where real-GNP-plus-inflation targeting was virtually absent from the rows of the table pertaining to variation in interest rates and exchange rates.) These results are consistent with the theoretical analysis in chapter 2 of interest-rate effects for productivity shocks under the YY and CC regimes (and with the analysis of the deterministic simulations in chapter 4).[30]

Table 5-8 illustrates this point by contrasting the root-mean-squared deviations for real-GNP-plus-inflation targeting with those for nominal-income targeting; the variables examined are the levels and period-to-period changes in the interest rate and the levels of bilateral dollar exchange rates. The entries in the table are again ratios of the *RMSD* or *RMS%D* for regime 2B/2BX divided by the corresponding root-mean-squared deviation for regime 2A/2AX. For example, for INTERMOD-C for the United States, level deviations from baseline for regime 2BX were 151 percent, and period-to-period changes were 223 percent, of those for regime 2AX. The table shows that, with only a few exceptions, regime 2B/2BX produced more variation in interest rates and exchange rates than did regime 2A/2AX. In many instances, the variability under 2B/2BX was a significant multiple of that for 2A/2AX. Judged by these empirical results, the real-GNP-plus-inflation targeting regime requires policymakers to accept significantly greater amounts of variability in interest rates, and perhaps also in exchange rates.

As pointed out earlier, the theoretical analysis in chapter 2 identifies productivity shocks as the primary reason that interest rates would be more variable under real-GNP-plus-inflation targeting (the CC regime) than under nominal-

---

30. Under most conditions (and in particular when oil is omitted from the analysis), goods-demand and money-demand shocks have identical interest-rate consequences under the YY and CC regimes. For productivity shocks, the source of the difference in interest-rate effects between the YY and CC regimes is that the price level does not return to baseline under the CC regime, whereas it must do so under the YY regime. The analysis in chapter 2 tends *not* to uncover differences in effects on exchange rates between the YY and CC regimes; hence the stochastic simulation results for exchange rates are not readily reconciled with the theory in chapter 2.

Table 5-8. *Interest-Rate and Exchange-Rate Variability: Real-GNP-plus-Inflation Targeting Contrasted with Nominal-Income Targeting*

Index value for RMS%D or RMSD of regime 2B/2BX (regime 2AX or 2A = 1.0)

Country and variable	Model								
	GEM	INTERMOD-A	INTERMOD-C	LIVERPOOL	MPS	MSG	MULTIMOD	MX3	TAYLOR
United States									
Short-term interest rate									
Level	0.98	0.77	1.51	14.49	1.13	0.72	3.04	2.61	1.00
Change	1.42	1.68	2.23	7.12	1.40	1.61	6.03	1.93	n.a.
Bilateral dollar exchange rate									
Level	n.a.	n.a.	n.a.	n.a.	n.a.	n.a.	n.a.	n.a.	n.a.
Japan									
Short-term interest rate									
Level	0.64	0.75	1.97	9.27	n.a.	0.92	4.37	2.28	1.10
Change	1.13	1.50	2.29	8.03	n.a.	1.03	7.04	2.74	n.a.
Bilateral dollar exchange rate									
Level	2.04	0.57	1.66	33.03	n.a.	1.90	2.02	1.22	0.93
Germany									
Short-term interest rate									
Level	1.59	0.88	1.55	37.27	n.a.	1.19	3.49	2.38	1.00
Change	1.33	1.49	1.81	12.19	n.a.	1.01	3.90	2.71	n.a.
Bilateral dollar exchange rate									
Level	1.25	0.82	1.43	40.71	n.a.	1.60	1.57	1.30	1.06
United Kingdom									
Short-term interest rate									
Level	n.a.	0.81	2.59	5.80	n.a.	n.a.	3.20	n.a.	1.00
Change	n.a.	1.24	2.11	6.41	n.a.	n.a.	4.19	n.a.	n.a.
Bilateral dollar exchange rate									
Level	n.a.	0.84	3.65	21.67	n.a.	n.a.	1.83	n.a.	0.98
Canada									
Short-term interest rate									
Level	n.a.	0.82	2.58	1.79	n.a.	n.a.	3.15	n.a.	1.11
Change	n.a.	1.37	2.33	8.46	n.a.	n.a.	5.77	n.a.	n.a.
Bilateral dollar exchange rate									
Level	n.a.	1.58	6.03	26.65	n.a.	n.a.	1.59	n.a.	1.04

Source: B-I tables in annex B, full-period (ten-year) simulations.
n.a.: Not available.

Table 5-9. *MPS Experimentation with Alternative Coefficients for Real-GNP-plus-Inflation Targeting Regime, U.S. Variables*

Index value for *RMS%D* or *RMSD* (base case of regime 2BX = 1.0)

U.S. variable	Base case (2BX) (1.50, 0.75)	Alternative coefficient values		
		(2.00, 0.50)	(1.00, 0.50)	(1.50, 0.25)
Real GNP				
Level	1.00	0.84	1.26	1.02
Growth rate	1.00	0.93	1.01	0.94
GNP deflator				
Level	1.00	1.04	1.19	1.20
Inflation rate	1.00	1.02	1.11	1.10
Short-term interest rate				
Level	1.00	1.02	0.90	0.95
Period-to-period change	1.00	1.00	0.70	0.75
Monetary base				
Level	1.00	1.06	1.15	1.19

Source: B-I tables in annex B, full-period (ten-year) simulations, and memorandum submitted to project organizers.

income targeting. It is tempting to interpret the data in table 5-8 as supporting the conjecture that supply-side shocks are quantitatively important in most or all of the model groups' variance-covariance matrices.

When the MPS model group submitted their stochastic simulations, they reported an extension of the analysis that sheds some further light on the variability of interest rates (and other variables) under real-GNP-plus-inflation targeting. The original guidelines for regime 2B specified that the real-GNP and inflation terms were to be assigned coefficients with the same value of 1.5 (see equations 3-1 in chapter 3). The MPS group experimented with alternative coefficients on the two terms. The MPS 2BX regime reported in table B-I-4 has a coefficient of 1.50 for real GNP and 0.75 for inflation. In addition, the MPS group reported simulations with other combinations of coefficients; for example, they performed simulations with pairs of coefficients for real GNP and inflation of (2.00, 0.50), (1.00, 0.50), and (1.50, 0.25). In their results it is thus possible to examine the effects of doubling the output coefficient while keeping the inflation coefficient unchanged at 0.50, and cutting the inflation coefficient by a factor of 3 while keeping the real-GNP coefficient unchanged at 1.50. Table 5-9 summarizes the results of this MPS experimentation for a few key variables.

The results in table 5-9 imply (not surprisingly) that policymakers using real-GNP-plus-inflation targeting could stabilize a combination of real GNP and inflation more effectively by adjusting the relative sizes of the coefficients on the two terms (from the arbitrary, identical values specified in the project guidelines). In the MPS model, at any rate, lower root-mean-squared deviations are obtained for key variables when a smaller coefficient is used for the inflation term than for the real GNP term.

Note, however, that the improved stabilization of output and inflation may come at a cost of increased volatility in interest rates. Adjusting the output coefficient in the regime upward and the inflation coefficient downward relative to the base case (going from column 1 to column 2 in the table) results in a better stabilization of output with only slightly worse inflation performance and little change in interest-rate volatility. But halving the output coefficient with no change in the inflation coefficient (column 3 versus 2) poses a more difficult trade-off; period-to-period interest-rate volatility falls significantly (by 30 percent), but at the cost of worse stabilization of both output and inflation. Another instance of difficult trade-off can be seen by comparing columns 1 and 4 of the table; cutting the MPS coefficient on inflation by a factor of 3 with the income coefficient kept at 1.5 slightly worsens output variability, significantly worsens inflation variability, but reduces period-to-period interest-rate variation by 25 percent.

To put the MPS figures about interest-rate variability in table 5-9 in perspective, remember that, even with the base case 2BX coefficients, the period-to-period variation for real-GNP-plus-inflation targeting was 4 percent greater than that for nominal-income targeting (table 5-8), which in turn was some 25 percent greater than under the MPS version of the money targeting regime (table B-I-4 in annex B). If policymakers were to use the MPS model as their analytical framework for describing the U.S. economy, it is thus possible that they could not adopt a real-GNP-plus-inflation targeting regime without being willing to tolerate more variation in interest rates than would be required under some other regimes.[31]

The MPS results in table 5-8 are model specific and apply only to the U.S. economy. Yet they suggest that qualitatively similar inferences may be applicable for other model/country combinations.

Comparison of Results for Whole and Final-Half Periods

Model groups were requested to submit results for the final half of the ten-year period as well as for the entire ten years. This request stemmed from a concern that the initial years of the full period might not be representative of the full period because the lagged effects of shocks would be limited during the initial

---

31. The empirical results for the MPS model are not definitive on this point. Although interest-rate variability was higher for the *reported* variants of real-GNP-plus-inflation targeting than for the *reported* variants of other regimes (including money targeting), this ranking might not hold for all variants of the regimes. In principle, one would want to compare regime variants that achieve comparable degrees of output and inflation variability and see which of those variants exhibit lower interest-rate volatility. The conjecture of the MPS model group is that research along these lines with the MPS model would show real-GNP-plus-inflation targeting proving to have *less* interest-rate variability than money targeting.

years of the simulation. (The models contain numerous lagged endogenous variables. Because of these lags, the draw of shocks for the initial year can have important effects on several subsequent years; in the initial year itself, however, there are no carryover effects from shocks drawn for earlier years.)

In the event, the empirical results for the final-half period turned out to be qualitatively little different from those for the full period. For example, for almost all model/country combinations, the identification of a preferred regime is the same regardless of which of the two periods is examined.[32]

For all the models except two, the root-mean-squared deviations for the final-half period tend to be marginally higher than those for the full period. This fact seems consistent with the presumption that, given the importance of lagged endogenous variables in the models, the effects of lagged shocks play a greater role in the later than in the initial years of the simulation period. The two models that are a partial exception are MSG and LIVERPOOL. For many variables for the United States and Germany, the *RMS%D*s or *RMSD*s of the MSG model are *smaller*, not larger, for the final five years.[33] In the LIVERPOOL model, the comparison is mixed, with the final-half period sometimes being smaller, sometimes larger.

We have not included summary tables for the final half of the simulation period analogous to tables 5-2, 5-6, and 5-7 because there are so few qualitative differences from the full-period results. For only a handful of cases is there a switch in preferred regime, and in those few cases the quantitative significance of the switch is usually small.[34]

Model-Consistent versus Adaptive Expectations

The role that expectations play in the efficacy of policy, and the empirical importance of forward-looking expectations, are questions that have arisen frequently in recent studies involving macroeconometric models. Earlier publications in this series of projects have addressed these issues.[35]

---

32. The bottom portions of the B-I tables in annex B give the results for the final-half period; they can be directly compared with the ten-year results in the top portions of the tables. Note again that the GEM model group conducted their simulations only for an initial five years; in this respect, the GEM results are not compatible with the results from the other models.

33. In a comment on a draft of this chapter, Warwick McKibbin conjectured that this difference of MSG from the other models might be due to price effects occurring "up front" in the MSG model (earlier in the simulation period than for other models).

34. The only really striking change is in the TAYLOR model for Canada: regime 2BX is preferred for the entire ten-year period, but regime 3X is preferred for the final five years.

35. For important contributions in the empirical literature, see for example Masson and Blundell-Wignall (1985), Haas and Masson (1986), and Taylor (1988). For comparisons in earlier publications in this series of projects, see Bryant, Henderson, and others (1988, pp. 53–57); and Bryant, Helliwell, and Hooper (1989, pp. 71–76).

For this project, a majority of the participating models made use of rational, model-consistent expectations when generating their simulations. The INTER-MOD model is the only one of the participating models that can be simulated with adaptive expectations (INTERMOD-A) as well as model-consistent expectations (INTERMOD-C). The INTERMOD group presented two complete sets of results for the core simulations, one for each of the expectation modes. The INTERMOD results thus provide an interesting, albeit model-specific, insight into the consequences of using alternative treatments of expectations.

Table 5-10 provides data summarizing the differences in results between INTERMOD-A and INTERMOD-C. The figures are again index values, with an index value greater (less) than unity indicating cases in which the adaptive-expectations simulation is associated with a higher (lower) *RMS%D* or *RMSD* than the consistent-expectations simulation. The shaded cells in the table indicate the minority of cases for which the performance of the adaptive-expectations mode is better than that for consistent expectations.

The typical result, which holds for nominal-income targeting and also for money targeting and exchange-rate targeting, is that model-consistent expectations significantly reduce the volatility of most variables relative to the adaptive-expectations case. Exceptions are minor, and for most cases the amount of the reduction is fairly substantial. This result is consistent with the results for the deterministic simulations in chapter 4.[36] The outcomes under real-GNP-plus-inflation targeting, however, are sharply different: for most variables, the *RMS%D*s or *RMSD*s for consistent expectations are *higher* than for adaptive expectations. The only variable under regime 2BX that shows smaller volatility for consistent expectations, the typical pattern for other regimes, is the level of real GNP; this case is, of course, an important exception.

The atypical INTERMOD-A results for regime 2BX evident in table 5-10 can be related to the atypical INTERMOD-A results for regime 2BX in table 5-8. In table 5-8—in contrast to almost all the other data in that table—INTERMOD-A exhibits *less* rather than more variation in the level of the interest rate for regime 2BX than for 2AX.[37] Variables such as interest rates and exchange rates "jump" toward new equilibrium values under the consistent-expectations mode but tend to move more sluggishly under adaptive expectations. This typical difference between consistent and adaptive expectations may help to explain the relative movements of the level of the interest rate under the 2BX and 2AX regimes for INTERMOD-A and INTERMOD-C.

---

36. Except in the case of real-GNP-plus-inflation targeting, INTERMOD-C generally produced noticeably smaller deviations from baseline paths for the various deterministic shocks than INTERMOD-A.

37. It remains true that the consistent-expectations solutions have less interest-rate variability than the adaptive-expectations solutions; the ranking of all four regimes in terms of interest-rate variability is $2AX^C < 2BX^C < 2BX^A < 2AX^A$, where the superscripts C and A indicate, respectively, INTERMOD-C and INTERMOD-A.

Table 5-10. *Contrast between INTERMOD-A and INTERMOD-C*

Index value for *RMS%D* or *RMSD* of INTERMOD-A (index value for INTERMOD-C = 1.0)

	Regime			
Variable and country	Money targeting (1)	Nominal-income targeting (2AX)	Real-GNP-plus-inflation targeting (2BX)	Exchange-rate targeting (3X)
Real GNP, level				
United States	1.45	1.49	1.19	1.51
Japan	1.30	1.34	1.33	1.01
Germany	1.21	1.28	1.07	1.42
United Kingdom	1.53	1.53	1.13	1.54
Canada	1.61	1.55	1.48	1.62
Real GNP, growth rate				
United States	0.95	1.02	0.91	0.97
Japan	0.99	1.00	0.96	0.96
Germany	0.81	0.94	0.89	0.92
United Kingdom	0.90	1.10	0.84	1.10
Canada	1.01	1.07	0.98	1.05
GNP deflator, level				
United States	1.57	1.84	0.69	1.56
Japan	1.70	1.63	0.60	1.48
Germany	2.08	2.37	0.52	2.58
United Kingdom	1.68	1.78	0.22	1.55
Canada	1.71	1.67	0.32	1.50
GNP deflator, change				
United States	1.44	1.54	0.68	1.40
Japan	1.46	1.42	0.67	1.20
Germany	1.70	1.51	0.52	1.65
United Kingdom	1.44	1.40	0.32	1.29
Canada	1.38	1.36	0.34	1.26
Short-term interest rate, level				
United States	1.42	2.07	1.06	1.49
Japan	1.72	1.99	0.75	1.43
Germany	1.20	1.63	0.93	1.38
United Kingdom	1.29	1.80	0.56	1.23
Canada	1.38	2.10	0.67	1.37
Short-term interest rate, period-to-period change				
United States	0.92	1.16	0.88	1.02
Japan	1.10	2.37	0.90	1.02
Germany	0.92	0.94	0.77	0.98
United Kingdom	0.99	1.17	0.69	0.98
Canada	1.04	1.45	0.67	0.96
Bilateral dollar exchange rate, level				
United States	n.a.	n.a.	n.a.	n.a.
Japan	1.05	1.01	0.35	1.42
Germany	0.88	0.88	0.50	1.37
United Kingdom	0.94	0.93	0.21	1.37
Canada	0.85	1.12	0.29	1.37

Source: B-I tables in annex B, full-period (ten-year) simulations. Shaded cells indicate cases for which the adaptive expectations mode (INTERMOD-A) has lower *RMS%D* or *RMSD* than the consistent-expectations mode (INTERMOD-C).
n.a.: Not available.

All things considered, the stochastic simulations for the two expectation modes of the INTERMOD model appear to confirm the inferences reached in earlier studies comparing adaptive and model-consistent expectations. If announcements of current and future policy actions are regarded as credible by private-sector economic agents and if the agents react promptly to the announcements, the consequences of the actions tend to be smoothed over time. In particular, correct anticipations of future actions shift some of the consequences back into the present. In the context of the stochastic simulations here, the results for the INTERMOD-C model suggest that credible policy acted on by forward-looking economic agents might significantly reduce volatility in macroeconomic variables of key importance to economic policy.

Changing Feedback Coefficients in the Regimes

As explained in chapter 3, in a few instances the model groups reported results for alternative as well as originally specified values of the feedback coefficients. We indicate briefly here the main points that emerge from those results.

Table 5-11 focuses on the effects on key macroeconomic variables in the United States, Japan, and Germany of increasing the feedback coefficient in the nominal-income targeting regime. The results—available for three of the participating models, INTERMOD-A, MX3, and MPS (the MPS data only for the United States)—are presented in index form, with the results for the regime with lower feedback coefficient as the base. An index value less (greater) than unity occurs when the increase in the feedback coefficient causes the variable to have a lower (higher) root-mean-squared deviation from baseline.[38]

As expected, an increase in the feedback coefficient for each of the three models decreases the variance of the variable being targeted, the level of nominal GNP. The consequences for the components of nominal GNP (output and prices) are mixed. For INTERMOD-A and MPS, increases in the feedback coefficient tend to reduce, by modest amounts, the root-mean-squared deviations for real GNP and prices (both the level and the inflation rate) as well as for nominal GNP itself. In the MX3 model, however, the reduction in the variance of nominal GNP tends not to reduce the variance of the two components separately; apparently, output and prices vary by similar amounts, as with the lower feedback coefficient, but somehow offset each other to a greater degree.

---

38. The figures in table 5-11 are derived from the tables in annex B; the data involve comparisons of results for regimes 2A and 2AX. For INTERMOD-A, the index is the ratio of 2A to 2AX (since the 2AX feedback coefficient for INTERMOD-A is *smaller* than that for 2A). For the MPS and MX3 models, the index is the ratio of 2AX to 2A (since the feedback coefficient for the 2AX regime in those models is *larger* than that for 2A).

Table 5-11. *Effects of Modest Increases in Feedback Coefficient for Nominal-Income Targeting Regime in Three Models: INTERMOD-A, MPS, and MX3*

Index value for *RMS%D* or *RMSD* of higher-coefficient case (lower-coefficient case = 1.0)[a]

	Country		
Variable and model	United States	Japan	Germany
Real GNP, level			
INTERMOD-A	0.97	1.01	0.90
MPS	0.93	n.a.	n.a.
MX3	1.02	0.96	1.14
Real GNP, growth rate			
INTERMOD-A	1.00	0.98	0.93
MPS	0.97	n.a.	n.a.
MX3	1.00	0.85	0.86
Nominal GNP, level			
INTERMOD-A	0.54	0.64	0.75
MPS	0.81	n.a.	n.a.
MX3	0.71	0.80	0.74
GNP deflator, level			
INTERMOD-A	0.70	0.76	0.72
MPS	0.92	n.a.	n.a.
MX3	1.00	1.00	1.00
GNP deflator, inflation rate			
INTERMOD-A	0.74	0.83	0.83
MPS	0.97	n.a.	n.a.
MX3	1.00	0.93	1.00
Short-term interest rate, level			
INTERMOD-A	1.31	1.33	1.40
MPS	1.08	n.a.	n.a.
MX3	1.42	1.60	1.49
Short-term interest rate, change			
INTERMOD-A	1.95	1.82	2.49
MPS	1.28	n.a.	n.a.
MX3	1.78	1.74	1.69
Bilateral dollar exchange rate, level			
INTERMOD-A	n.a.	1.10	1.41
MPS	n.a.	n.a.	n.a.
MX3	n.a.	1.04	1.05

Source: B-I tables in annex B, full-period (ten-year) simulations.

n.a.: Not available.

a. Feedback coefficient in INTERMOD-A model raised from 0.70 (2AX) to 1.50 (2A); in MPS model from 1.50 (2A) to 2.00 (2AX); and in MX3 model from 1.50 (2A) to 3.00 (2AX).

The most striking feature of table 5-11 is the tendency for greater stabilization of nominal GNP to be associated with an increase in the variance of short-term interest rates and exchange rates. This tendency (which has been observed throughout chapters 2, 4, and 5) is marked for the period-to-period change in interest rates: the *RMSD*s for the higher-coefficient case are augmented by 28 percent in the least extreme case (MPS for the United States) and by 149 percent in the most extreme (INTERMOD-A for Germany).[39]

39. Results for INTERMOD-A for the United Kingdom and Canada are also available, and they exhibit the same general pattern as for the three countries shown in table 5-11.

Table 5-12 contains results for the MSG model, for all four types of regime. The figures in the table are again index values for the *RMS%D* or *RMSD* of the higher-coefficient case (the lower-coefficient case equals unity). Unlike in table 5-11, however, the increases in feedback coefficients are very large rather than modest. In effect, McKibbin raised the coefficient value to as high a number as would be required to minimize the loss under a hypothetical loss function giving equal weight to the logarithm of real GNP and the rate of inflation. For three of the four regime types, that meant raising the coefficient virtually to infinity (thereby approximating the exact targeting assumed in the theoretical analysis of chapter 2).

Consider first the case of nominal-income targeting, the second of the four columns in table 5-12. When the feedback coefficient in that regime is increased in the MSG model, the model exhibits a similar pattern, qualitatively, to that of the three models shown in table 5-11. Indeed, because of the huge increase in the coefficient, the *RMS%D* for nominal GNP itself is driven all the way to zero—in effect, exact targeting. The stabilization of nominal GNP, however, is again purchased at the expense of substantially greater variation in interest rates and exchange rates.[40] Each of the three countries exhibits this pattern. The United States, however, differs from Japan and Germany: output and prices as well as nominal GNP have lower *RMS%D*s for the United States, whereas the lower *RMS%D*s for nominal GNP in Japan and Germany are accompanied by greater volatility in the two components of nominal GNP. In this respect, the MSG model results seem more akin to the MX3 results in table 5-11 than to the results for the INTERMOD-A and MPS models.

Examination of the columns for the three other regimes in table 5-12 reveals some other interesting consequences of increasing the feedback coefficients. Some of these are regime specific. For example, with exchange-rate targeting, not only exchange rates themselves but also interest rates have diminished variability when the feedback coefficient is increased; this outcome is consistent with the interest-parity conditions used in the models. Money targeting and real-GNP-plus-inflation targeting, however, exhibit the more typical pattern of greater interest-rate variability. Some differences in table 5-12 pertain more to countries. A large boost in the feedback coefficient for real-GNP-plus-inflation targeting destabilizes the price level and even the inflation rate in Japan; in contrast, for the United States and Germany an increase in the coefficient for that regime yields lower root-mean-squared deviations for both the price level and the inflation rate.

A more extensive examination of "optimized" feedback coefficients for different types of policy regime would, of course, require an experimental de-

---

40. Recall figure 4-1 in the preceding chapter and the discussion of the MSG deterministic simulations for the 2A and 2AX regimes.

Table 5-12. *MSG Model: Effects of Substantially Increasing Feedback Coefficient in All Four Regimes*

Index value for *RMS%D* or *RMSD* of higher-coefficient case (lower-coefficient case = 1.0)[a]

Country and variable	Regime			
	Money targeting	Nominal-income targeting	Real-GNP-plus-inflation targeting	Exchange-rate targeting
United States				
Real GNP, level	0.98	0.67	0.57	0.61
Real GNP, growth rate	0.99	0.70	0.87	0.65
Nominal GNP, level	0.82	0.00	0.75	0.60
GNP deflator, level	0.94	0.56	0.82	0.51
GNP deflator, inflation rate	0.97	0.56	0.40	0.52
Short-term interest rate, level	1.11	2.17	0.99	0.90
Short-term interest rate, change	1.14	1.75	1.23	0.67
Bilateral dollar exchange rate, level	n.a.	n.a.	n.a.	n.a.
Japan				
Real GNP, level	0.92	0.16	0.21	0.93
Real GNP, growth rate	0.93	1.76	0.29	1.15
Nominal GNP, level	0.89	0.00	0.85	1.55
GNP deflator, level	0.73	0.96	3.58	0.44
GNP deflator, inflation rate	0.82	1.17	1.69	1.20
Short-term interest rate, level	1.18	2.47	2.63	0.79
Short-term interest rate, change	1.20	2.76	2.37	0.60
Bilateral dollar exchange rate, level	1.27	3.03	1.90	0.00
Germany				
Real GNP, level	0.91	1.18	0.17	1.05
Real GNP, growth rate	0.95	1.45	0.27	0.82
Nominal GNP, level	0.88	0.00	0.20	2.86
GNP deflator, level	0.99	2.77	0.59	0.74
GNP deflator, inflation rate	1.00	3.23	0.61	0.63
Short-term interest rate, level	1.17	2.41	2.32	0.79
Short-term interest rate, change	1.21	3.18	2.63	0.60
Bilateral dollar exchange rate, level	1.24	3.35	0.95	0.00

Source: B-I tables in annex B, full-period (ten-year) simulations.

n.a.: Not available.

a. Feedback coefficient for the money-targeting regime was raised from −5 to −1,000,000; for the nominal-income targeting regime, from 1.5 to 1,000,000; for the real-GNP-plus-inflation targeting regime, from 1.5 to 105; and for the exchange-rate targeting regime, from 2.5 to 1,000,000.

sign different from the one chosen for this project. Rather than having model groups perform simulations given a particular specification of a policy regime, including the values for its feedback coefficients, model groups would be given one or more loss functions to use in evaluation and only the general specifications for regimes. Each model group would then derive the optimal value (for its model) of the feedback coefficients that would minimize a particular loss function.[41] In an exercise designed along these different lines, the focus of

41. For the exercise to be interesting, the loss function or functions used for evaluation would need to include more than a single ultimate-target variable, or the "intermediate-target" variable(s) in the equation for the policy regime should differ from the ultimate-target variables in the loss function (or both conditions should hold). If the same, single variable were to be used in both the loss function and the equation for the policy regime, all the model groups might typically find that a feedback coefficient of infinity would best minimize the single-objective loss function.

interest would be a cross-model or a cross-country comparison of the values of feedback coefficients for alternative regimes, and a comparison of alternative types of loss function.

The results for alternative feedback coefficients in tables 5-11 and 5-12 pertain to only a few variables for four models, and it would be risky to try to extract broad generalizations from them. We do not have enough information about the effects of altering the feedback coefficients in regimes, for example, to argue that increases in the coefficients will typically increase the volatility of a wide range of nontargeted variables. What can be said, however, is that the selective results here are fully consistent with the earlier discussion of interest-rate and exchange-rate volatility. If policymakers decide to give weight to variables such as interest rates or exchange rates in their loss functions, then they may have valid reasons to be wary of policy regimes that attempt singlemindedly to target one or two variables such as nominal GNP, output, or prices. High feedback coefficients that lead to more exact targeting of nominal GNP, output, or prices may entail acceptance of significantly greater variability in interest rates and exchange rates.

Summary Conclusions

This project has proven the feasibility of using stochastic simulation techniques in a large-scale model comparison exercise. Application of these techniques provides a valuable new dimension to the empirical analysis of macroeconomic policies in a global setting.

Stochastic simulation techniques raise new issues about the degree of comparability in the results that can be achieved across individual models, as we have forthrightly shown in chapter 3 and this chapter. Our project was only partially successful in standardizing the procedures applied by the participating model groups. Future model comparison exercises, benefiting from our identification of the problems encountered in this project, should aim to improve the degree of standardization achieved.

In addition to their differences in implementation of the stochastic simulations, the models participating in the project were constructed with differing theoretical specifications and differing estimation techniques. These differences lead, in ways not yet fully understood, to considerable diversity in the empirical results. This diversity, while it adds richness to the analysis, also tends to undermine the sharpness of conclusions about the relative performance of alternative policy regimes for the conduct of monetary policy.

Despite the diversity of results, several generalizations do emerge from the analysis of the stochastic simulations. With occasional exceptions, moreover, the stochastic simulations support the conclusions of the theoretical analysis in chapter 2 and the conclusions based on the deterministic simulations in chapter 4.

The broadest generalization pertains to the overall ranking of the regime types: for purposes of minimizing the variances of real GNP and the inflation rate in the face of stochastic shocks, nominal-income targeting and real-GNP-plus-inflation targeting are "preferred" over both money targeting and exchange-rate targeting. This preference emerges in a large majority—more than 80 percent—of the cases considered across various models and countries.

Consistent with the deterministic simulation results presented in chapter 4, real-GNP-plus-inflation targeting is most often the regime of choice for minimizing the variance of either real GNP or real GNP plus inflation, particularly in the United States and Japan. However, unlike the deterministic results, which sometimes show a preference for exchange-rate targeting in the case of Germany, the stochastic simulations for Germany show both nominal-income targeting and real-GNP-plus-inflation targeting to be consistently preferred over exchange-rate targeting.

Another departure from the deterministic results is that, for purposes of minimizing variance in inflation alone, the stochastic results show a moderate preference for nominal-income targeting, whereas the deterministic results had shown a more clear-cut preference for real-GNP-plus-inflation targeting. The stochastic results, however, do generally coincide with the deterministic results (as well as with the predictions of theory) in the choice of nominal-income targeting for purposes of minimizing variance in the price *level* (particularly in the cases of the United States and Japan).

If the variability of interest rates is a matter of concern to policymakers, the apparent dominance of nominal-income targeting and real-GNP-plus-inflation targeting is diminished, as was anticipated in the results presented in chapters 2 and 4. The stochastic simulations suggest that the variability of interest rates is minimized under exchange-rate targeting in both Japan and Germany, much the same as in the deterministic simulation results. Exchange-rate targeting also tends to minimize the variance in exchange rates in those countries. In the U.S. case, on the other hand, the results across models about interest-rate variability are too diverse to draw any generalizations, other than the fact that nominal-income targeting and real-GNP-plus-inflation targeting do not stand out one way or another. If interest-rate variability is given a weight equal to those of real GNP variability and inflation variability as matters of concern to policymakers, the regimes of nominal-income targeting and real-GNP-plus-inflation targeting still come out ahead, but they clearly lose ground to other regimes. Real-GNP-plus-inflation targeting loses the most ground, consistent with the fact that interest rates are clearly most variable under that regime.

Supplementary experiments carried out by several of the model groups suggest that the conclusions summarized here can be significantly influenced by modifications of the policy regimes or of the models' structures. The MPS group showed, for example, that the combination of real GNP and inflation can be stabilized more effectively in that model by raising the feedback coefficient on real GNP relative to the coefficient on inflation in the regime for real-GNP-plus-inflation targeting. That combined gain, however, is realized at the cost of higher variability in inflation. Several other model groups reported that when the feedback coefficient in a policy regime is increased (thereby reducing the degree of slippage between desired and actual values of the targeted variable or variables), the variance in real GNP and inflation combined is generally diminished but, again, usually at the cost of greater variability in interest rates. In yet another illustration, the INTERMOD group showed that the volatility of most variables is reduced when expectations are treated as model consistent rather than adaptive (reflecting the tendency for interest rates to jump to new equilibrium values under consistent expectations as opposed to moving gradually under adaptive expectations).

We conclude by returning to a familiar theme. The lack of full standardization for the stochastic simulation experiments and, still more important, the existence of wide diversity among the participating models require caution in digesting the empirical results. Throughout this and the preceding chapters, we have tried to strike the appropriate degree of caution. To find this balance is like steering between Scylla and Charybdis. Although we have frankly identified the problematic aspects of the empirical experiments, we have tried to guard against readers rushing to an incorrect judgment that the problems are so serious that they invalidate any conclusions based on the experiments. To avoid the opposite danger, we have resisted the natural temptation to extract generalizations from the empirical data except when it seemed likely that the conclusions can hold up under careful scrutiny or offer fruitful grounds for further research. Only after much future research has been completed will it be possible to tell whether we have in fact successfully steered a middle course between the hazardous rocks on the one side and the whirlpool on the other.

References

Bryant, R. C., D. A. Currie, J. A. Frenkel, P. R. Masson, and R. Portes, eds. 1989. *Macroeconomic Policies in an Interdependent World*. Washington: Brookings, Centre for Economic Policy Research, and International Monetary Fund.

Bryant, R. C., J. F. Helliwell, and P. Hooper. 1989. "Domestic and Cross-Border Consequences of U.S. Macroeconomic Policies." In Bryant, Currie, and others (1989), 59–115. Unabridged version available as Brookings Discussion Paper in International Economics 68 (January 1989).

Bryant, R. C., D. W. Henderson, G. Holtham, P. Hooper, and S. A. Symansky, eds. 1988. *Empirical Macroeconomics for Interdependent Economies*. Brookings.

Fair, R. C. 1984. *Specification, Estimation, and Analysis of Macroeconometric Models*. Harvard University Press.

———. 1988. "Optimal Choice of Monetary Policy Instruments in a Macroeconometric Model." *Journal of Monetary Economics* 22: 301–15.

Frenkel, J. A., M. Goldstein, and P. R. Masson. 1989. "Simulating the Effects of Some Simple Coordinated versus Uncoordinated Policy Rules." In Bryant, Currie, and others (1989), 203–39.

Haas, R., and P. R. Masson. 1986. "MINIMOD: Specification and Simulation Results." *IMF Staff Papers* 33: 722–67.

Holbrook, R. S. 1972. "Optimal Economic Policy and the Problem of Instrument Instability." *American Economic Review* 62: 57–65.

Masson, P. R., and A. Blundell-Wignall. 1985. "Fiscal Policy and the Exchange Rate in the Big Seven: Transmission of U.S. Government Spending Shocks." *European Economic Review* 28: 11–42.

McKibbin, W. J., and J. D. Sachs. 1989. "Implications of Policy Rules for the World Economy." In Bryant, Currie, and others (1989), 151–94.

Taylor, J. B. 1988. "The Treatment of Expectations in Large Multicountry Econometric Models." In Bryant, Henderson, and others (1988), 161–82.

———. 1989. "Policy Analysis with a Multicountry Model." In Bryant, Currie, and others (1989), 122–41.

———. 1993. *Macroeconomic Policy in a World Economy: From Econometric Design to Practical Operation*. Norton.

CHAPTER 6

Invited Contributors: Selected Comments and Reflections

John F. Helliwell

THIS VOLUME and the associated conference held in 1990 represent an impressive effort to combine model assessment and policy evaluation in a stochastic domain, an ambitious undertaking best assessed as one further step in a collaborative research project of long standing and wide scope. By the time of the conference presentations of the preliminary results from the first set of stochastic simulations, it became clear that the original project design was perhaps too ambitious: in a single set of experiments it tried to assess the efficiency of different monetary-policy regimes in reducing the variance of key endogenous variables subject to model-specific patterns of stochastic shocks. When the results from different models were compared, it was too difficult to disentangle the effects of the different patterns of stochastic shocks from differences in model structure and even in the specific forms of the policy regimes. In addition, because this was the first large-scale attempt to compare the operation of monetary-policy regimes across a range of model types, there were even many uncertainties about how best to define the timing and extent of the assumed information flows to policymakers, and about the extent to which policymakers are assumed to be willing and able to meet short-term targets for their chosen intermediate targets for monetary policy.

As a result of this information overload, the organizers and modelers agreed to perform further experiments designed to help make the stochastic results more understandable. The most important addition was of new simulations designed to reveal the basic characteristics of the models being used to compare the policy regimes—compared in a context free of model-specific aspects of shocks and policy responses. The deterministic shocks used were temporary in nature, whereas those used in earlier conferences had been sustained, so that analysts still lack the full information required to track the changes made in models as time has passed, and lack any easy means of guessing how models unrepresented in the current experiments might have behaved had they been included.

416

Another important piece of post-conference analysis related to the effect of imposing policy regimes that lean against the wind rather than achieve intermediate targets exactly. This was accomplished by the use of available results from a subset of the models, with results reported in tables 5-11 and 5-12. Qualitatively, the results of these experiments were predictable, in that attempting to hold the target variables unchanged made the assigned short-term instrument subject to very large variations. What is more, the resulting values achieved for the attainment of the target variables differed as a consequence, with greater attainment usually following from greater willingness to accept instrument instability.

In the remainder of these comments I attempt an overall evaluation of the sequence of experiments. I first summarize some of the conclusions and remaining problems related to experimental design and then assess the empirical results and their possible policy implications. Finally, I try to spell out some implications of the current experiments for future attempts to evaluate policy regimes, for future efforts to compare models, and for possible future developments of the models themselves.

Experimental Design

There are three distinctly different ways of setting up the experimental design dynamics for assessing policy regimes. The core simulation procedures, as applied by most of the model groups, assume full knowledge of the pattern and size of all contemporaneous disturbances. Having sufficient leverage of the policy instrument on the variable or variables in the policy regime permits the choice of feedback coefficients high enough to permit the target values of policy regime variables (such as money, exchange rates, or nominal income) to be hit exactly. A second and quite different approach assumes no contemporaneous knowledge of disturbances and their effects, with policymakers having to wait until the next period to choose policies to respond to the remaining effects of the past and expected current and future shocks. A third approach, which mediates between the first two, assumes contemporaneous knowledge of some quickly reported data, such as exchange rates, while forcing policymakers to wait longer for information about the real and price-level outcomes of both the disturbances and their offsetting policies. Which time pattern of the arrival of information is more realistic for evaluating policy regimes?

The answer depends on the nature of the regime being assessed and the policy instrument being used. When the policy instrument is the short-term interest rate, and the regime involves the setting of the exchange rate, there are grounds for believing the authorities will have sufficient knowledge to hit their exchange-rate target exactly (assuming the absence of policy-induced destabilizing expectations), since the interest-rate consequences of their open-market operations and the foreign exchange rate show up on the same screens at the same time.

The situation is more complicated for a monetary target, because excess bank reserves cannot be controlled exactly and bank balance sheets are not under the same continual scrutiny as the foreign-exchange market. Over a period as long as a quarter or a year, however, there are much stronger grounds for assuming a full policy response to within-period shocks and outcomes, even if no attempt is made to overshoot at the end of the period to meet a pre-set average target for the period as a whole.

The case for assuming that the information about the pattern of shocks is only available with a lag (as was assumed in a conference paper by Peter Pauly and Christian Petersen) becomes much stronger when the policy regime relates to nominal GNP, since even the preliminary figures for the period as a whole are not released until several weeks into the next period and are subject to substantial revision for many months after that. As was pointed out by several conference participants, the fact that nominal GNP cannot be targeted precisely, however great may be the contemporaneous power of the policy instrument, does not mean that the policymakers cannot be reacting during the period to actual or anticipated contemporaneous shocks that may cause nominal income to diverge from target. Nonetheless, because the release of the actual data for the preceding period is likely to lead to a reinterpretation of the current gap between actual and target values for nominal income, analysts may wish to build some interpretation and assimilation lags into the reaction to at least some kinds of shocks.

Interpretation of Results

In this section I consider mainly the stochastic simulation results in chapter 5, using the chapter 4 results only as a way to understand and evaluate the reliability of the stochastic results.

In their analysis of the stochastic simulation results, the editors note that more general reporting of employment results from the models would have eased the comparison of the chapter 5 results with the theoretical presumptions raised in chapter 2. The output-employment linkage, however, is one in which a large specification difference exists between the theoretical model and almost any empirical model. The theoretical model of chapter 2 assumes that employment is immediately and costlessly adjustable by firms, given current values for prices and wages. Yet all empirically estimated labor-demand equations show that employment and hours are quasi-fixed factors, so that employment is always less responsive than output to short-term changes in demand and always more sluggish in response to relative prices than is assumed in the theoretical analysis in chapter 2. Hence one would not expect to find empirical models replicating in many instances the relative patterns of changes in output and employment that would flow from the model of chapter 2. That said, it would nevertheless be interesting to collect employment and output data jointly when the pattern of shocks is subdivided to allow demand and supply shocks to be separately assessed.

The dominant result from the stochastic simulations appears to be that for most models, and for most loss functions, the nominal-income and real-GNP-plus-inflation regimes give the best results. In general, as might be expected, the more weight the loss function attaches to the variable that is the focus of the policy regime, the better that regime does relative to the alternatives. How is this ranking likely to be affected by the assumption that the results of current period shocks are available for immediate policy responses? Since monetary policy tends to operate first on real variables and only later on price levels (although this tendency is reduced when there are forward-looking price expectations and when prices are relatively flexible), the ability to respond immediately is probably of greater aid when the loss function attaches more weight to the variance of real GNP. In general, the modest preference for the nominal-income and real-GNP-plus-inflation regimes is likely to carry forward into an experimental domain where response is less immediate, although the interactions of expectations and model dynamics, and the complexities of the patterns of shocks, make caution necessary in any such assessments.

It would be interesting to see to what extent the preference for the nominal-income and real-GNP-plus-inflation regimes is contingent on the historical average of shocks. In particular, the theory suggests that the preference across regimes is likely to depend on the source of the shocks, and the models could indicate how great this margin of preference might be. If the differences are great, there is likely to be a policy payoff in attempting to determine the probable origins of contemporaneous shocks, and not merely to react to their net effects on a single chosen target variable. As a practical matter, important policy choices are often made in circumstances—for example, when stock markets drop, as in October 1987, when oil prices increase, or when an unexpected change in spending or money demand occurs—that provide at least some indication of the source of the shocks. Thus the assessment of regimes would be of most use to policymakers if it were conditional on the source of the shocks, so that the choice of regime could be altered appropriately to current circumstances.

Because of the undifferentiated nature of the shocks being used for the present experiments, the authors of chapter 5 are appropriately modest in the conclusions they draw about the rankings of the various policy regimes. They note the fairly robust dominance of nominal GNP and GNP-plus-inflation regimes over money targeting or exchange-rate targeting, and note the interest-rate and exchange-rate variability generally entailed thereby. As between money targeting and exchange-rate targeting, the rankings tend to vary by model and by country, and not in a way that invites easy conclusions about the extent of optimal currency areas.

Implications for the Assessment of Policy Regimes

The real test of a policy regime is its ability to smooth the economy in response to a sequence of disturbances, possibly cyclical in nature. Here arises a real possibility, particularly in the context of a feedback regime applied to lagged variables, that the execution and operation lags of the policy may be long enough to exacerbate rather than diminish the destabilizing effects of the shocks. Thus the stabilizing effectiveness of any policy regime is likely to depend not only on the source of the shock but also on its dynamic structure. This has implications for the future plan of research in three main areas: the types of shocks to be assessed, the regimes to be considered, and the methods used for obtaining results.

When assessing alternative regimes, it would be worthwhile to consider their relative efficiency when confronting different types and patterns of shocks. In particular, the alternative patterns of shocks should include the following:

— Sustained shocks representative of the main classes of exogenous shocks and policies to which the economy is likely to be subject.
— Temporary shocks of the same types (as was done in chapter 4 for policy changes, although not for representative foreign and domestic disturbances).
— Stochastic shocks to key variables, following typical sizes and dynamic patterns, with the same drawings of random variables being used for each model, to permit tighter distributions of intermodel differences, as proposed by Ray Fair in his comments. This need not preclude the use of model-specific distributions of shocks, as was done in the core simulations, since these would help to show the extent to which the ranking of regimes depends on the patterns of shocks employed.
— Stochastic shocks divided into bundles based on the real/monetary and foreign/domestic distinctions, with perhaps separate treatment of exchange-rate shocks. This bundling of the component shocks should permit closer matching of the empirical results with the theoretical results, as suggested during the 1990 conference by Dale Henderson and Koichi Hamada.

Because the results might well be expected to show that the alternative regimes have different relative efficiencies for the different types of shock, as predicted by the theoretical work, the question is raised again whether it is possible to make use of different regimes for different sorts of shock. This question is the familiar one of signal extraction: would it be possible to tell, at the time the policy reactions are needed, the origin of the shocks? In some cases, such as changes in oil prices, the separation of shocks would seem to be fairly straightforward. When it comes to shocks in real demand, productivity, and portfolio preferences, the decomposition may be less easy. In any event, the question of regime choice and policy design is logically subsequent to the gathering of information about the apparent efficacy of different types of policy regimes under different patterns of shocks.

On the choice of regimes to be assessed, a range of possibilities exists. At one extreme, there are simple regimes with fixed coefficients. Special forms of these include regimes focused on targeting exchange rates or money supplies, with feedback coefficients high enough to ensure the continual meeting of the targets. This effect has long been achieved in many models by treating either exchange rates or monetary quantities as exogenous, with the interest rate then being solved for, so as to clear the private markets consistently with one of these two policy regimes. Moving toward explicit policy optimization, there is first the choice of optimal feedback coefficients for a given form of regime, then the choice of alternative forms of regime, and then, at the further extreme, the unfettered choice of instrument values to maximize the expected value of some preference function. Given the current state of knowledge, the decision by the project organizers to stick to fairly basic policy regimes was the correct one.

The appropriate choice of policy regimes to assess should depend on the purpose of the research. At the current stage of research, the primary aim should be to learn more about model structure and properties, and to aid in the design and construction of more informative models. At the next stage, interest may well shift, given a reasonably well understood set or subset of available models, to an examination of alternative simple policy strategies. At a much later stage, which may always remain beyond the analyst's grasp, the intent may be to produce an optimal set of policies, whether in the form of particular settings or simple policy regimes. In the meantime, which may be long, full optimization exercises are best seen as ways of exposing the soft spots of the models under review. A computer with unbounded curiosity and lots of available power is without peer in exposing attractive policy options that may be found within the structure of a model but are not present in the real world, at least in an exploitable form.

Since the time taken by stochastic simulations was an important constraint on many of the model groups, much can be said for the use of linearized versions of models, as proposed by Warwick McKibbin in this volume, and by Pauly and Peterson in their conference paper, to speed up and increase the precision of the derivation of stochastic properties, especially if the capacity is maintained to ensure that the simplifications required are not systematically distorting the results. A slightly different set of considerations suggests that it might also be useful for more models to explore alternative forms for expectations formation, some of which can lead to faster model solutions than can be obtained under fully forward-looking expectations. On the other hand, as emphasized by John Taylor, many of the models have such a simple structure that the combination of efficient-solution algorithms and the regular annual 30 percent reductions in the cost of computing has made it feasible for them to be solved in their original structural forms, even with the use of forward-looking expectations for a wide range of their key variables. On research grounds, it is always useful to have some models evaluated in both linearized and their original nonlinear forms to provide continuing assessments of the consequences of linearization.

Implications for Model Evaluation

At the top of my priorities would be a methodical evaluation of the ability of alternative macroeconomic frameworks to explain macroeconomic reality, both within and beyond their sample estimation periods. As Ray Fair and Christopher Sims point out in their comments, evaluation of policy regimes presupposes some degree of confidence in the models being used. This issue arose in two forms in the experiments for the conference, because differences in the fit and structure of the models not only influenced the reactions of the models themselves to given shocks and policies but also altered the pattern of stochastic shocks used for policy assessment. This issue did not arise in the deterministic simulations reported in chapter 4, but it did complicate any attempts to use the model properties illustrated in chapter 4 to explain intermodel differences in the stochastic simulation results of chapter 5. As Ray Fair and I have both suggested, the difficulty could be reduced by using a common structure of stochastic disturbances, restricting it to key variables to ensure that the disturbances used actually have points of entry into all the models assessed. The restriction to key variables would also permit the overall pattern of shocks to be more easily decomposed into those of domestic and foreign origin, and in other ways that would permit easier comparison of the experimental results with theoretical presumptions based on more tightly constrainted model structures of the sort presented in chapter 2.

The second major gap in model evaluation relates to longer-term model properties and to the timing and nature of the transition paths from now to then. As some information, still relatively unsystematic, suggests, what appear to be minor or innocuous assumptions about terminal conditions and the properties of long-run steady-state growth paths can have important effects on even short-term model properties, especially in models that impose forward-looking expectations.

Implications for Model Development

Here I emphasize only three of the many implications for model development:

1. Most of the macroeconomic models under study in this volume, and most of theoretical and applied macroeconomics in general, are incomplete and often unconvincing in the determination of the level and rate of growth of productive capacity. Especially as models start to build in more constraints, forcing longer-run output levels toward some sort of supply-determined values, it is important to invest more resources in studying the domestic and international forces affecting the size and growth of potential output. Studies of comparative growth are accumulating evidence that rates of productivity growth are not constant, even after adjusting for cyclical disturbances, and that they continue to provide the largest shares of increases in per capita incomes. Furthermore, evidence and theoretical developments alike are starting to emphasize the international transfer of ideas as a principal source of whatever international convergence is taking place in growth rates and income levels. These longer-term aspects of interdependence on the supply side are of great importance for domestic and trade policies. The time is ripe for a new marriage between growth and cycles in both theory and empirical models.

2. International linkages are increasing in strength and pervasiveness, yet most theories and applied models still tend to represent growing trade shares (which doubled between 1960 and 1985, on average, for all industrial countries) as resulting from some combination of high-income elasticities of demand for imported goods combined with trends of uncertain duration. It will not be easy to explain the determinants of increasing openness, but the importance of the results is great, especially because of the likely links between openness and the rates of technical progress that are central to the determination of longer-term supply potential. Openness to capital movements is often assumed by applying something like uncovered interest parity to determine spot exchange rates. Yet the large and persistent departures from purchasing power parity, and the failure of forward rates to be predictors of future spot rates, suggest that the arbitrage condition is more a means of determining market forward rates than a means of tying down the spot exchange rate. The determinants of longer-term international capital movements, and the split between direct and portfolio investment, also remain ill understood. Movements of people are

more easily dealt with in a modeling context, chiefly because restrictions on immigration remain among the most used of the shrinking set of economic policies available to the nation-state. As for international linkages beyond the movements of goods, services, and population, they remain both ill measured and vaguely conceived. It is easier to speak in general of the dramatic changes in the potential and relative costs of global communications and transportation than it is to assess their impact on the evolution of national economies and of the linkages among them.

3. Most models usually treat expectations on an all-or-nothing basis, with participants assumed either to know all future values of key variables (insofar as they are determined by model structure and predictable trends and variances of exogenous variables) or to use current values as their only guides to an uncertain future. Most models mediate between these two extremes by imposing model-consistent solutions for some markets with easily adjusted prices, such as those for bonds and foreign exchange, while using alternative price-setting rules for other markets, such as those for many goods and services, including labor, where there are greater commitments and costs of adjustment and fewer available means for arbitraging discrepancies between current and expected future prices. The middle ground might be more fruitfully tilled by an application of intermediate cases that involve learning, with due allowance for information costs, sequential decisionmaking, and inherent uncertainties about economic structure. Because of the shortage of observable data on expectations and the likely sensitivity of model properties to expectational assumptions, it is inevitable that data will be almost powerless to distinguish among at least some classes of quite different expectations mechanisms. In these circumstances, sensitivity assessments of the effects of alternative ways of modeling expectations seem a useful part of the modeler's arsenal.

Was It Worth It?

An important part of any review of scientific research activity must be to assess whether the investment was and remains worth making. This is particularly true when the resources include redirecting empirical researchers' efforts, already spread rather thin among the projects competing for their attention. My overall judgment is highly favorable. The attempt to draw theorists, empirical modelers, and policymakers together in discussions and evaluations of both models and policy strategies provides useful disciplines for all. The theorists start to think more about the design of operational and testable forms for their propositions, the modelers are driven to a more methodical review of model properties, and policymakers gain a better understanding of the nature and quality of the information available about the response of the economy to their policies. If this is chastening for all parties, so much the better. If it leads to further rounds of fruitful collaboration, better still.

Finally, it is important to acknowledge the tireless patience of the organizers and editors in the design and execution of a very complex joint research project. Model evaluation is not a glamorous business, but it is nonetheless valuable and even necessary. Only systematic efforts of the kind they have been doing for several years can improve the understanding of the effects of different ways of modeling macroeconomic structure. Despite all the qualifications that have been and must be made, the evidence assembled in these chapters is likely to stand as the best and most comprehensive empirical record so far available of the effects of different monetary policy regimes in a stochastic environment.

John B. Taylor

The results reported in this volume are a valuable addition to our knowledge about macroeconomic policy. Whereas previous model-comparison exercises conducted by the Brookings Institution have looked at the effects on the economy of one-time changes in the instruments of monetary and fiscal policy—that is, *policy multipliers*—this exercise has emphasized comparisons of the response of the economy to monetary policy regimes that are simplified *policy rules*.[1] Such a comparison is welcome not only because it is the first of its kind and is in keeping with modern macroeconomic research, which characterizes macroeconomic policy in terms of policy rules, but also because it has the potential to be of great use in the actual formulation of policy. As this book makes clear, policy rules are not limited to a fixed setting for the policy instruments. However, policy rules are different from discretion in the sense that the response of the instrument of policy to economic events is given.

A comparison exercise such as this one is difficult because of the lack of experience most policy analysts have had with the econometric analysis of policy rules. As a result there has been less standardization of the methodology or of the experiments than is desirable in this type of exercise. For example, the stochastic simulations are done with different methods for creating the shocks (some models draw shocks from the fully estimated variance-covariance matrix, others use approximations), and the policy rules used by the different model groups are not exactly the same.

There are also arbitrary differences among models in what is treated as a "shock" and what is treated as an exogenous variable. These differences are much more important in evaluating policy rules than in comparing the effects of one-time instrument changes. Some models have equations with very few exogenous variables; hence the residuals, or shocks, are larger and the estimated noise is greater. For example, the price of oil might be treated as an exogenous variable in one model but not in another. The results of the stochastic simulations would be very different if the model with exogenous oil prices treated the future path of oil prices as known and the other assumed it was part of the random disturbance.

Many of these standardization problems arise because this type of policy analysis is so new. It is as though *Consumer Reports* did a comparison of different personal computers in 1977, when most PCs were still under development

---

1. A third type of model comparison exercise, one of which is now under way under the direction of Phil Howrey, looks at *forecasts* from different models.

in inventors' garages. Until recently very few econometric models had been used to evaluate different policy rules. Not until the rational-expectations revolution of the 1970s underlined the need to consider policy rules to deal with the Lucas critique, to model credibility, and to handle expectations generally did the impetus to such research begin. And most large models required fast algorithms and faster computers, which were developed in the 1980s. Most econometric modelers have focused on the effects of one-time changes in the instruments of policy. In the last few years, however, the number of researchers that have tried to use their models to evaluate policy rules has greatly increased. The type of econometric policy evaluation considered here is fundamentally different from traditional approaches and raises a host of issues that do not arise in the conventional use of econometric models. How to estimate a covariance matrix of a large rational-expectations model is only one example.

There are some advantages, however, to performing this comparison exercise at such an early stage. The comparison itself has greatly contributed to the diffusion of knowledge and has added an element of standardization to the methodology. The experience of different modeling groups has been shared. And in areas where there have been big differences in the results of different models, there has been an effort to uncover the reasons and make adjustments.

All the policy regimes evaluated in the comparison are simplified interest-rate rules. In other words, it is assumed that the central bank uses the interest rate, rather than reserves or the monetary base, as its short-run operating instrument. This is clearly appropriate, given the operating strategies used by most central banks today. The monetary authorities are assumed to adjust their interest rate in response to deviations of the money supply from some target, or deviations of the exchange rate from some target, or a weighted deviation of the inflation rate (or the price level) from some target and the deviation of real output from some target.

The results are very different from model to model. No particular policy rule with particular parameters emerges as optimal for any single country, let alone all countries. Because of the differences among the models and the methodology, I would have been surprised if a clear winner had presented itself.

Yet Ralph Bryant, Catherine Mann, and Peter Hooper in chapter 5 are able to see a consistent pattern emerging from their comparison for several key issues. They find that policies which focus on the exchange rate do not work as well as policies that focus on nominal GNP or on the sum of real output and inflation. They also find that policies which focus solely on the money supply do not work as well. In other words, monetary policy in which the short-term interest rate is raised by the monetary authorities if nominal income is above a target, and lowered if nominal income is below target, seems to work better than the other policies the authors consider. No consensus emerges on the important question of how much the interest rate should change (as a rule) in response to the state of the economy, but that a consensus is emerging about a functional form shows significant progress and is very promising for this kind of policy research.

That significant progress has been made can be seen by recalling the lack of agreement among some of the models in the 1989 volume *Macroeconomic Policies in an Interdependent World*, edited by Bryant and others. For example, the three papers by Taylor, by Jacob Frenkel, Morris Goldstein, and Paul Masson, and by Warwick McKibbin and Jeffrey Sachs in that volume did not all agree that targeting exchange rates as opposed to targeting domestic prices or nominal income would result in inferior economic performance. In his comments in that volume, Ralph Tryon noted, "It is puzzling, therefore, that two other papers... using similar, although not identical, methods, do not confirm Taylor's results.... The superiority of nominal income targeting reported by Taylor does not appear [in the other papers]" (p. 149). Tryon guessed that the differences were due to the different parameter values in the different models. Thanks to the work of this model comparison exercise we now know that these models and others are actually quite similar in showing the superiority of some type of nominal-income targeting and some of the difficulties associated with exchange-rate targeting.

Despite this progress we appear to have a long way to go with this general research program. I would emphasize two areas that need particular study. First is the lack of agreement about ranking particular rules and the differences in predicted economic outcomes from different rules—with the exceptions noted above. This lack of agreement makes it difficult to advise policymakers about which rule to use. In my view, achieving greater agreement (full agreement is unlikely) about these issues will probably require greater agreement among the models themselves. Perhaps it is time to talk about a cooperative effort in designing models to supplement the cooperative effort in comparing models. I believe some of the differences among models do not represent strong ideological differences. The example about how many exogenous variables to include is a case in point. We all agree that oil prices are important, but some models include them explicitly and others model them as part of the random disturbance. That makes a big difference in policy evaluation, but is something that could be handled in a cooperative model development effort.

Second is the need to study the practical operation of policy regimes, not just the formal design of simplified policy rules that is the main subject of this book. The operational problem can be put in this way. How could the researchers advise policymakers if the exercise said that one of the policy rules of those listed in chapter 3 was best? None of those policies is specified well enough to be fully operational; for example, the interest rate is a quarterly or even yearly average in some models. Where would one find the direction to lower the Federal Funds rate by 50 basis points on a given day? And how does the rule deal with obvious increases in inflation that have not yet shown up in the output deflator? The operational problem is even more difficult when researchers disagree about the form of the policy rule, a situation that is not likely to change soon.

Although such research on the operation of policy rules is important, I would argue that the recent focus of this model-comparison work on the design of policy rules is also important, and I hope it continues. There is a growing need to find ways to characterize good monetary policy as something besides pure discretion. A monetary policy that is determined from scratch each day or each month, or when people do not have any idea how the central bank will react to changes in economic conditions, is not a good policy. Economic theory shows that things work better if there is more certainty about the conduct of monetary policy. A good policy will ultimately be like the ones studied in this research—characterized by systematic, regular responses to economic shocks.

Christopher A. Sims

Macroeconomic ideas ought eventually to take on a form that can be part of a policy model—namely, a form relevant to the decisions about managing fiscal and monetary policy that continually need to be made, month to month and year to year. Macroeconomic ideas ought eventually to be confronted with data, not just casually but in the context of an interpretation, as complete as possible, of the full available multivariate history of macroeconomic variables. The work of getting ideas into a form relevant to real-time policy analysis and of seriously confronting them with data is difficult and, recently, only marginally rewarding professionally. Increasingly, the work is not being done, or not being done very well.

This volume is therefore a welcome step in what seems to me the right direction. It attempts to assemble, publicize, and interpret results from a variety of models that aim to be truly predictive. It should help us to understand how the models work and thus to understand better what we do and do not know about the way the world works.

But despite the virtues of the broad objectives of the project summarized in the volume, the specifics of its implementation seem badly flawed in several ways. Most of the reservations I had about the previous project, summarized in *Empirical Macroeconomics for Interdependent Economies (EMIE)*, are unresolved in this one, or even exacerbated. My objections fall under three main headings:

1. Puzzlement over how to interpret the project's specifications of policy. The explicit description of policies specifies monetary policy alone, without enough consideration of the essential interdependence of monetary and fiscal policies.

2. Dissatisfaction with the ISLM framework underlying most of these models—not because I think market-clearing equilibrium models should be used instead but because I think sticky-price modeling is important. ISLM is not a coherent starting point for such modeling.

3. Dismay at the total lack of attention to inference about the match of models to data. That the proportion of attention given to models that are only casually matched to data has gone up since *EMIE* is regrettable, though understandable, given the way the project is structured. Attending to such issues would have been difficult, but ignoring them may have resulted in a project that does more harm than good.

The first objection is the subject of my contribution to *EMIE* and has been elaborated in subsequent articles by Eric Leeper (1991) and me (1992). In these comments I try to show how much ambiguity this problem creates in the interpretation of results reported in this book by remaking the point in a deterministic continuous-time model that may be easier to grasp than the earlier stochastic frameworks. The second objection is really an extension of the first and is pursued below in the context of the same model.

The Match to Data

The third objection is perhaps an obvious point, of which not much can be said short of developing a prospectus for a different project. Some of these models claim to be based on a detailed examination of a large amount of data, but the nature of the statistical match between models and data is not discussed. Other models have very slim statistical foundations, being essentially theoretical models with coefficients chosen to be in some sense realistic.

Economists (or other social scientists, for that matter) can damage their credibility by describing the range of conclusions across an array of diverse, ostensibly empirical models that are not assessed for conformity with data. An instructive example of such damage, and of a response to it based on an attempt to assess fit across an array of already existing models, appears in work in progress by James Heckman. He shows that the apparent inability of econometric evaluations of a certain type of policy to deliver even a qualitative conclusion largely disappears when attention is focused on the best-fitting models.

Macroeconometric model builders in practice already give less attention than they should to questions of statistical fit. Every time their models' conclusions are taken seriously without any examination of the models' statistical credentials, this tendency is reinforced.

The Need for Complete, Joint Specification of Policies

A monetary policy that fixes the stock of high-powered money, or that raises interest rates in responses to deviations of a nominal variable like the money stock, price level, or exchange rate from a target value, is not feasible unless backed by a compatible fiscal policy. Compatible fiscal policies constitute a broad class, but they all include a positive response of taxation to either the level of the real value of public debt or the flow of real interest expenditures in the government budget. With neutral taxation (not a realistic assumption, but a useful benchmark), over a wide range of fiscal policies, the nature of equilibrium is unaffected by the particular form of the fiscal policy. On the face of it, this might justify the specification of fiscal policy requested by the organizers of this project, where fiscal policy is required not to respond to debt or interest expense for ten years but is allowed to respond thereafter.

The problem with this setup is that if fiscal-policy reactions to debt levels are postponed, the size of the eventual fiscal adjustment grows exponentially with the postponement. This makes analysis of policies with postponed fiscal adjustment problematic for two reasons—credibility problems and fiscal-neutrality problems. A policy that generates an unexpected rise or fall in public debt, but then reacts to that change with a large, long-delayed fiscal adjustment, cannot realistically be treated as credible. As recent U.S. political history makes clear, large, long-postponed fiscal adjustments are politically difficult and disruptive if they involve fiscal stringency. It therefore becomes hard to interpret the policy, because the fiscal adjustment is not inevitable. The alternative is to have a large, long-postponed adjustment in *monetary* policy—that is, abandonment of the nominal target that generated the need for fiscal adjustment in the first place. As imbalance between a government's fiscal system and its debt burden grows, sensible people will consider the possibility that the government's monetary commitment may crack before its fiscal commitment does. Thus even if the fiscal-policy adjustment does occur after the ten-year delay, the results of the policy in the meantime are likely to have been strongly affected by public uncertainty about whether the monetary policy being followed was sustainable. When the fiscal adjustment required is easing, it is even less realistic to imagine a long delay. That real governments will wait for ten years, allowing successor administrations to introduce large, long-delayed tax breaks or new spending, is unlikely.

Even aside from credibility problems, the fact that delayed fiscal adjustments will have to be large raises problems. To conclude that the exact nature of fiscal policy does not affect equilibrium depends on assuming that taxes are neutral. This is a bad enough assumption when one is considering small changes in taxation rates. Larger changes are likely to be more strongly nonneutral. Thus the sensitivity of policy conclusions to fiscal policy is likely to be stronger the more the fiscal responses to debt are delayed.

It is possible for monetary policy to forgo any attempt to hit a nominal target—for example, by simply committing to a nominal-interest-rate target. Contrary to what might be concluded from many simple macroeconomic models, this approach does not usually leave the price level indeterminate—it simply shifts its determination from monetary to fiscal policy. If fiscal policy makes real taxation respond positively to real debt, it leaves the price level indeterminate. Then and only then can monetary policy succeed in setting the price level. But if fiscal policy does not make real taxation respond to the level of real debt, the price level must adjust to keep revenue yields in line with the real debt burden. In this instance fiscal policy provides the "nominal anchor" and monetary policy is not needed—indeed cannot be used—to set the price level.

In this latter type of policy regime, in which the price level takes on the role of adjusting real debt to the flow of real revenues, the effects of monetary policy actions strongly depend on fiscal policy. Specifying such a regime with the requirement that tax rates and expenditures be fixed forever would be consistent. Allowing arbitrary adjustments in fiscal policies after ten years leaves the effects of any given monetary policy ambiguous.

These points have been made with formal models before in papers by Leeper and me, cited earlier. Those papers use stochastic, market-clearing, representative-agent rational-expectations models. The stochastic difference-equation models may appear inelegant and technically demanding. The assumptions of market clearing and rational expectations in all markets are inessential to the main results. So here I reproduce them in a model with sticky prices and sticky wages—Barro-Grossman wage and price dynamics in the terminology of chapter 2—a simple Phillips curve without expectational effects, and cost-based price adjustment. Also, the model is nonstochastic and has continuous time, making the solutions particularly simple in form and easy to understand.

A Model

Consider an economy in which a representative consumer faces the constraint

$$(6\text{-}1) \qquad C_t + \frac{\dot{M}_t + \dot{B}_t}{P_t} = r_t \frac{B_t}{P_t} + (1 - \tau)\frac{W_t L_t / P_t + \pi_t}{1 + \gamma V_t}.$$

The representative firm faces the constraint

$$(6\text{-}2) \qquad \pi_t = \Theta L_t^\alpha - \frac{W_t L_t}{P_t}.$$

The government faces the constraint

$$(6\text{-}3) \qquad \frac{\xi Y_t}{1 + \gamma V_t} + r_t \frac{B_t}{P_t} = \frac{\tau Y_t}{1 + \gamma V_t} + \frac{\dot{M}_t + \dot{B}_t}{P_t}.$$

Here C is consumption, M is money stock, B is government interest-bearing debt, P is the price level, r is the interest rate, τ is the tax rate, W is the wage, L is the level of employment, π is profits, and γ is a transactions-costs parameter,

$$(6\text{-}4) \qquad V_t = \frac{P_t Y_t (1 - \tau)}{M_t}.$$

is velocity,

(6-5) $$Y_t = \theta L_t^\alpha$$

is output, and ξY_t is government purchases, including their transactions-costs component, assumed proportional to output.

In equations 6-1 through 6-5, it is assumed that transactions costs are incurred for real expenditures but not for asset purchases or interest payments. Although different assumptions might be more realistic, they would not change the behavior of the model but would give it a less clean mathematical structure. It is also assumed that taxes fall on labor income and profits but not on interest income. As the model stands, taxes are almost neutral,[1] because desired labor supply is wage inelastic and short-run employment is not a choice variable. An income tax on interest earnings is in effect a change in the nominal interest rate on government debt. While the effect of taxes on equilibrium nominal interest rates, and therefore on velocity and on real resource availability, probably exists, it is small and complicated. A more ambitious version of the model would include realistic tax non-neutralities, among which this interest-tax effect is probably not very important.

The economy specified here has no capital, even in the form of inventories, and it has no foreign sector. These are important omissions and would probably affect conclusions if they were added to the model. But the objective here is not to duplicate chapter 2, but only to show that the conclusions from that chapter or any other model about the effects of policy regimes rest heavily on careful joint specification of monetary and fiscal policy regimes.

At this point I could proceed in the standard direction, giving firms and consumers dynamic utility functions, letting them optimize taking prices as given, and assuming prices adjust to clear markets. Instead, I begin by looking at a more interesting and probably more realistic model in which asset markets clear continuously but labor and product markets do not. More concretely, I assume that wage and price dynamics are generated by workers adjusting wages in a direction that reflects their preference for $L = 1$, whereas producers adjust prices in a direction that reflects their desire to have the real wage match the marginal product of labor. That is, I assume

(6-6) $$\dot{w} = vl$$

(6-7) $$\dot{p} = \mu \left[w - p - (\alpha - 1)l - \log(\alpha) - \theta \right].$$

Lower-case letters indicate natural logs [including $\theta = \log(\Theta)$]. Correspondingly, I assume that neither firms nor workers treat L as a choice variable.

----

1. As discussed later, the tax rate has a small effect on equilibrium velocity because transactions costs are assumed proportional to after-tax income.

Equation 6-6 is an old-fashioned Phillips curve, with no expectational terms, and equation 6-7 can be thought of as reflecting cost-based pricing behavior. To assume that equations 6-6 and 6-7 held true in an equilibrium with steady inflation would not make sense, because they would imply that firms and consumers could not measure and discount the steady inflation. But to assume that the two equations hold across equilibria with varying, but nonexplosive, inflation is a reasonable hypothesis to explore, despite its implication of "irrationality." In a nonexplosive equilibrium, the costs to agents of this irrationality may be small, comparable to the information-processing costs of implementing more subtle behavioral rules.

Though consumers assume they have no control over L, they do see in equation 6-1 an opportunity to shift consumption across time by buying and selling assets. Equations 6-1 and 6-3 together imply that for the economy as a whole there is no such opportunity, but individual consumers still behave as if there were a choice. They maximize

(6-8)
$$\int_0^\infty e^{-\beta t} \log(C_t) dt$$

subject to equation 6-1 (and equations 6-4 and 6-5), taking C, B, and M as choice variables.

Firms have no choice variables at all, once constraints are taken into account, though of course the aggregate price behavior specified in equation 6-7 is motivated by the notion that firms move prices in a direction that will tend to raise profits.

First-order conditions for the consumer's optimization problem are

(6-9)
$$\dot{p} + \dot{c} = r - \beta$$

(6-10)
$$r = \frac{\gamma V^2}{(1 + \gamma V)^2}.$$

In these two equations, I begin a convention that all non-Greek letters implicitly carry t-subscripts.

I have already specified fiscal policy, in making taxes and government purchases proportional to Y. To complete the model, it is necessary to specify monetary policy. Three possibilities are considered, matching as closely as possible the policies used in chapter 2:

(6-11a)
$$m = 1$$

(6-11b)
$$p_t + y_t = p_0 + y_0, \text{ all } t$$

(6-11c) $r = \beta.$

I could also consider the policy that keeps $\dot{p} + y$ (rather than $p + y$ as in equation 6-11b) constant, as in chapter 2, but the algebra is messy and does not contribute to the point of these comments. Constant-r policies with r fixed at values other than β would also yield well-behaved solutions, but they would involve steady-state inflation. This makes them harder to compare to equations 6-11a and 6-11b and also would require modification of the wage and price dynamics in equations 6-6 and 6-7 to keep the model reasonable.

From equations 6-1 and 6-3, one can derive the social-resource constraint

(6-12) $$C = \frac{1 - \xi}{1 + \gamma V} Y,$$

and then, using equation 6-4,

(6-13) $$PC = \frac{1 - \xi}{1 - \tau} \frac{VM}{1 + \gamma V}.$$

Now equations 6-9 and 6-10 can be combined with equation 6-13 to give

(6-14) $$\frac{d}{dt} \log\left(\frac{V}{1 + \gamma V}\right) - \dot{m} = \frac{\gamma V^2}{(1 + \gamma V)^2} - \beta.$$

Under the policy 6-11a, $m \equiv 1$, the $\dot{m}$ term in equation 6-14 vanishes, and it becomes an unstable difference equation in $V/(1 + \gamma V)$. Since $V/(1 + \gamma V)$ is bounded for positive V, exponential upward explosion in it is impossible. Exponential downward explosion would violate the transversality conditions of consumers—they would be maintaining bounded consumption while becoming unboundedly wealthy. (See my 1992 paper for a more detailed argument.) Thus with M fixed, equation 6-14 implies that V is also constant. Constancy of V implies, with equations 6-14 and 6-10, that r is also constant, and $r = \beta$.

With policy 6-11b, from the definition of V in equation 6-4, $\dot{m} = -\dot{v}$. This leaves equation 6-14 still an unstable difference equation in V and thus again implies that V is constant and $r \equiv \beta$.

With policy 6-11c, constancy of V follows immediately from equation 6-10, and then constancy of M follows from equation 6-14.

It may seem that I have now demonstrated that all the policies considered are equivalent. But though it is true that, from given initial conditions for its roman-character variables, the economy evolves the same way under all three policies, the response of the economy's initial values to a one-time, unanticipated change in $\tau, \xi, \theta,$ or γ is different under the different policy specifications. Also, as will be seen, policies that switch back and forth between those in equations 6-11a through 6-11c generate more complicated behavior.

Responses of a deterministic model to one-time, unanticipated disturbances are not as irrelevant to the actual behavior of a stochastic world as it might seem. For a linear-quadratic model, the dynamics of a stochastic system in which disturbances recur continually can be thought of as simply a linear combination of responses to one-time shocks, with the shape of the responses unaffected by whether the model is stochastic. In a nonlinear model the same interpretation holds approximately, for relatively small disturbances. Thus the fact that the shocks examined below are formally one-time deterministic disturbances does not impede their interpretation as approximate responses to small, recurring but unpredictable shocks.

Because with these policies V and M are constant, it is useful to note that

$$(6\text{-}15) \qquad l = \frac{v + m - p - \log(1 - \tau) - \theta}{\alpha}.$$

With p and l inversely linearly related in this way, one can reduce equations 6-6 and 6-7 to a two-equation system in the two variables p and w. This system contains all the model's dynamics, with other variables determined as functions of p and w. If one assumes that $\mu = v = 0.3$, $\alpha = 0.7$, $\gamma = 0.002$, $\beta = 0.05$, $\xi = 0.3$, and $\tau = 0.35$, the system has complex roots with period 6.75 years and an exponential decay rate of 0.21. The system's impulse responses are displayed in figures 6-1 and 6-2.

Now to consider the effects on the system of disturbances to parameter values, I begin with ξ, the fraction of output absorbed by government expenditure. Under policy 6-11b or 6-11a, V and M are both fixed, and the sticky-price assumption means that initial P is fixed in the face of the ξ increase. Thus by equation 6-4, Y is initially unchanged and therefore L is also initially unchanged. C simply adjusts immediately to its new, constant equilibrium level.

Note, however, that these conclusions are reached without attention to the government budget constraint. If the economy is in equilibrium to start with, with the surplus of taxes over expenditures matching interest payments, the rise in ξ generates a deficit, and from equation 6-3 it can be seen that in the new equilibrium real debt will explode, tending to grow at the exponential rate $r = \beta$. This path is not sustainable. If the initial increase in ξ is from 0.3 to 0.31 and other parameters are maintained at the values specified above for ten years, the debt grows by the factor $(0.01e^{0.5} + 0.04)/0.5 = 1.13$. The surplus of taxes over purchases, which is $(0.35 - 0.3)Y$, has to grow by the same factor. The government expenditures will have to be reduced by more than the initial increase, ending up at 0.2935. Thus the eventual permanent reduction in expenditure is 65 percent of the increase that was sustained over the ten years. A tax adjustment would have to be of similar magnitude.

Figure 6-1. *Responses of Prices to Price and Wage Shocks*

Natural logs

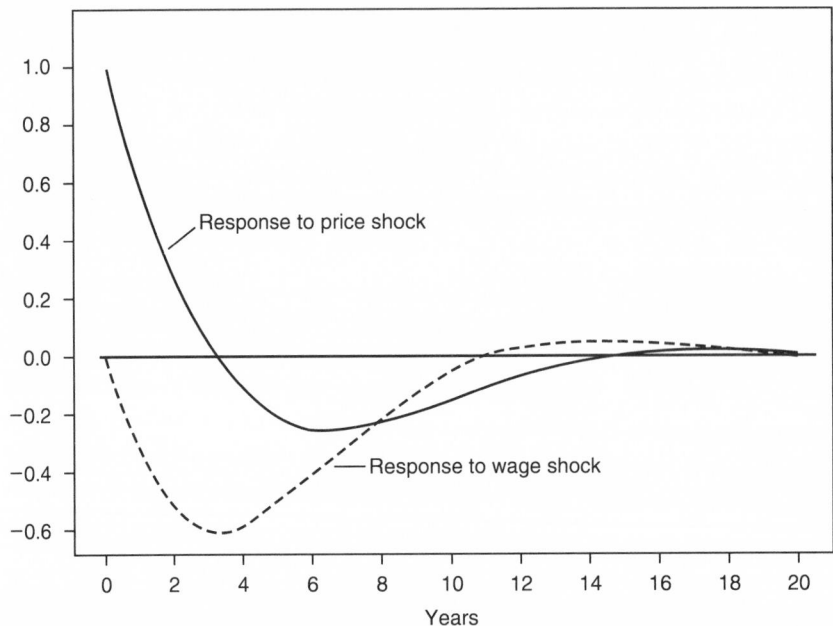

Response to price shock

Response to wage shock

Years

Figure 6-2. *Responses of Wages to Wage and Price Shocks*

Natural logs

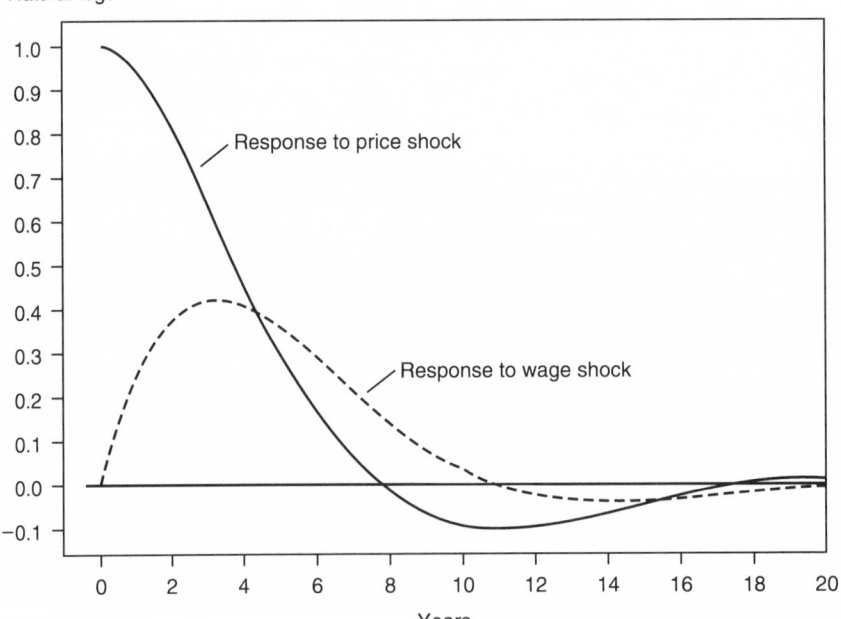

Response to price shock

Response to wage shock

Years

The response I have calculated to the initial expenditure increase rests on the assumption that consumers know that the unsustainable path of government debt will be cut short by *fiscal* policy. It could also be cut short by a period of monetary expansion and inflation. If consumers believed that to be even possible, the conclusion that V, r, P, and Y are constant during the ten years of high ξ would no longer hold, so that the effects of the fiscal expansion would be quite different.

Indeed suppose that M is kept constant for ten years, but then in the tenth year there is a switch to the $r \equiv 0.05$ policy, which is thereafter sustained forever with no fiscal adjustment. Then the paths of C and P are as displayed in figure 6-3. For the first ten years C remains 5 to 10 percent above its initial level, there is steady inflation of over 2 percent a year, and velocity, and thus nominal interest rates, rise above their steady-state values. Consumption finally falls back to its equilibrium only after the constant-r policy is implemented, falling steadily for more than five years thereafter.

I conclude that increased government spending, which has no effect on interest rates or employment under a constant-M policy backed by a credible

Figure 6-3. *Consumption and Price Level after Increase in Government Expenditures, with Money Stock Fixed for Ten Years*

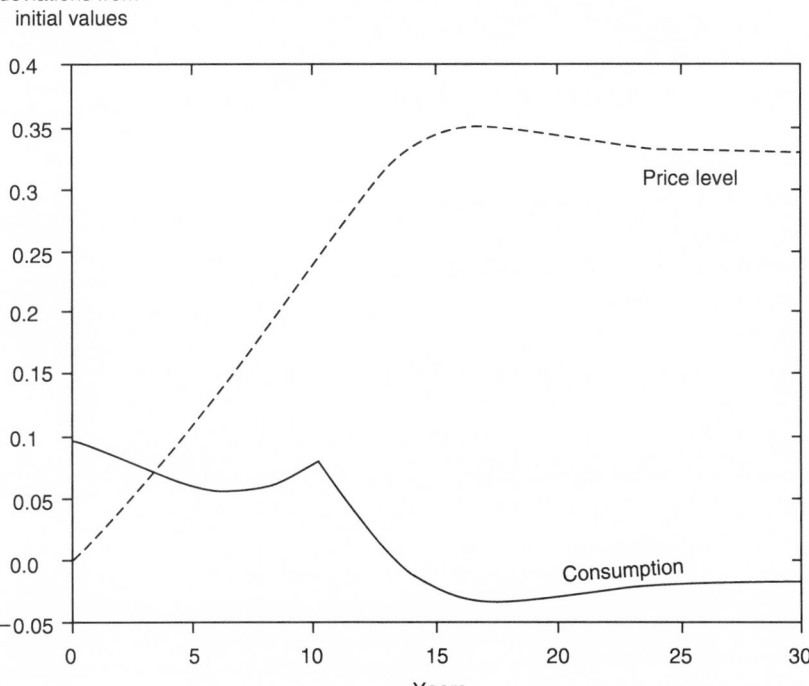

pledge to eventually restore fiscal balance, instead generates a strong inflationary expansion when it is expected that the commitment to fixed M will be
abandoned in ten years.

Under the constant-interest-rate policy 6-11c, an increase in ξ generates an
immediate response in M. The government budget constraint 6-3 implies that,
since M, r, and V are constant along the new equilibrium path, B is constant
also at the value

$$(6\text{-}16) \qquad\qquad B' = \frac{M'V(\tau - \xi')}{\beta(1 + \gamma V)}.$$

Here the prime mark indicates the value of a variable after the change in ξ.
But at the instant of the change in ξ, consumers can only exchange M for B;
they cannot change the total volume of their asset holdings. (This can occur
only over time as a flow of savings goes into increased asset holdings.) Thus

$$(6\text{-}17) \qquad\qquad B' + M' = B + M = A.$$

Equations 6-16 and 6-17 can be solved for B' and M' as functions of A. If
one assumes that the economy was initially in equilibrium with $M = 1$, then
with the assumed parameter values it had $B = 5$ initially. The increase in ξ
from 0.3 to 0.31 without any corresponding change in τ requires B to drop to
$B' = 4.8$, with a corresponding rise in M to $M' = 1.2$. Since these changes
occur with V fixed and P initially "stuck," Y initially rises in proportion to
the increase in M. This sets off inflation in w and p. Output returns to its
initial level after about one year, and then falls into a trough about two years
after the initial disturbance. Output then returns monotonically over the next
two years to approximately its equilibrium level and remains nearly constant
thereafter. Note that this response, while initially stronger than what was found
for fixed-M-for-ten-years-only, is considerably less persistent.

This calculated response is as dependent as the one for the fixed-M case
on assumptions about what consumers believe about future fiscal policy. The
difference is that here they are required to believe that the current policy of no
fiscal response to the size of the debt or deficit will persist forever, instead of
being required to believe in a drastic change in policy, of a politically difficult
type, far in the future.

Note that in this model the rough order of magnitude of the effect of a
fiscal expansion on "demand" is found not by a standard Keynesian multiplier
calculation but by observing the size of the proportional change in the net government surplus—revenues minus noninterest expenditures. The change from
government being 30 percent of output to its being 31 percent of output decreased the net surplus from 0.05 to 0.04, producing a 20 percent instantaneous
increase in output. Of course, in reality, the effects are not this large, because
people do not believe that government pays no attention to debt or deficits

in setting fiscal policies. But the strong contrasts among the three policies—fixed-M backed by future fiscal stringency, fixed-M for ten years only, and fixed-r—show how sensitive both the level of output and the fiscal "multiplier" can be to beliefs about fiscal and monetary policy commitments. Indeed the effects of a government expenditure increase are more similar across similar long-run fiscal policies than across similar ten-year monetary policies.

The contrast here between fixed-r and fixed-M-backed-by-fiscal-stringency policies does fit the standard conclusions, as reproduced in chapter 2: a fixed-M policy makes the effect of fiscal expansion or contraction on output negligible (here, precisely zero), whereas a fixed-r policy makes the effects very strong. But the standard conclusion rests on implicit assumptions about future fiscal policy.

Now consider the effects of a money-demand shock, here modeled as a rise in γ. Since r will have to remain at $\beta = 0.05$ after the change in γ, V will have to decline. With M fixed and P stuck, this requires an initial drop in Y proportional to the initial drop in V. A 5 percent increase in γ, from 0.002 to 0.0021, would produce a 2.4 percent drop in Y, followed by deflation and a return of Y to equilibrium on a path the same shape (though upside down) as that produced by a government expenditure expansion. If instead of keeping M fixed, the 6-11b policy of keeping nominal output constant is followed, the adjustment occurs instantly and entirely in M, with Y constant. There is no subsequent output or price fluctuation.

The fixed-M policy, because it produces a temporary drop in nominal income, causes a drop in tax revenue and an increase in government debt. As before, this will require that "ten years later" taxes be raised or expenditures be cut to finance the larger debt. The fixed-PY policy, because it jumps M upward to a new equilibrium level, jumps B downward by the same amount. Since government revenues and expenditures are unaffected, debt will start shrinking. The conclusions reached here about the effects of policy depend on fiscal authorities eventually undoing the debt decline with tax cuts or expenditure increases. If, instead, consumers thought the debt might be adjusted with tight money and high interest rates, the effects of the policy and the shock would be quite different. Note that, in effect, the fixed-M policy generates expected future fiscal stringency, corresponding to the contractionary effect on output, whereas the fixed-PY policy generates expected future fiscal easing, corresponding to its elimination of the negative effect on output of the increased demand for money.

With r fixed, an increase in γ from 0.002 to 0.0021 produces a 2.05 percent increase in M, while V decreases by 2.4 percent as with the other policies. Thus there is a slight initial decrease in output, about 0.35 percent, that dissipates through subsequent deflation. The fixed-r policy does not completely isolate the economy from the effects of the money-demand shift, because the required change in M implies a future excess of revenues over expenses and debt service at the equilibrium level of output, which is contractionary.

The standard sort of supply shock is a change in Θ, which simultaneously increases the level of output and the marginal product of labor. With M fixed, since V is constant, an increase in Θ must decrease L in order to keep Y constant. Because this simultaneously lowers marginal costs, both prices and wages start to move downward in response to the favorable productivity shock. The dynamics of the response is not quite the same as for a ξ shock, since the equilibrium p is lowered by more than the equilibrium w, but it again results in a rapidly damped oscillatory return to equilibrium in about four years. A fixed-PY policy produces the same result, as does the fixed-r policy.

It may be surprising that the policies are all equivalent for a supply shock. With the other two shocks, γ and ξ, there is under a fixed-r policy a direct impact on the long-run budget constraint, requiring an adjustment in the allocation of the public's portfolio between M and B. The same is true for a PY-constant policy under a γ shock. With a supply shock, the allocation of private-sector wealth between M and B does not shift under any of the three policies.

The model discussed here can easily be converted into a market-clearing version. One simply drops the price and wage adjustment equations 6-6 and 6-7 and replaces them with $L \equiv 1$ (inelastic labor supply) and $W/P = \Theta \alpha L^{\alpha-1}$ (real wage equals marginal product of labor). Obviously, in this case L is not affected by any shock; Y is affected only by the Θ shock; and C is affected by the Θ and ξ shocks. But in all these cases the effects of shocks on these real variables are the same under all three policies 6-11a through 6-11c. With market clearing, the differences in monetary and fiscal policies affect only wage and price responses to shocks.

The Limits of ISLM

The model presented here has a standard LM curve, derived in the standard way. It is equation 6-10. There is, however, no standard IS curve. Equation 6-9 relates the real interest rate to the rate of growth of consumption, not to "aggregate demand." Furthermore, as was verified at some length, the actual connection of what might be thought of as demand disturbances to output and interest rates depends strongly on mathematical boundary conditions determined by beliefs about future monetary and fiscal policies.

Those conditions ought to be a central characteristic of Keynesian macro-economic modeling. In market-clearing macro models, the payoff from getting the dynamic interaction of monetary and fiscal policies right is only in the better modeling of prices. The real equilibrium is insensitive to these issues. But in Keynesian modeling, price effects become real effects, and indeed are central to modeling the business cycle.

Yet when one looks at most models that attempt to incorporate the insights of rational-expectations theory into a Keynesian viewpoint, one sees, paradoxically, detailed treatment of the expectational elements of wage and price adjustment—the analogs of equations 6-6 and 6-7. The analog of equation 6-9 and its interaction with boundary conditions is stuffed into IS: $I(r, Y) = Y - G - C(r, Y)$. This seems to me to have it backward. Asset markets, particularly markets for paper assets, are thick and competitive and filled with speculators. Surely here taking careful account of expectations and assuming market clearing make sense as a first approximation. Labor and most product markets, however, are poorly approximated as continuously clearing competitive markets in homogeneous commodities. Treating price adjustment as sluggish and examining direct quantity responses to non-market-clearing allocations are an attractive first approximation here.

Insofar as the models examined in this volume are based on the ISLM framework, they cannot, in my view, give a useful assessment of the effects of large and truly permanent differences in monetary and fiscal policy rules. They will contain some version of an estimated IS curve relating real interest rates to "demand." Such a relation will not be stable under shifts in fiscal and monetary policy rules.

This is not to say that these models cannot give useful insights into the effects of variations in fiscal and monetary policies. Because the models have no facilities for considering changing expectations about distant future policies in asset valuation, they should not be asked to deal with such issues directly. They can be asked to project the effects of modest differences, sustained over modestly long periods, in settings of monetary and fiscal policy variables, with agents assuming that monetary and fiscal policy reaction functions will return to normal thereafter. Probably, despite the organizers' request for assessment of an unusual, unsustainable combination of monetary and fiscal policies to be maintained over ten years, many of the models have relied on estimated aggregate-demand relationships that reflect agents' continued belief in "normal" long-run policy. The results may therefore have some use as qualitative guides to the effects of less sustained policy changes in the direction of those specified by the organizers, if not to the specified changes themselves.

References

Leeper, E. M. 1991. "Equilibria under 'Active' and 'Passive' Monetary and Fiscal Policies." *Journal of Monetary Economics* 27:129–47.

Sims, C. 1992. "A Simple Model for Study of the Determination of the Price Level and the Interaction of Monetary and Fiscal Policy." Cowles Foundation Discussion Paper, Yale University.

Bennett T. McCallum

The basic objective of the enormous exercise reported in part 2 of this volume is to study the effects of alternative simplified monetary-policy regimes (hereafter referred to as rules) as predicted by a variety of multicountry econometric models. This objective is, I would argue, outstandingly praiseworthy. Understanding the effects of different potential policy regimes is what the subject of economics is fundamentally about, in my judgment, and in the macroeconomic area it is natural to focus on fluctuations. That can be done only with some type of quantitative model, and, given the profession's lack of agreement on the nature of fluctuations, it is important to consider the answers provided by different models with differing specifications. Furthermore, it may be a reasonable strategy to begin with monetary policy, leaving fiscal policy aside for the time being. If so, it makes good sense to consider alternative rules with the three types of variables that the organizers designated as targets: monetary aggregates, measures of nominal income, and average or "effective" exchange rates. For these reasons, then, I strongly support the organizer's basic conception as well as the spirit of the enterprise. But in my opinion the enterprise has several significant flaws or problems involving specific details of the experimental design—either the policy rules or other aspects of the simulation studies—that greatly reduce the usefulness of the simulation results.

The first problem is not with the design of the rules but with the study's inclusion of both quarterly and annual models. Both types can be extremely useful, of course, for various purposes, but it seems inappropriate to lump them together in an exercise of the present kind. For one reason, their generated root-mean-squared deviations are not directly comparable; for another, it is highly unlikely that the *same* policy rule is appropriate (even in a single model) for both time frames. Going further, one might even question whether annual models are in fact sensible for the type of exercise in question, which is supposed to represent policy processes as they would be carried out by actual central banks operating in a systematic, rule-like fashion. It seems implausible, that is, to suppose that short-term interest rates would be held fixed over an entire year. There is some difficulty in that regard even for quarterly models, but the match with reality is clearly much better than is the case with annual models.

The second problem pertains to the specification of the rules themselves. As a way of introducing this problem, let me mention that I have been doing some small-scale simulation work of my own, studying the properties of one particular monetary rule using quite rudimentary but contrasting models

444

for the United States alone.[1] These are quarterly models with which my rule sets each quarter's growth rate of the monetary base partly in response to the previous quarter's deviation of nominal GNP from a prespecified target path. The relevant point is that when I discuss these simulations, in seminars or at conferences, one of the main objections raised is that it seems unrealistic to suppose that the Federal Reserve obtains observations on GNP as promptly as the rule's one-quarter lag implies. In fact I would argue that this rule can be justified as reasonably operational, but I certainly do not think the same can be said for the GNP rules used in the simulations in part 2 of this volume, for they pretend that the monetary policymaker has observations on the *current period's* GNP—both nominal and real. Such observations are not available, of course, and Meltzer (1987) has documented that estimates of current-period GNP are highly inaccurate. By contrast, observations are available promptly on exchange rates, so the third category of rules is not subject to the same criticism. What about the first category, which includes money stock measures? I return to issues regarding that target variable below; the point being made here is that the organizers and model groups gave too little attention to specifying the rules under study in part 2 so as to make them *operational*.[2]

In that same regard a second aspect of the utilized rules is also troublesome—namely, their reliance on "baseline" values. The typical rule form relates deviations of instrument settings from some baseline reference path to departures of the relevant target variable from its baseline path.[3] What analysts actually want to study, of course, is the ability of policy rules to keep target variables close to target paths selected for their normative merits, which may not correspond to the baseline paths of the simulations in part 2.[4] Thus the utilized procedure involves a presumption that if a rule is effective in relation to an arbitrary baseline path, it will also be effective in relation to a normatively chosen baseline path. If the models in use were linear and the target variables were all "nominal," as opposed to "real," then this presumption would be justified. My conjecture is that nonlinearity is not a major problem but that emphasis on real target variables may be. That is a rather complex issue, however, to which I do not want to devote space in this comment.[5]

---

1. The basic study is McCallum (1988), with various extensions reported in McCallum (1990).

2. This argument should not be interpreted as a claim that *expectations* of current (or even future) variables are inappropriate for inclusion on the right-hand side of policy rules. But the argument does suggest that such expectations should be based on information sets that include current values only for asset prices, with only lagged values permitted for other variables.

3. See equations 3-1 in chapter 3.

4. I have not been able to find a general statement governing the selection of baseline values. For particular models some indications are provided in part 3.

5. For a detailed discussion, see McCallum (1992).

The point to be emphasized here is that rules expressed in terms of baseline values are inherently nonoperational. One way to express the problem is to note that, because the instrument-variable and target-variable baseline paths are related to each other by the model at hand, any rule specification involving these paths must be *model specific*. A given realization of the target-variable path in two models would, therefore, call for different instrument paths even with a single given rule. Thus comparisons across models are seriously compromised. Another way to express the problem is to note that giving a policymaker a parameterized rule of the type in question would not provide him with enough information to determine instrument settings in response to the economy's performance. The policymaker would also have to generate, by some unspecified process, baseline values for the instrument and target variables. Different choices of this process would then imply different policy actions in response to a given state of the economy. In sum, to be truly operational—something that is ready for a policymaker to implement—a rule needs to specify instrument settings in raw terms (rather than as deviations) and to be applicable for arbitrary target paths.

Of course, to be operational a rule must also be specified in terms of an instrument variable that is actually controllable. In this regard the organizers have demonstrated their concern for operationality by specifying that some short-term interest rate should be used as the instrument by each modeling group. That is highly commendable. I would add, nevertheless, that there is a case for believing that the monetary base (or some measure of bank reserves) would be a better instrument. It too is controllable and has the advantage that its growth rates are more easily interpreted in terms of monetary policy "tightness" or "ease" in a dynamic setting.[6] Thus it may lend itself more readily to use as an instrument in a simple policy rule. In my own situations for the U.S. economy, with a small Keynesian model and a small VAR system,[7] I found it necessary to use a more complex feedback rule with an interest-rate instrument, in comparison with the monetary base, to do a reasonable job of hitting nominal-GNP targets. Be that as it may, it would be very worthwhile to learn which of these two potential instruments would work better for nominal-GNP or price-level targets in ambitious multicountry models such as those considered in part 2. It is too bad that the opportunity was not taken.

6. The problem with interest rates is that "tight" monetary policy corresponds to high interest rates from a short-run perspective but to low interest rates from a long-run perspective. How to manage the transition is unclear. The problem cannot be overcome by pretending that actual policy actions are conducted "in the short run," as some economists have claimed. At any point of time the current situation is the resultant of "long-run" effects of policy actions taken at many points of time in the past as well as "short-run" effects of recent actions.

7. See the exercises reported on pp. 61–66 of McCallum (1990).

Having mentioned the monetary base, I should quickly emphasize that I consider it to be attractive as an *instrument*, not as a target variable. Indeed, one of the more questionable features of the symposium's experimental design is its specification of the base as a target variable in the first rule. There are two distinct reasons for objection. First, the combination of an interest-rate instrument with a base target seems almost bizarre. Since these two variables merely provide different signals about the extent of open-market operations, policymakers might as well work directly with the one they are interested in controlling. Second, using the base as the target variable in a rule that is supposed to represent money-stock targeting seems undesirable. Almost all proponents of money-stock targets would favor either M1 or M2 as the aggregate variable. I tend myself to advocate nominal-income targeting, but if I favored money-stock targets, I would claim that use of the base tends to misrepresent my position.

Finally, for several interrelated reasons I am somewhat uncomfortable with the "loss function" evaluations provided in chapters 4 and 5. This discomfort results mostly from the emphasis—not extreme but still present—given to deviations of real GNP from its baseline path. In terms of economic theory, those deviations would be an appropriate loss function only for a certain class of models—namely, flexible-price classical models. With one possible exception, however, the participating models are not of that class. And in terms of policy preferences or objectives, it would appear that the objectives of actual policymakers are dominated by a desire for output (or employment) to be high and inflation to be close to zero. Output above normal is avoided not because it is itself considered bad but only because of the fear that high output will bring on an inflationary spurt in the near future. Another reason for concern arises because the economics profession has demonstrated a large amount of disagreement over the mechanism that is supposed to make monetary policy actions have effects—temporary but important—on real aggregative variables. It is not just that various models have different parameter values but rather that there is no conceptual agreement among theorists about the mechanism at work or even its qualitative nature. That being the case, it seems undesirable to put much weight on real output variability when attempting to rank the various policy rules. Thus I consider it more important to know which, if any, of the rules are robust across models, robust in the sense of yielding effective achievement of target paths with the same numerical parameter values used in each of the models. But, as explained earlier, such comparisons are effectively ruled out by the use of baseline reference paths in the form of rules utilized.

In conclusion, it should be repeated that the foregoing objections to specific details of the experimental design do not imply disapproval of the basic objectives of the study. They reflect, instead, disappointment that the achievement of those praiseworthy objectives was undermined by the design flaws I have mentioned.

References

McCallum, B. T. 1988. "Robustness Properties of a Rule for Monetary Policy." In *Money, Cycles, and Exchange Rates: Essays in Honor of Allan H. Meltzer*, edited by K. Brunner and B. T. McCallum, 173–202. Carnegie-Rochester Conference Series on Public Policy 29. Amsterdam: North-Holland.

——. 1990. "Targets, Indicators, and Instruments of Monetary Policy." In *Monetary Policy for a Changing Financial Environment*, edited by W. S. Haraf and P. Cagan, 44–70. Washington: American Enterprise Institute.

——. 1992. "Specification of Policy Rules and Performance Measures in Multicountry Performance Studies." International Monetary Fund working paper, Washington.

Meltzer, A. H. 1987. "Limits of Short-Run Stabilization Policy." *Economic Inquiry* 25:1–14.

Ray C. Fair

An impressive amount of work has gone into the results described in this volume, and the organizers did an amazing job in directing and riding herd on the model builders. I do, however, have some serious reservations about both the general approach that was followed and the specifics of what was done. I discuss three specifics first.

1. In the chapter on deterministic simulations (chapter 4), the policy regimes were ranked according to how far the shocked path deviated from the baseline (base) path. The further the deviation (in a squared-error sense), the worse the policy regime is said to have done. But is that sensible? Consider the first experiment, a one-period increase in U.S. government expenditures. Why should the best policy regime be the one that minimizes the effect of this change? Say that one policy regime almost completely eliminated the output effects of this change, while a second regime led to a fairly large output increase and a drop in unemployment. Say also that inflation in both instances was very little affected, because the economy was operating considerably below full employment. In this case one would be unlikely to say the first policy regime was better.

Or take the case in which there is a positive supply shock, like an upward shift in a production function. Here one would not want to pick a policy regime that lessened as much as possible the effects of this shift. Even for a negative supply shock, if the economy were at full employment, one would probably not want a policy regime that tried to push the economy up to the old level. Generally, I think a confusion exists between wanting a policy regime that minimizes variances, which is what the stochastic simulation results are about, and wanting a policy regime that undoes the effects of some fiscal policy action or technological change. The first goal is usually desirable; the second is usually not.

2. For the stochastic simulation work (chapter 5), the aim is to compute variances and rank policy regimes on how well they do in minimizing the variances. As the authors note, they are not quite computing variances, because the base paths used are not the mean paths. They also average the variances across time to get a summary measure, which is not rigorous, because the variances are not constant across time.

My first concern about the stochastic simulation work is the use of the base path instead of the mean path. If variances are to be computed, why not use the mean path? Also, apparently the same base path was used for all the regimes even though the actual base paths differ across policy regimes. The model builders apparently got around this problem for a given policy regime by adding errors to the chosen base path so as to make the base path for the given policy regime in effect the chosen base path. The stochastic simulation work was then done with those errors always added in. At the time of this writing, however, it is not clear whether everyone did so, and in general the treatment of the base paths seems somewhat muddled. It would have been much more straightforward simply to have used the mean path.[1]

My second concern relates to the number of repetitions done per period: ten for quarterly models and forty for annual models. When one is trying to estimate the difference between two variances, this is a very small number of trials! I did a study (Fair 1988) using my U.S. model similar to that in chapter 5. For my model one policy regime used the money supply as the policy instrument and the other regime used the interest rate. Given the output from the repetitions, it is possible to compute not only the variances and the differences between the variances but also the variances of the variances and variances of the differences. I had to take 1,000 repetitions before the variances of the differences were small enough for me to place any confidence in the results. Even then, 1,000 repetitions were enough only because I used the trick of drawing the same set of errors for both policy regimes. Of course, many fewer repetitions are needed if one is interested only in the variances for a particular regime, but the work in chapter 5 is interested in differences. The problem with differences is that the difference between two variances is typically much smaller in absolute value than either of the variances, and many more repetitions are needed to get the stochastic simulation variances small relative to the size of the differences. From my experience, ten or forty repetitions are scarcely large enough to allow any confidence to be placed in the comparisons of the variances from the alternative policy regimes. It is possible to check this conclusion, however, by computing the variances of the differences. As just noted, that can be done by simply using the values from the repetitions.

3. The fact that the policy regimes the model builders were allowed to use are not exact makes the results somewhat murky. I think it would have made the comparisons sharper (to the extent that any of the comparisons are more than comparisons of stochastic simulation noise) to have extreme regimes to compare. Sometimes better insights can be obtained from extreme comparisons.

My reservation about the general approach concerns the lack of testing of the models. I think one should test before analyzing. If a model tests poorly and does not seem to be a good approximation of the world economy, its policy properties are of no interest. Many of the policy differences between two models may occur simply because one model is a good approximation and one is not. Since there is no way of knowing from the current results how good

---

1. See chapter 5, note 6. [Eds.]

any of the models are, not much can be made of the policy similarities and differences.

Some of the parameters of some of the models are calibrated rather than estimated in the usual ways. The MSG model is complete calibrated, and I believe some of the parameters of the rational-expectations models are calibrated. It is risky to draw policy inferences from calibrated models. Such models or parts of models are not as closedly tied to the historical data as conventional models are, and they may be way off. A few calibrated values that are inadvertently but seriously wrong might cause the overall model to be a poor approximation, and no one can test for that.

I also have reservations about the common use of the rational-expectations assumption among most of the model builders. As is well known, the properties of models can be quite sensitive to the use of the rational-expectations assumption. If the assumption is a poor approximation of the way that expectations are actually formed, the properties of the model may be very inaccurate. Having tested the rational-expectations assumption against simpler alternatives (Fair, forthcoming), I found it is not well supported by the data. My sense is that many of the model builders have imposed rational-expectations constraints without testing them against other alternatives—a risky approach. The properties of these models should not be trusted until the constraints have been adequately tested.

Testing alternative models is difficult because of the danger of data mining and because of differences in what is treated as exogenous. Nevertheless, testing methods are available, and I think the first step of the conference should have been to use some of those methods. At a minimum, each model could have been tested against simple autoregressive or vector-autoregressive models. Also, as discussed earlier, the rational-expectations assumption should have been tested against other alternatives. Some of the testing methods require rolling reestimation and some require stochastic simulation, but given the organizers' skill at directing the model builders, having each model perform a standard series of tests does not seem out of the question. If that were done in the future, we might be able to get down to, say, the final four, whose policy properties could then be compared.

References

Fair, R. C. 1988. "Optimal Choice of Monetary Policy Instruments in a Macroeconometric Model." *Journal of Monetary Economics* 22: 301–15.
———. Forthcoming. "Testing the Rational Expectations Hypothesis in Macroeconometric Models." *Oxford Economic Papers*.

Donald L. Kohn

My comments focus on the issues of the credibility and time consistency of monetary policy.[1] These topics are touched on in several papers in this volume, perhaps most prominently in those by Peter Klenow and by Paul Masson and Steven Symansky. I approach these issues from the perspective of the process of monetary policymaking in the United States during the latter part of the 1980s.

The credibility of monetary policy has become increasingly important to policymakers in recent years, partly because of the greater emphasis on price stability as an objective of monetary policy. Inflation is recognized as being uniquely under the control of the monetary authorities over the long run, and price stability as being the inflation result that will minimize distortions and uncertainties and improve the long-run growth of the economy. Members of the Federal Open Market Committee (FOMC) are aware that the greater the credibility of their price stability objective, the less costly will be the approach to that objective in terms of output forgone. They have been shown the results of model simulations under various credibility assumptions prepared by the Federal Reserve staff to illustrate this point. And they have read about the results of outside models that do not have credibility effects, which show very high unemployment rates accompanying a path to price stability in five years.

The price stability objective itself is part of the credibility equation. Not only does even low, steady inflation probably involve distortions and inefficiencies in a necessarily imperfectly indexed economy, but price stability seems an inherently more credible goal than, say, 4 1/2 percent inflation. The latter can too easily begin to slip to 5 or 5 1/2 percent—the differences look small. Only "price stability," or zero inflation, resonates in a way that makes it a target from which persistent deviations would be obvious and hard to explain away over time.

Increased concern about credibility can also be seen in the greater emphasis in policymaking on variables that reflect market expectations. Some policymakers have advocated attention to what they call "forward-looking" indicators of policy, such as yield curves, exchange rates, and commodity prices. These financial and related market variables embody market expectations of future inflation, and their movements may contain evidence of changes in such expectations that the central bank ought to be aware of. As they look at market variables and their response to policy, policymakers have emphasized "staying

---

1. These comments represent my own views and are not necessarily those of the Federal Reserve Board or other members of the Federal Reserve staff.

ahead of the curve." That is, policy actions should anticipate events sufficiently to encourage favorable changes in expectations, or at a minimum to forestall incipient movements in inflation expectations away from the direction intended by the Federal Reserve.

Those using market-based, expectations-driven indicators seem to recognize the limitations of such variables. For one, those indicators reflect market expectations about the Federal Reserve's own future actions as well as about the effect of those actions and other forces in the economy on output and inflation. For another, movements in these variables may be affected by actual and expected changes in real output and real interest rates as well as by prospective inflation. Moreover, stabilizing some of these variables would not tie down the price level—they are not nominal anchors. Rather, at best, they are measures of relative inflation rates—over time in the case of yield curves, and over countries in the case of exchange rates. Still, carefully interpreted in conjunction with other information, such variables do provide some feedback to policymakers on market expectations about inflation; they can therefore impose an element of discipline on the policy process and a reading on the credibility of the central bank's stated objectives.

Given that the policymakers recognize the importance of credibility, how have they gone about trying to gain some? One technique used, perhaps subconsciously, is escalating the rhetoric about the primacy of the price stability objective. The time-inconsistency literature recognizes the role of "reputation" in disciplining central bank actions to bring about price stability. By raising the visibility of price stability as an objective of monetary policy, policymakers have placed their reputations at risk if progress is not forthcoming, and awareness of this possibility can act as an important constraint on their decisions.

If reputation were not sufficient, a tighter form of discipline would be a law requiring the Federal Reserve to achieve price stability. Indeed, in 1989, Representative Stephen Neal of North Carolina proposed a congressional resolution along these lines, mandating price stability in five years. A favorable vote would have meant explicit political support for the Federal Reserve's price stability objective and the clarification of ambiguous and potentially contradictory directions in existing Acts. The Federal Reserve worked with Neal to fine-tune the language in his bill and testified in favor of the revised version. However, it did not gather much support.

The Federal Reserve has enunciated a general, medium-term strategy for going from moderate inflation to price stability. In his testimony to the Senate Banking Committee on February 22, 1990, a time of elevated resource utilization and modestly accelerating inflation, Chairman Alan Greenspan said:

> The strategy of the Federal Open Market Committee (FOMC) for moving toward this goal [price stability] remains the same—to restrain growth

in money and aggregate demand in coming years enough to establish a clear downward tilt to the trend of inflation and inflation expectations, while avoiding a recession. Approaching price stability may involve a period of expansion in activity at a rate below the growth of the economy's potential, thereby relieving pressures on resources. Once some slack develops, real output growth can pick up to around its potential growth rate, even as inflation continues to trend down. Later, as price stability is approached. real output growth can move still higher, until full resource utilization is restored.

This strategy, which attempts to avoid recession, implies some sensitivity about the degree of slack in the economy as it progresses toward price stability. Even if "sacrifice ratios" do not vary much over different unemployment rates, loss functions may not be linear, with large deviations from full employment considered disproportionately painful.

To enhance credibility, one could imagine announcing a "rule" or "regime" based on this strategy—that is, precommit to a reaction function containing both actual prices and output and desired paths for these variables. Of the regimes considered in this volume, such a strategy corresponds most closely to 2B, which targets both real GNP and inflation. That this regime proved superior in many of the simulations provides a degree of reassurance. In some others, however, particular specifications of regime 2B did not have a stable solution, which raises the issue of whether the Federal Reserve would risk perpetually accelerating inflation or deflation.

In practice, policy guards against such an outcome by varying the response to real or price data according to the state of the business cycle and the kinds of shocks affecting the economy. That is, coefficients in the reaction function change over time and economic states. One suspects that this type of flexible response gives superior results to an inflexible "rule"—even beyond minimizing potential economic instabilities. Even if there were a regime along the lines of 2B that dominated judgmental policy, its announcement, by itself, would probably not enhance credibility, since the specifications would be too complex and arcane to be comprehensible and convincing to the general public.

A money-supply or nominal-income regime might be considered a potential alternative to the complex specifications of something like regime 2B to accomplish many of the same objectives. Depending on how they are specified, such regimes can have the advantage relative to 2B of potentially tying down the price level over time and, in the context of credibility, of focusing on one variable and therefore communicating policy intent more clearly. The FOMC is aware of the potential for its money-supply targets to affect credibility and takes that into account in setting the long-run money supply targets it announces every February and July.

The usefulness, however, of preannounced money or nominal GDP targets in accomplishing the Federal Reserve's objectives or enhancing its credibility may be limited. The relationship of money growth—whatever measure of money is chosen—to price-level movements is complex, possibly evolving over time because of deregulation and innovation in financial systems, and subject as well to short-run money-demand shifts. Even without the complications of unanticipated variations in velocities, intermediate-term money-supply paths to achieve a gradual approach to price-level stability are not simple gradual decelerations. Such paths also need to take into account the effects on money demand of changing interest rates as inflation ebbs if they are to avoid over-shooting the stable price objective.

Nominal GNP paths consistent with attention both to inflation and real output would probably be less complex than those for money. Still, desired nominal GDP trajectories would depend on where the economy started relative to its potential, and could also require "fine-tuning" to take account of possible changes in the speed of adjustment in prices to shortfalls from potential output. Moreover, following a given nominal GDP path would imply a similar reaction to, say, a shortfall in output or in prices. In practice, depending on the nature and persistence of such a deviation, central bank strategies might well need to be adapted. Nominal GDP also suffers from being further removed from the control of the central bank, with uncertain relationships between central bank actions and GDP outcomes in regard to both timing and strength.

Partly for these reasons, it is doubtful that decisionmakers in labor or product markets would or should pay much attention to money or nominal-income paths announced by the central bank. Such paths might, however, serve to discipline the central bank as it reacts to incoming data, and market knowledge of central bank intentions comes from watching those reactions. From them the objectives of the central bank can be deduced—for example, the weight placed on prices and output over the intermediate term.

Developments during the latter 1980s provide an illustration of how Federal Reserve actions can reveal intentions and feed back on credibility and expectations. The very rapid increase in interest rates in 1988, when inflation data did not show much acceleration, along with the sluggish reduction in 1989, when some feared recession, probably won some credibility for the Federal Reserve's determination to at least keep inflation from accelerating—a marked contrast to the usual experience after long economic expansions. In this case, the actions were about in line with the rhetoric of the central bank. That the rise in short-term rates in 1988 was accompanied by unusually small increases in long-term rates reinforces the notion of some gain in damping inflation expectations.

In this period the difficulties in sending consistent signals to the market about policy intentions and the sensitivity of policymakers to those signals were also illustrated by attitudes toward foreign-exchange-market intervention. In late

1989 Governors Wayne Angell and Manuel Johnson dissented from a decision to raise the ceiling on the Federal Reserve's foreign currency holdings. They did so because they felt that selling dollars, especially to reduce the currency's value, would send conflicting signals to the market about the Federal Reserve's intentions regarding price stability. They were in a minority, but the strength of their reaction suggests the importance policymakers have come to place on the kind of signals they send to the public.

In light of the increased emphasis on price stability and the Federal Reserve's commitment to that objective, how is one to interpret the steady 4 to 5 percent inflation rates the United States experienced during the last half of the 1980s? From one perspective, as I already noted, maintaining inflation roughly within the same band as the economic expansion matured was unusual—perhaps a result of heightened attention to price stability. From another, the persistence of this rate prompted the question whether it had become the "time-consistent" inflation rate for the United States. This is an important question because it could have a major bearing on the difficulties and costs associated with achieving price stability.

If a 4 to 5 percent inflation, for example, is seen by the public as the time-consistent rate, it may be very difficult to change expectations, and the cost of moving to price stability could be relatively high. A public that perceived the inflation rate of the latter 1980s as the product of deeply rooted underlying forces and preferences acting on and within the central bank would be highly skeptical of an announced price stability goal. This public would view decreases in inflation as temporary and expect the central bank to raise output rather than to accept and maintain lower inflation. Private actions taken in anticipation of such a central bank response would tend to validate a return to the former inflation rate and result in substantial output losses if the central bank did not validate such expectations.

There is, however, an alternative explanation of the persistent 4 to 5 percent inflation performance of the 1980s—historical accident. In effect, that was the inflation rate when economic activity reached its potential. Because the rate was much lower than the double-digit rates of the late 1970s and early 1980s, and the costs associated with it were not very large by comparison, there was no imperative to undertake vigorous efforts to reduce it further. Nonetheless, it was not a rate the Federal Reserve was seeking, and it was not the result of a deliberate game-theoretic attempt to deceive economic agents in order to boost output for a time.

The second explanation appears more plausible than the first—a judgment that has been reinforced by the action of the Federal Reserve when recession occurred unexpectedly in the 1990s. The Federal Reserve has eased policy, at times aggressively, to counteract influences depressing economic activity. But it has done so in the context of accepting and encouraging the trend of moderat-ing inflation that accompanied the slack in resource utilization. The persistence of relatively high long-term interest rates, among other indicators, nonethe-less suggests that private decisionmakers have only slowly begun to recognize that inflation will persist below the previous band of 4 to 5 percent. This de-layed reaction may well have impeded the needed balance-sheet restructuring and contributed to sluggish economic expansion—underlining once again the importance of credibility in policymaking.

3

Stochastic Simulations of Monetary-Policy Regimes

CHAPTER 7

Evaluating Policy Regimes under Imperfect Credibility

Paul R. Masson and Steven A. Symansky

THE NUMERICAL results presented in part 2 of this volume concern policy regimes that are assumed to be credible: there is no question that the policies will be followed, and the private sector's expectations are formed accordingly. But in practice policy regimes or, more basic, operating rules—change.[1] These changes may occur because the monetary authorities change objectives to meet political exigencies or because there are shifts in public perceptions of what is economically important. They may also occur because altered circumstances make an announced path for a policy instrument, or a rule for that policy instrument, no longer optimal. There is an extensive literature, beginning with Kydland and Prescott (1977) and extended by Barro and Gordon (1983) and many others, that considers the "time inconsistency" of optimal policy; that is, the passage of time—even in the absence of shocks—changes the incentives to stick with the chosen policy. More recently authors have explained that, in a multiperiod context with stochastic shocks, the authorities' concern for their reputation might remove the temptation for them to renege on an announced policy (Backus and Driffill 1986 and Currie and Levine 1987). Uncertainty about the future, however, is likely to mean that no policy regime is perfectly credible: even for a policy that is "time consistent" in the absence of shocks, the subsequent occurrence of random shocks will change the attractiveness of that policy relative to alternative policies (Canzoneri and Henderson 1988).

In light of the nonzero probability that policy regimes or rules may be abandoned, it seems to be stacking the deck in favor of these policies to assume that expectations are formed on the basis of complete credibility. In

The authors are grateful to Matt Canzoneri, David Currie, Peter Isard, and Warwick McKibbin for background discussion and comments. The views expressed here are those of the authors alone and do not represent those of the International Monetary Fund.

1. In most places in this chapter, the authors use the word "rule" rather than "regime" when referring to the policies followed by monetary authorities. See chapter 1 for a discussion of terminology for the operating procedures used by policymakers. The alternative procedures considered here are analyzed at the level of technical discourse; they are relatively simple, without scope for discretionary instrument variation (in the conventional-language sense of chapter 1). [Eds.]

general, lack of credibility will tend to make a policy less effective in attaining policy goals. Monetary deceleration, for instance, may lead to a slower decline in inflation if wage and price behavior is not modified to reflect low expected inflation. Similarly, a policy of fixed exchange rates may not be tenable—or may involve prohibitively high interest rates—if expectations of a depreciation persist. It would seem to be important, therefore, to evaluate policies on the basis of an estimate of their credibility, if that credibility can be modeled.[2] Taking account of the private sector's assessment of the credibility of policy helps to meet the criticism made by Lucas (1976) concerning the use of models in this context.

This chapter is intended to provide an exploratory, rather than definitive, analysis of how credibility affects different policy regimes, limited here to different announced paths (or rules) for monetary deceleration. It is an attempt to implement, in a medium-size nonlinear model, an index of credibility that reflects the probability that the rule will be abandoned in favor of a simple alternative path for the money supply. The probability assessment is based on assumed knowledge of the authorities' objective function, of the parameters of the model, and of the distribution of shocks hitting the economy. It is thus a simple extension of the setup assumed in the stochastic simulations discussed elsewhere in this volume. Expectations are assumed to be formed on the basis of a linear combination of solutions of the model in future periods under the announced rule and under a single alternative rule. The weights applied to each are the assessments of the probability of the two policies being followed. One or the other policy is assumed to be chosen on the basis of whether the authorities' objective function yields a larger value if they stick to the rule or abandon it.

In our framework there is no question of trying to discover the "type" of government (that is, its objective function): it is assumed to be known by the private sector. Rather, given a particular objective function, for some shocks the announced path for policy will not be optimal, and both the government and the private sector realize this beforehand and can evaluate the probability of this occurring. As Canzoneri and Henderson (1988) have shown in the context of international cooperation, if shocks are unbounded, then the efficient point cannot be supported for all realizations.

There are several aspects of credibility that are not taken into account in our analysis.[3] In particular, as discussed above, we do not consider the possibility

2. If the ranking of rules is not affected by the introduction of less-than-perfect credibility, then the insights from the standard comparisons of outcomes may still be useful. But it is not obvious that this would be the case. Some rules, for instance, may be more dependent on credibility for their success than others, and rules may also differ in their degree of credibility for a given distribution of shocks affecting the economy.

3. See Blackburn and Christensen (1989) for a survey of issues related to the credibility of monetary policy.

that the private sector would not know the true preferences of the authorities, who might therefore have an incentive to signal or hide their characteristics and to invest in building "reputation."[4] Those preferences are assumed to be constant over time.[5] Likewise, we do not take into account the possibility of "private information" (Canzoneri 1985). Instead, here the authorities' preferences are assumed to be known, and it is assumed that the authorities and the private sector have the same information about current shocks. There is no distortion in the economy for which the authorities attempt to compensate by aiming for an overly expansionary target, as in Barro and Gordon (1983). We do not examine strategic behavior on the part of the private sector (as in Horn and Persson 1988) but instead assume that the private sector is made up of atomistic agents; the only issue is how they form their expectations.

Two strands of the literature that are closely related to our analysis have to do with the evaluation of simple policy rules in the face of stochastic shocks and with the formulation of policy rules that, although simple, allow for the possibility of abandoning a rule if shocks make it optimal to do so. In the first strand, Levine, Currie, and Gaines (1988) have examined the sustainability of simple policy rules in a stochastic context, showing that the degree of discounting and the nature of the shocks are important determinants of sustainability. Shocks are shown generally to support the sustainability of those policies, although these authors point out (p. 20) that, for some combination of shocks, temptation to renege on the rule exceeds the reputational benefits from sticking to it. They assume, however, that this probability is negligible and that expectations are formed on the basis of perfect policy credibility. Here, we explore the probability of going off the rule and endogenize expectations accordingly.

In the second strand, Flood and Isard (1989) considered simple policy rules with "escape clauses"—rules that take into account that particular draws of shocks may make the incentives to abandon the rule too great—at which point the authorities revert to discretion (that is, reoptimization). The private sector is assumed to form its expectations in a way that reflects this possibility. The model they consider is quite simple, and the distribution of shocks is assumed to be uniform, giving a bound on shocks and making an analytical solution possible. Their interest, moreover, is in designing policy rules with escape options rather than in modeling credibility. We extend the analysis to the question of imperfect credibility of a simple policy rule in the face of unbounded shocks drawn from a normal distribution and apply it to an empirical macroeconometric model.

---

4. Rogoff (1987) has surveyed some of the literature on reputation as it relates to monetary policy; he emphasizes how sensitive the results are to differences in information structure.

5. Cukierman and Meltzer (1986) assumed that preferences shift stochastically over time.

The size of this model, MULTIMOD, and its nonlinearity preclude calculating fully optimal feedback rules, which in any case would be too complex to
be realistic policy alternatives.[6] Our interest here is in modeling expectations
formation rather than a game between the private sector and the authorities
(or between various national governments). We restrict ourselves to a simple rule: an exogenous path for money growth. We do allow for feedback of
expectations formation to the authorities' optimal policy, however, since the
comparison of utility from sticking to the rule takes into account the negative
effects of loss of credibility that would result from going off the rule. In this
respect, then, our setup corresponds to a "trigger strategy equilibrium" in the
literature on game theory, with an infinite "punishment" period (Canzoneri and
Henderson 1991).

A Simple Theoretical Example

It is convenient to illustrate the issue, and to give a flavor of the numerical
simulations reported below, by setting out a model that is similar in some, but
not all, respects to that in Barro and Gordon (1983). We will work with a
two-period model in order to avoid the complications of solving a multiperiod
rational-expectations model (for instance, using the techniques of Blanchard
and Kahn 1980). In the first period the authorities announce a policy of lowering
the growth rate of money by x in the second period. In the second period
the authorities either lower money growth as announced or renege, keeping it
unchanged. How credible is the commitment to lower the rate of growth of
money by x?

The authorities decide between the two policies in period 2 on the basis of
a simple objective function V that depends only on the discounted present value
of inflation, π. In our analysis, only the objective function in period 2 plays
a role; it is assumed that in period 1 the announced policy yielded a lower
expected disutility than the alternative. In period 1 the private sector forms
expectations of inflation for the next period on the basis of the probability
of the two policies being carried out in period 2: sticking to the rule, with
probability ρ, and keeping money growth unchanged, with probability $1 - \rho$.

The model of inflation is simple, but unlike the model in Barro and Gordon
(1983) it contains the key feature that inflation in period 2 depends on inflation
in period 1, as well as on the policy choice in period 2.[7] Inflation in period 1

---

6. See Masson, Symansky, and Meredith (1990) for a description of the model.

7. In this section we also ignore the output target and the possibility that the authorities aim for a value
that would yield unemployment below the natural rate. In the next section, however, we relax the assumption
that only the discounted present value of inflation enters the objective function and include deviations from
full-capacity output.

is a weighted average of inflation in the previous period ($\pi_0 > 0$) and expected inflation in period 2, $E_1(\pi_2)$; such a model would result from staggered wage contracts, for instance (Taylor 1980 and Calvo 1983). Inflation in period 2 is equal to the change in money growth, μ, plus inflation in period 1;[8] μ takes on the value $-x$ or 0. We can write the model as follows:

$$(7\text{-}1) \qquad\qquad V_1 = \pi_1^2 + E_1(V_2)$$

$$(7\text{-}2) \qquad\qquad V_2 = \pi_2^2$$

$$(7\text{-}3) \qquad\qquad \pi_1 = [\pi_0 + E_1(\pi_2)]/2 + u_1$$

$$(7\text{-}4) \qquad\qquad \pi_2 = \pi_1 + \mu + u_2$$

$$(7\text{-}5) \qquad\qquad E_1(\pi_2) = \rho\pi_2(r) + (1 - \rho)\pi_2(n),$$

where $\pi_2(r)$ and $\pi_2(n)$ are, respectively, the expected outcomes for inflation, given information available in period 1, if the authorities stick to the rule, or not. It is clear that these outcomes depend on the value of ρ itself, since inflation in period 2 depends on inflation in period 1. It is also clear that the objective probability ρ depends on the distribution of the shocks, since the particular drawing for u_2 will cause $V_2(r)$ to be either greater or less than $V_2(n)$ and, hence, will lead the authorities to choose a value of μ equal to 0 or $-x$, respectively.

As a result of this relationship, the effects of the announced policy therefore depend on the credibility of that policy. To see how *actual* inflation in periods 1 and 2 depends on this credibility, for a given value of μ, substitute equation 7-5 into equations 7-3 and 7-4. Expected inflation for period 2 can be written as

$$(7\text{-}6) \qquad\qquad E_1(\pi_2) = \pi_1 - \rho x.$$

Hence inflation in period 1 is given by

$$(7\text{-}7) \qquad\qquad \pi_1 = \pi_0 - \rho x + 2u_1,$$

and actual inflation in period 2 will be equal to

$$(7\text{-}8) \qquad\qquad \pi_2 = \pi_0 - \rho x + 2u_1 + \mu + u_2.$$

The lower credibility is, the higher inflation will be in periods 1 and 2, whatever the policy actually chosen in period 2 (that is, whatever the value of μ).

8. Such an equation could also be the result of a multiperiod model in which no further changes in money growth were expected to occur and, hence, in which inflation was expected to continue at its period-2 rate in subsequent periods.

The incentives to stick to the rule also depend on credibility, in the following way. We assume in period 2 that the authorities chose to follow the announced rule—that is, to carry out a deceleration of money growth by x—provided that the disutility from doing so, $V_2(r)$, is less than the disutility of reverting to constant money growth, $V_2(n)$. The value of the objective function facing the authorities when choosing a value of μ in period 2 can be expressed as

$$(7\text{-}9) \qquad V_2 = (\pi_0 - \rho x + 2u_1 + \mu + u_2)^2.$$

Therefore, the values of V_2, should the authorities stick to the rule ($\mu = -x$) or keep money growth constant ($\mu = 0$), will respectively be

$$(7\text{-}10) \qquad V_2(r) = (\pi_0 - \rho x + 2u_1 - x + u_2)^2$$

and

$$(7\text{-}11) \qquad V_2(n) = (\pi_0 - \rho x + 2u_1 + u_2)^2.$$

We will call the difference in disutilities $R(\rho)$, where we make explicit the dependence on ρ:

$$(7\text{-}12) \qquad R(\rho) = V_2(r) - V_2(n) = (1 + 2\rho)x^2 - 2\pi_0 x - 2xu_2 - 4xu_1.$$

If $R > 0$, the authorities choose to abandon the rule. Thus a higher ρ increases the value of R, making it more likely that the rule will be abandoned. The reason is that, by lowering inflation in period 1, a higher value of ρ makes it less attractive to carry out the monetary disinflation when period 2 arrives because the inflation gains have already been achieved. This is the standard example of time inconsistency. For some realizations of u_2, therefore, the authorities will choose to leave money growth unchanged.

Credibility ρ should depend on a rational assessment of the likelihood that R is greater or less than zero and, hence, depends on the variance of the shocks in period 2. We can find a fixed point for ρ as follows. We assume for simplicity that $u_1 = 0$; the expected value of R is given by

$$(7\text{-}13) \qquad E_1[R(\rho)] = (1 + 2\rho)x^2 - 2\pi_0 x,$$

and its variance is given by

$$(7\text{-}14) \qquad \text{var}[R(\rho)] = 4x^2 \text{var}(u_2).$$

We can therefore evaluate credibility on the basis of the distribution of outcomes for $R(\rho)$. Figure 7-1 illustrates two possibilities. In the top panel the expected

Figure 7-1. *Calculation of Credibility Parameter ρ*

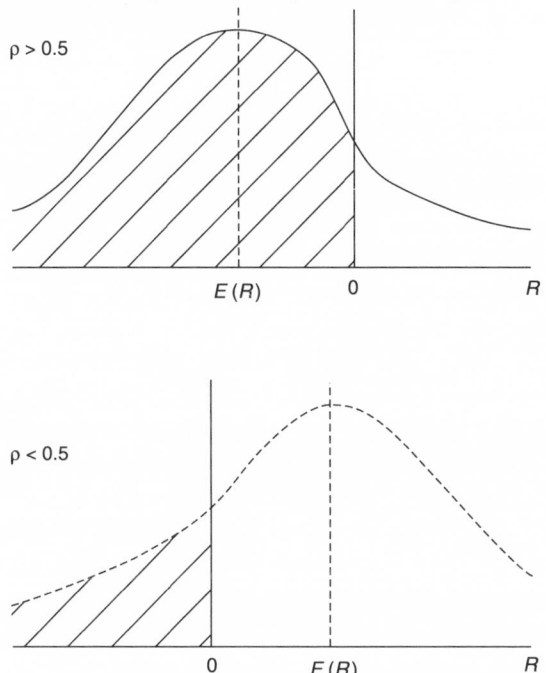

value for R is negative, so that, for the distribution shown, sticking to the regime is more probable than abandoning it. The shaded area is the estimate of credibility: it is the proportion of the outcomes where $R < 0$, so that the authorities stick to the rule. In the bottom panel the expected value for R is positive, giving a value for credibility that is less than 0.5.

Because the mean of the distribution depends positively on ρ from equation 7-12, and because the area to the left of the vertical axis depends negatively on the mean of the distribution, it follows that a fixed point for ρ exists. In the simulation examples reported in tables 7-1 through 7-4, we assume that shocks are normally distributed (as was done for the standard stochastic simulations performed for the conference); we therefore integrate under the normal distribution to calculate estimates of ρ. Starting from an initial value ρ_0, we calculate the expected value of R and, therefore, the likelihood that $R < 0$, yielding ρ_1. Iteration of this difference equation

$$(7\text{-}15) \qquad\qquad \rho_i = A(\rho_{i-1})$$

continues until values of ρ from one iteration to the next are arbitrarily close. Note that the values of R are not bounded—since a normal distribution is assumed—and credibility is neither complete nor zero. Instead, $\rho \in (0, 1)$.

Thus, imperfect credibility prevails, and this has an effect on expectations and on the effectiveness of policy rules.[9]

Simulation Examples

In what follows we make joint estimates of credibility and of the effects of policy rules by applying the methodology described above to a medium-size multiregion model, MULTIMOD. As in the discussion above, our illustration concerns a policy of disinflation, applied to the U.S. economy, that involves an announced path for the deceleration of money growth. The initial position in the baseline case involves 4 percent inflation and full utilization of capacity, as was roughly the case for the United States in 1989. The announced policy is for a deceleration of money growth of 1 percent a year, so that after four years money would be growing at a rate that would be consistent with price stability after lags in the economy had worked themselves out.

In the first example, the alternative policy, which we assume is relevant for expectations formation, is that the authorities allow money to grow at its most recent rate rather than pursue the announced deceleration. Thus, even if money growth has already declined, there is still doubt about whether the other staged reductions will take place. After four years of declines in the rate of money growth, however, the two policies converge.

To illustrate the importance of credibility, we begin by simulating the outcomes of the policy of monetary deceleration under alternative assumptions about credibility when credibility is exogenous. They are summarized in table 7-1. The first-year (1990) effects of the policy change differ widely, with declines in inflation ranging from 0.7 percent (the baseline contains a steady 4 percent inflation) to 1.6 percent. It is clear from table 7-1 that the more credible is the policy, the quicker is the deceleration of inflation, although price stability is achieved by 1993 under all three assumptions about credibility. Output losses, however, may be higher in the first few years if the announced policy is credible because forward-looking exchange rates and bond prices respond more in this case, leading to short-run declines in aggregate demand. This possibility results from the nature of the inflation model in MULTIMOD, for which the degree of inertia depends on average contract length. The parameter that captures contract length is assumed to be fixed; if contract length were to be endogenous

9. Currie and Levine (1987) showed that for bounded shocks there is a discount rate sufficiently low that there is no incentive with an infinite horizon to switch from the optimal policy. With unbounded shocks, the probability of a switch is nonzero but can be made arbitrarily low by choosing the discount rate low enough. Levine, Currie, and Gaines (1988) assumed that the effect on expectations is negligible (that is, that credibility is close to complete). This is not, however, the case in the simulations discussed below.

Table 7-1. *Effects of Monetary Deceleration*[a] *with Different Assumptions for Credibility, 1989–93*

Percent

Assumption	1989	1990	1991	1992	1993
Annual inflation					
$\rho = 0$	4.0	3.3	2.6	1.5	0.2
$\rho = 0.5$	3.5	2.9	2.0	1.0	−0.1
$\rho = 1.0$	2.9	2.4	1.4	0.4	−0.4
Deviation from full capacity utilization					
$\rho = 0$	...	−1.1	−2.5	−3.8	−4.8
$\rho = 0.5$	−0.7	−1.7	−2.7	−3.4	−3.9
$\rho = 1.0$	−1.5	−2.4	−2.9	−3.1	−2.9

a. The path for the rate of money growth is lowered relative to baseline by 1 percent in 1990, 2 percent in 1991, 3 percent in 1992, and 4 percent from 1993 onward. This path was announced in 1989.

(permitting recontracting when the disinflation policy is announced), output losses would be smaller (or even zero). *Cumulative* deviations from full capacity utilization over the period 1989–93 are in any case lower in the case of perfect credibility (−9.8 percent) than in the case of zero credibility (−12.2 percent).

The net effect on the authorities' objective function depends on how inflation and capacity utilization are weighted. Generalizing the welfare function posited above in the theoretical section, we assume that the authorities attempt to minimize the following function:

$$(7\text{-}16) \qquad V = E \sum_{i=0}^{\infty} \left[\pi_i^2 + \alpha (CU_i - 1)^2 \right] / (1.05)^i,$$

where π is the rate of change of absorption prices (as a decimal fraction), CU is capacity utilization (a value of unity indicates full utilization), and the assumed discount rate is 5 percent. A parameter that greatly affects credibility is the weight on output losses, α. In our first set of experiments, we assume that $\alpha = 2$.

Using this objective function, which is assumed to be known by the private sector, we then proceed to endogenize credibility, ρ. The first step is to calculate an estimate of the variance of the difference R in objective-function values under the two policies in response to random shocks. Using the same set of shocks as were generated for the stochastic simulations discussed elsewhere in this volume, we calculated the variance of R, which was used to generate values for credibility corresponding to particular expected values for R.

Table 7-2 shows how the credibility of the policy and outcomes for inflation and capacity utilization evolve over time in this case. It should be stressed here that, although we performed stochastic simulations to calculate the variance of R, we ran deterministic simulations of the model when calculating the effects

Table 7-2. *Effects of Monetary Deceleration with Endogenous Credibility, 1989–93*[a]

Item	1989	1990	1991	1992	1993
Annual inflation (percent)	3.0	2.7	1.9	0.9	−0.1
Deviation from full capacity utilization (percent)	−1.4	−1.9	−2.1	−2.7	−3.4
Expected welfare loss from following the rule[b]	6.1	6.1	5.8	5.1	4.5
Expected welfare loss from abandoning the rule[c]	11.5	7.4	4.5	3.4	4.5
Credibility of the rule	0.97	0.68	0.33	0.28	0.50

a. The path for the rate of money growth is lowered relative to baseline by 1 percent in 1990, 2 percent in 1991, 3 percent in 1992, and 4 percent from 1993 onward. This path was announced in 1989.
b. As defined in equation 7-16.
c. As defined in equation 7-16, the alternative policy is no further deceleration of money growth (that is, projected continuation of the current growth rate).

of policy, presented here. The announced policy, moreover, was in fact always carried out. This rather stylized example allows the effects of credibility to be explained more clearly. But a realistic comparison of alternative policies would include random shocks and would allow for the possibility of switching regimes.

Because random shocks are absent, the difference between what was expected and what actually occurred solely reflects lack of credibility of policy. In the example we give, credibility starts at a high level, with $\rho = 0.97$ when the path of monetary deceleration starting in 1990 is announced in 1989. This degree of credibility reflects an assessment of the probability that authorities would find it to their advantage to stay with the rule in 1990 instead of leaving money growth unchanged. For instance, negative output shocks would tend to make the further output losses implied by a tightened monetary policy too costly. In 1990 the authorities lower money growth by 1 percent. The credibility of their commitment to the announced path evolves over time: it has actually decreased, since the policy has already brought down inflation, and, given the momentum built into the economy, inflation would continue to decline even if money growth were not cut further. Because inflation is closer to zero, the quadratic objective function attributes a smaller gain from further declines in inflation; conversely, because capacity utilization is farther away from unity, the disutility of further output losses has increased.

As time progresses, therefore, the credibility of the disinflation policy declines in this example, even though the policy is actually carried out. In our simple example, the announced policy and the alternative policy—when the authorities abandon the announced rule—converge to the same money growth in 1993, so that the credibility of the policy commitment becomes indeterminate. We nevertheless calculate in table 7-2 the values implied for the objective function, which are of course equal in this case, so we indicate $\rho = 0.5$.

Table 7-3. *Effects of Monetary Deceleration: Outcomes for Various Objective Function Weights, 1989–93*[a]

Item	1989	1990	1991	1992	1993
			Weight: $\alpha = 4$		
Annual inflation (percent)	3.6	3.3	2.4	1.3	0.1
Deviation from full capacity utilization (percent)	−0.5	−1.0	−2.2	−3.4	−4.4
Credibility of the rule[b]	0.39	0.02	0.01	0.03	0.50
			Weight: $\alpha = 1$		
Annual inflation (percent)	3.0	2.4	1.6	0.8	−0.3
Deviation from full capacity utilization (percent)	−1.5	−2.2	−2.4	−2.6	−3.1
Credibility of the rule[b]	1.00	0.89	0.60	0.43	0.50
			Weight: $\alpha = 0.33$		
Annual inflation (percent)	2.9	2.4	1.5	0.7	−0.3
Deviation from full capacity utilization (percent)	−1.5	−2.3	−2.6	−2.7	−3.0
Credibility of the rule[b]	1.00	0.95	0.73	0.52	0.50

a. The path for the rate of money growth is lowered relative to baseline by 1 percent in 1990, 2 percent in 1991, 3 percent in 1992, and 4 percent from 1993 onward. This path was announced in 1989.

b. The alternative policy is no further deceleration of money growth (that is, projected continuation of the current growth rate).

The sensitivity of credibility to the objective function postulated for the authorities is illustrated in table 7-3, where the weight α on output losses is varied. The policy actually carried out by the authorities is the same as in table 7-2—a deceleration of money growth by 1 percentage point in each of the years 1990–93. The alternative policy is also the same: that the authorities would keep money growth constant at its most recent value, rather than continuing the deceleration to a rate of money growth consistent with zero inflation (achieved in 1993).

Putting a higher weight on output ($\alpha = 4$) than in table 7-2 reduces credibility considerably; from 1990–92, the probability that the authorities would find it in their interest to continue their policies is virtually zero in this case. It is interesting that, although the low credibility retards achievement of the deceleration of inflation, it also produces somewhat lower output losses through 1991 because the initial increase in the long-term real interest rate and appreciation of the real exchange rate are somewhat smaller. Conversely, much lower values of α improve credibility, which speeds disinflation, but initial output losses increase.

The importance of the alternative policy is illustrated in table 7-4, which also considers a range of α values. Here, the authorities choose between the same announced path for monetary deceleration as above and a policy of expanding the money supply at its initial (1989) rate, consistent with 4 percent inflation. In this case, the policy rules never converge. On the contrary, there is a widening difference between them because reversion to the initial policy in

Table 7-4. *Effects of Monetary Deceleration*[a] *with a Different Alternative Monetary Policy Rule: Outcomes for Various Objective Function Weights, 1989–93*[b]

Item	1989	1990	1991	1992	1993
			Weight: $\alpha = 3.5$		
Annual inflation (percent)	3.3	2.9	1.8	0.7	−0.1
Deviation from full capacity utilization (percent)	−1.0	−1.6	−2.7	−3.6	−3.7
Credibility of the rule	0.68	0.64	0.83	1.00	1.00
			Weight: $\alpha = 3$		
Annual inflation	3.1	2.4	1.4	0.5	−0.3
Deviation from full capacity utilization (percent)	−1.2	−2.2	−3.0	−3.2	−3.1
Credibility of the rule	0.84	0.92	0.99	1.00	1.00
			Weight: $\alpha = 2$		
Annual inflation	3.0	2.3	1.3	0.5	−0.4
Deviation from full capacity utilization (percent)	−1.4	−2.4	−2.9	−3.1	−2.9
Credibility of the rule	0.97	0.99	1.00	1.00	1.00

a. The path for the rate of money growth is lowered relative to baseline by 1 percent in 1990, 2 percent in 1991, 3 percent in 1992, and 4 percent from 1993 onward. This path was announced in 1989.

b. The alternative policy is money growth equal to that in the baseline case (that is, a growth rate consistent with 4 percent inflation in the steady state).

the later years would involve a large monetary acceleration, and inflation gains would be lost. As a result, credibility increases over time and converges to virtual unity in all simulations.[10] The weight on output losses influences the path; credibility is initially somewhat lower when α is large. Even larger values for α, which might cause the authorities to engineer a large monetary expansion in the later years of the simulation, caused the model not to converge.

Concluding Remarks and Suggested Extensions

This chapter presents a preliminary attempt to allow for imperfect credibility in evaluating policy regimes, limited here to rules for the deceleration of money growth. We have further simplified the problem by considering a simple alternative policy rule. In Flood and Isard (1989) and in game-theoretic discussions of policy, abandoning the rule involves reoptimizing. We have not attempted to calculate optimal policies in MULTIMOD because of the computational difficulty and also because fully optimal policies are too complex to be reasonable alternatives. But the question of what might constitute a reasonable benchmark regime for comparing simple policy rules is an important one. If one is considering disinflation policies, unchanged money growth seems a plausible

10. For very large shocks, of course, the authorities might choose to return to their initial expansionary policies, but such shocks are very unlikely.

alternative. If one is considering the credibility of a peg for the exchange rate, reversion to floating exchange rates with a money-supply target would also be the most natural alternative. Our framework is clearly less plausible when other situations are considered.

What our simple examples show is that, if the distribution of shocks is the same as in some historical period and if the objective function for the authorities puts plausible weights on output and inflation, credibility can be far short of complete. As a result, expectations can differ significantly from those in the case of full credibility. The implied performance of the money-targeting policy is thereby significantly affected. An interesting question is whether the ranking of simple rules—for instance, money targeting versus nominal-income or exchange-rate targeting—is modified by making the degree of credibility endogenous. It is also of interest to examine how other policies can affect the credibility of monetary policy; for instance, bond-financed fiscal expansion may destroy the credibility for an anti-inflationary monetary policy.[11] In principle this could be captured by our objective function, which takes into account expected future outcomes.

It could also be that some policy rules, because they give tolerable results in all circumstances, are more credible than others. It should be the case that loss of credibility from deviation from a policy commitment also depends on how the commitment is framed—that is, on how absolute the targets are and on how well the target variable is measured. These questions, however, take us well beyond the subject of this chapter.

References

Backus, D., and J. Driffill. 1986. "The Consistency of Optimal Policy in Stochastic Rational Expectations Models." Centre for Economic Policy Research Discussion Paper 124. London.

Barro, R. J., and D. B. Gordon. 1983. "A Positive Theory of Monetary Policy in a Natural Rate Model." *Journal of Political Economy* 91:589–610.

Blackburn, K., and M. Christensen. 1989. "Monetary Policy and Policy Credibility: Theories and Evidence." *Journal of Economic Literature* 27:1–45.

Blanchard, O. J., and C. M. Kahn. 1980. "The Solution of Linear Difference Models under Rational Expectations." *Econometrica* 48:1305–11.

Calvo, G. 1983. "Staggered Contracts and Exchange Rate Policy." In *Exchange Rates and International Macroeconomics*, edited by J. A. Frenkel, 235–52. University of Chicago Press.

---

11. An overlapping-generations model in which the probability of inflating away outstanding debt is made a function of the debt stock is presented in Masson (1985).

Canzoneri, M. B. 1985. "Monetary Policy Games and the Role of Private Information." *American Economic Review* 75:1056–70.

Canzoneri, M. B., and D. Henderson. 1988. "Is Sovereign Policymaking Bad?" In *Stabilization Policies and Labor Markets*, edited by K. Brunner and A Meltzer, 93–140. Carnegie-Rochester Conference Series on Public Policy 28. Amsterdam: North-Holland.

———. 1991. *Noncooperative Monetary Policies in Interdependent Economies*. MIT Press.

Cukierman, A., and A. H. Meltzer. 1986. "A Theory of Ambiguity, Credibility, and Inflation under Discretion and Asymmetric Information." *Econometrica* 54: 1099–1128.

Currie, D., and P. Levine. 1987. "Credibility and Time Consistency in a Stochastic World." *Journal of Economics/Zeitschrift für Nationalokonomie* 47:225–52.

Flood, R., and P. Isard. 1989. "Simple Rules, Discretion and Monetary Policy." National Bureau of Economic Research Working Paper 2934. Cambridge, Mass.

Horn, H., and T. Persson. 1988. "Exchange Rate Policy, Wage Formation, and Credibility." *European Economic Review* 32:1621–36.

Kydland, F. E., and E. C. Prescott. 1977. "Rules Rather Than Discretion: The Inconsistency of Optimal Plans." *Journal of Political Economy* 85: 473–91.

Levine, P., D. Currie, and J. Gaines. 1988. "Simple Rules for International Policy Agreements." Paper presented to a conference on International Regimes and Macroeconomic Policy, London, September 8–9.

Lucas, R. G., Jr. 1976. "Econometric Policy Evaluation: A Critique." *Journal of Monetary Economics* (Supplement) 1:19–46.

Masson, P. R. 1985. "The Sustainability of Fiscal Deficits." *Staff Papers* (International Monetary Fund) 32:577–605.

Masson, P. R., S. Symansky, and G. Meredith. 1990. *MULTIMOD Mark II: A Revised and Extended Model*. Occasional Paper 71. Washington: International Monetary Fund.

Rogoff, K. 1987. "Reputational Constraints on Monetary Policy." *In Bubbles and Other Essays*, edited by K. Brunnner and A. Meltzer, 141–82. Carnegie-Rochester Series on Public Policy 26. Amsterdam: North-Holland.

Taylor, J. B. 1980. "Aggregate Dynamics and Staggered Contracts." *Journal of Political Economy* 88:1–23.

CHAPTER 8

The Importance
of Federal Reserve Credibility:
Evidence from the TAYLOR Model

Peter J. Klenow

TIME INCONSISTENCY of optimal policy set by the Board of Governors of the Federal Reserve System (Federal Reserve Board, or the "Fed") has attracted a good deal of attention from macroeconomists since the seminal paper by Kydland and Prescott (1977).[1] For reasons of tractability, the subject has been examined almost exclusively in highly stylized models.[2] The empirical significance of time inconsistency has seldom been examined because these stylized models are too limited to confront with data.

Investigating time inconsistency with the TAYLOR multicountry model serves several purposes. The investigation will provide evidence about whether time inconsistency arises, given estimated relationships among macroeconomic variables. If time inconsistency does arise, the *magnitude* of the excess inflation that results if the Fed cannot credibly target a given inflation rate can be empirically gauged. Through this investigation, a better understanding of the properties of the TAYLOR model itself will also be gained.

The TAYLOR model provides an ideal setting in which to test for the existence and potential quantitative importance of Fed credibility. It is one of a growing number of large-scale empirical macroeconometric models that incorporate rational expectations. Models with adaptive expectations cannot be used to explore issues of time inconsistency because they do not possess a prerequisite for assessing time inconsistency: the dependence of current endogenous variables on expected future values of policy variables. If expectations

---

1. In what follows, "time inconsistency of optimal Fed policy" will be used interchangeably with "imperfect Fed credibility." The latter often connotes uncertainty about Fed preferences (for example, about inflation and real output). Here it is assumed that private agents know the Fed's preferences and thereby know the Fed's optimal policy. I refer to Fed credibility in the limited sense of whether the Fed adheres to the optimal policy rule conditional on private agents' expecting the Fed to follow the optimal policy rule. Rogoff (1989); Chari, Kehoe, and Prescott (1989); and Blackburn and Christensen (1989) have surveyed the literature on time inconsistency.

2. Masson and Symansky (chapter 7 in this volume) and Westaway and Wren-Lewis (1990a, b) are some other empirical examinations of time inconsistency.

are formed adaptively—that is, are determined by some arbitrary estimated function of lagged variables—the Fed will not be tempted to say one thing and do another. Given that the Fed follows policy rule x, the outcome will be the same whether the Fed announces policy rule x or some other policy rule y.[3]

Among rational-expectations models, the TAYLOR model is especially suitable for investigating time inconsistency because of the extent to which it incorporates rational expectations.[4] Because time inconsistency operates through expected future policy, it is crucial that the model capture many of the channels by which expected future policy affects current variables such as output and inflation. For example, the target inflation rate embedded in the Fed's policy rule should feed into the long-term interest rate by way of expected future short-term rates. The TAYLOR model includes expectations of future exchange rates (in the exchange-rate equations), short-term interest rates (in the term-structure equations), real output (in consumption, investment, and wage equations), inflation (in consumption, investment, and wage equations—the first two through the ex ante long-term real interest rate), and wages (in the wage equations). Pervaded by forward-looking expectations, the TAYLOR model promises to capture well the effect of anticipated policies.

Finally, as a multicountry model the TAYLOR model incorporates the effect of openness on the severity of time-consistent inflation. Rogoff (1985) has contended that international monetary policy coordination may generate higher time-consistent inflation. Without coordination, Rogoff argued, a country that unilaterally inflates will face exchange-rate depreciation. If exchange-rate depreciation raises the cost of inflating—say, because the trade balance enters the country's objective function—then time-consistent inflation will be lower. With coordination, all countries may inflate simultaneously, leaving exchange rates unaffected. Thus time-consistent inflation may be higher under coordination. Although I do not consider policy coordination here, the insight remains that one needs a multicountry model to capture the way exchange rates and trade alter the response of output to unexpected inflation. The Fed's desire to exploit (in vain in the rational-expectations equilibrium) the relationship between real output and unexpected inflation is the fundamental source of time inconsistency.

---

3. This chapter uses the word "rule" rather than "regime" to describe the general operating procedures followed by the Federal Reserve and the monetary authorities of other countries. See chapter 1 for a discussion of terminology. In the sense of chapter 1, the "rules" of this chapter could equally well be labeled "regimes." The core simulation rules referred to in this chapter are (with a few modifications) the regimes studied in chapters 3–5.

4. For a general description of the model, see Taylor (1989a). For a more detailed exposition of the model's structure, see Taylor (1988), especially appendix A. Taylor (1989b) contains insights into the reduced-form properties of the TAYLOR model (for example, the Phillips curve generated by data from stochastic simulations).

In the first section of this chapter I outline the procedure for testing for and gauging the quantitative significance of time inconsistency in the TAYLOR model. The second section provides a heuristic discussion of what these tests will reveal about the TAYLOR model. The third section summarizes the results of the stochastic simulations. Qualifying observations on the simulations are offered in the fourth section, and conclusions are made in the final section.

Testing for Time Inconsistency

Suppose that the Fed's objective function at time t has the form

$$(8\text{-}1) \qquad E_t \frac{1-\beta}{1-\beta^{T-t+1}} \sum_{s=t}^{T} \beta^{s-t} L_s, \quad 0 < \beta < 1$$

$$(8\text{-}2) \qquad L_t = \phi[\log(Y_t/Y_t^*)]^2 + (2-\phi)(\pi_t - \pi^*)^2 + \alpha(\Delta RS_t - \Delta RS_t^*)^2,$$

where L_t represents the momentary loss, β is the discount factor the Fed applies to future values of the momentary loss, Y is the level of real output, π is the inflation rate, and RS is the short-term nominal interest rate.[5] Asterisks denote "bliss" values, and ϕ ($0 < \phi < 2$) and α ($\alpha > 0$) are fixed Fed preference parameters. (For convenience, symbol definitions are presented in tabular form in table 8-1.) Throughout, it is assumed that private agents know the functional form and parameter values of the Fed's objective function.[6] To economize on stochastic simulations, I set $\pi^* = 0.01$ (4 percent annual inflation) and $\alpha = 0.10$ throughout. I presume that $T = \infty$ and simulate a finite number of periods to estimate equation 8-1.

The quadratic term in interest rate fluctuations captures the costs of instrument volatility. This cost should depend on the risk premium induced by uncertainty about future interest rates and the associated welfare loss, but incorporating such a risk premium would require an ad hoc extension of the TAYLOR model. Instead I arbitrarily set $\Delta RS_t^* = 0$ for all t, so that the Fed prefers no fluctuations in interest rates, other things being equal. As mentioned, I set $\alpha = 0.10$, the value suggested by the conference organizers for the core simulations.

---

5. Consider the more general time t loss function $L_t = f[\log(Y_t/Y_t^*)] + g(\pi_t - \pi^*) + h(\Delta RS_t - \Delta RS_t^*)$. The quadratic form chosen for g in equation 8-2 is arbitrary, but the existence of a consistent policy rule requires that $g'' > 0$ (at least over some subset of the domain) when $f' > 0$. Intuitively, the cost of inflation must eventually increase sharply with the level of inflation or the Fed will want to generate higher inflation than expected, no matter how high the expected inflation.

6. Because I posit full knowledge of Fed preferences, I also do not consider a role for reputation in obviating the time-inconsistency quandary. Rogoff (1989) has summarized and distilled much of the literature dealing with reputation under uncertainty about Fed preferences.

Table 8-1. *Definitions of Symbols*

Symbol	Definition
π	Inflation
π^*	The Federal Reserve's (Fed's) target for inflation
π^c	Private agents' expectations of inflation
Y	Real output
Y^*	The Fed's target for real output
Y^b	The baseline (or trend) value of output
RS	Short-term nominal interest rate
RS^*	The Fed's target for the short-term nominal interest rate
$E_t \frac{1-\beta}{1-\beta^{T-t+1}} \sum\limits_{s=t}^{T} \beta^{s-t} L_s$	The Fed's loss, with momentary loss $L_t = \phi[\log(Y_t/Y_t^*)]^2 + (2 - \phi)(\pi_t - \pi^*)^2 + \alpha(\Delta RS_t - \Delta RS_t^*)^2$
β	Discount factor the Fed applies to the momentary loss
ϕ	Weight the Fed places on real output relative to inflation

I choose $\pi^* > 0$ to reflect the government's desire for seignorage as part of optimal expenditure financing, but I do not attempt to relate π^* to the literature on optimal inflation. The inflation target is innocuous for this investigation in that mean-squared-percentage deviations from target paths in stochastic simulations do not depend much on the target inflation rate, despite the model's nonlinearity.

Let Y_t^b denote "baseline" output at time t. The sequence $\{Y_t^b\}_{t=1}^T$ constitutes an exogenously given trend path for real output in the TAYLOR model. The trend level of real output for each country in the Group of Seven (G7: the United States, Japan, Germany, France, the United Kingdom, Italy, and Canada) is determined by regressing the logarithm of output on a constant and a time trend over the quarterly sample for 1971:1 through 1986:4. Hence output is presumed to be trend stationary. Such deterministic "detrending" is controversial, given evidence of stochastic growth in output.[7]

The trend output path is designed to approximate a steady-state path determined by the interaction of consumer preferences and firm technology under perfectly flexible prices and wages, with the technology growing smoothly and exogenously with respect to macroeconomic policy.[8] This trend path corresponds to "potential" or "sustainable" output at each time t. In the TAYLOR

7. See Durlauf (1989) for evidence on unit roots in the real output series of G7 countries. The TAYLOR model could easily accommodate stochastic trends out of sample. Stochastic simulations would simply include shocks to the level of baseline real output. Interesting issues would arise, such as whether the Fed and private agents have full knowledge of the path of trend output. In-sample stochastic trends substantially complicate estimation in the TAYLOR model.

8. The Y_t^b process is exogenous to stabilization policy, a controversial proposition in light of models of endogenous growth that have been developed recently. See Durlauf (1989) for a model in which stabilization policy affects the level of trend output and King and Rebelo (1990) for a model in which policy (albeit tax, not stabilization, policy) affects the growth rate of sustainable output.

model, nominal wages respond positively to the percentage deviation of output from its trend path, so that the trend path may be interpreted as corresponding to a "natural rate of unemployment."

I posit $Y_t^* > Y_t^b$ for all t: the Fed's bliss path of real output lies strictly above the exogenously given trend path. The Fed prefers higher output because, say, taxes cause labor supply and the capital stock to be lower than is socially optimal. The possible existence of time inconsistency of optimal Fed policy depends crucially on this supposition. One might conjecture that the Fed prefers real output to be as high as possible, so that no bliss point $Y_t^* < \infty$ exists at each time t. Yet certainly the Fed does not want output to be as high as possible *conditional on* the production technology and the preferences of a given population. Higher output can be achieved through less leisure and more savings, but the Fed will prefer positive levels of consumption and leisure to any finite increment in real output. I thus maintain $Y_t^b < Y_t^* < \infty$ for all t.

Because the TAYLOR model has the property of long-run monetary neutrality (the long-run Phillips curve is vertical), the Fed cannot keep output above its trend path indefinitely. The Fed may be able to do so in the short run, but attempting to do so indefinitely will generate an explosive path for inflation. If the Fed must commit to a given rule and wishes to keep inflation below some finite bound for the indefinite future (and with a probability of unity), the Fed must settle for targeting trend output.

Given that the Fed must target trend output, the optimal fixed rule when the Fed's objective function is characterized by equations 8-1 and 8-2 will be as if $Y_t^* = Y_t^b$ for all t, regardless of the true path of Y_t^*.[9] Hence information about the optimal fixed rule (when $\beta = \phi = 1$ and $T = \infty$) can be culled from the core simulations conducted for the conference. For the core simulations I used the following versions of interest rate rules:

(Rule 1) $RS - RS^* = \pi^e - \pi^* - 0.5\log(M^*/M)$

(Rule 2a) $RS - RS^* = \pi^e - \pi^* + 1.5[\log(PY) - \log(P^*Y^b)]$

(Rule 2b) $RS - RS^* = \pi^e - \pi^* + 1.5[(\pi - \pi^*) + \log(Y/Y^b)]$

(Rule 3) $RS - RS^* = \pi^e - \pi^* + 1.5[\log(PY/P^*Y^b)] + 2.5\log(E^*/E)$.

The United States, Canada, Germany, Japan, and the United Kingdom simultaneously follow a given rule in each set of simulations for rules 1, 2a, and 2b; for rule 3 the United States targets nominal output, and the other countries

---

9. By "fixed rule" I mean the rule the Fed is precommitted to follow. The Fed cannot reoptimize conditional on private agents' expectations and on the state variables; instead it must follow the rule. What I, to avoid confusion, refer to as the "optimal fixed rule" is variously referred to as the "optimal rule" and the "precommitment rule" in the literature on time inconsistency.

follow regime 3, where E equals U.S. dollars per unit of foreign currency. The other two countries in the European Monetary System (EMS), France and Italy, mimic Germany's interest-rate movements to maintain a differential equal to the risk premium existing along the baseline path. The exchange rates between EMS countries fluctuate, despite constant interest-rate differentials, because of time-varying risk premiums (shocks hitting the exchange rate equations).

For each of the rules 1–3 I conducted ten stochastic simulations, each covering the forty quarters from 1990:1 through 1999:4. I obtained the rational-expectations equilibrium in each period of each simulation by the Fair-Taylor (1983) extended-path algorithm. For each rule I calculated the average value of equation 8-2 over the entire 400 periods. With $\beta = \phi = 1$ for each of the G7 countries, the U.S. preference ranking for the four interest-rate rules is

$$L_{(2a)} < L_{(3)} < L_{(2b)} < L_{(1)},$$

where subscripts indicate the various interest-rate rules.

The United States prefers to target nominal output, conditional on other countries' following the same rule as it does. Numerically the difference in the average loss under nominal-output targeting (rule 2a) and nominal-output-plus-exchange-rate targeting (rule 3) appears to be small. I do not propose a formal measure for comparing summary statistics for the loss function, in part because Fed preferences are presumably ordinal, not cardinal. If I had standard errors for the average of equation 8-2 in a sample of ten simulations of forty quarters each, I might test the null hypothesis of equality between the two numbers. Given the nonlinear structure of the TAYLOR model, obtaining such standard errors requires running more simulations, in which case one might prefer to compare the average of equation 8-2 over all of these simulations. Fair (1988) proposed a "bootstrap" approach to obtaining standard errors for the *difference* in summary statistics such as the average of equation 8-2 across stochastic simulations. His approach clearly warrants application to future work with stochastic simulations.

I treat rule 2a, nominal-output targeting, as the optimal fixed rule.[10] Now suppose that private agents believe the Fed is following the optimal fixed rule, but that the Fed has discretion to follow whatever rule it wishes. The Fed will then deviate from the optimal fixed rule if doing so will yield a lower expected loss, conditional on private agents' believing the Fed is adhering to the optimal fixed rule. If the Fed wishes to deviate, then the optimal fixed rule is time inconsistent in the TAYLOR model. To test for time inconsistency of

---

10. The results reported in the rest of this chapter depend little on the choice of rule 2a versus rule 2b as the optimal fixed rule.

the optimal fixed rule, I will carry out stochastic simulations over the forty quarters from 1990:1 through 1999:4, with the following structure:

Step 1: Private agents form expectations at each time t under the belief that the Fed is following the optimal fixed rule.

Step 2: The Fed chooses the optimal policy rule conditional on private agents' forming expectations as in step 1.

Note that private agents have full knowledge of past realizations of interest rates and other variables when they form their expectations in step 1. Thus, private agents continue to expect that the Fed will follow the optimal fixed rule, despite ample evidence that the Fed has not followed the optimal fixed rule in the past. Private agents are surely not so myopic, but presuming that they are helps to uncover whether the Fed can gain from fooling private agents.[11]

To recapitulate, if in step 2 the Fed attains a smaller loss by deviating from the optimal fixed rule, then optimal policy will be time inconsistent in the TAYLOR model. Rational private agents apprised of the structure of the economy will, however, recognize the Fed's incentive to deviate from the optimal fixed rule and will form their expectations accordingly. Suppose that private agents use the rule that emerges from step 2 in forming their expectations. Then the Fed will take these expectations as given and choose an optimal rule. Suppose that private agents in turn use this latest rule to form their expectations. Then the Fed, in turn, will condition its choice of a rule on these beliefs.

By iterating on steps 1 and 2, one hopefully will arrive at convergence on a fixed point. The fixed point, the "consistent" rule in Kydland and Prescott's (1977) terminology, has the classic rational-expectations feature: conditional on private agents believing that the Fed uses rule x, the Fed finds x to be the optimal rule. Exact convergence in a finite number of iterations will occur with a probability of zero. But if the Fed's loss function is ordinal, using a convergence criterion for the loss function would be inappropriate. I will instead obtain lower and upper bounds on the excess inflation generated by time inconsistency of the optimal fixed rule. I obtain an upper bound when the Fed gains from targeting a lower inflation rate in step 2 than private agents expect in step 1.

In the third section, below, I describe the results of these iterations and compare the loss under the time-consistent policy rule to the loss under the optimal fixed rule. I carry out this exercise for various specifications of equation

---

11. Alternatively, private agents might learn about the parameters of the Fed's policy rule as time advances—say, through least-squares learning. The Fed's gain from fooling private agents presumably shrinks when agents gradually infer the Fed's policy rule. The results in this chapter should therefore be considered an upper bound on the severity of the time-inconsistency problem.

8-2. In summary, I measure the cost of incomplete credibility by comparing the loss under perfect credibility with the loss under imperfect credibility for various values of β, ϕ, and $(Y^* - Y^b)/Y^b$.

Time Inconsistency and the Structure of the TAYLOR Model

Kydland and Prescott (1977) added a Lucas supply curve to equation 8-2 and demonstrated in a static environment the Fed's incentive to fool private agents into underestimating inflation. The story becomes much more complicated in dynamic contexts, as considered by Barro and Gordon (1983a, b) and Rogoff (1989), wherein issues of reputation arise. The problem of time inconsistency refuses to go away in dynamic contexts, where the outcome hinges on such specifics as whether T is finite or infinite, the values of β and ϕ, and the parameters of the Lucas supply function.

To frame the discussion of time inconsistency in the TAYLOR model, it will be useful to consider a simple version of a static model used in Kydland and Prescott (1977). Suppose that the Fed faces a structural relationship between real output and unexpected inflation:

$$(8\text{-}3) \qquad\qquad y = y^b + \psi(\pi - \pi^e) + v, \quad \psi > 0,$$

where lowercase letters denote natural logarithms of corresponding uppercase letters, π^e represents private agents' expectations of inflation, and v is a mean-zero random variable whose realization is not known to private agents or to the Fed when they choose π^e and π, respectively. The Fed has the quadratic objective function

$$(8\text{-}4) \quad L = E\{\phi(y - y^*)^2 + [(2 - \phi)(\pi - \pi^*)^2]\}, \quad y^* > y^b, \quad 0 < \phi < 2.$$

If the Fed precommits to a rule known to private agents, then $\pi^e = \pi$. Under precommitment, equation 8-3 gives $y = y^b + v$. Then, the Fed minimizes equation 8-4 by selecting

$$\text{(Optimal fixed rule)} \qquad\qquad \pi_{opt} = \pi^*.$$

If the Fed has discretion and if agents believe that the Fed will follow the optimal fixed rule, then $\pi^e = \pi^*$ and the Fed minimizes equation 8-4 by choosing

$$\text{(Inconsistent rule)} \quad \pi_{incons} = \pi^* + \frac{\phi\psi}{\phi\psi^2 + 2 - \phi}(y^* - y^b).$$

Since $\pi_{incons} > \pi_{opt}$, the optimal fixed rule is time inconsistent: the Fed will choose an inflation rate higher than π^* to surprise private agents and thereby push output above y^b. If private agents have rational expectations about the Fed's behavior under discretion, they will anticipate the Fed's desire to deviate from the optimal fixed rule. (Recall that private agents have full knowledge of the Fed's loss function.) Rational private agents will set $\pi^e = \pi_{cons}$, where π_{cons} is defined by the property that the Fed maximizes equation 8-4 conditional on $\pi^e = \pi_{cons}$ by choosing $\pi = \pi_{cons}$. Given equations 8-3 and 8-4, the unique value of π_{cons} is

(Consistent rule) $$\pi_{cons} = \pi^* + \frac{\phi\psi}{2 - \phi}(y^* - y^b).$$

From this expression it is readily apparent that the excess inflation caused by the Fed's inability to commit to the optimal fixed rule is higher the higher are ϕ, ψ, and $(y^* - y^b)$. One can see intuitively that, when the Fed cannot commit to the optimal fixed rule, the resulting inflation is higher the more weight the Fed places on real output in its objective function, the more stimulus unexpected inflation provides to real output, and the farther the Fed wishes to push real output above y^b.

The preceding static model covers familiar territory, but it provides a useful vocabulary for discussing time inconsistency in Taylor's dynamic multicountry model. For example, the TAYLOR model features a dynamic version of equation 8-3. The structural relationship between unexpected inflation and real output stems from staggered nominal-wage contracts in the TAYLOR model. As shown in Taylor (1980), monetary shocks have persistent real effects in the presence of staggered wage contracts.

Aside from being dynamic, the version of equation 8-3 in the TAYLOR model is more complicated in at least two respects. First, given simple policy rules such as those in the first section, above, the Fed imperfectly controls real output and π, the realized inflation rate, each period. The Fed manipulates short-term nominal interest rates (through open market operations) to influence inflation and real output, but it cannot exactly achieve bliss levels of output and inflation because of the nonlinear structure of the model and the shocks hitting the equations. That is, the Fed uses simple interest rate rules that influence, but do not yield precise control over, π and real output.

Second, private agents' expectations of inflation, π^e in equation 8-3, take on an unusual form because of staggered nominal-wage contracts. At the beginning of each time t, private agents form expectations of inflation, output, exchange rates, and interest rates conditional on time $t-1$ variables and the structure and parameters of the model, including the stickiness of nominal wages. That is, private agents choose current consumption, investment, and so forth on the basis of rational expectations of future variables. Yet current nominal wages are influenced by past nominal-wage contracts. These past contracts embed earlier beliefs about prices and output that are no longer "rational" in the sense that private agents hold different beliefs conditional on the latest information. Note that staggered setting of nominal-wage contracts implies that even the current nominal-wage contract will be influenced by earlier beliefs (see Taylor 1980). Hence the version of π^e in the TAYLOR model corresponding to π^e in equation 8-3 does not equal private agents' expectations of inflation at the beginning of time t but something more complicated.

Of keen interest is the parameter corresponding to ψ in equation 8-3, the percentage stimulus to real output provided by each percentage point of unexpected inflation. Because the TAYLOR model is a dynamic nonlinear model, there is no single value for ψ; the impact of unexpected inflation on real output at time t will depend on past and expected future values of other variables in the model. In principle, ψ depends on ϕ and $(y^* - y^b)$. One must consider various values of ϕ and $(y^* - y^b)$ to obtain a range of values of ψ. As equation 8-3 indicates, ψ directly affects the magnitude of the excess inflation resulting from Fed credibility problems. Some rough sense for the magnitude of ψ is the primary aim of this paper.

Results of Stochastic Simulations

With each policy rule I carried out ten stochastic simulations covering the forty quarters from 1990:1 through 1999:4. As noted above, the rational-expectations equilibrium is obtained for each period of each simulation by the Fair-Taylor (1983) extended-path algorithm. For each forty-quarter simulation, I calculated a sample version of equation 8-1, the Fed's loss. I then took the arithmetic average of equation 8-1 over the ten stochastic simulations. I calculated this average for several values of β, ϕ, and $(Y^* - Y^b)/Y^b$. For β, the Fed's discount factor, I considered 1.00, 0.995, 0.990, and 0.980. Because the TAYLOR model is quarterly, the corresponding annual discount factors are 1.00, 0.98, 0.96, and 0.92. For ϕ, the Fed's weight on real output relative to inflation, I considered 2/3, 1, and 4/3. For $(Y^* - Y^b)/Y^b$, the Fed's opinion on the difference between optimal and sustainable output, I considered 3 percent and 5 percent.

Table 8-2 shows the loss when the Fed follows the optimal fixed rule, nominal-output targeting, with the real-output target equal to Y^b. The loss increases monotonically in ϕ and $(Y^* - Y^b)/Y^b$. This outcome under the optimal fixed rule is not surprising, given $Y^* > Y^b$. The optimal fixed rule targets Y^b and P^* (the price path corresponding to inflation rates uniformly equal to π^*), so that real-output deviations naturally contribute more to the loss than do price

Table 8-2. *Loss under the Optimal Fixed Rule:*
$RS - RS^* = \pi^c - \pi^* + 1.5[\log(PY) - \log(P^*Y^b)]^a$

	ϕ		
β	2/3	1	4/3
		With $\frac{(Y^*-Y^b)}{Y^b}$ = 3 percent	
1.00	12.2	15.8	19.4
0.995	13.4	17.4	21.3
0.99	14.7	19.1	23.4
0.98	17.5	22.8	28.0
		With $\frac{(Y^*-Y^b)}{Y^b}$ = 5 percent	
1.00	22.7	31.6	40.5
0.995	25.0	34.8	44.6
0.99	27.5	38.2	48.9
0.98	32.8	45.6	58.5

a. Symbols are as defined in table 8-1.

fluctuations. Thus, the greater is the weight on real-output fluctuations and the farther is Y^* from Y^b, the greater is the Fed's loss under the optimal fixed rule.

Next I ran simulations in which private agents believe that the Fed follows the optimal fixed rule (rule 2a), but the Fed actually follows rule 2b:

(8-5) $RS - RS^* = \pi^e - \pi^* + 1.5[(\pi - \pi^*) + \log(Y/Y^*)].$

Because $Y^* > Y^b$, the Fed, unbeknown to private agents, is trying to keep real output above its baseline or "sustainable" path. Note the analogy between the rule in equation 8-5 and the inconsistent rule in the static Kydland and Prescott (1977) model discussed earlier. In the static model, private agents formed π^e before the Fed set π. The Fed found it optimal to follow the inconsistent rule conditional on $\pi^e = \pi^*$. Since the Fed found it optimal to set $\pi > \pi^e$ conditional on $\pi^e = \pi^*$, the optimal fixed rule was found to be time inconsistent. This logic did not require that private agents *could* be fooled into believing that the Fed would follow the optimal fixed rule when the Fed had discretion. Similarly, the stochastic simulations I conducted with the TAYLOR model in which private agents are fooled do not require that private agents *will* be fooled. The simulations merely establish whether the optimal fixed rule is time inconsistent.[12]

In table 8-3 I report the average Fed loss when the Fed fools private agents. I ran two sets of ten stochastic simulations to prepare table 8-3. The two sets had Y^* in equation 8-5 corresponding to $[(Y^* - Y^b)/Y^b] = 3$ percent and $[(Y^* - Y^b)/Y^b] = 5$ percent, respectively. Separate simulations were not

12. The caveat offered in footnote 10 applies here. The Fed's incentive to fool agents presumably diminishes the faster agents catch on to the policy rule that the Fed is actually following. Thus the tests carried out here, with no learning, provide an upper bound on the probability that time inconsistency will arise.

Table 8-3. *Loss When the Fed Fools Private Agent (Inconsistent Rule):* $RS - RS^* = \pi^c - \pi^* + 1.5[(\pi - \pi^*) + \log(Y/Y^*)]^a$

	ϕ		
β	2/3	1	4/3
	With $\frac{(Y^*-Y^b)}{Y^b}$ = 3 percent		
1.00	8.9	9.3	13.0
0.995	9.8	12.1	14.4
0.99	10.8	13.3	15.8
0.98	12.9	15.9	18.8
	With $\frac{(Y^*-Y^b)}{Y^b}$ = 5 percent		
1.00	15.2	21.2	27.2
0.995	16.7	23.3	30.0
0.99	18.4	25.6	32.9
0.98	21.9	30.6	39.3

a. Symbols are as defined in table 8-1.

necessary for the different values of β and ϕ because these parameters directly affect only the calculation of the loss.

Comparing tables 8-2 and 8-3 for each combination of β, ϕ, and $(Y^* - Y^b)/Y^b$ shows that the Fed attains a lower loss by deviating from the optimal fixed rule when private agents believe that the Fed is following the optimal fixed rule. This the optimal fixed rule is time inconsistent in the TAYLOR model. If the Fed's preferences are ordinal, it is not meaningful to compare numerically the Fed's gain from deviating across β, ϕ, and $(Y^* - Y^b)/Y^b$. If the Fed's preferences are cardinal, then I infer from tables 8-2 and 8-3 that the Fed's gain from deviating from the optimal fixed rule tends to be greater the more the Fed discounts the future, the more weight the Fed places on output, and the farther the Fed wishes to push real output above trend.

Next, I iterated on steps 1 and 2 as outlined in the first section of this chapter. The Fed chooses a rule conditional on agents forming their expectations on the basis of the rule in equation 8-5. If the Fed can gain by choosing a rule generating higher inflation than private agents expect, then I iterated on steps 1 and 2 once more. Reporting each iteration for each combination of β, ϕ, and $(Y^* - Y^b)/Y^b$ would require voluminous tables, so I report only the outcome of each set of iterations.

As anticipated in the first section, I did not achieve exact convergence of the loss function for the simple rules I tried for any of the combinations of β, ϕ, and $(Y^* - Y^b)/Y^b$. I did obtain lower and upper bounds on the loss under the consistent rule. In table 8-4 I report upper bounds on the Fed's loss under the consistent rule for each combination of β, ϕ, and $(Y^* - Y^b)/Y^b$. In each case, the loss under the consistent rule is strictly higher than the loss under the optimal fixed rule. Tables 8-2 through 8-4 show that, as in the static Kydland and Prescott (1977) model,

Table 8-4. *Upper Bounds on Loss under the Consistent Rule*[a]

	ϕ		
β	2/3	1	4/3
	With $\frac{(Y^*-Y^b)}{Y^b}$ = 3 percent		
1.00	21.9	30.4	38.9
0.995	24.1	33.5	42.8
0.99	26.5	36.7	47.0
0.98	31.6	43.9	56.2
	With $\frac{(Y^*-Y^b)}{Y^b}$ = 5 percent		
1.00	46.0	66.5	87.1
0.995	50.6	73.2	95.8
0.99	55.5	80.4	105.2
0.98	66.3	96.0	125.7

a. Symbols are as defined in table 8-1.

$$L_{incons} < L_{opt} < L_{cons}.$$

Because the Fed reverts from the optimal fixed rule to the consistent rule in its attempt to achieve the inconsistent (or fooling) solution, seeking the best becomes the enemy of attaining the good.

If the Fed's preferences are ordinal, then I can say something about how much the Fed prefers the optimal fixed rule to the consistent rule. A numerical comparison of tables 8-2 and 8-4 suggests that the cost to the Fed of reverting from the optimal fixed rule to the consistent rule is higher the more the Fed discounts the future, the more weight the Fed places on real output, and the further the Fed wishes to push real output above trend. The results for ϕ and $(Y^* - Y^b)/Y^b$, moreover, coincide with those of the static model in the preceding section.

If the Fed's preferences are ordinal, then I can still compare average inflation under each consistent rule with π^*. Recall that $\pi^* = 4$ percent annually. Table 8-5 reports the geometric mean inflation rate in excess of 4 percent under the consistent rule. Because convergence is not exact, I report upper and lower bounds on the "excess inflation" occurring under the consistent rule. The time-consistent inflation rate exceeds the optimal inflation rate by 0.5 percent to 2.4 percent. I was unable to obtain distinct bound intervals for each combination of β, ϕ, and $(Y^* - Y^b)/Y^b$. Yet the upper and lower bounds on excess inflation are nondecreasing in $1/\beta$, ϕ, and $(Y^* - Y^b)/Y^b$. As in the static model of the preceding section, time-consistent inflation tends to increase with ϕ and $(Y^* - Y^b)/Y^b$.

In all candor, my prior distribution on time-consistent inflation less optimal inflation placed substantial weight on inflation above 2.4 percent. If the range of 0.5 percent to 2.4 percent is accurate, then I find the problem of time

Table 8-5. *Bounds on* $(\pi - \pi*)$ *under the Consistent Rule*[a]

Time-consistent annual percentage inflation less optimal annual inflation

	ϕ		
β	2/3	1	4/3
	With $\frac{(Y^*-Y^b)}{Y^b}$ = 3 percent		
1.00	(0.5, 1.3)	(0.6, 1.6)	(0.6, 1.8)
0.995	(0.5, 1.3)	(0.6, 1.6)	(0.6, 1.8)
0.99	(0.6, 1.3)	(0.6, 1.6)	(0.6, 1.8)
0.98	(0.8, 1.3)	(0.9, 1.7)	(1.0, 2.0)
	With $\frac{(Y^*-Y^b)}{Y^b}$ = 5 percent		
1.00	(1.0, 1.4)	(1.0, 1.8)	(1.1, 2.2)
0.995	(1.0, 1.4)	(1.0, 1.8)	(1.1, 2.4)
0.99	(1.0, 1.4)	(1.0, 1.8)	(1.1, 2.4)
0.98	(1.0, 1.4)	(1.3, 2.0)	(1.1, 2.4)

a. Symbols are as defined in table 8-1.

inconsistency of optimal Fed policy less troublesome than expected. Because I considered the posited values of ϕ and $(Y^* - Y^b)/Y^b$ to be reasonable, the dynamic version of ψ—the responsiveness of real output to unexpected inflation—must be smaller than I anticipated. According to the TAYLOR model, the Fed's ability to stimulate output through "inflation surprises" is limited and translates into moderate inflation under the consistent rule.

Variation of time-consistent inflation with β, ϕ, and $(Y^* - Y^b)/Y^b$ in table 8-5 has intuitive appeal. Consider the finding that time-consistent inflation is higher the more the Fed discounts future momentary losses. The gains from generating surprise inflation are presumably greater in the short term than in the long term, so that the Fed will be more tempted to deviate the lower is its weight on future values of the momentary loss. The lower is β, the higher must be inflation under the consistent rule to ensure that the Fed does not wish to generate surprise inflation at the margin.

The consistent rule has the property that the marginal cost to the Fed from generating surprise inflation just equals the marginal benefit from pushing real output above trend. Given a quadratic loss in inflation, time-consistent inflation must be higher the higher is the "marginal-benefit schedule" of real output above trend and the lower is the "marginal-cost schedule" of inflation. Higher ϕ shifts the marginal-benefit schedule upward and the marginal-cost schedule downward. Higher $(Y^* - Y^b)/Y^b$ shifts the marginal-benefit schedule upward. Hence, higher ϕ and $(Y^* - Y^b)/Y^b$ imply higher time-consistent inflation.

As a final note, recall that Rogoff (1985) found time-consistent inflation higher under international coordination of monetary policy. If Rogoff's findings apply to the TAYLOR model, then the range of time-consistent inflation rates

I report in table 8-5 serve as lower bounds on the time-consistent inflation rate under coordination in the TAYLOR model.

Qualifications

Necessary qualifications to the foregoing concern the Lucas critique, closed-form solutions, and homogeneous policy regimes.

The Lucas Critique

The above tests for time inconsistency are subject to the Lucas critique (1976) in that the parameters of the TAYLOR model are treated as invariant to the Fed's choice of policy rule. The parameters and functional forms of equations in the TAYLOR model are not derived explicitly from individual consumers' utility maximization and individual producers' profit maximization, conditional on exogenous stochastic processes for government expenditures and the money supply. Thus, I cannot formally incorporate the dependence of model parameters on the Fed's policy rule.

There are two reasons that the Lucas critique may not apply with its usual force to the tests for time inconsistency I conducted with the TAYLOR model. First, expectations in the TAYLOR model are rational, or "model-consistent." The dependence of expectations on the Fed's policy rule is captured, at least conditional on the parameters and functional forms. For example, suppose that utility maximization yields the following structural equation for aggregate consumption of nondurable goods:

$$(8\text{-}6) \qquad C_t = \alpha_0 + \alpha_1 C_{t-1} + \alpha_2 Y_t^p + \alpha_3 RRL_t + \epsilon_t,$$

with

$$Y_t^p = \frac{1 - \delta_1}{1 - \delta_1^n} \sum_{j=0}^{n-1} \delta_1^j E_t Y_{t+j}$$

$$RRL_t = \frac{1 - \delta_2}{1 - \delta_2^m} \sum_{j=0}^{m-1} \delta_2^j E_t (RS_{t+j} - \pi_{t+j}),$$

where Y_t^p is a distributed lead of expected future income and RRL_t is a distributed lead of expected future short-term real interest rates. The α parameters in equation 8-6 are functions of parameters describing preferences, technology, and the policy rules governing real government expenditures and the money supply. The δ parameters embedded in Y_t^p and RRL_t are likewise functions of "deep structural" parameters. Yet—conditional on the α and δ parameters and the functional forms—the expectations of future income, interest rates, and inflation embedded in Y_t^p and RRL_t are calculated correctly. The sensitivity of expectations of future income to current shocks may change with the policy regime, for example, but this sensitivity will be captured because expectations are model consistent in the TAYLOR model. Of course, the Lucas critique does apply to the assumption that the α and δ parameters are invariant to the Fed's choice of policy rule.

A second reason that the Lucas critique is less detrimental to the above analysis of time inconsistency pertains to time inconsistency itself. The Fed's lack of credibility boosts average inflation without necessarily much affecting higher moments, such as the volatility of prices and output. Aside from the wage equations, the equations of the TAYLOR model are arguably invariant to the average rate of inflation. Changes in the policy rule that merely raise the target rate of inflation will less dramatically affect parameters and functional forms than will changes in the policy rule that affect higher moments. Insofar as time inconsistency affects first and not higher moments, treating parameters as invariant to the policy rule may not be a bad approximation.

Closed-Form Solutions

Because of the nonlinear structure of the TAYLOR model, I cannot analytically derive a closed-form solution for output and inflation. That is, I cannot express the variables in the Fed's objective function solely as functions of predetermined variables, current values of shocks, and the short-term interest rate (the Fed's policy instrument given the interest rate rules I consider). Hence I cannot analytically derive the optimal fixed rule or the time-consistent rule. I must instead conduct stochastic simulations to compare the performance of some simple rules.

The core simulations with the TAYLOR model suggested that nominal-output targeting is the optimal fixed rule for the United States. The exercise I carried out in the preceding section presumes that nominal-output targeting is the optimal fixed rule. With this presumption I found evidence of time inconsistency: the Fed can do better by abandoning the optimal fixed rule, given that private agents think the Fed is following the optimal fixed rule. But suppose that, rather than nominal-output targeting (with a particular reaction coefficient), some rule z is the optimal fixed rule. Rule z might actually be time consistent. At minimum the simulations reveal a relationship between unexpected inflation and real output that the Fed will be tempted to exploit (in vain in the rational-expectations equilibrium) under a wide set of policy rules.

Now consider the consistent rule. The true time-consistent inflation rate could be large or small compared with what I found when experimenting with a few simple rules in the preceding section. Nevertheless, the simulations illustrate how the time-consistent inflation rate is likely to vary with ϕ and β in the TAYLOR model. Likewise, in the language of the second section above, the simulations give us a sense for the *magnitude* of ψ in the TAYLOR model.

There are some alternatives to experimenting with simple rules to calculate the consistent rule. For example, one might take a linear-quadratic (LQ) approximation of the Fed's problem of maximizing equation 8-1 subject to the equations of the TAYLOR model (the constraints). The LQ form could be obtained by substituting the nonlinear equations of the TAYLOR model into the objective function and taking a second-order Taylor series approximation of the resulting objective function around the steady-state values of all endogenous and policy variables. Using techniques outlined in Sargent (1987), one could obtain a linear decision rule for the Fed's policy variables and linear stochastic processes for all of the endogenous variables. The decision rule would generally depend on *all* state variables, not just on a few endogenous variables, as in candidate rules 1–3 from the core simulations.

An LQ approximation imposes certainty equivalence. The TAYLOR model does not exhibit certainty equivalence even when the Fed's momentary loss function 8-2 is quadratic, since the equations of the TAYLOR model are not strictly linear. The Fair-Taylor (1983) extended-path algorithm I used to calculate rational-expectations solutions to the TAYLOR model imposes certainty equivalence when calculating private agents' expectations, but not more generally. Although more computationally involved than taking an LQ approximation, techniques developed by Judd (1990) could enable one to obtain a nonlinear approximation of the consistent policy rule. The Judd techniques do not impose certainty equivalence.

Homogeneous Policy Rules

I uniformly assumed that countries follow the same policy rule. Clearly, the optimal fixed rule and the consistent rule are unlikely to be the same in each country, given the varying parameters and (to a lesser extent) functional forms. Considering permutations of possible heterogeneous rules is computationally expensive, so I have neglected them here.

Conclusions

Evidence from the TAYLOR multicountry model suggests that the Federal Reserve will be tempted to deviate from nominal-output targeting, generating higher than optimal inflation. The intuition in a large empirical model parallels the intuition originally provided by Kydland and Prescott (1977): when the Fed prefers real output to be above its trend path and has the ability to stimulate output by surprise inflation, time-consistent inflation will exceed optimal inflation. Thus, the Fed may be unable to commit credibly to a nominal output target that is consistent with the optimal inflation rate and the exogenous trend in real output. I estimated the "excess inflation" resulting from the Fed's lack of credibility to be 0.5 percent to 2.4 percent annually. Excess inflation is higher the lower is the Fed's discount factor, the more the Fed cares about real output relative to inflation, and the farther the Fed wishes to push real output above trend.

These estimates of time-consistent inflation in the TAYLOR model are far from conclusive. First, the exercise is subject to the Lucas critique. The estimated parameters should depend on whether the Fed follows the optimal fixed rule or the consistent rule (these rules themselves being functions of the parameters).

Second, I have not obtained analytical solutions for the optimal or the consistent rule, but instead relied on results averaged over stochastic simulations with simple policy rules. Third, I did not consider the possibility of individual G7 countries following different policy rules. Heterogeneity of estimated parameters across G7 countries strongly suggests that optimal and consistent rules will differ across countries. The optimal and consistent rules for each country would, of course, have to be calculated simultaneously.

Fourth, I have not modeled private agents' uncertainty about the Fed's preferences, such as the value of the parameter ϕ in the Fed's momentary loss (equation 8-2). Much of the literature on the time inconsistency of optimal Fed policy seeks conditions under which reputation building will cause the optimal fixed rule to be time consistent, at least over some time interval. Finally, I did not consider international coordination of monetary policy. Rogoff (1985) has maintained that coordination raises the time-consistent inflation rate, so that the time-consistent inflation rate under coordination should be estimated with the TAYLOR model. In summary, much can be done to obtain results for time inconsistency that are more precise and general than those reported here.

References

Barro, R. J., and D. B. Gordon. 1983a. "Rules, Discretion, and Reputation in a Model of Monetary Policy." *Journal of Monetary Economics* 12:101–21.

——. 1983b. "A Positive Theory of Monetary Policy in a Natural Rate Model." *Journal of Political Economy* 91:589–610.

Blackburn, K., and M. Christensen. 1989. "Monetary Policy and Policy Credibility: Theories and Evidence." *Journal of Economic Literature* 27:1–45.

Chari, V. V., P. J. Kehoe, and E. C. Prescott. 1989. "Time Consistency and Policy." In *Modern Business Cycle Theory*, edited by R. J. Barro, 265–305. Harvard University Press.

Durlauf, S. N. 1989. "Output Persistence, Economic Structure, and the Choice of Stabilization Policy." *Brookings Papers on Economic Activity* 2:69–116.

Fair, R. C. 1988. "Source of Economic Fluctuations in the United States." *Quarterly Journal of Economics* 103:313–32.

Fair, R. C., and J. B. Taylor. 1983. "Solution and Maximum Likelihood Estimation of Dynamic Nonlinear Rational Expectations Models." *Econometrica* 51:1169–85.

Judd, K. L. 1990. "Minimum Weighted Residual Methods for Solving Dynamic Economic Models." Hoover Institution, Stanford University.

King, R. G., and S. T. Rebelo. 1990. "Public Policy and Economic Growth: Developing Neoclassical Implications." National Bureau of Economic Research Working Paper 3338. Cambridge, Mass.

Kydland, F. E., and E. C. Prescott. 1977. "Rules Rather Than Discretion: The Inconsistency of Optimal Plans." *Journal of Political Economy* 85:473–92.

Lucas, R. G., Jr. 1976. "Econometric Policy Evaluation: A Critique." *Journal of Monetary Economics* (Supplement) 1:19–46.

Rogoff, K. 1985. "Can International Monetary Policy Cooperation Be Counterproductive?" *Journal of International Economics* 18:199–217.

———. 1989. "Reputation, Coordination, and Monetary Policy." In *Modern Business Cycle Theory*, edited by R. J. Barro, 236–64. Harvard University Press.

Sargent, T. J. 1987. *Dynamic Macroeconomic Theory.* Harvard University Press.

Taylor, J. B. 1980. "Aggregate Dynamics and Staggered Contracts." *Journal of Political Economy* 88:1–23.

———.1988. "The Current Account and Macroeconomic Policy: An Econometric Analysis." In *The U.S. Trade Deficit: Causes, Consequences, and Cures*, edited by A. E. Burger, 131–85. Twelfth Annual Economic Policy Conference Proceedings, Federal Reserve Bank of St. Louis. Boston: Kluwer Academic.

———. 1989a. "Policy Analysis with a Multicountry Model." In *Macroeconomic Policies in an Interdependent World*, edited by R. C. Bryant, D. A. Currie, and others, 122–41. Washington: Brookings, Centre for Economic Policy Research, and International Monetary Fund.

———. 1989b. "Monetary Policy and the Stability of Macroeconomic Relationships." Phillips Lecture, Canberra, Australia, August 1988.

Westaway, P., and S. Wren-Lewis. 1990a. "Is There a Case for the MTFS?" Centre for Economic Policy Research Discussion Paper 411. London.

———. 1990b. "Forecasting Government Policy: An Example of the Importance of Time Inconsistency." *International Journal of Forecasting* 6:401–05.

CHAPTER 9

Stochastic Behavior of the World Economy under Alternative Policy Regimes

Joseph E. Gagnon and Ralph W. Tryon

THIS CHAPTER analyzes alternative regimes for monetary policy. The regimes considered are reaction functions that link the short-term nominal interest rate to targets for the monetary base, real output, and prices. We analyze these regimes by using stochastic simulations of a three-country macroeconomic model. An important feature of the model is that agents' expectations are forward looking, so that the future effects of different policy regimes are incorporated in current behavior.

This research follows the lead of Frenkel, Goldstein, and Masson (1989) and Taylor (1989b). As in these authors' studies, this chapter focuses on the stabilizing properties of alternative regimes in the face of shocks that are likely to hit the world economy in the future. As in Taylor, the distribution of the shocks is estimated by using the complete model structure and historical data.

A major innovation of this study, however, is its modeling of policy instruments in the historical sample. Taylor assumed that private agents had perfect foresight of exogenous future government spending and money supplies throughout the period 1972–86. Frenkel, Goldstein, and Masson did not need to make such a strong assumption because they used instrumental variables rather than the model's own structure to capture future expectations. Nevertheless, Frenkel, Goldstein, and Masson implicitly assumed that the process determining policy instruments was stable over the historical period. We believe that it is more reasonable to assume that policy regimes have undergone shifts during the past fifteen years. We also believe that it is more reasonable to assume that private agents did *not* have perfect foresight about the future values of policy instruments in the historical period.

Given an estimated distribution of the shocks in the historical period, we simulate the model over a future baseline period by using alternative regimes

We would like to thank Ralph Bryant, Peter Hooper, and participants in the Brookings conference for helpful comments. The views expressed in this chapter are those of the authors and should not be interpreted as reflecting the views of the Board of Governors of the Federal Reserve System or other members of its staff.

for monetary policy. The alternative regimes can be compared on the basis of their ability to stabilize key macroeconomic variables in the face of random shocks. An innovative feature of our simulations is that the baseline path in the absence of shocks is the model's ex ante prediction of the next ten years. In other words, we do not include "addfactors" in any equation to force the model to track a judgmental path. We followed this approach for two reasons. First, we believe that the addition of fixed addfactors would invalidate the use of random shocks based on a historical distribution that did not allow for addfactors. Second, as the model's ex ante prediction, the baseline path provides valuable information about the long-run properties of the model.

Because of the computational intensity of our simulations, we have ana- lyzed only a small subset of interesting monetary policy regimes. Nevertheless, we have found the results to be illuminating, despite their limitations, and they challenge us to seek ways to make a more exhaustive analysis feasible.

Simulation Framework

The model we use, MX3, is a quarterly macroeconomic model of the Group of Three (G3) economies: United States, Japan, and Germany.[1] The model is closed by a rest-of-world (ROW) sector by using national income accounts data from the rest of the Group of Seven (G7) industrial countries. Each country bloc in MX3 has twelve behavioral equations, nineteen identities, four gov- ernment policy rules, and two exogenous variables. The scale of MX3 is thus considerably smaller than that of the Multicountry Model (MCM) of the Board of Governors of the Federal Reserve System (Federal Reserve); the MCM has approximately 170 equations per country bloc.

Innovations and Structure of the MX3 Model

MX3 differs from traditional large-scale quantitative macroeconomic models in three important dimensions. The first, and most obvious, difference is that expectations are rational and forward looking rather than backward looking. When simulating MX3, expectations of future variables are taken to be rational in the sense that expectations are set equal to the model's own prediction of the future.[2]

---

1. For a more detailed description of the theory and estimation of the model, and a complete equation listing, see Gagnon (1991). The appendix to this chapter displays the structure of a typical country bloc in MX3.

2. Because it is not feasible to compute true expectations in a large stochastic nonlinear model, the expectations variables are solved under the assumption that future disturbances are identically zero; that is, the model solution enforces certainty equivalence. This procedure introduces an approximation error. Simply put, the model solves nonlinear functions of expectations when the theory calls for expectations of nonlinear functions.

The second innovation of MX3 lies in its treatment of lags in the structural relations. In MX3, the behavioral equations contain only one lagged dependent variable and no other lagged variables. (The appearance of a lagged dependent variable in the decision rule is a general result of optimizing behavior with costly adjustment.) Higher-order dynamics in the behavior of any individual time series are assumed to reflect the transmission and equilibration of shocks throughout the entire system of equations. In other words, a system of several first-order equations typically gives rise to time-series behavior of individual variables that is higher than first order. This research takes the view that the apparent significance of lagged variables in much empirical work can be traced to misspecification of the estimation equation and, in particular, to the lack of a good measure of expected future variables.

The third, and perhaps most significant, difference between MX3 and traditional models concerns the long-run properties of the model. MX3 is designed to exhibit the qualities of an optimal growth model in the long run. The ultimate sources of growth in this economy are exogenous increases in labor force and technology. MX3's parameters are carefully restricted to ensure that changes in government policy and permanent shocks to supply are consistent with steady-state growth paths.

MX3 is designed to be a structural model for analyzing fiscal and monetary policy. By allowing expectations to react endogenously to changes in policy rules, MX3 takes a large step toward addressing Lucas's (1976) critique of model-based policy analysis. The essence of the Lucas critique is that the "structural" equations of most macroeconometric models really are not capturing stable decision rules of economic agents. Instead, these equations are better characterized as reduced forms that combine the interactions of policymakers and private agents. Lucas demonstrated that one would not expect such a reduced-form relationship to hold constant in the face of a change in the policymakers' behavior.

Lucas's prescription for macroeconometric modeling is to consider the decision problem for each class of economic agents. Lucas argued that, for a wide range of decisionmaking environments, agents base their actions on expectations of future variables as well as on the realizations of current and past variables.[3] Only when modelers have correctly identified the optimal decision rules and information sets of each class of agents can they hope to gauge the effects of different policy rules accurately.

Unfortunately, a fully satisfactory analysis of macroeconomic dynamics based on optimizing behavior has yet to be developed, and it is likely to be

---

3. Rational expectations embody a simplifying assumption that ignores any process by which agents learn about the nature of the economy or the shocks that have occurred recently. Under rational expectations, agents know the true stochastic structure of the economy, including the rules of the policy regime in effect.

years away for models of the scale of MX3. The strategy behind MX3 was to build a tractable model now by appealing heuristically to the structural equations that might result from a suitably specified set of agents, tastes, and technologies.

The long-run structure of MX3 is that of an optimal growth model with Cobb-Douglas technology, perfectly competitive firms, and long-lived utility-maximizing households. In MX3, households and firms rationally forecast future income and real interest rates when making their consumption and investment plans. Growth in the model is driven exogenously by growth in the labor force and in technology. With Cobb-Douglas technology and perfect competition, the share of total output that accrues to capital is given by the exponent on capital in the production function. The capital-output ratio equates the returns to capital with the cost of capital, which in turn is dependent on the real rate of interest. The real interest rate serves to equilibrate consumption and investment at the level of output given by the production function.

Although it would be possible to build a model of the economy with only the simple relationships described above, such a model would not be able to explain the short- to medium-run dynamics evident in the data. The transmission of shocks throughout the economy is almost certainly influenced by adjustment costs, gestation lags, and delays in the assimilation of new information. These characteristics of the economic environment may prevent markets from behaving competitively in any given period, and yet market forces may move the economy to a competitive outcome over a longer horizon.

Only recently have economists begun to enrich the dynamics of growth models by solving the decision problems of agents with costs of adjustment or gestation lags. At present, this work has yielded only rudimentary models that require the assumption of continuously competitive market clearing in order to obtain a solution. The structure of MX3 reflects the view that economic theory in its present state yields clearer insights about the long-run behavior of the economy than about short-run dynamics. The approach taken in MX3 is to enforce a competitive steady state in the long run, but to allow (heuristically) for imperfect competition and costly adjustment in the short run. In several instances, the model's dynamics are inspired by optimal decision rules in the face of convex adjustment costs. These decision rules determine the control variable as a function of its previous value and the discounted expected future sum of the forcing variables. The structural equations of the model, however, are not derived from the maximization of specific objective functions.

Each country bloc in MX3 is composed of four different types of economic agents. Producers in each country produce a homogeneous good that is differentiated from the goods produced in the other countries. Productive capacity is modeled by a Cobb-Douglas function in terms of the capital stock and the labor force. Total production can deviate temporarily from capacity production, but these deviations will be associated with equilibrating price movements. Fixed investment responds to deviations between the rate of return on physical capital and the rate of return on other assets.

Traders do not utilize capital and labor; they are modeled as pure arbitragers. Domestic traders purchase goods from domestic producers to sell to foreigners. This trade is characterized by significant costs of transportation and adjustment that prevent the continuous equalization of prices across countries. The preferences of households, producers, and governments for foreign goods relative to domestic goods jointly determine the demand curve faced by foreign traders selling to the domestic market.

Households maximize utility from discounted future consumption subject to their budget constraints. Households own the firms that produce and trade goods, and the net income earned by these firms passes directly to the households. The notional labor supply of each household is constant, but actual labor supplied may fluctuate as output fluctuates around capacity. (The model, in other words, enforces equal capacity utilization of capital and labor.)

Governments determine the level of the monetary base and *real* government spending. The government budget constraint determines the level of bonds outstanding. Tax rates are modeled with an ad hoc adjustment mechanism to ensure that the ratio of bonds to taxable income returns to an exogenous target level. The target level of government debt and the speed of adjustment to that target may be considered as additional policy instruments of government.

Financial markets determine the levels of interest rates and exchange rates. These financial markets represent the combined behavior of the four sectors in the model. Production technology and the labor force are modeled as exogenous to the rest of the economy.

Ideally, all of the private sector's behavioral equations and the government's policy equations in MX3 should be estimated simultaneously by a technique such as full-information maximum likelihood (FIML).[4] Unfortunately, the computational requirements for FIML in all but the smallest rational-expectations models are prohibitive for standard estimation techniques. Therefore, MX3 was estimated by instrumental-variables techniques. One advantage of estimating each equation separately and using instruments for current and future endogenous variables is that the exact rules of the government's policy regimes

---

4. The advantages of FIML are especially important in the context of rational-expectations models because future expectations in the equations being estimated can be solved directly by the model's own structure. Moreover, the implied cross-equation restrictions of rational expectations can be tested, both jointly across all equations and individually in particular equations.

not be specified before estimating the private sector's behavioral equations. (These policy rules must be specified, however, in order to simulate the model.)

One significant change was made to MX3 before this study. The risk-premium coefficients in the fixed-investment equations were calibrated on the assumption that the capital stock in each country was close to its equilibrium level in 1988, given the outputs and real interest rates that prevailed. In no case did this adjustment set the risk-premium coefficient more than two standard deviations from its estimated value. This calibration was necessary because the long-run capital stock is very sensitive to the value of the risk premium, and the risk premium was not estimated very precisely. With 1988 chosen as the benchmark year, the model was able to project a reasonably smooth baseline path for each country over the period 1989–98.

Baseline Path

The stochastic simulations reported here were simulated over the period 1989:1–1998:4. The "baseline path" refers to the behavior of all the model variables over this period in the absence of any shocks. To create the baseline path the exogenous variables in the model were projected to grow at a constant rate from their year-end 1988 levels. Government policy instruments were also projected to grow at constant rates from their year-end 1988 levels. The model was then simulated dynamically from 1989:1 through 1998:4, with all shocks equal to zero.

The labor-force growth rates were taken from projections for the next five years in OECD (1989). Because the baseline goes ten years into the future, the labor-force growth rates were shaded up or down slightly in consultation with country desk officers for Japan and Germany and U.S. labor-market specialists at the Federal Reserve. Labor-force growth was arbitrarily set at a slightly higher rate in ROW to reflect the experience of non-OECD countries. The assumed labor-force growth rates are presented in table 9-1.

The level of production technology was estimated as a Hodrick-Prescott trend in the Solow residual for each country. The projected future growth rate of technology was constrained to be equal across countries and constant over time. The growth rate of technology in the 1989–98 baseline is slightly higher than the average rate over the estimation period but substantially lower than the rate over the last four years.

Given the long-run growth rates of technology and the labor force, it is possible to compute the implied long-run growth rates of potential output in each country:

(9-1)
$$\frac{\Delta CAP}{CAP} = \frac{\Delta LF}{LF} + \frac{\Delta Q}{Q(1 - \alpha)},$$

Table 9-1. *Properties of the Baseline Path, 1989–98*
Percent

Variable	Germany	Japan	ROW[a]	United States
Labor force (growth rate)	0.5	1.0	1.5	1.4
Technology (growth rate)	1.25	1.25	1.25	1.25
Long-run potential output (growth rate)	2.35	2.97	3.35	3.17
Real government spending (growth rate)	2.35	2.97	3.35	3.17
Target ratio of public-sector debt	26.8	24.9	55.2	31.3
Monetary base (growth rate)	4.35	4.97	7.35	7.17
1998 inflation rate	3.9	2.5	2.6	4.2
1998 interest rate	4.2	4.1	5.8	5.4
1998 GDP (growth rate)	2.2	3.4	4.1	3.3

a. Rest of the world.

where $CAP [= Q \cdot K^{\alpha} \cdot LF^{1-\alpha}]$ refers to production capacity, LF is the labor force, Q is the level of technology, and K is the capital stock. Equation 9-1 is valid whenever the long-run capital-output ratio is constant. The long-run capital-output ratio is constant in MX3 provided that the real interest rate, the depreciation rate, and the risk premium for holding capital are constant in the long run. Table 9-1 presents the implied long-run real growth rates for the countries of MX3.

Fiscal policy in MX3 is captured by the level of real government consumption and the target ratio of public-sector debt to national income. The baseline path assumes that real government spending grows at the long-run rate of real output growth, starting at the observed level of government spending at year-end 1988. The target ratio of public-sector debt to national income is fixed at the observed ratio of public-sector debt to national income at year-end 1988. An ad hoc tax-adjustment process gradually changes the tax rate to keep debt near its target level.

Monetary policy in the baseline path fixes a constant growth rate for the monetary base. The monetary base is assumed to grow at the long-run growth rate of nominal GDP, defined as the sum of the long-run growth rate of production capacity and the long-run inflation rate. The long-run inflation rate is assumed to be 4 percent in the United States and ROW and 2 percent in Germany and Japan.[5]

After some fluctuations and transitions in the first few years of the baseline, all the prices and real quantities of the model converge to smooth growth paths. Even though the paths are smooth, there is some evidence that the model has

---

5. Unfortunately, this procedure does not correct for the fact that the long-run income elasticity of money demand is not unity. Thus the long-run inflation rates in the baseline path are not equal to their originally assumed values.

not reached a steady state by the end of the baseline period. The interest rates and inflation rates are close to their long-run values in the United States and Japan by 1998. In Germany and ROW, however, the inflation rates and interest rates are still moving gradually toward their long-run levels by the end of the baseline path. The rate of growth of real output is close to its long-run value in Germany and the United States in 1998, but Japan and ROW still have further adjustments to make. Table 9-1 presents the values of these variables in the last year of the baseline path.

Historical Residuals

The final step before conducting stochastic simulations was to create the historical residuals in the stochastic equations. Residuals were created over forty-nine quarters, from 1976:4 through 1988:4. Because of the presence of rational expectations in many of the stochastic equations, the residuals of these equations are conditional on the assumptions about the rules of the policy regime and about the exogenous variables in the model. In creating the residuals, it was assumed that agents had perfect foresight about the future paths of the labor force and technology. It was also assumed that agents had perfect foresight about the residuals in the model identities and the trade-share equations, which do not involve future expectations.[6] Beginning in 1989:1 and extending into all later periods, all residuals are assumed to be zero.

Rather than assume perfect foresight about policy instruments, government spending and the monetary base were modeled as first-order (nonstationary) autoregressions. In other words, agents expected that the monetary base and government spending would grow at constant rates into the future, but they were surprised by innovations to the monetary base and government spending in the solution period. The target ratio of government debt was assumed to be constant.

We assume that there was an unanticipated shift in both the monetary and fiscal policy regimes during the historical period. The monetary regime shift consisted of a slowdown in the growth rate of the monetary base beginning in 1980:1 in all countries. The fiscal regime shift consisted of an increase in the growth rate of U.S. government spending and a decrease in the growth rate of government spending in the remaining countries beginning in 1981:1. In addition, the target ratio of government bonds to national income jumped up in the United States and ROW in 1981:1.

---

6. Residuals in the identities arise from statistical errors and omissions, from the lack of complete data for ROW, and from the use of a short-term interest rate and an aggregate depreciation rate in the stock-flow identities. The trade-share residuals are quite small; because of their relative unimportance, the trade shares have not been subjected to shocks in the stochastic simulations.

Table 9-2. *Policy Regimes in the Historical Period, 1976–88*
Percent

Instrument	Germany	Japan	ROW	United States
Monetary base (growth rate)				
1976–79	7.88	9.52	13.30	8.16
1980–88	6.44	7.60	9.08	7.52
Government expenditures (growth rate)				
1976–80	2.32	4.12	2.24	1.24
1981–88	1.52	2.28	1.96	3.12
Target debt ratio				
1976–80	26.80	24.90	41.50	20.50
1981–88	26.80	24.90	55.20	31.30
Policy residuals				
Monetary base				
Mean	−0.000	−0.000	0.000	0.000
Standard deviation	0.007	0.019	0.014	0.004
Autocorrelation	0.154	−0.288	−0.206	0.401
Government expenditure				
Mean	0.000	−0.000	0.000	0.000
Standard deviation	0.013	0.027	0.003	0.014
Autocorrelation	−0.544	−0.484	−0.230	−0.048
Tax rate				
Mean	−0.001	0.000	−0.002	−0.001
Standard deviation	0.004	0.005	0.013	0.006
Autocorrelation	−0.086	0.677	−0.293	−0.079

The assumed growth rates of the monetary base and government spending before the regime shifts were estimated as the average observed growth rates between 1976:1 and the dates of the regime shifts. The assumed growth rates after the regime shifts were estimated as the average observed growth rates between the regime shifts and 1988:4. The target ratios of public-sector debt to national income were assumed to be the observed values in 1988:4, except for the United States and ROW before 1981:1, when they were assumed to be the observed values in 1981:1. The rules of these government policy regimes are documented in table 9-2.

Table 9-2 also presents evidence on the goodness of fit of these assumed policy rules. For the observed policy instruments—government expenditure, monetary base, and tax rate—residuals were calculated over the historical period. In each case the dependent variable is expressed as a ratio to facilitate comparison across residuals. The target ratio of government debt is unobservable, so no residuals were calculated for that equation. According to table 9-2, the assumed policy rules appear to fit reasonably well. Although the table does not show it, the properties of the policy-rule residuals are very similar in each regime.

Table 9-3. *Properties of the Private-Sector Residuals*

Equations	Mean	Standard deviation	Autocorrelation
GX	0.002	0.012	0.663
GER	0.021	0.078	0.468
GC	−0.005	0.006	−0.362
GIF	0.004	0.011	0.346
GII	−0.002	0.016	0.743
GXGSNI	0.002	0.023	0.067
GPXGSNI	−0.001	0.004	0.027
GMB	0.001	0.012	0.602
JX	−0.005	0.013	0.714
JER	0.103	0.133	0.552
JC	−0.003	0.004	0.495
JIF	−0.008	0.021	0.834
JII	−0.005	0.018	0.784
JXGSNI	0.003	0.030	−0.141
JPXGSNI	−0.002	0.026	0.296
JMB	0.001	0.016	−0.234
RX	0.000	0.011	0.858
RER	0.012	0.026	0.426
RC	0.004	0.006	0.842
RIF	−0.008	0.012	0.915
RII	0.001	0.010	0.728
RXGSNI	0.001	0.017	0.041
RPXGSNI	−0.000	0.010	0.393
RMB	−0.001	0.012	−0.109
UX	−0.001	0.004	−0.085
UC	0.003	0.005	0.471
UIF	0.003	0.006	0.431
UII	0.004	0.013	0.610
UXGSNI	0.013	0.041	0.545
UPXGSNI	−0.000	0.009	0.118
UMB	0.003	0.006	0.187

There are thirty-one private-sector behavioral equations for which random shocks are to be drawn for the stochastic simulations. The equations are private consumption (*C*), fixed investment (*IF*), inventory investment (*II*), export volume (*XGSNI*), export price (*PXGSNI*), money demand (*MB*), and the contract price (*X*) in each of the four countries, plus the open-interest-rate-parity equations for the three exchange rates (*ER*). (Countries are identified by the prefixes *G, J, R,* and *U* for Germany, Japan, ROW, and the United States.) The mean, standard deviation (around zero), and first-order autocorrelation of these residuals are given in table 9-3. Table 9-4 presents the contemporaneous correlation matrix of the residuals. As can be seen from table 9-3, the residual means are very close to zero, except for some of the exchange-rate residuals.[7] The largest

7. All of the model equations are expressed in logarithms or ratios to capacity output, so that a residual value of 0.01 represents a 1 percent shock to an equation.

Table 9-4. *Residual Correlation Matrix*

Equations	GX	GER	GC	GIF	GII	GXGSNI	GPXGSNI	GMB
GX	1.00							
GER	0.64	1.00						
GC	−0.28	−0.09	1.00					
GIF	0.54	0.58	0.24	1.00				
GII	0.61	0.46	−0.30	0.49	1.00			
GXGSNI	0.12	0.14	0.10	0.26	0.03	1.00		
GPXGSNI	−0.15	0.15	−0.05	0.14	0.32	0.01	1.00	
GMB	0.24	0.01	−0.13	0.02	−0.13	0.20	−0.37	1.00
JX	0.61	0.54	0.03	0.44	0.28	0.04	−0.24	0.20
JER	0.39	0.69	−0.12	0.46	0.46	−0.07	0.34	−0.14
JC	−0.29	0.03	0.14	−0.11	−0.28	−0.24	0.12	−0.30
JIF	0.82	0.72	−0.11	0.63	0.48	0.26	−0.18	0.38
JII	0.69	0.64	−0.04	0.55	0.44	0.09	−0.06	0.09
JXGSNI	−0.16	0.06	0.03	0.05	0.20	0.03	0.28	−0.19
JPXGSNI	−0.36	0.10	0.01	−0.06	0.03	−0.12	0.60	−0.38
JMB	0.06	−0.06	−0.02	0.19	0.18	0.12	0.02	0.08
RX	0.51	0.48	−0.01	0.28	0.35	−0.10	−0.02	0.03
RER	0.31	0.65	−0.07	0.32	0.12	0.10	−0.07	0.22
RC	0.80	0.62	0.04	0.65	0.54	0.24	−0.14	0.43
RIF	0.70	0.50	−0.05	0.42	0.49	0.15	−0.15	0.31
RII	0.50	0.27	−0.07	0.34	0.48	0.08	−0.01	0.10
RXGSNI	0.23	0.13	0.02	0.22	0.07	0.36	−0.00	0.14
RPXGSNI	−0.22	0.04	−0.12	−0.20	0.12	−0.21	0.44	−0.42
RMB	−0.08	−0.04	−0.09	0.02	−0.06	−0.16	0.19	0.03
UX	0.59	0.67	−0.02	0.37	0.31	0.17	−0.02	0.05
UC	0.36	0.48	−0.02	0.40	0.24	0.06	−0.09	0.08
UIF	−0.04	0.25	0.08	0.08	−0.03	−0.07	−0.01	−0.23
UII	0.10	0.27	−0.02	0.13	0.18	0.47	0.12	−0.04
UXGSNI	0.13	−0.03	−0.27	0.04	0.17	0.40	0.12	0.32
UPXGSNI	−0.31	−0.23	0.24	−0.09	0.00	−0.34	0.20	−0.32
UMB	0.12	0.14	0.01	0.27	0.18	−0.17	0.09	0.09

standard deviations occur in the exchange-rate and U.S. export equations. Only four of the thirty-one residual series exhibit autocorrelation greater than 0.8. Another nine residuals, however, have autocorrelation coefficients between 0.5 and 0.8.

The autocorrelation in the estimated residuals suggests that there could be efficiency gains from estimation by FIML. The use of FIML in estimating rational-expectations models allows the model structure to determine the future expectations, as is the case when the model is simulated and when the model residuals are computed. The single-equation methods that were used to estimate MX3 do not capture all the model's information and restrictions in determining future expectations. The loss of information about expectations may be quite important: although only nineteen of the thirty-one stochastic equations contain future expectations, eleven of the thirteen residual series that were highly autocorrelated are in equations with future expectations.

Table 9-4 *(continued)*

Equations	JX	JER	JC	JIF	JII	JXGSNI	JPXGSNI	JMB
JX	1.00							
JER	0.34	1.00						
JC	0.13	0.35	1.00					
JIF	0.69	0.36	−0.26	1.00				
JII	0.86	0.52	0.17	0.75	1.00			
JXGSNI	0.15	0.07	−0.14	−0.07	−0.26	1.00		
JPXGSNI	−0.29	0.45	0.29	−0.36	−0.21	0.37	1.00	
JMB	0.14	−0.09	−0.36	−0.00	−0.24	0.17	−0.14	1.00
RX	0.67	0.44	0.22	0.38	0.63	−0.13	−0.04	−0.07
RER	0.58	0.54	0.20	0.50	0.49	0.10	0.13	−0.10
RC	0.71	0.38	−0.26	0.87	0.73	−0.03	−0.34	0.05
RIF	0.67	0.21	−0.31	0.70	0.65	0.03	−0.36	0.08
RII	0.51	0.18	−0.20	0.35	0.47	−0.02	−0.32	0.30
RXGSNI	0.05	−0.06	−0.27	0.26	0.05	0.05	−0.20	0.09
RPXGSNI	−0.28	0.40	0.29	−0.40	−0.20	0.28	0.74	−0.21
RMB	0.05	0.08	0.03	−0.07	−0.08	0.15	0.17	0.13
UX	0.26	0.29	−0.06	0.57	0.37	−0.12	−0.19	0.05
UC	0.54	0.47	0.22	0.43	0.58	−0.20	−0.07	−0.16
UIF	0.07	0.22	0.25	0.02	0.14	0.04	0.09	−0.18
UII	0.14	0.05	−0.06	0.30	0.21	0.10	−0.05	0.00
UXGSNI	0.23	−0.29	−0.50	0.18	−0.22	0.19	−0.06	0.20
UPXGSNI	−0.19	0.10	0.35	−0.29	−0.18	−0.01	0.31	0.04
UMB	0.16	0.26	−0.04	0.08	0.15	0.19	0.27	0.09

Equations	RX	RER	RC	RIF	RII	RXGSNI	RPXGSNI	RMB
RX	1.00							
RER	0.35	1.00						
RC	0.58	0.44	1.00					
RIF	0.71	0.36	0.86	1.00				
RII	0.59	0.17	0.60	0.75	1.00			
RXGSNI	−0.22	0.07	0.20	0.15	−0.07	1.00		
RPXGSNI	0.11	−0.01	−0.29	−0.25	−0.26	−0.05	1.00	
RMB	−0.06	−0.10	−0.13	−0.15	−0.18	0.10	0.13	1.00
UX	0.20	0.23	0.41	0.28	0.09	0.21	−0.26	−0.05
UC	0.55	0.51	0.47	0.45	0.35	0.04	−0.09	−0.03
UIF	0.20	0.27	0.01	0.06	−0.06	0.34	0.22	−0.01
UII	−0.04	0.30	0.17	0.11	0.09	0.32	−0.17	−0.08
UXGSNI	−0.36	−0.08	0.08	−0.03	−0.13	0.27	−0.14	0.04
UPXGSNI	−0.03	−0.14	−0.26	−0.36	−0.32	−0.21	0.31	0.03
UMB	0.28	0.19	0.17	0.20	0.03	−0.03	0.19	0.34

Equations	UX	UC	UIF	UII	UXGSNI	UPXGSNI	UMB
UX	1.00						
UC	0.24	1.00					
UIF	0.03	0.63	1.00				
UII	0.19	0.11	0.20	1.00			
UXGSNI	0.13	−0.37	−0.26	0.43	1.00		
UPXGSNI	−0.10	−0.10	0.11	−0.19	−0.15	1.00	
UMB	−0.13	0.18	0.07	−0.25	−0.03	0.09	1.00

Table 9-5. *Properties of the Private-Sector Residuals under the Assumption of Perfect Foresight of Policy Instruments*

Equations	Mean	Standard deviation	Autocorrelation
GX	0.003	0.009	0.379
GER	0.027	0.069	0.460
GC	−0.004	0.006	−0.199
GIF	0.006	0.009	−0.156
GII	0.001	0.013	0.648
GXGSNI	0.002	0.023	0.067
GPXGSNI	−0.001	0.004	0.027
GMB	0.001	0.012	0.602
JX	−0.001	0.007	0.462
JER	0.108	0.130	0.631
JC	−0.002	0.004	0.711
JIF	−0.002	0.010	0.566
JII	0.001	0.011	0.746
JXGSNI	0.003	0.030	−0.141
JPXGSNI	−0.002	0.026	0.296
JMB	0.001	0.016	−0.234
RX	0.006	0.009	0.779
RER	0.013	0.027	0.410
RC	0.005	0.007	0.848
RIF	−0.005	0.008	0.895
RII	0.005	0.010	0.675
RXGSNI	0.001	0.017	0.041
RPXGSNI	−0.000	0.010	0.393
RMB	−0.001	0.012	−0.109
UX	−0.001	0.004	−0.090
UC	0.004	0.005	0.276
UIF	0.003	0.006	0.411
UII	0.006	0.014	0.625
UXGSNI	0.013	0.041	0.545
UPXGSNI	−0.000	0.009	0.118
UMB	0.003	0.006	0.187

To test for implications of our assumptions about the policy regimes in the historical period, we recomputed the residuals under the assumption that agents had perfect foresight of future values of the policy instruments. This assumption is identical to that of Taylor (1989b). By looking at the actual values of the residuals, we did not identify any noticeable differences across the two sets of residuals, even in the quarters immediately surrounding the assumed regime shifts.

Table 9-5 lists some summary statistics of the residuals computed under perfect foresight. For most equations, the standard deviation and autocorrelation are less than or equal to the corresponding values in table 9-3. (The statistics are identical for equations without future expectations.) We also computed the log likelihood of the model by using the historical residuals. The log likelihood under the assumption of perfect foresight of policy instruments is 4,075.28. The log likelihood assuming stochastic policy rules and unanticipated regime shifts is 3,966.75.

These likelihood values are based only on the thirty-one private-sector residuals. We were surprised to find that the assumption of perfect foresight leads to a better fit of the behavioral equations. We can think of two reasons for this anomalous result. First, our assumed policy rules and regime shifts are not capturing the true policy rules and regime shifts in the historical period. But table 9-2 shows that the assumed policy rules do not perform badly. Second, the private-sector stochastic equations were estimated with instrumental variables that did not allow for regime shifts. If the second explanation is relevant, the estimated coefficients may be biased from their true values in a way that causes apparently better fit of the model when no regime shifts are assumed in the historical period. Once again, the best solution would be to estimate the model and the policy rules simultaneously by FIML, allowing for unanticipated regime shifts.

Stochastic Simulations

The stochastic simulations focus on alternative monetary policy regimes. The rules of the fiscal policy regime are always unchanged from their baseline specification.

Implementation

Six monetary policy regimes are considered. In each case the short-term interest rate is the policy instrument. Regimes 1 through 6 express the alternative policy rules (variables marked by an asterisk indicate baseline values; the interest rates and inflation rates are expressed in decimal form at annual rates, so that a 6 percent rate is 0.06):

(Regime 1) $\quad RS - RS^* = 5.0 \left[\log(MB) - \log(MB^*) \right]$

(Regime 2) $\quad RS - RS^* = 1.5 \left[\log(PGNP \cdot GDP) - \log(PGNP^* \cdot GDP^*) \right]$

(Regime 3) $\quad RS - RS^* = 3.0 \left[\log(PGNP \cdot GDP) - \log(PGNP^* \cdot GDP^*) \right]$

(Regime 4) $\quad RS - RS^* = 1.5 \left[DPGNP - DPGNP^* + \log(GDP) \right.$
$$\left. - \log(GDP^*) \right]$$

(Regime 5) $\quad RS - RS^* = 1.5 \left[\log(PGNP) - \log(PGNP^*) \right]$

(Regime 6) $\quad RS - RS^* = 2.5 \left[\log(ER) - \log(ER^*) \right].$

In regime 1 the monetary authority targets the monetary base. In regime 2 the monetary authority targets nominal *GDP*. Regime 3 also targets nominal *GDP*, but uses a much larger reaction coefficient on deviations of nominal *GDP* from target. In regime 4 the monetary authority attempts to minimize deviations of both the inflation rate and the level of output from their respective targets. Regime 5 targets the price level. Finally, regime 6 targets the exchange rate in Germany, Japan, and ROW. (To complete the model under regime 6 it is assumed that the United States follows regime 1.)

The stochastic simulations are conducted over the forty quarters from 1989:1 through 1998:4. To begin a stochastic simulation, thirty-one residuals are drawn from a random number generator according to a normal distribution with mean zero and the estimated variance-covariance matrix. The model is solved in 1989:1 by using these residuals and the fixed lags and exogenous variables. The future expectations are computed by the Fair-Taylor algorithm. Future residuals are assumed to be zero. The stochastic solution for 1989:1 is then used for the necessary lags in solving in 1989:2. When solving in 1989:2 a new draw of residuals is taken from their estimated distribution, but future residuals are again assumed to be zero. This process is repeated for forty quarters, thus completing one stochastic replication over the baseline period. Ten stochastic replications are conducted for each policy regime over the baseline period, for a total of 400 draws of the residuals.[8]

To economize on computation time, the Fair-Taylor algorithm is allowed only one type-III iteration over a forecast horizon of twenty quarters. The type-II convergence criterion is 0.02 percent. In most cases type-II convergence is achieved, but sometimes the solution stops at the iteration limit of 100. Some trial solutions indicated that these restrictions allow reasonably accurate results. Occasionally the model diverged during solution; when the model cannot be solved during any period of a given replication, the entire replication is restarted using a different seed for the random number generator. Regime 6 always led to solution divergence, and no results are available for this regime.

A Metric for Comparison

To compare the simulation results for different regimes, one needs a measure (or measures) of how well the regimes perform. The primary measure used here is the root-mean-squared deviation (RMSD) of key economic variables around their baseline values. In other words, the objective is stated in terms

8. These replications were conducted with TROLL 13.1 software using the new stochastic simulator package. Each replication requires about 75 minutes of processing (CPU) time on an Amdahl 5850.

of the second moments, rather than the first moments, of the data. This choice of objective reflects our conviction that the average levels of real economic variables are invariant to any well-specified monetary policy in the long run. Although nominal variables do depend on monetary policy, this study ignores the factors involved in choosing a long-run inflation rate and focuses solely on deviations from the long-run rate.

The transition from one policy regime to another is likely to involve significant costs as agents learn gradually about the new regime. It would be of interest to consider the problem of making such a regime shift less costly, but we do not pursue that topic here. The assumption behind all the stochastic simulations in this chapter is that the regime shift is understood perfectly by the private sector and is fully credible. Thus comparisons of economic performance across policy regimes reflect differences in the long-run stochastic behavior of the economy and not the short-run transition costs.

The use of second moments as measures of economic performance may be rationalized on two grounds. First, fluctuations of variables around their expected values give rise to adjustment costs as agents adapt their behavior to the new conditions. Second, agents may be risk averse, so that their utility is increased when monetary policy succeeds in reducing the variance of an important variable. Of course it is possible that, by reducing the variance of one variable, policy may increase the variance of some other variable. In conducting the analysis it is necessary to consider all of the most important variables. Implicitly or explicitly, policymakers may have to weigh stabilization of one variable against the destabilization of another.

Simulation Results

Table 9-6 summarizes the results of the stochastic simulations. This table shows the RMSD of each variable from its baseline path. The RMSDs were calculated over 400 observations, representing ten stochastic replications of forty quarters each. The variables are measured in logarithms, except for the interest rate and the current account ratio, which are in decimals. The growth rates shown are log changes for all variables except the interest rate and current account ratio, which are in first differences.

Because the RMSDs in table 9-6 were calculated over a finite number of observations, they are subject to sampling error; therefore, they may not equal the true RMSDs implied by the model structure and estimated residual covariance. Ideally, we would like to present a 95 percent confidence interval for each RMSD in table 9-6. Getting such a confidence interval by bootstrapping over the realizations of the deviations of each variable from

Table 9-6. *Summary of Stochastic Simulations of Policy Regimes*
Root-mean-squared deviation from baseline

Variables		Regime 1: MB	Regime 2: GDPV	Regime 3: GDPV1	Regime 4: DPGNP and GDP	Regime 5: PGNP
				United States		
GDP	(log)[a]	0.080	0.081	0.083	0.020	0.119
		(0.032–0.145)	(0.031–0.150)	(0.031–0.155)	(0.015–0.029)	(0.048–0.276)
GDP	(dlog)	0.020	0.018	0.018	0.017	0.029
PGNP	(log)	0.088	0.087	0.087	0.215	0.021
PGNP	(dlog)[a]	0.012	0.012	0.012	0.018	0.006
		(0.010–0.015)	(0.009–0.014)	(0.009–0.015)	(0.014–0.025)	(0.004–0.008)
GDPV	(log)	0.033	0.024	0.017	0.216	0.106
GDPV	(dlog)	0.021	0.018	0.016	0.024	0.025
CAB	(ratio)	0.004	0.004	0.004	0.005	0.005
CAB	(del)	0.002	0.001	0.002	0.002	0.002
RS	(level)	0.031	0.036	0.051	0.094	0.047
RS	(del)	0.015	0.027	0.048	0.052	0.014
MB	(log)	0.006	0.024	0.035	0.161	0.129
MB	(dlog)	0.003	0.011	0.017	0.024	0.020
				Germany		
GDP	(log)[a]	0.034	0.029	0.033	0.020	0.043
		(0.021–0.050)	(0.015–0.040)	(0.014–0.061)	(0.014–0.026)	(0.021–0.073)
GDP	(dlog)	0.026	0.021	0.018	0.018	0.025
PGNP	(log)	0.066	0.035	0.038	0.183	0.020
PGNP	(dlog)[a]	0.015	0.013	0.013	0.018	0.011
		(0.012–0.019)	(0.011–0.015)	(0.011–0.014)	(0.013–0.026)	(0.009–0.014)
GDPV	(log)	0.080	0.031	0.023	0.180	0.044
GDPV	(dlog)	0.036	0.028	0.024	0.027	0.029
ER	(log)	0.207	0.198	0.208	0.258	0.206
ER	(dlog)	0.118	0.110	0.109	0.105	0.127
CAB	(ratio)	0.020	0.018	0.020	0.021	0.019
CAB	(del)	0.024	0.023	0.025	0.027	0.026
RS	(level)	0.049	0.047	0.070	0.112	0.042
RS	(del)	0.052	0.042	0.071	0.114	0.024
MB	(log)	0.010	0.076	0.098	0.087	0.104
MB	(dlog)	0.010	0.030	0.037	0.042	0.037

baseline seemed impractical, both because of the large number of variables and stochastic draws and because of the high degree of autocorrelation present in the deviations within each stochastic replication.[9] Instead, we calculated the RMSD for the log of *GDP* and the growth rate of *PGNP* for each replication separately, rather than for all ten replications jointly. Below the overall RMSDs for these variables in table 9-6 we list the smallest and the largest RMSD from the ten separate replications of forty quarters each. These intervals are almost certainly larger than a 95 percent confidence interval for the overall RMSD because they include outliers and because the overall

9. The autocorrelation of the deviations from baseline is due solely to the dynamic specification of the model. The random shocks were serially independent.

Table 9-6 *(continued)*

Root-mean-squared deviation from baseline

Variables		Regime 1: MB	Regime 2: GDPV	Regime 3: GDPV1	Regime 4: DPGNP and GDP	Regime 5: PGNP
				Japan		
GDP	(log)[a]	0.030	0.023	0.022	0.021	0.029
		(0.021–0.035)	(0.018–0.028)	(0.016–0.029)	(0.017–0.032)	(0.023–0.037)
GDP	(dlog)	0.031	0.026	0.022	0.022	0.029
PGNP	(log)	0.031	0.024	0.024	0.092	0.020
PGNP	(dlog)[a]	0.015	0.014	0.013	0.016	0.013
		(0.012–0.017)	(0.012–0.016)	(0.010–0.016)	(0.013–0.020)	(0.011–0.016)
GDPV	(log)	0.053	0.035	0.028	0.099	0.039
GDPV	(dlog)	0.043	0.036	0.031	0.033	0.038
ER	(log)	0.267	0.265	0.276	0.323	0.265
ER	(dlog)	0.170	0.175	0.180	0.173	0.168
CAB	(ratio)	0.024	0.025	0.025	0.024	0.025
CAB	(del)	0.036	0.037	0.038	0.036	0.037
RS	(level)	0.025	0.053	0.085	0.121	0.037
RS	(del)	0.027	0.054	0.094	0.148	0.025
MB	(log)	0.005	0.084	0.137	0.135	0.082
MB	(dlog)	0.005	0.036	0.062	0.093	0.030
				ROW		
GDP	(log)[a]	0.023	0.022	0.022	0.016	0.028
		(0.017–0.027)	(0.014–0.032)	(0.013–0.033)	(0.011–0.021)	(0.019–0.039)
GDP	(dlog)	0.020	0.017	0.015	0.015	0.017
PGNP	(log)	0.047	0.029	0.028	0.160	0.019
PGNP	(dlog)[a]	0.012	0.011	0.011	0.015	0.011
		(0.010–0.015)	(0.010–0.012)	(0.009–0.013)	(0.011–0.022)	(0.009–0.012)
GDPV	(log)	0.052	0.028	0.023	0.160	0.026
GDPV	(dlog)	0.028	0.024	0.021	0.024	0.021
ER	(log)	0.136	0.126	0.127	0.320	0.121
ER	(dlog)	0.050	0.049	0.052	0.054	0.068
CAB	(ratio)	0.011	0.012	0.014	0.013	0.010
CAB	(del)	0.009	0.010	0.013	0.009	0.013
RS	(level)	0.026	0.042	0.068	0.098	0.060
RS	(del)	0.023	0.036	0.063	0.100	0.034
MB	(log)	0.005	0.053	0.086	0.097	0.103
MB	(dlog)	0.005	0.023	0.037	0.046	0.031

a. Numbers in parentheses are the smallest and largest RMSDs from ten separate replications of forty quarters each.

RMSD is calculated over a sample ten times larger than the RMSDs from the separate replications.

Regime 1: Monetary-Base Targeting

The first regime we consider is monetary-base targeting, using the reaction function given above in the equation for regime 1. This regime is roughly equivalent to a fixed monetary base, since the actual changes in the monetary base under this regime are quite small. As shown in table 9-6, the RMSD of the monetary base is less than 0.01, or about 1 percent, for each country.

The RMSD of the growth rate of the monetary base is of about the same magnitude.

It is striking that under this regime the variability of the (log) level of both output and prices in the United States is much higher than the variability of the growth rate. This is not the case in the other countries (except perhaps for the price level in Germany). Thus shocks appear to be more persistent in the United States than abroad. (Recall that the shocks to the price equation are serially correlated in the United States. Also, the estimated contract lengths are longer, and the sensitivity to excess demand is lower, in the United States.) Both the level and the growth rate of *nominal* output ($GDP \cdot PGNP$, labeled $GDPV$ in the tables), in contrast, are less variable in the United States than in any of the other countries.

The bilateral dollar exchange rates are by far the most volatile series reported. The deutsche mark and yen exchange rates have RMSDs of 0.207 and 0.267 respectively, whereas the RMSD in the ROW exchange rate is 0.136. The exchange-rate deviations from baseline are also highly serially correlated. The relatively high variability of the price level (and the monetary base) in Germany can probably be attributed to the exchange-rate shocks.

The differences in variability across countries tell something about the magnitudes of the shocks hitting the different economies (for example, exchange-rate and production-function shocks); they also reflect different degrees of equation error in the estimated equations. Differences in the parameters in the estimated money-demand functions (and other equations) also contribute—there is no particular reason for the same feedback rule to have the same effects in different countries.

Regimes 2 and 3: Nominal-GDP Targeting

In regime 2 monetary policy is set on a nominal-*GDP* target with a feedback coefficient of 1.5. As expected, the variability of the log level of nominal *GDP* is lower than when the target is the monetary base. In the United States, the RMSD of *GDPV* falls from 0.033 to 0.024, a reduction of about 30 percent. The variability of the growth rate of *GDPV* also falls, but only from 0.021 to 0.018. In Japan the reductions are of roughly comparable magnitudes, but in Germany and ROW the nominal-*GDP* regime has a stronger effect. In all countries the variability of the monetary base is significantly increased, since it is no longer a target, and in all countries except Germany the variability of nominal interest rates is also increased.

In the United States the regime has almost no effect on the variability of the *components* of nominal *GDP*, prices and real output. There is only a slight decrease in the RMSD of the growth rate of real output, from 0.02 to 0.018, whereas the RMSD of the inflation rate is unchanged. The other countries show a more pronounced reduction in price variability, although this reduction is more apparent in the price level than in the inflation rate. It is evident that stabilizing the level of a variable does not necessarily lead to a corresponding reduction in the variability of the growth rate.

The third column of table 9-6 shows the results for a nominal-*GDP* target using a feedback coefficient of 3.0 instead of 1.5. The variability of nominal *GDP* is further reduced in all cases, and the variability of interest rates and the monetary base is further increased. There is, however, essentially no further reduction in the variability of real output and prices, either in levels or in growth rates, and in the United States and Germany the variability of real output actually increases. Further, note that the variability of the money growth rate is quite high outside the United States, with a RMSD of 0.037 in Germany and ROW and 0.062 in Japan. These figures imply quite large changes in the quarterly growth rates of the monetary base. These results suggest that the returns to stabilization efforts may diminish sharply as the degree of control over the target is tightened.

Regime 4: Inflation and Output Targeting

This regime targets monetary policy on the sum of the inflation rate and the log level of real *GDP*. The motivation for this variant of a nominal income target is that agents may be less concerned about the price level than about the inflation rate—that is, they ignore past inflation—while they are concerned about the level of output.

The results summarized in table 9-6 show that regime 4 is quite effective in reducing the variability of real output but leads to greater price variability than any of the other regimes considered so far. In the United States, for example, the RMSD of *GDP* is reduced to 0.020, and the RMSD of the *GDP* growth rate is reduced to 0.017, whereas the RMSDs of the price level (*PGNP*) and the inflation rate rise to 0.215 and 0.018, respectively. The same pattern of results appears for the other three countries, but the size and significance of the changes are much lower for Japan and ROW. The variability of interest rates and the monetary base is very high in all countries.

These results conform to the intuitive basis for the regime, with variability in the price level being much greater than variability in inflation. The regime is not "balanced" very well, however, in that the reduction in the variability of output comes at the expense of an increase in the variability of inflation (relative to the other regimes). An obvious alternative would be to raise the weight on inflation in the constructed target in order to reduce the variability of both output and inflation. We tried a limited number of replications of regime 4 after doubling the coefficient on the inflation rate, and the RMSD for inflation decreased.

Regime 5: Price-Level Targeting

Regime 5 is a simple price-level target, for which the same feedback coefficient (1.5) is used as for the nominal-income target (regime 2). The regime is quite effective in reducing the variability of the price level (from 0.088 to 0.021 in the United States and from 0.066 to 0.020 in Germany) and also leads to some reduction in the variability of inflation. This improvement comes at the expense of much greater variability in output: in the United States the RMSD of the growth rate of output is 0.029, and the RMSD of the level of output is 0.119.

Regime 6: Exchange-Rate Targeting

Regime 6 failed to solve for any trial. Failure (that is, divergence, or in some cases violation of non-negativity constraints) typically occurred early in a given trial, often while we were solving for the first period, and in all cases by the fifth period. Numerous attempts to get modified versions of the regime to solve also failed, although we did ascertain that the source of the difficulty was the Japanese sector of the model. The model solved satisfactorily when the United States and Japan targeted their monetary bases and Germany and ROW targeted their exchange rates with the dollar. The model always diverged when any country targeted the Japanese exchange rate. We conjecture that either the initial conditions for the Japanese data or the parameters of the Japanese sector are such that the algorithm cannot find a stable solution with a fixed Japanese exchange rate, even though such a solution may exist.

Conclusion

Given the limitations of this study, we hesitate to draw firm conclusions about the stabilization properties of alternative monetary policy regimes. Nevertheless we were encouraged by our finding that increasing the feedback coefficient between the target and the policy instrument tends to stabilize the target variable, albeit at the cost of destabilizing other variables. We also note that stabilizing the level of a variable is not always equivalent to stabilizing its growth rate, even though the literature on macroeconomic policy analysis often ignores this distinction.

There are several dimensions in which this research can be extended. First, the policy regimes could be made more complex, and they could incorporate the signal extraction problem faced by central banks in trying to interpret the earliest available economic indicators as noisy measures of contemporaneous activity. Second, more care should be taken in distinguishing between permanent and temporary shocks to the economy. In this chapter, all shocks are assumed to be temporary, and agents are assumed to have perfect foresight of future growth in technology and labor. In reality, technology and labor are themselves stochastic processes, and shocks to these processes may have a permanent effect on the level of potential output, thus calling into question the advisability of a predetermined target for the level of output. Finally, there is evidence that the model's parameter estimates could be improved significantly by FIML estimation with well-specified monetary and fiscal policy rules in the historical period.

Appendix: An MX3 Country Bloc

This appendix presents the structure of a typical country bloc in the MX3 macroeconometric model.

Private Sector Behavior

Consumption:

$$\left\{ 1 + b / \left[1 + \frac{\Delta}{4} + (1 - TAU_t)\frac{RS_t}{4} - \frac{DPA_{t+1}}{4} \right] \right\} C_t$$

$$= b \cdot C_{t-1}$$

$$+ \left[C_{t+1} - (1 - b)\beta \left(\frac{GDEBT_t + MB_t}{PA_{t+1}} \right) \right]$$

$$/ \left[1 + \frac{\Delta}{4} + (1 - TAU_t)\frac{RS_t}{4} - \frac{DPA_{t+1}}{4} \right]$$

$$+ (1 - b)\beta \cdot YN_t$$

$$+ (1 - b)\beta \left(\frac{GDEBT_{t-1} + MB_{t-1}}{PA_t} \right) + \epsilon_{1t}.$$

Inventory investment: $II_t = e_0 + e_1(GDP_{t+1} - GDP_t)$

$$- e_3(RS_t - DPA_{t+1}) + \epsilon_{2t}.$$

Fixed investment: $(1 + c \cdot d)IF_t = c \cdot IF_{t-1} + d \cdot IF_{t+1}$

$$+ (1 - c)(1 - d)$$

$$[\alpha(1 - TAU_t)GDP_t/CC_t$$

$$- (1 - \delta)K_{t-1}] + \epsilon_{3t}.$$

Contract price: $\quad X_t = p_0 \cdot PGNP_t + p_1 \cdot PGNP_{t+1} + p_2 \cdot PGNP_{t+2}$
$$+ (1 - p_0 - p_1 - p_2)PGNP_{t+3}$$
$$+ p_3[p_0 \cdot \log(CU_t)$$
$$+ p_1 \cdot \log(CU_{t+1}) + p_2 \cdot \log(CU_{t+2})$$
$$+ (1 - p_0 - p_1 - p_2)\log(CU_{t+3})] + \epsilon_{4t}.$$

Money demand: $\quad \log(MB_t/PA_t) = r_0 + r_1 \cdot \log(MB_{t-1}/PA_{t_1-1})$
$$+ r_2 \cdot \log(A_t) + r_3 \cdot RS_t + \epsilon_{5t}.$$

Exchange rate: $\quad \left(ER_t^1 - ER_{t+1}^1\right)/ER_t^1 = \left(RS_t^1 - RS_t\right)/4 + ERRES_t.$

Exchange risk premium: $\quad ERRES_t = \rho_0 + \rho_1 \cdot ERRES_{t-1} + \epsilon_{6t}.$

Export volume: $\quad \log(XGSNI_t) = h_0 + h_1 \cdot \log(XGSNI_{t-1})$
$$+ h_2 \cdot \log(AW_t/CAPW_t) + h_3$$
$$\cdot \log(PXGSNI_t/PMGSNI_t)$$
$$+ h_4(1 - h_1)\log(CAPTOT_t) + \epsilon_{7t}.$$

Export price: $\quad \log(PXGSNI_t) = g_0 + g_1 \cdot \log(PXGSNI_{t-1})$
$$+ g_2 \cdot \log(PGNPW_t)$$
$$+ (1 - g_1 - g_2)\log(PGNP_t)$$
$$+ g_3 \cdot \log(PXGSNI_{t-1}/PXGSNI_{t-2})$$
$$- g_4(1 - g_1)TIME + \epsilon_{8t}.$$

Export share: $\quad X01S_t = \psi_1 + \Upsilon_{10} \cdot X01S_{t-1} + \Upsilon_{12}$
$$\cdot \log\left[\left(ER_t^1 \cdot PGNP_t^1\right)/\left(ER_t^2 \cdot PGNP_t^2\right)\right] + \Upsilon_{13}$$
$$\cdot \log\left[\left(ER_t^1 \cdot PGNP_t^1\right)/\left(ER_t^3 \cdot PGNP_t^3\right)\right].$$

Export share: $\quad X02S_t = \psi_2 - \Upsilon_{20} \cdot X02S_{t-1} - \Upsilon_{12}$
$$\cdot \log\left[\left(ER_t^1 \cdot PGNP_t^1\right)/\left(ER_t^2 \cdot PGNP_t^2\right)\right] + \Upsilon_{23}$$
$$\cdot \log\left[\left(ER_t^2 \cdot PGNP_t^2\right)/\left(ER_t^3 \cdot PGNP_t^3\right)\right].$$

Export share: $\quad X03S_t = (1 - \psi_1 - \psi_2) - \Upsilon_{10} \cdot X01S_{t-1} - \Upsilon_{20} \cdot X02S_{t-1}$
$$- \Upsilon_{13} \cdot \log\left[\left(ER_t^1 \cdot PGNP_t^1\right)/\left(ER_t^3 \cdot PGNP_t^3\right)\right]$$
$$- \Upsilon_{23} \cdot \log\left[\left(ER_t^2 \cdot PGNP_t^2\right)/\left(ER_t^3 \cdot PGNP_t^3\right)\right].$$

Government Policy

Money growth rate: $\quad MB_t = m \cdot MB_{t-1}.$

Tax rate: $\quad TAU_t = w \cdot TAU_{t-1} + (1 - w)TBAR_t.$

Government spending: $G_t = nG_{t-1}$.

Target debt ratio: $BRATIO_t = z$.

Identities and Definitions

Absorption: $A_t = C_t + IF_t + II_t + G_t$.

Gross domestic product: $GDP_t = A_t + XGSNI_t - MGSNI_t$.

Gross national product: $GNP_t = GDP_t + RS_t \cdot NFA_{t-1}/PGNP_t$.

Disposable income: $YN_t = PGNP_t \cdot GNP_t/PA_t$
$$- \delta \cdot K_{t-1} - TAX_t/PA_t.$$

GNP deflator: $PGNP_t = p_0 \cdot X_t + p_1 \cdot X_{t-1} + p_2 \cdot X_{t-2} + (1 - p_0 - p_1$
$$- p_2)X_{t-3}.$$

Absorption deflator: $PA_t \cdot A_t = PGNP_t \cdot GNP_t$
$$- PXGSNI_t \cdot XGSNI_t$$
$$+ PMGSNI_t \cdot MGSNI_t$$
$$- RS_t \cdot NFA_{t-1}.$$

Import volume: $MGSNI_t = X10S_t^1 \cdot XGSNI_t^1$
$$+ X20S_t^2 \cdot XGSNI_t^2 + X30S_t^3 \cdot XGSNI_t^3.$$

Import price: $PMGSNI_t = \bigl(ER_t^1 \cdot PXGSNI_t^1 \cdot X10S_t^1 \cdot XGSNI_t^1$
$$+ ER_t^2 \cdot PXGSNI_t^2 \cdot X20S_t^2 \cdot XGSNI_t^2$$
$$+ ER_t^3 \cdot PXGSNI_t^3 \cdot X30S_t^3 \cdot XGSNI_t^3\bigr)$$
$$/MGSNI_t.$$

Tax revenues: $TAX_t = TAU_t \cdot TI_t$.

Taxable income: $TI_t = PGNP_t \cdot GNP_t - \delta \cdot K_{t-1} \cdot PA_t + RS_t$
$$\cdot GDEBT_{t-1}.$$

Equilibrium tax rate: $TBAR_t = [G_t \cdot PA_t + RS_t \cdot GDEBT_{t-1}$
$$- 4(MB_t - MB_{t-1})]/TI_t - BRATIO_t$$
$$+ GDEBT_{t-1}/TI_t.$$

Capital accumulation: $K_t = \left(1 - \dfrac{\delta}{4}\right)K_{t-1} + \dfrac{IF_t}{4}$.

Government debt: $GDEBT_t = (1 + RS_t/4)\,GDEBT_{t-1}$
$$+ (PA_t \cdot G_t - TAX_t)$$
$$/4 - (MB_t - MB_{t-1})\,.$$

Net foreign assets: $NFA_t = (1 + RS_t/4)\,NFA_{t-1}$
$$+ PXGSNI_t \cdot XGSNI_t/4$$
$$- PMGSNI_t \cdot MGSNI_t/4\,.$$

Capacity output: $CAP_t = Q_t \cdot K_{t-1}^{\alpha} \cdot LF_{t-1}^{1-\alpha}\,.$

Capacity utilization: $CU_t = GDP_t/CAP_t\,.$

Cost of capital: $CC_t = (1 - TAU_t)(RS_t - DPA_{t+1} + \delta) + \pi\,.$

Inflation rate (absorption): $DPA_t = 4(PA_t - PA_{t-1})/PA_{t-1}\,.$

Inflation rate (GNP): $DPGNP_t = 4(PGNP_t - PGNP_{t-1})/PGNP_{t-1}\,.$

Exogenous Variables

Labor force: LF.

Production technology: Q.

References

Frenkel, J. A., M. Goldstein, and P. R. Masson. 1989. "Simulating the Effects of Some Simple Coordinated versus Uncoordinated Policy Rules." In *Macroeconomic Policies in an Interdependent World*, edited by R. C. Bryant, D. A. Currie, and others, 203–39. Brookings, Centre for Economic Policy Research, and International Monetary Fund.

Gagnon, J. E. 1991. "A Forward-Looking Multicountry Model for Policy Analysis: MX3." *Economic and Financial Computing* 1:311–61.

Lucas, R. E. 1976. "Econometric Policy Evaluation: A Critique." In *The Phillips Curve and Labor Markets*, edited by K. Brunner and A. Meltzer, 19–46. Carnegie-Rochester Conference Series on Public Policy 1. Amsterdam: North-Holland.

Organization for Economic Cooperation and Development (OECD). 1989. *Economic Outlook* 46. Paris. December.

Taylor, J. B. 1989a. "The Current Account and Macroeconomic Policy: An Econometric Analysis." In *U.S. Trade Deficit: Causes, Consequences, and Cures*, edited by A. E. Burger, 131–85. Boston: Kluwer Academic.

———. 1989b. "Policy Analysis with a Multicountry Model." In *Macroeconomic Policies*, ed. Bryant, Currie, and others, 122–41.

CHAPTER 10

Stochastic Simulations of Alternative Monetary Regimes Using the McKibbin-Sachs Global (MSG2) Model

Warwick J. McKibbin

THIS CHAPTER explores the performance of a number of international monetary regimes by applying stochastic simulation techniques to the McKibbin-Sachs (MSG2) multicountry model.[1] Previous studies that have used the model to evaluate the steady-state stochastic properties of regimes focused on the performance of alternative regimes in handling individual shocks.[2] This study estimates the variance-covariance matrix of a range of shocks over the historical period from 1973 to 1988. The performance of a number of regimes is then assessed given this matrix.

Although such an exercise is useful and has already been undertaken using other models,[3] it must be kept in perspective. The performance of each regime depends not only on the regime but also on the model and the variance-covariance matrix of residuals. The residuals can be interpreted as shocks to the economy (including expectation errors conditioned on the historical policy regime), measurement errors in the data, and specification errors in the model. Thus an evaluation of regimes based solely on this counterfactual exercise is fraught with danger. At a minimum, the evaluation should consider other information such as the performance of the regimes in the face of a given shock. In a 1989 study, Jeffrey Sachs and I (see McKibbin and Sachs 1989) evaluated regimes for individual shocks; that study is an essential companion to the results presented here.

---

1. See McKibbin and Sachs (1991) for a complete description of the version of the MSG2 model used in this paper. The regions covered are the United States, Japan, Germany, the rest of the European Monetary System (REMS), the rest of the Organization for Economic Cooperation and Development (ROECD), the oil-exporting developing countries (OPEC), and the nonoil developing countries (LDCs).

2. For example, see McKibbin and Sachs (1986) for a study using the earlier MSG1 model, which ignored supply-side considerations. Also see McKibbin and Sachs (1989) for a study using the current version of the MSG2 model.

3. See Frenkel, Goldstein, and Masson (1989) and Taylor (1989).

Methodological Overview

The biggest problem faced in generating the results in this paper was the construction of a time-series data base for the MSG model. Because the model is based on the computable general equilibrium (CGE) approach to modeling, a cross section of data for one year (1986) is used to calibrate the model. Because constructing a time-series data base took an immense amount of time, a full variance-covariance matrix of residuals has not yet been constructed. Rather, the procedure followed in this paper was to generate residuals for the Group of Three (G3) economies (United States, Japan, and Germany) only, focusing on the production function, aggregate consumption, and money-demand equations. Residuals have been calculated for these three equations for the United States, Japan, and Germany as well as for the OPEC price equation.[4] Data were used for the 1973–88 period.

A number of problems arise in calculating data for forward-looking variables. In the consumption and investment equations for each country, data are required for human wealth and Tobin's q, both forward-looking variables in the model. For example, human wealth is defined as the discounted present value of the future stream of real household disposable income. Human wealth is calculated by using the actual data for real household disposable income together with projected data generated by a first-order autoregressive forecasting equation for beyond 1988. The present value of this series was calculated using the human-wealth equation in the model, with the actual rather than model-generated data for disposable income. A similar procedure was followed to calculate Tobin's q. Future work will attempt to apply the approach used by Taylor (1989), in which period-by-period simulations of the model generate values of the forward-looking variables.

In implementing the regimes in this paper, several approaches are followed. Simple ad hoc rules are specified, and two approaches to calculating optimal rules are explored. The first calculates the optimal time-consistent rule that minimizes an intertemporal loss function. The second approach calculates the simple optimal feedback rule, where the policy instrument (that is, the short-term nominal interest rate) feeds back on a restricted set of variables. The size of the feedback coefficient is found by minimizing the loss function described below.

In calculating the complex optimal feedback rules, I assume the problem facing the policymaker in each country is to choose a closed-loop rule for a policy instrument (U) to minimize an expected loss function of a vector of

---

4. For a full listing of the equations, see McKibbin and Sachs (1991).

targets (τ), given the world economy represented by the MSG2 model. This can be expressed as

(10-1)
$$\min_{\mathbf{U}_s} \sum_{s=0}^{\infty} \delta_t^s (\tau_{t+s}, \Omega \tau_{t+s}),$$

subject to

(10-2)
$$\mathbf{X}_{t+1} = \alpha_1 \mathbf{X}_t + \alpha_2 \mathbf{e}_t + \alpha_3 \mathbf{U}_t + \alpha_4 \mathbf{E}_t + \alpha_5 \epsilon_t$$

(10-3)
$${}_t\mathbf{e}_{t+1} = \beta_1 \mathbf{X}_t + \beta_2 \mathbf{e}_t + \beta_3 \mathbf{U}_t + \beta_4 \mathbf{E}_t + \beta_5 \epsilon_t$$

(10-4)
$$\tau_t = \gamma_1 \mathbf{X}_t + \gamma_2 \mathbf{e}_t + \gamma_3 \mathbf{U}_t + \gamma_4 \mathbf{E}_t + \gamma_5 \epsilon_t,$$

where

- $\mathbf{U}$ = a vector of control variables
- τ = a vector of targets
- $\mathbf{X}$ = a vector of state variables (such as, asset stocks, wages)
- $\mathbf{e}$ = a vector of jumping variables (such as, asset prices), where ${}_t e_{t+1}$ is the rational expectation of $\mathbf{e}_{t+1}$ conditional on information in period t
- $\mathbf{E}$ = a vector of exogenous variables
- ϵ = a vector of stochastic shocks (which are linear combinations of the structural residuals)
- δ = the social discount rate (assumed to be 0.1).

As developed in other papers (see McKibbin 1987, McKibbin and Sachs 1991), the optimal time-consistent, closed-loop, policy rules that are calculated are written in the form:

(10-5)
$$\mathbf{U}_t = \Gamma_1 \mathbf{X}_t + \Gamma_2 \mathbf{E}_t + \Gamma_3 \epsilon_t + \Gamma_{4t},$$

where the vector Γ_{4t} is a cumulation of all expected future values of exogenous variables and shocks. Accompanying this feedback rule (assuming it is stable) is a feedback rule for the jumping variables in the form

(10-6)
$$\mathbf{e}_t = \mathbf{H}_1 \mathbf{X}_t + \mathbf{H}_2 \mathbf{E}_t + \mathbf{H}_3 \epsilon_t + \mathbf{H}_{4t},$$

The simple ad hoc rules explored in this paper are implemented by imposing constraints on the rule expressed in equation 10-5. Where the feedback is on current endogenous variables, one can still express the rule in the form of equation 10-5 by using the reduced-form relation between endogenous variables, state variables, and current and expected future exogenous variables and shocks. Accompanying the simple rule, there will also be unique paths for the jumping variables in the form of equation 10-6, which will keep the model on its seventy-eight–dimensional stable manifold.[5]

The optimal time-consistent rule will, in general, be a complex feedback rule on a range of variables; however, the simple rules specified by this conference are ad hoc. To bridge the gap between these approaches, I also calculate optimal simple rules.[6] This is done by imposing the form of the feedback rule specified by the conference and then searching for a feedback coefficient such that the loss function in equation 10-1 is minimized. Because this approach is meant to be illustrative, only one case is considered for each of the four feedback rules (money, nominal income, output plus inflation, and exchange rates). In the case considered, the optimal coefficients are calculated by minimizing a loss function that is a weighted averaged of the individual G3 country's loss functions, subject to the additional constraint that the coefficient be the *same* for all countries. This is a simple cooperative rule. An extension of this approach, which is in the process of being explored, is to calculate different optimal feedback parameters for each country.

To simplify the interpretation and implementation of the stochastic simulation methodology, the linearized version of the model is used. This enables the variance-covariance matrix of all variables conditioned on the variance-covariance matrix of the residuals to be calculated analytically, which, in turn, avoids the significant problems encountered when attempting to undertake the stochastic simulations numerically.

Assume for ease of exposition that the variables this paper wants to examine are contained in a vector $\boldsymbol{\Phi}$, which is related to the other variables in the system by

$$(10\text{-}7) \qquad \boldsymbol{\Phi}_t = \Theta_1 \mathbf{X}_t + \Theta_2 \mathbf{e}_t + \Theta_3 \mathbf{U}_t + \Theta_4 \mathbf{E}_t + \Theta_5 \boldsymbol{\epsilon}_t.$$

The rules for the control variables ($\mathbf{U}_t$) and jumping variables ($\mathbf{e}_t$) given in equations 10-5 and 10-6 can be substituted into equation 10-7 to write $\boldsymbol{\Phi}$ as a function of the state variables and the shocks (ignoring the exogenous variables for expositional convenience):

$$(10\text{-}8) \qquad \boldsymbol{\Phi}_t = \Theta_1^* \mathbf{X}_t + \Theta_5^* \boldsymbol{\epsilon}_t.$$

---

5. Consisting of twenty-eight jumping variables (such as exchange rates, human wealth, Tobin's q, and long real interest rates) and fifty state variables (debt stocks, capital stocks, and so forth).

6. Pauly and Petersen (1990) also calculate optimal simple rules. The difference here is that the criteria for optimality is based on the ultimate loss function rather than on the intermediate target.

The variance-covariance matrix of the variables contained in the $\mathbf{\Phi}$ vector can be calculated for the first year of the simulation as a function of the variance-covariance matrix of the residuals ($\mathbf{\Lambda_\epsilon}$):

$$\mathbf{\Lambda}_{\mathbf{\Phi}(1)} = (\Theta_5^*)\mathbf{\Lambda_\epsilon}(\Theta_5^{*\prime}).$$

Using a similar procedure, the variance-covariance matrix of the variables in $\mathbf{\Phi}$ can be calculated for period 2. Equation 10-8 can be rewritten:

(10-9) $$\mathbf{\Phi}_{t+1} = \Theta_1^*\mathbf{X}_{t+1} + \Theta_5^*\mathbf{\epsilon}_{t+1}.$$

Substituting equations 10-2, 10-5, and 10-6 into equation 10-9 obtains

$$\mathbf{\Phi}_{t+1} = \Theta_1^*(\boldsymbol{\alpha}_1 + \boldsymbol{\alpha}_2\mathbf{H}_1 + \boldsymbol{\alpha}_3\boldsymbol{\Gamma}_1)\mathbf{X}_t + \Theta_1^*(\boldsymbol{\alpha}_5 + \boldsymbol{\alpha}_2\mathbf{H}_2 + \boldsymbol{\alpha}_3\boldsymbol{\Gamma}_2)\mathbf{\epsilon}_t + \Theta_5^*\mathbf{\epsilon}_{t+1}.$$

Assuming that the shocks are independently distributed over time, it can be shown that

$$\mathbf{\Lambda}_{\mathbf{\Phi}(2)} = (\Theta^{**}_5)\mathbf{\Lambda_\epsilon}(\Theta^{**\prime}_5) + \mathbf{\Lambda}_{\mathbf{\Phi}(1)},$$

where

$$\Theta_5^{**} = \Theta_1^*(\boldsymbol{\alpha}_5 + \boldsymbol{\alpha}_2\mathbf{H}_2 + \boldsymbol{\alpha}_3\boldsymbol{\Gamma}_2),$$

This procedure is repeated to calculate the variance-covariance matrix for the variables contained in $\mathbf{\Phi}$ for the first ten years of the simulation period. The shocks are assumed to be independent over time. The ten- and five-year averages are calculated as the average of variances for each period.

The Regimes

The regimes were implemented following the guidelines supplied by the conference. As already mentioned, several alternative regimes were implemented, and they are discussed below. All regimes specified by the conference converged.[7] Stability of each regime was checked by calculating the eigenvalues of the model.

The regimes are numbered as follows:

(Regime 1) $i - i^* = -5 \log(M^*/M)$

(Regime 2a) $i - i^* = 1.5 [\log(PY) - \log(PY^*)]$

7. In the version of these results presented at the conference, the initial attempts at implementing rule 2 failed to converge. In these earlier attempts, output and inflation were included as separate targets in a quadratic loss function. The loss function was then minimized, given interest rates were the instruments. When the regime was subsequently implemented according to the simple feedback rule on the sum of output and inflation, this regime converged.

(Regime 2b) $i - i^* = 1.5[(\pi - \pi^*) + \log(Y) - \log(Y^*)]$
(Regime 3) $i - i^* = 2.5\log(E^*/E)$.

Regimes 1′–3′ are regimes 1–3 with perfect stabilization of the targets.

(Regime 1′) $i - i^* = -1000000\log(M^*/M)$
(Regime 2a′) $i - i^* = 1000000\,[\log(PY) - \log(PY^*)]$
(Regime 2b′) $i - i^* = 1000000[(\pi - \pi^*) + \log(Y) - \log(Y^*)]$
(Regime 3′) $i - i^* = 1000000\log(E^*/E)$.

In the MSG2 model, regimes 1′, 2a′, and 3′ were stable, with perfect stabilization of the variable in the feedback rule. Regime 2b′ was found to be unstable, and the results are not reported further for this regime.

   In addition to the perfect stabilization of targets shown in regimes 1′–3′, results are presented for regimes 1″–3″, where optimal simple feedback rules have been calculated.

(Regime 1″) $i - i^* = \mu_1\log(M^*/M)$
(Regime 2a″) $i - i^* = \mu_{2a}\,[\log(PY) - \log(PY^*)]$
(Regime 2b″) $i - i^* = \mu_{2b}[(\pi - \pi^*) + \log(Y) - \log(Y^*)]$
(Regime 3″) $i - i^* = \mu_3\log(E^*/E)$.

In each of regimes 1″–3″, the same coefficient in the feedback rule applies to each of the G3 economies.

   Finally, regime 4″ is the optimal time-consistent feedback rule linking the interest rates to the vector of state variables and expected values of shocks that minimize the loss function in equation 10-1. The vector of targets include inflation and output for each country with equal weight on the log of output and the rate of inflation.

   A two-stage procedure was followed to obtain the optimization rules as a feedback rule for the nominal interest rate. The loss function was minimized with the money stock as the policy instrument. The money-demand function was then inverted to write the feedback rule in terms of the short-term nominal interest rate.

   The conference also specified a loss function with a weight on interest-rate variability. Use of this loss function led to convergence problems. The interest rate cannot be the sole target in the loss function when undertaking an optimization exercise, because without any nominal magnitudes as targets the price level is indeterminant in the MSG model. This problem seems to occur even for small weights on interest-rate variability in the loss function. The alternative loss function, which included interest-rate variability, was not considered further.

Results

The results of the simulations are contained in appendix table 10A-1. The simulations are assumed to begin in 1989 and to end in 2029. To interpret the numbers, note that for each period the variance-covariance matrix for all variables conditional on the variance-covariance of shocks is calculated. This is equivalent to the forty draws a period that were specified in the guidelines for the conference. The average of the variance for each variable is calculated over the first ten years of the simulations and then over the second five years of the simulation.

The variance-covariance matrix of residuals is also given in table 10A-2. Note that shocks to oil prices and supply shocks in each region dominate the matrix. This is questionable; as I have shown in McKibbin (1989), shocks to actual and expected fiscal and monetary policies, as well as oil price shocks, go a substantial way toward explaining the experience of 1980s. Fiscal shocks are excluded from this exercise by the assumption that government expenditure is nonstochastic and because the model was not used to generate the expected variables in the model when calculating the residuals for each equation. Yet these demand shocks are crucial to the period over which the residuals are calculated.

Several interesting results emerge from these tables. As a rule of thumb, the loss function with equal weight on inflation and output deviations (but without discounting) can be used to evaluate the outcomes. It can be seen that the nominal-income target (regime 2a) specified in the ad hoc manner does not perform as well as the money target (regime 1) for the United States, yet the nominal-income target outperforms the money target in other countries. The outcome for the United States is deceptive, however, because in the results for regimes 2a' and 1', where one assumes perfect targeting of money and nominal income, the nominal-income rule outperforms the money-targeting rule. This highlights the arbitrary nature of the comparison of simple rules and the need to be careful to distinguish between the principle behind a given rule and the way it is implemented in practice. The fixed-exchange-rate rule (regime 3) performs the least well of the regimes for Japan and Germany even when a distinction is made between leaning against the wind and complete fixity of the exchange rate (regime 3'). However, this rule performs well for the United States when other countries are responsible for pegging to the dollar.

The results for the optimal cooperative simple rules given in regimes 1'' − 3'' are somewhat surprising. For regime 1'' (money target) and regime 3'' (the exchange-rate target), the optimal simple rule was complete targeting of the intermediate-target variables. The results therefore correspond to regimes 1' and 3' respectively and are not repeated. The results for regimes 2a' and 2b' are not exact targeting and are therefore presented in table 10A-1. The feedback coefficient that minimized the weighted average of each country's loss function was found to be 29.42 for regime 2a' and 105 for regime 2b'.

The results for regime 4" are based on using the optimal time-consistent feedback rule with countries taking the actions of other countries as given. There is not an unambiguous improvement from countries' following this complex rule. Part of the explanation is that, although policymakers are allowed to optimize in this regime, with fewer constraints on the form of the feedback rule, they optimize over a constrained space that may not span the space containing the arbitrary feedback rules. The simple rules are not necessarily in the set of time-consistent policy rules, whereas the results for regime 4' are constrained to be time consistent. In other words, these results show that if the policymaker is not arbitrarily constrained to follow the simple rules, then the simple rules are not attainable because they are not credible to the private agents in the model. Also, the equilibrium that is explored with the optimizing rules is a Nash equilibrium of a dynamic game between policymakers in the different regions, which may be also lead to an inferior outcome relative to the arbitrary rules.

A comparison of the optimal cooperative simple rules with the optimal time-consistent noncooperative rule (regime 4") illustrates that over ten years, the average variances of output in the United States, Japan, and Germany, and inflation in Germany and Japan, are lower under the simple rule. The average variance of inflation is higher in the United States. For the other regions a comparison is not illuminating, because in regime 4" all countries are optimizing whereas in the other regimes only the G3 coalition is assumed to be optimizing. The nonparticipants (that is, the ROECD and REMS regions) that are assumed to be following a money rule are worse off under the simple rule. This result for the G3 economies suggests that simple rules may be better than complex optimal rules if the simple rules can be made completely credible.

Conclusion

Although these results are preliminary, several interesting points emerge. First, the ranking of the regimes consisting of simple feedback rules with less than complete stabilization is different from the ranking of the regimes when there is complete, or an optimal amount of, stabilization. This suggests that some caution should be exercised when evaluating simple rules.

Second, the optimal time-consistent rule compared poorly with the simple rules. This suggests some possible gains may be achieved by following precommitted simple rules rather than the complex "optimal" rules considered in this chapter. The class of complex rules considered here are time consistent and impose the constraint that countries do not cooperate when setting policies.

Finally, the results suggest that the regime based on the optimal simple feedback rule, in which interest rates respond to the gap between actual and desired nominal income, performs well relative to the other regimes (in terms of minimizing the variance of output and inflation) for the United States, Japan, and Germany. When the G3 follow this regime, other regions of the model (that is, the ROECD and REMS regions) are also better off than when the G3 follow the alternative regimes considered.

Table 10A-1. *Stability of Alternative Policy Regimes*

Regime and variability	Real GNP (log)	Real GNP growth	GNP deflator (log)	Inflation	Nominal GNP	Change in nominal GNP	Short nominal interest rate	Change in nominal interest rate	Current account (%GNP)	Exchange rate (log)
United States										
Five-year variance										
Regime 1	0.00106	0.00046	0.00672	0.00116	0.00559	0.00016	0.01040	0.00025	0.00011	:::
Regime 2a	0.00218	0.00096	0.00877	0.00217	0.00380	0.00024	0.00855	0.00055	0.00014	:::
Regime 2b	0.00272	0.00007	0.16467	0.02541	0.19442	0.02292	0.09240	0.00091	0.00014	:::
Regime 3	0.00088	0.00043	0.00421	0.00087	0.00319	0.00008	0.01105	0.00021	0.00010	:::
Regime 1'	0.00097	0.00045	0.00483	0.00096	0.00360	0.00010	0.01238	0.00027	0.00012	:::
Regime 2a'	0.00099	0.00045	0.00099	0.00037	0.00000	0.00000	0.03971	0.00042	0.00023	:::
Regime 3'	0.00134	0.00064	0.00594	0.00113	0.00307	0.00011	0.01058	0.00032	0.00011	:::
Regime 2a''	0.00085	0.00039	0.00102	0.00041	0.00003	0.00000	0.02871	0.00037	0.00017	:::
Regime 2b''	0.00032	0.00010	0.07277	0.00040	0.07783	0.00026	0.07805	0.00030	0.00018	:::
Regime 4''	0.00045	0.02505	0.09166	0.00136	0.08913	0.00115	0.16145	0.00073	0.00029	:::
Ten-year variance										
Regime 1	0.00691	0.00197	0.00926	0.00228	0.00349	0.00026	0.00656	0.00046	0.00013	::::
Regime 2a	0.01146	0.00336	0.01819	0.00475	0.00270	0.00033	0.00607	0.00075	0.00019	::::
Regime 2b	0.00596	0.00133	0.09449	0.01507	0.10087	0.01243	0.05630	0.00172	0.00012	::::
Regime 3	0.00684	0.00206	0.00831	0.00224	0.00213	0.00018	0.00735	0.00060	0.00012	::::
Regime 1'	0.00664	0.00192	0.00821	0.00212	0.00232	0.00018	0.00804	0.00060	0.00013	::::
Regime 2a'	0.00565	0.00167	0.00565	0.00152	0.00000	0.00000	0.02857	0.00231	0.00018	::::
Regime 3'	0.00686	0.00226	0.00979	0.00249	0.00208	0.00022	0.00700	0.00070	0.00018	::::
Regime 2a''	0.00553	0.00162	0.00550	0.00160	0.00003	0.00000	0.02127	0.00197	0.00016	::::
Regime 2b''	0.00191	0.00101	0.06303	0.00248	0.05700	0.00195	0.05541	0.00260	0.00015	::::
Regime 4''	0.00195	0.01558	0.07506	0.00319	0.06420	0.00242	0.11022	0.00366	0.00021	::::

Japan

Five-year variance

Regime 1	0.14282	0.00000	0.00393	0.00007	0.19255	0.00009	0.30747	0.00014	0.00056	0.03006
Regime 2a	0.11992	0.00000	0.00431	0.00013	0.16799	0.00014	0.37798	0.00032	0.00052	0.03006
Regime 2b	0.14335	0.00001	0.01656	0.00089	0.12818	0.00076	0.28572	0.00005	0.00077	0.54954
Regime 3	0.25704	0.00002	0.00844	0.00078	0.19547	0.00056	0.01105	0.00021	0.00096	0.00000
Regime 1'	0.11979	0.00000	0.00189	0.00005	0.14977	0.00006	0.42637	0.00016	0.00050	0.05875
Regime 2a'	0.00078	0.03691	0.00078	0.00007	0.00000	0.00000	2.06939	0.00033	0.00005	0.61467
Regime 3'	0.30730	0.01338	0.01389	0.00193	0.24013	0.00145	0.01058	0.00032	0.00123	0.00000
Regime 2a''	0.01046	0.00000	0.00313	0.00001	0.00230	0.00000	1.98611	0.00023	0.00018	0.65790
Regime 2b''	0.00483	0.00001	0.26917	0.00324	0.20345	0.00355	2.03293	0.00010	0.00028	1.24206
Regime 4''	0.00621	0.81719	11.24897	0.44852	11.73310	0.49262	2.02124	0.00009	0.00005	13.90186

Ten-year variance

Regime 1	0.13764	0.01271	0.00359	0.00095	0.18134	0.01957	0.28967	0.03123	0.00060	0.07147
Regime 2a	0.11690	0.01103	0.00310	0.00082	0.15317	0.01657	0.34464	0.03729	0.00058	0.08776
Regime 2b	0.13660	0.01245	0.01248	0.00139	0.15605	0.01945	0.29246	0.03969	0.00072	0.31645
Regime 3	0.24274	0.02129	0.01226	0.00536	0.26944	0.04484	0.00735	0.00060	0.00091	0.00000
Regime 1'	0.11627	0.01093	0.00190	0.00063	0.14281	0.01583	0.40665	0.04502	0.00055	0.11470
Regime 2a'	0.00287	0.03432	0.00287	0.00112	0.00000	0.00000	2.09687	0.28325	0.00014	0.80395
Regime 3'	0.28248	0.03812	0.01738	0.00433	0.32481	0.04258	0.00700	0.00070	0.00116	0.00000
Regime 2a''	0.01235	0.00174	0.00421	0.00064	0.00230	0.00028	1.98564	0.24191	0.00027	0.84206
Regime 2b''	0.00629	0.00106	0.15944	0.00394	0.11389	0.00445	2.01801	0.22375	0.00034	1.14463
Regime 4''	0.00575	0.45800	6.00193	0.27160	6.21194	0.29842	2.02836	0.22937	0.00015	8.08613

(continued)

Table 10A-1 (continued)

Regime and variability	Real GNP (log)	Real GNP growth	GNP deflator (log)	Inflation	Nominal GNP	Change in nominal GNP	Short nominal interest rate	Change in nominal interest rate	Current account (%GNP)	Exchange rate (log)
Germany										
Five-year variance										
Regime 1	0.02352	0.00014	0.00192	0.00044	0.03304	0.00010	0.05087	0.00016	0.00410	0.00466
Regime 2a	0.01326	0.00004	0.00388	0.00029	0.02860	0.00017	0.06434	0.00037	0.00384	0.00819
Regime 2b	0.02538	0.00001	0.01330	0.00344	0.05600	0.00318	0.09088	0.00029	0.00331	0.14579
Regime 3	0.05204	0.00036	0.01458	0.00144	0.01660	0.00036	0.01105	0.00021	0.00373	0.00000
Regime 1'	0.01758	0.00017	0.00170	0.00042	0.02477	0.00007	0.06764	0.00018	0.00397	0.00760
Regime 2a'	0.02848	0.00053	0.02848	0.00270	0.00000	0.00000	0.30351	0.00031	0.00323	0.16551
Regime 3'	0.07777	0.00027	0.04197	0.00310	0.01166	0.00104	0.01058	0.00032	0.00452	0.00000
Regime 2a"	0.00357	0.00085	0.00521	0.00088	0.00032	0.00000	0.27851	0.00028	0.00321	0.09443
Regime 2b"	0.00107	0.00009	0.00519	0.00140	0.00217	0.00082	0.43867	0.00030	0.00169	0.05013
Regime 4"	0.05954	0.05378	0.09994	0.01160	0.25642	0.00589	0.80232	0.00403	0.00096	0.41903
Ten-year variance										
Regime 1	0.02612	0.00309	0.00234	0.00046	0.02772	0.00265	0.04262	0.00408	0.00387	0.00830
Regime 2a	0.01273	0.00149	0.00232	0.00025	0.02250	0.00220	0.05061	0.00494	0.00376	0.01236
Regime 2b	0.02556	0.00272	0.00941	0.00207	0.03763	0.00391	0.07231	0.00500	0.00331	0.07682
Regime 3	0.03846	0.00335	0.00966	0.00155	0.03186	0.00639	0.00735	0.00060	0.00381	0.00000
Regime 1'	0.02155	0.00280	0.00230	0.00046	0.02124	0.00217	0.05792	0.00591	0.00375	0.01277
Regime 2a'	0.01778	0.00313	0.01778	0.00257	0.00000	0.00000	0.29323	0.05012	0.00288	0.13906
Regime 3'	0.05996	0.00637	0.02420	0.00224	0.02978	0.00602	0.00700	0.00070	0.00446	0.00000
Regime 2a"	0.00574	0.00139	0.00543	0.00113	0.00031	0.00004	0.26451	0.03650	0.00295	0.09887
Regime 2b"	0.00076	0.00020	0.00330	0.00077	0.00155	0.00060	0.38894	0.03448	0.00177	0.06865
Regime 4"	0.03113	0.03222	0.08794	0.00907	0.16964	0.00804	0.58953	0.03236	0.00143	0.32042

Rest of OECD

Five-year variance

Regime 1	0.00167	0.00001	0.00311	0.00014	0.00789	0.00011	0.00398	0.00002	0.00076	0.00398
Regime 2a	0.00098	0.00001	0.00346	0.00024	0.00633	0.00018	0.00811	0.00004	0.00084	0.00811
Regime 2b	0.00355	0.00001	0.03381	0.00062	0.05776	0.00075	0.07805	0.01715	0.00027	0.07805
Regime 3	0.00075	0.00001	0.00283	0.00017	0.00130	0.00011	0.00000	0.00000	0.00093	0.00000
Regime 1'	0.00160	0.00001	0.00192	0.00009	0.00580	0.00007	0.00334	0.00002	0.00076	0.00334
Regime 2a'	0.00018	0.00066	0.00018	0.00001	0.00000	0.00000	0.05075	0.00090	0.00048	0.05075
Regime 3'	0.00033	0.00046	0.00492	0.00049	0.00551	0.00046	0.00000	0.00000	0.00141	0.00000
Regime 2a''	0.00625	0.00003	0.00122	0.00007	0.01056	0.00008	0.00986	0.00008	0.00071	0.00986
Regime 2b''	0.00002	0.00000	0.00279	0.00003	0.00248	0.00003	0.04615	0.00038	0.00069	0.04615
Regime 4''	0.01763	0.02189	0.38234	0.03855	0.56337	0.05742	0.50003	0.02851	0.00084	0.50003

Ten-year variance

Regime 1	0.00118	0.00010	0.00189	0.00014	0.00522	0.00033	0.00298	0.00030	0.00055	0.00298
Regime 2a	0.00069	0.00008	0.00188	0.00018	0.00376	0.00028	0.00558	0.00062	0.00055	0.00558
Regime 2b	0.00255	0.00011	0.02030	0.00060	0.03618	0.00102	0.05014	0.01055	0.00036	0.05014
Regime 3	0.00056	0.00009	0.00166	0.00018	0.00135	0.00033	0.00000	0.00000	0.00063	0.00000
Regime 1'	0.00111	0.00009	0.00124	0.00012	0.00399	0.00028	0.00280	0.00040	0.00055	0.00280
Regime 2a'	0.00014	0.00074	0.00014	0.00003	0.00000	0.00000	0.03478	0.00655	0.00041	0.03478
Regime 3'	0.00028	0.00034	0.00273	0.00032	0.00345	0.00051	0.00000	0.00000	0.00094	0.00000
Regime 2a''	0.00406	0.00023	0.00116	0.00026	0.00765	0.00058	0.00802	0.00104	0.00056	0.00802
Regime 2b''	0.00008	0.00004	0.00179	0.00005	0.00150	0.00010	0.03978	0.00865	0.00074	0.03978
Regime 4''	0.00895	0.01163	0.19240	0.01979	0.28344	0.02957	0.26908	0.02159	0.00079	0.26908

(continued)

Table 10A-1 (*continued*)

Regime and variability	Real GNP (log)	Real GNP growth	GNP deflator (log)	Inflation	Nominal GNP	Change in nominal GNP	Short nominal interest rate	Change in nominal interest rate	Current account (%GNP)	Exchange rate (log)
Rest of EMS										
Five-year variance										
Regime 1	0.00294	0.00008	0.00684	0.00053	0.00189	0.00022	0.05087	0.00016	0.00058	0.00565
Regime 2a	0.00813	0.00017	0.00981	0.00100	0.00122	0.00038	0.06434	0.00037	0.00044	0.00875
Regime 2b	0.00203	0.00004	0.02068	0.00325	0.01589	0.00336	0.09088	0.00029	0.00052	0.09898
Regime 3	0.00269	0.00007	0.00771	0.00041	0.00314	0.00015	0.01105	0.00021	0.00116	0.00000
Regime 1'	0.00572	0.00013	0.00633	0.00056	0.00099	0.00016	0.06764	0.00018	0.00053	0.00930
Regime 2a'	0.13952	0.00051	0.04447	0.00352	0.02961	0.00001	0.30350	0.00031	0.00046	0.26943
Regime 3'	0.01175	0.00045	0.02744	0.00212	0.00617	0.00067	0.01058	0.00032	0.00102	0.00585
Regime 2a"	0.06158	0.00104	0.01067	0.00134	0.02425	0.00002	0.27850	0.00028	0.00039	0.10004
Regime 2b"	0.05258	0.00055	0.01152	0.00299	0.02751	0.00105	0.43867	0.00030	0.00059	0.06003
Regime 4"	0.19801	0.05642	0.09216	0.01257	0.47269	0.00559	0.80230	0.00403	0.00257	0.97394
Ten-year variance										
Regime 1	0.00178	0.00009	0.00362	0.00034	0.00180	0.00028	0.04262	0.00408	0.00036	0.00719
Regime 2a	0.00517	0.00025	0.00545	0.00067	0.00362	0.00069	0.05061	0.00494	0.00032	0.01025
Regime 2b	0.00148	0.00011	0.01086	0.00174	0.00975	0.00197	0.07230	0.00500	0.00034	0.05189
Regime 3	0.00169	0.00020	0.00422	0.00036	0.00270	0.00053	0.00735	0.00060	0.00069	0.00000
Regime 1'	0.00346	0.00016	0.00346	0.00038	0.00203	0.00036	0.05792	0.00591	0.00034	0.01129
Regime 2a'	0.07894	0.00462	0.02535	0.00326	0.03291	0.00403	0.29323	0.05102	0.00033	0.20470
Regime 3'	0.00632	0.00219	0.01455	0.00140	0.00498	0.00075	0.00700	0.00070	0.00058	0.00649
Regime 2a"	0.03743	0.00206	0.00782	0.00146	0.02785	0.00332	0.26451	0.03650	0.00031	0.08824
Regime 2b"	0.03433	0.00178	0.00990	0.00216	0.03678	0.00403	0.38893	0.03448	0.00048	0.06087
Regime 4"	0.11551	0.03469	0.08208	0.00943	0.33635	0.01141	0.58952	0.03236	0.00144	0.63244

Table 10A-2. *Variance-Covariance Matrix of Residuals*

	United States			Japan			Germany			
Country	Consumption (% U.S. GNP)	Money demand (log)	Production (log)	Consumption (% U.S. GNP)	Money demand (log)	Production (log)	Consumption (% U.S. GNP)	Money demand (log)	Production (log)	OPEC prices (log)
United States										
Consumption (% U.S. GNP)	0.00012									
Money demand (log)	0.00015	0.00067								
Production (log)	0.00083	0.00249	0.01536							
Japan										
Consumption (% U.S. GNP)	0.00005	0.00021	0.00144	0.00018						
Money demand (log)	0.00078	0.00161	0.01069	0.00044	0.00844					
Production (log)	0.00039	0.00106	0.00633	0.00027	0.00446	0.00269				
Germany										
Consumption (% U.S. GNP)	−0.00006	−0.00009	−0.00072	−0.00005	−0.00063	−0.00032	0.00006			
Money demand (log)	0.00013	0.00040	0.00305	0.00014	0.00223	0.00121	−0.00004	0.00079		
Production (log)	0.00055	0.00164	0.00934	0.00040	0.00653	0.00388	−0.00009	0.00175	0.00579	
OPEC prices (log)	0.00012	0.00015	0.00083	0.00002	0.00078	0.00039	−0.00001	0.00013	0.00055	0.00012

References

Bryant, R. C., D. A. Currie, J. A. Frenkel, P. R. Masson, and R. Portes. 1989. *Macroeconomic Policies in an Interdependent World*. Washington: Brookings, Centre for Economic Policy Research, and International Monetary Fund.

Frenkel, J. A., M. Goldstein, and P. R. Masson. 1989. "Simulating the Effects of Some Simple Coordinated versus Uncoordinated Policy Rules." In Bryant, Currie, and others (1989), 203–39.

McKibbin, W. J. 1987. "Numerical Solution of Rational Expectations Models, with and without Strategic Behavior." Research Discussion Paper 8706. Canberra: Reserve Bank of Australia.

———. 1989. "The World Economy from 1979 to 1988: Results from the MSG2 Model." Brookings Discussion Paper in International Economics 72.

McKibbin, W. J., and J. D. Sachs. 1986. "Comparing the Global Performance of Alternative Exchange Arrangements." National Bureau of Economic Research Working Paper 2000. Revised in *Journal of International Money and Finance* 7:387–410.

———. 1989. "Implications of Policy Rules for the World Economy." In Bryant and others (1989), 151–94.

———. 1991. *Global Linkages: Macroeconomic Interdependence and Cooperation in the World Economy*. Brookings.

Pauly, P., and C. Petersen. 1990. "Feedback Rules for Nominal-Income Targeting." Paper prepared for Brookings Conference on Empirical Evaluation of Alternative Policy Regimes. Washington, March 8–9.

Taylor, J. B. 1989. "Policy Analysis with a Multi-Country Model." In Bryant, Currie, and others (1989), 122–41.

CHAPTER 11

Policy Analysis
and Model Reduction Techniques
with the Global Economic Model

Nicos Christodoulakis, David Currie, Anthony Garratt,
David Kemball-Cook, Paul Levine, Ray Barrell,
Jonathan Ireland, and Peter Westaway

THE DESIGN of robust, well-behaved policy rules is typically a complex, time-consuming, and computer-intensive process.[1] Ideally it involves the application of control theory to produce well-designed but simple policy rules; it involves designing rules that are robust in their performance with respect to different types of shocks, to variations in model specification (including alternative expectations schemes), and even to different models; and it involves examination of the incentive compatibility of the different rules, raising issues of time inconsistency and, in the international context, the sustainability of cooperative rules.

To investigate all these issues together is an ambitious task. To investigate them all in a nonlinear, large-scale macroeconometric model may well be grossly overambitious. The computer power and time required for such control exercises rise sharply with the scale of the model, and nonlinearity necessitates the use of Monte Carlo methods to determine the performance of alternative policy rules in the face of stochastic disturbances. With linear models, by contrast, it is possible to solve analytically for the stochastic properties. These features do not preclude the investigation of one or two of the above issues using a large nonlinear model, but they make it almost impossible to investigate all the issues together.

This chapter sets out and applies a methodology for developing a reduced, linearized version of a large-scale, nonlinear model that may be used for policy analysis and design. In our application, we use the large, nonlinear Global Economic Model (GEM), which is maintained jointly by the National Institute of Economic and Social Research and the London Business School and which is

---

1. The authors of this paper use the word "rule" rather than "regime" when referring to the analytical representations of operating procedures followed by national monetary authorities. See chapter 1 for a discussion of terminology. In the sense of chapter 1, the "rules" of this chapter could equally well be labeled "regimes." [Eds.]

used by both institutions (as well as other U.K. and international agencies) for forecasting world developments. Given its forecasting use, it is necessarily large, disaggregated, and nonlinear. These features make it difficult to undertake systematic policy analysis, although they by no means preclude it. (See, for example, the stochastic simulations reported elsewhere in this volume, and the policy exercises carried out by Currie and Wren-Lewis 1989, 1990.) The development of a reduced, linearized model, MINIGEM, that reproduces the key features of the parent model, GEM, will enormously enhance the range of policy design and analysis that can be undertaken with GEM. Validation of results derived from MINIGEM using the parent model will ensure that the model reduction and linearization are not biasing the results in any appreciable way.

Construction of MINIGEM

The linear representation, MINIGEM, of a three-bloc version of the parent model, GEM, comprises the following:

Bloc 1 (dollar bloc): United States
Bloc 2 (deutsche mark bloc): Germany, United Kingdom, France, and Italy
Bloc 3 (yen bloc): Japan.

Thus, we have focused on the Group of Six (G6) economies[2] and have assumed the rest of the world to be exogenous and passive. The aggregation of the countries into blocs was necessary in order to reduce the number of state variables in the linear model to a low number: preserving all the country detail of the parent model would produce a very large representation, contrary to the objective of this exercise.

The procedure that we followed includes several steps: to drop the exchange-rate equations of the parent model, to construct a reduced, linearized version of the main model with exchange rates exogenous, and then to reintroduce the exchange-rate equation into the linearized model and complete the representation of the main model. Model validation was carried out on the full model, including exchange-rate equations.

Before the linearization could be done, three preliminary stages had to be carried out. The first stage was to define the base run about which the model was linearized. The second stage was to identify and define the GEM variables (referred to as outputs) whose behavior when perturbed would be of interest in

---

2. The Group of Seven (G7), excluding Canada. Later versions may include the Benelux countries (Belgium, the Netherlands, and Luxembourg) in bloc 2 and the newly industrialized countries (NICs) in bloc 3.

the linear model. The third stage was to determine the GEM variables (known as inputs) to which the appropriate perturbations, or shocks, would be given. These disturbances, when applied to the nonlinear GEM, provided trajectories of the output variables, which were then used to generate multipliers (relative to base). In turn, the multipliers were used as the basis for linearization. This exercise as well as the stochastic realization and simulation of the next section was carried out using the software package LACES, which has been developed at the London Business School.

Implementing the Three Preliminary Stages

In the first stage of the linearization procedure, the definition of the base run, we required that the base run be smooth throughout the whole period, in order to minimize the degree of base dependency. The base run was formed using the National Institute world forecasts, published in the *National Institute Economic Review*. Forty quarterly periods, 1990:1–1999:4, were included. (For more detail see Barrell, Gurney, and Dulake 1990.)

In the second stage, definition of outputs, three output variables for each bloc were chosen, making a total of nine outputs. They were real output (Y), using GNP; inflation (IF), measured as the annual percentage increase in the GDP price deflator; and current balance to GNP ratio (CB), as a percentage. For blocs 1 and 3 the GEM variables used to define the outputs were individual country variables (the United States and Japan respectively); for bloc 2 the variables were defined in deutsche marks where appropriate and were weighted averages of the individual country variables.

In the third stage, GEM was subjected to a number of inputs or shocks in order to generate a series of multipliers for the outputs. In these exercises, forward expectations (which are treated as distinct inputs) were exogenized. The choice of inputs had to be sufficiently varied in order to represent as fully as possible the dynamic properties of the parent GEM, and needed to include monetary, fiscal, and exogenous inputs. Each perturbation was applied in turn, keeping all other input variables exogenous at their base values. All the perturbations were permanent. Multipliers were then obtained in two different ways, depending on the nature of the output. First, if the output variable represented a *stock* or a *flow*, the appropriate multiplier for each time period was obtained as the percentage difference of the perturbed value from the base value (both at the same time period); that is, the difference between the two divided by the base and multiplied by 100. A variable of this kind is output (Y). In the second method, if the output variable represented a *rate*, then the multiplier was calculated simply as the difference between the perturbed value and the base, expressed in percentage terms. Variables of this kind are inflation (IF) and current balance (CB). To help compensate for possible asymmetries and nonlinearities in the parent model, perturbations were applied in each case in both negative and positive directions. The mean of the absolute values from the positive and negative shocks was then used to produce one series of multipliers.

The exchange-rate variables were defined as inputs rather than outputs because the exchange-rate equations were dropped for the purpose of model reduction and then reintroduced into the reduced representation. The treatment of the exchange rate at the input stage is worth noting. We defined the exchange rate in real terms, whereas in GEM it is defined in nominal terms. The real exchange rate was defined in the base run, where the nominal exchange rates are defined according to the open-arbitrage condition with risk premiums. Interest rate paths were set to ensure that current account equilibrium was reached by the end of the forecast period. Countries with higher-than-average real interest rates depreciate in real terms in the base, and those with lower-than-average real interest rates appreciate. In addition, for all inputs, the nominal exchange rates were redefined as the reciprocal of the real rates, where real exchange rates are exogenous. Hence in the simulations on nonlinear GEM, nominal exchange rates moved according to price differentials between blocs, with real exchange rates fixed to base. The simulations reported below in figures 11-1–11-4 follow this procedure. In examining the effects of alternative policies, we treated the perturbations and associated inputs as follows:

Rules 1–3:   An increase in real government expenditure (GV), using government consumption in each of the blocs, such that the effect approximated a 1 percent increase in GNP. For bloc 2, the composite input involves each country in the bloc increasing government expenditure at the same time. Three separate inputs were defined, one for each of the blocs (GV_1, GV_2, and GV_3).

Rules 4–6:   A lowering of real interest rates (IT) by 2 percentage points in each of the blocs (1 percent in bloc 3). Each country in the deutsche mark bloc lowers interest rates at the same time and by the same amount. Three separate inputs are defined (IT_1, IT_2, IT_3).

Rule 7:   A 20 percent increase in commodity prices, excluding oil ($COMM$), for the four commodities: food, in both developed and undeveloped countries; minerals; ores and metals in developing countries; and wages and prices of nonfood agricultural products.

Rule 8:   A 20 percent increase in oil prices (OIL).

Rules 9–10:   A 5 percent increase in each of the two real exchange rates, where the rates are defined to be those of blocs 2 and 3 relative to bloc 1. They represent a depreciation for blocs 2 and 3 and define two additional inputs (R_{12}, R_{13}).

The Structure of the Linear Model

The multipliers in the linear model are defined as outcomes from a dynamic system that is determined from four matrices $\mathbf{A}$, $\mathbf{B}$, $\mathbf{C}$, and $\mathbf{D}$. (These matrices are the outcome of a linearization algorithm described in the appendix.) The system is defined in the following way:

$$(11\text{-}1) \qquad\qquad \mathbf{x}_{t+1} = \mathbf{A}\mathbf{x}_t + \mathbf{B} \begin{bmatrix} \mathbf{w}_t \\ \mathbf{v}_t \\ \mathbf{er}_t \end{bmatrix},$$

$$(11\text{-}2) \qquad\qquad \mathbf{y}_t = \mathbf{C}\mathbf{x}_t + \mathbf{D} \begin{bmatrix} \mathbf{w}_t \\ \mathbf{v}_t \\ \mathbf{er}_t \end{bmatrix},$$

where

$$\mathbf{w}_t = \text{instruments} = \begin{bmatrix} IT_1 \\ IT_2 \\ IT_3 \\ GV_1 \\ GV_2 \\ GV_3 \end{bmatrix}, \quad \mathbf{v}_t = \text{exogenous shocks} = \begin{bmatrix} COMM \\ OIL \end{bmatrix},$$

$$\mathbf{y}_t = \text{outputs} = \begin{bmatrix} Y_1 \\ Y_2 \\ Y_3 \\ IF_1 \\ IF_2 \\ IF_3 \\ CB_1 \\ CB_2 \\ CB_3 \end{bmatrix}, \quad \mathbf{er}_t = \text{real exchange rates} = \begin{bmatrix} R_{12} \\ R_{13} \end{bmatrix} = \mathbf{j}_t,$$

and IT_i and GV_i define fiscal and monetary instruments respectively, and Y_i, IF_i, and CB_i define output, inflation, and the current balance to GNP ratio for blocs $i = 1, 2, 3$ respectively. $COMM$ and OIL are the exogenous commodity and oil price shocks. R_{12} and R_{13} represent the real exchange rates of blocs 2 and 3 with respect to bloc 1, where an increase in either variable represents a bloc 2 or bloc 3 depreciation.

The input variables correspond to $\mathbf{w}_t$ and $\mathbf{v}_t$, and the outputs to $\mathbf{y}_t$; the state vector $\mathbf{x}_t$ is a compressed expression of the endogenous vector of the nonlinear model and bears no apparent economic interpretation. The state vector, $\mathbf{x}_t$, may be seen as analogous to the concept of principal components of the original system.

Comparison of Linear and Nonlinear GEM

A first step in the validation of linearization is the simple comparison of the multipliers derived from nonlinear GEM with those from MINIGEM. This comparison of backward-looking trajectories under fixed real exchange rates is reported in this section. Following that, we describe how MINIGEM is enhanced by the addition of exchange rates as jumping variables and report on further steps taken in the validation.

The linearization was carried out with an order of thirty-five and achieved a root-mean-squared error of 0.00003 in absolute terms, or 0.0016 as a percentage of the maximum value of the multipliers. To illustrate the accuracy of the linearization, we compare the multipliers of the parent model, GEM, with those of MINIGEM, for a subset of inputs and for the periods 1990:1–1999:4. Figures 11-1–11-4 plot the multipliers for output and inflation for the following inputs.

Figure 11-1 plots the effects of a 5 percent increase in bloc-1 real government consumption on the bloc-1 outputs defined above. As in all the simulations in figures 11-1–11-4, the real exchange rates and all other inputs are held exogenous (although in figure 11-4 real exchange rates are increased by 5 percent and then held exogenous). There are no appreciable differences in the multipliers of GEM and MINIGEM. The pattern of the multipliers is broadly consistent with both output and inflation increasing. Figure 11-2 plots the effects of a decrease of 2 percentage points in bloc-1 real interest rates on bloc-1 outputs, as defined above. The two sets of multipliers are virtually identical—the response to an expansionary monetary policy is to increase output and inflation. Figure 11-3

Figure 11-1. *The Effects of a 5 Percent Increase in Real Government Consumption (in Bloc 1)*

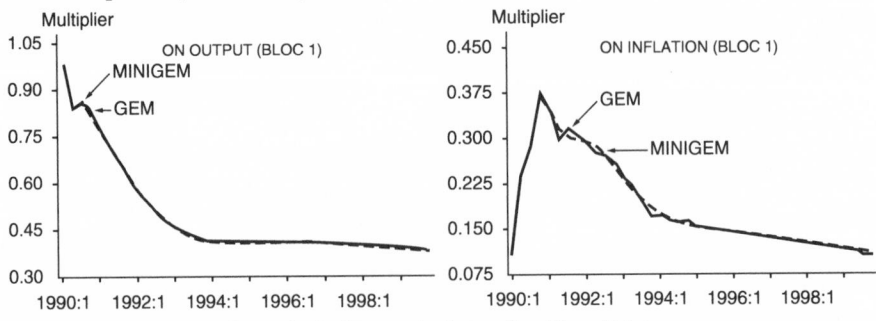

Source: Authors' calculations. See text for details concerning the formation of the multipliers.

Figure 11-2. *The Effects of a 2 Percentage Point Decrease in Real Interest Rates (in Bloc 1)*

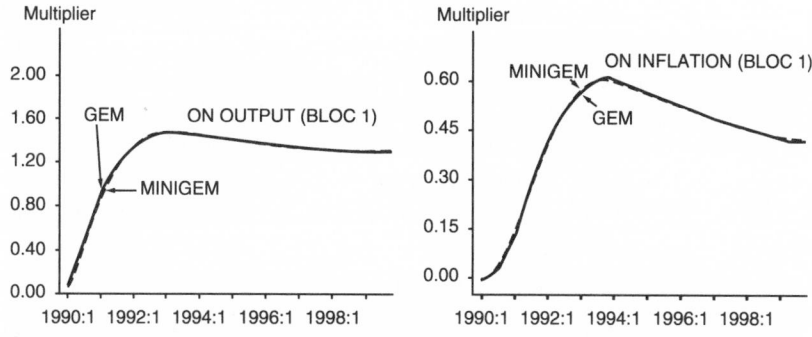

Source: Authors' calculations. See text for details concerning the formation of the multipliers.

Figure 11-3. *The Effects of a 20 Percent Increase in Commodity Prices (in Bloc 1)*

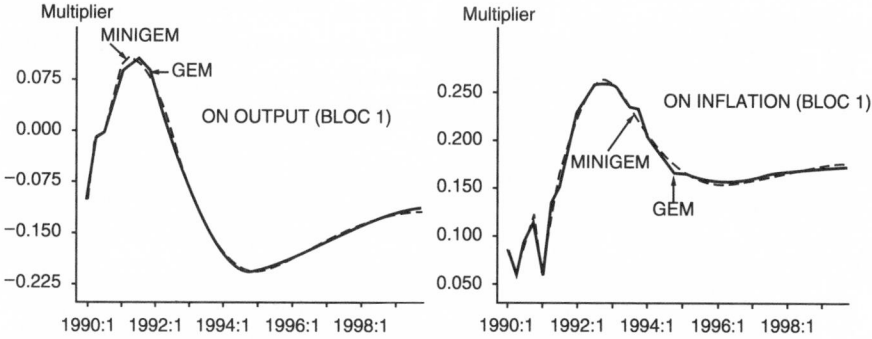

Source: Authors' calculations. See text for details concerning the formation of the multipliers.

Figure 11-4. *The Effects of a 5 Percent Depreciation of the Real Exchange Rate (between Bloc 2 and Bloc 1)*

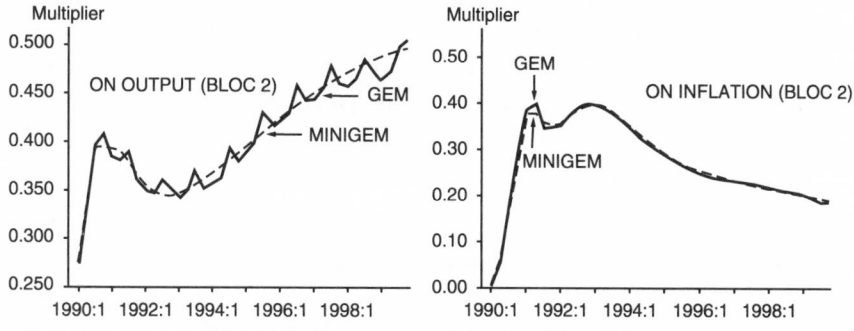

Source: Authors' calculations. See text for details concerning the formation of the multipliers.

plots the effects of a 20 percent increase in commodity prices (excluding oil) on bloc-1 outputs. The two sets of multipliers are very similar. The results are consistent with the observation that bloc 1 and the less-developed countries are the major commodity exporters and blocs 2 and 3 are major importers of commodities. Hence, a commodity-price increase causes inflation in bloc 1 with a small negative effect on output. Figure 11-4 plots the effects of a 5 percent depreciation of the real exchange rate between bloc 2 and bloc 1 (R_{12}) on bloc-2 outputs. The two sets of multipliers are virtually identical, with both output and inflation increasing as a result of an appreciating dollar or a depreciating deutsche mark.

The subset of multipliers in the four sets of figures are an attempt to show a range of outputs, subject to a range of fiscal, monetary, and exogenous inputs. The fits are very good and this applies to all of the output and input combinations used.

Exchange-Rate Equations

Having obtained a linearized version of GEM defined by the matrices **A**, **B**, **C**, and **D**, we then introduce the exchange-rate equations into MINIGEM. The exchange-rate equations, which define the two jumping variables, take the following form:

$$(11\text{-}3) \qquad R_{12,t+1} = R_{12,t} + 0.25(IT_{2,t} - IT_{1,t}) - \alpha_1 CB_{1,t} + \alpha_2 CB_{2,t}$$

$$(11\text{-}4) \qquad R_{13,t+1} = R_{13,t} + 0.25(IT_{3,t} - IT_{1,t}) - \alpha_3 CB_{1,t} + \alpha_4 CB_{3,t},$$

where IT_i for $i = 1, 2$, and 3 defines annual real interest rates for blocs 1, 2, and 3, and CB_1, CB_2, and CB_3 are ratios of current balances to nominal income for blocs 1, 2, and 3. Equations 11-3 and 11-4 represent basic UIP (uncovered interest parity) relationships with a risk premium related to the current account balance. The risk premiums were chosen to be small but to act to ensure current account balance in the long run. The choice of alternative formulations of the risk premium (for example, cumulated net asset positions in relation to income) would allow alternative long-run external terminal conditions to be imposed: the choice of current account balance was made here to be consistent with the current choice of terminal condition in the parent GEM.

Further Steps in Validation

A further stage in the validation is to compare forward-looking MINIGEM trajectories with those from forward-looking GEM. This is a very stringent validation exercise, since it involves the solution of the trajectories for the forward-looking exchange-rate variables using an extended Blanchard-Kahn solution method and comparing these trajectories with those for the parent model, solved using a nonlinear solution method. Because the long-run properties of the model influence the entire trajectory of the exchange rate and must therefore be sensible, this is a strong test for both the parent model and the reduction technique. For this exercise we examine a range of outputs, depicted in figure 11-5, in response to a positive shock to bloc 1's government consumption equal to 1 percent of its baseline GNP. The exchange-rate equations used in this exercise for both MINIGEM and nonlinear GEM are those described in equations 11-3 and 11-4.

Comparisons of the trajectories of endogenous variables in GEM with those in MINIGEM show that for blocs 1 and 2 the fits are very close. For bloc 3 the fit appears to be less good for the real exchange rate, but because the deviations of the variable are not large this error is not particularly significant. This test underscores the validity of MINIGEM as a linear approximation to the parent model, GEM.

Results from Policy Simulations on MINIGEM

Using GEM base-run data from 1979:1–1989:4 for output variables ($\mathbf{Y}_t$), a stochastic realization in deviation form was obtained (see appendix, equation 11A-16). Time trends and constants were removed as described above and noise covariance matrices were then evaluated. Welfare loss was defined as

$$(11\text{-}5) \qquad W_0 = \frac{1}{2} \sum_{t=0}^{\infty} \lambda^t \left(\sum_i Y_{i,t}^2 + \sum_i IF_{i,t}^2 + 0.1 \sum \Delta NIT_{i,t}^2 \right),$$

where Y_i, IF_i, and ΔNIT_i are real output, annual inflation (in percent), and quarterly change in nominal interest rate for bloc i. This form was chosen to be consistent with that specified by Brookings for the stochastic exercises reported elsewhere in this volume.

The investigations of policy rules were carried out in two stages. In the first stage the stochastic realization was used to evaluate rules according to asymptotic welfare loss where there was no deterministic shock, and the asymptotic covariance matrix of outputs was produced in each case. The optimization techniques available enabled the "optimal" simple rule of each form to be discovered (that which minimized asymptotic welfare loss). In the second stage the optimal rules in each class were evaluated in the face of certain deterministic shocks, both temporary and permanent.

Figure 11-5. *The Effects of a 5.14 Percent Increase in Government Consumption (in Bloc 1), or a 1 Percent Shock to GNP (in Bloc 1)*

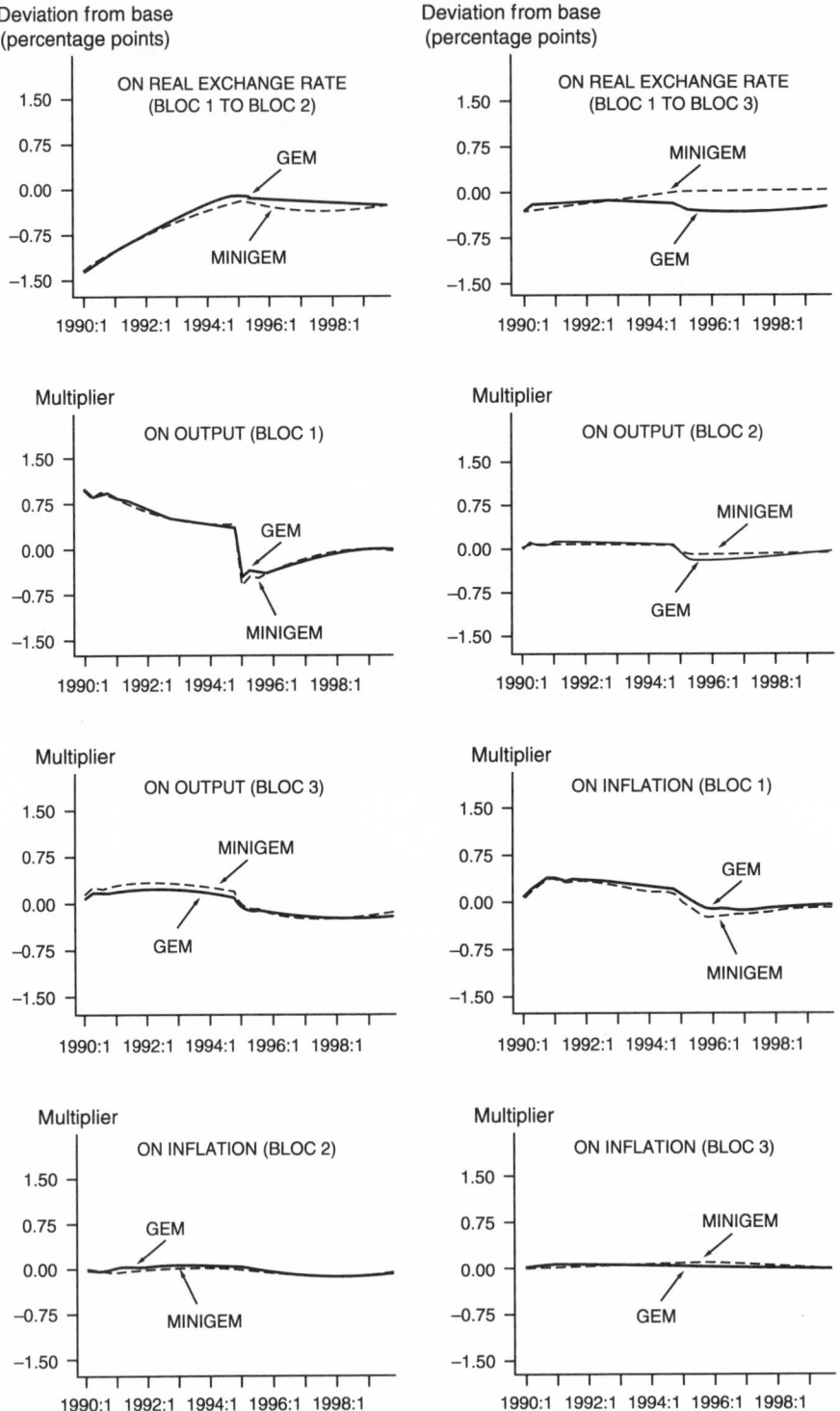

Source: Authors' calculations. See text for details concerning the formation of the multipliers.

Table 11-1. *Best Simple Rules and Optimal Policies*

Rule	Stochastic welfare loss	Coefficients of best simple rules
No control: fixed real interest rates	237.72	...
Monetary rule (1a)(αIF)	231.93	$\alpha =$ 0.232
Monetary rule (1b)($\alpha IF + \beta Y$)	202.65	$\alpha =$ 0.193
		$\beta =$ 1.067
Optimal monetary policy	168.24	...
Fiscal rule (2)($\gamma IF_{-1} + \delta Y_{-1}$)	202.41	$\gamma = -1.17$
		$\delta = -3.71$
Combined monetary and fiscal rule (3)	189.80	...
($IT = \alpha IF + \beta Y$,		$\alpha =$ 0.119
$GV = \gamma IF_{-1} + \delta Y_{-1}$)		$\beta =$ 0.759
Optimal monetary and fiscal policy	140.23	$\gamma = -0.918$
		$\delta = -3.338$
		...

Source: Authors' calculations.

The simple rules investigated included a subset of the rules proposed by Brookings, augmented by various fiscal rules; they follow:

Rule 1a: Monetary rule (feedback on inflation), $IT_{i,t} = \alpha IF_{i,t}$,

Rule 1b: Monetary rule (inflation and output), $IT_{i,t} = \alpha IF_{i,t} + \beta Y_{i,t}$,

Rule 2: Fiscal rule (lagged inflation and output), $GV_{i,t} = \gamma IF_{i,t-1} + \delta Y_{i,t-1}$,

Rule 3: Combined fiscal and monetary rule (inflation and output), $IT_{i,t} = \alpha IF_{i,t} + \beta Y_{i,t}, GV_{i,t} = \gamma IF_{i,t-1} + \delta Y_{i,t-1}$,

where all variables are expressed in appropriate deviation form as described in the preceding sections. IF_i is the inflation rate (in percent) in bloc i, Y_i is real GNP, IT_i is real interest rates (in percent), and GV_i is real government expenditure—all measured on an annual basis. Fiscal policy was allowed to respond only with a one-quarter delay, so as to allow for implementation lags. To provide a basis for comparison, full optimal rules were also computed, both for monetary policy alone and for the joint use of monetary and fiscal policy.

Table 11-1 reports the optimal coefficients for the various simple feedback rules, together with the associated welfare losses, and the results for optimal policy. The monetary rule 1a, where interest rates feed back on inflation, is virtually equivalent to a policy of fixed real interest rates: the feedback coefficient is small, and the welfare loss scarcely falls. When feedback on output is also allowed for, the performance of the monetary rule improves, with a significant drop in welfare loss. Note that the main feedback is on output; the coefficient on inflation remains small. Relative to the full optimal rules, this rule gives about one-half of the possible gain in performance.

Table 11-2. *Standard Deviations of Key Variables under Various Rules*

Standard deviations

		Monetary rule			Fiscal rule	Joint rule	
Variable	No control	(1a)	(1b)	Optimal	(2)	(3)	Optimal
Output							
United States (Y_1)	0.69	0.68	0.57	0.39	0.59	0.53	0.14
Europe (Y_2)	0.85	0.87	0.67	o.50	0.73	0.67	0.30
Japan (Y_3)	1.20	1.17	0.82	0.38	1.02	0.80	0.13
Inflation							
United States (IF_1)	0.51	0.65	0.65	0.51	0.63	0.65	0.49
Europe (IF_2)	1.30	1.26	1.30	1.00	1.27	1.29	0.85
Japan (IF_3)	0.92	0.90	0.94	0.84	0.92	0.93	0.80
Real interest rates							
United States (IT_1)	0.00	0.15	0.63	0.77	0.00	0.41	1.48
Europe (IT_2)	0.00	0.28	0.74	1.24	0.00	0.49	3.07
Japan (IT_3)	0.00	0.21	0.56	1.47	0.00	0.93	1.01
Government expenditure							
United States (GV_1)	0.00	0.00	0.00	0.00	1.82	1.36	7.98
Europe (GV_2)	0.00	0.00	0.00	0.00	1.87	1.43	8.72
Japan (GV_3)	0.00	0.00	0.00	0.00	3.48	2.33	5.72

Source: Authors' calculations using the following equations—monetary rule (1a): $IT_i = 0.23\ IF_i$; monetary rule (1b): $IT_i = 0.19\ IF_i + 1.07Y_i$; fiscal rule (2): $GV_i = -1.17IF_i(-1) - 3.71Y_i(-1)$; and combined monetary and fiscal rule (3): $IT_i = 0.20\ IF_i + 0.76Y_i$, $GV_i = -0.92IF_i(-1) - 3.34Y_i(-1)$.

Table 11-1 also reports on fiscal feedback rules. Rule 2 is a feedback including fiscal policy alone (that is, accompanied by fixed real interest rates). This gives a welfare performance similar to that for monetary policy obtained by strong fiscal feedbacks on both output and inflation. (On the unrealistic assumption of no implementation lag for fiscal policy, the fiscal feedback becomes very powerful with a large associated welfare gain.) Combining this with monetary feedback rule 3 gives a further gain in welfare, and comparison with the welfare loss under the full optimal monetary and fiscal policy shows that this simple rule obtains about one-half of the possible gain. Comparing β for rules 1b and 3 shows that the presence of fiscal feedback reduces somewhat the role for monetary feedback on output.

Table 11-2 reports the standard deviations of output, inflation, real interest rates, and government spending under the various rules. This shows that the main benefits of the rules accrue in terms of output stabilization: inflation variability is scarcely altered, and indeed in the United States it rises. It also shows that the benefits of the rules accrue differently to the different blocs: Japan, in particular, benefits more from output stabilization than the other blocs. This suggests that the sustainability of cooperation over rules of this type requires examination. The fact that simple monetary-policy rules give a rather low benefit in GEM in terms of stabilizing inflation and output requires some explanation.

The low benefit does *not* arise because monetary policy is ineffective in GEM: indeed, there are quite powerful interest rate effects operating in GEM, especially in Japan. (For a discussion of this, see Currie and Wren-Lewis 1990.) Rather, it arises because of the difficulties of timing interest rate changes so as to be stabilizing. (This is the case even if information and implementation lags are ignored, as in the exercise reported here.) It is perfectly possible to design a rule that stabilizes demand by interest-rate variation operating through the direct channels of influence on domestic demand. However, the exchange rate reacts to these interest-rate variations, and because of the UIP condition for the exchange rate, the exchange rate reacts to the expected forward cumulation of interest-rate deviations. This exchange-rate change then feeds through with significant lags to net export demand and prices. The problem is that these influences through the exchange rate are poorly timed to stabilize output and inflation, and this seems to be true for any feedback coefficient. Indeed, as the feedback coefficient rises, this exchange-rate feedback adds to volatility, and stabilization performance deteriorates. It is therefore not possible to find an interest-rate feedback rule of the form investigated here that successfully stabilizes output and inflation in the face of ongoing stochastic shocks, because the exchange-rate effects operate against the direct demand effects. The answer to this difficulty is to investigate more general dynamic specifications for the monetary feedback rule. A more general specification, still within the class of simple rules, should allow a better stabilization performance for monetary policy, since it can be chosen to prevent these two channels of influence (the direct demand effect of interest rates and the exchange-rate reaction) from interfering with one another. The investigation of more general rules of this kind will be the subject of further research.

Table 11-3 reports the performance of the various rules in the face of exogenous oil- and commodity-price shocks. (The coefficients are chosen as optimal for the stochastic case. The contrast to the stochastic case, which investigates the effects of endogenous uncertainty arising from the unexplained errors in model relationships, should be noted.) It should be noted that the welfare ranking of the various rules in the stochastic case does not carry over to the deterministic shocks. The combined monetary and fiscal rule 3 performs poorly in the face of temporary deterministic commodity- and oil-price shocks, though the welfare consequences are small. More significantly, the monetary rule 1b gives nearly as good a performance in the face of a permanent oil shock, compared with the joint rule 3. It also does better in the face of a permanent commodity-price shock (though both rules give a good performance compared with the other rules). These results suggest that simple rules may not be robust in performance, unless designed specifically with robustness in mind. Subsequent research will systematically investigate the design of simple robust rules in the context of MINIGEM.

Table 11-3. *Welfare Performance of Best Simple Rules and Optimal Policies*

| | Stochastic case | Deterministic case | | | |
| | | Oil price shock | | Commodity price shock | |
		Permanent	Temporary	Permanent	Temporary
No control	237.72	11.24	0.12	78.01	0.18
Monetary rule (1a)	231.93	12.73	0.12	46.98	0.18
Monetary rule (1b)	202.65	3.96	0.10	8.44	0.18
Optimal monetary policy	168.24	3.17	0.09	4.47	0.15
Fiscal rule (2)	202.41	8.04	0.17	30.41	0.26
Combined monetary and fiscal rule (3)	189.80	3.91	0.14	8.77	0.22
Optimal monetary and fiscal policy	140.23	3.88	0.06	3.06	0.10

Source: Authors' calculations.

Conclusion

This chapter has been concerned with demonstrating the feasibility of using model reduction and linearization methods to produce a faithful representation of a large-scale, nonlinear macroeconometric model, and then to use this representation to undertake policy analysis. The reduced-version global model, MINIGEM, was shown to reproduce reasonably faithfully the properties of the GEM parent model. (See the appendix for greater detail on our methodology.) The optimal policy rules and their performance are easily derived using MINIGEM, and the results suggest that the particular rules chosen in the Brookings exercise are not particularly robust with respect to different types of shocks. What is needed is the systematic design of simple rules with robustness explicitly considered, possibly involving somewhat more general dynamic forms for the rules. The investigation of robust policy rules in MINIGEM represents a current line of research enquiry.

Appendix: Methodology and Techniques

In this appendix, we set out the procedure used for obtaining a stochastic linearization of a given nonlinear model and for designing optimal simple rules given the variance-covariance of the stochastic terms. A full treatment of the techniques described here may be found in Christodoulakis (1989b) and Levine, Currie, and Gaines (1989).

Linearization Methodology

We first briefly summarize the linearization methodology. Nonlinear GEM has the general form:

(11A-1) $$f(\mathbf{Y}_t, \mathbf{U}_t, \mathbf{Z}_t, t) = 0,$$

where

> $\mathbf{Y}_t$ = a selected vector of M endogenous variables including lags
>
> $\mathbf{U}_t$ = a vector of N exogenous or exogenized variables, including both policy instruments and selected exogenous variables
>
> $\mathbf{Z}_t$ = the remaining endogenous and exogenous variables that are not explicitly represented by the linearization.

The first stage of the linearization exercise is to obtain a base run given by

(11A-2) $$f(\bar{\mathbf{Y}}_t, \bar{\mathbf{U}}_t, \bar{\mathbf{Z}}_t, t) + \bar{\mathbf{e}}_t = 0,$$

where, over the historical period, $\bar{\mathbf{Y}}_t$, $\bar{\mathbf{U}}_t$, and $\bar{\mathbf{Z}}_t$ consist of historical data and $\bar{\mathbf{e}}_t$ denotes single-equation residuals chosen so that endogenous variables take their historically observed values whereas, over the forecast period, exogenous variables and constant adjustments are fixed at predicted and judgmental values respectively.

The second stage is to perturb the N selected exogenous variables, $\mathbf{U}_t$, to obtain multipliers between $\mathbf{Y}_t$ and $\mathbf{U}_t$. The linearization procedure requires that the multipliers are carefully chosen so as to be stationary. Denoting perturbations about the base run using lowercase letters, we write

$$\mathbf{u}_t = \mathbf{U}_t - \bar{\mathbf{U}}_t \qquad \text{if } \mathbf{U}_t \text{ is a rate or ratio}$$

(11A-3) $$= (\mathbf{U}_t - \mathbf{U}_t)/\bar{\mathbf{U}}_t$$

$$\text{or} = \log \mathbf{U}_t - \log \mathbf{U}_t \qquad \text{otherwise,}$$

and similarly for perturbations $\mathbf{y}_i$ of endogenous variables.

The linearization algorithm is based on the "balanced realization" method, which has been used in engineering applications and more recently in time-series analysis (Aoki and Havenner 1986). The original algorithm is due to Kung (1978). Maciejowski and Vines (1984) were the first to apply the algorithm to large macroeconomic models. Christodoulakis (1989a) extends the algorithm in a number of ways, the most important of them to handle rational expectations.

The third stage, the linearization procedure, leads to a state-space representation of the form

(11A-4a) $$\mathbf{x}_{t+1} = \mathbf{A}\mathbf{x}_t + \mathbf{B}\mathbf{u}_t$$

(11A-4b) $$\mathbf{y}_t = \mathbf{C}\mathbf{x}_t + \mathbf{D}\mathbf{u}_t,$$

where $\mathbf{x}_t$ is a constructed state vector that has a number of important dynamic properties. First, it is asymptotically stable; that is, all the eigenvalues of matrix $\mathbf{A}$ lie strictly inside the unit disc in the complex plane. Second, the order of the system is minimal in the sense that it does not include superfluous dynamics. Third, the realization has the implication that the matrix pair $(\mathbf{A}, \mathbf{B})$ is controllable and $(\mathbf{C}, \mathbf{A})$ is observable. Another useful property of a balanced-model representation is the nesting of the system matrices, $\mathbf{A}, \mathbf{B}, \mathbf{C}, \mathbf{D}$; that is, any lower-dimensional model can be read by taking the leading principal submatrices of $\mathbf{A}$ and $\mathbf{C}$ and the corresponding upper bloc of $\mathbf{B}$. These lower-dimensional nested models have the stability properties of the original model.

The order of reduction in the linear approximation is the number of state variables in the linear representation. These variables model the dynamic behavior of the system, and their number is chosen to achieve (if possible) an acceptable trade-off between the need for a linear model of manageable size and that for minimizing the differences between the original (supplied) multipliers and the multipliers produced by the approximation. (The larger is the order, the more accurate the approximation becomes.) For an overall measure of the accuracy of the approximation, we use the root-mean-squared error, defined as follows:

$$\psi = \left\{ \sum_{j=1}^{N} \sum_{i=1}^{M} \sum_{t=1}^{T} \frac{[\mathbf{Y}_t(i, j) - \mathbf{y}_t(i, j)]^2}{M \times N \times T} \right\}^{1/2},$$

where

$$N = \text{number of inputs,}$$
$$M = \text{number of outputs,}$$
$$T = \text{number of time periods,}$$

and where $\mathbf{Y}$ is the full range of multipliers as a deviation from base, calculated as a result of the inputs or shocks to the nonlinear GEM, and $\mathbf{y}$ denotes the equivalent multipliers computed from the linear system.

A Deterministic Realization

Equations 11A-4a and 11A-4b are in deviation form about the base run. The linear deterministic approximation of the original model, equation 11A-1, in levels is of the form

(11A-5a) $$\mathbf{X}_{t+1} = \mathbf{A}\mathbf{X}_t + \mathbf{B}\mathbf{U}_t$$

(11A-5b) $$\mathbf{Y}_t = \mathbf{C}\mathbf{X}_t + \mathbf{D}\mathbf{U}_t + \mathbf{q} + \mathbf{f}(\mathbf{t}),$$

where capital letters are used to denote time-series in levels; $\mathbf{U}_t$ must be replaced with $\log \mathbf{U}_t$ if $\mathbf{U}_t$ corresponds to a proportional deviation in equation 11A-3 and similarly for $\mathbf{Y}_t$; $\mathbf{q}$ is an unknown vector for constant terms; and $\mathbf{f}(\mathbf{t})$ is a vector of time functionals that are postulated to represent the deterministic trend of the time series. Vector $\mathbf{f}(\mathbf{t})$ may include polynomial terms, logarithmic trends, and cyclic functionals.

The fourth stage of the procedure is to use the original data for $\mathbf{Y}_t$ and $\mathbf{U}_t$ to estimate $\mathbf{q}, \mathbf{f}(\mathbf{t})$ and the initial state vector $\mathbf{X}_1$. Vectors $\mathbf{q}$ and $\mathbf{f}(\mathbf{t})$ somehow account for the ignored time series, $\mathbf{Z}_t$, in equation 11A-1, whereas the role of $\mathbf{X}_1$ is to capture the effect of lags prior to the first period of the sample. Vectors $\mathbf{q}, \mathbf{f}(\mathbf{t})$, and $\mathbf{X}_1$ are chosen to minimize the errors $\epsilon_t = \bar{\mathbf{Y}}_t - \mathbf{Y}_t$ in the sum-of-squares sense.

The trend components in equation 11A-5b, in part, capture the characteristics of the ignored time series, $\mathbf{Z}_t$, in equation 11A-1. If these characteristics are more complex than simple time functionals, then more sophisticated methods should be adopted. Moreover, it is important to include sufficient exogenous variables, $\mathbf{U}_t$, to explain the key dynamics in $\mathbf{Y}_t$; otherwise, the fitting errors in equation 11A-5b may be exceedingly high. This will result in very high estimates of the variances of the noise terms, to which we now turn.

A Stochastic Realization

Using the deterministic realization, equation 11A-5b, we can evaluate the residuals

$$\begin{aligned} \epsilon_t &= \bar{\mathbf{Y}}_t - \mathbf{Y}_t \qquad && \text{if variable Y is a ratio, or} \\ &= \ln\bar{\mathbf{Y}}_t - \ln\mathbf{Y}_t \qquad && \text{otherwise.} \end{aligned}$$

Then, in order to produce stochastic simulations, we have to construct a realization for the above residual and incorporate it with the linear representation of the model from equation 11A-4. A first approach is to postulate a simple autoregressive process of the form

(11A-6) $\Phi(L)\boldsymbol{\epsilon}_t = \boldsymbol{\omega}_t,$

where L is the lag operator, $\Phi(L)$ is the autoregressive polynomial, and $\boldsymbol{\omega}_t$ is assumed to be a white-noise process. The covariance matrix is obtained by correlating the residuals $\boldsymbol{\omega}$, and system matrices $\mathbf{A}$ and $\mathbf{C}$ in equation 11A-4 should appropriately change to include the additional dynamics introduced by $\Phi(L)$. This approach has been employed by Frenkel, Goldstein, and Masson (1989) to produce stochastic simulations for the MULTIMOD world model (see also chapter 7 of this volume).

A second approach can be based on stochastic realization techniques developed by Faurre (1976), Maciejowski (1983), Aoki and Havenner (1986), and others. As described in Christodoulakis (1989b), the method can distinguish between the case where single-equation residuals, $\bar{\mathbf{e}}$, of the parent model are not serially correlated and the case where they are. When residuals $\bar{\mathbf{e}}$ are not serially correlated, it can be shown that residual $\boldsymbol{\epsilon}$ can be approximated by a compound white-noise process $[\zeta_1^T \zeta_2^T]^T$. The linear model takes the form:

(11A-7a) $\mathbf{X}_{t+1} = \mathbf{A}\mathbf{X}_t + \mathbf{B}\mathbf{U}_t + \boldsymbol{\zeta}_{1t}$

(11A-7b) $\mathbf{Y}_t = \mathbf{C}\mathbf{X}_t + \mathbf{D}\mathbf{U}_t + \mathbf{q} + \mathbf{f(t)} + \boldsymbol{\zeta}_{2t},$

where $\boldsymbol{\zeta}_{1t}$ and $\boldsymbol{\zeta}_{2t}$ are assumed to be stationary white-noise vectors with zero mean and covariance given by

(11A-8) $\mathrm{cov}\begin{bmatrix} \boldsymbol{\zeta}_{1t} \\ \boldsymbol{\zeta}_{2t} \end{bmatrix} = \begin{bmatrix} \mathbf{Q} & \mathbf{S} \\ \mathbf{S}^T & \mathbf{R} \end{bmatrix} \geq 0.$

In this formulation no extra dynamics are added to the model. The covariance matrix is estimated as follows. A sample covariance of order k, based upon a sample of length T, is first calculated from

(11A-9) $\mathbf{J}_k^d = \frac{1}{T} \sum_{t=1}^{T-k} (\bar{\mathbf{Y}}_{t+k} - \mathbf{Y}_{t+k})(\bar{\mathbf{Y}}_t - \mathbf{Y}_t),$

where $\bar{\mathbf{Y}}_t$ represents the least-squares trend. It can be shown that in the Markovian representation equation 11A-4, intertemporal variance-covariance matrices $\mathbf{J}_k$ are given by

(11A-10) $\mathbf{J}_k = \mathbf{C}\mathbf{A}^{k-1}(\mathbf{S} + \mathbf{A}\mathbf{P}\mathbf{C}^T),$ $k > 0,$

where $\mathbf{P}$ is the covariance matrix of $\mathbf{X}_t$. Matrix $\mathbf{P}$ is assumed to be constant and is the positive definite solution to the Lyapunov equation. Thus,

(11A-11) $$\mathbf{P} = \mathbf{APA}^T + \mathbf{Q}.$$

For $k = 0$, the contemporaneous variance-covariance matrix is given by

(11A-12) $$\mathbf{J}_0 = \mathbf{CPC}^T + \mathbf{R}.$$

The stochastic realization can now be formulated as follows:

Step 1: Let $\mathbf{G} = \mathbf{S} + \mathbf{APC}^T$ in equation 11A-10. Determine $\mathbf{G}$ so that $\mathbf{J}_k$ approximates $\mathbf{J}_k^d$ given by equation 11A-9 in the least-squares sense for $k > 0$.

Step 2: Use $\mathbf{S} = \mathbf{G} - \mathbf{APC}^T$, $\mathbf{R} = \mathbf{J}_0 - \mathbf{CPC}^T$, and equation 11A-11 to determine the covariance of the white-noise vectors, ζ_{1t} and ζ_{2t}. Matrix $\mathbf{Q}$ should be chosen so that both equation 11A-8 and matrix $\mathbf{R}$ are positive semidefinite. If we assume that ζ_{1t} and ζ_{2t} are related as in the Kalman filter, as has been considered by Maciejowski (1983) and Aoki and Havenner (1986), then we obtain an algorithm for calculating suitable covariance matrices. The innovation mechanism is assumed to be:

(11A-13) $$\zeta_{1t} = L_1 \zeta_{2t},$$

with $\mathbf{L}_1 = \mathbf{SR}^{-1}$. Then, taking covariances of equation 11A-13, we obtain

(11A-14) $$\mathbf{Q} = \mathbf{SR}^{-1}\mathbf{S}^T.$$

Step 3: With $\mathbf{Q}$ now given in this way, equation 11A-11 may be transformed into a Riccati-type equation for matrix $\mathbf{P}$:

(11A-15) $$\mathbf{P} = \mathbf{APA}^T + (\mathbf{G} - \mathbf{APC}^T)(\mathbf{J}_0 - \mathbf{CPC}^T)^{-1}(\mathbf{G} - \mathbf{APC}^T)^T,$$

and then matrices $\mathbf{S}$ and $\mathbf{R}$ are determined as above.

If equation 11A-15 in step 3 has a positive semidefinite solution $\mathbf{P}$, then the stochastic realization is unique and has the welcome property of giving a minimum covariance matrix. Unfortunately, a solution to equation 11A-15 may not exist and, if it does, iterative techniques suggested by Faurre (1976) do not guarantee convergence; also see Harvey (1989, chap. 3). Aoki (1987) states that a solution can always be found as long as $\mathbf{R} = \mathbf{J}_0 - \mathbf{CPC}^T$ is kept positive definite, but again this is conditional on convergence of an iterative process. A more promising approach, given by Desai and Pal (1984), is based on constructing and investing an infinite-dimensional matrix of the variance-covariances. This method allows a direct calculation of matrices $\mathbf{R}$ and $\mathbf{S}$, then $\mathbf{Q}$ is set according to equation 11A-14, and $\mathbf{P}$ is found as the positive definite solution of Lyapunov equation 11A-11. Because the number of sample variance-covariance matrices is limited by the number of observations, a finite-dimension approximation to the latter method was employed in this chapter.

The stochastic realization in deviation form can be written:

$$(11A\text{-}16a) \qquad\qquad \mathbf{x}_{t+1} = \mathbf{A}\mathbf{x}_t + \mathbf{B}\mathbf{u}_t + \boldsymbol{\zeta}_{1t}$$

$$(11A\text{-}16b) \qquad\qquad \mathbf{y}_t = \mathbf{C}\mathbf{x}_t + \mathbf{D}\mathbf{u}_t + \boldsymbol{\zeta}_{2t},$$

where $\mathrm{cov}\begin{bmatrix} \boldsymbol{\zeta}_{1t} \\ \boldsymbol{\zeta}_{2t} \end{bmatrix} = \begin{bmatrix} \mathbf{Q} & \mathbf{S} \\ \mathbf{S}^T & \mathbf{R} \end{bmatrix}$ is known.

When residuals $\bar{\mathbf{e}}$ of the parent model, equation 11A-1, cannot be assumed serially uncorrelated, then they should be approximated by a stochastic realization that takes the form

$$(11A\text{-}17a) \qquad\qquad \mathbf{z}_{t+1} = \mathbf{F}\mathbf{z}_t + \boldsymbol{\zeta}_{1t}$$

$$(11A\text{-}17b) \qquad\qquad \boldsymbol{\epsilon}_t = \mathbf{H}\mathbf{z}_t + \boldsymbol{\zeta}_{2t},$$

where $\mathbf{z}$ is an additional state vector and matrices $\mathbf{F}$, $\mathbf{H}$, and $\mathbf{Z}$ are determined in a way similar to that described earlier. The covariance matrix in equation 11A-8 is again determined by equations 11A-9 through 11A-15 with $\mathbf{F}$ and $\mathbf{H}$ substituting for matrices $\mathbf{A}$ and $\mathbf{B}$ respectively.

The dynamics of the model are now augmented to include equation 11A-17 and take the form

$$(11A\text{-}18a) \qquad\qquad \begin{bmatrix} \mathbf{x}_{t+1} \\ \mathbf{z}_{t+1} \end{bmatrix} = \begin{bmatrix} \mathbf{A} & \\ & \mathbf{F} \end{bmatrix}\begin{bmatrix} \mathbf{x}_t \\ \mathbf{z}_t \end{bmatrix} + \begin{bmatrix} \mathbf{B} \\ 0 \end{bmatrix}\mathbf{U}_t + \begin{bmatrix} 0 \\ \mathbf{I} \end{bmatrix}\boldsymbol{\zeta}_{1t}$$

$$(11A\text{-}18b) \qquad\qquad \mathbf{y}_t = [\mathbf{C}\ \mathbf{I}]\begin{bmatrix} \mathbf{x}_t \\ \mathbf{z}_t \end{bmatrix} + \mathbf{D}\mathbf{u}_t + \boldsymbol{\zeta}_{2t}.$$

The same approach can be used to estimate stochastic processes for the exogenous variables. However, such an application is beyond the specification set out for the contributors to this volume.

Optimal Simple Rules

After endogenizing the vector of the forward-looking jumping variable, $\mathbf{j}_t$, the final linear stochastic representation takes the form:

(11A-19a)
$$\begin{bmatrix} \mathbf{v}_{t+1} \\ \mathbf{x}_{t+1} \\ \mathbf{j}^e_{t+1,t} \end{bmatrix} = \tilde{\mathbf{A}} \begin{bmatrix} \mathbf{v}_t \\ \mathbf{x}_t \\ \mathbf{j}_t \end{bmatrix} + \tilde{\mathbf{B}}\mathbf{w}_t + E_1\boldsymbol{\zeta}_t$$

(11A-19b)
$$\mathbf{y}_t = \tilde{\mathbf{C}} \begin{bmatrix} \mathbf{v}_t \\ \mathbf{x}_t \\ \mathbf{j}_t \end{bmatrix} + \tilde{\mathbf{D}}\mathbf{w}_t + E_2\boldsymbol{\zeta}_t,$$

where $\boldsymbol{\zeta}_t = [\boldsymbol{\zeta}^T_{1t}, \boldsymbol{\zeta}^T_{2t}]^T$; $\mathbf{w}_t$ is a vector of policy instruments; $\mathbf{v}_t$ is a vector of exogenous variables with estimated or assumed exogenous processes; and $\boldsymbol{\zeta}_t$ is a vector representing estimation errors, linearization errors, and also, potentially, shocks to exogenous variables. From the procedure described above, we have an estimate for, say, $\text{cov}(\boldsymbol{\zeta}_t) = \Sigma$. The matrices in equations 11A-19a and 11A-19b are straightforwardly determined from their counterparts in equations 11A-16a and 11A-16b.

We now outline a procedure for designing optimal rules within the class of simple rules of the form

(11A-20)
$$\mathbf{w}_t = \mathbf{K}\mathbf{y}_t,$$

where $\mathbf{K}$ is constrained in some specified way so as to assign particular instruments to particular targets. Although equation 11A-20 appears to be a simple proportional rule, the formulation is more general. By suitably augmenting the state vector in equation 11A-19a, proportional-integral-derivative rules may be written in the form of equation 11A-20.

The criterion for choosing the best rule within the class of rules given by 11A-20 is to minimize an expected welfare loss, $E(W_0)$ at time $t = 0$, where W_0 is given by

(11A-21)
$$W_0 = \sum_{t=0}^{\infty} \lambda^t (\mathbf{y}^T_t \mathbf{Q}_1 \mathbf{y}_t + \mathbf{w}^T_t \mathbf{Q}_2 \mathbf{w}_t).$$

If at $t = 0$ the economy is displaced from its long-run equilibrium, then $E(W_0)$ will have deterministic plus stochastic components. If so, we have an imposed process for $\mathbf{v}_t$: $\mathbf{v}_{t+1} = \mathbf{F}^T \mathbf{v}_t$ with $\mathbf{v}_0$ given. For permanent shocks, $\mathbf{F} = \mathbf{I}$, the identity matrix. For the purely stochastic problem, the initial displacement of all state variables in equation 11A-19a is zero. Eliminating $\mathbf{v}_t$ from equation 11A-19b and substituting the rule allows equation 11A-19 to be written as an innovations model:

(11A-22a) $$\mathbf{s}_{t+1} = \mathbf{A}^*\mathbf{s}_t + \mathbf{B}^*\boldsymbol{\zeta}_t$$

(11A-22b) $$\mathbf{y}_t = \mathbf{C}^*\mathbf{s}_t + \mathbf{D}^*\boldsymbol{\zeta}_t,$$

where $\mathbf{s}_t = [\mathbf{v}_t^T \mathbf{x}_t^T \mathbf{j}_t^T]$, and $\mathbf{A}^*$, $\mathbf{B}^*$, $\mathbf{C}^*$, and $\mathbf{D}^*$ depend on the system matrices in equation 11A-18 and the feedback matrix, $\mathbf{K}$, in equation 11A-20. To ease the notational burden, we drop the asterisk in the system matrices $\mathbf{A}^*$, $\mathbf{B}^*$, $\mathbf{C}^*$, $\mathbf{D}^*$ while stressing that $\mathbf{A}$, $\mathbf{B}$, $\mathbf{C}$, and $\mathbf{D}$ do not now coincide with their previous use.

Substituting the rule into equation 11A-21 and taking the trace (tr), we arrive at

(11A-23) $$E(W_0) = \sum_{t=0}^{\infty} \lambda^{ts}\text{tr}\left\{(\mathbf{Q}_1 + \mathbf{K}^T\mathbf{Q}_2\mathbf{K})\left[E(\mathbf{y}_t)E(\mathbf{y}_t)^T + \text{cov}(\mathbf{y}_t)\right]\right\}.$$

From equation 11A-22b and the serial independence of the error term, we have

(11A-24) $$\text{cov}(\mathbf{y}_t) = \mathbf{C}\text{cov}(\mathbf{s}_t)\mathbf{C}^T + \mathbf{D}\text{cov}(\boldsymbol{\zeta}_t)\mathbf{D}^T,$$

where $\mathbf{s}_t = \begin{bmatrix} \mathbf{z}_t \\ \mathbf{j}_t \end{bmatrix}$ and $\mathbf{z}_t = \begin{bmatrix} \mathbf{v}_t \\ \mathbf{x}_t \end{bmatrix}$.

Then the saddlepath rational-expectations solution to the model under the rule of equation 11A-20 has the form

(11A-25) $$\mathbf{j}_t = -\mathbf{N}\mathbf{z}_t,$$

where $\mathbf{N} = \mathbf{N}(\mathbf{K})$. Thus

(11A-26) $$\text{cov}(\mathbf{s}_t) = \text{cov}\begin{bmatrix} \mathbf{z}_t \\ -\mathbf{N}\mathbf{z}_t \end{bmatrix} = \begin{bmatrix} \text{cov}(\mathbf{z}_t) & -\text{cov}(\mathbf{z}_t)\mathbf{N}^T \\ -\mathbf{N}\text{cov}(\mathbf{z}_t) & \mathbf{N}\text{cov}(\mathbf{z}_t)\mathbf{N}^T \end{bmatrix}.$$

It now remains to evaluate

(11A-27) $$\mathbf{V} = \sum_{t=0}^{\infty} \lambda^t [E(\mathbf{z}_t)E(\mathbf{z}_t)^T + \text{cov}(\mathbf{z}_t)],$$

where, from equations 11A-22a and 11A-25,

(11A-28) $$\mathbf{z}_{t+1} = (\mathbf{A} - \mathbf{A}_{12}\mathbf{N})\mathbf{z}_t + \mathbf{B}_1\boldsymbol{\zeta}_1,$$

and where

$$\mathbf{A} = \begin{bmatrix} \mathbf{A}_{11} & \mathbf{A}_{12} \\ \mathbf{A}_{21} & \mathbf{A}_{22} \end{bmatrix} \quad \text{and} \quad \mathbf{B} = \begin{bmatrix} \mathbf{B}_1 \\ \mathbf{B}_2 \end{bmatrix}$$

are partitioned conformably with

$$\begin{bmatrix} \mathbf{z}_t \\ \mathbf{j}_t \end{bmatrix}.$$

Let $\mathbf{H} = \mathbf{A}_{11} - \mathbf{A}_{12}\mathbf{N}$. Then it is a standard result that $\mathbf{V}$ satisfies the Lyapunov equation:

$$(11\text{A-}29) \qquad \mathbf{V} = \lambda \mathbf{H}\mathbf{V}\mathbf{H}^T + [\mathbf{z}_0\mathbf{z}_0^T + \frac{\lambda}{1-\lambda}\mathbf{B}_1\text{cov}(\boldsymbol{\zeta}_t)\mathbf{B}_1^T].$$

Taking equations 11A-23–24, 11A-26–27, and 11A-29 together, we can now evaluate $E(W_0)$ for a given rule $\mathbf{K}$, initial displacement $\mathbf{z}_0$, and covariance matrix $\text{cov}(\boldsymbol{\zeta}_1)$, using the matrix of penalties in appropriately reduced form. If we wish to calculate asymptotic welfare loss in the purely stochastic problem with zero initial displacement, then we solve for constant covariance matrix $\text{cov}(\mathbf{z}_t)$, and the Lyapunov equation 11A-29 is replaced with

$$(11\text{A-}30) \qquad \text{cov}(\mathbf{z}_t) = \mathbf{H}\text{cov}(\mathbf{z}_t)\mathbf{H}^T + \mathbf{B}_1\text{cov}(\boldsymbol{\zeta}_t)\mathbf{B}_1^T.$$

This is solved as a Lyapunov equation to yield $\mathbf{V}$. The welfare loss is obtained as before.

The optimal simple rule, within the class of rules defined by equation 11A-20 and the restrictions on $\mathbf{K}$, is then obtained by minimizing with respect to the free parameters in $\mathbf{K}$, using standard numerical optimization techniques. It should be stressed that simple rules (unlike fully optimal rules) are not certainty-equivalent; that is, the optimal rule depends on the noise covariance matrix in the stochastic realization and also on any deterministic shocks applied to the system.

References

Aoki, M. 1987. *State Space Methods of Time Series Analysis*. Berlin: Springer-Verlag.
Aoki, M., and A. Havenner. 1986. "Approximate State Space Models of Some Vector-Valued Macroeconomic Time Series for Cross-Country Comparisons." *Journal of Economic Dynamics and Control* 10:149–55.

Barrell, R. J., A. Gurney, and S. Dulake. 1990. "The World Economy." *National Institute Economic Review* 132:25–47.

Christodoulakis, N. 1989a. "Extensions of Linearisation to Large Econometric Models with Rational Expectations." *Computers, Mathematics and Applications* 18:629–42.

———. 1989b. "On Deterministic and Stochastic Approximations of Time-Series and Econometric Models." Discussion Paper. Centre for Economic Forecasting. London Business School.

Currie, D. A., and S. Wren-Lewis. 1989. "Evaluating Blueprints for the Conduct of International Macro Policy." *American Economic Review* 79 (*Papers and Proceedings*, 1988):264–69.

———. 1990. "Evaluating the Extended Target Zone Proposal for the G3." *Economic Journal* 100:105–23.

Desai, U. B., and D. Pal. 1984. "A Transformation Approach to Stochastic Model Reduction." *IEEE Transactions on Automatic Control*, AC-29:1097–1100.

Faurre, P. 1976. "Stochastic Realisation Algorithms." In *System Identification— Advances and Case Studies*, edited by R. Mehra and D. Lainiotis, 1–25. Academic Press.

Frenkel, J. A., M. Goldstein, and P. R. Masson. 1989. "Simulating the Effects of Some Simple Coordinated versus Uncoordinated Policy Rules." In *Macroeconomic Policies in an Interdependent World*, edited by R. C. Bryant, D. A. Currie, and others, 203–39. Washington: Brookings, Centre for Economic Policy Research, and International Monetary Fund.

Harvey, A. 1989. *Forecasting Structural Time Series Models and the Kalman Filter*. Cambridge University Press.

Kung, S. 1978. "A New Identification and Model Reduction Algorithm via Singular Value Decomposition." Proceedings of the Twelfth Asilomar Conference on Circuits, Systems and Computers. Pacific Grove, Calif. March.

Levine, P., D. Currie, and J. Gaines. 1989. "The Use of Simple Rules for International Policy Agreements." In *Blueprints for Exchange-Rate Management*, edited by M. Miller, B. Eichengreen, and R. Portes, 281-319. Academic Press.

Maciejowski, J. 1983. "Approximate Gauss-Markov Realisation of Multivariate Stochastic Processes." University of Cambridge.

Maciejowski, J., and D. Vines. 1984. "Decoupled Control of a Macroeconomic Model Using Frequency-Domain Methods." *Journal of Economic Dynamics and Control* 7: 55–77.

4
Other Approaches to Monetary-Policy Regimes

CHAPTER 12

Simulating the OECD INTERLINK Model under Alternative Monetary-Policy Regimes

Pete Richardson

THIS CHAPTER reviews the influence of various monetary regimes for the Group of Three (G3) economies (the United States, Japan, and Germany) on the comparative simulation properties of a recent version of the Organization for Economic Cooperation and Development's INTERLINK model.[1] The simulated shocks are global, and the main objective is to assess the relative effectiveness of alternative monetary policy settings in achieving a stable set of outcomes for main macroeconomic aggregates worldwide. Because the relative performance of different policies seems to depend on both the nature of the shocks and specific structural features of the model used, the chapter also examines the extent to which these results are likely to be empirically fragile.

Large empirical models are at a disadvantage, compared with those of some other participants, in carrying out the large volume of stochastic model solutions required for the "core" simulations of this conference. Indeed, the simulation capabilities and resource requirements of INTERLINK do not allow such an exercise, given the combination of model scale, country detail, and data base needs.[2] There are even more compelling reasons to think that the returns to a detailed stochastic simulation exercise with INTERLINK might be low.

The author thanks Andrew Dean, Thomas Egebo, Mike Feiner, Koichi Hamada, Richard Herd, and Jeff Shafer for comments on an early draft; Portia Eltvedt and Serge Petiteau for graphics; and Julie de Kerorguen and Laura Garcia for secretarial assistance. The late Rik Ford made an invaluable contribution in managing the OECD model and the data systems used.

1. The model used is the January 1990 version of INTERLINK. Basic accounts of its broad structure and simulation properties are given in Richardson (1987a, 1987b, and 1988) and the detailed lists of studies therein. More recent studies contributing to the system are described by Herd (1987); Torres, Jarrett, and Suyker (1989); Egebo, Richardson, and Lienert (1990); and Martin and Torres (1990). Recent revisions include changes to import and export prices of manufactures, import volumes of manufactures, housing investment for the major countries, supply blocs for the smaller countries, and measures of business-sector potential and U.S. consumption. Changes for the spring 1990 version included reestimated consumption functions and price blocs for the smaller-country models.

2. INTERLINK is a semiannual model combining twenty-three individual OECD countries with six non-OECD regional submodels. It involves approximately 5,000 equations and a twenty-year data base of 7,500 series.

First, although work examining forward-looking model-solution techniques is under way at the OECD, the main multicountry version of the model still lacks a forward-looking treatment of expectations in financial markets that would provide some of the key nonlinear elements important to stochastic simulation analyses.[3] Second, to policymakers, an analysis of model responses to stochastic shocks that are based on *sample historical residuals* is of only limited interest in relation to other elements of uncertainty. In particular, key uncertainties attach to both the appropriateness of model structure (parameter and structural uncertainty—hence, the key model mechanisms on which such simulations rely) and singular events leading to systematic shifts in variables that are either exogenous or, being only partially modeled, tend to get classified as "stylized assumptions." The experience of the past two decades suggests that some of the main trials for policymakers have been and will continue to be associated with discrete events falling into this latter category: the impact of debt crises and non-OECD behavior on world trade and payments, the effects of stock market fluctuations and consumer confidence on economic growth and stability, and the effects of worldwide inflationary pressures. Third, the results of stochastic simulations alone may be difficult to digest without first studying the implications of alternative policy regimes challenged by deterministic shocks.

The analysis in this chapter, therefore, follows a more restricted agenda. It examines the implications of alternative monetary policy assumptions confronted by various deterministic global shocks that are typical of the events faced by authorities and analysts. In particular, it looks at the differences in simulated outcomes for key policy variables associated with the use of different interest-rate reaction rules for the G3 economies and examines some of the key mechanisms involved.

Simulation Specification

This section provides a general description of the types of shocks used, the transmission mechanisms in INTERLINK, and the types of monetary-policy regimes considered.[4] The first part of the appendix provides more detail on the specific implementation of the shocks and the specification of the monetary-policy reaction functions, and the second part of the appendix presents in detail the specific transmission mechanisms for each of the combinations of shocks and regimes.

---

3. Preliminary work involves dynamic optimization and forward-looking solution techniques for single-country submodels on the basis of software developed in conjunction with the PROPE group at Imperial College, London.

4. A useful summary of the financial-sector relationships involved is given by Helliwell, Cockerline, and Lafrance (1990).

Shocks

Shocks used in simulation exercises can be generally classified as real or nominal, supply or demand, and global or country-specific. The shocks used in this chapter fall into a subset of these categories and are chosen for three reasons. First, these shocks are inherently interesting. Second, they match the types of shocks that are likely to be embodied in the matrix of residuals used by the modeling groups that participated in the stochastic simulation exercise. Finally, some of these shocks follow on the work of Bryant, Holtham, and Hooper (1988), *EMIE*.

Four shocks are considered, each exposing different linkages in the INTER-LINK model and each possibly eliciting a different optimal policy response. The first three shocks are real demand shocks originating in different parts of the world. The first, an increase in non-OECD import demand, is an experiment in the appropriate policy response of the G3 monetary authorities to an exogenous increase in non-OECD demand that may hit the countries differently depending on the shares of trade with the nonmember countries. The second, a fall in OECD private consumption, puts the shock within the industrial country group. The third, a U.S. fiscal contraction, allows a comparison of appropriate monetary policies when the shock is centered in one of the G3. The fourth shock is a global nominal supply shock, specified as an increase in OECD wages. Each of these shocks reveals transmission mechanisms of the INTERLINK model that will affect how the monetary policy regimes reduce instability in the target variables.

SHOCK 1: INCREASE IN NON-OECD IMPORT DEMAND. Independent of the monetary policy assumptions, the initial effects of 5 percent higher non-OECD imports operate in INTERLINK through a fairly conventional trade-multiplier process, with higher world exports (about $1\frac{3}{4}$ percent in the first year) distributed across individual countries according to market performance and specialization. The resulting demand stimulus raises output and factor demand in the OECD and puts upward pressure on wages and prices. Price levels are further stimulated by inflation transmitted through higher import costs.

The initial distribution of real GNP effects across countries reflects both geographical market specialization and the relative GNP shares of exports. Thus, although the increases in market-weighted world imports for the United States and Japan are typically higher than for Germany, a higher export share in GNP for Germany implies an effect on German GNP roughly twice that for the United States and marginally higher than that for Japan. Real GNP effects are thereafter modified by multiplier-accelerator responses operating through the supply sector, consumption, and global trade-multiplier effects.

The relative strength of price and wage responses between countries reflects the size and persistence of GNP disturbances, the degree of labor market adjustment, and the size of output- and labor-gap terms in the underlying wage and price equations. Resulting differentials in cost and price responses then modify the underlying distribution of trade through competitiveness. At the same time, price and interest-rate differentials influence exchange rates, with expected rates in INTERLINK being assumed to depend on price differentials.

SHOCK 2: FALL IN OECD CONSUMPTION. In the absence of monetary controls for the G3 countries, the effects on output of a global 1 percent reduction in OECD consumption levels are substantial and sustained, with real GNP reduced in the fifth year by $1\frac{1}{4}$, $2\frac{3}{4}$, and $1\frac{3}{4}$ percent for the United States, Japan, and Germany respectively. This contrasts with corresponding *single-country* results, where real GNP tends to recover substantially over the period. The main differences here reflect trade-linkage multipliers and competitiveness effects. In an unlinked case, competitor prices are assumed to be unchanged; with a global shock there is a common tendency for prices to fall—thereby eliminating the scope for gains in trade competitiveness. The trade-multiplier effects on GNP are also more pronounced for Japan and Germany, reflecting trade-multiplier effects.

The effects of the sustained reduction in demand on prices are large, with the annual inflation rate for the United States reduced by around 1 percent annually, and by $1\frac{1}{2}$ percent for Japan and Germany. As in the previous simulation, the paths of output and prices show little or no sign of longer-run stability with fixed nominal interest rates.

Over the simulation period, the dollar tends to depreciate while the yen and deutsche mark appreciate by 2 to $2\frac{1}{2}$ percent. For the OECD area, the short-term effects on trade balances are favorable, with lower import demand at the area level leading the collapse in world trade. A short-term improvement in OECD balances reflects an adjustment delay in non-OECD import behavior, which is assumed to be constrained by export revenue. Once movements in OECD demand stabilize, non-OECD imports catch up, and net area trade balances remain more or less unchanged. The distribution of changes in current balances reflects a combination of factors. For the United States, a higher-than-average import demand elasticity,[5] combined with an underlying baseline imbalance, ensures an overall improvement. Relatively high export share, low import demand elasticities, and a substantial baseline surplus imply an overall deterioration for Japan. For Germany, the current balance falls progressively over the period, reflecting a higher-than-average export share elasticity.

---

5. In the current version of INTERLINK, income elasticities for import demand of manufactures are $2\frac{1}{2}$, 2, and $1\frac{1}{2}$ for the United States, Germany, and Japan respectively.

SHOCK 3: U.S. FISCAL CONTRACTION. When a simulation with the model keeps nominal interest rates and floating exchange rates unchanged from baseline, a U.S. real fiscal contraction (equivalent to 1 percent of real GNP) produces a relatively high GNP multiplier, in the region of 1.9, and substantial and growing international spillovers. Trade-linkage effects contribute to steady reductions in exports and real GNP in all major trading partners, with average reductions of 1.5 and 0.7 percent for Japan and Germany respectively. At the same time, downward pressure on prices in both the U.S. and world markets leads to a general disinflation, averaging 0.8 percent annually for the OECD area as a whole. This in turn implies rising real interest rates and further downward output adjustments.

Given the origin and degree of demand contraction, U.S. prices take the lead in the disinflation. Given the form of exchange-rate expectations and a substantial improvement in U.S. net foreign assets, this puts upward pressure on the dollar, which is up by 5 percent by the end of the period. OECD-area current balances improve in the short run, with non-OECD countries adjusting slowly to lower export earnings.[6] The U.S. current balance improves substantially over the period ($20–$40 billion), with a rising proportion mirrored in lower Japanese and German surpluses as non-OECD imports also contract. Although favorable to the current configuration of trade imbalances, the international repercussions are large, both for output and employment, and the results show general signs of longer-term instability.

SHOCK 4: INCREASE IN OECD WAGE RATES. This supply-shock simulation assumes a single 2 percent ex ante increase in OECD wage rates (in the residuals for private sector wage-rate equations) in the starting period. The specific form of these equations (augmented Phillips curves, with backward-looking price expectations) and the price blocs (cost-plus–based equations with potential output-gap terms) imply a generally dynamic inflation response, modified or checked only by the endogenous reactions of output and employment. The presence of lagged price responses to increases in wage costs also implies a sustained increase in real wages and real labor costs until wage movements are curtailed by demand pressure. The effects on output and demand depend primarily on the responses of real disposable income and consumption; the influence of higher labor costs on profitability, output expectations, and factor demand; and the influence of inflation on real interest rates and investment. Trade-competitiveness effects are important only insofar as there are major divergences in price responses across countries.

---

6. The effect of a fiscal contraction originating in either Germany or Japan would not have the symmetric effect on the dollar; that is, under these circumstances the dollar still appreciates. This is due, in part, to the slope of the LM curves in the model and, in part, to the size of the net-asset term in the equations.

Monetary-Policy Regimes

In specifying the range of monetary-policy regimes considered for the individual G3 countries, an important distinction can be made between two broad classes of regimes: "exact" targeting versus a "looser" form of targeting that uses reaction functions. By and large, the monetary regimes considered here can be described as "exact" targeting rules, insofar as the instrument variable is usually set to achieve "exactly" stability in the policy target variable in each period.[7] This is typically achieved by inverting one or more behavioral equations in the models. For example, with a fixed money-supply target, short-term interest rates move in the simulation so as to give a path of money supply that is unchanged from the baseline path. In effect, money demand, which is determined by a behavioral equation, is equated to the fixed baseline path of money supply by "renormalizing" the equations in question to determine the market-clearing value of interest rates.

In contrast to exact targeting, "looser" monetary targeting—as used, for example, in the "core" set of stochastic simulations discussed in part 2 of this book—involves the addition to the model of an explicit reaction function linking the setting of the monetary instrument (short-term interest rates) to simulated movements in the policy target. For example, one might specify an x basis-point increase in interest rates per y percent increase above baseline in the monetary aggregate. The main advantages in adopting a looser form of monetary rule are that such rules may be simpler for economic agents to understand and also simpler for authorities to implement, since such rules do not assume a precise knowledge of the underlying behavioral model. With an *appropriate* choice of reaction-function coefficient, moreover, approximate control of the target variable may be achieved over a period of time. The principal disadvantage is the degree of imprecision, and therefore the amount of trial and error required to achieve satisfactory control over the target variable.

In practice the distinction between these two forms of rule is likely to be considerably less precise. As elaborated below, setting an "exact" money target through a demand-for-money relationship may well boil down to choosing a reaction function in which interest rates respond to calibrated changes in real and nominal income. The principal difference will concern the choice of reaction parameters and the amount of prior knowledge involved. In the real world outside econometric models, neither is likely to be particularly certain.

The following paragraphs elaborate further on the six alternative monetary policy rules considered for the G3 countries and the underlying reaction-function parameters involved. Further details are given in the first part of the appendix.

---

7. The terms "regime" and "rule" are used as synonyms in the following discussion and later in the chapter.

POLICY OPTION A: UNCHANGED NOMINAL INTEREST RATES. This is a model default option, whereby the money supply is assumed to accommodate endogenous movements in money demand fully. Maintaining unchanged nominal rates implies that real rates, which are key determinants of real investment and consumption, move inversely with inflation.

POLICY OPTION B: FIXED MONEY TARGETS. For this option, money supply is assumed to be held fixed at baseline values, with short-term interest rates endogenized to eliminate excess money demand.[8] This assumption implies an inversion of the corresponding money-demand equations. (See the first part of the appendix for equation specifics.) Because of the instability of available money-demand estimates, this rule may best be characterized as a simple monetary rule linking interest-rate reactions to a weighted function of income- and price-level movements, rather than as a precise control rule for money aggregates. Although some estimates suggest that the underlying dynamics of money-demand equations might give rise to instrument instability, the dynamics of the semiannual equations in INTERLINK are sufficiently straightforward to provide a stable trade-off between interest rates and nominal income effects.

POLICY OPTION C: EXCHANGE-RATE TARGETING. This option is implemented by assuming that the United States follows a fixed money rule, as in the preceding case, and that Japan and Germany use interest rates to hold exchange-rate parity with the dollar. This effectively involves the endogenization of short-term interest rates through the inversion of the model's exchange-rate equations, yielding an overall reaction function that relates domestic short-term rates directly to changes in foreign short-term rates, price-level differentials, and asset stocks. With a similar rule applying across most other OECD countries, the U.S. money target and corresponding interest rates act as primary anchors to the system.

This option, which is consistent with the corresponding exchange-rate-target rule applied in the core stochastic simulations, can be thought of as representing one of several possible forms of exchange-rate coordination. Because a range of different interest rate configurations for the G3 countries would be consistent with stable exchange rates, the choice of the United States as the country following independent monetary policy is essentially arbitrary. Equally feasible alternatives might involve Japan or Germany following a money-supply rule (with the United States targeting the dollar) or the choice of other coordinated targets based on a different nominal anchor.

---

8. The money-demand equations in INTERLINK relate to broad money aggregates: M2 for the United States, M2 plus certificates of deposit for Japan, and M3 for Germany.

POLICY OPTION D: FIXED REAL SHORT-TERM INTEREST RATES. Various measures of real short-term interest rates might be considered, depending largely on the choice of definition for expected inflation rates. For convenience, the current simulations use a relatively simple definition based on the actual GNP inflation rate. In simulation, nominal short-term rates move one-for-one with percentage deviations of the GNP inflation rate from baseline.

POLICY OPTION E: FIXED REAL LONG-TERM INTEREST RATES. Two features of INTERLINK suggest that targeting the long-term real interest rate might prove to be a more effective means of control than targeting a real short-term rate. First, it is typically inflation-adjusted long-term rates that enter the cost-of-capital and -borrowing terms in the model's investment and consumption equations. Second, since the interest-yield curve is typically represented as an error-correction process, the presence of significant adjustment lags between short- and long-term rates implies that changes in the former feed through only slowly to influence domestic demand. Thus, initial movements in short-term rates will be a *multiple* of the simulated change in the inflation rate rather than a strict one-for-one adjustment. In long-run equilibriums, however, both long- and short-term rates are constant in real terms (see the equations in the appendix for more detail). In effect, the choice of a real long-term interest rate as a target essentially accelerates the policy reactions to inflation signals.

Table 12-1 summarizes the corresponding rules for the G3 countries, evaluated on the basis of actual parameter values in the model.

NOMINAL-INCOME TARGETING. In addition to the five options outlined above, preliminary investigations were made using different forms of rules targeting nominal income. These revealed two major difficulties. First, the specific dynamics of the relationship between nominal income and interest rates for the G3 countries in INTERLINK imply severe instrument instability. Thus, the effects of a change in short-term rates are typically small in the current semester and build up over a two-year period to be four or five times as large. Under these circumstances, *exact* contemporaneous targeting gives oscillatory, explosive results for sustained shocks to output and prices, and some alternative form of iterative control rule is required to hit a nominal-income target at a future time.

This problem is compounded by the relative importance of exchange rates in INTERLINK as a means of adjusting future price levels. In common with several other macroeconometric models, the lags in the transmission of the direct effects of interest rates to demand and prices are sufficiently long that the main leverage of interest rates on prices operates through exchange rates. With a global shock, however, the stimulus to nominal income is often broadly similar across countries, and the exchange-rate mechanism therefore cannot be

Table 12-1. *INTERLINK Targeting Rules*

Targeting rule	Expression[a]		
A. Unchanged nominal interest rates	$r_s = 0$		
B. Fixed money supply	$r_s = a_1 y + a_2 p + a_3 p_{-1}$		
	a_1	a_2	a_3
United States	0.50	0.50	0.00
Japan	1.07	2.14	−1.41
Germany	0.89	3.05	−2.48
C. Exchange-rate targets	$r_s = r_f + b_1(p - p_f) + b_2 w$		
	b_1	b_2	
Japan	0.87	−7.84	
Germany	0.87	−2.52	
D. Fixed real short-term interest rates	$r_s = \dot{p}$		
E. Fixed real long-term interest rates	$r_s = c_1 \dot{p} + c_2 r_{s-1} + c_3 \dot{p}_{-1}$		
	c_1	c_2	c_3
United States	4.76	−0.14	−3.62
Japan	3.33	0.67	−3.00
Germany	3.70	−0.67	−3.37

a. All variables are expressed as deviations from the baseline. The short-term interest rate, r_s, is expressed in percentage points; all other variables are expressed as percentages.

readily exploited if the G3 countries *simultaneously* attempt to get back toward a baseline nominal-GNP path—unless, of course, the European Monetary System (EMS) assumption is dropped.

Preliminary experimentation suggested that it was always possible for nominal-income targets for two of the G3 countries to be met approximately within a year or so, but almost entirely at the expense of the third country. This suggests that, for global shocks of the kind considered here, uncoordinated nominal-income targeting is likely to exacerbate exchange-rate pressures unless a more diluted form of target is set—for example, one expressed in terms of nominal-income growth rather than income levels.

Comparative Evaluation of Policy Regimes

In drawing specific conclusions from the experiments outlined in the preceding section and fleshed out in the appendix, it is useful first to establish some basic criteria for assessing the relative effectiveness of the alternative policy regimes considered.[9] To this end, table 12-2 summarizes the simulation results classified by shock and policy option, concentrating narrowly on three key

9. The second section of the appendix analyzes in detail the simulation results, transmission mechanisms, and quantitative responses of the G3 countries to each combination of shock and monetary policy reaction function.

Table 12-2. *Summary Comparison of Policy Outcomes*[a]

Policy rule	1. Non-OECD import shock			2. OECD consumption shock			3. U.S. fiscal shock			4. OECD wage shock		
	United States	Japan	Germany	United States	Japan	Germany	United States	Japan	Germany	United States	Japan	Germany
A. Fixed nominal interest rates												
GNP level	0.38	1.16	1.76	−1.28	−2.00	−1.56	−1.86	−1.50	−0.70	0.66	0.44	0.30
Inflation	0.30	0.78	0.68	−1.02	−1.44	−1.52	−1.48	−0.86	−0.68	1.00	2.14	3.18
Current balance	4	9	5	11	−6	−7	28	−12	−8	−14	4	7
B. Fixed money targets												
GNP level	0.16	0.26	0.12	−0.24	−0.14	−0.14	−0.42	0.04	0.06	−0.36	−1.68	−1.80
Inflation	0.25	0.20	0.20	−0.56	−0.18	−0.32	−0.62	0	−0.08	0.64	0.56	1.12
Current balance	14	9	6	2	−6	−5	17	−4	−3	−4	3	6
C. Exchange-rate targets												
GNP level	0.16	0.52	0.22	−0.28	−0.52	−0.40	−0.42	−0.30	−0.24	−0.24	−1.80	−1.68
Inflation	0.22	0.40	0.30	−0.54	−0.48	−0.56	−0.58	−0.22	−0.28	0.62	0.42	1.18
Current balance	9	12	6	2	−4	−5	17	−3	−3	−4	6	9
D. Fixed real short-term interest rates												
GNP level	0.20	0.66	0.40	−0.54	−0.88	−0.80	−0.76	−0.28	−0.22	−0.10	−1.18	−1.24
Inflation	0.22	0.50	0.42	−0.64	−0.72	−0.84	−0.82	−0.22	−0.26	0.64	0.88	1.64
Current balance	8	11	6	5	−5	−6	20	−7	−4	−7	4	6
E. Fixed real long-term interest rates												
GNP level	0.14	0.48	0.24	−0.34	−0.50	−0.38	−0.56	−0.12	−0.12	−0.22	−1.54	−1.80
Inflation	0.20	0.34	0.30	−0.54	−0.44	−0.56	−0.62	−0.10	−0.16	0.60	0.064	1.10
Current balance	9	13	6	5	−5	−5	18	−5	−3	−5	4	6

a. Deviations from baseline are five-year averages; real GNP levels and inflation rates are percentages; current account balances are in billions of dollars.

economic variables for the G3 countries: the real-GNP level, the inflation rate, and the current account balance. In each case, these are averaged over the five-year simulation period and therefore largely abstract from short-term, period-to-period movements. To the extent that the latter are important (for example, where specific instabilities are present), the reader is referred to the appendix (figures 12A-1 through 12A-4).

Note that the evaluation criteria are symmetric with respect to the direction of the effect of the shock on the target variable. That is, since the objective of the monetary policy rule is to stabilize the target variables, any deviation from baseline, whether it be a positive increase in GNP or a decline in inflation, is treated as a loss and as a poorer monetary policy rule. Although the evaluation criteria used here are standard for the literature, one should nevertheless ponder the biases that the policymakers in control of the rules might impart as regards the effectiveness of the rules, given the policymakers' inherently asymmetric view of the impact of the shocks.

The general diversity of results obtained across the range of model simulations suggests that important trade-offs exist, and it is difficult to reject the notion that superior sets of incomes might be obtained by a combination of more flexible rules and a wider range of policy instruments. The concern here is not with issues of policy optimization, however, but with the relative stabilization performance and robustness of different monetary rules (with some emphasis also on the speed of adjustment and the potential instabilities involved). As a further guide to such an assessment, table 12-3 provides a classification by simulation of those rules that appear to be most effective in meeting three specific criteria: minimizing inflation effects, minimizing real-GNP effects, and minimizing a simple average of inflation and real-GNP effects.

To the extent that the emphasis of policy may also vary with the sign of the shock—inflation being the main focus with a positive demand shock, and GNP being the focus of a negative demand shock—both inflation and GNP criteria are useful. The rather arbitrary simple average of inflation and output attempts to provide a broader criterion of overall stability. Figure 12-1 illustrates this criterion by plotting the corresponding inflation and real GNP pairings for each policy, by country and simulation shock. "Preferred" options in figure 12-1 correspond to those lying closest to the respective axes and the point of origin. Several general points emerge from figure 12-1.

First, a general conclusion is that most of the alternative regimes considered appear to be effective stabilizers over a five-year period relative to the benchmark regime of fixed nominal-interest rates. This is because the IS curves in the relevant country models are moderately steep and because interest rates have significant effects on output and prices, more so in relation to a regime whereby movements in *real* interest rates are the uncontrolled outcome of fluctuations in

Table 12-3. *Classification of Alternative Policy Rules*

	Preferred policy rule[a]		
Shock	United States	Japan	Germany
1. Non-OECD import shock			
Inflation	D/C/E	B	B
GNP	B/C/E	B	B[C/E]
Both[b]	E	B	B
2. OECD consumption shock			
Inflation	B/C/E	B	B
GNP	B/C/E	B	B
Both[b]	B/C/E	B	B
3. U.S. fiscal shock			
Inflation	B/C/E	B	B
GNP	B/C[E]	B	B/E
Both[b]	B/C[E]	B	B
4. OECD wage shock			
Inflation	B/C/D/E	C	B/C/E
GNP	D	A	A
Both[b]	C/D/E[B]	D	D[B/C/E]

a. As defined in Tables 12-1 and 12-2. A slash (/) indicates clusters that are not significantly different; brackets indicate points that are inferior but not greatly so.
b. Gives equal weight to GNP and inflation responses in absolute terms.

inflation and are potentially destabilizing. Indeed, with INTERLINK, a regime of fixed nominal-interest rates seems to imply long-run price instability for all of the shocks considered.[10]

More specifically, interest-rate regimes based on money-supply targeting (policy option B) seem to have the most effective stabilizing influence across the broad range of global *demand-side* shocks. There are individual cases in which one or another of the G3 countries is better or no worse off under alternative rules, but usually it is at the expense of the other two.

The apparent effectiveness of the money-target regime, particularly for Japan and Germany, derives from two key features of the model: the particularly strong influence of interest rates on private sector demand, and the particular strength of the policy reactions implied by the steepness of the corresponding LM curves (illustrated by table 12-1). The former is a fairly robust feature of the model; the latter somewhat less so. Indeed, the empirical fragility of money-demand relationships suggests that the notion of precise "money-supply" targeting cannot be taken literally. The implied reaction functions linking short-term rates to a combination of real income and price levels appear nonetheless to be effective stabilizers, in the context of INTERLINK, for a broad range of demand shocks.

10. Although the analysis is confined to a five-year period, a possible longer-term stabilization of the simulated accelerations and decelerations in prices given with the unchanged nominal-interest rate assumption seems highly likely.

Figure 12-1. *Inflation and Real GNP-and-Inflation Outcomes under Alternative Policy Rules*[a]

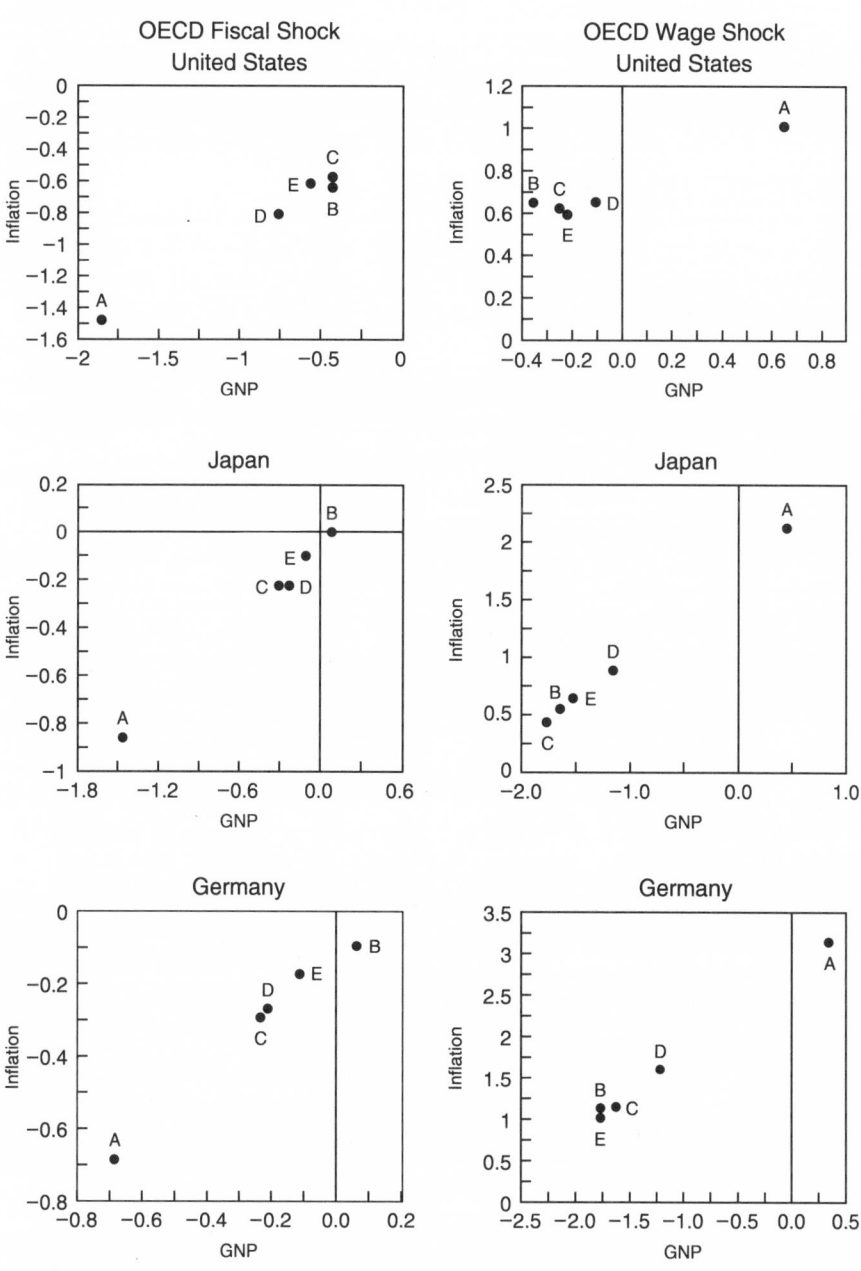

a. Outcomes for policies A–E are as defined in tables 12-1 and 12-2.

A third broad observation concerns the relative performance of regimes targeting money and exchange rates (rules B and C) for Japan and Germany. Here the results suggest an important trade-off between output and prices (figure 12-1). With a positive demand shock, both output and inflation appear to be higher with exchange-rate targeting than without, which suggests that such an option is less effective for these countries if the primary policy concern is stabilization. This in turn raises the issue of whether more optimal forms of exchange-rate coordination are possible.

It is important, however, to note that this result also reflects the specific model features that determine the configuration of exchange-rate movements with money-supply targeting (option B), since these essentially determine the subsequent adjustments to interest rates under option C. For the positive non-OECD shock (shock 1), it is the larger increases in Japanese and German interest rates relative to U.S. rates that are all important in producing the dollar depreciation. These in turn reflect the relative steepness of LM curves embodied in the models, the relative distribution of trade and output effects, and the strength of relative price movements. The first is clearly not a robust feature of empirical multicountry models, although the last probably is.[11]

The difference in LM-curve slopes is even more noticeable in the case of the reduction in OECD consumption (shock 2), where the pattern of changes in nominal income for all three countries is generally more similar in the short run, but U.S. interest-rate reductions are relatively smaller, implying dollar appreciation. In the case of the U.S. fiscal shock (shock 3), there is much less scope for disagreement about relative interest-rate movements, since the effects of a contraction on U.S. income are initially many times greater than for its G3 partners. Nonetheless, in INTERLINK the relative movements in interest differentials are too small to offset the combination of expectation effects (generated by relative price movements) and an improving U.S. net-asset position, so that the dollar appreciates unless monetary policies in Japan and Germany become more restrictive.[12] Again, this is not an empirically robust result.

A further important reservation in the case of exchange-rate targeting relates to the specification of expectations. To the extent that these are modeled as stable, backward-looking processes, it is hardly surprising that the benefits and costs of exchange-rate targeting are shown to be relatively slight. In the real world, one of the main objectives of exchange-rate coordination would be precisely to stabilize the otherwise volatile reactions of expectations.[13]

---

11. Confirmation of the general disagreement in country ranking of LM-slope coefficients for multi-country models is given by Helliwell, Cockerline, and Lafrance (1990) and by Brayton and Marquez (1990).

12. For some other multicountry models the reverse is true, so that exchange-rate targeting would imply a greater relaxation of interest rates in Japan and Germany.

13. An alternative way of proceeding in the context of INTERLINK would be to assess the effectiveness of alternative policies, subject also to systematic changes in exchange-rate expectations.

For most *demand-side* shocks, the maintenance of unchanged real interest rates—short- or long-term—gives some degree of stabilization, although for Japan and Germany money targeting is more effective. In general, a rule based on fixed real long-term rates (policy option E) appears to be a more effective stabilizer than one based on fixed short-term rates (option D). As illustrated earlier, an essential feature of this option is that it gives a relatively high weight to inflation as a signal and thereby brings forward the degree of policy action given by rules based on short-term rates or the money supply. The robustness of such results is therefore strongly dependent on the specification of the interest-yield curve in the model.

For the United States, the differential effects of alternative policy regimes are less clearly defined across demand shocks, and figure 12-1 illustrates a far greater degree of clustering of points, also reflected in the classification of "preferred policies" in table 12-3. For a non-OECD shock, whereby the United States is less affected than either Japan or Germany, fixed real interest rates are marginally more stabilizing, particularly with a real long-term rate target. For the consumption shock, the evidence is more mixed, with the minimum output disturbance given by a money target, and with little difference in inflation responses between a fixed real long-term rate and either of the money-target options. In the case of a U.S. fiscal shock, a money-target regime is generally most effective for the United States, with exchange-rate targeting being marginally superior (but largely at the expense of Japan and Germany).

The general pattern of results and ranking of rules differs for the *supply-side* OECD wage shock. For the benchmark case of fixed nominal interest rates, the output effects for Germany and Japan are minimized, since the stimulation of activity resulting from substantially reduced real interest rates more than outweighs the adverse effects of higher wage costs. This, however, is entirely at the expense of price stability.

Among the alternative policy rules, fixed real short-term rates in general perform best in terms of the combined output-inflation criterion. For the United States, there is very little to choose between regimes on inflation, although a fixed long-term real rate gives the greatest stabilization. For Japan, minimum inflation over the period is given by exchange-rate coordination, although this result appears to be influenced by the choice of terminal point (see the appendix, figure 12A-4). For most of the simulation period, a fixed long-term real rate provides the most stable path for prices, although in the longer run the inflation rate has yet to stabilize. This is also true for Germany, where there is little difference in terminal inflation values between the fixed real long-term rate and money-target regimes.

An important reservation in following a rule based on fixed real long-term rates is that the path of short-term rates is erratic in the case of a sustained inflation shock, a feature that reflects the specific dynamics of the rule (as shown in table 12-1). For Japan and Germany, the simulated movements in short-term rates necessary to achieve such a target simulation are not at all realistic, suggesting the need for an additional instrument-smoothing criterion. A fixed real short-term rate gives a generally more credible result, although with higher inflation costs.

Concluding Remarks

This chapter has presented simulation results from the OECD INTERLINK model that illustrate the implications of selecting alternative, simple monetary policy regimes for four simulated shocks of a global nature. The results, in general, suggest that simple monetary regimes might be used effectively to stabilize output and inflation responses, although important trade-offs exist that might be better mediated by a more flexible choice of targets and instruments.

For *demand-side* shocks, there is some evidence that rules based on money-supply targets are generally more effective for Japan and Germany, and that there are no stabilization gains to be made from the specific form of exchange-rate targeting considered here. This result is empirically fragile because it is sensitive to the precise specification of the exchange-rate model (one that in INTERLINK excludes important forward-looking elements) and the relative LM slopes for individual G3 countries (for which empirical evidence is mixed). For the United States, the results are mixed, and a regime based on fixed real long-term rates appears to be marginally more effective in some cases, although by relatively narrow margins.

In the case of a *supply-side* wage shock, regimes based on fixed real interest rates appear to be more effective, given a mixed inflation- and output-based criterion. With a sustained inflationary shock, however, a regime based on fixed real long-term rates may imply instrument instability for some countries.

In addition to the specific simulations presented, preliminary tests were made using rules based on alternative nominal-income targets. Exact targeting in this form proved to be unsuccessful on two counts: the specific dynamics of the relationship between interest rates and nominal income in the model imply severe instrument instability, and the relative importance of the exchange-rate mechanism in this relationship makes the simultaneous pursuit of precise nominal income targets by the G3 countries difficult, except at the expense of other OECD country objectives. Inspection of the exact money-target rules used, however, confirms that these are close to being looser forms of nominal-income-based regimes for interest rates.

Just how far these results conflict with other evidence on the effectiveness of monetary regimes—for example, that reported by Frenkel, Goldstein, and

Masson (1989)—is difficult to say. Specific model features are both influential and empirically fragile, and the absence of explicit forward-looking elements and credibility effects in the current version of INTERLINK may be a serious disadvantage. Global shocks differ from single-country shocks, however, by putting rather less emphasis on the exchange-rate mechanism and are also more likely to involve backward-looking expectations elements in the face of major one-of-a-kind shocks. In this respect, the conclusion that the relative performance of simple policy regimes varies with the nature of the shocks facing the economy is difficult to reject.

Appendix: Specifications and Detailed Simulation Results

The first part of this appendix provides more detail about the specification of shocks in this exercise and of the monetary policy reaction functions in INTERLINK.

Specification of Shocks

To illustrate the influence of alternative monetary policy regimes on INTER-LINK properties, the following four shocks were simulated over a five-year period (1987–91).

SHOCK 1: AN INCREASE IN NON-OECD IMPORT DEMAND. This case assumes a 5 percent, stepped increase in the volume level of non-OECD country imports. The normal mechanism within the model (whereby an ex ante change in non-OECD imports would progressively be modified by changes in interest-debt repayments and net export revenues) is shut off, although interest flows themselves are endogenous and affect service flows and the current balance.

SHOCK 2: A FALL IN OECD PRIVATE CONSUMPTION. This case assumes a simultaneous 1 percent, ex ante stepped reduction in the levels of private consumption for all OECD countries. The shock is administered through calibrated changes in consumption-equation residuals and therefore allows consumption to adjust endogenously to subsequent changes in income, prices, and financial-sector variables.

SHOCK 3: A U.S. FISCAL CONTRACTION. The case of a U.S. fiscal contraction (a reduction in real expenditure equivalent to 1 percent of GNP) has been featured in earlier studies, although without a great deal of experimentation in monetary policy assumptions.[14] As cuts in U.S. public expenditure become progressively real, the emphasis on appropriate monetary policy settings becomes more pressing. At the same time, an update of results for the U.S. fiscal shock provides a useful point of reference for the evolution of model properties.

SHOCK 4: AN INCREASE IN OECD WAGE RATES. This case assumes a common ex-ante increase in wage rates for all OECD countries, administered as a 2 percent increase in wage-equation residuals in the starting period. The subsequent scale of effects on wage rates is therefore conditioned by the strength of wage and price interactions and by the modifying influence of demand pressure in goods and labor markets.

OTHER ASSUMPTIONS. In addition, all simulations assume that real government expenditure and marginal tax rates will be maintained at baseline levels for OECD countries. Interest flows, taxes and social security, and the nominal values of expenditures are fully endogenous, implying that overall government balances are also endogenous in real and nominal terms.

Member countries of the EMS and the majority of other European economies (Austria, the countries of Scandinavia, Switzerland, and others) are assumed to target interest rates in order to maintain parity with the deutsche mark. The United Kingdom is treated as an exception and operates the same monetary policy options as the G3 countries, which are discussed below. The remaining OECD member countries are assumed either to operate a policy reaction function linking domestic interest rates to weighted foreign interest rates or to target a constant real exchange rate.

Specification of the Monetary Reaction Functions

POLICY OPTION A: UNCHANGED NOMINAL INTEREST RATES. The money supply is assumed to accommodate endogenous movements in money demand. This monetary regime is the benchmark case most often used in simulations of INTERLINK.

POLICY OPTION B: FIXED MONEY TARGETS. Money supply is assumed to be fixed at baseline values, with short-term interest rates endogenous to eliminate excess money demand. This inverted money-demand equation is

$$(12\text{-}1) \qquad (m^d - p) = ay - br_s + c(m^d - p)_{-1},$$

---

14. Useful comparative studies of empirical model properties for a U.S. fiscal shock are Bryant, Holtham, and Hooper (1988); Bryant, Helliwell, and Hooper (1989); Helliwell (1988); and, in the context of INTERLINK, Herd and Ballis (1988) and Herd (1989).

where $m^d = m^s = 0$. This implies a rule of the form

(12-2)
$$r_s = \frac{a}{b}y + \frac{p}{b} - \frac{c}{b}p_{-1},$$

where

> r_s = the absolute deviation of short-term rates from baseline
> y = the percentage deviation of real income levels from baseline
> p = the percentage deviation of price levels from baseline
> a = the income impact elasticity of money demand
> b = the interest-rate impact elasticity of money demand
> c = the lagged adjustment parameter.

POLICY OPTION C: EXCHANGE-RATE TARGETING. Japan and Germany use interest rates to hold exchange-rate parity with the dollar, whereas the United States is assumed to follow a fixed-money regime as in the preceding case. Short-term interest rates are endogenized through inversion of the model's exchange-rate equations. Broadly unchanged from the version described by Holtham (1984), the relevant relationships can be expressed in terms of deviations from baseline as

(12-3)
$$(e - e*) = c(r_s - r_f) + dw$$

(12-4)
$$e* = fe_{-1} - (1 - f)(p - p_f),$$

where p_f and r_f represent weighted foreign prices and interest rates and $e*$ is the expected exchange rate. Equation 12-3 determines the deviation between actual and expected rates as a function of interest differentials and the stock of foreign assets, w, expressed as a share of world wealth. Equation 12-4 represents a backward-looking adaptive expectations mechanism that is driven by relative price differentials. Substituting equation 12-4 into 12-3, and holding exchange rates unchanged at their baseline levels, implies an overall reaction function of the form

(12-5)
$$r_s = r_f + \frac{(1 - f)}{c}(p - p_f) - \frac{d}{c}w.$$

POLICY OPTION D: FIXED REAL SHORT-TERM INTEREST RATES. Expressed as deviations from baseline, the real rate is defined as

(12-6)
$$i_s = r_s - \dot{p}.$$

If the real short-term rate is held unchanged in simulation, this involves a simple rule of the form

(12-7)
$$r_s = \dot{p}.$$

POLICY OPTION E: FIXED REAL LONG-TERM INTEREST RATES. Defining the real long-term interest rate, i_ι, in a way analogous to the real short-term rate gives

(12-8) $$i_\iota = r_\iota - \dot{p},$$

which, along with the yield-curve relationship of the general form

(12-9) $$\Delta r_\iota = g\Delta r_s - h(r_\iota - r_s)_{-1},$$

gives an expression for the short-term interest-rate rule for unchanged long-term real rates as

(12-10) $$r_s = \frac{\dot{p}}{g} + \frac{(g - h)}{g} r_{s(-1)} - \frac{(1 - h)}{g} \dot{p}_{-1}.$$

Simulation Results in Detail

This part of the appendix provides extensive detail on the transmission mechanisms and quantitative responses of the G3 economies to the combination of shocks and monetary policy regimes.

Tables 12A-1 through 12A-4 are organized as follows.

Simulations

1. A 5 percent increase in non-OECD imports (table 12A-1)
2. A 1 percent ex ante reduction in OECD private consumption (table 12A-2)
3. U.S. real fiscal contraction equivalent to 1 percent of real GNP (table 12A-3)
4. A 2 percent ex ante increase in OECD wage rates (table 12A-4).

G3 Policy Options

A. Fixed nominal interest rates
B. Fixed money supply
C. Exchange-rate targets (Japan and Germany)
D. Unchanged real short-term interest rates
E. Unchanged real long-term interest rates.

In all the tables, changes in real GNP, the GNP deflator, and effective exchange rates are expressed as percentage deviations from baseline levels; changes in short-term interest rates are expressed as percentage points; current-account trade balances are expressed in billions of dollars.

Table 12A-1. *Five Percent Increase in Non-OECD Import Demand*

Policy option A: Fixed nominal interest rates

Variable[a]	Deviations from baseline				
	Year 1	Year 2	Year 3	Year 4	Year 5
Real GNP					
United States	0.3	0.4	0.4	0.4	0.4
Japan	0.5	0.9	1.1	1.3	1.5
Germany	0.6	0.7	0.6	0.6	0.8
OECD	0.3	0.5	0.6	0.7	0.8
GNP deflator					
United States	0.1	0.3	0.7	1.0	1.5
Japan	0.2	0.9	1.7	2.8	3.9
Germany	0.3	1.0	1.8	2.5	3.4
OECD	0.1	0.4	0.6	1.0	1.9
Short-term interest rate					
United States					
Japan			—Unchanged—		
Germany					
OECD					
Effective exchange rate					
United States	0.1	0.3	0.5	0.7	1.0
Japan	−0.1	−0.4	−0.8	−1.1	−1.5
Germany	−0.1	−0.3	−0.7	−1.2	−1.9
Current balances					
United States	3	4	5	5	4
Japan	7	9	9	10	12
Germany	3	3	5	7	8
OECD	21	24	28	32	36

Policy option B: Fixed monetary aggregates (broad)

Variable[a]	Deviations from baseline				
	Year 1	Year 2	Year 3	Year 4	Year 5
Real GNP					
United States	0.3	0.4	0.1	0	0
Japan	0.4	0.5	0.3	0.1	0
Germany	0.4	0.2	0	0	0
OECD	0.3	0.3	0.2	0.1	0.1
GNP deflator					
United States	0.1	0.4	0.7	1.0	1.3
Japan	0.2	0.6	0.9	1.0	1.0
Germany	0.2	0.6	0.7	0.8	1.0
OECD	0.1	0.4	0.6	0.8	1.0
Short-term interest rate					
United States	0.2	0.4	0.5	0.5	0.6
Japan	0.8	1.3	1.3	1.0	0.7
Germany	0.9	1.0	0.6	0.7	1.0
OECD	0.4	0.6	0.6	0.6	0.7
Effective exchange rate					
United States	−0.2	−0.4	−0.4	−0.5	−0.6
Japan	0.2	0.2	0.2	0.2	0.2
Germany	0.2	0.6	0.9	1.0	1.0
Current balances					
United States	4	6	10	13	14
Japan	8	11	14	17	21
Germany	4	5	6	7	9
OECD	25	33	41	50	59

a. Units are as defined in the text.

Table 12A-1 *(continued)*

Policy option C: United States maintains monetary aggregate; Germany and Japan target exchange rates

Variable[a]	Deviations from baseline				
	Year 1	Year 2	Year 3	Year 4	Year 5
Real GNP					
United States	0.3	0.3	0.2	0	0
Japan	0.5	0.7	0.6	0.5	0.3
Germany	0.5	0.4	0.1	0	0.1
OECD	0.3	0.4	0.3	0.2	0.2
GNP deflator					
United States	0.1	0.3	0.6	0.8	1.1
Japan	0.2	0.8	1.3	1.7	2.0
Germany	0.3	0.6	1.1	1.2	1.5
OECD	0.1	0.4	0.7	0.9	1.2
Short-term interest rate					
United States	0.1	0.3	0.4	0.5	0.5
Japan	0.2	0.7	0.9	1.0	0.9
Germany	0.4	0.9	0.9	0.7	0.8
OECD	0.1	0.4	0.5	0.5	0.6
Effective exchange rate					
United States					
Japan			——Unchanged——		
Germany					
Current balances					
United States	4	6	9	12	13
Japan	7	9	11	15	19
Germany	4	5	6	8	8
OECD	23	30	38	46	54

Policy option D: Unchanged real short-term interest rates

Variable[a]	Deviations from baseline				
	Year 1	Year 2	Year 3	Year 4	Year 5
Real GNP					
United States	0.3	0.3	0.2	0.1	0.1
Japan	0.5	0.7	0.7	0.7	0.7
Germany	0.5	0.5	0.3	0.3	0.4
OECD	0.3	0.4	0.4	0.3	0.4
GNP deflator					
United States	0.1	0.3	0.6	0.8	1.1
Japan	0.2	0.7	1.3	1.9	2.5
Germany	0.3	0.8	1.3	1.6	2.1
OECD	0.1	0.4	0.7	1.0	1.4
Short-term interest rate					
United States	0.1	0.3	0.3	0.3	0.3
Japan	0.3	0.5	0.6	0.6	0.5
Germany	0.4	0.5	0.4	0.4	0.6
OECD	0.2	0.2	0.2	0.2	0.2
Effective exchange rate					
United States	0	0.1	0.2	0.3	0.4
Japan	0	0.0	−0.1	−0.3	−0.4
Germany	0	−0.1	−0.3	−0.4	−0.5
Current balances					
United States	4	6	8	10	10
Japan	7	9	11	13	16
Germany	4	4	6	7	8
OECD	23	29	34	41	48

a. Units are as defined in the text.

Table 12A-1 *(continued)*

Policy option E: Unchanged real long-term interest rates

Variable[a]	Deviations from baseline				
	Year 1	Year 2	Year 3	Year 4	Year 5
Real GNP					
United States	0.2	0.2	0.1	0.1	0.1
Japan	0.4	0.5	0.5	0.5	0.5
Germany	0.4	0.2	0.2	0.2	0.2
OECD	0.3	0.3	0.2	0.2	0.2
GNP deflator					
United States	0.1	0.3	0.5	0.7	1.0
Japan	0.2	0.6	0.9	1.3	1.7
Germany	0.2	0.5	0.8	1.1	1.5
OECD	0.1	0.3	0.5	0.8	1.1
Short-term interest rate					
United States	0.4	0.3	0.3	0.4	0.4
Japan	0.9	0.8	0.6	0.5	0.5
Germany	1.1	0.4	0.4	0.5	0.6
OECD	0.6	0.4	0.3	0.4	0.3
Effective exchange rate					
United States	−0.2	−0.1	0	0	0.1
Japan	0.2	0.3	0.3	0.1	0
Germany	0.2	0.1	−0.1	−0.1	−0.1
Current balances					
United States	5	7	9	11	12
Japan	8	10	13	15	17
Germany	4	5	5	7	9
OECD	27	31	37	44	51

a. Units are as defined in the text.

SHOCK 1: INCREASE IN NON-OECD DEMAND (TABLE 12A-1 AND FIGURE 12A-1). With *unchanged nominal interest rates* (policy option A in the preceding section and in table 12A-1), the real-GNP effect for the total OECD area rises over the first two years by 0.5 percent and continues to drift upward to 0.8 percent above baseline after five years, with world trade about 2 percent higher. For the United States and Germany, real GNP levels off at 0.4 percent and 0.7 percent higher, respectively, whereas GNP in Japan rises more steadily over the period, to become 1.5 percent higher in the fifth year, reflecting a more dynamic trade performance.

With sustained increases in output and employment, inflationary pressures continue throughout the period, with price levels for the United States, Japan, and Germany respectively higher by 1.5, 3.9, and 3.4 percent by the end of the period—equivalent to average increases in annual inflation rates of 0.3, 0.8, and 0.7 percent. As illustrated in figure 12A-1, inflation rates accelerate throughout the period, consistent with long-run model instability under a fixed nominal interest-rate rule.

Figure 12A-1. *Five Percent Stepped Increase in Non-OECD Imports*

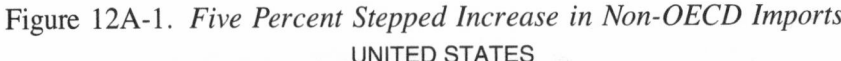

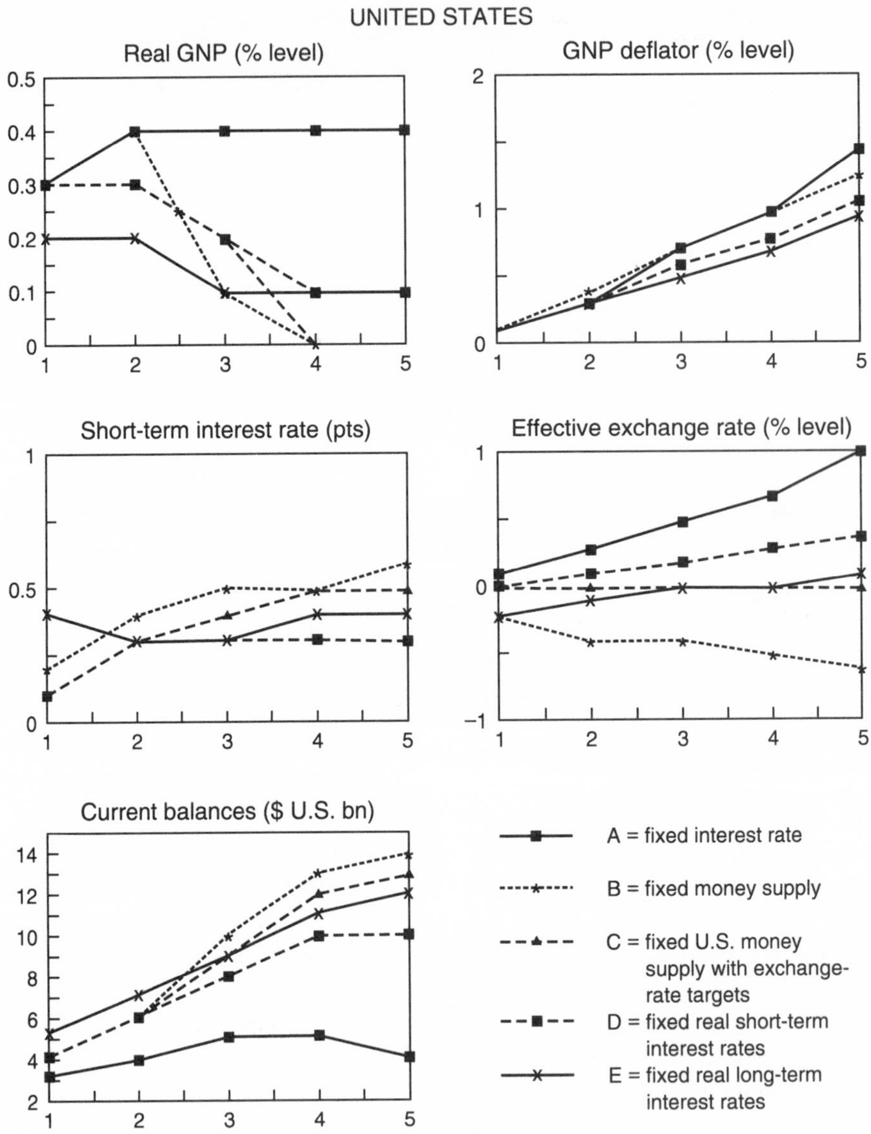

UNITED STATES

Figure 12A-1 *(continued)*

JAPAN

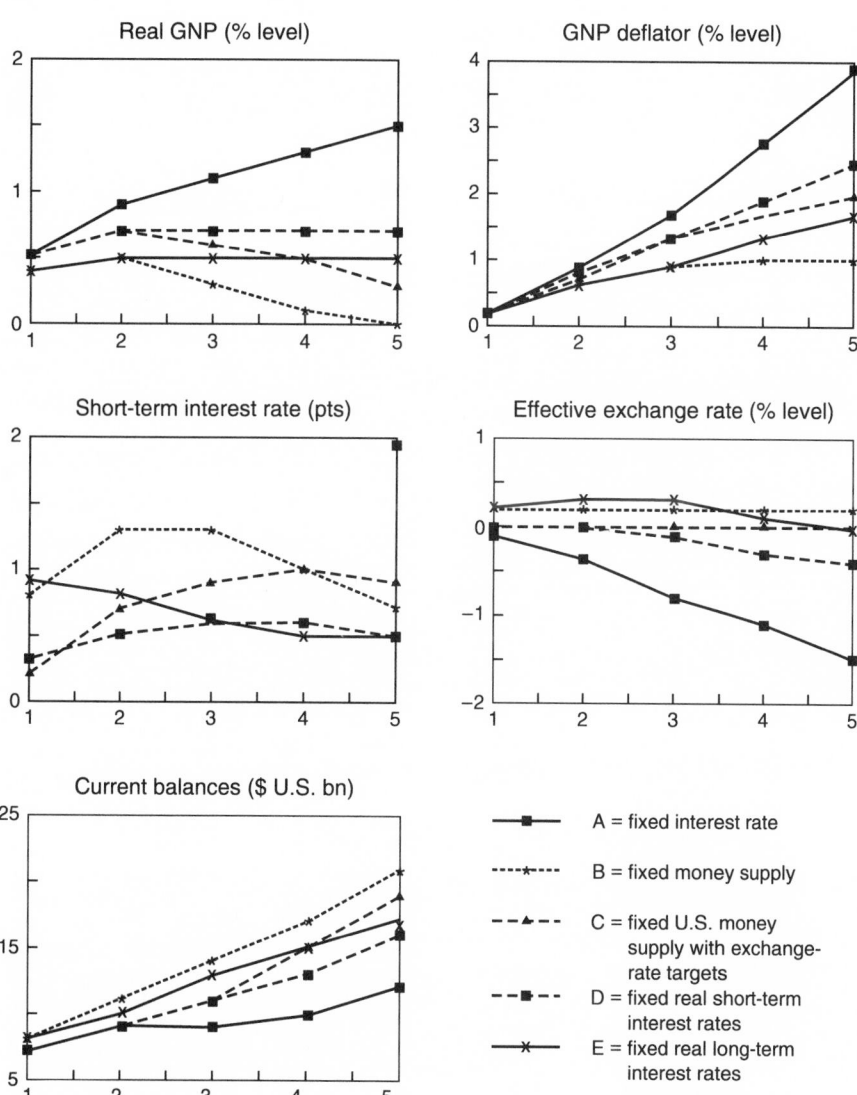

Figure 12A-1 *(continued)*

GERMANY

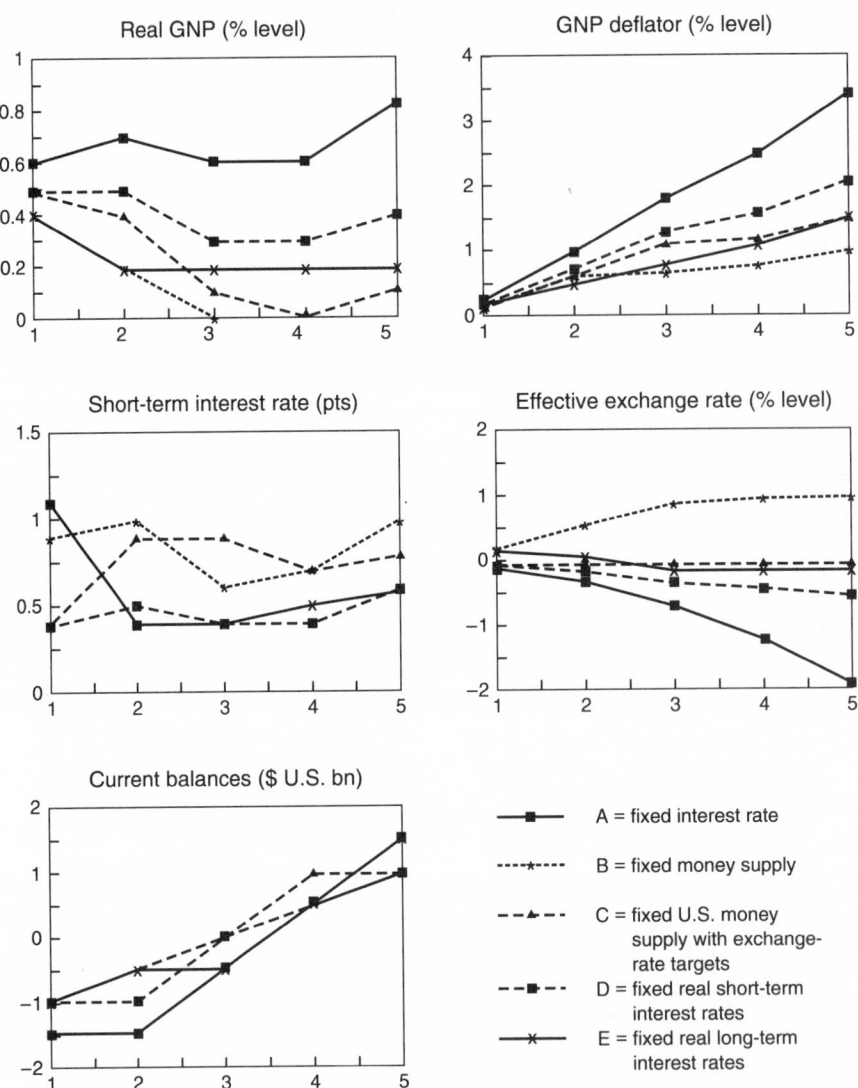

Figure 12A-1 *(continued)*

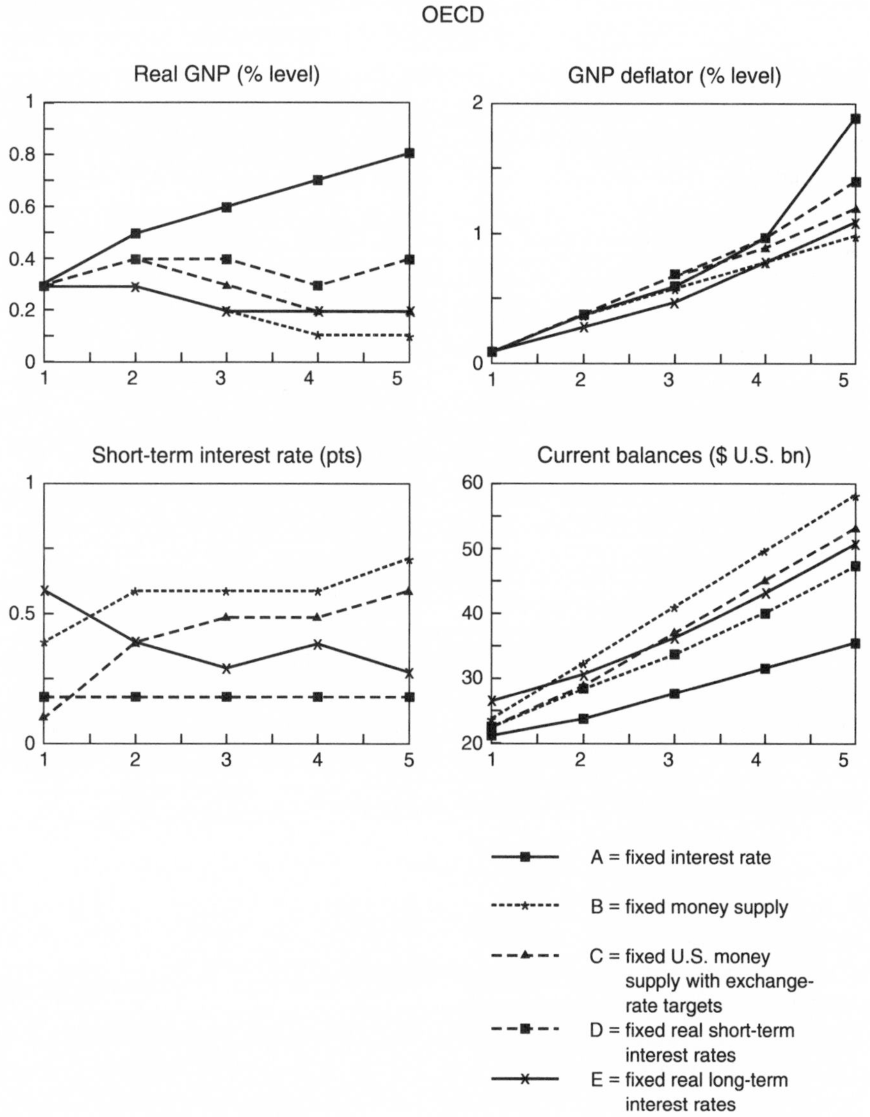
OECD
Real GNP (% level)
0
0.2
0.4
0.6
0.8
1
1
2
3
4
5
GNP deflator (% level)
0
1
2
1
2
3
4
5
Short-term interest rate (pts)
0
0.5
1
1
2
3
4
5
Current balances ($ U.S. bn)
20
30
40
50
60
1
2
3
4
5
A = fixed interest rate
B = fixed money supply
C = fixed U.S. money supply with exchange-rate targets
D = fixed real short-term interest rates
E = fixed real long-term interest rates

Although there is a common inflationary tendency, price differentials are further reinforced by the exchange-rate mechanism—a steady depreciation of the yen and deutsche mark against the dollar, resulting in correspondingly higher import costs. For the OECD area, the current trade balance improves steadily over the period, reflecting both the direct effect of higher exports and rising interest flows from the non-OECD area associated with rising debt accumulation. The adverse effect on the balance of the non-OECD area is nonetheless curtailed to the extent that this area, too, benefits from subsequently higher levels of world trade.

With *unchanged monetary aggregates* (policy option B, table 12A-1), the underlying excess demand for money drives up short-term interest rates so that the initial output effects are progressively crowded out, through lower consumption and investment. Despite a continuing higher level of world trade, the impact on OECD-area GNP is negligible by the fourth year. This reduction in demand pressure in turn tends to alleviate inflationary pressures. U.S. short-term rates remain 0.5 percent higher throughout, whereas for Japan and Germany short-term rates rise sharply in the first two years. For Japan they tend to fall back as real GNP and prices stabilize; for Germany there is some relaxation, but with a further tightening in the final year caused by a rebound in output.

Compared with policy option A, the patterns of price response are significantly altered. Given initially larger increases in real and nominal income for Japan and Germany, corresponding increases in short-term rates are proportionately larger than for the United States, implying a greater degree of crowding out and moderation in prices. With prices in all three countries tending to move in a broadly similar fashion and smaller increases in U.S. rates, the pattern of currency movements is reversed, with the yen and deutsche mark appreciating in dollar terms. For the United States, this implies little overall difference in price response compared with policy option A.

For the OECD area, the improvement in the current balance is significantly increased, by up to a further $23 billion in the fifth year. This reflects two principal features: the relative reduction in OECD domestic demand and imports, and higher interest flows associated with a higher non-OECD trade deficit and higher world interest rates. The United States and Japan benefit disproportionately, accounting jointly for about 80 percent of further improvement in the area's current balance.

For Japan and Germany, *targeting exchange rates* (policy option C, table 12A-1) implies looser monetary control than in the money-targeting case, with smaller short-run increases in interest rates being required to offset an incipient appreciation against the dollar. This implies a somewhat slower erosion of the gains to real GNP, but at the cost of higher prices. For Japan, where the initial demand stimulus is strongest, GNP remains above baseline throughout the period, albeit at a declining rate. Compared with the previous case, prices for Japan no longer stabilize, and there is an approximate doubling of the increase in the annual inflation rate. For Germany, the induced increase in short-term interest rates is sufficient to erode the GNP stimulus progressively, but prices continue to rise over the period.

The main implication for the United States is a somewhat slower erosion of the output effect, given both higher world demand and little overall change in the U.S. competitive position. The rate of increase in U.S. prices, however, is somewhat moderated, with the neutralization of the dollar's fall under policy option B more than compensating for a larger increase in world prices. Movements in the OECD current balance are marginally less favorable over the period, given higher activity and marginally lower interest rates.

Maintaining *unchanged real short-term interest rates* (policy option D, table 12A-1) effectively links movements in short-term rates to inflation in each of the G3 countries. Compared with having fixed money aggregates— where price and income *levels* provide the main stimulus to interest rates— this simulation involves a significant easing of policy. For Japan and Germany, short-term rates are raised by an average 0.5 points (roughly half of the increases under policy option B). For the United States, the degree of relaxation is somewhat less.

The overall consequences for output vary among the G3 countries. In the United States, the moderate increase in short-term rates is sufficient to permit a steady attenuation of the real GNP effects. For Japan, the increase in the real-GNP level stabilizes in the second year at around 0.7 percent; for Germany, initial increases are marginally reduced beyond the second year, to lie midway between those for the alternative accommodating and nonaccommodating policy assumptions (policy option C). Prices also show somewhat different relative movements. For Japan and Germany, continuing demand pressure results in larger increases in price levels, with inflation rates raised by an average 0.4 to 0.5 percent over the period. For the United States, prices continue to rise but at a slower rate compared with that for a fixed money target (policy option B). This result reflects the combination of price and interest rate movements, which cause an appreciation of the dollar. Looked at another way, the interest differentials arising in the case of fixed monetary aggregates significantly exceed the underlying inflation differentials.

As discussed in the preceding section for the simulation specifications, the case of *unchanged real long-term interest rates* (policy option E, table 12A-1) differs from policy option D largely in the speeds of response. The net result is a much quicker policy response, with short-term rates rising sharply in the first year, compared with policy options A–D, and output and prices are squeezed more in the earlier half of the simulation. Real GNP responses are therefore flatter, leveling off for Japan and Germany and being more quickly eroded for the United States. As a result, price responses for all three countries are also more subdued. For the United States, overall price increases are smaller than for fixed monetary aggregates (policy option B), reflecting the earlier squeeze on output. For all three countries, price responses are lower, and the output gains are smoother and more continuing, than under policy option C. By putting an early emphasis on inflation and accepting smaller short-term output increases, the overall result for the G3 countries is, arguably, superior to that under policy option C, although in the longer run it is more inflationary than under option B for Japan and Germany.

SHOCK 2: DECLINE IN OECD PRIVATE CONSUMPTION (TABLE 12A-2 AND FIGURE 12A-2). With no monetary controls for the G3 countries (table 12A-2, policy option A), the effects of a global 1 percent reduction in OECD consumption levels are substantial and sustained, with real GNP and inflation reduced more than one for one with the reduction in demand. As in the previous simulation, the paths of output and prices show little or no sign of longer-run stability with *fixed nominal interest rates*.

Introducing *fixed monetary aggregate targets* for the G3 countries (policy option B, table 12A-2) leads to a major stabilization of the situation. Short-term rates are driven down substantially to offset the fall in real and nominal demand. As indicated in table 12-1, significantly lower interest rate elasticities for Japan and Germany imply steeper LM slopes and, therefore, substantially larger movements in corresponding short-term rates. Interest-rate differentials for Germany and Japan thus move favorably vis-à-vis the United States, and effective exchange rates move in a direction opposite to that under policy option A, with the dollar appreciating against the deutsche mark and yen.

The reductions in short-term interest rates feed through fairly quickly to the real side, partially offsetting the initial disturbance to consumption and business and residential investment. For all three countries, the initial decline in GNP is stabilized by the second year, and then reversed by the end of the third year, with output rising above baseline thereafter. The cumulative movements in output and employment are nonetheless negative, implying sustained reductions in price levels, although for Japan and Germany the downward trend is reversed in later years. Differential movements in prices also reflect those of exchange rates, with dollar appreciation contributing to the above-average reduction in U.S. prices. For the OECD area as a whole, the GNP deflator is 1.9 percent lower by the fifth year, and real GNP is 0.3 percent higher.

Compared with policy option A, two general factors contribute to differences in current balance movements: lower interest rates imply a significant reduction in interest flows to the OECD countries, and more buoyant OECD domestic demand gives a smaller reduction in OECD imports.

Table 12A-2. *One Percent Ex Ante Reduction in OECD Private Consumption Levels*

Policy option A: Fixed nominal interest rates

Variable[a]	Deviations from baseline				
	Year 1	Year 2	Year 3	Year 4	Year 5
Real GNP					
United States	−1.2	−1.6	−1.3	−1.1	−1.2
Japan	−0.9	−1.7	−2.2	−2.5	−2.7
Germany	−1.2	−1.8	−1.6	−1.4	−1.8
OECD	−1.0	−1.5	−1.6	−1.6	−1.8
GNP deflator					
United States	−0.4	−1.4	−2.6	−3.8	−5.1
Japan	−0.4	−1.7	−3.4	−5.2	−7.2
Germany	−0.7	−2.4	−4.3	−5.9	−7.6
OECD	−0.4	−1.2	−2.4	−3.8	−4.8
Short-term interest rate			—All unchanged—		
Effective exchange rate					
United States	0.0	−0.2	−0.5	−0.7	−0.9
Japan	−0.1	0	0.5	1.2	2.0
Germany	0.1	0.8	1.6	2.2	2.7
Current balances					
United States	11	10	8	11	16
Japan	−3	−7	−6	−6	−8
Germany	−2	−3	−6	−11	−12
OECD	9	4	0	0	1
Corresponding real GNP responses (unlinked)					
United States	−0.9	−0.9	−0.5	−0.4	−0.3
Japan	−0.5	−0.7	−0.8	−0.8	−0.6
Germany	−0.5	−0.4	−0.2	−0.1	−0.1

Policy option B: Fixed monetary aggregates (broad)

Variable[a]	Deviations from baseline				
	Year 1	Year 2	Year 3	Year 4	Year 5
Real GNP					
United States	−1.2	−1.1	0	0.6	0.5
Japan	−0.7	−0.7	−0.2	0.3	0.6
Germany	−0.9	−0.5	0.2	0.3	0.2
OECD	−0.9	−0.8	−0.2	0.2	0.3
GNP deflator					
United States	−0.5	−1.4	−2.1	−2.4	−2.8
Japan	−0.4	−1.1	−1.4	−1.3	−0.9
Germany	−0.6	−1.4	−1.6	−1.5	−1.6
OECD	−0.3	−1.0	−1.5	−1.7	−1.9
Short-term interest rate					
United States	−0.6	−1.3	−1.2	−1.0	−1.2
Japan	−1.3	−2.1	−1.6	−0.5	0.2
Germany	−2.1	−2.3	−0.9	−0.6	−1.1
OECD	−1.2	−1.6	−1.1	−0.8	−0.9
Effective exchange rate					
United States	0.5	1.0	1.0	1.0	1.1
Japan	−0.4	−1.0	−1.2	−1.1	−0.9
Germany	−0.6	−0.7	−0.4	−0.4	−0.5
Current balances					
United States	9	5	−2	−2	2
Japan	−4	−7	−7	−6	−5
Germany	−3	−6	−6	−4	−4
OECD	1	−8	−7	−1	4

a. Units are as defined in the text.

Table 12A-2 *(continued)*

Policy option C: United States maintains monetary aggregate; Germany and Japan target exchange rates

Variable[a]	Deviations from baseline				
	Year 1	Year 2	Year 3	Year 4	Year 5
Real GNP					
United States	−1.1	−1.0	−0.1	0.4	0.4
Japan	−0.8	−1.0	−0.6	−0.3	0.1
Germany	−1.1	−1.1	−0.2	0.3	0.1
OECD	−1.0	−1.0	−0.5	−0.1	0
GNP deflator					
United States	−0.4	−1.3	−1.9	−2.3	−2.7
Japan	−0.4	−1.4	−2.1	−2.5	−2.4
Germany	−0.7	−1.9	−2.6	−2.6	−2.8
OECD	−0.4	−1.1	−1.7	−2.1	−2.3
Short-term interest rate					
United States	−0.6	−1.2	−1.2	−1.0	−1.2
Japan	−0.5	−1.2	−1.3	−1.2	−0.8
Germany	−0.8	−2.0	−1.8	−1.1	−1.1
OECD	−0.5	−0.9	−1.0	−0.9	−0.9
Effective exchange rate					
United States					
Japan			―Unchanged―		
Germany					
Current balances					
United States	9	4	−2	−2	2
Japan	−3	−5	−4	−4	−6
Germany	−2	−4	.−7	−8	−6
OECD	5	−4	−7	−3	0

Policy option D: Fixed real short-term interest rates

Variable[a]	Deviations from baseline				
	Year 1	Year 2	Year 3	Year 4	Year 5
Real GNP					
United States	−1.1	−1.0	−0.3	−0.1	−0.2
Japan	−0.8	−1.1	−1.0	−0.8	−0.7
Germany	−1.1	−1.1	−0.6	−0.6	−0.6
OECD	−0.9	−1.1	−0.7	−0.6	−0.6
GNP deflator					
United States	−0.5	−1.3	−1.9	−2.6	−3.2
Japan	−0.4	−1.3	−2.2	−2.9	−3.6
Germany	−0.6	−1.9	−2.8	−3.4	−4.2
OECD	−0.3	−1.0	−1.7	−2.3	−2.9
Short-term interest rate					
United States	−0.7	−0.9	−0.7	−0.6	−0.8
Japan	−0.6	−0.9	−0.9	−0.7	−0.6
Germany	−0.9	−1.3	−0.9	−0.6	−0.9
OECD	−0.5	−0.5	−0.4	−0.3	−0.3
Effective exchange rate					
United States	0	0	−0.1	−0.2	−0.2
Japan	0	−0.1	−0.1	0.1	0.2
Germany	0	0.1	0.5	0.7	0.8
Current balances					
United States	9	5	1	3	7
Japan	−3	−5	−5	−6	−7
Germany	−2	−4	−6	−8	−8
OECD	4	−1	−3	−1	1

a. Units are as defined in the text.

Table 12A-2 *(continued)*

Policy option E: Fixed real long-term interest rates

Variable[a]	Deviations from baseline				
	Year 1	Year 2	Year 3	Year 4	Year 5
Real GNP					
United States	−0.8	−0.5	−0.2	−0.1	−0.1
Japan	−0.5	−0.6	−0.6	−0.4	−0.4
Germany	−0.7	−0.5	−0.3	−0.2	−0.2
OECD	−0.7	−0.6	−0.4	−0.4	−0.3
GNP deflator					
United States	−0.4	−0.9	−1.5	−2.0	−2.7
Japan	−0.3	−0.9	−1.4	−1.9	−2.2
Germany	−0.5	−1.1	−1.7	−2.2	−2.8
OECD	−0.3	−0.8	−1.2	−1.8	−2.2
Short-term interest rate					
United States	−1.2	−0.7	−0.7	−0.8	−0.8
Japan	−1.3	−1.2	−0.7	−0.4	−0.3
Germany	−2.4	−0.8	−0.7	−0.7	−0.9
OECD	−1.5	−0.7	−0.5	−0.5	−0.5
Effective exchange rate					
United States	0.1	0.3	0.3	0.1	0.2
Japan	0.1	−0.5	−0.4	−0.1	−0.1
Germany	−0.4	−0.3	−0.1	0.1	0.1
Current balances					
United States	5	3	2	3	6
Japan	−4	−5	−5	−6	−6
Germany	−3	−4	−4	−6	−7
OECD	0	1	−1	0	2

a. Units are as defined in the text.

Exchange-rate targeting (policy option C, table 12A-2) implies smaller reductions in nominal interest rates compared with policy option B. For Japan and Germany, the process of recovery is significantly delayed, with real GNP getting back toward baseline only in the fourth and fifth years. Cumulative downward pressure on prices continues, with little sign of stabilization toward the end of the period. The results for prices and real GNP for the United States are only slightly affected. For output, a reversal of previously adverse short-term movement in trade competitiveness implies a smaller short-term loss of exports, although this effect is only temporary because of greater reductions in foreign prices beyond the second year. Weaker world demand also contributes to a smaller rebound in U.S. real GNP. U.S. prices are marginally less weak, given the absence of dollar appreciation.

Because the greater proportion of the short-term reduction in nominal income for the consumption shock comes from the real side, adopting a policy of *fixed real short-term interest rates* (policy option D, table 12A-2) gives smaller interest-rate reductions than under money-aggregate targets. This in turn gives a further weakening of the recovery phase, with real GNP staying

Figure 12A-2. *One Percent Ex Ante Reduction in Private Consumption*

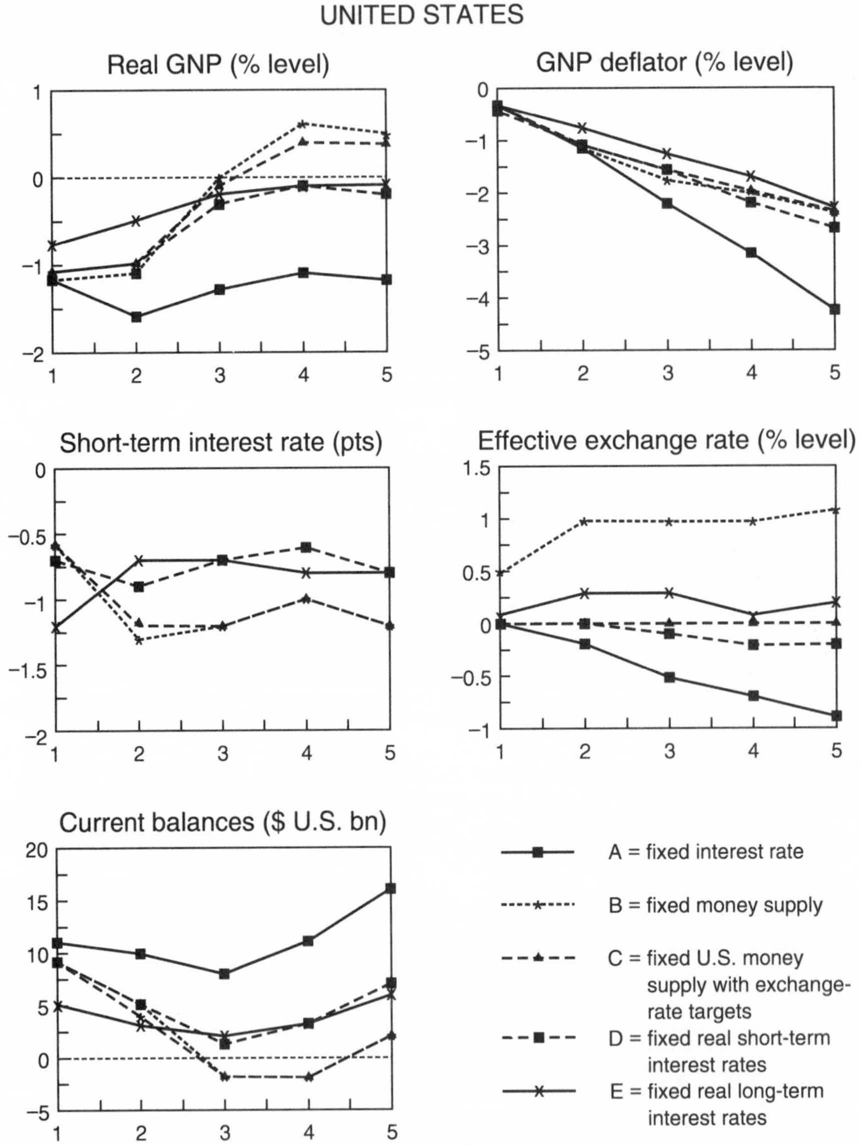

UNITED STATES

Real GNP (% level)

GNP deflator (% level)

Short-term interest rate (pts)

Effective exchange rate (% level)

Current balances ($ U.S. bn)

A = fixed interest rate

B = fixed money supply

C = fixed U.S. money supply with exchange-rate targets

D = fixed real short-term interest rates

E = fixed real long-term interest rates

Figure 12A-2 *(continued)*

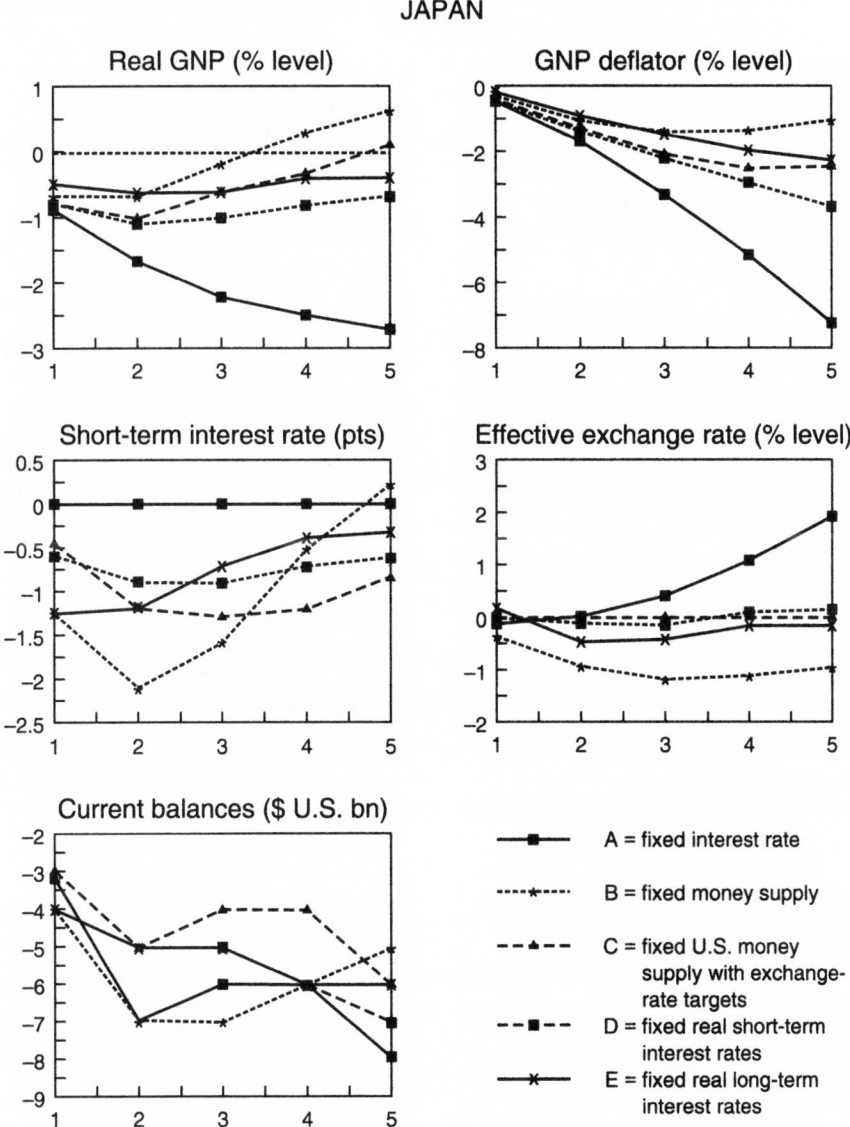

JAPAN

Figure 12A-2 *(continued)*

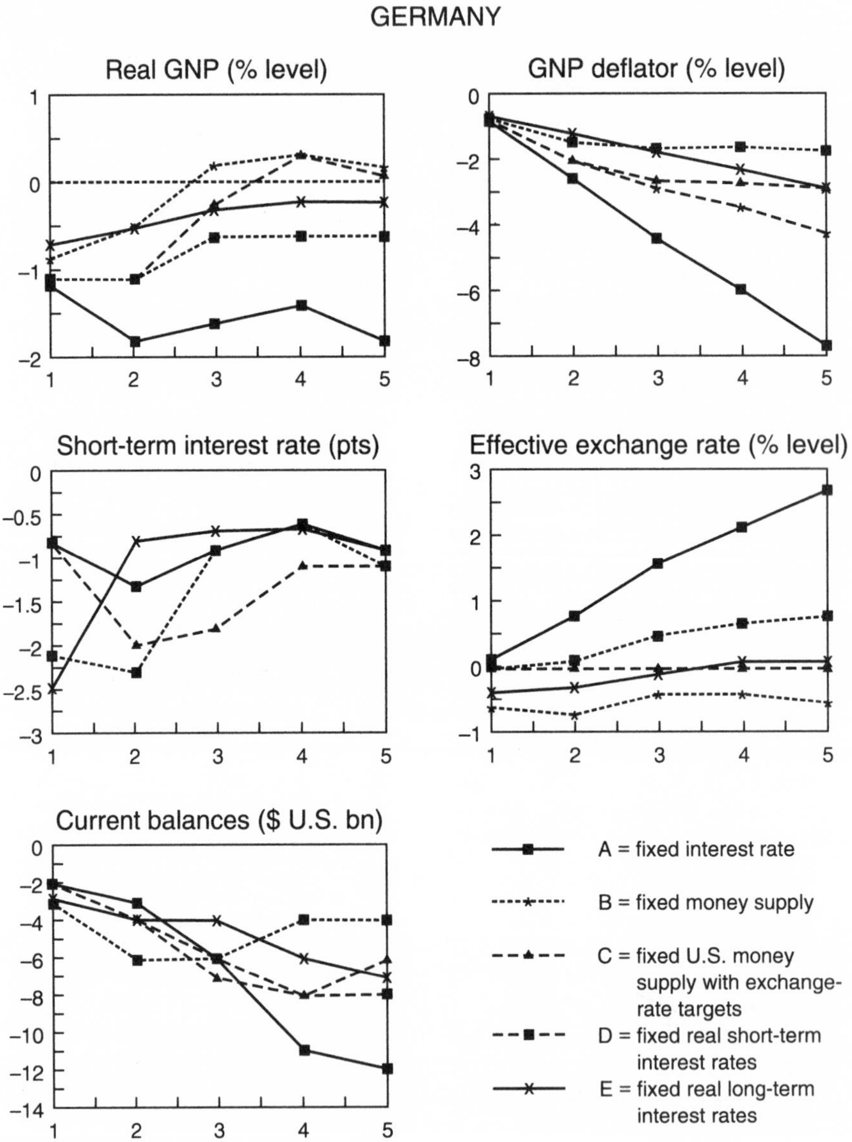

GERMANY

Real GNP (% level)

GNP deflator (% level)

Short-term interest rate (pts)

Effective exchange rate (% level)

Current balances ($ U.S. bn)

A = fixed interest rate

B = fixed money supply

C = fixed U.S. money supply with exchange-rate targets

D = fixed real short-term interest rates

E = fixed real long-term interest rates

Figure 12A-2 *(continued)*

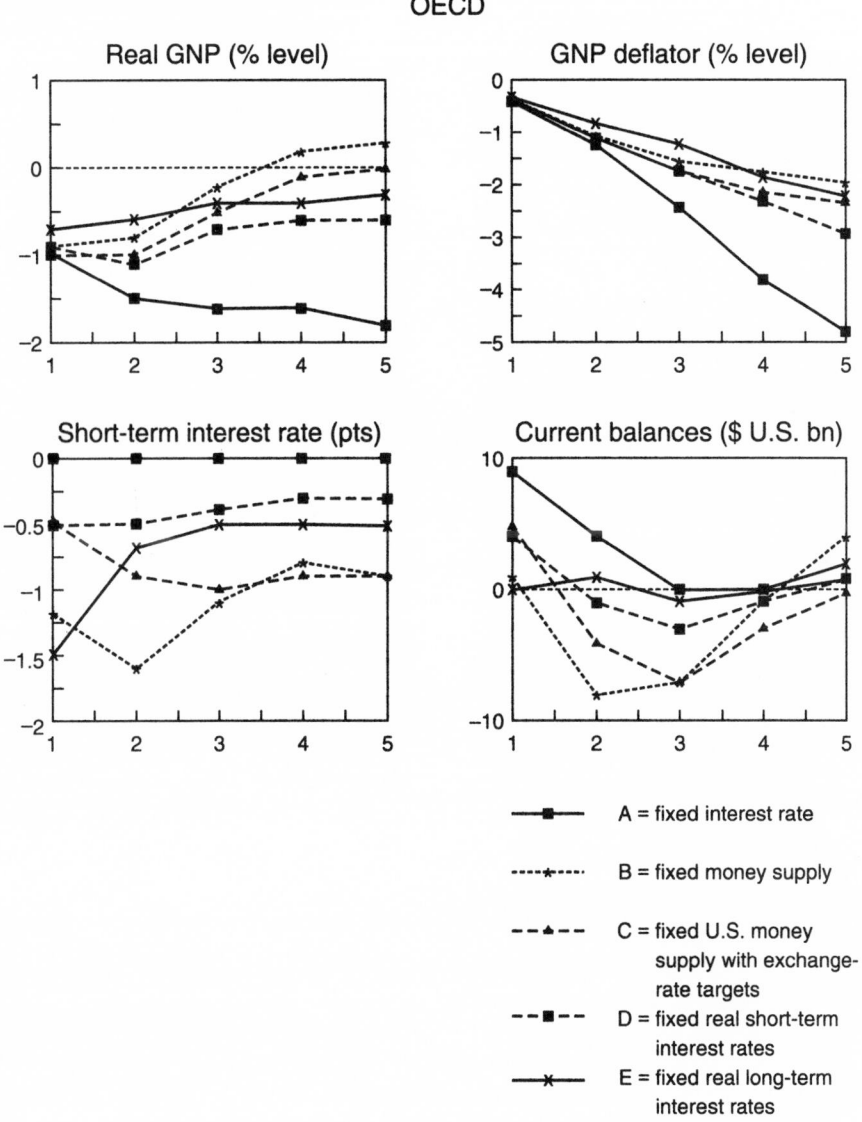

OECD

A = fixed interest rate

B = fixed money supply

C = fixed U.S. money supply with exchange-rate targets

D = fixed real short-term interest rates

E = fixed real long-term interest rates

below baseline throughout the period. For the United States, this implies a relatively soft landing; for Japan and Germany, sustained reductions in GNP levels. Prices and wages are therefore correspondingly weaker, with German prices being generally more responsive to the cumulative reductions in demand. The growing gap between Germany's and other countries' price levels largely offsets the influence of larger reductions in German short-term interest rates in first two years, resulting in a longer-term deutsche mark appreciation.

As in the case of the non-OECD demand shock, maintaining *unchanged real long-term interest rates* (policy option E, table 12A-2) puts a greater emphasis on the price inflation (deflation) signal and therefore gives a sharper initial reduction in short-term rates. For the first two years, this results in smaller GNP losses for all G3 countries than in any other case. The speed of recovery thereafter, however, is slower than with either money or exchange-rate targeting. Averaged over the period, the GNP losses for Germany and Japan are nonetheless marginally smaller than with an exchange-rate target. For the OECD area, GNP is reduced by an average 0.5 percent, compared with an average 0.8 percent under targeting of real short-term rates. The simulated fall in prices is also somewhat smaller, although there is no sign of stabilization.

SHOCK 3: U.S. FISCAL CONTRACTION (TABLE 12A-3, FIGURE 12A-3). With *unchanged nominal interest rates* (policy option A, table 12A-3) a U.S. real fiscal contraction produces substantial and growing international spillovers, with trade linkages contributing to a steady reduction in exports and real GNP in the United States and all major trading partners. At the same time, downward pressure on prices at home and abroad leads to a general disinflation, rising real interest rates, and further output adjustment.

In this context, a *money-targeting rule* (policy option B, table 12A-3) proves to be a very powerful force for stabilization. In the United States, the implied reduction in short-term interest rates (an average $1\frac{1}{4}$ percentage points) has a quick-acting effect on consumption and investment. The previously falling path for real GNP is checked by the second year and is effectively neutralized by the third year, and output bounces back thereafter. For the rest of the OECD, the trade-induced contraction is therefore quickly attenuated, and GNP is reduced by relatively little over the period.

With regard to prices, downward pressure on U.S. prices is somewhat alleviated, and exchange-rate pressures are significantly dampened, by the movement in interest-rate differentials. A smaller fall in the U.S. demand, combined with lower interest payments, implies more modest improvements in the U.S. current balance (by an average $17 billion) and correspondingly smaller adjustments in the imbalances.

Table 12A-3. *Reduction in U.S. Government Real Consumption Equivalent to 1 Percent of GNP*

Policy option A: Fixed nominal interest rates

Variable[a]	Deviations from baseline				
	Year 1	Year 2	Year 3	Year 4	Year 5
Real GNP					
United States	−1.6	−2.0	−1.8	−1.8	−2.1
Japan	−0.4	−0.9	−1.2	−1.5	−2.0
Germany	−0.4	−0.7	−0.7	−0.7	−1.0
OECD	−0.8	−1.1	−1.2	−1.3	−1.6
GNP deflator					
United States	−0.6	−1.8	−3.4	−5.2	−7.4
Japan	−0.2	−0.8	−1.7	−2.8	−4.3
Germany	−0.2	−0.8	−1.6	−2.4	−3.4
OECD	−0.3	−0.8	−1.8	−2.8	−4.1
Short-term interest rate					
United States					
Japan			Unchanged		
Germany					
OECD					
Effective exchange rate					
United States	0.3	1.2	2.2	3.4	4.9
Japan	−0.3	−1.6	−1.7	−2.1	−2.8
Germany	−0.1	−0.5	−0.9	−1.5	−2.1
Current balances					
United States	22	25	24	30	40
Japan	−6	−11	−12	−14	−19
Germany	−3	−4	−6	−11	−14
OECD	7	4	0	−1	−1

Policy option B: Fixed monetary aggregates (broad)

Variable[a]	Deviations from baseline				
	Year 1	Year 2	Year 3	Year 4	Year 5
Real GNP					
United States	−1.5	−1.2	0	0.4	0.2
Japan	−0.3	−0.2	0.1	0.3	0.3
Germany	−0.3	−0.2	0.1	0.1	0
OECD	−0.7	−0.6	0	0.2	0.2
GNP deflator					
United States	−0.5	−1.5	−2.2	−2.6	−3.1
Japan	−0.1	−0.4	−0.4	−0.2	0.1
Germany	−0.2	−0.4	−0.4	−0.4	−0.4
OECD	−0.3	−0.7	−1.0	−1.1	−1.3
Short-term interest rate					
United States	−0.8	−1.4	−1.3	−1.2	−1.5
Japan	−0.5	−0.7	−0.2	0.4	0.6
Germany	−0.6	−0.8	−0.1	0.1	−0.4
OECD	−0.4	−0.6	−0.2	−0.4	−0.1
Effective exchange rate					
United States	0.1	0.5	0.9	1.2	1.6
Japan	−0.1	−0.6	−0.9	−1.0	−1.2
Germany	−0.1	−0.4	−0.4	−0.6	−0.9
Current balances					
United States	19	17	12	15	22
Japan	−5	−7	−4	−3	−3
Germany	−3	−4	−3	−3	−4
OECD	5	−2	6	1	1

a. Units are as defined in the text.

Table 12A-3 (continued)

Policy option C: United States maintains fixed monetary aggregate; Germany and Japan target exchange rates

Variable[a]	Deviations from baseline				
	Year 1	Year 2	Year 3	Year 4	Year 5
Real GNP					
United States	-1.5	-1.1	0	0.3	0.2
Japan	-0.3	-0.4	-0.3	-0.2	-0.3
Germany	-0.3	-0.4	-0.1	-0.1	-0.3
OECD	-0.7	-0.6	-0.2	0	-0.1
GNP deflator					
United States	-0.5	-1.5	-2.1	-2.4	-2.9
Japan	-0.1	-0.5	-0.8	-0.9	-1.1
Germany	-0.2	-0.6	-0.9	-1.1	-1.4
OECD	-0.3	-0.7	-1.1	-1.3	-1.6
Short-term interest rate					
United States	-0.7	-1.4	-1.2	-1.1	-1.4
Japan	-0.2	0	0.3	0.4	0.4
Germany	-0.2	-0.3	0	0.2	0.6
OECD	-0.3	-0.5	-0.2	-0.1	-0.3
Effective exchange rate					
United States					
Japan			——————Unchanged——————		
Germany					
Current balances					
United States	19	17	12	15	21
Japan	-5	-5	-2	-1	-1
Germany	-2	-3	-3	-4	-4
OECD	4	1	2	0	1

Policy option D: Fixed short-term real interest rates

Variable[a]	Deviations from baseline				
	Year 1	Year 2	Year 3	Year 4	Year 5
Real GNP					
United States	-1.4	-1.2	-0.5	-0.3	-0.4
Japan	-0.3	-0.4	-0.3	-0.2	-0.2
Germany	-0.3	-0.4	-0.1	-0.1	-0.2
OECD	-0.7	-0.6	-0.3	-0.2	-0.3
GNP deflator					
United States	-0.5	-1.5	-2.3	-3.1	-4.1
Japan	-0.1	-0.5	-0.7	-0.9	-1.1
Germany	-0.2	-0.6	-0.9	-1.0	-1.3
OECD	-0.2	-0.7	-1.1	-1.5	-2.0
Short-term interest rate					
United States	-0.8	-1.0	-0.8	-0.9	-1.1
Japan	-0.2	-0.3	-0.2	-0.2	-0.2
Germany	-0.3	-0.4	-0.2	-0.2	-0.4
OECD	-0.4	-0.5	-0.3	-0.3	-0.4
Effective exchange rate					
United States	0	0.4	0.9	1.5	2.2
Japan	0	-0.4	-0.9	-1.2	-2.0
Germany	0	-0.2	-0.4	-0.7	-1.1
Current balances					
United States	19	18	16	20	27
Japan	-5	-7	-6	-7	-9
Germany	-2	-3	-4	-6	-7
OECD	4	0	0	0	1

a. Units are as defined in the text.

Table 12A-3 *(continued)*

Policy option E: Fixed long-term real interest rates

Variable[a]	Deviations from baseline				
	Year 1	Year 2	Year 3	Year 4	Year 5
Real GNP					
United States	−1.0	−0.7	−0.4	−0.4	−0.3
Japan	−0.1	−0.2	−0.1	−0.1	−0.1
Germany	−0.2	−0.1	−0.1	−0.1	−0.1
OECD	−0.5	−0.4	−0.2	−0.2	−0.2
GNP deflator					
United States	−0.4	−1.0	−1.6	−2.3	−3.1
Japan	−0.1	−0.2	−0.3	−0.4	−0.5
Germany	−0.1	−0.3	−0.4	−0.6	−0.8
OECD	−0.2	−0.5	−0.8	−1.1	−1.5
Short-term interest rate					
United States	−1.4	−0.7	−0.8	−1.0	−1.1
Japan	−0.3	−0.2	−0.1	−0.1	−0.1
Germany	−0.7	−0.1	−0.2	−0.3	−0.4
OECD	−0.7	−0.4	−0.4	−0.4	−0.5
Effective exchange rate					
United States	−0.5	0.2	0.7	1.1	1.7
Japan	0.5	−0.2	−0.6	−1.0	−1.5
Germany	0.2	−0.1	−0.4	−0.6	−0.9
Current balances					
United States	15	16	16	19	24
Japan	−3	−5	−5	−6	−7
Germany	−2	−2	−3	−4	−6
OECD	3	0	1	1	0

a. Units are as defined in the text.

The results for this particular simulation indicate some fairly substantial changes in model properties compared with earlier published results. This primarily reflects the incorporation of a revised U.S. consumption function, now incorporating an explicit effect from the value of household equity holdings. Being inversely related to long-term rates, this gives stronger stimulus to consumption as short- and long-term rates are reduced. Effectively, the U.S. model now incorporates full crowding out within two to three years.[15]

Compared with policy option A, *exchange-rate targeting* (policy option C, table 12A-3) implies little or no short-term adjustment in short-term rates for Japan and Germany and more competitiveness losses. For these countries, real GNP losses are therefore more long-lived. Indeed maintaining an exchange-rate target involves longer-term increases in short-term rates, coinciding with falling rates of inflation. For the United States, real GNP and price profiles are more or less unchanged.

15. Other important changes to the U.S. model include the incorporation of a stock-based housing-investment equation and a more dynamic equation for imports of manufactures. Neither of these changes significantly affects U.S. multipliers in this case.

Figure 12A-3. *Reduction in U.S. Government Expenditure Equivalent to 1 Percent of GNP*

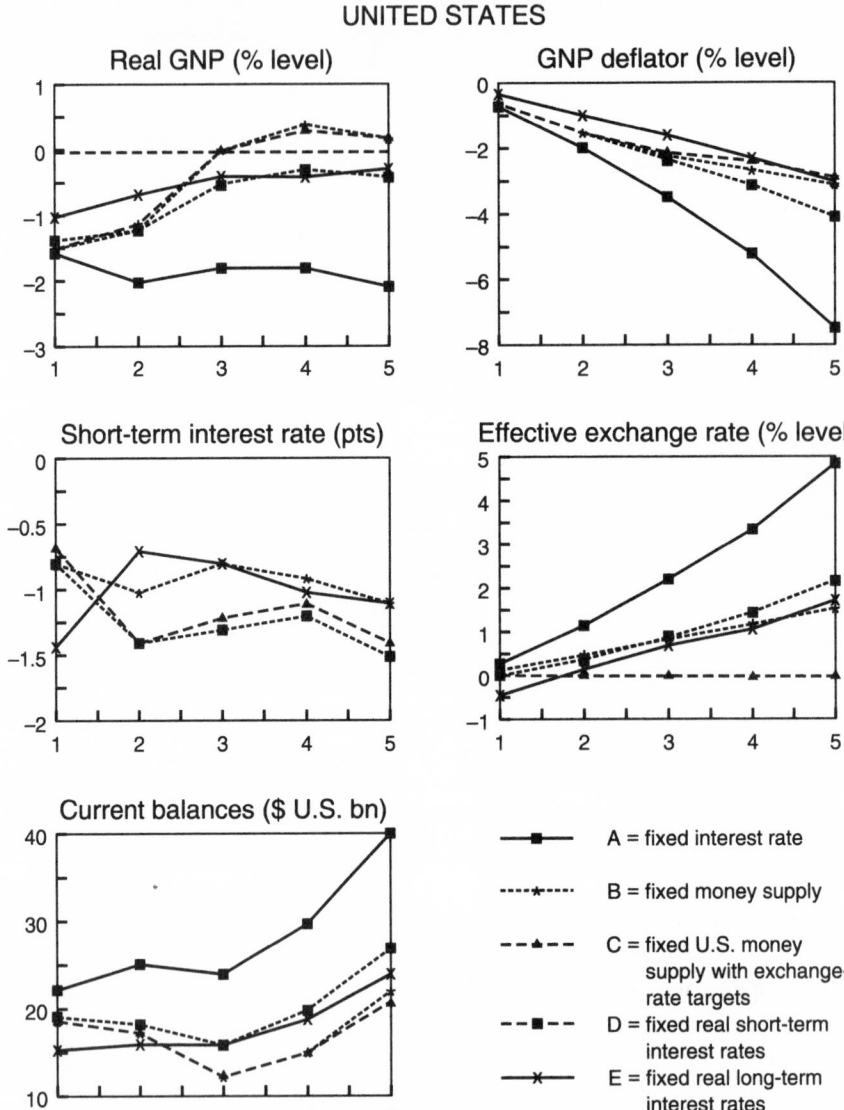

Figure 12A-3 *(continued)*

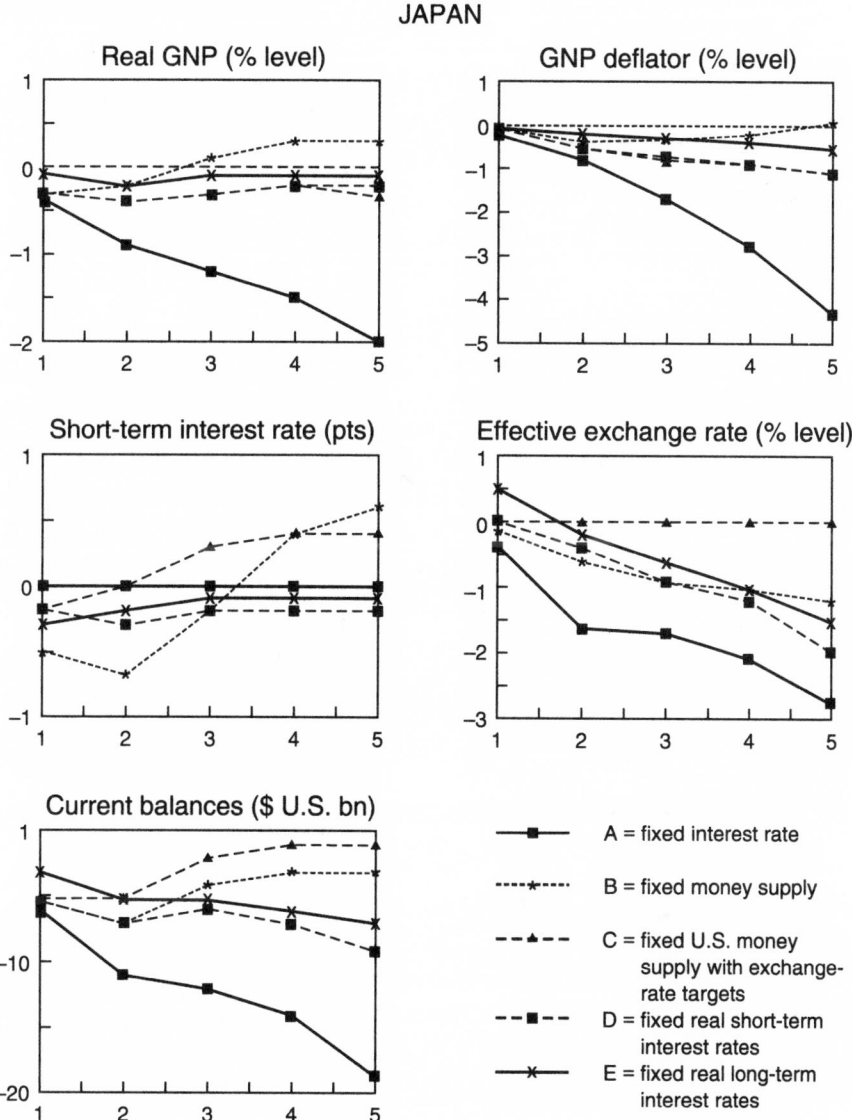

JAPAN

Real GNP (% level)

GNP deflator (% level)

Short-term interest rate (pts)

Effective exchange rate (% level)

Current balances ($ U.S. bn)

A = fixed interest rate

B = fixed money supply

C = fixed U.S. money supply with exchange-rate targets

D = fixed real short-term interest rates

E = fixed real long-term interest rates

Figure 12A-3 *(continued)*

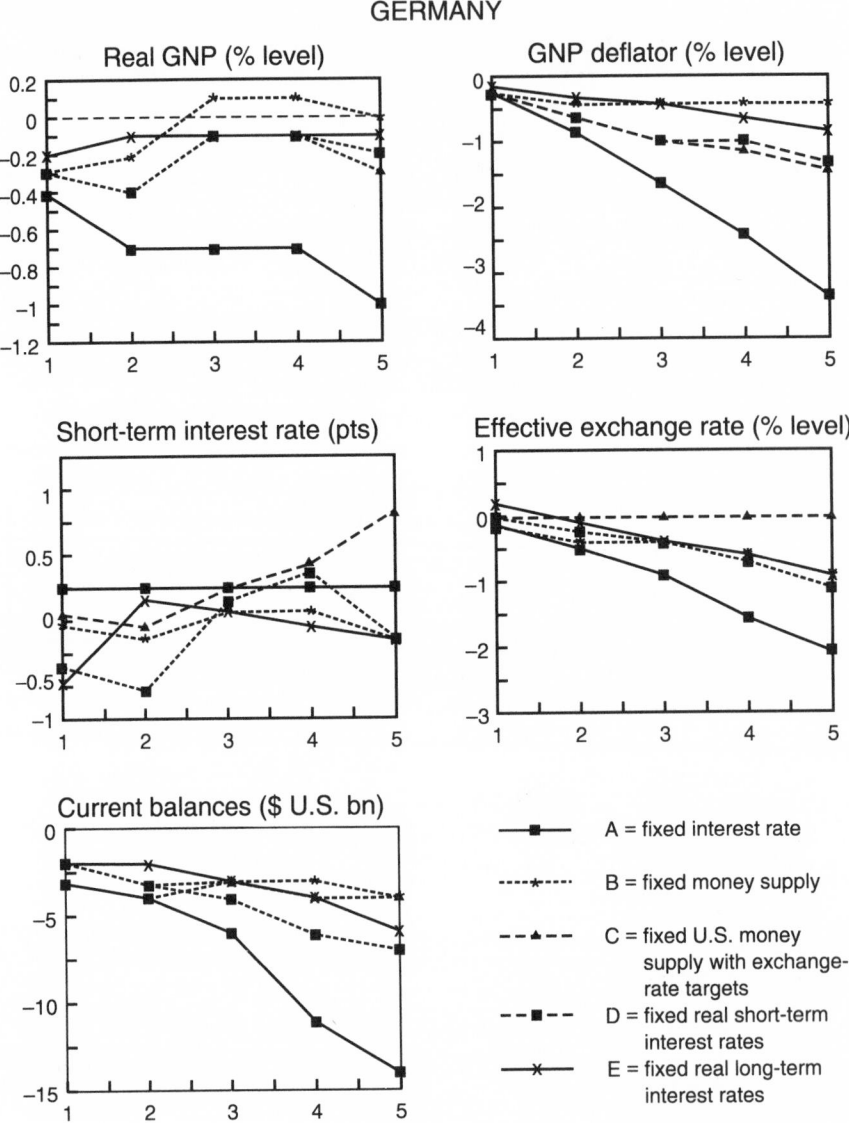

GERMANY

Real GNP (% level)

GNP deflator (% level)

Short-term interest rate (pts)

Effective exchange rate (% level)

Current balances ($ U.S. bn)

A = fixed interest rate

B = fixed money supply

C = fixed U.S. money supply with exchange-rate targets

D = fixed real short-term interest rates

E = fixed real long-term interest rates

Figure 12A-3 *(continued)*

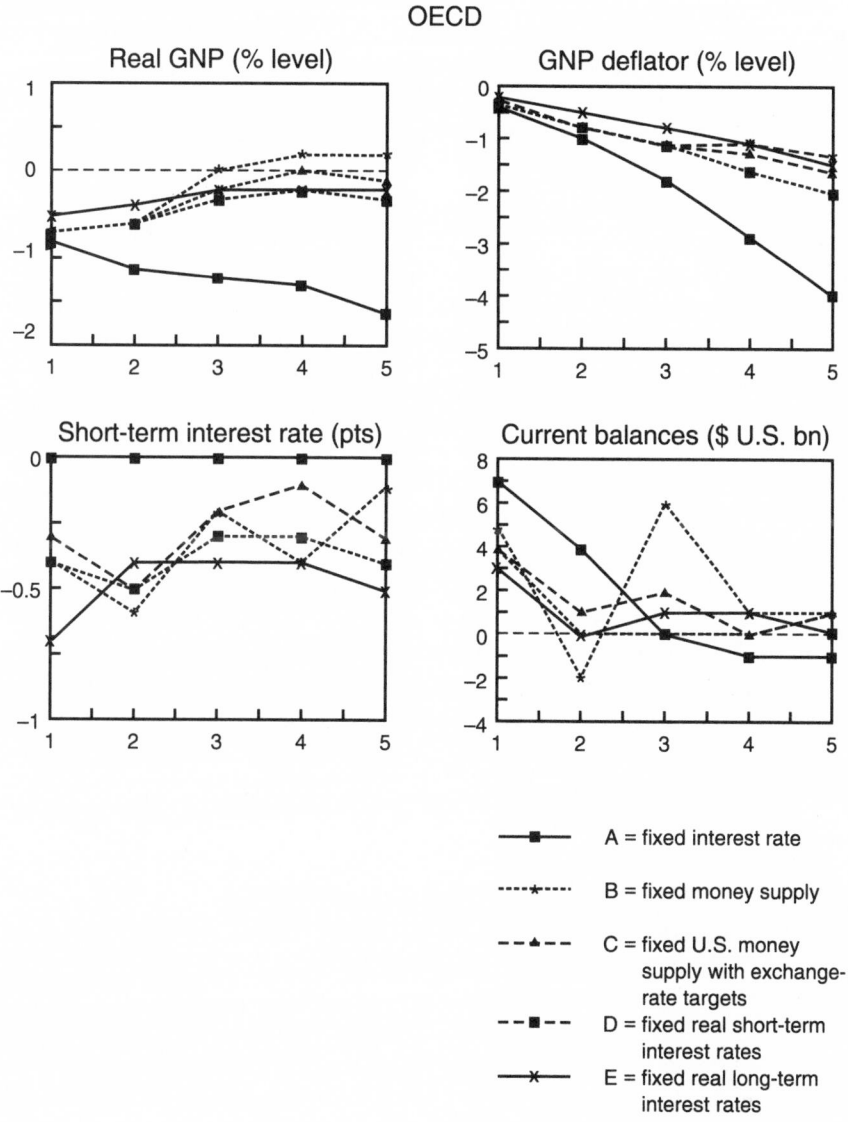

OECD

A = fixed interest rate

B = fixed money supply

C = fixed U.S. money supply with exchange-rate targets

D = fixed real short-term interest rates

E = fixed real long-term interest rates

As for the other shocks, an *unchanged real short-term rate* (policy option D, table 12A-3) generally implies somewhat smaller reductions in U.S. interest rates, a generally slower demand recovery, and a more pronounced fall in prices. For Japan and Germany, short-term rates fall relative to the exchange-rate-targeting case (option C), and, despite a more depressed U.S. economy, there is little difference in the outcomes for real GNP.

Targeting *real long-term interest rates* (policy option E, table 12A-3) again gives larger immediate reductions in U.S. short-term rates than any of the other policy options. For the United States, this has the result of giving a larger short-term stimulus to the real side and a smaller real GNP loss in the first two years of the simulation. The subsequent easing of nominal rates implied by the inflation path, however, means that full recovery is not achieved over the five-year period. Even so, for Japan and Germany the initial cuts in short-term rates are sufficiently stimulative to the domestic economy to offset much of the spillover from U.S. trade, and the GNP results are superior to those given by exchange-rate targeting.

Given the different profile for output, the fall in U.S. prices is generally smaller than with a fixed money supply. By the fifth year, however, the cumulative output loss is marginally greater, and the terminal price level is similar to that with money targets. Effective exchange-rate movements are also broadly in line with those under policy option B, with the effects of a narrow spread of interest-rate movements being offset by the narrower spread of price differentials. Averaged over the period, movements in the U.S. current balance are also broadly similar to those under money targeting, although the profile is more skewed.

SHOCK 4: RISE IN OECD WAGE RATES (TABLE 12A-4 AND FIGURE 12A-4). Assuming *unchanged nominal interest rates* (policy option A, table 12A-4), overall model responses prove to be highly unstable. Although higher wage costs lead to downward adjustments in employment levels and there is a significant weakening of consumption, there are also strong stimulative pressures coming from business and residential investment because real interest rates are substantially reduced. In general, the influence of reduced profitability entering directly into output expectations is too weak to offset these positive effects, and for the major countries there is a general tendency toward higher output over the medium term. The balance of these real effects varies across countries in the short run. U.S. real GNP remains unchanged in the first year but rises by an average 0.8 percent thereafter. For Japan and Germany there are particularly large reductions in consumption, and real GNP falls during the first year or so, but it increases thereafter because of rising investment and trade influences.

Although the labor market adjusts to give lower employment, the timing and influence of these effects are generally too weak to stabilize the wage and

Table 12A-4. *Two Percent Ex Ante Increase in OECD Wage Rates*

Policy option A: Fixed nominal interest rates

Variable[a]	Deviations from baseline				
	Year 1	Year 2	Year 3	Year 4	Year 5
Real GNP					
United States	0	0.8	1.0	0.8	0.5
Japan	−0.1	0.1	0.5	0.8	0.9
Germany	−0.2	−0.4	0.4	0.8	0.9
OECD	0	0.4	0.7	0.9	1.0
GNP deflator					
United States	0.8	2.0	3.0	4.0	5.0
Japan	2.0	4.6	6.8	8.9	10.7
Germany	1.9	4.9	8.3	12.1	15.9
OECD	1.3	3.0	4.4	5.8	7.1
Short-term interest rate					
United States					
Japan			Unchanged		
Germany					
OECD					
Effective exchange rate					
United States	0.7	1.8	3.1	4.4	5.7
Japan	−0.8	−2.0	−3.0	−3.7	−4.3
Germany	−0.5	−1.8	−3.4	−5.3	−7.2
Current balances					
United States	−2	−14	−17	−17	−20
Japan	1	4	5	5	5
Germany	3	7	7	8	12
OECD	1	−4	−6	−5	−6

Policy option B: Fixed monetary aggregates (broad)

Variable[a]	Deviations from baseline				
	Year 1	Year 2	Year 3	Year 4	Year 5
Real GNP					
United States	0.3	0.5	−0.3	−1.0	−1.3
Japan	−0.5	−1.3	−2.0	−2.4	−2.2
Germany	−0.8	−2.0	−1.8	−2.0	−2.4
OECD	−0.1	−0.4	−0.9	−1.3	−1.4
GNP deflator					
United States	1.0	2.3	3.0	3.3	3.2
Japan	1.9	3.5	3.9	3.5	2.8
Germany	1.6	3.3	4.4	5.3	5.6
OECD	1.3	2.7	3.4	3.6	3.5
Short-term interest rate					
United States	0.4	1.4	1.5	1.3	1.1
Japan	2.8	2.4	1.0	−0.4	−1.1
Germany	3.2	2.6	2.4	2.4	1.1
OECD	1.7	1.7	1.6	1.1	0.4
Effective exchange rate					
United States	−0.9	−0.5	0	0.2	0.8
Japan	0.6	0.2	−0.7	−1.3	−1.4
Germany	1.0	0.4	−0.2	−0.5	−1.2
Current balances					
United States	−2	−10	−4	−1	−4
Japan	4	8	5	2	−2
Germany	6	11	6	4	5
OECD	12	11	7	0	10

a. Units are as defined in the text.

Table 12A-4 *(continued)*

**Policy option C: United States maintains monetary aggregate:
Germany and Japan target exchange rates**

Variable[a]	Year 1	Year 2	Year 3	Year 4	Year 5
			Deviations from baseline		
Real GNP					
United States	0.1	0.6	−0.1	−0.8	−1.1
Japan	−0.3	−1.0	−1.9	−2.8	−3.0
Germany	−0.4	−1.4	−1.9	−2.2	−2.5
OECD	−0.1	−0.1	−0.6	−1.2	−1.5
GNP deflator					
United States	0.9	2.1	2.8	3.1	3.1
Japan	2.0	3.8	4.3	3.6	2.1
Germany	1.8	4.2	5.5	6.1	5.9
OECD	1.3	2.8	3.7	4.0	3.8
Short-term interest rate					
United States	0.3	1.3	1.5	1.3	1.1
Japan	1.8	3.0	2.6	0.9	−0.8
Germany	1.3	3.1	2.4	3.2	2.6
OECD	0.7	1.6	1.7	1.3	0.8
Effective exchange rate					
United States					
Japan			Unchanged		
Germany					
Current balances					
United States	−2	−9	−6	0	−2
Japan	3	8	8	7	4
Germany	4	11	11	9	9
OECD	6	12	13	10	2

Policy option D: Unchanged real short-term interest rates

Variable[a]	Year 1	Year 2	Year 3	Year 4	Year 5
			Deviations from baseline		
Real GNP					
United States	−0.1	−0.1	−0.1	0	−0.2
Japan	−0.6	−1.2	−1.4	−1.4	−1.3
Germany	−0.7	−1.8	−1.4	−1.0	−1.3
OECD	−0.3	−0.5	−0.5	−0.4	−0.4
GNP deflator					
United States	0.8	1.8	2.2	2.7	3.2
Japan	1.8	3.5	4.2	4.4	4.4
Germany	1.7	3.6	5.1	6.8	8.2
OECD	1.3	2.5	3.2	3.8	4.2
Short-term interest rate					
United States	1.1	0.7	0.5	0.5	0.4
Japan	2.3	1.4	0.6	0.2	−0.1
Germany	2.3	1.7	1.6	1.7	1.1
OECD	1.6	1.0	0.5	0.2	−0.2
Effective exchange rate					
United States	0.1	0.6	1.2	1.8	2.3
Japan	0	−0.8	−1.4	−1.5	−1.2
Germany	−0.1	−0.3	−0.9	−1.7	−2.6
Current balances					
United States	1	−8	−9	−9	−11
Japan	2	4	5	5	5
Germany	4	9	6	5	9
OECD	11	3	−2	−2	−3

a. Units are as defined in the text.

Table 12A-4 *(continued)*

Policy option E: Unchanged real long-term interest rates

Variable[a]	Deviations from baseline				
	Year 1	Year 2	Year 3	Year 4	Year 5
Real GNP					
United States	−0.6	−0.6	0.3	0	−0.2
Japan	−1.3	−2.0	−1.9	−1.5	−1.0
Germany	−1.7	−2.6	−1.4	−1.6	−1.7
OECD	−0.8	−1.1	−0.7	−0.6	−0.6
GNP deflator					
United States	0.7	1.3	1.9	2.5	3.0
Japan	1.5	2.3	2.6	2.9	3.2
Germany	1.3	2.0	3.2	4.6	5.5
OECD	1.1	2.0	2.6	3.1	3.5
Short-term interest rate					
United States	1.6	−0.5	1.9	0.6	0.3
Japan	4.8	0	−0.4	−0.2	0.1
Germany	4.9	0	3.5	1.0	0.1
OECD	3.5	0.1	1.8	0.2	0.2
Effective exchange rate					
United States	−0.9	−0.4	0.5	0.7	1.2
Japan	1.0	0.1	−1.8	−1.2	−0.3
Germany	1.2	0.4	0.5	−0.1	−1.3
Current balances					
United States	5	−8	−6	−8	−9
Japan	2	4	3	5	5
Germany	6	7	5	6	7
OECD	20	−6	4	−2	−4

a. Units are as defined in the text.

price spiral and result in a steady acceleration of global inflation. In the short run, the size of wage and price movements depends on the degree of current-period simultaneity. The largest inflation effects are for Germany and Japan (annual average rates of 2 percent and 3 percent respectively), reflecting quick wage and price adjustments and relatively weak feedback from unemployment to wages. For Germany there is a relatively low wage and unemployment elasticity; for Japan a more flexible labor supply response tends to lead to smaller changes in unemployment. For the United States, price inflation responds more weakly, with a 1 percent increase in the annual average rate. This reflects longer lags between wage and price adjustments, owing to what are assumed to be more rigid wage-contracting practices in North America. The gradual divergence in price behavior contributes to the significant dollar appreciation over the period, which in turn reinforces import-price pressures for Japan and Germany.

For the OECD area, the main influences on the current balance are adverse, coming from a loss of competitiveness vis-à-vis the non-OECD countries and from higher activity rates. The United States is generally adversely affected,

Figure 12A-4. *Increase in OECD Wage Rates*

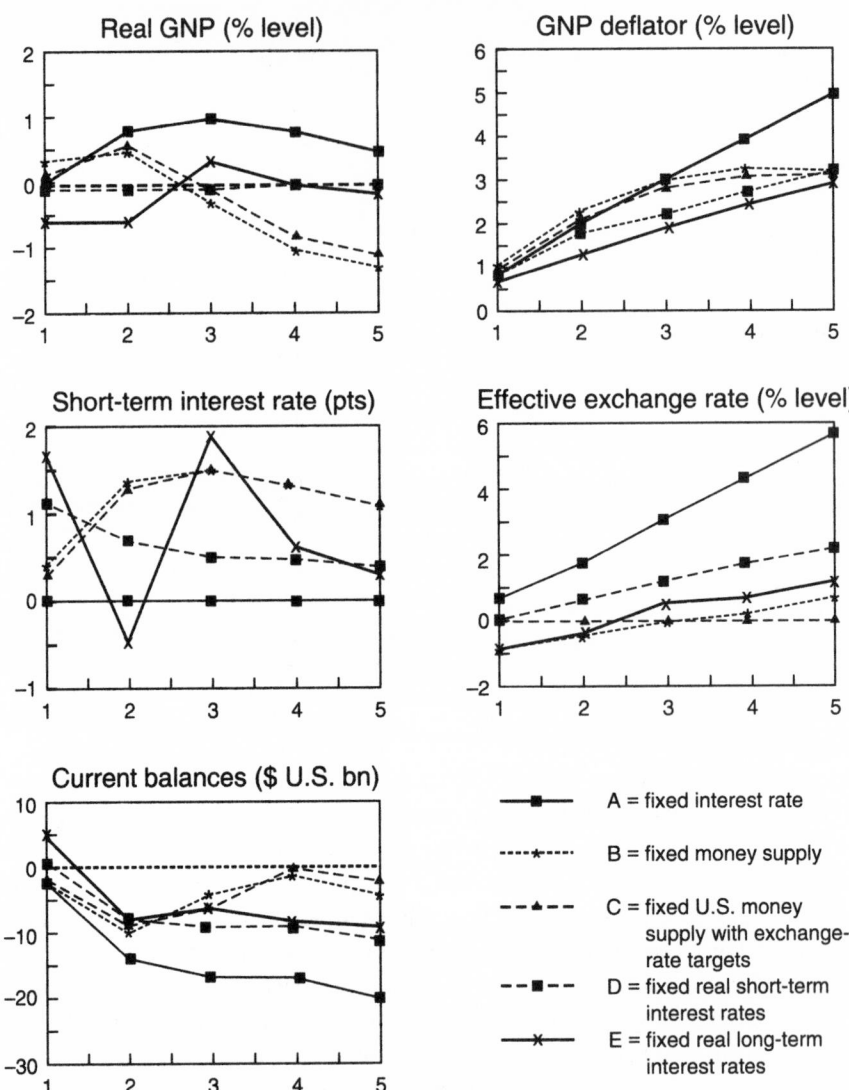

Figure 12A-4 *(continued)*

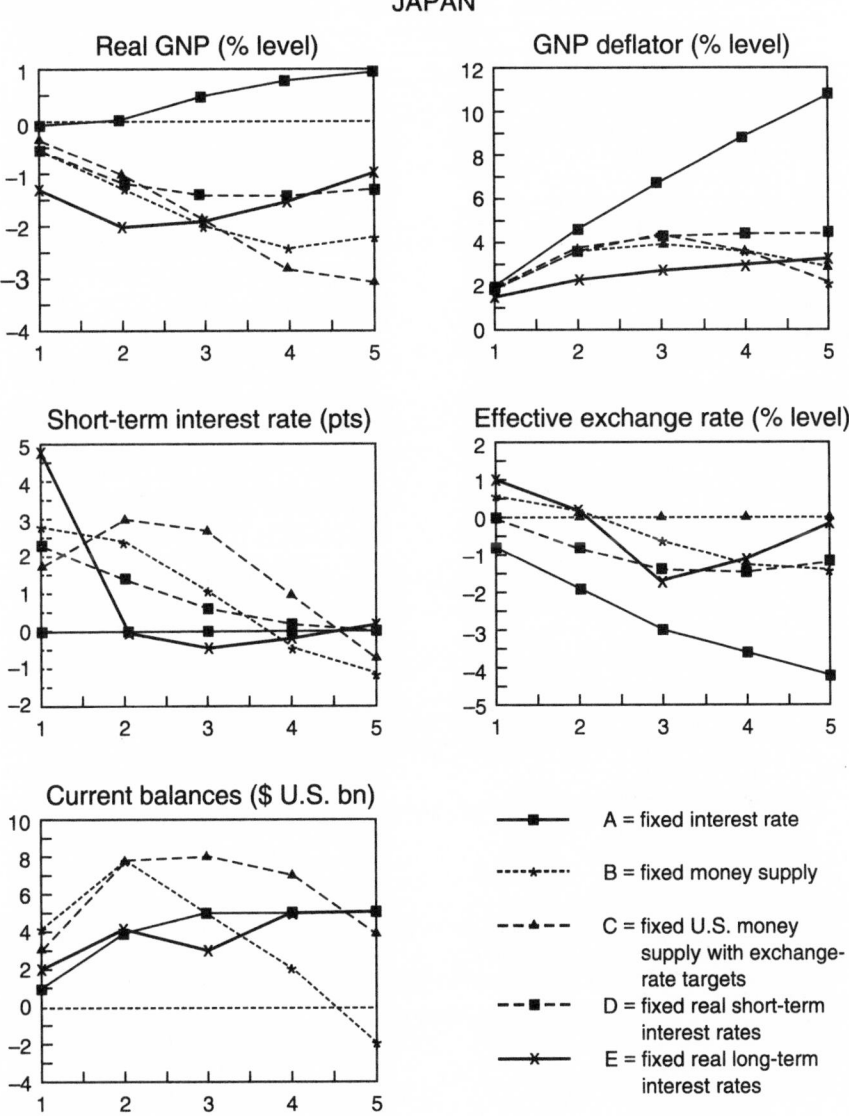

JAPAN

Figure 12A-4 *(continued)*

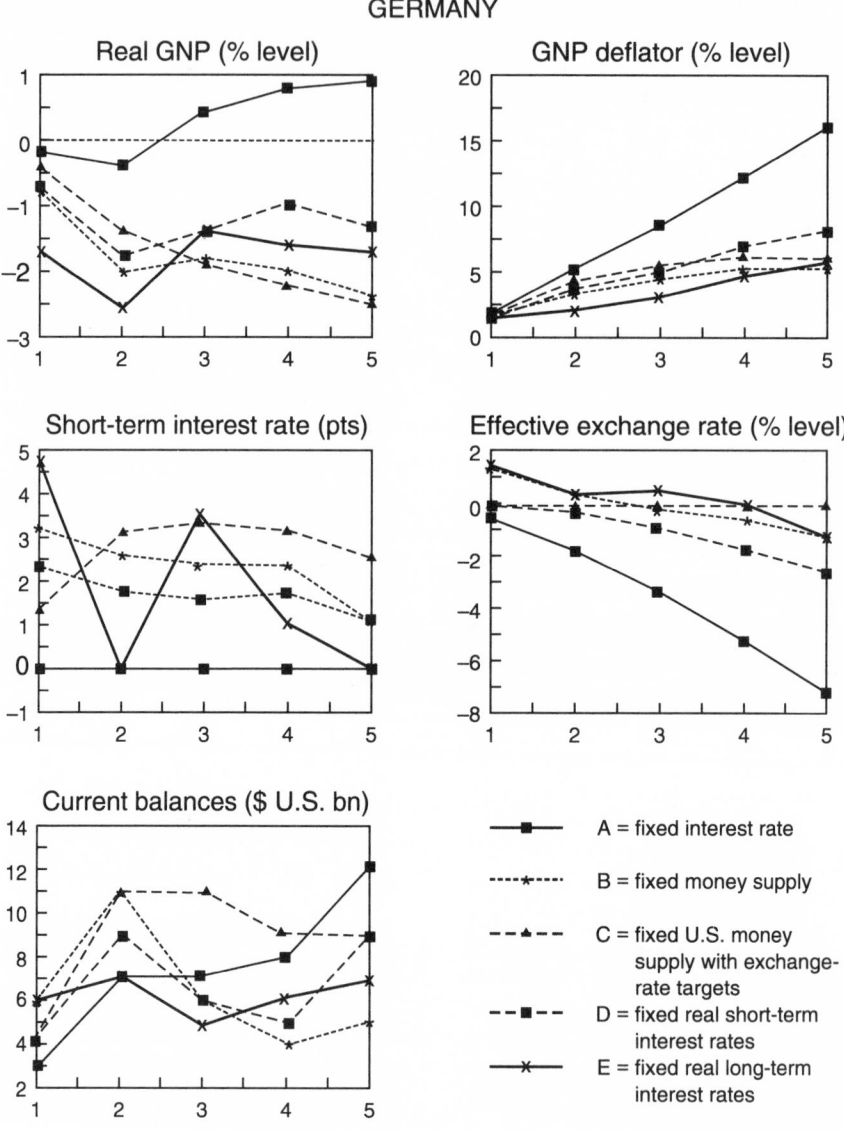

GERMANY

Figure 12A-4 *(continued)*

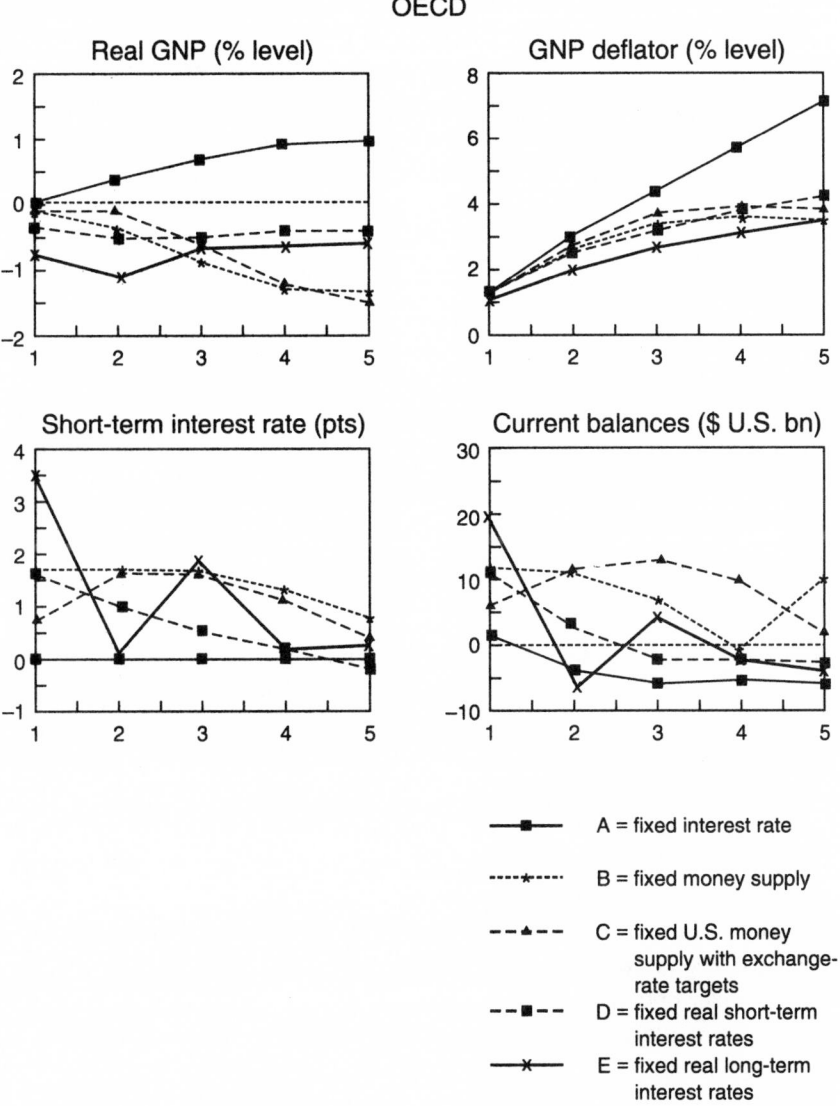

OECD

Real GNP (% level)

GNP deflator (% level)

Short-term interest rate (pts)

Current balances ($ U.S. bn)

───■─── A = fixed interest rate

----*---- B = fixed money supply

──▲── C = fixed U.S. money
supply with exchange-
rate targets

──■── D = fixed real short-term
interest rates

──*── E = fixed real long-term
interest rates

reflecting a higher GNP level. Japan and Germany benefit because of generally weaker demand and smaller import elasticities.

With a *fixed money supply* (policy option B, table 12A-4), interest rates rise significantly, reversing the fall in real interest rates and putting stronger downward pressure on demand. Proportionately larger initial increases in short-term rates for Japan and Germany again reflect correspondingly steeper LM slopes (as illustrated in table 12-1) and the larger increases in nominal demand coming from the higher price responses noted earlier. Although real GNP for the United States is higher in the first two years, demand is checked to give a moderation in inflationary pressure, and interest rates eventually rise sufficiently to give higher *real rates* and a resulting contraction in consumption and investment. The contractionary effects on real GNP are considerably larger for Japan and Germany than for the United States because of the correspondingly larger initial increases in short rates.

Compared with policy option A, there is a significant moderation in inflation, and increases in prices level off or decline during the last two years. For Japan, the balance of real and price adjustment is sufficiently favorable to imply a subsequent easing of interest rates, which eventually return to below baseline. For Germany, there a less favorable price adjustment, and therefore a more sustained increase in short-term rates, until the fifth year.

The fairly diverse interest-rate and price movements give a somewhat varied pattern of exchange-rate responses. For the United States, significantly smaller increases in interest rates and a deterioration in the balance of payments give an effective depreciation over the first two years. Thereafter the easing of Japanese rates and stability in U.S. price levels are sufficient to give an overall appreciation. This is mirrored by movements in the yen and deutsche-mark rates, which rise initially and then fall back as short-term rates are eased.

Given substantially higher interest rates and lower activity rates, the OECD current balance is favorably affected. For the United States, the general deterioration under option A is attenuated by higher interest rates and, eventually, reduced demand levels. The overall effects on current balances for Japan and Germany remain favorable.

Given the specific pattern of exchange-rate movements obtained under money targets, *exchange-rate targeting* for Japan and Germany (policy option C, table 12A-4) involves smaller increases in short-term rates in the first year of simulation, followed by sharper increases in the second and subsequent years. This at first implies a lesser brake on demand, followed by larger reductions in later years. Inflationary pressures are correspondingly stronger through most of the simulation period. For Japan, downward pressure on demand is sufficiently strong and sustained to give a smaller price response by the fifth year; for Germany, the later squeeze is too little and too late to give any improvement over money targeting. The outcomes for U.S. inflation and output, with exchange-rate targeting, are little affected from those under money targets, except in terms of marginal timing differences.

Compared with money targets, a rule based on *unchanged real short-term interest rates* (policy option D, table 12A-4) has more varied implications for each of the G3 countries. For the United States, there is a larger initial increase in short-term rates in the first year (1.1 compared with 0.4), followed by considerable easing as the inflation rate comes quickly under control. As a result, U.S. real GNP falls slightly in the first two years and remains at a slightly lower level over much of the period. Compared with policy options A–C, there is a more substantial easing of price pressures, although the increase in the price level in the fifth year is broadly the same. For Japan and Germany, increases in interest rates are generally smaller, implying smaller output losses but higher inflation, notably so for Germany.

Under *unchanged real long-term interest rates* (policy option E, table 12A-4), the inflation signal again gives accelerated and substantial increases in short-term rates. For Japan and Germany, interest-rate movements are unduly large and variable on an annual basis. The corresponding semiannual time paths are more erratic, with *unrealistically* large increases in short-term rates occurring in the initial period.

For the United States, the initial rise in short-term rates puts firm downward pressure on demand and real GNP. Price-level increases are generally lower than in all other cases, although by the final year the overall level is only marginally below that given by a money-supply rule (option B). For Germany and Japan, the bringing forward of short-term-rate increases again accelerates the process by which demand is squeezed. Short-run reductions in real GNP are therefore significantly larger, and price levels are more subdued. The resulting early slowdown in inflation rates, however, leads to a subsequent easing of short-term rates, and the squeeze on output is correspondingly smaller by the third year, so that prices continue to rise in the third and fourth years.

Although providing a substantial attenuation in inflationary pressures over the period for all G3 countries, the implied volatility in short-term rates needed to hold real long-term rates unchanged, notably for Japan and German, is clearly impractical and implies the need for additional smoothing of short-term rates.

References

Brayton, F., and J. Marquez. 1990. "The Behavior of Monetary Sectors and Monetary Policy: Evidence from Multicountry Models." In *Financial Sectors in Open Economies: Empirical Analysis and Policy Issues*, edited by P. Hooper and others, 365-93. Washington: Board of Governors of the Federal Reserve System.

Bryant, R. C., J. Helliwell, and P. Hooper. 1989. "Domestic and Cross-Border Consequences of U.S. Macroeconomic Policies." In *Macroeconomic Policies in an Interdependent World,* edited by R. C. Bryant and others, 59–115. Washington: Brookings,
Centre for Economic Policy Research, and International Monetary Fund.

Bryant, R. C., G. Holtham, and P. Hooper. 1988. "Consensus and Diversity in Model
Simulations." In *Empirical Macroeconomics for Interdependent Economics,* edited
by R. C. Bryant and others, 27–62. Brookings.

Egebo, T., P. Richardson, and I. Lienert. 1990. "A Model of Housing Investment for
the Major OECD Economies." *OECD Economic Studies* 14:151–88.

Frenkel, J. A., M. Goldstein, and P. R. Masson. 1989. "Simulating the Effects of
Some Simple Coordinated versus Uncoordinated Policy Rules." In *Macroeconomic
Policies in an Interdependent World,* edited by R. C. Bryant, D. A. Currie and others,
203–39. Washington: Brookings, Centre for Economic Policy Research, and International Monetary Fund.

Helliwell, J. 1988. "The Effects of Fiscal Policy on International Imbalances: Japan
and the United States." Papers and Proceedings of the Fourth Economic Planning
Agency. International Symposium. Tokyo: Economic Research Institute.

Helliwell, J., J. Cockerline, and R. Lafrance. 1990. "Multicountry Modelling of Financial Markets." In *Financial Sectors in Open Economies: Empirical Analysis and
Policy Issues*, edited by P. Hooper and others, 305-56. Washington: Board of Governors of the Federal Reserve System.

Herd, R. 1987. "Import and Export Price Equations for Manufactures." OECD ESD
Working Paper 43. Paris.

———. 1989. "The Impact of Increased Government Saving on the Economy." OECD
ESD Working Paper 68. Paris.

Herd, R., and B. Ballis. 1988. "Eliminating the U.S. Federal Budget Deficit by 1993:
The Interaction of Monetary and Fiscal Policy." OECD ESD Working Paper 59.
Paris.

Holtham, G. 1984. "Multinational Modelling of Financial Linkages and Exchange
Rates." *OECD Economic Studies* 2:51–92.

Martin, J. P., and R. Torres. 1990. "Measuring Potential Output in the Seven Major
OECD Countries." *OECD Economic Studies* 14:127–49.

Richardson, P. 1987a. "Recent Developments in OECD's Macroeconomic Model."
OECD ESD Working Paper 46. Paris.

———. 1987b. "A Review of the Simulation Properties of OECD's INTERLINK
Model." OECD ESD Working Paper 47. Paris.

———. 1988. "The Structure and Simulation Properties of OECD's INTERLINK
Model." *OECD Economic Studies* 10:57–122.

Torres, R., P. Jarrett, and W. Suyker. 1989. "Modeling Business Sector Supply for the
Smaller OECD Countries." OECD ESD Working Paper 71. Paris.

CHAPTER 13

The European Monetary System: Achievements and Survival

Andrew Hughes Hallett, Patrick Minford, and Anupam Rastogi

THE EUROPEAN MONETARY SYSTEM has been justified in one of at least four ways:

—as a device for reducing uncertainty, by reducing exchange-rate variability (especially within the EMS but also overall) and preferably without increasing the uncertainty surrounding other variables, such as interest rates or output;

—as an alternative to domestic monetary targets in achieving price discipline;

—as a route to the ultimate objective of European economic and monetary union (EMU) in the European Community (EC), the gains from which would take the form of lower monetary transactions costs, and the objective of which would be advanced by progressive reduction in exchange-rate variability;

—as a surrogate for explicit cooperation: cooperation would avoid "beggar-thy-neighbor" exchange-rate policies, whether of depreciation (for trade-balance–output reasons) or of appreciation (for inflation reasons). By its rules, the EMS prevents such policies.

In this chapter we try to shed some empirical light on these four arguments by using the method of model simulation and optimization. The alternative empirical method is to go directly to the facts and estimate the observable effects of the EMS. Neither method is free of difficulties. In direct estimation it is difficult to disentangle the EMS effect from other effects. Furthermore,

This work was financed by the ESRC Consortium for Modeling and Forecasting the economy. Andrew Hughes Hallett is at the University of Strathclyde; Patrick Minford and Anupam Rastogi are at the University of Liverpool. The authors are grateful for research assistance to Gary Hutson and Eric Nowell and thank for their comments Charles Adams, Matthew Canzoneri, Nicos Christodoulakis, Neil Ericsson, Michele Fratianni, Paul De Grauwe, Jurgen von Hagen, Catherine Mann, Manfred Neumann, Michael Parkin, Jean Pisani-Ferry, Roland Vaubel, Walter Wasserfallen, and Charles Wyplosz, as well as other participants in the 1989 Konstanz Seminar and the 1990 Brookings workshop on policy rules.

actual policies may not have been optimal, so that the EMS's relative *potential* performance is not gauged by estimation. Historical data can show only what did happen, not what could have happened.

Our optimization approach compares the performance of the EMS regime with that of exchange-rate floating (which we take as a benchmark), both at their best. Our approach is reliant on the parameters of the model, and these are vulnerable to estimation difficulties as well as instability under regime change. This vulnerability can be minimized by sensitivity analysis across parameter values, and we have done this here to a substantial degree.

The main advantage of our approach lies in the ability to explore, with the powerful techniques of stochastic simulation and optimal control, a wide variety of alternative EMS regimes and concomitant policy behavior. During the EMS period beginning in 1979, the actual regime followed has been in more or less continuous flux, starting with largely independent monetary policy, wide exchange-rate bands, and frequent parity changes supported by stringent capital controls, and ending today with narrow bands, rare realignments, substantial monetary cooperation, and no capital controls. In this chapter we ask how various EMS regimes would have withstood, in terms of stability, the shocks experienced during the estimation sample period, 1955–85.

Our concern is that the problems of market management induced by fixed-but-adjustable peg systems cause serious instability in the face of shocks above a certain threshold—just as a bridge may fail under heavy traffic. In this chapter we explore the features of an EMS regime that could be expected to avoid such instability. From that exploration we try to explain the EMS's survival for more than a decade, without the breakdown many predicted, and also to examine the claims for the EMS listed above.

Throughout the paper the LIVERPOOL world model (a linked system of nine country models, all similar in design to the LIVERPOOL model of the U.K. economy) is used as the empirical framework (see Minford, Agenor, and Nowell 1986 for a full account). Key features of this model, which has been estimated largely with annual data, are rational expectations, perfect capital mobility, and wealth effects on consumption; markets clear continuously in an annual framework subject to a range of nominal contracts (especially bonds and wages, although the latter have a maximum maturity of one year here). The latter feature distinguishes it from "disequilibrium" rational-expectations models with a high degree of nominal rigidity such as Taylor (1988); McKibbin-Sachs's MSG2 model (Ishii, McKibbin, and Sachs 1985); MINIMOD of Haas and Masson (1986); and, more recently, MULTIMOD of Masson and others (1988). (For more detailed comparisons emphasizing this distinction, see Bryant and others 1988.) The LIVERPOOL model has also been used regularly in forecasting since 1984; this cumulative experience has contributed substantially to its empirical learning curve. Appendix A to this chapter contains a brief outline of the model; appendix B gives a summary of its simulation properties and empirical performance.

As far as we know, earlier empirical work on the EMS has been exclusively along the lines of direct estimation, formal or informal, from the observed facts. Several early studies computed comparative descriptive statistics, pre- and post-EMS, on variables of interest and for EMS and non-EMS countries (the latter being a control). These include Collins (1990), De Grauwe (1990), Giavazzi and Giovannini (1989), and Ungerer and others (1986). Vaubel (1989) has offered a useful summary of these and of a number of German studies in the following negative terms:

> To sum up: the exchange rate mechanism of the EMS does not seem to have contributed to reducing nominal effective exchange rate variations, inflation, and inflation differences of the member currencies, or to increasing intra-ERM [exchange-rate mechanism of the EMS] trade, investment, and growth in the member countries.

Recently, two studies—Artis and Taylor (1988) and Fratianni and von Hagen (1990)—have used ARCH (autoregressive conditional heteroscedasticity) to examine whether there have been shifts in the (conditional) variances of the exchange-rate and other series. Both find that the bilateral intra-EMS exchange-rate variances, real and nominal, have fallen post-EMS. But the record on trade-weighted exchange rates, real and nominal, is ambiguous because the bilateral variances against non-EMS currencies have risen. Given that events other than the EMS have been at work since 1979 (shifts in monetary policies, swings in fiscal policy, oil-price developments) and that policies may have been suboptimal, this evidence sheds little light on whether the EMS has succeeded in its principal appointed task of lowering overall (as opposed to intra-EMS) exchange-rate uncertainty.

As for inflation, Fratianni and von Hagen found that its conditional variance (as well as its trend) has fallen post-EMS in the EMS countries but that this fall is matched in the non-EMS countries. There is also evidence of greater covariance within (but not between) EMS and non-EMS countries, suggesting some degree of policy coordination within (but again not between) each group.

The European Monetary System: Background

The EMS is a supplement to domestic monetary systems. How it has worked has depended on the countries involved and changes over time. For example, the Netherlands has consistently treated the deutsche-mark—guilder link as effectively fixed. Italy and France, in contrast, periodically allow devaluations after discussions with EMS partners, principally Germany; in recent years, however, none occurred until Italy left the system in 1992.

The Netherlands uses the EMS as a device for pegging its prices (at German levels) and for minimizing transaction costs in foreign trade, much of which is with Germany. The Netherlands is willing to relinquish any freedom to use domestic monetary policy to stabilize its economy; any stabilization that occurs comes from German monetary decisions. This is a kind of EMU, although asymmetrical in this case.

The United Kingdom (until October 1990, when it joined the ERM) had a fully floating system, apart from the usual temporary central bank intervention and some recent experimentation after the Louvre Accord with a shadow EMS link to the deutsche mark. In such a floating system, prices are set domestically; there are significant transaction costs in foreign trade with EC partners; and money can be used domestically to stabilize output.

As argued in Minford (1989a) fixed and floating-rate systems differ little in their transmission of real shocks. As for monetary shocks, although the direction of impact of foreign monetary shocks is altered, floating does not clearly insulate against these shocks because the exchange rate tends to move sharply in response. Thus, fixed rates eliminate any domestic monetary variance, and foreign monetary variance dominates, whereas floating provides a mixture of domestic and foreign monetary variance. The combination may be greater or less for prices or output than under fixed rates depending on model structure and on the variance-covariance structure of the shocks. This suggests that, abstracting from transitional costs, a country will be attracted to a fully fixed system if the dominant foreign money in the system exhibits low variance; in this case it is unlikely that the variance combination under floating will be as low. This seems to be the position of the Netherlands.

What then of EMS in less-than-fully-fixed systems? Here we face a problem of evaluating system behavior. It turns out (Hughes Hallett and Minford 1989, 1990) that behavior depends crucially on the parameters of flexibility; that is, on the size of the permitted parity changes, on the margins around those parities, and on how long the parities must be held. At the extreme where the margins are wide, the parity may be adjusted in small steps and frequently, and the system is indistinguishable from free floating. In the early days, for example, of Italy's association with the EMS, this was the regime Italy followed. But nowadays such a regime is not fashionable; even Spain, having entered on a wide band, has been unwilling to allow its parity to be devalued until forced to do so in the upheavals of 1992.

What can happen when the limits are set more tightly? In effect there is a clash between two monetary systems. Monetary growth may be set independently over the medium term, and yet exchange rates are not allowed to respond to this monetary divergence except discretely. Hence the length of time between realignments (and perhaps the size of the realignments) is likely to be crucial. Unfortunately there are no rules governing how realignments should be undertaken. The arguments between the French and the Germans in late 1989, and the confusion in September 1992, suggest that realignments are being put off as long as possible.

How do people expect this clash to be resolved? We may distinguish two cases: perfect capital mobility with only limited exchange controls (so that uncovered interest parity prevails, except at moments of speculative crisis when it is assumed, for a time at least, that controls must be binding); and fully and permanently effective exchange controls, where the central bank can use sterilized intervention to fix the exchange rate while setting interest rates through monetary policy. In contrast, under perfect capital mobility, during the period when the exchange rate is being pegged temporarily the central bank cannot fix the money supply as well; it has to let the money supply adjust to whatever the exchange-rate peg dictates. We will call the limited exchange control setup "no controls" in what follows, to indicate that uncovered interest parity holds.

In setting up the model of the EMS, we assume that German money supply growth is fixed by the Bundesbank, with no constraints from the monetary policies of other EMS countries. These others, however, are constrained by German money supply growth to the extent that their parity (assumed to be set against the deutsche mark) is held. The assumptions apply to the automatic workings of the EMS. But they do not rule out German strategic reactions to other EMS monetary policies in the short run when these can have spillover effects on Germany. Nor, of course, do they rule out short- and long-run independence from Germany for these other countries, both within the parity limits and through parity changes.

German dominance may seem over-strong in this view. Fratianni and von Hagen (1990) argued that Germany has not been dominant within the EMS. By dominance they mean that other EMS money supplies have had no independence of German money supply and that the German money supply has been independent of these others. They find from vector autoregression that other EMS money supplies are not exclusively affected by the German money supply in either the short or long run but respond to both world and other EMS money supplies. (De Grauwe 1988 showed that this is also true of their interest rates in relation to German and other interest rates.) Fratianni and von Hagen also found no effect of other EMS money supplies on Germany's in the long run, although some marginally significant effect was found in the short run.

It is clear that these results are entirely in line with our assumptions. It is the element of exchange-rate flexibility in the EMS that permits both some monetary independence by other EMS countries and some German strategic response to this independence.

The Basic EMS Version of the LIVERPOOL Model

In our "default" model we assume that, under the EMS regime, parities (initially set along an equilibrium trajectory, given anticipated events) must be held for at least one year after a shock has occurred. During this time, the exchange rate cannot move beyond the margins, set at plus or minus 3 percent around parity. A new parity trajectory may then be set to achieve expected exchange-rate equilibrium, given the shock and its anticipated consequences: the parity can only be moved in multiples of plus or minus 5 percent, but the expected exchange rate can move flexibly because parity change plus the margins spans the whole exchange-rate space. It has been suggested that the rules restrict not only the frequency of parity changes but also their size (say, to less than 10 percent); and that the frequency permitted may be diminishing (say, to two years between changes). Such restrictions are, we have found in previous work (Hughes Hallett and Minford 1989), potentially crucial to the system's stability. In that 1989 study we investigated a lower frequency of parity change: a two-year gap creates enormous instability because parity changes that are fully anticipated but stored up by the two-year rule actually exaggerate the current disequilibrium and trigger a future backlash. Here we look at this issue again within a stochastic framework, as well as at the consequences of imposing restrictions on the size of parity changes.

A regime change such as the EMS may provoke changes in supposedly structural equations (Lucas 1976). In particular, under the EMS the usual wage equation, which is not set up for policy conflict and sudden switches of regime, may need to be modified. It seems likely that, faced with the prospect of a sudden devaluation or price jump of uncertain timing, labor unions would take precautionary action to raise contracted wages in advance of the expected price jump. This is like the "peso problem": the model is set up as if, and so that, there is no parity change in year 1, whereas there is a positive probability that there will be one (which never actually happens). Another reason for preemptive action would be overlaps in contract periods. The model assumes that, in normal times of smooth price behavior, this is of no importance because such devices as bonus variation could iron out temporary anomalies in the contract as other workers get ahead or behind. But for extreme jumps such as those here, these devices would be inadequate and we could expect the contract to reflect the likely overlap. As Taylor (1979) has shown, this creates a serially correlated pattern of wage movements in response to a shock in expected prices, starting from the quarter of the shock.

Together these factors argue for a special adjustment of current wages in response to the prospect of future devaluation. The adjustment we make for illustrative purposes is equal to approximately one-third of the parity change expected in the following year. The effect of this anticipatory movement in wages is to push prices up faster than the exchange-rate peg would normally permit. Consequently the real exchange rate tends to be pushed up—very much a feature of the EMS experience of those other countries, notably France and Italy, whose underlying inflation has traditionally exceeded Germany's.

This adjustment is purely illustrative. As noted above, the EMS has been not one but a series of regimes that have differed both among countries and over time. It is in order to take Lucas's (1976) critique seriously that we have made this correction to our estimated structure for a hypothetical regime change. To allow for potential error in setting the parameter's size, we have checked for sensitivity: as we show (below), it turns out that our results do not vary much qualitatively, even if the parameter is not included at all.

We can find some empirical support for our correction in Italian and French experience since the EMS began in 1979. Italy has pursued monetary policy that has systematically and substantially generated more inflation than in Germany. Figure 13-1 (top panel) shows the static prediction (conditional on actual values for right-hand-side variables) of the Italian structural real wage equation as estimated up to 1978: real wages have turned out higher than predicted, indicating an effect from anticipated devaluation not allowed for in the equation. The case of France (figure 13-1, bottom panel) is an interesting contrast. In the early 1980s, President Mitterrand initiated his "dash for growth," which involved frequent devaluations of the franc. Then, from 1983, he changed tack and pursued a tough monetary policy, using the EMS as an excuse (Minford 1989c). To bring about convergence of inflation with Germany, the money supply in France was tightened more than in Germany so that by 1990 the two countries' inflation rates would be the same. Figure 13-1 shows that in the early period French real wages lie above the prediction based on pre-1979 data, whereas in the later period they lie below. Both results are consistent with our proposed correction.

In other respects, the model's setup can be quickly described under the two EMS regimes. Without exchange controls, the model is solved as if on fixed exchange rates (with the money supply temporarily endogenous) when the exchange rate hits the EMS limit; otherwise it solves in the standard floating-rate mode, with the money supply exogenous. With exchange controls, the model is solved with the money supply exogenous throughout; the exchange rate is fixed when it hits the EMS limit, and the uncovered interest parity condition is suspended. Interest rates are then set by the interaction of money demand (with prices being set by the exchange rate and wages) and money supply.

This describes how the EMS model adjusts in the year of the shock. For the year after—when the parity can change—the exchange rate moves to find an equilibrium within the limits, with the money supply exogenous; if it cannot find one, then the parity changes (by one or more multiples of a predetermined

Figure 13-1. *Italian and French Real Wages and Static Prediction, 1960–89*

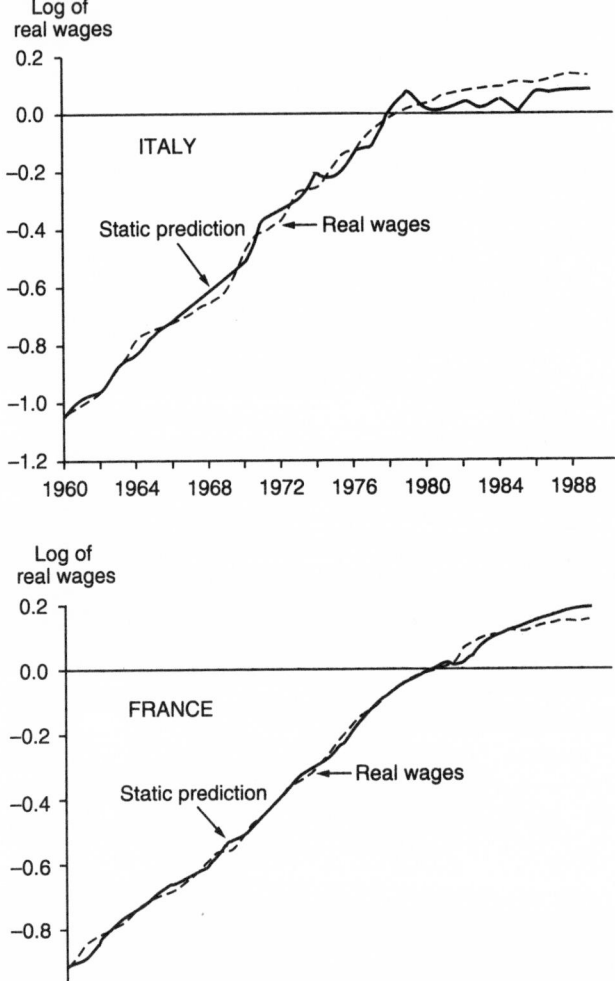

step size) until it does. Thereafter, the parity moves again whenever needed to find an equilibrium, with the money supply exogenous. This sequence is repeated every time a shock occurs: in year 1, adjustment without parity change; thereafter, parity change until an exchange-rate equilibrium is found.

The key difference between the two regimes is the behavior of interest rates (which then has impact elsewhere in the model). Under no controls, interest rates must rise sharply in response to the prospect of devaluation, as dictated by uncovered interest parity. This effect is obviously deflationary and creates pressure for exchange controls in this partially flexible EMS system. The authorities may be compelled, in Tobin's phrase, to throw sand in the machinery of international arbitrage. As the time of a parity change approaches, the system becomes unmanageable without controls. For this reason, in the "no-controls" case the authorities are assumed to deliberately create uncertainty about the exact timing within the year, as well as to use temporary controls ad hoc to boost manageability near the time, of parity changes.

If they do resort to total controls, then interest rates will be kept low by the monetary expansion, permitting a more reflationary impact; the resulting speculation against the currency is simply frustrated by the controls. The catch is that real interest rates are held below world rates, causing a micro distortion of the domestic capital market, subsidizing capital investment, and taxing saving. If the policy becomes systematic it could entail serious cost.

Simulations of Monetary Independence under the EMS

Several monetary policy simulations are shown for floating, EMS without controls, and EMS with controls in figures 13-2 through 13-4. In all cases, the country is assumed to pursue a policy of temporary reflation and two years of 4 percent annual growth in the money supply, and 8 percent money growth in total by year 2 (regardless of intervention in year 1) in the no-controls case.

Under floating (figure 13-2), this reflation has the familiar effects. Prices rise, the exchange rate falls—both rather sharply—and the real exchange rate falls as real wages are depressed by the unexpected inflation. Output rises because net exports are stimulated by higher competitiveness and domestic demand is stimulated by lower real interest rates, but lower real financial wealth restrains this effect (in some cases offsetting it).

The EMS without controls (figure 13-3, top panel) upsets this familiar scene. Now wages and prices rise, although not so much as under floating, because they are restrained by the exchange-rate limits. The real exchange-rate actually rises because prices are pushed up, relative to the exchange-rate depreciation, by the anticipatory wage pressure. Interest rates, both real and nominal, rise because of the need to maintain uncovered arbitrage, with nominal and real exchange rates expected to fall next year. Output falls because net exports are hit by the lower competitiveness and domestic demand is hit both by the higher real interest rate and by the drop in real financial wealth. Reflation is frustrated, even reversed, for real variables yet has inflationary effects on nominal variables; the mechanism of frustration is the exchange rate and its sympathetic link with interest rates. (See appendix B for more details of this simulation and further explanation.)

Figure 13-2. *The EMS under Floating Exchange Rates: Effects on the EMS3 of a 4 Percent Annual Increase in Money-Supply Growth for Two Years*

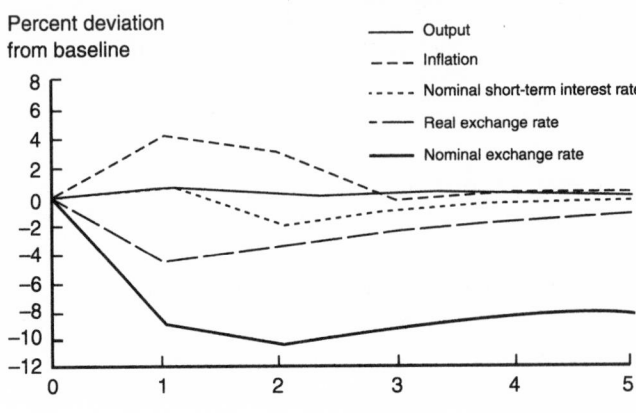

UNITED KINGDOM

Percent deviation from baseline

Output
Inflation
Nominal short-term interest rate
Real exchange rate
Nominal exchange rate

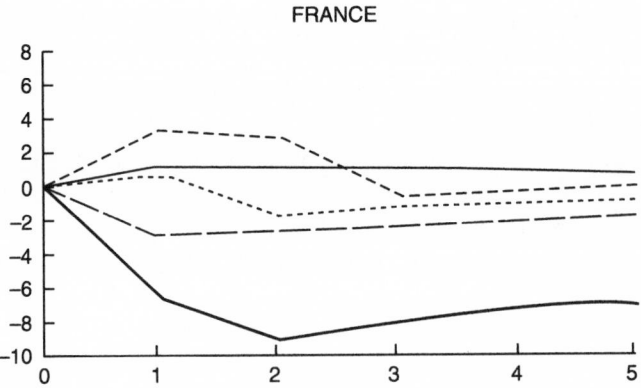

FRANCE

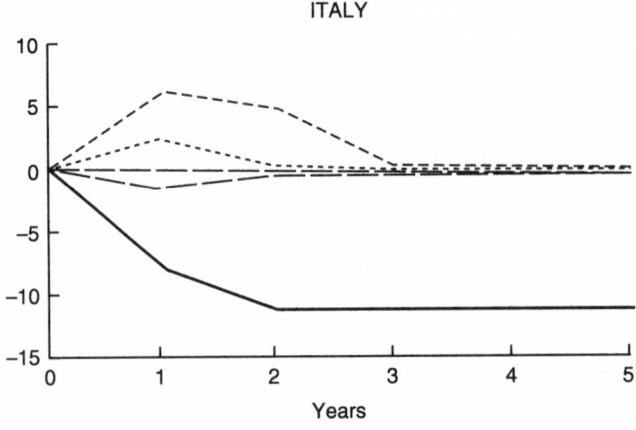

ITALY

Years

Figure 13-3. *The EMS with and without Exchange Controls: Effects on the EMS3 of a 4 Percent Annual Increase in Money-Supply Growth for Two Years*
A. Without Exchange Controls

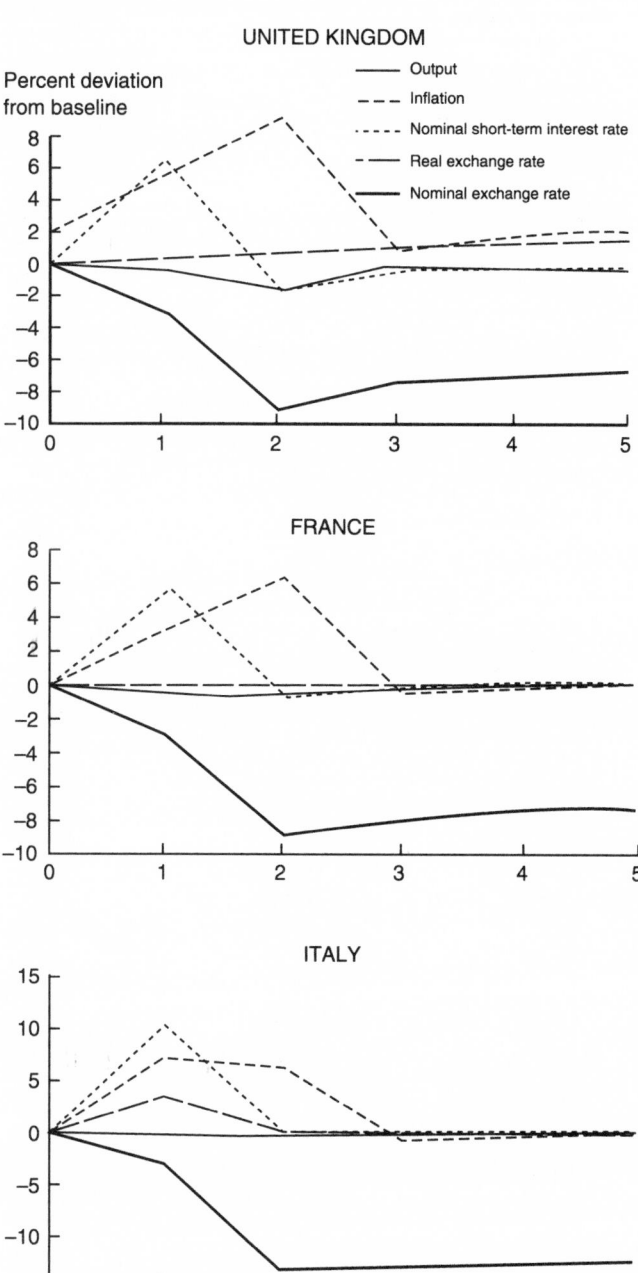

Figure 13-3 (*continued*)
B. With Exchange Controls

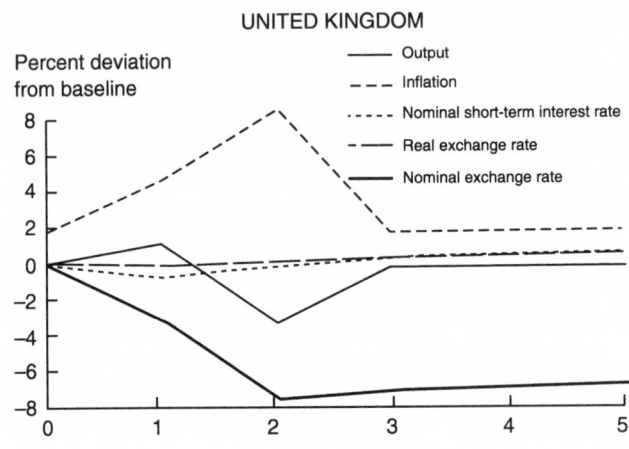

UNITED KINGDOM

Percent deviation
from baseline

Output
Inflation
Nominal short-term interest rate
Real exchange rate
Nominal exchange rate

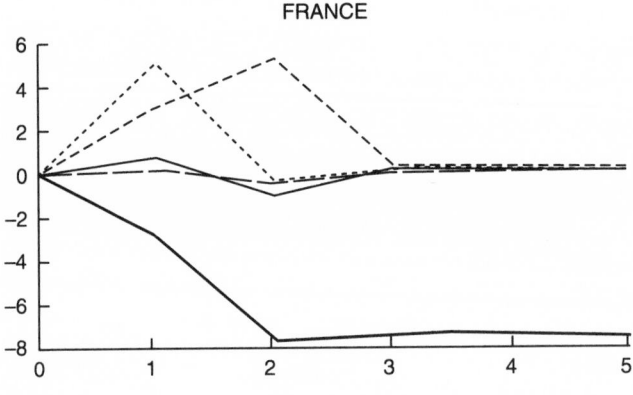

FRANCE

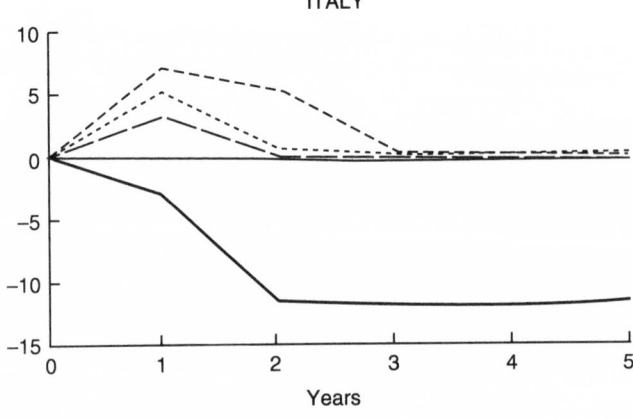

ITALY

Years

The EMS with exchange controls (figure 13-3, bottom panel) can at least cut this link. (The microeconomic costs of controls, of course, are not considered here.) Interest rates now move in line with domestic monetary conditions only, so with this reflation they rise less and may fall, which reduces the immediate deflationary effect on output compared with the no-control case. Output contracts in year 2, however, because the delayed inflation in that year causes a negative wealth effect and a fall in expenditure. The delay to inflation thus lessens the Phillips curve stimulus while leaving unchanged the overall expenditure contraction across years 1 and 2 as inflation reduces wealth.

Figure 13-4 shows the effects in the no-controls case when there is no adjustment of the wage parameter. Now the real exchange rate falls as under floating. But, as in the exchange-control case, the delayed inflation causes output to fall in year 2 after a stimulus in year 1. The output reaction (both up and down) is smaller because real interest rates fall much less than when exchange controls uncouple them from their link (through uncovered interest parity) to the real exchange rate.

In the default model, we assume the no-controls case, together with the wage adjustment discussed above. But, as we show below, the results are not at all sensitive to the assumptions about either wages or exchange controls. The essence of the ERM difference appears to lie in the way it delays the inflation shock.

One possible stylized representation of the model's operation (following Miller and Weller 1989) is given in figure 13-5, which may be set beside the essentially similar but stochastic ("smooth-pasted") and smaller model of Miller and Weller. The figure indicates that, under floating, a monetary reflation shock causes the real exchange rate to fall and thereafter to move along the saddlepath to equilibrium from below. Under the EMS (no controls, wage parameter included), the same shock forces the real exchange rate upward and then onto the saddlepath, which now approaches equilibrium from above. Hence the EMS alters both the model's impact effects and the location of its dynamic path (it does not alter its eigenvalues).

The essential difference between this model and that of Miller and Weller is in the anticipation of parity change. In their model the parity is assumed not to change, so that it acts as a stabilizing force. Here, a parity is expected to change in response to shocks that make that parity untenable; the only question is when and by how much. The smooth-pasting feature is only a minor difference.

The discussion of transmission has so far been informal. It is useful to recast it in a simplified analytic form, using familiar diagrams (figure 13-6). The model is represented by three curves in e, y space (e is the real exchange rate; y is output). The *ISBB* (aggregate demand) curve shows goods market equilibrium, assuming uncovered interest parity in asset markets (this allows us to substitute out real interest rates in favor of the real exchange rate,

Figure 13-4. *The EMS without Exchange Controls and Wage Adjustment Parameter: Effects on the EMS3 of a 4 Percent Annual Increase in Money-Supply Growth for Two Years*

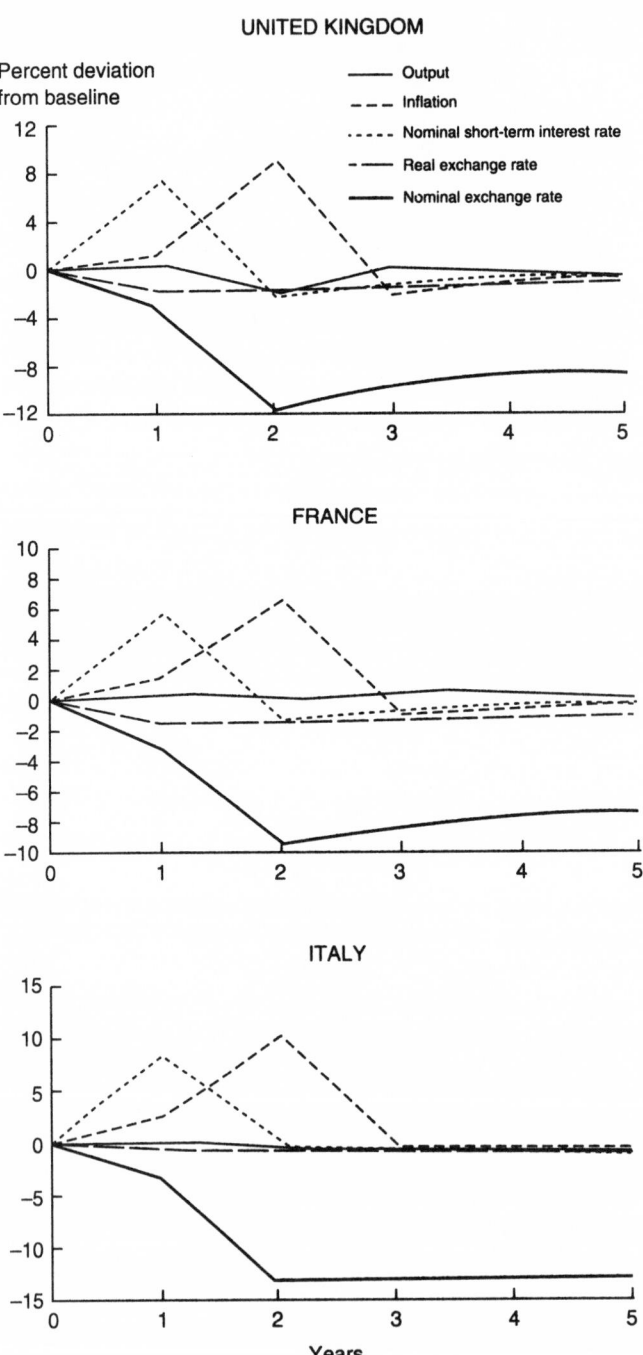

Figure 13-5. *Stylized Illustration of Model Path for Monetary
Reflation under Floating and the EMS*[a]

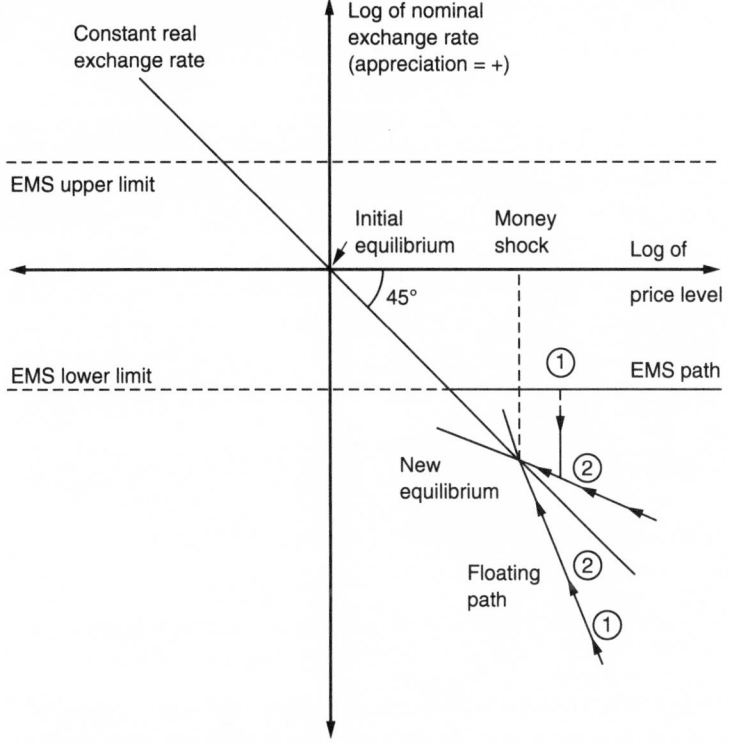

a. ① and ② indicate years 1 and 2 after shock.

Figure 13-6. *Transmission Mechanisms for the EMS3 under Floating
and the EMS (No Controls, Wage Adjustment Included)*

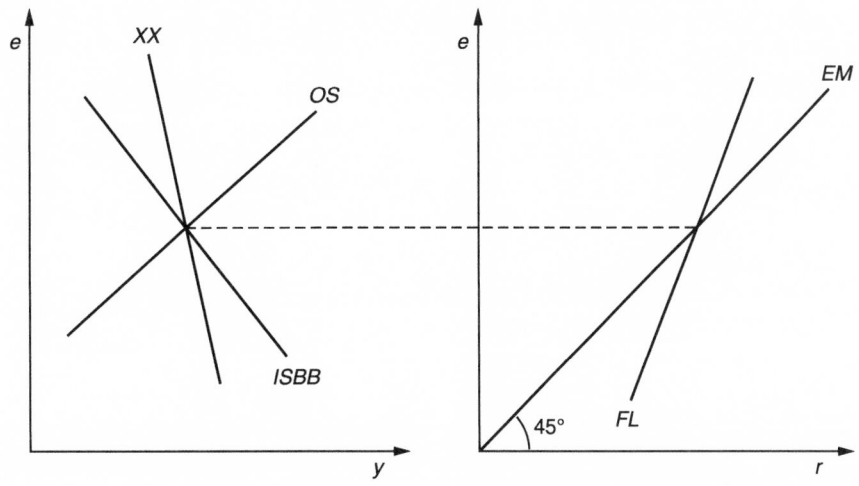

remembering that the expected real exchange rate is a function of the current rate and current shocks, in the usual saddlepath solution). The OS curve is the open-economy supply curve. It slopes upward in e because a rise in e raises consumer real wages relative to product real wages; it shifts rightward with an unanticipated rise in prices because this too raises expected consumer real wages relative to actual. In addition to the effect of p^{ue} on the OS curve, under EMS with the wage adjustment parameter there is a leftward shift from next period's expected devaluation, d^e_{+1}.

The $ISBB$ curve shifts left with higher prices (which lower nominally denominated wealth), as well as with other shifts in wealth. Real interest rates, r, vary with the real exchange rate, e, under uncovered interest parity, but if uncovered parity is broken by exchange controls then r can move independently, and a rise in r shifts the $ISBB$ curve leftward.

The XX curve is the locus for current account balance: to its left the economy acquires net foreign assets and spends more, and vice versa to its right. Adjustment in the model occurs in two main ways: wealth acquired or lost in this way shifts the $ISBB$ curve and real wages adjust to equilibrium, shifting the OS curve back to its original position. To simplify matters, we shall omit the XX curve and indicate adjustment after the impact effects by an arrow. We shall also relabel the $ISBB$ curve as AD and the OS curve as AS, to emphasize that in the open economy it is natural to regard the real exchange rate, e, as the key (relative) price affecting aggregate demand and supply.

The right-hand quadrant in e, p space displays the monetary sector. Under floating, prices (p) depend on the equality of money demand and supply: hence higher e means higher interest rates, lower money demand, and so higher prices. This defines an FL curve, which shifts rightward with lower output because that too lowers demand for money. Under EMS we exploit the identity that the nominal exchange rate, s, equals $e - p$; hence e and p must vary together along the 45 degree line (we assume zero bands here to simplify the diagram) for as long as the parity is unchanged. The money supply is endogenous during this period. When the parity is changed, the EMS is governed again by the floating solution, with the money supply exogenous, as parity moves until a floating solution can be found within the limits around it.

Figure 13-7 illustrates the difference for the money supply shock between floating (top panel) and EMS with no controls and wage adjustment (bottom panel). Take floating and the right-hand quadrant first (the monetary sector). Under floating, the 4 percent increase in money supply in year 1 shifts the FL curve to the right to FL'; in year 2 it shifts further to FL'' before eventually shifting out to $FL*$ as output falls back, lowering the real demand for money to normal. Prices rise most in year 1 (nominal interest rates rise in anticipation of inflation, lowering money demand at once), then somewhat further later. In the left-hand quadrant (the real sector), rising prices shift AD to AD' in year

Figure 13-7. *Money-Supply Expansion for the EMS3 under Floating and the EMS (No Controls, Wage Adjustment Included)*

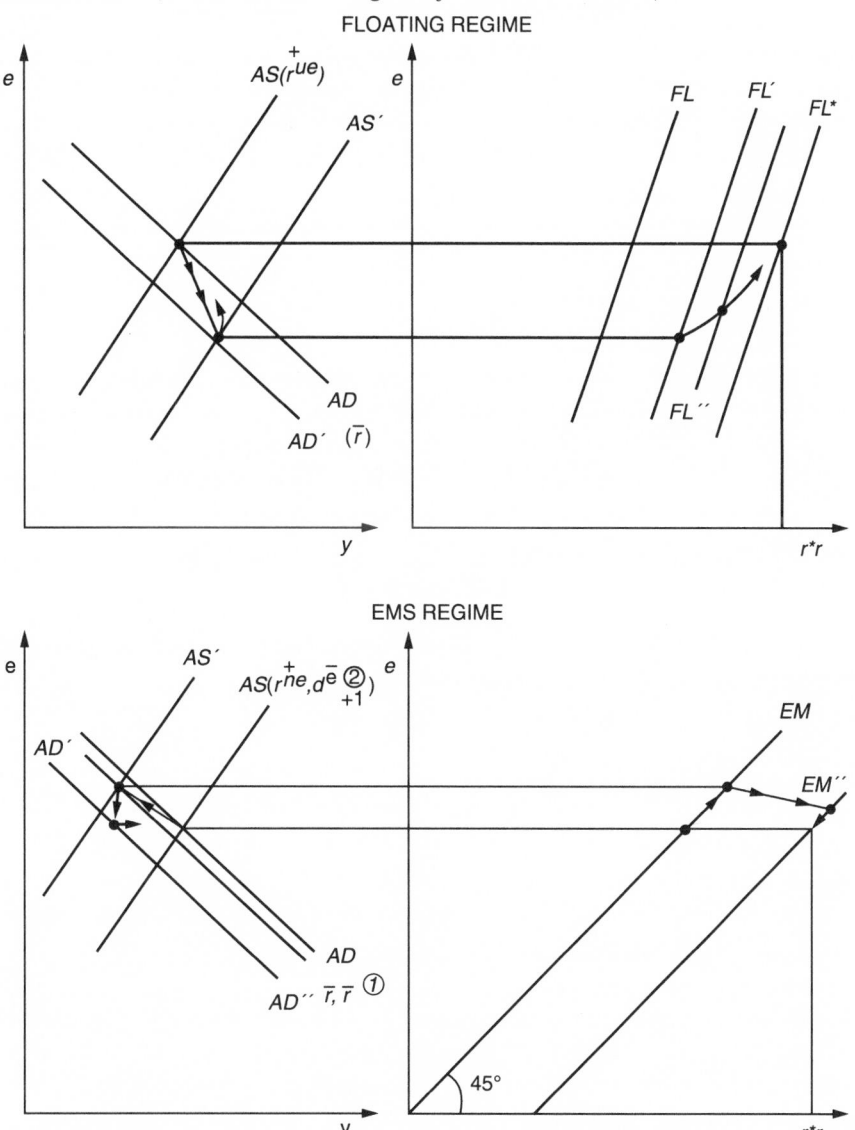

1, with a further small shift to AD'' in year 2. Surprise inflation shifts AS to the right, in the standard Phillips curve manner.

Under EMS (bottom panel of figure 13-7) the year-1 price rise is limited by the EM curve, but in year 2 devaluation shifts this to EM'', causing a substantial delayed price rise. As e falls back, prices fall back to $p*$. In the real sector, the AS curve is shifted leftward to AS' by the wage rise in anticipation of devaluation, which more than offsets the normal Phillips curve effect of p^{ue}. The *AD* curve shifts left slightly in year 1, but substantially more so in year 2, reflecting the delay in price rises.

We may use the same apparatus to understand the other permutations in our assumptions. For example, if there is no wage adjustment, its effect in shifting the *AS* curve leftward is removed. Or, if under EMS there are tough exchange controls, then real interest rates are detached from the real exchange rate and fall under the impact of (now exogenous) money-supply expansion; this shifts the *AD* curve rightward.

Evaluating the EMS

The simulations described above show the own-country responses to a standardized variation in the macroeconomic instrument under floating and under the EMS. For completeness, the appendix shows in part the responses of other countries to the same variation. These responses are now used as a set of multipliers to evaluate how the world will respond to a variety of situations under the two different regimes of floating and EMS. We will use these to judge whether the EMS achieves its four possible aims in terms of its operating properties. We begin with the aim of stabilization and then go on to discuss the extent to which the EMS acts as a source of price discipline, a promoter of EMU, and a surrogate for cooperation.

Stabilization Properties of the EMS

There are at least two ways in which a world regime under EMS or floating could be defined. There could be a general decision to follow fixed policies, with no reaction to shocks, or there could be strategic policymaking, with each country reacting to changes in the environment, including changes in other countries' policies (generating a noncooperative Nash equilibrium). Call these the fixed-rule and the Nash cases respectively.

In the Nash case, we do not permit time inconsistency (or "cheating"); a country is allowed to select one reaction to events (under perfect foresight and after iterating with the reactions of other countries), and it is then forced to stick to it by some penalty function (such as the fear of losing credibility). There are good reasons to suppose that such penalty functions do hold, in view of the disastrous results were they not to (an empirical assessment of just how disastrous, using the LIVERPOOL model of the United Kingdom, is reported in Minford 1989b; see also Hughes Hallett 1986 for a discussion of the international reasons).

We take the Nash case under floating as a benchmark. It may be regarded as the status quo, since countries are currently free to react as they please to domestic and foreign shocks, with no agreed constraints. It is true that the Louvre Accord exists, and some have argued that it represents a move toward exchange-rate limits (target zones). But because the Accord is not formally binding (and appears to have been forgotten since the 1987 crash), it is difficult to see its effect, and we ignore it here as second order. We therefore have four possible systems: fixed rule, floating with Nash, EMS fixed-rule, and EMS with Nash. Our primary interest, however, is in the Nash cases because these define the maximizing outcomes under the assumption of no cooperation.

We will consider later a last theoretical system: full cooperation. This is the ultimate in strategic policymaking, but it is obviously more relevant under the EMS than under floating. We find that the cooperative bargains that are feasible (that is, make all parties better off) involve different welfare weights and, of course, policies for each shock. The practical difficulties of identifying the shock and then of resetting the welfare weights are in our view likely to be insuperable when all the Group of Seven (G7) countries are involved. Brandsma and Hughes Hallett (1989) looked at this issue and found that cooperative policies are difficult to sustain as the distribution of gains keeps altering. The same argument may not apply, however, to a smaller coalition such as within the EMS, which is regarded as a cohesive group of countries committed to pegging their bilateral exchange rates. We consider this case carefully below.

We undertake two parallel simulation exercises. First, we consider a set of deterministic shocks in some detail to get a feel for the model effects and the policy reactions that may occur. Second, we carry out a set of stochastic simulations using the distributions of all the model's equation errors over the sample period (1955–85). We evaluate the effects of stability by the standard method of a quadratic welfare function, which in effect attaches penalty weights to the variances (around the baseline, treated as the desired trajectory) of output, the price level, real interest rates, the real exchange rate, and the monetary instrument. This function is also the maximand of each government.

The weights are set to penalize equally the following deviations from the desired trajectory in each period: 1 percent on the level of output and prices; 1 percent annually (1 percentage point) on the short-run real interest rate and the real exchange rate; and 3 percent annually (3 percentage points) on the rate of growth of the money supply. For France and Italy, we multiplied the weights on all targets other than prices by 2 and 10 respectively to dampen rather extreme instability in use of the monetary instrument (the standard control procedure for dealing with instrument instability; see Aoki 1976).

To those used to including only inflation and output among the targets, we must point out that the exchange-rate target in particular is of key importance in assessing the EMS, the objective of which, after all, is the stabilization of exchange rates. If this objective is removed, then—although floating still appears highly desirable relative to EMS—the ranking of different EMS regimes alters materially. This is discussed in the appendix. Whereas the size of weighting given to possible targets has therefore been found to matter little (Hughes Hallett 1987), in this particular case it appears essential to the spirit and substance of the exercise to include the exchange rate prominently among the targets.

We set the desired or ideal trajectories for this exercise equal to the baseline solution of the model in order to abstract entirely from the initial conditions, which might otherwise dominate the effects of the shocks and so bias the exercise.

Deterministic Shocks

In the deterministic exercise, we look at a basket of seven shocks: six of them are to individual EMS countries (France, Italy, and the United Kingdom)—a monetary shock each (a 4 percent reduction in real money demand for two years) and a real shock each (a 5 percent rise in the real exchange rate for one year); one shock is global (a 50 percent permanent rise in the dollar prices of oil and other commodities).

The results for this limited set of shocks, taken as a group, are shown in table 13-1. These results are fully detailed in the appendix, which displays the simulated effects of each shock under EMS and floating with fixed policies, as well as the welfare cost under each policy regime. The appendix also discusses (with reference to figure 13-9), the details of the direct multipliers and spillovers under the EMS and floating.

There are two sources of the instability found here with this EMS regime. The first is model instability when money supplies are held constant: for France and Italy, the EMS default regime produces larger reactions of the target variables to these shocks than does floating. This instability arises for a dependent-currency EMS country (one of the "EMS3": the United Kingdom, France, and Italy) whenever a shock produces a parity change; this occurs for France and Italy under their money-demand shocks, hence their poor results under the EMS. The other countries benefit because the spillovers on them from these two countries for these shocks are smaller under the EMS (see appendix table 13A-1).

Table 13-1. *Welfare Costs of Seven Shocks under EMS and Floating Regimes*

	Money fixed			Nash reaction		
Country	EMS	Floating	Ratio (E/F)	EMS	Floating	Ratio (E/F)
United States	552	522	1.06	540,446	2,325	232
Canada	1,587	1,375	1.15	476,487	411,305	1.16
Japan	194	165	1.18	66,316	21,103	3.14
Germany	11	9	1.22	394,834	3,862	102
France	4,833	1,296	3.73	613,191	5,059	121
Italy	7,346	2,636	2.79	126,447	440,646	0.29
United Kingdom	38	43	0.88	433,702	695	624

Source: Appendix table 13B-1.

The second source is instrument instability: EMS countries (and as a result some non-EMS countries too) are induced into large money-supply changes by the peculiar responses of their economies to the monetary instrument under the EMS. These changes in turn provoke sharp responses from other countries, notably the United States. The resulting large variability in relative money supplies causes massive variability in real exchange rates. Welfare costs consequently soar under the EMS compared with floating, as table 13-1 shows.

The one exception here is Italy, which experiences more instability under floating than under the EMS for the oil and Italian money-demand shocks. Its money supply reacts sharply under floating. The reason is discussed below. Figures 13-7 and 13-8 illustrate model instability within the EMS3. Figure 13-8 shows a negative supply shock—a leftward shift of the *AS* curve. Under floating (top panel), this produces a rightward shift of the *FL* curve as output falls, and this raises prices; the price rise shifts *AD* to *AD'* but also partially offsets the shift in the *AS* curve. The fall in output is thereby limited.

Under fixed rates (bottom panel), the rise in prices is confined to the 45-degree line; this gives less dampening to the *AS* curve, which consequently shifts further to the left. In addition, a parity change is expected for the following year, which allows prices to jump onto the *FL* curve. This expectation raises wages and shifts the *AS* curve further still to the left. The delay in price rises also causes a delayed shift in *AD* in year 2. The result is a displacement in price volatility over time (less in year 1 but more in year 2) and greater volatility in output and other real variables.

Figure 13-7 can be used, more or less as it stands, to understand a (permanent) money-demand shock. There too it was seen that, although delayed, there was greater price volatility under EMS than under floating.

In summary, the greater model instability under EMS arises from the one-year delay after a shock in the reaction of the exchange rate and so of prices. This delayed reaction both reduces the generally stabilizing Phillips curve shift in the *AS* curve in year 1 and also delays the shift in the *AD* curve, so putting back the adjustment process. Whereas under floating the impact effects of the shocks are concentrated (with offsetting effects) in year 1, the EMS delay creates a "double-whammy." The adjustment lags then damp down the economy from one year later than under floating.

We now turn to the issue of instrument instability. Figure 13-9 shows the Nash equilibrium for the case of the oil price shock, a negative supply shock that both depresses output and raises prices. The figures for the Nash equilibrium in the monetary instruments and for the "insular case" (where no monetary reaction is assumed for other countries) are taken from the deterministic simulation reported in the appendix. Two things can be seen. First, under EMS the slopes of the Nash reaction functions are positive instead of the normal

Figure 13-8. *Supply Shocks for the EMS3 under Floating and the EMS*

FLOATING REGIME

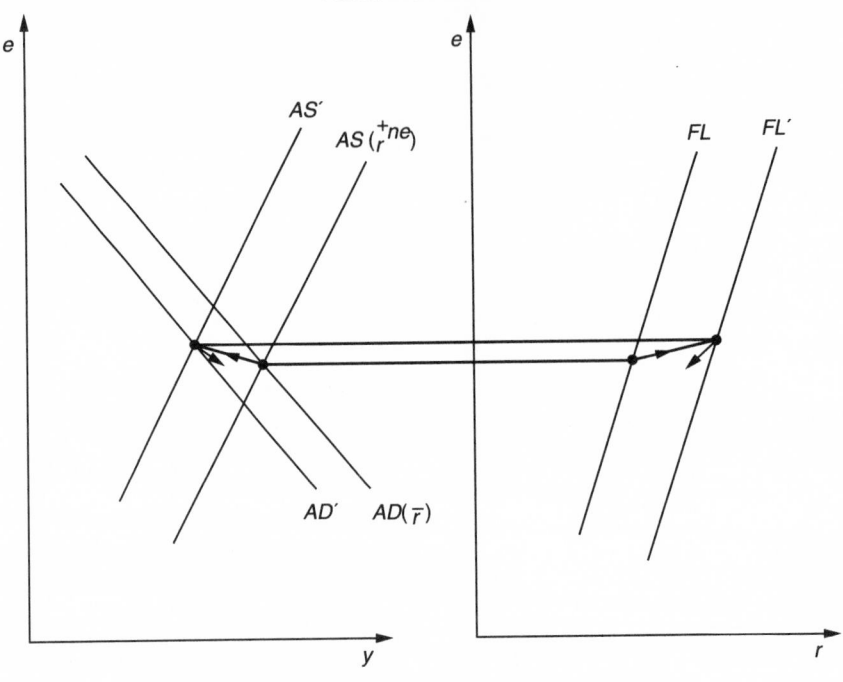

EMS REGIME

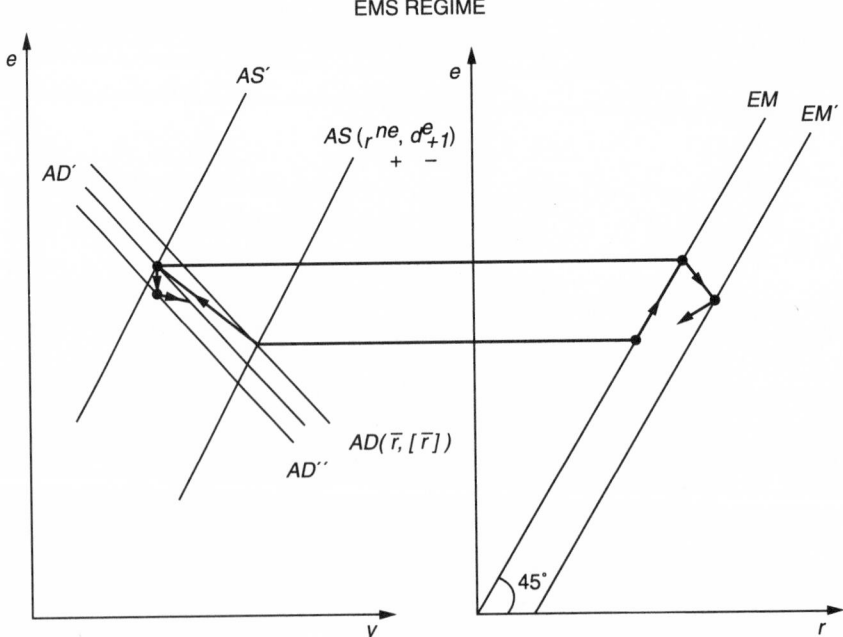

Figure 13-9. *Nash Reaction Functions: Oil Shock Intercepts*

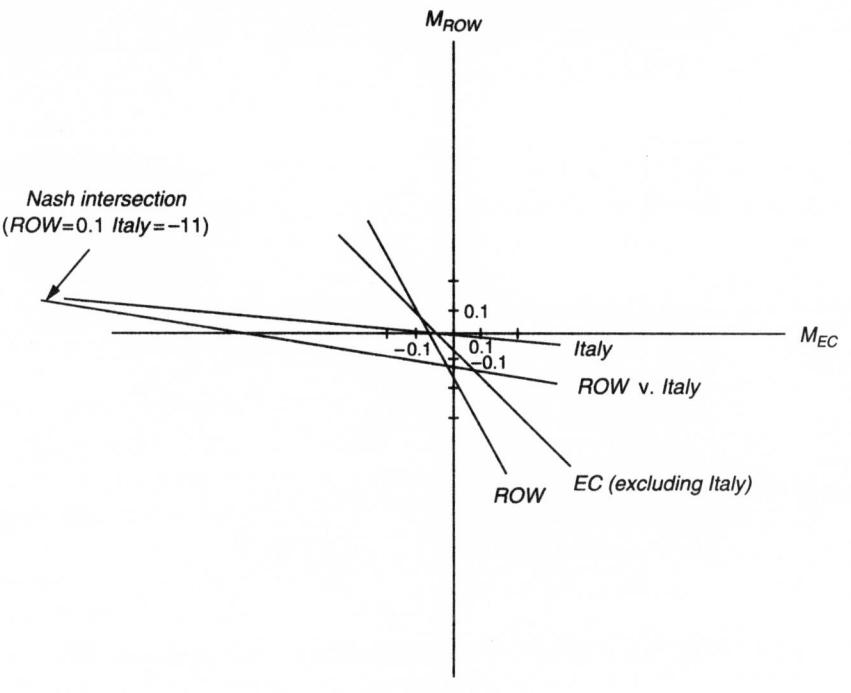

FLOATING REGIME

M_{ROW}

Nash intersection
(ROW=0.1 Italy=−11)

0.1

−0.1   0.1   Italy
        −0.1

ROW v. Italy

M_{EC}

ROW   EC (excluding Italy)

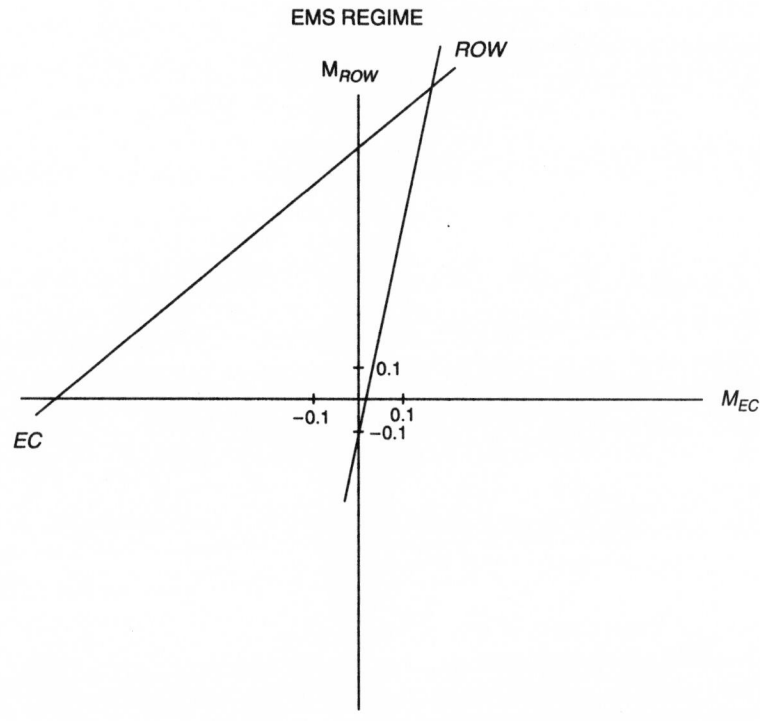

EMS REGIME

ROW

M_{ROW}

0.1

−0.1   0.1 M_{EC}
        −0.1

EC

negative, as under floating. Second, the insular reaction of EC countries is more deflationary under EMS than under floating for the oil shock.

The key to these two features lies in the perversity of the response to EMS3 monetary policy under the EMS, as seen in appendix table 13A-2 and figure 13-3. Under the EMS, monetary expansion by the EMS3 countries raises home prices normally enough, but it lowers home output (and raises the real exchange rate and interest rates) perversely. Abroad (even in other EMS countries), monetary expansion similarly lowers output (instead of the normal effect, under floating, of raising it). The effect on prices abroad under the EMS is mixed, but on average a slight lowering occurs compared with the more substantial lowering under floating.

This perversity under EMS—of both the direct effect of EC reflation on home output and the spillover effect on foreign output—means that the EC responds to more ROW (rest-of-the-world) reflation with more reflation at home (offsetting the foreign expansionary spillover on output). As for the ROW, it reacts to the negative spillover from more EC reflation by reflating more itself. Hence both positive slopes. Recall that the slopes of the Nash reaction functions depend solely on the instrument multipliers and spillovers and are therefore invariant to the shock. Hence the slopes shown in figure 13-9 are general for floating and EMS and illustrate the fundamental instrument instability of the EMS. The sharper insular deflation by the EC under the EMS arises from the need to offset the effects of the oil shock, which are negative for output and positive for prices: a large EC deflation now *raises* EC output while lowering prices, as usual.

The positively sloped reaction functions of the bottom panel of figure 13-9 result, of course, in a destabilized Nash equilibrium under the EMS. The case of Italy under floating has been shown separately in figure 13-9 (top panel). Italy has a near-vertical Phillips curve under floating—a very weak response of output to money—because of its high degree of wage indexation. Hence when Italy reacts (with normal slope) to ROW reflation, it takes much sharper deflationary action to obtain the necessary offset, and this is the cause of its instability under floating. Under the EMS, Italy's reaction function is similar to that of the other EC countries. The negative spillovers of fellow EMS members' Nash reflation largely offset the positive spillovers from the ROW; so Italy's own money supply is led to react little in the Nash equilibrium. Although Italy avoids domestic monetary instability under the EMS, it suffers from the instability induced among others. This will be apparent when we consider the wider range of stochastic simulations below.

Already we can see the outline of the EMS regime problem. The inelasticity of the current parity, combined with the anticipation of parity changes when there are no capital controls, destabilizes both the economy and policy responses. We now turn to stochastic simulations, where we find the problem dramatically confirmed.

Stochastic Simulations

Thirty-eight sets of sequential shocks for six years each were applied to the two regimes, EMS-Nash and floating-Nash (192 shocks in all for each regime). The shocks were drawings from the single-equation residuals estimated for the model over the sample period (1957–81 for the most part, see the appendix for technical details).

The average welfare cost for the thirty-eight sets is shown in table 13-2. Model instability is apparent in the EMS results when the money supply is held constant (first three columns); the third column shows the ratio of welfare costs under EMS and floating, with no policy responses. There is clearly a serious problem with the EMS regime. Nash instrument responses (second three columns) add materially to model instability because money supplies react in the way discussed in the deterministic case (figure 13-9). The last column highlights the extremely high ratio of the welfare costs of the EMS compared with floating, when money supplies do react.

As appendix table 13B-4 makes clear, the extraordinarily high welfare cost under the EMS-Nash default, compared with floating-Nash, arises from interactive overuse of the monetary instrument (and the associated real-exchange-rate instability). The relatively high fixed money cost of EMS versus floating arises from greater variance of both output and inflation, as well as of real exchange rates and real interest rates: in other words, there is a widely spread increase in variance across all countries and target variables.

The essential point of these results seems to be unavoidable. The EMS is a system prone to acute instability in the face of shocks. Particularly vulnerable are the EMS-dependent countries. The reason for this instability seems to lie in the nonlinearity of the fixed-but-adjustable system's response to shocks, with large shocks creating a sharp response, and in deflationary circumstances the perverse trade-off in EMS-dependent countries inducing monetary over-reaction. This systemic instability is not a feature of pure fixed systems, as indicated in our stochastic simulations for the Brookings exercise. Although these are not strictly comparable because they do not embody Nash reactions,

Table 13-2. *Average Welfare Costs across All Shocks, by Country*

Country	Fixed money			Nash reaction		
	Floating	EMS	Ratio (E/F)	Floating	EMS	Ratio (E/F)
United States	315	1,779	5.6	1,028	316,674	308
Canada	4,816	40,525	8.4	47,423	507,385	10.7
Japan	743	1,294	1.7	6,818	64,180	9.4
Germany	2,024	3,530	1.7	1,828	204,083	112
France	737	3,530	4.8	896	299,724	334
Italy	187	3,191	17.1	41,550	68,439	1.6
United Kingdom	79	2,048	25.9	201	211,743	1,053

preliminary work allowing such restrictions (reported in Minford 1989a) nevertheless suggests that the Nash element does not destabilize fixed rates.

Alternative EMS Regimes

It may well be said, in response to our analysis, that the fault must lie in our modeling of the EMS or our choice of EMS regime. Clearly, the EMS has survived since 1979, most recently without capital controls. One might argue that the shocks in the 1980s have been small, but this seems improbable; although there has been only a mild recession (1982), there was a large oil price shock in 1980, an international debt crisis, domestic crises in EMS3 countries (for example, Mitterrand's difficulties in 1982–83), and a gyrating dollar. On the other hand, the long period of fixed parities, ending in a crisis and partial collapse of the system in 1992, may actually prove our point.

We therefore examined the model's sensitivity to different assumptions. We looked at our anticipation parameter for wages and at the choice of regime. We examined variations in the rules of the regime: in the period of delay before the parity can be changed and in the size of the parity change permitted. We also considered capital controls. Finally, we considered variations in policy reactions that might have helped. Clearly, having no money supply reaction is no help against model instability, but it would, of course, prevent instrument instability. And cooperation—or a coalition among EMS members—could help to offset model instability.

Slightly lengthening the period of delay badly worsens instability: we tried raising it to two years from the default one year and encountered severe problems of convergence. This result also emerged from our earlier nonstochastic study (Hughes Hallett and Minford 1989). The reason is that putting adjustment off does not diminish the size of the adjustment necessary and may even increase it (if the EMS-induced price change goes in a direction opposite to the floating solution, it may go further before having to be reversed). This too was apparent in 1992. The expectation of adjustment is deferred one year, but that year's events still impinge on the current year's outcome through expectations.

What we found in addition is summarized in table 13-3. We focus here only on the aggregate welfare cost measure, but its decomposition is displayed and discussed in the appendix. In essence, when extreme instability occurs it is associated with high instrument variability and the resulting instability in the real exchange rate. When regimes exhibit moderate instability, the differences between them in the variances of the target variables are highly correlated: if one falls, they all tend to fall.

Table 13-3 is organized to show the welfare costs for different EMS regimes. It begins with the default EMS model, assuming Nash noncooperative reactions; then one assumption at a time is relaxed in turn. Not all permuta-

Table 13-3. *Average Welfare Cost of the EMS under Alternative Assumptions: Summary of Key Results*

Thousands of welfare-cost units, average for countries shown

Assumption	ROW[a]	EMS4[b]	All
Default EMS (Nash)	296	196	239
Model sensitivity			
No wage reaction parameter (NASH)	208	209	209
Parity rules			
Parity change limited (max. 5 percent) (Nash)	300	86	178
No parity change (Nash)	13	1.7	6.5
Capital controls (Nash)	228	170	195
Monetary policy rules			
High penalty on money			
(France, Italy, and United Kingdom only) (Nash)	41	37	39
Fixed money	16	3	8
Worldwide cooperation (default EMS)	10	2	5.4
EMS coalition (default EMS)	25	1	11
European Monetary Union (EMU)	8.5	0.5	3.9

Source: Appendix table13B-3.
a. Rest of the world.
b. The EMS4 are the United Kingdom, France, Italy, and Germany.

tions can be shown in a summary table, but in the following discussion we mention some that are of interest. Appendix table 13A-3 gives a full listing of the welfare costs by country for every permutation.

The default EMS under the Nash assumption recapitulates the dramatic instability shown earlier. Capital controls are in existence to some degree through all these model-regime combinations: as explained above, some controls are needed in periods preceding well-anticipated parity changes to avoid massive interest rate movements. Indeed the "abolition" of exchange controls that has just been effected within the EMS specifically provides for their temporary use in such circumstances. The fears of analysts such as Giavazzi and Spaventa (1990) are that this temporary use may not be effective: once deregulation has occurred in normal times, evasion may be much easier in times of crisis. We could not deal with this problem in our modeling efforts here because the model is annual (and so too time-aggregated).

What we have modeled is permanently tough exchange controls as opposed to temporarily invoked controls, our default assumption. Permanent controls make little difference to model instability across all countries, but under the Nash assumption they do slightly reduce instrument instability, presumably because the model has a less perverse Phillips curve trade-off. This shows that, provided that capital controls can be used effectively in crisis, they are not mandatory or desirable at other times within the EMS. The qualification must remain that the effectiveness of capital controls in a crisis may be impaired if they are only used in a crisis.

If the model is varied to eliminate the wage reaction, instability is somewhat reduced, but it is still serious. This shows that the parity delay itself alters the system's adjustment in a similar direction (toward a perverse Phillips curve trade-off) and thus destabilizes the Nash equilibrium.

Limits on the size of parity change are also not much help. They do markedly reduce instability for the EMS4 (the United Kingdom, France, Italy, and Germany), but they increase it for ROW. In any case, they leave marked instability because there is still substantial scope for conflicting policy even with these limits. Preventing parity change altogether transforms the situation. The reason is that it effectively prevents any independent use of monetary policy and, hence, the destabilizing Nash reactions. The margins are insignificant in this context.

Big gains therefore appear when Nash independence is effectively abandoned. As in the case of no parity change, fixed money supplies, which are unresponsive to shocks, reduce costs sharply. Worldwide cooperation reduces costs further, but (as argued earlier) such cooperation is probably infeasible. A coalition of the EMS countries (playing Nash games with other countries, the United States, Canada, and Japan) is far more realistic. For the EMS4, the prospects under such a coalition, worldwide cooperation, or fixed money are very similar. The EMS4 countries in fact fully maximize their collective welfare under EMU, the ultimately rigid system (modeled here as no parity change and zero margins). The ROW also prefers EMU because it effectively reduces the EMS propensity to instability. But this does not carry over to regimes whose exchange-rate stability is desired for its own sake (see appendix B).

What this analysis appears to indicate is that the EMS has survived by becoming more rigid (permitting less and less parity adjustment) and by the resulting monetary cooperation between member countries. The EMS could not afford for long the luxury of frequent parity changes and of independent monetary policies by member countries because these would destabilize it seriously. In short, in order to survive the EMS has had to become more than its overt rules; it has had to develop into a monetary coalition. There is no viable "halfway house" between full monetary integration and floating, as argued by Walters (1990). This conclusion validates the fears of many skeptics, voiced at the founding of the EMS, that the EMS could not survive without institutional change. The EMS has been forced into greater integration by the need to avoid the great potential instability of the original specification.

As regards exchange controls, temporary ones are recognized to be necessary to prevent EMS breakdown when parity changes are allowed. But whether controls are temporary or permanent, our work shows that they do not avoid the instability of the basic regime design. The weakening of controls in July 1990 has obviously been another factor hastening institutional change, but in a way we have not modeled here. Finally, we note in table 13-4 the comparison, regime by regime, of floating and its EMS equivalent. Throughout, the float-

Table 13-4. *Floating and EMS Regimes Compared*[a]

Item	ROW	EMS4	All
Fixed money (floating/EMS)	2.0/16.0	0.7/3.0	0.8/8.0
Nash (independence)	18.0/296.0	11.0/196.0	14.0/239.0
Nash (EMS coalition)	3.3/25.0	0.3/1.0	0.5/11.0
Worldwide cooperation	1.4/10.0	0.7/2.0	2.0/5.4

a. The numerator is welfare cost under floating; the denominator is welfare cost under the EMS.

ing regime dominates its equivalent; floating therefore provides a useful extra degree of freedom in economic adjustment.

The EMS as Creator of Price Discipline and Route to EMU

Our key finding is that the EMS creates greater instability for EMS-dependent countries than they would experience under floating. This property arises from the peculiar responses of EMS3 economies to their monetary instruments under the EMS. The monetary instrument is hobbled effectively by the EMS: a monetary stimulus fails to stimulate output, perversely strengthens the real exchange rate, and yet fails to prevent inflation.

There can be little doubt that this hobbling of monetary policy is precisely the intention of the EMS. It is the mechanism by which the EMS creates price discipline: deviations from monetary policy consistent with the inflation rate of the reserve currency are penalized by these unpleasant consequences. There is a parallel with the aversion therapy sometimes used for cigarette smokers or alcoholics, whereby a drug is taken that causes indulgence to be accompanied by nausea. Whether one undertakes such a style of cure depends on the alternatives. It has been argued for both France and Italy (Giavazzi and Pagano 1988 and Sachs and Wyplosz 1986) that the EMS made it politically possible to pursue tough monetary policies in a way that purely domestic mechanisms could not. The EMS appealed to pan-Europeanism; people would endure the hardships of tight money for the sake of preserving Europe.

This is a highly persuasive explanation for the acceptance of the EMS as a counterinflationary framework in continental Europe. The facts are also clear that the framework has produced convergence of French and (to some degree) Italian inflation to the German rate. Episodes of independent monetary expansion in these two countries have become rarer as the counterproductiveness of such moves has come to be appreciated. At the same time, there is some evidence that macroeconomic performance other than for inflation (figure 13-10) has worsened: growth has been slower, and unemployment has been higher, compared with these two countries' past and with performance elsewhere. De Grauwe (1989) has also argued plausibly that in practice the EMS exchange-rate discipline has acted in a more gradualistic way than the domestic monetary shock treatment used in the United States and the United Kingdom in the early

Figure 13-10. *Key Variables for the EMS3, 1960–90*

UNITED KINGDOM

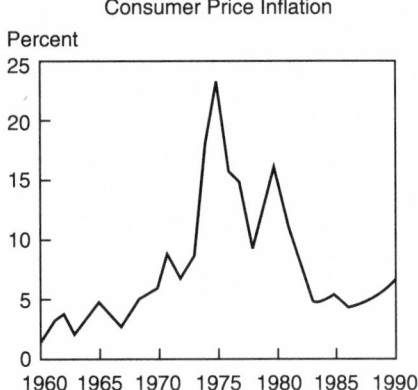

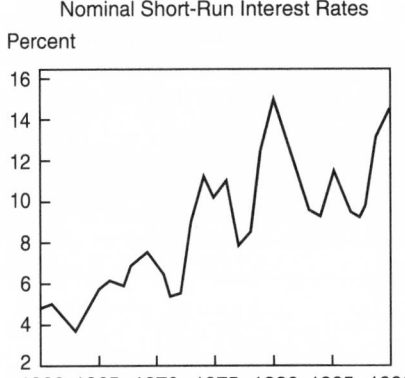

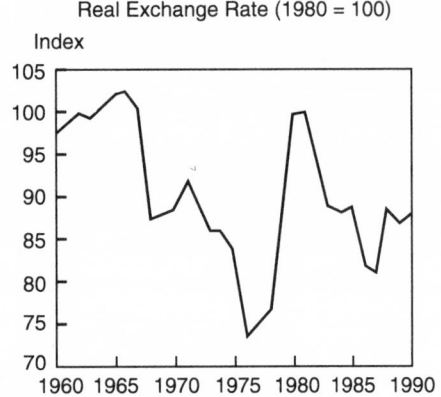

FRANCE

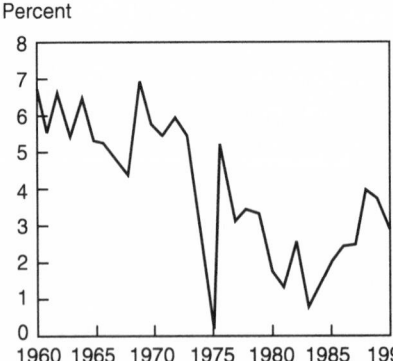

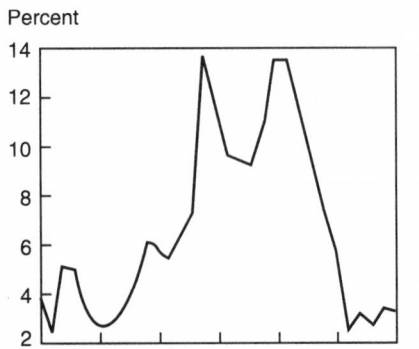

Figure 13-10 *(continued)*

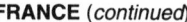

FRANCE *(continued)*

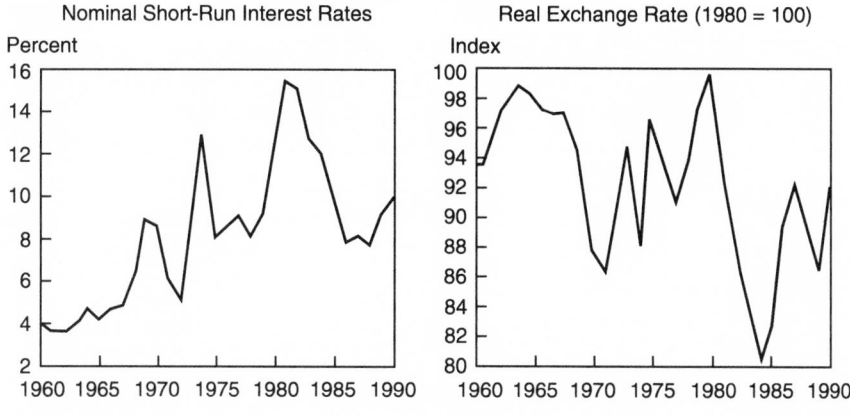

Nominal Short-Run Interest Rates

Real Exchange Rate (1980 = 100)

ITALY

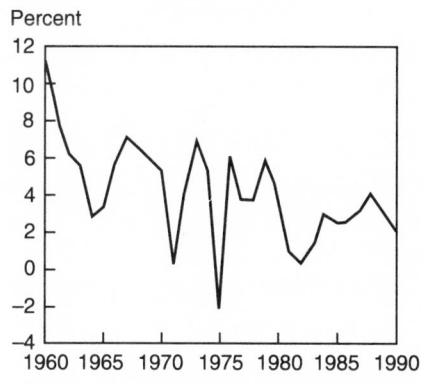

Real GDP Growth

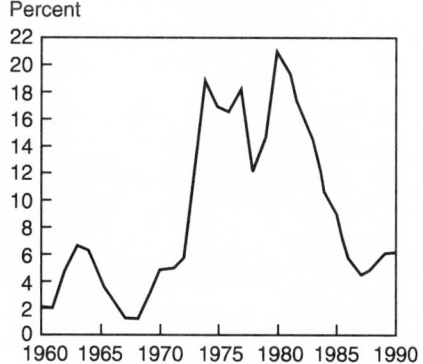

Consumer Price Inflation

Nominal Short-Run Interest Rates

Real Exchange Rate (1980 = 100)

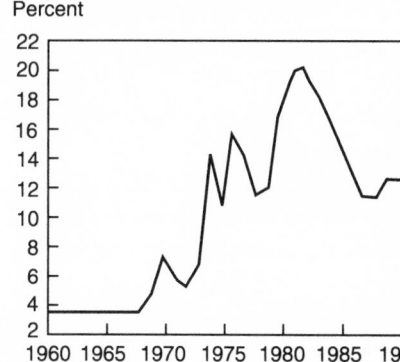

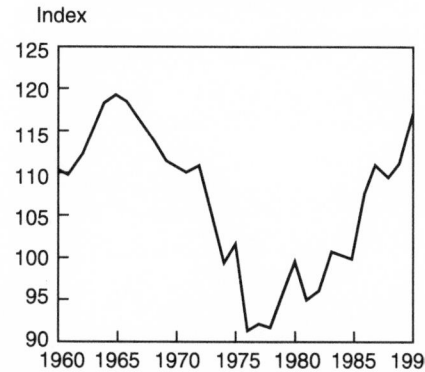

Sources: International Monetary Fund, *International Financial Statistics* (Washington, various years); and United Kingdom, Central Statistics Office, *Economic Trends* (London, various years).

1980s. It is well known that, faced with these choices, the United Kingdom has (until recently) preferred to use domestic monetary discipline. But this is not to deny that, compared with nothing at all, the EMS creates price discipline: the simulation analysis here clearly shows that it does, and by what means.

But most important of all, the joint challenges to EMS members posed by the system's potential instability seem to have forced their central banks to abandon independence and to cooperate to a degree never originally foreseen. In this respect, therefore, the EMS has been both a step toward EMU and a producer of cooperation. Albeit not a surrogate for cooperation, the existence of the EMS has certainly acted as a source of it. And EMU is certainly easier to achieve the more firmly such cooperation is established.

Conclusions

We have attempted to evaluate the EMS with the use of a full macroeconometric model, fitted to postwar data and adjusted in a few key coefficients to deal with the post-1979 existence of the EMS. We have used optimization methods to ascertain the overall effects that would occur under the EMS and under floating on the assumption that all governments react to events and, strategically, to each other. Although there are inevitably arbitrary assumptions in the work here, our overall conclusion is not enormously surprising: the EMS acts as a device to hobble the monetary policy of EMS countries that do not control the key currency (the deutsche mark). EMS-dependent countries find that monetary policy creates unpleasant and destabilizing results. This fact discourages them from using monetary policy—hence the encouragement of price convergence and discipline. By the same token, however, the behavior of these economies in response to shocks when they do use the monetary instrument under EMS is significantly worse than under floating.

The EMS suffers from severe system instability, moreover, that is induced partly by agents' responses to anticipations of parity change and partly by instability of money supply response. This very system instability has forced, even with tough exchange controls, greater rigidity in parities, but also greater cooperation and the abandonment of monetary independence. The recent July 1990 removal of permanent controls has undoubtedly been a factor further hastening rigidity, but in a way not modeled here. We found that an EMS with no parity change and fixed money supplies exhibited reasonable stability, although still less than a floating regime in which money supplies could be varied independently and noncooperatively.

This is not an entirely surprising conclusion. The stability problems of the EMS arise because parities can move and monetary independence is therefore exercised. To remove these problems requires the removal of both parity change and monetary independence. Yet such removal also takes away the ability of monetary policy to respond flexibly to shocks. Therefore floating, which preserves that ability without concomitant instability, appears from a general world viewpoint to be a superior regime.

The achievement of the EMS is to have survived by discovering how to alleviate these problems and, by that discovery, to have launched participating countries onto a fast track toward monetary unification. Nevertheless, it has done so at the cost of sacrificing the greater stability, both inside and outside the EMS, offered by the regime of floating.

Appendix A: Outline of the LIVERPOOL World Model and Summary of Results

The model consists of nine country models (all on floating exchange rates except the two Benelux countries fixed to a "basket") and three trade blocs (export and import prices and volumes for each bloc) to link those other countries not modeled closely.

Outline

We will discuss it now as if it were a two-country model ("United States" and "Europe," say), with a floating exchange rate between the two: the "home" country can be described (in log-linear form) by the following stylized equations:

(13A-1)
$$y = \delta_\theta \theta - \delta_r r - \delta_e e + \delta_F y_F$$
$$+ \delta_d d + \lambda_1 y_{-1} + \varepsilon_\delta \qquad (IS)(\delta_F < 1)$$

(13A-2)
$$y = \sigma_p(p - E p_{-1}) + \sigma_e(e - \lambda_2 e_{-1})$$
$$+ \lambda_3 y_{-1} + \varepsilon_s \qquad (PP) = \sigma_p$$

(13A-3)
$$m = \mu_y y + \mu_\theta 0 - \mu_R R + p$$
$$+ \lambda_4(m - p)_{-1} + \varepsilon_\mu \qquad (LM)$$

(13A-4)
$$\Delta m = \phi \overline{d} + \varepsilon_m \qquad \text{(money supply)}$$

(13A-5)
$$\Delta \overline{d} = \varepsilon_d \qquad \text{(deficit process)}$$

(13A-6)
$$x = -\beta_e e - \beta_y y + \beta_F y_F \qquad \text{(current balance)}$$

(13A-7)
$$\Delta \theta = \phi(x + \overline{d} - Ty) - q\Delta R - \Delta p \qquad \text{(balance-sheet constraint)}$$

$(13A - 8)$ $r = r_F - E e_{+1} - e$ (efficient market
condition)

$(13A - 9)$ $R = r + E p_{+1} - p,$ (nominal-real interest-rate
identity)

where

y = output (log)

θ = real value of financial index (log)

p = consumer price index (log)

m = money supply (log)

r = real interest rate (fraction per year)

R = nominal interest rate (fraction per year)

e = real exchange rate (fractional departure from equilibrium)

d = government deficit, including interest payments, as a fraction
of GDP $(= \bar{d} - T_y)$

$\bar{d}$ = cyclically adjusted d

x = current account balance (fraction of GDP)

E_{-i} = rational expectation on data through $t - i,$

and the F subscript denotes "foreign." All coefficients are positive. The ε_j are error terms, which may be autocorrelated. The constant terms have been set at zero, implying that all real variables (y, e, θ, r) can be treated as deviations from equilibrium (denoted by *).

Equations 13A-1 and 13A-3, IS and LM curves, come from interrelated private-sector demand functions for financial assets, physical assets, and non-durable consumption. The main point to note is the role of financial wealth, θ, in demand for both goods and money.

Equation 13A-2 is the PP, or Phillips, curve that relates output to unanticipated inflation (seen from the last year, on the grounds that there is a one-year wage-contracting lag for a significant unionized fraction of the labor force) and, the open economy aspect, the real exchange rate. The latter effect arises because as the terms of trade improve (the real exchange rate rises) the consumption real wage increases relative to the own-product real wage.

In equation 13A-4, the money-supply function, the assumption is that the government pursues monetary targets dictated by its expected equilibrium deficit, except for temporary spells (ε_m, which may be a process with auto-regressive and moving-average components) when it attempts exogenously to vary the fiscal-monetary mix. This long-run tendency to go for "balanced" monetary financing is the result of the intertemporal budget constraint on government, which prevents permanent "monetary" financing of a deficit.

The ratio of GDP to financial assets is denoted by ϕ; hence $\phi\overline{d}$ is the expected long-run rate of injection of financial assets into the economy arising from the government's deficit, and equation 13A-4 states that this will ultimately be matched by the rate of monetary injection. Since both $\overline{d}$ and such temporary spells are assumed to be exogenous, the level of M at any time is exogenously determined (by the history of d and these spells). Equations 13A-3 and 13A-4 give rise to the LM curve in the (p, y) domain in figure 13A.

Equation 13A-5 is the postulated process driving the exogenous cyclically adjusted deficit (tax rates and government spending as a fraction of GDP are thus exogenous, while the actual deficit is endogenous; it is treated as a random walk (as are tax rates and government spending by implication). The parameter T reflects the marginal (net) tax rate over the cycle.

Equation 13A-6 is a standard net exports (current balance) equation. Equation 13A-7 then equates changes in financial wealth with this current balance, the change in net foreign assets, plus the deficit, the change in government liabilities, minus the effects on asset values of inflation and interest rate changes.

Equation 13A-8 is the interest parity condition adjusted for expected exchange-rate change, in terms of real interest and exchange rates. The information available is assumed to be contemporaneous in this annual setup. This is identically equivalent with the usual formulation in terms of the nominal interest differential. Note that our definition of real interest rate uses the consumption deflator, p, and that of the real exchange rate uses the two countries' consumption deflators converted to a common currency. These deflators do, of course, include an effect of foreign prices through the prices of imports. Equation 13A-9 is the familiar Fisher identity.

The model for the other economy is a mirror image. Notice, however, that $x_F = -x$, and $e_F = -e$, so we can drop the equivalents of equations 13A-6 and 13A-8 to obtain

$$(13A\text{-}10) \qquad y_F = \delta_\theta^F \theta - \delta_r^F r_F + \delta_e^F e + \delta_y^F y + \delta_d^F \overline{d}_F + \lambda_1^F y_{F,-1} + \varepsilon_\delta^F$$

$$(13A\text{-}11) \qquad y_F = \sigma_p^F(p_F - E_{-1}p_F) - \sigma_e^F(e - \lambda_2^F e_{-1}) + \lambda_3^F y_{,-1} + \varepsilon_s^F$$

$$(13A\text{-}12) \qquad m_F = \mu_y^F y_F - \mu_\theta^F 0 - \mu_R^F R_F + p_F + \lambda_4^F(m_F - p_{F,-1}) + \varepsilon_\mu^F$$

$$(13A\text{-}13) \qquad \Delta m_F = \phi^F \overline{d}_F + \varepsilon_m^F$$

$$(13A\text{-}14) \qquad \Delta d_F = \varepsilon_d^F$$

$$(13A\text{-}15) \qquad \Delta \theta_F = \phi^F(-x + \overline{d}_F - T^F y_F) - q^F \Delta R_F - \Delta p_F$$

$$(13A\text{-}16) \qquad R_F = r_F + E p_{F+1} - p_F.$$

Figure 13A. *Full Macroeconomic Equilibrium in the World Economy*

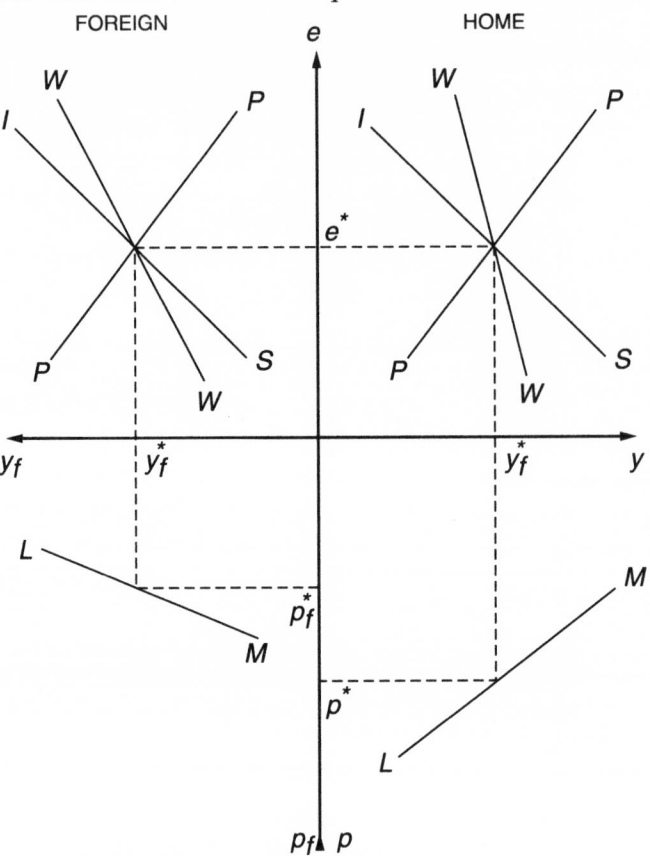

Rational-expectations models of this type have by now a rather familiar behavior in solution. There is, first, the impact effect of an unanticipated shock or "surprise." Second, there is the model's path back to equilibrium from this impact along its "stable manifold" (that is, as determined by the *stable* roots of the model's characteristic equation), which in a well-behaved model will be unique (the condition for uniqueness is that the number of nonstable roots be equal to the number of expected future variables). This path will in turn have two elements: a moving-average component (in which the economy "jumps" onto the stable manifold) and the effect of the stable roots (the stable manifold). Hence, an example of a final-form equation for an endogenous variable, z_t, will be $(1 - p_1 L)(1 - p_2 L)z_1 = \pi_1(1 - m_1 L)\varepsilon_1 + \pi_2(1 - m_2 L)_{\epsilon_2}$, where L is the lag operator, p_1, p_2 are the stable roots, and ε_1, ε_2 are the error terms in the structural equations.

It so happens that in the LIVERPOOL world model the final-form equation approximates to a first-order process $(1 - pL)z_t = \dots$, where p is of magnitude 0.7. Furthermore, for the real exchange rate, e, the net impact of the moving-average terms is very small, so that $(1 - 0.7L)e_s \simeq \eta_s$ where η_s is a composite "surprise" effect from all the various structural errors. This allows us to illustrate the model graphically in a rather simple way: since $Ee_{+1} \simeq 0.7e$, $r = r_F + (1 - 0.7)e$, whence we may eliminate r from the model in terms of r_F and e.

Figure 13A shows the IS and PP curves for the home country in (e, y) space in the upper right quadrant and the LM curve in (p, y) space in the lower right one. The WW curve shows values of e and y for which $\Delta\theta = 0$; that is, full stock equilibrium: to its right θ is falling, to its left θ is rising. Since the IS curve is shifted leftward by a fall in θ, the system equilibrates by pushing the IS/PP curves' intersection to the WW curve. Because $\phi\bar{d} = \Delta m* = \Delta p*$ (monetary equilibrium), $y*$ is determined as that level of supply (along the PP curve) at which there is current account balance. Prices then settle wherever this income intersects the LM curve.

For the foreign country, the same applies. (Of course the foreign price, p_F, is determined independently of p because the floating exchange rate interposes to make them consistent with each other and e.) Only the slopes of IS, PP, and WW curves change sign because $e = -e_F$. Clearly, e has to settle at the *same* value for both countries. This is achieved by r_E, the "world" real interest rate, which moves the IS curves of the two countries until aggregate supply equals aggregate demand in both countries at the common real exchange rate.

Appendix B: Details of Simulation and Optimization Results

This appendix provides a full listing of the welfare-cost values for all deterministic shocks, countries, and regimes (table 13B-1). Table 13B-2 shows the impact effects, in the average of years 1 and 2, on all countries of all shocks and of the monetary interventions under both floating and the EMS. Below, we discuss how these effects come about. Table 13B-3 shows a full listing of the welfare costs for different model-regime combinations under the thirty-eight sets of stochastic simulations. We then provide some notes on the assumptions and methodology, on the stochastic simulations methods, and on the LIVERPOOL model's forecasting performance. Finally, we consider the sensitivity of the results to alternative weights in country objective functions.

Table 13B-1. *Welfare Costs of the Seven Deterministic Shocks*[a]

Floating model: Fixed money							
Country	*FRDM*	*ITDM*	*UKDM*	*FRRXR*	*ITRXR*	*OILP*	*UKRXR*
United States	4.4	0.1	0.0	1.2	0.1	515.3	1.6
Canada	57.1	17.7	6.3	4.8	8.9	1,275.3	4.2
Japan	9.1	1.4	0.3	0.1	0.5	153.1	0.1
Germany	0.6	0.1	0.0	0.3	0.1	7.8	0.3
France	1,127.4	0.8	0.2	7.2	0.5	160.4	0.1
Italy	6.6	2,466.6	0.0	0.2	5.1	156.9	0.2
United Kingdom	0.4	0.0	8.6	0.2	0.1	17.9	15.1

Floating model: Nash							
Country	*FRDM*	*ITDM*	*UKDM*	*FRRXR*	*ITRXR*	*OILP*	*UKRXR*
United States	10.6	204.7	0.1	1.3	4.0	1.8	2,103.2
Canada	117.6	66,616.3	5.3	62.8	1,363.6	87.5	343,054.0
Japan	51.4	2,345.6	0.4	3.2	47.6	2.9	18,654.1
Germany	0.5	283.9	0.1	0.4	5.6	0.9	3,571.7
France	1,057.8	416.6	0.2	4.1	8.9	0.5	1,677.8
Italy	152.2	79,393.2	0.7	78.9	1,570.5	116.6	359,335.0
United Kingdom	0.7	24.3	3.2	0.2	0.5	4.7	662.8

EMS: Fixed money							
Country	*FRDM*	*ITDM*	*UKDM*	*FRRXR*	*ITRXR*	*OILP*	*UKRXR*
United States	6.2	1.2	0.2	0.5	0.1	543.2	0.7
Canada	5.5	13.3	0.7	4.6	0.7	1,562.4	0.5
Japan	2.0	1.8	0.2	0.2	0.1	190.1	0.1
Germany	1.2	1.4	0.0	0.4	0.0	8.2	0.1
France	4,578.9	2.9	0.1	12.7	0.1	242.7	0.6
Italy	3.7	7,137.4	0.2	0.2	5.8	198.7	0.2
United Kingdom	0.7	1.0	3.3	0.2	0.0	18.1	14.9

EMS: Nash							
Country	*FRDM*	*ITDM*	*UKDM*	*FRRXR*	*ITRXR*	*OILP*	*UKRXR*
United States	510,444.0	568.9	2.8	1,354.3	0.3	67.7	28,008.7
Canada	291,069.0	1,289.0	1.9	1,344.8	1.5	31.3	182,751.0
Japan	47,962.0	125.6	1.7	95.6	0.4	7.0	18,124.5
Germany	388,343.0	363.2	3.7	878.3	0.3	61.5	5,185.2
France	607,594.0	315.0	7.6	1,078.0	0.6	96.9	4,099.2
Italy	114,262.0	7,380.0	2.3	262.2	7.1	18.6	4,515.2
United Kingdom	429,598.0	233.2	6.5	829.3	0.4	32.2	3,003.1

a. FDRM, ITDM, UKDM: 4 percent reduction in real money demand for two years for France, Italy, United Kingdom, respectively.

FDRXR, ITRXR, UKRXR: 5 percent rise in the real exchange rate for Fance, Italy, United Kingdom, respectively.

OILP: 50 percent permanent rise in dollar price of oil and other commodities.

Impact Effects

Table 13B-2 shows all impact effects. The monetary policy effects are illustrated in figure 13B (for an explanation of the notation and the diagrammatic setup, see the preceding section).

Figure 13B (top panel) shows the effects of a monetary stimulus in the EMS3 countries under floating, the "normal" case. Unexpected inflation at

Table 13B-2 *Impact Effects of Policy and Shocks: Average of First and Second Years*

Money supply, United States					Money supply, Canada				
	Floating		EMS			Floating		EMS	
Country	GDP	Prices	GDP	Prices	Country	GDP	Prices	GDP	Prices
United States	0.87	5.79	0.84	6.27	United States	0.25	−0.19	0.25	−0.19
Canada	0.09	−0.83	−0.04	−1.12	Canada	0.41	3.05	0.41	3.05
Japan	0.03	−0.58	−0.01	−0.69	Japan	−0.01	−0.25	−0.01	−0.25
Germany	0.09	−0.34	0.05	−0.24	Germany	0.03	−0.05	0.03	−0.05
France	0.16	−0.23	0.06	−0.37	France	0.01	−0.13	0.01	−0.13
Italy	0.19	−0.38	0.18	−0.52	Italy	0.03	−0.19	0.03	−0.19
United Kingdom	0.11	−0.12	0.09	−0.18	United Kingdom	0.02	−0.06	0.02	−0.06

Money supply, Japan					Money supply, Germany				
	Floating		EMS			Floating		EMS	
Country	GDP	Prices	GDP	Prices	Country	GDP	Prices	GDP	Prices
United States	0.45	−0.37	0.45	−0.37	United States	0.31	−0.51	1.44	−2.27
Canada	0.01	−0.31	0.01	−0.31	Canada	−0.18	−2.39	−0.09	−4.68
Japan	0.37	5.60	0.37	5.60	Japan	−0.09	−1.40	0.04	−3.33
Germany	0.05	−0.12	0.05	−0.12	Germany	0.75	7.38	1.20	6.65
France	0.04	−0.14	0.04	−0.14	France	−0.14	−0.84	3.52	−3.99
Italy	0.06	−0.21	0.06	−0.21	Italy	0.03	−1.07	1.09	−4.15
United Kingdom	0.03	−0.12	0.03	−0.12	United Kingdom	0.14	−0.26	1.87	−2.19

Money supply, France					Money supply, Italy				
	Floating		EMS			Floating		EMS	
Country	GDP	Prices	GDP	Prices	Country	GDP	Prices	GDP	Prices
United States	0.23	−0.65	0.10	0.26	United States	−0.05	0.04	−0.13	0.20
Canada	0.05	−1.16	−0.16	−0.21	Canada	−0.05	−0.78	−0.10	−0.65
Japan	0.02	−0.78	−0.09	0.09	Japan	−0.06	−0.33	−0.08	−0.12
Germany	0.16	−0.19	−0.10	0.13	Germany	−0.09	0.11	0.02	0.10
France	1.02	4.67	−0.63	6.46	France	−0.09	−0.13	−0.09	−0.10
Italy	0.11	−0.55	−0.09	0.13	Italy	−0.04	9.32	−0.41	10.95
United Kingdom	0.11	−0.16	−0.06	0.04	United Kingdom	−0.04	0.05	−0.01	0.07

Money supply, United Kingdom					Money demand, France				
	Floating		EMS			Floating		EMS	
Country	GDP	Prices	GDP	Prices	Country	GDP	Prices	GDP	Prices
United States	0.21	−0.27	−0.10	0.22	United States	0.55	−1.36	−0.37	0.96
Canada	−0.02	−1.09	−0.05	−0.45	Canada	0.04	−2.80	−0.16	0.87
Japan	−0.01	−0.68	−0.02	−0.12	Japan	0.07	−2.01	−0.08	0.90
Germany	0.04	−0.04	−0.09	0.10	Germany	0.38	−0.39	−0.40	0.53
France	−0.01	−0.33	−0.07	0.01	France	3.14	14.08	−5.54	24.28
Italy	0.06	−0.48	−0.03	0.03	Italy	0.31	−1.65	−0.30	1.06
United Kingdom	0.20	5.38	−1.01	7.00	United Kingdom	0.36	−0.48	−0.38	0.38

(continued)

Table 13B-2 *(continued)*

Money demand, Italy				
	Floating		EMS	
Country	GDP	Prices	GDP	Prices
United States	−0.04	0.01	−0.79	0.29
Canada	−0.09	−0.92	−0.16	−1.54
Japan	−0.08	−0.41	−0.09	−0.35
Germany	−0.14	0.12	0.38	0.18
France	−0.13	−0.18	−0.11	−0.28
Italy	0.21	24.15	−1.46	44.89
United Kingdom	−0.07	0.04	0.14	0.26

Money demand, United Kingdom				
	Floating		EMS	
Country	GDP	Prices	GDP	Prices
United States	0.22	−0.04	0.14	0.13
Canada	−0.08	−0.84	−0.05	0.07
Japan	−0.04	−0.39	0.00	0.15
Germany	0.00	−0.02	−0.03	−0.03
France	−0.04	−0.22	−0.01	0.05
Italy	0.03	−0.26	0.02	0.12
United Kingdom	0.54	3.34	−0.12	4.03

Real exchange rate, France				
	Floating		EMS	
Country	GDP	Prices	GDP	Prices
United States	−0.21	0.81	−0.40	0.38
Canada	−0.16	0.49	−0.10	−0.78
Japan	−0.09	0.54	−0.13	0.00
Germany	−0.25	0.37	−0.23	0.31
France	−1.43	1.98	−1.65	1.62
Italy	−0.20	0.40	−0.19	0.31
United Kingdom	−0.18	0.24	−0.20	0.28

Real exchange rate, Italy				
	Floating		EMS	
Country	GDP	Prices	GDP	Prices
United States	−0.22	0.10	−0.24	0.12
Canada	0.02	−0.12	0.01	−0.25
Japan	0.00	−0.04	−0.01	−0.08
Germany	0.09	−0.08	0.09	−0.04
France	0.04	−0.02	0.03	−0.03
Italy	−0.25	2.02	−0.28	1.84
United Kingdom	0.04	−0.01	0.04	0.00

Real exchange rate, United Kingdom				
	Floating		EMS	
Country	GDP	Prices	GDP	Prices
United States	−0.21	0.39	−0.29	0.39
Canada	−0.02	0.32	−0.05	−0.24
Japan	−0.01	0.37	−0.06	0.14
Germany	−0.11	0.11	−0.15	0.18
France	−0.05	0.24	−0.07	0.33
Italy	−0.07	0.37	−0.11	0.30
United Kingdom	−0.93	1.29	−0.95	1.31

Oil/LDC prices				
	Floating		EMS	
Country	GDP	Prices	GDP	Prices
United States	−3.18	7.57	−3.33	7.94
Canada	−0.52	14.03	−0.68	15.15
Japan	0.66	6.70	0.65	7.58
Germany	−0.96	0.52	−1.03	0.65
France	0.44	4.48	−1.07	6.03
Italy	−0.04	5.44	−0.35	7.00
United Kingdom	−1.11	0.73	−1.22	0.85

home in the EMS3 occurs from the outward shift of the *LM* curve in p, y space (right-hand lower quadrant); this shifts the open economy supply curve, *PP*, to the right (right-hand upper quadrant) along the *IS* curve, creating a normal expansion, with the real exchange rate, *RXR*, falling. In the ROW there are resulting shifts in *IS*, *PP*, and *LM* curves as world real interest rates fall and EMS3 output rises. ROW output rises, and ROW prices fall. With labels reversed, the same diagram will apply to ROW monetary expansion and its spillovers onto EMS3. Figure 13B may also be used to give effects of ROW monetary expansion under the EMS, since the EMS barely affects ROW multipliers and spillovers.

The effects of EMS3 monetary expansion, however, are quite different under EMS (figure 13B, bottom panel). Here again the *LM* curve of EMS3 shifts out, and prices rise. But because of the pre-echo effect on wages, the *PP* curve shifts to the left, raising the real exchange rate and lowering output.

Table 13B-3. *Welfare Costs for All Model-Regime Permutations*

Country	Fixed money	Nash	High-penalty[a]	Cooperative	Coalition
		Default model			
United States	1,779.060	316,674.437	14,955.937	3,334.297	1,944.333
Canada	40,525.359	507,385.500	98,489.937	23,568.695	68,427.812
Japan	4,499.520	64,180.781	8,362.395	3,549.068	4,618.250
Germany	1,294.094	204,083.500	21,383.609	1,227.817	245.657
France	3,530.385	299,724.375	59,801.203	2,889.552	824.373
Italy	3,190.908	68,438.937	17,289.695	2,788.012	2,533.271
United Kingdom	2,048.628	211,743.437	47,556.160	1,679.236	525.834
		No parity change			
United States	2,323.277	2,401.401	2,414.721	3,448.365	2,237.114
Canada	33,681.324	35,075.031	34,924.707	19,289.738	29,208.676
Japan	4,418.449	10,963.266	12,466.668	3,466.013	4,138.898
Germany	1,131.931	1,596.664	1,665.610	1,220.965	252.059
France	3,492.545	6,819.359	7,034.309	2,847.261	711.427
Italy	1,900.978	2,441.609	2,449.112	1,999.209	612.201
United Kingdom	344.046	2,650.294	2,766.427	362.962	511.257
		Parity change limited to 5 percent			
United States	2,317.908	4,677.379	5,389.699	4,805.602	4,766.977
Canada	45,592.098	675,762.125	47,314.871	23,930.969	192,135.750
Japan	5,777.586	220,946.937	174,268.000	4,161.242	7,237.371
Germany	1,318.043	81,459.437	13,632.066	1,488.594	323.637
France	16,081.543	139,397.562	29,914.531	20,398.520	4,199.668
Italy	14,726.762	26,766.355	16,359.402	17,765.816	5,664.961
United Kingdom	4,020.050	96,753.375	13,717.945	4,437.242	819.227
		Capital controls			
United States	1,611.984	100,639.437	80,652.125	3,113.757	271,113.250
Canada	34,257.621	523,193.937	1,008,308.690	16,669.797	4,212,673.000
Japan	4,702.781	58,818.281	67,313.500	3,357.674	266,582.437
Germany	1,192.853	32,212.629	70,593.250	959.240	360.394
France	4,131.211	172,753.562	66,323.187	3,860.790	3,673.248
Italy	3,503.713	259,414.625	337,297.625	3,114.067	2,969.652
United Kingdom	2,801.759	214,716.750	83,505.437	2,175.149	1,889.502
		Low-wage-reaction parameter			
United States	1,807.666	7,375.105	12,496.355	3,726.984	2,148.365
Canada	34,065.320	594,732.000	1,135,140.000	23,112.160	23,750.664
Japan	4,141.637	20,920.113	36,143.711	2,879.448	3,947.729
Germany	1,099.288	1,076.252	1,121.961	825.248	183.392
France	3,872.583	831,321.062	1,673,016.000	3,715.405	859.219
Italy	3,346.087	3,434.534	3,987.982	3,509.991	2,439.351
United Kingdom	755.266	1,158.686	1,466.422	948.029	160.880

a. High penalty on money in the United Kingdom, Italy, and France only.

In the ROW, output now falls slightly as the effect of the fall in world real interest rates is offset by that of the fall in EMS3 output; falling ROW output shifts out, and prices rise. But because of the pre-echo effect on wages, the *PP* curve shifts to the left, raising the real exchange rate and lowering output. In the ROW, output now falls slightly as the effect of the fall in world real

Figure 13B. *Money-Supply Expansion under Floating and the EMS*

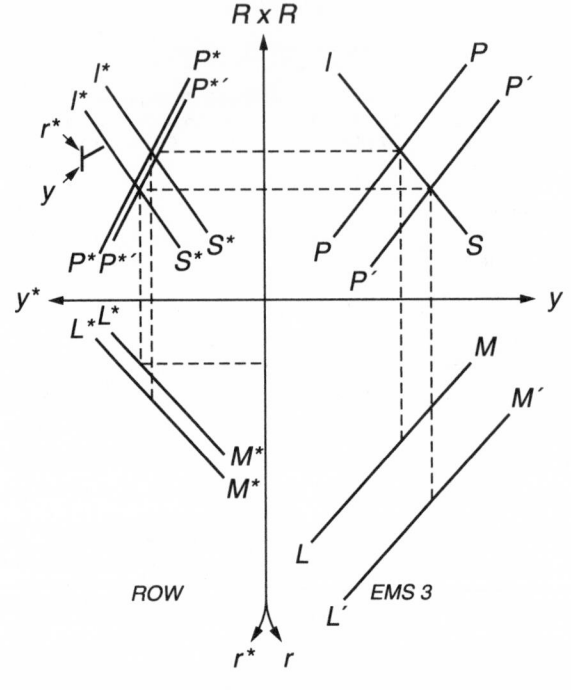

FLOATING REGIME

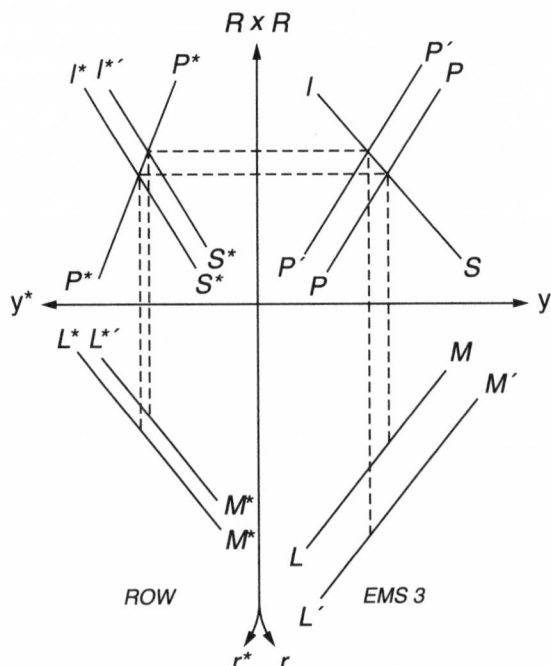

EMS REGIME

interest rates is offset by that of the fall in EMS3 output; falling ROW output also means that prices fall less with the fall in interest rates. Figure 13B (bottom panel) illustrates the topsy-turvy world of the EMS3 when monetary policy is hobbled by the EMS.

Notes on Assumptions and Methodology

The outcome is evaluated over a policy planning horizon of six years, inclusive of the year of the shock. Each country is assumed to have one instrument of response—money supply growth. It is allowed to plan the use of this instrument at the time that a shock occurs—that is, no lag is assumed in policy response or shock perception. The instrument can be altered for two years at a time. Whenever it is altered, the change is a surprise to the private sector. For example, suppose that the private sector had expected (in the "base run" excluding the shock) 2 percent money growth throughout. Then, in response to the shock, say, the government plans 3 percent money growth for two years, 5 percent for the next two, and 7 percent for the last two. The surprise is 1 percent in years 1 and 2, 3 percent in years 3 and 4, and 5 percent in years 5 and 6. Thus, the private sector in effect assumes that the government's policy changes are temporary.

This assumption probably understates the private sector's capacity to forecast future policy changes. On the one hand, a public with knowledge of the government's preferences and the model could rationally predict the government's intentions. On the other hand, the alternative assumption of fully credible and revealed policy intentions for six years ahead—the full rational-expectations policy scenario—is empirically difficult to sustain, presumably because our assumed government preference maximization is not a good model of government behavior, convenient as it may be for this exercise. This aspect is worth pursuing in future work. Meanwhile, the results should not be unduly sensitive because the parity changes that are the key to our findings occur in the year after the shock. These are influenced mainly by the shock and the change in money supply in the first two years.

The detailed assumptions about the EMS system in our default model are: margins of plus or minus 3 percent around a deutsche-mark parity, parity changes permitted in multiples of plus or minus 5 percent, and a gap of at least a year between them. In practice this means that the parity can change in the year after an initial shock and then once a year thereafter.

Nash strategies are determined at the time of the shock, with governments using the model and their knowledge of each other's welfare function to compute the equilibrium. (This assumes that governments have an information advantage over the private sector, as just discussed.) Both Nash and cooperative strategies are assessed using the algorithm of Brandsma and Hughes Hallett

Table 13B-4. *Single Equation Errors, LIVERPOOL World Model[a]*

Country and variable	Standard error	
United States		
log *M1*	0.057	
log *g*	0.003	
log *ndc*	0.003	
log(*RXR*)	0.079	
*xvol/y***	0.009	(1973–81)
Canada		
log *M1*	0.066	
log *g*	0.002	
log *ndc*	0.002	
log(*RXR*)	0.026	
*xvol/y***	0.016	(1973–81)
France		
log *M1*	0.029	
log *g*	0.002	
log *ndc*	0.006	
log(*RXR*)	0.132	
*xvol/y***	0.006	(1973–81)
Italy		
log *M1*	0.005	
log *g*	0.003	
log *ndc*	0.002	
log(*RXR*)	0.187	
*xvol/y***	0.027	(1973–81)
Japan (Source: Rastogi 1989)		
log *ndc*	0.0166	
log *g*	0.0139	
log *M1*	0.0618	
log(*RXR*)	0.0604	
log *Export*	0.0420	
log *Import*	0.0615	
*xvol/y***	0.009	
Germany (Source: Davis 1987)		
log *ndc*	0.012	
log *g*	0.006	
log *M1*	0.019	
log(*RXR*)	0.038	
*xvol/y***	0.037	
United Kingdom (Source: Minford and others 1984)		
log *M*	0.041	
log *g*	0.005	
log(*RXR*)	0.001	
log *ndc*	0.024	
log *RW*	0.006	
log *U*	0.005	
*xvol/y***	0.0175	

a. The sample period is 1957–81 for the United States, Canada, France, Italy, and the United Kingdom; 1956–85 for Japan; and 1961–83 for Germany. Notation is as follows:

    ndc = private-sector nondurable consumption
      g = private-sector stock of physical assets
     M1 = demand for real balances M1
     RW = real earnings
    RXR = real exchange rate
      U = unemployment, in thousands
   xvol = trade balance excluding terms of trade effects
    *y*** = equilibrium value of *y*.

(1989). This takes the multipliers from the LIVERPOOL model for policy and shock effects, computes the first-order conditions, and solves for the simultaneous strategy choices. To keep down the amount of computation, the model simulations and multipliers are for three periods: the averages respectively of years 1–2, 3–4, and 5–6.

Notes on the Stochastic Simulations

Thirty-eight sets of drawings of six random shocks were made from error distributions shown in table 13B-4. Because these are single equation estimates, there is no covariance estimated or assumed. The shocks were applied one year at a time, with lagged dependent variables from the first year's shock simulation used for the second year's shock and so on; shocks were applied to the first six years of the base run. The shocks are unanticipated on occurrence, and the model is solved forward to the terminal date ten years beyond year 6. Each set of shocks gives one complete alternative run of the model over the full time period (up to the terminal date). The shocks are reduced in size (divided by 100) in order to speed model convergence and to reduce the already enormous amounts of computer time required. The averages of years 1–2, 3–4, and 5–6 from the resulting model run are then input into the Brandsma and Hughes Hallett program described above to compute the Nash outcome. At the end, the results are scaled up to correspond to the size of the original shocks. This scaling procedure is likely to bias the results for the EMS toward greater stability because larger shocks will create greater strains within the fixed margins around parity. In any case, we get so much separation between regimes on instability that the ranking that is of key importance to us should not be seriously affected.

Forecasting Performance

Table 13B-5 reports the model's forecasting errors during 1984–89 up to two years ahead. As a benchmark, IMF forecasting errors over 1971–86 are shown (taken from Artis 1988). Errors for a strictly comparable period are not available, and the period since 1984 has been relatively stable. Nevertheless, the LIVERPOOL forecast errors appear to be of tolerable size.

NOTES ON DECOMPOSITION OF WELFARE COSTS. Tables 13B-6 and 13B-7 show, for selected regimes, the components going into the welfare cost: the standard deviations of output, the price level, real interest rates, the real exchange rate, and money supply growth.

What emerges is that, if one is comparing different exchange-rate regimes, then it does not matter which component of welfare is given most weight. All move in the same direction and are higher under EMS than under floating. The exchange-rate regime destabilizes the economy generally. That can be seen

Table 13B-5. *LIVERPOOL World Model Forecasting Errors (RMSE)[a]*

	Growth		Inflation	
Country	LPL	IMF	LPL	IMF

Zero-ahead errors

Country	LPL	IMF	LPL	IMF
United States	1.061	1.063	0.454	0.724
Canada	1.404	1.338	0.906	1.567
Japan	1.259	1.716	0.594	2.418
Germany	1.125	1.412	0.463	0.862
France	0.669	1.208	0.214	1.291
Italy	1.290	1.470	0.566	1.971

One-year-ahead errors

	Growth		Inflation	
Country	LPL	IMF	LPL	IMF
United States	1.284	2.047	1.494	1.725
Canada	0.887	2.238	1.613	2.731
Japan	1.476	3.217	0.955	4.200
Germany	1.488	2.207	1.378	0.686
France	0.933	1.085	1.671	1.200
Italy	1.053	2.482	1.771	3.574

Two-year-ahead errors (LPL)

Country	Growth	Inflation
United States	1.022	2.197
Canada	1.185	1.971
Japan	1.131	1.486
Germany	0.764	1.761
France	0.535	2.978
Italy	0.795	2.665

Sources: LPL forecasts are for 1984–89, from *Quarterly Economic Bulletin* (Liverpool Research Group in Macroeconomics), various issues; IMF forecasts are for 1971–86, from *World Economic Outlook,* various issues; and IMF forecast errors are from Artis (1988).
a. Root-mean-squared errors.

in the correlation matrix in table 13B-8, which shows the average correlation (for all countries) for each monetary regime across the different exchange-rate regimes is positive.

This table and table 13B-9 describe the average across all countries of the country correlation between the different cost components (for example, the y, p cell shows the average of the seven correlations between y and p components, one for each of the seven countries examined). Mnemonics for the two tables are as follows:

$$y = \text{output}$$

$$p = \text{price level}$$

$$rs = \text{real interest rate}$$

$$rxr = \text{real exchange rate}$$

$$m = \text{growth rate of money supply}$$

$$w = \text{aggregate welfare cost.}$$

Table 13B-6. *Welfare Cost Components: Floating*

Item	United States	Canada	Japan	Germany	France	Italy	United Kingdom
				Fixed money			
Real GNP (standard deviation; percent of base value)	9.166	2.523	8.715	6.215	4.643	3.912	1.545
Price level (standard deviation; percent of base value)	11.790	6.372	13.324	19.911	10.945	5.814	3.995
Short-term interest rate (percent)	3.168	7.219	7.232	18.522	12.356	4.818	4.069
Real exchange rate (percent)	4.060	7.284	6.508	18.760	11.765	4.006	4.142
Money instrument (percent growth)	0.000	0.000	0.000	0.000	0.000	0.000	0.000
Welfare cost	315.306	4,816.312	743.682	2,024.518	737.350	187.187	79.370
				Nash			
Real GNP (standard deviation; percent of base value)	8.076	2.420	8.579	5.402	4.111	3.707	1.404
Price level (standard deviation; percent of base value)	11.432	6.751	12.716	19.412	10.608	12.936	3.554
Short-term interest rate (percent)	2.785	7.101	6.901	18.653	11.755	4.468	3.604
Real exchange rate (percent)	21.745	130.252	62.205	14.602	14.303	117.905	9.094
Money instrument (percent growth)	0.199	0.121	1.410	0.147	0.264	4.154	0.127
Welfare cost	1,028.641	47,423.004	6,818.344	1,828.307	896.445	41,550.070	201.501
				EMS coalition			
Real GNP (standard deviation; percent of base value)	8.080	2.414	8.579	5.309	4.096	3.747	1.397
Price level (standard deviation; percent of base value)	10.681	6.178	13.259	17.197	10.645	6.241	4.343
Short-term interest rate (percent)	2.800	6.862	6.879	18.587	11.727	4.588	3.625
Real exchange rate (percent)	6.141	52.252	10.022	2.666	2.758	26.255	3.239
Money instrument (percent growth)	0.244	0.156	0.107	0.339	0.319	0.628	0.078
Welfare cost	334.692	8,604.617	879.570	295.637	140.456	683.073	16.668
				Worldwide cooperation			
Real GNP (standard deviation; percent of base value)	9.568	5.416	8.470	7.690	4.741	3.741	1.442
Price level (standard deviation; percent of base value)	13.090	9.523	15.690	16.776	10.540	6.213	3.696
Short-term interest rate (percent)	3.272	6.882	7.011	18.243	11.766	4.526	3.956
Real exchange rate (percent)	6.154	7.387	2.040	5.907	6.071	2.074	2.393
Money instrument (percent growth)	5.543	3.834	1.876	5.473	3.475	8.901	11.151
Welfare cost	473.209	3,432.971	376.738	1,275.401	562.940	163.837	102.599

Table 13B-7. *Welfare Cost Components: EMS Default Model*

Item	United States	Canada	Japan	Germany	France	Italy	United Kingdom
				Fixed money			
Real GNP (standard deviation; percent of base value)	23.113	10.915	15.091	24.030	20.241	15.336	14.900
Price level (standard deviation; percent of base value)	30.328	158.368	54.155	20.572	41.229	40.876	20.780
Short-term interest rate (percent)	9.218	69.960	20.875	15.052	22.479	28.672	20.144
Real exchange rate (percent)	13.194	115.008	21.875	21.799	24.639	18.624	20.681
Money instrument (percent growth)	0.000	0.000	0.000	0.000	0.000	0.000	0.000
Welfare cost	1,779.060	40,525.359	4,499.520	1,294.094	3,530.385	3,190.908	2,048.628
				Nash			
Real GNP (standard deviation; percent of base value)	16.006	9.650	13.609	14.934	17.288	11.465	11.309
Price level (standard deviation; percent of base value)	54.888	152.555	49.989	17.016	39.007	34.813	17.506
Short-term interest rate (percent)	6.401	47.698	15.190	11.728	15.925	20.407	15.595
Real exchange rate (percent)	392.073	501.395	188.953	319.369	395.259	190.005	332.999
Money instrument (percent growth)	10.496	0.437	2.043	1.468	0.919	0.388	0.139
Welfare cost	316,674.437	507,385.500	64,180.781	4,083.500	99,724.375	68,438.937	11,743.437
				EMS coalition			
Real GNP (standard deviation; percent of base value)	15.476	9.936	13.684	14.955	24.931	11.692	11.196
Price level (standard deviation; percent of base value)	28.052	153.101	49.865	16.245	34.931	34.889	41.018
Short-term interest rate (percent)	5.676	47.504	14.966	11.878	15.936	20.754	15.773
Real exchange rate (percent)	14.842	133.473	18.683	9.227	15.767	45.025	10.835
Money instrument (percent growth)	0.519	1.282	0.403	0.374	7.548	1.075	3.439
Welfare cost	1,944.333	68,427.812	4,618.250	245.657	824.373	2,533.271	525.834
				Worldwide cooperation			
Real GNP (standard deviation; percent of base value)	16.004	7.289	13.667	13.022	13.434	11.369	11.468
Price level (standard deviation; percent of base value)	27.565	134.288	39.945	18.691	36.395	32.552	27.121
Short-term interest rate (percent)	6.883	47.897	15.639	14.658	16.950	21.420	16.024
Real exchange rate (percent)	23.975	47.625	15.513	10.544	14.189	11.850	6.772
Money instrument (percent growth)	13.243	13.109	6.149	2.970	18.929	13.202	21.008
Welfare cost	3,334.297	23,568.695	3,549.068	1,227.817	2,889.552	2,788.012	1,679.236

Table 13B-8. *Average Correlation of Cost Components across Exchange-Rate Regimes*

	y	p	rs	rxr	m	w
			Cooperative monetary policy			
y	1.00000	...	...	...	...	...
p	0.63470	1.00000	...	...	...	...
rs	0.52532	0.68063	1.00000	...	...	...
rxr	0.57376	0.43664	0.47092	1.00000	...	...
m	0.21662	0.35047	0.42047	0.33687	1.00000	0.11859
w	0.59513	0.82864	0.75587	0.45764	...	1.00000
			Fixed money policy			
y	1.00000	...	...	...	...	...
p	0.83984	1.00000	...	...	...	...
rs	0.67194	0.67337	1.00000	...	...	...
rxr	0.88707	0.83911	0.72057	1.00000	...	...
m	0.00000	0.00000	0.00000	0.00000	0.00000	0.00000
w	0.60373	0.78461	0.81390	0.69294	...	1.00000
			Nash noncooperative monetary policy			
y	1.00000	...	...	...	...	...
p	0.66015	1.00000	...	...	...	...
rs	0.69719	0.68548	1.00000	...	...	...
rxr	0.19136	0.30441	0.01563	1.00000	...	...
m	0.07504	0.24905	0.00655	0.44639	1.00000	0.42996
w	0.20082	0.35105	0.11545	0.84701	...	1.00000

For the comparisons between EMS and floating, for given monetary regimes (as shown in table 13-4) there is therefore no sensitivity to the weights.

On the other hand, if one compares, within a given exchange-rate regime, the behavior of the different monetary regimes, fixed money and Nash, a more complex pattern emerges. The permitted variation in money supply tends to reduce output variance and (usually) price and interest-rate variance as well, but at the cost of much greater exchange-rate variance. The latter can be regarded as an implied instrument cost, in that it is associated with the movements of relative money supplies. As such, it appears reasonable to give it weight.

However, the relative ranking of fixed money and Nash monetary regimes, as of others such as Nash coalitions and cooperation, could be sensitive to the weight that is given to the exchange rate. To check this for the key comparison of interest to us—that between different EMS regimes—we include table 13B-9, which shows the correlation (the average of all the country correlations) between these components across all the Nash EMS regimes and models, the Nash EMS coalition, and EMS worldwide cooperation.

It is plain that within the EMS regimes, as monetary regimes are varied the exchange-rate cost is negatively correlated with output, interest rates and the money supply, namely, all the other components except prices where there

Table 13B-9. *Correlation between Cost Components for EMS Default Model across Different Monetary Policy Regimes*

	y	p	rs	rxr	m	w
y	1.00000	...	...	...	...	...
p	0.37296	1.00000	...	...	...	...
rs	0.73764	0.42758	1.00000	...	...	...
rxr	−0.22306	0.09646	−0.37603	1.00000	...	...
m	−0.48325	−0.36506	−0.17191	−0.19685	1.00000	0.11859
w	−0.20739	0.08389	−0.32681	0.97962	...	1.00000

Table 13B-10. *EMS and EMU Welfare Costs with All Except y, p Weights Set at Zero*

Thousands of welfare-cost units

Regime	ROW	EC	All
EMS default regime			
Fixed money	32	6.1	39
Nash	142	6.1	148
EMS coalition	33	561	594
Worldwide cooperation			
(given EMS coalition)	12	4.9	17
EMU	358.6	1.6	360

is no correlation. The variation in the overall welfare cost is dominated by the exchange-rate variation.

To confirm this we redo table 13-3 for the EMS, setting the weights on exchange rates, and interest rates and money supply to zero. The resulting table 13B-10 reveals that the extreme instability we have noted in the EMS without limits and monetary coordination is heavily associated with exchange-rate instability. The order of instability between regimes is substantially altered with this different welfare cost. The worst case here is EMS coalition, worse than the Nash case.

What this shows is that the evaluation of EMS regimes is extremely sensitive to weights on preferences. A government that cares little about exchange-rate variation per se would in particular prefer independent Nash to an EMS coalition. Hence, the desire for monetary coordination within the EMS is highly dependent on the desire for exchange-rate stability. It is true that compared with all the EMS regimes, EMU, with its total fixity, is preferred by EC countries. But it is a disaster for the ROW (Canada in particular), and it would be unlikely to survive the extreme hostility it would provoke. The general direction of evolution within the EMS—toward a high degree of fixity and coordination—would therefore not survive a welfare function of this sort. The desire for exchange-rate stability, perhaps not surprisingly, is a precondition for wishing to increase exchange-rate fixity.

References

Aoki, M. 1976. *Optimal Control and System Theory in Dynamic Economic Analysis.* New York: North-Holland.

Artis, M. 1988. "How Accurate Is the *World Economic Outlook?* A Post-Mortem on Short-Term Forecasting at the IMF." In *Staff Studies for the World Economic Outlook.* World Economic and Financial Surveys. Washington: International Monetary Fund.

Artis, M., and M. Taylor. 1988. "Exchange Rate, Interest Rates, Capital Controls, and the European Monetary System: Assessing the Track Record." In *The European Monetary System,* edited by F. Giavazzi, S. Micossi, and M. Miller, 185–206. Cambridge University Press.

Brandsma, A. S., and A. J. Hughes Hallett. 1989. "The Design of Interdependent Policies with Incomplete Information." *Economic Modelling* 6:432–46.

Bryant, R. C., D. W. Henderson, G. Holtham, P. Hooper, and S. A. Symansky, eds. 1988. *Empirical Macroeconomics for Interdependent Economies.* Brookings.

Collins, S. 1990. "PPP and the Peso Problem: Exchange Rates in the EMS." In *International and European Monetary Systems,* edited by E. M. Claassen, 99–117. Praeger.

Davis, J. 1987. "A Rational Expectations Model of the Federal Republic of Germany." Ph.D. dissertation, University of Liverpool.

De Grauwe, P. 1988. "Exchange Rate Variability and the Slowdown in Growth of International Trade." *Staff Papers* (International Monetary Fund) 35:63–84.

———. 1989. "The Cost of Disinflation and the European Monetary System." Center for European Policy Research Discussion Paper 326. London.

———. 1990. "Fiscal Policies in the EMS: A Strategic Analysis." In *International and European Monetary Systems,* edited by E. M. Claassen, 121–40. Praeger.

Fratianni, M., and J. von Hagen. 1990. "The European Monetary System Ten Years After." In *Unit Roots, Investment Measures and Other Essays,* edited by A. Meltzer, 173–241. Carnegie-Rochester Conference Series on Public Policy 32. Amsterdam: North-Holland.

Giavazzi, F., and A. Giovannini. 1989. *Limiting Exchange Rate Flexibility: The European Monetary System.* MIT Press.

Giavazzi, F., and M. Pagano. 1988. "The Advantage of Tying One's Hands: EMS Discipline and Central Bank Credibility." *European Economic Review* 32:1055–75.

Giavazzi, F., and L. Spaventa. 1990. "The 'New' EMS." Center for European Policy Research Discussion Paper 369. London.

Haas, R. D., and P. R. Masson. 1986. "MINIMOD: Specification and Simulation Results." *International Monetary Fund Staff Papers* 33:722–67.

Hughes Hallett, A. 1986. "Autonomy and the Choice of Policy in Asymmetrically Dependent Economies." *Oxford Economic Papers* 36:516–44.

———. 1987. "How Robust Are the Gains to Policy Coordination to Variations in the Model and Objectives?" *Ricerche Economiche* 41:341–72 (special issue on game theory and coordination).

Hughes Hallett, A., and P. Minford. 1989. "Exchange Rate Agreements as a Policy Regime: Their Performance and Design Characteristics." In *Dynamic Modeling and*

Control of National Economies, edited by N. Christodoulakis, 223–30. Oxford and New York: Pergamon.

———. 1990. "Target Zones and Exchange Rate Management: A Stability Analysis of the European Monetary System." *Open Economies Review* 1:175–200.

Ishii, N., W. McKibbin, and J. Sachs. 1985. "The Economic Policy Mix, Policy Cooperation, and Protectionism: Some Aspects of Macroeconomic Interdependence among the United States, Japan, and Other OECD Countries." *Journal of Policy Modelling* 7:533–72.

Lucas, R. E., Jr. 1976. "Econometric Policy Evaluation: A Critique." In *The Phillips Curve,* edited by A. H. Meltzer and K. Brunner, 19–46. Carnegie-Rochester Conference Series on Public Policy 1. Amsterdam: North-Holland.

Masson, P., and others. 1988. "MULTIMOD: A Multiregion Econometric Model." WP/88/23. Washington: International Monetary Fund.

Miller, M., and P. Weller. 1989. "Target Zones, Currency Options, and the Dollar." In *Blueprints for Exchange Rate Management,* edited by M. Miller, B. Eichengreen, and R. Portes. New York: Cambridge University Press.

Minford, P. 1989a. "Do Floating Exchange Rates Insulate?" In *Exchange Rates and Open Economy Macroeconomics,* edited by R. MacDonald and M. Taylor, 275–94. Oxford: Blackwell.

———. 1989b. "Ulysses and the Sirens: A Political Model of Credibility in an Open Economy." *Greek Economic Review* 11:1–18.

———. 1989c. "Exchange Rate Regimes and Policy Coordination." In *Blueprints for Exchange Rate Management,* edited by M. Miller, B. Eichengreen, and R. Portes, 207–35. Academic Press.

Minford, P., and others. 1984. "The LIVERPOOL Macroeconomic Model of the United Kingdom." *Economic Modelling* 1:24–62.

Minford, P., P. Agenor, and E. Nowell. 1986. "A New Classical Econometric Model of the World Economy." *Economic Modelling* 3:154–74.

Rastogi, A. B. 1989. "A Rational Expectations Model of the Japanese Economy 1955–1985." Ph.D. dissertation, University of Liverpool.

Sachs, J., and C. Wyplosz. 1986. "France under Mitterrand." *Economic Policy* 2:261–322.

Taylor, J. 1979. "Staggered Wage Setting in a Macro Model." *American Economic Review* 69 *(Papers and Proceedings, 1978)*: 108–13.

———. 1988. "The Treatment of Expectations in Large Multicountry Econometric Models—Appendix." In Bryant and others 1988, 173–79.

Ungerer, H., and others. 1986. "The European Monetary System: Recent Developments." Occasional Paper 48. Washington: International Monetary Fund.

Vaubel, R. 1989. "Comments." In *New Institutional Arrangements for the World Economy,* edited by H. J. Vosgerau, 119–23. New York and Berlin: Springer-Verlag.

Walters, A. 1990. *Sterling in Danger: The Economic Consequences of Pegged Exchange Rates.* London: Collins/Fontana with the Institute of Economic Affairs.

5
Applications
and Extensions
of Stochastic Simulation
Techniques to Particular
Economic Sectors

CHAPTER 14

Evaluating Forecasts
of the U.S. Trade Balance

Jaime Marquez and Neil R. Ericsson

Accepting these [forecast] errors and suitable frequencies, it would be healthier if economic forecasts were provided in probabilistic intervals. On several occasions, relevant errors have been estimated and tabulated, but prevailing practice is to provide only point estimates, with a number of decimal places. That exceeds the limits of our precision.

—Lawrence Klein (1981, p. 56)

A statistical prediction means simply a (probability) statement about the location of a sample point not yet observed. **—Trygve Haavelmo (1944, p. 105)**

MODEL-BASED FORECASTS of the U.S. trade balance are commonplace. Yet, despite the rocky track record of forecasts from econometric models, most existing analyses treat predictions from stochastic trade models as though they were outcomes of deterministic processes, taking their statistical accuracy for granted.[1] The statistical accuracy of forecasts *can* be measured easily, and its calculation has numerous uses. For example, statistical accuracy (or the lack thereof) is central to evaluating the likely consequences of policy actions. Depending on the actual uncertainty, fine tuning may be straightforward or completely unrealistic. A measure of statistical accuracy is also helpful when using forecasts to evaluate competing models. Statistical assessments of forecasts include the standard errors and confidence intervals of the forecasts, the means (and so the biases) of the forecasts, and ex post performance relative

The authors are staff economists in the Division of International Finance, Board of Governors of the Federal Reserve System. The views expressed in this paper are solely the responsibility of the authors and should not be interpreted as reflecting those of the Board of Governors of the Federal Reserve System or other members of its staff. The authors thank William Helkie for encouraging this project and providing the data for the Helkie-Hooper model; Ned Prescott and Lucia Foster for excellent research assistance; and Carlo Bianchi, Giorgio Calzolari, Julia Campos, Hali Edison, Ray Fair, William Helkie, David Hendry, Peter Hooper, Fred Joutz, James MacKinnon, Andy Rose, Charlie Thomas, and Ralph Tryon for valuable comments and suggestions. All numerical results in this paper were obtained using the econometrics software package TROLL Version 13 (Intex Solutions 1989).

1. See, for example, Feldstein (1986), Eichengreen (1989), Krugman and Baldwin (1987), Marris (1987), Bryant and Holtham (1988), Krugman (1988), Cline (1989a, b), Hooper (1988, 1989), Helliwell (1989), Howard (1989a, b), Meade (1988), U.S. Library of Congress (1988), and U.S. Congressional Budget Office (1989).

to forecast uncertainty. This chapter provides such measures for four structural econometric models of the U.S. merchandise trade balance, or "trade balance" for short. Each model differs in size, dynamic specification, estimation method, and level of country and commodity disaggregation. Two time-series models of the trade balance are included for comparison.

The analysis begins in the first section by describing these trade models and estimating their parameters. Estimated income elasticities for the structural models are positive and statistically significant, and, for some models, they are in line with the asymmetries in income elasticities noted by Houthakker and Magee (1969). The estimated price elasticities are negative and significant and satisfy the Marshall-Lerner (stability) condition; the pass-through of exchange rates to import prices is positive and significant. As a benchmark for later results, the analysis in the first section also generates deterministic forecasts of the trade balance from each model. Although widely used, deterministic forecasts may be biased by model nonlinearities such as those common to these trade models, even if the coefficient estimates are unbiased. In addition, deterministic forecasts often are presented without any measure of forecast uncertainty, thereby undermining their usefulness for studying the determinants of international trade, predicting the likely response of international trade to economic policies, and addressing other practical questions in which uncertainty plays a role.

To address these limitations, the second section calculates the distribution of trade-balance forecasts for these models. Two complications arise in doing so: multiple sources of uncertainty and the lack of an analytical solution.

Forecast uncertainty arises from many sources, including the inherently stochastic nature of the process generating the data (implying as yet unknown future shocks) and the imprecision of coefficient estimates in the model producing the forecasts. As an example of the latter, the trade elasticities estimated in the first section create a source of uncertainty in the forecasts of the trade balance because the elasticities are estimated rather than known. Although *exact* formulas for forecast distributions accounting for these two sources of uncertainty exist only for static models and the simplest of dynamic models, reasonable analytical approximations are available for general linear dynamic models.

Unfortunately, the nonlinearities typical to empirical trade and price equations preclude applying these analytical formulas, so we rely on stochastic simulation. Simulation begins with random draws of both model coefficients and disturbances from specified distributions to produce a simulated forecast. Many such forecasts are generated. From the resulting "sample" of forecasts, we obtain estimates of the mean forecast, the mean forecast error, the standard deviation of the sample of forecasts (which is the estimated standard error of the forecasts), and the 95 percent confidence interval. In effect, taking functions of these Monte Carlo replications (such as averaging) mirrors evaluating the integrals that would be required for an analytical solution.

Empirically, the associated forecast errors are large relative to the magnitude of the trade-balance forecasts and relative to the deviations between forecasts from the different models. Often the errors are systematic and increase in magnitude as the forecast horizon lengthens. The forecast *standard* errors tend to be large as well—ranging from approximately $13 billion to $30 billion for one-step-ahead forecasts from the structural models, and up to $36 billion for comparable s-step-ahead forecasts. This evidence leads naturally to an appraisal of ex post forecast performance, in which the realized outcomes of the trade balance are compared with the confidence regions around the forecasts to see whether the forecasts deviate (statistically) significantly from the outcomes. On the whole, confidence bands are so large that they embrace the path of actual realizations. This result, however, stems from the sizable uncertainty of the forecasts and is not necessarily indicative of predictive accuracy or of model reliability. Further, comparison of the root-mean-square forecast errors, the estimated standard errors of the forecasts, and the sample moments of the trade balance indicates inefficient use of the data by the structural models.

The third section considers two additional ways that stochastically generated forecasts can help to evaluate trade models: forecast-encompassing tests and estimation of the nonlinearity biases of deterministic forecasts. Different models may capture different aspects of the trade balance's behavior, in which case forecasts from one model are informative in explaining the forecast errors from another. Conversely, forecast encompassing, or the *lack* of additional information in another model's forecasts, is evidence in favor of one's own model. Chong and Hendry (1986) proposed this concept, and this section summarizes empirical results for the corresponding test statistic, generalized to multistep forecasts from nonlinear models with coefficient uncertainty. The statistics reveal misspecification in all models. Alternatively viewed, the forecast performance of each model indicates room for improved model specification, and the statistics may suggest ways in which that respecification could occur. For instance, the structural models fail against the time-series models, suggesting dynamic misspecification in the former. Failure of the time-series models against the structural models points to behavioral misspecification of the time-series models.

The third section also evaluates the contribution of model nonlinearities to deterministic forecast biases, using the Monte Carlo technique of antithetic variates in order to increase the numerical precision of the estimates of bias. Our analysis relaxes an assumption maintained in previous applications of antithetic variates to forecasts from econometric models: that the coefficient estimates are known with certainty. The results indicate that biases from model nonlinearity are statistically significant for all the models but are economically significant only for the model explaining trade on a bilateral basis and for the time-series models when predicting several periods ahead.

From the evidence in earlier sections, the final section draws implications for econometric practice, trade modeling, and policy analysis.

Econometric Models of the U.S. Trade Balance

This section summarizes the form of the four structural and two time-series models, reports estimates of certain elasticities from the structural models, describes the forecasting process, and calculates deterministic forecasts for all models. The first structural model is that developed in Helkie and Hooper (1988); the remaining three structural models are treated as variations on it.[2] The two time-series models are a univariate autoregression (AR) of the trade balance and a four-equation vector autoregression (VAR). Although the choice of models is not exhaustive, the Helkie-Hooper model is widely used in the literature, and VARs and univariate time-series models are often taken as "non-structural" alternatives.[3] A detailed description of the models appears in Marquez and Ericsson (1990, appendix E).

Model Structure

The form of the four structural models is summarized in equations 14-1 through 14-5:

$$(14\text{-}1) \qquad \ln(P_{xt}) = P_x(P_t, E_t, P_t^*) + upx_t$$

$$(14\text{-}2) \qquad \ln(X_t) = X[P_{xt}/(E_t P_t^*), Y_t^*] + ux_t$$

$$(14\text{-}3) \qquad \ln(P_{mt}) = P_m(E_t, P_t^*, P_{xt}) + upm_t$$

$$(14\text{-}4) \qquad \ln(M_t) = M(P_{mt}/P_t, Y_t) + um_t$$

$$(14\text{-}5) \qquad NX_t = P_{xt}X_t - P_{mt}M_t,$$

where P_m, P_x, and P are the prices of imports and exports and the general price level; E is the nominal exchange rate (domestic to foreign); M, X, NX,

2. In fact, the first model deviates from that in Helkie and Hooper (1988). Following advice from William Helkie, we reestimated the Helkie-Hooper model with a slighly different specification and data set. Even so, the coefficient estimates and other model properties remained virtually unchanged from the original model. See Helkie and Hooper (1987) for additional details on the Helkie-Hooper model.

3. For example, Krugman and Baldwin (1987), Bryant and Holtham (1988), Cline (1989a, 1989b), Helliwell (1989), and Howard (1989b) use forecasts from the "Helkie-Hooper" model and variants thereon to evaluate the policy implications of the U.S. external deficit. For recent perspectives on trade in general, see the issues "International Trade and Commercial Policy," vol. 3 (Spring 1987), and "Balance of Payments," vol. 6 (Autumn 1990), in the *Oxford Review of Economic Policy*.

and Y are the volume of imports, the volume of exports, the (nominal) trade balance, and real income; and the absence or presence of an asterisk (*) denotes a variable measured for the domestic (U.S.) or foreign country. Each model assumes that the errors $(upx_t, ux_t, upm_t, um_t)'$, denoted u_t, are normally and independently distributed:

$$(14\text{-}6) \qquad u_t \sim NI(0, \Omega),$$

conditional upon a given dynamic structure for equations 14-1 through 14-4. To distinguish the econometric models based upon equations 14-1 through 14-5 from the two time-series models, we will refer to the former as "structural": the structural models rely on an underlying economic theory to explain both trade flows and prices, whereas the time-series models do not.

Empirical implementation of equations 14-1 through 14-5 requires specification of exogeneity, dynamics, estimation technique, and level of trade disaggregation. The econometric model of U.S. trade in Helkie and Hooper (1988) makes (implicitly or explicitly) the following assumptions:

A1— Real incomes, the general domestic and foreign price levels, and the nominal exchange rates are super exogenous with respect to trade elasticities.

A2— International markets operate recursively: prices affect trade, but neither contemporaneous nor lagged trade affects prices.

A3— Trade prices follow the markup-pricing model (Hooper and Mann 1989).

A4— Internationally traded goods are imperfect substitutes for domestic products (Goldstein and Khan 1985).

A5— Exports are disaggregated into agricultural and nonagricultural exports, and imports are disaggregated into oil and non-oil imports; this disaggregation allows trade elasticities to vary with the commodity composition of trade.

A6— Trade elasticities are equal across trading partners and cross-price elasticities are zero.

A7— Trade flows are subject to nonprice rationing and supply shifts that are not adequately captured by price indices.

A8— In a given equation, the distributed-lag coefficients for nonnormalized (right-hand-side) variables are Almon polynomials, and lags on the normalized ("own" dependent) variable are excluded; however, several equations are estimated with autoregressive disturbances and thus implicitly include the lagged dependent variable, albeit with the common factor restriction imposed.

A9— The covariance matrix of contemporaneous structural disturbances, Ω, is diagonal.

Assumptions A1–A4 are standard in existing trade models; to keep the analysis manageable, the practical implications of modifying them will not be addressed.[4] The specific issues of concern to Helkie and Hooper (1988) bore directly on the choice of the level of commodity disaggregation (assumption A5).[5] The equality of parameters across trading partners (assumption A6) permits modeling trade on a multilateral basis. The use of a supply-shift variable (assumption A7) seeks to avoid inadequacies in the construction of price indices for international trade. Helkie and Hooper (1988) proxied nonprice rationing and supply shifts by relative capacity utilization and the ratio of U.S. to foreign capital stocks respectively. By excluding lags on the normalized endogenous variable from each equation's specification (assumption A8), this model rules out certain forms of persistence. Finally, recursive international markets and diagonal Ω (assumptions A4 and A9) may simplify parameter estimation.

This chapter examines the sensitivity of results from the Helkie-Hooper model to certain changes in assumptions A5–A9 using three additional structural models. Table 14-1 shows the form of these models, and table 14-2 contains the associated parametric restrictions. The Helkie-Hooper model is labeled as M1. Model M2 relaxes assumption A9 to allow for a (possibly) nondiagonal covariance matrix Ω, and so uses full-information maximum likelihood (FIML) to estimate the coefficients.[6] Model M3 modifies assumptions A7, A8, and A9, as follows:

A7a— Nonprice rationing and supply-shift variables are not included.

A8a— Dynamic adjustment is modeled as partial adjustment, generalized to include some lagged nonnormalized endogenous variables.

A9a— The covariance matrix Ω may be nondiagonal, so the coefficients are estimated by FIML.

---

4. On assumption A1, see Engle, Hendry, and Richard (1983) on four distinct concepts of exogeneity, some of which are used herein. Briefly, weak, strong, super, and strict exogeneity correspond to different notions of being "determined outside the model under consideration" according to the purposes of the inferences being conducted: conditional inference (estimation and hypothesis testing), prediction, policy analysis, and forecasting, respectively. It is not valid to make variables exogenous simply by not modeling them, but testing for the validity of the various exogeneity assumptions in the models examined is beyond the scope of this chapter. Although estimation of Helkie and Hooper's model requires only weak exogeneity, assumption A1 states super exogeneity because of the model's design for and use in policy analysis. The analysis of s-step-ahead forecasts assumes *strong* exogeneity. Baldwin (1988) and Krugman (1989) scrutinize assumption A3.

5. Oil trade relies on the perfect substitute model (see Goldstein and Khan 1985), with domestic oil production taken as strongly exogenous and oil consumption modeled as a function of real income and relative prices. Note that the perfect substitute model still implies that oil imports are a function of real income and prices, as in equation 14-4.

6. The FIML procedure in TROLL's Version 13 software does not handle autoregressive disturbances per se but does accept nonlinear equation specifications. Thus, equations in M1 that have autoregressive errors were coded as nonlinear equations with white-noise errors. Then all the equations in M1 were estimated by nonlinear FIML. We also estimated each nonlinear equation by TROLL's nonlinear least squares (NLS) routine and obtained virtually identical parameter estimates to those obtained by Helkie and Hooper (1988) using the Cochrane-Orcutt procedure.

Table 14-1. Alternative Econometric Models of the U.S. Trade Balance: Schematic Specifications[a]

Model	Specification

Commodity-disaggregated systems

M1, M2, M3

$$(1 - \alpha'_{0i}L)\ln X_{it} = \alpha_{1i} + \alpha_{2i}\ln Y^*_t + \alpha_{3i}(L)\ln[P_{xit}/(E_t P^*_t)] + \alpha_{4i}NP_{xit} + \alpha_{5i}T_{xit} + ux_{it}$$

$$(1 - \beta'_{0i}L)\ln M_{it} = \beta_{1i} + \beta_{2i}(L)\ln Y_t + \beta_{3i}(L)\ln[P_{mit}/P_t] + \beta_{4i}NP_{mit} + \beta_{5i}T_{mit} + um_{it}$$

$$(1 - \gamma'_{0i}L)\ln P_{xit} = \gamma_{1i} + \gamma_{2i}\ln C_t + \gamma_{3i}\ln[E_t P^*_t] + upx_{it}$$

$$(1 - \delta'_{0i}L)\ln P_{mit} = \delta_{1i} + \delta_{2i}(L)\ln E_t + \delta_{3i}(L)\ln P^*_t + upm_{it}$$

$$NX_t = \sum_i P_{xit}X_{it} - \sum_i P_{mit}M_{it}$$

Country-disaggregated system

M4

$$(1 - \alpha'_{0j}L)\ln X_{jt} = \alpha'_{1j} + \alpha'_{2j}\ln YP_{jt} + \alpha'_{3j}\ln YT_{jt} + \alpha'_{4j}(L)\ln[P_{xt}/(E_{jt}P_{jt})] + \alpha'_{5j}(L)(\sum_{r\neq j}\omega_r \ln[(E_{rt}P_{xrt})/(E_{jt}P_{jt})]) + ux_{jt}$$

$$(1 - \beta'_{0j}L)\ln M_{jt} = \beta'_{1j} + \beta'_{2j}\ln YP_t + \beta'_{3j}\ln YT_t + \beta'_{4j}(L)\ln[E_{jt}P_{xjt}/P_t] + \beta'_{5j}(L)(\sum_{r\neq j}\pi_r \ln[E_{rt}P_{xrt}/P_t]) + um_{jt}$$

$$(1 - \gamma'_0 L)\ln P_{xt} = \gamma'_1 + \gamma'_2\ln P_t + \gamma'_3[\sum_j \omega_j \ln(E_{jt}P_{xjt})] + upx_t$$

$$(1 - \delta'_{0j}L)\ln P_{xjt} = \delta'_{1j} + \delta'_{2j}\ln(P_{xt}/E_{jt}) + \delta'_{3j}\ln P_{jt} + upm_{jt}$$

$$NX_t = \sum_j P_{xt}X_{jt} - \sum_j E_{jt}P_{xjt}M_{jt}$$

Vector autoregressive system

M5

$$\ln X_t = \xi_{11} + \xi_{12}(L)\ln X_{t-1} + \xi_{13}(L)\ln M_{t-1} + \xi_{14}(L)\ln P_{x,t-1} + \xi_{15}(L)\ln P_{m,t-1} + ux_t$$

$$\ln M_t = \xi_{21} + \xi_{22}(L)\ln X_{t-1} + \xi_{23}(L)\ln M_{t-1} + \xi_{24}(L)\ln P_{x,t-1} + \xi_{25}(L)\ln P_{m,t-1} + um_t$$

$$\ln P_{xt} = \xi_{31} + \xi_{32}(L)\ln X_{t-1} + \xi_{33}(L)\ln M_{t-1} + \xi_{34}(L)\ln P_{x,t-1} + \xi_{35}(L)\ln P_{m,t-1} + upx_t$$

$$\ln P_{mt} = \xi_{41} + \xi_{42}(L)\ln X_{t-1} + \xi_{43}(L)\ln M_{t-1} + \xi_{44}(L)\ln P_{x,t-1} + \xi_{45}(L)\ln P_{m,t-1} + upm_t$$

$$NX_t = P_{xt}X_t - P_{mt}M_t$$

Univariate time-series equation

M6

$$NX_t = \lambda_0 + \lambda_1 NX_{t-1} + v_t$$

a. *Indexes and definitions:* Subscript i denotes the ith commodity; subscript j denotes the jth *foreign* country; subscript t denotes time; an asterisk (*) denotes foreign countries (aggregated); a prime ($'$) denotes a parameter from model M4; the natural logarithm is denoted ln; the lag operator is denoted L. *Endogenous variables:* M, real U.S. imports; NX, nominal trade balance; P_m, import price index; P_x, export price index; X, real U.S. exports. *Exogenous variables:* C, production costs; E, nominal exchange rate (US/foreign); NP_m, nonprice rationing of imports; NP_x, nonprice rationing of exports; T_m, trend factors affecting imports; T_x, trend factors affecting exports; P, GDP deflator; Y, real GDP; YP, estimated permanent income; YT, estimated transitory income. *Disturbances:* um, import disturbance; ux, export disturbance; upm, import price disturbance; upx, export price disturbance; v, trade balance disturbance.

Table 14-2. *Alternative Econometric Models of the U.S. Trade Balance: Parametric Configurations*

Attributes	Structural models[a]				Time-series models[b]	
	M1	M2	M3	M4	M5	M6
Number of coefficients[c]	51	51	45	127	68	2
Number of disturbances	8	8	8	21	4	1
Number of autoregressive disturbances	7	7	0	0	0	0
Parameter restrictions	$\alpha_{0i} = 0$	$\alpha_{0i} = 0$	$\alpha_{3i}(L) = \alpha_{3i}$			
	$\beta_{0i} = 0$	$\beta_{0i} = 0$	$\beta_{3i}(L) = \beta_{3i}$			
	$\gamma_{0i} = 0$	$\gamma_{0i} = 0$	$\alpha_{4i} = 0$			
	$\delta_{0i} = 0$	$\delta_{0i} = 0$	$\alpha_{5i} = 0$			
	Ω diagonal		$\beta_{4i} = 0$			
			$\beta_{5i} = 0$			

a. Model M1: Helkie and Hooper (1988); model M2: model M1 by full-information maximum likelihood (FIML); model M3: model M1 by FIML, with partial adjustment and without nonprice rationing; model M4: bilateral trade model by FIML.
b. Model M5: VAR(4) of import and export volumes and price indices; model M6: AR(1) of the nominal trade balance.
c. The number of coefficients excludes the number of variances and covariances for the model's vector of disturbances.

Model M4 is from Marquez (1989) and alters assumptions A5–A9.

A5b— Trade elasticities across commodities are equal. Thus, trade flows are aggregated across commodities.

A6b— Trade elasticities are not assumed to be equal across countries, and cross-price elasticities are not imposed to be zero. Thus, the model explains U.S. exports and imports on a bilateral basis with respect to Canada, Germany, Japan, the United Kingdom, the rest of the OECD countries (ROECD), non-OPEC developing countries (LDCs), and OPEC. Trade with centrally planned economies is assumed to be known.

A7b— Nonprice rationing and supply-shift variables are not included.

A8b— Dynamics appear as lagged endogenous variables and Almon polynomials on (some) other variables.

A9b— The covariance matrix Ω may be nondiagonal, so the coefficients are estimated by FIML.

Note that the behavioral equations in all of the structural models are logarithmic in form, implying that trade volumes and prices are nonlinear functions of the coefficient estimates and disturbances. These nonlinearities have important practical implications for the distribution of the forecasts from the trade balance, as subsequent sections will show.

The time-series models M5 and M6 are included in the analysis as benchmarks for the dynamic specification and forecasting performance of models M1–M4. Model M5 is a fourth-order, four-variable VAR for the logarithms of export and import volumes and price indices. From the logarithms, the trade balance is constructed by using the identity in equation 14-5. Thus, the VAR will have nonlinearities that are qualitatively similar to those in the structural models.

Model M6 is one of the simplest possible time-series specifications, a first-order univariate AR of the level of the trade balance:

$$(14\text{-}7) \qquad\qquad NX_t = \lambda_0 + \lambda_1 NX_{t-1} + v_t,$$

where λ_0 is the constant term, λ_1 is the autoregressive coefficient, and v_t is the error term. By construction, model M6 uses only past information on the trade balance in forecasting the trade balance. Similarly, model M5 uses only past information on export and import volumes and price indices.

In addition to differences in behavioral specification (or the lack thereof), these six models differ in size, whether measured by the number of equations or the number of parameters. For example, model M6 has one stochastic equation with two coefficients, whereas model M4 has 21 stochastic equations with 127 coefficients (see table 14-2). Taken as a whole, the diversity in model specification offers an opportunity to evaluate the consequences of both model structure and estimation technique on forecast performance.

Model Estimation and Data Properties

This subsection reports estimates of parameters associated with models M1–M6, using quarterly data ending in 1984:4 (to match Helkie and Hooper 1988). We focus on derived income, price, and pass-through elasticities. Estimated coefficients of individual model parameters and corresponding standard errors appear in Marquez and Ericsson (1990, appendix E). Empirical properties of the trade balance are briefly examined. Construction of, and sources for, all the data appear in the appendix.

Table 14-3 reports the estimated elasticities for models M1–M4. Several features are of particular interest, including the models' economic and statistical properties and their sensitivity to estimation method, model specification, and degree of disaggregation.

The estimated trade elasticities are consistent with standard theory. The income elasticities are positive, the price elasticities are negative, and the pass-through effect of exchange rates to import prices is positive. Also, the sum of the estimated price elasticities is more negative than -1, suggesting that these models satisfy the Marshall-Lerner condition.[7] Most estimated elasticities are economically and statistically significant and have small standard errors. One

---

7. The Marshall-Lerner condition states that the sum of the price elasticities for exports and imports should be less than -1 in order to avoid instability in market adjustments to changes in relative prices.

Table 14-3. *Alternative Structural Models of the U.S. Trade Balance: Long-Run Elasticity Estimates*

Attributes	Structural models[a]			
	M1	M2	M3	M4
Estimation				
Sample[b]	1969:3–1984:4	1969:3-1984:4	1969:3-1984:4	1973:1-1984:4
Method	NLS,OLS[c]	FIML	FIML	FIML
Import volume				
Income				
Non-oil	2.08 (0.11)	2.36 (0.68)	2.75 (0.08)	
Oil	3.62 (0.03)	3.55 (0.55)	1.36 (1.10)[d]	
Canada				1.64 (0.17)
Germany				2.92 (0.31)
Japan				3.70 (0.30)
United Kingdom				2.43 (0.52)
ROECD (rest of OECD)				2.32 (0.31)
LDCs (non-OPEC developing countries)				3.12 (0.21)
OPEC (Organization of Petroleum Exporting Countries)				5.19 (0.85)
Aggregate[e]	2.34 (0.18)	2.70 (0.49)	2.29 (0.33)	3.01 (0.16)
Price				
Non-oil	−1.12 (0.11)	−1.07 (0.08)	−0.97 (0.09)	
Oil	−2.58 (0.91)	−0.83 (0.36)	−0.61 (0.42)[e]	
Canada				−0.63 (0.17)
Germany				−1.41 (0.33)
Japan				−0.58 (0.23)
United Kingdom				−0.44 (0.39)
ROECD				−0.68 (0.14)
LDCs				−1.44 (0.43)
OPEC				−3.97 (1.95)
Aggregate	−1.56 (0.29)	−0.99 (0.36)	−0.85 (0.14)	−1.36 (0.31)
Export volume				
Income				
Agricultural	1.12 (0.34)	1.11 (0.08)	1.33 (0.10)	
Nonagricultural	2.24 (0.10)	2.15 (0.31)	1.27 (0.11)	
Canada				1.70 (0.21)
Germany				1.52 (0.17)
Japan				0.75 (0.17)
United Kingdom				3.41 (0.70)
ROECD				1.79 (0.29)
LDCs				0.40 (0.16)
OPEC				1.29 (0.47)
Aggregate	2.06 (0.29)	1.98 (0.26)	1.28 (0.09)	1.27 (0.01)

Table 14-3 *(continued)*

Attributes	Structural models[a]			
	M1	*M2*	*M3*	*M4*
Export volume				
Price				
Agricultural	−0.84 (0.14)	−0.88 (0.11)	−0.66 (0.17)	
Nonagricultural	−0.98 (0.11)	−0.92 (0.12)	−1.04 (0.26)	
Canada				−0.44 (0.34)
Germany				−0.99 (0.17)
Japan				−0.41 (0.28)
United Kingdom				−0.87 (0.36)
ROECD				−0.83 (0.22)
LDCs				−1.62 (0.62)
OPEC				−0.86 (0.17)
Aggregate	−0.96 (0.09)	−0.91 (0.10)	−0.98 (0.22)	−0.96 (0.21)
Pass-through coefficients				
Non-oil	0.82 (0.09)	0.83 (0.10)	0.94 (0.09)	
Canada				0.71 (0.17)
Germany				0.83 (0.03)
Japan				0.48 (0.08)
United Kingdom				0.41 (0.55)[d]
ROECD				1.10 (0.06)
LDCs				0.84 (0.16)
Marshall-Lerner				
condition	−2.52 (0.30)	−1.91 (0.37)	−1.83 (0.26)	−2.32 (0.33)
Houthakker-Magee				
asymmetry				
Canada				0.06 (0.27)
Germany				−1.40 (0.35)
Japan				−2.95 (0.34)
United Kingdom				0.98 (0.77)
ROECD				−0.53 (0.42)
LDCs				−2.72 (0.26)
OPEC				−3.00 (0.48)
Aggregate	−0.28 (0.34)	−0.72 (0.55)	−1.01 (0.34)	−1.74 (0.19)

a. See table 14-2, note a. The numbers in parentheses are standard errors.
b. The starting observation for estimation varies across equation in model M1; see Marquez and Ericsson (1990, appendix E).
c. NLS, nonlinear least squares; OLS, ordinary least squares.
d. For this elasticity, the measure of dispersion is the scaled median absolute deviation. See appendix tables 14A-2 and 14A-3 for the estimated standard error and the 95 percent confidence interval.
e. The elasticity estimates for aggregate trade are obtained as a weighted average of the disaggregated trade elasticities.

notable exception is the (derived) price elasticity of oil imports in model M3, which is small (−0.61) and statistically insignificant.[8]

Several examples illustrate the sensitivity of the estimated elasticities to the choice of estimation method, the dynamic specification of the behavioral relations, and their level of disaggregation by country and commodity. First,

8. Because the elasticities of models M3 and M4 are nonlinear functions of the estimated coefficients, both those elasticities and their standard errors must be derived. We do so by Monte Carlo simulation, as described in the appendix.

estimation of the Helkie-Hooper model by FIML (M2) rather than by NLS and ordinary least squares (OLS) (M1) changes the price elasticity for oil imports from -2.58 to -0.83. Second, income elasticities for aggregate exports and imports are not equal in models M3 and M4 but are equal in models M1 and M2.[9] Thus, models M3 and M4 imply a deterioration of the U.S. trade balance from equal increases in income throughout the world, other things being equal, whereas models M1 and M2 do not. Third, the price elasticity of imports for model M4 varies from -0.44 for the United Kingdom to -3.97 for OPEC, bringing into question the validity of assumption A6 in models M1–M3. Similarly, the pass-through coefficients in M4 vary from 0.41 for U.S. imports from the United Kingdom to 1.10 for U.S. imports from the ROECD bloc of countries. Finally, aggregating the data reduces the range of elasticity estimates. For example, the income elasticity for aggregate imports varies from 2.3 for M3 to 3.0 for M4, whereas elasticities for the components of these aggregates are more disperse.

Before turning to the models' forecasts themselves, we note some basic time-series properties of the trade-balance data. The first column of numbers in table 14-4 lists characteristics of the AR(1) model M6, estimated over 1969:3–1984:4. For comparison, the second column gives estimates for an AR(4) model over the same sample. Both models are estimated by OLS. Based on these estimates, the trade balance appears to be nonstationary, and possibly explosively so. That feature may stem from inclusion of the 1980–84 period in the estimation sample.[10] Because forecasts from dynamic models need not have finite moments, an examination of the empirical properties of forecasts from models such as M5 and M6 may contribute to the literature on their analytical properties.[11] The VAR (M5) is estimated over 1969:3–1984:4 by multivariate least squares, which is FIML here because the coefficients are unrestricted.

The estimated equation standard errors for models M1–M6 appear under the column heading $\hat{\sigma}$ in table 14-5 (in the next section) and range from $5.5 billion to $10.5 billion. These standard errors are calculated as the root-mean-squared deviations between the actual trade balance and its one-step-ahead deterministic simulation, in sample. Deterministic rather than stochastic simulation is used for computational savings and because the nonlinearity biases of one-step-ahead deterministic simulations for these models appear quite small (see the section on "Additional Applications," below, under "Nonlinearity Bias"). The *sample*

9. See Houthakker and Magee (1969). The asymmetry in income elasticities is measured as the income elasticity for exports minus the income elasticity for imports. Note the large elasticity asymmetries between the United States and Germany, Japan, and the LDCs.

10. If the estimation sample ends in 1979:4, then the $\Sigma \hat{\lambda}_q$ are 0.96 (0.06) and 0.94 (0.07) for the AR(1) and AR(4) models, respectively.

11. See Orcutt and Winokur (1969); Sargan (1982); Hoque, Magnus, and Pesaran (1988); Ericsson and Marquez (1989); and Magnus and Pesaran (1989).

Table 14-4. *Summary Statistics for Two Time-Series Models*

Summary statistic[a]	M6 (p = 1)	AR(4) (p = 4)
$\hat{\lambda}_0$	−0.91 (1.25)[b]	−0.87 (1.25)[b]
$\sum_{q=1}^{p} \hat{\lambda}_q$	1.044 (0.03)[b]	1.026 (0.05)[b]
$\hat{\sigma}$	7.805	7.64
$\bar{R}^2$	0.94	0.94
Durbin's h	0.30	−0.115

a. λ_0 is the constant term, $\{\lambda_q\}$ are the autoregressive coefficients, p is the order of the autoregression, σ is the equation standard error, and $\bar{R}^2$ is the adjusted multiple correlation coefficient.
b. The numbers in parentheses are standard errors.

standard errors of the level and change in the trade balance are $31.2 billion and $7.8 billion, respectively. Thus, in sample, the structural models offer marked improvement in fit over the unconditional variance of the trade balance, and (for M1–M3) some improvement over pure time-series models and over the unconditional variance of the change in the trade balance. Similar comparisons out-of-sample appear below.

Forecasting

Given the nonlinearities in the behavioral equations, forecasting the trade balance S periods ahead (say) involves solving the whole trade model for import and export prices and volumes, period by period. For notational simplicity, the entire model is represented as:

$$(14\text{-}8) \qquad f(y_t, y_{t-1}, z_t, \theta, u_t) = 0, \qquad t = 1, \dots, T + S,$$

where the first T observations are used in estimation (here, ending in 1984:4), the remaining S are forecast, $f(\cdot)$ is an $n \times 1$ vector of equations included in the model, y_t is an $n^+ \times 1$ vector of endogenous variables in period t, z_t is an $r \times 1$ vector of (assumedly) weakly exogenous variables, θ is a $c \times 1$ vector of parameters, and u_t is an $m \times 1$ vector of corresponding disturbances. For describing forecast procedures, it is more convenient to write equation 14-8 solved for y_t explicitly:

$$(14\text{-}9) \qquad y_{T+s} = g(y_{T+s-1}, z_{T+s}, \theta, u_{T+s}),$$

$$s = 1 - T, \dots, -1, 0, 1, \dots, S,$$

where $g(\cdot)$ is a suitable redefinition of $f(\cdot)$ above, and the time subscript is changed such that forecasts are calculated for positive s.

By assumption, equation 14-9 is the process generating y_{T+s}. Thus, this equation naturally serves for generating $\hat{y}_{T+s}$ (the forecast of y_{T+s}), given some choice of assumptions about y_{T+s-1}, θ, and u_{T+s}. The particular choice adopted determines the type of forecast. If the actual value of y_{T+s-1} is used, then the S forecasts $\{\hat{y}_{T+s}; s = 1, \ldots, S\}$ are one period ahead; that is, forecasts of the endogenous variables are conditional on the observed endogenous variables lagged one period. Alternatively, the previous forecast $\hat{y}_{T+s-1}$ could replace y_{T+s-1} in equation 14-9, but with observed y_T starting the forecast process. This sequential solution for $\hat{y}_{T+s}$ generates a set of s-period-ahead forecasts ($s = 1, \ldots, S$).

Given the class of forecasts (whether one period or s period ahead), the choice of θ and u_{T+s} in $g(\cdot)$ fully specifies the forecast procedure. Numerous choices of θ and u_{T+s} exist, the most common being "deterministic simulation" ($\theta = \hat{\theta}$ and $u_{T+s} = 0$) and "stochastic simulation" (θ and u_{T+s} random). The remainder of this section considers the former. The next section, "Stochastic Properties of the Trade-Balance Forecasts," calculates the latter by Monte Carlo methods and uses them for model evaluation via predictive failure tests. The section "Additional Applications of Stochastically Simulated Forecasts" uses stochastic simulation for model evaluation via forecast-encompassing tests and compares the numerical solutions for both deterministic and stochastic simulations. The analysis in the body of the chapter is conducted with one-period- and s-period-ahead forecasts, in both cases drawing sets of random values for θ and u_{T+s}; the appendix presents the results for which only u_{T+s} is treated as random. For brevity, analytical derivations below often are given for s-step-ahead forecasts only. However, the formal structure developed applies to both s-step and one-step forecasts, and both types of forecasts are examined empirically.

Before proceeding, we note that the term *simulation* carries different meanings in the econometric and Monte Carlo literatures. To avoid confusion, we use the definition in Howrey and Kelejian (1969, p. 207): "A simulation experiment is the solution sequence generated by a dynamic model under certain specified conditions in which the exogenous variables are usually taken as given and the model is used to generate the endogenous variables sequentially."

Deterministic Forecasts

In deterministic simulation, equation 14-9 is solved numerically, setting θ equal to its in-sample estimated value $\hat{\theta}$ and u_{T+s} equal to its expected value (usually zero). The associated one-step-ahead forecasts are

(14-10) $\delta_{T+s} = g(y_{T+s-1}, z_{T+s}, \hat{\theta}, 0)$, $s = 1, \ldots, S$.

The s-step-ahead forecasts use the same formula, but with δ_{T+s-1} replacing y_{T+s-1} ($s = 2, \ldots, S$). Equation 14-10 is computationally simple to implement for both one-step- and s-step-ahead forecasts, but, by ignoring $\hat{\theta}$ and u_{T+s} as sources of randomness, the extent of forecast uncertainty cannot be assessed. That precludes developing confidence intervals for the forecasts and evaluating the forecast performance of different models.[12]

To highlight these limitations, consider the deterministic one-step- and s-step-ahead trade-balance forecasts from equation 14-10 for the period 1985:1–1987:4, plotted in figure 14-1.[13] Two features are notable: the forecasts differ substantially in numerical terms across models, and the dispersion of model forecasts increases strikingly as the forecast horizon lengthens. On the former, s-step-ahead forecasts from models M1–M3 and M5 indicate a general improvement, whereas models M4 and M6 forecast continued deterioration. On the latter, the range of trade-balance forecasts increases from \$50 billion (annual rates) at one quarter ahead to \$140 billion (annual rates) at twelve quarters ahead. Hooper (1988) and Bryant and Holtham (1988) reported similar findings in comparing forecasts from different trade models and interpreted the increase in forecast dispersion as indicative of forecast uncertainty. This interpretation, however, unrealistically treats deterministic simulations from alternative models as though they were drawings from some (unspecified) distribution of outcomes.

Although forecast uncertainty may well increase with the forecast horizon, neither ex post nor ex ante measures of that uncertainty are related to the dispersion of deterministic simulations from alternative models, making the latter an unreliable estimate of forecast uncertainty. For instance, one model's forecasts might be always correct, yet the dispersion across different models' forecasts could be substantial because of misspecification in the other models. Conversely, all forecasts might be nearly identical (for instance, because of similar model design), yet all could have large uncertainty associated with them. Simply put, a set of *forecasts* from different models bears no relation to a sampling of possible *outcomes* of the variable forecast. For reasons discussed in the next section, descriptive statisics of model performance such as mean absolute error (MAE) and root-mean-square forecast error (RMSFE) also are unsatisfactory measures of forecast uncertainty.

Deterministic simulations are of potential interest but often lack a measure of uncertainty. Numerically large differences between forecasts from alternative

---

12. Equation 14-10 also gives biased forecasts for most nonlinear functions $g(\cdot)$ because the expectation of a nonlinear function generally is not equal to the function of the expectation. See the subsection "Nonlinearity Bias" below for a numerical analysis of such forecast biases.

13. For the structural models M1–M4, the forecasts of y are ex post in the sense that those forecasts are conditional upon the outcomes of the assumedly weakly exogenous variables z. However, the variables in y (import and export prices and volumes) *are* solved simultaneously at each period.

Figure 14-1. *Deterministic Forecasts of the Trade Balance, 1985–87*

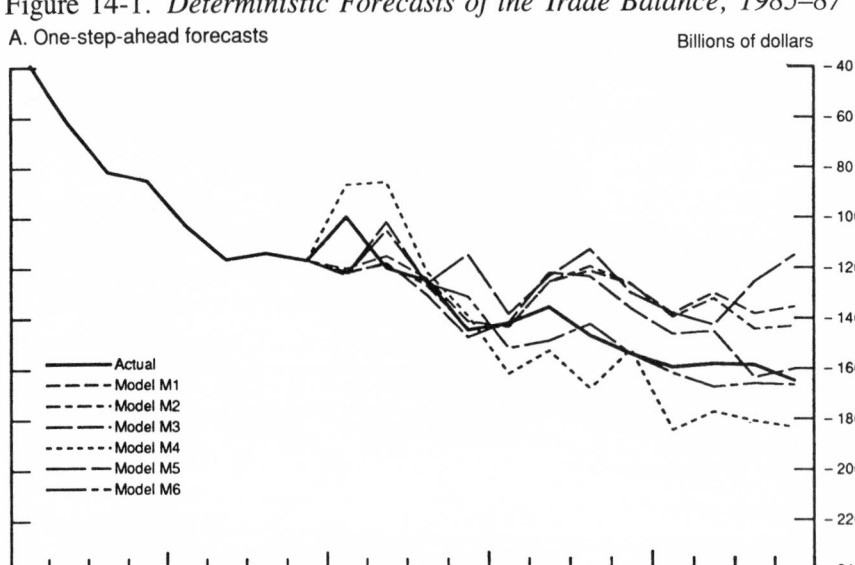

A. One-step-ahead forecasts

Billions of dollars

Actual
Model M1
Model M2
Model M3
Model M4
Model M5
Model M6

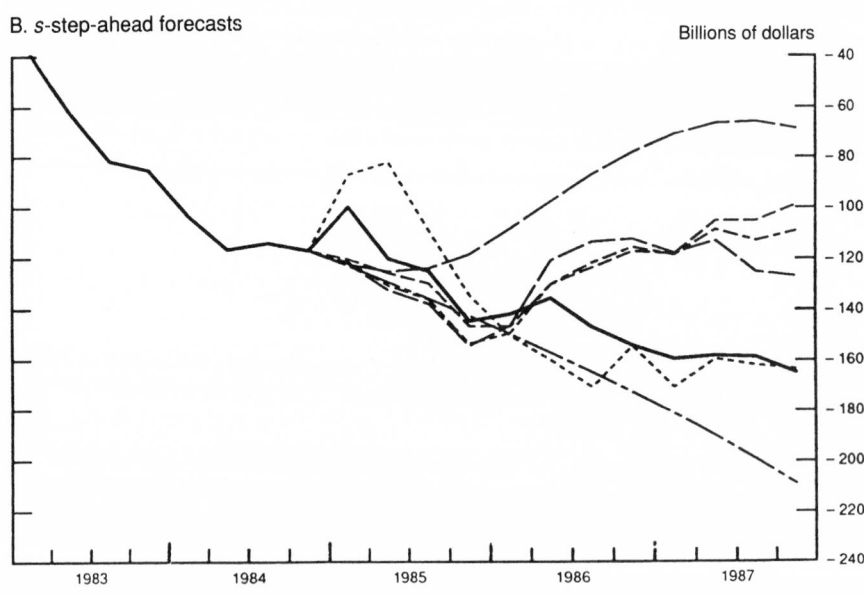

B. *s*-step-ahead forecasts

Billions of dollars

models (or between forecasts of a given model and actual outcomes) may or may not be statistically significant, and a measure of the distributional properties of the forecasts is necessary to find that out. Lacking such a measure undermines the value of deterministic simulation for studying international trade and evaluating policies. Thus, the next section assesses the uncertainty of trade-balance forecasts by means of stochastic simulation.

Stochastic Properties of the Trade-Balance Forecasts

In much the same way that coefficient estimates are *estimates* and hence are uncertain, so are forecasts. However, whereas the uncertainty of coefficient estimates in a well-specified model arises from only one source, namely, the disturbances over the estimation period, forecast uncertainty has two sources: "inherent" and "coefficient." That is, uncertainty arises from future disturbances and from the estimation of model parameters. In light of equation 14-9, those sources are $\{u_{T+s}, s = 1, \ldots, S\}$ and the estimated coefficients $\hat{\theta}$, the latter being a function of the in-sample disturbances $\{u_t, t = 1, \ldots, T\}$. Standard errors and confidence intervals can be constructed to reflect such uncertainty in forecasts, thereby permitting hypothesis testing.

For a linear static system, Goldberger, Nagar, and Odeh (1961) analytically obtained the variance-covariance matrix of the forecast, accounting for both sources of uncertainty. Schmidt (1974) and Baillie (1979) derived comparable formulas for linear dynamic systems, and Calzolari (1981, 1987a) proposed simplified methods for implementing those formulas. See Chong and Hendry (1986) for a summary and Monte Carlo analysis.

Equation 14-9 is nonlinear, so Schmidt and Baillie's formulas are not directly applicable. Instead, we solve a stochastic analog to those analytical formulas, simulating by Monte Carlo the effects of inherent and coefficient uncertainty, which are analytically derivable for linear models. Stochastic simulation is computationally simple, in effect being repeated deterministic simulation, with each deterministic simulation solving equation 14-9 for a different, stochastically generated value of θ and $\{u_{T+s}\}$ rather than for only $\hat{\theta}$ and $\{0\}$. The two subsections that follow describe the design of the stochastic simulation and analyze the results.

Experimental Design of the Stochastic Simulation

From equation 14-9, the forecast $\hat{y}_{T+s}$ (relative to the outcome y_{T+s}) depends on the realizations of two random variables, $\hat{\theta}$ and $\{u_{T+i}, i = 1, \ldots s\}$, so $\hat{y}_{T+s}$ is also a random variable. If the distribution of the forecast $\hat{y}_{T+s}$ were derived analytically, assumptions would be made about the distributional properties of those disturbances and of the coefficient estimates. Similar assumptions are made when solving for the distributional properties of forecasts by stochastic simulation. Values of $\{\hat{\theta}; u_{T+s}, s = 1, \ldots, S\}$ are randomly drawn according to those distributional assumptions, with each set of values generating a path of S forecasts. From the sample of forecast paths, distributional properties of the forecasts can be estimated, such as the sample mean, the standard deviation (which gives the estimated forecast standard error), and the 95 percent confidence interval. The remainder of this subsection describes the assumptions used, the procedure for generating the sample of forecasts, and some statistics derivable from that sample.

To generate random drawings for the errors u_{T+s}, we assume normality and independence for all u_t:

$$(14\text{-}11) \qquad u_t \sim NI(0, \Omega) \qquad t = 1, \ldots, T + S,$$

where Ω is an $m \times m$ covariance matrix independent of the time period t. Thus, the kth drawing of u_{T+s} (denoted $u_{k,T+s}$) is

$$(14\text{-}12) \qquad u_{k,T+s} = \hat{\Lambda}\eta_{k,s}, \qquad k = 1, \ldots, K; \; s = 1, \ldots, S,$$

where Λ is the (lower triangular) Cholesky decomposition of Ω (and so $\Lambda\Lambda' = \Omega$), $\hat{\Lambda}$ is the (empirical) in-sample estimate of Λ from $\hat{\Omega}$ (the in-sample estimate of Ω), $\eta_{k,s}$ is an $m \times 1$ vector of drawings from an independent standard normal distribution, and K is the number of replications (the number of times that the forecast is simulated). In this analysis, $K = 1,000$ and the forecast period is 1985:1–1987:4 ($S = 12$).

To generate random drawings for all the coefficients in the model, we assume that the asymptotic properties of $\hat{\theta}$ hold in finite samples:

$$(14\text{-}13) \qquad \hat{\theta} \sim N(\theta, \Sigma),$$

where Σ is the $c \times c$ asymptotic covariance matrix of $\hat{\theta}$.[14] Thus, the kth drawing of $\hat{\theta}$, denoted θ_k, is

$$(14\text{-}14) \qquad \theta_k = \hat{\theta} + \hat{\Gamma}\zeta_k, \qquad k = 1, \ldots, K; \; s = 1, \ldots, S,$$

where Γ is the Cholesky decomposition of Σ (and so $\Gamma\Gamma' = \Sigma$), $\hat{\Gamma}$ is the sample estimate of Γ from $\hat{\Sigma}$ (the empirical estimate of Σ), and ζ_k is a $c \times 1$ vector of drawings from an independent standard normal distribution.[15]

---

14. Note that the estimation procedure may have implications for the assumed structure of Σ—for example, block diagonality equation by equation for OLS and NLS.

15. As an illustration of the magnitudes involved in equations 14-12 and 14-14, the dimensions of Ω and Σ for model M4 are 21×21 and 127×127, respectively.

At the kth replication, S forecasts are solved sequentially by means of equation 14-9 by combining θ_k from equation 14-4, $\{u_{k,T+s}, s = 1, \ldots, S\}$ from equation 14-12, and the paths of the exogenous variables:

$$(14\text{-}15) \qquad \begin{aligned} y_{k,T+s} &= g(y_{k,T+s-1}, z_{T+s}, \theta_k, u_{k,T+s}) \\ &= g(y_{k,T+s-1}, z_{T+s}, \hat{\theta} + \hat{\Gamma}\zeta_k, \hat{\Lambda}\eta_{k,s}), \quad s = 1, \ldots, S, \end{aligned}$$

with the initial condition that $y_{k,T} \equiv y_T$. One element of equation 14-15 is the (kth) simulated trade-balance forecast $NX_{k,T+s}$.

The full stochastic simulation produces a random sample of K trade-balance forecasts, from which the mean forecast (μ_{T+s}), mean forecast error (ν_{T+s}), and standard deviation of the simulated forecasts (σ_{T+s}) are estimated by

$$(14\text{-}16) \qquad \tilde{\mu}_{T+s} = \sum_k NX_{k,T+s}/K$$

$$(14\text{-}17) \qquad \tilde{\nu}_{T+s} = NX_{T+s} - \tilde{\mu}_{T+s}$$

$$(14\text{-}18) \qquad \tilde{\sigma}_{T+s} = \left[\sum_k (NX_{k,T+s} - \tilde{\mu}_{T+s})^2/K \right]^{1/2}, \qquad s = 1, \ldots, S,$$

where NX_{T+s} is the recorded value of the trade balance, and these Monte Carlo estimators are denoted by a tilde ($\tilde{\ }$) in order to distinguish them from *empirical* estimators such as $\hat{\theta}$.[16] Thus, $\tilde{\sigma}_{T+s}^2$ is the estimated variance for a single s-period-ahead forecast. Unlike the deterministic forecasts from equation 14-10, the equations 14-16 through 14-18 recognize that both coefficient estimates and innovations are random variables that could take values other than their (estimated) means. That randomness affects the forecast's distribution and

---

See Bianchi and Calzolari (1983), Brown and Mariano (1984), Fair (1984), and Bianchi, Calzolari, and Brillet (1987) on alternative procedures for drawing coefficients and residuals.

At first blush, the assumption of normality in equations 14-11 and 14-13 may seem restrictive, and to a certain extent it is. However, analyses *without* forecast standard errors impose even more restrictive assumptions. Such analyses can be viewed as implicitly assuming normality and, in addition, setting $\Omega = 0$ and $\Sigma = 0$. Forecast standard errors from stochastic Monte Carlo simulation typically assume normality as well, with Ω equal to its estimated value (as above) but $\Sigma = 0$. Thus, our procedure is more general than those commonly used. Also, as the derivations in Schmidt (1974) and Baillie (1979) imply, finite sample deviations of the estimator's distribution from normality do not affect the distribution of the forecasts from *linear* models, to the order of approximation present. For instance, those deviations matter only for terms of $o(1/T)$ in the forecast error variance. *Residual-based* stochastic simulation sets $\Sigma = 0$ and randomizes (permutes) the estimated in-sample residuals to generate the simulated forecast errors, from which the estimated forecast standard errors are calculated. Although not quite a special case of our procedure, it omits coefficient uncertainty, and the randomized residuals need not approximate the underlying distribution of the *errors* any better than normality does. See Brown and Mariano (1989) for a comparative analysis of residual-based, deterministic, and Monte Carlo predictors.

16. To obtain an unbiased estimator of σ^2, the summation in equation 14-18 should be divided by $K - 1$ rather than K. We use K instead because the numerical differences are negligible for large K (and our choice of $K = 1,000$ seems large) and it is consistent with the matrix generalization, Φ, below.

is the basis for statistical inferences about the forecasts.[17] In fact, $\tilde{\sigma}^2_{T+s}$ (and its generalization $\tilde{\Phi}$ below) can be calculated accounting for the uncertainty either from future shocks *and* coefficient estimation or from future shocks alone. Paralleling analytical formulas for linear models, the two possible calculations are referred to as the "approximate" and "asymptotic" formulas respectively. The latter is asymptotic because it ignores uncertainty from estimation, which affects the variance σ^2_{T+s} in finite (estimation) samples only. The former is "approximate" because the assumption of $\hat{\theta}$ being exactly normal need not hold, even if the $\{u_t\}$ are normal; but this approximation affects σ^2_{T+s} to *only* order $o(1/T)$.

The matrix generalization of $\tilde{\sigma}^2_{T+s}$ follows immediately. Define ϕ_k as the vector of deviations between the kth stochastic simulation of the S forecasts and the estimated mean forecasts:

$$(14\text{-}19) \qquad \phi_k = [(NX_{k,T+1} - \tilde{\mu}_{T+1}), \ldots, (NX_{k,T+S} - \tilde{\mu}_{T+S})]'.$$

The standard Monte Carlo estimator for the variance of the vector of forecasts $(\tilde{\mu}_{T+1}, \ldots, \tilde{\mu}_{T+S})'$ is

$$(14\text{-}20) \qquad \tilde{\Phi} = \sum_k \phi_k \phi_k' / K.$$

Just as $\tilde{\sigma}^2_{T+s}$ provides a measure of the forecast uncertainty for the single forecast $\tilde{\mu}_{T+s}$, so does $\tilde{\Phi}$ for the vector of forecasts. Having constructed these measures of forecast uncertainty, we can formulate forecast-based test statistics.

A natural hypothesis to test is that the outcomes of the trade balance in the forecast period come from the same distribution as that assumed to generate the in-sample values—that is, the distribution implied by the function $g(\cdot)$ in equation 14-9. One approach to testing this hypothesis is to compare the forecast errors with their variance-covariance matrix derived from $g(\cdot)$ and see whether the errors are substantially larger than anticipated. For a forecast at $T + s$, the corresponding test statistic is the forecast error t-ratio, which is the mean forecast error $\tilde{\nu}_{T+s}$ divided by its estimated standard error $\tilde{\sigma}_{T+s}$. This statistic is approximately distributed as a standardized normal random variable under the null hypothesis; its square is approximately $\chi^2(1)$. For the static linear model, this statistic simplifies to one based on the one-step prediction interval (see Chow 1960, p. 593 on the latter).

---

17. Using stochastic simulation to estimate μ (rather than calculating it analytically) introduces a third source of uncertainty when forecasting from nonlinear models. Although estimates of the uncertainty contributed by simulation are feasible, we ignore this complication, assuming that K is large enough so that simulation uncertainty is negligible relative to inherent and coefficient uncertainty.

For the entire set of forecasts, the S forecast errors are compared with their measure of uncertainty. Denote the vector of mean forecast errors by:

$$(14\text{-}21) \qquad \tilde{\nu} = (\tilde{\nu}_{T+1}, \ldots, \tilde{\nu}_{T+S})'$$
$$= [(NX_{T+1} - \tilde{\mu}_{T+1}), \ldots, (NX_{T+S} - \tilde{\mu}_{T+S})]'.$$

Then the test statistic is

$$(14\text{-}22) \qquad \tau = \tilde{\nu}'[\tilde{\Phi}]^{-1}\tilde{\nu}.$$

Under the null hypothesis that the model is correctly specified over both the estimation and forecast samples, τ is approximately distributed as $\chi^2(S)$.[18] Large values of τ indicate misspecification of the model—such as that from omitted-variables bias, with that bias varying as the correlation between included and omitted variables changes. While the power of τ is often high against such parameter nonconstancy, τ may have little or no power against other forms of misspecification, as in the previous example but with no change in the intervariable correlation. For linear models, the distribution of τ is invariant (approximately invariant) to the use of one-step- or s-step-ahead forecasts with the asymptotic formula (approximate formula) (see Pagan 1989). The statistic τ is *not* invariant to the type of forecast from *non*linear models.

By allowing model nonlinearity, the statistic τ generalizes Chong and Hendry's (1986, p. 682, equation 31) χ^2 statistic for detecting predictive failure.[19] In contrast to the linear framework, analytical solutions for the forecasts and their variance-covariance matrix Φ are not usually available, so both are estimated by stochastic simulation.

Whereas τ may be a reasonable test statistic for detecting a wide class of deviations in forecast properties from those anticipated, more powerful tests exist for specific forms of deviation. For instance, forecasts can be systematically off, so it may be of interest to test whether or not forecast errors have a fixed bias. One test statistic for this is

$$(14\text{-}23) \qquad \tau^* = (\sqrt{S}) \cdot [\tilde{\nu}'(\tilde{\Phi}^{-1/2})\iota/S],$$

18. Note that the mean forecast errors $\tilde{\nu}$ are the discrepancies between *outcomes* and the mean forecasts, whereas the elements of ϕ_k are the discrepancies between the kth set of *simulated forecasts* and the mean forecasts, so being typical hypothesized forecast errors under the null of correct specification. The $\tilde{\nu}$ indicate the actual forecast performance of the model, whereas the ϕ_k (via $\tilde{\Phi}$) are the basis for estimating how well the model ought to have forecast if the model were well-specified.

19. Chong and Hendry's χ^2 statistic in turn generalizes Hendry's (1979) χ^2 statistic in two directions. The former accounts for coefficient uncertainty, making it similar to Chow's (1960, pp. 594–95) statistic; and it is applicable to s-step- as well as one-step-ahead forecasts.

where ι is an $S \times 1$ vector of ones. This statistic transforms the forecast errors into errors that (under the null hypothesis of correct model specification) are standardized and uncorrelated, averages those transformed errors, and rescales the average by $\sqrt{S}$. (By contrast, τ is the sum of *squares* of the transformed errors.) The τ^* statistic is approximately distributed as Student's t-statistic $t(S - 1)$ under the null of zero mean in the forecast error and is designed to have power against the alternative of a nonzero mean, constant across forecasts. For linear models, Chow (1960, p. 594, equation 11) and Hendry (1989, pp. 49–50) gave equivalent analytical solutions for τ^* including coefficient uncertainty. The invariance results for τ also apply to τ^*.

Criteria such as MAE and RMSFE often are used to measure the performance of alternative macroeconomic models. The usefulness of these statistics is questionable for dynamic and/or nonlinear models; even for static linear models, their purposes contrast with those of τ and τ^*. The issues are threefold.

First, to justify averaging a function of forecast errors over different forecast periods, these criteria assume that the moments of the forecast errors are constant across periods, but they are unlikely to be so in dynamic and/or nonlinear models. In general, the forecast-error variance for a dynamic and/or nonlinear model depends on the forecast period—that is, the diagonal elements of Φ are not identical (nor does Φ need to be diagonal). That invalidates model comparison with such statistics. Thus, although MAE and RMSFE are reported below, they appear with period-by-period estimates of forecast standard errors, which provide evidence on the constant-variance assumption. (Note that the constant-variance assumption is made, whether the forecasts are deterministic or stochastic.) Second, as Hendry and Richard (1982, pp. 26–31) and Fair (1984, pp. 264–65; 1986) noted, such measures do not account for differences in conditioning sets across models, so models with greater reliance on exogenous variables may have an "unfair" advantage in ex post forecasting. Specifically, Hendry and Richard showed analytically that a misspecified model with invalidly assumed exogenous variables can have a smaller RMSFE (or MAE) than the correctly specified model. Third, a model that does well (or poorly) in terms of its MAE or RMSFE may still have its forecasts falling outside (or within) a suitable measure of forecast uncertainty. Such "conflicting" results may arise even when forecast variances are constant and the sample size is large (as for static linear models with no coefficient uncertainty). The cause is that the two classes of statistics are being used to evaluate the models against different information sets: for τ and τ^*, different subsamples within a given data set, and, for MAE and RMSFE, different data sets over a given subsample (see Ericsson 1992 for details).

Empirical Forecast Performance

With the theoretical properties of the forecasts characterized and forecast-based test statistics formulated, the empirical forecasts generated by stochastic simulation may be interpreted. Table 14-5 lists the mean forecast error $\tilde{\nu}_{T+s}$, its estimated (approximate) standard error $\tilde{\sigma}_{T+s}$, and their ratio across models and forecast periods for one-step-ahead forecasts. Values of the MAE, RMSFE, and the test statistics τ and τ^* are also given for each model. Figure 14-2 presents the mean forecast $\tilde{\mu}_{T+s}$, an approximate 95 percent confidence interval given by $\tilde{\mu}_{T+s} \pm 2\tilde{\sigma}_{T+s}$, and the realized trade balance NX_{T+s}, one graph per set of one-step-ahead forecasts for a given model. Table 14-6 and figure 14-3 contain the corresponding information for s-step-ahead forecasts. From these summaries of the stochastic simulation, we analyze the models' ex post forecast performance, focusing on systematic biases in the forecasts, the economic and statistical magnitudes of forecast errors, the size of the forecast standard error, and statistical measures of forecast accuracy.

The one-step-ahead forecast errors for models M1–M3 and M5 are systematic and highly autocorrelated, tending to be positive and decreasing over the first four or so periods and negative and increasing in magnitude over the remainder. Forecasts from M4 reflect this pattern, but with opposite sign. Model M6 has relatively small, unsystematic forecast errors. The s-step-ahead forecast errors are (approximately) weighted cumulants of the one-step-ahead forecast errors, with the patterns for M1–M5 being approximately the same or accentuated. The forecast errors for M6 are systematic and positive, although small relative to the confidence intervals.

Numerically, the forecast errors are often large relative to the size of the trade balance. For example, model M1 underpredicts the trade *deficit* twelve periods ahead by $63 billion in 1987:4, that is, by approximately one-third of the actual deficit. One explanation of such large errors lies in what is being forecast: the difference of two large quantities, similar in magnitude, which themselves must be forecast. Even if imports and exports are determined independently and the forecast errors for imports and exports are small relative to their actual values, the forecast errors for their difference may well be of the same order as the difference itself. Many economic variables (such as savings, inventories, net investment, profits, and budget deficits) have similar characteristics. This problem need not appear when forecasting functions of the relevant variables other than their difference; for instance, the export-import ratio might be forecast with a high degree of accuracy.

For all models, the s-step-ahead forecast standard error tends to increase as the forecast horizon lengthens. The sharpest increase—from $9 billion in 1985:1 to $87 billion in 1987:4 with model M6—is due both to the omission

Table 14-5. *Forecast Performance for Models of the U.S. Trade Balance: One Step Ahead, Approximate Formula, 1985–87*

	1985 (quarter)				1986 (quarter)				1987 (quarter)				Summary measures of forecast performance[b]			
Model[a]	1	2	3	4	1	2	3	4	1	2	3	4	MAE	RMS FE	τ	τ*
Historical trade balance (billions of dollars)	−99.5	−119.8	−124.8	−144.5	−141.7	−135.4	−146.9	−154.1	−159.5	−158.2	−158.7	−164.8				
Mean forecast error (billions of dollars)																
M1	21.4	−4.1	−0.3	−3.0	2.4	−9.2	−25.0	−25.9	−19.7	−25.4	−17.9	−27.1	15.1	18.2	10.7	−1.6
M2	22.7	−0.7	2.6	0.1	2.4	−9.3	−27.1	−26.7	−18.7	−23.7	−12.2	−20.0	13.8	17.1	15.5	−1.8
M3	23.4	−1.5	6.2	2.9	−0.1	−13.6	−23.8	−17.8	−12.9	−12.0	5.5	−5.0	10.4	13.0	10.7	−0.9
M4	−15.8	−33.0	−3.2	0.1	20.0	23.2	24.6	−3.2	25.5	11.4	11.3	9.8	15.1	18.0	9.1	0.8
M5	23.6	−17.6	1.8	−30.2	−2.7	−11.9	−32.9	−24.2	−20.5	−14.8	−31.9	−49.0	21.8	25.3	17.2	−2.1
M6	23.0	−15.3	0.9	−12.9	10.1	13.0	−4.4	−0.1	2.5	8.9	7.5	1.7	8.4	10.7	19.7	0.3
Estimated standard error of the mean forecast error (billions of dollars)													σ̂			
M1	13.2	13.0	13.7	14.3	14.5	14.3	15.2	16.1	17.3	18.8	20.1	21.5	5.7			
M2	12.9	13.0	12.8	14.0	14.4	13.4	13.7	14.4	15.7	17.0	19.1	21.5	5.5			
M3	14.0	13.5	13.5	13.8	14.1	13.7	14.4	14.5	15.6	16.1	17.2	17.8	6.4			
M4	18.3	19.1	20.1	22.2	23.3	21.8	22.7	22.0	26.4	27.4	28.8	30.8	10.5			
M5	14.8	14.8	15.2	15.0	16.7	16.1	16.0	19.3	21.3	20.7	21.4	22.4	6.7			
M6	8.9	8.6	8.3	8.6	9.3	9.1	8.9	9.1	8.7	9.1	9.3	9.1	7.8			
Forecast error "t" ratio																
M1	1.6	−0.3	−0.0	−0.2	0.2	−0.6	−1.6	−1.6	−1.1	−1.4	−0.9	−1.3				
M2	1.8	−0.1	0.2	0.0	0.2	−0.7	−2.0	−1.9	−1.2	−1.4	−0.6	−0.9				
M3	1.7	−0.1	0.5	0.2	−0.0	−1.0	−1.7	−1.2	−0.8	−0.7	0.3	−0.3				
M4	−0.9	−1.7	−0.2	0.0	0.9	1.1	1.1	−0.1	1.0	0.4	0.4	0.3				
M5	1.6	−1.2	0.1	−2.0	−0.2	−0.7	−2.1	−1.3	−1.0	−0.7	−1.5	−2.2				
M6	2.6	−1.8	0.1	−1.5	1.1	1.4	−0.5	−0.0	0.3	1.0	0.8	0.2				

a. See table14-2, notes a and b.
b. MAE, mean absolute error; RMSFE, root-mean-square forecast error; σ̂, the estimated equation standard error of the implied equation for the trade balance, *in sample*; τ, the $\chi^2(12)$ statistic testing against predictive failure (its 5 percent and 10 percent levels are 21.0 and 18.5); τ*, the *t*-statistic testing against nonzero mean forecast error (its 5 percent and 10 percent levels for a two-tailed test are 2.2 and 1.8).

Figure 14-2. *Ninety-five Percent Confidence Intervals for Trade-Balance Forecasts: One Step Ahead, Approximate Formula, 1985–87*

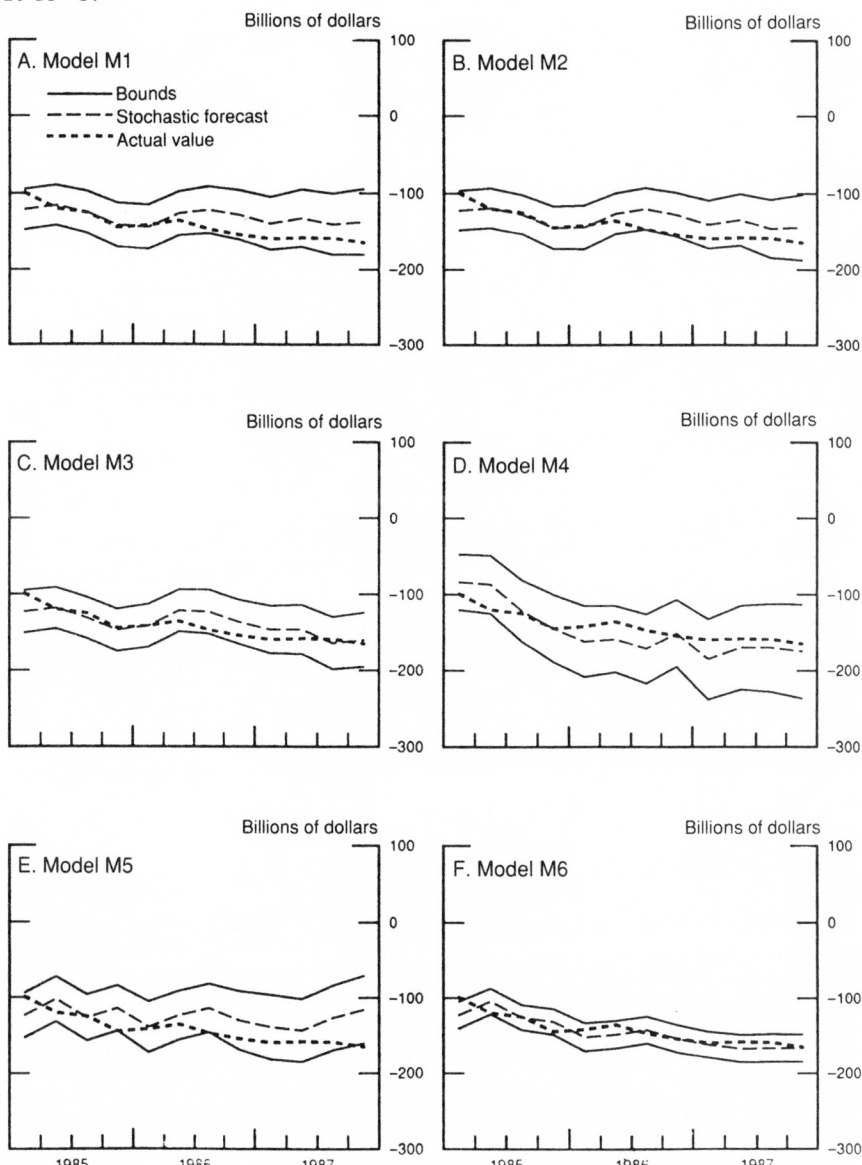

Table 14-6. *Forecast Performance for Models of the U.S. Trade Balance: s-Step Ahead, Approximate Formula, 1985–87*

Model[a]	1985 (quarter)				1986 (quarter)				1987 (quarter)				Summary measures of forecast performance[b]			
	1	2	3	4	1	2	3	4	1	2	3	4	MAE	RMSFE	τ	τ*
Historical trade balance (billions of dollars)																
	−99.5	−119.8	−124.8	−144.5	−141.7	−135.4	−146.9	−154.1	−159.5	−158.2	−158.7	−164.8				
Mean forecast error (billions of dollars)																
M1	21.4	6.5	5.6	2.7	5.8	−4.6	−22.8	−36.0	−40.0	−50.3	−50.5	−63.1	25.8	33.0	11.0	−1.7
M2	22.7	11.5	11.9	9.7	8.3	−4.8	−25.2	−38.3	−40.6	−48.1	−43.6	−53.5	26.5	31.4	13.8	−1.8
M3	23.4	13.7	14.1	10.9	5.8	−13.8	−32.8	−40.7	−40.4	−42.9	−31.0	−36.3	25.5	28.5	11.4	−1.4
M4	−15.8	−36.6	−15.9	−5.1	7.8	29.6	27.5	−0.1	13.0	−4.9	−7.4	−10.4	14.5	18.1	7.7	−0.2
M5	23.6	6.8	0.5	−25.6	−32.2	−36.5	−56.9	−73.4	−85.2	−87.7	−87.6	−90.3	50.5	59.9	7.9	−1.0
M6	23.0	8.8	10.3	−1.7	8.8	23.0	20.5	22.4	27.2	38.9	50.0	56.0	24.2	29.1	20.1	0.6
Estimated standard error of the mean forecast error (billions of dollars)																
M1	13.2	15.7	17.3	19.2	19.5	19.7	20.7	22.7	25.6	28.5	31.1	33.9				
M2	12.9	15.2	15.9	18.0	19.2	18.4	19.3	20.8	23.7	26.3	29.7	33.6				
M3	14.0	16.9	18.6	20.8	21.4	20.7	21.8	22.7	26.0	26.8	28.9	30.3				
M4	18.3	19.8	21.2	24.1	25.4	26.0	26.9	27.1	30.4	33.3	34.4	36.0				
M5	14.8	23.8	28.9	33.6	40.4	50.2	58.6	67.0	72.4	77.5	82.9	88.4				
M6	8.9	14.1	18.5	23.2	29.0	35.4	41.9	49.1	56.8	65.9	75.8	86.7				
Forecast error "t" ratio																
M1	1.6	0.4	0.3	0.1	0.3	−0.2	−1.1	−1.6	−1.6	−1.8	−1.6	−1.9				
M2	1.8	0.8	0.7	0.5	0.4	−0.3	−1.3	−1.8	−1.7	−1.8	−1.5	−1.6				
M3	1.7	0.8	0.8	0.5	0.3	−0.7	−1.5	−1.8	−1.6	−1.6	−1.1	−1.2				
M4	−0.9	−1.8	−0.7	−0.2	0.3	1.1	1.0	−0.0	0.4	−0.1	−0.2	−0.3				
M5	1.6	0.3	0.0	−0.8	−0.8	−0.7	−1.0	−1.1	−1.2	−1.1	−1.1	−1.0				
M6	2.6	0.6	0.6	−0.1	0.3	0.6	0.5	0.5	0.5	0.6	0.7	0.6				

a. See table 14-2, notes a and b.
b. See table 14-5, note b.

Figure 14-3. *Ninety-five Percent Confidence Intervals for Trade-Balance Forecasts: s Step Ahead, Approximate Formula, 1985–87*

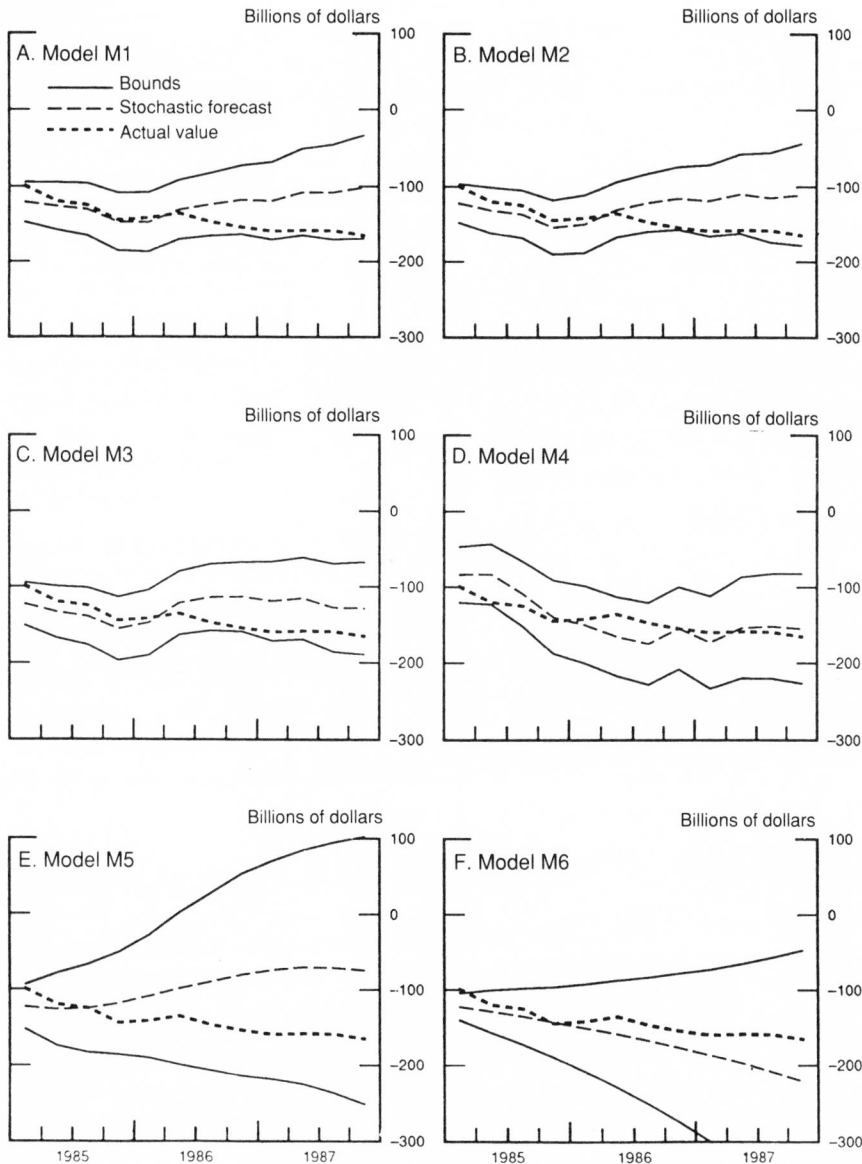

of "exogenous" variables in the model and to the presence of an estimated dynamic root close to unity. The tendency of forecast uncertainty to increase is robust to model specification, although it is less pronounced in the other models. The numerical size of the forecast standard error *is* sensitive to model specification: standard errors range from $8.9 billion (M6) to $18.3 billion (M4) in the first quarter and from $30 billion (M3) to $88 billion (M5) in the twelfth quarter (all figures in annual rates). FIML yields only small gains in precision, with the forecast standard errors for model M2 typically being 5–10 percent smaller than those for M1. Finally, the confidence intervals are not monotonically increasing in the forecast horizon, nor need they be (see Chong and Hendry 1986, p. 685; Calzolari 1987b, pp. 211–20; Hall and Henry 1988, pp. 251–58; and Ericsson and Marquez 1989).

The 95 percent s-step-ahead confidence intervals displayed in figure 14-3 often are larger than the realized trade balance itself. For models M1–M4, their confidence intervals are large despite taking "future" production costs, degree of rationing, trend factors, real incomes, GDP deflators, and *nominal exchange rates* as known. Standard errors for comparable ex ante forecasts of the trade balance would almost invariably be larger, perhaps similar to those for the (ex ante) time-series forecasts from models M5 and M6.

The numbers for the analysis above are all calculated using the approximate formula—that is, accounting for uncertainty from future shocks and estimation. The component from estimation can be substantial, as indicated by figures 14-4 and 14-5, which respecively plot one-step and s-step $\tilde{\sigma}_{T+s}$ from both the asymptotic and approximate formulas. In the extreme, the twelve-step-ahead forecast standard errors of M1, M2, and M5 nearly double, and that of M6 more than doubles, by accounting for the uncertainty from estimation.

The statistics τ and τ^* provide two measures of parameter constancy (equivalently, predictive failure) for the six models over the twelve quarters forecast. From the values of τ in tables 14-5 and 14-6, significant predictive failure is apparent in model M6 only. The one-step and s-step values of τ for model M6 are 19.7 and 20.1 respectively, slightly larger than their 10 percent critical value of 18.5 and slightly smaller than their 5 percent critical value of 21.0. Still, model M6 has smaller one-step-ahead MAE and RMSFE than do models M1–M5, reflecting its often small mean forecast errors. The statistic τ is significant for model M6 because model M6 *as estimated* implies that its forecast errors should have been even smaller. The statistic τ^* is statistically insignificant, except for model M5 with one-step-ahead forecasts.

The validity of the χ^2 and t distributions for τ and τ^* depends on the forecast errors being normally distributed under the null hypothesis. The errors are asymptotically normal for linear models, but need not be so for nonlinear ones. To examine the closeness to normality of the distribution of the forecast errors under the null, we have calculated Jarque and Bera's (1980) $\chi^2(2)$ statistic for the K simulated values of each forecast period of each model. The Jarque-Bera statistic tests whether skewness and excess kurtosis are zero (that is, whether they are what they would be if the error distribution were normal). If the number of replications is large, the statistic will have unit power for trivially small nonzero values of skewness and excess kurtosis, so the values of the sample moments are of interest as well. Tables 14A-6 through 14A-9 in the appendix report values of the Jarque-Bera statistic and the corresponding measures of skewness and excess kurtosis. Very little skewness and excess kurtosis are apparent in the stochastic forecasts for models M1–M4, whether statistically or numerically assessed. By contrast, considerable nonnormality is apparent in the s-step-ahead forecast errors from models M5 and M6 using the approximate formula, especially at longer horizons. This is not so surprising, given that all coefficient variation (constant term aside) is in the dynamics for these two models, and the dynamic coefficients enter nonlinearly for forecast horizons of more than one period, all the more nonlinearly for longer horizons. Thus, the assumption of normality of the ϕ_k appears reasonable for the most part, supporting the use of standard critical values for τ and τ^*.

The sample standard errors of the trade balance and its quarterly change are useful benchmarks against which to compare the estimated standard errors of the *one-step*-ahead forecasts. The sample standard error of the trade balance is interpretable as the one-step-ahead forecast standard error from a model in which the trade balance is a constant plus an independent, identically distributed error. Likewise, the sample standard error of the quarterly change in the trade balance is interpretable as the one-step-ahead forecast standard error from a model in which the trade balance is a (known) random walk with drift. These two sample standard errors measure actual trade-balance variation over the forecast period, whereas the estimated forecast standard errors measure the variation anticipated, given a specific model, and so given an information set from which to construct forecasts. The sample standard errors are respectively $19.5 billion and $10.5 billion at annual rates for 1985:1–1987:4, and correspond to two simple time-series models: a constant-mean, independent, identically distributed process and a random walk with drift. Also, these sample standard errors can be interpreted as measuring the unconditional variation of the trade balance and its change.

The sample standard error for the quarterly change in the trade balance is less than the estimated standard error for any forecast period of any structural model, even when using the asymptotic rather than approximate formula (see table 14A-4 in the appendix). This is surprising because the additional information used by models M1–M4 in forecasting (such as future incomes

Figure 14-4. *Standard Errors for One-Step-Ahead Forecasts, 1985–87*

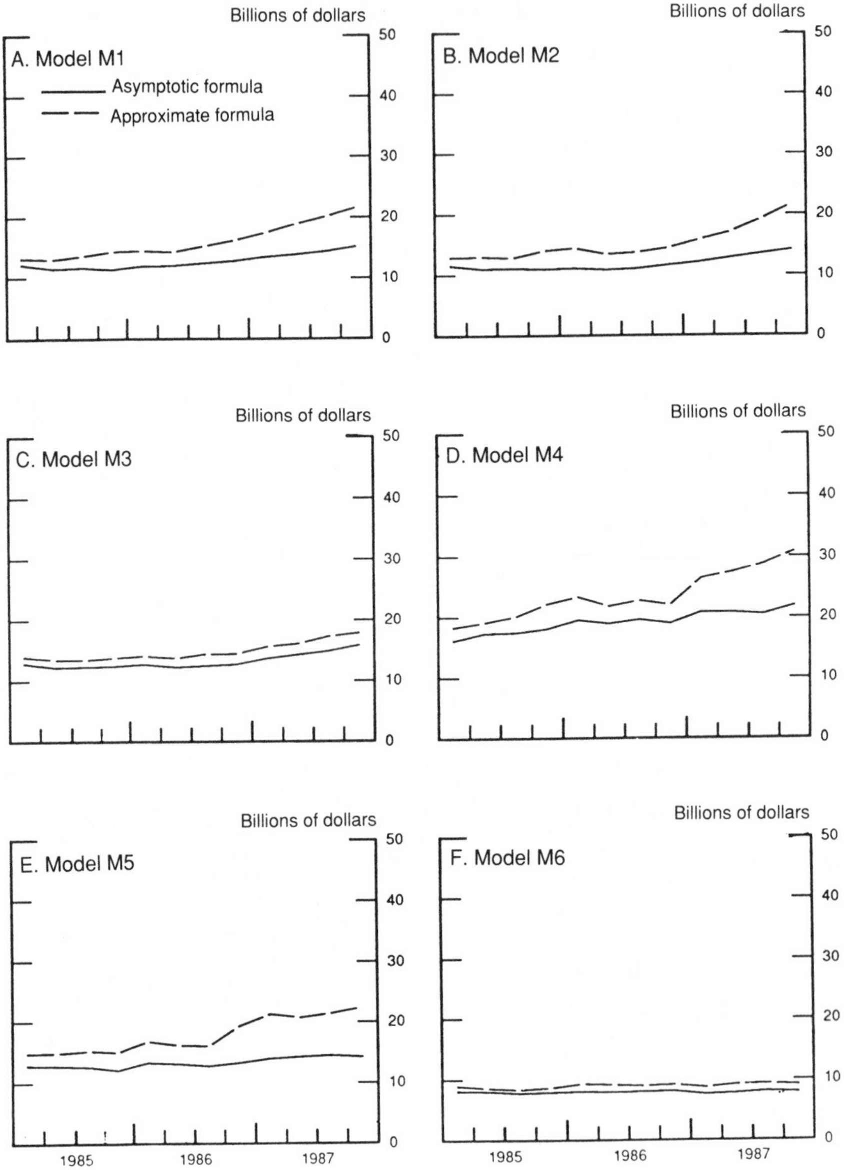

Billions of dollars

A. Model M1
——— Asymptotic formula
– – – Approximate formula

Billions of dollars

B. Model M2

Billions of dollars

C. Model M3

Billions of dollars

D. Model M4

Billions of dollars

E. Model M5

Billions of dollars

F. Model M6

1985   1986   1987

1985   1986   1987

Figure 14-5. *Standard Errors for s-Step-Ahead Forecasts, 1985–87*

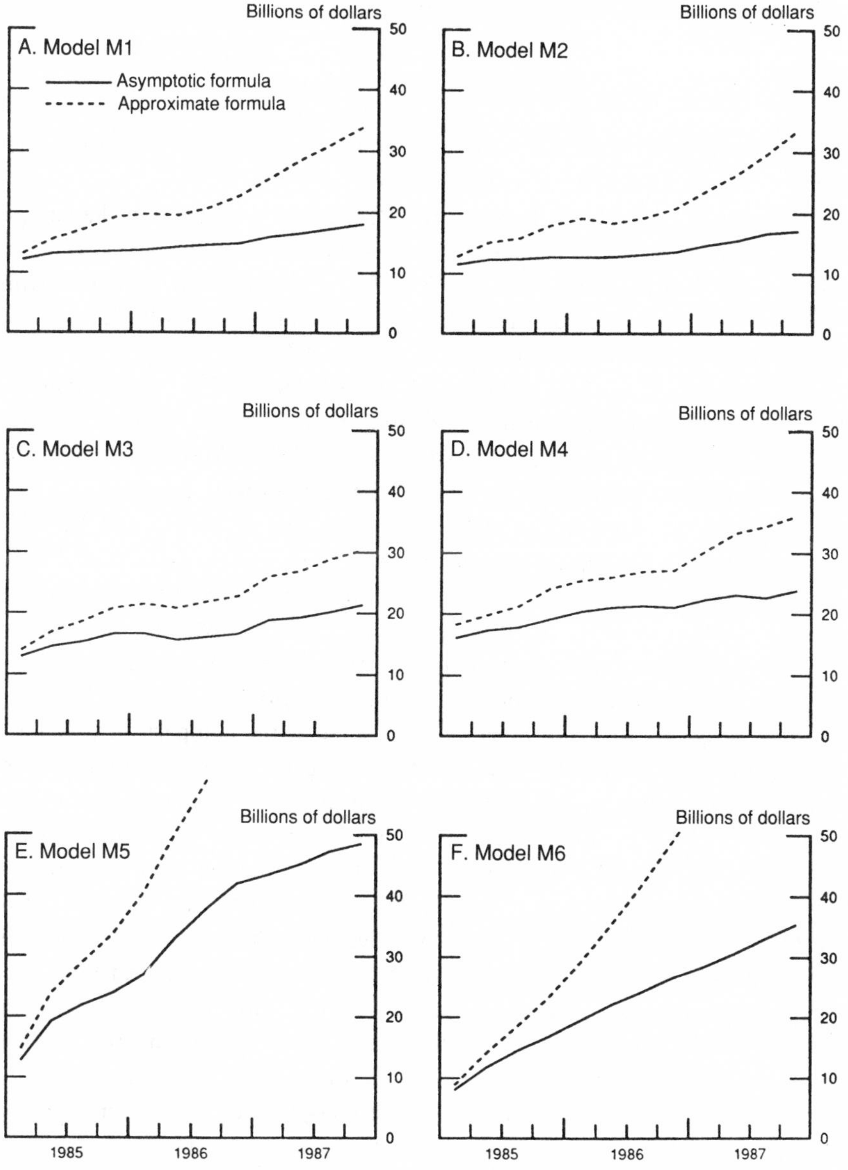

and exchange rates) should not increase the inherent forecast uncertainty and in general should reduce it. In statistical terms,

$$\text{var}(NX_t|I_t) \le \text{var}(NX_t),$$

where I_t is an information set, and the inequality often is strict. An interpretation of this empirical puzzle is given below.

A second comparison is between the RMSFE of a model and the sample standard errors of either the trade balance or its quarterly change, keeping in mind the caveats associated with the RMSFE. The estimated standard errors of the one-step-ahead forecasts are relatively constant (certainly by comparison to those of the s-step-ahead forecasts), so the RMSFE measures (roughly) the observed *conditional* variation of the trade balance. The sample standard error for the quarterly change measures the observed *unconditional* variation of that change and is less than any structural model's RMSFE. Alternatively interpreted, the one-step-ahead RMSFE of the random-walk model is less than that of any of the structural models, paralleling one of Meese and Rogoff's (1983) results for forecasts of exchange rates.[20] However, as implied by the forecast-encompassing results in the next section, the random-walk model for the trade balance is *not* the best forecasting model on the available information set. That contrasts with the (now) conventional wisdom for exchange rates.

These two sets of comparisons suggest that the information set for modeling and forecasting is not used efficiently. In particular, the comparison of sample standard errors and RMSFEs shows that ignoring all that information, except the lagged trade balance, produces better forecasts over this period than those actually obtained using that information. Equally, from the variance inequality above, a model could be constructed from the information set of any one of the structural models, such that that resulting model's estimated standard error and RMSFE would be as small as (or smaller than) the sample standard error for the quarterly change. These results do not specify how to construct such a model, but only that one could be constructed with those properties. As described below, lack of forecast encompassing has a similar constructive role.

Two general conclusions are evident for the models examined. First, the trade-balance forecasts are subject to a wide margin of error, even in the short run. Yet, despite the large confidence intervals implied, forecast errors from some models are detectably larger than anticipated, as indicated by rejection using τ and τ^*. Second, forecast uncertainty is time dependent, with both

---

20. The sample standard errors and the RMSFEs are themselves estimates, so the difference between the sample standard error of the quarterly change and a given RMSFE might be statistically insignificant. Even so, the RMSFE often is 50 percent or 100 percent (or more) larger than the sample standard error. Such numerically large discrepancies warrant concern, irrespective of their statistical properties.

dynamics and model nonlinearity as contributing factors. Although not mono-tonic, the forecast variance tends to increase with the forecast horizon, par-ticularly so for s-step-ahead forecasts. Nonconstancy of the forecast variance implies that the MAE and RMSFE may be unreliable evaluation criteria, even when interpreted in what would be a sensible manner for static linear mod-els. By contrast, the statistics τ and τ^* are robust to time-dependent forecast uncertainty.

Additional Applications of Stochastically Simulated Forecasts

This section considers two additional ways that stochastically generated fore-casts can help evaluate trade models: forecast-encompassing tests and estima-tion of the nonlinearity biases of deterministic forecasts.

Forecast Encompassing

As seen in the preceding section, model-based forecasts can help evaluate model performance by comparing characteristics of a given model across *dif-ferent* subsamples (for example, with the test statistics τ and τ^*). With fore-casts from more than one model, models may be evaluated with a different criterion—forecast encompassing—in which a model's forecasts over a given period are compared with another model's forecasts over the *same* period.

Intuitively, the question of interest is whether or not the forecast *errors* of a given model (model h, say) may be explained (at least in part) by the *forecasts* of another model (model l). Under the null hypothesis of model h being correctly specified, the forecast errors from model h are innovations, unpredictable by any information available at the time the forecasts were made, including the data of model l, and hence the forecasts of model l. If in fact model h's forecast errors are not predictable by model l's forecasts, then model h "forecast-encompasses" model l. That is, given model h's forecasts, model l's forecasts are redundant for predicting the variable of interest. However, if model l's forecasts *are* informative, model h is inadequate for forecasting, having predictable forecast errors. Model l then has useful information that model h does not have. Equivalently, relying on model h alone entails a loss of information.

Tests of forecast encompassing are simple to calculate because they are based on a regression of the forecast errors of one model on the forecasts of another. We generalize Chong and Hendry's (1986) forecast-encompassing statistic in several directions: (1) inclusion of a constant term, to detect sys-tematic biases in the forecast; (2) comparison against several models at once, rather than just one; (3) allowance for model nonlinearity, and so forecast-error heteroscedasticity; (4) allowance for multistep-ahead forecasts, which have inherently autocorrelated forecast errors, as shown by Chong and Hendry (1986, equation 26) and Hendry (forthcoming, chap. 10); and (5) accounting for the uncertainty from estimating rather than knowing model coefficients.[21] The last three are more complicated technically and are solved by feasible generalized least squares (GLS) estimation using $\hat{\Phi}(h)$, the (Monte Carlo-based) estimated variance-covariance matrix of model h's forecast errors. White's (1980) heteroscedasticity-consistent standard errors offer a computationally convenient alternative approach for conducting inference under (3), and can be easily generalized to address the autocorrelation arising from (4), as in Fair and Shiller (1990). Still, "correcting" only the standard error generally results in a less powerful procedure than that from GLS, so we use GLS.

All models fail the forecast-encompassing tests, notably so with s-step-ahead forecasts. The mean forecasts from the structural models help explain the mean forecast errors of each of the time-series models, suggesting that the latter lack important economic determinants. Conversely, the value of forecasts from the time-series models in explaining the forecast errors of the structural models suggests dynamic misspecification of the structural models. To summarize, every model contains information that would be valuable in improving the other models, and every model could be improved (see Marquez and Ericsson 1990, section 4 and appendix C, and Ericsson and Marquez 1993, for further details).

For expositions on forecast encompassing, see Chong and Hendry (1986), who developed the concept of forecast encompassing and clarified its relationship to the pooling (or combination) of forecasts; and Ericsson (1992), who established parallels between forecast encompassing and the testing of nonnested hypotheses. On encompassing in general, see Mizon and Richard (1986), Hendry and Richard (1989), and Ericsson and Hendry (1989).

Nonlinearity Bias

In general, deterministic forecasts from nonlinear models are biased: the expectation of a nonlinear function is not usually equal to the function of the expectations. Here, the mean forecast is a nonlinear function of the future disturbances and the coefficient estimates. In principle, the mean of the trade-balance forecast from any of models M1–M6 may be computed by numerically integrating equation 14-9 over these random variables, but practical difficulties

---

21. After presenting this paper at the Brookings conference in March 1990, we learned that Fisher and Wallis (1990) had independently proposed the first two generalizations.

arise from both the number of random variables and the absence of a closed-form solution. As an alternative to numerical integration, we estimate the expectation by Monte Carlo simulation, using the variance-reduction technique antithetic variates. By exploiting the symmetry of the distribution of ($\{\eta_{k,s}\}$, ζ_k) (the random drawings in the preceding section), this method provides a much more precise estimate of the expectation than that offered by the standard Monte Carlo estimator. Specifically, the values ($\{\eta_{k,s}\}$, ζ_k) and ($\{-\eta_{k,s}\}$, $-\zeta_k$) are equally likely (by symmetry). Little additional computational expense is required to calculate a simulated trade balance from each, rather than from just the first, so that *pairs* of trade-balance forecasts are generated from these pairs of sets of random numbers. Each of the two forecasts of a given pair is unbiased, and the two forecasts of a pair tend to be negatively correlated because they are functions of oppositely signed random numbers. Thus, the average of the two forecasts is also unbiased, but generally has a much smaller variance than either of the individual forecasts. The final estimate of the mean forecast is constructed as the average over the 1,000 replications of the averaged pairs of forecasts. That estimate, less the deterministic forecast, is the estimated nonlinearity bias.

Some deterministic forecasts from each model have statistically significant nonlinearity biases. For models M1–M3, however, the biases typically are less than \$2 billion, so their economic significance is minor. The considerable accuracy with which antithetic variates estimate the mean of the trade-balance forecasts makes such numerically small departures from unbiasedness statistically significant. Specifically, using antithetic variates rather than averages from standard Monte Carlo simulation increases the precision of the estimated nonlinearity bias by fourfold to over 2,000-fold. That is, the variance of the estimated bias from antithetic variates ranges from 1/4 to less than 1/2,000 of the variance of the estimated bias from standard Monte Carlo simulation. Comparable gains in efficiency were obtained by Hendry and Trivedi (1972) in a Monte Carlo study of econometric estimators and by Calzolari (1979) and Fisher and Salmon (1986) for nonlinearity biases.

Models M4–M6 have much larger and economically potentially important biases: for instance, approximately \$10 billion at twelve periods ahead. These biases appear to arise because of dynamics for M5 and M6 and because of country disaggregation for M4. With such substantive nonlinearity biases, deterministic forecasts will be at an inherent disadvantage in forecasting performance relative to (unbiased) stochastic forecasts (see Marquez and Ericsson 1990, section 5 and appendixes C and D, for further details).

For concise discussions of Monte Carlo analysis, including the use of antithetic variates, see Hammersley and Handscomb (1964) and Hendry (1984). See Nagar (1969) and Howrey and Kelejian (1969), among others, for early studies that recognized systematic biases in deterministic forecasts arising from model nonlinearities. More recently, Mariano and Brown (1983) and Fair (1984, 1988) estimated such biases by standard Monte Carlo techniques; and Calzolari (1979), Fisher and Salmon (1986), and Mariano and Brown (1989) did so by antithetic variates.

Conclusions

This chapter has generalized existing methodology for evaluating forecasts and applied it to forecasts over 1985:1–1987:4 from six econometric models of the U.S. trade balance. The predictive performance of these models has implications for econometric practice, trade modeling, and the role of these models in policymaking.

Deterministic forecasts are shown to be an unreliable basis for assessing model performance, both because they typically lack a measure of forecast uncertainty and because they tend to be biased for nonlinear models. Forecasts generated by stochastic simulation are a simple, computationally feasible alternative without these problems and can allow for uncertainty not only from the disturbances but also from coefficient estimation. Confidence intervals for the forecasts are immediately obtainable from stochastic simulation.

Measures of forecast uncertainty aid the interpretation of forecasts in many situations, including ex ante prediction, counterfactual policy simulation, and the evaluation of the forecasting models themselves. For the last, intramodel and intermodel analyses based on stochastic forecasts are easily conducted with parameter constancy and forecast-encompassing test statistics, and each of these statistics provides unique information about the models. Stochastic simulation with antithetic variates offers an efficient, reliable technique for detecting and assessing nonlinearity biases.

Empirically, the confidence intervals of the trade-balance forecasts are very large and are generally increasing with the forecast horizon. Both features are common across the models, even though the models differ in several basic attributes that might have influenced the results: model size, dynamic specification, choice of "exogenous" variables, estimation method, and level of country and commodity aggregation. The forecast errors are large and systematic, and the 95 percent confidence interval of even a one-step-ahead forecast is often an order of magnitude greater than the quarter-to-quarter (or month-to-month) trade-balance fluctuations receiving attention by policymakers. The uncertainty of the model-based forecasts clearly tempers the role of these models in formulating policy.

Despite this large uncertainty, the forecast-encompassing tests indicate that forecast errors from each of the six trade-balance models examined are in part predictable by the forecasts (and so the data) of the other models. That is, each model involves a loss of information relative to the other models. Conversely, those tests imply that better forecasts *are* obtainable from the data currently used in modeling. However, to assess the *magnitude* of the implied feasible reduction in forecast uncertainty, we must await the development of an improved model.

Finally, the deterministic forecasts of several models are subject to substantial biases from model nonlinearity. As a rule, ignoring such biases degrades forecast performance.

The numerical results of the stochastic simulation depend only in part on the estimation and forecast samples chosen. Specifically, confidence intervals for other forecast periods should be similar to those obtained for 1985:1–1987:4 because models M1–M6 are very nearly linear. The forecast confidence interval of a well-specified model shrinks with longer estimation periods, but this need not occur for models M1–M6, given the misspecification evident from the forecast-encompassing tests. The values of the predictive failure tests τ and τ^* and the forecast-encompassing tests could be either larger or smaller for other estimation and forecast samples.

As currently implemented, the models in this analysis are subject to many limitations. Two of the most important are the chosen dynamic specifications and the assumed weak exogeneity of income, GDP deflators, and the exchange rate. Testing these and other assumptions and redesigning the models in light of the outcomes almost certainly would modify the numerical results obtained above. Even so, the message of this chapter remains the same: model-based forecasts are random variables, and accounting for their distributional properties is essential for interpreting the forecasts properly, whether in policy analysis, model evaluation, or ex ante prediction exercises.

Appendix: Description of Data, Calculation of Standard Errors for Trade Elasticities, and Additional Results

This appendix describes data for the Helkie-Hooper model and its closest variants (M1–M3), the bilateral trade model (M4), the VAR (M5), and the univariate AR model (M6). Data sources appear as italicized abbreviations and are described under "Data Sources," below. The appendix also describes our calculation of standard errors for trade elasticities and presents additional results.

Data for Models M1–M3

All series for these models are maintained in the data bank of the trade model developed in Helkie and Hooper (1988). Unless otherwise noted, all dollars are U.S. dollars.

EXPORTS, IMPORTS, THEIR DEFLATORS, AND THE TRADE BALANCE. The nominal values of agricultural exports and nonagricultural exports are in billions of dollars, quarterly at annual rates, and come from *NIA* table 4.3. Real exports are in billions of (constant) 1982 dollars, quarterly at annual rates, and come from *NIA* table 4.4. The price deflators for agricultural and nonagricultural exports are obtained as the ratios between the respective nominal and real exports.

Nominal and real values of non-oil imports are in billions of (current and 1982) dollars, quarterly at annual rates, and come from *NIA* tables 4.3 and 4.4 respectively. The non-oil import deflator is constructed as the ratio between nominal and real non-oil imports.

The nominal value of oil imports is in billions of dollars, quarterly at annual rates, and comes from *NIA* table 4.3. The volume of oil imports, quarterly in billions of barrels per year, is constructed as the excess of domestic consumption over the sum of domestic production and inventory drawdowns:

$$MQFL = FLC - FLQ + FLSCN,$$

where $MQFL$, FLC, FLQ, and $FLSCN$ are respectively oil imports, oil consumption, oil production, and the change in oil inventories (all quarterly in billions of barrels per year, taken from *DOE*). The unit value of oil imports is obtained as the ratio between the nominal value and the volume of oil imports.

The nominal trade balance, in billions of dollars, quarterly at annual rates, is constructed as the difference between the nominal value of exports and the nominal value of imports.

GNP AND CPI. Real U.S. GNP comes from *NIA* table 1.2. The U.S. GNP and consumption deflators are constructed as ratios between nominal magnitudes (*NIA* table 1.1) and real variables (*NIA* table 1.2). U.S. capacity utilization comes from *FRB* table 2.12.

Foreign GNP is constructed as a geometric mean of the levels of foreign GNPs, using the weights in table 14A-1. The sources for foreign GNPs are *CSR* (Canada); *BOJ* (Japan); *ET* (United Kingdom); *Statistical Supplement, DBB* (Germany); *Comptes Nationales, INSEE* (France); *INSTAT* (Italy); *Bulletin de Statistique,* Institute National de Statistique (Belgium); *Kwartaalrekeningen,* Central Bureau of Statistics (Netherlands); *Reflets de L'Economie,* Office Fédéral de la Statistique (Switzerland); and *National Accounts,* National Central Bureau of Statistics (Sweden).

The foreign consumer price index (CPI) is constructed as a geometric mean of the country-specific consumer price indices, using the trade weights in table 14A-1. The sources for the individual CPIs are *CSR* (Canada); *BOJ*

Table 14A-1. *1978–83 Average Trade Weights for the G10 Countries*

Percent

Country	Trade weight	Country	Trade weight
Canada	9.1	Belgium	6.4
Japan	13.6	Netherlands	8.3
United Kingdom	11.9	Switzerland	3.6
Germany	20.8	Sweden	4.2
France	13.1		
Italy	9.0	Total	100.0

(Japan); *Employment Gazette,* Department of Employment (United Kingdom); *DBB* (Germany); *Bulletin Mensuel de Statistique, INSEE* (France); *INSTAT* (Italy); *Bulletin de la Banque Nationale,* National Bank of Belgium (Belgium); *Maandstatistiek, van de Pryzen,* Central Bureau of Statistics (Netherlands); *La Vie Economique,* Département Fédéral de l'Economie Publique (Switzerland); and *Allman Manadsstatistik,* Swedish Official Statistical Office (Sweden). Each trade weight is the average over 1978–83 of the given country's share in the group's total imports. The source of these nominal imports is *IFS,* line 77abd.

COMMODITY PRICE. The world nonfuel commodity price comes from the *IFS* commodity price table (line 001).

CAPITAL STOCK. Relative capital stocks are constructed as ratios between the U.S. capital stock and the respective foreign capital stocks. For every country, the (real) capital stock equals cumulated real gross fixed investment. Real investment equals nominal investment deflated by the GNP (GDP) deflator. Nominal investment comes from *IFS* (line 93e), and the GNP (GDP) deflator is obtained as the ratio between nominal and real GNP (GDP), with both nominal and real variables taken from *IFS,* typically lines 99a (99b) and 99a.r (99b.r). Capital stocks for foreign industrialized countries (*KDC*) and for developing countries (*KLDC*) are constructed as geometric means of the capital stocks of selected countries, where the weights are 1978–83 multilateral trade weights. For *KDC,* the countries and weights are Belgium (0.061), Canada (0.068), France (0.112), Germany (0.151), Italy (0.081), Japan (0.132), Netherlands (0.069), Sweden (0.029), Switzerland (0.030), United Kingdom (0.102), Australia (0.023), Austria (0.019), Denmark (0.017), Finland (0.014), Greece (0.007), Ireland (0.009), New Zealand (0.005), Norway (0.016), Portugal (0.006), Spain (0.025), Turkey (0.006), and South Africa (0.018). For *KLDC,* the countries and weights are Brazil (0.142), India (0.076), Israel (0.051), South Korea (0.149), Malaysia (0.079), Mexico (0.108), Philippines (0.044), Singapore (0.149), Taiwan (0.149), and Thailand (0.053). An overall foreign capital stock is constructed as the geometric mean of *KDC* and *KLDC*:

$$KFOREIGN = KDC^{0.767}KLDC^{0.233}.$$

The country-specific weights and the weights on *KDC* and *KLDC* are the country's (or countries') average share(s) in the corresponding group's total imports. The source of these imports is *IFS* (line 77abd).

EXCHANGE RATES AND U.S. PRODUCER PRICE INDICES. The weighted average of the dollar relative to G10 currencies is constructed as a geometric mean of the bilateral exchange rates, using the weights in table 14A-1. The bilateral exchange rates are from *FRB* table 3.28.

The U.S. producer price index (PPI), with export weights, is constructed as a geometric mean of the PPIs for durable manufacturing, nondurable manufacturing, and petroleum products. The weights are the 1982 shares of these products in their combined export value. The source of the individual PPIs is the "PPI Press Release" of the Bureau of Labor Statistics, U.S. Department of Labor. The source of the weights is *Highlights of Exports and Imports Trade* (FT990) from the Bureau of Economic Analysis, U.S. Department of Commerce.

Data for Model M4

Model M4 is described in Marquez (1989). All of the series for M4 are maintained in the data bank of the Federal Reserve Board's Multicountry Model (see Edison, Marquez, and Tryon 1987). The countries modeled in M4 are Canada, Germany, Japan, the United Kingdom, the rest of the OECD countries (ROECD), non-OPEC developing countries (LDCs), and OPEC.

EXPORTS, IMPORTS, THEIR DEFLATORS, AND THE TRADE BALANCE. All (nominal) bilateral trade flows are in billions of dollars, f.o.b. (free on board), quarterly at annual rates, and come from *DOT* (1987).

To estimate the value of imports in 1972 dollars from each of Canada, Germany, Japan, and the United Kingdom, the nominal dollar value of U.S. (bilateral) imports from a given country s is deflated by P_sE_s, where P_s is the *multilateral export* unit value of country s in local currency (with 1972 = 1.00) and E_s is the dollar exchange rate index (dollars per local currency, with 1972 = 1.00). The value P_sE_s estimates the associated dollar import price. It uses the multilateral export price rather than the bilateral trade price because long series of quarterly data for the latter are not publicly available.

Thus, the deflator for *imports* from country s is $P_s E_s$ (1972 = 1.00). The sources for the multilateral export unit values of the four countries involved are *CSR*, D50501×100/D40587 (Canada); *DBB*, XU0110 (Germany); *IFS*, line 74 divided by its value in 1972 (Japan); and *ET*, CGTO (United Kingdom).

The export price for the ROECD is measured as a geometric mean of the country-specific *dollar* export prices of the countries in this aggregate, where those prices come from the *IFS*. The weight on each export price is the sample mean of the same country's export share in total exports of the ROECD. The countries in the ROECD are as follows, with the corresponding weight and *IFS* line number in parentheses: Austria (5 percent, 122), Belgium (15 percent, 126), France (26 percent, 132), Italy (18 percent, 136), Netherlands (17 percent, 138), Norway (4 percent, 142), Sweden (8 percent, 144), and Switzerland (7 percent, 146). For these export prices and for the LDC export price (below), the line numbers are from *IFS* table 74d of "Export Unit Values," whereas other *IFS* data are from the *IFS* country-specific tables. The source for the LDC export price is *IFS* (line 201). For OPEC, the export price is the oil market price, in dollars, as reported by the *IEA*. The value of U.S. exports in 1972 dollars is estimated as the nominal value of total bilateral exports deflated by the U.S. *multilateral* export unit value P_{US}. The source for P_{US} is the "U.S. Import/Export Unit Value Press Release" (discontinued as of June 1989), published by the U.S. Department of Commerce, Bureau of the Census.

The procedures used for constructing real trade flows assume that the commodity mix of country s's exports to the United States is (and remains) the same as that to other countries, and likewise for U.S. exports to country s. The nominal trade balance (billions of dollars, quarterly at annual rates) is constructed as the difference between the sum of the nominal values of bilateral exports and the sum of the nominal values of bilateral imports.

Two caveats on the trade balance for M4 must be noted for the forecast analysis in this chapter. First, the numerical values of the trade balance for M1–M3 are not the same as those for M4 because the sources are different (*NIA* versus *DOT*). To standardize the forecast analysis, we use the numbers from the *NIA,* which are those for the Helkie-Hooper (1988) model. The percentage discrepancies between the two trade-balance series can be substantial, the maximum over the forecast period being 26.5 percent ($31.8 billion) in 1985:2. Even so, *estimation* of M4 uses the *DOT* numbers. Second, trade with countries not modeled in M4 are aggregated into a rest-of-world sector (ROW), whose imports and exports are treated as known in forecasting. By contrast, M1–M3 treat all imports and exports as endogenous. This difference should not give M4 much of an inherent advantage in forecasting, noting that the maximum percentages over the forecast period of ROW imports, exports, and trade balance (in absolute value) out of total figures are 6.8 percent, 4.3 percent, and 11.1 percent respectively.

TARIFFS. Goods imported are often subject to tariffs, which in turn affect the price paid by the consumer. The imputed price (P_{ks}) of country k's imports from country s is constructed as $P_{ks} = E_{ks}(1 + \tau_k)P_s$, where E_{ks} is the bilateral exchange rate between countries k and s (see below), τ_k is the average ad valorem tariff rate of country k, and P_s is the multilateral export unit value of country s in local currency (described above). These imputed prices determine (in part) the demand for different bilateral imports in M4.

The tariff rate is available only for the United States and is constructed as the share of total (multilateral) tariff receipts in total U.S. imports. (Hence, the tariff rates on goods imported by countries other than the United States are assumed to be zero.) The source for tariff receipts is the *Monthly Bulletin,* U.S. Department of the Treasury.

THIRD-COUNTRY IMPORT PRICES. Imports from one country often face competition by imports from another country. For instance, U.S. imports of Japanese cars face competition by U.S. imports of German cars. Thus, the bilateral trade equations include third-country import prices. For instance, the equation for country k's imports from country s includes a geometrically weighted average of country k's import prices from country q ($q \neq s, k$), constructed as

$$P_{k|s} = \prod_{q \neq s, k} [E_{kq}P_q]^{\omega_q},$$

where ω_q is the share of the qth country in the group's total exports, and P_q is the multilateral export unit value of country q in local currency (described above). The aggregation of export prices of various countries into a single index makes two important assumptions: first, country k's imports from country s are strongly separable from country k's imports from countries other than s; second, the elasticity of substitution among imports from countries other than s is unity.

REAL INCOME, AND GNP (GDP) DEFLATORS. Real incomes for Canada, Germany, Japan, the United Kingdom, and the United States are defined as real GNP (or GDP) measured in domestic currency. The sources are *CSR,* Series D40593 (Canada); *DIW* (Germany); *BOJ* (Japan); *ET* (United Kingdom); and *NIA,* table 1.2 (United States). For the ROECD and the LDCs, real income is measured as a geometric mean of industrial production, using the means of trade shares as weights. For ROECD, industrial production is from *IFS* (line 66), and the countries and weights are the same as for export prices above. The countries included as LDCs are as follows, with weights and *IFS* line numbers in parentheses: South Korea (32 percent, 66), Mexico (36 percent, 66), and Taiwan (32 percent). Taiwan's industrial production is reported in *Financial Statistics* (Bank of China, Taiwan District), line 66. In view of data difficulties, the model assumes that OPEC's income equals OPEC's real exports.

Each GNP (GDP) deflator is constructed as the nominal value of GNP (GDP) divided by the corresponding real value. The sources are *CSR*, table 1.2 (Canada); *DIW* (Germany); *BOJ* (Japan); *ET*, table 2 (United Kingdom); and *NIA,* table 7.1 (United States). In view of data difficulties, the model assumes that the deflators for the ROECD, LDCs, and OPEC are their export prices. For instance, the equation for U.S. exports to OPEC uses OPEC's export price as a proxy for OPEC's GNP price deflator.

POTENTIAL OUTPUT. Potential output for Canada, Germany, Japan, the United Kingdom, and the United States is generated using Cobb-Douglas production functions. These functions include labor, capital, oil, and imports as inputs, and the associated parameters are estimated econometrically. The estimated elasticities are 4 percent to 14 percent for the share of capital, 60 percent to 80 percent for the share of labor, 4 percent to 7 percent for the share of oil, and 8 percent to 18 percent for the share of imports. See Edison, Marquez, and Tryon (1987) for details. Potential output paths for the LDCs and the ROECD are generated as fitted trends to actual output.

EXCHANGE RATES. Only four bilateral exchange rates are used: the Canadian dollar, the West German deutsche mark, the pound sterling, and the Japanese yen, all as quarterly averages against the U.S. dollar. The source is *FRB,* table 3.28. Export prices for the ROECD, LDCs, and OPEC are in U.S. dollars, as are the values of U.S. bilateral trade with them, so it is not necessary to calculate exchange rates for them.

Data for Model M5

Model M5 is a logarithmic VAR explaining real exports and imports by the United States and the price deflators for these two trade flows. The nominal values of multilateral exports and imports are in billions of dollars, quarterly at annual rates, and come from *NIA* table 4.3. Real exports and imports are in billions of (constant) 1982 dollars, quarterly at annual rates, and come from *NIA* table 4.4. The associated price deflators for these trade flows are obtained as the ratios between the respective nominal and real exports. The nominal trade balance (billions of dollars, quarterly at annual rates) is constructed as the difference between the nominal value of exports and the nominal value of imports.

Data for Model M6

Model M6 explains the nominal trade balance by its lagged value alone. The only variable involved is the trade balance itself, and it is constructed as the difference between the nominal values of exports and imports, both in billions of dollars, quarterly at annual rates. See the first subsection in this appendix for details.

Data Sources

Principal sources of data used in the analysis are as follows:

BOJ   *Economic Statistics Monthly,* Bank of Japan (Tokyo), monthly

CSR   *Canadian Statistical Review,* Statistics Canada (Ottawa), quarterly

DBB   *Monthly Report,* Deutsche Bundesbank (Frankfurt am Main), monthly

DIW   *Lange Reihen der vierteljahrlichen volkswirtschaftlichen Gesamtrechnung für die Bundesrepublik Deutschland,* Deutsches Institute für Wirtschaftsforshung (Berlin), quarterly

DOE   *Monthly Petroleum Statistics,* U.S. Department of Energy (Washington, D.C.), monthly

DOT   *Direction of Trade Statistics,* International Monetary Fund (Washington, D.C.), monthly

ET   *Economic Trends,* U.K. Central Statistical Office (London), monthly

FRB   *Federal Reserve Bulletin,* Board of Governors of the Federal Reserve System (Washington, D.C.), monthly

IEA   "End of Month Oil Market Report," International Energy Agency (Paris), monthly

IFS   *International Financial Statistics,* International Monetary Fund (Washington, D.C.), monthly

INSEE   *Comptes Nationales* and *Bulletin Mensuel de Statistique,* Institute National de la Statistique et des Etudes Economiques (Paris), quarterly and monthly respectively

INSTAT   *Indicatori Mensili,* Instituto Centrale di Statistica (Rome), monthly

NIA   "National Income Accounts," in *Survey of Current Business,* U.S. Department of Commerce, Bureau of Economic Analysis (Washington, D.C.), monthly.

Calculation of Standard Errors for Trade Elasticities

Because of model design, the long-run elasticities for models M3 and M4 are nonlinear functions of the estimated coefficients. For example, the estimate of the long-run income elasticity for exports of model M4 is constructed as

$$\hat{a}'_{2j} = \hat{\alpha}'_{2j}/(1 - \hat{\alpha}'_{0j}),$$

where the notation follows that in table 14-1. By being the ratio of two estimates, each of which is approximately normally distributed, the distribution of $\hat{a}'_{2j}$ is difficult to handle analytically (see Marsaglia 1965). So, to estimate the properties of $\hat{a}'_{2j}$, we assume that the coefficient estimates have an exact joint normal distribution with a mean and covariance matrix given by the estimated coefficients and their estimated covariance matrix. We generate a random sample of values for $(\hat{\alpha}'_{2j}, \hat{\alpha}'_{0j})$ following that distribution and, for each set of values, calculate the corresponding elasticity by substitution into the equation above. From that sample of simulated elasticities, estimates of the mean and the standard deviation of the simulated $\hat{a}_{2j}$ are calculated, and they appear in table 14-3. This procedure generates standard errors for the estimated elasticities similar to those from the standard analytical formula for asymptotic standard errors of a nonlinear function of estimates, which are themselves asymptotically normally distributed (see Silvey 1975, pp. 115–16). We use the 1,000 replications of the coefficient estimates from the stochastic simulation as the random sample of values for $(\hat{\alpha}'_{2j}, \hat{\alpha}'_{0j})$.

Strictly speaking, the moments of $\hat{a}'_{2j}$ as simulated in *this* Monte Carlo study do not exist because $(\hat{\alpha}'_{2j}, \hat{\alpha}'_{0j})$ is assumed normally distributed. However, the lack of moments may be relatively unimportant. First, provided that $[1 - E(\hat{\alpha}'_{0j})]/\sqrt{\text{var}(\hat{\alpha}'_{0j})}$ is relatively large (for example, 3 or 4), this Monte Carlo simulation is unlikely to generate "extreme" values of $\hat{a}'_{2j}$, so the finite-*replication* Monte Carlo estimates of the mean and variance of $\hat{a}'_{2j}$ may be well-behaved (see Sargan 1982). Second, the econometric (rather than Monte Carlo) finite-sample moments of $\hat{a}'_{2j}$ may or may not exist, regardless. Third, alternative measures are easily calculated from the Monte Carlo simulation (for example, the median simulated elasticities and their 95 percent confidence intervals).

Tables 14A-2 and 14A-3 summarize the statistical properties of the Monte Carlo distributions for the elasticity estimates of models M3 and M4 respectively. The statistics reported are the mean, median, standard deviation, scaled median absolute deviation, minimum, maximum, and the critical values for the 95 percent confidence interval. Overall, the evidence reveals that the distributions are well behaved; that is, they are fairly symmetrical and have few extreme values. Exceptions to this pattern are oil consumption in model M3 and the U.K. export price (and so U.K. pass-through) in model M4. For the former, the ratio $[1 - \hat{E}(\hat{\alpha}'_{0j})]/\sqrt{\text{vâr}(\hat{\alpha}'_{0j})}$ is 2.4, whereas for the latter this ratio is even smaller (1.4). These relatively low values are consistent with a "high" probability of generating extreme values.

Table 14A-2. *Empirical Distribution of Long-Run Elasticities: Model M3*[a]

Item	Mean	Median	Standard deviation	Scaled deviation[b]	Minimum	Maximum	Approximate 95 percent confidence interval[c]	
							Lower bound	Upper bound
Oil consumption[d]								
Price	0.104	−0.223	12.185	0.153	−33.502	382.451	−0.979	0.022
Income	0.165	0.493	15.989	0.383	−495.329	77.597	−0.410	1.793
Non-oil imports								
Price	−0.974	−0.970	0.089	0.082	−1.351	−0.672	−1.170	−0.819
Income	2.754	2.749	0.084	0.085	2.515	3.126	2.571	2.958
Export volume								
Agricultural								
Price	−0.657	−0.658	0.171	0.161	−1.385	0.006	−1.037	−0.319
Income	1.330	1.337	0.100	0.099	0.727	1.628	1.110	1.511
Nonagricultural								
Price	−1.035	−1.011	0.255	0.223	−3.979	−0.452	−1.559	−0.609
Income	1.271	1.281	0.113	0.104	0.578	1.566	1.003	1.480
Non-oil import price								
Pass-through	0.938	0.940	0.093	0.085	0.544	1.241	0.749	1.139

a. The empirical distribution is based on a sample of 1,000 elasticity estimates.
b. The scaled median absolute deviation is constructed as median(|x − median(x)|)/0.6745 where x is an observation of the empirically generated sample of long-run elasticities.
c. The 1,000 sample points are grouped in 100 intervals of equal length, and the upper and lower bounds for the 95 percent confidence interval correspond to the midpoint of the intervals associated with 2.5 percent and 97.5 percent probability, respectively.
d. The coefficient for the lagged dependent variable is 0.88, with a standard error of 0.05; see Marquez and Ericsson (1990, appendix E, model M3, equation 21). The elasticities for oil consumption differ from those for oil imports because of domestic production.

Table 14A-3. *Empirical Distribution of Long-Run Elasticities: Model M4*[a]

Item	Mean	Median	Standard deviation	Scaled deviation[b]	Minimum	Maximum	Approximate 95 percent confidence interval[c] Lower bound	Upper bound
Price elasticities								
Export volume								
Canada	-0.440	-0.429	0.335	0.323	-1.526	0.949	-1.140	0.216
Germany	-0.986	-0.987	0.172	0.169	-1.512	-0.433	-1.336	-0.650
Japan	-0.405	-0.395	0.283	0.247	-1.815	1.049	-1.020	0.100
United Kingdom	-0.868	-0.860	0.361	0.342	-1.917	0.704	-1.602	-0.118
ROECD	-0.834	-0.831	0.218	0.199	-1.809	0.003	-1.311	-0.383
LDCs	-1.621	-1.620	0.615	0.589	-5.518	0.372	-2.814	-0.403
OPEC	-0.857	-0.846	0.173	0.136	-1.992	0.999	-1.235	-0.596
Import volume[d]								
Canada	-0.632	-0.631	0.168	0.160	-1.235	-0.145	-0.972	-0.283
Germany	-1.410	-1.407	0.328	0.307	-2.454	-0.401	-2.084	-0.741
Japan	-0.581	-0.589	0.228	0.229	-1.471	0.035	-1.031	-0.104
United Kingdom	-0.436	-0.489	0.394	0.322	-1.197	3.720	-1.076	0.404
ROECD	-0.681	-0.681	0.141	0.139	-1.110	-0.150	-0.953	-0.405
LDCs	-1.438	-1.402	0.428	0.400	-3.009	-0.336	-2.351	-0.625
Income elasticities								
Export volume								
Canada	1.697	1.693	0.210	0.207	0.872	2.339	1.273	2.136
Germany	1.523	1.515	0.173	0.169	1.024	2.080	1.172	1.871
Japan	0.751	0.759	0.171	0.145	-0.140	1.355	0.396	1.070
United Kingdom	3.409	3.323	0.695	0.620	1.532	6.595	2.275	5.125
ROECD	1.788	1.772	0.291	0.285	0.943	3.056	1.237	2.389
LDCs	0.395	0.409	0.159	0.149	-0.226	0.983	0.036	0.699
OPEC	1.289	1.214	0.468	0.319	0.564	8.259	0.737	2.193

(continued)

Table 14A-3 (continued)

Item	Mean	Median	Standard deviation	Scaled deviation[b]	Minimum	Maximum	Approximate 95 percent confidence interval[c]	
							Lower bound	Upper bound
Import volume								
Canada	1.639	1.636	0.171	0.159	1.157	2.169	1.311	2.015
Germany	2.918	2.925	0.309	0.292	1.964	3.907	2.322	3.598
Japan	3.696	3.683	0.296	0.296	2.893	4.683	3.133	4.332
United Kingdom	2.427	2.357	0.517	0.464	−0.109	4.864	1.870	3.482
ROECD	2.318	2.319	0.311	0.305	1.251	3.470	1.701	2.956
LDCs	3.122	3.121	0.209	0.217	2.482	3.807	2.691	3.784
Import prices[e]								
Pass-through								
Canada	0.713	0.726	0.173	0.159	0.277	1.130	0.294	0.776
Germany	0.827	0.826	0.026	0.025	0.713	0.914	0.772	0.880
Japan	0.479	0.480	0.075	0.076	0.251	0.689	0.319	0.621
United Kingdom	0.411	0.221	8.228	0.551	−55.043	124.299	−4.429	4.219
ROECD	1.100	1.098	0.058	0.060	0.949	1.303	1.051	1.214
LDCs	0.839	0.842	0.163	0.143	0.138	1.307	0.437	1.233

a–c. See table 14A-2.
d. The equation for oil consumption does not include the normalized variable lagged one period as an explanatory variable.
e. The coefficient of the lagged dependent variable for the United Kingdom is 0.94, with a standard error of 0.04; see Marquez and Ericsson (1990, appendix E, model M4, equation 29).

Additional Results

In many instances, results exist for four distinct cases: one-step-ahead and *s*-step-ahead, each with either the approximate or the asymptotic formula. For ease of presentation, often results for only the approximate formula are reported in the text (as in tables 14-5 and 14-6, and figures 14-2 and 14-3). Tables 14A-4 and 14A-5 and figures 14A-1 and 14A-2 are comparable tables and figures for the asymptotic formula. Further, tables 14A-6 through 14A-9 include numerical results for all four cases on higher moments of the forecast errors.

Table 14A-4. *Forecast Performance for Models of the U.S. Trade Balance: One Step Ahead, Asymptotic Formula, 1985–87*

| | Forecast period | | | | | | | | | | | | Summary measures of forecast performance[b] | | | |
| | 1985 (quarter) | | | | 1986 (quarter) | | | | 1987 (quarter) | | | | | | | |
Model[a]	1	2	3	4	1	2	3	4	1	2	3	4	MAE	RMSFE	τ	τ^*
Historical trade balance (billions of dollars)	−99.5	−119.8	−124.8	−144.5	−141.7	−135.4	−146.9	−154.1	−159.5	−158.2	−158.7	−164.8				
Mean forecast error (billions of dollars)																
M1	21.1	−4.4	−0.8	−3.6	1.8	−9.8	−26.0	−27.0	−21.1	−26.9	−19.7	−29.2	15.9	19.1	25.6	−3.2
M2	22.4	−1.0	2.2	−0.4	1.7	−9.9	−27.8	−27.5	−19.7	−24.8	−13.5	−21.6	14.4	17.8	28.5	−2.9
M3	23.1	−1.6	6.0	2.9	−0.2	−13.6	−23.8	−17.7	−12.8	−11.8	5.7	−4.8	10.3	12.9	12.7	−1.2
M4	−16.2	−33.4	−3.6	−0.3	19.4	23.0	24.3	−3.5	24.8	10.6	10.1	8.3	14.8	17.8	10.8	0.8
M5	23.5	−17.7	1.7	−30.6	−3.1	−12.3	−33.2	−24.6	−20.9	−15.3	−32.5	−49.6	22.1	25.6	43.5	−4.5
M6	23.0	−15.3	0.9	−12.9	10.1	13.0	−4.4	−0.1	2.5	8.9	7.5	1.7	8.4	10.7	21.3	1.2
Estimated standard error of the mean forecast error (billions of dollars)																
M1	12.2	11.5	11.7	11.4	12.0	12.0	12.4	12.8	13.4	13.8	14.4	15.1				
M2	11.5	11.0	11.1	10.9	11.1	10.9	11.0	11.6	12.1	12.8	13.4	14.1				
M3	12.9	12.2	12.3	12.4	12.7	12.3	12.5	12.7	13.7	14.3	14.9	15.8				
M4	16.1	17.3	17.4	18.0	19.5	18.9	19.6	18.9	20.8	20.8	20.5	21.9				
M5	12.8	12.7	12.6	12.1	13.3	13.1	12.7	13.2	13.9	14.2	14.5	14.2				
M6	8.1	8.0	7.7	7.9	8.0	7.9	8.0	8.0	7.5	7.7	8.0	7.9				
Forecast error "t" ratio																
M1	1.7	−0.4	−0.1	−0.3	0.1	−0.8	−2.1	−2.1	−1.6	−1.9	−1.4	−1.9				
M2	1.9	−0.1	0.2	−0.0	0.2	−0.9	−2.5	−2.4	−1.6	−1.9	−1.0	−1.5				
M3	1.8	−0.1	0.5	0.2	−0.0	−1.1	−1.9	−1.4	−0.9	−0.8	0.4	−0.3				
M4	−1.0	−1.9	−0.2	−0.0	1.0	1.2	1.2	−0.2	1.2	0.5	0.5	0.4				
M5	1.8	−1.4	0.1	−2.5	−0.2	−0.9	−2.6	−1.9	−1.5	−1.1	−2.3	−3.5				
M6	2.8	−1.9	0.1	−1.6	1.3	1.7	−0.5	−0.0	0.3	1.2	0.9	0.2				

a. Model M1: Helkie and Hooper (1988). Model M2: model M1 by FIML. Model M3: model M1 by FIML, with partial adjustment and without nonprice rationing. Model M4: bilateral trade model by FIML. Model M5: VAR(4) of import and export volumes and price indices. Model M6: AR(1) of the nominal trade balance.

b. MAE, mean absolute error; RMSFE, root-mean-square forecast error; τ, the $\chi^2(12)$ statistic testing against predictive failure (its 5 percent and 10 percent levels are 21.0 and 18.5); τ^*, the t-statistic testing against nonzero mean forecast error (its 5 percent and 10 percent levels for a two-tailed test are 2.2 and 1.8).

Table 14A-5. Forecast Performance for Models of the U.S. Trade Balance: s Step Ahead, Asymptotic Formula, 1985–87

						Forecast period							Summary measures of forecast performance[b]			
	1985 (quarter)				1986 (quarter)				1987 (quarter)							
Model[a]	1	2	3	4	1	2	3	4	1	2	3	4	MAE	RMSFE	τ	τ*
Historical trade balance (billions of dollars)	−99.5	−119.8	−124.8	−144.5	−141.7	−135.4	−146.9	−154.1	−159.5	−158.2	−158.7	−164.8				
Mean forecast error (billions of dollars)																
M1	21.1	6.3	5.0	1.9	5.0	−5.3	−23.7	−36.9	−41.2	−51.8	−52.4	−65.2	26.3	34.0	26.4	−3.0
M2	22.4	11.1	11.4	9.1	7.6	−5.4	−25.7	−38.8	−41.0	−48.8	−44.7	−55.1	26.8	31.9	27.4	−2.6
M3	23.1	13.2	13.5	10.2	5.0	−14.8	−34.0	−41.9	−41.6	−44.1	−32.2	−37.4	25.9	29.2	15.8	−1.8
M4	−16.2	−37.2	−16.5	−5.6	7.4	29.5	27.5	0.0	12.7	−4.8	−7.1	−10.3	14.6	18.2	9.0	−0.5
M5	23.5	6.5	0.4	−25.8	−32.8	−37.1	−57.4	−74.3	−86.9	−90.1	−90.6	−94.0	51.6	61.4	13.5	−2.0
M6	23.0	8.7	10.0	−2.5	7.6	20.9	17.5	18.1	21.4	31.2	40.1	43.6	20.4	23.8	21.3	1.2
Estimated standard error of the mean forecast error (billions of dollars)																
M1	12.2	13.2	13.4	13.6	13.8	14.3	14.6	14.9	16.0	16.6	17.3	18.0				
M2	11.5	12.3	12.4	12.8	12.7	12.8	13.2	13.6	14.7	15.5	16.7	17.1				
M3	12.9	14.5	15.2	16.5	16.5	15.5	16.0	16.6	18.8	19.3	20.2	21.3				
M4	16.1	17.3	17.8	19.1	20.4	21.1	21.3	21.1	22.4	23.1	22.7	23.8				
M5	12.8	19.2	21.8	23.8	27.0	32.9	37.8	41.9	43.3	45.0	47.2	48.4				
M6	8.1	11.7	14.5	16.7	19.4	22.1	24.2	26.6	28.4	30.7	33.1	35.4				
Forecast error "t" ratio																
M1	1.7	0.5	0.4	0.1	0.4	−0.4	−1.6	−2.5	−2.6	−3.1	−3.0	−3.6				
M2	1.9	0.9	0.9	0.7	0.6	−0.4	−2.0	−2.8	−2.8	−3.2	−2.7	−3.2				
M3	1.8	0.9	0.9	0.6	0.3	−1.0	−2.1	−2.5	−2.2	−2.3	−1.6	−1.8				
M4	−1.0	−2.2	−0.9	−0.3	0.4	1.4	1.3	0.0	0.6	−0.2	−0.3	−0.4				
M5	1.8	0.3	0.0	−1.1	−1.2	−1.1	−1.5	−1.8	−2.0	−2.0	−1.9	−1.9				
M6	2.8	0.7	0.7	−0.1	0.4	0.9	0.7	0.7	0.8	1.0	1.2	1.2				

a. See table 14A-4.
b. See table 14A-4.

Table 14A-6. *Further Statistical Properties of the Stochastic Trade-Balance Forecasts: One Step Ahead, Approximate Formula, 1985–87*

								Forecast period					
	1985 (quarter)				1986 (quarter)				1987 (quarter)			
Model[a]	1	2	3	4	1	2	3	4	1	2	3	4
Historical trade balance (billions of dollars)	−99.5	−119.8	−124.8	−144.5	−141.7	−135.4	−146.9	−154.1	−159.5	−158.2	−158.7	−164.8
Skewness												
M1	−0.28	−0.01	−0.11	−0.17	−0.16	−0.15	−0.03	−0.07	−0.09	−0.13	−0.06	−0.05
M2	−0.19	0.00	−0.08	−0.02	−0.02	−0.14	−0.08	−0.08	0.02	−0.12	−0.02	−0.05
M3	−0.11	−0.00	−0.08	−0.01	0.09	−0.07	−0.08	0.01	0.11	−0.16	−0.08	0.08
M4	−0.07	−0.11	−0.05	−0.13	−0.11	−0.27	−0.10	−0.05	−0.15	−0.20	−0.20	−0.26
M5	−0.21	−0.10	−0.13	−0.14	−0.13	−0.19	0.02	−0.41	−0.16	−0.27	−0.22	−0.06
M6	0.08	0.07	−0.03	0.09	−0.01	0.04	0.01	−0.01	−0.02	0.08	0.00	0.14
Excess kurtosis												
M1	0.07	0.18	−0.02	0.16	0.08	−0.02	−0.09	−0.21	−0.15	0.18	−0.00	0.24
M2	0.01	0.03	−0.03	0.23	−0.33	−0.05	−0.04	0.24	−0.29	−0.19	−0.26	0.20
M3	0.02	0.13	−0.16	0.07	0.25	−0.27	−0.17	−0.14	−0.12	0.09	−0.02	−0.05
M4	0.10	0.01	0.04	−0.01	0.00	0.09	0.14	0.33	−0.00	0.29	−0.04	0.13
M5	0.13	−0.16	0.25	0.05	−0.25	0.14	0.03	0.60	0.03	0.17	0.13	0.11
M6	0.17	0.15	−0.09	0.01	0.00	0.14	0.04	0.03	−0.03	−0.22	0.12	−0.18
Jarque-Bera $\chi^2(2)$ statistic												
M1	13.57	1.44	2.12	5.97	4.29	3.96	0.52	2.54	2.33	4.08	0.68	2.78
M2	6.16	0.05	1.18	2.19	4.68	3.58	1.05	3.42	3.62	3.96	2.78	2.10
M3	1.96	0.75	2.09	0.25	3.92	3.83	2.38	0.84	2.46	4.78	1.04	1.06
M4	1.22	1.92	0.44	3.00	1.96	12.33	2.62	4.90	3.78	10.26	6.45	11.67
M5	8.23	2.91	5.45	3.59	5.42	6.87	0.10	43.28	4.05	13.68	8.74	1.04
M6	2.29	1.81	0.53	1.25	0.03	1.08	0.06	0.06	0.12	2.99	0.62	4.73

a. See table 14A-4.

Table 14A-7. Further Statistical Properties of the Stochastic Trade-Balance Forecasts: s Step Ahead, Approximate Formula, 1985–87

	Forecast period											
	1985 (quarter)				1986 (quarter)				1987 (quarter)			
Model[a]	1	2	3	4	1	2	3	4	1	2	3	4
Historical trade balance (billions of dollars)	−99.5	−119.8	−124.8	−144.5	−141.7	−135.4	−146.9	−154.1	−159.5	−158.2	−158.7	−164.8
Skewness												
M1	−0.28	−0.08	−0.08	−0.14	−0.18	−0.17	−0.12	−0.13	−0.10	−0.22	−0.16	−0.03
M2	−0.19	0.03	0.04	0.04	0.01	−0.00	0.07	−0.03	0.04	−0.00	0.10	0.05
M3	−0.11	−0.06	−0.03	−0.10	−0.03	−0.16	−0.07	−0.19	−0.16	−0.21	−0.12	−0.01
M4	−0.07	−0.08	−0.09	−0.09	−0.08	−0.20	−0.19	−0.26	−0.13	0.01	−0.07	−0.08
M5	−0.21	−0.21	−0.26	−0.20	−0.15	−0.20	−0.23	−0.39	−0.32	−0.23	−0.31	−0.41
M6	0.08	−0.00	−0.05	−0.13	−0.29	−0.39	−0.57	−0.68	−0.84	−0.95	−1.07	−1.22
Excess kurtosis												
M1	0.07	0.38	0.29	0.10	0.09	0.22	−0.06	−0.09	−0.17	−0.10	−0.02	−0.12
M2	0.01	−0.03	−0.03	0.10	−0.29	−0.10	0.14	0.38	−0.11	−0.14	−0.08	0.17
M3	0.02	0.01	0.13	0.00	0.17	0.08	−0.09	0.22	0.76	0.62	0.74	0.36
M4	0.10	0.02	−0.00	−0.06	−0.01	−0.04	0.18	0.46	0.22	0.69	0.24	0.08
M5	0.13	0.18	0.77	0.34	0.33	0.68	0.99	1.74	2.01	2.35	2.96	3.25
M6	0.17	−0.06	−0.13	0.02	0.17	0.41	0.72	0.99	1.41	1.78	2.22	2.91
Jarque-Bera $\chi^2(2)$ statistic												
M1	13.57	7.16	4.62	3.51	6.03	6.92	2.53	3.31	2.98	8.15	4.17	0.76
M2	6.16	0.20	0.35	0.72	3.48	0.39	1.57	6.16	0.72	0.86	1.79	1.66
M3	1.96	0.64	0.85	1.57	1.42	4.30	1.26	7.98	27.98	23.67	25.05	5.39
M4	1.22	1.17	1.31	1.63	0.95	6.95	7.19	19.54	5.05	19.71	3.31	1.37
M5	8.23	8.39	35.74	11.62	8.29	26.09	49.69	151.03	185.48	238.32	382.44	467.52
M6	2.29	0.14	1.21	2.84	15.21	32.84	75.96	117.23	200.04	282.77	397.03	600.06

a. See table 14A-4.

Table 14A-8. *Further Statistical Properties of the Stochastic Trade-Balance Forecasts: One Step Ahead, Asymptotic Formula, 1985–87*

	Forecast period											
	1985 (quarter)				1986 (quarter)				1987 (quarter)			
Model[a]	1	2	3	4	1	2	3	4	1	2	3	4
Historical trade balance (billions of dollars)	−99.5	−119.8	−124.8	−144.5	−141.7	−135.4	−146.9	−154.1	−159.5	−158.2	−158.7	−164.8
Skewness												
M1	−0.28	0.04	−0.01	−0.05	0.01	−0.05	−0.09	0.04	−0.05	−0.06	−0.05	−0.05
M2	−0.16	0.04	−0.02	−0.04	−0.06	−0.07	−0.01	0.05	0.05	−0.04	−0.05	0.03
M3	−0.23	0.00	−0.06	−0.08	−0.07	−0.08	−0.06	0.00	0.05	−0.11	−0.05	0.02
M4	−0.07	−0.17	0.00	−0.11	−0.20	−0.26	−0.01	−0.07	−0.07	−0.04	−0.19	−0.19
M5	−0.13	−0.09	−0.10	−0.22	−0.05	−0.12	0.09	−0.14	0.04	−0.20	−0.32	−0.14
M6	0.05	0.08	−0.08	0.07	0.10	0.08	0.16	−0.05	−0.04	0.09	0.01	0.15
Excess kurtosis												
M1	0.19	0.00	−0.21	0.19	0.08	−0.03	−0.32	−0.13	−0.22	0.21	0.14	−0.08
M2	0.07	0.11	−0.14	0.19	0.13	0.00	−0.24	−0.07	−0.41	0.21	−0.01	−0.14
M3	0.03	0.07	−0.21	0.15	0.03	−0.05	−0.18	−0.10	−0.38	0.19	−0.09	−0.14
M4	0.12	0.27	0.24	−0.01	0.05	0.22	−0.01	0.18	−0.01	−0.15	0.06	−0.15
M5	0.01	−0.16	0.18	−0.03	−0.16	−0.12	0.16	0.16	−0.20	−0.05	0.09	−0.13
M6	0.31	−0.01	−0.11	0.01	−0.09	−0.00	−0.03	−0.18	−0.05	−0.17	0.27	−0.00
Jarque-Bera $\chi^2(2)$ statistic												
M1	14.50	0.21	1.80	1.94	0.30	0.45	5.38	0.93	2.40	2.32	1.30	0.72
M2	4.60	0.73	0.87	1.77	1.22	0.82	2.43	0.61	7.25	2.10	0.35	1.01
M3	8.84	0.20	2.40	2.11	0.78	1.16	1.91	0.44	6.33	3.38	0.76	0.91
M4	1.33	7.63	2.39	1.97	6.60	13.40	0.03	2.27	0.80	1.33	5.93	6.96
M5	2.80	2.53	3.02	8.45	1.47	3.12	2.36	4.16	1.97	6.65	17.36	3.86
M6	4.26	0.99	1.50	0.88	2.01	1.10	4.34	1.81	0.37	2.65	2.96	3.74

a. See table 14A-4.

Table 14A-9. *Further Statistical Properties of the Stochastic Trade-Balance Forecasts: s Step Ahead, Asymptotic Formula, 1985–87*

Model[a]	1985 (quarter)				1986 (quarter)				1987 (quarter)			
	1	*2*	*3*	*4*	*1*	*2*	*3*	*4*	*1*	*2*	*3*	*4*
Historical trade balance (billions of dollars)	−99.5	−119.8	−124.8	−144.5	−141.7	−135.4	−146.9	−154.1	−159.5	−158.2	−158.7	−164.8
Skewness												
M1	−0.28	0.02	0.02	−0.04	0.03	−0.05	−0.07	−0.04	−0.01	−0.22	0.00	−0.05
M2	−0.16	0.04	0.08	−0.03	−0.06	−0.05	0.04	−0.06	0.08	−0.13	0.07	0.09
M3	−0.23	−0.03	0.06	−0.13	−0.08	−0.03	0.03	0.02	0.01	−0.15	0.02	0.11
M4	−0.07	−0.12	−0.04	−0.17	−0.20	−0.16	−0.01	−0.08	−0.01	−0.01	−0.17	−0.17
M5	−0.13	−0.03	−0.04	−0.22	−0.10	−0.16	−0.13	−0.22	−0.20	−0.27	−0.27	−0.21
M6	0.05	0.09	0.04	0.02	−0.04	0.05	−0.01	0.02	−0.01	0.05	0.07	0.08
Excess kurtosis												
M1	0.19	0.04	0.10	0.16	0.17	0.01	−0.21	0.32	−0.11	0.06	0.39	−0.17
M2	0.07	0.04	0.09	0.11	0.08	−0.10	−0.31	0.25	−0.13	0.05	0.31	−0.12
M3	0.03	−0.08	−0.02	0.05	0.02	0.07	−0.16	0.16	−0.15	−0.03	0.11	−0.13
M4	0.12	0.27	0.22	0.18	0.09	−0.04	−0.14	0.11	−0.10	−0.04	−0.02	−0.13
M5	0.01	0.06	−0.02	0.05	−0.12	−0.12	0.12	0.15	0.10	0.15	0.39	0.10
M6	0.31	−0.10	−0.20	−0.04	0.07	0.01	−0.08	−0.10	−0.00	−0.10	−0.13	−0.30
Jarque–Bera $\chi^2(2)$ statistic												
M1	14.50	0.12	0.50	1.33	1.39	0.47	2.53	4.64	0.47	8.12	6.49	1.63
M2	4.60	0.29	1.39	0.72	0.89	0.90	4.22	3.20	1.71	2.89	4.81	1.88
M3	8.84	0.46	0.54	2.80	1.17	0.31	1.25	1.22	1.01	3.96	0.51	2.66
M4	1.33	5.28	2.39	6.17	6.97	4.44	0.82	1.48	0.42	0.07	4.95	5.48
M5	2.80	0.25	0.26	8.27	2.25	5.14	3.30	8.77	6.98	13.23	18.49	8.03
M6	4.26	1.73	1.85	0.13	0.55	0.44	0.27	0.47	0.03	0.77	1.55	4.69

Forecast period

a. See table 14A-4.

Figure 14A-1. *Ninety-five Percent Confidence Intervals for Trade-Balance Forecasts: One Step Ahead, Asymptotic Formula, 1985–87*

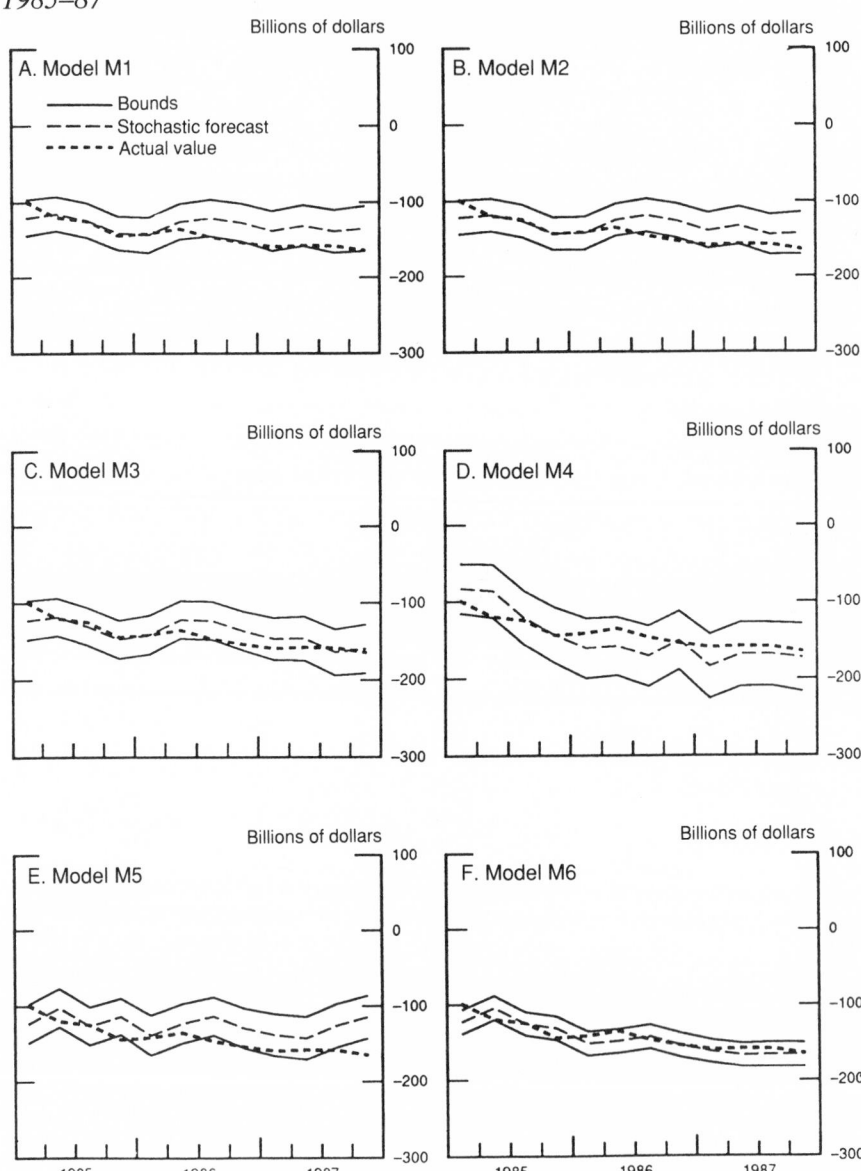

Figure 14A-2. *Ninety-five Percent Confidence Intervals for Trade-Balance Forecasts: s Step Ahead, Asymptotic Formula, 1985–87*

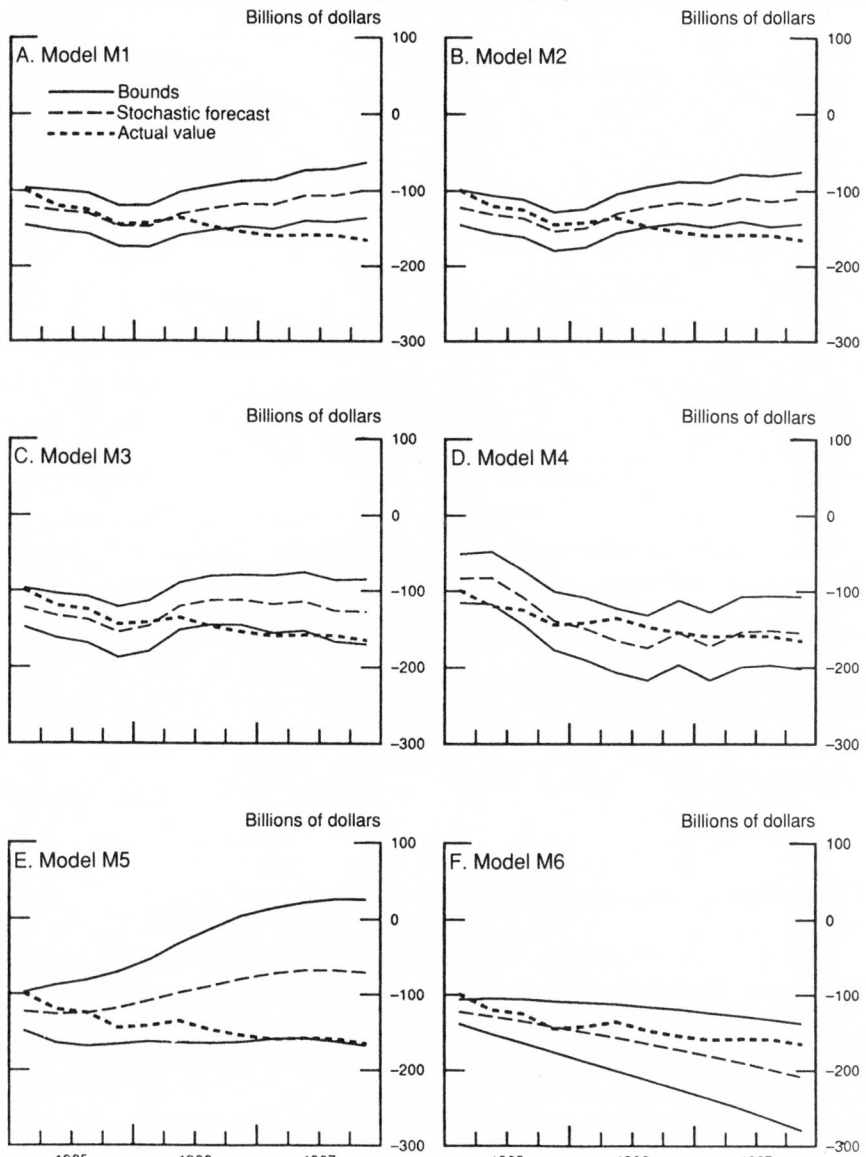

References

Baillie, R. T. 1979. "Asymptotic Prediction Mean Squared Error for Vector Autoregressive Models." *Biometrika* 66:675–78.

Baldwin, R. 1988. "Hysteresis in Import Prices: The Beachhead Effect." *American Economic Review* 78:773–85.

Bianchi, C., and G. Calzolari. 1983. "Standard Errors of Forecasts in Dynamic Simulation of Nonlinear Econometric Models: Some Empirical Results." In *Time Series Analysis: Theory and Practice 3,* edited by O. D. Anderson, 177–98. Amsterdam: North-Holland.

Bianchi, C., G. Calzolari, and J.-L. Brillet. 1987. "Measuring Forecast Uncertainty: A Review with Evaluation Based on a Macro Model of the French Economy." *International Journal of Forecasting* 3:211–27.

Brown, B. W., and R. S. Mariano. 1984. "Residual-based Procedures for Prediction and Estimation in a Nonlinear Simultaneous System." *Econometrica* 52: 321–43.

———. 1989. "Predictors in Dynamic Nonlinear Models: Large-Sample Behavior." *Econometric Theory* 5:430–52.

Bryant, R. C., and G. Holtham. 1988. "The U.S. External Deficit: Diagnosis, Prognosis, and Cure." In *External Deficits and the Dollar: The Pit and the Pendulum,* edited by R. C. Bryant, G. Holtham, and P. Hooper, 57–81. Brookings.

Calzolari, G. 1979. "Antithetic Variates to Estimate the Simulation Bias in Nonlinear Models." *Economics Letters* 4:323–28.

———. 1981. "A Note on the Variance of Ex-Post Forecasts in Econometric Models." *Econometrica* 49:1593–95.

———. 1987a. "Forecast Variance in Dynamic Simulation of Simultaneous Equation Models." *Econometrica* 55:1473–76.

———. 1987b. *La varianza delle previsioni nei modelli econometrici.* Padova, Italy: Cleup Editore.

Chong, Y. Y., and D. F. Hendry. 1986. "Econometric Evaluation of Linear Macroeconomic Models." *Review of Economic Studies* 53:671–90.

Chow, G. C. 1960. "Tests of Equality between Sets of Coefficients in Two Linear Regressions." *Econometrica* 28:591–605.

Cline, W. R. 1989a. "Macroeconomic Influences on Trade Policy." *American Economic Review 79 (Papers and Proceedings,* 1988):123–27.

———. 1989b. *United States External Adjustment and the World Economy.* Washington: Institute for International Economics.

Edison, H. J., J. R. Marquez, and R. W. Tryon. 1987. "The Structure and Properties of the Federal Reserve Board Multicountry Model." *Economic Modelling* 4:115–315.

Eichengreen, B. J. 1989. "Trade Deficits in the Long Run." In *U.S. Trade Deficit: Causes, Consequences, and Cures,* edited by A. E. Burger, 239–78. Boston: Kluwer Academic.

Engle, R. F., D. F. Hendry, and J.-F. Richard. 1983. "Exogeneity." *Econometrica* 51:277–304.

Ericsson, N. R. 1992. "Parameter Constancy, Mean Square Forecast Errors, and Measuring Forecast Performance: An Exposition, Extensions, and Illustration." *Journal of Policy Modeling* 14:465–95.

Ericsson, N. R., and D. F. Hendry. 1989. "Encompassing and Rational Expectations: How Sequential Corroboration Can Imply Refutation." International Finance Discussion Paper 354. Board of Governors of the Federal Reserve System.

Ericsson, N. R., and J. R. Marquez. 1989. "Exact and Approximate Multi-Period Mean-Square Forecast Errors for Dynamic Econometric Models." International Finance Discussion Paper 348. Board of Governors of the Federal Reserve System.

——. 1993. "Encompassing the Forecasts of U. S. Trade Balance Models." *Review of Economics and Statistics* 75:19–31.

Fair, R. C. 1984. *Specification, Estimation, and Analysis of Macroeconometric Models.* Harvard University Press.

——. 1986. "Evaluating the Predictive Accuracy of Models." In *Handbook of Econometrics,* edited by Z. Griliches and M. D. Intriligator, 3:1979–95. Amsterdam: North-Holland.

——. 1988. "Sources of Economic Fluctuations in the United States." *Quarterly Journal of Economics* 53:313–32.

Fair, R. C., and R. J. Shiller. 1990. "Comparing Information in Forecasts from Econometric Models." *American Economic Review* 80:375–89.

Feldstein, M. 1986. "Correcting the World Trade Imbalance." Unpublished, Harvard University.

Fisher, P., and M. Salmon. 1986. "On Evaluating the Importance of Nonlinearity in Large Macroeconometric Models." *International Economic Review* 27:625–46.

Fisher, P. G., and K. F. Wallis. 1990. "The Historical Tracking Performance of UK Macroeconometric Models 1978–85." *Economic Modelling* 7:179–97.

Goldberger, A. S., A. L. Nagar, and H. S. Odeh. 1961. "The Covariance Matrices of Reduced-Form Coefficients and of Forecasts for a Structural Econometric Model." *Econometrica* 29:556–73.

Goldstein, M., and M. S. Khan. 1985. "Income and Price Effects in Foreign Trade." In *Handbook of International Economics,* edited by R. W. Jones and P. B. Kenen, 2:1041–1105. Amsterdam: North-Holland.

Haavelmo, T. 1944. "The Probability Approach in Econometrics." *Econometrica* 12 (Supplement).

Hall, S. G., and S. G. B. Henry. 1988. *Macroeconomic Modelling.* Amsterdam: North-Holland.

Hammersley, J. M., and D. C. Handscomb. 1964. *Monte Carlo Methods.* London: Chapman and Hall.

Helkie, W. L., and P. Hooper. 1987. "The U.S. External Deficit in the 1980s: An Empirical Analysis." International Finance Discussion Paper 304. Board of Governors of the Federal Reserve System.

——. 1988. "An Empirical Analysis of the External Deficit, 1980–86." In *External Deficits and the Dollar: The Pit and the Pendulum,* edited by R. C. Bryant, G. Holtham, and P. Hooper, 10–56. Brookings.

Helliwell, J. F. 1989. "Reducing International Imbalances: Evidence from Multicountry Models." *American Economic Review 79 (Papers and Proceedings*, 1988):258–63.

Hendry, D. F. 1979. "Predictive Failure and Econometric Modelling in Macroeconomics: The Transactions Demand for Money." In *Economic Modelling*, edited by P. Ormerod, 217–42. London: Heinemann.

———. 1984. "Monte Carlo Experimentation in Econometrics." In *Handbook of Econometrics*, edited by Z. Griliches and M. D. Intriligator, 2:937–76. Amsterdam: North-Holland.

———. 1989. *PC-GIVE: An Interactive Econometric Modelling System*. Version 6.0/6.01. Oxford: Institute of Economics and Statistics and Nuffield College, University of Oxford.

———. Forthcoming. *Lectures on Econometric Methodology*. Oxford: Oxford University Press (with Duo Qin and Carlo Favero).

Hendry, D. F., and J.-F. Richard. 1982. "On the Formulation of Empirical Models in Dynamic Econometrics." *Journal of Econometrics* 20:3–33.

———. 1989. "Recent Developments in the Theory of Encompassing." In *Contributions to Operations Research and Economics: The Twentieth Anniversary of CORE*, edited by B. Cornet and H. Tulkens, 393–440. MIT Press.

Hendry, D. F., and P. K. Trivedi. 1972. "Maximum Likelihood Estimation of Difference Equations with Moving Average Errors: A Simulation Study." *Review of Economic Studies* 39:117–45.

Hooper, P. 1988. "The Dollar, External Imbalance, and the U.S. Economy." *Journal of Economic and Monetary Affairs* 2:30–53.

———. 1989. "Exchange Rates and U.S. External Adjustment in the Short Run and the Long Run." International Finance Discussion Paper 346. Board of Governors of the Federal Reserve System.

Hooper, P., and C. L. Mann. 1989. "Exchange Rate Pass-Through in the 1980s: The Case of U.S. Imports of Manufactures." *Brookings Papers on Economic Activity* 1:297–337 (with discussion).

Hoque, A., J. R. Magnus, and B. Pesaran. 1988. "The Exact Multi-Period Mean-Square Forecast Error for the First-Order Autoregressive Model." *Journal of Econometrics* 39:327–46.

Houthakker, H. S., and S. P. Magee. 1969. "Income and Price Elasticities in World Trade." *Review of Economics and Statistics* 51:111–25.

Howard, D. H. 1989a. "Implications of the U.S. Current Account Deficit." *Journal of Economic Perspectives* 3:153–65.

———. 1989b. "The United States As a Heavily Indebted Country." International Finance Discussion Paper 353. Board of Governors of the Federal Reserve System.

Howrey, P., and H. H. Kelejian. 1969. "Simulation versus Analytical Solutions." In *The Design of Computer Simulation Experiments*, edited by T. H. Naylor, 207–31. Duke University Press.

Intex Solutions. 1989. *TROLL Version 13*. Reference manuals, vols. 1–6 and updates. Needham, Mass.

Jarque, C. M., and A. K. Bera. 1980. "Efficient Tests for Normality, Homoscedasticity and Serial Independence of Regression Residuals." *Economics Letters* 6:255–59.

Klein, L. R. 1981. *Econometric Models as Guides for Decision-Making.* Charles C. Moskowitz Memorial Lectures 22. New York: Free Press.

Krugman, P. R. 1988. "U.S. External Adjustment." Paper prepared for the meeting of academic advisers to the Board of Governors of the Federal Reserve System, November 3. 1988.

———. 1989. *Exchange-Rate Instability.* MIT Press.

Krugman, P. R., and R. E. Baldwin. 1987. "The Persistence of the U.S. Trade Deficit." *Brookings Papers on Economic Activity* 1:1–55 (with discussion).

Magnus, J. R., and B. Pesaran. 1989. "The Exact Multi-Period Mean-Square Forecast Error for the First-Order Autoregressive Model with an Intercept." *Journal of Econometrics* 42:157–79.

Mariano, R. S., and B. W. Brown. 1983. "Asymptotic Behavior of Predictors in a Nonlinear Simultaneous System." *International Economic Review* 24:523–36.

———. 1989. "Stochastic Simulation, Prediction and Validation of Nonlinear Models." In *Economics in Theory and Practice: An Eclectic Approach,* edited by L. R. Klein and J. Marquez, 17–36. Dordrecht, Netherlands: Kluwer Academic.

Marquez, J. 1989. "Income and Price Elasticities of Foreign Trade Flows: Econometric Estimation and Analysis of the US Trade Deficit." In *Economics in Theory and Practice: An Eclectic Approach,* edited by L. R. Klein and J. Marquez, 129–76. Dordrecht, Netherlands: Kluwer Academic.

Marquez, J., and N. R. Ericsson. 1990. "Evaluating the Predictive Performance of Trade-Account Models." International Finance Discussion Paper 377. Board of Governors of the Federal Reserve System.

Marris, S. 1987. *Deficits and the Dollar: The World Economy at Risk.* Policy Analyses in International Economics 14. Updated edition. Washington: Institute for International Economics.

Marsaglia, G. 1965. "Ratios of Normal Variables and Ratios of Sums of Uniform Variables." *Journal of the American Statistical Association* 60:193–204.

Meade, E. E. 1988. "Exchange Rates, Adjustment, and the J-curve." *Federal Reserve Bulletin* 74:633–44.

Meese, R. A., and K. Rogoff. 1983. "Empirical Exchange Rate Models of the Seventies: Do They Fit Out of Sample?" *Journal of International Economics* 14:3–24.

Mizon, G. E., and J.-F. Richard. 1986. "The Encompassing Principle and Its Application to Testing Non-Nested Hypotheses." *Econometrica* 54:657–78.

Nagar, A. L. 1969. "Stochastic Simulation of the Brookings Econometric Model." In *The Brookings Model: Some Further Results,* edited by J. S. Duesenberry, G. Fromm, L. R. Klein, and E. Kuh, 425–56. Amsterdam: North-Holland.

Orcutt, G. H., and H. S. Winokur, Jr. 1969. "First Order Autoregression: Inference, Estimation, and Prediction." *Econometrica* 37:1–14.

Pagan, A. 1989. "On the Role of Simulation in the Statistical Evaluation of Econometric Models." *Journal of Econometrics* 40:125–39.

Sargan, J. D. 1982. "On Monte Carlo Estimates of Moments That Are Infinite." In *Advances in Econometrics: A Research Annual,* edited by R. L. Basmann and G. F. Rhodes, Jr., 267–99. Greenwich, Conn.: JAI Press.

Schmidt, P. 1974. "The Asymptotic Distribution of Forecasts in the Dynamic Simulation of an Econometric Model." *Econometrica* 42:303–09.

Silvey, S. D. 1975. *Statistical Inference.* London: Chapman and Hall.

U.S. Congressional Budget Office. 1989. *Policies for Reducing the Current-Account Deficit.* Government Printing Office.

U.S. Library of Congress. 1988. *The Dollar and the Trade Deficit: What's to Be Done?* Congressional Research Service Report for Congress.

White, H. 1980. "A Heteroskedasticity-Consistent Covariance Matrix Estimator and a Direct Test for Heteroskedasticity." *Econometrica* 48:817–38.

CHAPTER 15

Modeling and Policy Use
of Auction Price Expectations

Flint Brayton, William Kan, Peter A. Tinsley,
and Peter von zur Muehlen

A STANDARD theoretical assumption of present-value models of asset prices is that agents' expectations of future inflation are embedded in auction prices such as primary commodity prices and the term structure of interest rates.[1] The aim of this paper is to provide an empirical assessment of use of auction price information in short-run monetary policy, using the Board of Governors of the Federal Reserve System quarterly econometric model (FRB/MPS) as a stochastic simulation vehicle.

The first section of the chapter discusses a common modeling framework to represent movements of auction prices and the related issue of simulating policy-consistent expectations in large-scale modeling systems. Under general assumptions, the trajectories of state variables in a multivariate economic model have univariate autoregressive moving average (ARMA) representations. Long autoregressions (LARs) are proposed as a practical way to approximate the information sets of simulated agents in large modeling systems, so long as it is recognized that the parameters of the LAR approximations depend on the structure of the model(s) perceived by the simulated agents (including the monetary policy regime).

The generic modeling framework is applied to the corporate bond rate and dividend-price ratio in the second section and to several primary commodity price indexes in the third section. Although theory suggests that the relevant present-value arbitrage conditions should hold at each point of time, the empirical estimates indicate that these conditions are better interpreted as cointegrating attractors, holding reasonably well on average but subject to lengthy deviations from estimated "fundamentals."

The authors thank D. Battenberg and T. Grunwald for expert programming assistance. The views presented are those of the authors and do not necessarily represent those of the Federal Reserve Board or other members of its staff.

1. Recent empirical explorations of the inflation-indicator properties of auction prices include analyses of primary commodity prices by Baillie (1989), Boughton and Branson (1988), and Durand and Blöndal (1988) and of the term structure of interest rates by Mishkin (1990a, 1990b).

The fourth section discusses policy simulations with the FRB/MPS model, augmented to include the estimated auction-price equations. The simulated outcomes provide gauges of the effects of using primary commodity prices as policy indicators and of the quantitative importance of accounting for the policy dependence of agents' expectations. The final section offers conclusions.

Modeling and Simulating Expectations in Auction Prices

In comparing competing models, it is often difficult to separate differences in simulated responses that are due only to alternative assumptions about the formation of agents' expectations from differences that are due to variations in the general scope and complexity of the competing model specifications.

Auction prices provide a useful arena for assessing the realism and effects of modeler's assumptions about agents' expectations. Auction prices, specifically those of bonds and equity shares, provide key transmission channels for monetary policy in most macroeconomic policy models. Under the conditions of efficient markets and forward-looking agents, auction prices are also direct measures of agents' forecasts of future events. Thus, the only stochastic errors that are introduced into models of auction prices are the modelers' errors in the specifications of agents' expectations. Models that assert that auction-price movements are defined by postulated arbitrage conditions generally assume that the model representations differ, at most, from agents' expectations by white-noise discrepancies. As demonstrated below, that prospect appears to be most unlikely.

Generic Auction-Price Modeling

In a standard intertemporal optimization subject to quadratic adjustment costs or dynamic instrument uncertainty, the first-order condition for a quasi-fixed instrument or response variable, y_t, controlled by the representative agent is the second-order difference equation

$$(15\text{-}1) \qquad {}_t y_{t+1} - (\rho_1 + \rho_2)_t y_t + \rho_1 \rho_2 y_{t-1} - (1 - \rho_1)(1 - \rho_2) x_t = 0,$$

where the leading subscript convention, as in ${}_t y_{t+i}$, indicates the agent's expectation of y_{t+i} formed in time t; and x_t denotes a stochastic forcing term that generally is not under the control of the agent.

Under the convention that the characteristic roots of equation 15-1 conform to the saddlepoint restrictions, $0 \le \rho_1 \le 1 \le \rho_2$, the agent's planned response may be characterized by a partial adjustment toward a turnpike trajectory, $\hat{y}_t$:

(15-2)
$$\Delta y_t = (1 - \rho_1)(_t \hat{y}_t - y_{t-1}),$$

$$_t \hat{y}_t = (1 - \rho_2^{-1}) \sum_{i=0}^{\infty} \rho_2^{-i}(_t x_{t+i}).$$

No stochastic error term is attached to either equation 15-1 or 15-2 because it is presumed that planned actions of the representative agent are executed.

Under the assumption of negligible transaction costs, risk-neutral arbitrage conditions for auction prices are, essentially, a first-order (single-root) variant of equation 15-1:

(15-3)
$$_t y_{t+1} - \rho y_t - (1 - \rho)x_t = 0.$$

In the absence of stochastic bubbles, the "fundamentals" solution of equation 15-3 is the familiar present value[2]

(15-4)
$$y_t = (1 - \lambda) \sum_{i=0}^{\infty} \lambda_t^i x_{t+i}, \qquad \lambda = \rho^{-1},$$

where y_t is the asset price; x_t denotes expected payments not captured by expected capital gains, such as dividends in the case of equity prices; and λ is the relevant discount factor. Again, the fundamentals solution does not contain a stochastic error term because auction prices are direct measurements of agents' expectation of the present value of the forward trajectory $\{x_{t+i}\}$.

Descriptions of Agents' Expectations by Long Autoregression

In general, the forcing variable, x_t, is not exogenous but an instrument controlled by other agents. In a linear system, where all information conditioned in t is captured by variables dated t or earlier, the trajectories of all state variables, z_t, both exogenous variables and endogenous instruments of agents, can be represented by a vector ARMA process:

(15-5)
$$A(L)z_t = B(L)e_t,$$

where $A(.)$ and $B(.)$ are matrix polynomials in the lag operator, L; and e_t is the vector of stochastic innovations attributable to intrinsic disturbances, such

2. Economically meaningful solutions to equations 15-1 and 15-3 are subject to terminal or "transversality" conditions. Optimal solutions for variables subject to dynamic adjustment costs satisfy both terminal and initial conditions; the role of two-point boundary problems (solutions to 15-1 that satisfy split end-point requirements) in characterizing agents' intertemporal optimizations is discussed in Tinsley (1970). Because initial conditions are generally not required in the absence of adjustment costs, auction prices are sometimes called "jumping" variables.

as unpredictable weather, and agents' forecast errors in predicting the behavior of other agents.[3]

Following Zellner and Palm (1974), the *final equation* for the ith element of z_t, say x_t, is the univariate ARMA representation

$$(15\text{-}6) \qquad\qquad \alpha(L)x_t = \beta(L)a_{x,t},$$

where $\alpha(L)$ is the scalar polynomial $|A(L)|$, and the right-hand side of equation 15-6 denotes the appropriate row of $A^*(L)B(L)e_t$, where A^* is the adjoint of A.

This paper explores modeler's characterizations of agents' expectations of forward forcing terms $\{x_{t+i}\}$ that use LAR approximations of the relevant ARMA final equations,

$$(15\text{-}7) \qquad\qquad \phi(L)x_t = a_{x,t},$$

where $\phi(L)$ is a high-order truncation of $\beta(L)^{-1}a(L)$. In practice, most forcing variables that are the principal arguments of agents' expectations in this chapter contain a unit root, so it is convenient to reformulate equation 15-7 in the stationary format:

$$(15\text{-}7a) \qquad\qquad \Delta x_t = b_0 + \sum_{j=1}^{k} b_j \Delta x_{t-j} + a_{x,t}.$$

The set of k characteristic roots of equation 15-7a will be denoted by $\{\rho_1, \ldots, \rho_k\}$.[4]

In the case of auction prices, the modeler's task is to provide an approximation of agents' present-value expectation, y_t, as defined in equation 15-4, subject to the autoregressive depiction 15-7a of the dynamic behavior of the relevant forcing term(s), x_t. The modeler's present-value approximation will be denoted by $_t\tilde{y}$, to distinguish it from the agents' present-value expectation,

---

3. Vector ARMA representations of linear, rational-expectations models are obtained by replacing representative agents' expectations by model-consistent, certainty-equivalent projections. Derivation and illustrations, using the Wiener-Hopf-Kolmogorov annihilation operator discussed by Whittle (1963), may be found in Hansen and Sargent (1980), Whiteman (1983), and Dagli and Taylor (1984).

4. Use of a LAR as an initial "reduced-form" approximation of an ARMA process is discussed in Koreisha and Pukkila (1990). For the autoregressions referenced in this chapter, $k = 16$, which is somewhat larger than the square root of the sample size, as suggested by Koreisha and Pukkila. Tests of integration orders of the basic data used in this study are displayed in table 15-1, in some cases for both a postwar quarterly sample and an annual sample that includes prewar observations. It will be noted that the estimated integration orders of two variables, the equity dividend-price ratio, and the consumer inflation rate differ in the two samples. Unfortunately, current methods of descriptive time-series analysis do not readily accommodate intermittent changes in integration orders. In the case of normative analysis, as noted in Tinsley, Krieger, and Kan (1990), a characteristic of controlled economic systems is that the integration order of endogenous variables may be altered by the optimization objectives of private or public agents.

y_t. Note that the LARs, as in equation 15-7a, are used as *auxiliary descriptors* of the dynamic behavior of given forcing terms and coexist in the model with "structural" or feedback-equation descriptions of the same state variables.

The LAR descriptors are incorporated in two simulation phases that identify the characteristic roots and the "initial" conditions of the LAR representation 15-7a:

The parameters of autoregressive final-form representations of forcing variables, as in equation 15-7a, are constructed in an *estimation phase*. If the final forms are directly fit to historical data, the effective information set of simulated agents will resemble the so-called weak-form implementation of rational expectations.[5] By contrast, if the autoregressions are fit to prior simulated output of the model, they will incorporate modeler's restrictions imposed by the model characterizations of agents' behavior, including any counterfactual specifications such as alterations in monetary policy. As seen below, the principal objective in the estimation phase is to extract the characteristic roots, $\{\rho_1\}$, of the approximating LAR regressions.

In the second phase, after estimating the relevant LAR regressions 15-7a, the modeler generates an approximation of the auction-price expectation 15-4 in the *forecast phase*. A kth-order polynomial interpolation of the present-value summation in 15-4 is obtained by selecting any k historical or projected observations in the infinite set $\{_t\Delta x_{t+i}\}$.[6] The relative positions of the k elements in this "observation" vector impose conditions on the information set of the simulated agents. We discuss briefly two versions of the forecast phase: back-history and projected-history.

The infinite summation in equation 15-4 is evaluated by exploiting the finite truncation provided by the LAR approximation in 15-7a. Back-history and projected-history variants differ only in the degree of full model information used by simulated agents to estimate the "initial conditions" of 15-7a. In the case of autoregressive *back-history* (equation numbers denoted by the suffix b) representations, modelers confine the agent's information set to the (simulated or historical) prior history, $\Delta x_{t-\theta}(\theta \geq 0)$. If agents are postulated to observe concurrent observations, x_t, the modelers' representation, $_t\tilde{y}$, of agents' present-value expectation, y_t, as defined in equation 15-4 and subject to forecasts based on equation 15-7a, is

$$(15\text{-}8ab) \qquad _t\tilde{y} = \beta_0 + x_t + \sum_{j=1}^{k} \beta_j \Delta x_{t-j+1},$$

---

5. The format of the historically based models can range from simple univariate models to multivariate vector autoregression (VAR) models, depending on the extent of information ascribed to agents.

6. Polynomial interpolation of the present-value summation is analogous to a finite-order integration by parts; see discussion in Tinsley (1970).

where

(15-8bb) $\beta_j = \sum_{i=1}^{k} V_{i,j}^{-} \left(\dfrac{\lambda \rho_i^{k+1}}{(1 - \lambda \rho_i)} \right)$

(15-8cb) $V_{j,*} = \left(\rho_1^{k-j+1}, \ldots, \rho_k^{k-j+1} \right)$

(15-8db) $\beta_0 = \left[\dfrac{b_0}{(1 - \sum_{j=1}^{k} b_j)} \right] \left[\dfrac{\lambda}{(1 - \lambda)} - \sum_{j=1}^{k} \beta_j \right].$

Alternatively, modelers may position the k "observations" of $\{_t \Delta x_\tau\}$ within the model's simulation trajectory of *projected-history* (equation numbers denoted by the suffix f, for "forward"), such as

(15-8af) $_t \tilde{y} = \beta_0 + x_t + \sum_{j=1}^{k} \beta_j [_t \Delta x_{t+j}],$

where

(15-8bf) $\beta_j = \sum_{i=1}^{k} V_{i,j}^{-} \left[\dfrac{\lambda \rho_i}{(1 - \lambda \rho_i)} \right].$

The remaining equations in the projected-history equation set (15-8cf, df) are the same as those shown for the back-history equation set (15-8cb,db). In the projected-history variant, the k "initial conditions" or interpolation points, $\{_t \Delta x_{t+i}, i = 1, \ldots, k\}$, of the present-value summation 15-4 are now positioned in simulated future time, ahead of the current period, t, in which agents' expectations are being formed. By using full-model simulation solutions, the projected-history case is similar to a "strong-form" implementation of rational expectations.[7] Expectations based on projected-history implementations will resemble those generated by extended-path estimators, as in Fair and Taylor (1983).

Unless the LAR descriptors are applied only to exogenous variables or are restricted to using only historical data, implementation requires alternating cycles of multiperiod model simulations using the LAR regressions estimated

---

7. The interpolation points $\{_t \Delta x_\tau\}$ of the autoregression need not be adjacent and may be positioned far ahead of the current period, t, so long as one makes suitable adjustments to the rows of the Vandermonde matrix, **V**.

in the previous iteration and reestimation of the LAR regressions until stable estimates of the LAR descriptors are obtained.[8]

Calibrating Modeler's Characterizations of Agent Expectations

Agents' expectations are what they are. The "rationality" of agents' expectations cannot be evaluated because both the agents' information set and the agents' processing ("model") of that information are generally unknown to the modeler. It is useful, however, to calibrate the performance of alternative characterizations of agents' expectations, $_t\tilde{y}$, against the given history of agents' expectations, y_t. If a model's characterizations of agent expectations are not well calibrated, in dimensions that are yet to be defined, one might be cautious in interpreting the policy implications of counterfactual simulations produced by that model.

The empirical relationship between the modeler's present-value approximation, $_t\tilde{y}$, and agents' present-value expectation, y_t, will be described by the linear projection

$$(15\text{-}9) \qquad\qquad y_t = a_0 + a_1[_t\tilde{y}] + u_t,$$

where u_t is a stochastic disturbance containing the modeler's errors in capturing the formation of agents' expectations. In the case of I(0) agent expectations, y_t, equation 15-9 resembles standard regression tests of market "efficiency" in the finance literature, where efficient calibration is associated with a zero intercept and a unit slope. Equation 15-9, however, is a gauge of the accuracy of the modeler's descriptions of historical realizations of agents' expectations, not the accuracy of agents' expectations in predicting future events.

Typically, in the case of auction prices in postwar samples, y_t is I(1). In this case, equation 15-9 is a linear cointegration regression, which suggests two calibration yardsticks. First, a desirable "weak-form" calibration property of a modeler's characterization, $_t\tilde{y}$, is that the stochastic disturbance of 15-9, u_t, be stationary, or I(0). We will use the standard augmented Dickey-Fuller (ADF) statistic to assess the integration order of u_t. Second, in addition to any long-run association between y_t and $_t\tilde{y}$ indicated by the cointegration regression 15-9, it is useful to determine if the modeler's characterization, $_t\tilde{y}$, also replicates short-run movements in agents' expectations, Δy_t.

---

8. There are several routine modifications of equations 15-8ab–db or 15-8af–df that depend on the observation lags assumed for the agents' effective information set; the integration order of the forcing variables; or, in the case of n-period instruments such as bonds, finite truncations of the present-value infinite summation. Although noted where appropriate, these variations will not be discussed explicitly in the remainder of the chapter.

Using $_t\hat{y}(= y_t - u_t)$ to denote the right-hand-side predictor in the cointegrating regression 15-9, a linear projection of Δy_t on the modelers' projected change from last period, $_t\hat{y} - y_{t-1}$, and lagged first differences of both Δy_t and $_t\Delta\hat{y}$ is[9]

$$(15\text{-}10) \quad \Delta y_t = d_0 + \theta[_t\hat{y} - y_{t-1}] + \sum_{i=1}^{n} d_{1,i}\Delta y_{t-i} + \sum_{i=1}^{m} d_{2,i}[_{t-i}\Delta\hat{y}] + a_t.$$

If the model is dynamically well-calibrated, one might expect $\theta = 1$ and $d_{1,i} = d_{2,i} = 0$ for all i. By contrast, if θ is not significantly different from zero, then the information in the modeler's construction may be "stale"—in the sense that it is cointegrated with past levels of $y_{t-h}(h > 0)$—but not very helpful in explaining current-period movements of agents' expectations, Δy_t.

Expectational Models of the Corporate Bond Rate and Dividend-Price Ratio

Two key transmission channels for monetary policy in the FRB/MPS model are the responses of the corporate bond rate and the price of equity to agents' perceptions of future short-term interest rates. Cointegration equations are developed and estimated for bond and equity variants of the auction price "fundamentals" equation 15-4.

The Corporate Bond Rate

A present-value expression used for the corporate bond rate, R, is based on Shiller's (1979) linear expansion of the bond price:

$$(15\text{-}11) \qquad _t\tilde{R} \cong \frac{(1 - \lambda)}{(1 - \lambda^n)} \sum_{i=0}^{n-1} \lambda^i(_t r_{t+i}).$$

The estimated discount rate is based on the sample mean of the corporate bond rate, $\lambda = (1 + \bar{R})^{-1}$, and the t-period expectations of the forward funds rates, $_t r_\tau(\tau > t)$, are initially generated by applying the back-history projection system outlined in equations 15-8 ab–db above to historical observations,

Table 15-1. *Testing Integration Orders of Basic Data*

Variable[a]	Span	Null: I(2)		Null: I(1)	
		ADF[b]	$\tilde{Q}^c$	ADF[d]	$\tilde{Q}^c$
		Quarterly data			
π	1958:4–1989:3	−7.51***	0.84	−2.16	0.79
dp	1958:4–1989:3	−5.86***	0.92	1.56	0.94
d	1958:4–1989:3	−3.53***	0.52	0.12	0.79
R	1958:4–1989:3	−6.53***	0.80	−1.53	0.81
r	1958:4–1989:3	−5.95***	0.66	−2.22	0.78
$r - \pi$	1958:4–1989:3	−6.06***	0.64	−2.23	0.77
pr^{fd}	1958:4–1988:2	−4.57***	0.33	−1.04	0.32
pr^{met}	1958:4–1988:2	−4.58***	0.70	−2.93**	0.74
pr^{mat}	1958:4–1988:2	−4.06***	0.71	−1.57	0.93
pr^{gold}	1958:4–1988:2	−4.30***	0.91	−1.64	0.88
p^{fd}	1958:4–1988:2	−4.32***	0.26	−0.71	0.31
p^{met}	1958:4–1988:2	−4.33***	0.66	−0.46	0.77
p^{mat}	1958:4–1988:2	−3.10**	0.92	0.22	0.96
p^{gold}	1958:4–1988:2	−4.18***	0.88	−0.87	0.89
		Annual data			
q^{fd}	1928–88	−4.88***	0.27	−1.18	0.34
q^{met}	1928–88	−5.67***	0.31	−1.45	0.37
q^{mat}	1928–88	−4.94***	0.78	1.82	0.87
q^{gold}	1928–88	−4.67***	0.54	1.01	0.52
q^a	1928–88	−5.38***	0.48	−1.08	0.50
dp	1928–88	−6.89***	0.27	−3.41**	0.04
R	1928–88	−5.52***	0.20	−0.88	0.33
r	1928–88	−7.37***	0.53	−1.67	0.46
$r - \pi$	1928–88	−7.35***	0.05	−1.66	0.45
π	1928–88	−9.38***	0.28	−4.23***	0.77

a. See table 15-2.
b. ADF, augmented Dickey-Fuller test. Alternative hypothesis of a single unit root I(1), accepted at 90 percent (*), 95 percent (**), and 99 percent (***) confidence level, using critical values in Engle and Yoo (1987).
c. Confidence levels of a Ljung-Box test for residual autocorrelation.
d. Alternative hypothesis of stationarity, I(0), accepted at 90 percent (*), 95 percent (**), and 99 percent (***) confidence level.

assuming that the current-period funds rate, r_t, is known by agents at the beginning of period t.[10]

As shown in table 15-1, both the corporate bond rate, R, and the federal funds rate, r, appear to be I(1) over the quarterly sample period, 1958:4–1989:3 (symbols in table 15-1 are defined in table 15-2). Consequently, a long-run relationship between the historical record of agents' expectations, R_t, and the modeler's approximation, $_t\tilde{R}$, is provided by the cointegrating regression

$$(15\text{-}12) \qquad R_t = \beta_0 + \beta_1[_t\tilde{R}] + u_t.$$

Estimates of the cointegrating regression (15-12) are listed in table 15-3, where the kth-order autoregression of the first-difference of the funds rate,

10. Equations 15-8ab–db are modified to account for the n-period summation in 15-11, where n is assumed to be 100 (twenty-five years). Although the average maturity of seasoned AAA industrials was about twenty-five years in both 1978 and 1982, it has fallen in recent years (averaging about sixteen years in 1989).

Table 15-2. *Symbols Used in Testing Integration Orders of Basic Data*

Variable	Description
	Quarterly data
π	Consumption-deflator inflation
dp	Logarithm of dividend-price ratio
d	Log of real dividends (nominal dividends deflated by the consumption deflator)
R	Corporate bond rate
r	Federal funds rate
$r - \pi$	Real rate (federal funds rate less consumption-deflator inflation)
pr^{fd}	Log of food commodity price index less the log of the consumption deflator
pr^{met}	Log of industrial metals commodity price index less the log of the consumption deflator
pr^{mat}	Log of industrial materials commodity price index less the log of the consumption deflator
pr^{gold}	Log of precious metals commodity price index less the log of the consumption deflator
p^{fd}	Log of food commodity price index
p^{met}	Log of industrial metals commodity price index
p^{mat}	Log of industrial materials commodity price index
p^{gold}	Log of the precious metals commodity price index
	Annual data
q^{fd}	Log of food productivity less the log of nonfarm productivity
q^{met}	Log of industrial metals productivity less the log of nonfarm productivity
q^{mat}	Log of industrial materials productivity less the log of nonfarm productivity
q^{gold}	Log of precious metals productivity less the log of nonfarm productivity
q^{a}	Log of nonfarm productivity
dp	Log of dividend-price ratio (Standard & Poor's)
R	Corporate bond rate (Moody's seasoned AAA bonds)
r	Six-month commercial paper rate
$r - \pi$	Six-month commercial paper rate less consumer-price-index–wage (CPI-W) inflation
π	CPI-W inflation

equation 15-7a, was fit only to the sample interval before the 1979 shift in monetary policy, 1958:4–1979:3, while suppressing the intercept.[11] As shown in lines 1 and 2 of table 15-3, the modeler's approximation, $_t\tilde{R}$, appears to have satisfactory long-run calibration properties. The relationship is cointegrated at a 1 percent level of significance in both the full-sample and the pre-Volcker sample, and the estimated cointegration coefficients appear to be relatively stable through the full sample. This is visually confirmed also by the time-series plots of the historical bond rate, R_t, and the cointegration predictor, $_t\hat{R}$, in the top panel of figure 15-1.

11. As a general rule, the intercepts of all autoregressions in the first differences of I(1) variables were suppressed, forcing the estimated roots to approximate any apparent historical or simulated sample trends. This model format is extremely adaptable; a Chow test of subsamples before and after the 1979 shift in monetary policy was not able to detect shifts in the LAR model of either the funds rate or the inflation rate. The purpose of adopting a flexible format was to specify a generic autoregression format that could be used without operator intervention in automated contraction mapping sequences. We also tried a generic I(0) format (apparently paralleling the interesting work reported in Sims 1989), even for I(1) variables, since the solution method in equations 15-8 does not require stable roots (as long as they do not dominate the discount rate). Unfortunately, the I(0) format appeared to run afoul of the singularity in the format of particular solutions as the sum of the estimated autoregression coefficients passes through unity.

Table 15-3. *Long-Run and Short-Run Characteristics of Corporate Bond Rate and Dividend-Price Models*

Regression estimate (equation 15-12)	Span	ADF[a]	R^2	RMSE[b]	$\bar{Q}$[c]
Corporate bond rate regressions[d]					
Long run					
(1) $R_t = .005 + .899_t\bar{R} \equiv {}_t\hat{R}$	1958:4–1989:3	−4.90***	0.950	0.0016	0.61
(2) $R_t = .004 + .918_t\bar{R} \equiv {}_t\hat{R}$	1958:4–1979:3	−4.58***	0.940	0.0011	0.33
Short run ($\hat{R}$ defined by equation 1 cointegration coefficients; intercepts not reported)					
(3) $\Delta R_t = \underset{(8.2)}{.499}({}_t\hat{R} - R_{t-1}) + \underset{(4.4)}{1.40} \sum_{i=1}^{7} d_{1,i}\Delta R_{t-i} - \underset{(-1.8)}{.551} \sum_{i=1}^{7} d_{2,i}\Delta_{(t-i}\hat{R})$	1961:3–1989:3	…	0.564	0.0008	0.94
(4) $\Delta R_t = \underset{(5.9)}{.211}({}_t\hat{R} - R_{t-1}) + \underset{(4.6)}{438}\Delta R_{t-1} - \underset{(-1.8)}{.121}\Delta_{(t-i}\hat{R})$	1960:1–1979:3	…	0.439	0.0004	0.67
(5) $\Delta R_t = \underset{(5.0)}{.664}({}_t\hat{R} - R_{t-1}) + \underset{(2.3)}{1.88} \sum_{i=1}^{8} d_{1,i}\Delta R_{t-i} - \underset{(-1.1)}{.797} \sum_{i=1}^{8} d_{2,i}\Delta_{(t-i}\hat{R})$	1980:1–1989:3	…	0.749	0.0011	0.62
Dividend-price regressions[e]					
Long run					
(6) $dp_t = -6.44 + .217(\mu_t r\bar{r}) + .016(\mu\Psi_t) \equiv {}_t d\hat{p}$	1961:1–1988:3	−4.62***	0.541	0.084	0.30
(7) $dp_t = -4.28 + .251(\mu_t r\bar{r}) - .005(\mu\Psi_t) \equiv {}_t d\hat{p}$	1961:1–1970:4	−3.67*	0.327	0.071	0.64
Short run ($d\hat{p}$ defined by equation 6 cointegration coefficients; intercepts not reported)					
(8) $\Delta dp_t = \underset{(2.1)}{.096}({}_t d\hat{p} - dp_{t-1}) + \underset{(3.9)}{.374}\Delta dp_{t-1} - \underset{(-0.1)}{.093}\Delta_{(t-1} d\hat{p})$	1961:1–1988:3	…	0.138	0.063	0.75
(9) $\Delta dp_t = \underset{(1.7)}{.147}({}_t d\hat{p} - dp_{t-1}) + \underset{(2.9)}{.526}\Delta dp_{t-1} - \underset{(-0.3)}{.078}\Delta_{(t-1} d\hat{p})$	1961:1–1970:4	…	0.204	0.050	0.04
($d\hat{p}$ defined by equation 7 cointegration coefficients; intercept not reported)					
(10) $\Delta dp_t = \underset{(4.9)}{.429}({}_t d\hat{p} - dp_{t-1}) + \underset{(4.2)}{.549}\Delta dp_{t-1} - \underset{(0.3)}{.083}\Delta_{(t-1} d\hat{p})$	1961:1–1970:4	…	0.484	0.040	0.66

a. ADF test accepts cointegration at 90 percent (*), 95 percent (**), and 99 percent (***) level of confidence.
b. Root-mean-squared errors.
c. Confidence level of a Ljung-Box test for residual autocorrelation; in the case of long-run regressions, the statistic is associated with the relevant ADF regression.
d. R denotes the corporate bond ratio; $\hat{R}$, the present value expectation; and $\bar{R}$, the cointegration predictor.
e. The log dividend-price ratio is denoted dp; $r\bar{r}$ is the real funds rate, present value expectation (adjusted for the expected growth of real dividends); Ψ is a twelve-quarter, rolling sample, risk-premium proxy (see text); μ, a constant, equals 49.9; and $d\bar{p}$ is the cointegration predictor.

Figure 15-1. *Corporate Bond Yield and the Dividend-Price Ratio, 1960–88*

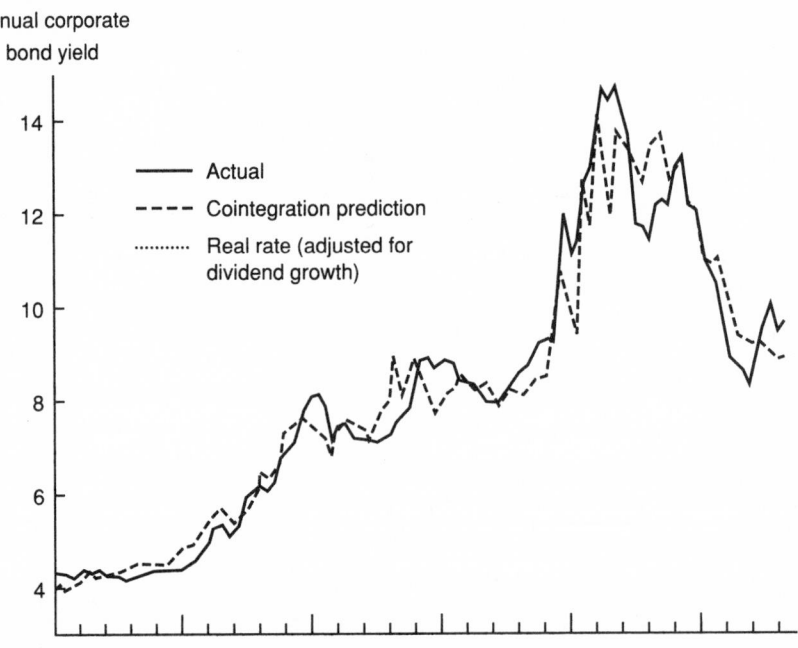

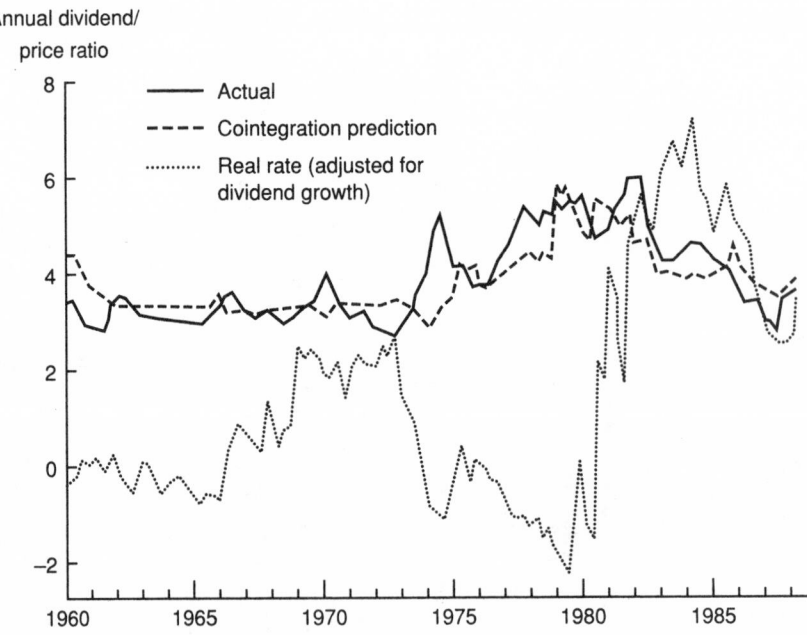

As suggested by equation 15-10, short-run associations of agents' and modelers' expectations can be calibrated by regressions of the historical changes in the corporate bond rate, ΔR_t, on the modelers' projected changes, $_t\hat{R} - R_{t-1}$, and lags in both ΔR and $\Delta \hat{R}$, where $\hat{R}$ is the cointegration predictor. Changes in the dynamic association of R and $\hat{R}$ are evident in lines 3–5 of table 15-3. This is not surprising, perhaps, given the marked change in monetary policy in late 1979. It seems plausible that some of the shifting of these short-run regressions can be attributed to the use of back-history observation sets of the funds rate $\{\Delta r_{t-j}, j = 1, \ldots, 16\}$ in the early quarters of the 1980s, rather than use of projected-history observation sets $\{_t\Delta r_{t+j}, j = 1, \ldots, 16\}$.[12]

In contrast to the expectation that efficient auction prices behave approximately like random walks or martingales, at least in high-frequency data, the lagged values of differences of agents' prior expectations, the $d_{1,\,i}\Delta y_{t-i}$ terms in equation 15-10, are generally significant in all the short-run regressions presented in this chapter. In all cases, the mean lag of the bivariate transfer function between the modeler's approximation, $_t\hat{y}$, and the agents' realizations, y_t, defined by the short-run regression 15-10 is

(15-13)
$$ML = [1 - \theta - \sum_{i=1}^{n} d_{1,i} - \sum_{i=1}^{m} d_{2,i}]/\theta.$$

In all of the auction-price models estimated in this chapter, the sum of the $d_{1,i}$ coefficients is positive and provides an acceleration of the mean lag that would be provided by θ alone. In the case of line 4 of table 15-3, the pre-1980s sample, the mean lag between movements of $\hat{R}$ and subsequent movements of R is a little over two quarters.

The Dividend-Price Ratio

The present-value relationship for the dividend-price ratio is based on Campbell and Shiller's (1989) log linearization

(15-14)
$$dp_t \cong m + \sum_{i=1}^{\infty} \lambda^i (_t r_{t+1} -_t \pi_{t+i} -_t g_{d,t+i}),$$
$$= m + \mu(_t rr),$$

---

12. If modelers make persistent errors in approximating agents' expectations, the cointegrating error should be autocorrelated. Although we have not tried formal testing for common factors, as in Sargan (1980), one might expect to find something like the pattern of coefficients implied by the following regression format

(15-10a)
$$\Delta y_t = d_0 + (_t\hat{y} - y_{t-1}) + \sum_{i=1}^{n} d_i[\Delta y_{t-i} - (_{t-i}\Delta\hat{y})] + a_t.$$

However, it is invariably the case that the estimated coefficients on lagged first differences of the cointegrating predictor, $_{t-i}\Delta y$, are not statistically different from zero.

where dp denotes the log of the dividend-price ratio; r is the federal funds rate; π is the quarterly inflation rate of an aggregate consumption deflator; g_d is the growth rate of real dividends; and m and μ are functions of the sample discount rate, λ: $m = \ln(1 - \lambda)$ and $\mu = \lambda/(1 - \lambda)$. Thus, $_t rr$ can be interpreted as the expectation in period t of the present value of the future trajectory of the I(1) real funds rate, adjusted for the growth rate of dividends, and normalized to a convenient real-rate dimension by multiplying by the inverse of μ.

The modeler's approximation, $_t r\tilde{r}$, is constructed by LAR approximations for r, π, and g_d in the infinite summation 15-14 by using the appropriate variants of the back-history projection system 15-8ab–db. It is assumed that agents know the current funds rate, but information on other variables (such as the inflation rate) is lagged one quarter. The discount rate, λ, is approximated by the sample mean of the holding period return to equity, $\overline{h}^e$, less the mean inflation rate, $\overline{\pi}$, and mean growth rate of real dividends, $\overline{g}_d$, as in $\lambda = \exp(-[\overline{h}^e - \overline{\pi} - \overline{g}_d])$.[13]

Although both the real interest rate, $r - \pi$, and the log dividend-price ratio, dp, appear to be I(1) in the postwar sample shown in table 15-1, initial tests suggested that dp and $r\tilde{r}$ are not cointegrated over the postwar sample. Consequently, the cointegrating regression between the historical dividend-price ratio, dp, and the modeler's approximation, $r\tilde{r}$, was augmented to include, Ψ, an approximation of a CAPM (capital asset pricing model) risk premium.[14]

$$(15\text{-}15) \qquad dp_t = \beta_0 + \beta_1 \mu[_t r\tilde{r}] + \beta_2 \mu[\Psi_t] + \mu_t.$$

Specifically, the CAPM price of risk is assumed to vary with Ψ, the ratio of the standard deviation of the return to equity, $\sigma(h^e)$, relative to the standard deviation of the return to household wealth, $\sigma(h^w)$. As available from data in the FRB/MPS model, h^w includes the returns to financial assets, equity, and land but excludes capital gains on government bonds. A time-varying estimate of the risk premium is generated by twelve-quarter, rolling-sample estimates of the standard deviation components of Ψ.

---

13. One would not expect a Taylor's series expansion around a fixed sample mean to hold up over an extended simulation horizon for an I(1) series. Campbell and Shiller (1989) used annual data from 1871–1986 and 1926–86 samples and suggested that the log dividend-price ratio is I(0). Indeed, as shown in table 15-1, the log dividend-price ratio appears to be I(0) if one uses a sample that includes prewar data but appears to be I(1) for the postwar sample in table 15-1. We experimented with time-varying expansions. Although the cointegration regressions had much higher coefficients on the real rate, the net impact of the real rate was considerably reduced under a time-varying discount rate.

14. Note that the parameters of equation 15-15, β_1 and β_2, are arbitrary normalizations of the effective cointegrating parameters, $(\mu\beta_1)$ and $(\mu\beta_2)$, using the sample estimate of μ. In the absence of an error in measuring the effective discount rate used by agents, one would expect $\beta_1 \cong (1 - t_y)/(1 - t_{cg})$, where t_y is the marginal tax rate on income and t_{cg} is the marginal tax rate on capital gains.

Empirical estimates of the cointegrating equation (15-15) for the log dividend-price ratio, dp, are listed in lines 6 and 7 of table 15-3 for the full sample, 1961:1–1988:3, and for an abbreviated sample ending in 1970:4. Both regressions indicate that the modeler's prediction, $d\hat{p}$, exhibits long-run calibration, in the sense that cointegration is maintained (albeit at a 10 percent level of significance in the case of the shorter sample) throughout the sample. Although estimates of the β_1 coefficient on the expected present-value of the growth-adjusted real rate, $_t r \tilde{r}$, appears to be relatively invariant over the sample, the estimate of the β_2 coefficient on the risk premium, Ψ, is reduced, in absolute terms, by an order of magnitude and is negative in the pre-1971 sample.

The shifting relative importance of the two cointegrating regressors is displayed in the bottom panel of figure 15-1, which includes the time profiles of the historical dividend-price ratio, $\exp(dp_t)$; the antilog of the cointegration predictor, $\exp(d\hat{p}_t)$; and the normalized real rate expectation, $_t r \tilde{r}$. It is evident from this plot that the expected real rate appears to move *inversely* to the dividend-price ratio during the 1970s and early 1980s and that the risk premium regressor is carrying most of the explanatory load during this interval.

Calibration of the short-run association between dp and $d\hat{p}$ is examined in lines 8–10 of table 15-3. The short-run associations of the historical dividend-price ratio and the cointegrating predictor supplied by line 6 are examined for the full sample in line 8 and for the sample ending in 1970:4 in line 9. Although the coefficients of the two equations do not appear to vary greatly, the implied dynamic structure is rather different, at least as evaluated by mean-lag calculations. The mean lag of the full sample equation in line 8 is 6.5 quarters, whereas the mean lag of the sample estimate ending in 1970, in line 9, is 2.8 quarters. If the role of the risk premium is downgraded in the pre-1971 sample, as in line 10, which uses the cointegrating predictor from line 7, the mean lag is approximately zero.

In summary, using what we believe are representative expectational models of two important auction markets, the expectations model of the corporate bond rate appears to be reasonably well-calibrated over our postwar sample, whereas the ability of the expectations model of the equity market to mimic the expectations of agents is more questionable. As shown in the bottom panel of figure 15-1, movements of the modeler's approximation of agents' expectations of the real rate of interest do not dominate the historical movements of the dividend-price ratio. Consequently, to the extent that models with policy-dependent expectations specify policy-transmission channels that rely significantly on wealth or cost of capital effects of equity valuations, one might interpret simulations of counterfactual policy implications with a significant degree of caution.

Table 15-4. *Components of the Primary Commodity Price Indexes*

Index grouping	Components
Food[a]	Bananas, barley, broilers, cocoa, coffee, corn, eggs, hogs, lamb, oats, oranges, pork, potatoes, rice, rye, steers, sugar, tea, wheat
Industrial materials[b]	Ammonia, benzene, corrugated boxes, burlap, Portland cement, chlorine, copra, cotton, caustic soda, cotton printcloth, cottonseed oil, ethylene, flaxseed, gravel, hides, lumber, nylon, phosphate rock, plywood, rubber, sand, soda ash, soybeans, stone, synthetic rubber, tallow, wool
Industrial metals	Aluminum, copper, lead, nickel, steel, tin, zinc
Precious metals	Gold, platinum, silver

a. Productivity values for cocoa, coffee, and tea were unavailable.
b. Productivity values for hides, phosphate rock, and rubber were unavailable.

An Expectational Model for Commodity Prices

In theory, commodity prices behave like auction prices.[15] Although casual evidence suggests that a strict interpretation of this supposition is an oversimplification,[16] it is useful to describe a model based on the assumption of perfect arbitrage in primary commodity markets.

Primary commodities consist mainly of foodstuffs, industrial materials, and either industrial or precious metals (table 15-4). Most primary commodities, therefore, are industrial inputs, although precious metals and food have utility in individuals' consumption. Because there is limited substitutability in their usage, shortfalls in the production of these commodities tend to have immediate effects on their prices, and the effect may be magnified or diminished depending on the level of current commodity stocks.

The assumption of efficient auction-market behavior suggests that current asset prices embody agents' forecasts of future sticky-price inflation. Arbitrage ensures that the expected rate of return to carrying a commodity stock into the next period cannot exceed the nominal interest rate because agents would immediately bid up its current price and, thereby, lower the expected capital gain. But, as noted in the literature, this effect is asymmetric: an unusually large anticipated supply will drive the future price below the current-use value of the commodity, possibly in a downward freefall if desired current stocks are

---

15. Early discussions of commodity-price determination include the work of Gustafson (1958), who analyzed commodity demand, and Muth (1961), who introduced rational expectations. Important subsequent contributions include Samuelson (1971), who showed that the theory of competitive storage yields a nonlinear first-order Markov process for prices, and Newberry and Stiglitz (1981, 1982), who derived results for strategic stockpiling and commodity-price stabilization in models featuring risk aversion. Recent empirical examinations of the use of commodity price indexes as policy indicators were spurred by Angell (1987).

16. The prices of selected commodities—such as lumber, tin, and agricultural products—are under the influence of international cartels or government price stabilization and subsidy programs. Nevertheless, since many factors such as weather and final demand cannot be fully anticipated, there is a role for fluctuating prices and market arbitrage.

zero, because it is impossible to borrow against future production by carrying negative inventories. Crops cannot be eaten before they are grown. Because episodes in which stockouts followed by production shortfalls are not unprecedented, one should expect periodic flares in commodity-price behavior.

In addition to interest opportunity costs and physical storage charges, each commodity yields a direct utility in consumption or production. This use value or convenience yield is the analogue of the coupon yield of a bond or the dividend of an equity share. A simple stock-out model, for example, implies an inverse relationship between the expected real convenience yield and the ratio of beginning-of-period inventories to expected sales: the expectation of increased demand raises the intrinsic value of maintaining a stock, since a potential shortfall would deprive the owner of additional profit. Thus, as noted in Tinsley, Krieger, and Kan (1990), commodity prices reflect cyclical changes in convenience yields, lending them the property of price dual reflections of cyclical swings in real business activity that, in turn, are known to lead turning points in the inflation rates of final demand prices.

Finally, if the equilibrium commodity price level is determined by a markup on unit labor costs, then improvements in labor productivity in the primary-commodity-producing industry will tend to drive down equilibrium commodity prices. As suggested in Tinsley, Krieger, and Kan (1990), the equilibrium (log) commodity price may be represented as a markup on unit labor costs,

(15-16) $$p_t^c = \eta + w_t^c - q_t^c,$$

where η is the producer price markup, q^c is (log) labor productivity in the producing industry, and w^c is the (log) industry wage. If the supply price of labor is proportional to a weighted average of the demand price for labor in the commodity-producing industry (superscript c) and in alternative industries (superscript a),

(15-17) $$w_t^c = (1 - \gamma)(p_t^c + q_t^c) + \gamma(p_t^a + q_t^a),$$

the relative (log) commodity price is a linear function of the industry productivity differential,

(15-18) $$p_t^c - p_t^a = \eta/\gamma - (q_t^c - q_t^a).$$

To combine all these ingredients into an explicit commodity-price model, we begin with the risk-neutral arbitrage condition for a generic primary-commodity price:

(15-19) $$_tP_{t+1}^c + C_tP_t \le (1 + r_t)P_t^c,$$

where $_tP_{t+1}^c$ is the expectation in period t of next period's commodity price; r is the short-term interest rate; C is the real convenience yield; and P_t is a price index of consumer expenditures (that is, the price dual of the revealed expenditure preferences of representative agents). Competitive arbitrage requires that (15-19) is either an equality or the desired stock of the commodity is zero.

Assuming an absence of speculative bubbles and commodity dumping, forward integration of 15-19 gives the fundamentals solution for the commodity price, P_t^c, as a convolution of the term structure of interest rates, r_{t+i}, with expected consumer price inflation, π_{t+i}, and the expected growth in real convenience yields, $g_{c,t+i}$:

$$(15\text{-}20) \quad P_t^c = C_t P_t \{ 1 + \sum_{i=1}^{\infty} \exp[-\sum_{j=1}^{i} (_t r_{t+j} -_t \pi_{t+j} - g_{c,t+j})] \},$$

$$= C_t P_t M_t.$$

Taking logs and expanding around the sample mean of the commodity-specific, growth-adjusted real yield in the (.) term of equation 15-20 yields an equation for the *relative* commodity price, $p_t^c - p_t \equiv pr_t^c$,

$$(15\text{-}21) \qquad pr_t^c = m + c_t - \sum_{i=1}^{\infty} \lambda^i (_t r_{t+i} -_t \pi_{t+i} -_t g_{c,t+i}),$$

$$= m + c_t - \mu(_t \tilde{r} -_t \tilde{\pi} -_t \tilde{g}_c),$$

where c_t denotes the log of C_t; $_t \tilde{r}$ is the discounted equivalent of a long-term bond rate; $_t \tilde{\pi}$ is the discounted, expected inflation rate; $_t \tilde{g}_c$ is the discounted, expected growth in c_{t+i}; μ is a normalization constant based on the discount rate, $\mu = \lambda/(1 - \lambda)$; and the discount rate is the mean expansion point, $\lambda = \exp[-$ sample mean $(r - \pi - g_c)]$.

In implementing the generic log commodity-price model, equation 15-21, we have made several simplifying assumptions. First, our initial estimates assume that movements in the log convenience yield, c, are adequately captured by (inverse) movements in the log productivity differential, $q = q^c - q^a$. Thus, c_t will be replaced by $-q_t$, and the corresponding growth rate, g_c, will be replaced by $-g_q$. Second, on the supposition that the risk premium associated with a primary commodity is not unlike that of an all-equity producer of that commodity, we assume that the effective discount rate for primary commodities is approximated by $-\ln(\lambda) \cong$ sample mean $(h^e - \pi + g_q)$, where h^e is the quarterly return to equity defined in the preceding section. Third, individual primary commodity prices are aggregated into four subgroups: food (*fd*), industrial materials (*mat*), industrial metals (*met*), and precious metals (*gold*). Group indexes of both prices and productivity were constructed by Tornquist aggregators (see Diewert 1978), using quarterly interpolations of annual share weights based on nominal world production estimates. Fourth, we replaced the discounted expected interest rates in equation 15-21 by the current-period corporate bond rate, R_t.

Taking these simplifications into account, the expected long-run model of a commodity price index is

$$(15\text{-}22) \qquad pr_t^c = \beta_0 - \beta_1 q_t - \beta_2 \mu [R_t -_t \tilde{\pi} +_t \tilde{g}_q^c] + u_t^c,$$

where u_t^c is the relevant cointegrating error, and it is expected that both cointegrating coefficients, β_1 and β_2, will be positive. As indicated in 15-22, β_2 is a convenient but arbitrary normalization of the estimated coefficient $(\beta_2 \mu)$, based on the sample estimate of $\mu = \lambda/(1 - \lambda)$.

Estimated Commodity Price Models

As shown in table 15-1, the hypothesis that the relative commodity prices, pr_t^c, are nonstationary cannot be rejected, except possibly in the case of the industrial materials price index. This conclusion conforms with findings in several studies, such as Baillie (1989), Boughton and Branson (1988), and Durand and Blöndal (1988). But, in contrast to the conclusion of these studies that commodity prices do not have stable long-run relationships with consumer or producer prices, equation 15-22 suggests that a long-run relationship might exist if either the differential productivity index, q_i, or the real interest rate, $r - \pi$, is I(1). As shown in table 15-1, the differential productivity series and the real interest rate appear to be I(1) in both the shorter postwar samples and the longer samples including prewar data.[17]

Estimated cointegrating relationships between relative commodity prices and growth-adjusted real rates, as in equation 15-22, are presented in table 15-5 for each of the four primary-commodity groups. Note at the outset that there does not appear to be a reliable long-term relationship between the precious metals (log) price index, p^{gold}, and the consumer (log) price index, p, where $pr^{gold} = p^{gold} - p$. As seen in the fourth line of table 15-5, the ADF test for cointegration is insignificant, and the cointegration coefficient of

---

17. Boughton, Branson, and Muttardy (1989) appear to suggest that the level of I(1) jumping variables, such as commodity prices, should be cointegrated with the inflation rates of I(2) sticky-price indexes and provide evidence based on a postwar sample. As seen in equation 15-22, the appropriate model appears to be a possible cointegrating relationship between an I(1) relative price and a growth-adjusted I(1) real rate. The formulation of Boughton, Branson, and Muttardy is empirically consistent with postwar samples of consumer price indexes that indicate I(2) behavior, but not with samples including prewar consumer price indexes that indicate I(1) behavior, as noted in table 15-1. It is difficult to square their formulation with producer price indexes that, as noted in Tinsley, Krieger, and Kan (1990), appear to be I(1) in both prewar and postwar samples.

Table 15-5. *Long-Run and Short-Run Characteristics of Relative Commodity Price Models*

Regression	Span	ADF[a]	R^2	RMSE	$\bar{Q}$[b]
Long run[c]					
(1) $pr_t^{mat} = .207 - .255\mu(R_t - {}_t\bar{\pi}) - .672\mu({}_t\bar{g}_q^{mat}) - .142q_t^{mat} \equiv {}_t\hat{p}^{mat}$	1959:3–1988:2	-3.13	0.636	0.065	0.41
(2) $pr_t^{met} = .350 - .511\mu R_t + .834\mu({}_t\bar{\pi}) \equiv {}_t\hat{p}^{met}$	1957:4–1988:3	-4.75***	0.371	0.199	0.94
(3) $pr_t^{fd} = .323 - .512\mu(R_t - {}_t\bar{\pi} + {}_t\bar{g}_q^{fd}) - .205q_t^{fd} \equiv {}_t\hat{p}^{fd}$	1959:3–1988:3	-4.08**	0.597	0.127	0.68
(4) $pr_t^{gold} = -.916 + .848\mu(R_t - {}_t\bar{\pi}) \equiv {}_t\hat{p}^{gold}$	1957:4–1988:3	-2.14	0.127	0.512	0.65
Short run (${}_t\hat{p}^c$ defined by relevant cointegrations; intercepts not reported)					
(5) $\Delta pr_t^{mat} = .097({}_t\hat{p}^{mat}) - .084 pr_{t-1}^{mat} - .027\Delta({}_{t-1}\hat{p}^{mat}) + .177\Delta pr_{t-1}^{mat}$ $\qquad$ (2.96) $\qquad$ (-.315) $\qquad$ (-.333) $\qquad$ (1.89)	1960:4–1988:3	...	0.333	0.018	0.56
(6) $\Delta pr_t^{met} = .152({}_t\hat{p}^{met}) - .180 pr_{t-1}^{met} + .424\Delta({}_{t-1}\hat{p}^{met}) + .464\Delta pr_{t-1}^{met}$ $\qquad$ (2.13) $\qquad$ (-4.10) $\qquad$ (-2.87) $\qquad$ (5.75)	1958:4–1988:3	...	0.431	0.090	0.93
(7) $\Delta pr_t^{fd} = .097({}_t\hat{p}^{fd}) - .084 pr_{t-1}^{fd} + .125 \sum_{i=1}^{3} d_{1,i}\Delta({}_{t-i}\hat{p}^{fd}) + .555 \sum_{i=1}^{3} d_{2,i}\Delta(pr_{t-1}^{fd})$ $\qquad$ (2.94) $\qquad$ (-3.41) $\qquad$ (-2.87) $\qquad$ (3.98)	1960:4–1988:3	...	0.329	0.042	0.90

a. ADF test accepts cointegration at 90 percent level of confidence.
b. Confidence level of a Ljung-Box test for residual autocorrelation; in the case of long-run regressions, the statistic is associated with the relevant ADF regression.
c. The relative price superscripts indicate the primary commodity group: industrial materials (*mat*), industrial metals (*met*), food (*fd*), and precious metals (*gold*); R_t denotes the corporate bond rate; ${}_t\bar{\pi}$ is the present-value expectation of consumer price inflation; q_t^c is the productivity differential of the relevant commodity group; and ${}_t\bar{g}_q^c$ is the present-value expectation of the growth of the relevant productivity differential.

the real rate is positive, contrary to our theoretical prior for the auction-price model, equation 15-22. Consequently, precious metals have been dropped from further consideration in this paper. One caveat is that we have not tested measures of the convenience yield for precious metals on the basis of the demand for currency-risk hedges.

Empirical estimates of the cointegrating relationship 15-22 for the remaining indexes (industrial materials, industrial metals, and food) are listed in the first three lines of table 15-5. As indicated by the ADF test for stationarity of the residual, u_t, cointegration is accepted for both the industrial metals and food-price indexes. Although the ADF statistic is not quite large enough for a strict interpretation of cointegration for the industrial materials price index, this appears to be a relatively well-behaved equation.

The estimated cointegrating coefficients on the real rate components have the expected signs. For food and industrial metals, the semi-elasticities of the interest rate are 0.5, and half that amount for industrial materials. The level and growth rates of differential productivity appear in the cointegrating equations for both industrial materials and food with the expected signs. In general, the long-run regressions in table 15-5 appear to be well calibrated, indicating that movements in the real rate of interest tend to change equilibrium asset prices in the opposite direction.

This is borne out also in the plots of the cointegrating equations in figure 15-2, where the historical relative price series, pr_t^c, are contrasted with the cointegrating predictors, $_t\hat{p}r^c$. The plots show a reasonably close correspondence between predictions and actual outcomes; the major misses occur during the period of supply-side shocks in the early 1970s. One should expect that back-history approximations of agents' formation of expectations would perform more poorly in periods of large unanticipated shocks. As might be expected for jumping variables, the plots in figure 15-2 indicate that the historical relative commodity prices have a tendency to overshoot significant turning points in the modelers' approximations when these are based on back-history LAR descriptors.

Calibration of short-run associations between the cointegrating predictors and the historical relative prices are evaluated by the remaining short-run regressions in table 15-5. The mean lags for industrial materials and food are rather lengthy (approximately 7 and 5 quarters, respectively), whereas the mean lag for industrial metals is approximately zero.

Unraveling the Inflation Signal of Commodity Prices

Primary commodity prices have the potential to be operationally useful policy indicators, not only because measurements are available on a continuous basis but also because auction prices contain, in principle, anticipations of

Figure 15-2. *Relative Commodity Prices, 1960–88*

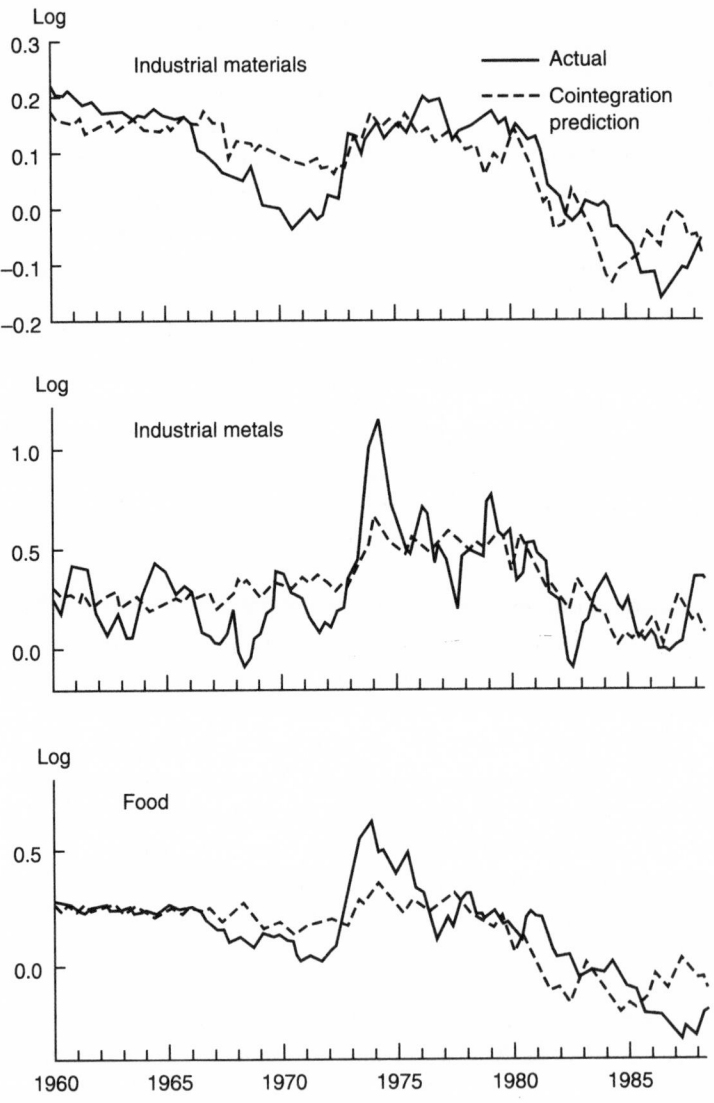

the expected inflation trajectory of sticky prices, such as the consumer deflator, p_t. However, some care must be taken to adjust observed movements in
commodity prices for shifts in differential productivity, policy-induced shifts
in interest rates, or other influences on the commodity-specific convenience
yields. In other words, direct measures of commodity-price movements are
only the outer layer of the most relevant estimate of agents' predictions of
inflation.

By construction, the cointegration errors of the three commodity price
indexes, the u_t^c of equation 15-22, contain the modeler's errors in representing
agents' expectations. Because each of the cointegrating errors contains the same
(unobserved) error in modeling expected inflation, a multivariate filter of the
cointegrating errors of the several commodity price indexes can be used to
estimate the common error.

A simple unobserved-components filter was constructed for the estimated
cointegrating errors of the three commodity price indexes (industrial materials,
industrial metals, and food):

$$(15\text{-}23) \qquad {}_t\overset{\star}{\pi} - {}_t\tilde{\pi} = \mathbf{G_\pi}\mathbf{u_t}, \qquad \mathbf{G_\pi} = [.5, .2, .3],$$

where ${}_t\overset{\star}{\pi}$ denotes the agents' unobserved forecast of the discounted present-
value of expected inflation, ${}_t\tilde{\pi}$ is the modelers' back-history approximation of
agents' inflation expectation, and $\mathbf{u_t}$ is the 3×1 vector of estimated cointegrating errors. The 1×3 vector, $\mathbf{G_\pi}$, is a static filter gain and is identified
by the simplifying assumption that each cointegrating error contains only two
unobserved components, an idiosyncratic component and a component that is
common to all three cointegrating errors. The idiosyncratic component includes
modelers' errors in characterizing the differential productivity trends, and the
common component is the modelers' error in representing expected inflation.
Each unobserved component is assumed to be independently distributed with
a fixed variance.

Now consider the following hierarchical ordering of inflation indicators:
First, one could construct an inflation prediction on the basis of unadjusted
relative commodity prices by applying the filter gain in equation 15-23 directly to the three observed primary-commodity relative price indexes. This is
quite a crude measure of expected inflation because it does not abstract from
known policy-dependent effects, such as interest rates, or from idiosyncratic
events, such as industry-specific productivity and demand shifts, to which national monetary policy might not wish to respond. This measure, however,
does capture the flavor of most published primary-commodity aggregate price
indexes.

In the lower panel of figure 15-3, the solid line depicts a measure of ex-
pected inflation, $\overset{\star}{\pi}$, constructed by applying the estimated filter-gain in equation

Figure 15-3. *Alternative Inflation Expectations, 1960–88*

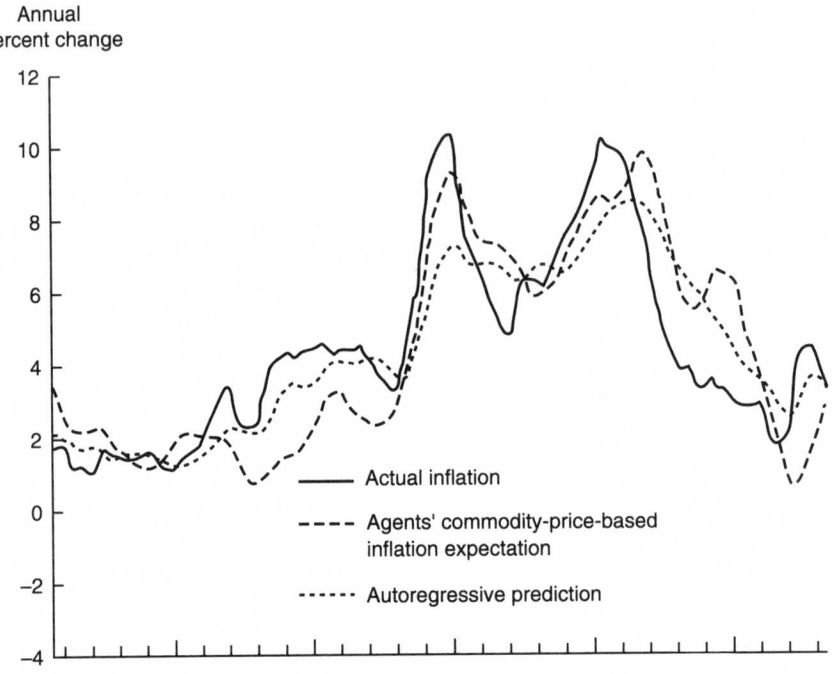

Annual
percent change

Actual inflation

Agents' commodity-price-based
inflation expectation

Autoregressive prediction

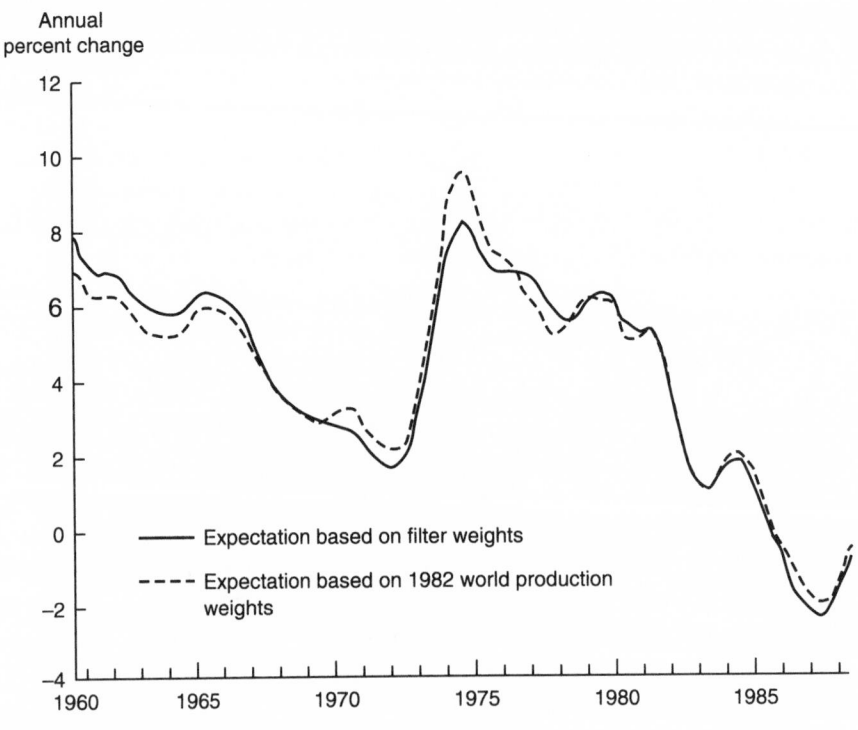

Annual
percent change

Expectation based on filter weights

Expectation based on 1982 world production
weights

15-23 to the observed relative commodity-price indexes; the dotted line is constructed using the share weights associated with 1982 world production of the associated commodities. Clearly, these two views of expected inflation are very similar, except perhaps in 1974 when, in the aftermath of world-wide supply-side shocks, food and metals prices shot up, causing the world production index (which places more emphasis on these two commodity groups) to overshoot relative to the estimate based on the filter weights.

The panels of figure 15-4 show a succession of "filtered" constructions of expected inflation, $_t\overset{*}{\pi}$, plotted against the historical series of quarterly inflation, π_t, of the consumption price. The top panel in figure 15-4 again reproduces the expected inflation estimate, conditioned only on the relative commodity prices; as indicated, this estimate overstates historical inflation at the beginning of the sample period and understates inflation after 1976.

The middle panel of figure 15-4 adjusts the filtered estimate for the impacts of the expected level, q_t, and growth rates, $_t g_q$, of differential productivity. There is some change in the overall tilt of the expected inflation plot, but the improvement is not dramatic.

Finally, the bottom panel of figure 15-4 also removes agents' expectation of future interest rates, as represented by the corporate bond rate. Because the corporate bond rate is responsive to expected movements in the short-term interest rate, policymakers should unravel the direct impact of expected interest rates to reduce the risk of confusing agents' expectations about the interest-rate effects of expected policy with agents' expectation of inflation. In other words, neither nominal interest rates nor primary commodity prices alone are sufficient statistics for expected inflation, but both may be combined to identify agents' inflation expectations.

One interesting characteristic of the bottom panel in figure 15-4 is that removing the interest-rate effect reveals a pronounced lag in agents' expected inflation, relative to actual quarterly inflation. Any apparent tendency of turning points in commodity prices to lead turning points in consumer price inflation appears to be due largely to the direct impact of movements in the corporate bond rate.

Stochastic Simulations with the FRB/MPS Quarterly Model

This section reports on stochastic simulation experiments with the FRB/MPS quarterly model, which was modified to incorporate the estimated equations for the corporate bond rate, the dividend-price ratio on common stock, and the three indexes of primary commodity prices. The objectives of the simulations are to assess the potential value of commodity prices as monetary policy indicators and to gauge the quantitative importance of accounting for the

Figure 15-4. *Actual and Filtered Inflation, 1960–88*

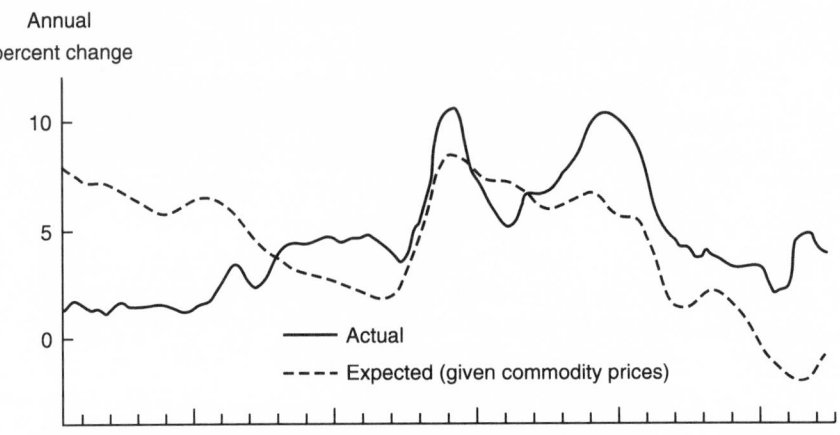

Annual
percent change

— Actual

- - - Expected (given commodity prices)

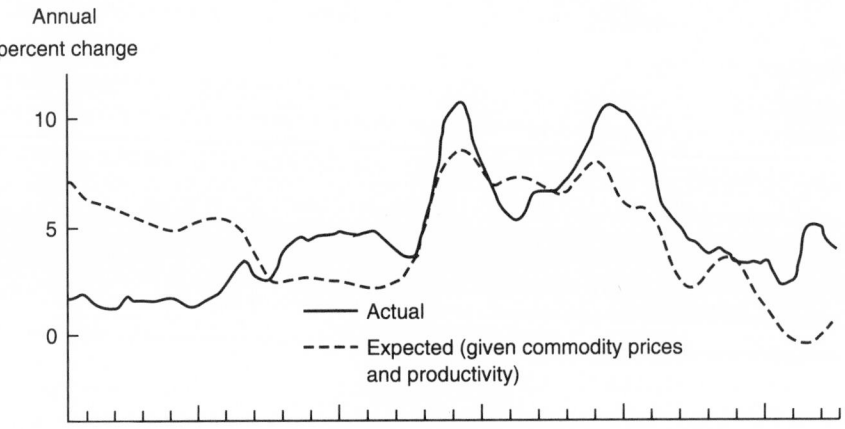

Annual
percent change

— Actual

- - - Expected (given commodity prices
and productivity)

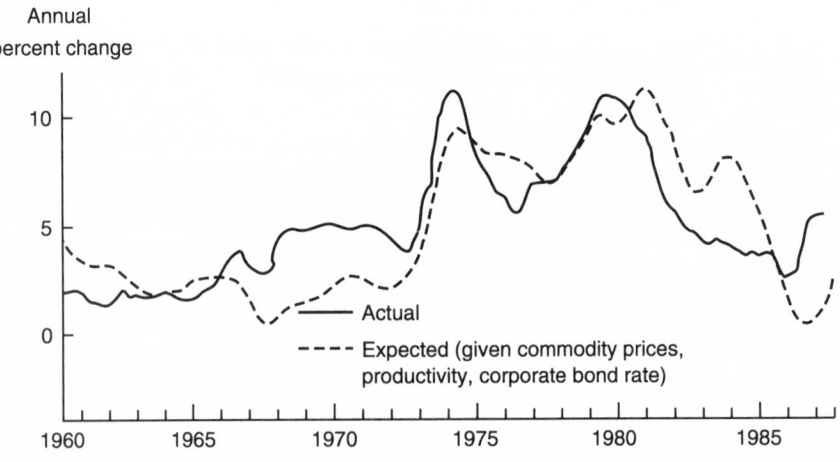

Annual
percent change

— Actual

- - - Expected (given commodity prices,
productivity, corporate bond rate)

policy dependence of the autoregressive representations of expectations.[18] In the structure of the FRB/MPS model, the bond- and equity-price equations are important channels for the transmission of monetary policy.[19] Primary-commodity prices, in contrast, do not appear explicitly elsewhere in the FRB/MPS model; consequently, their only possible effect is through feedback responses by the simulated policymakers.

Expectations Based on Historical Long Autoregressions

In each experiment, the augmented FRB/MPS model is stochastically simulated over a forty-quarter horizon. In general, the design of these stochastic simulations is the same as that used in the core simulations for this conference: the simulation horizon is the ten-year period, 1989:4–1999:3; the policy feedback rule is specified in terms of deviations from a deterministic baseline containing fairly neutral projections of key macroeconomic variables; 100 stochastic replications are undertaken for each policy; and stochastic shocks are generated by a bootstrap procedure—sampling, with replacement, from the estimated model residuals in the 1960:1–1984:4 interval.[20]

The first set of simulation experiments generates expectations of the federal funds rate and inflation by the back-history projection system (equations 15-8ab–db) through use of historical LAR descriptors of the funds rate and inflation. Thus, in this set of simulation experiments, the characteristic roots of the LAR regressions used to form expectations are conditioned only by historical monetary policy and are invariant to counterfactual policies.

Alternative monetary policies are defined by selecting a specific set of policy indicators. The pool of potential policy indicators is restricted to y (the log of real GNP), p (the log of the GNP deflator), π (the annual rate of

18. Policy-dependent LAR descriptors were run only for the auction-price bloc of equations. Agents' dynamic behavior in real-expenditure equations is assumed to be dominated by adjustment costs, and we made no attempt to disentangle the lag structures of agents' expectations and adjustment costs in nonfinancial blocs of the model.

19. For a description of the FRB/MPS quarterly model, see Brayton and Mauskopf (1985, 1987). To avoid a major shift in the relative importance of the principal channels of monetary policy, the simulations reported here use a version of the dividend-price ratio equation 15-15 estimated through 1970 only, with properties similar to that shown in lines 7 and 10 of table 15-3.

20. All exogenous variables in the core simulations are deterministic; however, in the simulations described here, the world price of oil is subjected to stochastic disturbances associated with an historical ARIMA (autoregressive-integrated-moving-average) oil price regression. The reason for this altered simulation procedure is that price inflation driven by demand disturbances appears to be contained sufficiently by policies that respond to real output departures from baseline projections. That is, in the absence of oil-price disturbances, supply-side price shocks are confined to random draws from the relatively small historical residuals of the model wage and price markup equations. Consequently, the policy-loss function (defined below in equation 15-25) is relatively insensitive to supplemental feedback responses to sticky-price indicators, such as the level of the GNP deflator, given the long estimated lags from changes in resource utilization to subsequent sticky-price responses.

Table 15-6. *Stochastic Policy Simulations with Historical Long Autoregression (LAR) Descriptors (LAR-H) of Expectations*

Simulation	Policy feedback coefficients							RMSE[a]			Policy criterion		Feedback price indicator
	y_t	y_{t-1}	p_t	p_{t-1}	p_t^c	π_t	$\overset{*}{\pi}(p_t^c)$	y	π	Δr	Loss	Rank	
	Feedback with contemporaneous output and price indicators												
(1)	1.5	...	0.25	...	...	...	...	2.08	2.41	1.38	12.0	1	GNP price level
(2)	1.5	...	...	...	...	0.25	...	2.07	2.56	1.39	12.8	4	GNP price inflation
(3)	2.0	...	...	...	0.10	...	...	1.72	2.45	1.81	12.2	2	Commodity price level
(4)	2.0	...	...	...	...	...	0.10	1.77	2.50	1.83	12.7	3	Commodity price inflation filter
	Feedback with lagged output and inertial price indicators												
(5)	...	2.0	...	0.25	...	...	...	2.41	2.51	2.22	17.0	6	GNP price level
(6)	...	2.0	...	...	0.20	...	...	2.31	2.40	2.33	16.5	5	Commodity price level

a. Root-mean-squared errors of deviations from deterministic baseline projections in the second half of forty-quarter simulations, using a sample of 100 stochastic replications. RMSEs for the level of real GNP, y, are measured in percent; those for GNP price inflation, π, and the first-difference of the federal funds rate, Δr, are in percentage points.

change of the GNP deflator), $\overline{p}^c$ (the log of a weighted average of the three commodity price indexes), and $\overset{*}{\pi}$ (an estimate of expected inflation based on the commodity-based inflation filter, as cited in equation 15-23).[21] All variables are measured as deviations from baseline values.

The influence of the selected policy indicators on the policy instrument is summarized by a generic feedback rule,

$$(15\text{-}24) \qquad 0.01 \cdot r_t = \beta_{y,i} y_{t-i} + \beta_{p,i} p_{t-i} + \beta_\pi \pi_t + \beta_{pc} \overline{p}^c_t + \beta_{\overset{*}{\pi}} \overset{*}{\pi}_t,$$

where r denotes the federal funds rate. The federal funds rate may respond to either current ($i = 0$) or lagged ($i = 1$) values of the levels of real GNP and the GNP price deflator.

For a given set of policy indicators, the coefficients, β_x, of indicators excluded from the feedback rule are set to zero, and the coefficients of the included indicators are determined by a grid search to minimize the policy loss function,

$$(15\text{-}25) \qquad\qquad L = \text{var}(y) + \text{var}(\pi) + \text{var}(\Delta r).$$

This criterion is an unweighted average of the quarterly variances of the log level of real GNP, y; the aggregate rate of inertial price inflation, π; and the change in the federal funds rate, Δr. The last argument penalizes policies that require unusually active use of the policy instrument. Variances are calculated for departures from the deterministic baseline projection and measured over the second-half of the forty-quarter simulation horizon to capture better the steady-state implications of alternative policies.

Results of simulations in which policymakers are assumed to respond to measures of current-quarter ($i = 0$) macroeconomic activity—real GNP and the GNP deflator—are shown in the upper part of table 15-6. The policy underlying the first experiment, line 1, moves the federal funds rate 1.5 percentage points (relative to baseline) for each 1 percent deviation of the level of real output and 1/4 percentage point for each 1 percent deviation of the level in the GNP deflator. A second policy (line 2), which substitutes the inflation-rate indicator for the price-level indicator, leads to an outcome that is slightly worse than targeting the price level. This is somewhat surprising because the policy-loss function depends on the inflation rate, not the price level, and may be an

---

21. The same weights used to aggregate the three commodity price indexes in the commodity-based inflation filter, $\overset{*}{\pi}$, are used to aggregate the raw commodity-price indexes in construction p^c. The gross volatility of commodity prices is somewhat understated in the present stochastic simulations by the deterministic characterizations of most exogenous variables. As indicated by the overbar, the filter estimate of inflation, $\overset{*}{\pi}$, is smoothed by a two-quarter moving average as a crude adjustment for the dynamics implied by the short-run regressions estimated for the commodity-price indexes.

instance of the importance of "integral" feedback control whereby the policy planner aims to narrow the cumulative sum of past target misses in inflation rates (see Phillips 1957).

To examine the policy value of the inflation information embedded in commodity prices, the next policy (line 3) substitutes the weighted aggregate commodity-price level for the GNP deflator. The performance of the commodity-price rule is bracketed by the outcomes of the first two experiments, where the policy loss is better than that associated with targeting GNP inflation and not much worse than that obtained by targeting the GNP price level.

A final experiment with current-quarter indicators uses the expected-inflation filter based on commodity prices, $\overset{*}{\pi}_t$, as the price measure in the policy rule. By construction, the information set of the commodity price filter does not include direct measurement of the current-quarter inflation rate, π_t, as noted earlier. As can be seen in line 4 of table 15-6, however, the policy loss in this case is slightly better than the performance of the feedback response to the direct measure of current-quarter inflation (line 2).[22]

One advantage of primary-commodity prices is that they are observed immediately, whereas measurements of aggregate macroeconomic activity are released with lengthy lags and are subject to subsequent revisions. Simulations of policies that reflect more realistic timing of information available to policymakers are reported in the lower portion of table 15-6. In line 5, the funds rate responds to one-quarter lags in real GNP and in the level of the GNP deflator; the incremental policy loss associated with this lag in measurements is about 40 percent of the policy loss shown in line 1. Line 6 reports a test of the value of the more timely information in commodity prices. Here, the *current-quarter* commodity price level replaces the *one-quarter lag* of the GNP deflator as an indicator in the policy reaction. The net result is a modest reduction in the simulated policy loss. Relative to the policy in line 5, the root-mean-squared errors (RMSEs) of real GNP and aggregate inflation are each reduced by about 5 percent, whereas the RMSE of the funds-rate change is higher.

Expectations Based on Policy-dependent Long Autoregressions

A second set of experiments simulates the impact of counterfactual changes in monetary policy on the LAR characterizations of agents' expectations, notably of future inflation rates and federal funds rates. For a given policy,

---

22. A key premise of the filtering approach—that there is useful information in the stochastic disturbances of the commodity price equations—is supported by the results of an additional set of stochastic simulations in which these residuals are set to zero. In a repeat of the experiment summarized in line 3 of table 15-6, where the feedback indicators include the level of the commodity-price index, the loss function is boosted from $L = 12.2$ to $L = 12.9$ when the simulated commodity prices do not incorporate the relevant stochastic disturbances.

Table 15-7. *Selected Characteristics of Policy-Dependent LAR Descriptors (LAR-PD) of Expectations*

Simulation	Policy feedback coefficients			Bond rate response to sustained increase in funds rate[a] (quarter after increase)				Expected inflation response to sustained increase in observed inflation[b] (quarter after increase)			
	y_t	p_t	p_t^c	1	2	4	8	1	2	4	8
Feedback with contemporaneous GNP price indicator											
(1)	1.0	0.25	$\cdots$	0.32	0.77	1.32	1.20	0.0	1.2	1.7	2.0
(2)	1.5	0.25	$\cdots$	0.25	0.59	1.00	1.11	0.0	0.9	1.1	1.4
(3)	2.0	0.25	$\cdots$	0.22	0.51	0.87	1.05	0.0	0.8	1.0	1.2
(4)	2.5	0.25	$\cdots$	0.20	0.46	0.61	0.78	0.0	0.8	1.0	1.2
Feedback with contemporaneous commodity price indicator											
(5)	1.0	$\cdots$	0.10	0.25	0.61	1.12	1.14	0.0	0.9	1.3	1.5
(6)	1.5	$\cdots$	0.10	0.23	0.54	0.94	1.03	0.0	0.8	1.2	1.3
(7)	2.0	$\cdots$	0.10	0.21	0.49	0.83	0.93	0.0	0.8	1.1	1.1

a. Partial model simulation of corporate bond rate, R_t, response to a permanent 1.0 percentage point increase in the federal funds rate, r_t.
b. Partial model simulation of discounted, expected inflation rate, $_t\bar{\pi}$, response to a permanent 1.0 percentage point increase in the GNP price inflation rate, π_t.

policy-dependent LAR descriptors (LAR-PD) of the relevant forcing terms in the auction-price models are estimated by a procedure that iterates between stochastic simulation and estimation stages. The simulation stage is a lengthy (1973:1–1989:4) stochastic simulation of the FRB/MPS model under the selected counterfactual monetary policy rule. In the estimation stage, the relevant LAR descriptors are refit to the simulated counterfactual "history." The old LARs are replaced by the revised LARs in the auction-price sector of the FRB/MPS model, and the two stages are repeated until the coefficients of the LAR descriptors converge. This contraction-mapping procedure yields a set of policy-dependent LARs. These LAR-PD autoregressions are then used in a full set of 100 stochastic replications of the ten-year projection horizon.

Two of the feedback policies cited in table 15-6 have been repeated, using the LAR-PD procedure: in one policy, the feedback rule responds to readings on current real output and the GNP deflator; in the other, the feedback rule responds to measurements of current output and the index of primary-commodity prices.

Table 15-7 provides a short summary of the policy sensitivity of LAR-PD expectations, focusing on two key policy-transmission channels that depend on agents' perceptions of policy. The three left-hand columns of table 15-7 identify the coefficients of the policy feedback rule; basically, for a given price indicator (p or p^c), policy is more active in targeting real output in successive rows.[23] The middle four columns of the table indicate the cumulative response of the corporate bond rate, R, to movements in the funds rate, r. The remaining four

23. Line 2 of table 15-7 is the GNP-price policy rule reported for the historical autoregressions (LAR-H) in line 1 of table 15-6, and line 7 is the commodity-price policy rule reported in line 3 of table 15-6.

right-hand columns of the table indicate the response of expected inflation, $_t\tilde{\pi}$, to movements in the current inflation rate, π_t. In both cases, because of the unit-root specification in equation 15-7a of the LARs, the cumulative long-run response of expectations is unity.[24]

The results in table 15-7 suggest a nontrivial interaction between the policy stance and the short-term responsiveness of long-term expectations. When the policy response of the funds rate to real output is more cautious, as in line 1 of the table, changes in the funds rate are more persistent or less likely to be reversed; therefore, the bond rate responds relatively quickly to observed changes in the funds rate under this policy. By contrast, the more aggressive policy shown in line 4 of the table responds to a larger proportion of transient disturbances in real output, and this in turn induces more frequent reversals of the funds rate (larger negative autocorrelations). Consequently, the bond rate is slower to respond to movements in the funds rate because a given change is perceived as less persistent. After four quarters, for example, the bond-rate response under the more active policy in line 4 is less than half of the bond-rate response under the less active policy in line 1.

Similarly, as seen in the right-hand columns of table 15-7, more active policies lead to faster damping of movements in inflation caused by changes in real output. This reduces the positive autocorrelations in observed rates of inflation and leads to a somewhat slower response of expected inflation.

In general, the results displayed in table 15-7 for policy-dependent LAR expectations indicate that more cautious policy responses to real output are associated with relatively fast expectational responses, whereas more aggressive policy responses to real output are associated with slower responses in long-term expectations. In other words, the short-term "bang per buck" is less for aggressive policies because agents are more conditioned to rapid reversals of policy stances. Thus, although the bond rate is less likely to reinforce the intended policy effects of movements in the short-term interest rate, agents' expectations are less likely to exacerbate the persistence of short-term movements in inflation, given the estimated "perception" of the effectiveness of more aggressive policy in containing inflation. *Thus, the net impact of policy-dependent expectations on the effectiveness of counterinflationary policies appears to be a wash: real long-term interest rates are relatively invariant to the alternative characterizations of expectations.*

Indeed, this is the bottom line of the simulations reported in table 15-8. Two sets of loss functions are reported in table 15-8 for each of the seven policy settings reviewed in table 15-7. The LAR-H columns indicate the policy losses

---

24. Strictly speaking, in the case of the corporate bond rate, the cumulative weight sum for the modeler's expectation, $\tilde{R}$, is unity, but the estimated cumulative sum for the historical bond rate, R, is about 0.9, as shown in table 15-3.

Table 15-8. *Policy Loss Contrasts of Historical (LAR-H) and Policy-Dependent (LAR-PD) Descriptors of Expectations*

Simulation	Indicator feedback coefficients			LAR-H		LAR-PD	
	y_t	p_t	p_t^c	Loss	Rank	Loss	Rank
	Feedback with contemporaneous GNP price indicator						
(1)	1.0	0.25	$\cdots$	14.4	7	13.4	5
(2)	1.5	0.25	$\cdots$	**12.0**	1	**12.3**	1
(3)	2.0	0.25	$\cdots$	12.5	4	13.2	4
(4)	2.5	0.25	$\cdots$	13.6	5	14.4	6
	Feedback with contemporaneous commodity price indicator						
(5)	1.0	$\cdots$	0.10	14.2	6	**12.8**	2
(6)	1.5	$\cdots$	0.10	12.4	3	14.5	7
(7)	2.0	$\cdots$	0.10	**12.2**	2	13.1	3

associated with expectations based on historical autoregressions. (The results in lines 2 and 7 of the LAR-H columns of table 15-8 are the same as those reported for lines 1 and 3 in table 15-6.) The LAR-PD columns contain the policy losses for the relevant feedback rules generated by the policy-dependent variants of the LAR regressions.

In general, the relative ranking of policies does not appear to be significantly altered by the introduction of policy-dependent expectations. For policies responding to current observations on real output and the GNP price level, shown in the upper portion of table 15-8, the policy that minimizes the loss function under the historical LAR descriptors, LAR-H (as reported in line 1 of table 15-6), also minimizes the loss under policy-dependent expectations, LAR-PD. This is not true in the lower panel, where a less active policy (line 5) has a lower loss under LAR-PD than the policy (line 7) that minimized the loss under LAR-H expectations. The difference in losses of the two commodity-price policies, however, is remarkably small.

To summarize the effects of introducing policy-dependent expectations, the results of table 15-7 indicate that the conduct of policy can induce nontrivial alterations in the expectation structure and associated policy-transmission channels. The relative invariance of policy rankings in table 15-8, however, suggest that the net impact of accounting for the policy dependence of expectations on the design of optimizing policies is modest, at least in the context of the policy feedback rules employed in this study.

Conclusions

This chapter has explored the policy usefulness of auction-price indicators. The general methodology is to exploit present-value formulations of auction prices that contain agents' expectations of forward rates of interest and inflation.

The computational approach to expectations uses long autoregression (LAR) descriptors of agents' information sets, recognizing that the coefficients in LAR approximations depend on the structure of the models perceived by agents.

Present-value formulations are estimated for the corporate bond rate, the dividend yield on equity, and several primary commodity price indexes. Although theory suggests that arbitrage conditions should hold in each period, the empirical estimates resemble cointegrating attractors, holding reasonably well on average but subject to stationary departures from estimated "fundamentals." The cointegrating regression for the corporate bond rate fits well, and arbitrage deviations are short in duration. The long-run model for the dividend yield on equity requires a rolling-sample risk premium to achieve cointegration; the estimated coefficient of the risk premium, however, exhibits subsample instability. Acceptable long-run relationships are estimated for three groups of primary commodity price indexes—food, industrial materials, and industrial metals. No reliable long-run relationship is found for an index of precious metals prices, however, that contains the price of gold.

One set of stochastic policy experiments with the FRB/MPS quarterly model uses historical LAR descriptors to generate agents' expectations. Commodity-price indexes appear to be moderately useful as policy indicators, particularly when aggregate measurements of current economic activity are reported with a lag.

A second set of simulation experiments explores the effect of policy-dependent expectations, generated by a contraction-mapping procedure that iterates between model simulations and LAR estimations based on the simulated outcomes. The results indicate that accounting for agents' perceptions of the current policy rule can induce nontrivial alterations in the dynamic structure of agents' expectations. The net impact on long-term real interest rates is modest, however, because of the offsetting effects of changes in the expected persistence of movements in inflation and nominal interest rates. Thus, accounting for the policy dependence of agents' expectations did not appreciably alter the performance rankings of the alternative feedback policies examined.

References

Angell, W. 1987. "A Commodity Price Guide to Monetary Aggregate Targeting." Paper presented at the Lehrman Institute, New York, December 10.

Baillie, R. 1989. "Commodity Prices and Aggregate Inflation: Would a Commodity Price Rule Be Worthwhile?" In *IMF Policy Advice Market Volatility, Commodity Price Rules and Other Essays,* edited by K. Brunner and A. H. Meltzer, 186–240. Carnegie-Rochester Conference Series on Public Policy 31. Amsterdam: North-Holland.

Boughton, J. M., and W. Branson. 1988. "Commodity Prices as a Leading Indicator of Inflation." International Monetary Fund Working Paper.

Boughton, J. M., W. Branson, and A. Muttardy. 1989. "Commodity Prices and Inflation: Evidence from Seven Large Industrial Countries." NBER Working Paper 3158. Cambridge, Mass.: National Bureau of Economic Research.

Brayton, F., and E. Mauskopf. 1985. "The Federal Reserve Board MPS Quarterly Econometric Model of the U.S. Economy." *Economic Modelling* 2:170–292.

———. 1987. "Structure and Uses of the MPS Quarterly Econometric Model of the United States." *Federal Reserve Bulletin,* February, 93–109.

Campbell, J., and R. Shiller. 1989. "The Dividend-Price Ratio and Expectations of Future Dividends and Discount Factors." *Review of Financial Studies* 2:195–228.

Dagli, C. A., and J. B. Taylor. 1984. "Estimation and Solution of Linear Rational Expectations Models Using a Polynomial Matrix Factorization." *Journal of Economic Dynamics and Control* 8:341–48.

Diewert, W. E. 1978. "Superlative Index Numbers and Consistency in Aggregation." *Econometrica* 46:883–900.

Durand, M., and S. Blöndal. 1988. "Are Commodity Prices Leading Indicators of OECD Prices?" OECD Department of Economics and Statistics Working Paper 49. Paris.

Engle, R. F., and C. W. I. Granger. 1987. "Co-Integration and Error Correction: Representation, Estimation, and Testing." *Econometrica* 55:251–76.

Engle, R. F., and B. S. Yoo. 1987. "Forecasting and Testing in Co-Integrated Systems." *Journal of Econometrics* 35:143–59.

Fair, R. C., and J. B. Taylor. 1983. "Solution and Maximum Likelihood Estimation of Dynamic Rational Expectations Model." *Econometrica* 51:1169–85.

Fuller, W. 1976. *Introduction to Statistical Time Series*. New York: Wiley.

Granger, C., and A. Escribano. 1989. "The Long-Run Relationship between Prices from an Efficient Market: The Case of Gold and Silver." University of California at San Diego, Department of Economics.

Gustafson, R. 1958. "Carryover Levels for Grains: A Method for Determining Amounts That Are Optimal under Specific Conditions." U.S. Department of Agriculture Technical Bulletin 1178.

Hansen, L. P., and T. J. Sargent. 1980. "Formulating and Estimating Dynamic Linear Rational Expectations Models." *Journal of Economic Dynamics and Control* 2:7–46.

Koreisha, S., and T. Pukkila. 1990. "A Generalized Least-Squares Approach for Estimation of Autoregressive Moving-Average Models." *Journal of Time Series Analysis* 11:139–51.

Mishkin, F. 1990a. "What Does the Term Structure Tell Us about Future Inflation?" *Journal of Monetary Economics* 25:77–95.

———. 1990b. "The Information in the Longer Maturity Term Structure about Future Inflation." *Quarterly Journal of Economics* 105:815–28.

Muth, J. F. 1961. "Rational Expectations and the Theory of Price Movements." *Econometrica* 29:315–35.

Newberry, D. M. G., and J. E. Stiglitz. 1981. *The Theory of Commodity Price Stabilization: A Study in the Economics of Risk.* Oxford: Oxford University Press.

———. 1982. "Optimal Commodity Stockpiling Rules." *Oxford Economic Papers* 34:403–27.

Phillips, A. 1957. "Stabilization Policy and the Time-Form of Lagged Responses." *Economic Journal* 67:265–77.

Samuelson, P. 1971. "Stochastic Speculative Price." *Proceedings of the National Academy of Sciences* 68:335–37.

Sargan, J. D. 1980. "Some Tests of Dynamic Specification for a Single Equation." *Econometrica* 48:879–97.

Shiller, R. J. 1979. "The Volatility of Long-Term Interest Rates and Expectations Models of the Term Structure." *Journal of Political Economy* 87:1190–1219.

Sims, C. 1989. "Modeling Trends." Institute for Empirical Macroeconomics Discussion Paper 22. Federal Reserve Bank of Minneapolis. December.

Stock, J. H. 1987. "Asymptotic Properties of Least Squares Estimates of Cointegration Vectors." *Econometrica* 55:1035–56.

Tinsley, P. 1970. "On Ramps, Turnpikes, and Distributed Lag Approximations of Optimal Intertemporal Adjustment." *Western Economic Journal* 8:397–411.

Tinsley, P., R. Krieger, and W. Kan. 1990. "The Long and Short of Industry Pricing: A Proximate Cause of Business Cycles." Federal Reserve Staff Working Paper.

Whiteman, C. 1983. *Linear Rational Expectations Models: A User's Guide.* Minneapolis: University of Minnesota Press.

Whittle, P. 1963. *Prediction and Regulation by Linear Least-Square Methods.* London: English University Press.

Zellner, A., and F. Palm. 1974. "Time Series Analysis and Simultaneous Equation Econometric Models." *Journal of Econometrics* 2:17–54.

CHAPTER 16

Using External Sustainability
to Forecast the Dollar

Ellen E. Meade and Charles P. Thomas

THE INCREASE in U.S. external debt since the early 1980s has prompted many
to ask whether continued current account deficits of the magnitude witnessed
can be sustained. The long-run sustainability of the current account has been
examined by Hooper (1989), Krugman (1985, 1988), and Marris (1985, 1987).
In these studies the authors used partial equilibrium models of the U.S. current
account, in which the dollar is predetermined, to draw inferences about the path
that the dollar must follow to guarantee external sustainability. When model
extrapolations of the current account, given a path for the dollar, imply an ever-
increasing U.S. net demand for foreign capital, these authors concluded that
the given path of the dollar is unsustainable. This is because, in their view, it is
unlikely that the net supply of foreign capital available to finance such deficits
would be forthcoming.

The conclusion drawn in these earlier papers about sustainability is sharp
and does not allow for the substantial uncertainty that surrounds this issue.
There is uncertainty about the estimated model of the U.S. current account
that is used to generate the net demand for foreign assets for a given path of
the dollar. There is considerable uncertainty about the preferences of foreign
investors for U.S. assets. Finally, there is uncertainty about the mechanics of
exchange-rate determination, which yields uncertainty about the particular path
for the dollar.

In this chapter we develop a way to link the long-run net demand for and
supply of foreign capital to the path of the dollar that explicitly addresses these
sources of uncertainty. We find that, for any given assumption about foreign
preferences or the willingness of foreigners to supply net capital, there is a
range of sustainable exchange rates. That range of sustainable exchange rates

The authors thank Brian Cody, Craig Hakkio, David Howard, Eric Leeper, and participants of the Brookings
conference, especially Mike Gavin and Dale Henderson, and of a workshop at the Federal Reserve Board for
comments on an earlier version. The views expressed are those of the authors and do not necessarily reflect
the views of the Board of Governors of the Federal Reserve System or its staff. Virginia Carper provided
expert research assistance.

769

varies considerably, moreover, with changes in the assumption about foreign preferences. Using our framework, we can recast the earlier studies in terms of the likelihood that particular levels of the dollar would be consistent with sustainability.

The chapter is organized as follows: in the first section we present a partial equilibrium model of the current account and discuss the cumulative net demand for foreign assets that is generated using that model. We also present estimates of a cumulative net demand schedule. This is in the spirit of the earlier work on sustainability; however, we attempt to quantify some of the uncertainty associated with the cumulative net demand schedule. The second section addresses the cumulative net supply of foreign funds available to the United States. Rather than estimate a cumulative net supply schedule, we impose a set of priors over the supply of funds. In the third section, we present a method for combining the demand schedule generated by the current account model with the priors on the supply of foreign funds to produce a forecast for sustainable exchange rates. We then discuss, in the fourth section, the initial distribution for the dollar and the posterior "sustainable" distribution that results from the interaction of demand and supply. Conclusions are presented in the final section.

The Current Account and the Cumulative Net Demand Curve

As in earlier papers on sustainability, the net demand for foreign capital is evaluated by using a partial equilibrium model of the U.S. current account. Before discussing the results of simulations with that model, we first review the dynamics of net foreign asset accumulation in a stylized model.

Stylized Model

A minimum requirement for sustainability is that, for a fixed exchange rate, the current account balance adjust to ensure that the long-run ratio of net foreign assets to nominal GNP is bounded. The net foreign asset (NFA) position influences the current account through two effects in our model, one direct and one indirect. The direct effect is simply the service-income component of the current account balance. As the NFA position deteriorates, service payments increase, the current account worsens, and the NFA position deteriorates further. This effect is destabilizing.

The second, or indirect, effect is stabilizing. When the NFA position declines and service payments on the position increase, the level of income declines, for a given level of production. With imports determined by income, such a decline in income will reduce imports. Similarly, when exports are specified to depend on foreign income, a decline in the home NFA position will increase foreign income and home exports. This effect is incorporated in the simulation model by exogenizing GDP and endogenizing GNP for both the United States and foreign countries.[1]

The essential structure of our partial equilibrium model is as follows. We assume that real production (GDP) in the United States and foreign countries, g and g^*, grows at a common exogenous rate γ and that prices, p and p^*, grow at a common rate π. Nominal income (GNP) in the United States and foreign countries, Y and Y^*, is the value of domestic production plus net factor income:[2]

(16-1a) $$Y = g\,p + Dr$$

(16-1b) $$Y^* = g^* p^* - DrE,$$

where

D = the NFA position of the United States, denominated in dollars
  ($D < 0$ is a debtor position)

r = the rate of interest

E = the nominal exchange rate, in units of foreign currency per dollar.

Real incomes, y and y^*, are given as

(16-2a) $$y = Y/p$$

(16-2b) $$y^* = Y^*/p^*.$$

Real exports from the United States, x, depend on real foreign income and the real exchange rate, R, whereas real imports, m, depend on real domestic income and the real exchange rate:

(16-3a) $$x = a(R)y^*$$

(16-3b) $$m = b(R)y,$$

where

$$R = (p/p^*)E$$
$$a[] \geq 0,\ b[] \geq 0,\ a'[] < 0,\ b'[] > 0.[3]$$

1. There are other indirect effects that are not captured in the model: the effect of changes in wealth on consumption and income and the effect of changes in net exports on income.

2. The assumption that real productive capacity is identical to GDP is a strong one and implies that changes in the current account must be accommodated by changes in absorption. A more complicated model would allow deviations of output from capacity both in the United States and in foreign countries.

3. Note that the stylized trade equations are specified in share form, which imposes a unitary income elasticity. Long-run analysis, such as that in the following note, requires unitary income elasticities in the long run. Otherwise, trade shares explode or fall to zero.

The change in the NFA position for the United States, or the current account balance, is given by the trade balance plus net factor income:[4]

(16-4) $\dot{D} = CA = x\,p - m\,p^*/E + Dr$.

Empirical Model

The empirical model of the current account is a modified version of the Helkie-Hooper model used in several recent studies (Helkie and Hooper 1988, Cline 1989, Hooper and Mann 1989). The most significant modification of the Helkie-Hooper model is the incorporation of the indirect income effect discussed above. Without this indirect effect, the Helkie-Hooper model is inherently unstable because there is no internal mechanism to limit debt or wealth accumulation. For example, in the case of an overvalued dollar, there is nothing to stop the NFA position from deteriorating to the point where net factor payments exceed GDP. In the modified Helkie-Hooper model, GDP is predetermined for the United States and foreign industrial countries. GNP is computed endogenously, given GDP and U.S. net factor payments. For the United States, the computation of GNP is straightforward. The computation of GNP for foreign countries is analogous, although it requires an assumption about the distribution of factor payments across creditor countries.[5]

To the Helkie-Hooper equations for merchandise trade and nonfactor services we append identities to calculate net investment income, the current account, net capital flows, and the NFA position for the United States.[6] For simplicity, we treat net investment income as the product of a single rate of

---

4. This stylized model is bounded in the sense that the stabilizing influence of the indirect effect is sufficient to offset the destabilizing influence of the direct effect, keeping the NFA-GNP ratio from exploding for an arbitrary level of the real exchange rate. Thomas (1991) has demonstrated that

$$\lim_{t \to \infty}[D/Y] = Z/[(\rho - \delta r)g_0 + Zr],$$

provided that $(\rho - \delta r) > 0$, where

$$\rho = \pi + \gamma$$
$$\delta = (1 - aE - b/E)$$
$$Z = (ag_0 - bg_0/E),$$

and g_0, $g*_0$ are the initial levels of production in the United States and foreign countries. Since δ is less than unity, the condition that $(\rho - \delta r) > 0$ says that, so long as the nominal interest rate is not too much larger than the nominal growth rate of the economies, the ratio of NFA to GNP will stabilize even for a fixed real exchange rate.

5. The computation of the "indirect" income effects is outlined in the first section of the appendix to this chapter.

6. Complete documentation of the modified Helkie-Hooper model used here is available from the authors on request.

return and the NFA position. Historically, the rate of return received on U.S. investment claims has exceeded the rate of return paid on U.S. liabilities.[7] Because of this difference in gross rates of return, the measured implicit net rate of return on the recent U.S. net foreign liability position has been quite low. In the simulations that follow, we assume that the low net rate of return continues to apply to the initial or historical NFA position (which we label "old" NFA). Any future additions to the initial net position that arise in simulations with the model are assumed to pay market rates of return (we term the NFA position cumulated over the simulation horizon "new" NFA.) This distinction between "old" NFA and "new" NFA positions allows us to impose the long-run property that the rate of return on the net position equal the rate of growth of nominal GNP.[8]

Equation 16-5 describes net investment service income:[9]

$$(16\text{-}5) \quad NSYV = (RORNFA_{old})(NFA_{old}) + (RORNFA_{new})(NFA_{new}),$$

where

$$NSYV = \text{net investment service income}$$
$$RORNFA_{old(new)} = \text{the rate of return on old (new) NFA position}$$
$$NFA_{old(new)} = \text{the old (new) NFA position cumulated over the historical (simulation) period.}$$

To close the model, we include an identity for the current account balance and add to the "new" NFA position the capital flows necessary to finance the current account:[10]

$$(16\text{-}6) \quad CABAL = GBAL + NSYOV + NSYV + TRAN$$

$$(16\text{-}7) \quad \Delta NFA_{new} = CABAL,$$

---

7. Several factors contribute to this rate of return differential. First, direct investment (DI) positions are recorded at "book" value. Since U.S. DI claims abroad are generally older than foreign DI claims in the United States, the use of book value tends to overstate the net liability position (by as much as $300 billion; see Stekler and Stevens 1991). Second, U.S.- and foreign-based multinationals both have tax incentives to adjust the prices they charge affiliates so as to report profits outside of the United States. Finally, the return on portfolio claims includes some fee income that is not included in the imputed return on portfolio liabilities.

8. In the early years of the simulations, the average rate of return on the *total* NFA is less than the marginal rate of return, since the "new" net position is a small fraction of the total net position. By the end of the thirty-year simulation horizon we consider, however, the average and marginal returns are approximately equal.

9. This formulation assumes that the NFA position and the factor payments associated with it are denominated in dollars.

10. In the simulations we assume that an imbalance in the current account represents a change in NFAs. That is, we abstract from such factors as capital gains and the statistical discrepancy in the balance of payments accounts that, historically, have caused the measured change in NFAs to differ from the current account.

where

$CABAL$ = the current account balance

$GBAL$ = net exports of goods

$NSYOV$ = net service income other than investment services

$NSYV$ = net investment service income

$TRAN$ = net unilateral transfers

ΔNFA_{new} = the change in NFA_{new}.

Each behavioral equation in the model was estimated through 1989:2 (the last quarter of data available when this research was undertaken).[11] The simulations reported cover a post-sample period that begins in 1989:3 and ends in 2020:4. Although the simulation horizon examined in this paper is much longer (thirty years) than studies in previous work, we deemed such a lengthy horizon necessary in order to address adequately the long-run nature of sustainability. Before turning to the results of several simulation experiments, it is important to review the baseline assumptions used to extrapolate the predetermined variables.

—The weighted-average dollar (an index of the currencies of the G10 countries aggregated using weights in multilateral trade from 1972–76) was held unchanged at its value in 1989:2.

—All prices in the model, both domestic and foreign (except for export and import prices, which are endogenous), were extrapolated at 3.5 percent per year (note that the real exchange rate and the price of oil relative to the price of other imports remain unchanged over the simulation horizon).

—The growth of real GDP in the United States and foreign industrial countries on average was extrapolated at 2.5 percent per year (roughly in line with recent estimates of potential GDP growth), and the real growth rate in developing countries was assumed to be 4 percent (overall foreign growth averages about 3 percent per year, outpacing activity in the United States by about $\frac{1}{2}$ percentage point).

—U.S. short-term interest rates were assumed to ease gradually to 6 percent by the end of 1990. The rate of return on the "old" NFA position was assumed to remain at its 1989:2 average of 3.5 percent; the rate of return on the "new" NFA position was assumed to increase gradually from 3.5 percent to 6 percent by 1990:4.

Baseline Simulation

Simulation of the model through 2020, given the baseline paths for the predetermined variables, yields a predicted path for the current account. We call this

---

11. Most of the equations in the model were estimated by using a correction for first-order serial correlation, as in the original Helkie-Hooper work (1988).

Figure 16-1. *Ratio of Net Foreign Assets (NFA) to GNP, 1989–2020*

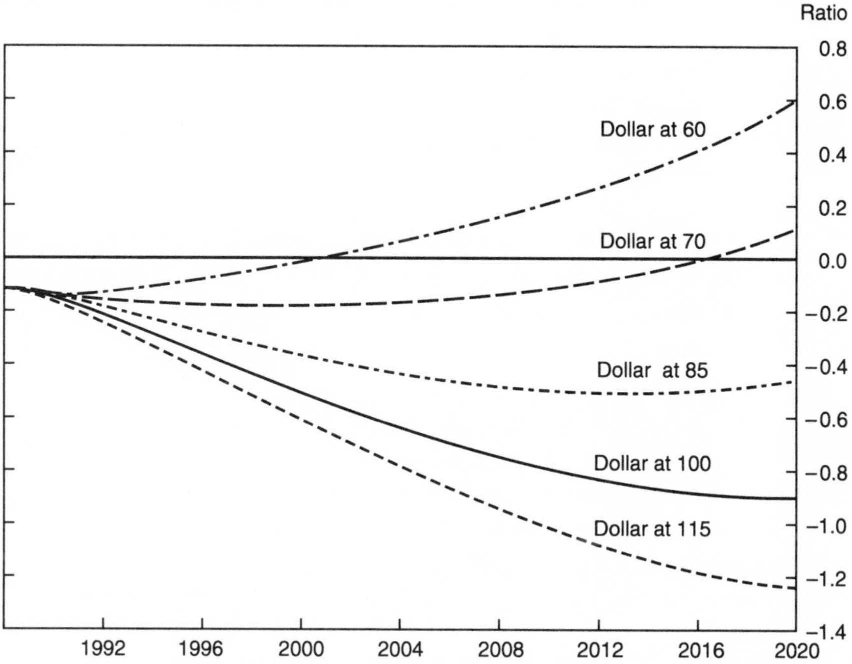

the net demand for foreign assets. We focus our analysis on the cumulative net demand for foreign assets (or the NFA position) relative to nominal GNP. The simulation suggests that if the weighted-average dollar were to have remained unchanged at its level in 1989:2 (about 100), the ratio of the NFA position to nominal GNP would decline from −12 percent to −90 percent in 2020 (shown by the solid line in figure 16-1).[12] The current account deficit as a share of nominal GNP grows from 2 percent in 1989:2 to 5.4 percent at the end of the simulation. The implication of this increase in the current account deficit is that domestic absorption is reduced.

This simulation experiment is practically identical to the exercise performed in the earlier studies of current account sustainability. Both Hooper (1989) and Marris (1985, 1987) conditioned their analyses on particular values for the dollar; Krugman (1985, 1988) assumed that the dollar would follow the path dictated by the differential between U.S. and foreign interest rates. For the exchange rates considered in these earlier studies, the current account, if simulated over a sufficiently long horizon, would have grown without bound. Because of the inclusion of the indirect income effects described above, our

---

12. We discuss simulation results only for the year 2020, an arbitrarily chosen date in the distant future.

simulation would eventually converge to a stable ratio of the NFA position to
nominal GNP. (In fact, a dollar of about 100 appears to yield a relatively stable
NFA-GNP ratio, roughly −90 percent, by 2020.)

Model simulations conditioned on alternative paths of the dollar result in
different net demands for foreign assets. (This is demonstrated in figure 16-1
for a weighted-average dollar unchanged at 115, 85, 70, and 60.) These
alternative simulations can be viewed as generating a demand schedule for
cumulative NFAs in 2020, shown graphically as the downward-sloping line
labeled "baseline" in figure 16-2. Each point on the cumulative net demand
schedule represents the level of the dollar on which each simulation is conditioned, and the ratio of the NFA position to nominal GNP that results in
2020.[13]

Uncertainty

Considerable uncertainty surrounds the estimated cumulative net demand curve,
however. One source of uncertainty arises from the assumptions for the predetermined variables in the system. To illustrate this, we have considered a "faster
foreign growth" alternative, in which, for example, the opening of markets in
Eastern Europe leads to annual average growth in foreign industrial countries
of 3.3 percent (almost 1 percentage point higher than in the baseline case).
This faster growth is allowed to persist through 1993 before returning to the
pace of 2.5 percent assumed in the baseline. This temporary increase in the
rate of foreign growth results in a significant shift out in the cumulative net
demand schedule, as shown in figure 16-2.

Another source of uncertainty about the cumulative net demand curve arises
from the uncertainty associated with the parameters and residuals in the model
equations. To quantify this uncertainty, we performed 1,000 stochastic simulations in which the residuals and estimated parameters of the model were
chosen from their sample distributions (the stochastic simulation technique is
described in the third section of the appendix). This exercise was performed
for each of five different paths of the dollar used to generate figures 16-1 and
16-2 (an unchanged dollar at 60, 70, 85, 100, and 115).

When model uncertainty is included, a given level of the dollar yields
a probability distribution over the NFA-GNP ratio rather than a single value
for that ratio. Figure 16-3 illustrates this distribution by plotting the one-sixth
quantile, the median, and the five-sixths quantile of the NFA-GNP ratio for
various levels of the dollar. For a given level of the dollar, two-thirds of the

---

13. If the simulation horizon is extended beyond 2020, the cumulative net demand schedule rotates
counterclockwise. For very high (low) values of the dollar, the NFA-GNP ratio worsens (improves) as the
simulation horizon lengthens.

Figure 16-2. *Cumulative Net Demand for Foreign Capital in 2020*

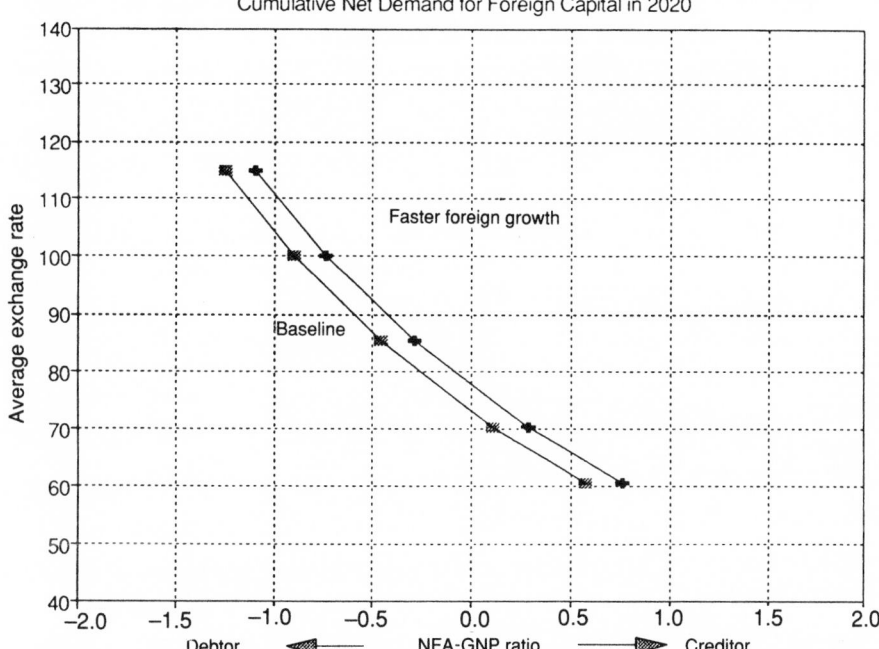

Figure 16-3. *Effect of Model Uncertainty on Cumulative Net Demand Curve in 2020*

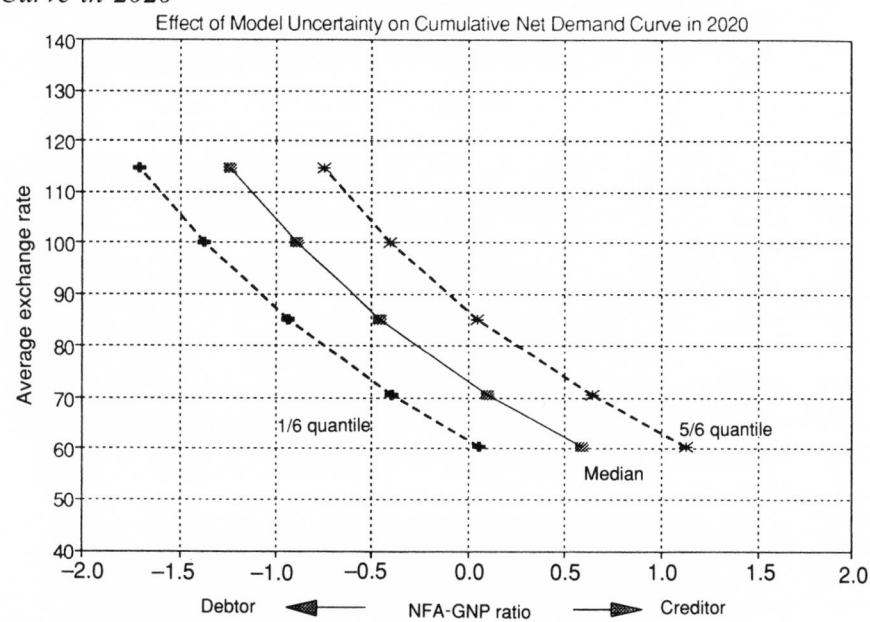

simulated values for the ratio of the NFA position to nominal GNP fall within
the band formed by the one-sixth and five-sixths quantiles.

The uncertainty associated with the cumulative net demand schedule has
obvious implications for the analysis of sustainability. Because there is a range
of NFA-GNP ratios consistent with any value of the dollar, it is impossible
to draw sharp conclusions about sustainability for any particular level of the
dollar. Put another way, any given level of the NFA-GNP ratio is consistent
with a wide range of paths for the dollar.

Cumulative Net Supply Curve

In the earlier studies on sustainability, no explicit assumptions about asset
preferences were made. Judgments about the sustainability of the demand for
foreign capital generated by a partial equilibrium model of the current account
were based on an implicit notion of foreign preferences for holding U.S. assets. In this section, foreign preferences for U.S. assets and the uncertainty
surrounding those preferences are considered explicitly. We do this by postulat-
ing a specific set of priors over the supply of funds available from foreigners.[14]

We postulate priors over the supply of funds rather than estimate asset-
demand equations, for two reasons. First, equations of foreign asset demands
have generally failed to measure parameters precisely or to pass standard specification tests. The literature on portfolio-balance models offers little hard empirical evidence on the preferences of foreigners for U.S. assets.[15] Second,
even if we had a well-specified system to describe foreign portfolio choices, it
would undoubtedly depend on variables not modeled here. Uncertainty about
these unmodeled variables would lead to a distribution for holdings that would
result in a set of priors analogous to those we postulate.

Our priors over the supply of foreign capital are expressed in terms of a
distribution over the NFA-GNP ratio. Scaling the NFA position by nominal
GNP is certainly simple to compute and may be the measure most appropriate
for capturing default risk, but is not the only conceivable measure of external
imbalance. Alternatively, scaling the NFA position by foreign wealth may
better measure the degree of concentration in foreign portfolios and thus may
be a better measure of external imbalance. Another alternative is to consider
the share of dollar-denominated assets in foreign portfolios (that is, the total
outstanding stock of dollar-denominated liabilities worldwide, not just claims

---

14. For expositional reasons, the discussion of the net supply of funds is in terms of foreign preferences.
Portfolio preferences of domestic residents are equally important, and it is the net supply of funds, including
both domestic and foreign investors, that determines whether a particular NFA position is sustainable.

15. Levich (1985) provides a summary of empirical work. See also Dooley and Isard (1983), Isard
(1987).

Figure 16-4. *Prior Distribution on Cumulative Net Supply Curve*

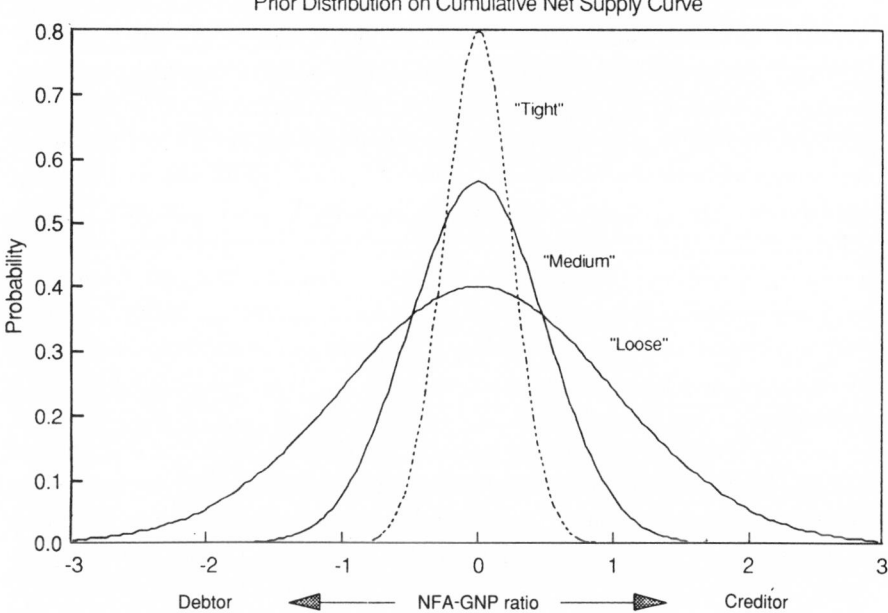

on U.S. residents) in order to measure currency risk.[16] Although there are several different measures that might be considered, most of these are extremely difficult to compute. For that reason, our analysis centers on the ratio of the NFA position to nominal GNP.[17]

The priors are described by a probability distribution over the potential cumulative net supply of capital (the ratio of the NFA position to nominal GNP) consistent with foreign preferences. We consider three alternative prior distributions, shown in figure 16-4. Each prior is normally distributed with a mean of zero; the priors differ in the degree of concentration about the mean. The "tight," "medium," and "loose" prior distributions have standard deviations of 0.25, 0.5, and 1.0 respectively.[18]

16. See Dealtry and Van't dack (1989) for a discussion of the difficulties in computing the share of dollar-denominated assets in the portfolios of non-U.S. residents.

17. Even this relatively straightforward measure is subject to severe error, owing to the difficulty in computing the NFA position. See Scholl (1990) and the references therein for a discussion of the issues in valuing the U.S. NFA position. It is worth noting that the United States is not the largest world debtor, even among industrial nations. In 1988, the NFA-GNP ratio was about −10 percent for the United States. This compares with a NFA-GDP ratio in 1988 of −38 percent for Canada (he largest debtor among industrial countries). The external debt position in a number of developing countries exceeded that of the United States in 1988 (for example, the NFA-GDP ratio was −103 percent for Ecuador, −71 percent for Argentina, −59 percent for Chile, and so on).

18. Although we think these priors are reasonable, they are certainly not exhaustive. An advantage of the method used here is that it is easily adapted to alternative priors, including those not centered at zero.

The Interaction of Demand and Supply

Similar to the earlier studies on sustainability, we believe it unlikely that a very high cumulative net demand for foreign capital, such as that associated with a debtor position in excess of 100 percent, for example, would be forthcoming from foreign suppliers. Because every point on the cumulative net supply schedule is not equally likely, we can use the priors on the supply of foreign capital to shed light on the distribution of "sustainable" exchange rates. Specifically, each point on the cumulative net demand curve represents the outcome of a simulation with the current account model, given an initial path for the dollar. Each simulated demand outcome is measured against the prior distribution over supply and assigned a probability. The posterior "sustainable" distribution of exchange rates results from weighting each initial exchange-rate path by its probability.

The method for obtaining the posterior distribution of the dollar is outlined in figure 16-5. The "medium" prior over supply is illustrated by the arrows that project from the x-axis up to the demand schedule. The solid arrow projects from the mean of the supply prior; the broken arrows project from the one-sixth and five-sixth quantiles, encompassing two-thirds of the distribution. The value for the dollar associated with each point on the demand curve (shown on the y-axis) is then weighted by its probability of occurrence, as determined by the prior distribution over supply. This method yields a posterior "sustainable" distribution of exchange rates, as opposed to a single value for the dollar that was the focus of earlier studies.

Although we abstract from the effects of model uncertainty in the discussion that follows, it is nevertheless important to keep in mind that the "sustainable" distribution would be significantly wider were we to consider explicitly the effects of model uncertainty on the cumulative net demand schedule.

Sustainable Paths for the Dollar

So far we have described the derivation of the cumulative net demand schedule (given a path for the dollar), the use of a prior distribution for the cumulative net supply schedule, and the interaction of demand and supply. What remains is the discussion of the initial distribution for the dollar on which the demand schedule is conditioned. We then turn to a discussion of the posterior "sustainable" distribution for exchange rates.

There are many plausible initial distributions for the dollar. The exchange-rate paths used to derive the cumulative net demand schedule pictured in figures 16-2, 16-3, and 16-5 were unchanged at a particular level of the dollar. For the analysis of the sustainable paths, we want to condition on an initial

Figure 16-5. *Interaction of Demand and Supply*

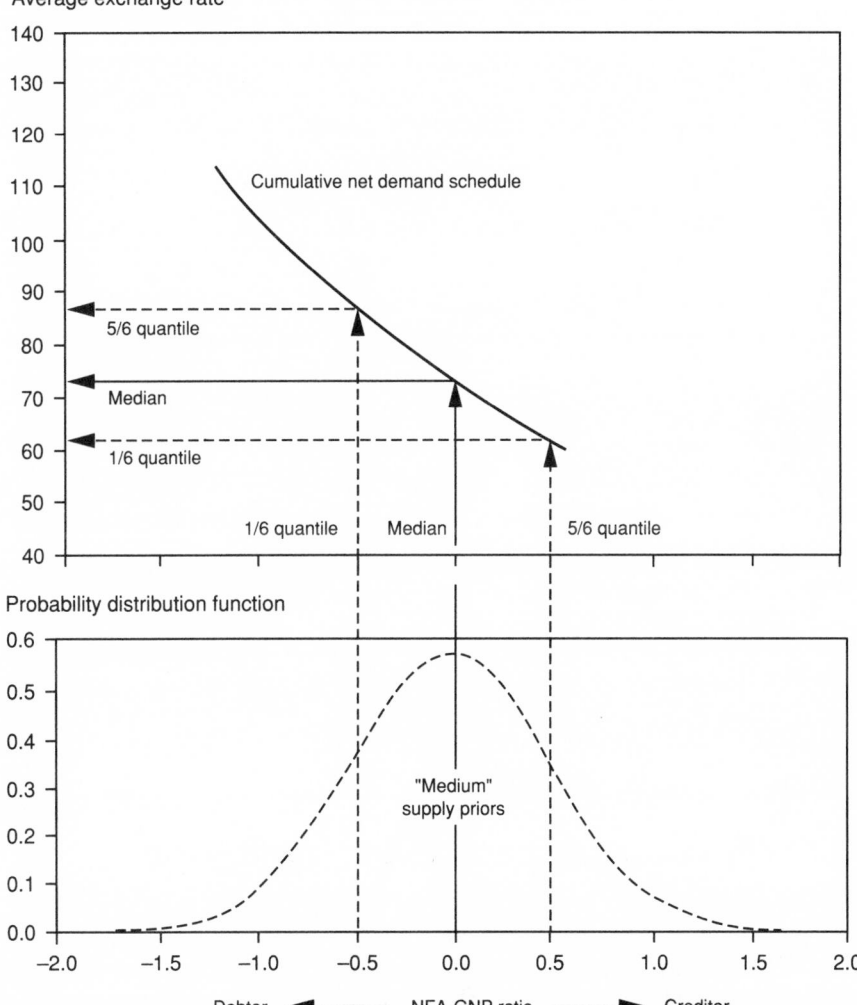

distribution for the dollar that is empirically sensible. For this, we have looked to the literature on exchange-rate behavior and have generated the initial distribution from a random-walk process that mimics the historical volatility of the dollar.[19] Meese and Rogoff (1983) were the first to suggest that a random-walk model of the dollar outperformed other models of exchange-rate behavior;[20] since that time, many other studies have favored the random-walk model in comparison with other models of exchange-rate determination (see Boughton

19. The initial distribution consists of 1,000 paths for the dollar that begin in 1989:3 and continue through 2020.

20. The Meese-Rogoff (1983) results covered out-sample simulation performance.

Figure 16-6. *Sample Distribution of Random-Walk Dollar, 1989–2020*

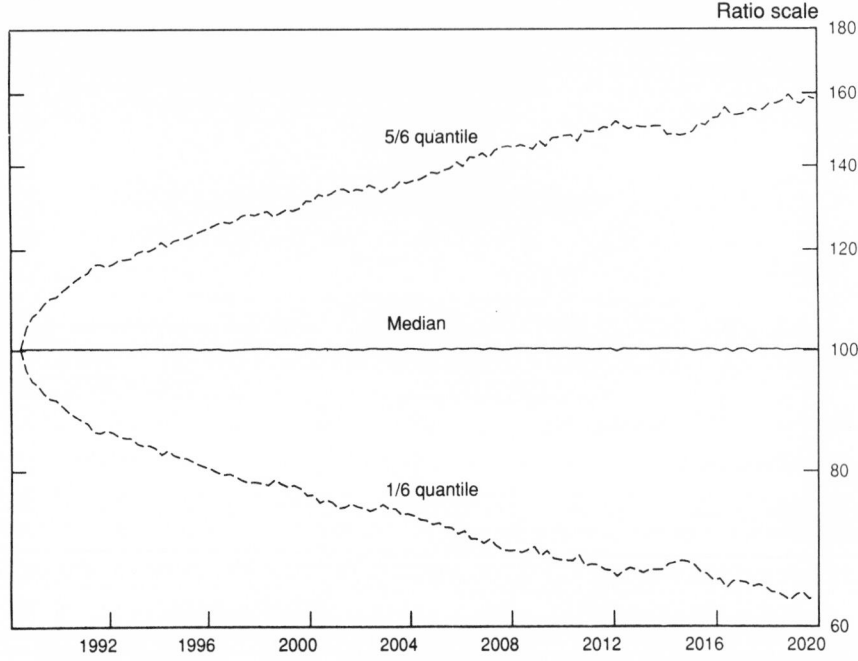

Figure 16-7. *Simulation Results and Priors*

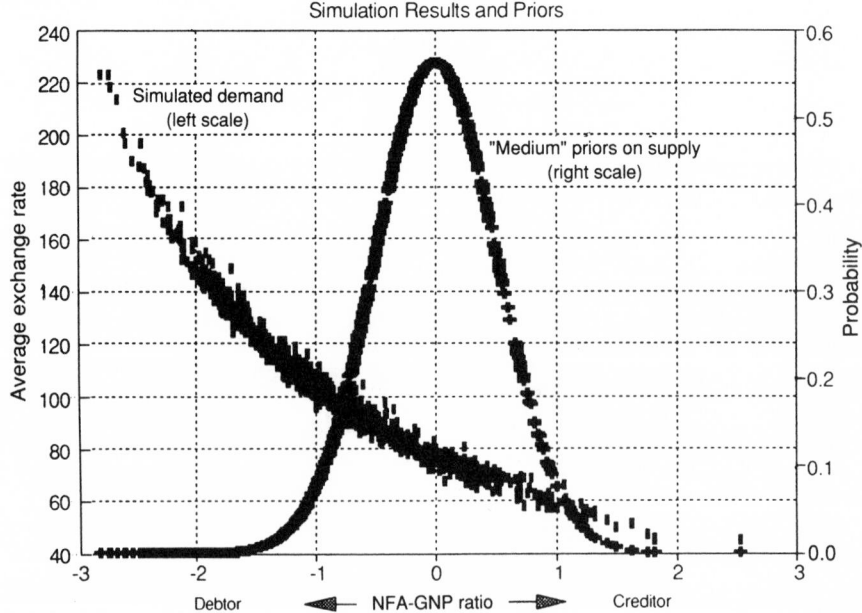

Figure 16-8. *Posterior Distribution of the Dollar: "Medium" Supply Priors, 1989–2020*

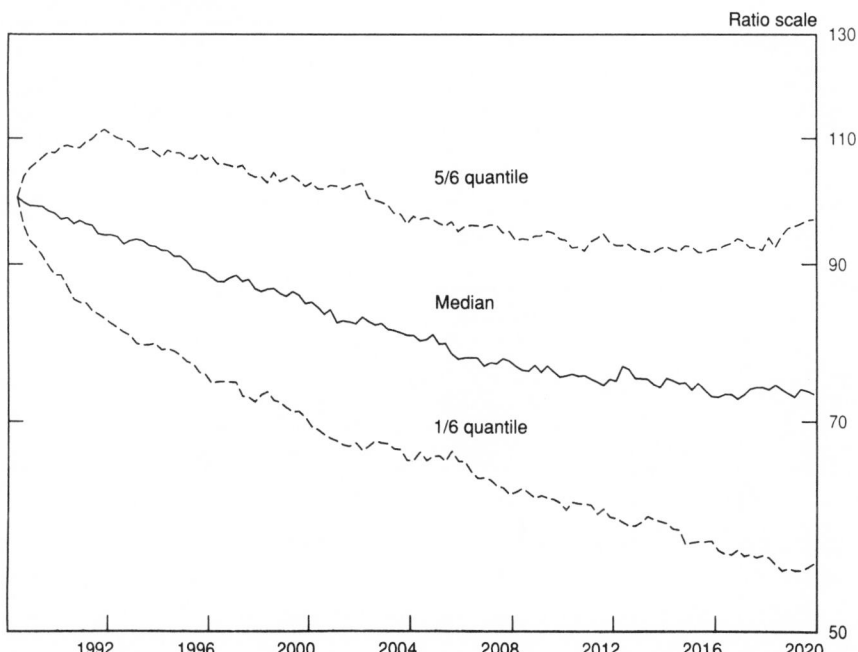

1987, Diebold and Nason 1990, Edison 1985, 1991, Meese and Rose 1989, and Schinasi and Swamy 1989). Because of wide acceptance in the literature, we chose to model the dollar initially as a random-walk process.

Each of the random-walk paths over T time periods was generated from T independent random draws from a normal distribution, with a mean of zero and a variance equal to that of the actual dollar between 1975:1 and 1989:2. To avoid any sampling bias in the initial distribution of 1,000 paths, we drew 500 independent exchange-rate paths and applied antithetics. This means that the final sample of 1,000 paths included 500 independent random-walk paths and the mirror image of each path.[21]

The initial distribution of random-walk exchange-rate paths for the simulation period beginning in 1989:3 and ending in 2020 is summarized in figure 16-6. Early on, the distribution of exchange-rate values is concentrated

21. The rth exchange-rate path and its mirror image (denoted by a "+") were generated as follows:

$$\ln(E_{r,t}) = \ln(E_{r,t-1}) + \epsilon_{r,t}$$

and

$$\ln(E_{r,t}^{+}) = \ln(E_{r,t-1}^{+}) - \epsilon_{r,t},$$

where $\epsilon_{r,t} \sim N(0, \sigma_E)$, $t = (1, \ldots, T)$, $r = (1, \ldots, 500)$. For further details, see Marquez and Ericsson (1990).

Figure 16-9. *Distribution of Dollar in 2020*

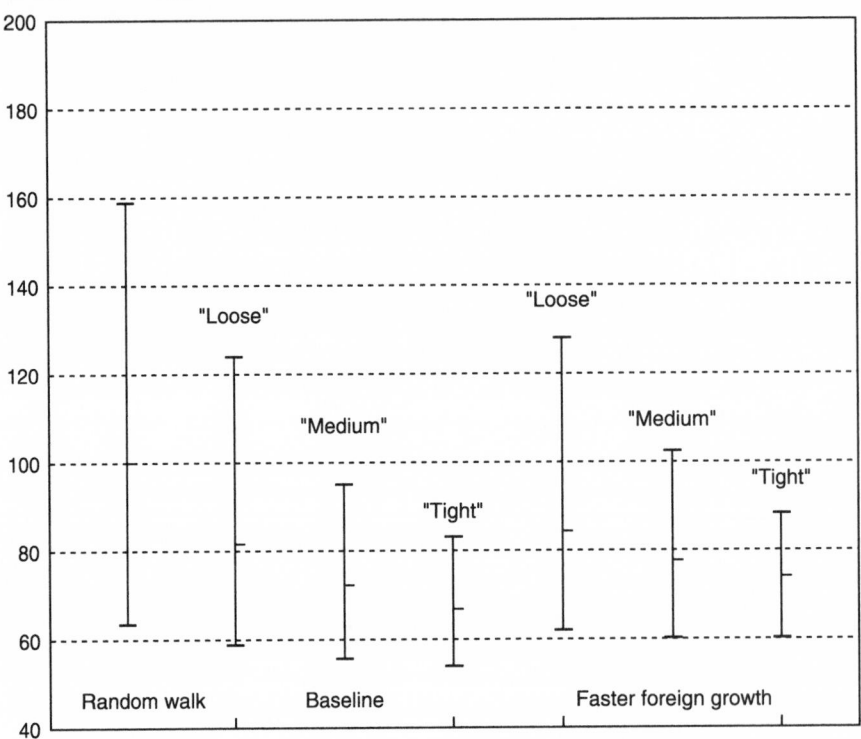

around the initial value of 100; by 2020, the distribution has disbursed sub-stantially around its original median, is symmetric, and is approximately log-normal.

These random-walk paths for the dollar were used in simulations with the current account model to generate conditional forecasts of the NFA-GNP ratio, shown in figure 16-7 for the year 2020. Each dot on the downward-sloping line labeled "simulated demand" represents the outcome of a single simulation. In isolation, these results suggest that the NFA-GNP ratio in 2020 could vary from a debtor position of almost 300 percent to a creditor position of almost 300 percent.

Imposition of the "medium" supply prior that is pictured in figure 16-7 on the simulated demand schedule results in a posterior distribution of the dollar, as described in the preceding section. This posterior distribution, shown in figure 16-8, indicates that it is likely that "sustainable" paths involve some depreciation of the dollar. More specifically, two-thirds of the posterior distri-bution (defined by the one-sixth and five-sixth quantiles) indicate that the dollar must either remain roughly unchanged at its level in mid-1989 (about 100) or depreciate in order to be consistent with external sustainability.

The range of sustainable values for the dollar depends on the concentration of the prior distribution on supply, as illustrated in figure 16-9. "Loose" priors on the supply of foreign capital widen the range of posterior exchange rates considerably and imply that appreciating paths are sustainable. "Tight" priors, in contrast, narrow the range of sustainable dollar values. If foreign industrial countries are allowed to grow more rapidly than the United States, then the range of sustainable exchange rates involves somewhat less depreciation, regardless of the prior distribution on supply.

Two important points emerge from this exercise. First, unlike the earlier literature on sustainability, these results emphasize the range of sustainable paths for the dollar and the uncertainty involved in selecting any particular path. Second, paths for the dollar previously dismissed as unsustainable emerge from this exercise as potentially sustainable. Clearly the choice of prior distribution over the supply of foreign capital is important in the results presented here; in earlier studies, the supply of foreign capital was simply ignored.

Conclusions

External sustainability is a complicated issue. In this chapter we have integrated two important facets of sustainability—the cumulative net demand for (as identified by the current account model) and the net supply of (as determined by factors that influence asset preferences) foreign capital—to derive a distribution of "sustainable" exchange rates. We demonstrated that for any analysis, even one based on these two facets alone, it is appropriate to discuss external sustainability not in terms of a particular value for the dollar, as in earlier studies, but in terms of a range of values. This emphasizes the importance of uncertainty—about estimated model equations and foreign preferences—for conclusions about "sustainable" exchange rates. Our results indicate that current levels of the dollar are likely to be well within the "sustainable" range.

Appendix: Indirect Income Effects, Foreign Wealth, and Stochastic Simulations

Incorporating Indirect Income Effects

For the United States, going from GDP to GNP is an identity, with the deflator for net factor payments assumed to grow at the same rate as other prices. The equation used in the simulation model is

$$GNP = GDP + NSYV/(PGNP/100),$$

where

GNP = U.S. real GNP

GDP = U.S. real GDP

$NSYV$ = the value of U.S. net factor payments

$PGNP$ = U.S. GNP implicit deflator.

To incorporate U.S. net factor payments into foreign income, we translate U.S. nominal factor payments into units of real foreign income and augment foreign income by this amount. Specifically, we assume that all U.S. factor payments are denominated in dollars and are paid to the other G10 countries. To compute the share of U.S. factor payments in G10 GNP, we compute that ratio for 1988 and apply index changes for later years. The nominal, dollar-denominated factor payments are converted into foreign currency using the G10 exchange-rate index and then are deflated by the G10 price. The adjustment factor for the indirect income effects is computed as follows:

$$FIA = \frac{NSYV}{\$FGNPV(88)} \cdot \frac{E}{E(88)} \cdot \frac{FPCPI(88)}{FPCPI} \cdot \frac{FGNP(88)}{FGNP},$$

where

FIA = foreign income adjustment

$FGNPV(88)$ = the value of G10 GNP in 1988

E = a G10 exchange-rate index, units of foreign currency per dollar

$FPCPI$ = G10 index of consumer prices

$FGNP$ = real G10 GNP.

In 1988 U.S. net factor payments were about 0.113 percent of foreign G10 GNP. The foreign-income adjustment is used in the simulations to augment the G10 activity variables as they enter the U.S. export equations.

Including these income effects in the model makes a sizable difference in the NFA-GNP ratio by 2020. Table 16A-1 compares the NFA-GNP ratio in 2020 for simulations with and without indirect income effects for various levels of the dollar.

Measures of Foreign Wealth

The willingness of foreigners to hold a given stock of net claims on the United States depends on foreign wealth and the return structure of the claims on

Table 16A-1. *Importance of Indirect Income Effects for Simulated NFA-GNP Ratio in 2020 for Various Levels of the Exchange Rate*

	NFA-GNP ratio (percent)	
Exchange rate	With indirect income effects	Without indirect income effects
115	−125	−175
100	−90	−131
85	−45	−72
70	11	4
60	58	72

the United States, including default risk. A common indicator of default risk is the portion of income that is required to meet interest obligations. In the extrapolations in the chapter, the rate of return on U.S. claims is assumed to be constant at 6 percent; therefore, net service payments as a share of income are simply 0.06 times the ratio of the NFA position to GNP. Service payments as a share of GNP for the criteria used in the text are shown in column 2 of table 16A-2.

To compute the share that the U.S. NFA position represents in foreign portfolios, it is necessary to project a relevant measure of foreign wealth. Using OECD data for 1977 and 1978, we estimate that the financial wealth (excluding land) of the G10 countries plus Switzerland but excluding the United States was on the order of $16.8 trillion at the end of 1988. This represents about $3\frac{1}{3}$ times U.S. GNP for that year. If we assume that the ratio of foreign wealth to foreign GNP remains roughly constant and that foreign GNP growth is equal to U.S. GNP growth, then we can project that this measure of foreign wealth will remain about $3\frac{1}{3}$ times U.S. GNP. Column 3 of table 16A-2 restates the criteria used in the text in terms of the NFA position of the United States relative to foreign financial wealth, under the assumptions given above.

Stochastic Simulation Technique

In a deterministic simulation of the modified Helkie-Hooper (1988) model, the equation parameters equal their point estimates, and the equation residuals equal their expected values.[22] "Model" uncertainty can be quantified through stochastic simulations. For each simulation, shocks are added to the estimated parameters and residuals of each behavioral equation in the model.[23] The shocked parameters are held unchanged over the simulation range. In contrast, different shocks to the residuals are drawn for each time period in the simulation. Thus,

22. Because most of the model equations were estimated with a correction for first-order serial correlation, the expected value of the residual for a given equation is: $\epsilon_t = \rho\epsilon_{t-1} + \eta_t$, where ρ is the estimate of persistence and η_t is a white-noise (mean zero) error.

23. Unlike the other estimates in the model, the coefficient for first-order serial correlation, ρ, remains equal to its point estimate throughout the stochastic simulations.

Table 16A-2. *Sustainability Measures*

Percent

U.S. NFA / U.S. GNP (1)	NSYV / U.S. GNP (2)	U.S. NFA / G10 Wealth (3)
10	0.6	3
50	3.0	15
100	6.0	30
200	12.0	60

given N estimated parameters in the model and M behavioral equations, one stochastic simulation over T time periods involves drawing N shocks for the parameters from the distribution of those parameters, and $M \cdot T$ shocks for the equation from the distribution of the equation residuals.[24] Note that R replications of a stochastic simulation involve drawing $R \cdot N$ parameter shocks and $R(M \cdot T)$ residual shocks.

The shocks to the equation parameters are drawn from a normal distribution with a mean of zero and are scaled by the variance-covariance matrix of the parameter estimates in the individual equation. The residual shocks are drawn from a normal distribution, with a mean of zero and a variance equal to the variance of the historical equation errors between 1975:1 and 1989:2. The variance of the residuals is computed over the most recent fifteen-year period rather than over the estimation range of each equation, for two reasons. First, it was deemed desirable to compute the residual variances over a common time period (and the estimation range of all equations is not identical). Second, the variance over the past fifteen years may be a better approximation to the variance over the simulation horizon than the variance over the entire estimation range.[25]

References

Boughton, J. 1987. "Tests of the Performance of Reduced-Form Exchange Rate Models." *Journal of International Economics* 23:41–56.

Cline, W. R. 1989. *American Trade Adjustment: The Global Impact.* Policy Analyses in International Economics 26. Washington: Institute for International Economics.

Dealtry, M., and J. Van't dack. 1989. "The U.S. External Deficit and Associated Shifts in International Portfolios." Bank for International Settlement Economic Papers 25. Basle, Switzerland.

24. Although the description of the technique is rather brief here, Marquez and Ericsson (1990) contains additional details.

25. Implicit in this method is the assumption that the parameters and residuals of the estimated model will remain stationary over the lengthy simulation horizon (1989:3–2020:4). Note that, although the variance of the parameters is characterized by the entire estimation range of each equation, the variance of the residuals is not.

Diebold, F. X., and J. M. Nason. 1990. "Nonparametric Exchange Rate Prediction?" *Journal of International Economics* 28:315–22.

Dooley, M. P., and P. Isard. 1983. "The Portfolio-Balance Model of Exchange Rates and Some Structural Estimates of the Risk Premium." *International Monetary Fund Staff Papers* 30:683–702.

Edison, H. 1985. "The Rise and Fall of Sterling: Testing Alternative Models of Exchange Rate Determination." *Applied Economics* 17:1003–21.

———. 1991. "Forecast Performance of Exchange Rate Models Revisited." *Applied Economics* 23:187–96.

Helkie, W., and P. Hooper. 1988. "An Empirical Analysis of the External Deficit, 1980–86." In *External Deficits and the Dollar: The Pit and the Pendulum*, edited by R. C. Bryant, G. Holtham, and P. Hooper, 10–56. Brookings.

Hooper, P. 1989. "Exchange Rates and U.S. External Adjustment in the Short Run and the Long Run." International Financial Discussion Paper 346. Board of Governors of the Federal Reserve System.

Hooper, P., and C. Mann. 1989. "The Emergence and Persistence of the U.S. External Imbalance, 1980–87." *Princeton Studies in International Finance* 65. Princeton University.

Isard, P. 1987. "Lessons from Empirical Models of Exchange Rates." *International Monetary Fund Staff Papers* 34:1–28.

Krugman, P. R. 1985. "Is the Strong Dollar Sustainable?" National Bureau of Economic Research Working Paper 1644. Cambridge, Mass.

———. 1988. "Sustainability and the Decline of the Dollar." In *External Deficits and the Dollar: The Pit and the Pendulum*, edited by R. C. Bryant, G. Holtham, and P. Hooper, 82–99. Brookings.

Levich, R. M. 1985. "Empirical Studies of Exchange Rates." In *Handbook of International Economics,* edited by R. W. Jones and P. B. Kenen, 979–1041. New York: North Holland Press.

Marquez, J. R., and N. R. Ericsson. 1990. "Evaluating the Predictive Performance of Trade-Account Models." International Finance Discussion Paper 377. Board of Governors of the Federal Reserve System.

Marris, S. 1985. *Deficits and the Dollar*. Policy Analyses in International Economics 14. Washington: Institute for International Economics.

———. 1987. *Deficits and the Dollar*. Policy Analyses in International Economics 14, rev. Washington: Institute for International Economics.

Meese, R., and K. Rogoff. 1983. "Empirical Exchange Rate Models of the Seventies: Do They Fit Out of Sample?" *Journal of International Economics* 14:3–24.

Meese, R., and A. K. Rose. 1989. "An Empirical Assessment of Non-Linearities in Models of Exchange Rate Determination." International Finance Discussion Paper 367. Board of Governors of the Federal Reserve System.

Schinasi, G. J., and P. A. V. B. Swamy. 1989. "The Out-of-Sample Performance of Exchange Rate Models When Coefficients Are Allowed to Change." *Journal of International Money and Finance* 8:375-90.

Scholl, R. B. 1990. "International Investment Position: Component Detail for 1989." *Survey of Current Business* 70:54–65.

Stekler, L., and G. Stevens. 1991. "The Adequacy of U.S. Direct Investment Data." In *International Economic Transactions: Issues in Measurement and Empirical Research*, edited by P. Hooper and J. D. Richardson, 321–50. University of Chicago Press.

Thomas, C. P. 1991. "A Very Short Note on the Stability of External Debt." Board of Governors of the Federal Reserve System.

Annexes

Reference Tables for Deterministic Simulations

THE REFERENCE TABLES included in this annex present raw data from the deterministic simulations carried out for the project by participating model groups. Chapter 3 provides detailed background on the simulations, including descriptions of the shocks and the alternative monetary-policy regimes.

The tables in this annex share a common format. They are ordered by model, and then by country within the tables for a particular model. Available data are reported for selected variables and time periods for the three countries with the largest economies—the United States, Japan, and Germany. A typical set of model tables is numbered A-XXX-1 through A-XXX-7, where XXX is a three-letter mnemonic for the individual model. The models and their mnemonics (see chapter 3 for more detail) are

GEM: a version of the Global Economic Model developed by the National Institute for Economic and Social Research (NIESR) in London and jointly maintained with the London Business School (LBS).

INA: the adaptive-expectations version of the INTERMOD policy simulation model originally developed by a Canadian team under the direction of John Helliwell (following the IMF effort to construct MULTIMOD), sponsored by the Canadian Department of Finance and subsequently supported by the Bank of Canada.

INC: the model-consistent e⁻ pectations version of the INTERMOD policy simulation model.

LIV: the multicountry model developed by Patrick Minford and several associates at the University of Liverpool.

MCM: the multicountry model developed by the staff of the Division of International Finance of the Federal Reserve Board.

MPS: the model, primarily of the U.S. economy but also with an external sector, developed by the domestic divisions of the Federal Reserve Board (following earlier work by teams of economists at MIT, the

University of Pennsylvania, and the Federal Reserve, financed by the Social Science Research Council).

MSG: an updated version of a multicountry policy simulation model originally developed by Warwick McKibbin and Jeffrey Sachs at Harvard University, maintained by McKibbin at the Brookings Institution.

MUL: the MULTIMOD multicountry policy simulation model developed in the Research Department of the International Monetary Fund.

MX3: a multicountry policy simulation model developed in the Division of International Finance of the Federal Reserve Board by Joseph Gagnon and Ralph Tryon.

TAY: the multicountry policy simulation model developed by John Taylor and associates at Stanford University.

The selected variables reported are real GNP, the GNP deflator as a measure of the price level, and the rate of inflation in the GNP deflator (tables 1, 3, and 5); the short-term interest rate, the long-term interest rate, and the ratio of the current-account balance to nominal GNP (tables 2, 4, and 6);[1] and bilateral nominal exchange rates of the U.S. dollar against the yen and the deutsche mark (table 7).[2] Data for the real GNPs, the GNP deflators, and the bilateral dollar exchange rates are measured as percentage deviations of the variable from baseline values. Data for the inflation rates, the interest rates, and the ratios of current-account balances to nominal GNPs are measured as deviations from baseline values in percentage points.

Four data observations are shown for each variable in each simulation. Data points for annual models are reported for the first (initial-impact), second, fifth, and tenth year of the simulations. For quarterly models, the data points are for the first, sixth, eighteenth, and thirty-eighth quarters: the first quarter is the initial-impact period, and the sixth, eighteenth, and thirty-eighth quarters correspond roughly with the counterpart observations from the annual models for the second, fifth, and tenth years of the simulation.[3]

Each table in this annex is divided horizontally into panels, one for each type of shock. Data are reported for up to twelve types of shock (see chapter 3): four transitory aggregate demand shocks, three transitory aggregate supply shocks, three transitory money-demand shocks, a transitory increase in the price

1. The distinction between GNP (gross national product) and GDP (gross domestic product) is not made in all the participating models. The tables substitute GDP for GNP when the latter is not available.

2. For all the models, the bilateral exchange rates are measured as U.S. dollars per yen or deutsche mark, so that a minus sign indicates an appreciation of the U.S. dollar and a positive sign indicates a dollar depreciation. (The column headings in the tables, somewhat misleadingly, are labeled as the "DM/$" and the "Yen/$" exchange rates; notwithstanding this labeling, the exchange rates are measured as dollars per deutsche mark or dollars per yen.)

3. The MCM model reported simulation results for only thirty-six quarters (nine rather than ten years), and the final observation in the MCM tables is therefore the thirty-sixth rather than the thirty-eighth quarter.

of oil, and a permanent increase in the U.S. stock of money. If a particular panel is blank in a table, that model group did not submit results for that shock.

Within each horizontal panel, the individual rows refer to regime types. Simulations are available for up to eight regimes, four original ("O") and four variant ("X") specifications. As elsewhere in the volume, the acronyms for regimes are 1 and 1X for money targeting, 2A and 2AX for nominal-income targeting, 2B and 2BX for real-GNP-plus-inflation targeting, and 3 and 3X for exchange-rate targeting. When an individual row in a panel is blank, the model group did not submit results for that regime specification.

Shock and Regime	Real GNP				GNP Deflator				Inflation Rate			
	1st Qtr	6th Qtr	18th Qtr	38th Qtr	1st Qtr	6th Qtr	18th Qtr	38th Qtr	1st Qtr	6th Qtr	18th Qtr	38th Qtr
Shock A. US Aggregate Demand												
1												
1X	0.998	-0.023	-0.025	-0.008	0.108	0.098	0.065	0.029	0.040	-0.056	-0.014	-0.004
2A												
2AX	0.992	-0.040	-0.023	-0.005	0.109	0.087	0.042	0.015	0.273	-0.066	-0.015	-0.002
2B												
2BX	0.992	-0.033	-0.006	-0.003	0.108	0.087	0.066	0.059	0.274	-0.064	-0.006	-0.001
3												
3X												
Shock I. Japanese Aggregate Demand												
1												
1X	0.008	0.002	0.000	-0.004	-0.001	0.005	0.011	0.011	0.000	0.006	0.001	-0.001
2A												
2AX	0.007	0.000	-0.001	-0.003	-0.001	0.005	0.008	0.007	0.002	0.006	0.001	-0.001
2B												
2BX	0.007	-0.001	-0.001	-0.000	-0.001	0.005	0.005	0.006	0.002	0.005	-0.000	-0.000
3												
3X												
Shock G. German Aggregate Demand												
1												
1X	0.020	0.002	-0.002	-0.002	-0.005	0.005	0.010	0.005	0.001	0.002	0.001	-0.001
2A												
2AX	0.019	0.001	-0.002	-0.001	-0.006	0.004	0.008	0.003	0.003	0.000	0.001	-0.001
2B												
2BX	0.020	-0.002	0.000	-0.000	-0.004	0.003	0.001	0.002	0.004	-0.002	-0.001	0.000
3												
3X												
Shock B. Global Aggregate Demand												
1												
1X	1.025	-0.018	-0.026	-0.013	0.102	0.108	0.086	0.045	0.041	-0.048	-0.012	-0.007
2A												
2AX	1.018	-0.038	-0.025	-0.008	0.102	0.096	0.058	0.025	0.278	-0.060	-0.014	-0.004
2B												
2BX	1.019	-0.036	-0.007	-0.003	0.103	0.095	0.071	0.066	0.279	-0.061	-0.007	-0.001
3												
3X												
Shock C. US Aggregate Supply												
1												
1X	-0.001	-0.012	0.007	0.001	-0.000	0.007	-0.001	0.006	0.000	-0.030	0.003	0.001
2A												
2AX	-0.001	-0.015	0.007	0.000	-0.000	0.007	-0.002	0.005	-0.000	-0.031	0.003	0.000
2B												
2BX	-0.001	-0.014	0.007	0.001	-0.000	0.006	0.001	0.007	-0.000	-0.031	0.004	0.000
3												
3X												
Shock J. Japanese Aggregate Supply												
1												
1X												
2A												
2AX												
2B												
2BX												
3												
3X												

Shock and	Real GNP				GNP Deflator				Inflation Rate			
Regime	1st Qtr	6th Qtr	18th Qtr	38th Qtr	1st Qtr	6th Qtr	18th Qtr	38th Qtr	1st Qtr	6th Qtr	18th Qtr	38th Qtr

Shock H. German Aggregate Supply

1												
1X	-0.001	0.000	-0.001	-0.001	-0.000	-0.000	0.003	0.001	0.000	-0.000	0.001	-0.001
2A												
2AX	-0.001	0.001	-0.001	-0.001	-0.000	-0.000	0.004	0.001	-0.000	-0.000	0.001	-0.001
2B												
2BX	0.000	-0.001	0.001	-0.001	0.000	-0.001	0.000	0.000	0.000	-0.001	0.001	-0.000
3												
3X												

Shock E. Oil Price Increase

1												
1X	-0.181	0.012	-0.012	-0.013	0.052	0.066	0.101	0.063	0.015	-0.022	0.004	-0.008
2A												
2AX	-0.180	0.011	-0.019	-0.015	0.049	0.069	0.106	0.064	-0.033	-0.018	0.003	-0.008
2B												
2BX	-0.178	0.009	-0.001	0.001	0.051	0.067	0.111	0.109	-0.032	-0.020	0.008	-0.001
3												
3X												

Shock L. U.S. Money Demand
1
1X
2A
2AX
2B
2BX
3
3X

Shock D. Japanese Money Demand
1
1X
2A
2AX
2B
2BX
3
3X

Shock K. German Money Demand
1
1X
2A
2AX
2B
2BX
3
3X

Shock F. U.S. Money Supply-Permanent
FIXM
1
1X

GEM MODEL
EFFECTS ON U.S. INTEREST RATES AND U.S. CURRENT ACCOUNT/GNP RATIO
(Deviations from Baseline)

Shock and Regime	Short Interest Rate				Long Interest Rate				Current Account/GNP Ratio			
	1st Qtr	6th Qtr	18th Qtr	38th Qtr	1st Qtr	6th Qtr	18th Qtr	38th Qtr	1st Qtr	6th Qtr	18th Qtr	38th Qtr

Shock A. US Aggregate Demand

	1st Qtr	6th Qtr	18th Qtr	38th Qtr	1st Qtr	6th Qtr	18th Qtr	38th Qtr	1st Qtr	6th Qtr	18th Qtr	38th Qtr
1												
1X	0.012	0.013	0.007	0.004	-0.002	0.007	0.004	0.002	-0.002	0.000	0.000	0.000
2A												
2AX	0.082	0.012	0.005	0.003	-0.002	0.006	0.002	0.001	-0.002	0.000	0.000	0.000
2B												
2BX	0.082	-0.024	-0.003	-0.001	-0.002	-0.007	-0.002	-0.000	-0.002	0.000	0.000	0.000
3												
3X												

Shock I. Japanese Aggregate Demand

	1st Qtr	6th Qtr	18th Qtr	38th Qtr	1st Qtr	6th Qtr	18th Qtr	38th Qtr	1st Qtr	6th Qtr	18th Qtr	38th Qtr
1												
1X	0.000	0.001	0.002	0.002	0.000	0.001	0.001	0.001	0.000	0.000	0.000	0.000
2A												
2AX	0.001	0.001	0.002	0.001	0.000	0.001	0.001	0.001	0.000	0.000	0.000	0.000
2B												
2BX	0.001	0.001	-0.000	-0.000	0.000	0.001	-0.000	0.000	0.000	0.000	0.000	0.000
3												
3X												

Shock G. German Aggregate Demand

	1st Qtr	6th Qtr	18th Qtr	38th Qtr	1st Qtr	6th Qtr	18th Qtr	38th Qtr	1st Qtr	6th Qtr	18th Qtr	38th Qtr
1												
1X	0.000	0.001	0.001	0.001	0.000	0.001	0.001	0.000	0.000	0.000	0.000	0.000
2A												
2AX	0.001	0.001	0.002	0.001	0.000	0.001	0.001	0.000	0.000	0.000	0.000	0.000
2B												
2BX	0.001	-0.001	-0.000	0.000	0.000	-0.000	-0.000	0.000	0.000	0.000	0.000	0.000
3												
3X												

Shock B. Global Aggregate Demand

	1st Qtr	6th Qtr	18th Qtr	38th Qtr	1st Qtr	6th Qtr	18th Qtr	38th Qtr	1st Qtr	6th Qtr	18th Qtr	38th Qtr
1												
1X	0.012	0.015	0.011	0.007	-0.002	0.008	0.005	0.004	-0.002	0.000	0.000	0.000
2A												
2AX	0.083	0.014	0.008	0.004	-0.002	0.007	0.004	0.002	-0.002	0.000	0.000	0.000
2B												
2BX	0.084	-0.024	-0.003	-0.001	-0.002	-0.007	-0.002	-0.001	-0.002	0.000	0.000	0.000
3												
3X												

Shock C. US Aggregate Supply

	1st Qtr	6th Qtr	18th Qtr	38th Qtr	1st Qtr	6th Qtr	18th Qtr	38th Qtr	1st Qtr	6th Qtr	18th Qtr	38th Qtr
1												
1X	0.000	0.000	0.001	0.001	0.000	0.000	0.000	0.001	0.000	0.000	0.000	0.000
2A												
2AX	0.000	-0.002	0.001	0.001	0.000	-0.000	0.001	0.001	0.000	0.000	0.000	0.000
2B												
2BX	0.000	-0.011	0.003	0.000	0.000	-0.003	0.002	0.000	0.000	0.000	0.000	0.000
3												
3X												

Shock J. Japanese Aggregate Supply

1												
1X												
2A												
2AX												
2B												
2BX												
3												
3X												

798

Shock and Regime	Short Interest Rate				Long Interest Rate				Current Account/GNP Ratio			
	1st Qtr	6th Qtr	18th Qtr	38th Qtr	1st Qtr	6th Qtr	18th Qtr	38th Qtr	1st Qtr	6th Qtr	18th Qtr	38th Qtr

Shock H. German Aggregate Supply

1												
1X	0.000	0.000	0.001	0.000	0.000	0.000	0.000	0.000	0.000	0.000	0.000	0.000
2A												
2AX	-0.000	0.000	0.001	0.000	0.000	0.000	0.000	0.000	0.000	0.000	0.000	0.000
2B												
2BX	0.000	-0.001	0.000	-0.000	0.000	-0.000	0.000	-0.000	0.000	0.000	0.000	0.000
3												
3X												

Shock E. Oil Price Increase

1												
1X	0.004	0.012	0.014	0.010	-0.002	0.006	0.007	0.005	-0.003	0.000	0.000	0.000
2A												
2AX	-0.010	0.020	0.022	0.012	-0.002	0.012	0.011	0.006	-0.003	0.000	0.000	0.000
2B												
2BX	-0.010	-0.003	0.002	0.000	-0.002	0.004	0.001	0.000	-0.003	0.000	0.000	0.000
3												
3X												

Shock L. U.S. Money Demand

1
1X
2A
2AX
2B
2BX
3
3X

Shock D. Japanese Money Demand

1
1X
2A
2AX
2B
2BX
3
3X

Shock K. German Money Demand

1
1X
2A
2AX
2B
2BX
3
3X

Shock F. U.S. Money Supply-Permanent

FIXM
1
1X

GEM MODEL
EFFECTS ON JAPANESE REAL GNP, JAPANESE PRICE LEVEL, JAPANESE INFLATION RATE
(Deviations from Baseline)

Shock and Regime	Real GNP				GNP Deflator				Inflation Rate			
	1st Qtr	6th Qtr	18th Qtr	38th Qtr	1st Qtr	6th Qtr	18th Qtr	38th Qtr	1st Qtr	6th Qtr	18th Qtr	38th Qtr
Shock A. US Aggregate Demand												
1												
1X	0.170	0.041	0.001	-0.014	-0.002	0.013	0.036	0.033	0.002	0.012	0.008	-0.004
2A												
2AX	0.163	0.023	-0.015	-0.009	-0.002	0.010	0.021	0.003	0.040	0.009	0.003	-0.005
2B												
2BX	0.158	0.014	-0.008	-0.002	-0.002	0.008	0.017	0.010	0.039	0.007	0.003	-0.002
3												
3X												
Shock I. Japanese Aggregate Demand												
1												
1X	0.953	0.042	-0.022	-0.033	-0.000	0.015	0.059	0.027	0.000	0.017	0.011	-0.011
2A												
2AX	0.904	0.038	-0.027	-0.028	-0.000	0.013	0.048	0.010	0.225	0.016	0.007	-0.011
2B												
2BX	0.907	0.044	-0.012	-0.016	-0.000	0.015	0.054	0.036	0.226	0.018	0.009	-0.006
3												
3X												
Shock G. German Aggregate Demand												
1												
1X	0.034	0.010	0.001	-0.003	-0.001	0.004	0.009	0.006	0.000	0.004	0.002	-0.001
2A												
2AX	0.032	0.006	-0.003	-0.002	-0.001	0.003	0.007	0.001	0.008	0.003	0.001	-0.002
2B												
2BX	0.033	0.001	-0.004	0.000	-0.000	0.002	0.002	-0.002	0.008	0.001	0.000	-0.000
3												
3X												
Shock B. Global Aggregate Demand												
1												
1X	1.157	0.092	-0.021	-0.050	-0.003	0.032	0.104	0.067	0.002	0.033	0.020	-0.016
2A												
2AX	1.099	0.066	-0.045	-0.040	-0.003	0.027	0.076	0.014	0.273	0.028	0.010	-0.017
2B												
2BX	1.098	0.059	-0.023	-0.018	-0.003	0.024	0.074	0.044	0.272	0.025	0.012	-0.008
3												
3X												
Shock C. US Aggregate Supply												
1												
1X	-0.001	0.010	0.008	-0.001	-0.000	0.003	0.004	0.011	0.000	0.003	0.001	0.001
2A												
2AX	-0.001	0.008	0.005	-0.002	0.000	0.003	0.003	0.006	-0.000	0.003	0.001	0.000
2B												
2BX	-0.001	0.007	0.007	-0.002	0.000	0.002	0.003	0.008	-0.000	0.003	0.001	0.001
3												
3X												
Shock J. Japanese Aggregate Supply												
1												
1X												
2A												
2AX												
2B												
2BX												
3												
3X												

Shock and Regime	Real GNP				GNP Deflator				Inflation Rate			
	1st Qtr	6th Qtr	18th Qtr	38th Qtr	1st Qtr	6th Qtr	18th Qtr	38th Qtr	1st Qtr	6th Qtr	18th Qtr	38th Qtr
Shock H. German Aggregate Supply												
1												
1X	-0.001	0.001	0.001	-0.001	-0.000	0.001	0.001	0.001	0.000	0.001	-0.000	-0.000
2A												
2AX	-0.001	0.002	0.000	-0.002	-0.000	0.001	0.001	0.000	-0.000	0.001	-0.000	-0.000
2B												
2BX	-0.000	-0.001	0.001	-0.000	0.000	-0.000	-0.000	0.000	0.000	-0.000	-0.000	0.000
3												
3X												
Shock E. Oil Price Increase												
1												
1X	-0.257	0.149	0.106	0.068	-0.065	0.056	0.084	0.197	0.043	-0.061	0.020	0.020
2A												
2AX	-0.242	0.109	0.044	0.036	-0.064	0.052	0.062	0.102	-0.076	-0.065	0.011	0.005
2B												
2BX	-0.243	0.096	0.050	0.071	-0.063	0.045	0.049	0.108	-0.077	-0.070	0.010	0.012
3												
3X												
Shock L. U.S. Money Demand												
1												
1X												
2A												
2AX												
2B												
2BX												
3												
3X												
Shock D. Japanese Money Demand												
1												
1X												
2A												
2AX												
2B												
2BX												
3												
3X												
Shock K. German Money Demand												
1												
1X												
2A												
2AX												
2B												
2BX												
3												
3X												
Shock F. U.S. Money Supply-Permanent												
FIXM												
1												
1X												

Table A-GEM-4
GEM MODEL
EFFECTS ON JAPANESE INTEREST RATES AND JAPANESE CURRENT ACCOUNT/GNP RATIO
(Deviations from Baseline)

Shock and Regime	Short Interest Rate				Long Interest Rate				Current Account/GNP Ratio			
	1st Qtr	6th Qtr	18th Qtr	38th Qtr	1st Qtr	6th Qtr	18th Qtr	38th Qtr	1st Qtr	6th Qtr	18th Qtr	38th Qtr
Shock A. US Aggregate Demand												
1												
1X	0.000	0.004	0.005	0.002	0.001	0.003	0.002	0.001	0.001	0.000	0.000	0.000
2A												
2AX	0.012	0.008	0.002	-0.001	0.001	0.004	0.001	-0.001	0.001	0.000	-0.000	0.000
2B												
2BX	0.012	0.005	-0.001	-0.001	0.001	0.003	-0.001	-0.001	0.001	0.000	0.000	0.000
3												
3X												
Shock I. Japanese Aggregate Demand												
1												
1X	0.000	-0.001	0.007	-0.001	-0.001	0.001	0.004	-0.001	-0.001	0.000	0.000	0.000
2A												
2AX	0.068	0.013	0.005	-0.004	-0.001	0.003	0.003	-0.002	-0.001	0.000	0.000	0.000
2B												
2BX	0.068	0.015	-0.001	-0.005	-0.001	0.004	-0.000	-0.003	-0.001	0.000	0.000	0.000
3												
3X												
Shock G. German Aggregate Demand												
1												
1X	0.000	0.002	0.001	0.000	0.000	0.001	0.001	0.000	0.000	0.000	0.000	0.000
2A												
2AX	0.002	0.002	0.001	-0.000	0.000	0.001	0.001	-0.000	0.000	0.000	0.000	0.000
2B												
2BX	0.003	0.001	-0.001	-0.000	0.000	0.000	-0.000	-0.000	0.000	0.000	0.000	0.000
3												
3X												
Shock B. Global Aggregate Demand												
1												
1X	0.001	0.004	0.013	0.001	0.001	0.005	0.007	0.000	0.001	0.000	-0.000	0.000
2A												
2AX	0.082	0.023	0.008	-0.006	0.001	0.008	0.004	-0.003	0.001	0.000	-0.000	0.000
2B												
2BX	0.082	0.021	-0.003	-0.007	0.001	0.007	-0.001	-0.003	0.001	0.000	-0.000	0.000
3												
3X												
Shock C. US Aggregate Supply												
1												
1X	0.000	0.001	0.001	0.001	0.000	0.000	0.001	0.001	0.000	0.000	0.000	0.000
2A												
2AX	-0.000	0.003	0.002	0.001	0.000	0.001	0.001	0.001	0.000	0.000	0.000	0.000
2B												
2BX	-0.000	0.003	0.002	-0.000	0.000	0.001	0.001	-0.000	0.000	0.000	0.000	0.000
3												
3X												
Shock J. Japanese Aggregate Supply												
1												
1X												
2A												
2AX												
2B												
2BX												
3												
3X												

Shock and	Short Interest Rate				Long Interest Rate				Current Account/GNP Ratio			
Regime	1st Qtr	6th Qtr	18th Qtr	38th Qtr	1st Qtr	6th Qtr	18th Qtr	38th Qtr	1st Qtr	6th Qtr	18th Qtr	38th Qtr

Shock H. German Aggregate Supply

1												
1X	0.000	0.000	0.000	0.000	0.000	0.000	0.000	0.000	0.000	0.000	0.000	0.000
2A												
2AX	-0.000	0.001	0.001	-0.000	0.000	0.000	0.000	-0.000	0.000	0.000	0.000	0.000
2B												
2BX	0.000	-0.000	0.000	0.000	0.000	-0.000	0.000	0.000	0.000	0.000	0.000	0.000
3												
3X												

Shock E. Oil Price Increase

1												
1X	0.013	0.016	0.015	0.026	0.001	0.012	0.008	0.013	-0.006	0.001	0.000	0.000
2A												
2AX	-0.023	0.040	0.026	0.034	0.001	0.023	0.013	0.017	-0.006	0.001	0.000	0.000
2B												
2BX	-0.023	0.007	0.015	0.021	0.001	0.014	0.007	0.010	-0.006	0.001	0.000	0.000
3												
3X												

Shock L. U.S. Money Demand

1
1X
2A
2AX
2B
2BX
3
3X

Shock D. Japanese Money Demand

1
1X
2A
2AX
2B
2BX
3
3X

Shock K. German Money Demand

1
1X
2A
2AX
2B
2BX
3
3X

Shock F. U.S. Money Supply-Permanent

FIXM
1
1X

GEM MODEL
EFFECTS ON GERMAN REAL GNP, GERMAN PRICE LEVEL, GERMAN INFLATION RATE
(Deviations from Baseline)

Shock and Regime	Real GNP				GNP Deflator				Inflation Rate			
	1st Qtr	6th Qtr	18th Qtr	38th Qtr	1st Qtr	6th Qtr	18th Qtr	38th Qtr	1st Qtr	6th Qtr	18th Qtr	38th Qtr
Shock A. US Aggregate Demand												
1												
1X	0.171	-0.006	-0.017	-0.005	-0.004	0.030	0.022	-0.012	0.001	0.024	-0.013	-0.003
2A												
2AX	0.175	-0.015	-0.015	-0.003	-0.004	0.028	0.011	-0.013	0.043	0.021	-0.014	-0.001
2B												
2BX	0.171	-0.016	-0.004	0.000	-0.004	0.026	0.017	0.010	0.042	0.020	-0.009	0.000
3												
3X												
Shock I. Japanese Aggregate Demand												
1												
1X	0.013	-0.004	-0.001	-0.004	-0.001	0.007	0.008	-0.001	0.000	0.006	-0.001	-0.003
2A												
2AX	0.013	-0.005	-0.001	-0.003	-0.001	0.006	0.005	-0.003	0.003	0.006	-0.002	-0.002
2B												
2BX	0.014	-0.006	-0.001	-0.001	-0.001	0.006	0.004	0.001	0.003	0.006	-0.002	-0.001
3												
3X												
Shock G. German Aggregate Demand												
1												
1X	0.934	-0.047	-0.030	-0.004	-0.000	0.079	0.038	-0.011	0.000	0.050	-0.037	-0.001
2A												
2AX	0.930	-0.054	-0.029	-0.003	-0.000	0.076	0.028	-0.016	0.232	0.047	-0.037	0.000
2B												
2BX	0.938	-0.046	-0.019	-0.004	-0.001	0.081	0.048	0.011	0.233	0.051	-0.032	-0.001
3												
3X												
Shock B. Global Aggregate Demand												
1												
1X	1.116	-0.056	-0.047	-0.013	-0.005	0.116	0.067	-0.022	0.002	0.080	-0.051	-0.006
2A												
2AX	1.117	-0.074	-0.045	-0.010	-0.005	0.110	0.045	-0.032	0.277	0.074	-0.053	-0.003
2B												
2BX	1.121	-0.067	-0.023	-0.004	-0.005	0.113	0.069	0.023	0.278	0.076	-0.043	-0.002
3												
3X												
Shock C. US Aggregate Supply												
1												
1X	-0.002	0.007	-0.001	-0.001	0.000	0.002	0.005	-0.000	0.000	0.002	0.001	-0.001
2A												
2AX	-0.001	0.006	-0.001	-0.002	0.000	0.002	0.005	-0.001	-0.000	0.002	0.001	-0.001
2B												
2BX	-0.002	0.006	-0.000	-0.001	0.000	0.002	0.008	0.002	-0.000	0.002	0.002	-0.001
3												
3X												
Shock J. Japanese Aggregate Supply												
1												
1X												
2A												
2AX												
2B												
2BX												
3												
3X												

Shock and Regime	Real GNP				GNP Deflator				Inflation Rate			
	1st Qtr	6th Qtr	18th Qtr	38th Qtr	1st Qtr	6th Qtr	18th Qtr	38th Qtr	1st Qtr	6th Qtr	18th Qtr	38th Qtr
Shock H. German Aggregate Supply												
1												
1X	-0.002	-0.038	0.000	0.001	0.000	0.076	0.009	0.000	0.000	-0.018	-0.011	-0.000
2A												
2AX	-0.003	-0.039	-0.003	0.000	0.000	0.076	0.008	0.000	-0.001	-0.018	-0.011	-0.000
2B												
2BX	0.002	-0.033	0.008	0.004	-0.000	0.077	0.009	0.001	0.001	-0.017	-0.011	-0.000
3												
3X												
Shock E. Oil Price Increase												
1												
1X	-0.134	0.112	-0.029	-0.004	-0.085	0.080	0.138	0.055	0.027	-0.017	-0.000	-0.008
2A												
2AX	-0.140	0.104	-0.038	-0.011	-0.085	0.078	0.123	0.022	-0.056	-0.018	-0.006	-0.010
2B												
2BX	-0.127	0.119	-0.007	0.010	-0.086	0.086	0.169	0.130	-0.053	-0.011	0.009	-0.002
3												
3X												
Shock L. U.S. Money Demand												
1												
1X												
2A												
2AX												
2B												
2BX												
3												
3X												
Shock D. Japanese Money Demand												
1												
1X												
2A												
2AX												
2B												
2BX												
3												
3X												
Shock K. German Money Demand												
1												
1X												
2A												
2AX												
2B												
2BX												
3												
3X												
Shock F. U.S. Money Supply-Permanent												
FIXM												
1												
1X												

GEM MODEL
EFFECTS ON GERMAN INTEREST RATES AND GERMAN CURRENT ACCOUNT/GNP RATIO
(Deviations from Baseline)

Shock and Regime	Short Interest Rate				Long Interest Rate				Current Account/GNP Ratio			
	1st Qtr	6th Qtr	18th Qtr	38th Qtr	1st Qtr	6th Qtr	18th Qtr	38th Qtr	1st Qtr	6th Qtr	18th Qtr	38th Qtr

Shock A. US Aggregate Demand

1												
1X	0.000	0.006	0.001	-0.003	0.001	0.004	0.001	-0.001	0.001	0.000	0.000	0.000
2A												
2AX	0.013	0.003	-0.001	-0.004	0.001	0.002	-0.000	-0.002	0.001	0.000	0.000	0.000
2B												
2BX	0.013	0.001	-0.003	0.000	0.001	0.002	-0.002	0.000	0.001	0.000	0.000	0.000
3												
3X												

Shock I. Japanese Aggregate Demand

1												
1X	0.000	0.002	0.001	-0.001	0.000	0.001	0.001	-0.000	0.000	0.000	0.000	0.000
2A												
2AX	0.001	0.000	0.001	-0.002	0.000	0.001	0.001	-0.001	0.000	0.000	0.000	0.000
2B												
2BX	0.001	-0.000	-0.001	-0.000	0.000	0.001	-0.000	-0.000	0.000	0.000	0.000	0.000
3												
3X												

Shock G. German Aggregate Demand

1												
1X	0.000	0.014	0.000	-0.003	-0.004	0.009	0.001	-0.001	-0.004	0.000	0.000	0.000
2A												
2AX	0.069	0.006	-0.000	-0.005	-0.004	0.003	0.000	-0.003	-0.004	0.000	0.000	0.000
2B												
2BX	0.070	0.001	-0.013	-0.001	-0.004	0.002	-0.007	-0.001	-0.004	0.000	0.000	0.000
3												
3X												

Shock B. Global Aggregate Demand

1												
1X	0.000	0.022	0.002	-0.006	-0.004	0.014	0.002	-0.003	-0.004	0.000	0.000	0.000
2A												
2AX	0.083	0.009	0.000	-0.010	-0.004	0.006	0.001	-0.005	-0.004	0.000	0.000	0.000
2B												
2BX	0.083	0.002	-0.017	-0.002	-0.004	0.004	-0.009	-0.001	-0.004	0.000	0.000	0.000
3												
3X												

Shock C. US Aggregate Supply

1												
1X	0.000	0.000	0.001	-0.000	0.000	0.000	0.000	-0.000	0.000	0.000	0.000	0.000
2A												
2AX	-0.000	0.002	0.001	-0.001	0.000	0.001	0.001	-0.000	0.000	0.000	0.000	0.000
2B												
2BX	-0.000	0.002	0.001	-0.001	0.000	0.001	0.000	-0.000	0.000	0.000	0.000	0.000
3												
3X												

Shock J. Japanese Aggregate Supply

1												
1X												
2A												
2AX												
2B												
2BX												
3												
3X												

Shock and Regime	Short Interest Rate				Long Interest Rate				Current Account/GNP Ratio			
	1st Qtr	6th Qtr	18th Qtr	38th Qtr	1st Qtr	6th Qtr	18th Qtr	38th Qtr	1st Qtr	6th Qtr	18th Qtr	38th Qtr

Shock H. German Aggregate Supply

1												
1X	0.000	0.006	-0.000	-0.000	0.000	0.004	-0.000	-0.000	0.000	0.000	0.000	0.000
2A												
2AX	-0.000	0.009	0.001	0.000	0.000	0.005	0.001	0.000	0.000	0.000	0.000	0.000
2B												
2BX	0.000	-0.013	-0.001	0.001	0.000	-0.001	-0.001	0.001	0.000	0.000	0.000	0.000
3												
3X												

Shock E. Oil Price Increase

1												
1X	0.008	0.025	0.018	0.005	-0.004	0.011	0.009	0.003	-0.004	0.000	0.000	0.000
2A												
2AX	-0.017	0.046	0.021	0.003	-0.004	0.024	0.011	0.002	-0.004	0.000	0.000	0.000
2B												
2BX	-0.016	0.027	0.001	0.002	-0.004	0.021	0.001	0.001	-0.004	0.000	0.000	0.000
3												
3X												

Shock L. U.S. Money Demand

1
1X
2A
2AX
2B
2BX
3
3X

Shock D. Japanese Money Demand

1
1X
2A
2AX
2B
2BX
3
3X

Shock K. German Money Demand

1
1X
2A
2AX
2B
2BX
3
3X

Shock F. U.S. Money Supply-Permanent

FIXM
1
1X

807

GEM MODEL
BILATERAL DOLLAR EXCHANGE RATES
(Deviations from Baseline)

Shock and Regime	Bilateral DM/$ Exchange Rate				Bilateral Yen/$ Exchange Rate			
	1st Qtr	6th Qtr	18th Qtr	38th Qtr	1st Qtr	6th Qtr	18th Qtr	38th Qtr
Shock A. US Aggregate Demand								
1								
1X	-0.009	-0.024	-0.039	-0.074	0.050	0.035	0.022	0.012
2A								
2AX	0.033	-0.020	-0.034	-0.065	0.061	0.008	-0.001	-0.018
2B								
2BX	-0.012	-0.060	-0.045	-0.042	-0.012	-0.062	-0.038	-0.040
3								
3X								
Shock I. Japanese Aggregate Demand								
1								
1X	-0.016	-0.015	-0.015	-0.023	-0.010	0.007	0.017	0.020
2A								
2AX	-0.015	-0.013	-0.015	-0.023	-0.048	-0.004	0.009	0.000
2B								
2BX	-0.006	-0.004	-0.006	-0.007	-0.009	0.037	0.049	0.025
3								
3X								
Shock G. German Aggregate Demand								
1								
1X	-0.043	-0.017	0.003	-0.015	0.007	0.008	0.009	0.006
2A								
2AX	-0.076	-0.016	-0.005	-0.029	-0.000	0.001	0.002	-0.002
2B								
2BX	-0.006	0.057	0.034	0.012	-0.001	0.000	0.001	-0.002
3								
3X								
Shock B. Global Aggregate Demand								
1								
1X	-0.070	-0.057	-0.053	-0.113	0.043	0.047	0.044	0.035
2A								
2AX	-0.058	-0.049	-0.054	-0.117	0.011	0.004	0.009	-0.022
2B								
2BX	-0.022	-0.006	-0.016	-0.036	-0.021	-0.026	0.012	-0.018
3								
3X								
Shock C. US Aggregate Supply								
1								
1X	-0.008	-0.011	-0.009	-0.013	0.002	0.001	0.002	0.004
2A								
2AX	-0.007	-0.015	-0.010	-0.015	-0.001	-0.009	-0.003	-0.002
2B								
2BX	-0.010	-0.018	-0.004	-0.011	-0.009	-0.017	-0.002	-0.003
3								
3X								
Shock J. Japanese Aggregate Supply								
1								
1X								
2A								
2AX								
2B								
2BX								
3								
3X								

Shock and Regime	Bilateral DM/$ Exchange Rate				Bilateral Yen/$ Exchange Rate			
	1st Qtr	6th Qtr	18th Qtr	38th Qtr	1st Qtr	6th Qtr	18th Qtr	38th Qtr
Shock H. German Aggregate Supply								
1								
1X	-0.010	0.001	0.006	0.001	0.002	0.002	0.002	0.000
2A								
2AX	-0.021	-0.011	0.001	0.001	0.001	0.001	0.001	-0.001
2B								
2BX	0.024	0.037	0.014	0.018	0.001	0.001	0.001	0.002
3								
3X								
Shock E. Oil Price Increase								
1								
1X	0.028	0.036	0.062	0.050	0.176	0.199	0.206	0.256
2A								
2AX	-0.043	-0.029	-0.005	-0.035	0.042	0.058	0.083	0.142
2B								
2BX	0.066	0.092	0.130	0.125	-0.017	0.001	0.025	0.098
3								
3X								
Shock L. U.S. Money Demand								
1								
1X								
2A								
2AX								
2B								
2BX								
3								
3X								
Shock D. Japanese Money Demand								
1								
1X								
2A								
2AX								
2B								
2BX								
3								
3X								
Shock K. German Money Demand								
1								
1X								
2A								
2AX								
2B								
2BX								
3								
3X								
Shock F. U.S. Money Supply-Permanent								
FIXM								
1								
1X								

809

Table A-INA-1
INTERMOD (ADAPTIVE) MODEL
EFFECTS ON U.S. REAL GNP, U.S. PRICE LEVEL, U.S. INFLATION RATE
(Deviations from Baseline)

Shock and Regime	Real GNP				GNP Deflator				Inflation Rate			
	1st Yr	2nd Yr	5th Yr	10th Yr	1st Yr	2nd Yr	5th Yr	10th Yr	1st Yr	2nd Yr	5th Yr	10th Yr
Shock A. US Aggregate Demand												
1	1.088	-0.171	-0.293	-0.114	0.077	0.209	0.360	0.038	0.080	0.137	-0.007	-0.073
1X												
2A	0.916	-0.539	-0.181	0.073	0.070	0.091	0.129	-0.126	0.072	0.022	-0.034	-0.025
2AX												
2B	0.927	-0.488	-0.074	0.009	0.070	0.112	0.201	0.153	0.072	0.044	-0.004	0.003
2BX												
3	1.078	-0.138	-0.345	-0.138	0.076	0.233	0.367	-0.141	0.079	0.162	-0.021	-0.121
3X												
Shock I. Japanese Aggregate Demand												
1	0.046	0.042	0.005	-0.056	-0.004	0.022	0.086	0.127	-0.004	0.026	0.022	-0.005
1X												
2A	0.036	0.049	-0.058	-0.001	-0.004	0.030	0.055	-0.022	-0.004	0.035	-0.001	-0.018
2AX												
2B	0.030	0.037	-0.017	0.005	-0.004	0.025	0.058	0.069	-0.005	0.031	0.005	0.004
2BX												
3	0.048	0.023	0.014	-0.032	-0.004	0.015	0.066	0.151	-0.004	0.019	0.019	0.012
3X												
Shock G. German Aggregate Demand												
1	0.011	0.040	-0.004	-0.039	-0.001	0.016	0.063	0.059	-0.001	0.018	0.015	-0.011
1X												
2A	0.010	0.061	-0.078	0.020	-0.002	0.037	0.034	-0.014	-0.002	0.040	-0.012	-0.006
2AX												
2B	0.003	0.050	-0.032	0.007	-0.002	0.032	0.036	0.045	-0.002	0.035	-0.007	0.005
2BX												
3	0.011	0.020	0.012	-0.030	-0.001	0.006	0.047	0.100	-0.001	0.007	0.016	0.004
3X												
Shock B. Global Aggregate Demand												
1	1.146	-0.090	-0.292	-0.209	0.072	0.248	0.510	0.224	0.075	0.181	0.030	-0.089
1X												
2A	0.963	-0.431	-0.314	0.096	0.064	0.155	0.213	-0.165	0.066	0.094	-0.048	-0.047
2AX												
2B	0.961	-0.403	-0.123	0.021	0.063	0.169	0.291	0.261	0.065	0.109	-0.006	0.012
2BX												
3	1.137	-0.096	-0.319	-0.200	0.072	0.254	0.482	0.111	0.074	0.189	0.015	-0.105
3X												
Shock C. US Aggregate Supply												
1	-0.405	-0.619	-0.188	-0.156	1.306	0.133	0.267	0.123	1.350	-1.197	0.022	-0.060
1X												
2A	-0.547	-0.853	-0.213	-0.045	1.300	0.031	0.159	-0.031	1.344	-1.296	-0.007	-0.051
2AX												
2B	-0.504	-0.539	-0.068	-0.045	1.301	0.088	0.520	0.790	1.345	-1.238	0.095	0.029
2BX												
3	-0.413	-0.577	-0.205	-0.174	1.305	0.159	0.265	0.022	1.349	-1.170	0.020	-0.087
3X												
Shock J. Japanese Aggregate Supply												
1	-0.015	0.042	0.007	-0.019	0.001	0.013	0.029	0.064	0.001	0.012	0.012	0.004
1X												
2A	-0.015	0.053	-0.007	-0.018	0.001	0.018	0.019	0.009	0.001	0.018	0.006	-0.006
2AX												
2B	-0.019	0.055	0.014	0.001	0.001	0.016	0.010	0.065	0.001	0.016	0.010	0.011
2BX												
3	-0.013	0.032	0.005	-0.011	0.001	0.010	0.025	0.066	0.001	0.009	0.010	0.007
3X												

Shock and Regime	Real GNP				GNP Deflator				Inflation Rate			
	1st Yr	2nd Yr	5th Yr	10th Yr	1st Yr	2nd Yr	5th Yr	10th Yr	1st Yr	2nd Yr	5th Yr	10th Yr
Shock H. German Aggregate Supply												
1	-0.004	0.049	0.005	-0.034	-0.000	0.025	0.047	0.058	-0.000	0.026	0.012	-0.005
1X												
2A	-0.003	0.060	-0.013	-0.014	-0.000	0.038	0.032	-0.011	-0.001	0.040	0.012	-0.013
2AX												
2B	-0.009	0.054	0.008	-0.005	-0.001	0.036	0.030	0.072	-0.001	0.039	0.018	0.005
2BX												
3	-0.003	0.035	0.003	-0.023	-0.000	0.018	0.039	0.074	-0.000	0.018	0.009	0.004
3X												
Shock E. Oil Price Increase												
1	1.146	-0.090	-0.292	-0.209	0.072	0.248	0.510	0.224	0.075	0.181	0.030	-0.089
1X												
2A	0.963	-0.431	-0.314	0.096	0.064	0.155	0.213	-0.165	0.066	0.094	-0.048	-0.047
2AX												
2B	0.961	-0.403	-0.123	0.021	0.063	0.169	0.291	0.261	0.065	0.109	-0.006	0.012
2BX												
3	1.137	-0.096	-0.319	-0.200	0.072	0.254	0.482	0.111	0.074	0.189	0.015	-0.105
3X												
Shock L. U.S. Money Demand												
1	-0.060	-0.191	-0.001	0.078	-0.002	-0.057	-0.144	-0.166	-0.002	-0.057	-0.029	0.011
1X												
2A	0.009	-0.004	-0.002	0.001	0.001	0.001	0.001	-0.002	0.001	0.000	-0.000	-0.000
2AX												
2B	0.009	-0.004	-0.001	0.000	0.001	0.001	0.002	0.001	0.001	0.000	-0.000	-0.000
2BX												
3	-0.069	-0.149	-0.040	0.090	-0.003	-0.031	-0.145	-0.278	-0.003	-0.029	-0.044	-0.010
3X												
Shock D. Japanese Money Demand												
1	-0.002	0.015	-0.009	-0.006	-0.000	0.004	0.008	-0.023	-0.000	0.005	-0.001	-0.008
1X												
2A	0.001	0.001	-0.001	0.000	-0.000	0.000	0.000	-0.001	-0.000	0.000	-0.000	-0.001
2AX												
2B	0.000	0.001	-0.000	0.000	0.000	0.000	0.001	-0.000	0.000	0.000	-0.000	-0.000
2BX												
3	0.001	0.001	0.000	-0.000	0.000	0.000	0.001	0.001	0.000	0.000	0.000	-0.000
3X												
Shock K. German Money Demand												
1	-0.000	0.013	-0.009	0.002	-0.000	0.006	0.003	-0.018	-0.000	0.007	-0.003	-0.004
1X												
2A	0.000	0.001	-0.001	0.001	-0.000	0.000	0.000	-0.001	-0.000	0.000	-0.000	-0.001
2AX												
2B	-0.000	0.001	-0.000	-0.000	-0.000	0.000	0.000	-0.000	-0.000	0.000	-0.000	-0.000
2BX												
3	0.000	0.001	-0.000	-0.000	0.000	-0.000	0.001	0.000	0.000	-0.000	0.000	-0.000
3X												
Shock F. U.S. Money Supply-Permanent												
FIXM												
1	-0.000	0.000	-0.000	0.000	0.000	-0.000	-0.000	-0.001	0.000	-0.000	0.000	-0.000
1X												

INTERMOD (ADAPTIVE) MODEL
EFFECTS ON U.S. INTEREST RATES AND U.S. CURRENT ACCOUNT/GNP RATIO
(Deviations from Baseline)

Shock and Regime	Short Interest Rate				Long Interest Rate				Current Account/GNP Ratio			
	1st Yr	2nd Yr	5th Yr	10th Yr	1st Yr	2nd Yr	5th Yr	10th Yr	1st Yr	2nd Yr	5th Yr	10th Yr
Shock A. US Aggregate Demand												
1	0.456	0.037	0.042	-0.019	0.151	0.113	0.068	0.009	-0.108	-0.021	-0.029	-0.023
1X												
2A	1.397	-0.473	-0.067	-0.093	0.461	0.153	-0.027	-0.093	-0.031	-0.241	0.029	0.008
2AX												
2B	1.348	-0.480	-0.140	0.021	0.445	0.140	-0.102	-0.009	-0.047	-0.198	0.033	-0.010
2BX												
3	0.493	0.067	0.028	-0.115	0.163	0.131	0.070	-0.056	-0.133	0.006	-0.040	-0.029
3X												
Shock I. Japanese Aggregate Demand												
1	0.017	0.026	0.038	0.033	0.005	0.012	0.028	0.037	0.012	0.017	0.002	-0.009
1X												
2A	0.046	0.118	0.010	-0.040	0.015	0.049	0.036	-0.022	-0.000	0.036	-0.010	0.002
2AX												
2B	0.086	0.064	-0.018	0.014	0.028	0.040	0.007	0.008	0.004	0.025	-0.002	0.002
2BX												
3	0.019	0.017	0.036	0.057	0.006	0.010	0.025	0.051	0.020	0.008	0.005	-0.002
3X												
Shock G. German Aggregate Demand												
1	0.004	0.023	0.025	0.011	0.001	0.008	0.020	0.017	-0.008	0.018	-0.002	-0.006
1X												
2A	0.012	0.145	-0.047	0.002	0.004	0.051	0.013	-0.007	-0.026	0.061	-0.035	0.013
2AX												
2B	0.060	0.048	-0.033	0.014	0.020	0.029	-0.003	0.007	-0.021	0.045	-0.017	0.003
2BX												
3	0.004	0.011	0.027	0.035	0.001	0.005	0.018	0.033	0.002	0.006	0.002	-0.004
3X												
Shock B. Global Aggregate Demand												
1	0.476	0.085	0.106	0.024	0.157	0.133	0.116	0.062	-0.103	0.013	-0.029	-0.038
1X												
2A	1.454	-0.214	-0.110	-0.130	0.480	0.251	0.017	-0.124	-0.057	-0.143	-0.016	0.024
2AX												
2B	1.492	-0.371	-0.192	0.047	0.492	0.208	-0.099	0.005	-0.065	-0.129	0.014	-0.005
2BX												
3	0.516	0.094	0.092	-0.022	0.170	0.145	0.112	0.028	-0.111	0.020	-0.033	-0.036
3X												
Shock C. US Aggregate Supply												
1	0.374	-0.181	0.045	-0.004	0.124	0.023	0.060	0.022	0.148	-0.206	-0.019	-0.016
1X												
2A	1.143	-1.066	-0.018	-0.115	0.377	-0.099	0.069	-0.070	0.220	-0.459	-0.041	0.005
2AX												
2B	0.929	-2.022	0.066	-0.020	0.307	-0.462	0.071	-0.016	0.185	-0.451	-0.037	-0.020
2BX												
3	0.404	-0.167	0.041	-0.059	0.134	0.035	0.062	-0.014	0.122	-0.158	-0.014	-0.021
3X												
Shock J. Japanese Aggregate Supply												
1	-0.006	0.022	0.016	0.021	-0.002	0.006	0.011	0.020	-0.024	0.025	0.004	-0.003
1X												
2A	-0.020	0.104	0.026	-0.009	-0.007	0.030	0.018	0.003	-0.031	0.045	0.006	-0.002
2AX												
2B	0.008	0.043	0.030	0.017	0.003	0.016	0.014	0.020	-0.029	0.051	0.009	0.003
2BX												
3	-0.005	0.018	0.014	0.027	-0.002	0.005	0.010	0.023	-0.019	0.018	0.002	-0.001
3X												

Shock and Regime	Short Interest Rate				Long Interest Rate				Current Account/GNP Ratio			
	1st Yr	2nd Yr	5th Yr	10th Yr	1st Yr	2nd Yr	5th Yr	10th Yr	1st Yr	2nd Yr	5th Yr	10th Yr
Shock H. German Aggregate Supply												
1	-0.002	0.030	0.023	0.012	-0.001	0.010	0.015	0.017	-0.024	0.028	0.007	-0.006
1X												
2A	-0.005	0.145	0.040	-0.036	-0.002	0.047	0.026	-0.014	-0.037	0.063	0.015	-0.004
2AX												
2B	0.046	0.005	0.019	0.004	0.015	0.012	0.018	0.009	-0.032	0.068	0.009	-0.001
2BX												
3	-0.002	0.023	0.020	0.026	-0.001	0.007	0.014	0.025	-0.018	0.018	0.002	-0.003
3X												
Shock E. Oil Price Increase												
1	0.476	0.085	0.106	0.024	0.157	0.133	0.116	0.062	-0.103	0.013	-0.029	-0.038
1X												
2A	1.454	-0.214	-0.110	-0.130	0.480	0.251	0.017	-0.124	-0.057	-0.143	-0.016	0.024
2AX												
2B	1.492	-0.371	-0.192	0.047	0.492	0.208	-0.099	0.005	-0.065	-0.129	0.014	-0.005
2BX												
3	0.516	0.094	0.092	-0.022	0.170	0.145	0.112	0.028	-0.111	0.020	-0.033	-0.036
3X												
Shock L. U.S. Money Demand												
1	0.390	-0.088	-0.060	-0.043	0.129	0.057	-0.025	-0.046	0.039	-0.085	0.005	0.018
1X												
2A	0.014	-0.003	-0.001	-0.001	0.005	0.002	0.000	-0.001	-0.000	-0.002	0.000	0.000
2AX												
2B	0.013	-0.003	-0.002	0.000	0.004	0.002	-0.001	-0.000	-0.001	-0.002	0.000	-0.000
2BX												
3	0.422	-0.064	-0.083	-0.094	0.139	0.072	-0.032	-0.087	0.012	-0.050	-0.001	0.019
3X												
Shock D. Japanese Money Demand												
1	-0.001	0.008	-0.000	-0.012	-0.000	0.002	0.002	-0.008	-0.006	0.008	-0.002	-0.002
1X												
2A	0.001	0.002	-0.000	-0.001	0.000	0.001	0.000	-0.001	0.000	0.001	-0.000	0.000
2AX												
2B	0.001	0.001	-0.001	0.000	0.000	0.001	0.000	0.000	0.000	0.000	0.000	0.000
2BX												
3	0.000	0.000	0.000	0.001	0.000	0.000	0.000	0.001	0.000	0.000	0.000	0.000
3X												
Shock K. German Money Demand												
1	-0.000	0.008	-0.002	-0.007	-0.000	0.003	0.000	-0.005	-0.006	0.009	-0.002	0.000
1X												
2A	0.000	0.002	-0.001	-0.000	0.000	0.001	0.000	-0.000	-0.000	0.001	-0.001	0.000
2AX												
2B	0.001	0.001	-0.000	-0.000	0.000	0.000	0.000	0.000	-0.000	0.001	-0.000	0.000
2BX												
3	0.000	0.000	0.000	0.000	0.000	0.000	0.000	0.000	0.000	0.000	0.000	0.000
3X												
Shock F. U.S. Money Supply-Permanent												
FIXM												
1	-0.000	0.000	-0.000	-0.000	0.000	0.000	-0.000	-0.000	0.000	0.000	0.000	0.000
1X												

Table A-INA-3
INTERMOD (ADAPTIVE) MODEL
EFFECTS ON JAPANESE REAL GNP, JAPANESE PRICE LEVEL, JAPANESE INFLATION RATE
(Deviations from Baseline)

Shock and Regime	Real GNP				GNP Deflator				Inflation Rate			
	1st Yr	2nd Yr	5th Yr	10th Yr	1st Yr	2nd Yr	5th Yr	10th Yr	1st Yr	2nd Yr	5th Yr	10th Yr
Shock A. US Aggregate Demand												
1	0.167	0.083	0.023	-0.071	0.003	0.064	0.178	0.206	0.003	0.063	0.034	-0.018
1X												
2A	0.180	0.122	-0.094	-0.011	0.021	0.063	0.089	-0.058	0.021	0.043	-0.006	-0.026
2AX												
2B	0.149	0.096	-0.055	0.011	0.015	0.041	0.066	0.076	0.015	0.027	-0.001	0.010
2BX												
3	0.084	-0.016	-0.059	-0.013	-0.012	0.029	-0.014	-0.243	-0.013	0.043	-0.029	-0.051
3X												
Shock I. Japanese Aggregate Demand												
1	1.006	-0.157	-0.260	-0.077	0.097	0.218	0.323	-0.039	0.100	0.125	-0.009	-0.082
1X												
2A	0.804	-0.343	-0.178	0.037	-0.008	0.173	0.106	-0.098	-0.009	0.188	-0.046	-0.022
2AX												
2B	0.843	-0.325	-0.112	0.003	0.015	0.168	0.178	0.130	0.016	0.158	-0.014	0.000
2BX												
3	1.127	0.009	-0.166	-0.198	0.162	0.279	0.609	0.466	0.167	0.121	0.070	-0.073
3X												
Shock G. German Aggregate Demand												
1	0.024	0.035	0.000	-0.021	0.013	0.017	0.067	0.052	0.013	0.005	0.014	-0.012
1X												
2A	0.014	0.033	-0.020	0.005	0.030	0.009	0.034	-0.013	0.031	-0.021	0.001	-0.008
2AX												
2B	0.015	0.034	-0.014	0.007	0.030	0.006	0.037	0.034	0.031	-0.025	0.010	0.001
2BX												
3	0.026	0.033	0.018	-0.009	0.002	0.014	0.071	0.134	0.002	0.012	0.021	0.005
3X												
Shock B. Global Aggregate Demand												
1	1.197	-0.039	-0.237	-0.169	0.112	0.299	0.570	0.221	0.116	0.193	0.039	-0.111
1X												
2A	0.998	-0.185	-0.288	0.032	0.040	0.240	0.223	-0.170	0.042	0.206	-0.051	-0.054
2AX												
2B	1.008	-0.194	-0.180	0.022	0.058	0.211	0.276	0.233	0.060	0.157	-0.006	0.011
2BX												
3	1.236	0.026	-0.208	-0.221	0.151	0.321	0.668	0.357	0.157	0.176	0.063	-0.118
3X												
Shock C. US Aggregate Supply												
1	-0.014	0.120	0.043	-0.043	0.057	0.008	0.099	0.174	0.059	-0.051	0.036	-0.002
1X												
2A	0.015	0.139	0.009	-0.040	0.073	0.007	0.057	-0.005	0.076	-0.069	0.015	-0.023
2AX												
2B	-0.015	0.095	0.047	-0.005	0.070	-0.034	0.063	0.186	0.073	-0.108	0.040	0.022
2BX												
3	-0.092	0.074	-0.006	-0.019	0.044	-0.019	-0.015	-0.108	0.046	-0.065	0.004	-0.028
3X												
Shock J. Japanese Aggregate Supply												
1	-0.528	-0.447	-0.154	-0.135	1.141	0.086	0.205	0.126	1.180	-1.078	0.038	-0.046
1X												
2A	-0.643	-0.479	-0.179	-0.093	1.077	0.104	0.166	0.050	1.114	-0.996	0.069	-0.041
2AX												
2B	-0.622	-0.223	-0.097	-0.086	1.090	0.238	0.494	0.751	1.127	-0.872	0.150	0.023
2BX												
3	-0.456	-0.396	-0.112	-0.144	1.180	0.097	0.288	0.335	1.221	-1.107	0.041	-0.026
3X												

814

Shock and Regime	Real GNP				GNP Deflator				Inflation Rate			
	1st Yr	2nd Yr	5th Yr	10th Yr	1st Yr	2nd Yr	5th Yr	10th Yr	1st Yr	2nd Yr	5th Yr	10th Yr
Shock H. German Aggregate Supply												
1	-0.005	0.012	0.016	-0.015	0.029	0.013	0.033	0.057	0.030	-0.016	0.003	-0.002
1X												
2A	-0.013	0.014	0.011	-0.010	0.039	0.007	0.012	-0.005	0.040	-0.033	-0.019	-0.009
2AX												
2B	-0.007	0.020	0.030	-0.001	0.042	-0.023	0.018	0.061	0.044	-0.067	-0.007	0.006
2BX												
3	-0.003	0.008	0.020	-0.000	0.023	0.012	0.032	0.089	0.023	-0.011	0.009	0.009
3X												
Shock E. Oil Price Increase												
1	1.197	-0.039	-0.237	-0.169	0.112	0.299	0.570	0.221	0.116	0.193	0.039	-0.111
1X												
2A	0.998	-0.185	-0.288	0.032	0.040	0.240	0.223	-0.170	0.042	0.206	-0.051	-0.054
2AX												
2B	1.008	-0.194	-0.180	0.022	0.058	0.211	0.276	0.233	0.060	0.157	-0.006	0.011
2BX												
3	1.236	0.026	-0.208	-0.221	0.151	0.321	0.668	0.357	0.157	0.176	0.063	-0.118
3X												
Shock L. U.S. Money Demand												
1	0.025	0.050	-0.023	-0.032	0.010	0.009	0.014	-0.061	0.011	-0.002	-0.004	-0.020
1X												
2A	0.001	0.001	-0.000	0.000	0.000	0.000	0.001	-0.001	0.000	0.000	0.000	-0.000
2AX												
2B	0.001	0.001	-0.000	0.000	0.000	0.000	0.000	-0.000	0.000	0.000	-0.000	0.000
2BX												
3	-0.058	-0.031	-0.047	0.026	-0.005	-0.022	-0.126	-0.282	-0.005	-0.018	-0.042	-0.018
3X												
Shock D. Japanese Money Demand												
1	-0.082	-0.115	0.007	0.076	-0.052	-0.036	-0.142	-0.118	-0.053	0.016	-0.027	0.024
1X												
2A	0.012	-0.005	-0.002	0.001	-0.000	0.002	0.001	-0.002	-0.000	0.003	-0.001	-0.000
2AX												
2B	0.013	-0.005	-0.002	0.000	0.000	0.002	0.002	0.001	0.000	0.002	-0.000	-0.000
2BX												
3	0.017	-0.000	-0.003	-0.002	0.003	0.004	0.008	0.005	0.003	0.002	0.001	-0.001
3X												
Shock K. German Money Demand												
1	0.000	0.003	-0.005	0.000	0.007	0.001	-0.001	-0.016	0.007	-0.006	-0.003	-0.002
1X												
2A	0.000	0.001	-0.000	0.000	0.001	0.000	0.000	-0.001	0.001	-0.000	0.000	-0.000
2AX												
2B	0.000	0.000	-0.000	0.000	0.001	0.000	0.000	-0.001	0.001	-0.001	0.000	-0.000
2BX												
3	0.000	0.000	0.000	0.000	0.000	0.000	0.000	0.001	0.000	0.000	0.000	0.000
3X												
Shock F. U.S. Money Supply-Permanent												
FIXM												
1	-0.000	-0.000	0.000	0.000	0.000	-0.000	-0.001	0.000	0.000	-0.000	-0.000	0.000
1X												

INTERMOD (ADAPTIVE) MODEL
EFFECTS ON JAPANESE INTEREST RATES AND JAPANESE CURRENT ACCOUNT/GNP RATIO
(Deviations from Baseline)

Shock and Regime	Short Interest Rate 1st Yr	2nd Yr	5th Yr	10th Yr	Long Interest Rate 1st Yr	2nd Yr	5th Yr	10th Yr	Current Account/GNP Ratio 1st Yr	2nd Yr	5th Yr	10th Yr
Shock A. US Aggregate Demand												
1	0.068	0.041	0.074	0.050	0.022	0.028	0.056	0.062	0.061	0.054	0.023	0.011
1X												
2A	0.273	0.078	0.007	-0.077	0.090	0.086	0.048	-0.051	0.065	0.156	-0.023	-0.019
2AX												
2B	0.383	0.009	-0.065	0.030	0.127	0.088	-0.014	0.014	0.066	0.149	-0.037	0.000
2BX												
3	0.379	0.078	0.041	-0.089	0.125	0.109	0.072	-0.036	0.062	0.048	0.028	0.011
3X												
Shock I. Japanese Aggregate Demand												
1	0.459	0.030	0.031	-0.048	0.151	0.111	0.062	-0.018	-0.152	-0.031	-0.017	0.005
1X												
2A	1.216	-0.251	-0.105	-0.077	0.401	0.186	-0.023	-0.083	-0.139	-0.065	0.009	-0.009
2AX												
2B	1.085	-0.125	-0.188	0.005	0.358	0.199	-0.086	-0.033	-0.142	-0.051	-0.002	-0.016
2BX												
3	0.014	0.014	0.031	0.054	0.005	0.008	0.021	0.046	-0.160	-0.012	-0.034	-0.023
3X												
Shock G. German Aggregate Demand												
1	0.015	0.021	0.026	0.010	0.005	0.010	0.021	0.016	0.008	0.012	0.003	0.008
1X												
2A	0.067	0.058	-0.000	-0.011	0.022	0.034	0.021	-0.008	0.008	0.011	0.018	-0.004
2AX												
2B	0.085	0.021	-0.016	0.014	0.028	0.026	0.003	0.007	0.007	0.019	0.002	0.004
2BX												
3	0.003	0.009	0.023	0.033	0.001	0.004	0.015	0.030	0.007	0.013	0.004	0.009
3X												
Shock B. Global Aggregate Demand												
1	0.541	0.092	0.131	0.012	0.178	0.150	0.140	0.060	-0.084	0.035	0.008	0.023
1X												
2A	1.553	-0.118	-0.102	-0.163	0.512	0.305	0.043	-0.141	-0.068	0.103	0.004	-0.033
2AX												
2B	1.550	-0.096	-0.268	0.048	0.512	0.311	-0.097	-0.012	-0.070	0.117	-0.036	-0.011
2BX												
3	0.397	0.100	0.096	-0.002	0.131	0.121	0.108	0.041	-0.092	0.049	-0.001	-0.003
3X												
Shock C. US Aggregate Supply												
1	0.016	0.041	0.048	0.049	0.005	0.017	0.037	0.052	-0.040	0.088	0.032	0.011
1X												
2A	0.109	0.086	0.039	-0.054	0.036	0.052	0.055	-0.016	-0.037	0.170	0.047	-0.012
2AX												
2B	0.185	-0.249	0.094	0.027	0.061	-0.042	0.053	0.035	-0.037	0.136	0.041	-0.003
2BX												
3	0.311	-0.107	0.045	-0.041	0.103	0.034	0.056	-0.003	-0.039	0.082	0.033	0.012
3X												
Shock J. Japanese Aggregate Supply												
1	0.259	-0.152	0.022	-0.004	0.085	0.007	0.035	0.015	0.048	-0.050	-0.005	0.002
1X												
2A	0.677	-0.582	-0.025	-0.067	0.223	-0.043	0.050	-0.026	0.055	-0.079	-0.017	0.003
2AX												
2B	0.612	-1.430	0.096	-0.093	0.202	-0.337	0.055	-0.062	0.054	-0.088	-0.040	-0.028
2BX												
3	-0.004	0.014	0.013	0.025	-0.001	0.004	0.009	0.020	0.043	-0.036	-0.002	-0.009
3X												

816

Shock and Regime	Short Interest Rate				Long Interest Rate				Current Account/GNP Ratio			
	1st Yr	2nd Yr	5th Yr	10th Yr	1st Yr	2nd Yr	5th Yr	10th Yr	1st Yr	2nd Yr	5th Yr	10th Yr
Shock H. German Aggregate Supply												
1	0.010	0.011	0.020	0.015	0.003	0.006	0.013	0.018	-0.000	-0.003	0.007	0.005
1X												
2A	0.042	0.030	0.024	-0.024	0.014	0.019	0.021	-0.007	-0.000	-0.006	0.015	0.002
2AX												
2B	0.054	-0.047	0.033	0.007	0.018	-0.004	0.022	0.013	-0.001	0.005	0.020	0.006
2BX												
3	-0.001	0.018	0.017	0.025	-0.000	0.006	0.012	0.023	-0.001	-0.002	0.009	0.007
3X												
Shock E. Oil Price Increase												
1	0.541	0.092	0.131	0.012	0.178	0.150	0.140	0.060	-0.084	0.035	0.008	0.023
1X												
2A	1.553	-0.118	-0.102	-0.163	0.512	0.305	0.043	-0.141	-0.068	0.103	0.004	-0.033
2AX												
2B	1.550	-0.096	-0.268	0.048	0.512	0.311	-0.097	-0.012	-0.070	0.117	-0.036	-0.011
2BX												
3	0.397	0.100	0.096	-0.002	0.131	0.121	0.108	0.041	-0.092	0.049	-0.001	-0.003
3X												
Shock L. U.S. Money Demand												
1	0.012	0.009	-0.002	-0.033	0.004	0.006	0.002	-0.022	0.002	0.046	-0.007	-0.018
1X												
2A	0.003	0.001	0.000	-0.001	0.001	0.001	0.001	-0.000	0.001	0.002	0.000	-0.000
2AX												
2B	0.004	0.001	-0.001	0.001	0.001	0.001	0.000	0.000	0.001	0.002	-0.000	0.000
2BX												
3	0.324	-0.027	-0.062	-0.088	0.107	0.063	-0.018	-0.077	0.002	0.040	-0.003	-0.020
3X												
Shock D. Japanese Money Demand												
1	0.362	-0.063	-0.058	-0.019	0.119	0.059	-0.024	-0.030	0.004	-0.017	0.011	0.006
1X												
2A	0.019	-0.004	-0.002	-0.001	0.006	0.003	-0.001	-0.001	-0.002	-0.001	0.000	-0.000
2AX												
2B	0.016	-0.002	-0.003	0.000	0.005	0.003	-0.001	-0.001	-0.002	-0.001	0.000	-0.000
2BX												
3	0.000	0.000	0.000	0.001	0.000	0.000	0.000	0.001	-0.003	-0.000	-0.000	-0.000
3X												
Shock K. German Money Demand												
1	0.003	0.002	-0.003	-0.006	0.001	0.001	-0.001	-0.005	0.000	-0.000	-0.001	-0.001
1X												
2A	0.001	0.001	-0.001	-0.000	0.000	0.001	0.000	-0.000	0.000	0.000	0.000	-0.000
2AX												
2B	0.001	0.000	0.000	0.000	0.000	0.000	0.000	0.000	0.000	0.000	0.000	0.000
2BX												
3	0.000	0.000	0.000	0.000	0.000	0.000	0.000	0.000	0.000	0.000	0.000	0.000
3X												
Shock F. U.S. Money Supply-Permanent												
FIXM												
1	-0.000	-0.000	-0.000	0.000	-0.000	-0.000	-0.000	0.000	0.000	0.000	0.000	0.000
1X												

INTERMOD (ADAPTIVE) MODEL
EFFECTS ON GERMAN REAL GNP, GERMAN PRICE LEVEL, GERMAN INFLATION RATE
(Deviations from Baseline)

Shock and Regime	Real GNP				GNP Deflator				Inflation Rate			
	1st Yr	2nd Yr	5th Yr	10th Yr	1st Yr	2nd Yr	5th Yr	10th Yr	1st Yr	2nd Yr	5th Yr	10th Yr
Shock A. US Aggregate Demand												
1	0.150	0.108	0.013	-0.065	-0.013	0.074	0.166	0.176	-0.014	0.091	0.029	-0.018
1X												
2A	0.201	0.132	-0.116	-0.006	-0.054	0.156	0.056	-0.037	-0.056	0.217	-0.063	0.004
2AX												
2B	0.156	0.072	-0.064	0.009	-0.050	0.136	0.020	0.083	-0.051	0.192	-0.067	0.019
2BX												
3	0.021	-0.038	-0.089	0.026	-0.012	0.010	-0.104	-0.355	-0.013	0.023	-0.050	-0.046
3X												
Shock I. Japanese Aggregate Demand												
1	0.043	0.046	0.003	-0.022	-0.003	0.033	0.086	0.102	-0.003	0.037	0.017	-0.007
1X												
2A	0.035	0.046	-0.035	0.006	-0.006	0.040	0.045	-0.014	-0.006	0.047	-0.011	-0.005
2AX												
2B	0.031	0.036	-0.016	0.010	-0.008	0.041	0.044	0.049	-0.008	0.050	-0.005	0.004
2BX												
3	0.044	0.038	0.018	-0.009	-0.002	0.027	0.078	0.151	-0.003	0.030	0.020	0.009
3X												
Shock G. German Aggregate Demand												
1	0.970	-0.453	-0.163	0.021	0.201	0.088	0.123	-0.039	0.208	-0.118	-0.015	-0.012
1X												
2A	0.602	-0.396	-0.011	-0.111	0.263	-0.390	0.403	-0.133	0.272	-0.673	0.679	-0.358
2AX												
2B	0.769	-0.536	0.036	-0.024	0.227	-0.131	0.147	0.110	0.235	-0.369	0.143	-0.008
2BX												
3	1.185	-0.260	-0.240	-0.049	0.164	0.333	0.326	0.120	0.170	0.174	-0.047	-0.028
3X												
Shock B. Global Aggregate Demand												
1	1.163	-0.297	-0.148	-0.065	0.185	0.194	0.374	0.239	0.191	0.010	0.030	-0.036
1X												
2A	0.840	-0.211	-0.153	-0.103	0.202	-0.198	0.491	-0.192	0.209	-0.413	0.602	-0.356
2AX												
2B	0.958	-0.425	-0.041	-0.005	0.169	0.044	0.200	0.225	0.175	-0.129	0.070	0.013
2BX												
3	1.250	-0.260	-0.312	-0.031	0.150	0.369	0.299	-0.088	0.155	0.227	-0.078	-0.065
3X												
Shock C. US Aggregate Supply												
1	0.004	0.139	0.028	-0.044	-0.024	0.069	0.112	0.146	-0.025	0.096	0.040	-0.007
1X												
2A	0.081	0.120	-0.010	-0.025	-0.060	0.182	0.032	0.016	-0.062	0.250	-0.048	0.033
2AX												
2B	0.032	0.009	-0.023	0.002	-0.050	0.191	0.038	0.170	-0.052	0.249	-0.097	0.032
2BX												
3	-0.121	0.069	-0.020	-0.014	-0.022	0.002	-0.038	-0.181	-0.023	0.025	0.000	-0.035
3X												
Shock J. Japanese Aggregate Supply												
1	-0.015	0.026	0.010	-0.008	-0.000	0.007	0.029	0.057	-0.001	0.007	0.014	0.003
1X												
2A	-0.015	0.039	0.002	-0.009	-0.001	0.010	0.017	0.011	-0.001	0.011	0.011	-0.003
2AX												
2B	-0.013	0.031	0.017	0.005	-0.002	0.018	0.014	0.050	-0.003	0.022	0.025	0.006
2BX												
3	-0.014	0.013	0.013	-0.001	-0.000	0.004	0.024	0.061	-0.000	0.005	0.014	0.006
3X												

Shock and Regime	Real GNP				GNP Deflator				Inflation Rate			
	1st Yr	2nd Yr	5th Yr	10th Yr	1st Yr	2nd Yr	5th Yr	10th Yr	1st Yr	2nd Yr	5th Yr	10th Yr
Shock H. German Aggregate Supply												
1	-0.928	-0.647	-0.194	-0.026	1.723	0.035	0.113	0.000	1.782	-1.716	-0.055	-0.032
1X												
2A	-1.182	-0.464	-0.131	0.032	1.766	-0.333	0.035	0.008	1.827	-2.134	0.034	0.072
2AX												
2B	-0.954	-0.183	-0.193	-0.034	1.718	-0.055	0.479	0.622	1.777	-1.802	-0.024	0.024
2BX												
3	-0.776	-0.597	-0.109	-0.096	1.696	0.227	0.265	0.171	1.754	-1.495	0.112	-0.042
3X												
Shock E. Oil Price Increase												
1	1.163	-0.297	-0.148	-0.065	0.185	0.194	0.374	0.239	0.191	0.010	0.030	-0.036
1X												
2A	0.840	-0.211	-0.153	-0.103	0.202	-0.198	0.491	-0.192	0.209	-0.413	0.602	-0.356
2AX												
2B	0.958	-0.425	-0.041	-0.005	0.169	0.044	0.200	0.225	0.175	-0.129	0.070	0.013
2BX												
3	1.250	-0.260	-0.312	-0.031	0.150	0.369	0.299	-0.088	0.155	0.227	-0.078	-0.065
3X												
Shock L. U.S. Money Demand												
1	0.035	0.058	-0.033	-0.026	-0.016	0.028	0.018	-0.064	-0.016	0.045	-0.007	-0.018
1X												
2A	0.002	0.001	-0.001	0.000	-0.001	0.002	0.001	-0.001	-0.001	0.002	-0.000	-0.000
2AX												
2B	0.001	0.001	-0.001	0.001	-0.001	0.001	0.000	0.001	-0.001	0.002	-0.000	0.000
2BX												
3	-0.088	-0.054	-0.042	0.057	-0.014	-0.034	-0.163	-0.270	-0.015	-0.021	-0.044	-0.003
3X												
Shock D. Japanese Money Demand												
1	-0.002	0.010	-0.008	-0.004	-0.000	0.003	0.007	-0.024	-0.001	0.004	-0.002	-0.007
1X												
2A	0.001	0.001	-0.000	0.000	-0.000	0.001	0.001	-0.001	-0.000	0.001	0.001	-0.001
2AX												
2B	0.000	0.000	-0.001	0.000	-0.000	0.001	0.000	0.000	-0.000	0.001	-0.000	-0.000
2BX												
3	0.001	0.001	0.000	-0.000	-0.000	0.001	0.001	0.003	-0.000	0.001	0.001	0.000
3X												
Shock K. German Money Demand												
1	-0.153	-0.147	0.073	0.032	0.032	-0.190	-0.127	-0.056	0.033	-0.230	0.007	0.016
1X												
2A	0.009	-0.005	0.000	-0.001	0.003	-0.005	0.005	-0.003	0.004	-0.009	0.009	-0.005
2AX												
2B	0.010	-0.007	0.001	-0.000	0.003	-0.002	0.002	0.001	0.003	-0.005	0.002	-0.000
2BX												
3	0.016	-0.003	-0.003	-0.001	0.002	0.005	0.005	0.002	0.002	0.003	-0.000	-0.000
3X												
Shock F. U.S. Money Supply-Permanent												
FIXM												
1	-0.000	-0.000	0.000	0.000	-0.000	-0.000	0.000	0.000	-0.000	0.000	0.000	-0.000
1X												

INTERMOD (ADAPTIVE) MODEL
EFFECTS ON GERMAN INTEREST RATES AND GERMAN CURRENT ACCOUNT/GNP RATIO
(Deviations from Baseline)

Shock and Regime	Short Interest Rate				Long Interest Rate				Current Account/GNP Ratio			
	1st Yr	2nd Yr	5th Yr	10th Yr	1st Yr	2nd Yr	5th Yr	10th Yr	1st Yr	2nd Yr	5th Yr	10th Yr
Shock A. US Aggregate Demand												
1	0.053	0.052	0.063	0.039	0.018	0.029	0.051	0.050	0.048	0.062	0.023	0.016
1X												
2A	0.186	0.208	-0.068	-0.017	0.061	0.110	0.019	-0.025	0.044	0.184	-0.036	-0.023
2AX												
2B	0.325	0.112	-0.112	0.032	0.107	0.109	-0.026	0.016	0.050	0.184	-0.064	-0.003
2BX												
3	0.379	0.078	0.041	-0.089	0.125	0.109	0.072	-0.036	0.043	0.060	0.038	0.008
3X												
Shock I. Japanese Aggregate Demand												
1	0.017	0.032	0.033	0.026	0.005	0.014	0.027	0.029	0.009	0.016	0.005	0.020
1X												
2A	0.043	0.121	-0.011	-0.012	0.014	0.050	0.026	-0.010	0.002	0.029	0.011	0.003
2AX												
2B	0.081	0.086	-0.027	0.021	0.027	0.046	0.005	0.012	0.004	0.032	0.003	0.007
2BX												
3	0.014	0.014	0.031	0.054	0.005	0.008	0.021	0.046	0.013	0.014	0.006	0.022
3X												
Shock G. German Aggregate Demand												
1	0.489	-0.147	-0.008	-0.006	0.161	0.059	0.007	-0.011	-0.203	-0.219	0.050	-0.003
1X												
2A	1.337	-1.224	0.649	-0.371	0.441	-0.108	0.095	-0.081	-0.110	-0.440	0.300	-0.163
2AX												
2B	1.033	-0.632	0.044	-0.020	0.341	0.020	-0.056	-0.017	-0.155	-0.303	0.089	-0.032
2BX												
3	0.003	0.009	0.023	0.033	0.001	0.004	0.015	0.030	-0.260	-0.153	0.021	0.002
3X												
Shock B. Global Aggregate Demand												
1	0.558	-0.063	0.087	0.059	0.184	0.103	0.085	0.068	-0.146	-0.140	0.078	0.033
1X												
2A	1.566	-0.892	0.563	-0.399	0.517	0.052	0.136	-0.116	-0.065	-0.220	0.274	-0.182
2AX												
2B	1.438	-0.432	-0.093	0.031	0.474	0.175	-0.075	0.012	-0.103	-0.083	0.031	-0.026
2BX												
3	0.397	0.100	0.096	-0.002	0.131	0.121	0.107	0.041	-0.205	-0.079	0.065	0.032
3X												
Shock C. US Aggregate Supply												
1	-0.011	0.072	0.045	0.035	-0.004	0.021	0.037	0.041	-0.037	0.089	0.031	0.016
1X												
2A	-0.002	0.307	-0.045	0.015	-0.001	0.101	0.030	-0.003	-0.044	0.198	0.024	0.003
2AX												
2B	0.138	-0.076	-0.034	0.037	0.045	0.005	0.035	0.029	-0.036	0.157	-0.020	-0.006
2BX												
3	0.311	-0.107	0.045	-0.041	0.103	0.034	0.056	-0.003	-0.038	0.087	0.037	0.014
3X												
Shock J. Japanese Aggregate Supply												
1	-0.007	0.014	0.015	0.018	-0.002	0.003	0.010	0.017	-0.014	0.006	0.003	0.006
1X												
2A	-0.024	0.080	0.020	-0.002	-0.008	0.021	0.014	0.005	-0.019	0.014	0.010	0.005
2AX												
2B	-0.000	0.047	0.048	0.016	-0.000	0.015	0.016	0.021	-0.017	0.024	0.016	0.010
2BX												
3	-0.004	0.014	0.012	0.025	-0.001	0.004	0.009	0.020	-0.011	0.002	0.004	0.008
3X												

Shock and Regime	Short Interest Rate				Long Interest Rate				Current Account/GNP Ratio			
	1st Yr	2nd Yr	5th Yr	10th Yr	1st Yr	2nd Yr	5th Yr	10th Yr	1st Yr	2nd Yr	5th Yr	10th Yr
Shock H. German Aggregate Supply												
1	0.334	-0.265	-0.042	-0.019	0.110	-0.014	0.034	-0.005	0.241	-0.148	-0.107	0.034
1X												
2A	0.905	-1.287	-0.186	0.048	0.299	-0.225	0.025	-0.022	0.305	-0.342	-0.082	0.056
2AX												
2B	0.511	-1.608	-0.116	-0.038	0.169	-0.418	0.012	-0.064	0.246	-0.294	-0.171	-0.019
2BX												
3	-0.001	0.018	0.017	0.025	-0.000	0.006	0.012	0.023	0.201	-0.079	-0.056	0.028
3X												
Shock E. Oil Price Increase												
1	0.558	-0.063	0.087	0.059	0.184	0.103	0.085	0.068	-0.146	-0.140	0.078	0.033
1X												
2A	1.566	-0.892	0.563	-0.399	0.517	0.052	0.136	-0.116	-0.065	-0.220	0.274	-0.182
2AX												
2B	1.438	-0.432	-0.093	0.031	0.474	0.175	-0.075	0.012	-0.103	-0.083	0.031	-0.026
2BX												
3	0.397	0.100	0.096	-0.002	0.131	0.121	0.107	0.041	-0.205	-0.079	0.065	0.032
3X												
Shock L. U.S. Money Demand												
1	0.005	0.018	-0.005	-0.029	0.002	0.007	0.002	-0.021	0.001	0.049	-0.010	-0.020
1X												
2A	0.002	0.002	0.000	0.000	0.001	0.001	0.001	-0.000	0.001	0.002	0.000	-0.001
2AX												
2B	0.003	0.001	-0.001	0.001	0.001	0.001	0.000	0.000	0.001	0.002	-0.001	-0.000
2BX												
3	0.324	-0.027	-0.062	-0.088	0.107	0.063	-0.018	-0.076	-0.003	0.047	0.000	-0.033
3X												
Shock D. Japanese Money Demand												
1	-0.001	0.006	-0.001	-0.011	-0.000	0.002	0.001	-0.008	-0.003	0.003	-0.001	-0.001
1X												
2A	0.000	0.002	0.001	-0.000	0.000	0.001	0.001	-0.000	0.000	0.001	0.000	-0.000
2AX												
2B	0.001	0.001	-0.001	0.000	0.000	0.001	0.000	0.000	0.000	0.001	-0.000	-0.000
2BX												
3	0.000	0.000	0.000	0.001	0.000	0.000	0.000	0.001	0.000	0.000	0.000	0.000
3X												
Shock K. German Money Demand												
1	0.368	-0.143	-0.025	-0.011	0.121	0.034	-0.014	-0.014	0.042	-0.052	0.008	-0.002
1X												
2A	0.019	-0.016	0.008	-0.005	0.006	-0.001	0.001	-0.001	-0.001	-0.006	0.004	-0.002
2AX												
2B	0.014	-0.008	0.001	-0.000	0.005	0.000	-0.001	-0.000	-0.002	-0.004	0.001	-0.000
2BX												
3	0.000	0.000	0.000	0.000	0.000	0.000	0.000	0.000	-0.004	-0.002	0.000	-0.000
3X												
Shock F. U.S. Money Supply-Permanent												
FIXM												
1	-0.000	0.000	0.000	0.000	0.000	0.000	0.000	0.000	0.000	0.000	0.000	-0.000
1X												

Table A-INA-7
INTERMOD (ADAPTIVE) MODEL
BILATERAL DOLLAR EXCHANGE RATES
(Deviations from Baseline)

Shock and Regime	Bilateral DM/$ Exchange Rate				Bilateral Yen/$ Exchange Rate			
	1st Yr	2nd Yr	5th Yr	10th Yr	1st Yr	2nd Yr	5th Yr	10th Yr
Shock A. US Aggregate Demand								
1	-0.536	-0.140	-0.127	-0.004	-0.516	-0.149	-0.109	0.043
1X								
2A	-1.592	0.434	-0.115	0.122	-1.478	0.293	0.001	0.062
2AX								
2B	-1.346	0.390	0.005	0.055	-1.269	0.274	0.072	0.053
2BX								
3	-0.152	-0.031	-0.016	0.036	-0.152	-0.031	-0.017	0.036
3X								
Shock I. Japanese Aggregate Demand								
1	0.000	0.008	-0.003	-0.022	0.593	0.183	0.190	0.003
1X								
2A	-0.003	0.003	-0.033	0.030	1.572	-0.022	0.049	-0.030
2AX								
2B	-0.007	0.026	-0.007	0.015	1.341	0.148	-0.079	-0.033
2BX								
3	-0.006	-0.006	-0.013	-0.021	-0.006	-0.006	-0.013	-0.021
3X								
Shock G. German Aggregate Demand								
1	0.650	-0.033	0.060	-0.003	0.015	0.003	0.005	0.002
1X								
2A	1.781	-1.292	0.857	-0.354	0.074	-0.093	0.053	-0.008
2AX								
2B	1.307	-0.517	0.112	-0.060	0.034	-0.026	0.028	0.007
2BX								
3	-0.001	-0.004	-0.009	-0.013	-0.001	-0.004	-0.009	-0.013
3X								
Shock B. Global Aggregate Demand								
1	0.109	-0.164	-0.073	-0.030	0.086	0.035	0.086	0.048
1X								
2A	0.147	-0.862	0.698	-0.211	0.130	0.168	0.099	0.020
2AX								
2B	-0.072	-0.104	0.107	0.011	0.077	0.391	0.019	0.026
2BX								
3	-0.159	-0.040	-0.038	0.001	-0.159	-0.040	-0.038	0.001
3X								
Shock C. US Aggregate Supply								
1	-0.513	0.185	-0.090	-0.020	-0.477	0.154	-0.088	0.016
1X								
2A	-1.510	1.403	-0.148	0.146	-1.364	1.146	-0.038	0.088
2AX								
2B	-1.047	2.349	-0.023	0.245	-0.985	2.129	0.114	0.262
2BX								
3	-0.124	0.043	-0.018	0.016	-0.124	0.043	-0.018	0.016
3X								
Shock J. Japanese Aggregate Supply								
1	-0.001	-0.011	-0.003	-0.010	0.354	-0.127	0.076	0.050
1X								
2A	-0.006	-0.034	-0.014	0.002	0.934	-0.636	0.047	-0.003
2AX								
2B	-0.011	0.002	0.017	0.003	0.810	-1.718	-0.017	-0.350
2BX								
3	0.002	-0.006	-0.005	-0.010	0.002	-0.006	-0.005	-0.010
3X								

822

Shock and Regime	Bilateral DM/$ Exchange Rate				Bilateral Yen/$ Exchange Rate			
	1st Yr	2nd Yr	5th Yr	10th Yr	1st Yr	2nd Yr	5th Yr	10th Yr

Shock H. German Aggregate Supply

	1st Yr	2nd Yr	5th Yr	10th Yr	1st Yr	2nd Yr	5th Yr	10th Yr
1 1X	0.450	-0.259	0.006	0.002	0.016	-0.021	-0.008	0.000
2A 2AX	1.222	-1.540	-0.141	0.127	0.063	-0.135	-0.025	0.018
2B 2BX	0.622	-1.958	-0.263	-0.351	0.010	-0.067	0.017	0.018
3 3X	0.000	-0.007	-0.007	-0.010	0.000	-0.007	-0.007	-0.010

Shock E. Oil Price Increase

	1st Yr	2nd Yr	5th Yr	10th Yr	1st Yr	2nd Yr	5th Yr	10th Yr
1 1X	-0.048	0.137	-0.049	-0.126	0.026	-0.038	-0.051	-0.065
2A 2AX	-0.113	0.414	-0.359	0.146	0.083	-0.172	-0.057	-0.006
2B 2BX	0.005	0.257	-0.077	0.030	0.071	-0.210	-0.008	-0.010
3 3X	-0.008	-0.048	-0.058	-0.053	-0.008	-0.048	-0.058	-0.053

Shock L. U.S. Money Demand

	1st Yr	2nd Yr	5th Yr	10th Yr	1st Yr	2nd Yr	5th Yr	10th Yr
1 1X	-0.513	-0.013	0.015	0.037	-0.503	-0.022	0.016	0.035
2A 2AX	-0.016	0.002	-0.001	0.002	-0.015	0.001	-0.001	0.001
2B 2BX	-0.014	0.002	0.001	0.001	-0.013	0.001	0.001	0.001
3 3X	-0.130	0.011	0.025	0.035	-0.130	0.011	0.025	0.035

Shock D. Japanese Money Demand

	1st Yr	2nd Yr	5th Yr	10th Yr	1st Yr	2nd Yr	5th Yr	10th Yr
1 1X	-0.000	-0.003	-0.001	-0.000	0.485	0.051	-0.010	-0.022
2A 2AX	-0.001	-0.000	0.001	0.001	0.024	-0.001	-0.000	0.001
2B 2BX	0.000	0.000	0.000	0.001	0.020	0.002	-0.001	-0.000
3 3X	0.000	-0.000	-0.000	-0.000	-0.000	-0.000	-0.000	-0.000

Shock K. German Money Demand

	1st Yr	2nd Yr	5th Yr	10th Yr	1st Yr	2nd Yr	5th Yr	10th Yr
1 1X	0.493	-0.054	0.023	0.020	0.004	-0.007	-0.002	0.000
2A 2AX	0.025	-0.017	0.011	-0.004	0.001	-0.001	0.001	0.001
2B 2BX	0.018	-0.006	0.002	0.000	0.001	-0.001	0.000	0.001
3 3X	0.000	0.000	-0.000	-0.000	-0.000	-0.000	-0.000	-0.000

Shock F. U.S. Money Supply-Permanent

FIXM

	1st Yr	2nd Yr	5th Yr	10th Yr	1st Yr	2nd Yr	5th Yr	10th Yr
1 1X	0.000	0.000	0.001	0.000	-0.000	-0.000	-0.000	0.000

823

Table A-INC-1
INTERMOD (CONSISTENT) MODEL
EFFECTS ON U.S. REAL GNP, U.S. PRICE LEVEL, U.S. INFLATION RATE
(Deviations from Baseline)

Shock and Regime	Real GNP				GNP Deflator				Inflation Rate			
	1st Yr	2nd Yr	5th Yr	10th Yr	1st Yr	2nd Yr	5th Yr	10th Yr	1st Yr	2nd Yr	5th Yr	10th Yr
Shock A. US Aggregate Demand												
1	0.949	-0.355	-0.147	-0.039	0.108	0.246	0.281	0.050	0.112	0.142	-0.032	-0.042
1X												
2A	0.848	-0.534	-0.130	-0.014	0.117	0.180	0.170	-0.015	0.121	0.065	-0.044	-0.019
2AX	0.916	-0.412	-0.146	-0.028	0.109	0.223	0.233	0.017	0.113	0.117	-0.039	-0.033
2B	0.916	-0.430	-0.046	-0.034	0.139	0.289	0.661	1.073	0.144	0.154	0.101	0.077
2BX												
3	0.949	-0.321	-0.146	-0.027	0.102	0.259	0.285	0.030	0.105	0.162	-0.036	-0.043
3X												
Shock I. Japanese Aggregate Demand												
1	0.042	-0.001	-0.004	-0.015	-0.003	0.024	0.053	0.052	-0.003	0.028	0.010	-0.007
1X												
2A	0.033	0.008	-0.008	0.001	-0.007	0.021	0.026	0.003	-0.008	0.030	0.001	-0.007
2AX	0.037	0.001	-0.007	-0.007	0.035	0.002	-0.003	-0.004	-0.004	0.023	0.041	0.021
2B	0.038	0.006	0.001	-0.000	-0.007	0.022	0.044	0.113	-0.007	0.030	0.010	0.016
2BX												
3	0.041	-0.016	-0.005	-0.014	-0.002	0.020	0.042	0.057	-0.003	0.023	0.008	-0.002
3X												
Shock G. German Aggregate Demand												
1	0.012	0.007	-0.003	-0.000	-0.003	0.009	0.008	0.001	-0.003	0.013	-0.001	-0.002
1X												
2A	0.013	0.018	-0.002	0.002	-0.008	0.011	-0.002	-0.002	-0.008	0.019	-0.002	0.001
2AX	0.012	0.011	-0.003	0.002	-0.004	0.010	0.003	-0.003	-0.005	0.015	-0.002	-0.001
2B	0.012	0.014	-0.001	0.001	-0.008	0.010	-0.003	0.008	-0.009	0.019	-0.002	0.003
2BX												
3	0.013	0.002	-0.003	-0.004	-0.001	0.007	0.015	0.015	-0.001	0.009	0.001	-0.001
3X												
Shock B. Global Aggregate Demand												
1	1.001	-0.350	-0.153	-0.043	0.102	0.277	0.331	0.074	0.105	0.182	-0.027	-0.054
1X												
2A	0.895	-0.508	-0.138	-0.008	0.101	0.212	0.191	-0.017	0.105	0.114	-0.046	-0.024
2AX	0.966	-0.403	-0.151	-0.027	0.912	-0.326	-0.094	0.012	0.100	0.253	0.271	0.029
2B	0.965	-0.412	-0.045	-0.034	0.124	0.319	0.692	1.174	0.128	0.201	0.106	0.095
2BX												
3	0.999	-0.338	-0.155	-0.044	0.099	0.285	0.338	0.084	0.102	0.193	-0.028	-0.050
3X												
Shock C. US Aggregate Supply												
1	0.067	0.030	0.153	0.051	0.840	-0.480	-0.385	-0.084	0.869	-1.354	0.034	0.065
1X												
2A	0.014	-0.060	0.194	0.009	0.865	-0.483	-0.266	0.008	0.895	-1.382	0.073	0.037
2AX	0.057	0.011	0.164	0.031	1.052	0.043	0.092	-0.007	0.848	-0.475	-0.330	-0.037
2B	-0.022	-0.008	0.069	0.042	0.837	-0.557	-0.759	-1.275	0.865	-1.429	-0.109	-0.094
2BX												
3	0.064	0.007	0.162	0.039	0.835	-0.497	-0.423	-0.063	0.863	-1.366	0.038	0.072
3X												
Shock J. Japanese Aggregate Supply												
1	0.003	0.037	-0.007	0.011	-0.005	0.004	-0.016	-0.043	-0.005	0.009	-0.010	-0.002
1X												
2A	0.008	0.051	0.005	0.006	-0.008	0.002	-0.021	-0.007	-0.008	0.010	-0.008	0.007
2AX	0.007	0.042	0.001	0.012	0.006	0.039	-0.002	0.007	-0.006	0.001	-0.023	-0.024
2B	0.000	0.035	-0.001	-0.001	-0.008	-0.002	-0.029	-0.051	-0.009	0.007	-0.007	-0.004
2BX												
3	0.003	0.032	-0.005	0.010	-0.004	0.004	-0.012	-0.043	-0.004	0.008	-0.009	-0.004
3X												

824

Shock and Regime	Real GNP				GNP Deflator				Inflation Rate			
	1st Yr	2nd Yr	5th Yr	10th Yr	1st Yr	2nd Yr	5th Yr	10th Yr	1st Yr	2nd Yr	5th Yr	10th Yr
Shock H. German Aggregate Supply												
1	0.003	0.007	0.011	0.005	-0.006	-0.010	-0.036	-0.011	-0.006	-0.004	-0.002	0.008
1X												
2A	0.005	0.013	0.011	-0.003	-0.006	-0.007	-0.023	0.004	-0.007	-0.000	0.004	0.005
2AX	0.004	0.009	0.012	0.000	-0.006	-0.009	-0.031	-0.002	-0.006	-0.003	0.000	0.007
2B	-0.002	0.003	-0.003	0.001	-0.007	-0.010	-0.048	-0.095	-0.007	-0.003	-0.011	-0.009
2BX												
3	0.004	0.011	0.010	0.010	-0.006	-0.006	-0.032	-0.017	-0.006	-0.001	-0.004	0.007
3X												
Shock E. Oil Price Increase												
1	1.001	-0.350	-0.153	-0.043	0.102	0.277	0.331	0.074	0.105	0.182	-0.027	-0.054
1X												
2A	0.895	-0.508	-0.138	-0.008	0.101	0.212	0.191	-0.017	0.105	0.114	-0.046	-0.024
2AX	0.966	-0.403	-0.151	-0.027	0.912	-0.326	-0.094	0.012	0.100	0.253	0.271	0.029
2B	0.965	-0.412	-0.045	-0.034	0.124	0.319	0.692	1.174	0.128	0.201	0.106	0.095
2BX												
3	0.999	-0.338	-0.155	-0.044	0.099	0.285	0.338	0.084	0.102	0.193	-0.028	-0.050
3X												
Shock L. U.S. Money Demand												
1	-0.037	-0.100	0.010	0.004	0.007	-0.028	-0.035	-0.018	0.007	-0.036	-0.002	0.004
1X												
2A	0.009	-0.007	-0.000	0.001	0.001	0.001	0.000	-0.001	0.001	0.000	-0.001	-0.000
2AX	0.010	-0.006	-0.001	0.000	0.009	-0.005	-0.001	0.001	0.001	0.001	0.000	-0.001
2B	0.009	-0.007	0.000	0.000	0.001	0.001	0.001	-0.000	0.001	0.000	-0.000	-0.000
2BX												
3	-0.037	-0.078	0.011	0.010	-0.000	-0.021	-0.046	-0.029	-0.000	-0.021	-0.005	0.006
3X												
Shock D. Japanese Money Demand												
1	-0.000	0.010	-0.002	0.001	-0.001	0.002	0.001	-0.004	-0.001	0.003	-0.001	-0.001
1X												
2A	0.001	0.000	-0.000	0.000	-0.000	0.000	-0.000	-0.000	-0.000	0.000	-0.000	0.000
2AX	0.001	0.000	0.000	0.000	0.001	-0.000	-0.000	0.000	-0.000	0.000	-0.000	-0.000
2B	0.001	0.000	-0.000	-0.000	-0.000	0.000	-0.000	-0.001	-0.000	0.000	-0.000	-0.000
2BX												
3	0.001	-0.001	0.000	0.000	-0.000	0.000	-0.000	-0.000	-0.000	0.000	-0.000	-0.000
3X												
Shock K. German Money Demand												
1	0.000	0.005	-0.000	0.001	-0.001	0.001	-0.002	-0.003	-0.001	0.003	-0.001	-0.000
1X												
2A	-0.000	0.001	-0.000	0.000	-0.000	-0.000	-0.001	-0.000	-0.000	0.000	-0.000	-0.000
2AX	0.000	0.001	-0.001	-0.000	0.000	0.000	-0.001	-0.000	-0.000	0.000	-0.000	-0.001
2B	0.000	0.001	-0.001	0.000	-0.000	0.000	-0.000	-0.001	-0.000	0.000	-0.000	-0.000
2BX												
3	0.000	0.000	-0.000	-0.000	0.000	-0.000	-0.000	-0.000	0.000	-0.000	-0.000	-0.000
3X												
Shock F. U.S. Money Supply-Permanent												
FIXM												
1	0.000	0.027	-0.022	-0.015	0.003	0.032	0.084	0.074	0.003	0.030	0.012	-0.008
1X												

INTERMOD (CONSISTENT) MODEL
EFFECTS ON U.S. INTEREST RATES AND U.S. CURRENT ACCOUNT/GNP RATIO
(Deviations from Baseline)

Shock and Regime	Short Interest Rate				Long Interest Rate				Current Account/GNP Ratio			
	1st Yr	2nd Yr	5th Yr	10th Yr	1st Yr	2nd Yr	5th Yr	10th Yr	1st Yr	2nd Yr	5th Yr	10th Yr
Shock A. US Aggregate Demand												
1	0.415	-0.023	0.065	0.015	0.078	0.037	0.027	-0.014	-0.088	-0.014	-0.038	-0.028
1X												
2A	1.371	-0.344	0.102	-0.003	0.149	0.011	0.023	-0.013	-0.049	-0.162	-0.038	-0.027
2AX	0.679	-0.081	0.080	0.011	0.105	0.037	0.029	-0.015	-0.076	-0.055	-0.042	-0.029
2B	1.500	-0.291	0.077	0.066	0.176	0.031	0.059	-0.004	-0.074	-0.159	-0.025	-0.045
2BX												
3	0.449	-0.003	0.073	0.012	0.083	0.039	0.025	-0.006	-0.107	0.011	-0.034	-0.026
3X												
Shock I. Japanese Aggregate Demand												
1	0.015	0.010	0.021	0.016	0.018	0.018	0.017	0.004	0.016	0.005	0.004	0.001
1X												
2A	0.036	0.046	0.031	0.004	0.025	0.021	0.011	-0.005	0.010	0.019	0.003	0.002
2AX	-0.005	0.028	0.005	-0.009	0.022	0.018	0.025	0.010	0.020	0.019	0.014	-0.003
2B	0.087	0.010	0.017	0.024	0.024	0.018	0.023	0.026	0.013	0.012	0.001	0.002
2BX												
3	0.016	0.002	0.017	0.021	0.017	0.018	0.020	0.010	0.022	-0.004	0.002	0.002
3X												
Shock G. German Aggregate Demand												
1	0.004	0.007	0.002	0.000	0.003	0.003	0.002	-0.001	0.000	0.009	0.000	0.001
1X												
2A	0.007	0.042	-0.005	0.000	0.003	0.002	-0.001	0.001	-0.006	0.022	-0.002	0.001
2AX	0.005	0.014	0.001	-0.001	0.003	0.003	0.000	-0.001	-0.002	0.013	-0.000	0.001
2B	0.037	-0.000	0.000	0.005	0.005	0.002	0.004	0.004	-0.005	0.019	-0.002	0.001
2BX												
3	0.005	0.004	0.006	0.005	0.005	0.006	0.006	0.006	0.004	0.002	0.000	0.000
3X												
Shock B. Global Aggregate Demand												
1	0.432	-0.008	0.084	0.023	0.093	0.051	0.035	-0.021	-0.071	0.000	-0.033	-0.024
1X												
2A	1.414	-0.256	0.124	-0.001	0.172	0.029	0.030	-0.015	-0.046	-0.120	-0.037	-0.023
2AX	0.103	0.158	-0.038	-0.041	0.706	-0.053	0.103	0.019	0.123	0.053	0.038	-0.020
2B	1.619	-0.288	0.091	0.091	0.200	0.046	0.083	0.029	-0.066	-0.129	-0.025	-0.042
2BX												
3	0.469	0.001	0.094	0.030	0.105	0.060	0.044	-0.009	-0.082	0.008	-0.033	-0.025
3X												
Shock C. US Aggregate Supply												
1	0.370	-0.176	-0.104	-0.021	-0.044	-0.081	-0.036	0.022	0.035	-0.176	0.044	0.021
1X												
2A	1.302	-0.680	-0.167	0.004	-0.029	-0.157	-0.037	0.022	0.059	-0.317	0.079	0.015
2AX	0.877	-1.357	0.048	0.053	0.624	-0.295	-0.134	-0.016	-0.044	-0.106	-0.039	0.023
2B	1.140	-1.783	-0.087	-0.077	-0.117	-0.237	-0.075	-0.003	0.051	-0.278	0.066	0.036
2BX												
3	0.400	-0.209	-0.127	-0.018	-0.053	-0.093	-0.037	0.011	0.044	-0.176	0.039	0.021
3X												
Shock J. Japanese Aggregate Supply												
1	-0.001	0.016	-0.010	-0.014	-0.005	-0.007	-0.011	-0.010	-0.009	0.031	-0.003	0.001
1X												
2A	-0.001	0.076	-0.029	-0.005	-0.011	-0.012	-0.010	0.005	-0.013	0.042	-0.003	0.002
2AX	-0.007	0.008	-0.010	0.005	-0.000	0.029	-0.017	-0.010	-0.010	-0.011	-0.012	-0.000
2B	0.008	0.020	-0.011	-0.006	-0.007	-0.009	-0.005	-0.003	-0.009	0.036	-0.002	-0.001
2BX												
3	-0.000	0.016	-0.008	-0.016	-0.006	-0.007	-0.013	-0.014	-0.007	0.025	-0.002	0.000
3X												

Shock and Regime	Short Interest Rate				Long Interest Rate				Current Account/GNP Ratio			
	1st Yr	2nd Yr	5th Yr	10th Yr	1st Yr	2nd Yr	5th Yr	10th Yr	1st Yr	2nd Yr	5th Yr	10th Yr
Shock H. German Aggregate Supply												
1	-0.001	-0.002	-0.011	-0.003	-0.009	-0.009	-0.005	0.005	-0.001	0.011	0.000	0.001
1X												
2A	-0.003	0.008	-0.023	0.001	-0.014	-0.013	-0.004	0.003	-0.002	0.017	0.001	-0.000
2AX	-0.001	-0.001	-0.015	-0.002	-0.011	-0.011	-0.005	0.006	-0.001	0.012	0.001	0.000
2B	-0.014	-0.029	-0.017	-0.012	-0.015	-0.015	-0.011	-0.007	-0.001	0.015	-0.003	0.001
2BX												
3	-0.001	0.002	-0.011	-0.004	-0.010	-0.010	-0.008	0.001	-0.002	0.012	0.001	0.002
3X												
Shock E. Oil Price Increase												
1	0.432	-0.008	0.084	0.023	0.093	0.051	0.035	-0.021	-0.071	0.000	-0.033	-0.024
1X												
2A	1.414	-0.256	0.124	-0.001	0.172	0.029	0.030	-0.015	-0.046	-0.120	-0.037	-0.023
2AX	0.103	0.158	-0.038	-0.041	0.706	-0.053	0.103	0.019	0.123	0.053	0.038	-0.020
2B	1.619	-0.288	0.091	0.091	0.200	0.046	0.083	0.029	-0.066	-0.129	-0.025	-0.042
2BX												
3	0.469	0.001	0.094	0.030	0.105	0.060	0.044	-0.009	-0.082	0.008	-0.033	-0.025
3X												
Shock L. U.S. Money Demand												
1	0.403	-0.040	-0.010	-0.005	0.031	-0.011	-0.006	-0.003	0.021	-0.070	0.001	0.000
1X												
2A	0.014	-0.007	-0.000	-0.000	0.001	-0.001	0.000	0.000	-0.001	-0.002	0.000	0.000
2AX	0.001	0.001	-0.001	-0.000	0.007	-0.002	-0.000	0.000	0.001	-0.000	0.000	0.000
2B	0.014	-0.008	-0.001	0.000	0.001	-0.001	-0.000	0.000	-0.001	-0.002	0.000	-0.000
2BX												
3	0.436	-0.030	-0.016	-0.009	0.032	-0.013	-0.010	-0.005	0.008	-0.047	0.001	0.002
3X												
Shock D. Japanese Money Demand												
1	-0.000	0.005	-0.001	-0.002	0.000	0.000	-0.001	-0.001	-0.003	0.007	-0.000	0.000
1X												
2A	0.001	0.001	-0.001	-0.000	0.000	0.000	-0.000	-0.000	0.000	0.000	0.000	0.000
2AX	-0.000	0.000	-0.000	-0.000	0.001	0.000	-0.000	-0.000	0.000	0.000	0.000	0.000
2B	0.002	-0.000	-0.001	-0.000	0.000	0.000	0.000	0.000	0.000	0.000	0.000	0.000
2BX												
3	0.000	-0.000	-0.000	-0.000	0.000	0.000	0.000	0.000	0.000	-0.000	0.000	0.000
3X												
Shock K. German Money Demand												
1	-0.001	0.003	-0.001	-0.001	-0.000	-0.000	-0.001	-0.001	-0.003	0.005	0.000	0.000
1X												
2A	-0.000	0.001	-0.001	-0.000	-0.000	-0.000	-0.000	-0.000	-0.000	0.000	0.000	0.000
2AX	-0.000	0.000	-0.000	-0.000	0.000	0.000	-0.000	-0.000	0.000	0.000	-0.000	-0.000
2B	0.000	0.001	-0.001	0.000	0.000	0.000	-0.000	0.000	-0.000	0.000	0.000	0.000
2BX												
3	0.000	0.000	-0.000	-0.000	0.000	0.000	0.000	0.000	0.000	0.000	0.000	0.000
3X												
Shock F. U.S. Money Supply-Permanent												
FIXM												
1	0.001	0.024	0.027	0.026	0.030	0.033	0.031	0.032	-0.014	0.020	0.008	0.008
1X												

Table A-INC-3
INTERMOD (CONSISTENT) MODEL
EFFECTS ON JAPANESE REAL GNP, JAPANESE PRICE LEVEL, JAPANESE INFLATION RATE
(Deviations from Baseline)

Shock and Regime	Real GNP				GNP Deflator				Inflation Rate			
	1st Yr	2nd Yr	5th Yr	10th Yr	1st Yr	2nd Yr	5th Yr	10th Yr	1st Yr	2nd Yr	5th Yr	10th Yr
Shock A. US Aggregate Demand												
1	0.141	-0.015	0.016	-0.014	-0.004	0.056	0.087	0.069	-0.005	0.062	0.013	-0.016
1X												
2A	0.129	0.090	0.022	0.013	-0.007	0.024	0.033	0.005	-0.007	0.032	0.004	-0.008
2AX	0.136	0.014	0.021	-0.002	-0.006	0.045	0.065	0.043	-0.006	0.052	0.008	-0.013
2B	0.109	0.048	0.011	0.022	-0.023	0.005	-0.020	-0.013	-0.024	0.029	-0.006	0.009
2BX												
3	0.092	-0.058	0.036	0.038	-0.017	0.034	0.009	0.063	-0.018	0.053	0.000	0.017
3X												
Shock I. Japanese Aggregate Demand												
1	0.883	-0.338	-0.160	-0.045	0.118	0.230	0.281	0.094	0.122	0.116	-0.010	-0.040
1X												
2A	0.759	-0.409	-0.151	-0.019	0.071	0.235	0.195	0.019	0.074	0.169	-0.026	-0.027
2AX	0.839	-0.369	-0.155	-0.030	0.849	-0.356	-0.104	0.005	0.100	0.224	0.235	0.052
2B	0.843	-0.309	-0.053	-0.035	0.112	0.320	0.582	0.925	0.116	0.214	0.093	0.060
2BX												
3	0.978	-0.250	-0.148	-0.105	0.162	0.264	0.441	0.283	0.167	0.106	0.025	-0.057
3X												
Shock G. German Aggregate Demand												
1	0.026	-0.001	-0.002	0.001	0.003	0.008	0.010	0.003	0.004	0.005	-0.001	-0.002
1X												
2A	0.026	-0.002	0.001	0.003	0.008	0.001	0.001	-0.002	0.008	-0.008	-0.002	0.000
2AX	0.025	-0.002	-0.001	0.003	0.005	0.006	0.006	-0.002	0.005	0.001	-0.001	-0.001
2B	0.026	0.000	0.001	0.003	0.007	-0.001	0.002	0.003	0.007	-0.009	-0.000	0.001
2BX												
3	0.027	0.003	0.001	-0.000	0.000	0.012	0.022	0.026	0.000	0.012	0.002	0.000
3X												
Shock B. Global Aggregate Demand												
1	1.044	-0.363	-0.143	-0.052	0.111	0.286	0.356	0.141	0.115	0.181	-0.003	-0.055
1X												
2A	0.917	-0.320	-0.126	-0.001	0.070	0.255	0.221	0.017	0.072	0.192	-0.025	-0.034
2AX	1.002	-0.357	-0.136	-0.028	1.003	-0.413	-0.103	-0.003	0.097	0.272	0.300	0.082
2B	0.979	-0.256	-0.037	-0.007	0.099	0.326	0.584	0.994	0.102	0.234	0.094	0.084
2BX												
3	1.084	-0.318	-0.120	-0.061	0.142	0.303	0.443	0.308	0.147	0.166	0.020	-0.046
3X												
Shock C. US Aggregate Supply												
1	0.012	0.081	-0.022	0.029	-0.007	-0.064	-0.102	-0.083	-0.007	-0.060	-0.023	0.023
1X												
2A	0.022	0.180	-0.043	0.001	-0.006	-0.073	-0.061	-0.011	-0.006	-0.069	0.001	0.017
2AX	0.017	0.108	-0.026	0.015	0.017	0.063	-0.002	0.015	-0.006	-0.066	-0.084	-0.046
2B	0.016	0.146	-0.040	-0.018	-0.004	-0.054	-0.027	-0.100	-0.004	-0.052	0.017	-0.022
2BX												
3	0.033	0.143	-0.039	-0.040	0.009	-0.032	0.010	-0.047	0.009	-0.041	0.000	-0.018
3X												
Shock J. Japanese Aggregate Supply												
1	-0.059	0.024	0.067	0.032	0.915	-0.237	-0.190	-0.079	0.946	-1.180	0.013	0.025
1X												
2A	-0.120	0.026	0.075	0.003	0.896	-0.189	-0.132	-0.011	0.927	-1.113	0.029	0.016
2AX	-0.061	0.042	0.072	0.013	0.957	0.028	0.035	-0.003	0.913	-0.218	-0.153	-0.034
2B	-0.093	0.162	-0.000	0.015	0.939	-0.159	-0.159	-0.179	0.971	-1.125	-0.003	-0.002
2BX												
3	-0.035	0.014	0.045	0.059	0.919	-0.272	-0.265	-0.201	0.951	-1.221	-0.008	0.026
3X												

Shock and Regime	Real GNP 1st Yr	2nd Yr	5th Yr	10th Yr	GNP Deflator 1st Yr	2nd Yr	5th Yr	10th Yr	Inflation Rate 1st Yr	2nd Yr	5th Yr	10th Yr
Shock H. German Aggregate Supply												
1	0.004	0.001	-0.000	0.004	-0.004	-0.021	-0.027	-0.015	-0.004	-0.018	-0.004	0.006
1X												
2A	0.007	0.004	-0.003	-0.004	-0.002	-0.023	-0.017	0.000	-0.002	-0.022	-0.000	0.004
2AX	0.006	0.002	-0.000	0.001	-0.004	-0.022	-0.023	-0.007	-0.004	-0.019	-0.002	0.005
2B	0.002	-0.003	-0.002	-0.003	-0.003	-0.023	-0.022	-0.043	-0.004	-0.021	-0.005	-0.004
2BX												
3	0.007	0.003	0.001	0.006	-0.000	-0.016	-0.025	-0.027	-0.000	-0.016	-0.005	0.003
3X												
Shock E. Oil Price Increase												
1	1.044	-0.363	-0.143	-0.052	0.111	0.286	0.356	0.141	0.115	0.181	-0.003	-0.055
1X												
2A	0.917	-0.320	-0.126	-0.001	0.070	0.255	0.221	0.017	0.072	0.192	-0.025	-0.034
2AX	1.002	-0.357	-0.136	-0.028	1.003	-0.413	-0.103	-0.003	0.097	0.272	0.300	0.082
2B	0.979	-0.256	-0.037	-0.007	0.099	0.326	0.584	0.994	0.102	0.234	0.094	0.084
2BX												
3	1.084	-0.318	-0.120	-0.061	0.142	0.303	0.443	0.308	0.147	0.166	0.020	-0.046
3X												
Shock L. U.S. Money Demand												
1	0.004	0.053	-0.001	0.003	0.002	-0.010	-0.008	-0.013	0.002	-0.012	-0.002	-0.000
1X												
2A	0.001	0.001	-0.000	0.000	0.000	0.000	0.000	-0.000	0.000	0.000	-0.000	-0.000
2AX	0.002	-0.000	0.000	0.000	0.002	-0.001	0.000	0.000	0.000	0.001	-0.000	-0.000
2B	0.001	0.000	-0.000	0.000	0.000	0.000	-0.000	-0.000	0.000	0.000	-0.000	0.000
2BX												
3	-0.030	0.034	0.008	0.007	-0.004	-0.015	-0.029	-0.023	-0.004	-0.012	-0.003	0.004
3X												
Shock D. Japanese Money Demand												
1	-0.043	-0.049	0.011	0.005	-0.025	0.003	-0.025	-0.011	-0.025	0.029	-0.002	0.004
1X												
2A	0.013	-0.008	-0.001	0.001	0.001	0.003	0.001	-0.001	0.001	0.002	-0.001	0.000
2AX	0.015	-0.008	-0.001	0.001	0.015	-0.009	-0.001	0.001	0.001	0.003	0.001	-0.001
2B	0.013	-0.008	-0.001	0.000	0.001	0.003	0.002	0.001	0.001	0.002	-0.001	-0.000
2BX												
3	0.016	-0.007	-0.002	0.001	0.002	0.003	0.002	-0.001	0.002	0.000	-0.001	-0.000
3X												
Shock K. German Money Demand												
1	0.001	-0.001	0.000	0.001	0.003	-0.001	-0.002	-0.003	0.003	-0.004	-0.001	0.000
1X												
2A	0.000	-0.000	-0.000	0.000	0.000	0.000	-0.000	-0.001	0.000	-0.000	-0.000	0.000
2AX	0.000	-0.000	-0.000	0.000	0.000	-0.000	-0.000	0.000	0.000	0.000	-0.000	-0.001
2B	0.000	0.000	-0.000	-0.000	0.000	0.000	-0.000	-0.001	0.000	-0.000	-0.000	0.000
2BX												
3	0.000	-0.000	-0.000	0.000	0.000	0.000	-0.000	-0.000	0.000	0.000	-0.000	0.000
3X												
Shock F. U.S. Money Supply-Permanent												
FIXM												
1	-0.010	-0.025	0.010	0.015	-0.005	-0.004	-0.033	-0.054	-0.005	0.000	-0.009	-0.002
1X												

Table A-INC-4
INTERMOD (CONSISTENT) MODEL
EFFECTS ON JAPANESE INTEREST RATES AND JAPANESE CURRENT ACCOUNT/GNP RATIO
(Deviations from Baseline)

Shock and Regime	Short Interest Rate				Long Interest Rate				Current Account/GNP Ratio			
	1st Yr	2nd Yr	5th Yr	10th Yr	1st Yr	2nd Yr	5th Yr	10th Yr	1st Yr	2nd Yr	5th Yr	10th Yr
Shock A. US Aggregate Demand												
1	0.054	-0.001	0.035	0.017	0.032	0.028	0.023	-0.005	0.063	0.024	0.028	0.012
1X												
2A	0.164	-0.017	0.049	0.001	0.043	0.026	0.016	-0.008	0.055	0.131	0.028	0.013
2AX	0.086	-0.006	0.045	0.017	0.039	0.032	0.025	-0.004	0.061	0.054	0.031	0.014
2B	0.219	-0.032	0.013	0.048	0.038	0.021	0.044	0.068	0.060	0.125	0.015	0.024
2BX												
3	0.319	0.014	0.070	0.009	0.070	0.038	0.021	-0.009	0.066	0.011	0.025	0.017
3X												
Shock I. Japanese Aggregate Demand												
1	0.416	-0.041	0.055	0.026	0.075	0.035	0.032	0.001	-0.124	-0.012	-0.028	-0.020
1X												
2A	1.261	-0.257	0.081	0.020	0.143	0.017	0.033	-0.004	-0.116	-0.044	-0.028	-0.019
2AX	0.103	0.129	-0.019	-0.033	0.661	-0.096	0.064	0.025	0.094	0.029	0.031	-0.003
2B	1.285	-0.025	0.052	0.038	0.153	0.027	0.032	-0.025	-0.124	-0.033	-0.017	-0.029
2BX												
3	0.013	0.005	0.018	0.021	0.017	0.018	0.020	0.011	-0.131	0.010	-0.023	-0.025
3X												
Shock G. German Aggregate Demand												
1	0.012	0.002	0.003	0.001	0.004	0.003	0.002	0.000	0.012	0.003	0.001	0.001
1X												
2A	0.052	-0.005	-0.001	0.000	0.005	-0.000	0.000	0.001	0.014	-0.001	0.002	0.002
2AX	0.021	0.002	0.002	0.000	0.004	0.002	0.001	-0.001	0.013	0.002	0.001	0.001
2B	0.066	-0.025	0.002	0.006	0.007	0.000	0.005	0.006	0.014	0.003	0.003	0.004
2BX												
3	0.004	0.004	0.006	0.005	0.005	0.005	0.005	0.005	0.011	0.005	0.002	0.003
3X												
Shock B. Global Aggregate Demand												
1	0.477	-0.047	0.085	0.036	0.099	0.054	0.046	-0.013	-0.050	0.012	-0.001	-0.009
1X												
2A	1.476	-0.283	0.122	0.017	0.183	0.035	0.042	-0.011	-0.048	0.086	0.001	-0.006
2AX	0.100	0.181	-0.014	-0.047	0.767	-0.102	0.106	0.036	0.132	0.057	0.051	-0.012
2B	1.576	-0.073	0.083	0.117	0.217	0.071	0.106	0.066	-0.051	0.098	0.004	0.002
2BX												
3	0.335	0.022	0.093	0.027	0.093	0.062	0.043	-0.008	-0.055	0.025	0.006	-0.006
3X												
Shock C. US Aggregate Supply												
1	0.003	-0.004	-0.043	-0.018	-0.033	-0.035	-0.024	0.015	-0.006	0.079	-0.038	-0.008
1X												
2A	0.020	0.013	-0.090	0.000	-0.051	-0.052	-0.020	0.017	-0.013	0.174	-0.066	-0.004
2AX	-0.007	-0.061	-0.014	0.022	0.008	-0.002	-0.057	-0.014	-0.040	-0.042	-0.024	0.017
2B	0.049	0.047	-0.039	-0.061	-0.040	-0.052	-0.059	-0.081	-0.011	0.152	-0.051	-0.020
2BX												
3	0.223	-0.189	-0.118	-0.011	-0.062	-0.084	-0.031	0.014	-0.006	0.089	-0.036	-0.017
3X												
Shock J. Japanese Aggregate Supply												
1	0.359	-0.091	-0.051	-0.019	-0.008	-0.045	-0.026	-0.007	-0.008	-0.082	0.015	0.005
1X												
2A	1.184	-0.264	-0.083	-0.010	0.044	-0.074	-0.025	0.005	-0.004	-0.103	0.018	0.001
2AX	0.944	-1.159	0.023	0.020	0.603	-0.130	-0.056	-0.014	0.010	-0.050	-0.022	0.001
2B	1.230	-1.293	-0.007	0.018	0.012	-0.108	0.019	0.027	-0.002	-0.079	0.012	0.010
2BX												
3	0.003	0.010	-0.008	-0.015	-0.005	-0.007	-0.011	-0.013	-0.008	-0.069	0.013	0.009
3X												

830

Shock and Regime	Short Interest Rate				Long Interest Rate				Current Account/GNP Ratio			
	1st Yr	2nd Yr	5th Yr	10th Yr	1st Yr	2nd Yr	5th Yr	10th Yr	1st Yr	2nd Yr	5th Yr	10th Yr
Shock H. German Aggregate Supply												
1	0.000	-0.008	-0.010	-0.004	-0.009	-0.009	-0.006	0.003	0.002	-0.003	-0.005	-0.002
1X												
2A	0.008	-0.028	-0.022	-0.001	-0.014	-0.014	-0.005	0.003	0.003	-0.005	-0.006	-0.002
2AX	0.002	-0.014	-0.014	-0.003	-0.011	-0.012	-0.006	0.005	0.002	-0.003	-0.006	-0.002
2B	-0.006	-0.031	-0.011	-0.011	-0.012	-0.013	-0.011	-0.012	0.001	-0.006	-0.003	-0.006
2BX												
3	-0.002	-0.003	-0.012	-0.005	-0.011	-0.011	-0.009	-0.001	0.003	-0.001	-0.004	-0.002
3X												
Shock E. Oil Price Increase												
1	0.477	-0.047	0.085	0.036	0.099	0.054	0.046	-0.013	-0.050	0.012	-0.001	-0.009
1X												
2A	1.476	-0.283	0.122	0.017	0.183	0.035	0.042	-0.011	-0.048	0.086	0.001	-0.006
2AX	0.100	0.181	-0.014	-0.047	0.767	-0.102	0.106	0.036	0.132	0.057	0.051	-0.012
2B	1.576	-0.073	0.083	0.117	0.217	0.071	0.106	0.066	-0.051	0.098	0.004	0.002
2BX												
3	0.335	0.022	0.093	0.027	0.093	0.062	0.043	-0.008	-0.055	0.025	0.006	-0.006
3X												
Shock L. U.S. Money Demand												
1	0.001	0.004	-0.004	-0.004	-0.001	-0.002	-0.003	-0.003	-0.005	0.049	-0.001	-0.000
1X												
2A	0.002	-0.000	0.000	-0.000	0.000	0.000	0.000	0.000	0.001	0.001	-0.000	0.000
2AX	0.000	0.001	-0.000	0.000	0.001	-0.000	0.000	-0.000	0.000	0.000	0.000	0.000
2B	0.003	-0.001	-0.000	0.000	0.000	-0.000	0.000	0.000	0.001	0.001	-0.000	0.000
2BX												
3	0.299	-0.024	-0.014	-0.008	0.020	-0.011	-0.008	-0.005	-0.002	0.041	-0.001	-0.001
3X												
Shock D. Japanese Money Demand												
1	0.388	-0.019	-0.006	-0.002	0.032	-0.007	-0.004	-0.001	0.001	-0.017	0.001	0.001
1X												
2A	0.021	-0.007	-0.000	-0.001	0.001	-0.001	-0.000	-0.000	-0.002	0.000	0.000	0.000
2AX	0.001	0.002	-0.001	-0.000	0.011	-0.004	-0.000	-0.000	0.001	-0.000	0.000	0.000
2B	0.020	-0.006	-0.002	-0.000	0.001	-0.001	-0.000	0.000	-0.002	0.000	0.000	-0.000
2BX												
3	0.000	-0.000	0.000	0.000	0.000	0.000	0.000	0.000	-0.002	0.001	-0.000	-0.000
3X												
Shock K. German Money Demand												
1	0.002	-0.001	-0.001	-0.001	-0.000	-0.001	-0.001	-0.001	0.001	-0.001	-0.000	-0.000
1X												
2A	0.001	0.000	-0.001	-0.000	0.000	-0.000	-0.000	-0.000	0.000	-0.000	-0.000	0.000
2AX	0.000	-0.000	-0.000	0.000	0.000	0.000	-0.000	-0.000	0.000	0.000	-0.000	-0.000
2B	0.001	-0.000	-0.001	-0.000	0.000	0.000	0.000	0.000	0.000	0.000	0.000	0.000
2BX												
3	0.000	0.000	0.000	-0.000	0.000	0.000	0.000	0.000	0.000	0.000	0.000	0.000
3X												
Shock F. U.S. Money Supply-Permanent												
FIXM												
1	-0.005	-0.011	-0.011	-0.018	-0.016	-0.017	-0.021	-0.038	0.000	-0.013	-0.002	0.001
1X												

INTERMOD (CONSISTENT) MODEL
EFFECTS ON GERMAN REAL GNP, GERMAN PRICE LEVEL, GERMAN INFLATION RATE
(Deviations from Baseline)

Shock and Regime	Real GNP				GNP Deflator				Inflation Rate			
	1st Yr	2nd Yr	5th Yr	10th Yr	1st Yr	2nd Yr	5th Yr	10th Yr	1st Yr	2nd Yr	5th Yr	10th Yr
Shock A. US Aggregate Demand												
1	0.120	-0.008	0.028	0.023	0.003	0.070	0.071	0.005	0.004	0.069	0.001	-0.017
1X												
2A	0.121	0.114	0.035	0.029	-0.036	0.051	0.017	-0.018	-0.037	0.090	0.001	-0.004
2AX	0.118	0.027	0.033	0.025	-0.011	0.058	0.050	-0.001	-0.012	0.072	0.001	-0.012
2B	0.077	0.038	-0.012	0.002	-0.035	0.051	0.061	0.219	-0.037	0.089	0.009	0.041
2BX												
3	0.043	-0.050	0.033	0.031	-0.022	-0.009	0.000	0.085	-0.023	0.013	0.014	0.018
3X												
Shock I. Japanese Aggregate Demand												
1	0.045	-0.014	0.008	0.010	0.004	0.033	0.043	0.026	0.004	0.030	0.005	-0.007
1X												
2A	0.041	-0.003	0.017	0.017	-0.002	0.022	0.012	-0.010	-0.002	0.025	-0.001	-0.003
2AX	0.043	-0.011	0.011	0.016	0.043	-0.015	0.004	0.007	0.003	0.031	0.028	-0.001
2B	0.041	-0.007	0.002	0.009	-0.007	0.018	0.016	0.028	-0.008	0.026	0.005	0.000
2BX												
3	0.036	-0.026	0.001	0.009	0.001	0.023	0.030	0.028	0.001	0.023	0.005	-0.003
3X												
Shock G. German Aggregate Demand												
1	0.889	-0.490	-0.026	-0.024	0.189	0.095	0.009	0.006	0.196	-0.098	-0.002	-0.002
1X												
2A	0.712	-0.509	-0.006	-0.036	0.289	-0.043	0.048	0.015	0.299	-0.342	0.087	-0.003
2AX	0.834	-0.505	-0.021	-0.025	0.219	0.059	0.009	0.005	0.227	-0.166	0.007	-0.001
2B	0.799	-0.485	0.015	-0.015	0.308	0.121	0.204	0.248	0.318	-0.193	0.036	0.010
2BX												
3	0.991	-0.455	-0.032	-0.030	0.161	0.192	0.055	0.044	0.166	0.033	-0.006	-0.004
3X												
Shock B. Global Aggregate Demand												
1	1.065	-0.503	0.015	0.016	0.191	0.193	0.109	-0.000	0.197	0.002	-0.002	-0.027
1X												
2A	0.881	-0.392	0.053	0.009	0.251	0.026	0.065	-0.017	0.259	-0.232	0.086	-0.009
2AX	1.007	-0.479	0.024	0.017	1.007	-0.559	0.018	0.014	0.204	0.141	0.081	-0.006
2B	0.916	-0.454	0.001	-0.007	0.274	0.214	0.359	0.649	0.283	-0.061	0.068	0.064
2BX												
3	1.051	-0.530	0.008	0.027	0.110	0.143	0.020	0.069	0.114	0.035	0.013	0.009
3X												
Shock C. US Aggregate Supply												
1	0.002	0.075	-0.036	-0.029	-0.038	-0.059	-0.095	0.016	-0.039	-0.022	0.010	0.024
1X												
2A	0.004	0.170	-0.089	-0.027	-0.042	-0.021	-0.033	0.029	-0.044	0.022	0.018	0.005
2AX	0.003	0.099	-0.052	-0.033	0.004	0.046	-0.015	-0.015	-0.036	-0.044	-0.067	0.026
2B	0.015	0.135	-0.049	0.005	-0.019	0.015	-0.143	-0.363	-0.020	0.036	-0.091	-0.056
2BX												
3	0.039	0.134	-0.033	-0.032	0.004	0.037	0.008	-0.082	0.004	0.034	-0.010	-0.020
3X												
Shock J. Japanese Aggregate Supply												
1	0.006	0.023	-0.000	-0.000	-0.003	-0.007	-0.028	-0.032	-0.003	-0.004	-0.004	-0.000
1X												
2A	0.017	0.039	-0.004	-0.009	-0.008	-0.017	-0.020	0.004	-0.008	-0.010	0.006	0.003
2AX	0.014	0.031	0.001	-0.005	0.014	0.030	0.003	-0.000	-0.007	-0.015	-0.029	-0.009
2B	0.003	0.019	-0.004	-0.004	-0.010	-0.014	-0.019	-0.025	-0.010	-0.004	0.003	-0.002
2BX												
3	0.003	0.016	0.001	-0.001	-0.003	-0.008	-0.028	-0.033	-0.003	-0.005	-0.004	-0.000
3X												

832

Shock and Regime	Real GNP				GNP Deflator				Inflation Rate			
	1st Yr	2nd Yr	5th Yr	10th Yr	1st Yr	2nd Yr	5th Yr	10th Yr	1st Yr	2nd Yr	5th Yr	10th Yr
Shock H. German Aggregate Supply												
1	0.034	0.278	0.067	0.037	0.534	-0.758	-0.138	-0.054	0.552	-1.329	0.031	0.015
1X												
2A	-0.036	0.342	0.094	0.044	0.606	-0.816	-0.096	-0.049	0.626	-1.461	0.087	0.007
2AX	0.026	0.302	0.071	0.036	0.552	-0.768	-0.119	-0.045	0.571	-1.358	0.037	0.012
2B	-0.052	0.316	0.012	0.009	0.395	-1.143	-0.702	-0.728	0.408	-1.584	0.049	0.001
2BX												
3	0.022	0.204	0.060	0.035	0.486	-0.802	-0.205	-0.081	0.502	-1.325	0.040	0.023
3X												
Shock E. Oil Price Increase												
1	1.065	-0.503	0.015	0.016	0.191	0.193	0.109	-0.000	0.197	0.002	-0.002	-0.027
1X												
2A	0.881	-0.392	0.053	0.009	0.251	0.026	0.065	-0.017	0.259	-0.232	0.086	-0.009
2AX	1.007	-0.479	0.024	0.017	1.007	-0.559	0.018	0.014	0.204	0.141	0.081	-0.006
2B	0.916	-0.454	0.001	-0.007	0.274	0.214	0.359	0.649	0.283	-0.061	0.068	0.064
2BX												
3	1.051	-0.530	0.008	0.027	0.110	0.143	0.020	0.069	0.114	0.035	0.013	0.009
3X												
Shock L. U.S. Money Demand												
1	0.003	0.055	-0.002	0.001	-0.012	0.004	-0.009	-0.010	-0.012	0.016	-0.002	-0.000
1X												
2A	0.001	0.001	-0.001	0.000	-0.000	0.001	-0.000	-0.000	-0.000	0.002	-0.001	-0.000
2AX	0.001	0.000	0.000	0.000	0.001	-0.001	0.000	0.000	-0.000	0.001	0.000	-0.000
2B	0.001	0.000	-0.000	0.000	-0.000	0.001	-0.000	-0.000	-0.000	0.002	-0.001	-0.000
2BX												
3	-0.040	0.042	0.004	0.001	-0.013	-0.016	-0.014	-0.007	-0.013	-0.003	0.002	0.001
3X												
Shock D. Japanese Money Demand												
1	0.000	0.004	-0.000	-0.000	0.001	0.002	-0.002	-0.003	0.001	0.001	-0.001	-0.000
1X												
2A	0.001	-0.001	0.000	0.001	0.000	0.001	-0.000	-0.000	0.000	0.001	-0.000	-0.000
2AX	0.001	-0.000	-0.000	0.000	0.001	-0.001	-0.000	0.001	0.000	0.001	-0.000	-0.000
2B	0.001	-0.000	-0.001	0.000	0.000	0.001	-0.000	-0.001	0.000	0.001	-0.000	-0.000
2BX												
3	0.001	-0.000	-0.000	0.000	0.000	0.001	-0.000	-0.000	0.000	0.001	-0.000	-0.000
3X												
Shock K. German Money Demand												
1	-0.090	-0.080	-0.003	-0.005	0.048	-0.053	0.006	0.006	0.049	-0.104	-0.002	-0.001
1X												
2A	0.010	-0.011	0.000	0.000	0.004	-0.000	-0.001	0.000	0.005	-0.005	-0.001	0.001
2AX	0.012	-0.010	-0.000	0.000	0.012	-0.011	0.000	0.001	0.003	0.001	-0.000	-0.000
2B	0.011	-0.010	-0.000	0.000	0.004	0.000	0.000	-0.000	0.004	-0.004	0.000	-0.000
2BX												
3	0.015	-0.011	-0.001	0.001	0.002	0.003	-0.000	0.000	0.002	0.001	-0.000	-0.000
3X												
Shock F. U.S. Money Supply-Permanent												
FIXM												
1	-0.016	-0.024	0.003	0.013	-0.006	-0.029	-0.038	-0.046	-0.006	-0.024	-0.001	-0.002
1X												

INTERMOD (CONSISTENT) MODEL
EFFECTS ON GERMAN INTEREST RATES AND GERMAN CURRENT ACCOUNT/GNP RATIO
(Deviations from Baseline)

Shock and Regime	Short Interest Rate				Long Interest Rate				Current Account/GNP Ratio			
	1st Yr	2nd Yr	5th Yr	10th Yr	1st Yr	2nd Yr	5th Yr	10th Yr	1st Yr	2nd Yr	5th Yr	10th Yr
Shock A. US Aggregate Demand												
1	0.049	0.005	0.032	0.004	0.026	0.022	0.014	-0.009	0.053	0.023	0.026	0.018
1X												
2A	0.104	0.029	0.040	-0.009	0.033	0.022	0.007	-0.011	0.040	0.145	0.027	0.015
2AX	0.068	0.006	0.041	0.004	0.031	0.026	0.016	-0.008	0.049	0.058	0.030	0.019
2B	0.128	0.039	0.020	0.064	0.048	0.041	0.056	0.053	0.054	0.149	0.007	0.015
2BX												
3	0.319	0.014	0.070	0.008	0.070	0.038	0.021	-0.009	0.052	0.016	0.024	0.013
3X												
Shock I. Japanese Aggregate Demand												
1	0.020	0.007	0.019	0.011	0.015	0.014	0.013	0.004	0.018	-0.003	0.007	0.012
1X												
2A	0.059	0.020	0.029	-0.002	0.022	0.016	0.007	-0.006	0.016	0.004	0.011	0.009
2AX	0.003	0.029	0.000	-0.007	0.032	0.011	0.022	0.004	0.017	0.015	0.009	-0.004
2B	0.085	-0.008	0.013	0.015	0.018	0.011	0.017	0.031	0.019	0.010	0.008	0.017
2BX												
3	0.013	0.005	0.018	0.021	0.017	0.018	0.020	0.011	0.020	-0.005	0.006	0.011
3X												
Shock G. German Aggregate Demand												
1	0.449	-0.161	0.001	0.002	0.033	-0.012	0.002	-0.002	-0.186	-0.152	-0.011	-0.024
1X												
2A	1.520	-0.838	0.097	0.005	0.091	-0.060	0.011	0.004	-0.133	-0.267	0.021	-0.027
2AX	0.742	-0.310	0.005	0.002	0.051	-0.024	0.002	-0.003	-0.169	-0.185	-0.008	-0.026
2B	1.345	-0.509	0.016	-0.005	0.076	-0.059	-0.009	-0.025	-0.156	-0.242	0.000	-0.032
2BX												
3	0.004	0.004	0.005	0.005	0.004	0.005	0.005	0.005	-0.213	-0.101	-0.015	-0.022
3X												
Shock B. Global Aggregate Demand												
1	0.518	-0.148	0.049	0.006	0.069	0.017	0.018	-0.020	-0.116	-0.130	0.021	0.003
1X												
2A	1.692	-0.789	0.160	-0.014	0.141	-0.029	0.017	-0.012	-0.077	-0.118	0.058	-0.006
2AX	0.211	-0.065	0.007	-0.018	0.844	-0.291	0.066	0.006	0.095	0.011	0.021	-0.018
2B	1.572	-0.457	0.071	0.089	0.163	0.014	0.081	0.060	-0.085	-0.078	0.016	-0.001
2BX												
3	0.335	0.022	0.093	0.027	0.093	0.062	0.043	-0.008	-0.143	-0.088	0.020	0.004
3X												
Shock C. US Aggregate Supply												
1	-0.014	-0.006	-0.043	0.001	-0.030	-0.028	-0.011	0.022	-0.004	0.073	-0.035	-0.018
1X												
2A	-0.062	0.053	-0.096	0.021	-0.048	-0.039	-0.005	0.019	-0.013	0.183	-0.077	-0.011
2AX	-0.037	-0.008	0.014	0.016	-0.023	0.002	-0.058	0.006	-0.036	-0.034	-0.010	0.023
2B	-0.006	0.158	-0.138	-0.081	-0.055	-0.063	-0.079	-0.063	-0.009	0.152	-0.079	-0.009
2BX												
3	0.223	-0.189	-0.118	-0.011	-0.062	-0.084	-0.031	0.014	-0.003	0.079	-0.037	-0.013
3X												
Shock J. Japanese Aggregate Supply												
1	0.001	0.007	-0.011	-0.011	-0.005	-0.007	-0.009	-0.009	-0.002	0.011	-0.001	-0.006
1X												
2A	0.013	0.032	-0.028	-0.000	-0.012	-0.013	-0.007	0.005	-0.004	0.014	-0.006	-0.005
2AX	-0.007	-0.008	0.001	0.005	0.005	0.011	-0.017	-0.006	-0.010	-0.011	-0.009	0.000
2B	-0.002	0.011	-0.002	-0.009	-0.008	-0.009	-0.007	-0.008	-0.003	0.014	-0.002	-0.004
2BX												
3	0.003	0.010	-0.008	-0.015	-0.005	-0.007	-0.011	-0.013	-0.002	0.008	-0.001	-0.006
3X												

Shock and Regime	Short Interest Rate				Long Interest Rate				Current Account/GNP Ratio			
	1st Yr	2nd Yr	5th Yr	10th Yr	1st Yr	2nd Yr	5th Yr	10th Yr	1st Yr	2nd Yr	5th Yr	10th Yr
Shock H. German Aggregate Supply												
1	0.238	-0.208	-0.028	-0.008	-0.015	-0.039	-0.012	0.001	-0.002	-0.196	0.022	0.015
1X												
2A	0.865	-0.758	0.009	-0.015	-0.001	-0.088	-0.014	-0.004	0.018	-0.262	0.039	0.016
2AX	0.408	-0.343	-0.031	-0.009	-0.012	-0.053	-0.012	0.003	0.002	-0.214	0.023	0.016
2B	0.351	-1.240	0.050	0.014	-0.050	-0.084	0.016	0.041	0.016	-0.203	0.041	0.014
2BX												
3	-0.002	-0.003	-0.012	-0.005	-0.011	-0.012	-0.009	-0.001	0.003	-0.178	0.019	0.009
3X												
Shock E. Oil Price Increase												
1	0.518	-0.148	0.049	0.006	0.069	0.017	0.018	-0.020	-0.116	-0.130	0.021	0.003
1X												
2A	1.692	-0.789	0.160	-0.014	0.141	-0.029	0.017	-0.012	-0.077	-0.118	0.058	-0.006
2AX	0.211	-0.065	0.007	-0.018	0.844	-0.291	0.066	0.006	0.095	0.011	0.021	-0.018
2B	1.572	-0.457	0.071	0.089	0.163	0.014	0.081	0.060	-0.085	-0.078	0.016	-0.001
2BX												
3	0.335	0.022	0.093	0.027	0.093	0.062	0.043	-0.008	-0.143	-0.088	0.020	0.004
3X												
Shock L. U.S. Money Demand												
1	-0.006	0.008	-0.004	-0.004	-0.002	-0.001	-0.003	-0.002	-0.006	0.053	-0.002	-0.001
1X												
2A	0.001	0.001	-0.001	0.000	0.000	0.000	-0.000	0.000	0.000	0.002	-0.000	-0.000
2AX	-0.000	0.001	-0.000	-0.000	0.001	0.001	0.000	0.000	0.000	0.000	0.000	0.000
2B	0.003	0.000	-0.001	0.000	0.000	0.000	-0.000	0.000	0.001	0.001	-0.001	0.000
2BX												
3	0.299	-0.024	-0.014	-0.008	0.020	-0.011	-0.008	-0.005	-0.006	0.047	-0.003	-0.003
3X												
Shock D. Japanese Money Demand												
1	0.001	0.003	-0.001	-0.001	0.000	-0.000	-0.001	-0.001	-0.001	0.002	0.000	-0.001
1X												
2A	0.001	0.000	-0.000	0.001	0.000	0.000	-0.000	0.000	0.000	0.000	0.000	0.000
2AX	0.000	0.001	-0.000	-0.000	0.001	0.000	0.000	0.000	0.000	0.000	0.000	0.000
2B	0.002	-0.000	-0.001	0.000	0.000	0.000	-0.000	0.000	0.000	0.000	0.000	-0.000
2BX												
3	0.000	-0.000	-0.000	0.000	0.000	0.000	0.000	0.000	0.000	-0.000	0.000	0.000
3X												
Shock K. German Money Demand												
1	0.400	-0.057	0.002	0.001	0.036	-0.005	0.000	-0.000	0.027	-0.053	-0.003	-0.003
1X												
2A	0.022	-0.016	-0.001	0.002	0.001	-0.001	-0.000	0.000	-0.002	-0.003	0.000	0.000
2AX	0.003	-0.002	-0.000	-0.001	0.011	-0.006	-0.000	-0.000	0.001	-0.001	0.000	-0.000
2B	0.018	-0.012	-0.002	-0.000	0.001	-0.001	-0.000	0.000	-0.002	-0.003	0.001	-0.000
2BX												
3	0.000	0.000	-0.000	-0.000	0.000	0.000	0.000	0.000	-0.003	-0.001	0.001	-0.000
3X												
Shock F. U.S. Money Supply-Permanent												
FIXM												
1	-0.008	-0.021	-0.017	-0.017	-0.018	-0.019	-0.021	-0.039	0.001	-0.011	0.001	0.001
1X												

835

INTERMOD (CONSISTENT) MODEL
BILATERAL DOLLAR EXCHANGE RATES
(Deviations from Baseline)

Shock and Regime	Bilateral DM/$ Exchange Rate				Bilateral Yen/$ Exchange Rate			
	1st Yr	2nd Yr	5th Yr	10th Yr	1st Yr	2nd Yr	5th Yr	10th Yr
Shock A. US Aggregate Demand								
1	-0.488	-0.159	-0.161	0.022	-0.459	-0.131	-0.100	0.078
1X								
2A	-1.083	0.087	-0.169	0.060	-1.016	0.100	-0.099	0.096
2AX	-0.672	-0.119	-0.173	0.031	-0.632	-0.093	-0.114	0.081
2B	-0.680	0.599	0.427	0.650	-0.624	0.572	0.497	0.819
2BX								
3	-0.127	-0.006	-0.028	-0.003	-0.127	-0.006	-0.028	-0.003
3X								
Shock I. Japanese Aggregate Demand								
1	-0.009	-0.015	-0.022	-0.019	0.471	0.122	0.175	0.008
1X								
2A	-0.017	-0.038	-0.028	-0.006	1.109	-0.030	0.218	-0.008
2AX	-0.013	-0.029	0.000	0.000	0.698	0.193	0.000	0.000
2B	-0.006	-0.004	0.026	0.065	0.839	-0.292	-0.329	-0.587
2BX								
3	-0.005	-0.002	-0.007	-0.008	-0.005	-0.002	-0.007	-0.008
3X								
Shock G. German Aggregate Demand								
1	0.298	-0.125	0.021	0.008	0.006	-0.001	0.004	0.003
1X								
2A	0.846	-0.564	0.106	0.020	0.022	-0.020	0.010	0.001
2AX	0.467	-0.231	0.033	0.013	0.009	-0.006	0.005	0.004
2B	0.643	-0.587	-0.144	-0.203	0.018	-0.008	0.005	0.011
2BX								
3	-0.002	-0.002	-0.002	-0.002	-0.002	-0.002	-0.002	-0.002
3X								
Shock B. Global Aggregate Demand								
1	-0.227	-0.316	-0.167	0.018	0.051	0.015	0.079	0.083
1X								
2A	-0.260	-0.515	-0.082	0.079	0.108	0.057	0.137	0.092
2AX	-0.248	-0.164	0.000	0.000	0.066	0.098	0.000	0.000
2B	-0.077	-0.032	0.219	0.337	0.180	0.221	0.100	0.124
2BX								
3	-0.134	-0.009	-0.037	-0.011	-0.134	-0.009	-0.037	-0.011
3X								
Shock C. US Aggregate Supply								
1	0.124	0.499	0.245	-0.012	0.130	0.479	0.162	-0.095
1X								
2A	-0.216	1.068	0.272	-0.056	-0.195	0.999	0.157	-0.101
2AX	0.048	0.269	0.000	0.000	0.057	0.173	0.000	0.000
2B	0.032	1.101	-0.525	-0.679	0.017	1.034	-0.522	-0.862
2BX								
3	-0.089	0.076	0.047	0.004	-0.089	0.076	0.047	0.004
3X								
Shock J. Japanese Aggregate Supply								
1	-0.011	-0.016	-0.002	0.008	0.181	-0.196	-0.098	-0.026
1X								
2A	-0.026	-0.037	0.018	0.005	0.538	-0.578	-0.145	0.005
2AX	-0.019	0.008	0.000	0.000	0.234	-0.130	0.000	0.000
2B	-0.003	0.009	0.008	-0.007	0.044	-1.087	0.013	0.046
2BX								
3	-0.001	-0.004	0.003	0.006	-0.001	-0.004	0.003	0.006
3X								

Shock and Regime	Bilateral DM/$ Exchange Rate				Bilateral Yen/$ Exchange Rate			
	1st Yr	2nd Yr	5th Yr	10th Yr	1st Yr	2nd Yr	5th Yr	10th Yr
Shock H. German Aggregate Supply								
1	-0.103	-0.324	-0.099	-0.040	0.003	0.002	-0.000	-0.010
1X								
2A	0.065	-0.740	-0.111	-0.077	0.001	-0.011	-0.011	-0.016
2AX	-0.076	-0.452	-0.117	-0.054	0.004	0.001	-0.002	-0.014
2B	0.038	-0.294	0.595	0.575	-0.005	-0.012	-0.027	-0.045
2BX								
3	0.001	0.001	0.005	0.002	0.001	0.001	0.005	0.002
3X								
Shock E. Oil Price Increase								
1	-0.131	-0.138	-0.092	-0.040	-0.055	-0.091	-0.082	-0.052
1X								
2A	-0.238	-0.212	-0.107	-0.041	-0.083	-0.178	-0.101	-0.066
2AX	-0.193	-0.100	0.000	0.000	-0.080	-0.098	0.000	0.000
2B	-0.030	-0.039	0.029	0.036	-0.088	-0.228	-0.039	0.038
2BX								
3	-0.011	-0.017	-0.001	0.004	-0.011	-0.017	-0.001	0.004
3X								
Shock L. U.S. Money Demand								
1	-0.336	0.054	0.017	0.006	-0.333	0.051	0.017	0.004
1X								
2A	-0.012	0.008	-0.001	0.000	-0.011	0.006	0.000	0.000
2AX	-0.006	0.000	0.000	0.000	-0.006	0.000	0.000	0.000
2B	-0.010	0.007	-0.000	-0.000	-0.010	0.006	0.000	-0.000
2BX								
3	-0.120	0.010	0.006	0.003	-0.120	0.010	0.006	0.003
3X								
Shock D. Japanese Money Demand								
1	-0.000	-0.002	-0.001	0.001	0.341	-0.033	-0.014	-0.003
1X								
2A	0.000	0.000	0.000	0.001	0.015	-0.009	0.000	-0.000
2AX	-0.000	0.000	0.000	0.000	0.010	-0.000	0.000	0.000
2B	0.000	-0.000	-0.001	0.000	0.014	-0.008	-0.002	0.000
2BX								
3	0.000	0.000	0.000	0.000	-0.000	0.000	0.000	0.000
3X								
Shock K. German Money Demand								
1	0.328	-0.044	0.002	0.002	0.000	-0.002	0.000	-0.000
1X								
2A	0.011	-0.010	-0.002	0.002	0.001	-0.000	0.000	0.000
2AX	0.006	0.000	0.000	0.000	0.000	0.000	0.000	0.000
2B	0.010	-0.011	-0.001	-0.000	0.000	-0.001	0.000	-0.001
2BX								
3	0.000	0.000	0.000	0.000	0.000	0.000	0.000	0.000
3X								
Shock F. U.S. Money Supply-Permanent								
FIXM								
1	0.315	0.271	0.257	0.269	0.285	0.234	0.200	0.233
1X								

LIVERPOOL MODEL
EFFECTS ON U.S. REAL GNP, U.S. PRICE LEVEL, U.S. INFLATION RATE
(Deviations from Baseline)

Shock and Regime	Real GNP				GNP Deflator				Inflation Rate			
	1st Yr	2nd Yr	5th Yr	10th Yr	1st Yr	2nd Yr	5th Yr	10th Yr	1st Yr	2nd Yr	5th Yr	10th Yr
Shock A. US Aggregate Demand												
1	0.10	0.05	0.02	0.01	0.16	0.04	0.03	0.06	0.16	-0.12	0.00	0.00
1X	0.03	0.01	0.00	0.00	0.04	0.09	0.06	0.06	0.05	0.04	0.00	0.00
2A	0.10	0.06	0.02	0.02	0.16	-0.05	0.02	0.03	0.17	-0.22	0.01	0.00
2AX	-0.04	-0.02	0.00	0.00	-0.06	0.08	0.04	0.03	-0.06	0.14	-0.01	0.00
2B	0.18	0.11	0.07	-0.21	0.02	-0.09	-0.14	1.06	0.02	-0.11	0.02	0.40
2BX	0.42	0.15	0.17	0.20	-0.40	-0.38	-0.54	-0.93	-0.41	0.01	-0.08	-0.06
3	0.10	0.06	0.02	0.02	0.16	0.01	0.03	0.04	0.16	-0.15	0.00	0.00
3X	0.02	0.02	0.02	0.01	0.03	0.03	0.04	0.06	0.03	0.00	0.00	0.03
Shock I. Japanese Aggregate Demand												
1	-0.02	-0.12	-0.18	-0.25	0.18	0.35	0.66	0.92	0.18	0.18	0.08	0.02
1X	-0.05	-0.14	-0.21	-0.30	0.17	0.34	0.68	1.01	0.17	0.18	0.09	0.04
2A	-0.11	-0.15	-0.16	-0.23	0.15	0.19	0.22	0.28	0.15	0.04	0.01	0.01
2AX	-0.14	-0.15	-0.24	-0.33	0.16	0.29	0.53	0.77	0.16	0.14	0.06	0.03
2B	-0.06	-0.10	-0.08	0.07	0.17	0.38	0.91	0.70	0.17	0.22	0.16	-0.17
2BX	0.20	-0.06	0.01	0.11	-0.15	-0.12	-0.20	-0.68	-0.16	0.03	-0.08	-0.09
3	-0.08	-0.13	-0.12	-0.15	0.00	0.01	0.05	0.08	0.00	0.01	0.02	0.01
3X	-0.14	-0.19	-0.16	-0.15	-0.04	-0.06	0.04	0.04	-0.05	-0.01	0.07	0.01
Shock G. German Aggregate Demand												
1	-0.01	-0.07	-0.10	-0.18	0.16	0.29	0.52	0.81	0.17	0.14	0.07	0.04
1X	-0.13	-0.14	-0.08	-0.11	0.07	0.14	0.20	0.31	0.08	0.07	0.01	0.03
2A	-0.06	-0.11	-0.09	-0.12	0.12	0.15	0.15	0.18	0.12	0.04	0.01	-0.01
2AX	-0.15	-0.14	-0.08	-0.09	0.08	0.13	0.13	0.17	0.09	0.04	0.00	0.00
2B	-0.02	-0.02	0.08	0.32	0.15	0.25	0.20	-1.19	0.15	0.10	-0.06	-0.42
2BX	0.30	0.04	0.10	0.13	-0.19	-0.17	-0.19	-0.47	-0.20	0.02	-0.05	-0.05
3	-0.05	-0.14	-0.07	-0.09	0.04	0.05	0.06	0.09	0.04	0.01	-0.01	0.01
3X	-0.14	-0.19	-0.08	-0.06	-0.04	-0.07	0.05	0.08	-0.05	-0.02	0.06	0.03
Shock B. Global Aggregate Demand												
1	0.10	0.06	0.17	0.20	0.16	0.06	-0.13	-0.29	0.16	-0.10	-0.07	-0.02
1X	0.03	0.06	0.21	0.24	0.04	0.06	-0.19	-0.40	0.05	0.02	-0.09	-0.02
2A	0.01	-0.13	-0.15	-0.28	0.27	0.23	0.27	0.41	0.28	-0.04	0.02	0.01
2AX	-0.04	0.11	0.31	0.33	-0.06	-0.02	-0.32	-0.49	-0.06	0.04	-0.08	-0.01
2B	0.13	0.07	0.17	0.06	0.18	0.16	-0.33	-1.02	0.19	-0.02	-0.22	-0.07
2BX	0.26	-0.03	0.09	0.16	-0.24	-0.02	-0.01	-0.50	-0.25	0.23	-0.09	-0.08
3	0.12	-0.10	-0.07	-0.09	0.31	0.18	0.10	0.08	0.32	-0.13	-0.03	0.02
3X	-0.22	-0.27	-0.10	-0.05	-0.09	-0.07	-0.03	-0.09	-0.10	0.02	0.01	-0.01
Shock C. US Aggregate Supply												
1	-0.68	-0.37	-0.05	0.05	0.54	0.62	0.36	-0.01	0.56	0.09	-0.11	-0.04
1X	-0.60	-0.34	-0.17	-0.21	0.42	0.56	0.48	0.57	0.44	0.14	-0.03	0.03
2A	-0.54	-0.29	-0.12	-0.16	0.57	0.31	0.14	0.19	0.59	-0.27	-0.01	-0.01
2AX	-0.58	-0.32	-0.14	-0.18	0.42	0.43	0.34	0.41	0.43	0.01	-0.02	0.01
2B	-0.42	-0.25	-0.12	-0.25	0.81	1.33	2.33	4.48	0.84	0.53	0.31	0.50
2BX	-0.24	-0.18	0.11	0.17	0.07	0.06	-0.41	-0.93	0.07	-0.01	-0.19	-0.06
3	-0.71	-0.38	-0.13	-0.14	0.27	0.11	-0.05	-0.13	0.28	-0.16	-0.03	-0.01
3X	-0.90	-0.50	-0.17	-0.17	0.07	0.04	-0.04	-0.10	0.07	-0.03	-0.02	0.01
Shock J. Japanese Aggregate Supply												
1	-0.22	-0.01	-0.02	-0.13	0.12	0.05	0.00	0.22	0.13	-0.08	0.03	0.02
1X	0.15	0.09	0.19	0.29	-0.15	-0.23	-0.44	-0.71	-0.15	-0.08	-0.08	-0.04
2A	-0.15	0.12	0.12	0.06	0.11	-0.15	-0.12	-0.07	0.12	-0.27	0.02	-0.01
2AX	0.14	0.09	0.15	0.22	-0.11	-0.14	-0.26	-0.43	-0.12	-0.03	-0.05	-0.02
2B	-0.19	0.00	-0.10	-0.26	0.19	0.16	0.47	1.86	0.20	-0.03	0.17	0.31
2BX	0.46	0.13	0.11	0.15	-0.33	-0.44	-0.55	-0.86	-0.34	-0.11	-0.05	-0.05
3	-0.17	0.04	0.03	0.03	0.00	0.01	-0.02	-0.02	0.00	0.01	-0.01	0.00
3X	0.24	0.13	0.13	0.17	0.12	0.05	-0.02	-0.06	0.13	-0.07	-0.03	0.00

Shock and Regime	Real GNP				GNP Deflator				Inflation Rate			
	1st Yr	2nd Yr	5th Yr	10th Yr	1st Yr	2nd Yr	5th Yr	10th Yr	1st Yr	2nd Yr	5th Yr	10th Yr
Shock H. German Aggregate Supply												
1	-0.48	-0.04	-0.20	-0.32	0.34	0.25	0.43	0.84	0.35	-0.10	0.10	0.05
1X	0.18	-0.02	0.02	0.06	-0.09	-0.04	0.03	-0.07	-0.10	0.05	-0.02	-0.01
2A	-0.48	-0.04	-0.20	-0.35	0.41	0.04	0.24	0.39	0.43	-0.38	0.08	0.01
2AX	0.19	-0.03	-0.01	0.01	-0.12	-0.02	0.04	0.01	-0.12	0.10	-0.02	0.00
2B	-0.32	-0.05	-0.13	-0.36	0.45	0.60	1.34	3.84	0.47	0.15	0.28	0.68
2BX	0.46	0.04	0.09	0.15	-0.33	-0.37	-0.46	-0.88	-0.34	-0.04	-0.08	-0.06
3	-0.38	0.06	0.09	0.01	0.27	0.09	0.01	-0.03	0.28	-0.18	-0.04	0.07
3X	0.27	0.05	-0.02	-0.02	0.14	0.01	0.02	-0.01	0.15	-0.13	0.01	0.00
Shock E. Oil Price Increase												
1	0.10	0.06	0.17	0.20	0.16	0.06	-0.13	-0.29	0.16	-0.10	-0.07	-0.02
1X	0.03	0.06	0.21	0.24	0.04	0.06	-0.19	-0.40	0.05	0.02	-0.09	-0.02
2A	0.01	-0.13	-0.15	-0.28	0.27	0.23	0.27	0.41	0.28	-0.04	0.02	0.01
2AX	-0.04	0.11	0.31	0.33	-0.06	-0.02	-0.32	-0.49	-0.06	0.04	-0.08	-0.01
2B	0.13	0.07	0.17	0.06	0.18	0.16	-0.33	-1.02	0.19	-0.02	-0.22	-0.07
2BX	0.26	-0.03	0.09	0.16	-0.24	-0.02	-0.01	-0.50	-0.25	0.23	-0.09	-0.08
3	0.12	-0.10	-0.07	-0.09	0.31	0.18	0.10	0.08	0.32	-0.13	-0.03	0.02
3X	-0.22	-0.27	-0.10	-0.05	-0.09	-0.07	-0.03	-0.09	-0.10	0.02	0.01	-0.01
Shock L. U.S. Money Demand												
1	-0.40	-0.20	-0.05	-0.03	-0.67	-0.32	0.02	0.07	-0.69	0.36	0.05	0.00
1X	-0.32	-0.21	-0.12	-0.09	-0.70	-0.24	0.21	0.31	-0.72	0.47	0.07	0.00
2A	0.00	0.00	0.00	0.00	0.00	0.00	0.00	0.00	0.00	0.00	0.00	0.00
2AX	-0.26	-0.14	-0.06	-0.04	-0.42	-0.23	0.00	0.06	-0.44	0.20	0.04	0.00
2B	0.00	0.00	0.00	0.00	0.00	0.00	0.00	0.00	0.00	0.00	0.00	0.00
2BX	0.13	-0.01	0.08	0.13	-0.66	-0.76	-0.68	-0.94	-0.69	-0.10	-0.01	-0.05
3	0.00	0.00	0.00	0.00	0.00	0.00	0.00	0.00	0.00	0.00	0.00	0.00
3X	0.00	0.00	-0.01	-0.01	0.02	0.03	0.06	0.07	0.02	0.01	0.01	0.01
Shock D. Japanese Money Demand												
1	-0.08	-0.05	-0.10	-0.15	0.08	0.11	0.22	0.35	0.08	0.03	0.05	0.01
1X	-0.11	-0.07	-0.14	-0.19	0.10	0.15	0.28	0.42	0.10	0.05	0.05	0.02
2A	0.00	0.00	0.00	0.00	0.00	0.00	0.00	0.00	0.00	0.00	0.00	0.00
2AX	-0.11	-0.09	-0.03	-0.06	0.06	0.07	0.03	0.06	0.06	0.01	-0.02	0.00
2B	0.00	0.00	0.00	0.00	0.00	0.00	0.00	0.00	0.00	0.00	0.00	0.00
2BX	0.27	0.06	0.10	0.14	-0.22	-0.30	-0.48	-0.82	-0.23	-0.08	-0.08	-0.06
3	0.00	0.00	0.00	0.00	0.00	0.00	0.00	0.00	0.00	0.00	0.00	0.00
3X	0.00	0.00	-0.01	-0.01	0.02	0.03	0.06	0.07	0.02	0.01	0.01	0.01
Shock K. German Money Demand												
1	-0.05	0.00	0.01	0.01	0.03	0.02	0.00	-0.01	0.03	-0.02	0.00	-0.01
1X	-0.05	0.01	0.00	-0.01	0.03	0.01	-0.01	0.02	0.03	-0.02	0.00	0.00
2A	0.00	0.00	0.00	0.00	0.00	0.00	0.00	0.00	0.00	0.00	0.00	0.00
2AX	-0.05	0.00	-0.01	-0.03	0.03	0.01	0.00	0.03	0.04	-0.02	0.01	0.00
2B	0.00	0.00	0.00	0.00	0.00	0.00	0.00	0.00	0.00	0.00	0.00	0.00
2BX	0.29	0.09	0.10	0.15	-0.24	-0.34	-0.52	-0.88	-0.24	-0.10	-0.07	-0.06
3	0.00	0.00	0.00	0.00	0.00	0.00	0.00	0.00	0.00	0.00	0.00	0.00
3X	0.00	0.00	-0.01	-0.01	0.02	0.03	0.06	0.07	0.02	0.01	0.01	0.01
Shock F. U.S. Money Supply-Permanent												
FIXM												
1	0.00	0.00	0.00	-0.01	0.00	0.00	0.02	0.25	0.00	0.00	0.01	0.09
1X	-0.02	-0.04	-0.08	-0.11	0.04	0.09	0.24	0.50	0.04	0.05	0.05	0.04

LIVERPOOL MODEL
EFFECTS ON U.S. INTEREST RATES AND U.S. CURRENT ACCOUNT/GNP RATIO
(Deviations from Baseline)

Shock and Regime	Short Interest Rate				Long Interest Rate				Current Account/GNP Ratio			
	1st Yr	2nd Yr	5th Yr	10th Yr	1st Yr	2nd Yr	5th Yr	10th Yr	1st Yr	2nd Yr	5th Yr	10th Yr
Shock A. US Aggregate Demand												
1	0.39	0.03	0.06	0.07	0.08	0.01	0.01	0.01	0.00	0.00	0.00	0.00
1X	0.42	0.04	0.06	0.07	0.08	0.01	0.01	0.01	0.00	-0.01	-0.01	-0.01
2A	0.39	0.03	0.06	0.07	0.08	0.01	0.01	0.01	0.00	0.00	0.00	0.00
2AX	0.45	0.05	0.07	0.07	0.09	0.01	0.01	0.01	0.00	-0.01	-0.01	-0.01
2B	0.31	0.01	0.13	0.27	0.14	0.11	0.22	0.27	-0.05	-0.02	-0.01	-0.07
2BX	0.32	0.01	-0.07	-0.10	0.04	-0.04	-0.08	-0.12	-0.01	-0.04	-0.09	-0.09
3	0.39	0.03	0.06	0.07	0.08	0.01	0.01	0.01	0.00	0.00	0.00	0.00
3X	0.43	0.04	0.06	0.09	0.09	0.01	0.02	0.01	-0.01	-0.01	0.00	0.00
Shock I. Japanese Aggregate Demand												
1	0.07	0.10	0.09	0.07	0.09	0.09	0.09	0.09	0.00	0.03	0.01	-0.05
1X	0.08	0.11	0.10	0.10	0.09	0.09	0.09	0.09	0.01	0.04	0.00	-0.07
2A	0.06	0.05	0.08	0.07	0.06	0.06	0.06	0.07	0.01	0.03	0.00	-0.05
2AX	0.11	0.11	0.11	0.10	0.09	0.09	0.10	0.10	0.02	0.04	-0.01	-0.07
2B	0.16	0.17	0.11	-0.15	0.12	0.09	-0.06	-0.37	-0.01	0.00	-0.01	0.04
2BX	-0.03	0.08	-0.09	-0.12	-0.01	-0.02	-0.09	-0.12	0.03	0.01	-0.05	-0.06
3	0.03	0.08	0.06	0.07	0.04	0.04	0.04	0.03	0.01	0.04	0.01	-0.02
3X	0.08	0.11	0.08	0.10	0.02	0.02	0.01	0.00	0.02	0.03	0.00	-0.01
Shock G. German Aggregate Demand												
1	0.10	0.10	0.09	0.10	0.08	0.08	0.08	0.10	0.13	0.11	0.05	-0.01
1X	0.10	0.08	0.06	0.08	0.01	0.01	0.02	0.03	0.12	0.09	0.04	0.00
2A	0.08	0.07	0.09	0.09	0.05	0.05	0.06	0.07	0.12	0.10	0.05	0.00
2AX	0.10	0.08	0.07	0.08	0.01	0.01	0.01	0.02	0.12	0.09	0.04	0.00
2B	0.18	0.12	0.04	-0.13	0.08	0.04	-0.08	-0.25	0.15	0.12	0.09	0.11
2BX	-0.01	0.11	-0.02	-0.04	0.03	0.03	-0.02	-0.05	0.18	0.12	0.02	-0.03
3	0.06	0.12	0.08	0.09	0.06	0.06	0.05	0.05	0.12	0.11	0.05	0.01
3X	0.11	0.14	0.08	0.10	0.03	0.03	0.02	0.00	0.11	0.08	0.03	0.02
Shock B. Global Aggregate Demand												
1	0.39	0.08	0.05	0.04	0.08	0.02	0.01	0.01	0.00	0.13	0.06	0.03
1X	0.42	0.07	0.03	0.01	0.08	0.01	0.01	0.00	0.00	0.12	0.05	0.02
2A	0.42	0.15	0.18	0.19	0.18	0.13	0.14	0.17	0.08	0.12	0.04	-0.05
2AX	0.45	0.05	-0.02	-0.04	0.09	0.01	0.00	-0.01	0.00	0.10	0.04	0.01
2B	0.47	0.07	-0.07	-0.01	0.10	-0.01	-0.01	0.19	0.07	0.08	0.04	-0.03
2BX	0.61	0.24	-0.01	-0.03	0.20	0.07	-0.02	-0.05	0.12	0.08	-0.03	-0.07
3	0.39	0.14	0.15	0.19	0.14	0.09	0.10	0.11	0.10	0.13	0.08	0.02
3X	0.58	0.21	0.17	0.12	0.20	0.12	0.10	0.11	0.11	0.12	0.06	0.01
Shock C. US Aggregate Supply												
1	0.25	0.13	0.03	-0.01	0.05	0.03	0.01	0.00	-0.01	-0.01	-0.01	-0.01
1X	0.29	0.10	0.02	0.06	0.08	0.02	0.02	0.04	0.04	-0.01	-0.04	-0.05
2A	0.04	0.02	0.03	0.05	0.01	0.02	0.03	0.04	0.03	0.00	-0.03	-0.04
2AX	0.22	0.07	0.02	0.05	0.06	0.03	0.03	0.05	0.04	0.00	-0.04	-0.05
2B	0.58	0.38	0.26	0.35	0.37	0.31	0.34	0.43	0.02	-0.01	-0.01	-0.06
2BX	0.12	-0.01	-0.16	-0.11	-0.06	-0.11	-0.12	-0.13	0.08	0.02	-0.04	-0.07
3	0.22	0.11	0.03	0.04	0.07	0.04	0.03	0.03	0.06	0.00	-0.05	-0.05
3X	0.34	0.16	0.06	0.08	0.09	0.05	0.03	0.02	0.04	-0.03	-0.06	-0.04
Shock J. Japanese Aggregate Supply												
1	0.04	-0.03	0.03	0.06	-0.01	-0.02	0.00	0.00	-0.04	-0.02	0.03	0.00
1X	-0.08	-0.03	-0.07	-0.07	-0.04	-0.04	-0.05	-0.05	-0.02	0.01	0.04	0.04
2A	-0.05	-0.05	-0.01	-0.02	0.00	0.01	0.01	0.00	-0.03	-0.02	0.04	0.01
2AX	-0.05	-0.02	-0.05	-0.06	-0.03	-0.03	-0.04	-0.05	-0.02	0.01	0.03	0.03
2B	0.00	-0.04	0.11	0.07	0.05	0.08	0.11	0.13	0.00	-0.02	0.00	-0.06
2BX	-0.24	-0.03	-0.08	-0.11	-0.08	-0.05	-0.09	-0.12	0.03	0.02	-0.05	-0.05
3	0.11	-0.03	0.00	0.01	0.01	-0.01	0.00	0.00	0.00	-0.04	0.02	0.03
3X	-0.14	-0.05	-0.04	-0.06	-0.05	-0.03	-0.02	-0.02	-0.02	0.03	0.04	0.04

Shock and Regime	Short Interest Rate				Long Interest Rate				Current Account/GNP Ratio			
	1st Yr	2nd Yr	5th Yr	10th Yr	1st Yr	2nd Yr	5th Yr	10th Yr	1st Yr	2nd Yr	5th Yr	10th Yr
Shock H. German Aggregate Supply												
1	0.09	-0.06	0.05	0.05	0.02	0.01	0.05	0.06	0.01	-0.04	-0.08	-0.11
1X	-0.05	0.02	-0.02	-0.03	0.00	0.01	0.00	0.00	0.00	0.00	-0.01	0.01
2A	-0.10	0.01	0.05	0.07	-0.01	0.02	0.03	0.04	-0.01	-0.04	-0.08	-0.09
2AX	-0.05	0.02	-0.01	-0.01	0.00	0.01	0.00	0.01	0.00	0.00	-0.01	0.00
2B	0.20	0.13	0.22	0.45	0.21	0.23	0.38	0.59	-0.07	-0.10	-0.06	-0.11
2BX	-0.18	0.05	-0.10	-0.11	-0.06	-0.04	-0.11	-0.13	0.02	0.01	-0.04	-0.05
3	0.05	-0.05	-0.08	-0.01	-0.04	-0.07	-0.08	-0.02	-0.04	-0.04	-0.02	-0.04
3X	-0.13	-0.01	0.00	0.02	-0.02	0.01	0.01	0.00	0.00	0.00	-0.01	0.00
Shock E. Oil Price Increase												
1	0.39	0.08	0.05	0.04	0.08	0.02	0.01	0.01	0.00	0.13	0.06	0.03
1X	0.42	0.07	0.03	0.01	0.08	0.01	0.01	0.00	0.00	0.12	0.05	0.02
2A	0.42	0.15	0.18	0.19	0.18	0.13	0.14	0.17	0.08	0.12	0.04	-0.05
2AX	0.45	0.05	-0.02	-0.04	0.09	0.01	0.00	-0.01	0.00	0.10	0.04	0.01
2B	0.47	0.07	-0.07	-0.01	0.10	-0.01	-0.01	0.19	0.07	0.08	0.04	-0.03
2BX	0.61	0.24	-0.01	-0.03	0.20	0.07	-0.02	-0.05	0.12	0.08	-0.03	-0.07
3	0.39	0.14	0.15	0.19	0.14	0.09	0.10	0.11	0.10	0.13	0.08	0.02
3X	0.58	0.21	0.17	0.12	0.20	0.12	0.10	0.11	0.11	0.12	0.06	0.01
Shock L. U.S. Money Demand												
1	0.17	0.07	0.03	0.02	0.03	0.01	0.01	0.00	-0.01	-0.02	-0.01	-0.01
1X	0.25	0.14	0.05	0.03	0.09	0.06	0.03	0.03	0.02	-0.02	-0.03	-0.03
2A	0.00	0.00	0.00	0.00	0.00	0.00	0.00	0.00	0.00	0.00	0.00	0.00
2AX	0.11	0.06	0.03	0.02	0.02	0.01	0.01	0.00	0.00	-0.01	-0.01	-0.01
2B	0.00	0.00	0.00	0.00	0.00	0.00	0.00	0.00	0.00	0.00	0.00	0.00
2BX	-0.10	0.09	-0.08	-0.14	-0.02	-0.02	-0.12	-0.15	0.07	0.02	-0.07	-0.10
3	0.00	0.00	0.00	0.00	0.00	0.00	0.00	0.00	0.00	0.00	0.00	0.00
3X	0.00	0.01	0.00	0.03	0.00	0.00	0.00	-0.01	0.00	0.00	0.00	0.00
Shock D. Japanese Money Demand												
1	0.03	0.01	0.03	0.03	0.02	0.02	0.02	0.01	0.02	-0.01	-0.03	-0.03
1X	0.06	0.02	0.04	0.04	0.02	0.02	0.03	0.02	0.02	-0.01	-0.04	-0.03
2A	0.00	0.00	0.00	0.00	0.00	0.00	0.00	0.00	0.00	0.00	0.00	0.00
2AX	0.03	0.01	0.00	0.02	-0.01	-0.02	-0.01	-0.01	-0.01	-0.03	-0.01	-0.01
2B	0.00	0.00	0.00	0.00	0.00	0.00	0.00	0.00	0.00	0.00	0.00	0.00
2BX	-0.13	-0.02	-0.09	-0.11	-0.07	-0.06	-0.09	-0.13	0.05	0.01	-0.05	-0.06
3	0.00	0.00	0.00	0.00	0.00	0.00	0.00	0.00	0.00	0.00	0.00	0.00
3X	0.00	0.01	0.00	0.03	0.00	0.00	0.00	-0.01	0.00	0.00	0.00	0.00
Shock K. German Money Demand												
1	0.01	-0.01	0.00	0.00	0.00	0.00	0.00	0.00	0.00	-0.01	0.00	0.00
1X	0.01	-0.02	0.00	0.00	0.00	0.00	0.00	0.00	0.00	-0.01	0.00	0.00
2A	0.00	0.00	0.00	0.00	0.00	0.00	0.00	0.00	0.00	0.00	0.00	0.00
2AX	0.01	0.00	0.01	0.01	0.00	0.00	0.00	0.00	0.00	0.00	0.00	0.00
2B	0.00	0.00	0.00	0.00	0.00	0.00	0.00	0.00	0.00	0.00	0.00	0.00
2BX	-0.16	-0.05	-0.09	-0.12	-0.08	-0.07	-0.09	-0.13	0.04	0.01	-0.05	-0.05
3	0.00	0.00	0.00	0.00	0.00	0.00	0.00	0.00	0.00	0.00	0.00	0.00
3X	0.00	0.01	0.00	0.03	0.00	0.00	0.00	-0.01	0.00	0.00	0.00	0.00
Shock F. U.S. Money Supply-Permanent FIXM												
1	0.00	0.00	0.00	0.01	0.00	0.00	0.01	0.08	0.00	0.00	0.00	0.00
1X	0.03	0.03	0.06	0.11	0.02	0.02	0.04	0.07	0.03	0.04	0.04	0.05

Table A-LIV-3
LIVERPOOL MODEL
EFFECTS ON JAPANESE REAL GNP, JAPANESE PRICE LEVEL, JAPANESE INFLATION RATE
(Deviations from Baseline)

Shock and Regime	Real GNP				GNP Deflator				Inflation Rate			
	1st Yr	2nd Yr	5th Yr	10th Yr	1st Yr	2nd Yr	5th Yr	10th Yr	1st Yr	2nd Yr	5th Yr	10th Yr
Shock A. US Aggregate Demand												
1	0.00	-0.01	-0.02	-0.01	0.00	0.00	0.01	0.01	0.00	0.00	0.00	0.00
1X	0.00	-0.02	-0.01	-0.01	0.00	0.00	0.01	0.00	0.00	0.00	0.00	0.00
2A	0.00	-0.01	-0.02	-0.01	0.00	0.02	0.02	0.02	0.00	0.02	0.00	0.00
2AX	0.00	-0.02	-0.01	-0.01	0.00	0.00	0.00	0.00	0.00	0.00	0.00	0.00
2B	-0.13	0.08	-0.08	-0.16	0.13	-0.04	-0.01	0.37	0.13	-0.17	0.05	0.10
2BX	1.78	0.96	0.05	0.07	-0.52	-0.66	-0.23	-0.04	-0.54	-0.15	0.15	0.00
3	0.00	-0.01	-0.01	-0.01	0.00	-0.03	-0.04	-0.06	0.00	-0.03	-0.01	0.00
3X	0.02	-0.01	-0.01	-0.01	0.02	0.02	0.01	0.03	0.02	-0.01	-0.01	0.02
Shock I. Japanese Aggregate Demand												
1	0.87	0.22	-0.03	-0.04	0.03	0.08	0.02	-0.06	0.03	0.04	-0.03	-0.02
1X	0.82	0.20	-0.03	-0.05	-0.02	-0.01	-0.02	-0.08	-0.02	0.01	-0.02	0.00
2A	0.59	0.07	-0.03	-0.02	-0.22	0.15	0.13	0.10	-0.23	0.38	-0.03	0.00
2AX	0.50	0.03	-0.04	-0.06	-0.33	-0.08	-0.02	-0.07	-0.34	0.26	-0.01	0.03
2B	0.51	-0.01	-0.01	0.14	-0.17	0.22	1.05	1.26	-0.18	0.39	0.17	-0.01
2BX	2.65	0.95	0.00	0.06	-0.85	-0.91	-0.25	-0.12	-0.87	-0.06	0.17	0.00
3	1.03	0.30	-0.02	0.01	0.28	0.45	0.35	0.31	0.28	0.17	-0.03	0.00
3X	0.98	0.29	-0.01	0.01	0.24	0.38	0.38	0.33	0.24	0.14	0.03	0.00
Shock G. German Aggregate Demand												
1	-0.13	-0.08	0.00	-0.06	0.03	0.03	0.01	0.02	0.03	0.00	0.00	-0.01
1X	-0.05	-0.01	0.02	-0.03	0.00	0.01	0.01	0.01	0.00	0.01	0.00	0.00
2A	-0.06	-0.04	0.00	-0.06	0.07	0.05	0.00	0.07	0.07	-0.02	0.01	0.00
2AX	-0.05	0.00	0.03	-0.02	0.01	0.00	-0.02	-0.01	0.01	-0.01	0.00	0.00
2B	-0.19	-0.10	-0.01	0.03	0.24	0.32	0.32	0.66	0.24	0.09	0.02	0.05
2BX	1.78	0.73	0.05	0.03	-0.49	-0.59	-0.19	-0.03	-0.50	-0.11	0.13	0.00
3	-0.06	-0.08	0.02	-0.03	0.02	0.04	-0.02	0.03	0.02	0.01	0.00	0.00
3X	0.00	-0.03	0.01	0.00	0.02	0.03	0.10	0.13	0.02	0.01	0.06	0.03
Shock B. Global Aggregate Demand												
1	0.84	0.10	0.01	0.03	0.11	0.21	0.13	0.01	0.11	0.10	-0.04	-0.02
1X	0.75	0.06	0.02	0.04	0.00	0.04	0.03	-0.10	0.00	0.05	-0.03	-0.02
2A	0.41	0.09	-0.05	-0.08	0.00	0.13	0.17	0.19	0.00	0.13	-0.02	0.00
2AX	0.47	-0.13	0.04	0.07	-0.36	-0.08	-0.09	-0.21	-0.36	0.28	-0.04	-0.01
2B	0.10	-0.08	-0.16	-0.24	0.29	0.65	1.64	3.11	0.30	0.36	0.30	0.30
2BX	2.08	0.87	0.05	0.06	-0.72	-0.77	-0.26	-0.18	-0.74	-0.06	0.13	-0.01
3	0.82	0.22	-0.02	-0.07	0.33	0.44	0.16	0.00	0.34	0.10	-0.08	-0.04
3X	0.52	0.10	0.01	-0.05	0.13	0.24	0.13	-0.01	0.13	0.10	-0.02	-0.05
Shock C. US Aggregate Supply												
1	0.00	0.00	0.00	0.01	0.00	0.00	0.00	0.01	0.00	0.00	0.00	0.00
1X	-0.16	-0.06	0.02	-0.02	0.01	0.01	0.00	0.01	0.01	0.01	0.00	0.00
2A	-0.09	-0.01	0.01	-0.03	0.06	-0.02	-0.02	0.04	0.06	-0.09	0.01	0.02
2AX	-0.12	-0.03	0.01	-0.04	0.05	0.03	0.00	0.02	0.05	-0.02	0.00	0.02
2B	-0.03	0.02	-0.04	-0.17	0.00	-0.08	-0.20	-0.09	0.00	-0.09	0.00	0.09
2BX	1.83	0.85	0.06	0.05	-0.52	-0.64	-0.22	-0.01	-0.53	-0.13	0.14	0.01
3	-0.18	-0.03	0.02	-0.01	0.01	-0.11	-0.08	-0.05	0.01	-0.12	0.02	-0.01
3X	-0.22	-0.07	0.02	0.00	-0.04	-0.07	-0.01	0.06	-0.04	-0.03	0.02	0.02
Shock J. Japanese Aggregate Supply												
1	-1.00	-0.01	0.23	-0.02	0.33	0.12	-0.06	-0.02	0.34	-0.21	-0.01	0.01
1X	1.25	0.64	-0.02	0.00	-0.08	-0.19	-0.08	0.01	-0.08	-0.11	0.05	0.01
2A	-1.01	0.38	0.27	0.00	1.04	-0.52	-0.32	-0.08	1.05	-1.56	0.23	-0.04
2AX	1.03	0.51	-0.01	0.02	-0.30	-0.23	-0.02	0.02	-0.30	0.07	0.04	-0.01
2B	-0.99	0.63	0.39	-0.05	0.94	-0.52	-3.36	-3.11	0.95	-1.46	-0.44	0.10
2BX	3.14	1.42	0.02	0.04	-0.88	-1.08	-0.33	0.00	-0.90	-0.21	0.25	0.01
3	-1.00	0.21	0.27	-0.02	0.72	-0.18	-0.16	-0.09	0.73	-0.91	0.07	-0.01
3X	0.90	0.43	-0.02	0.01	-0.52	-0.26	-0.22	-0.29	-0.52	0.26	-0.04	0.01

842

Shock and Regime	Real GNP				GNP Deflator				Inflation Rate			
	1st Yr	2nd Yr	5th Yr	10th Yr	1st Yr	2nd Yr	5th Yr	10th Yr	1st Yr	2nd Yr	5th Yr	10th Yr
Shock H. German Aggregate Supply												
1	-0.31	0.22	0.07	0.00	0.13	-0.01	-0.01	0.03	0.13	-0.14	0.01	-0.02
1X	0.02	-0.03	0.00	0.01	0.00	0.00	0.00	0.00	0.00	0.00	0.00	0.00
2A	-0.20	0.28	0.07	-0.02	0.19	-0.31	-0.04	0.08	0.20	-0.50	0.06	0.01
2AX	0.02	-0.04	0.00	0.00	0.00	0.01	0.00	0.00	0.00	0.01	0.00	0.00
2B	-0.09	0.27	-0.02	-0.19	-0.05	-0.54	-0.94	-0.78	-0.05	-0.50	-0.04	0.09
2BX	2.18	0.80	0.04	0.05	-0.59	-0.69	-0.21	-0.02	-0.60	-0.11	0.14	0.00
3	-0.12	0.33	0.10	0.04	0.28	-0.06	0.07	0.12	0.28	-0.34	0.00	0.10
3X	0.02	-0.02	-0.01	0.00	0.01	0.01	0.03	0.01	0.01	0.00	-0.01	0.00
Shock E. Oil Price Increase												
1	0.84	0.10	0.01	0.03	0.11	0.21	0.13	0.01	0.11	0.10	-0.04	-0.02
1X	0.75	0.06	0.02	0.04	0.00	0.04	0.03	-0.10	0.00	0.05	-0.03	-0.02
2A	0.41	0.09	-0.05	-0.08	0.00	0.13	0.17	0.19	0.00	0.13	-0.02	0.00
2AX	0.47	-0.13	0.04	0.07	-0.36	-0.08	-0.09	-0.21	-0.36	0.28	-0.04	-0.01
2B	0.10	-0.08	-0.16	-0.24	0.29	0.65	1.64	3.11	0.30	0.36	0.30	0.30
2BX	2.08	0.87	0.05	0.06	-0.72	-0.77	-0.26	-0.18	-0.74	-0.06	0.13	-0.01
3	0.82	0.22	-0.02	-0.07	0.33	0.44	0.16	0.00	0.34	0.10	-0.08	-0.04
3X	0.52	0.10	0.01	-0.05	0.13	0.24	0.13	-0.01	0.13	0.10	-0.02	-0.05
Shock L. U.S. Money Demand												
1	0.00	-0.02	0.01	0.00	0.00	0.01	0.01	0.01	0.00	0.01	0.00	0.00
1X	-0.06	-0.03	0.01	-0.01	0.00	0.01	0.01	0.01	0.00	0.00	0.00	0.00
2A	0.00	0.00	0.00	0.00	0.00	0.00	0.00	0.00	0.00	0.00	0.00	0.00
2AX	0.00	-0.01	0.00	-0.01	0.00	0.00	0.00	0.00	0.00	0.00	0.00	0.00
2B	0.00	0.00	0.00	0.00	0.00	0.00	0.00	0.00	0.00	0.00	0.00	0.00
2BX	2.02	0.90	0.07	0.06	-0.56	-0.70	-0.24	-0.02	-0.58	-0.14	0.15	0.02
3	0.00	0.00	0.00	0.00	0.00	0.00	0.00	0.00	0.00	0.00	0.00	0.00
3X	0.01	0.00	-0.01	0.00	0.02	0.04	0.06	0.08	0.02	0.02	0.01	0.01
Shock D. Japanese Money Demand												
1	-0.65	-0.36	0.00	0.00	-0.71	-0.38	-0.05	0.01	-0.71	0.33	0.05	0.00
1X	-0.87	-0.48	0.01	0.00	-0.94	-0.46	-0.07	-0.02	-0.95	0.49	0.05	0.00
2A	0.00	0.00	0.00	0.00	0.00	0.00	0.00	0.00	0.00	0.00	0.00	0.00
2AX	-0.44	-0.25	0.01	0.00	-0.53	-0.29	-0.09	-0.04	-0.53	0.24	0.04	0.00
2B	0.00	0.00	0.00	0.00	0.00	0.00	0.00	0.00	0.00	0.00	0.00	0.00
2BX	1.61	0.64	0.01	0.04	-1.03	-1.19	-0.39	-0.03	-1.06	-0.16	0.25	0.02
3	0.00	0.00	0.00	0.00	0.00	0.00	0.00	0.00	0.00	0.00	0.00	0.00
3X	0.01	0.00	-0.01	0.00	0.02	0.04	0.06	0.08	0.02	0.02	0.01	0.01
Shock K. German Money Demand												
1	-0.02	0.02	-0.01	0.00	0.01	0.00	0.00	0.00	0.01	-0.01	0.00	0.00
1X	-0.03	0.02	0.00	0.00	0.00	0.00	0.00	0.00	0.00	0.00	0.00	0.00
2A	0.00	0.00	0.00	0.00	0.00	0.00	0.00	0.00	0.00	0.00	0.00	0.00
2AX	-0.01	0.01	0.00	0.00	0.00	0.00	0.00	0.00	0.00	0.00	0.00	0.00
2B	0.00	0.00	0.00	0.00	0.00	0.00	0.00	0.00	0.00	0.00	0.00	0.00
2BX	2.03	0.92	0.02	0.05	-0.57	-0.70	-0.22	-0.01	-0.59	-0.14	0.16	0.00
3	0.00	0.00	0.00	0.00	0.00	0.00	0.00	0.00	0.00	0.00	0.00	0.00
3X	0.01	0.00	-0.01	0.00	0.02	0.04	0.06	0.08	0.02	0.02	0.01	0.01
Shock F. U.S. Money Supply-Permanent FIXM												
1	0.00	0.00	0.00	0.01	0.00	0.00	0.00	0.00	0.00	0.00	0.00	0.00
1X	-0.03	-0.02	-0.02	-0.08	0.00	0.00	0.01	0.02	0.00	0.00	0.00	0.00

Table A-LIV-4

LIVERPOOL MODEL

EFFECTS ON JAPANESE INTEREST RATES AND JAPANESE CURRENT ACCOUNT/GNP RATIO

(Deviations from Baseline)

Shock and Regime	Short Interest Rate				Long Interest Rate				Current Account/GNP Ratio			
	1st Yr	2nd Yr	5th Yr	10th Yr	1st Yr	2nd Yr	5th Yr	10th Yr	1st Yr	2nd Yr	5th Yr	10th Yr
Shock A. US Aggregate Demand												
1	0.00	0.01	0.01	0.01	0.00	0.00	0.00	0.00	0.00	0.00	0.00	0.00
1X	0.00	0.01	0.01	0.02	0.00	0.00	0.00	0.00	0.00	0.00	0.00	0.00
2A	0.00	0.01	0.00	0.00	0.00	0.00	0.00	0.00	0.00	0.00	0.00	0.00
2AX	0.00	0.02	0.02	0.03	0.00	0.00	0.00	0.01	0.00	0.00	0.01	0.01
2B	-0.01	-0.13	-0.04	-0.08	0.03	0.02	0.05	0.06	0.04	0.02	0.02	0.03
2BX	-0.88	-0.25	0.01	-0.06	-0.16	0.01	-0.01	-0.08	-0.25	-0.16	0.02	-0.06
3	0.00	0.01	0.01	0.01	0.00	0.00	0.00	0.00	0.00	0.00	0.00	0.00
3X	-0.01	0.02	0.01	0.04	0.00	0.00	0.01	-0.01	0.00	0.00	0.01	0.00
Shock I. Japanese Aggregate Demand												
1	0.12	0.22	0.12	0.06	0.06	0.07	0.04	0.06	-0.18	-0.13	-0.08	-0.03
1X	0.15	0.26	0.15	0.11	0.07	0.08	0.05	0.06	-0.18	-0.13	-0.08	-0.02
2A	0.55	0.32	0.14	0.12	0.15	0.09	0.06	0.07	-0.14	-0.09	-0.07	-0.02
2AX	0.50	0.37	0.15	0.15	0.16	0.10	0.06	0.07	-0.13	-0.10	-0.08	-0.01
2B	0.51	0.58	0.24	0.20	0.35	0.28	0.06	-0.04	-0.12	-0.06	-0.05	-0.06
2BX	-1.00	0.09	0.07	-0.04	-0.04	0.16	0.03	-0.05	-0.45	-0.27	-0.09	-0.15
3	0.14	0.21	0.17	0.15	0.03	0.04	0.03	0.02	-0.21	-0.14	-0.06	-0.03
3X	0.19	0.28	0.23	0.23	0.04	0.05	0.04	0.01	-0.20	-0.13	-0.04	-0.03
Shock G. German Aggregate Demand												
1	0.05	0.03	-0.01	0.02	0.03	0.02	0.02	0.04	0.04	0.04	0.02	0.04
1X	0.06	0.04	0.05	0.10	0.01	0.00	0.00	0.01	0.01	0.01	0.02	0.03
2A	0.02	0.01	0.01	0.01	0.01	0.01	0.02	0.03	0.02	0.02	0.02	0.04
2AX	0.07	0.04	0.06	0.09	0.01	0.00	0.00	0.01	0.01	0.01	0.01	0.03
2B	0.08	-0.02	0.02	0.12	0.04	0.03	0.08	0.04	0.06	0.07	0.09	0.07
2BX	-1.02	-0.13	0.02	-0.01	-0.16	0.04	0.01	-0.03	-0.24	-0.09	0.06	-0.01
3	0.03	0.05	0.03	0.04	0.01	0.02	0.01	0.01	0.02	0.03	0.01	0.03
3X	0.03	0.06	0.05	0.09	0.00	0.00	0.00	-0.02	0.00	0.01	0.01	0.01
Shock B. Global Aggregate Demand												
1	0.28	0.44	0.26	0.25	0.06	0.09	0.05	0.05	-0.18	-0.10	-0.04	-0.02
1X	0.36	0.50	0.30	0.30	0.07	0.10	0.06	0.06	-0.17	-0.09	-0.03	-0.01
2A	0.60	0.32	0.17	0.17	0.17	0.10	0.09	0.11	-0.08	-0.05	-0.03	0.02
2AX	0.63	0.66	0.38	0.40	0.13	0.13	0.08	0.08	-0.12	-0.04	-0.01	0.01
2B	0.60	0.41	0.21	0.09	0.45	0.38	0.31	0.22	0.01	0.07	0.14	0.16
2BX	-0.58	0.09	0.11	0.07	0.03	0.16	0.07	0.01	-0.32	-0.18	0.00	-0.08
3	0.30	0.23	0.17	0.12	0.05	0.05	0.05	0.06	-0.15	-0.09	-0.06	-0.04
3X	0.47	0.31	0.21	0.10	0.11	0.08	0.06	0.08	-0.10	-0.07	-0.04	-0.02
Shock C. US Aggregate Supply												
1	0.00	0.00	0.01	0.02	0.00	0.00	0.00	0.00	0.00	0.00	0.00	0.02
1X	0.05	-0.03	-0.01	0.03	0.02	0.00	0.00	0.01	-0.01	-0.03	0.01	0.04
2A	-0.03	-0.05	-0.02	0.01	0.00	0.00	0.01	0.01	-0.01	-0.03	0.01	0.03
2AX	0.00	-0.05	-0.02	0.01	0.01	-0.01	0.00	0.02	-0.01	-0.03	0.01	0.05
2B	-0.05	-0.11	-0.06	-0.11	-0.04	-0.04	0.00	0.05	-0.02	-0.05	-0.04	-0.01
2BX	-1.00	-0.19	-0.01	-0.07	-0.19	0.00	-0.03	-0.09	-0.31	-0.20	-0.02	-0.05
3	0.04	-0.02	0.02	0.04	0.02	0.00	0.01	0.03	-0.01	-0.03	0.02	0.06
3X	0.12	0.02	0.03	0.09	0.03	0.01	0.01	0.01	0.00	-0.02	0.03	0.06
Shock J. Japanese Aggregate Supply												
1	0.65	-0.02	-0.07	0.00	0.13	-0.01	-0.01	0.00	0.13	-0.01	-0.01	0.00
1X	-0.78	-0.31	-0.07	-0.13	-0.17	-0.05	-0.01	-0.03	-0.17	-0.05	-0.01	-0.03
2A	0.04	-0.21	-0.08	-0.12	0.03	0.00	0.00	-0.01	0.03	0.00	0.00	-0.01
2AX	-0.53	-0.18	-0.05	-0.11	-0.09	-0.02	-0.02	-0.03	-0.09	-0.02	-0.02	-0.03
2B	-0.07	-1.24	-0.08	0.08	-0.61	-0.55	0.11	0.11	-0.61	-0.55	0.11	0.11
2BX	-1.70	-0.30	0.04	-0.09	-0.29	0.04	-0.01	-0.09	-0.29	0.04	-0.01	-0.09
3	0.27	-0.10	-0.07	-0.05	0.05	-0.02	-0.01	-0.01	0.05	-0.02	-0.01	-0.01
3X	-0.36	-0.16	-0.10	-0.13	-0.09	-0.05	-0.02	-0.02	-0.09	-0.05	-0.02	-0.02

844

Shock and Regime	Short Interest Rate				Long Interest Rate				Current Account/GNP Ratio			
	1st Yr	2nd Yr	5th Yr	10th Yr	1st Yr	2nd Yr	5th Yr	10th Yr	1st Yr	2nd Yr	5th Yr	10th Yr
Shock H. German Aggregate Supply												
1	0.26	-0.12	0.00	0.04	0.02	-0.04	-0.01	0.01	0.01	-0.07	0.01	0.09
1X	-0.02	0.02	0.00	-0.02	0.00	0.00	0.00	0.00	0.00	0.00	0.00	0.00
2A	-0.01	-0.04	0.03	0.08	0.00	-0.01	0.00	0.01	0.00	-0.07	0.02	0.09
2AX	-0.02	0.02	0.00	0.00	0.00	0.00	0.00	0.00	0.00	0.00	0.00	0.01
2B	-0.20	-0.34	-0.08	-0.15	-0.15	-0.10	0.02	0.05	-0.03	-0.10	-0.09	-0.03
2BX	-1.30	-0.13	0.00	-0.06	-0.21	0.04	-0.02	-0.09	-0.32	-0.15	-0.01	-0.06
3	-0.01	-0.03	-0.04	-0.01	-0.03	-0.04	-0.04	-0.01	-0.01	-0.09	-0.04	0.02
3X	-0.01	0.02	0.00	0.02	0.00	0.00	0.00	0.00	0.00	0.00	0.00	0.00
Shock E. Oil Price Increase												
1	0.28	0.44	0.26	0.25	0.06	0.09	0.05	0.05	-0.18	-0.10	-0.04	-0.02
1X	0.36	0.50	0.30	0.30	0.07	0.10	0.06	0.06	-0.17	-0.09	-0.03	-0.01
2A	0.60	0.32	0.17	0.17	0.17	0.10	0.09	0.11	-0.08	-0.05	-0.03	0.02
2AX	0.63	0.66	0.38	0.40	0.13	0.13	0.08	0.08	-0.12	-0.04	-0.01	0.01
2B	0.60	0.41	0.21	0.09	0.45	0.38	0.31	0.22	0.01	0.07	0.14	0.16
2BX	-0.58	0.09	0.11	0.07	0.03	0.16	0.07	0.01	-0.32	-0.18	0.00	-0.08
3	0.30	0.23	0.17	0.12	0.05	0.05	0.05	0.06	-0.15	-0.09	-0.06	-0.04
3X	0.47	0.31	0.21	0.10	0.11	0.08	0.06	0.08	-0.10	-0.07	-0.04	-0.02
Shock L. U.S. Money Demand												
1	0.00	0.02	0.01	0.02	0.00	0.00	0.00	0.00	0.00	0.01	0.01	0.01
1X	0.03	0.01	0.01	0.02	0.01	0.00	0.00	0.01	0.00	0.00	0.01	0.02
2A	0.00	0.00	0.00	0.00	0.00	0.00	0.00	0.00	0.00	0.00	0.00	0.00
2AX	0.00	0.01	0.01	0.02	0.00	0.00	0.00	0.00	0.00	0.00	0.00	0.01
2B	0.00	0.00	0.00	0.00	0.00	0.00	0.00	0.00	0.00	0.00	0.00	0.00
2BX	-1.13	-0.18	-0.02	-0.10	-0.20	0.01	-0.03	-0.10	-0.32	-0.19	-0.02	-0.05
3	0.00	0.00	0.00	0.00	0.00	0.00	0.00	0.00	0.00	0.00	0.00	0.00
3X	0.00	0.00	-0.01	0.01	0.00	0.00	0.00	-0.01	0.00	0.00	0.00	0.00
Shock D. Japanese Money Demand												
1	0.62	0.31	0.07	0.08	0.20	0.10	0.02	0.02	0.10	0.06	0.00	0.01
1X	0.85	0.41	0.09	0.10	0.26	0.12	0.02	0.02	0.13	0.08	0.00	0.01
2A	0.00	0.00	0.00	0.00	0.00	0.00	0.00	0.00	0.00	0.00	0.00	0.00
2AX	0.43	0.23	0.08	0.11	0.10	0.05	0.01	0.01	0.07	0.06	0.00	0.00
2B	0.00	0.00	0.00	0.00	0.00	0.00	0.00	0.00	0.00	0.00	0.00	0.00
2BX	-0.97	0.02	0.08	-0.07	-0.05	0.14	0.02	-0.08	-0.25	-0.13	-0.01	-0.07
3	0.00	0.00	0.00	0.00	0.00	0.00	0.00	0.00	0.00	0.00	0.00	0.00
3X	0.00	0.00	-0.01	0.01	0.00	0.00	0.00	-0.01	0.00	0.00	0.00	0.00
Shock K. German Money Demand												
1	0.01	-0.01	0.00	0.00	0.00	0.00	0.00	0.00	0.00	0.00	0.00	0.00
1X	0.03	-0.01	0.00	0.00	0.00	0.00	0.00	0.00	0.00	0.00	0.00	0.00
2A	0.00	0.00	0.00	0.00	0.00	0.00	0.00	0.00	0.00	0.00	0.00	0.00
2AX	0.01	-0.01	0.00	0.01	0.00	0.00	0.00	0.00	0.00	0.00	0.00	0.00
2B	0.00	0.00	0.00	0.00	0.00	0.00	0.00	0.00	0.00	0.00	0.00	0.00
2BX	-1.12	-0.21	0.00	-0.07	-0.19	0.02	-0.02	-0.09	-0.31	-0.18	0.00	-0.07
3	0.00	0.00	0.00	0.00	0.00	0.00	0.00	0.00	0.00	0.00	0.00	0.00
3X	0.00	0.00	-0.01	0.01	0.00	0.00	0.00	-0.01	0.00	0.00	0.00	0.00
Shock F. U.S. Money Supply-Permanent FIXM												
1	0.00	0.00	0.00	0.00	0.00	0.00	0.00	0.00	0.00	0.00	0.00	0.00
1X	0.02	0.01	0.02	0.05	0.01	0.01	0.01	0.03	0.01	0.01	0.01	0.04

Table A-LIV-5
LIVERPOOL MODEL
EFFECTS ON GERMAN REAL GNP, GERMAN PRICE LEVEL, GERMAN INFLATION RATE
(Deviations from Baseline)

Shock and Regime	Real GNP				GNP Deflator				Inflation Rate			
	1st Yr	2nd Yr	5th Yr	10th Yr	1st Yr	2nd Yr	5th Yr	10th Yr	1st Yr	2nd Yr	5th Yr	10th Yr
Shock A. US Aggregate Demand												
1	0.00	0.00	-0.01	-0.02	0.00	0.01	0.02	0.03	0.00	0.01	0.00	0.00
1X	0.00	0.00	-0.01	-0.01	0.00	0.00	0.01	0.01	0.00	0.00	0.00	0.00
2A	0.00	0.00	-0.01	-0.02	0.00	0.01	0.03	0.04	0.00	0.01	0.00	0.00
2AX	0.00	0.00	0.00	-0.01	0.00	0.00	-0.01	-0.01	0.00	0.00	0.00	0.00
2B	-0.01	-0.01	-0.07	-0.15	0.13	0.14	0.40	1.13	0.13	0.02	0.09	0.19
2BX	0.46	-0.17	-0.51	-0.74	-0.21	0.08	0.74	1.11	-0.22	0.30	0.16	0.02
3	0.00	0.00	-0.01	-0.01	0.00	-0.03	-0.03	-0.03	0.00	-0.03	0.00	0.00
3X	0.00	0.00	0.00	0.00	0.00	-0.01	0.00	0.05	0.00	0.00	0.00	0.03
Shock I. Japanese Aggregate Demand												
1	0.02	-0.05	-0.07	-0.10	0.03	0.10	0.11	0.16	0.03	0.07	0.01	0.02
1X	0.01	-0.06	-0.07	-0.09	0.01	0.07	0.09	0.13	0.01	0.06	0.01	0.04
2A	0.00	-0.06	-0.06	-0.08	0.07	0.11	0.10	0.13	0.07	0.04	0.01	0.00
2AX	-0.04	-0.08	-0.07	-0.10	0.00	0.06	0.07	0.10	0.00	0.07	0.00	0.04
2B	0.00	-0.05	-0.05	-0.03	0.10	0.26	0.66	1.31	0.10	0.16	0.13	0.15
2BX	0.50	-0.22	-0.54	-0.75	-0.16	0.12	0.80	1.14	-0.17	0.29	0.16	0.02
3	0.04	-0.03	-0.03	-0.02	0.07	0.08	0.08	0.13	0.07	0.02	0.02	0.01
3X	0.03	-0.01	0.00	0.01	0.04	0.06	0.16	0.18	0.04	0.02	0.07	0.01
Shock G. German Aggregate Demand												
1	0.62	0.48	0.33	0.14	-0.38	-0.30	-0.24	-0.04	-0.38	0.07	0.03	0.04
1X	0.51	0.41	0.28	0.15	-0.46	-0.43	-0.30	-0.15	-0.47	0.03	0.04	0.03
2A	0.60	0.46	0.32	0.14	-0.33	-0.20	-0.20	-0.05	-0.34	0.14	0.02	0.01
2AX	0.49	0.41	0.28	0.15	-0.61	-0.54	-0.34	-0.20	-0.62	0.07	0.06	0.02
2B	0.78	0.72	0.60	0.38	-1.01	-1.95	-4.67	-7.61	-1.02	-0.97	-0.89	-0.48
2BX	1.34	0.56	0.13	-0.32	-0.83	-0.92	-0.37	0.38	-0.86	-0.10	0.21	0.10
3	0.66	0.44	0.31	0.14	0.44	0.74	0.26	0.20	0.45	0.30	-0.13	-0.01
3X	0.56	0.39	0.26	0.15	0.31	0.49	0.24	0.21	0.31	0.18	-0.03	0.03
Shock B. Global Aggregate Demand												
1	0.45	0.31	0.19	0.09	-0.27	-0.15	-0.14	-0.04	-0.28	0.12	0.01	0.01
1X	0.44	0.31	0.21	0.10	-0.43	-0.35	-0.22	-0.10	-0.44	0.08	0.04	0.01
2A	0.57	0.37	0.20	0.00	-0.13	-0.05	-0.04	0.14	-0.13	0.08	0.02	0.02
2AX	0.43	0.33	0.23	0.13	-0.56	-0.50	-0.29	-0.17	-0.58	0.07	0.05	0.01
2B	0.73	0.64	0.44	0.12	-0.79	-1.58	-3.58	-4.67	-0.80	-0.82	-0.59	-0.05
2BX	1.15	0.37	-0.14	-0.65	-0.75	-0.68	0.09	0.94	-0.79	0.08	0.26	0.10
3	0.65	0.35	0.19	0.02	0.60	0.83	0.17	0.05	0.61	0.24	-0.16	-0.02
3X	0.57	0.36	0.21	0.04	0.30	0.50	0.12	-0.03	0.31	0.20	-0.09	-0.04
Shock C. US Aggregate Supply												
1	0.00	0.00	0.01	0.01	0.00	0.00	0.00	-0.01	0.00	0.00	0.00	0.00
1X	-0.13	-0.05	0.00	-0.03	0.13	0.07	0.01	0.04	0.13	-0.06	0.00	0.02
2A	-0.11	-0.03	-0.01	-0.03	0.08	0.02	0.03	0.05	0.09	-0.07	0.00	0.01
2AX	-0.12	-0.04	-0.01	-0.04	0.14	0.07	0.00	0.04	0.15	-0.07	0.00	0.02
2B	-0.07	-0.04	-0.05	-0.12	0.11	0.15	0.33	0.86	0.11	0.05	0.07	0.15
2BX	0.43	-0.16	-0.40	-0.59	-0.13	0.08	0.58	0.85	-0.13	0.22	0.12	0.02
3	-0.16	-0.04	0.00	-0.02	-0.01	-0.08	0.02	-0.04	-0.01	-0.07	0.00	-0.01
3X	-0.17	-0.02	0.02	0.01	-0.07	-0.05	0.07	0.06	-0.07	0.01	0.00	0.02
Shock J. Japanese Aggregate Supply												
1	-0.02	0.03	0.00	-0.01	0.03	-0.03	-0.01	0.01	0.03	-0.06	0.00	0.01
1X	0.13	0.06	0.00	0.01	-0.11	-0.07	0.00	-0.01	-0.11	0.04	0.01	-0.01
2A	-0.06	0.08	-0.02	-0.02	0.05	-0.08	-0.01	0.00	0.05	-0.14	0.00	-0.02
2AX	0.11	0.05	0.00	0.01	-0.09	-0.06	0.02	0.01	-0.09	0.03	0.01	-0.02
2B	-0.17	-0.02	-0.07	-0.08	0.18	0.13	0.49	1.32	0.18	-0.05	0.17	0.13
2BX	0.69	-0.04	-0.33	-0.50	-0.30	-0.13	0.43	0.72	-0.31	0.17	0.14	0.02
3	-0.10	0.06	0.01	-0.02	0.02	-0.03	-0.02	-0.03	0.02	-0.05	-0.05	0.00
3X	0.11	0.02	-0.01	0.01	0.06	0.04	-0.13	-0.20	0.06	-0.02	-0.04	0.00
	0.12	0.05	0.00	0.01	-0.10	-0.05	-0.02	-0.03	-0.10	0.05	0.01	-0.01

Shock and Regime	Real GNP				GNP Deflator				Inflation Rate			
	1st Yr	2nd Yr	5th Yr	10th Yr	1st Yr	2nd Yr	5th Yr	10th Yr	1st Yr	2nd Yr	5th Yr	10th Yr
Shock H. German Aggregate Supply												
1	-1.00	-0.37	-0.14	-0.02	1.72	0.62	0.17	0.04	1.75	-1.10	-0.09	0.00
1X	0.15	0.00	0.00	-0.01	-0.14	-0.03	0.01	0.01	-0.14	0.11	-0.02	0.00
2A	-0.99	-0.37	-0.14	-0.02	2.15	0.57	0.18	0.07	2.19	-1.58	-0.09	0.00
2AX	0.17	-0.01	0.00	-0.01	0.05	-0.02	-0.01	0.01	0.05	-0.07	0.01	0.00
2B	-1.01	-0.59	-0.41	-0.28	2.97	4.29	7.03	9.17	3.02	1.31	0.69	0.33
2BX	0.80	-0.12	-0.38	-0.56	-0.20	0.02	0.54	0.81	-0.21	0.23	0.11	0.02
3	-1.01	-0.47	-0.24	-0.05	3.24	0.77	0.03	-0.01	3.30	-2.43	-0.21	0.12
3X	0.13	0.00	0.00	0.01	-0.49	0.03	0.07	0.02	-0.50	0.52	-0.06	0.00
Shock E. Oil Price Increase												
1	0.45	0.31	0.19	0.09	-0.27	-0.15	-0.14	-0.04	-0.28	0.12	0.01	0.01
1X	0.44	0.31	0.21	0.10	-0.43	-0.35	-0.22	-0.10	-0.44	0.08	0.04	0.01
2A	0.57	0.37	0.20	0.00	-0.13	-0.05	-0.04	0.14	-0.13	0.08	0.02	0.02
2AX	0.43	0.33	0.23	0.13	-0.56	-0.50	-0.29	-0.17	-0.58	0.07	0.05	0.01
2B	0.73	0.64	0.44	0.12	-0.79	-1.58	-3.58	-4.67	-0.80	-0.82	-0.59	-0.05
2BX	1.15	0.37	-0.14	-0.65	-0.75	-0.68	0.09	0.94	-0.79	0.08	0.26	0.10
3	0.65	0.35	0.19	0.02	0.60	0.83	0.17	0.05	0.61	0.24	-0.16	-0.02
3X	0.57	0.36	0.21	0.04	0.30	0.50	0.12	-0.03	0.31	0.20	-0.09	-0.04
Shock L. U.S. Money Demand												
1	0.00	0.00	0.00	0.00	0.00	0.01	0.00	0.01	0.00	0.01	0.00	0.00
1X	-0.05	0.00	0.00	-0.01	0.05	0.01	0.00	0.02	0.05	-0.04	0.00	0.01
2A	0.00	0.00	0.00	0.00	0.00	0.00	0.00	0.00	0.00	0.00	0.00	0.00
2AX	0.00	0.00	0.00	0.00	0.00	0.00	0.00	0.00	0.00	0.00	0.00	0.00
2B	0.00	0.00	0.00	0.00	0.00	0.00	0.00	0.00	0.00	0.00	0.00	0.00
2BX	0.49	-0.17	-0.47	-0.69	-0.15	0.07	0.67	1.00	-0.16	0.24	0.14	0.04
3	0.00	0.00	0.00	0.00	0.00	0.00	0.00	0.00	0.00	0.00	0.00	0.00
3X	0.01	0.00	0.00	0.01	0.03	0.04	0.07	0.09	0.03	0.02	0.01	0.01
Shock D. Japanese Money Demand												
1	-0.07	-0.03	0.00	-0.01	0.07	0.03	0.02	0.04	0.07	-0.03	0.00	0.01
1X	-0.09	-0.04	0.00	-0.01	0.08	0.05	0.00	0.01	0.08	-0.03	-0.01	0.01
2A	0.00	0.00	0.00	0.00	0.00	0.00	0.00	0.00	0.00	0.00	0.00	0.00
2AX	-0.03	0.01	0.01	0.02	0.02	-0.01	-0.02	-0.05	0.02	-0.03	0.01	0.00
2B	0.00	0.00	0.00	0.00	0.00	0.00	0.00	0.00	0.00	0.00	0.00	0.00
2BX	0.53	-0.12	-0.39	-0.57	-0.19	0.01	0.55	0.84	-0.20	0.21	0.13	0.02
3	0.00	0.00	0.00	0.00	0.00	0.00	0.00	0.00	0.00	0.00	0.00	0.00
3X	0.01	0.00	0.00	0.01	0.03	0.04	0.07	0.09	0.03	0.02	0.01	0.01
Shock K. German Money Demand												
1	-0.07	0.01	0.00	0.00	-0.74	-0.12	0.00	0.01	-0.76	0.64	0.02	0.00
1X	-0.09	0.01	0.00	0.00	-0.90	-0.13	0.00	0.00	-0.92	0.80	0.02	0.00
2A	0.00	0.00	0.00	0.00	0.00	0.00	0.00	0.00	0.00	0.00	0.00	0.00
2AX	-0.05	0.00	0.00	0.00	-0.63	-0.08	0.00	0.00	-0.64	0.56	0.00	0.00
2B	0.00	0.00	0.00	0.00	0.00	0.00	0.00	0.00	0.00	0.00	0.00	0.00
2BX	0.49	-0.10	-0.39	-0.58	-0.85	-0.40	0.50	0.84	-0.89	0.48	0.19	0.02
3	0.00	0.00	0.00	0.00	0.00	0.00	0.00	0.00	0.00	0.00	0.00	0.00
3X	0.01	0.00	0.00	0.01	0.03	0.04	0.07	0.09	0.03	0.02	0.01	0.01
Shock F. U.S. Money Supply-Permanent FIXM												
1	0.00	0.00	0.00	0.00	0.00	0.00	0.00	0.00	0.00	0.00	0.00	0.00
1X	0.15	0.17	0.25	0.39	-0.15	-0.19	-0.27	-0.34	-0.15	-0.04	-0.02	0.00

Table A-LIV-6
LIVERPOOL MODEL
EFFECTS ON GERMAN INTEREST RATES AND GERMAN CURRENT ACCOUNT/GNP RATIO
(Deviations from Baseline)

Shock and Regime	Short Interest Rate				Long Interest Rate				Current Account/GNP Ratio			
	1st Yr	2nd Yr	5th Yr	10th Yr	1st Yr	2nd Yr	5th Yr	10th Yr	1st Yr	2nd Yr	5th Yr	10th Yr
Shock A. US Aggregate Demand												
1	0.00	0.01	0.02	0.03	0.00	0.00	0.01	0.01	0.00	0.00	0.00	0.00
1X	0.00	0.02	0.03	0.04	0.00	0.00	0.01	0.01	0.00	0.00	0.01	0.01
2A	0.00	0.01	0.02	0.03	0.00	0.00	0.01	0.01	0.00	0.00	0.00	0.00
2AX	0.00	0.02	0.04	0.05	0.00	0.01	0.01	0.01	0.00	0.00	0.01	0.01
2B	0.17	0.01	0.03	0.07	0.09	0.06	0.09	0.14	0.06	0.04	0.03	0.09
2BX	-0.35	0.31	0.17	0.07	0.17	0.26	0.09	-0.05	0.14	0.28	0.46	0.63
3	0.00	0.01	0.02	0.03	0.00	0.00	0.01	0.01	0.00	0.00	0.00	0.00
3X	-0.01	0.03	0.00	0.06	0.00	0.01	0.00	0.00	0.00	0.00	0.00	-0.01
Shock I. Japanese Aggregate Demand												
1	0.09	0.08	0.03	0.04	0.04	0.03	0.03	0.06	0.06	0.01	0.02	0.10
1X	0.12	0.09	0.04	0.09	0.04	0.03	0.03	0.06	0.05	0.00	0.03	0.11
2A	0.10	0.07	0.06	0.08	0.04	0.03	0.03	0.05	0.03	0.00	0.04	0.10
2AX	0.17	0.09	0.06	0.11	0.04	0.02	0.04	0.07	0.02	0.00	0.05	0.13
2B	0.15	0.17	0.12	0.17	0.12	0.11	0.09	0.05	0.04	0.01	0.03	0.04
2BX	-0.61	0.42	0.17	0.06	0.15	0.29	0.09	-0.05	0.13	0.24	0.43	0.62
3	0.05	0.07	0.07	0.09	0.02	0.02	0.01	0.01	0.04	-0.01	0.01	0.03
3X	0.05	0.04	0.06	0.12	0.01	0.01	0.00	-0.01	0.02	0.00	0.00	0.00
Shock G. German Aggregate Demand												
1	0.34	0.40	0.17	0.14	0.16	0.15	0.08	0.08	-0.57	-0.48	-0.29	-0.12
1X	0.47	0.44	0.17	0.17	0.13	0.11	0.03	0.03	-0.49	-0.39	-0.22	-0.11
2A	0.40	0.40	0.17	0.12	0.14	0.13	0.06	0.06	-0.55	-0.46	-0.27	-0.11
2AX	0.55	0.45	0.18	0.17	0.15	0.12	0.03	0.03	-0.49	-0.39	-0.22	-0.11
2B	-0.38	-0.38	-0.43	-0.16	-0.48	-0.48	-0.38	-0.15	-0.73	-0.66	-0.48	-0.34
2BX	-0.90	0.48	0.34	0.22	0.19	0.43	0.23	0.07	-0.65	-0.43	-0.08	0.27
3	0.22	0.32	0.15	0.13	0.04	0.06	0.04	0.03	-0.54	-0.46	-0.26	-0.12
3X	0.25	0.41	0.16	0.17	0.05	0.08	0.02	0.00	-0.47	-0.39	-0.21	-0.13
Shock B. Global Aggregate Demand												
1	0.42	0.50	0.16	0.13	0.08	0.10	0.03	0.03	-0.43	-0.34	-0.16	-0.07
1X	0.47	0.51	0.16	0.14	0.09	0.10	0.03	0.03	-0.43	-0.33	-0.15	-0.06
2A	0.67	0.49	0.24	0.22	0.21	0.17	0.11	0.12	-0.45	-0.41	-0.20	0.02
2AX	0.51	0.53	0.18	0.16	0.10	0.11	0.04	0.03	-0.43	-0.31	-0.13	-0.04
2B	-0.11	-0.27	-0.23	0.11	-0.25	-0.26	-0.07	0.16	-0.60	-0.55	-0.34	-0.11
2BX	-0.34	0.64	0.42	0.24	0.41	0.54	0.29	0.09	-0.49	-0.27	0.15	0.55
3	0.45	0.42	0.19	0.16	0.08	0.08	0.06	0.07	-0.43	-0.42	-0.22	-0.06
3X	0.58	0.48	0.22	0.10	0.14	0.12	0.07	0.08	-0.46	-0.41	-0.21	-0.05
Shock C. US Aggregate Supply												
1	0.00	0.00	0.01	0.01	0.00	0.00	0.00	0.00	0.00	0.00	0.01	0.01
1X	-0.05	-0.05	0.05	0.04	-0.01	0.00	0.02	0.02	-0.08	-0.01	0.05	0.05
2A	-0.04	-0.02	0.04	0.04	0.00	0.00	0.02	0.02	-0.07	-0.01	0.04	0.04
2AX	-0.07	-0.05	0.05	0.03	-0.01	0.00	0.02	0.03	-0.08	-0.01	0.05	0.06
2B	0.05	0.01	0.03	0.05	0.04	0.04	0.06	0.12	-0.08	-0.05	-0.01	0.04
2BX	-0.64	0.25	0.13	0.07	0.06	0.20	0.05	-0.07	-0.05	0.14	0.35	0.50
3	0.03	0.01	0.07	0.05	0.02	0.01	0.02	0.03	-0.09	-0.01	0.06	0.06
3X	0.10	0.03	0.09	0.09	0.02	0.01	0.02	0.01	-0.09	0.00	0.05	0.04
Shock J. Japanese Aggregate Supply												
1	0.01	0.00	-0.02	0.02	0.00	0.00	0.00	0.00	-0.01	0.02	-0.01	-0.01
1X	-0.03	0.05	-0.06	-0.09	0.01	0.01	-0.02	-0.02	0.08	0.03	-0.05	-0.05
2A	-0.02	-0.01	-0.04	-0.04	0.00	0.00	0.00	0.01	-0.03	0.06	-0.02	0.00
2AX	-0.02	0.05	-0.05	-0.08	0.01	0.01	-0.01	-0.02	0.07	0.02	-0.04	-0.04
2B	0.02	-0.10	0.15	0.07	0.06	0.09	0.14	0.09	-0.02	0.11	0.10	0.09
2BX	-0.89	0.29	0.12	0.06	0.03	0.22	0.04	-0.06	0.12	0.19	0.29	0.42
3	0.03	-0.02	-0.01	-0.01	0.00	-0.01	0.00	0.00	-0.05	0.05	0.00	-0.02
3X	-0.09	-0.01	-0.08	-0.10	-0.03	-0.02	-0.01	-0.01	0.06	0.00	-0.04	-0.04
	-0.02	0.05	-0.04	-0.07	0.01	0.01	-0.02	-0.02	0.08	0.03	-0.04	-0.04

Shock and Regime	Short Interest Rate				Long Interest Rate				Current Account/GNP Ratio			
	1st Yr	2nd Yr	5th Yr	10th Yr	1st Yr	2nd Yr	5th Yr	10th Yr	1st Yr	2nd Yr	5th Yr	10th Yr
Shock H. German Aggregate Supply												
1	1.88	0.18	0.06	0.04	0.38	0.04	0.00	0.02	0.05	0.22	0.18	0.11
1X	-0.64	0.02	0.04	-0.02	-0.13	0.01	0.01	0.00	-0.01	-0.03	0.00	0.00
2A	1.69	0.30	0.07	0.09	0.35	0.06	0.00	0.01	0.06	0.23	0.17	0.09
2AX	-0.73	0.01	0.04	0.00	-0.14	0.01	0.01	0.01	-0.01	-0.03	0.00	0.01
2B	3.01	1.08	0.41	0.07	1.23	0.68	0.28	0.14	0.27	0.38	0.27	0.20
2BX	-1.60	0.16	0.16	0.08	-0.11	0.23	0.05	-0.06	0.07	0.16	0.32	0.46
3	0.12	-0.05	-0.11	-0.02	-0.02	-0.05	-0.05	-0.01	0.13	0.28	0.19	0.08
3X	-0.44	0.03	0.03	0.02	-0.08	0.01	0.01	0.00	0.00	-0.02	0.00	-0.01
Shock E. Oil Price Increase												
1	0.42	0.50	0.16	0.13	0.08	0.10	0.03	0.03	-0.43	-0.34	-0.16	-0.07
1X	0.47	0.51	0.16	0.14	0.09	0.10	0.03	0.03	-0.43	-0.33	-0.15	-0.06
2A	0.67	0.49	0.24	0.22	0.21	0.17	0.11	0.12	-0.45	-0.41	-0.20	0.02
2AX	0.51	0.53	0.18	0.16	0.10	0.11	0.04	0.03	-0.43	-0.31	-0.13	-0.04
2B	-0.11	-0.27	-0.23	0.11	-0.25	-0.26	-0.07	0.16	-0.60	-0.55	-0.34	-0.11
2BX	-0.34	0.64	0.42	0.24	0.41	0.54	0.29	0.09	-0.49	-0.27	0.15	0.55
3	0.45	0.42	0.19	0.16	0.08	0.08	0.06	0.07	-0.43	-0.42	-0.22	-0.06
3X	0.58	0.48	0.22	0.10	0.14	0.12	0.07	0.08	-0.46	-0.41	-0.21	-0.05
Shock L. U.S. Money Demand												
1	0.00	0.03	0.01	0.02	0.00	0.01	0.00	0.00	0.00	0.01	0.01	0.01
1X	-0.01	0.03	0.04	0.03	0.00	0.01	0.01	0.02	-0.03	0.01	0.02	0.03
2A	0.00	0.00	0.00	0.00	0.00	0.00	0.00	0.00	0.00	0.00	0.00	0.00
2AX	0.00	0.01	0.01	0.02	0.00	0.00	0.00	0.00	0.00	0.00	0.00	0.01
2B	0.00	0.00	0.00	0.00	0.00	0.00	0.00	0.00	0.00	0.00	0.00	0.00
2BX	-0.68	0.32	0.16	0.08	0.08	0.23	0.06	-0.07	0.06	0.22	0.42	0.61
3	0.00	0.00	0.00	0.00	0.00	0.00	0.00	0.00	0.00	0.00	0.00	0.00
3X	0.01	0.00	0.00	0.02	0.00	0.00	0.01	-0.01	0.00	0.00	-0.01	-0.01
Shock D. Japanese Money Demand												
1	0.02	-0.01	0.04	0.06	0.00	0.00	0.01	0.02	-0.04	-0.01	0.03	0.03
1X	0.03	-0.02	0.05	0.07	0.00	-0.01	0.01	0.02	-0.05	-0.01	0.04	0.04
2A	0.00	0.00	0.00	0.00	0.00	0.00	0.00	0.00	0.00	0.00	0.00	0.00
2AX	0.02	0.01	0.01	0.07	0.00	0.00	0.00	0.00	-0.01	0.01	0.01	0.01
2B	0.00	0.00	0.00	0.00	0.00	0.00	0.00	0.00	0.00	0.00	0.00	0.00
2BX	-0.71	0.28	0.14	0.07	0.06	0.22	0.05	-0.06	0.02	0.16	0.33	0.48
3	0.00	0.00	0.00	0.00	0.00	0.00	0.00	0.00	0.00	0.00	0.00	0.00
3X	0.01	0.00	0.00	0.02	0.00	0.00	0.01	-0.01	0.00	0.00	-0.01	-0.01
Shock K. German Money Demand												
1	0.45	0.03	-0.01	0.00	0.10	0.00	0.00	0.00	0.00	0.01	0.00	0.00
1X	0.63	0.05	-0.01	0.00	0.14	0.01	0.00	0.00	0.01	0.01	0.00	0.00
2A	0.00	0.00	0.00	0.00	0.00	0.00	0.00	0.00	0.00	0.00	0.00	0.00
2AX	0.29	0.01	-0.01	0.01	0.06	0.00	0.00	0.00	0.01	0.01	0.00	0.00
2B	0.00	0.00	0.00	0.00	0.00	0.00	0.00	0.00	0.00	0.00	0.00	0.00
2BX	-0.24	0.51	0.15	0.07	0.23	0.29	0.06	-0.06	0.06	0.19	0.33	0.48
3	0.00	0.00	0.00	0.00	0.00	0.00	0.00	0.00	0.00	0.00	0.00	0.00
3X	0.01	0.00	0.00	0.02	0.00	0.00	0.01	-0.01	0.00	0.00	-0.01	-0.01
Shock F. U.S. Money Supply-Permanent **FIXM**												
1	0.00	0.00	0.00	0.00	0.00	0.00	0.00	0.00	0.00	0.00	0.00	0.00
1X	0.09	0.11	0.13	0.25	0.01	0.01	0.01	0.09	-0.14	-0.16	-0.23	-0.35

Table A-LIV-7
LIVERPOOL MODEL
BILATERAL DOLLAR EXCHANGE RATES
(Deviations from Baseline)

Shock and Regime	Bilateral DM/$ Exchange Rate				Bilateral Yen/$ Exchange Rate			
	1st Yr	2nd Yr	5th Yr	10th Yr	1st Yr	2nd Yr	5th Yr	10th Yr
Shock A. US Aggregate Demand								
1	0.16	0.02	0.00	0.02	0.16	0.03	0.00	0.01
1X	0.04	0.08	0.04	0.04	0.04	0.08	0.02	0.03
2A	0.16	-0.06	-0.03	-0.03	0.16	-0.07	-0.04	-0.03
2AX	-0.06	0.08	0.04	0.03	-0.06	0.06	0.01	0.01
2B	-0.29	-0.32	-0.64	-0.04	-0.44	-0.27	-0.34	0.50
2BX	-1.52	-0.81	-1.89	-2.73	-1.65	-0.46	-0.54	-0.99
3	0.16	0.04	0.04	0.05	0.16	0.04	0.05	0.06
3X	0.00	0.00	0.00	0.00	0.00	0.00	0.00	0.00
Shock I. Japanese Aggregate Demand								
1	0.24	0.35	0.61	0.85	0.61	0.84	1.04	1.27
1X	0.28	0.37	0.68	1.00	0.70	0.94	1.14	1.42
2A	0.19	0.17	0.18	0.24	1.05	0.69	0.49	0.49
2AX	0.31	0.34	0.56	0.80	1.28	1.10	1.03	1.20
2B	0.14	0.18	0.27	-0.67	0.89	0.66	0.13	-0.34
2BX	-1.03	-0.41	-1.52	-2.44	-0.02	0.93	0.32	-0.40
3	-0.01	0.01	0.03	0.03	-0.04	-0.05	-0.01	0.01
3X	0.00	0.00	-0.01	-0.03	0.00	0.00	-0.01	-0.03
Shock G. German Aggregate Demand								
1	1.18	1.21	0.99	1.03	0.11	0.23	0.49	0.79
1X	1.18	1.12	0.68	0.62	0.17	0.21	0.25	0.38
2A	1.08	0.96	0.56	0.38	0.04	0.09	0.13	0.08
2AX	1.41	1.23	0.66	0.51	0.19	0.21	0.22	0.24
2B	2.14	2.97	5.15	6.51	-0.36	-0.40	-0.44	-2.26
2BX	0.34	1.30	0.03	-1.21	-1.34	-0.35	-0.31	-0.59
3	-0.07	-0.07	0.01	0.02	0.01	0.04	0.06	0.06
3X	0.01	0.01	0.00	-0.01	0.00	0.00	-0.01	-0.01
Shock B. Global Aggregate Demand								
1	0.84	0.56	-0.02	-0.33	0.33	0.15	-0.18	-0.27
1X	0.93	0.74	-0.02	-0.39	0.41	0.34	-0.14	-0.24
2A	0.95	0.87	0.48	0.43	0.59	0.49	0.29	0.36
2AX	1.01	0.75	-0.13	-0.45	0.92	0.46	-0.13	-0.18
2B	1.74	2.41	3.37	3.70	-0.41	-0.78	-2.51	-4.83
2BX	0.08	1.07	-0.45	-2.06	-0.74	0.46	0.23	-0.29
3	-0.03	-0.07	0.05	0.08	0.04	0.01	0.06	0.10
3X	0.01	0.01	-0.01	-0.02	0.00	0.00	-0.01	-0.02
Shock C. US Aggregate Supply								
1	0.53	0.62	0.35	-0.03	0.53	0.62	0.34	-0.04
1X	0.04	0.36	0.56	0.64	0.22	0.39	0.50	0.67
2A	0.28	0.18	0.17	0.21	0.30	0.17	0.15	0.21
2AX	0.01	0.22	0.41	0.44	0.13	0.22	0.33	0.44
2B	0.54	1.09	1.99	3.54	0.72	1.36	2.51	4.33
2BX	-1.21	-0.41	-1.49	-2.34	-1.21	-0.12	-0.45	-1.02
3	0.07	0.06	0.00	-0.02	0.07	0.07	0.02	-0.01
3X	0.00	0.00	-0.01	-0.05	0.00	0.00	-0.01	-0.05
Shock J. Japanese Aggregate Supply								
1	0.29	0.12	0.03	0.29	0.65	-0.05	0.04	0.31
1X	-0.09	-0.18	-0.60	-0.89	-1.11	-0.59	-0.71	-1.09
2A	0.16	-0.11	-0.21	-0.12	-0.22	0.13	-0.04	-0.16
2AX	-0.07	-0.10	-0.41	-0.58	-0.68	-0.38	-0.52	-0.71
2B	0.06	0.00	0.02	0.64	0.60	1.01	4.12	5.14
2BX	-1.16	-0.45	-1.41	-2.05	-1.73	-0.29	-0.50	-1.02
3	0.03	0.01	-0.01	-0.02	-0.06	0.04	0.02	0.00
3X	0.00	0.00	0.00	0.04	0.00	0.00	0.01	0.04

850

Shock and	Bilateral DM/$ Exchange Rate				Bilateral Yen/$ Exchange Rate			
Regime	1st Yr	2nd Yr	5th Yr	10th Yr	1st Yr	2nd Yr	5th Yr	10th Yr

Shock H. German Aggregate Supply

1	1.69	0.33	0.51	0.98	0.42	0.19	0.62	1.08
1X	-0.75	0.00	0.03	-0.13	-0.25	-0.05	-0.01	-0.12
2A	1.53	0.28	0.32	0.54	0.45	0.31	0.48	0.59
2AX	-1.05	0.01	0.07	-0.01	-0.29	-0.04	0.02	-0.01
2B	-0.15	-3.15	-5.61	-5.06	0.95	1.40	2.50	4.56
2BX	-2.01	-0.53	-1.42	-2.21	-1.25	-0.16	-0.40	-0.92
3	-0.03	0.00	-0.01	-0.04	0.02	-0.01	-0.04	-0.05
3X	-0.01	0.01	0.00	-0.01	0.00	0.00	0.00	-0.02

Shock E. Oil Price Increase

1	2.34	0.47	-0.07	-0.27	2.78	0.36	-0.08	-0.27
1X	2.03	0.47	-0.10	-0.30	2.66	0.34	-0.15	-0.34
2A	2.63	-0.21	-0.09	-0.25	2.83	-0.26	-0.13	-0.28
2AX	1.98	-0.17	-0.49	-0.65	2.63	-0.25	-0.60	-0.71
2B	3.06	1.10	0.42	-0.01	3.37	1.33	0.69	0.26
2BX	0.93	-0.38	-1.88	-2.56	1.57	0.17	-0.74	-1.13
3	0.62	0.04	0.03	0.00	0.64	0.07	0.00	-0.02
3X	2.08	0.49	0.53	0.43	2.09	0.45	0.45	0.37

Shock L. U.S. Money Demand

1	-0.67	-0.35	0.04	0.08	-0.67	-0.36	0.03	0.08
1X	-0.88	-0.29	0.27	0.33	-0.81	-0.31	0.23	0.33
2A	0.00	0.00	0.00	0.00	0.00	0.00	0.00	0.00
2AX	-0.43	-0.23	0.02	0.09	-0.43	-0.24	0.02	0.09
2B	0.00	0.00	0.00	0.00	0.00	0.00	0.00	0.00
2BX	-1.75	-1.13	-1.86	-2.54	-1.63	-0.65	-0.54	-0.91
3	0.00	0.00	0.00	0.00	0.00	0.00	0.00	0.00
3X	0.00	0.00	0.00	-0.01	0.00	0.00	0.00	-0.01

Shock D. Japanese Money Demand

1	0.04	0.08	0.29	0.40	1.36	0.79	0.45	0.50
1X	0.05	0.11	0.39	0.52	1.79	1.01	0.58	0.67
2A	0.00	0.00	0.00	0.00	0.00	0.00	0.00	0.00
2AX	0.12	0.15	0.08	0.16	1.07	0.65	0.25	0.22
2B	0.00	0.00	0.00	0.00	0.00	0.00	0.00	0.00
2BX	-1.12	-0.49	-1.47	-2.18	-0.26	0.55	-0.16	-0.82
3	0.00	0.00	0.00	0.00	0.00	0.00	0.00	0.00
3X	0.00	0.00	0.00	-0.01	0.00	0.00	0.00	-0.01

Shock K. German Money Demand

1	1.06	0.14	-0.01	-0.02	0.06	0.02	0.00	-0.02
1X	1.26	0.13	-0.02	0.02	0.06	0.00	0.00	0.03
2A	0.00	0.00	0.00	0.00	0.00	0.00	0.00	0.00
2AX	0.92	0.10	0.00	0.05	0.08	0.02	0.02	0.05
2B	0.00	0.00	0.00	0.00	0.00	0.00	0.00	0.00
2BX	-0.25	-0.14	-1.49	-2.24	-1.10	-0.18	-0.43	-0.92
3	0.00	0.00	0.00	0.00	0.00	0.00	0.00	0.00
3X	0.00	0.00	0.00	-0.01	0.00	0.00	0.00	-0.01

Shock F. U.S. Money Supply-Permanent
FIXM

1	0.00	0.00	0.01	0.25	0.00	0.00	0.02	0.26
1X	0.38	0.49	0.76	1.18	0.05	0.10	0.25	0.45

Table A-MCM-1
MCM MODEL
EFFECTS ON U.S. REAL GNP, U.S. PRICE LEVEL, U.S. INFLATION RATE
(Deviations from Baseline)

Shock and Regime	Real GNP				GNP Deflator				Inflation Rate			
	1st Qtr	6th Qtr	18th Qtr	36th Qtr	1st Qtr	6th Qtr	18th Qtr	36th Qtr	1st Qtr	6th Qtr	18th Qtr	36th Qtr
Shock A. US Aggregate Demand												
1												
1X	1.305	0.070	-0.011	-0.088	-0.059	0.098	0.269	0.452	-0.061	0.131	0.055	0.019
2A												
2AX	1.320	0.175	0.081	0.307	-0.072	0.134	0.441	0.931	-0.075	0.171	0.114	0.071
2B												
2BX	1.326	0.167	0.129	0.193	-0.075	0.131	0.445	1.168	-0.078	0.166	0.123	0.180
3												
3X	1.332	0.231	0.055	0.117	-0.080	0.143	0.492	1.060	-0.084	0.183	0.124	0.126
Shock I. Japanese Aggregate Demand												
1												
1X												
2A												
2AX												
2B												
2BX												
3												
3X												
Shock G. German Aggregate Demand												
1												
1X												
2A												
2AX												
2B												
2BX												
3												
3X												
Shock B. Global Aggregate Demand												
1												
1X	1.427	0.105	-0.035	-0.108	-0.066	0.131	0.314	0.462	-0.068	0.153	0.054	0.004
2A												
2AX	1.442	0.233	0.065	0.433	-0.078	0.169	0.522	1.003	-0.080	0.199	0.128	0.045
2B												
2BX	1.448	0.223	0.124	0.196	-0.080	0.165	0.528	1.311	-0.083	0.192	0.139	0.191
3												
3X	1.445	0.299	0.063	0.109	-0.081	0.174	0.598	1.247	-0.084	0.207	0.150	0.138
Shock C. US Aggregate Supply												
1												
1X	-0.053	-0.003	-0.011	-0.024	-0.048	0.060	0.146	0.287	-0.050	0.037	0.030	0.023
2A												
2AX	-0.056	-0.005	0.036	-0.072	-0.047	0.057	0.163	0.426	-0.048	0.036	0.042	0.066
2B												
2BX	-0.055	-0.003	0.057	0.073	-0.047	0.056	0.168	0.478	-0.049	0.033	0.047	0.072
3												
3X	-0.056	-0.018	0.024	0.069	-0.046	0.055	0.137	0.363	-0.048	0.033	0.032	0.052
Shock J. Japanese Aggregate Supply												
1												
1X												
2A												
2AX												
2B												
2BX												
3												
3X												

852

Shock and Regime	Real GNP				GNP Deflator				Inflation Rate			
	1st Qtr	6th Qtr	18th Qtr	36th Qtr	1st Qtr	6th Qtr	18th Qtr	36th Qtr	1st Qtr	6th Qtr	18th Qtr	36th Qtr

Shock H. German Aggregate Supply

1
1X
2A
2AX
2B
2BX
3
3X

Shock E. Oil Price Increase												
1												
1X	-0.257	-0.040	-0.008	0.031	-0.207	-0.010	-0.047	-0.013	-0.215	-0.647	-0.010	0.016
2A												
2AX	-0.257	0.004	-0.025	-0.009	-0.212	0.002	-0.057	-0.068	-0.220	-0.624	-0.023	0.007
2B												
2BX	-0.261	-0.005	-0.024	0.001	-0.206	-0.001	-0.052	-0.072	-0.215	-0.630	-0.020	-0.001
3												
3X	-0.264	-0.045	0.020	-0.018	-0.205	-0.014	-0.074	-0.069	-0.214	-0.652	-0.015	0.003

Shock L. U.S. Money Demand

1
1X
2A
2AX
2B
2BX
3
3X

Shock D. Japanese Money Demand												
1												
1X	0.038	-0.005	0.005	0.007	-0.024	-0.001	-0.032	-0.053	-0.025	-0.002	-0.013	-0.005
2A												
2AX	-0.000	-0.000	0.000	-0.000	-0.000	-0.000	-0.000	0.000	-0.000	-0.000	-0.000	0.000
2B												
2BX	0.000	-0.000	-0.000	-0.001	-0.000	0.000	-0.000	-0.001	-0.000	-0.000	0.000	-0.000
3												
3X	0.000	0.000	0.000	-0.000	0.000	0.000	0.000	0.000	-0.000	-0.000	-0.000	-0.000

Shock K. German Money Demand

1
1X
2A
2AX
2B
2BX
3
3X

Shock F. U.S. Money Supply-Permanent

FIXM
1
1X

MCM MODEL
EFFECTS ON U.S. INTEREST RATES AND U.S. CURRENT ACCOUNT/GNP RATIO
(Deviations from Baseline)

Shock and Regime	Short Interest Rate				Long Interest Rate				Current Account/GNP Ratio			
	1st Qtr	6th Qtr	18th Qtr	36th Qtr	1st Qtr	6th Qtr	18th Qtr	36th Qtr	1st Qtr	6th Qtr	18th Qtr	36th Qtr
Shock A. US Aggregate Demand												
1												
1X	0.674	0.102	0.140	0.188	0.083	0.145	0.106	0.153	-0.175	-0.044	-0.045	-0.073
2A												
2AX	0.248	0.062	0.104	0.247	0.029	0.069	0.096	0.174	-0.157	-0.018	-0.014	0.145
2B												
2BX	0.219	0.048	0.046	0.098	0.025	0.072	0.059	0.097	-0.154	-0.024	-0.012	0.008
3												
3X	-0.011	0.055	0.129	0.108	-0.004	0.030	0.125	0.120	-0.144	-0.019	-0.013	0.002
Shock I. Japanese Aggregate Demand												
1												
1X												
2A												
2AX												
2B												
2BX												
3												
3X												
Shock G. German Aggregate Demand												
1												
1X												
2A												
2AX												
2B												
2BX												
3												
3X												
Shock B. GlobAJ Aggregate Demand												
1												
1X	0.736	0.144	0.148	0.181	0.091	0.178	0.113	0.147	-0.096	-0.041	-0.052	-0.078
2A												
2AX	0.271	0.080	0.117	0.286	0.031	0.084	0.110	0.186	-0.076	-0.015	-0.021	0.234
2B												
2BX	0.239	0.063	0.047	0.103	0.027	0.088	0.066	0.103	-0.072	-0.022	-0.018	0.006
3												
3X	-0.012	0.042	0.141	0.108	-0.005	0.032	0.134	0.126	-0.065	-0.015	-0.017	0.002
Shock C. US Aggregate Supply												
1												
1X	-0.085	0.034	0.076	0.138	-0.013	0.009	0.067	0.099	0.007	-0.002	-0.014	-0.018
2A												
2AX	-0.021	0.010	0.040	0.071	-0.004	0.009	0.038	0.071	0.004	0.003	-0.003	-0.069
2B												
2BX	-0.048	-0.002	0.019	0.048	-0.008	0.007	0.023	0.040	0.005	0.001	-0.003	0.004
3												
3X	-0.010	0.039	0.042	0.048	-0.003	0.022	0.043	0.047	0.003	0.002	-0.001	0.005
Shock J. Japanese Aggregate Supply												
1												
1X												
2A												
2AX												
2B												
2BX												
3												
3X												

854

Shock and Regime	Short Interest Rate				Long Interest Rate				Current Account/GNP Ratio			
	1st Qtr	6th Qtr	18th Qtr	38th Qtr	1st Qtr	6th Qtr	18th Qtr	38th Qtr	1st Qtr	6th Qtr	18th Qtr	38th Qtr

Shock H. German Aggregate Supply

1												
1X												
2A												
2AX												
2B												
2BX												
3												
3X												

Shock E. Oil Price Increase

1	0.05	0.06	0.01	-0.07	0.05	0.02	0.07	-0.06	-0.13	0.00	0.03	-0.03
1X	0.05	0.05	0.05	0.00	0.05	0.02	0.08	0.00	-0.13	0.00	0.02	0.01
2A	0.04	0.04	-0.04	-0.01	0.04	0.02	0.02	0.00	-0.13	0.01	0.01	0.00
2AX	0.05	0.03	-0.04	-0.01	0.05	0.02	0.02	0.00	-0.13	0.01	0.01	0.00
2B	0.01	-0.04	-0.06	-0.01	0.01	-0.02	0.03	0.02	-0.13	0.02	0.00	0.02
2BX	0.05	0.12	-0.04	0.05	0.05	0.02	0.03	0.05	-0.13	0.01	0.00	0.03
3												
3X												

Shock L. U.S. Money Demand

1	0.44	-0.51	-0.13	0.53	-0.02	-0.03	-0.40	0.26	-0.02	0.15	-0.21	0.08
1X	0.27	-0.34	-0.07	0.06	-0.01	-0.02	-0.23	-0.01	-0.01	0.07	-0.11	-0.02
2A	0.00	0.00	0.00	0.00	0.00	0.00	0.00	0.00	0.00	0.00	0.00	0.00
2AX	0.00	0.00	0.00	0.00	0.00	0.00	0.00	0.00	0.00	0.00	0.00	0.00
2B	0.00	0.00	0.00	0.00	0.00	0.00	0.00	0.00	0.00	0.00	0.00	0.00
2BX	0.00	0.00	0.00	0.00	0.00	0.00	0.00	0.00	0.00	0.00	0.00	0.00
3												
3X												

Shock D. Japanese Money Demand

1												
1X												
2A												
2AX												
2B												
2BX												
3												
3X												

Shock K. German Money Demand

1												
1X												
2A												
2AX												
2B												
2BX												
3												
3X												

Shock F. U.S. Money Supply-Permanent

FIXM	-2.11	-0.14	0.32	0.37	-0.39	-0.08	0.31	0.27	0.02	-0.05	0.08	0.12
1												
1X												

MCM MODEL
EFFECTS ON JAPANESE REAL GNP, JAPANESE PRICE LEVEL, JAPANESE INFLATION RATE
(Deviations from Baseline)

Shock and Regime	Real GNP				GNP Deflator				Inflation Rate			
	1st Qtr	6th Qtr	18th Qtr	36th Qtr	1st Qtr	6th Qtr	18th Qtr	36th Qtr	1st Qtr	6th Qtr	18th Qtr	36th Qtr

Shock A. US Aggregate Demand

1												
1X	0.308	0.143	0.016	0.037	-0.184	0.007	0.032	0.060	-0.186	0.021	0.004	-0.003
2A												
2AX	0.248	0.094	-0.017	-0.217	-0.124	0.011	0.055	0.237	-0.125	0.032	0.011	0.126
2B												
2BX	0.241	0.090	-0.034	-0.148	-0.116	0.007	0.055	0.136	-0.117	0.034	0.014	0.023
3												
3X	0.218	0.107	0.205	0.430	-0.095	0.003	0.088	0.366	-0.096	0.026	0.038	0.079

Shock I. Japanese Aggregate Demand

1
1X
2A
2AX
2B
2BX
3
3X

Shock G. German Aggregate Demand

1
1X
2A
2AX
2B
2BX
3
3X

Shock B. Global Aggregate Demand

1												
1X	1.265	0.167	-0.085	-0.007	-0.060	0.079	0.045	0.057	-0.060	0.038	-0.015	0.002
2A												
2AX	1.223	0.154	-0.121	-0.376	-0.021	0.098	0.099	0.305	-0.021	0.056	-0.006	0.179
2B												
2BX	1.217	0.154	-0.111	-0.229	-0.016	0.094	0.110	0.164	-0.016	0.053	0.002	0.019
3												
3X	1.216	0.213	0.145	0.489	-0.019	0.100	0.158	0.453	-0.019	0.054	0.024	0.093

Shock C. US Aggregate Supply

1												
1X	-0.019	-0.009	0.029	0.116	0.013	-0.004	-0.002	-0.054	0.014	-0.003	0.002	-0.039
2A												
2AX	-0.010	-0.014	0.005	0.065	0.005	0.003	0.006	-0.034	0.005	-0.003	0.002	-0.043
2B												
2BX	-0.013	-0.011	-0.006	-0.049	0.008	0.002	0.009	0.033	0.008	0.002	0.004	0.008
3												
3X	-0.009	-0.003	0.065	0.141	0.005	-0.003	0.010	0.083	0.005	-0.010	0.009	0.023

Shock J. Japanese Aggregate Supply

1
1X
2A
2AX
2B
2BX
3
3X

856

Shock and Regime	Real GNP 1st Qtr	6th Qtr	18th Qtr	36th Qtr	GNP Deflator 1st Qtr	6th Qtr	18th Qtr	36th Qtr	Inflation Rate 1st Qtr	6th Qtr	18th Qtr	36th Qtr
Shock H. German Aggregate Supply												
1												
1X												
2A												
2AX												
2B												
2BX												
3												
3X												
Shock E. Oil Price Increase												
1												
1X	-0.200	-0.065	0.059	-0.069	-0.510	-0.004	0.014	0.082	-0.515	0.071	0.025	0.027
2A												
2AX	-0.249	-0.053	0.065	-0.001	-0.456	-0.050	-0.010	0.025	-0.460	0.014	0.020	-0.002
2B												
2BX	-0.206	-0.100	0.054	0.042	-0.503	-0.035	-0.027	0.010	-0.508	-0.015	0.015	0.007
3												
3X	-0.239	0.012	0.031	-0.096	-0.464	-0.036	0.026	-0.016	-0.469	0.071	0.017	-0.020
Shock L. U.S. Money Demand												
1												
1X												
2A												
2AX												
2B												
2BX												
3												
3X												
Shock D. Japanese Money Demand												
1												
1X	-0.202	-0.373	0.000	0.035	0.227	-0.078	-0.160	-0.040	0.229	-0.025	0.001	0.049
2A												
2AX	0.000	-0.000	0.000	0.001	-0.000	-0.000	-0.000	-0.001	-0.000	-0.000	0.000	-0.001
2B												
2BX	0.000	0.000	-0.000	0.000	0.000	-0.000	-0.000	-0.000	0.000	0.000	0.000	0.000
3												
3X	0.000	0.000	0.000	-0.000	0.000	0.000	0.000	0.000	0.000	-0.000	-0.000	-0.000
Shock K. German Money Demand												
1												
1X												
2A												
2AX												
2B												
2BX												
3												
3X												
Shock F. U.S. Money Supply-Permanent												
FIXM												
1												
1X												

MCM MODEL
EFFECTS ON JAPANESE INTEREST RATES AND JAPANESE CURRENT ACCOUNT/GNP RATIO
(Deviations from Baseline)

Shock and Regime	Short Interest Rate				Long Interest Rate				Current Account/GNP Ratio			
	1st Qtr	6th Qtr	18th Qtr	36th Qtr	1st Qtr	6th Qtr	18th Qtr	36th Qtr	1st Qtr	6th Qtr	18th Qtr	36th Qtr

Shock A. US Aggregate Demand

1												
1X	0.030	0.060	0.015	0.025	0.000	0.038	0.005	0.022	0.030	0.047	0.030	0.040
2A												
2AX	0.025	0.021	0.008	0.004	-0.000	0.015	0.005	0.007	0.080	0.032	0.021	0.171
2B												
2BX	0.061	0.018	-0.004	-0.029	0.000	0.020	-0.005	-0.020	0.087	0.029	0.014	-0.012
3												
3X	-0.009	-0.034	-0.082	-0.128	-0.000	-0.016	-0.058	-0.083	0.103	0.021	0.010	0.009

Shock I. Japanese Aggregate Demand

1
1X
2A
2AX
2B
2BX
3
3X

Shock G. German Aggregate Demand

1
1X
2A
2AX
2B
2BX
3
3X

Shock B. GlobAJ Aggregate Demand

1												
1X	0.399	0.093	-0.013	0.014	0.000	0.115	-0.013	0.008	-0.007	0.030	0.042	0.050
2A												
2AX	0.239	0.050	-0.004	-0.014	-0.000	0.065	0.000	-0.004	0.021	0.019	0.030	0.248
2B												
2BX	0.252	0.035	-0.021	-0.047	0.000	0.065	-0.018	-0.033	0.026	0.018	0.018	-0.018
3												
3X	-0.000	0.004	-0.117	-0.167	-0.000	0.003	-0.073	-0.115	0.018	0.009	0.016	0.007

Shock C. US Aggregate Supply

1												
1X	-0.000	-0.005	0.008	-0.008	0.000	-0.003	0.007	0.016	0.004	-0.006	0.003	-0.016
2A												
2AX	-0.001	-0.002	0.002	0.006	-0.000	-0.002	0.001	0.004	-0.003	0.002	0.004	-0.049
2B												
2BX	-0.005	0.001	0.002	-0.008	0.000	-0.004	-0.002	-0.007	-0.001	0.000	0.001	-0.005
3												
3X	0.003	-0.017	-0.015	-0.042	-0.000	-0.003	-0.013	-0.024	-0.004	0.003	0.005	0.011

Shock J. Japanese Aggregate Supply

1
1X
2A
2AX
2B
2BX
3
3X

Shock and Regime	Short Interest Rate				Long Interest Rate				Current Account/GNP Ratio			
	1st Qtr	6th Qtr	18th Qtr	36th Qtr	1st Qtr	6th Qtr	18th Qtr	36th Qtr	1st Qtr	6th Qtr	18th Qtr	36th Qtr

Shock H. German Aggregate Supply

1												
1X												
2A												
2AX												
2B												
2BX												
3												
3X												

Shock E. Oil Price Increase

	1st Qtr	6th Qtr	18th Qtr	36th Qtr	1st Qtr	6th Qtr	18th Qtr	36th Qtr	1st Qtr	6th Qtr	18th Qtr	36th Qtr
1												
1X	-0.211	-0.029	0.025	0.022	0.000	-0.035	0.015	0.003	-0.465	-0.008	-0.012	0.018
2A												
2AX	-0.141	-0.021	0.011	0.005	-0.000	-0.022	0.005	0.005	-0.417	-0.026	-0.007	-0.025
2B												
2BX	-0.198	-0.039	0.012	0.007	0.000	-0.009	0.010	0.008	-0.459	-0.035	-0.006	0.001
3												
3X	-0.043	-0.047	0.040	0.040	-0.000	-0.068	0.033	0.028	-0.420	-0.005	-0.014	-0.002

Shock L. U.S. Money Demand

1												
1X												
2A												
2AX												
2B												
2BX												
3												
3X												

Shock D. Japanese Money Demand

	1st Qtr	6th Qtr	18th Qtr	36th Qtr	1st Qtr	6th Qtr	18th Qtr	36th Qtr	1st Qtr	6th Qtr	18th Qtr	36th Qtr
1												
1X	1.453	-0.155	-0.055	0.016	0.000	0.134	-0.058	-0.008	0.224	-0.004	0.001	0.035
2A												
2AX	-0.000	-0.000	0.000	0.000	-0.000	-0.000	-0.000	0.000	0.000	-0.000	-0.000	-0.000
2B												
2BX	0.000	-0.000	-0.000	0.000	0.000	0.000	0.000	-0.000	-0.000	-0.000	-0.000	-0.000
3												
3X	-0.000	0.000	-0.000	0.000	-0.000	0.000	-0.000	-0.000	-0.000	-0.000	0.000	-0.000

Shock K. German Money Demand

1												
1X												
2A												
2AX												
2B												
2BX												
3												
3X												

Shock F. U.S. Money Supply-Permanent

FIXM												
1												
1X												

859

MCM MODEL
EFFECTS ON GERMAN REAL GNP, GERMAN PRICE LEVEL, GERMAN INFLATION RATE
(Deviations from Baseline)

Shock and Regime	Real GNP				GNP Deflator				Inflation Rate			
	1st Qtr	6th Qtr	18th Qtr	36th Qtr	1st Qtr	6th Qtr	18th Qtr	36th Qtr	1st Qtr	6th Qtr	18th Qtr	36th Qtr
Shock A. US Aggregate Demand												
1												
1X	0.054	0.045	-0.015	-0.020	-0.055	0.005	0.050	0.041	-0.057	-0.032	0.014	-0.020
2A												
2AX	0.102	0.070	-0.019	-0.524	-0.029	0.038	0.113	0.908	-0.030	0.006	0.034	0.571
2B												
2BX	0.107	0.067	-0.011	-0.064	-0.018	0.027	0.116	0.480	-0.019	0.010	0.040	0.127
3												
3X	0.120	0.064	0.067	0.240	0.005	0.026	0.073	0.282	0.006	0.021	0.021	0.079
Shock I. Japanese Aggregate Demand												
1												
1X												
2A												
2AX												
2B												
2BX												
3												
3X												
Shock G. German Aggregate Demand												
1												
1X												
2A												
2AX												
2B												
2BX												
3												
3X												
Shock B. Global Aggregate Demand												
1												
1X	0.977	0.067	-0.088	-0.103	-0.024	0.087	0.190	0.231	-0.025	0.050	0.033	-0.012
2A												
2AX	1.012	0.092	-0.064	-0.890	0.017	0.111	0.256	1.474	0.017	0.073	0.056	0.881
2B												
2BX	1.020	0.089	-0.039	-0.093	0.022	0.102	0.254	0.732	0.023	0.070	0.061	0.155
3												
3X	1.028	0.111	0.010	0.186	0.028	0.101	0.224	0.512	0.030	0.073	0.046	0.090
Shock C. US Aggregate Supply												
1												
1X	0.003	-0.003	0.007	0.066	0.006	-0.004	0.001	-0.094	0.006	0.005	0.001	-0.070
2A												
2AX	-0.005	-0.002	0.009	0.126	0.001	0.003	0.022	-0.124	0.001	0.006	0.009	-0.171
2B												
2BX	-0.003	-0.000	0.010	-0.010	0.004	-0.001	0.028	0.170	0.004	0.008	0.014	0.049
3												
3X	-0.005	-0.002	0.031	0.086	0.000	-0.002	0.002	0.056	0.000	-0.000	0.004	0.023
Shock J. Japanese Aggregate Supply												
1												
1X												
2A												
2AX												
2B												
2BX												
3												
3X												

Shock and Regime	Real GNP				GNP Deflator				Inflation Rate			
	1st Qtr	6th Qtr	18th Qtr	36th Qtr	1st Qtr	6th Qtr	18th Qtr	36th Qtr	1st Qtr	6th Qtr	18th Qtr	36th Qtr

Shock H. German Aggregate Supply

1
1X
2A
2AX
2B
2BX
3
3X

Shock E. Oil Price Increase

1												
1X	0.030	-0.079	0.046	-0.007	-0.346	-0.035	-0.062	0.067	-0.362	0.078	0.018	0.068
2A												
2AX	0.073	-0.063	0.043	0.048	-0.377	-0.022	-0.070	-0.081	-0.395	0.001	0.016	-0.025
2B												
2BX	0.037	-0.077	0.036	0.020	-0.366	-0.040	-0.072	-0.075	-0.384	0.048	0.013	0.003
3												
3X	0.064	-0.050	0.041	0.011	-0.398	-0.055	-0.056	-0.012	-0.416	-0.026	0.016	0.014

Shock L. U.S. Money Demand

1
1X
2A
2AX
2B
2BX
3
3X

Shock D. Japanese Money Demand

1												
1X	0.108	-0.007	-0.009	-0.072	-0.011	0.009	0.019	0.082	-0.012	-0.049	0.001	0.045
2A												
2AX	-0.000	-0.000	0.000	0.001	0.000	0.000	0.001	0.000	0.000	0.000	0.000	-0.001
2B												
2BX	0.000	-0.000	-0.000	-0.000	0.000	0.001	0.001	0.001	0.000	0.000	0.000	-0.000
3												
3X	0.000	-0.000	-0.000	0.000	0.000	0.000	0.000	0.000	-0.000	0.000	0.000	0.000

Shock K. German Money Demand

1
1X
2A
2AX
2B
2BX
3
3X

Shock F. U.S. Money Supply-Permanent

FIXM
1
1X

Table A-MCM-6
MCM MODEL
EFFECTS ON GERMAN INTEREST RATES AND GERMAN CURRENT ACCOUNT/GNP RATIO
(Deviations from Baseline)

Shock and Regime	Short Interest Rate				Long Interest Rate				Current Account/GNP Ratio			
	1st Qtr	6th Qtr	18th Qtr	36th Qtr	1st Qtr	6th Qtr	18th Qtr	36th Qtr	1st Qtr	6th Qtr	18th Qtr	36th Qtr

Shock A. US Aggregate Demand

1												
1X	0.219	0.005	0.032	0.043	0.057	0.018	0.011	0.021	-0.043	0.014	0.006	0.005
2A												
2AX	0.015	0.021	0.019	0.076	0.004	0.009	0.010	0.031	0.014	0.042	0.045	0.137
2B												
2BX	0.062	0.004	0.004	0.008	0.016	0.005	0.002	0.003	0.045	0.028	0.050	0.140
3												
3X	0.006	-0.027	-0.098	-0.160	0.002	-0.007	-0.050	-0.088	0.098	0.015	0.022	0.026

Shock I. Japanese Aggregate Demand

1
1X
2A
2AX
2B
2BX
3
3X

Shock G. German Aggregate Demand

1
1X
2A
2AX
2B
2BX
3
3X

Shock B. Global Aggregate Demand

1												
1X	0.371	0.104	0.069	0.055	0.097	0.054	0.035	0.035	-0.345	-0.001	0.017	0.020
2A												
2AX	0.205	0.041	0.038	0.114	0.053	0.025	0.020	0.049	-0.257	0.011	0.059	0.145
2B												
2BX	0.217	0.020	-0.002	0.010	0.057	0.021	-0.001	0.002	-0.241	-0.001	0.059	0.157
3												
3X	0.007	-0.012	-0.080	-0.156	0.002	-0.002	-0.039	-0.083	-0.244	0.003	0.036	0.044

Shock C. US Aggregate Supply

1												
1X	-0.024	-0.002	0.013	0.093	-0.006	-0.002	0.006	0.029	0.013	-0.002	-0.001	0.018
2A												
2AX	-0.001	0.000	0.006	0.001	-0.000	-0.000	0.003	0.005	0.000	0.011	0.012	-0.000
2B												
2BX	-0.008	0.001	0.005	0.010	-0.002	-0.001	0.002	0.004	0.006	0.008	0.017	0.053
3												
3X	0.003	-0.019	-0.020	-0.052	0.001	-0.006	-0.011	-0.026	-0.002	0.001	0.003	0.006

Shock J. Japanese Aggregate Supply

1
1X
2A
2AX
2B
2BX
3
3X

Shock and Regime	Short Interest Rate				Long Interest Rate				Current Account/GNP Ratio			
	1st Qtr	6th Qtr	18th Qtr	36th Qtr	1st Qtr	6th Qtr	18th Qtr	36th Qtr	1st Qtr	6th Qtr	18th Qtr	36th Qtr

Shock H. German Aggregate Supply

1
1X
2A
2AX
2B
2BX
3
3X

Shock E. Oil Price Increase

1												
1X	0.318	-0.105	-0.010	-0.039	0.083	-0.029	-0.011	-0.009	-0.304	-0.012	-0.027	-0.015
2A												
2AX	-0.061	-0.017	-0.005	-0.007	-0.016	-0.011	-0.005	-0.004	-0.395	0.058	-0.029	-0.031
2B												
2BX	0.190	-0.042	0.008	-0.002	0.049	-0.014	0.002	0.001	-0.363	-0.006	-0.027	-0.025
3												
3X	-0.035	-0.086	-0.008	0.059	-0.009	-0.032	-0.007	0.027	-0.438	0.002	-0.028	0.004

Shock L. U.S. Money Demand

1
1X
2A
2AX
2B
2BX
3
3X

Shock D. Japanese Money Demand

1												
1X	0.132	-0.003	-0.001	-0.059	0.034	0.004	-0.002	-0.014	0.040	-0.023	0.006	-0.023
2A												
2AX	0.000	0.000	0.000	0.000	0.000	0.000	0.000	0.000	-0.000	0.000	0.000	0.000
2B												
2BX	0.000	0.000	0.000	0.000	0.000	0.000	0.000	0.000	0.000	0.000	-0.000	-0.000
3												
3X	-0.000	0.000	0.000	-0.000	-0.000	0.000	-0.000	-0.000	0.000	0.000	-0.000	0.000

Shock K. German Money Demand

1
1X
2A
2AX
2B
2BX
3
3X

Shock F. U.S. Money Supply-Permanent

FIXM
1
1X

MCM MODEL
BILATERAL DOLLAR EXCHANGE RATES
(Deviations from Baseline)

Shock and Regime	Bilateral DM/$ Exchange Rate				Bilateral Yen/$ Exchange Rate			
	1st Qtr	6th Qtr	18th Qtr	36th Qtr	1st Qtr	6th Qtr	18th Qtr	36th Qtr
Shock A. US Aggregate Demand								
1								
1X	-1.173	-0.174	-0.000	-0.197	-1.667	0.076	-0.039	-0.266
2A								
2AX	-0.641	0.080	0.480	4.483	-0.564	0.136	0.498	4.717
2B								
2BX	-0.439	-0.003	0.588	1.422	-0.396	0.100	0.624	1.781
3								
3X	-0.005	0.024	0.067	0.079	-0.000	0.028	0.065	0.074
Shock I. Japanese Aggregate Demand								
1								
1X								
2A								
2AX								
2B								
2BX								
3								
3X								
Shock G. German Aggregate Demand								
1								
1X								
2A								
2AX								
2B								
2BX								
3								
3X								
Shock B. Global Aggregate Demand								
1								
1X	-0.912	-0.203	-0.016	-0.130	-0.813	-0.135	0.000	-0.082
2A								
2AX	-0.186	0.028	0.469	6.490	-0.065	0.032	0.605	6.948
2B								
2BX	-0.063	-0.061	0.521	1.461	0.063	-0.038	0.709	2.064
3								
3X	-0.006	0.016	0.065	0.078	-0.003	0.011	0.080	0.087
Shock C. US Aggregate Supply								
1								
1X	0.108	0.029	-0.031	-0.576	0.175	0.009	-0.041	-0.921
2A								
2AX	0.007	0.133	0.156	-1.170	0.005	0.118	0.166	-1.107
2B								
2BX	0.058	0.135	0.242	0.504	0.066	0.129	0.255	0.646
3								
3X	-0.004	0.017	0.018	0.029	-0.004	0.017	0.017	0.028
Shock J. Japanese Aggregate Supply								
1								
1X								
2A								
2AX								
2B								
2BX								
3								
3X								

Shock and Regime	Bilateral DM/$ Exchange Rate				Bilateral Yen/$ Exchange Rate			
	1st Qtr	6th Qtr	18th Qtr	36th Qtr	1st Qtr	6th Qtr	18th Qtr	36th Qtr
Shock H. German Aggregate Supply								
1								
1X								
2A								
2AX								
2B								
2BX								
3								
3X								
Shock E. Oil Price Increase								
1								
1X	0.851	-0.092	0.033	0.405	-0.660	-0.013	-0.001	0.619
2A								
2AX	0.413	0.082	-0.057	-0.260	0.206	-0.081	-0.116	-0.296
2B								
2BX	0.513	-0.075	-0.042	-0.058	-0.587	-0.136	-0.120	-0.135
3								
3X	0.030	-0.009	-0.004	0.012	0.033	-0.018	-0.019	0.016
Shock L. U.S. Money Demand								
1								
1X								
2A								
2AX								
2B								
2BX								
3								
3X								
Shock D. Japanese Money Demand								
1								
1X	0.318	-0.042	0.053	0.327	4.251	-0.313	0.179	0.617
2A								
2AX	-0.001	-0.000	-0.001	-0.010	0.000	0.000	0.000	-0.009
2B								
2BX	-0.000	-0.001	-0.003	-0.004	0.001	-0.001	-0.001	-0.002
3								
3X	0.000	-0.000	-0.000	0.000	0.000	-0.000	0.000	0.000
Shock K. German Money Demand								
1								
1X								
2A								
2AX								
2B								
2BX								
3								
3X								
Shock F. U.S. Money Supply-Permanent								
FIXM								
1								
1X								

MPS MODEL
EFFECTS ON U.S. REAL GNP, U.S. PRICE LEVEL, U.S. INFLATION RATE
(Deviations from Baseline)

Shock and Regime	Real GNP				GNP Deflator				Inflation Rate			
	1st Qtr	6th Qtr	18th Qtr	38th Qtr	1st Qtr	6th Qtr	18th Qtr	38th Qtr	1st Qtr	6th Qtr	18th Qtr	38th Qtr
Shock A. US Aggregate Demand												
1	1.08	0.00	-0.10	-0.13	-0.17	0.18	0.16	-0.06	0.14	0.20	-0.06	-0.08
1X	1.08	0.06	-0.08	-0.13	-0.17	0.19	0.32	0.23	0.09	0.21	0.00	-0.06
2A	0.94	-0.17	0.09	0.05	-0.21	0.09	-0.01	-0.03	1.32	0.07	0.00	0.00
2AX	0.89	-0.18	0.05	0.04	-0.22	0.06	-0.01	-0.02	1.67	0.03	0.02	0.02
2B	0.96	-0.19	0.06	-0.01	-0.20	0.09	0.06	0.10	1.13	0.09	0.04	0.02
2BX	0.89	-0.14	0.01	0.00	-0.22	0.06	0.04	0.03	1.67	0.04	0.03	0.00
3												
3X												
Shock I. Japanese Aggregate Demand												
1												
1X												
2A												
2AX												
2B												
2BX												
3												
3X												
Shock G. German Aggregate Demand												
1												
1X												
2A												
2AX												
2B												
2BX												
3												
3X												
Shock B. Global Aggregate Demand												
1												
1X												
2A												
2AX												
2B												
2BX												
3												
3X												
Shock C. US Aggregate Supply												
1	0.22	-0.15	-0.12	0.14	0.27	0.30	0.12	-0.36	0.23	0.16	-0.08	-0.06
1X	0.23	-0.10	-0.07	-0.05	0.27	0.32	0.27	-0.11	0.14	0.18	-0.01	-0.11
2A	0.20	-0.29	0.04	0.10	0.26	0.27	-0.01	-0.10	0.40	0.12	-0.06	0.04
2AX	0.19	-0.30	0.03	0.09	0.26	0.26	-0.01	-0.08	0.51	0.11	-0.05	0.04
2B	0.17	-0.26	-0.03	-0.05	0.25	0.26	0.20	0.15	0.65	0.11	0.06	0.01
2BX	0.19	-0.13	-0.01	-0.01	0.26	0.29	0.32	0.36	0.51	0.15	0.05	0.00
3												
3X												
Shock J. Japanese Aggregate Supply												
1												
1X												
2A												
2AX												
2B												
2BX												
3												
3X												

866

Shock and	Real GNP				GNP Deflator				Inflation Rate			
Regime	1st Qtr	6th Qtr	18th Qtr	38th Qtr	1st Qtr	6th Qtr	18th Qtr	38th Qtr	1st Qtr	6th Qtr	18th Qtr	38th Qtr

Shock H. German Aggregate Supply
1
1X
2A
2AX
2B
2BX
3
3X

Shock E. Oil Price Increase

1	0.06	0.00	-0.19	0.12	-0.21	0.11	0.19	-0.23	0.09	-0.01	-0.01	-0.05
1X	0.07	0.01	-0.10	-0.01	-0.21	0.11	0.28	0.05	0.06	0.00	0.05	-0.06
2A	0.07	-0.07	-0.08	0.01	-0.21	0.09	0.05	-0.03	0.03	-0.02	-0.05	0.01
2AX	0.07	-0.08	-0.05	0.01	-0.21	0.09	0.03	-0.02	0.04	-0.03	-0.04	0.01
2B	0.09	0.05	-0.06	-0.01	-0.20	0.08	0.15	0.19	-0.16	-0.08	0.01	0.00
2BX	0.07	0.07	-0.02	0.02	-0.21	0.11	0.21	0.34	0.04	-0.03	0.02	0.02
3												
3X												

Shock L. U.S. Money Demand

1	-0.28	-0.94	1.26	-0.13	-0.08	-0.31	-1.48	1.03	2.25	-0.44	-0.10	0.55
1X	-0.16	-0.61	0.54	0.11	-0.05	-0.19	-1.06	-0.13	1.41	-0.23	-0.16	0.27
2A	0.00	0.00	0.00	0.00	0.00	0.00	0.00	-0.01	0.00	0.00	0.00	0.00
2AX	0.00	0.00	0.00	0.00	0.00	0.00	0.00	0.00	0.00	0.00	0.00	0.00
2B	0.00	0.00	0.00	0.00	0.00	0.00	0.00	0.00	0.00	0.00	0.00	0.00
2BX	0.00	0.00	0.00	0.00	0.00	0.00	0.00	0.00	0.00	0.00	0.00	0.00
3												
3X												

Shock D. Japanese Money Demand
1
1X
2A
2AX
2B
2BX
3
3X

Shock K. German Money Demand
1
1X
2A
2AX
2B
2BX
3
3X

Shock F. U.S. Money Supply-Permanent

FIXM	0.24	0.63	-0.13	-0.24	0.02	0.18	1.54	1.55	0.08	0.19	0.50	-0.20
1												
1X												

Table A-MPS-2
MPS MODEL
EFFECTS ON U.S. INTEREST RATES AND U.S. CURRENT ACCOUNT/GNP RATIO
(Deviations from Baseline)

Shock and Regime	Short Interest Rate				Long Interest Rate				Current Account/GNP Ratio			
	1st Qtr	6th Qtr	18th Qtr	38th Qtr	1st Qtr	6th Qtr	18th Qtr	38th Qtr	1st Qtr	6th Qtr	18th Qtr	38th Qtr

Shock A. US Aggregate Demand
1	0.03	0.09	0.05	-0.11	-0.13	0.06	0.03	-0.02	-0.13	0.01	0.03	0.04
1X	0.02	0.05	0.09	-0.01	-0.13	0.05	0.06	0.04	-0.13	0.00	0.03	0.05
2A	0.26	-0.13	0.12	0.03	-0.14	0.03	0.01	-0.01	-0.14	0.03	0.00	0.00
2AX	0.33	-0.23	0.08	0.03	-0.15	0.00	0.01	-0.01	-0.15	0.05	-0.01	-0.02
2B	0.22	-0.15	0.15	0.02	-0.14	0.03	0.04	0.01	-0.14	0.02	0.01	0.00
2BX	0.32	-0.26	0.04	0.00	-0.15	-0.01	0.01	0.00	-0.15	0.05	-0.01	0.00
3												
3X												

Shock I. Japanese Aggregate Demand
1												
1X												
2A												
2AX												
2B												
2BX												
3												
3X												

Shock G. German Aggregate Demand
1												
1X												
2A												
2AX												
2B												
2BX												
3												
3X												

Shock B. Global Aggregate Demand
1												
1X												
2A												
2AX												
2B												
2BX												
3												
3X												

Shock C. US Aggregate Supply
1	0.06	0.06	0.02	-0.15	-0.06	0.04	0.04	-0.10	-0.06	0.03	0.00	-0.03
1X	0.05	0.04	0.07	-0.08	-0.06	0.03	0.06	-0.04	-0.06	0.02	0.00	0.02
2A	0.09	-0.02	0.05	0.01	-0.06	0.04	0.01	-0.03	-0.06	0.04	-0.01	-0.02
2AX	0.11	-0.09	0.04	0.01	-0.06	0.03	0.01	-0.03	-0.06	0.04	-0.01	-0.02
2B	0.14	-0.22	0.05	-0.07	-0.06	0.00	0.06	0.00	-0.06	0.05	0.00	0.00
2BX	0.12	-0.18	0.00	-0.01	-0.06	0.00	0.05	0.03	-0.06	0.04	0.00	0.03
3												
3X												

Shock J. Japanese Aggregate Supply
1												
1X												
2A												
2AX												
2B												
2BX												
3												
3X												

Shock and Regime	Short Interest Rate				Long Interest Rate				Current Account/GNP Ratio			
	1st Qtr	6th Qtr	18th Qtr	38th Qtr	1st Qtr	6th Qtr	18th Qtr	38th Qtr	1st Qtr	6th Qtr	18th Qtr	38th Qtr

Shock H. German Aggregate Supply

Regime												
1												
1X												
2A												
2AX												
2B												
2BX												
3												
3X												

Shock E. Oil Price Increase

Regime												
1	0.05	0.06	0.01	-0.07	0.05	0.02	0.07	-0.06	-0.13	0.00	0.03	-0.03
1X	0.05	0.05	0.05	0.00	0.05	0.02	0.08	0.00	-0.13	0.00	0.02	0.01
2A	0.04	0.04	-0.04	-0.01	0.04	0.02	0.02	0.00	-0.13	0.01	0.01	0.00
2AX	0.05	0.03	-0.04	-0.01	0.05	0.02	0.02	0.00	-0.13	0.01	0.01	0.00
2B	0.01	-0.04	-0.06	-0.01	0.01	-0.02	0.03	0.02	-0.13	0.02	0.00	0.02
2BX	0.05	0.12	-0.04	0.05	0.05	0.02	0.03	0.05	-0.13	0.01	0.00	0.03
3												
3X												

Shock L. U.S. Money Demand

Regime												
1	0.44	-0.51	-0.13	0.53	-0.02	-0.03	-0.40	0.26	-0.02	0.15	-0.21	0.08
1X	0.27	-0.34	-0.07	0.06	-0.01	-0.02	-0.23	-0.01	-0.01	0.07	-0.11	-0.02
2A	0.00	0.00	0.00	0.00	0.00	0.00	0.00	0.00	0.00	0.00	0.00	0.00
2AX	0.00	0.00	0.00	0.00	0.00	0.00	0.00	0.00	0.00	0.00	0.00	0.00
2B	0.00	0.00	0.00	0.00	0.00	0.00	0.00	0.00	0.00	0.00	0.00	0.00
2BX	0.00	0.00	0.00	0.00	0.00	0.00	0.00	0.00	0.00	0.00	0.00	0.00
3												
3X												

Shock D. Japanese Money Demand

Regime												
1												
1X												
2A												
2AX												
2B												
2BX												
3												
3X												

Shock K. German Money Demand

Regime												
1												
1X												
2A												
2AX												
2B												
2BX												
3												
3X												

Shock F. U.S. Money Supply-Permanent

Regime												
FIXM	-2.11	-0.14	0.32	0.37	-0.39	-0.08	0.31	0.27	0.02	-0.05	0.08	0.12
1												
1X												

MSG MODEL
EFFECTS ON U.S. REAL GNP, U.S. PRICE LEVEL, U.S. INFLATION RATE
(Deviations from Baseline)

Shock and Regime	Real GNP				GNP Deflator				Inflation Rate			
	1st Yr	2nd Yr	5th Yr	10th Yr	1st Yr	2nd Yr	5th Yr	10th Yr	1st Yr	2nd Yr	5th Yr	10th Yr
Shock A. US Aggregate Demand												
1	1.466	-0.253	-0.020	0.043	0.673	0.424	0.020	-0.096	0.673	-0.250	-0.092	0.003
1X	1.324	-0.242	-0.024	0.033	0.583	0.368	0.025	-0.070	0.583	-0.215	-0.078	0.003
2A	1.377	-0.247	-0.022	0.037	0.617	0.389	0.023	-0.079	0.617	-0.228	-0.083	0.003
2AX	0.128	-0.027	-0.125	-0.046	-0.128	0.027	0.125	0.046	-0.128	0.156	-0.002	-0.013
2B	1.500	-0.043	-0.021	-0.011	0.703	0.682	0.729	0.829	0.703	-0.021	0.021	0.018
2BX	0.209	-0.103	-0.064	-0.040	-0.079	-0.015	0.184	0.422	-0.079	0.064	0.061	0.039
3	1.450	-0.247	-0.014	0.037	0.689	0.419	0.015	-0.080	0.689	-0.270	-0.086	0.003
3X	1.292	-0.236	-0.010	0.026	0.633	0.381	0.010	-0.047	0.633	-0.252	-0.075	0.007
Shock I. Japanese Aggregate Demand												
1	0.061	-0.016	0.032	0.026	0.102	0.065	-0.045	-0.049	0.102	-0.037	-0.024	0.006
1X	0.047	-0.017	0.034	0.026	0.100	0.063	-0.045	-0.044	0.100	-0.038	-0.022	0.007
2A	0.052	-0.017	0.033	0.026	0.101	0.064	-0.045	-0.046	0.101	-0.038	-0.023	0.007
2AX	-0.082	-0.031	0.062	0.026	0.082	0.031	-0.062	-0.026	0.082	-0.051	-0.012	0.008
2B	0.056	0.022	0.010	0.007	0.099	0.099	0.001	-0.160	0.099	0.000	-0.036	-0.029
2BX	-0.124	0.035	0.027	0.014	0.053	0.067	0.002	-0.088	0.053	0.013	-0.024	-0.014
3	0.072	-0.019	0.023	0.018	0.075	0.044	-0.034	-0.035	0.075	-0.032	-0.014	0.004
3X	0.061	-0.019	0.024	0.017	0.072	0.041	-0.033	-0.029	0.072	-0.031	-0.012	0.004
Shock G. German Aggregate Demand												
1	0.035	-0.007	0.014	0.011	0.068	0.043	-0.022	-0.020	0.068	-0.025	-0.015	0.005
1X	0.024	-0.008	0.015	0.008	0.067	0.038	-0.021	-0.011	0.067	-0.029	-0.012	0.005
2A	0.028	-0.008	0.015	0.009	0.068	0.040	-0.021	-0.014	0.068	-0.028	-0.013	0.005
2AX	-0.074	0.002	0.012	-0.023	0.074	-0.002	-0.012	0.023	0.074	-0.076	0.010	0.003
2B	0.033	0.016	0.005	0.003	0.064	0.055	0.029	0.021	0.064	-0.009	-0.007	0.002
2BX	-0.087	0.030	0.005	-0.004	0.054	0.044	0.023	0.030	0.054	-0.010	-0.004	0.004
3	0.054	-0.010	0.009	0.022	0.046	0.038	-0.014	-0.049	0.046	-0.008	-0.017	-0.001
3X	0.046	-0.011	0.010	0.022	0.043	0.035	-0.014	-0.042	0.043	-0.008	-0.016	0.000
Shock B. Global Aggregate Demand												
1	1.562	-0.277	0.026	0.080	0.844	0.531	-0.047	-0.165	0.844	-0.312	-0.130	0.014
1X	1.394	-0.267	0.025	0.066	0.751	0.469	-0.042	-0.124	0.751	-0.282	-0.112	0.015
2A	1.457	-0.271	0.026	0.071	0.785	0.492	-0.044	-0.138	0.785	-0.293	-0.118	0.015
2AX	-0.027	-0.056	-0.051	-0.043	0.027	0.056	0.051	0.043	0.027	0.028	-0.003	-0.002
2B	1.588	-0.006	-0.006	-0.001	0.866	0.835	0.758	0.690	0.866	-0.030	-0.022	-0.009
2BX	-0.002	-0.038	-0.032	-0.030	0.029	0.096	0.209	0.364	0.029	0.067	0.032	0.030
3	1.576	-0.277	0.018	0.077	0.811	0.501	-0.033	-0.164	0.811	-0.310	-0.117	0.006
3X	1.399	-0.267	0.025	0.064	0.748	0.457	-0.037	-0.119	0.748	-0.291	-0.103	0.011
Shock C. US Aggregate Supply												
1	-0.646	-0.168	0.280	0.142	1.196	0.404	-0.424	-0.243	1.196	-0.792	-0.113	0.063
1X	-0.685	-0.173	0.287	0.133	1.172	0.381	-0.402	-0.207	1.172	-0.791	-0.098	0.060
2A	-0.671	-0.171	0.284	0.137	1.181	0.390	-0.410	-0.220	1.181	-0.791	-0.103	0.061
2AX	-0.995	-0.210	0.315	0.085	0.995	0.210	-0.315	-0.085	0.995	-0.785	-0.018	0.037
2B	-0.527	0.087	0.096	0.070	1.288	0.765	-0.395	-1.816	1.288	-0.523	-0.348	-0.249
2BX	-0.952	0.228	0.147	0.070	1.042	0.742	0.196	-0.279	1.042	-0.300	-0.148	-0.069
3	-0.650	-0.163	0.281	0.136	1.188	0.386	-0.426	-0.230	1.188	-0.802	-0.103	0.061
3X	-0.690	-0.170	0.292	0.127	1.174	0.371	-0.413	-0.194	1.174	-0.803	-0.091	0.060
Shock J. Japanese Aggregate Supply												
1	0.011	-0.007	0.014	0.009	0.029	0.025	-0.020	-0.016	0.029	-0.004	-0.008	0.003
1X	0.008	-0.008	0.015	0.009	0.029	0.024	-0.019	-0.014	0.029	-0.004	-0.008	0.003
2A	0.009	-0.008	0.014	0.009	0.029	0.025	-0.019	-0.015	0.029	-0.004	-0.008	0.003
2AX	-0.021	-0.014	0.022	0.008	0.021	0.014	-0.022	-0.008	0.021	-0.008	-0.004	0.003
2B	0.006	0.010	0.003	0.002	0.016	0.028	0.002	-0.046	0.016	0.012	-0.011	-0.008
2BX	-0.041	0.011	0.009	0.004	0.006	0.018	0.000	-0.029	0.006	0.012	-0.008	-0.004
3	0.013	-0.007	0.012	0.007	0.024	0.021	-0.017	-0.013	0.024	-0.003	-0.006	0.002
3X	0.010	-0.008	0.013	0.007	0.023	0.020	-0.017	-0.011	0.023	-0.003	-0.005	0.002

Shock and Regime	Real GNP				GNP Deflator				Inflation Rate			
	1st Yr	2nd Yr	5th Yr	10th Yr	1st Yr	2nd Yr	5th Yr	10th Yr	1st Yr	2nd Yr	5th Yr	10th Yr
Shock H. German Aggregate Supply												
1	0.003	-0.003	0.011	0.020	0.018	0.022	-0.022	-0.045	0.018	0.003	-0.015	0.000
1X	0.001	-0.004	0.012	0.019	0.018	0.021	-0.020	-0.037	0.018	0.003	-0.014	0.001
2A	0.002	-0.003	0.011	0.019	0.018	0.021	-0.021	-0.040	0.018	0.003	-0.014	0.001
2AX	-0.017	-0.011	0.018	0.013	0.017	0.011	-0.018	-0.013	0.017	-0.006	-0.005	0.002
2B	-0.006	0.007	-0.002	0.000	-0.003	-0.012	-0.007	0.061	-0.003	-0.009	0.006	0.018
2BX	-0.016	0.032	0.003	0.000	0.005	-0.014	-0.034	-0.039	0.005	-0.019	-0.004	0.000
3	0.005	-0.002	0.007	0.020	0.012	0.018	-0.014	-0.047	0.012	0.006	-0.013	-0.002
3X	0.004	-0.003	0.009	0.021	0.012	0.017	-0.014	-0.041	0.012	0.005	-0.012	-0.001
Shock E. Oil Price Increase												
1	1.562	-0.277	0.026	0.080	0.844	0.531	-0.047	-0.165	0.844	-0.312	-0.130	0.014
1X	1.394	-0.267	0.025	0.066	0.751	0.469	-0.042	-0.124	0.751	-0.282	-0.112	0.015
2A	1.457	-0.271	0.026	0.071	0.785	0.492	-0.044	-0.138	0.785	-0.293	-0.118	0.015
2AX	-0.027	-0.056	-0.051	-0.043	0.027	0.056	0.051	0.043	0.027	0.028	-0.003	-0.002
2B	1.588	-0.006	-0.006	-0.001	0.866	0.835	0.758	0.690	0.866	-0.030	-0.022	-0.009
2BX	-0.002	-0.038	-0.032	-0.030	0.029	0.096	0.209	0.364	0.029	0.067	0.032	0.030
3	1.576	-0.277	0.018	0.077	0.811	0.501	-0.033	-0.164	0.811	-0.310	-0.117	0.006
3X	1.399	-0.267	0.025	0.064	0.748	0.457	-0.037	-0.119	0.748	-0.291	-0.103	0.011
Shock L. U.S. Money Demand												
1	-0.202	0.030	-0.018	-0.012	-0.147	-0.074	0.018	0.015	-0.147	0.072	0.015	-0.004
1X	-0.242	0.039	-0.023	-0.014	-0.174	-0.085	0.023	0.017	-0.174	0.089	0.017	-0.005
2A	0.008	-0.002	0.000	0.000	0.004	0.002	0.000	-0.001	0.004	-0.001	-0.001	0.000
2AX	0.001	0.000	-0.001	0.000	-0.001	0.000	0.001	0.000	-0.001	0.001	0.000	0.000
2B	0.009	0.000	0.000	0.000	0.004	0.004	0.004	0.005	0.004	0.000	0.000	0.000
2BX	0.001	-0.001	0.000	0.000	0.000	0.000	0.001	0.003	0.000	0.000	0.000	0.000
3	-0.210	0.032	-0.016	-0.013	-0.133	-0.069	0.017	0.020	-0.133	0.064	0.015	-0.003
3X	-0.257	0.042	-0.018	-0.016	-0.150	-0.076	0.020	0.026	-0.150	0.074	0.017	-0.003
Shock D. Japanese Money Demand												
1	-0.003	0.001	0.003	0.002	0.008	0.006	-0.003	-0.004	0.008	-0.002	-0.003	0.001
1X	-0.004	0.001	0.003	0.003	0.009	0.006	-0.004	-0.004	0.009	-0.003	-0.003	0.001
2A	0.000	0.000	0.000	0.000	0.001	0.000	0.000	0.000	0.001	0.000	0.000	0.000
2AX	0.000	0.000	0.000	0.000	0.000	0.000	0.000	0.000	0.000	0.000	0.000	0.000
2B	0.000	0.000	0.000	0.000	0.001	0.001	0.000	-0.001	0.001	0.000	0.000	0.000
2BX	-0.001	0.000	0.000	0.000	0.000	0.000	0.000	-0.001	0.000	0.000	0.000	0.000
3	0.000	0.000	0.000	0.000	0.000	0.000	0.000	0.000	0.000	0.000	0.000	0.000
3X	0.000	0.000	0.000	0.000	0.000	0.000	0.000	0.000	0.000	0.000	0.000	0.000
Shock K. German Money Demand												
1	-0.011	0.002	0.001	-0.007	0.010	0.001	0.001	0.018	0.010	-0.009	0.003	0.002
1X	-0.013	0.002	0.001	-0.008	0.012	0.001	0.001	0.019	0.012	-0.011	0.003	0.002
2A	0.000	0.000	0.000	0.000	0.000	0.000	0.000	0.000	0.000	0.000	0.000	0.000
2AX	0.000	0.000	0.000	0.000	0.000	0.000	0.000	0.000	0.000	0.000	0.000	0.000
2B	0.000	0.000	0.000	0.000	0.000	0.000	0.000	0.000	0.000	0.000	0.000	0.000
2BX	-0.001	0.000	0.000	0.000	0.000	0.000	0.000	0.000	0.000	0.000	0.000	0.000
3	0.000	0.000	0.000	0.000	0.000	0.000	0.000	0.000	0.000	0.000	0.000	0.000
3X	0.000	0.000	0.000	0.000	0.000	0.000	0.000	0.000	0.000	0.000	0.000	0.000
Shock F. U.S. Money Supply-Permanent												
FIXM	0.415	0.261	0.017	-0.030	0.309	0.564	0.971	1.052	0.309	0.255	0.086	-0.006
1												
1X												

Shock and Regime	Short Interest Rate				Long Interest Rate				Current Account/GNP Ratio			
	1st Yr	2nd Yr	5th Yr	10th Yr	1st Yr	2nd Yr	5th Yr	10th Yr	1st Yr	2nd Yr	5th Yr	10th Yr
Shock A. US Aggregate Demand												
1	2.674	0.213	0.000	-0.067	0.274	0.003	-0.051	-0.050	-0.399	-0.028	-0.022	-0.014
1X	3.179	0.211	0.000	-0.061	0.325	0.006	-0.047	-0.046	-0.423	-0.026	-0.023	-0.015
2A	2.990	0.213	0.000	-0.063	0.306	0.005	-0.049	-0.048	-0.414	-0.027	-0.023	-0.014
2AX	7.647	-0.179	0.035	0.030	0.739	0.002	0.031	0.008	-0.626	0.003	-0.029	-0.022
2B	3.206	-0.033	0.004	0.012	0.317	0.002	0.010	0.009	-0.407	-0.001	-0.011	-0.011
2BX	7.193	0.135	0.036	0.052	0.749	0.056	0.047	0.034	-0.608	-0.013	-0.023	-0.020
3	2.675	0.215	0.002	-0.053	0.279	0.010	-0.041	-0.041	-0.400	-0.035	-0.019	-0.012
3X	3.208	0.241	0.001	-0.036	0.340	0.020	-0.028	-0.021	-0.419	-0.038	-0.019	-0.011
Shock I. Japanese Aggregate Demand												
1	0.204	0.061	-0.016	-0.029	0.012	-0.011	-0.026	-0.018	0.023	-0.009	0.000	0.001
1X	0.245	0.076	-0.018	-0.030	0.018	-0.009	-0.027	-0.018	0.021	-0.010	0.000	0.001
2A	0.230	0.070	-0.017	-0.030	0.016	-0.010	-0.026	-0.018	0.021	-0.010	0.000	0.001
2AX	0.597	0.246	-0.042	-0.033	0.066	0.004	-0.037	-0.019	0.006	-0.026	0.000	0.001
2B	0.298	-0.015	-0.040	-0.034	-0.001	-0.034	-0.034	-0.027	0.019	-0.004	0.002	0.001
2BX	0.895	0.055	-0.041	-0.025	0.070	-0.021	-0.028	-0.016	-0.006	-0.014	0.000	0.001
3	0.184	0.030	-0.014	-0.022	0.010	-0.011	-0.020	-0.015	0.022	-0.003	0.001	0.000
3X	0.221	0.036	-0.015	-0.021	0.014	-0.010	-0.019	-0.014	0.021	-0.003	0.001	0.001
Shock G. German Aggregate Demand												
1	0.129	0.044	-0.009	-0.011	0.011	-0.002	-0.010	-0.001	0.006	-0.009	0.004	0.006
1X	0.152	0.051	-0.009	-0.005	0.016	0.001	-0.005	0.005	0.005	-0.010	0.005	0.007
2A	0.143	0.049	-0.009	-0.007	0.014	0.000	-0.007	0.002	0.005	-0.010	0.005	0.007
2AX	0.301	0.100	-0.003	0.056	0.058	0.033	0.043	0.061	-0.005	-0.016	0.014	0.013
2B	0.170	-0.005	-0.004	0.008	0.016	0.000	0.006	0.015	0.004	-0.006	0.006	0.007
2BX	0.527	0.003	0.009	0.029	0.065	0.016	0.025	0.034	-0.007	-0.011	0.007	0.008
3	0.125	0.034	-0.006	-0.034	0.004	-0.011	-0.027	-0.031	0.007	-0.007	0.000	0.002
3X	0.149	0.040	-0.006	-0.034	0.008	-0.011	-0.027	-0.030	0.006	-0.007	0.001	0.003
Shock B. Global Aggregate Demand												
1	3.007	0.318	-0.025	-0.107	0.297	-0.010	-0.087	-0.070	-0.370	-0.046	-0.017	-0.006
1X	3.575	0.338	-0.027	-0.096	0.358	-0.003	-0.079	-0.060	-0.397	-0.046	-0.018	-0.006
2A	3.363	0.331	-0.026	-0.100	0.335	-0.005	-0.082	-0.064	-0.387	-0.046	-0.017	-0.006
2AX	8.545	0.167	-0.010	0.052	0.857	0.039	0.038	0.051	-0.625	-0.039	-0.014	-0.008
2B	3.674	-0.054	-0.040	-0.014	0.331	-0.032	-0.018	-0.004	-0.384	-0.011	-0.003	-0.002
2BX	8.616	0.193	0.004	0.057	0.875	0.050	0.044	0.052	-0.622	-0.038	-0.016	-0.011
3	2.983	0.280	-0.019	-0.109	0.293	-0.012	-0.088	-0.087	-0.371	-0.044	-0.017	-0.009
3X	3.578	0.317	-0.020	-0.090	0.360	0.000	-0.074	-0.065	-0.393	-0.049	-0.017	-0.008
Shock C. US Aggregate Supply												
1	0.688	0.295	-0.180	-0.126	-0.014	-0.092	-0.133	-0.051	-0.081	-0.032	0.012	0.011
1X	0.812	0.347	-0.193	-0.123	0.001	-0.089	-0.134	-0.048	-0.087	-0.033	0.012	0.010
2A	0.766	0.328	-0.188	-0.125	-0.004	-0.090	-0.134	-0.049	-0.085	-0.033	0.012	0.010
2AX	1.791	0.684	-0.285	-0.081	0.118	-0.065	-0.129	-0.025	-0.133	-0.046	0.017	0.007
2B	1.040	-0.560	-0.377	-0.272	-0.231	-0.362	-0.287	-0.215	-0.075	0.011	-0.003	0.001
2BX	2.922	-0.545	-0.264	-0.112	0.062	-0.245	-0.138	-0.067	-0.151	0.027	0.003	0.002
3	0.672	0.278	-0.182	-0.118	-0.015	-0.091	-0.128	-0.051	-0.085	-0.034	0.015	0.010
3X	0.807	0.335	-0.201	-0.111	-0.001	-0.090	-0.128	-0.043	-0.089	-0.038	0.015	0.011
Shock J. Japanese Aggregate Supply												
1	0.051	0.023	-0.007	-0.009	0.002	-0.004	-0.008	-0.005	-0.003	-0.003	0.000	0.000
1X	0.060	0.027	-0.008	-0.009	0.004	-0.003	-0.008	-0.005	-0.004	-0.003	0.000	0.000
2A	0.057	0.026	-0.008	-0.009	0.003	-0.003	-0.008	-0.005	-0.004	-0.003	0.000	0.000
2AX	0.141	0.074	-0.016	-0.010	0.015	0.000	-0.012	-0.005	-0.007	-0.006	0.000	0.000
2B	0.072	0.007	-0.013	-0.009	-0.001	-0.009	-0.010	-0.007	-0.006	-0.003	0.000	0.000
2BX	0.219	0.040	-0.016	-0.008	0.018	-0.005	-0.009	-0.005	-0.013	-0.007	0.000	0.000
3	0.046	0.016	-0.006	-0.007	0.002	-0.003	-0.006	-0.004	-0.004	-0.002	0.000	0.000
3X	0.055	0.019	-0.007	-0.006	0.003	-0.003	-0.006	-0.003	-0.004	-0.002	0.001	0.000

Shock and Regime	Short Interest Rate				Long Interest Rate				Current Account/GNP Ratio			
	1st Yr	2nd Yr	5th Yr	10th Yr	1st Yr	2nd Yr	5th Yr	10th Yr	1st Yr	2nd Yr	5th Yr	10th Yr
Shock H. German Aggregate Supply												
1	0.027	0.023	-0.014	-0.032	-0.010	-0.015	-0.027	-0.028	-0.032	-0.013	0.001	0.005
1X	0.032	0.028	-0.014	-0.031	-0.008	-0.014	-0.027	-0.027	-0.032	-0.013	0.001	0.005
2A	0.030	0.027	-0.014	-0.031	-0.009	-0.015	-0.027	-0.028	-0.032	-0.013	0.001	0.005
2AX	0.069	0.063	-0.019	-0.022	0.001	-0.008	-0.022	-0.018	-0.033	-0.015	0.003	0.006
2B	-0.003	-0.015	0.007	0.027	0.008	0.012	0.024	0.038	-0.036	-0.008	0.008	0.011
2BX	0.015	-0.073	-0.018	-0.001	-0.018	-0.019	-0.004	0.004	-0.043	-0.012	0.007	0.009
3	0.022	0.020	-0.009	-0.033	-0.009	-0.014	-0.028	-0.033	-0.033	-0.012	0.001	0.004
3X	0.026	0.024	-0.009	-0.034	-0.008	-0.014	-0.028	-0.033	-0.033	-0.012	0.001	0.004
Shock E. Oil Price Increase												
1	3.007	0.318	-0.025	-0.107	0.297	-0.010	-0.087	-0.070	-0.370	-0.046	-0.017	-0.006
1X	3.575	0.338	-0.027	-0.096	0.358	-0.003	-0.079	-0.060	-0.397	-0.046	-0.018	-0.006
2A	3.363	0.331	-0.026	-0.100	0.335	-0.005	-0.082	-0.064	-0.387	-0.046	-0.017	-0.006
2AX	8.545	0.167	-0.010	0.052	0.857	0.039	0.038	0.051	-0.625	-0.039	-0.014	-0.008
2B	3.674	-0.054	-0.040	-0.014	0.331	-0.032	-0.018	-0.004	-0.384	-0.011	-0.003	-0.002
2BX	8.616	0.193	0.004	0.057	0.875	0.050	0.044	0.052	-0.622	-0.038	-0.016	-0.011
3	2.983	0.280	-0.019	-0.109	0.293	-0.012	-0.088	-0.087	-0.371	-0.044	-0.017	-0.009
3X	3.578	0.317	-0.020	-0.090	0.360	0.000	-0.074	-0.065	-0.393	-0.049	-0.017	-0.008
Shock L. U.S. Money Demand												
1	0.814	-0.055	-0.001	0.004	0.074	-0.007	0.003	-0.002	-0.042	0.007	-0.003	-0.003
1X	0.974	-0.075	0.000	0.005	0.088	-0.009	0.004	-0.002	-0.049	0.009	-0.003	-0.003
2A	0.018	0.001	0.000	0.000	0.002	0.000	0.000	0.000	-0.002	0.000	0.000	0.000
2AX	0.046	-0.001	0.000	0.000	0.005	0.000	0.000	0.000	-0.004	0.000	0.000	0.000
2B	0.019	0.000	0.000	0.000	0.002	0.000	0.000	0.000	-0.002	0.000	0.000	0.000
2BX	0.043	0.001	0.000	0.000	0.005	0.000	0.000	0.000	-0.004	0.000	0.000	0.000
3	0.821	-0.046	0.002	0.009	0.079	-0.002	0.008	0.004	-0.041	0.005	-0.002	-0.002
3X	0.989	-0.057	0.004	0.016	0.097	0.000	0.013	0.010	-0.047	0.004	-0.002	-0.002
Shock D. Japanese Money Demand												
1	0.006	0.008	-0.001	-0.002	0.001	0.000	-0.002	-0.001	0.000	-0.002	0.000	0.000
1X	0.008	0.011	-0.001	-0.003	0.001	0.000	-0.002	-0.002	0.000	-0.002	0.000	0.000
2A	0.001	0.000	0.000	0.000	0.000	0.000	0.000	0.000	0.000	0.000	0.000	0.000
2AX	0.004	0.001	0.000	0.000	0.000	0.000	0.000	0.000	0.000	0.000	0.000	0.000
2B	0.002	0.000	0.000	0.000	0.000	0.000	0.000	0.000	0.000	0.000	0.000	0.000
2BX	0.005	0.000	0.000	0.000	0.000	0.000	0.000	0.000	0.000	0.000	0.000	0.000
3	0.001	0.000	0.000	0.000	0.000	0.000	0.000	0.000	0.000	0.000	0.000	0.000
3X	0.001	0.000	0.000	0.000	0.000	0.000	0.000	0.000	0.000	0.000	0.000	0.000
Shock K. German Money Demand												
1	0.000	0.004	0.002	0.014	0.005	0.007	0.012	0.016	-0.001	-0.001	0.002	0.002
1X	-0.002	0.005	0.002	0.017	0.006	0.008	0.014	0.019	-0.001	-0.001	0.003	0.002
2A	0.001	0.000	0.000	0.000	0.000	0.000	0.000	0.000	0.000	0.000	0.000	0.000
2AX	0.002	0.001	0.000	0.000	0.000	0.000	0.000	0.000	0.000	0.000	0.000	0.000
2B	0.001	0.000	0.000	0.000	0.000	0.000	0.000	0.000	0.000	0.000	0.000	0.000
2BX	0.003	0.000	0.000	0.000	0.000	0.000	0.000	0.000	0.000	0.000	0.000	0.000
3	0.000	0.000	0.000	0.000	0.000	0.000	0.000	0.000	0.000	0.000	0.000	0.000
3X	0.001	0.000	0.000	0.000	0.000	0.000	0.000	0.000	0.000	0.000	0.000	0.000
Shock F. U.S. Money Supply-Permanent												
FIXM	-0.461	-0.292	-0.020	0.036	-0.086	-0.036	0.024	0.019	0.059	0.034	0.007	0.000
1												
1X												

Table A-MSG-3
MSG MODEL
EFFECTS ON JAPANESE REAL GNP, JAPANESE PRICE LEVEL, JAPANESE INFLATION RATE
(Deviations from Baseline)

Shock and Regime	Real GNP				GNP Deflator				Inflation Rate			
	1st Yr	2nd Yr	5th Yr	10th Yr	1st Yr	2nd Yr	5th Yr	10th Yr	1st Yr	2nd Yr	5th Yr	10th Yr
Shock A. US Aggregate Demand												
1	0.468	0.005	0.008	0.014	0.313	0.190	-0.014	-0.063	0.313	-0.123	-0.040	0.000
1X	0.422	0.003	0.007	0.012	0.292	0.160	-0.011	-0.046	0.292	-0.132	-0.031	0.000
2A	0.440	0.004	0.007	0.013	0.300	0.171	-0.012	-0.052	0.300	-0.129	-0.034	0.000
2AX	-0.082	0.001	-0.017	-0.012	0.082	-0.001	0.017	0.012	0.082	-0.084	0.001	-0.001
2B	0.469	0.015	0.007	0.005	0.311	0.425	0.319	0.173	0.311	0.114	-0.040	-0.026
2BX	-0.105	-0.006	-0.013	-0.009	0.054	0.143	0.185	0.241	0.054	0.089	0.014	0.010
3	0.230	-0.003	0.000	0.008	0.157	0.292	0.127	0.073	0.157	0.135	-0.031	-0.005
3X	-0.128	-0.019	-0.011	-0.001	-0.062	0.140	0.129	0.128	-0.062	0.202	0.004	-0.003
Shock I. Japanese Aggregate Demand												
1	1.681	0.011	0.022	0.016	0.719	-0.106	-0.044	-0.037	0.719	-0.825	0.001	0.003
1X	1.546	0.003	0.019	0.014	0.620	-0.097	-0.038	-0.030	0.620	-0.717	0.001	0.003
2A	1.597	0.006	0.020	0.015	0.657	-0.101	-0.040	-0.032	0.657	-0.758	0.001	0.003
2AX	0.297	-0.077	-0.012	-0.002	-0.297	0.077	0.012	0.002	-0.297	0.374	-0.008	-0.001
2B	1.685	0.010	0.022	0.012	0.722	0.293	-0.025	-0.271	0.722	-0.429	-0.071	-0.039
2BX	0.447	-0.054	-0.012	-0.005	-0.170	-0.312	-0.262	-0.231	-0.170	-0.142	0.011	0.004
3	2.330	0.051	0.039	0.024	1.200	-0.114	-0.105	-0.101	1.200	-1.314	-0.003	0.003
3X	2.305	0.050	0.038	0.024	1.185	-0.129	-0.098	-0.087	1.185	-1.314	0.002	0.003
Shock G. German Aggregate Demand												
1	0.023	0.002	0.001	0.001	0.053	0.023	-0.007	-0.007	0.053	-0.030	-0.007	0.002
1X	0.009	0.003	0.000	-0.001	0.051	0.020	-0.004	-0.001	0.051	-0.031	-0.005	0.002
2A	0.014	0.002	0.001	0.000	0.051	0.021	-0.005	-0.003	0.051	-0.030	-0.006	0.002
2AX	-0.078	0.020	-0.011	-0.017	0.078	-0.020	0.011	0.017	0.078	-0.098	0.003	0.001
2B	0.017	0.006	-0.002	-0.002	0.049	0.076	0.107	0.182	0.049	0.027	0.011	0.018
2BX	-0.090	0.009	-0.008	-0.009	0.051	0.084	0.097	0.142	0.051	0.034	0.008	0.009
3	0.080	0.000	0.005	0.008	0.058	0.037	0.010	-0.028	0.058	-0.021	-0.012	-0.005
3X	0.063	-0.001	0.004	0.008	0.047	0.021	0.015	-0.008	0.047	-0.027	-0.005	-0.004
Shock B. Global Aggregate Demand												
1	2.172	0.018	0.032	0.031	1.084	0.106	-0.065	-0.107	1.084	-0.978	-0.046	0.006
1X	1.977	0.009	0.026	0.026	0.962	0.083	-0.053	-0.077	0.962	-0.880	-0.035	0.005
2A	2.050	0.012	0.028	0.028	1.008	0.091	-0.057	-0.087	1.008	-0.917	-0.039	0.006
2AX	0.136	-0.056	-0.040	-0.031	-0.136	0.056	0.040	0.031	-0.136	0.192	-0.004	-0.001
2B	2.172	0.031	0.027	0.015	1.082	0.793	0.401	0.084	1.082	-0.288	-0.100	-0.048
2BX	0.252	-0.051	-0.033	-0.023	-0.066	-0.085	0.021	0.152	-0.066	-0.019	0.032	0.023
3	2.640	0.048	0.044	0.041	1.415	0.215	0.032	-0.056	1.415	-1.200	-0.046	-0.007
3X	2.240	0.030	0.031	0.030	1.170	0.031	0.046	0.034	1.170	-1.139	0.002	-0.005
Shock C. US Aggregate Supply												
1	0.148	0.004	0.014	0.020	0.106	0.169	-0.134	-0.101	0.106	0.063	-0.052	0.019
1X	0.131	0.003	0.014	0.019	0.099	0.151	-0.110	-0.078	0.099	0.052	-0.043	0.016
2A	0.138	0.003	0.014	0.019	0.101	0.158	-0.118	-0.086	0.101	0.056	-0.046	0.017
2AX	-0.027	-0.006	0.011	0.010	0.027	0.006	-0.011	-0.010	0.027	-0.020	-0.002	0.001
2B	0.117	0.009	0.004	0.007	0.081	0.112	-0.239	-0.755	0.081	0.031	-0.121	-0.094
2BX	-0.047	0.011	0.003	0.006	0.015	0.057	0.040	0.006	0.015	0.042	-0.006	-0.007
3	0.145	0.006	0.014	0.020	0.101	0.355	0.059	-0.046	0.101	0.254	-0.072	-0.005
3X	0.053	0.001	0.012	0.017	0.044	0.247	0.152	0.029	0.044	0.203	-0.037	-0.018
Shock J. Japanese Aggregate Supply												
1	-0.676	-0.027	-0.016	-0.008	1.143	0.020	0.011	0.003	1.143	-1.123	-0.004	0.000
1X	-0.702	-0.028	-0.017	-0.008	1.124	0.020	0.012	0.005	1.124	-1.104	-0.004	0.000
2A	-0.692	-0.028	-0.016	-0.008	1.131	0.020	0.012	0.004	1.131	-1.111	-0.004	0.000
2AX	-0.945	-0.045	-0.022	-0.011	0.945	0.045	0.022	0.011	0.945	-0.900	-0.004	-0.002
2B	-0.482	-0.027	-0.010	-0.005	1.288	1.150	1.169	1.263	1.288	-0.137	0.020	0.015
2BX	-0.887	-0.048	-0.021	-0.011	0.992	0.965	1.040	1.108	0.992	-0.027	0.020	0.010
3	-0.540	-0.018	-0.013	-0.006	1.244	0.063	0.037	0.016	1.244	-1.181	-0.008	-0.003
3X	-0.547	-0.019	-0.013	-0.007	1.240	0.056	0.041	0.020	1.240	-1.184	-0.006	-0.003

Shock and Regime	Real GNP				GNP Deflator				Inflation Rate			
	1st Yr	2nd Yr	5th Yr	10th Yr	1st Yr	2nd Yr	5th Yr	10th Yr	1st Yr	2nd Yr	5th Yr	10th Yr
Shock H. German Aggregate Supply												
1	-0.004	-0.002	0.004	0.007	0.012	0.013	-0.015	-0.029	0.012	0.001	-0.008	0.000
1X	-0.006	-0.002	0.004	0.007	0.012	0.012	-0.012	-0.023	0.012	0.000	-0.007	0.000
2A	-0.005	-0.002	0.004	0.007	0.012	0.012	-0.013	-0.025	0.012	0.001	-0.007	0.000
2AX	-0.017	-0.003	0.003	0.004	0.017	0.003	-0.003	-0.004	0.017	-0.014	0.000	0.000
2B	-0.024	0.006	-0.004	-0.004	-0.011	-0.004	0.026	0.160	-0.011	0.007	0.016	0.032
2BX	-0.026	0.018	0.000	-0.001	0.010	0.014	0.001	0.004	0.010	0.004	0.000	0.001
3	0.001	-0.002	0.004	0.008	0.009	0.025	0.005	-0.029	0.009	0.016	-0.009	-0.005
3X	-0.002	-0.002	0.004	0.008	0.007	0.017	0.011	-0.010	0.007	0.010	-0.004	-0.004
Shock E. Oil Price Increase												
1	2.172	0.018	0.032	0.031	1.084	0.106	-0.065	-0.107	1.084	-0.978	-0.046	0.006
1X	1.977	0.009	0.026	0.026	0.962	0.083	-0.053	-0.077	0.962	-0.880	-0.035	0.005
2A	2.050	0.012	0.028	0.028	1.008	0.091	-0.057	-0.087	1.008	-0.917	-0.039	0.006
2AX	0.136	-0.056	-0.040	-0.031	-0.136	0.056	0.040	0.031	-0.136	0.192	-0.004	-0.001
2B	2.172	0.031	0.027	0.015	1.082	0.793	0.401	0.084	1.082	-0.288	-0.100	-0.048
2BX	0.252	-0.051	-0.033	-0.023	-0.066	-0.085	0.021	0.152	-0.066	-0.019	0.032	0.023
3	2.640	0.048	0.044	0.041	1.415	0.215	0.032	-0.056	1.415	-1.200	-0.046	-0.007
3X	2.240	0.030	0.031	0.030	1.170	0.031	0.046	0.034	1.170	-1.139	0.002	-0.005
Shock L. U.S. Money Demand												
1	0.024	0.002	0.001	0.000	0.024	0.003	0.000	0.001	0.024	-0.021	0.004	-0.001
1X	0.023	0.003	0.001	0.000	0.025	0.002	0.000	0.001	0.025	-0.024	0.004	-0.001
2A	0.003	0.000	0.000	0.000	0.002	0.001	0.000	0.000	0.002	-0.001	0.000	0.000
2AX	0.000	0.000	0.000	0.000	0.000	0.000	0.000	0.000	0.000	-0.001	0.000	0.000
2B	0.003	0.000	0.000	0.000	0.002	0.003	0.002	0.001	0.002	0.001	0.000	0.000
2BX	-0.001	0.000	0.000	0.000	0.000	0.001	0.001	0.001	0.000	0.001	0.000	0.000
3	-0.113	-0.004	-0.004	-0.003	-0.064	0.016	-0.002	0.011	-0.064	0.079	0.005	0.000
3X	-0.220	-0.008	-0.007	-0.006	-0.129	0.014	-0.002	0.013	-0.129	0.143	0.004	0.002
Shock D. Japanese Money Demand												
1	-0.183	-0.012	-0.005	-0.002	-0.140	-0.018	0.002	0.001	-0.140	0.121	0.001	0.000
1X	-0.221	-0.014	-0.006	-0.003	-0.168	-0.016	0.003	0.002	-0.168	0.152	0.001	0.000
2A	0.010	0.000	0.000	0.000	0.004	-0.001	0.000	0.000	0.004	-0.005	0.000	0.000
2AX	0.002	0.000	0.000	0.000	-0.002	0.000	0.000	0.000	-0.002	0.002	0.000	0.000
2B	0.010	0.000	0.000	0.000	0.004	0.002	0.000	-0.002	0.004	-0.003	0.000	0.000
2BX	0.003	0.000	0.000	0.000	-0.001	-0.002	-0.002	-0.001	-0.001	-0.001	0.000	0.000
3	0.014	0.000	0.000	0.000	0.007	0.000	0.000	0.000	0.007	-0.008	0.000	0.000
3X	0.014	0.000	0.000	0.000	0.007	-0.001	-0.001	-0.001	0.007	-0.008	0.000	0.000
Shock K. German Money Demand												
1	-0.023	0.002	-0.002	-0.004	0.002	0.002	0.005	0.015	0.002	0.000	0.002	0.001
1X	-0.027	0.002	-0.003	-0.005	0.003	0.002	0.005	0.015	0.003	-0.001	0.002	0.001
2A	0.000	0.000	0.000	0.000	0.000	0.000	0.000	0.000	0.000	0.000	0.000	0.000
2AX	0.000	0.000	0.000	0.000	0.000	0.000	0.000	0.000	0.000	-0.001	0.000	0.000
2B	0.000	0.000	0.000	0.000	0.000	0.000	0.001	0.001	0.000	0.000	0.000	0.000
2BX	-0.001	0.000	0.000	0.000	0.000	0.001	0.001	0.001	0.000	0.000	0.000	0.000
3	0.000	0.000	0.000	0.000	0.000	0.000	0.000	0.000	0.000	0.000	0.000	0.000
3X	0.000	0.000	0.000	0.000	0.000	0.000	0.000	0.000	0.000	0.000	0.000	0.000
Shock F. U.S. Money Supply-Permanent												
FIXM	-0.031	0.006	0.001	-0.003	-0.041	-0.102	-0.007	0.020	-0.041	-0.060	0.025	-0.001
1												
1X												

875

Table A-MSG-4
MSG MODEL
EFFECTS ON JAPANESE INTEREST RATES AND JAPANESE CURRENT ACCOUNT/GNP RATIO
(Deviations from Baseline)

Shock and Regime	Short Interest Rate				Long Interest Rate				Current Account/GNP Ratio			
	1st Yr	2nd Yr	5th Yr	10th Yr	1st Yr	2nd Yr	5th Yr	10th Yr	1st Yr	2nd Yr	5th Yr	10th Yr
Shock A. US Aggregate Demand												
1	0.976	0.244	-0.007	-0.061	0.109	0.006	-0.049	-0.047	0.084	0.001	-0.003	-0.001
1X	1.190	0.273	-0.007	-0.056	0.136	0.012	-0.046	-0.044	0.086	0.000	-0.003	-0.001
2A	1.109	0.262	-0.007	-0.058	0.126	0.010	-0.047	-0.045	0.085	0.000	-0.003	-0.001
2AX	3.137	0.378	0.022	0.021	0.373	0.065	0.021	0.004	0.088	-0.007	-0.002	0.002
2B	1.223	0.139	-0.050	-0.031	0.106	-0.019	-0.034	-0.028	0.081	-0.001	0.001	0.003
2BX	3.459	0.403	-0.009	0.021	0.396	0.057	0.013	0.011	0.090	-0.005	-0.003	0.002
3	1.962	0.180	-0.008	-0.052	0.200	0.000	-0.042	-0.040	0.082	0.002	-0.001	0.000
3X	3.208	0.241	0.001	-0.036	0.340	0.020	-0.028	-0.021	0.083	0.003	-0.001	0.002
Shock I. Japanese Aggregate Demand												
1	3.000	-0.119	-0.028	-0.025	0.259	-0.039	-0.025	-0.016	-0.080	0.005	-0.002	-0.003
1X	3.609	-0.158	-0.032	-0.026	0.311	-0.046	-0.026	-0.016	-0.079	0.007	-0.002	-0.003
2A	3.380	-0.143	-0.030	-0.026	0.292	-0.043	-0.025	-0.016	-0.079	0.006	-0.002	-0.003
2AX	9.385	-0.619	-0.072	-0.025	0.778	-0.124	-0.034	-0.014	-0.065	0.019	-0.004	-0.004
2B	3.455	-0.473	-0.074	-0.041	0.230	-0.114	-0.045	-0.028	-0.080	0.006	-0.002	-0.002
2BX	8.091	-0.461	-0.038	-0.006	0.699	-0.082	-0.011	-0.003	-0.073	0.014	-0.001	-0.002
3	0.138	0.023	-0.016	-0.021	0.003	-0.012	-0.020	-0.015	-0.086	-0.001	-0.002	-0.003
3X	0.221	0.036	-0.015	-0.021	0.014	-0.010	-0.019	-0.014	-0.086	-0.001	-0.002	-0.002
Shock G. German Aggregate Demand												
1	0.095	0.031	-0.007	-0.008	0.008	-0.002	-0.007	0.000	0.010	-0.001	0.000	0.000
1X	0.100	0.038	-0.007	-0.002	0.011	0.002	-0.003	0.006	0.009	-0.001	0.000	0.001
2A	0.099	0.035	-0.007	-0.004	0.010	0.000	-0.004	0.004	0.009	-0.001	0.000	0.001
2AX	-0.257	0.146	0.006	0.055	0.013	0.045	0.044	0.060	-0.006	-0.001	0.004	0.006
2B	0.119	0.028	0.014	0.023	0.029	0.019	0.022	0.028	0.008	0.000	0.001	0.002
2BX	0.175	0.068	0.021	0.034	0.047	0.033	0.031	0.036	0.002	-0.001	0.002	0.003
3	0.097	0.029	-0.010	-0.034	0.000	-0.014	-0.028	-0.030	0.014	0.000	-0.001	-0.002
3X	0.149	0.040	-0.006	-0.034	0.008	-0.011	-0.027	-0.030	0.014	0.000	-0.001	-0.002
Shock B. Global Aggregate Demand												
1	4.070	0.156	-0.042	-0.095	0.374	-0.035	-0.081	-0.064	0.014	0.005	-0.005	-0.003
1X	4.899	0.153	-0.045	-0.085	0.455	-0.032	-0.074	-0.054	0.016	0.006	-0.005	-0.003
2A	4.588	0.155	-0.044	-0.089	0.425	-0.033	-0.077	-0.058	0.015	0.006	-0.005	-0.003
2AX	12.266	-0.095	-0.044	0.051	1.145	-0.014	0.031	0.050	0.018	0.010	-0.001	0.005
2B	4.798	-0.307	-0.110	-0.048	0.360	-0.113	-0.058	-0.027	0.010	0.004	0.001	0.002
2BX	11.724	0.011	-0.025	0.050	1.118	0.008	0.033	0.044	0.019	0.007	-0.003	0.002
3	2.197	0.232	-0.034	-0.107	0.202	-0.025	-0.090	-0.085	0.010	0.000	-0.004	-0.005
3X	3.578	0.317	-0.020	-0.090	0.360	0.000	-0.074	-0.065	0.011	0.002	-0.004	-0.003
Shock C. US Aggregate Supply												
1	0.317	0.216	-0.150	-0.101	-0.039	-0.078	-0.108	-0.042	0.001	0.001	-0.004	0.000
1X	0.383	0.256	-0.160	-0.098	-0.030	-0.076	-0.109	-0.040	0.002	0.001	-0.004	0.000
2A	0.358	0.242	-0.156	-0.099	-0.033	-0.077	-0.109	-0.040	0.002	0.001	-0.004	0.000
2AX	0.999	0.498	-0.224	-0.063	0.051	-0.053	-0.102	-0.020	0.007	-0.001	-0.005	0.002
2B	0.331	0.019	-0.175	-0.130	-0.088	-0.134	-0.137	-0.107	0.000	-0.002	0.001	0.001
2BX	1.053	0.136	-0.122	-0.052	0.048	-0.062	-0.064	-0.032	0.002	-0.006	0.000	0.001
3	0.535	0.193	-0.186	-0.108	-0.040	-0.102	-0.122	-0.048	0.000	0.000	-0.003	0.000
3X	0.807	0.335	-0.201	-0.111	-0.001	-0.090	-0.128	-0.043	0.001	0.001	-0.003	0.000
Shock J. Japanese Aggregate Supply												
1	0.584	-0.008	-0.006	-0.006	0.052	-0.006	-0.006	-0.003	0.005	0.001	-0.001	-0.001
1X	0.703	-0.014	-0.007	-0.006	0.063	-0.008	-0.006	-0.003	0.005	0.001	-0.001	-0.001
2A	0.658	-0.012	-0.007	-0.006	0.059	-0.007	-0.006	-0.003	0.005	0.001	-0.001	-0.001
2AX	1.834	-0.094	-0.018	-0.006	0.160	-0.022	-0.009	-0.003	0.009	0.003	-0.001	-0.001
2B	1.139	-0.183	0.016	0.015	0.103	-0.010	0.015	0.010	0.009	0.004	-0.001	0.000
2BX	2.688	-0.200	0.000	0.011	0.249	-0.022	0.009	0.007	0.012	0.007	-0.001	-0.001
3	0.036	0.012	-0.007	-0.006	0.000	-0.004	-0.006	-0.004	0.004	0.000	0.000	0.000
3X	0.055	0.019	-0.007	-0.006	0.003	-0.003	-0.006	-0.003	0.004	-0.001	-0.001	-0.001

Shock and	Short Interest Rate				Long Interest Rate				Current Account/GNP Ratio			
Regime	1st Yr	2nd Yr	5th Yr	10th Yr	1st Yr	2nd Yr	5th Yr	10th Yr	1st Yr	2nd Yr	5th Yr	10th Yr
Shock H. German Aggregate Supply												
1	0.009	0.014	-0.014	-0.028	-0.012	-0.015	-0.025	-0.026	-0.001	-0.002	-0.002	-0.002
1X	0.010	0.017	-0.014	-0.027	-0.011	-0.015	-0.024	-0.024	-0.001	-0.002	-0.002	-0.002
2A	0.010	0.016	-0.014	-0.028	-0.011	-0.015	-0.024	-0.025	-0.001	-0.002	-0.002	-0.002
2AX	0.006	0.032	-0.016	-0.019	-0.007	-0.009	-0.019	-0.016	-0.001	-0.002	-0.002	-0.001
2B	-0.047	0.009	0.018	0.042	0.017	0.026	0.039	0.054	-0.006	0.000	0.002	0.002
2BX	-0.249	0.000	-0.014	0.001	-0.032	-0.007	-0.001	0.006	-0.014	-0.002	0.000	0.001
3	0.020	0.017	-0.012	-0.033	-0.011	-0.016	-0.028	-0.033	0.000	0.000	-0.002	-0.003
3X	0.026	0.024	-0.009	-0.034	-0.008	-0.014	-0.028	-0.033	-0.001	-0.001	-0.002	-0.003
Shock E. Oil Price Increase												
1	4.070	0.156	-0.042	-0.095	0.374	-0.035	-0.081	-0.064	0.014	0.005	-0.005	-0.003
1X	4.899	0.153	-0.045	-0.085	0.455	-0.032	-0.074	-0.054	0.016	0.006	-0.005	-0.003
2A	4.588	0.155	-0.044	-0.089	0.425	-0.033	-0.077	-0.058	0.015	0.006	-0.005	-0.003
2AX	12.266	-0.095	-0.044	0.051	1.145	-0.014	0.031	0.050	0.018	0.010	-0.001	0.005
2B	4.798	-0.307	-0.110	-0.048	0.360	-0.113	-0.058	-0.027	0.010	0.004	0.001	0.002
2BX	11.724	0.011	-0.025	0.050	1.118	0.008	0.033	0.044	0.019	0.007	-0.003	0.002
3	2.197	0.232	-0.034	-0.107	0.202	-0.025	-0.090	-0.085	0.010	0.000	-0.004	-0.005
3X	3.578	0.317	-0.020	-0.090	0.360	0.000	-0.074	-0.065	0.011	0.002	-0.004	-0.003
Shock L. U.S. Money Demand												
1	0.059	0.007	0.000	0.002	0.007	0.001	0.001	-0.003	0.003	-0.001	-0.001	-0.001
1X	0.081	0.007	0.001	0.003	0.010	0.002	0.002	-0.003	0.003	-0.002	-0.001	-0.001
2A	0.007	0.002	0.000	0.000	0.001	0.000	0.000	0.000	0.001	0.000	0.000	0.000
2AX	0.019	0.002	0.000	0.000	0.002	0.000	0.000	0.000	0.001	0.000	0.000	0.000
2B	0.007	0.001	0.000	0.000	0.001	0.000	0.000	0.000	0.000	0.000	0.000	0.000
2BX	0.021	0.002	0.000	0.000	0.002	0.000	0.000	0.000	0.001	0.000	0.000	0.000
3	0.576	-0.038	0.004	0.009	0.057	0.000	0.007	0.004	0.002	0.000	0.000	0.000
3X	0.989	-0.057	0.004	0.016	0.097	0.000	0.013	0.010	0.002	0.000	0.000	0.000
Shock D. Japanese Money Demand												
1	0.847	-0.037	-0.004	-0.001	0.077	-0.008	-0.002	-0.001	0.001	0.002	0.000	0.000
1X	1.019	-0.049	-0.005	-0.002	0.092	-0.010	-0.002	-0.001	0.001	0.002	0.000	0.000
2A	0.020	-0.001	0.000	0.000	0.002	0.000	0.000	0.000	0.000	0.000	0.000	0.000
2AX	0.057	-0.004	0.000	0.000	0.005	-0.001	0.000	0.000	0.000	0.000	0.000	0.000
2B	0.021	-0.003	0.000	0.000	0.001	-0.001	0.000	0.000	0.000	0.000	0.000	0.000
2BX	0.049	-0.003	0.000	0.000	0.004	-0.001	0.000	0.000	0.000	0.000	0.000	0.000
3	0.000	0.000	0.000	0.000	0.000	0.000	0.000	0.000	0.000	0.000	0.000	0.000
3X	0.001	0.000	0.000	0.000	0.000	0.000	0.000	0.000	-0.001	0.000	0.000	0.000
Shock K. German Money Demand												
1	-0.026	0.005	0.003	0.014	0.004	0.008	0.012	0.016	-0.002	0.000	0.001	0.001
1X	-0.040	0.007	0.004	0.016	0.004	0.009	0.014	0.018	-0.003	0.000	0.001	0.002
2A	0.001	0.000	0.000	0.000	0.000	0.000	0.000	0.000	0.000	0.000	0.000	0.000
2AX	-0.002	0.001	0.000	0.000	0.000	0.000	0.000	0.000	0.000	0.000	0.000	0.000
2B	0.001	0.000	0.000	0.000	0.000	0.000	0.000	0.000	0.000	0.000	0.000	0.000
2BX	0.001	0.000	0.000	0.000	0.000	0.000	0.000	0.000	0.000	0.000	0.000	0.000
3	0.000	0.000	0.000	0.000	0.000	0.000	0.000	0.000	0.000	0.000	0.000	0.000
3X	0.001	0.000	0.000	0.000	0.000	0.000	0.000	0.000	0.000	0.000	0.000	0.000
Shock F. U.S. Money Supply-Permanent												
FIXM	-0.121	-0.160	-0.009	0.028	-0.031	-0.016	0.020	0.015	-0.004	-0.002	0.003	0.001
1												
1X												

MSG MODEL
EFFECTS ON GERMAN REAL GNP, GERMAN PRICE LEVEL, GERMAN INFLATION RATE
(Deviations from Baseline)

Shock and Regime	Real GNP				GNP Deflator				Inflation Rate			
	1st Yr	2nd Yr	5th Yr	10th Yr	1st Yr	2nd Yr	5th Yr	10th Yr	1st Yr	2nd Yr	5th Yr	10th Yr
Shock A. US Aggregate Demand												
1	0.561	-0.015	0.078	0.160	0.361	0.262	-0.066	-0.212	0.361	-0.098	-0.080	-0.009
1X	0.536	-0.029	0.078	0.153	0.344	0.238	-0.071	-0.189	0.344	-0.106	-0.070	-0.007
2A	0.546	-0.024	0.078	0.156	0.351	0.247	-0.070	-0.197	0.351	-0.104	-0.074	-0.008
2AX	0.021	-0.015	-0.051	-0.030	-0.021	0.015	0.051	0.030	-0.021	0.036	-0.001	-0.004
2B	0.606	0.046	0.039	0.043	0.379	0.320	-0.096	-0.786	0.379	-0.059	-0.142	-0.136
2BX	0.057	-0.021	-0.014	-0.002	0.011	0.026	0.081	0.111	0.011	0.015	0.014	0.002
3	0.436	0.056	0.049	0.116	0.279	0.279	0.060	-0.120	0.279	0.000	-0.071	-0.017
3X	0.176	0.041	0.015	0.050	0.111	0.153	0.109	0.054	0.111	0.042	-0.021	-0.006
Shock I. Japanese Aggregate Demand												
1	0.052	-0.008	0.036	0.060	0.088	0.066	-0.042	-0.082	0.088	-0.022	-0.024	-0.001
1X	0.039	-0.010	0.038	0.061	0.086	0.064	-0.042	-0.078	0.086	-0.022	-0.023	-0.001
2A	0.044	-0.009	0.037	0.061	0.087	0.065	-0.042	-0.079	0.087	-0.022	-0.024	-0.001
2AX	-0.075	-0.039	0.059	0.074	0.075	0.039	-0.059	-0.074	0.075	-0.037	-0.009	-0.002
2B	0.059	0.018	0.014	0.013	0.090	0.090	-0.050	-0.292	0.090	-0.001	-0.047	-0.048
2BX	-0.108	0.033	0.022	0.025	0.035	0.085	0.015	-0.110	0.035	0.050	-0.023	-0.026
3	0.107	-0.004	0.027	0.048	0.091	0.067	-0.033	-0.100	0.091	-0.024	-0.027	-0.006
3X	0.088	-0.006	0.027	0.044	0.079	0.057	-0.027	-0.078	0.079	-0.022	-0.022	-0.004
Shock G. German Aggregate Demand												
1	0.908	-0.111	0.054	0.061	0.388	0.105	-0.065	-0.069	0.388	-0.283	-0.015	0.002
1X	0.835	-0.099	0.034	0.035	0.335	0.078	-0.044	-0.038	0.335	-0.257	-0.008	0.003
2A	0.862	-0.104	0.042	0.045	0.355	0.088	-0.052	-0.049	0.355	-0.267	-0.011	0.003
2AX	0.160	0.086	-0.176	-0.218	-0.160	-0.086	0.176	0.218	-0.160	0.074	0.028	0.006
2B	0.941	-0.061	0.022	0.022	0.408	0.170	-0.094	-0.357	0.408	-0.238	-0.065	-0.048
2BX	0.325	-0.084	-0.078	-0.080	-0.032	-0.170	0.025	0.425	-0.032	-0.138	0.076	0.081
3	1.277	-0.155	0.132	0.183	0.654	0.257	-0.225	-0.356	0.654	-0.397	-0.077	-0.012
3X	1.263	-0.158	0.133	0.182	0.645	0.248	-0.223	-0.334	0.645	-0.397	-0.072	-0.009
Shock B. Global Aggregate Demand												
1	1.521	-0.134	0.168	0.281	0.836	0.433	-0.173	-0.363	0.836	-0.403	-0.120	-0.008
1X	1.410	-0.138	0.150	0.249	0.765	0.380	-0.157	-0.305	0.765	-0.385	-0.102	-0.005
2A	1.452	-0.137	0.157	0.261	0.792	0.400	-0.164	-0.326	0.792	-0.392	-0.109	-0.006
2AX	0.105	0.033	-0.169	-0.175	-0.105	-0.033	0.169	0.175	-0.105	0.073	0.018	0.000
2B	1.606	0.002	0.075	0.078	0.877	0.579	-0.240	-1.436	0.877	-0.298	-0.254	-0.233
2BX	0.273	-0.073	-0.069	-0.057	0.014	-0.059	0.121	0.427	0.014	-0.072	0.067	0.057
3	1.819	-0.103	0.209	0.347	1.024	0.604	-0.199	-0.576	1.024	-0.420	-0.176	-0.035
3X	1.527	-0.124	0.175	0.275	0.835	0.458	-0.140	-0.357	0.835	-0.376	-0.115	-0.019
Shock C. US Aggregate Supply												
1	0.212	0.055	0.016	0.111	0.135	0.152	-0.116	-0.203	0.135	0.017	-0.088	0.012
1X	0.196	0.049	0.021	0.105	0.125	0.139	-0.104	-0.172	0.125	0.014	-0.077	0.011
2A	0.202	0.051	0.020	0.107	0.129	0.144	-0.108	-0.183	0.129	0.015	-0.081	0.012
2AX	0.004	0.001	0.021	0.033	-0.004	-0.001	-0.021	-0.033	-0.004	0.003	-0.008	0.001
2B	0.209	0.015	-0.009	0.001	0.126	0.103	-0.138	-0.542	0.126	-0.023	-0.085	-0.078
2BX	0.029	0.003	0.006	0.010	-0.004	-0.003	-0.017	-0.069	-0.004	0.001	-0.008	-0.011
3	0.262	0.124	0.015	0.103	0.168	0.243	-0.004	-0.248	0.168	0.075	-0.107	-0.012
3X	0.189	0.107	0.028	0.082	0.121	0.194	0.052	-0.129	0.121	0.073	-0.070	-0.014
Shock J. Japanese Aggregate Supply												
1	-0.007	-0.003	0.009	0.019	0.020	0.025	-0.013	-0.025	0.020	0.005	-0.009	0.000
1X	-0.009	-0.004	0.010	0.019	0.020	0.024	-0.013	-0.024	0.020	0.004	-0.008	0.000
2A	-0.008	-0.004	0.010	0.019	0.020	0.025	-0.013	-0.025	0.020	0.005	-0.008	0.000
2AX	-0.024	-0.016	0.019	0.024	0.024	0.016	-0.019	-0.024	0.024	-0.007	-0.004	-0.001
2B	-0.005	0.009	0.002	0.002	0.012	0.022	-0.005	-0.055	0.012	0.010	-0.010	-0.010
2BX	-0.040	0.013	0.007	0.008	0.008	0.028	0.006	-0.033	0.008	0.020	-0.007	-0.008
3	0.000	0.000	0.006	0.014	0.017	0.025	-0.008	-0.029	0.017	0.008	-0.009	-0.002
3X	-0.005	-0.001	0.006	0.013	0.014	0.021	-0.006	-0.022	0.014	0.008	-0.007	-0.001

Shock and Regime	Real GNP				GNP Deflator				Inflation Rate			
	1st Yr	2nd Yr	5th Yr	10th Yr	1st Yr	2nd Yr	5th Yr	10th Yr	1st Yr	2nd Yr	5th Yr	10th Yr

Shock H. German Aggregate Supply

1	-0.864	-0.226	0.189	0.259	1.061	0.310	-0.195	-0.281	1.061	-0.751	-0.055	-0.009
1X	-0.878	-0.228	0.187	0.255	1.051	0.300	-0.192	-0.271	1.051	-0.751	-0.052	-0.009
2A	-0.873	-0.227	0.188	0.256	1.055	0.304	-0.193	-0.275	1.055	-0.751	-0.053	-0.009
2AX	-0.979	-0.238	0.168	0.220	0.979	0.238	-0.168	-0.220	0.979	-0.742	-0.033	-0.007
2B	-0.651	-0.005	0.090	0.099	1.203	0.653	-0.236	-1.557	1.203	-0.550	-0.267	-0.265
2BX	-0.813	0.133	0.137	0.146	1.079	0.706	0.247	-0.482	1.079	-0.374	-0.142	-0.148
3	-0.789	-0.217	0.188	0.274	1.114	0.360	-0.251	-0.420	1.114	-0.754	-0.086	-0.020
3X	-0.792	-0.219	0.190	0.275	1.112	0.357	-0.249	-0.403	1.112	-0.756	-0.083	-0.018

Shock E. Oil Price Increase

1	1.521	-0.134	0.168	0.281	0.836	0.433	-0.173	-0.363	0.836	-0.403	-0.120	-0.008
1X	1.410	-0.138	0.150	0.249	0.765	0.380	-0.157	-0.305	0.765	-0.385	-0.102	-0.005
2A	1.452	-0.137	0.157	0.261	0.792	0.400	-0.164	-0.326	0.792	-0.392	-0.109	-0.006
2AX	0.105	0.033	-0.169	-0.175	-0.105	-0.033	0.169	0.175	-0.105	0.073	0.018	0.000
2B	1.606	0.002	0.075	0.078	0.877	0.579	-0.240	-1.436	0.877	-0.298	-0.254	-0.233
2BX	0.273	-0.073	-0.069	-0.057	0.014	-0.059	0.121	0.427	0.014	-0.072	0.067	0.057
3	1.819	-0.103	0.209	0.347	1.024	0.604	-0.199	-0.576	1.024	-0.420	-0.176	-0.035
3X	1.527	-0.124	0.175	0.275	0.835	0.458	-0.140	-0.357	0.835	-0.376	-0.115	-0.019

Shock L. U.S. Money Demand

1	0.067	-0.013	0.016	0.018	0.044	0.019	-0.018	-0.017	0.044	-0.025	-0.003	-0.001
1X	0.072	-0.015	0.017	0.019	0.047	0.019	-0.019	-0.017	0.047	-0.028	-0.002	-0.001
2A	0.003	0.000	0.000	0.001	0.002	0.001	0.000	-0.001	0.002	-0.001	0.000	0.000
2AX	0.000	0.000	0.000	0.000	0.000	0.000	0.000	0.000	0.000	0.000	0.000	0.000
2B	0.004	0.000	0.000	0.000	0.002	0.002	-0.001	-0.005	0.002	0.000	-0.001	-0.001
2BX	0.000	0.000	0.000	0.000	0.000	0.000	0.000	0.001	0.000	0.000	0.000	0.000
3	-0.028	0.000	-0.004	-0.007	-0.018	-0.009	0.003	0.029	-0.018	0.008	0.006	0.002
3X	-0.102	0.006	-0.018	-0.028	-0.066	-0.035	0.027	0.069	-0.066	0.031	0.016	0.004

Shock D. Japanese Money Demand

1	-0.009	0.001	0.002	0.005	0.004	0.006	-0.003	-0.006	0.004	0.002	-0.002	0.000
1X	-0.011	0.001	0.003	0.006	0.005	0.007	-0.003	-0.007	0.005	0.001	-0.002	0.000
2A	0.000	0.000	0.000	0.000	0.001	0.000	0.000	0.000	0.001	0.000	0.000	0.000
2AX	0.000	0.000	0.000	0.000	0.000	0.000	0.000	0.000	0.000	0.000	0.000	0.000
2B	0.000	0.000	0.000	0.000	0.001	0.001	0.000	-0.002	0.001	0.000	0.000	0.000
2BX	-0.001	0.000	0.000	0.000	0.000	0.001	0.000	-0.001	0.000	0.000	0.000	0.000
3	0.000	0.000	0.000	0.000	0.000	0.000	0.000	0.000	0.000	0.000	0.000	0.000
3X	0.001	0.000	0.000	0.000	0.000	0.000	0.000	0.000	0.000	0.000	0.000	0.000

Shock K. German Money Demand

1	-0.194	0.026	-0.055	-0.072	-0.142	-0.081	0.051	0.083	-0.142	0.061	0.020	0.003
1X	-0.230	0.035	-0.066	-0.086	-0.169	-0.091	0.063	0.096	-0.169	0.077	0.022	0.004
2A	0.005	-0.001	0.000	0.000	0.002	0.001	0.000	0.000	0.002	-0.002	0.000	0.000
2AX	0.001	0.001	-0.001	-0.001	-0.001	-0.001	0.001	0.001	-0.001	0.000	0.000	0.000
2B	0.006	0.000	0.000	0.000	0.002	0.001	-0.001	-0.002	0.002	-0.001	0.000	0.000
2BX	0.002	-0.001	0.000	0.000	0.000	-0.001	0.000	0.003	0.000	-0.001	0.000	0.000
3	0.008	-0.001	0.000	0.001	0.004	0.002	-0.001	-0.002	0.004	-0.002	0.000	0.000
3X	0.008	-0.001	0.001	0.001	0.004	0.001	-0.001	-0.002	0.004	-0.002	0.000	0.000

Shock F. U.S. Money Supply-Permanent

FIXM	-0.065	-0.029	0.007	-0.028	-0.053	-0.083	-0.021	0.046	-0.053	-0.029	0.030	0.003
1												
1X												

Table A-MSG-6
MSG MODEL
EFFECTS ON GERMAN INTEREST RATES AND GERMAN CURRENT ACCOUNT/GNP RATIO
(Deviations from Baseline)

Shock and Regime	Short Interest Rate				Long Interest Rate				Current Account/GNP Ratio			
	1st Yr	2nd Yr	5th Yr	10th Yr	1st Yr	2nd Yr	5th Yr	10th Yr	1st Yr	2nd Yr	5th Yr	10th Yr
Shock A. US Aggregate Demand												
1	1.152	0.310	0.014	-0.065	0.145	0.024	-0.048	-0.051	0.052	0.009	0.003	0.002
1X	1.467	0.349	0.012	-0.060	0.182	0.031	-0.045	-0.048	0.058	0.010	0.002	0.003
2A	1.345	0.335	0.013	-0.062	0.168	0.028	-0.046	-0.049	0.056	0.010	0.002	0.002
2AX	6.164	0.121	-0.001	0.026	0.616	0.018	0.022	0.007	0.129	0.005	0.001	0.004
2B	1.499	-0.037	-0.156	-0.140	0.027	-0.135	-0.143	-0.138	0.057	0.003	0.000	0.002
2BX	5.688	0.355	-0.039	0.015	0.587	0.033	0.002	0.003	0.122	0.008	0.000	0.004
3	1.962	0.180	-0.008	-0.052	0.200	0.000	-0.042	-0.040	0.060	0.006	0.002	0.003
3X	3.208	0.241	0.001	-0.036	0.340	0.020	-0.028	-0.021	0.076	0.007	0.002	0.003
Shock I. Japanese Aggregate Demand												
1	0.175	0.072	-0.007	-0.027	0.016	-0.004	-0.022	-0.018	0.006	0.002	0.001	0.000
1X	0.208	0.090	-0.008	-0.028	0.021	-0.002	-0.024	-0.018	0.006	0.002	0.001	0.000
2A	0.196	0.083	-0.008	-0.028	0.019	-0.003	-0.023	-0.018	0.006	0.002	0.001	0.000
2AX	0.391	0.345	-0.034	-0.031	0.064	0.023	-0.035	-0.018	0.005	0.005	0.000	0.001
2B	0.288	-0.041	-0.050	-0.053	-0.016	-0.050	-0.052	-0.051	0.007	0.000	0.000	0.000
2BX	1.125	0.000	-0.037	-0.037	0.086	-0.030	-0.038	-0.034	0.015	0.000	0.000	0.000
3	0.138	0.023	-0.016	-0.021	0.003	-0.012	-0.020	-0.015	0.009	0.001	0.000	0.000
3X	0.221	0.036	-0.015	-0.021	0.014	-0.010	-0.019	-0.014	0.010	0.002	0.001	0.000
Shock G. German Aggregate Demand												
1	1.620	-0.007	-0.014	-0.010	0.150	-0.011	-0.010	-0.001	-0.096	0.002	-0.002	-0.002
1X	1.951	-0.035	-0.017	-0.004	0.179	-0.014	-0.006	0.006	-0.092	0.002	-0.002	-0.002
2A	1.826	-0.024	-0.016	-0.006	0.168	-0.013	-0.007	0.003	-0.094	0.002	-0.002	-0.002
2AX	5.508	-0.666	-0.025	0.058	0.455	-0.076	0.042	0.065	-0.057	-0.004	-0.003	-0.002
2B	1.767	-0.227	-0.060	-0.039	0.103	-0.076	-0.042	-0.033	-0.094	-0.001	-0.002	-0.002
2BX	4.274	-0.292	0.076	0.107	0.448	0.039	0.102	0.111	-0.067	-0.002	-0.001	-0.001
3	0.097	0.029	-0.010	-0.034	0.000	-0.014	-0.028	-0.030	-0.109	0.001	0.000	-0.001
3X	0.149	0.040	-0.006	-0.034	0.008	-0.011	-0.027	-0.030	-0.108	0.001	-0.001	-0.001
Shock B. Global Aggregate Demand												
1	2.947	0.374	-0.007	-0.102	0.310	0.009	-0.080	-0.070	-0.037	0.013	0.002	0.001
1X	3.626	0.404	-0.013	-0.093	0.380	0.015	-0.074	-0.060	-0.029	0.014	0.001	0.001
2A	3.367	0.395	-0.010	-0.096	0.353	0.013	-0.076	-0.064	-0.032	0.014	0.002	0.001
2AX	12.062	-0.199	-0.061	0.053	1.104	-0.035	0.030	0.054	0.077	0.006	-0.002	0.003
2B	3.555	-0.306	-0.266	-0.233	0.111	-0.261	-0.238	-0.223	-0.029	0.002	-0.001	0.000
2BX	11.087	0.064	0.000	0.084	1.091	0.042	0.066	0.081	0.070	0.006	0.000	0.003
3	2.197	0.232	-0.034	-0.107	0.202	-0.025	-0.090	-0.085	-0.040	0.009	0.002	0.002
3X	3.578	0.317	-0.020	-0.090	0.360	0.000	-0.074	-0.065	-0.023	0.009	0.002	0.002
Shock C. US Aggregate Supply												
1	0.434	0.258	-0.125	-0.114	-0.014	-0.066	-0.112	-0.049	0.010	0.008	0.000	0.000
1X	0.534	0.314	-0.138	-0.112	-0.001	-0.063	-0.114	-0.046	0.012	0.009	-0.001	0.000
2A	0.496	0.293	-0.133	-0.113	-0.006	-0.064	-0.114	-0.047	0.011	0.008	-0.001	0.000
2AX	1.565	0.778	-0.255	-0.071	0.130	-0.030	-0.116	-0.022	0.028	0.015	-0.003	0.001
2B	0.520	-0.032	-0.142	-0.115	-0.054	-0.118	-0.119	-0.101	0.013	0.000	-0.001	0.000
2BX	2.189	0.052	-0.142	-0.055	0.141	-0.086	-0.070	-0.035	0.040	0.001	-0.002	0.001
3	0.535	0.193	-0.186	-0.108	-0.040	-0.102	-0.122	-0.048	0.011	0.006	0.000	0.000
3X	0.807	0.335	-0.201	-0.111	-0.001	-0.090	-0.128	-0.043	0.014	0.008	-0.001	0.000
Shock J. Japanese Aggregate Supply												
1	0.016	0.027	-0.004	-0.008	0.001†	-0.001	-0.007	-0.005	-0.002	0.001	0.000	0.000
1X	0.019	0.034	-0.004	-0.008	0.002	0.000	-0.007	-0.005	-0.002	0.001	0.000	0.000
2A	0.018	0.032	-0.004	-0.008	0.002	-0.001	-0.007	-0.005	-0.002	0.001	0.000	0.000
2AX	-0.003	0.121	-0.014	-0.009	0.008	0.007	-0.011	-0.005	-0.002	0.002	0.000	0.000
2B	0.039	0.002	-0.012	-0.011	-0.005	-0.010	-0.011	-0.011	-0.001	0.000	0.000	0.000
2BX	0.193	0.028	-0.014	-0.012	0.014	-0.007	-0.012	-0.011	-0.001	0.000	0.000	0.000
3	0.036	0.012	-0.007	-0.006	0.000	-0.004	-0.006	-0.004	0.000	0.000	0.000	0.000
3X	0.055	0.019	-0.007	-0.006	0.003	-0.003	-0.006	-0.003	-0.001	0.001	0.000	0.000

880

Shock and Regime	Short Interest Rate				Long Interest Rate				Current Account/GNP Ratio			
	1st Yr	2nd Yr	5th Yr	10th Yr	1st Yr	2nd Yr	5th Yr	10th Yr	1st Yr	2nd Yr	5th Yr	10th Yr
Shock H. German Aggregate Supply												
1	0.247	0.106	-0.008	-0.028	0.027	0.000	-0.024	-0.026	0.009	0.006	0.002	0.002
1X	0.290	0.121	-0.009	-0.027	0.033	0.001	-0.023	-0.025	0.009	0.006	0.002	0.002
2A	0.274	0.115	-0.008	-0.027	0.031	0.001	-0.023	-0.025	0.009	0.006	0.002	0.002
2AX	0.649	0.207	-0.022	-0.018	0.076	0.010	-0.020	-0.016	0.013	0.007	0.002	0.002
2B	0.499	-0.549	-0.260	0.248	-0.219	-0.294	-0.250	0.244	0.012	0.000	-0.002	0.000
2BX	1.748	-0.710	-0.158	-0.143	-0.031	-0.222	-0.145	-0.140	0.024	-0.002	0.000	0.001
3	0.020	0.017	-0.012	-0.033	-0.011	-0.016	-0.028	-0.033	0.006	0.005	0.002	0.002
3X	0.026	0.024	-0.009	-0.034	-0.008	-0.014	-0.028	-0.033	0.007	0.005	0.002	0.002
Shock E. Oil Price Increase												
1	2.947	0.374	-0.007	-0.102	0.310	0.009	-0.080	-0.070	-0.037	0.013	0.002	0.001
1X	3.626	0.404	-0.013	-0.093	0.380	0.015	-0.074	-0.060	-0.029	0.014	0.001	0.001
2A	3.367	0.395	-0.010	-0.096	0.353	0.013	-0.076	-0.064	-0.032	0.014	0.002	0.001
2AX	12.062	-0.199	-0.061	0.053	1.104	-0.035	0.030	0.054	0.077	0.006	-0.002	0.003
2B	3.555	-0.306	-0.266	-0.233	0.111	-0.261	-0.238	-0.223	-0.029	0.002	-0.001	0.000
2BX	11.087	0.064	0.000	0.084	1.091	0.042	0.066	0.081	0.070	0.006	0.000	0.003
3	2.197	0.232	-0.034	-0.107	0.202	-0.025	-0.090	-0.085	-0.040	0.009	0.002	0.002
3X	3.578	0.317	-0.020	-0.090	0.360	0.000	-0.074	-0.065	-0.023	0.009	0.002	0.002
Shock L. U.S. Money Demand												
1	0.139	0.007	-0.002	0.002	0.014	0.000	0.001	-0.003	0.005	0.000	0.000	0.000
1X	0.198	0.006	-0.003	0.003	0.020	0.000	0.001	-0.003	0.007	0.000	0.000	0.000
2A	0.008	0.002	0.000	0.000	0.001	0.000	0.000	0.000	0.000	0.000	0.000	0.000
2AX	0.037	0.001	0.000	0.000	0.004	0.000	0.000	0.000	0.001	0.000	0.000	0.000
2B	0.009	0.000	-0.001	-0.001	0.000	-0.001	-0.001	-0.001	0.000	0.000	0.000	0.000
2BX	0.034	0.002	0.000	0.000	0.004	0.000	0.000	0.000	0.001	0.000	0.000	0.000
3	0.576	-0.038	0.004	0.009	0.057	0.000	0.007	0.004	0.010	0.000	0.000	0.000
3X	0.989	-0.057	0.004	0.016	0.097	0.000	0.013	0.010	0.015	-0.001	0.000	0.000
Shock D. Japanese Money Demand												
1	-0.006	0.009	0.000	-0.002	0.000	0.000	-0.002	-0.001	-0.001	0.000	0.000	0.000
1X	-0.009	0.013	0.000	-0.003	0.000	0.001	-0.002	-0.001	-0.001	0.000	0.000	0.000
2A	0.001	0.000	0.000	0.000	0.000	0.000	0.000	0.000	0.000	0.000	0.000	0.000
2AX	0.002	0.002	0.000	0.000	0.000	0.000	0.000	0.000	0.000	0.000	0.000	0.000
2B	0.002	0.000	0.000	0.000	0.000	0.000	0.000	0.000	0.000	0.000	0.000	0.000
2BX	0.007	0.000	0.000	0.000	0.001	0.000	0.000	0.000	0.000	0.000	0.000	0.000
3	0.000	0.000	0.000	0.000	0.000	0.000	0.000	0.000	0.000	0.000	0.000	0.000
3X	0.001	0.000	0.000	0.000	0.000	0.000	0.000	0.000	0.000	0.000	0.000	0.000
Shock K. German Money Demand												
1	0.830	-0.069	-0.004	0.014	0.075	-0.006	0.010	0.017	0.006	0.000	0.000	0.000
1X	1.002	-0.095	-0.005	0.017	0.089	-0.009	0.013	0.020	0.008	0.000	0.000	0.000
2A	0.011	0.000	0.000	0.000	0.001	0.000	0.000	0.000	-0.001	0.000	0.000	0.000
2AX	0.033	-0.004	0.000	0.000	0.003	0.000	0.000	0.000	0.000	0.000	0.000	0.000
2B	0.011	-0.001	0.000	0.000	0.001	0.000	0.000	0.000	-0.001	0.000	0.000	0.000
2BX	0.026	-0.002	0.000	0.001	0.003	0.000	0.001	0.001	0.000	0.000	0.000	0.000
3	0.000	0.000	0.000	0.000	0.000	0.000	0.000	0.000	0.000	0.000	0.000	0.000
3X	0.001	0.000	0.000	0.000	0.000	0.000	0.000	0.000	-0.001	0.000	0.000	0.000
Shock F. U.S. Money Supply-Permanent												
FIXM	-0.198	-0.185	-0.023	0.031	-0.048	-0.025	0.019	0.017	-0.003	-0.004	0.000	0.000
1												
1X												

Table A-MSG-7
MSG MODEL
BILATERAL DOLLAR EXCHANGE RATES
(Deviations from Baseline)

Shock and Regime	Bilateral DM/$ Exchange Rate				Bilateral Yen/$ Exchange Rate			
	1st Yr	2nd Yr	5th Yr	10th Yr	1st Yr	2nd Yr	5th Yr	10th Yr
Shock A. US Aggregate Demand								
1	-1.299	0.222	0.051	0.015	-1.547	0.151	0.132	0.132
1X	-1.438	0.274	0.048	0.024	-1.799	0.189	0.127	0.129
2A	-1.390	0.255	0.049	0.021	-1.707	0.174	0.129	0.130
2AX	-1.106	0.376	0.121	0.205	-3.758	0.751	0.025	0.101
2B	-1.098	0.897	0.000	0.000	-1.376	0.490	0.000	0.000
2BX	-1.198	0.185	0.000	0.000	-3.399	0.056	0.000	0.000
3	-0.785	0.003	0.000	0.000	-0.785	0.003	0.000	0.000
3X	0.000	0.000	0.000	0.000	0.000	0.000	0.000	0.000
Shock I. Japanese Aggregate Demand								
1	0.003	0.032	-0.004	-0.032	2.483	-0.313	-0.026	-0.021
1X	0.003	0.040	-0.004	-0.032	2.974	-0.390	-0.021	-0.015
2A	0.003	0.037	-0.004	-0.032	2.790	-0.361	-0.023	-0.017
2AX	-0.052	0.155	-0.014	-0.031	7.532	-1.256	0.032	0.035
2B	0.009	0.060	0.000	0.000	2.452	-0.018	0.000	0.000
2BX	0.192	0.001	0.000	0.000	6.727	0.259	0.000	0.000
3	-0.055	0.006	0.000	0.000	-0.055	0.006	0.000	0.000
3X	0.000	0.000	0.000	0.000	0.000	0.000	0.000	0.000
Shock G. German Aggregate Demand								
1	1.367	-0.124	-0.036	-0.033	-0.032	0.002	0.019	0.004
1X	1.636	-0.164	-0.020	-0.012	-0.049	0.002	0.018	0.001
2A	1.535	-0.148	-0.026	-0.020	-0.042	0.002	0.018	0.002
2AX	4.302	-0.904	0.168	0.194	-0.467	0.091	-0.009	-0.025
2B	1.301	0.122	0.000	0.000	-0.045	-0.072	0.000	0.000
2BX	3.573	0.119	0.000	0.000	-0.305	-0.070	0.000	0.000
3	-0.039	0.004	0.000	0.000	-0.039	0.004	0.000	0.000
3X	0.000	0.000	0.000	0.000	0.000	0.000	0.000	0.000
Shock B. Global Aggregate Demand								
1	0.071	0.130	0.010	-0.050	0.903	-0.160	0.125	0.115
1X	0.201	0.150	0.024	-0.020	1.125	-0.199	0.124	0.114
2A	0.148	0.144	0.018	-0.032	1.040	-0.184	0.125	0.115
2AX	3.144	-0.373	0.275	0.368	3.307	-0.414	0.048	0.111
2B	0.212	1.079	0.000	0.000	1.032	0.401	0.000	0.000
2BX	2.567	0.305	0.000	0.000	3.022	0.246	0.000	0.000
3	-0.879	0.014	0.000	0.000	-0.879	0.014	0.000	0.000
3X	0.000	0.000	0.000	0.000	0.000	0.000	0.000	0.000
Shock C. US Aggregate Supply								
1	-0.042	0.212	0.151	-0.028	-0.198	0.173	0.253	0.083
1X	-0.050	0.228	0.153	-0.021	-0.256	0.172	0.260	0.081
2A	-0.048	0.222	0.152	-0.024	-0.235	0.172	0.258	0.081
2AX	0.158	0.385	0.146	0.052	-0.639	0.153	0.286	0.064
2B	0.424	-0.198	0.000	0.000	0.313	-0.108	0.000	0.000
2BX	0.648	0.352	0.000	0.000	-0.338	0.324	0.000	0.000
3	-0.214	0.074	0.000	0.000	-0.214	0.074	0.000	0.000
3X	0.000	0.000	0.000	0.000	0.000	0.000	0.000	0.000
Shock J. Japanese Aggregate Supply								
1	-0.021	0.013	-0.001	-0.011	0.521	-0.012	0.033	0.021
1X	-0.026	0.016	-0.001	-0.011	0.616	-0.027	0.035	0.022
2A	-0.024	0.015	-0.001	-0.011	0.580	-0.021	0.034	0.022
2AX	-0.080	0.064	-0.008	-0.012	1.498	-0.194	0.048	0.033
2B	-0.024	0.010	0.000	0.000	-0.265	-1.121	0.000	0.000
2BX	-0.033	-0.003	0.000	0.000	1.185	-0.968	0.000	0.000
3	-0.014	0.003	0.000	0.000	-0.014	0.003	0.000	0.000
3X	0.000	0.000	0.000	0.000	0.000	0.000	0.000	0.000

882

Shock and Regime	Bilateral DM/$ Exchange Rate				Bilateral Yen/$ Exchange Rate			
	1st Yr	2nd Yr	5th Yr	10th Yr	1st Yr	2nd Yr	5th Yr	10th Yr
Shock H. German Aggregate Supply								
1	0.269	0.049	-0.071	-0.095	-0.013	0.004	0.021	0.011
1X	0.318	0.061	-0.069	-0.091	-0.019	0.003	0.022	0.011
2A	0.300	0.056	-0.070	-0.092	-0.017	0.003	0.022	0.011
2AX	0.685	0.105	-0.053	-0.061	-0.075	-0.011	0.026	0.007
2B	-0.366	0.292	0.000	0.000	-0.022	-0.026	0.000	0.000
2BX	0.338	-0.341	0.000	0.000	-0.191	-0.033	0.000	0.000
3	-0.008	0.005	0.000	0.000	-0.008	0.005	0.000	0.000
3X	0.000	0.000	0.000	0.000	0.000	0.000	0.000	0.000
Shock E. Oil Price Increase								
1	0.296	0.230	-0.066	-0.238	0.119	0.152	0.304	0.122
1X	0.368	0.273	-0.064	-0.227	0.114	0.137	0.314	0.119
2A	0.341	0.257	-0.064	-0.231	0.115	0.143	0.311	0.120
2AX	1.158	0.579	-0.063	-0.115	0.215	-0.025	0.360	0.102
2B	0.396	-0.128	0.000	0.000	0.036	-0.768	0.000	0.000
2BX	1.645	-0.013	0.000	0.000	0.142	-0.386	0.000	0.000
3	-0.234	0.085	0.000	0.000	-0.234	0.085	0.000	0.000
3X	0.000	0.000	0.000	0.000	0.000	0.000	0.000	0.000
Shock L. U.S. Money Demand								
1	-0.611	0.064	-0.024	-0.010	-0.676	0.079	-0.011	-0.004
1X	-0.692	0.083	-0.028	-0.010	-0.789	0.104	-0.015	-0.005
2A	-0.008	0.002	0.000	0.000	-0.010	0.001	0.001	0.001
2AX	-0.007	0.002	0.001	0.001	-0.023	0.005	0.000	0.001
2B	-0.007	0.005	0.000	0.000	-0.008	0.003	0.000	0.000
2BX	-0.007	0.001	0.000	0.000	-0.020	0.000	0.000	0.000
3	-0.230	-0.002	0.000	0.000	-0.230	-0.002	0.000	0.000
3X	0.000	0.000	0.000	0.000	0.000	0.000	0.000	0.000
Shock D. Japanese Money Demand								
1	-0.011	0.001	-0.001	-0.003	0.773	-0.068	0.006	0.009
1X	-0.015	0.002	-0.001	-0.003	0.921	-0.090	0.008	0.010
2A	0.000	0.000	0.000	0.000	0.017	-0.002	0.000	0.000
2AX	0.000	0.001	0.000	0.000	0.045	-0.008	0.000	0.000
2B	0.000	0.000	0.000	0.000	0.015	0.000	0.000	0.000
2BX	0.001	0.000	0.000	0.000	0.040	0.001	0.000	0.000
3	0.000	0.000	0.000	0.000	0.000	0.000	0.000	0.000
3X	0.000	0.000	0.000	0.000	0.000	0.000	0.000	0.000
Shock K. German Money Demand								
1	0.757	-0.074	0.044	0.056	-0.025	0.001	-0.004	-0.007
1X	0.898	-0.105	0.053	0.067	-0.036	0.002	-0.005	-0.008
2A	0.009	-0.001	0.000	0.000	0.000	0.000	0.000	0.000
2AX	0.026	-0.006	0.001	0.001	-0.003	0.001	0.000	0.000
2B	0.008	0.001	0.000	0.000	0.000	0.000	0.000	0.000
2BX	0.021	0.001	0.000	0.000	-0.002	0.000	0.000	0.000
3	0.000	0.000	0.000	0.000	0.000	0.000	0.000	0.000
3X	0.000	0.000	0.000	0.000	0.000	0.000	0.000	0.000
Shock F. U.S. Money Supply-Permanent								
FIXM 1 1X	1.350	0.934	0.000	0.000	1.498	0.934	0.000	0.000

Table A-MUL-1
MULTIMOD MODEL
EFFECTS ON U.S. REAL GNP, U.S. PRICE LEVEL, U.S. INFLATION RATE
(Deviations from Baseline)

Shock and Regime	Real GNP				GNP Deflator				Inflation Rate			
	1st Yr	2nd Yr	5th Yr	10th Yr	1st Yr	2nd Yr	5th Yr	10th Yr	1st Yr	2nd Yr	5th Yr	10th Yr
Shock A. US Aggregate Demand												
1	0.994	-0.283	-0.226	0.087	0.142	0.286	0.300	-0.109	0.149	0.150	-0.062	-0.049
1X	0.986	-0.299	-0.226	0.117	0.132	0.252	0.179	-0.083	0.138	0.125	-0.086	0.004
2A												
2AX	1.002	-0.259	-0.273	0.130	0.149	0.296	0.260	-0.235	0.156	0.153	-0.091	-0.031
2B												
2BX	0.871	-0.443	-0.103	0.010	0.113	0.221	0.228	0.181	0.118	0.112	-0.034	0.010
3												
3X	0.986	-0.280	-0.205	0.103	0.129	0.241	0.156	-0.074	0.135	0.117	-0.087	0.009
Shock I. Japanese Aggregate Demand												
1	0.041	-0.007	0.004	0.001	0.003	0.003	-0.003	-0.004	0.003	0.001	-0.003	0.002
1X	0.037	-0.014	0.008	-0.002	0.003	0.003	-0.009	0.002	0.003	0.000	-0.004	0.004
2A												
2AX	0.044	-0.007	0.002	0.001	0.001	0.002	-0.005	-0.002	0.002	0.001	-0.003	0.003
2B												
2BX	0.036	0.003	0.002	0.001	0.005	0.007	0.016	0.014	0.005	0.002	0.004	-0.002
3												
3X	0.040	-0.015	0.004	-0.001	0.002	0.002	-0.004	0.001	0.002	0.001	-0.002	0.001
Shock G. German Aggregate Demand												
1	0.028	0.002	0.000	0.000	0.001	0.001	-0.002	0.000	0.001	-0.000	-0.001	0.001
1X	0.024	-0.003	0.005	-0.003	0.001	0.000	-0.006	0.003	0.001	-0.001	-0.001	0.002
2A												
2AX	0.030	0.000	0.001	0.002	-0.000	-0.001	-0.004	0.001	-0.000	-0.001	-0.001	0.002
2B												
2BX	0.021	0.013	0.002	0.004	0.003	0.005	0.013	0.009	0.003	0.002	0.004	-0.003
3												
3X	0.028	-0.005	-0.002	0.001	0.000	0.001	-0.001	0.000	0.000	0.001	-0.001	0.000
Shock B. Global Aggregate Demand												
1	1.063	-0.288	-0.221	0.088	0.145	0.289	0.293	-0.113	0.152	0.150	-0.066	-0.046
1X	1.046	-0.318	-0.222	0.112	0.136	0.257	0.174	-0.075	0.143	0.126	-0.089	0.005
2A												
2AX	1.073	-0.268	-0.275	0.138	0.151	0.299	0.254	-0.246	0.158	0.154	-0.095	-0.029
2B												
2BX	0.931	-0.419	-0.107	0.018	0.121	0.231	0.256	0.204	0.127	0.114	-0.025	0.006
3												
3X	1.048	-0.306	-0.199	0.104	0.133	0.248	0.149	-0.074	0.139	0.120	-0.093	0.013
Shock C. US Aggregate Supply												
1	-0.175	0.076	0.145	-0.074	0.796	-0.268	-0.229	0.101	0.833	-1.101	0.058	0.038
1X	-0.170	0.037	0.235	-0.143	0.782	-0.285	-0.199	0.116	0.818	-1.104	0.080	0.008
2A												
2AX	-0.191	0.011	0.211	-0.091	0.776	-0.309	-0.284	0.196	0.812	-1.123	0.067	0.051
2B												
2BX	-0.300	0.128	-0.020	-0.020	0.875	-0.097	0.083	0.154	0.915	-1.005	0.079	-0.011
3												
3X	-0.160	0.040	0.220	-0.134	0.779	-0.287	-0.189	0.108	0.815	-1.104	0.084	0.003
Shock J. Japanese Aggregate Supply												
1	0.012	0.014	0.000	-0.002	-0.010	-0.014	-0.007	0.005	-0.010	-0.005	0.003	0.001
1X	0.014	0.021	-0.003	-0.002	-0.007	-0.012	-0.000	0.002	-0.007	-0.005	0.006	-0.003
2A												
2AX	0.008	0.013	0.001	-0.001	-0.007	-0.012	-0.004	0.007	-0.007	-0.006	0.005	-0.001
2B												
2BX	0.036	0.043	-0.009	-0.003	-0.025	-0.032	-0.034	-0.035	-0.026	-0.007	-0.007	0.002
3												
3X	0.005	0.010	-0.001	-0.000	-0.003	-0.005	0.001	-0.000	-0.003	-0.002	0.002	-0.001

Shock and Regime	Real GNP				GNP Deflator				Inflation Rate			
	1st Yr	2nd Yr	5th Yr	10th Yr	1st Yr	2nd Yr	5th Yr	10th Yr	1st Yr	2nd Yr	5th Yr	10th Yr
Shock H. German Aggregate Supply												
1	0.016	-0.002	0.001	0.001	-0.007	-0.010	-0.005	0.001	-0.008	-0.003	0.001	0.001
1X	0.016	0.010	-0.002	0.000	-0.005	-0.008	0.000	-0.001	-0.005	-0.003	0.004	-0.002
2A												
2AX	0.010	0.003	0.001	-0.002	-0.005	-0.008	-0.003	0.004	-0.005	-0.003	0.003	-0.001
2B												
2BX	0.065	0.047	-0.041	-0.002	-0.027	-0.043	-0.046	-0.045	-0.028	-0.016	-0.011	0.007
3												
3X	0.007	0.004	0.001	-0.001	-0.002	-0.004	0.001	0.000	-0.002	-0.001	0.001	-0.001
Shock E. Oil Price Increase												
1	1.063	-0.288	-0.221	0.088	0.145	0.289	0.293	-0.113	0.152	0.150	-0.066	-0.046
1X	1.046	-0.318	-0.222	0.112	0.136	0.257	0.174	-0.075	0.143	0.126	-0.089	0.005
2A												
2AX	1.073	-0.268	-0.275	0.138	0.151	0.299	0.254	-0.246	0.158	0.154	-0.095	-0.029
2B												
2BX	0.931	-0.419	-0.107	0.018	0.121	0.231	0.256	0.204	0.127	0.114	-0.025	0.006
3												
3X	1.048	-0.306	-0.199	0.104	0.133	0.248	0.149	-0.074	0.139	0.120	-0.093	0.013
Shock L. U.S. Money Demand												
1	-0.246	-0.288	0.071	-0.009	-0.021	-0.059	-0.196	-0.027	-0.022	-0.040	-0.029	0.054
1X	-0.260	-0.339	0.122	-0.046	-0.048	-0.129	-0.347	0.025	-0.050	-0.084	-0.039	0.091
2A												
2AX	0.000	0.007	-0.001	-0.001	-0.000	0.000	0.001	-0.001	-0.000	0.001	-0.000	-0.000
2B												
2BX	0.000	0.006	-0.002	-0.000	-0.000	0.000	0.001	-0.001	-0.000	0.001	-0.000	0.000
3												
3X	-0.256	-0.296	0.118	-0.065	-0.052	-0.144	-0.349	0.051	-0.055	-0.096	-0.026	0.083
Shock D. Japanese Money Demand												
1	0.008	0.020	-0.001	-0.001	-0.004	-0.009	-0.005	0.002	-0.004	-0.005	0.003	0.000
1X	0.003	0.017	0.004	-0.005	-0.001	-0.006	-0.009	0.006	-0.001	-0.005	0.002	0.001
2A												
2AX	0.000	0.001	0.000	0.000	-0.000	-0.000	-0.000	-0.000	-0.000	0.000	0.000	0.000
2B												
2BX	0.000	0.000	0.001	0.000	-0.000	-0.000	-0.000	-0.000	-0.000	0.000	-0.000	-0.000
3												
3X	0.000	0.001	0.000	0.000	-0.000	-0.000	-0.000	-0.000	-0.000	0.000	0.000	0.000
Shock K. German Money Demand												
1	0.010	0.030	0.002	-0.004	-0.004	-0.013	-0.010	0.006	-0.004	-0.009	0.004	0.001
1X	-0.001	0.023	0.013	-0.013	-0.002	-0.010	-0.014	0.012	-0.002	-0.008	0.003	0.000
2A												
2AX	0.000	0.000	0.000	0.000	-0.000	-0.000	-0.000	0.000	-0.000	0.000	0.000	0.000
2B												
2BX	0.000	0.000	0.000	-0.001	-0.000	-0.000	-0.001	-0.001	-0.000	0.000	-0.000	-0.000
3												
3X	0.000	0.001	0.000	0.000	-0.000	-0.000	-0.000	-0.000	-0.000	0.000	0.000	0.000
Shock F. U.S. Money Supply-Permanent												
FIXM												
1	0.384	0.499	0.001	-0.160	0.067	0.202	0.856	1.256	0.071	0.141	0.228	-0.021
1X	0.408	0.558	-0.053	-0.127	0.094	0.274	1.022	1.134	0.099	0.188	0.239	-0.080

885

MULTIMOD MODEL
EFFECTS ON U.S. INTEREST RATES AND U.S. CURRENT ACCOUNT/GNP RATIO
(Deviations from Baseline)

Shock and Regime	Short Interest Rate				Long Interest Rate				Current Account/GNP Ratio			
	1st Yr	2nd Yr	5th Yr	10th Yr	1st Yr	2nd Yr	5th Yr	10th Yr	1st Yr	2nd Yr	5th Yr	10th Yr
Shock A. US Aggregate Demand												
1	0.366	0.265	-0.018	-0.076	0.159	0.073	-0.078	-0.019	-0.122	0.013	-0.017	0.017
1X	0.124	0.214	0.042	-0.084	0.146	0.110	-0.084	0.006	-0.123	0.040	-0.032	0.026
2A												
2AX	0.573	0.018	-0.007	-0.053	0.120	-0.001	-0.043	-0.008	-0.122	-0.011	-0.007	0.010
2B												
2BX	0.586	0.712	-0.113	0.011	0.322	0.172	-0.106	0.025	-0.105	-0.002	-0.034	-0.001
3												
3X	0.129	0.216	0.022	-0.064	0.139	0.098	-0.092	0.018	-0.131	0.043	-0.026	0.019
Shock I. Japanese Aggregate Demand												
1	0.039	0.003	-0.008	0.001	0.005	-0.004	-0.005	0.003	0.021	-0.011	0.002	-0.000
1X	0.012	0.014	-0.006	0.003	0.007	0.002	-0.009	0.006	0.022	-0.010	0.003	-0.001
2A												
2AX	0.023	-0.003	-0.002	-0.000	0.003	-0.002	-0.002	0.001	0.021	-0.007	0.002	0.000
2B												
2BX	0.240	0.013	-0.009	-0.002	0.018	-0.027	0.009	-0.002	0.017	-0.029	0.009	-0.002
3												
3X	0.008	0.009	-0.002	0.001	0.004	0.001	-0.003	0.002	0.026	-0.009	0.008	0.004
Shock G. German Aggregate Demand												
1	0.028	-0.002	-0.005	0.002	0.002	-0.004	-0.001	0.002	0.012	-0.003	0.002	-0.001
1X	0.009	0.009	-0.006	0.004	0.003	-0.000	-0.006	0.004	0.012	-0.003	0.002	-0.002
2A												
2AX	0.015	-0.000	-0.001	0.002	0.002	-0.002	-0.002	-0.000	0.012	-0.001	0.002	0.000
2B												
2BX	0.187	0.000	-0.026	0.000	0.010	-0.024	0.014	-0.009	0.005	-0.017	0.015	-0.005
3												
3X	0.006	0.005	-0.002	0.001	0.001	0.001	-0.000	0.000	0.015	-0.003	-0.000	0.001
Shock B. Global Aggregate Demand												
1	0.431	0.264	-0.031	-0.072	0.165	0.063	-0.083	-0.015	-0.090	0.000	-0.013	0.016
1X	0.145	0.237	0.031	-0.076	0.158	0.113	-0.097	0.013	-0.090	0.027	-0.029	0.024
2A												
2AX	0.609	0.015	-0.011	-0.055	0.125	-0.004	-0.048	-0.007	-0.091	-0.019	-0.003	0.010
2B												
2BX	1.050	0.688	-0.124	0.005	0.349	0.116	-0.078	0.015	-0.087	-0.048	-0.012	-0.006
3												
3X	0.144	0.233	0.019	-0.065	0.149	0.102	-0.100	0.022	-0.092	0.029	-0.025	0.021
Shock C. US Aggregate Supply												
1	0.923	-0.807	0.002	0.063	-0.041	-0.215	0.059	0.014	0.034	-0.155	0.023	-0.021
1X	0.313	0.044	-0.160	0.118	-0.024	-0.101	0.010	0.022	0.034	-0.090	0.035	-0.035
2A												
2AX	0.291	-0.149	-0.037	0.053	-0.013	-0.072	0.017	0.018	0.034	-0.086	0.017	-0.015
2B												
2BX	4.896	-4.068	0.281	-0.028	0.102	-0.799	0.171	-0.025	0.067	-0.577	0.021	-0.017
3												
3X	0.311	0.038	-0.150	0.106	-0.027	-0.098	0.023	0.011	0.038	-0.085	0.028	-0.029
Shock J. Japanese Aggregate Supply												
1	0.008	-0.049	0.006	0.003	-0.007	-0.007	0.006	-0.001	-0.005	0.017	-0.003	0.000
1X	0.005	-0.006	-0.006	0.006	-0.007	-0.007	0.007	-0.003	-0.005	0.014	-0.003	0.000
2A												
2AX	0.001	0.000	-0.002	0.003	-0.003	-0.003	0.002	0.000	-0.005	0.013	-0.002	0.000
2B												
2BX	0.064	-0.756	0.017	0.009	-0.031	-0.051	-0.018	0.005	-0.011	0.042	-0.022	0.003
3												
3X	0.005	-0.000	-0.003	0.001	0.000	-0.001	-0.000	0.000	-0.006	0.010	-0.001	-0.000

Shock and Regime	Short Interest Rate				Long Interest Rate				Current Account/GNP Ratio			
	1st Yr	2nd Yr	5th Yr	10th Yr	1st Yr	2nd Yr	5th Yr	10th Yr	1st Yr	2nd Yr	5th Yr	10th Yr
Shock H. German Aggregate Supply												
1	0.001	-0.041	0.009	-0.001	-0.005	-0.004	0.004	-0.001	0.005	0.009	-0.006	0.002
1X	0.003	-0.005	-0.002	0.002	-0.004	-0.004	0.006	-0.004	0.002	0.008	-0.003	0.001
2A												
2AX	0.003	-0.002	-0.001	0.001	-0.002	-0.002	0.002	0.000	0.001	0.006	-0.003	-0.001
2B												
2BX	0.104	-0.887	0.125	0.002	-0.026	-0.054	-0.031	0.023	0.009	0.048	-0.064	0.018
3												
3X	0.004	-0.001	-0.002	0.001	-0.000	-0.002	-0.000	0.000	-0.002	0.005	-0.001	-0.000
Shock E. Oil Price Increase												
1	0.431	0.264	-0.031	-0.072	0.165	0.063	-0.083	-0.015	-0.090	0.000	-0.013	0.016
1X	0.145	0.237	0.031	-0.076	0.158	0.113	-0.097	0.013	-0.090	0.027	-0.029	0.024
2A												
2AX	0.609	0.015	-0.011	-0.055	0.125	-0.004	-0.048	-0.007	-0.091	-0.019	-0.003	0.010
2B												
2BX	1.050	0.688	-0.124	0.005	0.349	0.116	-0.078	0.015	-0.087	-0.048	-0.012	-0.006
3												
3X	0.144	0.233	0.019	-0.065	0.149	0.102	-0.100	0.022	-0.092	0.029	-0.025	0.021
Shock L. U.S. Money Demand												
1	1.145	0.183	-0.080	0.047	0.222	-0.015	-0.017	0.034	0.043	-0.131	0.010	-0.011
1X	0.390	0.451	-0.078	0.088	0.236	0.126	-0.091	0.090	0.042	-0.045	-0.026	-0.004
2A												
2AX	0.000	0.004	-0.000	-0.001	-0.000	0.001	-0.000	-0.000	0.000	-0.001	-0.000	0.000
2B												
2BX	-0.001	0.005	-0.002	-0.001	0.000	0.001	0.000	0.000	0.000	-0.001	-0.001	0.001
3												
3X	0.409	0.471	-0.092	0.108	0.240	0.125	-0.086	0.086	0.014	-0.037	-0.020	-0.009
Shock D. Japanese Money Demand												
1	0.026	-0.014	-0.001	0.002	-0.000	-0.005	0.002	0.000	-0.010	0.007	-0.001	-0.001
1X	0.008	0.010	-0.010	0.010	0.002	-0.002	-0.005	0.005	-0.088	0.003	0.002	-0.002
2A												
2AX	0.000	0.000	0.000	0.000	-0.000	-0.000	-0.000	0.000	0.000	0.000	0.000	0.000
2B												
2BX	-0.001	0.002	-0.002	-0.000	-0.000	0.000	-0.001	-0.000	0.000	0.000	0.000	-0.000
3												
3X	-0.000	-0.000	0.000	-0.000	-0.000	-0.000	0.000	0.000	0.000	0.000	0.000	0.000
Shock K. German Money Demand												
1	0.039	-0.018	-0.004	0.006	-0.003	-0.010	0.004	0.002	-0.016	0.008	0.003	-0.003
1X	0.011	0.011	-0.016	0.016	-0.000	-0.005	-0.005	0.008	-0.017	0.003	0.007	-0.006
2A												
2AX	0.000	0.000	0.000	0.000	-0.000	-0.000	-0.000	0.000	0.000	0.000	0.000	-0.000
2B												
2BX	-0.001	0.001	-0.002	-0.000	0.000	0.000	-0.000	0.000	0.000	0.000	-0.000	0.000
3												
3X	-0.000	0.000	0.000	-0.000	-0.000	-0.000	0.000	0.000	0.000	0.000	0.000	0.000
Shock F. U.S. Money Supply-Permanent **FIXM**												
1	-0.999	-0.216	0.202	0.029	-0.162	0.079	0.159	-0.037	-0.062	0.110	-0.021	-0.017
1X	-0.335	-0.403	0.158	0.004	-0.180	-0.056	0.219	-0.093	-0.062	0.037	0.018	-0.029

MULTIMOD MODEL

EFFECTS ON JAPANESE REAL GNP, JAPANESE PRICE LEVEL, JAPANESE INFLATION RATE

(Deviations from Baseline)

Shock and Regime	Real GNP				GNP Deflator				Inflation Rate			
	1st Yr	2nd Yr	5th Yr	10th Yr	1st Yr	2nd Yr	5th Yr	10th Yr	1st Yr	2nd Yr	5th Yr	10th Yr
Shock A. US Aggregate Demand												
1	0.142	0.031	0.014	-0.019	-0.003	-0.002	-0.026	0.002	-0.003	0.001	-0.008	0.011
1X	0.130	-0.002	0.035	-0.035	-0.002	-0.002	-0.036	0.020	-0.002	-0.000	-0.009	0.012
2A												
2AX	0.142	0.029	0.006	-0.008	-0.006	-0.004	-0.027	0.003	-0.006	0.003	-0.009	0.014
2B												
2BX	0.144	0.127	0.015	0.002	0.002	0.007	0.009	0.003	0.002	0.004	0.001	-0.002
3												
3X	0.076	-0.040	0.127	-0.033	-0.009	-0.019	-0.012	0.099	-0.009	-0.010	0.020	-0.010
Shock I. Japanese Aggregate Demand												
1	0.936	-0.269	-0.122	0.034	0.162	0.324	0.211	-0.083	0.164	0.163	-0.095	-0.006
1X	0.940	-0.303	-0.120	0.033	0.146	0.280	0.108	-0.028	0.148	0.134	-0.100	0.019
2A												
2AX	0.944	-0.216	-0.142	0.032	0.152	0.289	0.100	-0.068	0.154	0.138	-0.113	0.030
2B												
2BX	0.761	-0.444	-0.040	-0.010	0.136	0.269	0.245	0.222	0.138	0.134	-0.029	0.006
3												
3X	1.084	-0.123	-0.116	-0.005	0.117	0.218	0.041	-0.030	0.119	0.102	-0.085	0.019
Shock G. German Aggregate Demand												
1	0.025	0.006	-0.003	0.002	-0.000	0.002	0.000	-0.002	-0.000	0.002	-0.001	0.001
1X	0.021	0.001	-0.001	0.000	-0.000	0.001	-0.002	0.000	-0.000	0.001	-0.001	0.001
2A												
2AX	0.026	0.003	-0.002	0.002	-0.000	0.001	-0.001	-0.001	-0.000	0.001	-0.001	0.001
2B												
2BX	0.026	0.028	-0.013	0.008	-0.001	0.001	0.005	0.001	-0.001	0.002	0.000	0.000
3												
3X	0.023	0.003	-0.001	0.001	-0.001	-0.000	-0.000	-0.000	-0.001	0.001	-0.000	0.000
Shock B. Global Aggregate Demand												
1	1.098	-0.237	-0.119	0.018	0.161	0.328	0.200	-0.081	0.163	0.168	-0.101	-0.000
1X	1.087	-0.311	-0.093	0.002	0.146	0.283	0.079	-0.008	0.148	0.138	-0.110	0.031
2A												
2AX	1.105	-0.203	-0.174	0.053	0.159	0.319	0.125	-0.119	0.161	0.162	-0.130	0.038
2B												
2BX	0.933	-0.287	-0.038	-0.002	0.137	0.276	0.259	0.228	0.139	0.140	-0.028	0.004
3												
3X	1.157	-0.217	-0.082	-0.007	0.154	0.306	0.115	-0.039	0.156	0.153	-0.114	0.023
Shock C. US Aggregate Supply												
1	0.032	0.066	-0.016	0.019	-0.025	-0.025	0.002	0.001	-0.025	-0.001	0.010	-0.006
1X	0.033	0.053	-0.034	0.031	-0.017	-0.024	0.007	-0.006	-0.018	-0.007	0.015	-0.013
2A												
2AX	0.021	0.036	-0.007	0.011	-0.018	-0.024	-0.001	0.010	-0.018	-0.006	0.012	-0.008
2B												
2BX	0.126	0.324	0.005	0.008	-0.076	-0.074	-0.067	-0.071	-0.077	0.002	-0.005	0.002
3												
3X	0.069	0.117	-0.066	0.015	-0.004	0.011	0.065	-0.075	-0.004	0.016	0.006	-0.019
Shock J. Japanese Aggregate Supply												
1	-0.109	0.313	0.108	-0.032	0.658	-0.455	-0.264	0.075	0.666	-1.117	0.112	0.013
1X	-0.110	0.204	0.175	-0.060	0.650	-0.452	-0.198	0.050	0.658	-1.106	0.136	-0.018
2A												
2AX	-0.139	0.160	0.160	-0.040	0.649	-0.459	-0.203	0.096	0.657	-1.112	0.142	-0.019
2B												
2BX	-0.193	0.965	-0.039	0.018	0.761	-0.280	-0.024	0.003	0.770	-1.044	0.070	-0.007
3												
3X	-0.180	0.026	0.048	-0.002	0.706	-0.328	-0.075	0.022	0.715	-1.037	0.095	-0.012

Shock and Regime	Real GNP				GNP Deflator				Inflation Rate			
	1st Yr	2nd Yr	5th Yr	10th Yr	1st Yr	2nd Yr	5th Yr	10th Yr	1st Yr	2nd Yr	5th Yr	10th Yr
Shock H. German Aggregate Supply												
1	0.009	-0.012	0.005	-0.000	-0.001	-0.002	-0.005	0.001	-0.001	-0.001	0.000	0.001
1X	0.010	-0.002	0.000	0.001	0.000	-0.001	-0.002	-0.000	0.000	-0.001	0.001	-0.001
2A												
2AX	0.007	-0.005	-0.001	0.000	0.000	-0.001	-0.002	0.001	0.000	-0.001	0.000	0.000
2B												
2BX	0.030	-0.052	0.060	-0.018	-0.007	-0.001	-0.012	-0.007	-0.007	0.006	-0.005	0.000
3												
3X	0.007	-0.003	-0.000	0.001	0.001	0.001	-0.000	-0.000	0.001	0.000	-0.000	0.000
Shock E. Oil Price Increase												
1	1.098	-0.237	-0.119	0.018	0.161	0.328	0.200	-0.081	0.163	0.168	-0.101	-0.000
1X	1.087	-0.311	-0.093	0.002	0.146	0.283	0.079	-0.008	0.148	0.138	-0.110	0.031
2A												
2AX	1.105	-0.203	-0.174	0.053	0.159	0.319	0.125	-0.119	0.161	0.162	-0.130	0.038
2B												
2BX	0.933	-0.287	-0.038	-0.002	0.137	0.276	0.259	0.228	0.139	0.140	-0.028	0.004
3												
3X	1.157	-0.217	-0.082	-0.007	0.154	0.306	0.115	-0.039	0.156	0.153	-0.114	0.023
Shock L. U.S. Money Demand												
1	0.042	0.115	-0.005	0.010	-0.018	-0.032	-0.029	0.007	-0.018	-0.014	0.008	0.001
1X	0.023	0.070	0.028	-0.002	-0.010	-0.026	-0.042	0.019	-0.010	-0.016	0.005	-0.001
2A												
2AX	0.000	0.001	0.000	-0.000	-0.000	-0.000	-0.000	-0.000	-0.000	0.000	0.000	0.000
2B												
2BX	-0.000	0.000	-0.000	-0.002	-0.000	-0.000	-0.001	-0.000	-0.000	-0.000	0.000	0.000
3												
3X	-0.136	-0.062	0.088	-0.064	-0.036	-0.095	-0.142	0.021	-0.036	-0.061	0.021	-0.001
Shock D. Japanese Money Demand												
1	-0.291	-0.137	0.018	-0.014	-0.025	-0.080	-0.139	0.002	-0.026	-0.055	0.006	0.021
1X	-0.282	-0.261	0.094	-0.049	-0.058	-0.158	-0.292	0.034	-0.059	-0.101	0.008	0.042
2A												
2AX	0.000	0.009	-0.001	-0.001	-0.000	0.001	0.001	-0.001	-0.000	0.001	-0.001	0.000
2B												
2BX	-0.001	0.008	-0.000	0.001	-0.000	0.001	0.002	-0.001	-0.000	0.001	-0.000	-0.000
3												
3X	0.000	0.011	-0.001	-0.002	-0.000	0.001	0.002	-0.001	-0.000	0.001	-0.000	-0.000
Shock K. German Money Demand												
1	0.014	0.006	-0.005	0.004	0.001	0.002	0.001	-0.002	0.001	0.001	-0.001	-0.000
1X	0.007	0.007	-0.004	0.005	0.001	0.001	-0.002	0.000	0.001	0.001	-0.001	0.000
2A												
2AX	0.000	0.000	0.000	0.000	-0.000	-0.000	-0.000	-0.000	-0.000	0.000	0.000	0.000
2B												
2BX	-0.000	-0.001	-0.001	-0.001	-0.000	-0.000	-0.000	-0.001	-0.000	-0.000	0.000	0.000
3												
3X	0.000	0.000	0.000	0.000	-0.000	-0.000	-0.000	-0.000	-0.000	0.000	0.000	0.000
Shock F. U.S. Money Supply-Permanent												
FIXM												
1	-0.045	-0.119	0.004	0.022	0.018	0.036	0.046	-0.029	0.019	0.018	-0.005	-0.011
1X	-0.025	-0.070	-0.032	0.045	0.011	0.031	0.057	-0.050	0.011	0.020	-0.004	-0.007

Table A-MUL-4
MULTIMOD MODEL
EFFECTS ON JAPANESE INTEREST RATES AND JAPANESE CURRENT ACCOUNT/GNP RATIO
(Deviations from Baseline)

Shock and Regime	Short Interest Rate				Long Interest Rate				Current Account/GNP Ratio			
	1st Yr	2nd Yr	5th Yr	10th Yr	1st Yr	2nd Yr	5th Yr	10th Yr	1st Yr	2nd Yr	5th Yr	10th Yr
Shock A. US Aggregate Demand												
1	0.100	-0.002	-0.020	0.006	0.010	-0.014	-0.012	0.009	0.072	0.030	0.001	-0.021
1X	0.032	0.033	-0.018	0.009	0.014	0.002	-0.019	0.014	0.071	0.009	0.016	-0.027
2A												
2AX	0.068	0.013	-0.010	-0.003	0.010	-0.006	-0.010	0.005	0.073	0.044	-0.004	-0.013
2B												
2BX	0.525	-0.075	-0.064	0.017	0.028	-0.080	0.004	0.004	0.073	0.058	0.006	0.000
3												
3X	0.146	0.174	-0.034	-0.025	0.092	0.043	-0.087	0.026	0.071	0.008	0.015	-0.026
Shock I. Japanese Aggregate Demand												
1	0.370	0.325	-0.060	-0.036	0.153	0.060	-0.084	0.005	-0.189	0.030	0.009	0.003
1X	0.124	0.230	0.028	-0.053	0.148	0.109	-0.081	0.009	-0.183	0.033	0.010	0.003
2A												
2AX	0.546	0.036	-0.021	-0.018	0.115	-0.002	-0.033	0.001	-0.191	0.029	0.004	0.003
2B												
2BX	0.594	1.070	-0.133	0.003	0.359	0.213	-0.095	0.015	-0.195	0.032	0.014	0.002
3												
3X	0.006	0.006	-0.002	0.001	0.002	0.001	-0.002	0.001	-0.185	0.032	0.001	0.000
Shock G. German Aggregate Demand												
1	0.017	0.001	-0.003	0.001	0.002	-0.002	-0.002	0.001	0.013	0.005	-0.002	0.001
1X	0.005	0.005	-0.003	0.001	0.003	0.001	-0.003	0.002	0.011	0.003	-0.002	0.000
2A												
2AX	0.013	0.002	-0.001	0.001	0.003	-0.001	-0.001	-0.000	0.013	0.003	-0.000	0.001
2B												
2BX	0.086	-0.029	0.005	-0.004	0.010	-0.005	0.004	-0.002	0.015	0.022	-0.006	0.005
3												
3X	0.003	0.003	-0.001	0.001	0.001	0.001	-0.000	0.000	0.011	0.002	0.000	0.000
Shock B. Global Aggregate Demand												
1	0.488	0.327	-0.078	-0.034	0.169	0.049	-0.096	0.010	-0.106	0.064	0.009	-0.017
1X	0.161	0.269	0.008	-0.043	0.166	0.113	-0.105	0.026	-0.103	0.043	0.023	-0.022
2A												
2AX	0.629	0.058	-0.025	-0.033	0.137	0.001	-0.050	0.003	-0.106	0.078	0.004	-0.009
2B												
2BX	1.208	0.953	-0.183	0.017	0.396	0.126	-0.087	0.017	-0.108	0.115	0.014	0.005
3												
3X	0.159	0.185	-0.039	-0.024	0.097	0.044	-0.093	0.030	-0.105	0.044	0.019	-0.021
Shock C. US Aggregate Supply												
1	0.013	-0.066	0.013	0.002	-0.010	-0.009	0.014	-0.003	-0.006	0.079	-0.012	0.021
1X	0.008	-0.005	-0.009	0.013	-0.008	-0.008	0.012	-0.005	-0.005	0.038	-0.028	0.033
2A												
2AX	0.002	0.006	-0.004	0.010	-0.005	-0.005	0.007	0.002	-0.007	0.033	-0.009	0.015
2B												
2BX	0.059	-1.288	0.107	-0.013	-0.062	-0.074	-0.009	0.001	0.008	0.378	0.004	0.010
3												
3X	0.145	-0.041	-0.075	0.065	-0.047	-0.075	0.043	-0.007	-0.006	0.037	-0.028	0.033
Shock J. Japanese Aggregate Supply												
1	0.810	-0.931	0.048	0.043	-0.077	-0.220	0.082	0.001	-0.010	0.002	-0.002	-0.007
1X	0.273	-0.034	-0.141	0.091	-0.064	-0.123	0.036	0.008	-0.012	-0.014	0.001	-0.009
2A												
2AX	0.254	-0.150	-0.022	0.028	-0.019	-0.066	0.021	0.004	-0.007	-0.007	0.005	-0.008
2B												
2BX	4.744	-4.802	0.315	-0.017	-0.022	-0.900	0.153	-0.013	-0.027	0.047	-0.006	-0.006
3												
3X	0.003	-0.001	-0.002	0.001	0.000	-0.001	-0.000	0.000	-0.006	-0.010	0.005	-0.001

890

Shock and Regime	Short Interest Rate				Long Interest Rate				Current Account/GNP Ratio			
	1st Yr	2nd Yr	5th Yr	10th Yr	1st Yr	2nd Yr	5th Yr	10th Yr	1st Yr	2nd Yr	5th Yr	10th Yr
Shock H. German Aggregate Supply												
1	0.001	-0.008	0.002	0.001	-0.003	-0.002	0.003	-0.001	0.005	-0.008	0.002	0.001
1X	0.001	0.001	-0.002	0.002	-0.001	-0.001	0.002	-0.001	0.006	-0.002	-0.001	0.002
2A												
2AX	0.004	-0.003	-0.001	0.001	-0.001	-0.002	0.000	0.000	0.005	-0.004	-0.002	0.001
2B												
2BX	-0.050	-0.182	-0.033	0.016	-0.010	-0.010	-0.020	0.007	0.018	-0.018	0.036	-0.011
3												
3X	0.002	-0.001	-0.001	0.001	-0.000	-0.001	-0.000	0.000	0.005	-0.002	-0.001	0.001
Shock E. Oil Price Increase												
1	0.488	0.327	-0.078	-0.034	0.169	0.049	-0.096	0.010	-0.106	0.064	0.009	-0.017
1X	0.161	0.269	0.008	-0.043	0.166	0.113	-0.105	0.026	-0.103	0.043	0.023	-0.022
2A												
2AX	0.629	0.058	-0.025	-0.033	0.137	0.001	-0.050	0.003	-0.106	0.078	0.004	-0.009
2B												
2BX	1.208	0.953	-0.183	0.017	0.396	0.126	-0.087	0.017	-0.108	0.115	0.014	0.005
3												
3X	0.159	0.185	-0.039	-0.024	0.097	0.044	-0.093	0.030	-0.105	0.044	0.019	-0.021
Shock L. U.S. Money Demand												
1	0.036	-0.023	-0.007	0.011	-0.007	-0.014	0.007	0.004	0.007	0.104	-0.012	0.014
1X	0.011	0.011	-0.025	0.030	-0.004	-0.010	-0.007	0.016	0.003	0.046	0.012	0.011
2A												
2AX	-0.000	0.000	0.000	-0.000	0.000	0.000	0.000	0.000	0.000	0.001	0.000	-0.000
2B												
2BX	-0.000	0.001	-0.001	-0.000	0.000	0.001	0.000	0.001	0.000	0.001	0.000	-0.000
3												
3X	0.366	0.327	-0.106	0.104	0.154	0.055	-0.053	0.059	0.001	0.040	0.017	0.016
Shock D. Japanese Money Demand												
1	1.171	0.177	-0.038	0.021	0.245	0.010	0.002	0.008	-0.016	-0.010	0.010	0.002
1X	0.394	0.451	-0.046	0.058	0.246	0.144	-0.058	0.045	-0.006	-0.014	0.010	0.001
2A												
2AX	-0.000	0.005	0.000	-0.001	0.000	0.001	0.000	-0.000	0.000	-0.002	-0.000	0.000
2B												
2BX	-0.002	0.004	0.002	-0.002	0.002	0.002	-0.003	-0.000	0.000	-0.002	-0.000	0.000
3												
3X	-0.000	-0.000	0.000	-0.000	-0.000	-0.000	0.000	0.000	0.000	-0.002	0.000	0.000
Shock K. German Money Demand												
1	0.008	0.003	-0.002	0.001	0.001	-0.001	-0.001	0.001	0.009	0.006	-0.003	0.002
1X	0.002	0.004	-0.002	0.004	0.002	0.001	-0.003	0.004	0.005	0.005	-0.003	0.005
2A												
2AX	-0.000	0.000	0.000	0.000	0.000	0.000	0.000	0.000	0.000	0.000	0.000	0.000
2B												
2BX	-0.000	0.000	-0.000	-0.000	0.000	0.001	0.001	0.001	0.000	0.000	0.000	0.000
3												
3X	-0.000	-0.000	0.000	-0.000	-0.000	-0.000	0.000	0.000	0.000	0.000	0.000	-0.000
Shock F. U.S. Money Supply-Permanent FIXM												
1	-0.050	0.018	0.025	-0.021	0.011	0.024	0.001	-0.013	-0.004	-0.090	0.031	0.013
1X	-0.015	-0.015	0.037	-0.040	0.005	0.016	0.016	-0.025	-0.000	-0.037	0.006	0.018

Table A-MUL-5

MULTIMOD MODEL

EFFECTS ON GERMAN REAL GNP, GERMAN PRICE LEVEL, GERMAN INFLATION RATE

(Deviations from Baseline)

Shock and Regime	Real GNP				GNP Deflator				Inflation Rate			
	1st Yr	2nd Yr	5th Yr	10th Yr	1st Yr	2nd Yr	5th Yr	10th Yr	1st Yr	2nd Yr	5th Yr	10th Yr
Shock A. US Aggregate Demand												
1	0.169	0.001	0.023	-0.031	-0.003	-0.007	-0.020	0.009	-0.004	-0.004	0.002	0.004
1X	0.156	-0.041	0.048	-0.043	-0.004	-0.007	-0.025	0.017	-0.004	-0.004	0.002	0.004
2A												
2AX	0.166	-0.007	0.017	-0.021	-0.007	-0.007	-0.019	0.004	-0.007	-0.000	0.001	0.004
2B												
2BX	0.155	0.097	0.027	0.009	0.011	0.013	0.009	-0.002	0.012	0.002	0.003	-0.005
3												
3X	0.090	-0.072	0.172	-0.060	-0.013	-0.025	0.025	0.067	-0.013	-0.013	0.039	-0.032
Shock I. Japanese Aggregate Demand												
1	0.053	-0.017	0.008	-0.003	0.006	0.007	-0.010	0.001	0.007	0.001	-0.004	0.003
1X	0.050	-0.025	0.013	-0.006	0.006	0.005	-0.014	0.006	0.006	-0.001	-0.003	0.002
2A												
2AX	0.056	-0.018	0.004	-0.002	0.005	0.005	-0.010	0.002	0.005	0.000	-0.003	0.002
2B												
2BX	0.046	0.008	0.004	-0.004	0.008	0.009	0.007	0.006	0.008	0.002	0.001	-0.001
3												
3X	0.056	-0.021	0.004	-0.001	0.005	0.005	-0.005	0.001	0.005	0.000	-0.001	0.000
Shock G. German Aggregate Demand												
1	0.703	-0.238	-0.062	-0.001	0.122	0.227	0.091	-0.012	0.126	0.107	-0.073	0.009
1X	0.713	-0.268	-0.083	0.005	0.105	0.195	0.071	0.001	0.108	0.092	-0.062	0.008
2A												
2AX	0.692	-0.198	-0.088	0.003	0.128	0.212	0.051	-0.010	0.131	0.086	-0.073	0.015
2B												
2BX	0.586	-0.382	-0.026	-0.051	0.095	0.191	0.142	0.128	0.097	0.099	-0.030	0.003
3												
3X	0.855	-0.094	-0.061	-0.013	0.051	0.095	0.008	-0.003	0.053	0.045	-0.029	0.004
Shock B. Global Aggregate Demand												
1	0.922	-0.260	-0.047	-0.032	0.128	0.236	0.089	-0.004	0.132	0.110	-0.071	0.009
1X	0.918	-0.329	-0.018	-0.047	0.106	0.190	0.033	0.030	0.108	0.086	-0.061	0.013
2A												
2AX	0.906	-0.237	-0.083	-0.015	0.132	0.225	0.039	-0.013	0.135	0.095	-0.081	0.025
2B												
2BX	0.794	-0.236	-0.006	-0.037	0.113	0.208	0.161	0.132	0.116	0.097	-0.021	-0.005
3												
3X	0.951	-0.266	0.054	-0.065	0.102	0.184	0.067	0.033	0.105	0.084	-0.041	-0.014
Shock C. US Aggregate Supply												
1	0.043	0.089	-0.024	0.029	-0.025	-0.012	0.006	-0.004	-0.026	0.013	0.002	-0.003
1X	0.043	0.078	-0.058	0.051	-0.017	-0.014	0.012	-0.010	-0.018	0.003	0.007	-0.007
2A												
2AX	0.028	0.057	-0.022	0.023	-0.016	-0.010	0.004	0.001	-0.016	0.006	0.003	-0.003
2B												
2BX	0.199	0.447	-0.019	0.010	-0.093	-0.084	-0.064	-0.071	-0.095	0.009	-0.007	0.004
3												
3X	0.095	0.154	-0.119	0.057	0.001	0.029	0.049	-0.069	0.001	0.029	-0.017	0.006
Shock J. Japanese Aggregate Supply												
1	0.017	0.002	-0.007	0.004	-0.013	-0.012	0.005	-0.000	-0.014	0.002	0.004	-0.002
1X	0.019	0.010	-0.012	0.009	-0.011	-0.011	0.009	-0.005	-0.011	-0.001	0.006	-0.003
2A												
2AX	0.013	0.004	-0.005	0.004	-0.011	-0.011	0.005	-0.001	-0.011	-0.001	0.005	-0.002
2B												
2BX	0.043	0.014	0.014	-0.002	-0.032	-0.026	-0.018	-0.018	-0.032	0.006	-0.004	0.002
3												
3X	0.009	0.002	-0.003	0.002	-0.006	-0.005	0.002	-0.001	-0.007	0.001	0.001	0.000

Shock and Regime	Real GNP				GNP Deflator				Inflation Rate			
	1st Yr	2nd Yr	5th Yr	10th Yr	1st Yr	2nd Yr	5th Yr	10th Yr	1st Yr	2nd Yr	5th Yr	10th Yr
Shock H. German Aggregate Supply												
1	-0.218	0.346	0.076	-0.007	0.666	-0.437	-0.185	0.021	0.682	-1.121	0.120	-0.004
1X	-0.210	0.227	0.162	-0.039	0.637	-0.433	-0.176	0.012	0.653	-1.087	0.116	-0.006
2A												
2AX	-0.233	0.196	0.140	-0.023	0.634	-0.445	-0.156	0.040	0.650	-1.097	0.131	-0.014
2B												
2BX	-0.411	0.813	-0.074	0.127	0.843	-0.215	0.008	0.041	0.864	-1.074	0.068	0.007
3												
3X	-0.270	0.061	0.060	0.001	0.680	-0.332	-0.062	0.011	0.696	-1.027	0.087	-0.007
Shock E. Oil Price Increase												
1	0.922	-0.260	-0.047	-0.032	0.128	0.236	0.089	-0.004	0.132	0.110	-0.071	0.009
1X	0.918	-0.329	-0.018	-0.047	0.106	0.190	0.033	0.030	0.108	0.086	-0.061	0.013
2A												
2AX	0.906	-0.237	-0.083	-0.015	0.132	0.225	0.039	-0.013	0.135	0.095	-0.081	0.025
2B												
2BX	0.794	-0.236	-0.006	-0.037	0.113	0.208	0.161	0.132	0.116	0.097	-0.021	-0.005
3												
3X	0.951	-0.266	0.054	-0.065	0.102	0.184	0.067	0.033	0.105	0.084	-0.041	-0.014
Shock L. U.S. Money Demand												
1	0.058	0.155	-0.021	0.019	-0.023	-0.031	-0.015	-0.005	-0.024	-0.008	0.007	-0.000
1X	0.033	0.105	0.008	0.017	-0.014	-0.027	-0.027	0.001	-0.014	-0.014	0.007	-0.002
2A												
2AX	0.000	0.001	0.000	-0.000	-0.000	-0.000	-0.000	-0.000	0.000	0.000	0.000	0.000
2B												
2BX	-0.000	0.000	-0.000	-0.002	0.000	0.000	-0.000	-0.000	0.000	0.000	-0.000	0.000
3												
3X	-0.184	-0.041	0.087	-0.059	-0.049	-0.115	-0.102	-0.009	-0.050	-0.068	0.044	-0.018
Shock D. Japanese Money Demand												
1	0.013	0.012	-0.004	0.001	-0.007	-0.011	-0.002	-0.000	-0.008	-0.003	0.004	-0.001
1X	0.007	0.013	0.003	-0.001	-0.005	-0.011	-0.006	0.003	-0.005	-0.006	0.005	-0.003
2A												
2AX	0.000	0.001	0.000	0.000	-0.000	-0.000	-0.000	-0.000	0.000	0.000	-0.000	0.000
2B												
2BX	-0.000	0.000	0.001	-0.000	0.000	0.000	-0.000	-0.000	0.000	0.000	-0.000	0.000
3												
3X	0.000	0.001	0.000	0.000	0.000	0.000	-0.000	-0.000	0.000	0.000	-0.000	0.000
Shock K. German Money Demand												
1	-0.420	-0.204	0.041	-0.022	0.018	-0.035	-0.133	0.009	0.018	-0.054	-0.001	0.018
1X	-0.386	-0.335	0.085	-0.051	-0.053	-0.141	-0.227	0.038	-0.054	-0.091	0.021	0.025
2A												
2AX	0.000	0.007	-0.002	-0.001	-0.000	0.001	0.001	-0.001	0.000	0.001	-0.001	0.000
2B												
2BX	-0.000	0.008	-0.003	-0.001	0.000	0.001	0.001	-0.001	0.000	0.001	-0.001	0.000
3												
3X	0.000	0.009	-0.001	-0.001	0.000	0.001	0.001	-0.001	0.000	0.001	-0.001	0.000
Shock F. U.S. Money Supply-Permanent												
FIXM												
1	-0.059	-0.169	0.041	0.031	0.023	0.032	0.005	-0.015	0.024	0.009	-0.012	0.001
1X	-0.036	-0.119	0.006	0.039	0.015	0.029	0.021	-0.025	0.015	0.014	-0.011	0.003

MULTIMOD MODEL
EFFECTS ON GERMAN INTEREST RATES AND GERMAN CURRENT ACCOUNT/GNP RATIO
(Deviations from Baseline)

Shock and Regime	Short Interest Rate				Long Interest Rate				Current Account/GNP Ratio			
	1st Yr	2nd Yr	5th Yr	10th Yr	1st Yr	2nd Yr	5th Yr	10th Yr	1st Yr	2nd Yr	5th Yr	10th Yr
Shock A. US Aggregate Demand												
1	0.095	-0.013	-0.008	-0.003	0.010	-0.010	-0.006	0.001	0.099	0.014	0.015	-0.030
1X	0.030	0.026	-0.008	-0.002	0.013	0.005	-0.010	0.004	0.095	-0.012	0.036	-0.038
2A												
2AX	0.079	-0.007	-0.001	-0.009	0.013	-0.003	-0.006	-0.001	0.100	0.026	0.009	-0.022
2B												
2BX	0.423	0.050	-0.085	0.020	0.030	-0.059	-0.001	-0.004	0.104	0.055	0.014	-0.001
3												
3X	0.148	0.175	-0.034	-0.025	0.093	0.044	-0.087	0.027	0.084	-0.019	0.042	-0.043
Shock I. Japanese Aggregate Demand												
1	0.032	0.012	-0.011	0.003	0.004	-0.004	-0.005	0.003	0.036	-0.012	-0.001	-0.001
1X	0.010	0.014	-0.007	0.003	0.005	0.001	-0.007	0.004	0.035	-0.015	0.001	-0.001
2A												
2AX	0.030	-0.006	-0.003	0.000	0.003	-0.003	-0.002	0.001	0.037	-0.013	0.000	-0.001
2B												
2BX	0.131	0.061	-0.027	0.008	0.016	-0.012	-0.003	0.003	0.035	0.005	-0.008	-0.002
3												
3X	0.006	0.006	-0.002	0.001	0.002	0.001	-0.002	0.001	0.038	-0.013	0.002	0.000
Shock G. German Aggregate Demand												
1	0.245	0.180	-0.056	-0.002	0.080	0.019	-0.043	0.006	-0.402	0.037	0.009	-0.008
1X	0.083	0.134	0.009	-0.023	0.084	0.059	-0.040	0.003	-0.399	0.041	0.007	-0.010
2A												
2AX	0.409	0.007	-0.018	-0.003	0.077	-0.009	-0.017	-0.001	-0.401	0.034	0.009	-0.007
2B												
2BX	0.214	0.468	-0.077	0.040	0.198	0.132	-0.065	0.036	-0.409	0.045	0.013	-0.016
3												
3X	0.003	0.003	-0.001	0.001	0.000	0.000	-0.000	0.000	-0.411	0.033	0.002	-0.014
Shock B. Global Aggregate Demand												
1	0.378	0.184	-0.065	-0.004	0.102	0.012	-0.053	0.010	-0.268	0.041	0.025	-0.040
1X	0.123	0.173	-0.008	-0.014	0.099	0.061	-0.057	0.014	-0.272	0.013	0.044	-0.049
2A												
2AX	0.517	-0.007	-0.022	-0.014	0.094	-0.015	-0.027	0.002	-0.267	0.049	0.022	-0.033
2B												
2BX	0.891	0.573	-0.177	0.065	0.240	0.037	-0.053	0.029	-0.278	0.108	0.021	-0.018
3												
3X	0.161	0.186	-0.040	-0.024	0.098	0.045	-0.093	0.030	-0.283	0.011	0.051	-0.053
Shock C. US Aggregate Supply												
1	0.009	-0.050	0.003	0.007	-0.009	-0.009	0.007	0.002	0.005	0.103	-0.020	0.030
1X	0.008	-0.001	-0.009	0.013	-0.004	-0.006	0.003	0.004	0.007	0.063	-0.049	0.051
2A												
2AX	0.006	0.024	-0.009	0.012	-0.003	-0.005	0.002	0.006	0.002	0.055	-0.021	0.026
2B												
2BX	0.113	-1.261	0.194	-0.038	-0.067	-0.081	0.006	0.004	0.040	0.463	0.009	0.019
3												
3X	0.146	-0.042	-0.075	0.065	-0.048	-0.075	0.044	-0.007	0.011	0.070	-0.057	0.057
Shock J. Japanese Aggregate Supply												
1	0.004	-0.038	0.008	-0.001	-0.004	-0.003	0.005	-0.001	-0.002	0.005	-0.000	0.003
1X	0.003	-0.006	-0.001	0.002	-0.004	-0.004	0.006	-0.002	-0.001	0.006	-0.003	0.005
2A												
2AX	0.001	-0.004	0.000	0.002	-0.001	-0.001	0.002	0.000	-0.002	0.004	-0.001	0.003
2B												
2BX	0.040	-0.481	0.041	-0.007	-0.019	-0.029	-0.008	0.003	-0.005	0.011	0.019	0.003
3												
3X	0.003	-0.001	-0.002	0.001	0.000	-0.001	-0.000	0.000	-0.003	0.003	-0.002	0.001

Shock and Regime	Short Interest Rate				Long Interest Rate				Current Account/GNP Ratio			
	1st Yr	2nd Yr	5th Yr	10th Yr	1st Yr	2nd Yr	5th Yr	10th Yr	1st Yr	2nd Yr	5th Yr	10th Yr
Shock H. German Aggregate Supply												
1	0.641	-0.675	0.071	0.007	-0.042	-0.152	0.064	-0.006	0.031	-0.047	-0.002	-0.001
1X	0.217	-0.025	-0.091	0.050	-0.037	-0.083	0.020	0.009	0.020	-0.054	0.004	-0.006
2A												
2AX	0.200	-0.125	-0.008	0.009	-0.009	-0.046	0.012	-0.000	0.021	-0.051	0.005	-0.009
2B												
2BX	3.626	-2.479	0.314	-0.128	0.063	-0.585	0.170	-0.083	0.049	-0.008	0.001	0.003
3												
3X	0.002	-0.001	-0.001	0.001	-0.000	-0.001	-0.000	0.000	0.024	-0.043	0.006	-0.002
Shock E. Oil Price Increase												
1	0.378	0.184	-0.065	-0.004	0.102	0.012	-0.053	0.010	-0.268	0.041	0.025	-0.040
1X	0.123	0.173	-0.008	-0.014	0.099	0.061	-0.057	0.014	-0.272	0.013	0.044	-0.049
2A												
2AX	0.517	-0.007	-0.022	-0.014	0.094	-0.015	-0.027	0.002	-0.267	0.049	0.022	-0.033
2B												
2BX	0.891	0.573	-0.177	0.065	0.240	0.037	-0.053	0.029	-0.278	0.108	0.021	-0.018
3												
3X	0.161	0.186	-0.040	-0.024	0.098	0.045	-0.093	0.030	-0.283	0.011	0.051	-0.053
Shock L. U.S. Money Demand												
1	0.033	-0.018	-0.003	0.006	-0.000	-0.007	0.001	0.006	0.023	0.147	-0.022	0.019
1X	0.011	0.013	-0.014	0.013	0.004	-0.002	-0.010	0.014	0.015	0.082	0.006	0.018
2A												
2AX	0.000	0.001	0.000	-0.000	-0.000	0.000	0.000	-0.000	0.000	0.001	0.000	-0.001
2B												
2BX	-0.000	0.002	-0.001	-0.000	0.000	0.001	0.000	0.000	-0.000	0.001	0.001	-0.001
3												
3X	0.369	0.329	-0.107	0.104	0.155	0.056	-0.052	0.059	-0.015	0.056	0.017	0.016
Shock D. Japanese Money Demand												
1	0.016	-0.013	0.001	0.000	-0.001	-0.004	0.001	0.000	-0.003	0.003	-0.002	0.000
1X	0.005	0.004	-0.008	0.007	-0.001	-0.003	-0.002	0.003	-0.005	-0.000	0.000	0.001
2A												
2AX	0.000	0.000	0.000	0.000	-0.000	0.000	0.000	0.000	0.000	0.000	0.000	-0.000
2B												
2BX	-0.000	0.001	-0.001	-0.000	-0.000	-0.000	-0.000	0.000	-0.000	0.000	0.000	-0.000
3												
3X	-0.000	-0.000	0.000	-0.000	-0.000	-0.000	0.000	0.000	0.000	0.000	0.000	-0.000
Shock K. German Money Demand												
1	1.063	0.263	-0.060	0.027	0.237	0.020	-0.009	0.013	-0.008	-0.031	0.016	-0.000
1X	0.353	0.405	-0.009	0.034	0.233	0.148	-0.038	0.033	-0.006	-0.028	0.018	0.000
2A												
2AX	0.000	0.004	-0.000	-0.001	-0.000	0.001	0.000	-0.000	0.000	-0.005	0.000	0.001
2B												
2BX	-0.000	0.003	-0.001	-0.001	0.000	0.001	0.000	0.000	-0.000	-0.005	0.000	0.001
3												
3X	-0.000	0.000	0.000	-0.000	-0.000	-0.000	0.000	0.000	0.000	-0.005	-0.000	0.001
Shock F. U.S. Money Supply-Permanent												
FIXM												
1	-0.043	0.008	0.002	-0.002	-0.006	0.004	0.002	-0.005	-0.022	-0.145	0.048	0.033
1X	-0.013	-0.016	0.008	-0.008	-0.007	-0.001	0.009	-0.010	-0.015	-0.085	0.018	0.039

Table A-MUL-7
MULTIMOD MODEL
BILATERAL DOLLAR EXCHANGE RATES
(Deviations from Baseline)

Shock and Regime	Bilateral DM/$ Exchange Rate				Bilateral Yen/$ Exchange Rate			
	1st Yr	2nd Yr	5th Yr	10th Yr	1st Yr	2nd Yr	5th Yr	10th Yr
Shock A. US Aggregate Demand								
1	-0.376	-0.131	0.330	0.028	-0.377	-0.136	0.323	0.044
1X	-0.290	-0.195	0.285	-0.018	-0.299	-0.212	0.265	0.014
2A								
2AX	-0.363	0.095	0.173	0.019	-0.378	0.092	0.165	0.033
2B								
2BX	-0.766	-0.627	0.586	0.090	-0.769	-0.729	0.619	0.096
3								
3X	-0.118	-0.140	0.027	0.020	-0.117	-0.139	0.027	0.020
Shock I. Japanese Aggregate Demand								
1	-0.001	0.004	-0.000	-0.000	0.461	0.144	-0.322	0.015
1X	-0.000	0.005	0.004	-0.006	0.359	0.245	-0.279	0.010
2A								
2AX	0.002	-0.006	-0.001	-0.000	0.498	-0.008	-0.118	-0.010
2B								
2BX	-0.025	0.072	-0.032	0.026	1.085	0.741	-0.646	-0.140
3								
3X	-0.005	-0.005	0.002	-0.001	-0.005	-0.005	0.002	-0.001
Shock G. German Aggregate Demand								
1	0.288	0.078	-0.168	0.010	0.001	0.011	-0.001	-0.002
1X	0.228	0.155	-0.149	-0.010	0.003	0.007	0.005	-0.008
2A								
2AX	0.326	-0.048	-0.068	-0.008	0.002	0.004	0.000	-0.002
2B								
2BX	0.548	0.520	-0.373	-0.005	-0.048	0.042	-0.017	0.033
3								
3X	-0.003	-0.002	0.001	-0.001	-0.003	-0.002	0.001	-0.001
Shock B. Global Aggregate Demand								
1	-0.106	-0.065	0.148	0.035	0.080	0.016	-0.014	0.051
1X	-0.071	-0.064	0.133	-0.016	0.063	0.049	-0.009	0.021
2A								
2AX	-0.049	0.031	0.099	0.010	0.088	0.053	0.004	0.019
2B								
2BX	-0.216	-0.087	0.207	0.087	0.259	0.082	-0.065	-0.005
3								
3X	-0.129	-0.149	0.032	0.019	-0.127	-0.148	0.032	0.019
Shock C. US Aggregate Supply								
1	-0.043	0.790	-0.219	-0.018	-0.045	0.787	-0.206	-0.033
1X	-0.038	0.210	-0.052	-0.043	-0.050	0.205	-0.023	-0.076
2A								
2AX	-0.008	0.247	-0.072	-0.040	-0.013	0.247	-0.063	-0.053
2B								
2BX	-1.126	3.210	-0.423	0.346	-1.116	3.287	-0.511	0.331
3								
3X	-0.116	0.034	0.060	-0.052	-0.116	0.033	0.060	-0.052
Shock J. Japanese Aggregate Supply								
1	0.008	0.011	-0.005	-0.001	-0.087	-0.842	0.319	0.003
1X	0.004	0.002	-0.005	0.002	-0.022	-0.268	0.124	0.041
2A								
2AX	0.003	0.004	-0.000	-0.001	-0.039	-0.280	0.063	0.027
2B								
2BX	0.059	0.080	0.031	-0.020	0.447	-3.827	0.692	-0.118
3								
3X	-0.003	0.000	0.001	-0.001	-0.003	0.000	0.001	-0.001

Shock and Regime	Bilateral DM/$ Exchange Rate				Bilateral Yen/$ Exchange Rate			
	1st Yr	2nd Yr	5th Yr	10th Yr	1st Yr	2nd Yr	5th Yr	10th Yr
Shock H. German Aggregate Supply								
1	-0.041	-0.630	0.241	-0.018	0.006	0.007	-0.009	0.001
1X	-0.009	-0.209	0.083	0.036	-0.002	0.001	-0.012	0.008
2A								
2AX	-0.005	-0.189	0.046	0.010	0.003	0.001	-0.005	-0.001
2B								
2BX	0.807	-2.409	0.572	-0.364	0.167	0.311	-0.051	-0.106
3								
3X	-0.002	0.001	0.001	-0.001	-0.002	0.001	0.001	-0.001
Shock E. Oil Price Increase								
1	-0.076	0.090	-0.023	-0.063	-0.091	0.106	-0.021	-0.049
1X	-0.061	-0.028	-0.017	-0.055	-0.078	-0.015	0.014	-0.061
2A								
2AX	-0.101	0.029	-0.023	-0.040	-0.141	0.031	-0.012	-0.036
2B								
2BX	-0.319	0.546	0.060	-0.094	-0.391	0.480	-0.068	0.053
3								
3X	-0.072	0.011	0.031	-0.041	-0.072	0.011	0.031	-0.041
Shock L. U.S. Money Demand								
1	-1.028	-0.019	0.044	-0.084	-1.048	-0.036	0.063	-0.091
1X	-0.840	-0.532	0.185	-0.225	-0.876	-0.565	0.211	-0.229
2A								
2AX	0.000	-0.003	0.000	0.001	0.000	-0.003	0.000	0.001
2B								
2BX	0.000	-0.003	0.001	0.000	-0.000	-0.003	0.001	0.001
3								
3X	-0.295	-0.263	0.085	-0.083	-0.293	-0.261	0.085	-0.083
Shock D. Japanese Money Demand								
1	-0.005	0.004	-0.001	-0.001	1.188	0.085	-0.020	0.028
1X	0.002	-0.001	0.001	-0.005	1.009	0.671	-0.150	0.139
2A								
2AX	0.000	0.000	0.000	-0.000	0.000	0.005	0.000	-0.001
2B								
2BX	-0.000	-0.001	0.001	0.000	0.002	0.009	0.000	-0.002
3								
3X	0.000	0.000	-0.000	0.000	0.000	0.000	-0.000	0.000
Shock K. German Money Demand								
1	1.136	0.170	-0.044	0.046	0.007	0.034	-0.016	-0.000
1X	0.974	0.646	-0.108	0.098	-0.002	0.004	0.005	-0.015
2A								
2AX	0.000	0.004	0.000	-0.001	0.000	0.000	0.000	-0.000
2B								
2BX	0.000	0.001	0.001	-0.002	-0.000	-0.001	0.002	0.000
3								
3X	0.000	0.000	-0.000	0.000	0.000	0.000	-0.000	0.000
Shock F. U.S. Money Supply-Permanent								
FIXM								
1	1.430	0.540	0.511	1.244	1.446	0.560	0.473	1.212
1X	1.317	1.020	0.370	1.351	1.321	1.014	0.346	1.307

897

MX3 MODEL
EFFECTS ON U.S. REAL GNP, U.S. PRICE LEVEL, U.S. INFLATION RATE
(Deviations from Baseline)

Shock and Regime	Real GNP				GNP Deflator				Inflation Rate			
	1st Qtr	6th Qtr	18th Qtr	38th Qtr	1st Qtr	6th Qtr	18th Qtr	38th Qtr	1st Qtr	6th Qtr	18th Qtr	38th Qtr
Shock A. US Aggregate Demand												
1	0.652	-0.006	-0.010	0.019	0.003	0.002	-0.001	-0.009	0.011	-0.001	-0.005	0.003
1X												
2A	0.604	-0.006	-0.007	0.014	0.003	0.004	0.001	-0.008	0.012	0.000	-0.002	0.001
2AX												
2B	0.605	-0.005	-0.002	0.005	0.003	0.004	0.002	-0.018	0.011	0.000	-0.002	-0.002
2BX												
3												
3X												
Shock I. Japanese Aggregate Demand												
1	0.008	0.001	-0.006	0.017	0.000	0.002	0.001	-0.011	0.001	0.002	-0.004	0.003
1X												
2A	0.007	0.002	-0.004	0.014	0.000	0.003	0.001	-0.010	0.001	0.002	-0.003	0.002
2AX												
2B	0.006	0.002	0.001	0.004	0.000	0.002	0.002	-0.021	0.001	0.002	-0.002	-0.001
2BX												
3												
3X												
Shock G. German Aggregate Demand												
1	-0.000	0.000	-0.006	0.018	0.000	0.001	0.000	-0.011	0.000	0.002	-0.005	0.003
1X												
2A	0.001	0.002	-0.004	0.014	0.000	0.003	0.001	-0.010	0.000	0.002	-0.003	0.002
2AX												
2B	0.000	0.001	0.001	0.004	0.000	0.002	0.002	-0.022	0.000	0.002	-0.003	-0.002
2BX												
3												
3X												
Shock B. Global Aggregate Demand												
1	0.658	-0.009	-0.011	0.019	0.003	0.002	-0.002	-0.009	0.012	-0.001	-0.004	0.004
1X												
2A	0.609	-0.008	-0.006	0.015	0.003	0.003	0.000	-0.008	0.012	-0.000	-0.002	0.002
2AX												
2B	0.610	-0.007	-0.002	0.005	0.003	0.003	0.001	-0.018	0.011	-0.000	-0.002	-0.002
2BX												
3												
3X												
Shock C. US Aggregate Supply												
1	-0.829	-0.037	-0.017	0.010	0.000	0.000	0.008	-0.001	0.001	0.003	-0.001	0.001
1X												
2A	-0.758	-0.022	-0.011	0.008	0.001	0.003	0.010	-0.002	0.004	0.004	-0.001	0.001
2AX												
2B	-0.758	-0.023	-0.001	0.005	0.001	0.003	0.017	-0.002	0.004	0.003	0.002	-0.003
2BX												
3												
3X												
Shock J. Japanese Aggregate Supply												
1	0.011	0.004	-0.009	0.018	0.001	0.006	-0.001	-0.011	0.004	0.002	-0.005	0.003
1X												
2A	0.009	-0.002	-0.004	0.014	0.001	0.004	0.002	-0.010	0.002	0.002	-0.003	0.002
2AX												
2B	0.009	-0.001	0.003	0.001	0.001	0.005	0.004	-0.051	0.002	0.003	-0.004	-0.008
2BX												
3												
3X												

Shock and Regime	Real GNP				GNP Deflator				Inflation Rate			
	1st Qtr	6th Qtr	18th Qtr	38th Qtr	1st Qtr	6th Qtr	18th Qtr	38th Qtr	1st Qtr	6th Qtr	18th Qtr	38th Qtr
Shock H. German Aggregate Supply												
1	-0.003	0.002	-0.006	0.017	0.000	0.002	0.001	-0.011	0.000	0.002	-0.004	0.003
1X												
2A	-0.002	0.003	-0.004	0.014	0.000	0.003	0.001	-0.010	0.000	0.002	-0.003	0.002
2AX												
2B	-0.003	0.002	0.001	0.003	0.000	0.002	0.002	-0.022	-0.000	0.003	-0.002	-0.002
2BX												
3												
3X												
Shock E. Oil Price Increase												
1												
1X												
2A												
2AX												
2B												
2BX												
3												
3X												
Shock L. U.S. Money Demand												
1	-0.134	-0.018	-0.010	0.017	-0.001	-0.002	-0.000	-0.008	-0.004	0.002	-0.003	0.003
1X												
2A	0.001	0.003	-0.004	0.014	0.000	0.003	0.001	-0.010	0.000	0.002	-0.003	0.002
2AX												
2B	0.000	0.002	0.001	0.004	0.000	0.002	0.002	-0.022	0.000	0.002	-0.003	-0.002
2BX												
3												
3X												
Shock D. Japanese Money Demand												
1	-0.002	0.004	-0.006	0.018	0.000	0.003	0.001	-0.011	0.000	0.003	-0.005	0.003
1X												
2A	0.001	0.003	-0.004	0.014	0.000	0.003	0.001	-0.010	0.001	0.002	-0.003	0.002
2AX												
2B	0.000	0.002	0.001	0.003	0.000	0.002	0.002	-0.021	0.000	0.002	-0.003	-0.001
2BX												
3												
3X												
Shock K. German Money Demand												
1	0.001	0.004	-0.006	0.017	0.000	0.003	0.001	-0.011	0.001	0.002	-0.005	0.002
1X												
2A	0.001	0.003	-0.004	0.014	0.000	0.003	0.001	-0.010	0.001	0.003	-0.003	0.002
2AX												
2B	0.000	0.002	0.001	0.004	0.000	0.002	0.002	-0.022	0.000	0.002	-0.003	-0.002
2BX												
3												
3X												
Shock F. U.S. Money Supply-Permanent												
FIXM	0.318	0.298	0.116	0.039	0.066	0.521	0.926	0.959	0.265	0.310	0.043	0.003
1	0.304	0.427	0.195	-0.149	0.037	0.386	0.888	0.355	0.147	0.298	0.062	-0.176
1X												

MX3 MODEL
EFFECTS ON U.S. INTEREST RATES AND U.S. CURRENT ACCOUNT/GNP RATIO
(Deviations from Baseline)

Shock and Regime	Short Interest Rate				Long Interest Rate				Current Account/GNP Ratio			
	1st Qtr	6th Qtr	18th Qtr	38th Qtr	1st Qtr	6th Qtr	18th Qtr	38th Qtr	2ndt Qtr	6th Qtr	18th Qtr	38th Qtr
Shock A. US Aggregate Demand												
1	0.199	0.002	-0.006	0.008	NA	NA	NA	NA	-0.015	-0.008	-0.006	-0.010
1X												
2A	0.908	-0.003	-0.008	0.010	NA	NA	NA	NA	-0.019	-0.012	-0.003	-0.014
2AX												
2B	0.921	-0.007	-0.007	0.005	NA	NA	NA	NA	-0.019	-0.011	-0.001	-0.018
2BX												
3												
3X												
Shock I. Japanese Aggregate Demand												
1	0.007	0.003	-0.003	0.006	NA	NA	NA	NA	0.001	-0.003	-0.005	-0.008
1X												
2A	0.010	0.007	-0.003	0.007	NA	NA	NA	NA	-0.000	-0.006	-0.003	-0.012
2AX												
2B	0.010	0.006	-0.001	0.003	NA	NA	NA	NA	0.001	-0.005	-0.001	-0.016
2BX												
3												
3X												
Shock G. German Aggregate Demand												
1	0.004	0.003	-0.003	0.006	NA	NA	NA	NA	-0.004	-0.004	-0.005	-0.008
1X												
2A	0.001	0.007	-0.004	0.007	NA	NA	NA	NA	-0.006	-0.008	-0.003	-0.012
2AX												
2B	0.001	0.005	-0.003	0.003	NA	NA	NA	NA	-0.005	-0.007	-0.001	-0.016
2BX												
3												
3X												
Shock B. Global Aggregate Demand												
1	0.204	0.002	-0.006	0.008	NA	NA	NA	NA	-0.014	-0.012	-0.007	-0.010
1X												
2A	0.916	-0.007	-0.009	0.010	NA	NA	NA	NA	-0.019	-0.015	-0.004	-0.014
2AX												
2B	0.929	-0.010	-0.007	0.004	NA	NA	NA	NA	-0.018	-0.014	-0.002	-0.019
2BX												
3												
3X												
Shock C. US Aggregate Supply												
1	-0.227	-0.022	-0.004	0.007	NA	NA	NA	NA	-0.007	0.006	-0.004	-0.009
1X												
2A	-1.139	-0.028	-0.002	0.008	NA	NA	NA	NA	-0.000	0.006	0.000	-0.012
2AX												
2B	-1.135	-0.029	0.002	0.002	NA	NA	NA	NA	-0.001	0.007	0.003	-0.015
2BX												
3												
3X												
Shock J. Japanese Aggregate Supply												
1	0.032	0.001	-0.003	0.006	NA	NA	NA	NA	0.001	-0.001	-0.012	-0.008
1X												
2A	0.015	0.004	-0.003	0.007	NA	NA	NA	NA	-0.010	-0.004	-0.004	-0.013
2AX												
2B	0.017	0.002	-0.002	-0.010	NA	NA	NA	NA	-0.010	-0.001	-0.004	-0.031
2BX												
3												
3X												

Shock and Regime	Short Interest Rate				Long Interest Rate				Current Account/GNP Ratio			
	1st Qtr	6th Qtr	18th Qtr	38th Qtr	1st Qtr	6th Qtr	18th Qtr	38th Qtr	2ndt Qtr	6th Qtr	18th Qtr	38th Qtr
Shock H. German Aggregate Supply												
1	0.000	0.004	-0.003	0.006	NA	NA	NA	NA	-0.004	-0.003	-0.005	-0.008
1X												
2A	-0.003	0.008	-0.004	0.007	NA	NA	NA	NA	-0.006	-0.006	-0.003	-0.012
2AX												
2B	-0.005	0.007	-0.002	0.002	NA	NA	NA	NA	-0.005	-0.006	0.000	-0.016
2BX												
3												
3X												
Shock E. Oil Price Increase												
1												
1X												
2A												
2AX												
2B												
2BX												
3												
3X												
Shock L. U.S. Money Demand												
1	1.559	-0.003	-0.005	0.007	NA	NA	NA	NA	-0.041	-0.008	-0.007	-0.010
1X												
2A	0.002	0.009	-0.004	0.007	NA	NA	NA	NA	-0.003	-0.006	-0.003	-0.012
2AX												
2B	0.001	0.006	-0.003	0.002	NA	NA	NA	NA	-0.002	-0.005	0.000	-0.016
2BX												
3												
3X												
Shock D. Japanese Money Demand												
1	0.012	0.003	-0.003	0.006	NA	NA	NA	NA	-0.003	-0.001	-0.006	-0.008
1X												
2A	0.002	0.009	-0.004	0.007	NA	NA	NA	NA	-0.003	-0.006	-0.003	-0.012
2AX												
2B	0.001	0.006	-0.003	0.003	NA	NA	NA	NA	-0.002	-0.005	0.000	-0.016
2BX												
3												
3X												
Shock K. German Money Demand												
1	0.007	0.003	-0.003	0.006	NA	NA	NA	NA	-0.001	-0.001	-0.006	-0.008
1X												
2A	0.002	0.009	-0.004	0.007	NA	NA	NA	NA	-0.003	-0.006	-0.003	-0.012
2AX												
2B	0.001	0.007	-0.003	0.003	NA	NA	NA	NA	-0.002	-0.005	0.000	-0.016
2BX												
3												
3X												
Shock F. U.S. Money Supply-Permanent												
FIXM	-1.836	0.005	0.026	-0.000	NA	NA	NA	NA	-3.500	-3.596	-2.461	-1.140
1	-1.224	-0.043	0.037	-0.464	NA	NA	NA	NA	0.006	0.041	0.012	0.052
1X												

MX3 MODEL
EFFECTS ON JAPANESE REAL GNP, JAPANESE PRICE LEVEL, JAPANESE INFLATION RATE
(Deviations from Baseline)

Shock and Regime	Real GNP				GNP Deflator				Inflation Rate			
	1st Qtr	6th Qtr	18th Qtr	36th Qtr	1st Qtr	6th Qtr	18th Qtr	38th Qtr	1st Qtr	6th Qtr	18th Qtr	38th Qtr
Shock A. US Aggregate Demand												
1	0.001	0.034	-0.152	0.146	-0.001	0.025	-0.014	0.061	-0.005	0.064	-0.288	0.172
1X												
2A	0.000	0.019	-0.068	0.072	-0.002	0.044	0.050	-0.048	-0.006	0.073	-0.069	0.061
2AX												
2B	0.002	0.016	0.012	0.001	-0.001	0.038	0.288	-0.442	-0.005	0.083	-0.050	0.028
2BX												
3												
3X												
Shock I. Japanese Aggregate Demand												
1	0.649	0.020	-0.153	0.145	0.025	0.028	-0.021	0.064	0.100	0.047	-0.280	0.170
1X												
2A	0.578	0.001	-0.072	0.069	0.022	0.041	0.053	-0.044	0.088	0.063	-0.068	0.061
2AX												
2B	0.588	0.004	0.009	0.001	0.022	0.041	0.300	-0.411	0.088	0.074	-0.048	0.029
2BX												
3												
3X												
Shock G. German Aggregate Demand												
1	-0.008	0.029	-0.148	0.147	-0.002	0.020	-0.006	0.059	-0.007	0.060	-0.282	0.171
1X												
2A	-0.008	0.020	-0.068	0.073	-0.003	0.042	0.050	-0.050	-0.010	0.074	-0.069	0.062
2AX												
2B	-0.006	0.015	0.013	0.000	-0.002	0.035	0.283	-0.450	-0.007	0.081	-0.051	0.027
2BX												
3												
3X												
Shock B. Global Aggregate Demand												
1	0.648	0.021	-0.151	0.146	0.024	0.029	-0.007	0.066	0.100	0.050	-0.279	0.171
1X												
2A	0.578	0.001	-0.073	0.069	0.022	0.042	0.054	-0.043	0.088	0.064	-0.068	0.061
2AX												
2B	0.587	0.004	0.009	0.002	0.022	0.042	0.303	-0.411	0.088	0.076	-0.048	0.031
2BX												
3												
3X												
Shock C. US Aggregate Supply												
1	0.006	0.091	-0.170	0.145	0.001	0.125	-0.062	0.058	0.005	0.169	-0.288	0.171
1X												
2A	0.002	0.017	-0.067	0.072	-0.000	0.056	0.050	-0.048	-0.001	0.074	-0.067	0.062
2AX												
2B	0.000	0.019	0.013	0.003	-0.001	0.068	0.330	-0.424	-0.003	0.109	-0.056	0.024
2BX												
3												
3X												
Shock J. Japanese Aggregate Supply												
1	-0.085	0.300	-0.114	0.203	0.175	0.589	-0.221	-0.016	0.708	0.024	-0.261	0.179
1X												
2A	-0.295	0.068	-0.018	0.115	0.073	0.156	-0.008	-0.094	0.297	-0.037	-0.067	0.063
2AX												
2B	-0.310	0.157	0.047	0.039	0.089	0.317	0.246	-1.287	0.360	0.106	-0.210	-0.086
2BX												
3												
3X												

Shock and Regime	Real GNP				GNP Deflator				Inflation Rate			
	1st Qtr	6th Qtr	18th Qtr	36th Qtr	1st Qtr	6th Qtr	18th Qtr	38th Qtr	1st Qtr	6th Qtr	18th Qtr	38th Qtr
Shock H. German Aggregate Supply												
1	-0.003	0.030	-0.151	0.146	-0.001	0.022	-0.016	0.059	-0.005	0.061	-0.283	0.170
1X												
2A	-0.004	0.020	-0.068	0.073	-0.002	0.042	0.050	-0.049	-0.008	0.073	-0.069	0.061
2AX												
2B	-0.002	0.015	0.012	0.001	-0.002	0.034	0.278	-0.461	-0.006	0.074	-0.051	0.026
2BX												
3												
3X												
Shock E. Oil Price Increase												
1												
1X												
2A												
2AX												
2B												
2BX												
3												
3X												
Shock L. U.S. Money Demand												
1	-0.002	0.056	-0.162	0.146	-0.002	0.057	-0.042	0.057	-0.008	0.115	-0.291	0.171
1X												
2A	-0.004	0.020	-0.068	0.073	-0.002	0.042	0.050	-0.049	-0.008	0.073	-0.069	0.061
2AX												
2B	-0.002	0.015	0.013	0.001	-0.001	0.036	0.284	-0.450	-0.006	0.082	-0.051	0.026
2BX												
3												
3X												
Shock D. Japanese Money Demand												
1	-0.096	0.033	-0.164	0.142	-0.008	0.037	-0.022	0.064	-0.033	0.117	-0.286	0.171
1X												
2A	-0.004	0.020	-0.068	0.073	-0.002	0.042	0.050	-0.049	-0.008	0.074	-0.069	0.062
2AX												
2B	-0.001	0.014	0.012	0.001	-0.001	0.031	0.277	-0.455	-0.003	0.076	-0.050	0.027
2BX												
3												
3X												
Shock K. German Money Demand												
1	-0.004	0.058	-0.162	0.146	-0.002	0.058	-0.029	0.058	-0.008	0.116	-0.291	0.171
1X												
2A	-0.004	0.020	-0.068	0.073	-0.002	0.042	0.050	-0.049	-0.008	0.073	-0.070	0.061
2AX												
2B	-0.001	0.014	0.012	-0.001	-0.001	0.031	0.277	-0.449	-0.003	0.076	-0.050	0.027
2BX												
3												
3X												
Shock F. U.S. Money Supply-Permanent												
FIXM	0.010	0.105	-0.153	0.138	0.010	0.202	-0.012	0.062	0.042	0.191	-0.258	0.172
1	0.009	0.113	-0.167	0.100	0.011	0.218	-0.018	0.061	0.044	0.205	-0.308	0.105
1X												

MX3 MODEL
EFFECTS ON JAPANESE INTEREST RATES AND JAPANESE CURRENT ACCOUNT/GNP RATIO
(Deviations from Baseline)

Shock and Regime	Short Interest Rate				Long Interest Rate				Current Account/GNP Ratio			
	1st Qtr	6th Qtr	18th Qtr	36th Qtr	1st Qtr	6th Qtr	18th Qtr	38th Qtr	2nd Qtr	6th Qtr	18th Qtr	38th Qtr
Shock A. US Aggregate Demand												
1	-0.006	0.028	-0.105	0.099	NA	NA	NA	NA	0.159	0.043	-0.039	-0.063
1X												
2A	-0.002	0.095	-0.027	0.035	NA	NA	NA	NA	0.142	0.073	-0.063	0.071
2AX												
2B	-0.004	0.149	-0.057	0.043	NA	NA	NA	NA	0.112	0.076	-0.084	0.133
2BX												
3												
3X												
Shock I. Japanese Aggregate Demand												
1	0.196	0.023	-0.105	0.100	NA	NA	NA	NA	0.031	-0.001	-0.053	-0.089
1X												
2A	0.897	0.062	-0.028	0.038	NA	NA	NA	NA	0.046	0.029	-0.073	0.039
2AX												
2B	1.011	0.116	-0.059	0.046	NA	NA	NA	NA	-0.007	0.035	-0.082	0.105
2BX												
3												
3X												
Shock G. German Aggregate Demand												
1	-0.009	0.026	-0.099	0.099	NA	NA	NA	NA	0.045	0.001	-0.065	-0.087
1X												
2A	-0.016	0.093	-0.027	0.035	NA	NA	NA	NA	0.090	0.036	-0.079	0.040
2AX												
2B	-0.020	0.145	-0.058	0.040	NA	NA	NA	NA	0.060	0.042	-0.101	0.108
2BX												
3												
3X												
Shock B. Global Aggregate Demand												
1	0.195	0.023	-0.100	0.100	NA	NA	NA	NA	0.110	0.021	-0.051	-0.072
1X												
2A	0.897	0.064	-0.028	0.038	NA	NA	NA	NA	0.052	0.049	-0.062	0.063
2AX												
2B	1.010	0.120	-0.059	0.049	NA	NA	NA	NA	-0.004	0.050	-0.071	0.121
2BX												
3												
3X												
Shock C. US Aggregate Supply												
1	-0.014	0.104	-0.126	0.098	NA	NA	NA	NA	0.085	-0.209	-0.036	-0.092
1X												
2A	0.002	0.109	-0.026	0.036	NA	NA	NA	NA	0.108	-0.107	-0.086	0.037
2AX												
2B	-0.004	0.192	-0.065	0.040	NA	NA	NA	NA	0.117	-0.153	-0.101	0.093
2BX												
3												
3X												
Shock J. Japanese Aggregate Supply												
1	0.103	0.280	-0.148	0.099	NA	NA	NA	NA	-0.096	-0.516	-0.029	-0.137
1X												
2A	-0.334	0.336	-0.038	0.032	NA	NA	NA	NA	0.353	-0.374	-0.108	0.003
2AX												
2B	0.074	0.395	-0.244	-0.070	NA	NA	NA	NA	0.301	-0.481	-0.065	-0.188
2BX												
3												
3X												

904

Shock and Regime	Short Interest Rate				Long Interest Rate				Current Account/GNP Ratio			
	1st Qtr	6th Qtr	18th Qtr	36th Qtr	1st Qtr	6th Qtr	18th Qtr	38th Qtr	2nd Qtr	6th Qtr	18th Qtr	38th Qtr
Shock H. German Aggregate Supply												
1	-0.007	0.027	-0.104	0.099	NA	NA	NA	NA	0.059	0.010	-0.054	-0.085
1X												
2A	-0.009	0.092	-0.027	0.035	NA	NA	NA	NA	0.106	0.042	-0.078	0.041
2AX												
2B	-0.012	0.133	-0.058	0.042	NA	NA	NA	NA	0.077	0.047	-0.105	0.099
2BX												
3												
3X												
Shock E. Oil Price Increase												
1												
1X												
2A												
2AX												
2B												
2BX												
3												
3X												
Shock L. U.S. Money Demand												
1	-0.003	0.058	-0.117	0.099	NA	NA	NA	NA	0.548	-0.037	-0.027	-0.069
1X												
2A	-0.008	0.092	-0.027	0.035	NA	NA	NA	NA	0.113	0.044	-0.076	0.043
2AX												
2B	-0.012	0.146	-0.058	0.042	NA	NA	NA	NA	0.085	0.048	-0.098	0.106
2BX												
3												
3X												
Shock D. Japanese Money Demand												
1	0.905	0.046	-0.111	0.099	NA	NA	NA	NA	0.100	-0.049	-0.041	-0.090
1X												
2A	-0.008	0.093	-0.027	0.035	NA	NA	NA	NA	0.113	0.044	-0.077	0.043
2AX												
2B	-0.006	0.135	-0.057	0.041	NA	NA	NA	NA	0.067	0.069	-0.099	0.109
2BX												
3												
3X												
Shock K. German Money Demand												
1	-0.008	0.059	-0.113	0.099	NA	NA	NA	NA	0.101	-0.047	-0.045	-0.092
1X												
2A	-0.008	0.093	-0.027	0.035	NA	NA	NA	NA	0.114	0.044	-0.077	0.044
2AX												
2B	-0.006	0.135	-0.056	0.040	NA	NA	NA	NA	0.067	0.070	-0.098	0.117
2BX												
3												
3X												
Shock F. U.S. Money Supply-Permanent												
FIXM	-0.044	0.145	-0.114	0.102	NA	NA	NA	NA	0.187	-0.017	0.144	0.165
1	-0.041	0.146	-0.110	0.074	NA	NA	NA	NA	0.021	-0.120	0.184	-0.951
1X												

Table A-MX3-5
MX3 MODEL
EFFECTS ON GERMAN REAL GNP, GERMAN PRICE LEVEL, GERMAN INFLATION RATE
(Deviations from Baseline)

Shock and Regime	Real GNP				GNP Deflator				Inflation Rate			
	1st Qtr	6th Qtr	18th Qtr	38th Qtr	1st Qtr	6th Qtr	18th Qtr	38th Qtr	1st Qtr	6th Qtr	18th Qtr	38th Qtr
Shock A. US Aggregate Demand												
1	-0.009	-0.009	0.005	0.023	-0.000	-0.006	-0.038	-0.064	-0.002	-0.007	-0.008	-0.003
1X												
2A	-0.003	0.001	0.017	0.038	-0.001	-0.006	-0.027	-0.036	-0.002	-0.006	-0.005	-0.005
2AX												
2B	-0.005	-0.002	0.000	0.005	-0.000	-0.005	-0.054	-0.125	-0.001	-0.007	-0.018	-0.023
2BX												
3												
3X												
Shock I. Japanese Aggregate Demand												
1	-0.007	-0.004	0.005	0.023	-0.000	-0.004	-0.035	-0.064	-0.001	-0.005	-0.008	-0.003
1X												
2A	-0.005	0.003	0.016	0.037	-0.000	-0.004	-0.025	-0.035	-0.002	-0.005	-0.005	-0.004
2AX												
2B	-0.006	0.000	0.001	0.005	-0.000	-0.005	-0.055	-0.122	-0.001	-0.006	-0.019	-0.022
2BX												
3												
3X												
Shock G. German Aggregate Demand												
1	0.624	-0.017	0.003	0.022	0.010	-0.003	-0.037	-0.061	0.039	-0.012	-0.006	-0.003
1X												
2A	0.588	-0.008	0.014	0.036	0.009	-0.003	-0.026	-0.033	0.037	-0.010	-0.005	-0.005
2AX												
2B	0.588	-0.007	-0.003	0.007	0.009	-0.003	-0.053	-0.116	0.036	-0.010	-0.018	-0.020
2BX												
3												
3X												
Shock B. Global Aggregate Demand												
1	0.606	-0.029	0.002	0.022	0.009	-0.007	-0.041	-0.061	0.036	-0.014	-0.005	-0.003
1X												
2A	0.577	-0.010	0.015	0.037	0.009	-0.005	-0.027	-0.033	0.035	-0.011	-0.004	-0.005
2AX												
2B	0.576	-0.011	-0.003	0.007	0.009	-0.006	-0.061	-0.124	0.034	-0.012	-0.018	-0.024
2BX												
3												
3X												
Shock C. US Aggregate Supply												
1	-0.014	-0.005	0.009	0.024	-0.001	-0.009	-0.038	-0.066	-0.005	-0.009	-0.008	-0.003
1X												
2A	-0.014	0.001	0.018	0.038	-0.001	-0.006	-0.026	-0.036	-0.003	-0.006	-0.005	-0.005
2AX												
2B	-0.014	-0.003	0.002	0.006	-0.001	-0.008	-0.059	-0.129	-0.003	-0.009	-0.018	-0.024
2BX												
3												
3X												
Shock J. Japanese Aggregate Supply												
1	-0.019	-0.019	0.006	0.028	-0.005	-0.031	-0.055	-0.069	-0.018	-0.019	-0.008	0.000
1X												
2A	-0.005	-0.001	0.019	0.041	-0.001	-0.008	-0.029	-0.040	-0.004	-0.008	-0.003	-0.004
2AX												
2B	-0.004	-0.006	0.004	0.014	-0.001	-0.015	-0.083	-0.403	-0.005	-0.016	-0.031	-0.093
2BX												
3												
3X												

906

Shock and Regime	Real GNP				GNP Deflator				Inflation Rate			
	1st Qtr	6th Qtr	18th Qtr	38th Qtr	1st Qtr	6th Qtr	18th Qtr	38th Qtr	1st Qtr	6th Qtr	18th Qtr	38th Qtr
Shock H. German Aggregate Supply												
1	-0.686	-0.003	0.004	0.022	0.005	-0.001	-0.035	-0.063	0.020	-0.008	-0.009	-0.003
1X												
2A	-0.644	0.003	0.016	0.037	0.007	0.001	-0.026	-0.035	0.026	-0.009	-0.006	-0.003
2AX												
2B	-0.647	0.004	0.001	0.006	0.006	0.001	-0.050	-0.127	0.023	-0.008	-0.020	-0.026
2BX												
3												
3X												
Shock E. Oil Price Increase												
1												
1X												
2A												
2AX												
2B												
2BX												
3												
3X												
Shock L. U.S. Money Demand												
1	0.011	-0.003	0.006	0.024	0.000	-0.005	-0.038	-0.065	0.001	-0.009	-0.008	-0.002
1X												
2A	0.001	0.003	0.016	0.037	-0.000	-0.004	-0.025	-0.035	-0.001	-0.005	-0.006	-0.005
2AX												
2B	0.001	0.001	0.000	0.006	0.000	-0.004	-0.052	-0.123	0.000	-0.007	-0.018	-0.026
2BX												
3												
3X												
Shock D. Japanese Money Demand												
1	0.001	-0.001	0.006	0.023	-0.000	-0.004	-0.037	-0.065	0.000	-0.008	-0.008	-0.003
1X												
2A	0.001	0.003	0.016	0.037	-0.000	-0.004	-0.025	-0.035	-0.001	-0.005	-0.005	-0.004
2AX												
2B	0.000	0.001	0.001	0.005	0.000	-0.003	-0.052	-0.122	-0.000	-0.006	-0.019	-0.023
2BX												
3												
3X												
Shock K. German Money Demand												
1	-0.096	-0.016	0.006	0.022	-0.003	-0.012	-0.036	-0.063	-0.011	-0.007	-0.006	-0.003
1X												
2A	0.001	0.003	0.016	0.037	-0.000	-0.003	-0.025	-0.035	-0.001	-0.006	-0.005	-0.004
2AX												
2B	0.000	0.001	0.000	0.005	0.000	-0.003	-0.051	-0.119	-0.000	-0.006	-0.019	-0.021
2BX												
3												
3X												
Shock F. U.S. Money Supply-Permanent												
FIXM	-0.048	-0.045	0.030	0.023	-0.005	-0.028	-0.018	-0.059	-0.020	-0.010	0.002	-0.007
1	-0.068	-0.057	0.050	0.019	-0.012	-0.063	-0.033	-0.128	-0.047	-0.023	0.010	-0.044
1X												

MX3 MODEL
EFFECTS ON GERMAN INTEREST RATES AND GERMAN CURRENT ACCOUNT/GNP RATIO
(Deviations from Baseline)

Shock and Regime	Short Interest Rate				Long Interest Rate				Current Account/GNP Ratio			
	1st Qtr	6th Qtr	18th Qtr	38th Qtr	1st Qtr	6th Qtr	18th Qtr	38th Qtr	2nd Qtr	6th Qtr	18th Qtr	38th Qtr
Shock A. US Aggregate Demand												
1	0.001	-0.003	-0.010	0.003	NA	NA	NA	NA	0.002	-0.007	-0.007	-0.029
1X												
2A	-0.006	-0.006	-0.015	0.003	NA	NA	NA	NA	-0.010	-0.008	-0.005	-0.026
2AX												
2B	-0.009	-0.014	-0.027	-0.026	NA	NA	NA	NA	-0.010	-0.008	-0.008	-0.035
2BX												
3												
3X												
Shock I. Japanese Aggregate Demand												
1	0.002	-0.002	-0.009	0.003	NA	NA	NA	NA	-0.004	-0.003	-0.005	-0.029
1X												
2A	-0.008	-0.001	-0.014	0.003	NA	NA	NA	NA	-0.004	-0.003	-0.004	-0.027
2AX												
2B	-0.011	-0.009	-0.027	-0.025	NA	NA	NA	NA	-0.004	-0.003	-0.008	-0.037
2BX												
3												
3X												
Shock G. German Aggregate Demand												
1	0.363	-0.007	-0.013	0.005	NA	NA	NA	NA	-0.013	-0.009	-0.005	-0.030
1X												
2A	0.893	-0.016	-0.018	0.005	NA	NA	NA	NA	-0.025	-0.008	-0.004	-0.029
2AX												
2B	0.934	-0.026	-0.030	-0.020	NA	NA	NA	NA	-0.027	-0.008	-0.007	-0.038
2BX												
3												
3X												
Shock B. Global Aggregate Demand												
1	0.361	-0.009	-0.013	0.005	NA	NA	NA	NA	-0.014	-0.017	-0.008	-0.031
1X												
2A	0.876	-0.023	-0.019	0.006	NA	NA	NA	NA	-0.037	-0.015	-0.006	-0.029
2AX												
2B	0.913	-0.035	-0.031	-0.026	NA	NA	NA	NA	-0.039	-0.015	-0.010	-0.039
2BX												
3												
3X												
Shock C. US Aggregate Supply												
1	0.009	-0.011	-0.007	0.003	NA	NA	NA	NA	-0.023	-0.006	-0.007	-0.030
1X												
2A	-0.023	-0.007	-0.012	0.003	NA	NA	NA	NA	-0.025	-0.009	-0.006	-0.030
2AX												
2B	-0.026	-0.018	-0.024	-0.028	NA	NA	NA	NA	-0.025	-0.008	-0.010	-0.039
2BX												
3												
3X												
Shock J. Japanese Aggregate Supply												
1	0.018	-0.021	-0.008	0.005	NA	NA	NA	NA	-0.016	-0.013	-0.019	-0.033
1X												
2A	-0.009	-0.014	-0.014	0.002	NA	NA	NA	NA	-0.018	-0.006	-0.009	-0.031
2AX												
2B	-0.013	-0.034	-0.040	-0.118	NA	NA	NA	NA	-0.018	-0.005	-0.017	-0.081
2BX												
3												
3X												

908

Shock and Regime	Short Interest Rate				Long Interest Rate				Current Account/GNP Ratio			
	1st Qtr	6th Qtr	18th Qtr	38th Qtr	1st Qtr	6th Qtr	18th Qtr	38th Qtr	2nd Qtr	6th Qtr	18th Qtr	38th Qtr
Shock H. German Aggregate Supply												
1	-0.367	-0.002	-0.010	0.003	NA	NA	NA	NA	-0.001	-0.002	-0.005	-0.029
1X												
2A	-0.959	0.005	-0.015	0.003	NA	NA	NA	NA	0.007	-0.004	-0.004	-0.027
2AX												
2B	-0.940	-0.006	-0.030	-0.029	NA	NA	NA	NA	0.007	-0.002	-0.006	-0.037
2BX												
3												
3X												
Shock E. Oil Price Increase												
1												
1X												
2A												
2AX												
2B												
2BX												
3												
3X												
Shock L. U.S. Money Demand												
1	0.011	-0.006	-0.008	0.003	NA	NA	NA	NA	0.064	0.000	-0.004	-0.025
1X												
2A	0.001	-0.000	-0.014	0.003	NA	NA	NA	NA	-0.002	-0.002	-0.004	-0.027
2AX												
2B	0.001	-0.008	-0.027	-0.030	NA	NA	NA	NA	-0.001	-0.002	-0.006	-0.036
2BX												
3												
3X												
Shock D. Japanese Money Demand												
1	0.008	-0.005	-0.009	0.003	NA	NA	NA	NA	-0.001	0.000	-0.006	-0.028
1X												
2A	0.001	-0.000	-0.014	0.003	NA	NA	NA	NA	-0.002	-0.002	-0.004	-0.027
2AX												
2B	0.000	-0.007	-0.028	-0.027	NA	NA	NA	NA	-0.001	-0.002	-0.006	-0.036
2BX												
3												
3X												
Shock K. German Money Demand												
1	1.028	-0.015	-0.009	0.003	NA	NA	NA	NA	-0.013	-0.006	-0.006	-0.029
1X												
2A	0.001	-0.000	-0.014	0.003	NA	NA	NA	NA	-0.002	-0.002	-0.004	-0.027
2AX												
2B	0.000	-0.007	-0.028	-0.024	NA	NA	NA	NA	-0.001	-0.002	-0.006	-0.036
2BX												
3												
3X												
Shock F. U.S. Money Supply-Permanent												
FIXM	-0.062	-0.019	0.005	-0.001	NA	NA	NA	NA	-0.040	-0.031	-0.013	-0.018
1	-0.067	-0.033	0.012	-0.033	NA	NA	NA	NA	-0.075	-0.050	-0.011	-0.067
1X												

Table A-MX3-7
MX3 MODEL
BILATERAL DOLLAR EXCHANGE RATES
(Deviations from Baseline)

Shock and Regime	Bilateral DM/$ Exchange Rate				Bilateral Yen/$ Exchange Rate			
	1st Qtr	6th Qtr	18th Qtr	38th Qtr	1st Qtr	6th Qtr	18th Qtr	38th Qtr
Shock A. US Aggregate Demand								
1	-0.068	-0.011	0.067	-0.005	0.012	0.178	-0.832	0.585
1X								
2A	-0.226	-0.015	0.034	-0.030	-0.057	0.400	-0.827	0.657
2AX								
2B	-0.225	-0.011	0.081	0.034	-0.139	0.350	-1.077	1.034
2BX								
3								
3X								
Shock I. Japanese Aggregate Demand								
1	-0.007	-0.012	0.062	-0.001	0.126	0.171	-0.835	0.590
1X								
2A	-0.019	-0.025	0.027	-0.026	0.340	0.337	-0.838	0.664
2AX								
2B	-0.013	-0.020	0.075	0.034	0.298	0.295	-1.096	1.011
2BX								
3								
3X								
Shock G. German Aggregate Demand								
1	0.095	-0.017	0.057	0.003	0.072	0.174	-0.824	0.588
1X								
2A	0.183	-0.045	0.022	-0.021	0.138	0.375	-0.835	0.661
2AX								
2B	0.207	-0.041	0.069	0.035	0.068	0.327	-1.082	1.037
2BX								
3								
3X								
Shock B. Global Aggregate Demand								
1	0.032	-0.017	0.063	-0.001	0.064	0.174	-0.820	0.587
1X								
2A	-0.041	-0.033	0.030	-0.026	0.138	0.369	-0.829	0.659
2AX								
2B	-0.020	-0.028	0.081	0.036	0.085	0.323	-1.092	1.023
2BX								
3								
3X								
Shock C. US Aggregate Supply								
1	0.085	0.024	0.074	0.003	0.399	0.129	-0.837	0.593
1X								
2A	0.292	0.023	0.038	-0.021	0.605	0.378	-0.823	0.668
2AX								
2B	0.291	0.029	0.104	0.059	0.615	0.285	-1.101	1.047
2BX								
3								
3X								
Shock J. Japanese Aggregate Supply								
1	-0.053	-0.014	0.075	0.008	0.755	0.116	-0.805	0.620
1X								
2A	-0.054	-0.028	0.030	-0.022	0.765	0.329	-0.862	0.675
2AX								
2B	-0.063	-0.027	0.103	0.219	1.009	0.105	-1.178	1.819
2BX								
3								
3X								

910

Shock and Regime	Bilateral DM/$ Exchange Rate				Bilateral Yen/$ Exchange Rate			
	1st Qtr	6th Qtr	18th Qtr	38th Qtr	1st Qtr	6th Qtr	18th Qtr	38th Qtr
Shock H. German Aggregate Supply								
1	-0.108	-0.012	0.062	-0.000	0.073	0.174	-0.835	0.589
1X								
2A	-0.226	-0.023	0.026	-0.025	0.144	0.372	-0.836	0.660
2AX								
2B	-0.227	-0.023	0.071	0.035	0.073	0.320	-1.079	1.061
2BX								
3								
3X								
Shock E. Oil Price Increase								
1								
1X								
2A								
2AX								
2B								
2BX								
3								
3X								
Shock L. U.S. Money Demand								
1	-0.516	-0.005	0.069	-0.001	-0.396	0.191	-0.840	0.588
1X								
2A	-0.011	-0.026	0.026	-0.026	0.141	0.371	-0.835	0.661
2AX								
2B	-0.006	-0.021	0.073	0.031	0.071	0.325	-1.083	1.051
2BX								
3								
3X								
Shock D. Japanese Money Demand								
1	-0.009	-0.014	0.063	-0.001	0.361	0.174	-0.836	0.587
1X								
2A	-0.011	-0.026	0.026	-0.025	0.141	0.371	-0.836	0.661
2AX								
2B	-0.003	-0.021	0.071	0.033	0.036	0.321	-1.078	1.049
2BX								
3								
3X								
Shock K. German Money Demand								
1	0.293	-0.022	0.063	-0.001	0.107	0.185	-0.836	0.589
1X								
2A	-0.011	-0.026	0.027	-0.024	0.141	0.371	-0.836	0.662
2AX								
2B	-0.003	-0.021	0.071	0.031	0.036	0.322	-1.076	1.033
2BX								
3								
3X								
Shock F. U.S. Money Supply-Permanent								
FIXM	1.408	0.906	1.007	0.979	1.861	1.026	0.118	1.595
1	1.636	0.878	0.862	-0.065	2.138	1.023	-0.079	0.374

TAYLOR MODEL
EFFECTS ON U.S. REAL GNP, U.S. PRICE LEVEL, U.S. INFLATION RATE
(Deviations from Baseline)

Shock and Regime	Real GNP				GNP Deflator				Inflation Rate			
	1st Qtr	6th Qtr	18th Qtr	38th Qtr	1st Qtr	6th Qtr	18th Qtr	38th Qtr	1st Qtr	6th Qtr	18th Qtr	38th Qtr

Shock A. US Aggregate Demand

1												
1X	1.070	-0.003	0.001	0.000	0.001	0.000	-0.000	0.000	0.005	-0.001	0.000	0.000
2A	0.990	-0.004	-0.000	-0.000	0.001	-0.000	-0.000	-0.000	0.006	-0.001	0.000	0.000
2AX	0.988	-0.006	-0.000	-0.000	0.002	0.000	-0.000	-0.000	0.006	-0.002	0.000	0.000
2B	0.993	0.002	0.008	0.009	0.001	-0.000	0.000	0.000	0.006	-0.001	0.000	0.000
2BX	0.993	0.002	0.008	0.009	0.001	-0.000	0.000	0.000	0.006	-0.001	0.000	0.000
3												
3X	1.390	0.685	0.446	0.621	0.034	0.477	0.990	0.879	0.136	0.373	0.052	-0.116

Shock I. Japanese Aggregate Demand

1	
1X	
2A	
2AX	
2B	
2BX	
3	
3X	

Shock G. German Aggregate Demand

1	
1X	
2A	
2AX	
2B	
2BX	
3	
3X	

Shock B. Global Aggregate Demand

1												
1X	1.080	0.002	0.002	0.001	0.001	0.000	0.000	0.000	0.005	-0.001	-0.000	-0.000
2A	0.998	-0.004	-0.001	-0.000	0.001	0.000	-0.000	-0.000	0.006	-0.002	-0.000	0.000
2AX	0.998	-0.002	0.001	0.001	0.002	0.000	-0.000	-0.000	0.006	-0.002	0.000	0.000
2B	1.000	0.003	0.007	0.005	0.002	0.001	0.000	0.000	0.006	-0.002	0.000	-0.000
2BX	1.000	0.003	0.007	0.005	0.002	0.001	0.000	0.000	0.006	-0.002	0.000	-0.000
3												
3X	1.400	0.689	0.455	0.623	0.034	0.474	0.979	0.872	0.135	0.373	0.048	-0.116

Shock C. US Aggregate Supply

1												
1X	0.902	-0.174	-0.046	-0.016	0.454	0.125	-0.001	-0.000	1.816	-0.277	-0.000	0.000
2A	0.747	-0.151	-0.006	0.001	0.451	0.093	-0.004	-0.000	1.804	-0.286	0.004	0.000
2AX	0.804	-0.116	-0.001	0.002	0.453	0.117	0.000	0.000	1.812	-0.273	0.000	-0.000
2B	0.825	-0.067	-0.006	-0.001	0.454	0.126	0.003	0.001	1.816	-0.273	-0.001	-0.000
2BX	0.878	-0.019	0.001	0.002	0.455	0.135	0.005	0.001	1.820	-0.269	-0.002	-0.000
3												
3X	1.220	0.702	0.797	0.945	0.469	0.326	0.383	0.399	1.876	-0.128	0.020	-0.024

Shock J. Japanese Aggregate Supply

1	
1X	
2A	
2AX	
2B	
2BX	
3	
3X	

Shock and Regime	Real GNP				GNP Deflator				Inflation Rate			
	1st Qtr	6th Qtr	18th Qtr	38th Qtr	1st Qtr	6th Qtr	18th Qtr	38th Qtr	1st Qtr	6th Qtr	18th Qtr	38th Qtr

Shock H. German Aggregate Supply

1												
1X												
2A												
2AX												
2B												
2BX												
3												
3X												

Shock E. Oil Price Increase

1												
1X												
2A												
2AX												
2B												
2BX												
3												
3X												

Shock L. U.S. Money Demand

1												
1X												
2A												
2AX												
2B												
2BX												
3												
3X												

Shock D. Japanese Money Demand

1												
1X	0.000	-0.001	-0.001	-0.000	0.000	0.000	0.000	-0.000	0.000	0.000	-0.000	0.000
2A	0.000	0.000	0.000	0.000	0.000	0.000	0.000	0.000	0.000	0.000	0.000	0.000
2AX	0.000	0.000	0.000	0.000	0.000	0.000	0.000	0.000	0.000	0.000	0.000	0.000
2B	0.000	0.000	0.000	0.000	0.000	0.000	0.000	0.000	0.000	0.000	0.000	0.000
2BX	0.000	0.000	0.000	0.000	0.000	0.000	0.000	0.000	0.000	0.000	0.000	0.000
3												
3X	0.000	0.000	0.000	0.000	0.000	0.000	0.000	0.000	0.000	0.000	0.000	0.000

Shock K. German Money Demand

1												
1X												
2A												
2AX												
2B												
2BX												
3												
3X												

Shock F. U.S. Money Supply-Permanent

FIXM	0.360	0.192	0.103	0.052	0.019	0.287	0.742	0.953	0.076	0.233	0.096	0.020
1												
1X												

TAYLOR MODEL
EFFECTS ON U.S. INTEREST RATES AND U.S. CURRENT ACCOUNT/GNP RATIO
(Deviations from Baseline)

Shock and Regime	Short Interest Rate				Long Interest Rate				Current Account/GNP Ratio			
	1st Qtr	6th Qtr	18th Qtr	38th Qtr	1st Qtr	6th Qtr	18th Qtr	38th Qtr	1st Qtr	6th Qtr	18th Qtr	38th Qtr

Shock A. US Aggregate Demand

1												
1X	0.019	0.006	0.001	0.000	0.012	0.005	0.001	0.000	-0.120	0.001	-0.000	-0.000
2A	1.480	-0.006	-0.001	-0.000	0.324	-0.005	-0.002	-0.001	-0.110	0.001	0.000	0.000
2AX	1.480	-0.009	-0.001	-0.000	0.325	-0.005	-0.001	-0.001	-0.109	0.002	0.000	0.000
2B	1.480	-0.005	0.004	0.005	0.321	-0.004	0.001	0.003	-0.110	0.000	-0.001	-0.001
2BX	1.480	-0.004	0.004	0.005	0.320	-0.005	0.001	0.003	-0.110	0.000	-0.001	-0.001
3												
3X	0.353	-0.100	0.044	-0.079	-0.247	-0.012	0.021	-0.357	-0.153	-0.111	-0.115	-0.110

Shock I. Japanese Aggregate Demand

1
1X
2A
2AX
2B
2BX
3
3X

Shock G. German Aggregate Demand

1
1X
2A
2AX
2B
2BX
3
3X

Shock B. Global Aggregate Demand

1												
1X	0.019	0.007	0.001	0.000	0.013	0.005	0.001	0.000	-0.113	0.003	-0.000	-0.000
2A	1.490	-0.006	-0.002	-0.001	0.329	-0.007	-0.004	-0.001	-0.106	0.003	0.000	0.000
2AX	1.490	-0.003	0.002	0.001	0.335	-0.002	-0.000	-0.000	-0.106	0.002	-0.000	-0.000
2B	1.490	-0.004	0.002	0.000	0.334	-0.000	0.004	0.002	-0.106	0.001	-0.001	-0.001
2BX	1.490	-0.005	0.002	0.000	0.333	-0.000	0.004	0.002	-0.106	0.001	-0.001	-0.001
3												
3X	0.365	-0.103	0.041	-0.084	-0.240	-0.011	0.025	-0.359	-0.149	-0.111	-0.115	-0.114

Shock C. US Aggregate Supply

1												
1X	-0.028	-0.026	-0.003	-0.003	-0.059	-0.009	-0.002	-0.002	0.064	0.042	0.009	0.003
2A	1.790	-0.087	-0.015	0.000	0.528	-0.083	-0.018	-0.005	0.085	0.039	-0.000	0.000
2AX	1.610	-0.102	-0.002	0.003	0.403	-0.062	0.000	0.003	0.078	0.030	-0.001	-0.001
2B	1.900	-0.210	-0.017	-0.008	0.331	-0.116	-0.008	-0.006	0.074	0.016	0.000	0.001
2BX	1.730	-0.246	-0.009	-0.006	0.173	-0.134	-0.006	-0.006	0.066	0.002	-0.000	0.000
3												
3X	0.294	-0.606	-0.365	-0.189	-0.467	-0.489	-0.351	-0.553	0.031	-0.105	-0.135	-0.173

Shock J. Japanese Aggregate Supply

1
1X
2A
2AX
2B
2BX
3
3X

Shock and Regime	Short Interest Rate				Long Interest Rate				Current Account/GNP Ratio			
	1st Qtr	6th Qtr	18th Qtr	38th Qtr	1st Qtr	6th Qtr	18th Qtr	38th Qtr	1st Qtr	6th Qtr	18th Qtr	38th Qtr

Shock H. German Aggregate Supply
1
1X
2A
2AX
2B
2BX
3
3X

Shock E. Oil Price Increase
1
1X
2A
2AX
2B
2BX
3
3X

Shock L. U.S. Money Demand
1
1X
2A
2AX
2B
2BX
3
3X

Shock D. Japanese Money Demand

1												
1X	0.000	-0.000	-0.000	-0.000	0.000	-0.000	-0.000	-0.000	-0.000	-0.001	-0.000	0.000
2A	0.000	0.000	0.000	0.000	0.000	0.000	0.000	0.000	0.000	0.000	0.000	0.000
2AX	0.000	0.000	0.000	0.000	0.000	0.000	0.000	0.000	0.000	0.000	0.000	0.000
2B	0.000	0.000	0.000	0.000	0.000	0.000	0.000	0.000	0.000	0.000	0.000	0.000
2BX	0.000	0.000	0.000	0.000	0.000	0.000	0.000	0.000	0.000	0.000	0.000	0.000
3												
3X	0.000	0.000	0.000	0.000	0.000	0.000	0.000	0.000	0.000	0.000	0.000	0.000

Shock K. German Money Demand
1
1X
2A
2AX
2B
2BX
3
3X

Shock F. U.S. Money Supply-Permanent

FIXM	-4.290	0.130	0.063	0.017	-1.090	0.119	0.053	0.016	-0.053	-0.046	-0.022	-0.013
1												
1X												

TAYLOR MODEL
EFFECTS ON JAPANESE REAL GNP, JAPANESE PRICE LEVEL, JAPANESE INFLATION RATE
(Deviations from Baseline)

Shock and	Real GNP				GNP Deflator				Inflation Rate			
Regime	1st Qtr	6th Qtr	18th Qtr	38th Qtr	1st Qtr	6th Qtr	18th Qtr	38th Qtr	1st Qtr	6th Qtr	18th Qtr	38th Qtr
Shock A. US Aggregate Demand												
1												
1X	0.021	0.012	0.002	0.000	0.000	0.001	0.001	0.000	0.000	0.000	-0.000	-0.000
2A	0.015	-0.000	-0.001	0.000	0.000	0.001	0.000	-0.000	0.000	-0.000	-0.000	0.000
2AX	0.016	0.001	0.000	0.002	0.000	0.002	0.001	-0.001	0.000	0.001	-0.001	0.000
2B	0.018	0.008	0.010	0.009	0.000	0.002	0.002	0.003	0.000	0.000	0.000	0.000
2BX	0.018	0.009	0.010	0.009	0.000	0.002	0.002	0.003	0.000	0.001	0.000	0.000
3												
3X	0.450	1.230	-1.550	1.270	0.025	0.872	2.260	-0.686	0.101	0.977	-0.515	0.265
Shock I. Japanese Aggregate Demand												
1												
1X												
2A												
2AX												
2B												
2BX												
3												
3X												
Shock G. German Aggregate Demand												
1												
1X												
2A												
2AX												
2B												
2BX												
3												
3X												
Shock B. Global Aggregate Demand												
1												
1X	0.814	0.026	-0.002	-0.001	0.000	0.005	0.003	0.001	0.002	0.001	-0.001	-0.000
2A	0.738	-0.012	0.005	0.002	0.000	0.002	-0.002	-0.001	0.002	0.000	-0.000	0.000
2AX	0.744	0.004	0.010	0.002	0.001	0.002	-0.002	-0.001	0.002	0.000	-0.001	0.000
2B	0.746	0.009	0.012	-0.001	0.001	0.003	0.001	0.004	0.002	0.001	0.000	0.000
2BX	0.746	0.009	0.012	-0.001	0.001	0.003	0.001	0.004	0.002	0.001	0.000	0.000
3												
3X	1.200	1.220	-1.480	1.110	0.026	0.866	2.290	-0.602	0.102	0.965	-0.435	0.204
Shock C. US Aggregate Supply												
1												
1X	-0.001	-0.010	-0.014	-0.007	0.000	0.006	0.005	0.000	0.000	0.004	-0.001	-0.000
2A	-0.000	-0.003	0.037	0.037	-0.000	0.002	-0.012	-0.005	-0.001	-0.004	-0.000	0.001
2AX	0.001	0.003	0.012	0.006	-0.000	0.004	-0.003	-0.002	-0.000	-0.001	-0.001	0.000
2B	-0.001	-0.011	-0.009	0.004	0.000	0.003	0.004	0.005	0.000	0.000	0.001	-0.000
2BX	-0.001	-0.004	0.004	0.012	0.000	0.001	0.003	0.005	0.000	-0.000	0.001	0.000
3												
3X	0.270	0.981	0.354	0.080	0.009	0.319	1.200	1.120	0.036	0.350	0.160	-0.080
Shock J. Japanese Aggregate Supply												
1												
1X												
2A												
2AX												
2B												
2BX												
3												
3X												

Shock and	Real GNP				GNP Deflator				Inflation Rate			
Regime	1st Qtr	6th Qtr	18th Qtr	38th Qtr	1st Qtr	6th Qtr	18th Qtr	38th Qtr	1st Qtr	6th Qtr	18th Qtr	38th Qtr

Shock H. German Aggregate Supply

1
1X
2A
2AX
2B
2BX
3
3X

Shock E. Oil Price Increase

1
1X
2A
2AX
2B
2BX
3
3X

Shock L. U.S. Money Demand

1
1X
2A
2AX
2B
2BX
3
3X

Shock D. Japanese Money Demand

1												
1X	-0.044	-0.060	-0.013	-0.000	-0.000	-0.007	-0.006	-0.002	-0.000	-0.003	0.001	0.000
2A	0.000	0.000	0.000	0.000	0.000	0.000	0.000	0.000	0.000	0.000	0.000	0.000
2AX	0.000	0.000	0.000	0.000	0.000	0.000	0.000	0.000	0.000	0.000	0.000	0.000
2B	0.000	0.000	0.000	0.000	0.000	0.000	0.000	0.000	0.000	0.000	0.000	0.000
2BX	0.000	0.000	0.000	0.000	0.000	0.000	0.000	0.000	0.000	0.000	0.000	0.000
3												
3X	0.000	0.000	0.000	0.000	0.000	0.000	0.000	0.000	0.000	0.000	0.000	0.000

Shock K. German Money Demand

1
1X
2A
2AX
2B
2BX
3
3X

Shock F. U.S. Money Supply-Permanent

FIXM	0.003	0.014	-0.011	0.020	0.000	0.005	0.037	0.001	0.001	0.013	-0.002	0.007
1												
1X												

917

Table A-TAY-4
TAYLOR MODEL
EFFECTS ON JAPANESE INTEREST RATES AND JAPANESE CURRENT ACCOUNT/GNP RATIO
(Deviations from Baseline)

Shock and Regime	Short Interest Rate				Long Interest Rate				Current Account/GNP Ratio			
	1st Qtr	6th Qtr	18th Qtr	38th Qtr	1st Qtr	6th Qtr	18th Qtr	38th Qtr	1st Qtr	6th Qtr	18th Qtr	38th Qtr

Shock A. US Aggregate Demand

1												
1X	0.001	0.002	0.000	-0.000	0.002	0.001	0.000	-0.000	0.015	0.003	0.000	-0.000
2A	0.023	0.001	-0.001	-0.000	0.011	-0.005	-0.004	-0.001	0.014	0.003	0.000	0.000
2AX	0.026	0.005	0.001	0.003	0.016	0.001	-0.003	0.000	0.014	0.003	0.000	-0.000
2B	0.019	0.005	0.007	0.006	0.010	0.000	0.005	0.007	0.014	0.003	0.000	-0.000
2BX	0.020	0.006	0.006	0.005	0.011	0.001	0.005	0.007	0.014	0.003	0.000	-0.000
3												
3X	-1.230	-0.186	0.464	-0.304	-0.895	0.149	0.244	-0.314	0.013	0.003	-0.025	0.143

Shock I. Japanese Aggregate Demand

1												
1X												
2A												
2AX												
2B												
2BX												
3												
3X												

Shock G. German Aggregate Demand

1												
1X												
2A												
2AX												
2B												
2BX												
3												
3X												

Shock B. Global Aggregate Demand

1												
1X	0.045	0.009	-0.001	-0.000	0.029	0.005	-0.000	-0.000	-0.008	0.000	-0.001	-0.000
2A	1.100	-0.016	0.004	0.000	0.325	-0.040	-0.007	-0.001	-0.010	-0.001	-0.001	-0.000
2AX	1.110	0.007	0.012	0.001	0.352	-0.004	0.009	0.001	-0.011	-0.003	-0.002	-0.001
2B	1.110	0.006	0.011	-0.009	0.350	-0.001	0.016	0.002	-0.011	-0.002	-0.002	-0.001
2BX	1.110	0.005	0.009	-0.012	0.351	-0.000	0.018	0.001	-0.011	-0.002	-0.002	-0.001
3												
3X	-0.569	-0.191	0.442	-0.315	-0.677	0.134	0.238	-0.336	-0.011	-0.001	-0.030	0.140

Shock C. US Aggregate Supply

1												
1X	0.004	0.001	-0.001	-0.001	0.003	0.001	-0.000	-0.000	-0.001	-0.007	-0.004	-0.001
2A	-0.001	-0.002	0.037	0.047	-0.014	-0.023	0.001	0.016	-0.003	-0.009	-0.004	-0.004
2AX	0.006	0.008	0.012	0.004	0.004	0.008	0.016	0.007	-0.003	-0.007	-0.003	-0.001
2B	-0.009	-0.023	-0.021	-0.001	-0.007	-0.013	-0.016	-0.010	-0.002	-0.004	0.000	0.001
2BX	-0.008	-0.012	0.001	0.012	-0.010	-0.013	-0.009	-0.004	-0.002	-0.002	0.001	0.000
3												
3X	-0.768	-0.424	0.089	0.305	-0.775	-0.361	-0.265	-0.387	0.004	0.049	0.031	0.059

Shock J. Japanese Aggregate Supply

1												
1X												
2A												
2AX												
2B												
2BX												
3												
3X												

Shock and Regime	Short Interest Rate				Long Interest Rate				Current Account/GNP Ratio			
	1st Qtr	6th Qtr	18th Qtr	38th Qtr	1st Qtr	6th Qtr	18th Qtr	38th Qtr	1st Qtr	6th Qtr	18th Qtr	38th Qtr

Shock H. German Aggregate Supply
1
1X
2A
2AX
2B
2BX
3
3X

Shock E. Oil Price Increase
1
1X
2A
2AX
2B
2BX
3
3X

Shock L. U.S. Money Demand
1
1X
2A
2AX
2B
2BX
3
3X

Shock D. Japanese Money Demand

Shock and Regime	1st Qtr	6th Qtr	18th Qtr	38th Qtr	1st Qtr	6th Qtr	18th Qtr	38th Qtr	1st Qtr	6th Qtr	18th Qtr	38th Qtr
1												
1X	0.397	0.024	-0.002	0.000	0.199	0.012	-0.001	0.000	0.002	0.001	0.002	0.001
2A	0.000	0.000	0.000	0.000	0.000	0.000	0.000	0.000	0.000	0.000	0.000	0.000
2AX	0.000	0.000	0.000	0.000	0.000	0.000	0.000	0.000	0.000	0.000	0.000	0.000
2B	0.000	0.000	0.000	0.000	0.000	0.000	0.000	0.000	0.000	0.000	0.000	0.000
2BX	0.000	0.000	0.000	0.000	0.000	0.000	0.000	0.000	0.000	0.000	0.000	0.000
3												
3X	0.000	0.000	0.000	0.000	0.000	0.000	0.000	0.000	0.000	0.000	0.000	0.000

Shock K. German Money Demand
1
1X
2A
2AX
2B
2BX
3
3X

Shock F. U.S. Money Supply-Permanent

Shock and Regime	1st Qtr	6th Qtr	18th Qtr	38th Qtr	1st Qtr	6th Qtr	18th Qtr	38th Qtr	1st Qtr	6th Qtr	18th Qtr	38th Qtr
FIXM	0.002	0.012	0.016	0.009	0.004	0.016	0.011	0.012	0.004	0.007	0.004	0.003
1												
1X												

TAYLOR MODEL
EFFECTS ON GERMAN REAL GNP, GERMAN PRICE LEVEL, GERMAN INFLATION RATE
(Deviations from Baseline)

Shock and Regime	Real GNP				GNP Deflator				Inflation Rate			
	1st Qtr	6th Qtr	18th Qtr	38th Qtr	1st Qtr	6th Qtr	18th Qtr	38th Qtr	1st Qtr	6th Qtr	18th Qtr	38th Qtr
Shock A. US Aggregate Demand												
1												
1X	0.076	0.002	0.001	0.000	0.000	0.000	0.000	0.000	0.000	-0.000	-0.000	-0.000
2A	0.059	0.002	0.001	0.000	0.000	0.000	-0.000	-0.000	0.000	-0.000	-0.000	0.000
2AX	0.057	-0.000	0.001	0.001	0.000	0.001	-0.000	-0.000	0.001	-0.000	-0.000	0.000
2B	0.062	0.009	0.007	0.006	0.000	0.001	0.000	0.001	0.001	-0.000	0.000	0.000
2BX	0.062	0.008	0.007	0.006	0.000	0.001	0.000	0.001	0.001	-0.000	0.000	0.000
3												
3X	0.575	0.798	-0.104	0.531	0.021	0.332	0.745	0.565	0.085	0.311	-0.028	-0.004
Shock I. Japanese Aggregate Demand												
1												
1X												
2A												
2AX												
2B												
2BX												
3												
3X												
Shock G. German Aggregate Demand												
1												
1X												
2A												
2AX												
2B												
2BX												
3												
3X												
Shock B. Global Aggregate Demand												
1												
1X	0.946	0.002	0.000	0.000	0.001	0.001	0.000	0.000	0.005	-0.000	-0.000	-0.000
2A	0.802	0.008	0.005	0.000	0.001	0.001	-0.000	-0.000	0.005	-0.002	-0.000	0.000
2AX	0.793	-0.004	0.000	0.000	0.001	0.002	-0.000	-0.000	0.006	-0.002	-0.000	0.000
2B	0.795	-0.002	-0.001	-0.003	0.001	0.002	0.001	0.001	0.006	-0.001	-0.000	0.000
2BX	0.795	-0.002	-0.002	-0.003	0.001	0.002	0.001	0.001	0.006	-0.001	-0.000	0.000
3												
3X	1.350	0.791	-0.091	0.514	0.022	0.330	0.741	0.562	0.090	0.307	-0.024	-0.008
Shock C. US Aggregate Supply												
1												
1X	-0.006	-0.022	-0.011	-0.004	-0.000	0.007	0.002	-0.000	-0.000	0.001	-0.001	-0.000
2A	-0.005	-0.011	-0.002	0.003	-0.000	0.004	-0.004	-0.001	-0.001	-0.006	0.001	0.000
2AX	-0.005	-0.012	-0.004	-0.001	-0.000	0.006	-0.000	-0.000	-0.000	-0.003	-0.000	0.000
2B	-0.008	-0.008	0.004	0.011	-0.000	0.002	0.001	0.001	-0.000	-0.002	-0.000	0.000
2BX	-0.003	0.005	0.011	0.013	-0.000	-0.000	0.001	0.001	-0.000	-0.001	0.000	-0.000
3												
3X	0.526	1.110	0.754	0.955	0.009	0.125	0.286	0.264	0.037	0.107	0.016	-0.004
Shock J. Japanese Aggregate Supply												
1												
1X												
2A												
2AX												
2B												
2BX												
3												
3X												

920

Shock and Regime	Real GNP				GNP Deflator				Inflation Rate			
	1st Qtr	6th Qtr	18th Qtr	38th Qtr	1st Qtr	6th Qtr	18th Qtr	38th Qtr	1st Qtr	6th Qtr	18th Qtr	38th Qtr

Shock H. German Aggregate Supply
1
1X
2A
2AX
2B
2BX
3
3X

Shock E. Oil Price Increase
1
1X
2A
2AX
2B
2BX
3
3X

Shock L. U.S. Money Demand
1
1X
2A
2AX
2B
2BX
3
3X

Shock D. Japanese Money Demand

1												
1X	-0.001	-0.004	-0.002	-0.000	-0.000	0.001	0.000	-0.000	-0.000	-0.000	-0.000	0.000
2A	0.000	0.000	0.000	0.000	0.000	0.000	0.000	0.000	0.000	0.000	0.000	0.000
2AX	0.000	0.000	0.000	0.000	0.000	0.000	0.000	0.000	0.000	0.000	0.000	0.000
2B	0.000	0.000	0.000	0.000	0.000	0.000	0.000	0.000	0.000	0.000	0.000	0.000
2BX	0.000	0.000	0.000	0.000	0.000	0.000	0.000	0.000	0.000	0.000	0.000	0.000
3												
3X	0.000	0.000	0.000	0.000	0.000	0.000	0.000	0.000	0.000	0.000	0.000	0.000

Shock K. German Money Demand
1
1X
2A
2AX
2B
2BX
3
3X

Shock F. U.S. Money Supply-Permanent

FIXM	0.017	0.020	-0.012	-0.017	0.001	0.006	0.043	0.036	0.004	0.016	0.005	-0.002
1												
1X												

TAYLOR MODEL
EFFECTS ON GERMAN INTEREST RATES AND GERMAN CURRENT ACCOUNT/GNP RATIO
(Deviations from Baseline)

Shock and Regime	Short Interest Rate				Long Interest Rate				Current Account/GNP Ratio			
	1st Qtr	6th Qtr	18th Qtr	38th Qtr	1st Qtr	6th Qtr	18th Qtr	38th Qtr	1st Qtr	6th Qtr	18th Qtr	38th Qtr

Shock A. US Aggregate Demand

1												
1X	0.012	0.001	0.000	0.000	0.008	0.001	0.000	0.000	0.053	0.001	0.000	0.000
2A	0.089	0.004	0.002	0.000	0.032	-0.002	-0.000	-0.000	0.051	-0.001	-0.001	-0.000
2AX	0.086	0.000	0.001	0.001	0.036	0.001	0.002	0.001	0.051	0.000	-0.001	-0.000
2B	0.086	0.005	0.004	0.001	0.033	0.003	0.006	0.005	0.050	-0.002	-0.001	-0.000
2BX	0.087	0.005	0.003	0.001	0.033	0.003	0.006	0.005	0.050	-0.002	-0.001	-0.000
3												
3X	-0.585	0.033	0.079	-0.110	-0.483	0.110	0.039	-0.187	-0.056	-0.099	-0.002	-0.044

Shock I. Japanese Aggregate Demand

1
1X
2A
2AX
2B
2BX
3
3X

Shock G. German Aggregate Demand

1
1X
2A
2AX
2B
2BX
3
3X

Shock B. Global Aggregate Demand

1												
1X	0.143	0.005	0.000	0.000	0.075	0.004	0.000	0.000	-0.241	0.005	0.000	0.000
2A	1.200	0.014	0.006	0.000	0.374	-0.005	0.000	-0.000	-0.208	-0.004	-0.002	-0.000
2AX	1.190	-0.004	0.000	0.000	0.392	0.008	0.003	0.000	-0.205	0.003	-0.000	-0.000
2B	1.180	-0.010	-0.010	-0.012	0.390	0.008	0.002	-0.004	-0.206	0.003	0.002	0.002
2BX	1.180	-0.013	-0.011	-0.012	0.391	0.007	0.001	-0.005	-0.205	0.003	0.002	0.002
3												
3X	0.193	0.023	0.077	-0.114	-0.232	0.100	0.039	-0.193	-0.321	-0.095	0.002	-0.050

Shock C. US Aggregate Supply

1												
1X	0.004	-0.006	-0.003	-0.001	0.001	-0.005	-0.002	-0.001	-0.007	-0.020	-0.005	-0.002
2A	-0.007	-0.011	-0.008	0.002	0.002	0.014	0.015	0.010	-0.021	-0.026	0.002	0.002
2AX	-0.001	-0.012	-0.007	-0.002	0.008	0.009	0.005	0.002	-0.016	-0.017	0.001	0.001
2B	-0.020	-0.020	-0.001	0.009	-0.023	-0.023	-0.009	0.001	-0.012	-0.010	-0.003	-0.004
2BX	-0.012	0.000	0.010	0.012	-0.018	-0.010	-0.001	0.004	-0.009	-0.007	-0.004	-0.004
3												
3X	-0.631	-0.222	0.159	0.315	-0.684	-0.267	-0.085	0.004	-0.135	-0.245	-0.103	-0.229

Shock J. Japanese Aggregate Supply

1
1X
2A
2AX
2B
2BX
3
3X

Shock and Regime	Short Interest Rate				Long Interest Rate				Current Account/GNP Ratio			
	1st Qtr	6th Qtr	18th Qtr	38th Qtr	1st Qtr	6th Qtr	18th Qtr	38th Qtr	1st Qtr	6th Qtr	18th Qtr	38th Qtr

Shock H. German Aggregate Supply
1
1X
2A
2AX
2B
2BX
3
3X

Shock E. Oil Price Increase
1
1X
2A
2AX
2B
2BX
3
3X

Shock L. U.S. Money Demand
1
1X
2A
2AX
2B
2BX
3
3X

Shock D. Japanese Money Demand

Regime	1st Qtr	6th Qtr	18th Qtr	38th Qtr	1st Qtr	6th Qtr	18th Qtr	38th Qtr	1st Qtr	6th Qtr	18th Qtr	38th Qtr
1												
1X	0.001	-0.001	-0.001	-0.000	0.000	-0.001	-0.000	-0.000	-0.002	-0.004	-0.001	0.000
2A	0.000	0.000	0.000	0.000	0.000	0.000	0.000	0.000	0.000	0.000	0.000	0.000
2AX	0.000	0.000	0.000	0.000	0.000	0.000	0.000	0.000	0.000	0.000	0.000	0.000
2B	0.000	0.000	0.000	0.000	0.000	0.000	0.000	0.000	0.000	0.000	0.000	0.000
2BX	0.000	0.000	0.000	0.000	0.000	0.000	0.000	0.000	0.000	0.000	0.000	0.000
3												
3X	0.000	0.000	0.000	0.000	0.000	0.000	0.000	0.000	0.000	0.000	0.000	0.000

Shock K. German Money Demand
1
1X
2A
2AX
2B
2BX
3
3X

Shock F. U.S. Money Supply-Permanent

Regime	1st Qtr	6th Qtr	18th Qtr	38th Qtr	1st Qtr	6th Qtr	18th Qtr	38th Qtr	1st Qtr	6th Qtr	18th Qtr	38th Qtr
FIXM	0.012	0.019	0.014	0.006	0.012	0.020	0.012	0.006	0.026	0.025	0.015	0.010
1												
1X												

Table A-TAY-7
TAYLOR MODEL
BILATERAL DOLLAR EXCHANGE RATES
(Deviations from Baseline)

Shock and Regime	Bilateral DM/$ Exchange Rate				Bilateral Yen/$ Exchange Rate			
	1st Qtr	6th Qtr	18th Qtr	38th Qtr	1st Qtr	6th Qtr	18th Qtr	38th Qtr
Shock A. US Aggregate Demand								
1								
1X	-0.003	-0.002	-0.000	-0.000	-0.007	-0.002	-0.001	-0.000
2A	-0.247	0.004	0.001	0.000	-0.251	0.007	-0.001	0.000
2AX	-0.243	0.004	0.001	0.001	-0.243	0.007	-0.001	0.001
2B	-0.246	0.006	0.002	0.001	-0.252	0.008	0.002	0.002
2BX	-0.245	0.005	0.002	0.001	-0.251	0.008	0.002	0.002
3								
3X	0.685	0.770	0.329	0.685	1.020	1.740	-0.059	0.617
Shock I. Japanese Aggregate Demand								
1								
1X								
2A								
2AX								
2B								
2BX								
3								
3X								
Shock G. German Aggregate Demand								
1								
1X								
2A								
2AX								
2B								
2BX								
3								
3X								
Shock B. Global Aggregate Demand								
1								
1X	0.043	-0.001	-0.001	-0.000	0.012	0.001	-0.001	-0.000
2A	-0.051	-0.003	0.001	0.001	0.062	-0.022	-0.004	0.000
2AX	-0.050	-0.003	0.001	0.000	0.058	-0.021	0.000	0.001
2B	-0.049	-0.002	0.000	-0.002	0.057	-0.020	0.003	0.001
2BX	-0.048	-0.003	-0.000	-0.002	0.059	-0.020	0.003	0.000
3								
3X	0.834	0.767	0.336	0.674	1.200	1.730	0.030	0.560
Shock C. US Aggregate Supply								
1								
1X	0.081	-0.000	-0.002	0.001	0.082	0.003	-0.001	0.001
2A	-0.410	0.168	0.040	0.010	-0.406	0.146	0.035	0.014
2AX	-0.320	0.113	0.018	0.004	-0.305	0.112	0.019	0.005
2B	-0.115	0.148	0.008	0.005	-0.104	0.149	0.006	0.001
2BX	0.119	0.164	0.002	0.004	0.126	0.161	0.001	0.002
3								
3X	0.607	0.857	0.558	0.597	0.559	1.080	0.916	0.609
Shock J. Japanese Aggregate Supply								
1								
1X								
2A								
2AX								
2B								
2BX								
3								
3X								

924

Shock and Regime	Bilateral DM/$ Exchange Rate				Bilateral Yen/$ Exchange Rate			
	1st Qtr	6th Qtr	18th Qtr	38th Qtr	1st Qtr	6th Qtr	18th Qtr	38th Qtr
Shock H. German Aggregate Supply								
1								
1X								
2A								
2AX								
2B								
2BX								
3								
3X								
Shock E. Oil Price Increase								
1								
1X								
2A								
2AX								
2B								
2BX								
3								
3X								
Shock L. U.S. Money Demand								
1								
1X								
2A								
2AX								
2B								
2BX								
3								
3X								
Shock D. Japanese Money Demand								
1								
1X	0.000	-0.000	-0.000	-0.000	0.196	0.013	-0.001	0.000
2A	0.000	0.000	0.000	0.000	0.000	0.000	0.000	0.000
2AX	0.000	0.000	0.000	0.000	0.000	0.000	0.000	0.000
2B	0.000	0.000	0.000	0.000	0.000	0.000	0.000	0.000
2BX	0.000	0.000	0.000	0.000	0.000	0.000	0.000	0.000
3								
3X	0.000	0.000	0.000	0.000	0.000	0.000	0.000	0.000
Shock K. German Money Demand								
1								
1X								
2A								
2AX								
2B								
2BX								
3								
3X								
F. U.S. Money Supply-Permanent								
FIXM	1.530	0.514	0.763	0.937	1.510	0.516	0.733	0.927
1								
1X								

Reference Tables for Stochastic Simulations

THE TABLES in the first part of this annex, numbered B-I-1 to B-I-35, report the summary data for the stochastic simulation results submitted to the project organizers. Each of these tables presents the results of one model for a particular country across all types of policy regime implemented in that model.

Stochastic simulation results are available for the following models:

INTERMOD-A: the adaptive-expectations version of the INTERMOD policy simulation model originally developed by a Canadian team under the direction of John Helliwell (following the IMF effort to construct MULTIMOD), sponsored by the Canadian Department of Finance and subsequently also supported by the Bank of Canada.

INTERMOD-C: the model-consistent expectations version of the INTERMOD policy simulation model.

LIVERPOOL: the multicountry model developed by Patrick Minford and several associates at the University of Liverpool.

MPS: the model, primarily of the U.S. economy but also with an external sector, developed by the domestic divisions of the Federal Reserve Board (following earlier work by teams of economists at MIT, the University of Pennsylvania, and the Federal Reserve, financed by the Social Science Research Council).

MSG: an updated version of a multicountry policy simulation model originally developed by Warwick McKibbin and Jeffrey Sachs at Harvard University, maintained by McKibbin at the Brookings Institution.

MULTIMOD: the multicountry policy simulation model developed in the Research Department of the International Monetary Fund.

MX3: a multicountry policy simulation model developed in the Division of International Finance of the Federal Reserve Board by Joseph Gagnon and Ralph Tryon.

TAYLOR: the multicountry policy simulation model developed by John Taylor and associates at Stanford University.

GEM: a version of the Global Economic Model developed by the National Institute for Economic and Social Research (NIESR) in London and jointly maintained with the London Business School (LBS).

Tables B-I-1 to B-I-35 are ordered by country and, within the country, by model. For example, the nine different model results for the United States are in tables B-I-1 to B-I-9, and the eight for Japan are in tables B-I-10 to B-I-17. For most of the models, results are available for five major countries: the United States, Japan, Germany, the United Kingdom, and Canada. MPS results are available only for the United States. The MSG and MX3 results are limited to the United States, Japan, and Germany.

With four types of monetary-policy regimes and with a model group possibly implementing both the original "O" specification and its own "X" variant, as many as eight sets of results per country may be available. As elsewhere in the book, the regimes are labeled 1 and 1X for money targeting, 2A and 2AX for nominal-income targeting, 2B and 2BX for real-GNP-plus-inflation targeting, and 3 and 3X for exchange-rate targeting. For exchange-rate targeting, the MPS model does not have results because of that model's structure, the MX3 model does not have results because the model was unstable for that regime, and the GEM model did not report results for that regime. See chapter 3 for further discussion.

The statistics in the tables, except for the final two rows in the upper and the lower panels, are average root mean-squared deviations of variables from baseline, either percentage deviations (RMS%Ds) for real GNP, nominal GNP, and the GNP price deflator, or absolute deviations measured in percentage points (RMSDs) for growth in real GNP, growth in nominal GNP, the inflation rate for the GNP deflator, the level and the change in the short-term interest rate, and the ratio of the current account in the balance of payments to nominal GNP. Detailed definitions of these summary statistics are given in chapter 5. The upper panels of the tables show average root mean-squared deviations for the whole simulation period of ten years. The lower panels report comparable statistics for the second half of the simulation (years six through ten).

As explained in chapter 5, one method of interpreting these data is to focus on a few highly simplified "loss functions," calibrating the relative disutility of outcomes under the different regimes. The two simplest are the RMS%D for real GNP alone (first row of data in each panel of the tables) and the RMSD for inflation alone (sixth row of data in each panel). A focus on these two measures gives exclusive weight to either output variability or inflation variability. Two further illustrative functions include more than one variable, but without complex weighting of the relative importance of the variables. The third function is merely the unweighted sum of the RMS%D for real GNP and the RMSD of the inflation rate. The fourth function adds to the third (again with an equal weight) the RMSD of the period-to-period change in the short-term interest rate. The calculations for these third and fourth loss functions are shown in the final two rows of each panel in the tables.

For each row in tables B-I-1 to B-I-35, a particular entry on the row is enclosed in a rectangular box. This box indicates which regime—for that particular variable-model-country combination—yields the lowest average root mean-squared deviation (RMS%D or RMSD) from baseline. The box identifies, in other words, the regime that best insulated the particular variable, on average, from the full array of stochastic shocks.

The amount of detail in the B-I tables makes comparisons across countries or models difficult (quite apart from the underlying problem of differences between the O and the X regimes, and among the various X regimes). Annex B therefore includes some additional summary tables that recompile or process further some of the data from the B-I tables.

The set of tables numbered B-II-1 to B-II-9 facilitate, for each model separately, a comparison across countries and regimes of the values of the four illustrative loss functions (real GNP alone, the inflation rate alone, real GNP plus inflation, and the unweighted sum of real GNP, inflation, and the change in the short-term interest rate). The rectangular boxes, carried over from the B-I tables, again indicate which regime, for that loss function, had the lowest average root mean-squared deviation from baseline.

Finally, this annex includes a set of tables numbered B-III-1 to B-III-5, one each for five countries: the United States, Japan, Germany, the United Kingdom, and Canada. These tables again report the results for the four illustrative loss functions but are constructed so as to give money targeting an index value of unity. These tables give a better sense of the cardinal magnitudes of the values of loss functions across regimes and facilitate a rough-and-ready comparison of the results across the models. The rectangular boxes continue to identify the regime that results in the lowest average root mean-squared deviation from baseline for the particular country, loss function, and model combination in a row of the tables.

The symbol "n.a." or "N.A." in the tables indicates "not available."

TABLE B-1-1 INTERMOD (ADAPTIVE) MODEL : UNITED STATES

(Root Mean Squared Deviation from Baseline)

		Money Targeting (1X) (1)	Nominal GNP Targeting (2A)	(2AX)	Real GNP and Inflation Targeting (2B)	(2BX)	Exchange Rate Targeting (3) (3X)
Full Period (Ten Years)							
Real GNP	(level, %)	4.38	4.09	4.21	2.71	2.93	4.35
	(growth, % pts.)	2.70	2.73	2.74	2.43	2.45	2.69
Nominal GNP	(level, %)	9.03	4.05	7.52	5.86	6.53	8.59
	(growth, % pts.)	2.72	2.47	2.61	2.42	2.46	2.67
GNP Deflator	(level, %)	7.83	5.02	7.20	5.62	6.06	7.73
	(change, % pts.)	2.04	1.36	1.83	1.41	1.51	1.98
Short-Term Interest Rate	(level, % pts.)	4.08	7.03	5.37	4.59	4.15	4.32
	(change, % pts.)	1.92	3.22	1.65	3.37	2.78	2.09
Current Account / GNP	(level, % pts.)	0.91	1.31	1.01	1.00	0.93	0.91
Loss: GNP + Inflation		6.42	5.45	6.04	4.12	4.44	6.33
Loss: GNP + Inflation + Change in Interest Rate		8.34	8.67	7.69	7.49	7.22	8.42
Final Half-Period (Five Years)							
Real GNP	(level, %)	4.79	4.86	4.71	2.69	2.96	4.78
	(growth, % pts.)	2.74	2.91	2.88	2.43	2.45	2.75
Nominal GNP	(level, %)	11.79	4.66	9.61	7.51	8.42	11.03
	(growth, % pts.)	2.77	2.56	2.64	2.48	2.52	2.66
GNP Deflator	(level, %)	10.68	6.62	9.76	7.47	8.09	10.46
	(change, % pts.)	2.57	1.52	2.22	1.64	1.80	2.43
Short-Term Interest Rate	(level, % pts.)	5.26	8.44	6.88	4.82	4.44	5.53
	(change, % pts.)	1.93	3.31	1.69	3.35	2.77	2.09
Current Account / GNP	(level, % pts.)	1.13	1.66	1.27	1.18	1.11	1.16
Loss: GNP + Inflation		7.36	6.38	6.93	4.33	4.75	7.21
Loss: GNP + Inflation + Change in Interest Rate		9.29	9.69	8.62	7.68	7.52	9.30

TABLE B-2 INTERMOD (CONSISTENT) MODEL : UNITED STATES

(Root Mean Squared Deviation from Baseline)

		Money Targeting (1) (1X)	Nominal GNP Targeting (2A) (2AX)	Real GNP and Inflation Targeting (2B)	(2BX)	Exchange Rate Targeting (3) (3X)
Full Period (Ten Years)						
Real GNP	(level, %)	3.03	2.82	2.31	2.46	2.88
	(growth, % pts.)	2.85	2.69	2.53	2.69	2.76
Nominal GNP	(level, %)	4.56	3.53	8.08	8.68	4.43
	(growth, % pts.)	2.48	2.31	2.85	3.05	2.42
GNP Deflator	(level, %)	5.00	3.92	8.27	8.78	4.94
	(change, % pts.)	1.42	1.19	2.02	2.23	1.41
Short-Term Interest Rate	(level, % pts.)	2.88	2.59	4.37	3.92	2.90
	(change, % pts.)	2.08	1.42	3.70	3.17	2.05
Current Account / GNP	(level, % pts.)	0.82	0.81	1.04	0.98	0.68
Loss: GNP + Inflation		4.45	4.01	4.33	4.69	4.29
Loss: GNP + Inflation + Change in Interest Rate		6.53	5.43	8.03	7.96	6.34
Final Half-Period (Five Years)						
Real GNP	(level, %)	3.17	3.00	2.31	2.55	3.05
	(growth, % pts.)	2.82	2.70	2.55	2.73	2.77
Nominal GNP	(level, %)	5.54	4.23	10.87	11.64	5.33
	(growth, % pts.)	2.43	2.31	3.22	3.39	2.39
GNP Deflator	(level, %)	6.53	5.05	11.22	11.89	6.42
	(change, % pts.)	1.59	1.35	2.51	2.80	1.54
Short-Term Interest Rate	(level, % pts.)	3.33	3.15	4.84	4.50	3.44
	(change, % pts.)	1.93	1.43	3.75	3.25	2.02
Current Account / GNP	(level, % pts.)	0.99	0.99	1.23	1.18	0.83
Loss: GNP + Inflation		4.76	4.35	4.82	5.35	4.59
Loss: GNP + Inflation + Change in Interest Rate		6.69	5.78	8.57	8.60	6.61

TABLE B-I3

LIVERPOOL MODEL: UNITED STATES

(Root Mean Squared Deviation from Baseline)

Full Period (Ten Years)

		Money Targeting (1)	(1X)	Nominal GNP Targeting (2A)	(2AX)	Real GNP (2B)	Real GNP and Inflation Targeting (2BX)	Exchange Rate Targeting (3)	(3X)
Real GNP	(level, %)	10.36	8.04	6.69	5.60	24.39	19.04	102.88	5.07
	(growth, % pts.)	12.07	10.90	5.57	7.19	15.45	13.66	148.18	5.93
Nominal GNP	(level, %)	24.05	13.72	3.20	5.55	273.04	48.76	386.53	10.85
	(growth, % pts.)	21.16	14.86	4.13	5.37	66.25	18.95	253.49	6.99
GNP Deflator	(level, %)	22.14	13.86	8.81	7.99	287.35	38.71	329.51	9.13
	(change, % pts.)	13.79	8.49	8.09	6.43	70.37	11.46	124.83	3.12
Short-Term Interest Rate	(level, % pts.)	5.40	4.60	4.87	5.68	70.55	11.56	22.77	3.23
	(change, % pts.)	5.32	5.98	5.83	9.77	41.53	9.76	27.79	3.97
Current Account / GNP	(level, % pts.)	2.28	1.99	1.82	1.71	13.35	3.73	22.14	1.61
Loss: GNP + Inflation		24.15	16.53	14.78	12.03	94.75	30.50	227.71	8.19
Loss: GNP + Inflation + Change in Interest Rate		29.47	22.50	20.60	21.80	136.28	40.26	255.51	12.16

Final Half-Period (Five Years)

		Money Targeting (1)	(1X)	Nominal GNP Targeting (2A)	(2AX)	Real GNP (2B)	Real GNP and Inflation Targeting (2BX)	Exchange Rate Targeting (3)	(3X)
Real GNP	(level, %)	11.23	9.71	8.45	6.91	24.44	14.95	90.57	6.24
	(growth, % pts.)	10.52	12.92	6.24	8.12	12.14	9.88	135.53	6.82
Nominal GNP	(level, %)	32.26	17.51	3.69	6.68	405.78	53.53	496.79	16.04
	(growth, % pts.)	19.35	16.87	3.88	5.46	53.96	9.83	208.56	7.93
GNP Deflator	(level, %)	30.18	16.79	10.95	9.39	401.71	45.18	440.41	13.44
	(change, % pts.)	14.09	8.49	8.77	6.16	54.17	7.93	101.25	3.39
Short-Term Interest Rate	(level, % pts.)	6.13	4.73	4.93	5.09	53.50	7.55	21.90	3.65
	(change, % pts.)	5.09	6.33	5.49	9.14	25.46	6.53	28.76	4.29
Current Account / GNP	(level, % pts.)	2.55	1.89	2.14	1.64	16.42	2.17	21.05	1.91
Loss: GNP + Inflation		25.32	18.20	17.22	13.07	78.61	22.88	191.82	9.63
Loss: GNP + Inflation + Change in Interest Rate		30.41	24.53	22.71	22.20	104.07	29.40	220.58	13.91

TABLE B-I-4   MPS MODEL : UNITED STATES

(Root Mean Squared Deviation from Baseline)

		Money Targeting (1) / (1X)	Nominal GNP Targeting (2A) / (2AX)		Real GNP and Inflation Targeting (2B) / (2BX)		Exchange Rate Targeting (3) / (3X)
		(1X)	(2A)	(2AX)	(2B)	(2BX)	(3X)
Full Period (Ten Years)							
Real GNP	(level, %)	3.30	2.39	2.24	1.64		
	(growth, % pts.)	4.33	3.94	3.83	3.98		
Nominal GNP	(level, %)	6.03	1.66	1.35	5.22		
	(growth, % pts.)	4.34	3.55	3.42	3.86		
GNP Deflator	(level, %)	5.27	2.39	2.19	4.64		
	(change, % pts.)	2.50	1.92	1.87	2.00		
Short-Term Interest Rate	(level, % pts.)	7.54	2.47	2.65	2.80		
	(change, % pts.)	0.99	1.24	1.58	1.74		
Exchange Rate	(level, %)	11.16	9.02	9.37	11.54		
Current Account / GNP	(level, % pts.)	1.21	1.13	1.12	1.15		
Loss: GNP + Inflation		5.80	4.31	4.11	3.64		
Loss: GNP + Inflation + Change in Interest Rate		6.79	5.55	5.69	5.38		
Final Half-Period (Five Years)							
Real GNP	(level, %)	4.23	3.06	2.86	1.99		
	(growth, % pts.)	4.76	4.36	4.23	4.38		
Nominal GNP	(level, %)	8.41	1.96	1.56	8.19		
	(growth, % pts.)	4.88	3.81	3.66	4.29		
GNP Deflator	(level, %)	7.94	3.15	2.88	7.34		
	(change, % pts.)	3.03	2.18	2.11	2.32		
Short-Term Interest Rate	(level, % pts.)	3.19	2.89	2.65	3.45		
	(change, % pts.)	1.05	1.32	1.58	1.84		
Exchange Rate	(level, %)	14.85	10.48	10.80	14.75		
Current Account / GNP	(level, % pts.)	1.63	1.47	1.44	1.51		
Loss: GNP + Inflation		7.26	5.24	4.97	4.31		
Loss: GNP + Inflation + Change in Interest Rate		8.31	6.56	6.55	6.15		

933

TABLE B-I-5 MSG MODEL : UNITED STATES

(Root Mean Squared Deviation from Baseline)

		Money Targeting (1)	Money Targeting (1X)	Nominal GNP Targeting (2A)	Nominal GNP Targeting (2AX)	Real GNP and Inflation Targeting (2B)	Real GNP and Inflation Targeting (2BX)	Exchange Rate Targeting (3)	Exchange Rate Targeting (3X)
					Full Period (Ten Years)				
Real GNP	(level, %)	8.31	8.15	10.7	7.16	7.72	4.37	13.55	8.28
	(growth, % pts.)	4.44	4.38	5.80	4.08	3.65	3.18	7.29	4.76
Nominal GNP	(level, %)	5.90	4.81	5.19	0.00	31.75	23.88	7.57	4.57
	(growth, % pts.)	1.60	1.35	1.82	0.00	11.15	4.41	2.99	1.49
GNP Deflator	(level, %)	9.62	9.06	13.49	7.52	30.73	25.11	19.55	9.99
	(change, % pts.)	4.77	4.61	6.99	3.99	12.27	4.98	9.61	4.99
Short-Term Interest Rate	(level, % pts.)	8.09	8.97	7.79	16.90	23.72	23.54	9.29	8.36
	(change, % pts.)	2.14	2.45	2.74	4.80	4.14	5.10	3.95	2.65
Current Account / GNP	(level, % pts.)	1.14	1.15	1.37	1.34	1.07	1.21	2.26	1.33
Loss: GNP + Inflation		13.08	12.76	17.59	11.05	19.99	9.34	23.16	13.27
Loss: GNP + Inflation + Change in Interest Rate		15.22	15.21	20.32	15.96	24.14	14.44	27.11	15.92
					Final Half-Period (Five Years)				
Real GNP	(level, %)	3.26	3.11	4.67	3.15	5.22	1.78	8.59	3.66
	(growth, % pts.)	2.14	2.11	3.09	2.12	0.86	0.99	4.49	2.54
Nominal GNP	(level, %)	7.48	6.00	6.17	0.00	44.08	27.90	8.62	5.54
	(growth, % pts.)	1.26	0.99	1.56	0.00	15.13	1.60	2.82	1.07
GNP Deflator	(level, %)	8.20	6.95	9.36	3.15	40.56	26.98	16.30	7.70
	(change, % pts.)	3.40	3.10	4.65	1.92	15.94	1.99	7.30	3.37
Short-Term Interest Rate	(level, % pts.)	10.20	11.12	9.25	19.93	30.39	27.94	9.19	10.29
	(change, % pts.)	1.57	1.64	2.35	2.04	3.01	1.72	3.52	1.78
Current Account / GNP	(level, % pts.)	1.04	1.07	1.16	1.53	1.17	1.32	1.63	1.04
Loss: GNP + Inflation		6.66	6.21	9.32	5.07	21.15	3.76	15.89	7.03
Loss: GNP + Inflation + Change in Interest Rate		8.23	7.86	11.67	7.11	24.16	5.49	19.41	8.81

TABLE B-I-6

MULTIMOD MODEL : UNITED STATES

(Root Mean Squared Deviation from Baseline)

		Money Targeting		Nominal GNP Targeting	Real GNP and Inflation Targeting	Exchange Rate Targeting
		(1)	(1X)	(2AX)	(2BX)	(3X)
Full Period (Ten Years)						
Real GNP	(level, %)	3.93	3.69	3.55	3.10	3.54
	(growth, % pts.)	2.56	2.70	2.55	2.46	2.61
Nominal GNP	(level, %)	3.61	3.53	3.93	2.66	3.53
	(growth, % pts.)	2.48	2.61	2.57	2.22	2.56
GNP Deflator	(level, %)	5.12	4.76	5.66	3.02	4.68
	(change, % pts.)	1.97	1.81	2.15	1.23	1.79
Short-Term Interest Rate	(level, % pts.)	3.72	2.69	1.93	5.87	2.72
	(change, % pts.)	3.70	1.42	1.20	7.24	1.47
Current Account / GNP	(level, % pts.)	1.34	1.40	1.32	1.33	1.40
Loss: GNP + Inflation		5.90	5.51	5.70	4.32	5.33
Loss: GNP + Inflation + Change in Interest Rate		9.60	6.93	6.90	11.56	6.80
Final Half-Period (Five Years)						
Real GNP	(level, %)	4.30	4.70	4.54	3.69	4.51
	(growth, % pts.)	2.87	3.03	2.87	2.71	2.92
Nominal GNP	(level, %)	4.19	4.01	4.38	3.27	4.01
	(growth, % pts.)	2.68	2.82	2.76	2.42	2.76
GNP Deflator	(level, %)	6.66	6.14	7.32	3.80	6.02
	(change, % pts.)	2.23	1.98	2.40	1.33	1.95
Short-Term Interest Rate	(level, % pts.)	3.93	3.05	2.16	6.13	3.07
	(change, % pts.)	3.66	1.53	1.29	7.53	1.59
Current Account / GNP	(level, % pts.)	1.54	1.62	1.50	1.51	1.62
Loss: GNP + Inflation		6.54	6.68	6.93	5.02	6.46
Loss: GNP + Inflation + Change in Interest Rate		10.20	8.22	8.23	12.55	8.04

935

TABLE B-I-7   MX3 MODEL : UNITED STATES   (Root Mean Squared Deviation from Baseline)

		Money Targeting		Nominal GNP Targeting		Real GNP and Inflation Targeting		Exchange Rate Targeting	
		(1)	(1X)	(2A)	(2AX)	(2B)	(2BX)	(3)	(3X)
		Full Period (Ten Years)							
Real GNP	(level, %)	7.96		8.10	8.30	1.99			
	(growth, % pts.)	2.00		1.80	1.80	1.70			
Nominal GNP	(level, %)	3.28		2.38	1.71	21.55			
	(growth, % pts.)	2.10		1.80	1.60	2.40			
GNP Deflator	(level, %)	8.81		8.66	8.74	21.52			
	(change, % pts.)	1.22		1.17	1.15	1.77			
Short-Term Interest Rate	(level, % pts.)	3.10		3.57	5.14	9.43			
	(change, % pts.)	1.52		2.72	4.79	5.24			
Current Account / GNP	(level, % pts.)	0.43		0.41	0.44	0.52			
Loss: GNP + Inflation		9.18		9.27	9.45	3.76			
Loss: GNP + Inflation + Change in Interest Rate		10.71		12.00	14.23	9.00			
		Final Half-Period (Five Years)							
Real GNP	(level, %)	9.22		9.38	9.61	2.01			
	(growth, % pts.)	2.03		1.84	1.73	1.57			
Nominal GNP	(level, %)	3.31		2.25	1.65	27.87			
	(growth, % pts.)	2.11		1.85	1.60	2.26			
GNP Deflator	(level, %)	9.68		9.57	9.83	27.60			
	(change, % pts.)	1.16		1.11	1.15	1.72			
Short-Term Interest Rate	(level, % pts.)	2.95		3.37	4.96	9.30			
	(change, % pts.)	1.57		2.78	4.80	5.40			
Current Account / GNP	(level, % pts.)	0.53		0.50	0.54	0.62			
Loss: GNP + Inflation		10.38		10.49	10.76	3.73			
Loss: GNP + Inflation + Change in Interest Rate		11.96		13.27	15.56	9.13			

TABLE B-18 TAYLOR: UNITED STATES

(Root Mean Squared Deviation from Baseline)

		Money Targeting (1X)	Nominal GNP Targeting (2AX)	Real GNP and Inflation Targeting (2BX)	Exchange Rate Targeting (3X)
Full Period (Ten Years)					
Real GNP	(level, %)	5.15	1.95	2.59	2.24
	(growth, % pts.)	1.66	1.40	1.44	1.40
Nominal GNP	(level, %)	9.19	5.90	6.47	5.70
	(growth, % pts.)	2.08	2.00	1.92	1.95
GNP Deflator	(level, %)	2.26	1.52	1.42	1.59
	(change, % pts.)	1.14	1.32	1.13	1.27
Short-Term Interest Rate	(level, % pts.)	0.01	0.03	0.03	0.03
	(change, % pts.)	n.a.	n.a.	n.a.	n.a.
Current Account / GNP	(level, % pts.)	1.09	0.55	0.63	0.65
Loss: GNP + Inflation		6.29	3.27	3.72	3.51
Loss: GNP + Inflation + Change in Interest Rate		n.a.	n.a.	n.a.	n.a.
Final Half-Period (Five Years)					
Real GNP	(level, %)	5.97	1.68	2.71	2.01
	(growth, % pts.)	1.59	1.35	1.40	1.35
Nominal GNP	(level, %)	11.15	6.11	7.18	6.11
	(growth, % pts.)	2.07	1.94	1.87	1.90
GNP Deflator	(level, %)	2.87	1.54	1.70	1.74
	(change, % pts.)	1.19	1.37	1.13	1.32
Short-Term Interest Rate	(level, % pts.)	0.01	0.03	0.03	0.03
	(change, % pts.)	n.a.	n.a.	n.a.	n.a.
Current Account / GNP	(level, % pts.)	1.25	0.53	0.65	0.64
Loss: GNP + Inflation		7.16	3.05	3.84	3.33
Loss: GNP + Inflation + Change in Interest Rate		n.a.	n.a.	n.a.	n.a.

GEM: UNITED STATES

(Root Mean Squared Deviation from Baseline)

		Money Targeting (1X)/(1)	Nominal GNP Targeting (2A)	(2AX)	Real GNP and Inflation Targeting (2B)	(2BX)	Exchange Rate Targeting (3)	(3X)
			Full Period (Ten Years)					
Real GNP	(level, %)	1.61	1.21		1.12			
	(growth, % pts.)	0.83	0.88		0.83			
Nominal GNP	(level, %)	2.59	1.63		1.56			
	(growth, % pts.)	1.00	0.99		0.99			
GNP Deflator	(level, %)	1.65	1.35		1.32			
	(change, % pts.)	1.47	1.40		1.37			
Short-Term Interest Rate	(level, % pts.)	0.94	0.41		0.40			
	(change, % pts.)	0.21	0.24		0.34			
Current Account / GNP	(level, % pts.)	0.34	0.36		0.32			
Loss: GNP + Inflation		3.08	2.61		2.49			
Loss: GNP + Inflation + Change in Interest Rate		3.29	2.85		2.83			

938

TABLE B-I-10 — INTERMOD (ADAPTIVE) MODEL: JAPAN

(Root Mean Squared Deviation from Baseline)

		Money Targeting (1X)	Nominal GNP Targeting (2AX)		Real GNP and Inflation Targeting (2BX)		Exchange Rate Targeting (3X)
		(1)	(2A)	(2AX)	(2B)	(2BX)	(3)
Full Period (Ten Years)							
Real GNP	(level, %)	7.02	7.61	7.50	3.84	3.97	5.18
	(growth, % pts.)	3.75	3.78	3.84	3.13	3.18	3.65
Nominal GNP	(level, %)	15.35	7.76	12.12	16.07	16.86	22.88
	(growth, % pts.)	5.79	4.54	5.41	4.90	5.11	6.58
GNP Deflator	(level, %)	19.38	12.63	16.57	19.11	19.82	25.33
	(change, % pts.)	4.27	3.17	3.81	3.84	3.97	4.99
Short-Term Interest Rate	(level, % pts.)	6.29	10.32	7.77	6.60	5.81	3.72
	(change, % pts.)	3.61	6.52	3.59	6.32	5.38	1.83
Bilateral US $Exchange Rate	(level, %)	10.74	14.23	12.97	8.09	7.40	1.48
Current Account / GNP	(level, % pts.)	1.63	2.00	1.82	1.63	1.60	1.76
Loss: GNP + Inflation		11.29	10.78	11.31	7.68	7.94	10.17
Loss: GNP + Inflation + Change in Interest Rate		14.90	17.30	14.90	14.00	13.32	12.00
Final Half-Period (Five Years)							
Real GNP	(level, %)	9.32	9.93	9.92	4.77	4.94	6.51
	(growth, % pts.)	4.26	4.31	4.36	3.42	3.47	4.01
Nominal GNP	(level, %)	19.60	9.34	15.23	21.11	22.14	29.99
	(growth, % pts.)	6.16	4.82	5.76	5.15	5.37	6.92
GNP Deflator	(level, %)	25.71	16.17	21.72	25.46	26.44	34.16
	(change, % pts.)	4.81	3.41	4.24	4.22	4.39	5.69
Short-Term Interest Rate	(level, % pts.)	7.82	11.96	9.55	7.30	6.50	4.78
	(change, % pts.)	3.91	6.89	3.82	6.69	5.72	1.82
Bilateral US $Exchange Rate	(level, %)	13.63	16.84	15.93	8.98	8.25	1.91
Current Account / GNP	(level, % pts.)	2.07	2.54	2.30	1.99	1.97	2.27
Loss: GNP + Inflation		14.13	13.34	14.16	8.99	9.33	12.20
Loss: GNP + Inflation + Change in Interest Rate		18.04	20.23	17.98	15.68	15.05	14.02

TABLE B-I-11

INTERMOD (CONSISTENT) MODEL: JAPAN

(Root Mean Squared Deviation from Baseline)

		Money Targeting (1)	(1X)	Nominal GNP Targeting (2A)	(2AX)	Real GNP and Inflation Targeting (2B)	(2BX)	Exchange Rate Targeting (3)	(3X)
Full Period (Ten Years)									
Real GNP	(level, %)	5.38		5.61		2.94	2.99	5.15	
	(growth, % pts.)	3.80		3.85		3.24	3.31	3.79	
Nominal GNP	(level, %)	7.09		5.66		27.41	31.24	13.13	
	(growth, % pts.)	4.12		3.85		6.39	6.80	5.41	
GNP Deflator	(level, %)	11.38		10.16		29.31	32.88	17.09	
	(change, % pts.)	2.93		2.69		5.50	5.92	4.17	
Short-Term Interest Rate	(level, % pts.)	3.66		3.91		8.32	7.71	2.60	
	(change, % pts.)	3.27		2.62		7.01	5.99	1.79	
Bilateral US $Exchange Rate	(level, %)	10.25		12.82		20.83	21.26	1.04	
Current Account / GNP	(level, % pts.)	1.35		1.50		1.31	1.12	1.14	
Loss: GNP + Inflation		8.31		8.30		8.44	8.91	9.32	
Loss: GNP + Inflation + Change in Interest Rate		11.58		10.92		15.45	14.90	11.11	
Final Half-Period (Five Years)									
Real GNP	(level, %)	6.54		6.72		3.19	3.15	6.46	
	(growth, % pts.)	4.02		4.09		3.35	3.48	4.03	
Nominal GNP	(level, %)	8.74		6.91		37.11	42.39	16.58	
	(growth, % pts.)	4.33		4.11		7.26	7.70	5.68	
GNP Deflator	(level, %)	14.47		12.84		39.91	44.90	22.37	
	(change, % pts.)	3.11		2.90		6.53	7.02	4.56	
Short-Term Interest Rate	(level, % pts.)	4.30		4.74		9.14	8.67	3.11	
	(change, % pts.)	3.53		2.80		7.22	6.39	1.78	
Bilateral US $Exchange Rate	(level, %)	11.53		14.47		28.01	28.53	1.24	
Current Account / GNP	(level, % pts.)	1.69		1.85		1.62	1.34	1.43	
Loss: GNP + Inflation		9.65		9.62		9.72	10.17	11.02	
Loss: GNP + Inflation + Change in Interest Rate		13.18		12.42		16.94	16.56	12.80	

TABLE B-I-12

LIVERPOOL MODEL: JAPAN

(Root Mean Squared Deviation from Baseline)

		Money Targeting (1)	Money Targeting (1X)	Nominal GNP Targeting (2A)	Nominal GNP Targeting (2AX)	Real GNP and Inflation Targeting (2B)	Real GNP and Inflation Targeting (2BX)	Exchange Rate Targeting (3)	Exchange Rate Targeting (3X)
					Full Period (Ten Years)				
Real GNP	(level, %)	11.97	10.81	8.60	9.06	44.96	21.22	144.46	15.60
	(growth, % pts.)	12.60	12.67	8.77	10.37	52.00	11.51	211.38	21.36
Nominal GNP	(level, %)	14.43	11.61	4.31	6.11	255.22	161.86	329.15	18.00
	(growth, % pts.)	14.82	14.03	4.02	7.88	76.47	30.21	240.83	23.18
GNP Deflator	(level, %)	6.72	5.05	6.96	5.29	268.65	172.44	290.64	6.92
	(change, % pts.)	5.36	4.20	6.54	6.35	75.56	30.77	105.47	4.46
Short-Term Interest Rate	(level, % pts.)	7.53	6.74	6.45	8.23	59.77	26.75	20.19	3.33
	(change, % pts.)	7.42	9.19	5.71	13.62	45.86	11.19	25.32	3.62
Bilateral US $Exchange Rate	(level, %)	27.75	18.63	19.00	19.05	627.54	222.90	7.05	0.32
Current Account / GNP	(level, % pts.)	2.52	2.31	1.98	1.92	30.00	15.12	29.62	2.44
Loss: GNP + Inflation		17.33	15.01	15.13	15.40	120.52	51.99	249.94	20.05
Loss: GNP + Inflation + Change in Interest Rate		24.75	24.20	20.85	29.02	166.39	63.18	275.26	23.67
					Final Half-Period (Five Years)				
Real GNP	(level, %)	14.26	12.76	9.84	10.78	36.38	25.12	145.83	19.40
	(growth, % pts.)	12.98	13.39	8.29	12.04	34.64	9.90	201.16	25.18
Nominal GNP	(level, %)	17.94	14.23	5.25	7.41	356.60	263.15	415.46	23.11
	(growth, % pts.)	15.30	15.23	3.58	8.25	64.33	32.80	206.81	27.06
GNP Deflator	(level, %)	7.14	5.13	7.47	5.32	334.25	262.22	383.19	9.20
	(change, % pts.)	5.42	4.21	6.67	5.88	52.63	30.95	101.61	5.41
Short-Term Interest Rate	(level, % pts.)	9.42	7.78	7.04	6.52	49.12	26.12	21.02	4.03
	(change, % pts.)	7.46	10.34	5.08	10.23	32.10	8.84	29.23	4.29
Bilateral US $Exchange Rate	(level, %)	34.75	22.21	19.76	21.76	696.68	315.98	9.61	0.46
Current Account / GNP	(level, % pts.)	2.84	2.70	2.17	2.18	33.52	18.74	36.59	2.62
Loss: GNP + Inflation		19.68	16.98	16.51	16.66	89.01	56.07	247.44	24.81
Loss: GNP + Inflation + Change in Interest Rate		27.14	27.32	21.59	26.89	121.10	64.91	275.67	29.10

TABLE B-I-13   **MSG MODEL: JAPAN**

(Root Mean Squared Deviation from Baseline)

		Money Targeting		Nominal GNP Targeting		Real GNP and Inflation Targeting		Exchange Rate Targeting	
		(1)	(1X)	(2A)	(2AX)	(2B)	(2BX)	(3)	(3X)
Full Period (Ten Years)									
Real GNP	(level, %)	37.10	34.10	34.19	5.36	36.96	7.93	56.96	53.15
	(growth, % pts.)	11.28	10.46	10.50	18.52	11.16	3.25	16.93	19.52
Nominal GNP	(level, %)	42.58	37.79	39.14	0.00	39.52	33.75	36.68	56.99
	(growth, % pts.)	13.99	12.58	12.87	0.00	13.95	6.67	18.38	20.63
GNP Deflator	(level, %)	5.99	4.36	5.57	5.36	11.16	39.93	29.66	13.18
	(change, % pts.)	3.08	2.52	2.86	3.34	3.72	6.27	5.47	6.58
Short-Term Interest Rate	(level, % pts.)	53.82	63.77	58.71	144.81	54.09	142.06	10.64	8.36
	(change, % pts.)	17.67	21.22	19.31	53.22	19.93	47.30	4.43	2.65
Bilateral US $Exchange Rate	(level, %)	26.73	33.87	29.62	89.66	56.22	106.99	4.25	0.00
Current Account / GNP	(level, % pts.)	2.45	2.34	2.40	1.20	2.68	1.84	2.57	3.41
Loss: GNP + Inflation		40.18	36.61	37.05	8.70	40.69	14.20	62.43	59.73
Loss: GNP + Inflation + Change in Interest Rate		57.85	57.83	56.36	61.92	60.61	61.50	66.86	62.37
Final Half-Period (Five Years)									
Real GNP	(level, %)	37.79	34.61	34.63	2.79	37.87	6.95	58.28	55.43
	(growth, % pts.)	0.21	0.16	0.13	19.21	0.30	0.29	0.32	11.57
Nominal GNP	(level, %)	43.88	38.70	40.99	0.00	35.82	45.11	23.38	49.00
	(growth, % pts.)	0.95	0.75	1.20	0.00	2.75	5.96	4.33	3.81
GNP Deflator	(level, %)	6.27	4.34	6.57	2.79	12.85	51.88	39.20	11.78
	(change, % pts.)	0.83	0.67	1.14	0.83	2.96	5.69	4.62	4.40
Short-Term Interest Rate	(level, % pts.)	55.45	65.30	61.48	143.85	53.47	142.58	8.92	10.29
	(change, % pts.)	1.19	1.25	1.80	1.82	0.67	0.99	3.69	1.78
Bilateral US $Exchange Rate	(level, %)	17.34	24.24	17.34	78.40	74.08	111.45	3.57	0.00
Current Account / GNP	(level, % pts.)	2.36	2.23	2.28	0.73	2.77	1.68	2.26	3.51
Loss: GNP + Inflation		38.62	35.28	35.77	3.63	40.85	12.64	62.90	59.83
Loss: GNP + Inflation + Change in Interest Rate		39.81	36.53	37.57	5.45	41.52	13.63	66.59	61.61

MULTIMOD MODEL: JAPAN

		Money Targeting		(Root Mean Squared Deviation from Baseline) Nominal GNP Targeting		Real GNP and Inflation Targeting		Exchange Rate Targeting	
		(1)	(1X)	(2A)	(2AX)	(2B)	(2BX)	(3)	(3X)
Full Period (Ten Years)									
Real GNP	(level, %)	3.32	3.76	4.01	4.35			5.14	
	(growth, % pts.)	2.59	2.79	2.76	3.80			3.89	
Nominal GNP	(level, %)	5.85	4.91	5.06	5.39			10.52	
	(growth, % pts.)	3.68	3.78	3.87	2.61			6.10	
GNP Deflator	(level, %)	7.61	7.04	6.88	7.13			10.67	
	(change, % pts.)	3.11	2.92	3.03	2.93			4.24	
Short-Term Interest Rate	(level, % pts.)	4.85	3.37	2.54	11.11			2.65	
	(change, % pts.)	4.99	1.80	1.82	12.81			1.97	
Bilateral US $Exchange Rate	(level, %)	9.61	9.61	8.47	17.14			2.11	
Current Account / GNP	(level, % pts.)	1.60	1.57	1.49	1.47			1.62	
Loss: GNP + Inflation		6.44	6.68	7.04	7.28			9.37	
Loss: GNP + Inflation + Change in Interest Rate		11.43	8.48	8.86	20.09			11.34	
Final Half-Period (Five Years)									
Real GNP	(level, %)	3.59	4.03	4.38	4.52			5.97	
	(growth, % pts.)	2.64	2.92	2.86	3.93			4.10	
Nominal GNP	(level, %)	6.50	5.33	5.20	6.90			11.88	
	(growth, % pts.)	3.95	4.15	4.26	2.71			6.87	
GNP Deflator	(level, %)	8.68	7.85	7.49	8.37			12.47	
	(change, % pts.)	2.67	2.58	2.71	2.76			3.91	
Short-Term Interest Rate	(level, % pts.)	4.81	3.49	2.57	11.12			2.95	
	(change, % pts.)	5.18	1.96	1.99	13.57			2.01	
Bilateral US $Exchange Rate	(level, %)	10.91	10.74	9.26	19.77			2.35	
Current Account / GNP	(level, % pts.)	1.85	1.81	1.70	1.70			1.90	
Loss: GNP + Inflation		6.26	6.61	7.10	7.28			9.88	
Loss: GNP + Inflation + Change in Interest Rate		11.43	8.57	9.08	20.85			11.89	

TABLE B-I-15

MX3 MODEL: JAPAN

(Root Mean Squared Deviation from Baseline)

		Money Targeting (1)	(1X)	Nominal GNP Targeting (2A)	(2AX)	Real GNP and Inflation Targeting (2B)	(2BX)	Exchange Rate Targeting (3)	(3X)
				Full Period (Ten Years)					
Real GNP	(level, %)	2.99		2.30	2.16	2.07			
	(growth, % pts.)	3.10		2.60	2.20	2.20			
Nominal GNP	(level, %)	5.28		3.55	2.85	9.93			
	(growth, % pts.)	4.30		3.60	3.10	3.30			
GNP Deflator	(level, %)	3.09		2.44	2.44	9.24			
	(change, % pts.)	1.54		1.40	1.34	1.65			
Short-Term Interest Rate	(level, % pts.)	2.51		5.32	8.55	12.06			
	(change, % pts.)	2.74		5.42	9.39	14.77			
Bilateral US $Exchange Rate	(level, %)	26.67		26.53	27.64	32.34			
Current Account / GNP	(level, % pts.)	2.38		2.48	2.51	2.43			
Loss: GNP + Inflation		4.53		3.70	3.50	3.72			
Loss: GNP + Inflation + Change in Interest Rate		7.27		9.12	12.89	18.49			
				Final Half-Period (Five Years)					
Real GNP	(level, %)	2.97		2.35	2.39	2.09			
	(growth, % pts.)	3.08		2.57	2.22	2.12			
Nominal GNP	(level, %)	5.27		3.47	2.83	12.37			
	(growth, % pts.)	4.18		3.53	3.12	3.20			
GNP Deflator	(level, %)	3.22		2.59	2.66	11.88			
	(change, % pts.)	1.52		1.39	1.35	1.66			
Short-Term Interest Rate	(level, % pts.)	2.47		5.21	8.48	11.81			
	(change, % pts.)	2.71		5.29	9.35	13.93			
Bilateral US $Exchange Rate	(level, %)	29.68		29.24	30.80	34.62			
Current Account / GNP	(level, % pts.)	2.38		2.48	2.47	2.07			
Loss: GNP + Inflation		4.49		3.74	3.74	3.74			
Loss: GNP + Inflation + Change in Interest Rate		7.20		9.03	13.09	17.67			

TABLE B-I-16

TAYLOR MODEL: JAPAN

(Root Mean Squared Deviation from Baseline)

		Money Targeting (1)	Nominal GNP Targeting (2A)(2AX)	Real GNP and Inflation Targeting (2B)(2BX)	Exchange Rate Targeting (3)(3X)
Full Period (Ten Years)					
Real GNP	(level, %)	5.44	2.91	2.43	7.68
	(growth, % pts.)	1.03	0.73	0.68	1.89
Nominal GNP	(level, %)	6.55	4.95	6.08	7.78
	(growth, % pts.)	1.87	1.73	1.73	2.25
GNP Deflator	(level, %)	11.74	5.23	12.63	8.07
	(change, % pts.)	1.42	1.45	1.41	1.37
Short-Term Interest Rate	(level, % pts.)	0.04	0.04	0.04	0.14
	(change, % pts.)	n.a.	n.a.	n.a.	n.a.
Bilateral US $Exchange Rate	(level, %)	19.33	21.75	23.30	17.98
Current Account / GNP	(level, % pts.)	0.90	0.89	0.83	0.95
Loss: GNP + Inflation		6.86	4.36	3.84	9.05
Loss: GNP + Inflation + Change in Interest Rate		n.a.	n.a.	n.a.	n.a.
Final Half-Period (Five Years)					
Real GNP	(level, %)	6.65	3.31	2.66	9.32
	(growth, % pts.)	1.08	0.74	0.64	2.19
Nominal GNP	(level, %)	7.38	5.43	7.00	9.20
	(growth, % pts.)	1.80	1.77	1.68	2.42
GNP Deflator	(level, %)	6.30	5.50	16.12	8.67
	(change, % pts.)	1.46	1.51	1.43	1.39
Short-Term Interest Rate	(level, % pts.)	0.04	0.04	0.05	0.14
	(change, % pts.)	n.a.	n.a.	n.a.	n.a.
Bilateral US $Exchange Rate	(level, %)	18.25	20.69	24.54	17.04
Current Account / GNP	(level, % pts.)	0.98	0.98	0.89	1.10
Loss: GNP + Inflation		8.11	4.82	4.09	10.71
Loss: GNP + Inflation + Change in Interest Rate		n.a.	n.a.	n.a.	n.a.

TABLE B-I-17 — GEM MODEL: JAPAN

(Root Mean Squared Deviation from Baseline)

		Money Targeting (1)	(1X)	Nominal GNP Targeting (2A)	(2AX)	Real GNP and Inflation Targeting (2B)	(2BX)	Exchange Rate Targeting (3)	(3X)
				Full Period (Ten Years)					
Real GNP	(level, %)		3.12		2.29		1.89		
	(growth, % pts.)		1.36		1.27		1.33		
Nominal GNP	(level, %)		3.61		2.25		3.39		
	(growth, % pts.)		1.83		1.79		1.86		
GNP Deflator	(level, %)		3.16		2.85		2.97		
	(change, % pts.)		1.90		1.81		1.95		
Short-Term Interest Rate	(level, % pts.)		0.87		0.56		0.67		
	(change, % pts.)		0.39		0.44		0.51		
Bilateral US $Exchange Rate	(level, %)		14.45		3.81		7.76		
Current Account / GNP	(level, % pts.)		0.55		0.43		0.42		
Loss: GNP + Inflation			5.02		4.10		3.84		
Loss: GNP + Inflation + Change in Interest Rate			5.41		4.54		4.35		

TABLE B-I-18 — INTERMOD (ADAPTIVE) MODEL: GERMANY

(Root Mean Squared Deviation from Baseline)

		Money Targeting (1X)	Nominal GNP Targeting		Real GNP and Inflation Targeting		Exchange Rate Targeting (3X)
		(1)	(2A)	(2AX)	(2B)	(2BX)	(3)
Full Period (Ten Years)							
Real GNP	(level, %)	4.84	4.29	4.77	3.26	3.49	5.38
	(growth, % pts.)	3.60	3.36	3.63	3.18	3.22	3.93
Nominal GNP	(level, %)	9.51	6.68	8.88	5.62	6.29	11.55
	(growth, % pts.)	4.27	4.50	3.99	3.63	3.61	4.31
GNP Deflator	(level, %)	7.44	5.03	6.97	4.79	5.23	9.51
	(change, % pts.)	2.14	1.51	1.83	1.17	1.26	2.18
Short-Term Interest Rate	(level, % pts.)	4.65	7.53	5.36	5.33	4.72	3.81
	(change, % pts.)	3.77	6.56	2.63	4.79	3.92	2.03
Bilateral US $Exchange Rate	(level, %)	6.31	8.85	6.26	5.74	5.11	1.52
Current Account / GNP	(level, % pts.)	2.29	3.17	2.39	2.46	2.35	2.36
Loss: GNP + Inflation		6.98	5.80	6.60	4.43	4.75	7.56
Loss: GNP + Inflation + Change in Interest Rate		10.75	12.36	9.23	9.22	8.67	9.59
Final Half-Period (Five Years)							
Real GNP	(level, %)	5.63	4.90	5.37	3.44	3.70	6.05
	(growth, % pts.)	3.83	3.61	3.83	3.25	3.28	4.15
Nominal GNP	(level, %)	12.50	8.33	11.26	6.87	7.76	14.55
	(growth, % pts.)	4.54	5.01	4.17	3.77	3.73	4.51
GNP Deflator	(level, %)	10.18	6.50	9.31	6.25	6.86	12.75
	(change, % pts.)	2.68	1.63	2.11	1.30	1.41	2.55
Short-Term Interest Rate	(level, % pts.)	5.51	8.68	6.58	5.69	5.09	4.89
	(change, % pts.)	3.79	7.34	2.74	5.04	4.12	2.05
Bilateral US $Exchange Rate	(level, %)	7.63	10.34	7.48	6.71	5.99	1.95
Current Account / GNP	(level, % pts.)	2.62	4.08	2.96	3.01	2.85	2.76
Loss: GNP + Inflation		8.31	6.53	7.48	4.74	5.11	8.60
Loss: GNP + Inflation + Change in Interest Rate		12.10	13.87	10.22	9.78	9.23	10.65

TABLE B-I-19 — INTERMOD (CONSISTENT) MODEL: GERMANY

(Root Mean Squared Deviation from Baseline)

		Money Targeting		Nominal GNP Targeting		Real GNP and Inflation Targeting		Exchange Rate Targeting	
		(1)	(1X)	(2A)	(2AX)	(2B)	(2BX)	(3)	(3X)
Full Period (Ten Years)									
Real GNP	(level, %)	4.00		3.74		3.17	3.26	3.79	
	(growth, % pts.)	4.43		3.86		3.40	3.62	4.26	
Nominal GNP	(level, %)	5.96		5.28		10.33	10.91	6.23	
	(growth, % pts.)	4.76		4.15		4.72	4.83	4.67	
GNP Deflator	(level, %)	3.58		2.71		9.81	10.10	3.69	
	(change, % pts.)	1.26		1.21		2.57	2.44	1.32	
Short-Term Interest Rate	(level, % pts.)	3.86		3.28		5.94	5.09	2.77	
	(change, % pts.)	4.08		2.81		5.85	5.09	2.07	
Bilateral US $Exchange Rate	(level, %)	7.21		7.10		11.35	10.13	1.11	
Current Account / GNP	(level, % pts.)	2.16		2.03		2.19	2.19	1.88	
Loss: GNP + Inflation		5.26		4.95		5.74	5.70	5.11	
Loss: GNP + Inflation + Change in Interest Rate		9.34		7.76		11.59	10.79	7.18	
Final Half-Period (Five Years)									
Real GNP	(level, %)	4.23		4.07		3.15	3.25	3.97	
	(growth, % pts.)	4.45		3.83		3.37	3.58	4.29	
Nominal GNP	(level, %)	6.87		6.08		13.39	13.89	7.20	
	(growth, % pts.)	4.70		4.07		4.96	4.79	4.72	
GNP Deflator	(change, % pts.)	4.28		3.25		13.00	13.19	4.53	
	(change, % pts.)	1.41		1.37		3.01	2.56	1.46	
Short-Term Interest Rate	(level, % pts.)	3.97		3.59		6.15	5.09	3.26	
	(change, % pts.)	4.04		2.78		5.82	5.06	2.03	
Bilateral US $Exchange Rate	(level, %)	8.23		7.87		13.87	12.27	1.30	
Current Account / GNP	(level, % pts.)	2.37		2.41		2.61	2.61	2.13	
Loss: GNP + Inflation		5.64		5.44		6.16	5.81	5.43	
Loss: GNP + Inflation + Change in Interest Rate		9.68		8.22		11.98	10.87	7.46	

TABLE B-I-20 LIVERPOOL MODEL: GERMANY

(Root Mean Squared Deviation from Baseline)

		Money Targeting (1)	(1X)	Nominal GNP Targeting (2A)	(2AX)	Real GNP and Inflation Targeting (2B)	(2BX)	Exchange Rate Targeting (3)	(3X)
Full Period (Ten Years)									
Real GNP	(level, %)	6.50	5.12	5.76	4.70	81.20	31.65	102.07	6.04
	(growth, % pts.)	3.33	3.94	3.06	3.10	23.63	6.91	87.95	5.30
Nominal GNP	(level, %)	2.94	2.58	3.60	2.90	754.79	251.63	497.79	13.87
	(growth, % pts.)	3.08	3.41	3.72	5.05	193.80	42.03	188.62	7.93
GNP Deflator	(level, %)	8.06	5.89	7.02	5.57	802.66	208.85	396.12	10.40
	(change, % pts.)	4.68	4.03	5.24	5.25	203.73	36.27	140.39	4.95
Short-Term Interest Rate	(level, % pts.)	7.21	4.77	5.31	6.85	187.29	28.90	24.79	3.57
	(change, % pts.)	6.93	6.24	5.35	11.57	65.23	9.49	33.04	4.17
Bilateral US $Exchange Rate	(level, %)	22.27	16.68	14.23	15.31	579.37	183.24	5.49	0.49
Current Account / GNP	(level, % pts.)	4.03	3.22	3.49	3.10	66.43	22.54	61.59	3.68
Loss: GNP + Inflation		11.18	9.16	10.99	9.95	284.92	67.91	242.45	10.98
Loss: GNP + Inflation + Change in Interest Rate		18.11	15.40	16.34	21.52	350.15	77.40	275.49	15.15
Final Half-Period (Five Years)									
Real GNP	(level, %)	9.07	6.45	7.32	6.22	115.17	42.99	120.31	8.12
	(growth, % pts.)	3.38	4.10	3.02	3.40	18.42	4.81	74.65	6.19
Nominal GNP	(level, %)	3.34	3.18	4.58	2.81	1344.60	388.29	682.18	20.28
	(growth, % pts.)	3.19	3.79	3.94	4.17	271.82	41.92	151.23	8.97
GNP Deflator	(level, %)	10.22	7.24	8.49	6.61	1378.92	316.12	526.63	14.54
	(change, % pts.)	4.72	4.20	5.47	4.80	268.03	37.11	129.68	5.53
Short-Term Interest Rate	(level, % pts.)	9.01	5.31	6.20	5.20	240.60	30.70	22.73	4.06
	(change, % pts.)	7.18	6.47	5.65	8.57	55.69	6.63	34.72	4.65
Bilateral US $Exchange Rate	(level, %)	29.23	18.92	17.01	17.84	983.70	265.67	7.29	0.69
Current Account / GNP	(level, % pts.)	5.50	4.18	4.40	4.28	89.57	33.20	85.69	5.10
Loss: GNP + Inflation		13.79	10.65	12.79	11.02	383.20	80.10	250.00	13.64
Loss: GNP + Inflation + Change in Interest Rate		20.97	17.13	18.44	19.59	438.88	86.73	284.71	18.30

TABLE B-1-21   MSG MODEL: GERMANY

(Root Mean Squared Deviation from Baseline)

		Money Targeting		Nominal GNP Targeting		Real GNP and Inflation Targeting		Exchange Rate Targeting	
		(1)	(1X)	(2A)	(2AX)	(2B)	(2BX)	(3)	(3X)
Full Period (Ten Years)									
Real GNP	(level, %)	16.16	14.68	11.28	13.34	15.98	2.76	23.32	24.49
	(growth, % pts.)	5.56	5.29	3.86	5.60	5.21	1.41	9.76	7.98
Nominal GNP	(level, %)	16.65	14.57	15.00	0.00	19.39	3.94	6.03	17.26
	(growth, % pts.)	5.15	4.65	4.69	0.00	6.25	2.45	10.64	7.76
GNP Deflator	(level, %)	4.83	4.80	4.81	13.34	9.70	5.74	20.97	15.56
	(change, % pts.)	2.15	2.14	1.57	5.07	4.54	2.78	7.47	4.73
Short-Term Interest Rate	(level, % pts.)	20.65	24.07	22.50	54.15	26.88	62.36	10.64	8.36
	(change, % pts.)	6.38	7.69	7.03	22.39	7.07	18.57	4.43	2.65
Bilateral US $Exchange Rate	(level, %)	9.11	11.30	11.12	37.29	27.71	26.20	4.25	0.00
Current Account / GNP	(level, %)	6.22	6.12	6.13	5.37	5.75	4.21	7.96	6.68
Loss: GNP + Inflation		18.31	16.83	12.85	18.40	20.53	5.54	30.79	29.21
Loss: GNP + Inflation + Change in Interest Rate		24.69	24.51	19.88	40.79	27.59	24.11	35.22	31.86
Final Half-Period (Five Years)									
Real GNP	(level, %)	15.34	13.26	11.51	16.88	15.93	3.28	18.00	27.89
	(growth, % pts.)	1.18	1.30	0.61	2.30	0.26	0.96	4.60	1.65
Nominal GNP	(level, %)	18.18	15.74	16.91	0.00	23.65	4.66	10.82	10.80
	(growth, % pts.)	1.01	0.81	1.28	0.00	5.64	2.87	1.35	3.23
GNP Deflator	(level, %)	4.38	4.12	6.23	16.88	11.52	7.21	15.36	20.49
	(change, % pts.)	2.10	2.05	1.71	5.19	5.86	3.74	5.41	5.57
Short-Term Interest Rate	(level, % pts.)	22.55	26.01	25.37	55.09	30.14	66.23	8.92	10.29
	(change, % pts.)	1.27	1.34	1.93	1.77	1.71	1.72	3.69	1.78
Bilateral US $Exchange Rate	(level, %)	6.83	8.72	9.05	40.68	38.17	22.39	3.57	0.00
Current Account / GNP	(level, %)	6.40	6.30	6.20	5.68	5.75	4.11	8.34	6.72
Loss: GNP + Inflation		17.44	15.31	13.23	22.07	21.79	7.02	23.41	33.45
Loss: GNP + Inflation + Change in Interest Rate		18.70	16.65	15.15	23.84	23.50	8.73	27.10	35.23

TABLE B-I-22

MULTIMOD MODEL: GERMANY

(Root Mean Squared Deviation from Baseline)

		Money Targeting		Nominal GNP Targeting		Real GNP and Inflation Targeting		Exchange Rate Targeting	
		(1)	(1X)	(2A)	(2AX)	(2B)	(2BX)	(3)	(3X)
Full Period (Ten Years)									
Real GNP	(level, %)	3.37	3.57		2.89		3.31		3.90
	(growth, % pts.)	3.94	3.87		2.85		3.06		3.85
Nominal GNP	(level, %)	4.05	4.28		3.04		2.94		5.20
	(growth, % pts.)	3.90	3.88		2.85		2.70		3.90
GNP Deflator	(level, %)	3.86	3.92		3.43		2.85		4.38
	(change, % pts.)	1.59	1.60		1.47		1.19		1.93
Short-Term Interest Rate	(level, % pts.)	4.43	2.87		1.52		5.31		2.38
	(change, % pts.)	4.48	1.73		1.35		5.27		1.54
Bilateral US $Exchange Rate	(level, %)	8.69	8.39		5.20		8.14		1.89
Current Account / GNP	(level, % pts.)	2.30	2.35		2.17		2.16		2.27
Loss: GNP + Inflation		4.96	5.17		4.36		4.49		5.83
Loss: GNP + Inflation + Change in Interest Rate		9.43	6.90		5.71		9.77		7.37
Final Half-Period (Five Years)									
Real GNP	(level, %)	3.77	4.05		3.32		3.81		4.32
	(growth, % pts.)	4.26	4.17		3.10		3.33		4.04
Nominal GNP	(level, %)	4.53	4.68		3.14		3.49		5.79
	(growth, % pts.)	4.13	4.11		3.01		2.97		4.05
GNP Deflator	(level, %)	4.78	4.79		4.11		3.43		5.37
	(change, % pts.)	1.68	1.62		1.50		1.21		2.08
Short-Term Interest Rate	(level, % pts.)	4.71	3.22		1.58		5.52		2.63
	(change, % pts.)	4.53	1.90		1.41		5.34		1.59
Bilateral US $Exchange Rate	(level, %)	9.43	9.35		5.69		9.01		2.09
Current Account / GNP	(level, % pts.)	2.57	2.49		2.42		2.37		2.55
Loss: GNP + Inflation		5.44	5.68		4.83		5.02		6.40
Loss: GNP + Inflation + Change in Interest Rate		9.97	7.58		6.23		10.36		7.99

TABLE B-I-23 — MX3 MODEL: GERMANY

(Root Mean Squared Deviation from Baseline)

		Money Targeting (1) (1X)	Nominal GNP Targeting (2A) (2AX)		Real GNP and Inflation Targeting (2B) (2BX)		Exchange Rate Targeting (3) (3X)	

Full Period (Ten Years)

		(1)	(2A)	(2AX)	(2B)	(2BX)	(3)	(3X)
Real GNP	(level, %)	3.35	2.95	3.29	1.95			
	(growth, % pts.)	2.60	2.80	1.80	1.80			
Nominal GNP	(level, %)	8.01	3.10	2.34	18.01			
	(growth, % pts.)	3.60	2.80	2.40	2.70			
GNP Deflator	(level, %)	6.61	3.46	3.77	18.26			
	(change, % pts.)	1.54	1.34	1.30	1.77			
Short-Term Interest Rate	(level, % pts.)	4.91	4.66	7.03	11.24			
	(change, % pts.)	5.17	4.21	7.12	11.42			
Bilateral US $Exchange Rate	(level, %)	20.66	19.76	20.81	25.78			
Current Account / GNP	(level, % pts.)	2.00	1.85	1.98	2.15			
Loss: GNP + Inflation		4.90	4.29	4.59	3.72			
Loss: GNP + Inflation + Change in Interest Rate		10.06	8.50	11.71	15.14			

Final Half-Period (Five Years)

		(1)	(2A)	(2AX)	(2B)	(2BX)	(3)	(3X)
Real GNP	(level, %)	3.58	3.48	3.96	2.17			
	(growth, % pts.)	2.74	2.21	1.85	1.92			
Nominal GNP	(level, %)	8.80	3.20	2.39	24.66			
	(growth, % pts.)	3.74	2.93	2.45	2.99			
GNP Deflator	(level, %)	7.81	4.05	4.42	25.10			
	(change, % pts.)	1.54	1.36	1.31	2.04			
Short-Term Interest Rate	(level, % pts.)	4.94	4.80	7.17	12.57			
	(change, % pts.)	5.45	4.39	7.36	11.84			
Bilateral US $Exchange Rate	(level, %)	2.15	21.09	22.28	30.77			
Current Account / GNP	(level, % pts.)	2.14	1.94	2.14	2.47			
Loss: GNP + Inflation		5.12	4.84	5.27	4.21			
Loss: GNP + Inflation + Change in Interest Rate		10.57	9.23	12.63	16.05			

TABLE B-1-24

TAYLOR MODEL: GERMANY

(Root Mean Squared Deviation from Baseline)

		Money Targeting (1)	Nominal GNP Targeting (2A) (2AX)	Real GNP and Inflation Targeting (2B) (2BX)	Exchange Rate Targeting (3) (3X)
Full Period (Ten Years)					
Real GNP	(level, %)	3.79	1.73	1.83	6.41
	(growth, % pts.)	1.89	1.56	1.58	3.56
Nominal GNP	(level, %)	7.61	9.26	6.07	9.61
	(growth, % pts.)	3.03	3.03	2.77	4.01
GNP Deflator	(level, %)	2.07	1.85	2.00	2.33
	(change, % pts.)	1.96	2.37	1.98	2.33
Short-Term Interest Rate	(level, % pts.)	0.02	0.03	0.03	0.16
	(change, % pts.)	n.a.	n.a.	n.a.	n.a.
Bilateral US $Exchange Rate	(level, %)	21.60	23.33	21.51	18.78
Current Account / GNP	(level, % pts.)	1.79	1.40	1.49	2.76
Loss: GNP + Inflation		5.75	4.10	3.81	8.74
Loss: GNP + Inflation + Change in Interest Rate		n.a.	n.a.	n.a.	n.a.
Final Half-Period (Five Years)					
Real GNP	(level, %)	4.26	1.81	1.90	7.39
	(growth, % pts.)	1.80	1.47	1.41	3.71
Nominal GNP	(level, %)	9.00	10.68	6.72	11.46
	(growth, % pts.)	3.05	3.16	2.73	4.10
GNP Deflator	(level, %)	2.21	1.81	1.99	2.65
	(change, % pts.)	2.01	2.52	2.02	2.46
Short-Term Interest Rate	(level, % pts.)	0.02	0.03	0.03	0.17
	(change, % pts.)	n.a.	n.a.	n.a.	n.a.
Bilateral US $Exchange Rate	(level, %)	21.08	23.07	21.34	18.18
Current Account / GNP	(level, % pts.)	1.90	1.49	1.59	3.15
Loss: GNP + Inflation		6.27	4.33	3.92	9.85
Loss: GNP + Inflation + Change in Interest Rate		n.a.	n.a.	n.a.	n.a.

953

TABLE B-I-25 — GEM MODEL: GERMANY

(Root Mean Squared Deviation from Baseline)

		Money Targeting (1)	(1X)	Nominal GNP Targeting (2A)	(2AX)	Real GNP and Inflation Targeting (2B)	(2BX)	Exchange Rate Targeting (3)	(3X)
				Full Period (Ten Years)					
Real GNP	(level, %)	2.78			2.60		2.48		
	(growth, % pts.)		2.10		2.04		2.20		
Nominal GNP	(level, %)	2.87			2.75		3.84		
	(growth, % pts.)	2.07			2.01		2.19		
GNP Deflator	(level, %)	2.21			1.92		3.06		
	(change, % pts.)	1.30			1.24		1.65		
Short-Term Interest Rate	(level, % pts.)		0.36		0.69		0.75		
	(change, % pts.)		0.15		0.46		0.55		
Bilateral US $Exchange Rate	(level, %)	10.27			6.58		8.21		
Current Account / GNP	(level, % pts.)		0.37		0.38		0.38		
Loss: GNP + Inflation			4.08		3.84		4.13		
Loss: GNP + Inflation + Change in Interest Rate			4.23		4.30		4.68		

TABLE B-I-26

INTERMOD (ADAPTIVE) MODEL: UNITED KINGDOM

(Root Mean Squared Deviation from Baseline)

		Money Targeting		Nominal GNP Targeting		Real GNP and Inflation Targeting		Exchange Rate Targeting	
		(1)	(1X)	(2A)	(2AX)	(2B)	(2BX)	(3)	(3X)
Full Period (Ten Years)									
Real GNP	(level, %)	5.93		4.67	5.37	3.39	3.67	6.33	
	(growth, % pts.)	4.85		3.55	4.35	3.16	3.36	5.60	
Nominal GNP	(level, %)	11.05		5.26	9.01	7.82	8.49	13.54	
	(growth, % pts.)	6.42		4.69	5.77	5.03	5.21	7.00	
GNP Deflator	(level, %)	10.58		6.56	9.47	8.25	8.73	13.05	
	(change, % pts.)	3.13		1.93	2.56	2.03	2.17	3.42	
Short-Term Interest Rate	(level, % pts.)	5.33		8.46	6.35	5.67	5.14	3.83	
	(change, % pts.)	4.47		6.57	3.81	5.40	4.74	2.10	
Bilateral US $Exchange Rate	(level, %)	6.06		8.55	6.72	6.22	5.62	1.53	
Current Account / GNP	(level, % pts.)	2.15		2.38	2.19	2.21	2.20	2.23	
Loss: GNP + Inflation		9.06		6.60	7.93	5.42	5.84	9.75	
Loss: GNP + Inflation + Change in Interest Rate		13.53		13.17	11.74	10.82	10.58	11.85	
Final Half-Period (Five Years)									
Real GNP	(level, %)	6.44		5.37	5.89	3.46	3.76	6.72	
	(growth, % pts.)	5.12		3.83	4.64	3.23	3.41	5.80	
Nominal GNP	(level, %)	14.24		6.09	11.33	9.97	10.87	17.36	
	(growth, % pts.)	6.54		4.79	5.83	5.04	5.25	7.14	
GNP Deflator	(level, %)	14.17		8.52	12.74	10.82	11.51	17.41	
	(change, % pts.)	3.86		2.13	2.99	2.43	2.61	4.14	
Short-Term Interest Rate	(level, % pts.)	6.38		10.01	7.98	6.01	5.52	4.93	
	(change, % pts.)	4.37		6.59	3.82	5.43	4.76	2.05	
Bilateral US $Exchange Rate	(level, %)	7.21		9.52	7.90	6.99	6.33	1.96	
Current Account / GNP	(level, % pts.)	2.22		2.63	2.30	2.30	2.28	2.31	
Loss: GNP + Inflation		10.30		7.50	8.88	5.89	6.37	10.86	
Loss: GNP + Inflation + Change in Interest Rate		14.67		14.09	12.70	11.32	11.13	12.91	

TABLE B-1-27

INTERMOD (CONSISTENT) MODEL: UNITED KINGDOM

(Root Mean Squared Deviation from Baseline)

		Money Targeting (1)	Nominal GNP Targeting (2A)	Real GNP and Inflation Targeting (2B)	Real GNP and Inflation Targeting (2BX)	Exchange Rate Targeting (3)
Full Period (Ten Years)						
Real GNP	(level, %)	3.88	3.50	2.92	3.25	4.12
	(growth, % pts.)	4.94	3.95	3.52	4.00	5.09
Nominal GNP	(level, %)	6.39	5.09	32.86	38.63	8.57
	(growth, % pts.)	5.90	4.92	7.39	7.94	6.27
GNP Deflator	(level, %)	6.28	5.32	34.59	39.76	8.41
	(change, % pts.)	2.17	1.83	6.30	6.73	2.66
Short-Term Interest Rate	(level, % pts.)	4.12	3.53	9.81	9.13	2.79
	(change, % pts.)	4.53	3.26	7.41	6.88	2.15
Bilateral US $Exchange Rate	(level, %)	6.46	7.21	19.93	26.32	1.12
Current Account / GNP	(level, % pts.)	2.40	2.26	2.34	2.42	2.41
Loss: GNP + Inflation		6.05	5.33	9.22	9.98	6.78
Loss: GNP + Inflation + Change in Interest Rate		10.58	8.59	16.63	16.86	8.93
Final Half-Period (Five Years)						
Real GNP	(level, %)	4.02	3.76	2.96	3.26	4.22
	(growth, % pts.)	5.09	4.02	3.49	3.95	5.18
Nominal GNP	(level, %)	7.33	5.78	44.63	51.76	10.17
	(growth, % pts.)	5.88	4.84	8.40	8.39	6.30
GNP Deflator	(level, %)	7.93	6.59	47.16	53.47	10.70
	(change, % pts.)	2.37	1.94	7.48	7.35	2.87
Short-Term Interest Rate	(level, % pts.)	4.28	3.98	10.79	9.37	3.33
	(change, % pts.)	4.27	3.17	7.09	6.53	2.10
Bilateral US $Exchange Rate	(level, %)	7.42	7.97	26.88	35.53	1.33
Current Account / GNP	(level, % pts.)	2.40	2.30	2.37	2.40	2.39
Loss: GNP + Inflation		6.39	5.70	10.44	10.61	7.09
Loss: GNP + Inflation + Change in Interest Rate		10.66	8.87	17.53	17.14	9.19

TABLE B-I-28 LIVERPOOL MODEL: UNITED KINGDOM

(Root Mean Squared Deviation from Baseline)

		Money Targeting		Nominal GNP Targeting		Real GNP and Inflation Targeting		Exchange Rate Targeting	
		(1)	(1X)	(2A)	(2AX)	(2B)	(2BX)	(3)	(3X)
				Full Period (Ten Years)					
Real GNP	(level, %)	3.40	2.41	2.20	1.78	8.79	4.93	41.77	2.71
	(growth, % pts.)	2.23	2.55	1.54	1.80	4.62	4.86	66.96	3.62
Nominal GNP	(level, %)	6.57	4.36	1.77	2.70	55.36	526.24	320.83	9.16
	(growth, % pts.)	4.63	3.83	1.13	3.68	14.32	74.73	104.68	4.39
GNP Deflator	(level, %)	6.35	4.86	2.64	3.00	59.76	497.12	298.83	8.44
	(change, % pts.)	4.40	3.70	1.72	4.19	15.24	71.99	93.29	2.37
Short-Term Interest Rate	(level, % pts.)	5.29	5.02	2.54	9.23	14.72	48.24	19.24	3.60
	(change, % pts.)	5.04	7.05	1.59	14.68	10.19	30.94	21.26	3.81
Bilateral US $Exchange Rate	(level, %)	21.72	13.53	10.16	34.66	220.15	549.70	8.28	1.19
Current Account / GNP	(level, % pts.)	1.01	0.66	0.56	2.98	3.05	10.43	12.38	0.47
Loss: GNP + Inflation		7.80	6.11	3.92	5.97	24.02	76.92	135.06	5.09
Loss: GNP + Inflation + Change in Interest Rate		12.84	13.16	5.52	20.65	34.22	107.86	156.32	8.89
				Final Half-Period (Five Years)					
Real GNP	(level, %)	4.96	3.05	2.67	2.18	11.01	4.13	37.57	3.39
	(growth, % pts.)	2.30	2.71	1.47	2.01	3.81	3.52	62.83	4.22
Nominal GNP	(level, %)	9.47	5.40	2.58	3.24	91.02	810.75	468.29	14.05
	(growth, % pts.)	4.96	4.20	1.28	3.90	15.93	52.23	88.32	4.91
GNP Deflator	(level, %)	8.09	5.57	3.34	3.18	91.94	731.99	419.68	12.48
	(change, % pts.)	4.16	3.97	2.04	4.76	15.58	50.74	93.49	2.74
Short-Term Interest Rate	(level, % pts.)	6.61	5.48	3.36	9.14	15.83	37.95	22.02	4.15
	(change, % pts.)	4.87	7.52	1.81	13.91	9.54	22.82	26.56	4.26
Bilateral US $Exchange Rate	(level, %)	32.12	16.63	14.29	60.64	293.73	804.22	11.52	1.61
Current Account / GNP	(level, % pts.)	1.17	0.71	0.64	4.97	2.73	5.96	9.17	0.51
Loss: GNP + Inflation		9.12	7.02	4.72	6.94	26.58	54.86	131.06	6.13
Loss: GNP + Inflation + Change in Interest Rate		13.99	14.54	6.52	20.86	36.12	77.68	157.62	10.39

957

TABLE B-I-29 MULTIMOD MODEL: UNITED KINGDOM (Root Mean Squared Deviation from Baseline)

		Money Targeting		Nominal GNP Targeting		Real GNP and Inflation Targeting		Exchange Rate Targeting	
		(1)	(1X)	(2A)	(2AX)	(2B)	(2BX)	(3)	(3X)
Full Period (Ten Years)									
Real GNP	(level, %)	5.33	5.29		5.37		6.97		4.56
	(growth, % pts.)	3.34	3.37		3.12		3.57		2.87
Nominal GNP	(level, %)	5.92	5.60		5.16		3.58		7.56
	(growth, % pts.)	3.97	4.16		3.76		3.15		4.45
GNP Deflator	(level, %)	9.77	8.64		8.76		7.88		8.85
	(change, % pts.)	3.95	3.64		3.73		3.11		3.90
Short-Term Interest Rate	(level, % pts.)	8.17	4.57		2.58		8.26		2.84
	(change, % pts.)	9.75	2.89		1.76		7.38		2.16
Bilateral US $Exchange Rate	(level, %)	9.74	9.33		7.30		13.33		2.26
Current Account / GNP	(level, % pts.)	4.33	4.34		4.37		4.74		4.24
Loss: GNP + Inflation		9.29	8.93		9.10		10.08		8.47
Loss: GNP + Inflation + Change in Interest Rate		19.04	11.82		10.86		17.46		10.62
Final Half-Period (Five Years)									
Real GNP	(level, %)	6.58	6.57		6.64		8.50		5.61
	(growth, % pts.)	3.62	3.72		3.40		4.00		3.04
Nominal GNP	(level, %)	7.08	6.60		6.03		4.30		9.30
	(growth, % pts.)	4.11	4.39		4.10		3.33		4.96
GNP Deflator	(level, %)	12.25	10.68		10.88		9.80		11.05
	(change, % pts.)	4.16	3.86		3.99		3.06		4.27
Short-Term Interest Rate	(level, % pts.)	9.02	5.47		3.02		9.30		3.13
	(change, % pts.)	10.27	3.13		1.92		7.56		2.20
Bilateral US $Exchange Rate	(level, %)	11.45	11.10		8.46		16.15		2.49
Current Account / GNP	(level, % pts.)	5.01	5.15		5.10		5.23		4.99
Loss: GNP + Inflation		10.74	10.43		10.63		11.56		9.87
Loss: GNP + Inflation + Change in Interest Rate		21.01	13.56		12.56		19.12		12.07

TAYLOR MODEL: UNITED KINGDOM

(Root Mean Squared Deviation from Baseline)

		Money Targeting		Nominal GNP Targeting		Real GNP and Inflation Targeting		Exchange Rate Targeting	
		(1)	(1X)	(2A)	(2AX)	(2B)	(2BX)	(3)	(3X)
Full Period (Ten Years)									
Real GNP	(level, %)		3.94		2.44		2.82		3.10
	(growth, % pts.)		1.70		1.61		1.59		1.77
Nominal GNP	(level, %)		15.24		11.58		12.96		12.55
	(growth, % pts.)		3.41		3.23		3.25		3.37
GNP Deflator	(level, %)		4.92		4.42		4.49		3.89
	(change, % pts.)		2.78		2.73		2.72		2.67
Short-Term Interest Rate	(level, % pts.)		0.02		0.06		0.06		0.22
	(change, % pts.)		n.a.		n.a.		n.a.		n.a.
Bilateral US $Exchange Rate	(level, %)		21.08		23.07		21.34		18.18
Current Account / GNP	(level, %)		1.98		1.94		1.90		2.04
Loss: GNP + Inflation			6.72		5.17		5.54		5.77
Loss: GNP + Inflation + Change in Interest Rate			n.a.		n.a.		n.a.		n.a.
Final Half-Period (Five Years)									
Real GNP	(level, %)		4.40		2.52		3.11		3.25
	(growth, % pts.)		1.66		1.58		1.55		1.81
Nominal GNP	(level, %)		18.29		13.78		15.44		14.79
	(growth, % pts.)		3.33		3.22		3.17		3.36
GNP Deflator	(level, %)		5.93		5.02		5.19		4.32
	(change, % pts.)		2.73		2.73		2.68		2.61
Short-Term Interest Rate	(level, % pts.)		0.02		0.07		0.07		0.25
	(change, % pts.)		n.a.		n.a.		n.a.		n.a.
Bilateral US $Exchange Rate	(level, %)		21.08		23.07		21.34		18.18
Current Account / GNP	(level, %)		2.14		2.00		1.98		2.14
Loss: GNP + Inflation			7.13		5.25		5.79		5.86
Loss: GNP + Inflation + Change in Interest Rate			n.a.		n.a.		n.a.		n.a.

TABLE B-I-31

INTERMOD (ADAPTIVE): CANADA

(Root Mean Squared Deviation from Baseline)

		Money Targeting (1X) (1)	Nominal GNP Targeting (2A)	Nominal GNP Targeting (2AX)	Real GNP and Inflation Targeting (2B)	Real GNP and Inflation Targeting (2BX)	Exchange Rate Targeting (3)
			Full Period (Ten Years)				
Real GNP	(level, %)	5.75	5.16	5.31	3.26	3.50	5.63
	(growth, % pts.)	3.35	3.13	3.23	2.61	2.67	3.32
Nominal GNP	(level, %)	8.87	3.92	7.41	6.82	7.10	8.76
	(growth, % pts.)	3.67	2.99	3.37	3.00	3.05	3.64
GNP Deflator	(level, %)	8.62	6.09	8.13	7.96	8.04	8.88
	(change, % pts.)	2.56	1.85	2.20	1.87	1.91	2.50
Short-Term Interest Rate	(level, % pts.)	4.21	7.12	5.34	4.82	4.40	3.83
	(change, % pts.)	2.56	4.18	2.20	3.54	3.02	1.99
Bilateral US $Exchange Rate	(level, %)	2.77	4.39	3.24	5.56	5.11	1.53
Current Account / GNP	(level, % pts.)	1.77	2.16	1.88	1.98	1.93	1.80
Loss: GNP + Inflation		8.31	7.01	7.51	5.13	5.41	8.13
Loss: GNP + Inflation + Change in Interest Rate		10.87	11.19	9.71	8.67	8.43	10.02
			Final Half-Period (Five Years)				
Real GNP	(level, %)	6.31	6.02	5.87	3.34	3.62	6.22
	(growth, % pts.)	3.56	3.39	3.49	2.70	2.77	3.55
Nominal GNP	(level, %)	11.61	4.51	9.47	8.88	9.27	11.36
	(growth, % pts.)	3.98	3.14	3.61	3.18	3.25	3.95
GNP Deflator	(level, %)	11.29	7.67	10.69	10.10	10.26	11.67
	(change, % pts.)	3.18	2.09	2.66	2.06	2.16	3.05
Short-Term Interest Rate	(level, % pts.)	5.24	8.58	6.85	5.17	4.80	4.91
	(change, % pts.)	2.52	4.43	2.37	3.53	3.03	1.87
Bilateral US $Exchange Rate	(level, %)	3.32	4.96	3.76	6.84	6.30	1.95
Current Account / GNP	(level, % pts.)	1.77	2.38	1.95	2.05	1.99	1.83
Loss: GNP + Inflation		9.49	8.11	8.53	5.40	5.78	9.27
Loss: GNP + Inflation + Change in Interest Rate		12.01	12.54	10.90	8.93	8.81	11.14

TABLE B-I-32

INTERMOD (CONSISTENT): CANADA

(Root Mean Squared Deviation from Baseline)

Measure		Money Targeting		Nominal GNP Targeting		Real GNP and Inflation Targeting		Exchange Rate Targeting	
		(1)	(1X)	(2A)	(2AX)	(2B)	(2BX)	(3)	(3X)
Full Period (Ten Years)									
Real GNP	(level, %)	3.58		3.42		2.34	2.37	3.48	
	(growth, % pts.)	3.31		3.02		2.62	2.73	3.17	
Nominal GNP	(level, %)	3.89		3.43		22.92	23.85	4.77	
	(growth, % pts.)	3.23		2.96		5.60	6.07	3.17	
GNP Deflator	(level, %)	5.04		4.88		24.56	25.04	5.92	
	(change, % pts.)	1.86		1.62		5.11	5.64	1.99	
Short-Term Interest Rate	(level, % pts.)	3.06		2.54		6.78	6.55	2.80	
	(change, % pts.)	2.45		1.92		5.12	4.48	1.97	
Bilateral US $Exchange Rate	(level, %)	3.27		2.89		15.78	17.43	1.12	
Current Account / GNP	(level, % pts.)	2.18		2.17		2.16	2.17	2.13	
Loss: GNP + Inflation		5.44		5.04		7.45	8.01	5.47	
Loss: GNP + Inflation + Change in Interest Rate		7.89		6.96		12.57	12.49	7.44	
Final Half-Period (Five Years)									
Real GNP	(level, %)	3.78		3.68		2.58	2.63	3.67	
	(growth, % pts.)	3.57		3.34		2.84	3.06	3.42	
Nominal GNP	(level, %)	4.70		4.05		31.17	32.48	5.77	
	(growth, % pts.)	3.47		3.19		6.79	7.45	3.33	
GNP Deflator	(level, %)	6.07		5.74		33.41	34.10	7.32	
	(change, % pts.)	2.11		1.82		6.32	7.05	2.21	
Short-Term Interest Rate	(level, % pts.)	3.47		3.05		8.03	7.90	3.32	
	(change, % pts.)	2.42		2.09		5.28	4.69	1.92	
Bilateral US $Exchange Rate	(level, %)	3.43		3.22		20.53	22.70	1.33	
Current Account / GNP	(level, % pts.)	2.25		2.19		2.19	2.27	2.14	
Loss: GNP + Inflation		5.89		5.50		8.90	9.68	5.88	
Loss: GNP + Inflation + Change in Interest Rate		8.31		7.59		14.18	14.37	7.80	

961

TABLE B-1-33

LIVERPOOL MODEL: CANADA

(Root Mean Squared Deviation from Baseline)

		Money Targeting (1)	(1X)	Nominal GNP Targeting (2A)	(2AX)	Real GNP and Inflation Targeting (2B)	(2BX)	Exchange Rate Targeting (3)	(3X)
Full Period (Ten Years)									
Real GNP	(level, %)	5.37	6.55	3.14	3.82	15.33	11.56	27.53	2.95
	(growth, % pts.)	4.79	6.38	1.75	3.87	13.81	6.92	32.61	3.14
Nominal GNP	(level, %)	75.17	63.80	1.94	32.48	96.77	70.33	310.16	8.77
	(growth, % pts.)	28.53	34.32	1.37	22.33	32.34	31.30	101.14	4.51
GNP Deflator	(level, %)	72.84	62.63	3.44	32.01	98.47	69.28	288.98	8.18
	(change, % pts.)	26.56	30.60	1.73	19.37	30.61	26.76	91.10	2.68
Short-Term Interest Rate	(level, % pts.)	30.39	26.24	2.78	29.13	29.29	35.92	20.36	3.63
	(change, % pts.)	30.11	37.58	1.93	50.44	16.32	46.19	23.21	3.80
Bilateral US $Exchange Rate	(level, %)	114.23	101.50	10.68	55.57	284.62	96.64	5.00	0.15
Current Account / GNP	(level, % pts.)	3.72	8.31	2.07	4.97	16.01	6.69	19.74	1.69
Loss: GNP + Inflation		31.93	37.16	4.86	23.19	45.94	38.32	118.63	5.63
Loss: GNP + Inflation + Change in Interest Rate		62.04	74.73	6.79	73.63	62.25	84.51	141.83	9.43
Final Half-Period (Five Years)									
Real GNP	(level, %)	6.41	5.82	4.02	3.48	16.50	10.53	30.23	3.74
	(growth, % pts.)	4.11	3.71	1.59	2.51	11.26	3.74	33.84	3.64
Nominal GNP	(level, %)	104.37	80.41	2.71	41.29	158.49	92.18	458.37	13.56
	(growth, % pts.)	22.67	26.71	1.48	15.48	41.35	23.06	97.93	5.33
GNP Deflator	(level, %)	97.93	76.49	4.72	39.53	152.57	87.18	415.81	12.19
	(change, % pts.)	21.39	24.59	1.97	13.93	36.10	21.47	93.69	3.20
Short-Term Interest Rate	(level, % pts.)	31.46	22.63	3.48	19.77	38.94	24.42	23.03	4.43
	(change, % pts.)	25.11	32.02	2.09	36.19	17.13	30.94	28.34	4.31
Bilateral US $Exchange Rate	(level, %)	124.42	103.31	13.82	56.37	388.46	104.98	5.91	0.20
Current Account / GNP	(level, % pts.)	4.39	5.45	2.21	3.42	17.03	4.39	14.95	1.96
Loss: GNP + Inflation		27.80	30.41	5.99	17.40	52.60	32.00	123.91	6.94
Loss: GNP + Inflation + Change in Interest Rate		52.92	62.43	8.08	53.59	69.73	62.94	152.25	11.25

TABLE B-I-34 MULTIMOD MODEL: CANADA

(Root Mean Squared Deviation from Baseline)

		Money Targeting		Nominal GNP Targeting		Real GNP and Inflation Targeting		Exchange Rate Targeting	
		(1)	(1X)	(2A)	(2AX)	(2B)	(2BX)	(3)	(3X)
Full Period (Ten Years)									
Real GNP	(level, %)	3.81	3.73		3.71		4.69		4.24
	(growth, % pts.)	2.40	2.48		2.37		2.74		2.55
Nominal GNP	(level, %)	5.45	4.85		4.72		3.05		9.95
	(growth, % pts.)	2.85	2.84		2.79		2.28		3.64
GNP Deflator	(level, %)	7.92	7.00		7.03		5.27		10.41
	(change, % pts.)	2.99	2.69		2.76		2.04		4.22
Short-Term Interest Rate	(level, % pts.)	3.44	2.61		2.31		7.28		2.48
	(change, % pts.)	2.97	1.22		1.30		7.50		1.66
Bilateral US $Exchange Rate	(level, %)	8.25	7.87		7.16		11.35		1.97
Current Account / GNP	(level, % pts.)	2.58	2.67		2.59		3.37		3.00
Loss: GNP + Inflation		6.80	6.42		6.46		6.73		8.46
Loss: GNP + Inflation + Change in Interest Rate		9.77	7.64		7.77		14.23		10.12
Final Half-Period (Five Years)									
Real GNP	(level, %)	4.73	4.56		4.55		5.31		5.17
	(growth, % pts.)	2.61	2.73		2.58		2.89		2.78
Nominal GNP	(level, %)	6.72	5.82		5.50		3.84		12.80
	(growth, % pts.)	3.01	3.00		3.00		2.35		4.02
GNP Deflator	(level, %)	9.97	8.67		8.61		6.59		13.57
	(change, % pts.)	3.11	2.73		2.80		2.14		5.04
Short-Term Interest Rate	(level, % pts.)	3.72	3.02		2.71		7.40		2.70
	(change, % pts.)	3.06	1.39		1.40		7.80		1.70
Bilateral US $Exchange Rate	(level, %)	9.70	9.31		8.56		14.13		2.15
Current Account / GNP	(level, % pts.)	3.04	3.17		3.12		4.02		3.58
Loss: GNP + Inflation		7.84	7.29		7.35		7.45		10.21
Loss: GNP + Inflation + Change in Interest Rate		10.90	8.68		8.75		15.25		11.91

TABLE B-I-35

TAYLOR MODEL: CANADA

		Money Targeting (1)	Nominal GNP Targeting (2A)	(Root Mean Squared Deviation from Baseline) Real GNP and Inflation Targeting (2B)	Exchange Rate Targeting (3)
		(1X)	(2AX)	(2BX)	(3X)
			Full Period (Ten Years)		
Real GNP	(level, %)	9.36	5.19	3.10	7.81
	(growth, % pts.)	2.58	1.93	1.91	2.95
Nominal GNP	(level, %)	13.03	8.99	6.92	10.97
	(growth, % pts.)	2.52	1.91	1.90	2.95
GNP Deflator	(level, %)	5.26	5.65	5.47	5.54
	(change, % pts.)	0.87	0.96	0.86	0.87
Short-Term Interest Rate	(level, % pts.)	0.02	0.05	0.05	0.06
	(change, % pts.)	n.a.	n.a.	n.a.	n.a.
Bilateral US $Exchange Rate	(level, %)	8.29	12.13	12.66	7.34
Current Account / GNP	(level, % pts.)	2.70	2.25	1.68	2.73
Loss: GNP + Inflation		10.23	6.15	3.96	8.68
Loss: GNP + Inflation + Change in Interest Rate		n.a.	n.a.	n.a.	n.a.
			Final Half-Period (Five Years)		
Real GNP	(level, %)	11.19	5.95	2.71	2.01
	(growth, % pts.)	2.55	1.98	1.89	3.18
Nominal GNP	(level, %)	16.34	11.24	8.72	13.31
	(growth, % pts.)	2.48	1.95	1.87	3.15
GNP Deflator	(level, %)	6.19	6.47	6.18	6.54
	(change, % pts.)	0.96	1.04	0.96	0.94
Short-Term Interest Rate	(level, % pts.)	0.02	0.05	0.06	0.07
	(change, % pts.)	n.a.	n.a.	n.a.	n.a.
Bilateral US $Exchange Rate	(level, %)	8.62	13.12	14.61	8.03
Current Account / GNP	(level, % pts.)	2.71	2.32	1.67	2.96
Loss: GNP + Inflation		12.15	6.99	3.66	2.95
Loss: GNP + Inflation + Change in Interest Rate		n.a.	n.a.	n.a.	n.a.

TABLE B-II-1   INTERMOD (ADAPTIVE) MODEL

Summary of Losses Across Regimes and Countries
(Root Mean Squared Deviation from Baseline: Ten-Year Period)

	U.S.	Japan	Germany	U.K.	Canada
Orig. Money Targeting (1):					
Loss: Real GNP alone	4.38	7.02	4.84	5.93	5.75
Loss: Inflation alone	2.04	4.27	2.14	3.13	2.56
Loss: Real GNP + Inflation	6.42	11.29	6.98	9.06	8.31
Loss: Real GNP + Inflation + Chg. Int. Rate	8.34	14.90	10.75	13.53	10.87
Alt. Money Targeting (1X):					
Loss: Real GNP alone					
Loss: Inflation alone					
Loss: Real GNP + Inflation					
Loss: Real GNP + Inflation + Chg. Int. Rate					
Orig. Simple Nominal GNP Targeting (2A):					
Loss: Real GNP alone	4.09	7.61	4.29	4.67	5.16
Loss: Inflation alone	1.36	3.17	1.51	1.93	1.85
Loss: Real GNP + Inflation	5.45	10.78	5.80	6.60	7.01
Loss: Real GNP + Inflation + Chg. Int. Rate	8.67	17.30	12.36	13.17	11.19
Alt. Simple Nominal GNP Targeting (2AX):					
Loss: Real GNP alone	4.21	7.50	4.77	5.37	5.31
Loss: Inflation alone	1.83	3.81	1.83	2.56	2.20
Loss: Real GNP + Inflation	6.04	11.31	6.60	7.93	7.51
Loss: Real GNP + Inflation + Chg. Int. Rate	7.69	14.90	9.23	11.74	9.71
Orig. Real GNP plus Inflation Targeting (2B):					
Loss: Real GNP alone	2.71	3.84	3.26	3.39	3.26
Loss: Inflation alone	1.41	3.84	1.17	2.03	1.87
Loss: Real GNP + Inflation	4.12	7.68	4.43	5.42	5.13
Loss: Real GNP + Inflation + Chg. Int. Rate	7.49	14.00	9.22	10.82	8.67
Alt. Real GNP and Inflation Targeting (2BX):					
Loss: Real GNP alone	2.93	3.97	3.49	3.67	3.50
Loss: Inflation alone	1.51	3.97	1.26	2.17	1.91
Loss: Real GNP + Inflation	4.44	7.94	4.75	5.84	5.41
Loss: Real GNP + Inflation + Chg. Int. Rate	7.22	13.32	8.67	10.58	8.43
Orig. Exchange Rate Targeting (3):					
Loss: Real GNP alone	4.35	5.18	5.38	6.33	5.63
Loss: Inflation alone	1.98	4.99	2.18	3.42	2.50
Loss: Real GNP + Inflation	6.33	10.17	7.56	9.75	8.13
Loss: Real GNP + Inflation + Chg. Int. Rate	8.42	12.00	9.59	11.85	10.02
Alt. Exchange Rate Targeting (3X):					
Loss: Real GNP alone					
Loss: Inflation alone					
Loss: Real GNP + Inflation					
Loss: Real GNP + Inflation + Chg. Int. Rate					

Source: B-I tables.

965

Summary of Losses Across Regimes and Countries
(Root Mean Squared Deviation from Baseline: Ten-Year Period)

	U.S.	Japan	Germany	U.K.	Canada
Orig. Money Targeting (1):					
Loss: Real GNP alone	3.03	5.38	4.00	3.88	3.58
Loss: Inflation alone	1.42	2.93	1.26	2.17	1.86
Loss: Real GNP + Inflation	4.45	8.31	5.26	6.05	5.40
Loss: Real GNP + Inflation + Chg. Int. Rate	6.53	11.58	9.34	10.58	7.89
Alt. Money Targeting (1X):					
Loss: Real GNP alone					
Loss: Inflation alone					
Loss: Real GNP + Inflation					
Loss: Real GNP + Inflation + Chg. Int. Rate					
Orig. Simple Nominal GNP Targeting (2A):					
Loss: Real GNP alone					
Loss: Inflation alone					
Loss: Real GNP + Inflation					
Loss: Real GNP + Inflation + Chg. Int. Rate					
Alt. Simple Nominal GNP Targeting (2AX):					
Loss: Real GNP alone	2.82	5.61	3.74	3.50	3.42
Loss: Inflation alone	1.19	2.69	1.21	1.83	1.62
Loss: Real GNP + Inflation	4.01	8.30	4.95	5.33	5.04
Loss: Real GNP + Inflation + Chg. Int. Rate	5.43	10.92	7.76	8.59	6.96
Orig. Real GNP plus Inflation Targeting (2B):					
Loss: Real GNP alone	2.31	2.94	3.17	2.92	2.34
Loss: Inflation alone	2.02	5.50	2.57	6.30	5.11
Loss: Real GNP + Inflation	4.33	8.44	5.74	9.22	7.45
Loss: Real GNP + Inflation + Chg. Int. Rate	8.03	15.45	11.59	16.63	12.57
Alt. Real GNP and Inflation Targeting (2BX):					
Loss: Real GNP alone	2.46	2.99	3.26	3.25	2.37
Loss: Inflation alone	2.23	5.92	2.44	6.73	5.64
Loss: Real GNP + Inflation	4.69	8.91	5.70	9.98	8.01
Loss: Real GNP + Inflation + Chg. Int. Rate	7.86	14.90	10.79	16.86	12.49
Orig. Exchange Rate Targeting (3):					
Loss: Real GNP alone	2.88	5.15	3.79	4.12	3.48
Loss: Inflation alone	1.41	4.17	1.32	2.66	1.99
Loss: Real GNP + Inflation	4.29	9.32	5.11	6.78	5.47
Loss: Real GNP + Inflation + Chg. Int. Rate	6.34	11.11	7.18	8.93	7.44
Alt. Exchange Rate Targeting (3X):					
Loss: Real GNP alone					
Loss: Inflation alone					
Loss: Real GNP + Inflation					
Loss: Real GNP + Inflation + Chg. Int. Rate					

Source: B-I tables.

TABLE B-II-3   LIVERPOOL MODEL

Summary of Losses Across Regimes and Countries
(Root Mean Squared Deviation from Baseline: Ten-Year Period)

	U.S.	Japan	Germany	U.K.	Canada
Orig. Money Targeting (1):					
Loss: Real GNP alone	10.36	11.97	6.50	3.40	5.37
Loss: Inflation alone	13.79	5.36	4.68	4.40	26.56
Loss: Real GNP + Inflation	24.15	17.33	11.18	7.80	31.93
Loss: Real GNP + Inflation + Chg. Int. Rate	29.47	24.75	18.11	12.84	62.04
Alt. Money Targeting (1X):					
Loss: Real GNP alone	8.04	10.81	5.12	2.41	6.55
Loss: Inflation alone	8.49	4.20	4.03	3.70	30.60
Loss: Real GNP + Inflation	16.53	15.01	9.16	6.11	37.16
Loss: Real GNP + Inflation + Chg. Int. Rate	22.50	24.20	15.40	13.16	74.73
Orig. Simple Nominal GNP Targeting (2A):					
Loss: Real GNP alone	6.69	8.60	5.76	2.20	3.14
Loss: Inflation alone	8.09	6.54	5.24	1.72	1.73
Loss: Real GNP + Inflation	14.78	15.13	10.99	3.92	4.86
Loss: Real GNP + Inflation + Chg. Int. Rate	20.60	20.85	16.34	5.52	6.79
Alt. Simple Nominal GNP Targeting (2AX):					
Loss: Real GNP alone	5.60	9.06	4.70	1.78	3.82
Loss: Inflation alone	6.43	6.35	5.25	4.19	19.37
Loss: Real GNP + Inflation	12.03	15.40	9.95	5.97	23.19
Loss: Real GNP + Inflation + Chg. Int. Rate	21.80	29.02	21.52	20.65	73.63
Orig. Real GNP plus Inflation Targeting (2B):					
Loss: Real GNP alone	24.39	44.96	81.20	8.79	15.33
Loss: Inflation alone	70.37	75.56	203.73	15.24	30.61
Loss: Real GNP + Inflation	94.75	120.52	284.92	24.02	45.94
Loss: Real GNP + Inflation + Chg. Int. Rate	136.28	166.39	350.15	34.22	62.25
Alt. Real GNP and Inflation Targeting (2BX):					
Loss: Real GNP alone	19.04	21.22	31.65	4.93	11.56
Loss: Inflation alone	11.46	30.77	36.27	71.99	26.76
Loss: Real GNP + Inflation	30.50	51.99	67.91	76.92	38.32
Loss: Real GNP + Inflation + Chg. Int. Rate	40.26	63.18	77.40	107.86	84.51
Orig. Exchange Rate Targeting (3):					
Loss: Real GNP alone	102.88	144.46	102.07	41.77	27.53
Loss: Inflation alone	124.83	105.47	140.39	93.29	91.10
Loss: Real GNP + Inflation	227.71	249.94	242.45	135.06	118.63
Loss: Real GNP + Inflation + Chg. Int. Rate	255.51	275.26	275.49	156.32	141.83
Alt. Exchange Rate Targeting (3X):					
Loss: Real GNP alone	5.07	15.60	6.04	2.71	2.95
Loss: Inflation alone	3.12	4.46	4.95	2.37	2.68
Loss: Real GNP + Inflation	8.19	20.05	10.98	5.09	5.63
Loss: Real GNP + Inflation + Chg. Int. Rate	12.16	23.67	15.15	8.89	9.43

Source: B-I tables.

967

TABLE B-II-4   MPS MODEL

Summary of Losses Across Regimes and Countries
(Root Mean Squared Deviation from Baseline: Ten-Year Period)

	U.S.	Japan	Germany	U.K.	Canada
Orig. Money Targeting (1):					
Loss: Real GNP alone					
Loss: Inflation alone					
Loss: Real GNP + Inflation					
Loss: Real GNP + Inflation + Chg. Int. Rate					
Alt. Money Targeting (1X):					
Loss: Real GNP alone	3.30				
Loss: Inflation alone	2.50				
Loss: Real GNP + Inflation	5.80				
Loss: Real GNP + Inflation + Chg. Int. Rate	6.79				
Orig. Simple Nominal GNP Targeting (2A):					
Loss: Real GNP alone	2.39				
Loss: Inflation alone	1.92				
Loss: Real GNP + Inflation	4.31				
Loss: Real GNP + Inflation + Chg. Int. Rate	5.55				
Alt. Simple Nominal GNP Targeting (2AX):					
Loss: Real GNP alone	2.24				
Loss: Inflation alone	1.87				
Loss: Real GNP + Inflation	4.11				
Loss: Real GNP + Inflation + Chg. Int. Rate	5.69				
Orig. Real GNP plus Inflation Targeting (2B):					
Loss: Real GNP alone					
Loss: Inflation alone					
Loss: Real GNP + Inflation					
Loss: Real GNP + Inflation + Chg. Int. Rate					
Alt. Real GNP and Inflation Targeting (2BX):					
Loss: Real GNP alone	1.64				
Loss: Inflation alone	2.00				
Loss: Real GNP + Inflation	3.64				
Loss: Real GNP + Inflation + Chg. Int. Rate	5.38				
Orig. Exchange Rate Targeting (3):					
Loss: Real GNP alone					
Loss: Inflation alone					
Loss: Real GNP + Inflation					
Loss: Real GNP + Inflation + Chg. Int. Rate					
Alt. Exchange Rate Targeting (3X):					
Loss: Real GNP alone					
Loss: Inflation alone					
Loss: Real GNP + Inflation					
Loss: Real GNP + Inflation + Chg. Int. Rate					

Source: B-I tables.

TABLE B-II-5   MSG MODEL

Summary of Losses Across Regimes and Countries
(Root Mean Squared Deviation from Baseline: Ten-Year Period)

	U.S.	Japan	Germany	U.K.	Canada
Orig. Money Targeting (1):					
Loss: Real GNP alone	8.31	37.10	16.16		
Loss: Inflation alone	4.77	3.08	2.15		
Loss: Real GNP + Inflation	13.08	40.18	18.31		
Loss: Real GNP + Inflation + Chg. Int. Rate	15.22	57.85	24.69		
Alt. Money Targeting (1X):					
Loss: Real GNP alone	8.15	34.10	14.68		
Loss: Inflation alone	4.61	2.52	2.15		
Loss: Real GNP + Inflation	12.76	36.61	16.83		
Loss: Real GNP + Inflation + Chg. Int. Rate	15.21	57.83	24.51		
Orig. Simple Nominal GNP Targeting (2A):					
Loss: Real GNP alone	10.70	34.19	11.28		
Loss: Inflation alone	6.89	2.86	1.57		
Loss: Real GNP + Inflation	17.59	37.05	12.85		
Loss: Real GNP + Inflation + Chg. Int. Rate	20.33	56.36	19.88		
Alt. Simple Nominal GNP Targeting (2AX):					
Loss: Real GNP alone	7.16	5.36	13.34		
Loss: Inflation alone	3.89	3.34	5.07		
Loss: Real GNP + Inflation	11.05	8.70	18.40		
Loss: Real GNP + Inflation + Chg. Int. Rate	15.86	61.92	40.79		
Orig. Real GNP plus Inflation Targeting (2B):					
Loss: Real GNP alone	7.72	36.96	15.98		
Loss: Inflation alone	12.27	3.72	4.54		
Loss: Real GNP + Inflation	19.99	40.69	20.53		
Loss: Real GNP + Inflation + Chg. Int. Rate	24.14	60.61	27.59		
Alt. Real GNP and Inflation Targeting (2BX):					
Loss: Real GNP alone	4.37	7.93	2.76		
Loss: Inflation alone	4.98	6.27	2.78		
Loss: Real GNP + Inflation	9.34	14.20	5.54		
Loss: Real GNP + Inflation + Chg. Int. Rate	14.44	61.50	24.11		
Orig. Exchange Rate Targeting (3):					
Loss: Real GNP alone	13.55	56.96	23.32		
Loss: Inflation alone	9.61	5.47	7.47		
Loss: Real GNP + Inflation	23.16	62.43	30.79		
Loss: Real GNP + Inflation + Chg. Int. Rate	27.11	66.86	35.22		
Alt. Exchange Rate Targeting (3X):					
Loss: Real GNP alone	8.28	53.15	24.49		
Loss: Inflation alone	4.99	6.58	4.73		
Loss: Real GNP + Inflation	13.27	59.73	29.22		
Loss: Real GNP + Inflation + Chg. Int. Rate	15.92	62.37	31.86		

Source: B-I tables.

969

TABLE B-II-6   MULTIMOD MODEL

Summary of Losses Across Regimes and Countries
(Root Mean Squared Deviation from Baseline: Ten-Year Period)

	U.S.	Japan	Germany	U.K.	Canada
Orig. Money Targeting (1):					
Loss: Real GNP alone	3.93	3.32	3.37	5.33	3.81
Loss: Inflation alone	1.97	3.11	1.59	3.95	2.99
Loss: Real GNP + Inflation	5.90	6.44	4.95	9.29	6.80
Loss: Real GNP + Inflation + Chg. Int. Rate	9.60	11.43	9.43	19.04	9.77
Alt. Money Targeting (1X):					
Loss: Real GNP alone	3.69	3.76	3.57	5.29	3.73
Loss: Inflation alone	1.81	2.92	1.60	3.64	2.69
Loss: Real GNP + Inflation	5.51	6.68	5.17	8.93	6.42
Loss: Real GNP + Inflation + Chg. Int. Rate	6.93	8.48	6.90	11.82	7.64
Orig. Simple Nominal GNP Targeting (2A):					
Loss: Real GNP alone					
Loss: Inflation alone					
Loss: Real GNP + Inflation					
Loss: Real GNP + Inflation + Chg. Int. Rate					
Alt. Simple Nominal GNP Targeting (2AX):					
Loss: Real GNP alone	3.55	4.01	2.89	5.37	3.71
Loss: Inflation alone	2.15	3.03	1.47	3.74	2.76
Loss: Real GNP + Inflation	5.70	7.04	4.36	9.10	6.47
Loss: Real GNP + Inflation + Chg. Int. Rate	6.90	8.86	5.71	10.86	7.77
Orig. Real GNP plus Inflation Targeting (2B):					
Loss: Real GNP alone					
Loss: Inflation alone					
Loss: Real GNP + Inflation					
Loss: Real GNP + Inflation + Chg. Int. Rate					
Alt. Real GNP and Inflation Targeting (2BX):					
Loss: Real GNP alone	3.10	4.35	3.31	6.97	4.69
Loss: Inflation alone	1.23	2.93	1.19	3.11	2.04
Loss: Real GNP + Inflation	4.32	7.28	4.50	10.08	6.73
Loss: Real GNP + Inflation + Chg. Int. Rate	11.56	20.09	9.77	17.46	14.23
Orig. Exchange Rate Targeting (3):					
Loss: Real GNP alone					
Loss: Inflation alone					
Loss: Real GNP + Inflation					
Loss: Real GNP + Inflation + Chg. Int. Rate					
Alt. Exchange Rate Targeting (3X):					
Loss: Real GNP alone	3.54	5.14	3.90	4.56	4.24
Loss: Inflation alone	1.79	4.24	1.93	3.90	4.22
Loss: Real GNP + Inflation	5.33	9.37	5.83	8.47	8.46
Loss: Real GNP + Inflation + Chg. Int. Rate	6.80	11.34	7.37	10.62	10.12

Source: B-I tables.

970

TABLE B-II-7   MX3 MODEL

Summary of Losses Across Regimes and Countries
(Root Mean Squared Deviation from Baseline: Ten-Year Period)

	U.S.	Japan	Germany	U.K.	Canada
Orig. Money Targeting (1):					
Loss: Real GNP alone	7.96	2.99	3.35		
Loss: Inflation alone	1.22	1.54	1.54		
Loss: Real GNP + Inflation	9.18	4.53	4.90		
Loss: Real GNP + Inflation + Chg. Int. Rate	10.71	7.27	10.06		
Alt. Money Targeting (1X):					
Loss: Real GNP alone					
Loss: Inflation alone					
Loss: Real GNP + Inflation					
Loss: Real GNP + Inflation + Chg. Int. Rate					
Orig. Simple Nominal GNP Targeting (2A):					
Loss: Real GNP alone	8.10	2.30	2.95		
Loss: Inflation alone	1.17	1.40	1.34		
Loss: Real GNP + Inflation	9.27	3.70	4.29		
Loss: Real GNP + Inflation + Chg. Int. Rate	12.00	9.12	8.50		
Alt. Simple Nominal GNP Targeting (2AX):					
Loss: Real GNP alone	8.30	2.16	3.29		
Loss: Inflation alone	1.15	1.34	1.30		
Loss: Real GNP + Inflation	9.45	3.50	4.59		
Loss: Real GNP + Inflation + Chg. Int. Rate	14.23	12.89	11.71		
Orig. Real GNP plus Inflation Targeting (2B):					
Loss: Real GNP alone	1.99	2.07	1.95		
Loss: Inflation alone	1.77	1.65	1.77		
Loss: Real GNP + Inflation	3.76	3.72	3.72		
Loss: Real GNP + Inflation + Chg. Int. Rate	9.00	18.49	15.14		
Alt. Real GNP and Inflation Targeting (2BX):					
Loss: Real GNP alone					
Loss: Inflation alone					
Loss: Real GNP + Inflation					
Loss: Real GNP + Inflation + Chg. Int. Rate					
Orig. Exchange Rate Targeting (3):					
Loss: Real GNP alone					
Loss: Inflation alone					
Loss: Real GNP + Inflation					
Loss: Real GNP + Inflation + Chg. Int. Rate					
Alt. Exchange Rate Targeting (3X):					
Loss: Real GNP alone					
Loss: Inflation alone					
Loss: Real GNP + Inflation					
Loss: Real GNP + Inflation + Chg. Int. Rate					

Source: B-I tables.

Summary of Losses Across Regimes and Countries
(Root Mean Squared Deviation from Baseline: Ten-Year Period)

	U.S.	Japan	Germany	U.K.	Canada
Orig. Money Targeting (1):					
Loss: Real GNP alone					
Loss: Inflation alone					
Loss: Real GNP + Inflation					
Loss: Real GNP + Inflation + Chg. Int. Rate					
Alt. Money Targeting (1X):					
Loss: Real GNP alone	5.15	5.44	3.79	3.94	9.36
Loss: Inflation alone	1.14	1.42	1.96	2.78	0.87
Loss: Real GNP + Inflation	6.29	6.86	5.75	6.72	10.23
Loss: Real GNP + Inflation + Chg. Int. Rate	N.A.	N.A.	N.A.	N.A.	N.A.
Orig. Simple Nominal GNP Targeting (2A):					
Loss: Real GNP alone					
Loss: Inflation alone					
Loss: Real GNP + Inflation					
Loss: Real GNP + Inflation + Chg. Int. Rate					
Alt. Simple Nominal GNP Targeting (2AX):					
Loss: Real GNP alone	1.95	2.91	1.73	2.44	5.19
Loss: Inflation alone	1.32	1.45	2.37	2.73	0.96
Loss: Real GNP + Inflation	3.27	4.36	4.10	5.17	6.15
Loss: Real GNP + Inflation + Chg. Int. Rate	N.A.	N.A.	N.A.	N.A.	N.A.
Orig. Real GNP plus Inflation Targeting (2B):					
Loss: Real GNP alone					
Loss: Inflation alone					
Loss: Real GNP + Inflation					
Loss: Real GNP + Inflation + Chg. Int. Rate					
Alt. Real GNP and Inflation Targeting (2BX):					
Loss: Real GNP alone	2.59	2.43	1.83	2.82	3.10
Loss: Inflation alone	1.13	1.41	1.98	2.72	0.86
Loss: Real GNP + Inflation	3.72	3.84	3.81	5.54	3.96
Loss: Real GNP + Inflation + Chg. Int. Rate	N.A.	N.A.	N.A.	N.A.	N.A.
Orig. Exchange Rate Targeting (3):					
Loss: Real GNP alone					
Loss: Inflation alone					
Loss: Real GNP + Inflation					
Loss: Real GNP + Inflation + Chg. Int. Rate					
Alt. Exchange Rate Targeting (3X):					
Loss: Real GNP alone	2.24	7.68	6.41	3.10	7.81
Loss: Inflation alone	1.27	1.37	2.33	2.67	0.87
Loss: Real GNP + Inflation	3.51	9.05	8.74	5.77	8.68
Loss: Real GNP + Inflation + Chg. Int. Rate	N.A.	N.A.	N.A.	N.A.	N.A.

Source: B-I tables.

TABLE B-II-9   GEM MODEL

Summary of Losses Across Regimes and Countries
(Root Mean Squared Deviation from Baseline: Ten-Year Period)

	U.S.	Japan	Germany	U.K.	Canada
Orig. Money Targeting (1):					
Loss: Real GNP alone					
Loss: Inflation alone					
Loss: Real GNP + Inflation					
Loss: Real GNP + Inflation + Chg. Int. Rate					
Alt. Money Targeting (1X):					
Loss: Real GNP alone	1.61	3.12	2.78		
Loss: Inflation alone	1.47	1.90	1.30		
Loss: Real GNP + Inflation	3.08	5.02	4.08		
Loss: Real GNP + Inflation + Chg. Int. Rate	3.29	5.41	4.23		
Orig. Simple Nominal GNP Targeting (2A):					
Loss: Real GNP alone					
Loss: Inflation alone					
Loss: Real GNP + Inflation					
Loss: Real GNP + Inflation + Chg. Int. Rate					
Alt. Simple Nominal GNP Targeting (2AX):					
Loss: Real GNP alone	1.21	2.29	2.60		
Loss: Inflation alone	1.40	1.81	1.24		
Loss: Real GNP + Inflation	2.61	4.10	3.84		
Loss: Real GNP + Inflation + Chg. Int. Rate	2.85	4.54	4.30		
Orig. Real GNP plus Inflation Targeting (2B):					
Loss: Real GNP alone					
Loss: Inflation alone					
Loss: Real GNP + Inflation					
Loss: Real GNP + Inflation + Chg. Int. Rate					
Alt. Real GNP and Inflation Targeting (2BX):					
Loss: Real GNP alone	1.12	1.89	2.48		
Loss: Inflation alone	1.37	1.95	1.65		
Loss: Real GNP + Inflation	2.49	3.84	4.13		
Loss: Real GNP + Inflation + Chg. Int. Rate	2.83	4.35	4.68		
Orig. Exchange Rate Targeting (3):					
Loss: Real GNP alone					
Loss: Inflation alone					
Loss: Real GNP + Inflation					
Loss: Real GNP + Inflation + Chg. Int. Rate					
Alt. Exchange Rate Targeting (3X):					
Loss: Real GNP alone					
Loss: Inflation alone					
Loss: Real GNP + Inflation					
Loss: Real GNP + Inflation + Chg. Int. Rate					

Source: B-I tables.

973

TABLE B-III-1

UNITED STATES: LOSSES INDEXED ACROSS RULES
Money Targeting = 1.00

	Money Targeting		Nominal GNP Targeting		Real GNP and Inflation Targeting		Exchange Rate Targeting	
	(1)	(1X)	(2A)	(2AX)	(2B)	(2BX)	(3)	(3X)
Real GNP alone:								
INTERMOD-Adaptive	1.00	na	0.93	0.98	0.62	0.67	0.99	na
INTERMOD-Consistent	1.00	na	na	0.93	0.76	0.81	0.95	na
LIVERPOOL	1.00	0.78	0.65	0.54	2.35	1.84	9.93	0.49
MPS	na	1.00	0.72	0.68	na	0.50	na	na
GEM	na	1.00	na	0.75	na	0.70	na	na
MSG	1.00	0.98	1.29	0.86	0.93	0.53	1.63	1.00
MULTIMOD	1.00	0.94	na	0.90	na	0.79	na	0.90
MX3	1.00	na	1.02	1.04	0.25	na	na	na
TAYLOR	na	1.00	na	0.38	na	0.50	na	0.43
Inflation alone:								
INTERMOD-Adaptive	1.00	na	0.67	0.90	0.69	0.74	0.97	na
INTERMOD-Consistent	1.00	na	na	0.84	1.42	1.57	0.99	na
LIVERPOOL	1.00	0.62	0.59	0.47	5.10	0.83	9.05	0.23
MPS	na	1.00	0.77	0.75	na	0.80	na	na
GEM	na	1.00	na	0.95	na	0.93	na	na
MSG	1.00	0.97	1.44	0.82	2.57	1.04	2.01	1.05
MULTIMOD	1.00	0.92	na	1.09	na	0.62	na	0.91
MX3	1.0o	na	0.96	0.94	1.45	na	na	na
TAYLOR	na	1.00	na	1.16	na	0.99	na	1.11
Real GNP + Inflation:								
INTERMOD-Adaptive	1.00	na	0.85	0.94	0.64	0.69	0.99	na
INTERMOD-Consistent	1.00	na	na	0.90	0.97	1.05	0.96	na
LIVERPOOL	1.00	0.68	0.61	0.50	3.92	1.26	9.43	0.34
MPS	na	1.00	0.74	0.71	na	0.63	na	na
GEM	na	1.00	na	0.85	na	0.81	na	na
MSG	1.00	0.98	1.34	0.85	1.53	0.71	1.77	1.01
MULTIMOD	1.00	0.93	na	0.97	na	0.73	na	0.90
MX3	1.00	na	1.01	1.03	0.41	na	na	na
TAYLOR	na	1.00	na	0.50	na	0.58	na	0.60
Real GNP + Inflation + Change in Interest Rates:								
INTERMOD-Adaptive	1.00	na	1.04	0.92	0.90	0.87	1.01	na
INTERMOD-Consistent	1.00	na	na	0.83	1.23	1.20	0.97	na
LIVERPOOL	1.00	0.76	0.70	0.74	4.62	1.37	8.67	0.41
MPS	na	1.00	0.82	0.84	na	0.79	na	na
GEM	na	1.00	na	0.87	na	0.86	na	na
MSG	1.00	1.00	1.34	1.04	1.59	0.95	1.78	1.05
MULTIMOD	1.00	0.72	na	0.72	na	1.20	na	0.71
MX3	1.00	na	1.12	1.33	0.84	na	na	na
TAYLOR	na	na	na	na	na	na	na	na

Source: Calculated from B-I tables.

TABLE B-III-2

JAPAN : LOSSES INDEXED ACROSS RULES
Money Targeting = 1.00

	Money Targeting		Nominal GNP Targeting		Real GNP and Inflation Targeting		Exchange Rate Targeting	
	(1)	(1X)	(2A)	(2AX)	(2B)	(2BX)	(3)	(3X)
Real GNP alone:								
INTERMOD-Adaptive	1.00	na	1.08	1.07	0.55	0.57	0.74	na
INTERMOD-Consistent	1.00	na	na	1.04	0.55	0.56	0.96	na
LIVERPOOL	1.00	0.90	0.72	0.76	3.75	1.77	12.06	1.30
MPS	na	na	na	na	na	na	na	na
GEM	na	1.00	na	0.73	na	0.61	na	na
MSG	1.00	0.92	0.92	0.14	1.00	0.21	1.54	1.43
MULTIMOD	1.00	1.13	na	1.21	na	1.31	na	1.55
MX3	1.00	na	0.77	0.72	0.69	na	na	na
TAYLOR	na	1.00	na	0.53	na	0.45	na	1.41
Inflation alone:								
INTERMOD-Adaptive	1.00	na	0.74	0.89	0.90	0.93	1.17	na
INTERMOD-Consistent	1.00	na	na	0.92	1.88	2.02	1.42	na
LIVERPOOL	1.00	0.78	1.22	1.18	14.10	5.74	19.68	0.83
MPS	na	na	na	na	na	na	na	na
GEM	na	1.00	na	0.95	na	1.03	na	na
MSG	1.00	0.82	0.93	1.08	1.21	2.04	1.78	2.14
MULTIMOD	1.00	0.94	na	0.97	na	0.94	na	1.36
MX3	1.00	na	0.91	0.87	1.07	na	na	na
TAYLOR	na	1.00	na	1.02	na	0.99	na	0.96
Real GNP + Inflation:								
INTERMOD-Adaptive	1.00	na	0.95	1.00	0.68	0.70	0.90	na
INTERMOD-Consistent	1.00	na	na	1.00	1.02	1.07	1.12	na
LIVERPOOL	1.00	0.87	0.87	0.89	6.95	3.00	14.42	1.16
MPS	na	na	na	na	na	na	na	na
GEM	na	1.00	na	0.82	na	0.76	na	na
MSG	1.00	0.91	0.92	0.22	1.01	0.35	1.55	1.49
MULTIMOD	1.00	1.04	na	1.09	na	1.13	na	1.46
MX3	1.00	na	0.82	0.77	0.82	na	na	na
TAYLOR	na	1.00	na	0.64	na	0.56	na	1.32
Real GNP + Inflation + Change in Interest Rates:								
INTERMOD-Adaptive	1.00	na	1.16	1.00	0.94	0.89	0.81	na
INTERMOD-Consistent	1.00	na	na	0.94	1.33	1.29	0.96	na
LIVERPOOL	1.00	0.98	0.84	1.17	6.72	2.55	11.12	0.96
MPS	na	na	na	na	na	na	na	na
GEM	na	1.00	na	0.84	na	0.80	na	na
MSG	1.00	1.00	0.97	1.07	1.05	1.06	1.16	1.08
MULTIMOD	1.00	0.74	na	0.78	na	1.76	na	0.99
MX3	1.00	na	1.25	1.77	2.54	na	na	na
TAYLOR	na	na	na	na	na	na	na	na

Source: Calculated from B-I tables.

GERMANY : LOSSES INDEXED ACROSS RULES
Money Targeting = 1.00

	Money Targeting		Nominal GNP Targeting		Real GNP and Inflation Targeting		Exchange Rate Targeting	
	(1)	(1X)	(2A)	(2AX)	(2B)	(2BX)	(3)	(3X)
Real GNP alone:								
INTERMOD-Adaptive	1.00	na	0.89	0.99	0.67	0.72	1.11	na
INTERMOD-Consistent	1.00	na	na	0.94	0.79	0.82	0.95	na
LIVERPOOL	1.00	0.79	0.89	0.72	12.50	4.87	15.71	0.93
MPS	na	na	na	na	na	na	na	na
GEM	na	1.00	na	0.94	na	0.89	na	na
MSG	1.00	0.91	0.70	0.83	0.98	0.17	1.44	1.52
MULTIMOD	1.00	1.06	na	0.86	na	0.98	na	1.16
MX3	1.00	na	0.88	0.98	0.58	na	na	na
TAYLOR	na	1.00	na	0.46	na	0.48	na	1.69
Inflation alone:								
INTERMOD-Adaptive	1.00	na	0.71	0.86	0.55	0.59	1.02	na
INTERMOD-Consistent	1.00	na	na	0.96	2.04	1.94	1.05	na
LIVERPOOL	1.00	0.86	1.12	1.12	43.53	7.75	30.00	1.06
MPS	na	na	na	na	na	na	na	na
GEM	na	1.00	na	0.95	na	1.27	na	na
MSG	1.00	1.00	0.73	2.36	2.11	1.29	3.47	2.20
MULTIMOD	1.00	1.01	na	0.92	na	0.75	na	1.21
MX3	1.00	na	0.87	0.84	1.15	na	na	na
TAYLOR	na	1.00	na	1.21	na	1.01	na	1.19
Real GNP + Inflation:								
INTERMOD-Adaptive	1.00	na	0.83	0.95	0.63	0.68	1.08	na
INTERMOD-Consistent	1.00	na	na	0.94	1.09	1.08	0.97	na
LIVERPOOL	1.00	0.82	0.98	0.89	25.48	6.07	21.68	0.98
MPS	na	na	na	na	na	na	na	na
GEM	na	1.00	na	0.94	na	1.01	na	na
MSG	1.00	0.92	0.70	1.01	1.12	0.30	1.68	1.60
MULTIMOD	1.00	1.04	na	0.88	na	0.91	na	1.18
MX3	1.00	na	0.88	0.94	0.76	na	na	na
TAYLOR	na	1.00	na	0.71	na	0.66	na	1.52
Real GNP + Inflation + Change in Interest Rates:								
INTERMOD-Adaptive	1.00	na	1.15	0.86	0.86	0.81	0.89	na
INTERMOD-Consistent	1.00	na	na	0.83	1.24	1.16	0.77	na
LIVERPOOL	1.00	0.85	0.90	1.19	19.34	4.27	15.21	0.84
MPS	na	na	na	na	na	na	na	na
GEM	na	1.00	na	1.02	na	1.11	na	na
MSG	1.00	0.99	0.81	1.65	1.12	0.98	1.43	1.29
MULTIMOD	1.00	0.73	na	0.61	na	1.04	na	0.78
MX3	1.00	na	0.84	1.16	1.50	na	na	na
TAYLOR	na	na	na	na	na	na	na	na

Source: Calculated from B-I tables.

UNITED KINGDOM : LOSSES INDEXED ACROSS RULES
Money Targeting = 1.00

	Money Targeting		Nominal GNP Targeting		Real GNP and Inflation Targeting		Exchange Rate Targeting	
	(1)	(1X)	(2A)	(2AX)	(2B)	(2BX)	(3)	(3X)
Real GNP alone:								
INTERMOD-Adaptive	1.00	na	0.79	0.91	0.57	0.62	1.07	na
INTERMOD-Consistent	1.00	na	na	0.90	0.75	0.84	1.06	na
LIVERPOOL	1.00	0.71	0.65	0.52	2.58	1.45	12.28	0.80
MPS	na	na	na	na	na	na	na	na
GEM	na	na	na	na	na	na	na	na
MSG	na	na	na	na	na	na	na	na
MULTIMOD	1.00	0.99	na	1.01	na	1.31	na	0.86
MX3	na	na	na	na	na	na	na	na
TAYLOR	na	1.00	na	0.62	na	0.72	na	0.79
Inflation alone:								
INTERMOD-Adaptive	1.00	na	0.62	0.82	0.65	0.69	1.09	na
INTERMOD-Consistent	1.00	na	na	0.84	2.90	3.10	1.23	na
LIVERPOOL	1.00	0.84	0.39	0.95	3.46	16.36	21.20	0.54
MPS	na	na	na	na	na	na	na	na
GEM	na	na	na	na	na	na	na	na
MSG	na	na	na	na	na	na	na	na
MULTIMOD	1.00	0.92	na	0.95	na	0.79	na	0.99
MX3	na	na	na	na	na	na	na	na
TAYLOR	na	1.00	na	0.98	na	0.98	na	0.96
Real GNP + Inflation:								
INTERMOD-Adaptive	1.00	na	0.73	0.88	0.60	0.64	1.08	na
INTERMOD-Consistent	1.00	na	na	0.88	1.52	1.65	1.12	na
LIVERPOOL	1.00	0.78	0.50	0.77	3.08	9.86	17.32	0.65
MPS	na	na	na	na	na	na	na	na
GEM	na	na	na	na	na	na	na	na
MSG	na	na	na	na	na	na	na	na
MULTIMOD	1.00	0.96	na	0.98	na	1.09	na	0.91
MX3	na	na	na	na	na	na	na	na
TAYLOR	na	1.00	na	0.77	na	0.82	na	0.86
Real GNP + Inflation + Change in Interest Rates:								
INTERMOD-Adaptive	1.00	na	0.97	0.87	0.80	0.78	0.88	na
INTERMOD-Consistent	1.00	na	na	0.81	1.57	1.59	0.84	na
LIVERPOOL	1.00	1.02	0.43	1.61	2.67	8.40	12.18	0.69
MPS	na	na	na	na	na	na	na	na
GEM	na	na	na	na	na	na	na	na
MSG	na	na	na	na	na	na	na	na
MULTIMOD	1.00	0.62	na	0.57	na	0.92	na	0.56
MX3	na	na	na	na	na	na	na	na
TAYLOR	na	na	na	na	na	na	na	na

Source: Calculated from B-I tables.

TABLE B-III-5   CANADA : LOSSES INDEXED ACROSS RULES
Money Targeting = 1.00

	Money Targeting		Nominal GNP Targeting		Real GNP and Inflation Targeting		Exchange Rate Targeting	
	(1)	(1X)	(2A)	(2AX)	(2B)	(2BX)	(3)	(3X)
Real GNP alone:								
INTERMOD-Adaptive	1.00	na	0.90	0.92	[0.57]	0.61	0.98	na
INTERMOD-Consistent	1.00	na	na	0.96	[0.65]	0.66	0.97	na
LIVERPOOL	1.00	1.22	0.58	0.71	2.85	2.15	5.13	[0.55]
MPS	na	na	na	na	na	na	na	na
GEM	na	na	na	na	na	na	na	na
MSG	na	na	na	na	na	na	na	na
MULTIMOD	1.00	0.98	na	[0.97]	na	1.23	na	1.11
MX3	na	na	na	na	na	na	na	na
TAYLOR	na	1.00	na	0.55	na	[0.33]	na	0.83
Inflation alone:								
INTERMOD-Adaptive	1.00	na	[0.72]	0.86	0.73	0.75	0.98	na
INTERMOD-Consistent	1.00	na	na	[0.87]	2.75	3.03	1.07	na
LIVERPOOL	1.00	1.15	[0.07]	0.73	1.15	1.01	3.43	0.10
MPS	na	na	na	na	na	na	na	na
GEM	na	na	na	na	na	na	na	na
MSG	na	na	na	na	na	na	na	na
MULTIMOD	1.00	0.90	na	0.92	na	[0.68]	na	1.41
MX3	na	na	na	na	na	na	na	na
TAYLOR	na	1.00	na	1.10	na	[0.99]	na	1.00
Real GNP + Inflation:								
INTERMOD-Adaptive	1.00	na	0.84	0.90	[0.62]	0.65	0.98	na
INTERMOD-Consistent	1.00	na	na	[0.93]	1.37	1.47	1.01	na
LIVERPOOL	1.00	1.16	[0.15]	0.73	1.44	1.20	3.72	0.18
MPS	na	na	na	na	na	na	na	na
GEM	na	na	na	na	na	na	na	na
MSG	na	na	na	na	na	na	na	na
MULTIMOD	1.00	[0.94]	na	0.95	na	0.99	na	1.24
MX3	na	na	na	na	na	na	na	na
TAYLOR	na	1.00	na	0.60	na	[0.39]	na	0.85
Real GNP + Inflation + Change in Interest Rates:								
INTERMOD-Adaptive	1.00	na	1.03	0.89	0.80	[0.78]	0.92	na
INTERMOD-Consistent	1.00	na	na	[0.88]	1.59	1.58	0.94	na
LIVERPOOL	1.00	1.20	[0.11]	1.19	1.00	1.36	2.29	0.15
MPS	na	na	na	na	na	na	na	na
GEM	na	na	na	na	na	na	na	na
MSG	na	na	na	na	na	na	na	na
MULTIMOD	1.00	[0.78]	na	0.80	na	1.46	na	1.04
MX3	na	na	na	na	na	na	na	na
TAYLOR	na	na	na	na	na	na	na	na

Source: Calculated from B-I tables.

978

Contributors

RAY BARRELL
*National Institute of Economic and
  Social Research*

FLINT BRAYTON
Federal Reserve Board

RALPH C. BRYANT
Brookings Institution

NICOS CHRISTODOULAKIS
London Business School

DAVID CURRIE
London Business School

NEIL R. ERICSSON
Federal Reserve Board

RAY C. FAIR
Yale University

JOSEPH E. GAGNON
Federal Reserve Board

ANTHONY GARRATT
London Business School

JOHN F. HELLIWELL
*University of British Columbia
  and Harvard University*

DALE W. HENDERSON
Federal Reserve Board

ANDREW HUGHES HALLETT
University of Strathclyde

PETER HOOPER
Federal Reserve Board

JONATHAN IRELAND
*National Institute of Economic and
  Social Research*

WILLIAM KAN
Federal Reserve Board

DAVID KEMBALL-COOK
London Business School

PETER J. KLENOW
*Stanford University and University
  of Chicago*

DONALD L. KOHN
Federal Reserve Board

PAUL LEVINE
London Business School

BENNETT T. MCCALLUM
Carnegie-Mellon University

WARWICK J. MCKIBBIN
Brookings Institution

CATHERINE L. MANN
Federal Reserve Board

JAIME MARQUEZ
Federal Reserve Board

PAUL R. MASSON
International Monetary Fund

979

ELLEN E. MEADE
Federal Reserve Board

PATRICK MINFORD
University of Liverpool

ANUPAM RASTOGI
University of Liverpool

PETE RICHARDSON
*Organization for European
    Cooperation and Development*

CHRISTOPHER A. SIMS
Yale University

STEVEN A. SYMANSKY
International Monetary Fund

JOHN B. TAYLOR
Stanford University

CHARLES P. THOMAS
Federal Reserve Board

PETER A. TINSLEY
Federal Reserve Board

RALPH W. TRYON
Federal Reserve Board

PETER VON ZUR MUEHLEN
Federal Reserve Board

PETER WESTAWAY
*National Institute of Economic and
    Social Research*

Index